Short Story Criticism

Guide to Gale Literary Criticism Series

For criticism on	Consult these Gale series
Authors now living or who died after December 31, 1999	*CONTEMPORARY LITERARY CRITICISM (CLC)*
Authors who died between 1900 and 1999	*TWENTIETH-CENTURY LITERARY CRITICISM (TCLC)*
Authors who died between 1800 and 1899	*NINETEENTH-CENTURY LITERATURE CRITICISM (NCLC)*
Authors who died between 1400 and 1799	*LITERATURE CRITICISM FROM 1400 TO 1800 (LC)* *SHAKESPEAREAN CRITICISM (SC)*
Authors who died before 1400	*CLASSICAL AND MEDIEVAL LITERATURE CRITICISM (CMLC)*
Authors of books for children and young adults	*CHILDREN'S LITERATURE REVIEW (CLR)*
Dramatists	*DRAMA CRITICISM (DC)*
Poets	*POETRY CRITICISM (PC)*
Short story writers	*SHORT STORY CRITICISM (SSC)*
Literary topics and movements	*HARLEM RENAISSANCE: A GALE CRITICAL COMPANION (HR)* *THE BEAT GENERATION: A GALE CRITICAL COMPANION (BG)* *FEMINISM IN LITERATURE: A GALE CRITICAL COMPANION (FL)* *GOTHIC LITERATURE: A GALE CRITICAL COMPANION (GL)*
Asian American writers of the last two hundred years	*ASIAN AMERICAN LITERATURE (AAL)*
Black writers of the past two hundred years	*BLACK LITERATURE CRITICISM (BLC)* *BLACK LITERATURE CRITICISM SUPPLEMENT (BLCS)*
Hispanic writers of the late nineteenth and twentieth centuries	*HISPANIC LITERATURE CRITICISM (HLC)* *HISPANIC LITERATURE CRITICISM SUPPLEMENT (HLCS)*
Native North American writers and orators of the eighteenth, nineteenth, and twentieth centuries	*NATIVE NORTH AMERICAN LITERATURE (NNAL)*
Major authors from the Renaissance to the present	*WORLD LITERATURE CRITICISM, 1500 TO THE PRESENT (WLC)* *WORLD LITERATURE CRITICISM SUPPLEMENT (WLCS)*

ISSN 0895-9439

Volume 111

Short Story Criticism

Criticism of the Works of Short Fiction Writers

Jelana Krstović
Project Editor

GALE
CENGAGE Learning™

Detroit • New York • San Francisco • New Haven, Conn • Waterville, Maine • London

Short Story Criticism, Vol. 111

Project Editor: Jelena O. Krstović

Editorial: Dana Ramel Barnes, Tom Burns, Elizabeth A. Cranston, Kathy D. Darrow, Kristen A. Dorsch, Jeffrey W. Hunter, Jelena O. Krstović, Michelle Lee, Thomas J. Schoenberg, Lawrence J. Trudeau, and Russel Whitaker

Data Capture: Frances Monroe, Gwen Tucker

Indexing Services: Factiva®, a Dow Jones and Reuters Company

Rights and Acquisitions: Jaqueline Key, Mardell Schultz

Composition and Electronic Capture: Gary Leach

Manufacturing: Cynde Bishop

Associate Product Manager: Marc Cormier

Gale
27500 Drake Rd.
Farmington Hills, MI, 48331-3535

LIBRARY OF CONGRESS CATALOG CARD NUMBER 88-641014

ISBN-13: 978-1-4144-1895-7
ISBN-10: 1-4144-1895-7

ISSN 0895-9439

Printed in the United States of America
1 2 3 4 5 6 7 12 11 10 09 08

Contents

Preface

Short Story Criticism (*SSC*) presents significant criticism of the world's greatest short-story writers and provides supplementary biographical and bibliographical materials to guide the interested reader to a greater understanding of the authors of short fiction. This series was developed in response to suggestions from librarians serving high school, college, and public library patrons, who had noted a considerable number of requests for critical material on short-story writers. Although major short-story writers are covered in such Gale series as *Contemporary Literary Criticism* (*CLC*), *Twentieth-Century Literary Criticism* (*TCLC*), *Nineteenth-Century Literature Criticism* (*NCLC*), and *Literature Criticism from 1400 to 1800* (*LC*), librarians perceived the need for a series devoted solely to writers of the short-story genre.

Scope of the Series

SSC is designed to serve as an introduction to major short-story writers of all eras and nationalities. Since these authors have inspired a great deal of relevant critical material, *SSC* is necessarily selective, and the editors have chosen the most important published criticism to aid readers and students in their research.

Approximately three to six authors, works, or topics are included in each volume, and each entry presents a historical survey of the critical response to the work. The length of an entry is intended to reflect the amount of critical attention the author has received from critics writing in English and from foreign critics in translation. Every attempt has been made to identify and include the most significant essays on each author's work. In order to provide these important critical pieces, the editors sometimes reprint essays that have appeared elsewhere in Gale's Literary Criticism Series. Such duplication, however, never exceeds twenty percent of an *SSC* volume.

Organization of the Book

An *SSC* entry consists of the following elements:

- The **Author Heading** cites the name under which the author most commonly wrote, followed by birth and death dates. Also located here are any name variations under which an author wrote, including transliterated forms for authors whose native languages use nonroman alphabets. If the author wrote consistently under a pseudonym, the pseudonym will be listed in the author heading and the author's actual name given in parentheses on the first line of the biographical and critical introduction. Uncertain birth or death dates are indicated by question marks. Single-work entries are preceded by the title of the work and its date of publication.

- The **Introduction** contains background information that introduces the reader to the author and the critical debates surrounding his or her work.

- The list of **Principal Works** is ordered chronologically by date of first publication and lists the most important works by the author. The first section comprises short-story collections, novellas, and novella collections. The second section gives information on other major works by the author. For foreign authors, the editors have provided original foreign-language publication information and have selected what are considered the best and most complete English-language editions of their works.

- Reprinted **Criticism** is arranged chronologically in each entry to provide a useful perspective on changes in critical evaluation over time. All short-story, novella, and collection titles by the author featured in the entry are printed in boldface type. The critic's name and the date of composition or publication of the critical work are given at the beginning of each piece of criticism. Unsigned criticism is preceded by the title of the source in which it appeared. Footnotes are reprinted at the end of each essay or excerpt. In the case of excerpted criticism, only those footnotes that pertain to the excerpted texts are included.

- Critical essays are prefaced by brief **Annotations** explicating each piece.

- A complete **Bibliographical Citation** of the original essay or book precedes each piece of criticism. Source citations in the Literary Criticism Series follow University of Chicago Press style, as outlined in *The Chicago Manual of Style,* 15th ed. (Chicago: The University of Chicago Press, 2006).

- An annotated bibliography of **Further Reading** appears at the end of each entry and suggests resources for additional study. In some cases, significant essays for which the editors could not obtain reprint rights are included here. Boxed material following the further reading list provides references to other biographical and critical sources on the author in series published by Gale.

Indexes

A **Cumulative Author Index** lists all of the authors that appear in a wide variety of reference sources published by Gale, including *SSC.* A complete list of these sources is found facing the first page of the Author Index. The index also includes birth and death dates and cross references between pseudonyms and actual names.

A **Cumulative Nationality Index** lists all authors featured in *SSC* by nationality, followed by the number of the *SSC* volume in which their entry appears.

An alphabetical **Title Index** lists all short-story, novella, and collection titles contained in the *SSC* series. Titles of short-story collections, separately published novellas, and novella collections are printed in italics, while titles of individual short stories are printed in roman type with quotation marks. Each title is followed by the author's last name and corresponding volume and page numbers where commentary on the work is located. English-language translations of original foreign-language titles are cross-referenced to the foreign titles so that all references to discussion of a work are combined in one listing.

In response to numerous suggestions from librarians, Gale also produces an annual paperbound edition of the SSC cumulative title index. This annual cumulation, which alphabetically lists all titles reviewed in the series, is available to all customers. Additional copies of this index are available upon request. Librarians and patrons will welcome this separate index; it saves shelf space, is easy to use, and is recyclable upon receipt of the next edition.

Citing *Short Story Criticism*

When citing criticism reprinted in the Literary Criticism Series, students should provide complete bibliographic information so that the cited essay can be located in the original print or electronic source. Students who quote directly from reprinted criticism may use any accepted bibliographic format, such as University of Chicago Press style or Modern Language Association (MLA) style. Both the MLA and the University of Chicago formats are acceptable and recognized as being the current standards for citations. It is important, however, to choose one format for all citations; do not mix the two formats within a list of citations.

The examples below follow recommendations for preparing a bibliography set forth in *The Chicago Manual of Style,* 15th ed. (Chicago: The University of Chicago Press, 2006); the first example pertains to material drawn from periodicals, the second to material reprinted from books:

Morrison, Jago. "Narration and Unease in Ian McEwan's Later Fiction." *Critique* 42, no. 3 (spring 2001): 253-68. Reprinted in *Short Story Criticism.* Vol. 57, edited by Jelena Krstovic, 212-20. Detroit: Gale, 2003.

Brossard, Nicole. "Poetic Politics." In *The Politics of Poetic Form: Poetry and Public Policy,* edited by Charles Bernstein, 73-82. New York: Roof Books, 1990. Reprinted in *Short Story Criticism.* Vol. 57, edited by Jelena Krstovic, 3-8. Detroit: Gale, 2003.

The examples below follow recommendations for preparing a works cited list set forth in the *MLA Handbook for Writers of Research Papers,* 6th ed. (New York: The Modern Language Association of America, 2003); the first example pertains to material drawn from periodicals, the second to material reprinted from books:

Morrison, Jago. "Narration and Unease in Ian McEwan's Later Fiction." *Critique* 42.3 (spring 2001): 253-68. Reprinted in *Short Story Criticism.* Ed. Jelena Krstovic. Vol. 57. Detroit: Gale, 2003. 212-20.

Brossard, Nicole. "Poetic Politics." *The Politics of Poetic Form: Poetry and Public Policy.* Ed. Charles Bernstein. New York: Roof Books, 1990. 73-82. Reprinted in *Short Story Criticism.* Ed. Jelena Krstovic. Vol. 57. Detroit: Gale, 2003. 3-8.

Suggestions are Welcome

Readers who wish to suggest new features, topics, or authors to appear in future volumes, or who have other suggestions or comments are cordially invited to call, write, or fax the Associate Product Manager:

Associate Product Manager, Literary Criticism Series

Gale

27500 Drake Road

Farmington Hills, MI 48331-3535

1-800-347-4253 (GALE)

Fax: 248-699-8054

Acknowledgments

The editors wish to thank the copyright holders of the excerpted criticism included in this volume and the permissions managers of many book and magazine publishing companies for assisting us in securing reproduction rights. Following is a list of the copyright holders who have granted us permission to reproduce material in this volume of *SSC.* Every effort has been made to trace copyright, but if omissions have been made, please let us know.

COPYRIGHTED MATERIAL IN *SSC,* VOLUME 111, WAS REPRODUCED FROM THE FOLLOWING PERIODICALS:

American Transcendental Quarterly, v. 17, March, 2003; v. 20, June, 2006 Copyright © 2003, 2006 by The University of Rhode Island. Both reproduced by permission.—***ANQ,*** v. 16, winter, 2003. Copyright © 2003 by Helen Dwight Reid Educational Foundation. Reproduced with permission of the Helen Dwight Reid Educational Foundation, published by Heldref Publications, 1319 18th Street, NW, Washington, DC 20036-1802.—***Christianity and Literature,*** v. 56, fall, 2006; v. 56, summer, 2007. Both reproduced by permission.—***Clues,*** v. 25, fall, 2006. Copyright © 2006 by Helen Dwight Reid Educational Foundation. Reproduced with permission of the Helen Dwight Reid Educational Foundation, published by Heldref Publications, 1319 18th Street, NW, Washington, DC 20036-1802.—***College Literature,*** v. 30, summer, 2003. Copyright © 2003 by West Chester University. Reproduced by permission.—***Comparative Literature Studies,*** v. 41, 2004. Copyright © 2004 by The Pennsylvania State University. Reproduced by permission of the publisher.—***ELH,*** v. 72, fall, 2005. Copyright © 2005 by The Johns Hopkins University Press. Reproduced by permission.—***Eudora Welty Newsletter,*** v. 30, summer, 2006. Reproduced by permission of the publisher and author.—***Explicator,*** v. 56, spring, 1998; v. 62, summer, 2004; v. 64, fall, 2005; v. 65, fall, 2006; v. 65, winter, 2007. Copyright © 1998, 2004, 2005, 2006, 2007 by Helen Dwight Reid Educational Foundation. All reproduced with permission of the Helen Dwight Reid Educational Foundation, published by Heldref Publications, 1319 18th Street, NW, Washington, DC 20036-1802.— ***GLQ,*** v. 12, 2006. Copyright © 2006 Duke University Press. All rights reserved. Used by permission of the publisher.—***International Fiction Review,*** v. 28, 2001. Copyright © 2001 International Fiction Association. Reproduced by permission.—***Journal of the Short Story in English,*** autumn, 2000. Copyright © Presses de l'Université d'Angers, 2000. Reproduced by permission.—***Midwest Quarterly,*** v. 46, spring, 2005; v. 47, spring, 2006. Copyright © 2005, 2006 by *The Midwest Quarterly*, Pittsburgh State University. Both reproduced by permission.—***Mississippi Quarterly,*** v. 55, summer, 2002; v. 56, spring, 2003; v. 56, summer, 2003; v. 56, fall, 2003; v. 57, spring, 2004; v. 57, summer, 2004; v. 59, winter-spring, 2005. Copyright © 2002, 2003, 2004, 2005 by *The Midwest Quarterly*, Pittsburgh State University. All reproduced by permission.—***Papers on Language & Literature,*** v. 39, summer, 2003. Copyright © 2003 by The Board of Trustees, Southern Illinois University at Edwardsville. Reproduced by permission.—***Perspectives on Political Science,*** v. 34, fall, 2005. Copyright © 2005 by Helen Dwight Reid Educational Foundation. Reproduced with permission of the Helen Dwight Reid Educational Foundation, published by Heldref Publications, 1319 18th Street, NW, Washington, DC 20036-1802.—***Renascence,*** v. 57, fall, 2004; v. 59, spring, 2007 Copyright © 2004, 2007 Marquette University Press. Both reproduced by permission.—***Rocky Mountain Review,*** v. 58, fall, 2004. Copyright © 2004 by the Rocky Mountain Modern Language Association. Reproduced by permission.—***South Central Review,*** v. 14, summer, 1997. Copyright © 1997 South Central Review. Reproduced by permission.—***Southern Literary Journal,*** v. 35, spring, 2003; v. 37, spring, 2005; v. 38, fall, 2005; v. 39, fall, 2006 Copyright © 2003, m2005, 2006 by the University of North Carolina Press. All used by permission.—***Southern Quarterly,*** v. 40, fall, 2001; v. 40, summer, 2002 Copyright © 2001, 2002 by the University of Southern Mississippi. Both reproduced by permission.—***Southern Review,*** v. 41, spring, 2005 for "Consenting to Love: Autobiographical Roots of 'Good Country People'" by Mark Bosco. Copyright © 2005 by Louisiana State University. Reproduced by permission of the author.—***Studies in Short Fiction,*** v. 33, fall, 1996: v. 35, fall, 1998 Copyright © 1996, 1998 by Newberry College. Both reproduced by permission.—***Theory, Culture & Society,*** v. 22, spring, 2005 for "On the Critique of Secular Ethics: An Essay with Flannery O'Connor and Hannah Arendt," by Vikki Bell.Theory, Culture & Society, Ltd. Reproduced with permission of Sage Publications and the author.

COPYRIGHTED MATERIAL IN *SSC,* VOLUME 111, WAS REPRODUCED FROM THE FOLLOWING BOOKS:

Jarrell, Donna. From "The Challenge of 'June Recital': Generic Considerations in the Structure of ***The Golden Apples,*** in ***Postmodern Approaches to the Short Story.*** Edited by Farhat Iftekharrudin, Joseph Boyden, Joseph Longo, and Mary Rohrberger. Praeger, 2003. Copyright © 2003 by The Society for the Study of the Short Story. All rights reserved. Reproduced by permission of Greenwood Publishing Group, Inc., Westport, CT.—Tiegreen, Helen Hurt. From "Mothers, Daughters, and ***The Golden Apples,***" in ***Southern Mothers: Fact and Fictions in Southern Women's Writing.*** Edited by Nagueyalti Warren and Sally Wolff. Louisiana State University Press, 1999. Copyright © 1999 by Louisiana State University Press. All rights reserved. Reproduced by permission.

Gale Literature Product Advisory Board

The members of the Gale Literature Product Advisory Board—reference librarians from public and academic library systems—represent a cross-section of our customer base and offer a variety of informed perspectives on both the presentation and content of our literature products. Advisory board members assess and define such quality issues as the relevance, currency, and usefulness of the author coverage, critical content, and literary topics included in our series; evaluate the layout, presentation, and general quality of our printed volumes; provide feedback on the criteria used for selecting authors and topics covered in our series; provide suggestions for potential enhancements to our series; identify any gaps in our coverage of authors or literary topics, recommending authors or topics for inclusion; analyze the appropriateness of our content and presentation for various user audiences, such as high school students, undergraduates, graduate students, librarians, and educators; and offer feedback on any proposed changes/enhancements to our series. We wish to thank the following advisors for their advice throughout the year.

Barbara M. Bibel
Librarian
Oakland Public Library
Oakland, California

Dr. Toby Burrows
Principal Librarian
The Scholars' Centre
University of Western Australia Library
Nedlands, Western Australia

Celia C. Daniel
Associate Reference Librarian
Howard University Libraries
Washington, D.C.

David M. Durant
Reference Librarian
Joyner Library
East Carolina University
Greenville, North Carolina

Nancy T. Guidry
Librarian
Bakersfield Community College
Bakersfield, California

Heather Martin
Arts & Humanities Librarian
University of Alabama at Birmingham, Sterne Library
Birmingham, Alabama

Susan Mikula
Librarian
Indiana Free Library
Indiana, Pennsylvania

Thomas Nixon
Humanities Reference Librarian
University of North Carolina at Chapel Hill, Davis Library
Chapel Hill, North Carolina

Mark Schumacher
Jackson Library
University of North Carolina at Greensboro
Greensboro, North Carolina

Gwen Scott-Miller
Assistant Director
Sno-Isle Regional Library System
Marysville, Washington

Flannery O'Connor
1925-1964

(Full name Mary Flannery O'Connor) American short story writer, novelist, essayist, and critic.

The following entry provides an overview of O'Connor's short fiction. For additional information on her short fiction career, see *SSC,* Volumes 1 and 61; for discussion of the short story "A Good Man Is Hard to Find" (1953), see *SSC,* Volume 23; for discussion of the short story collection *Everything That Rises Must Converge* (1965), see *SSC,* Volume 82.

INTRODUCTION

Recognized as a seminal figure in American short fiction, O'Connor infused her stories with the rich detail of her native South while critiquing materialism and spiritual apathy in contemporary society. A Roman Catholic whose stated purpose was to reveal the mystery of God's grace in everyday life, O'Connor was an anomaly among post-World War II authors and her choice to depict salvation through shocking, often violent plots sparked controversy during her lifetime. Although her narrative tone of ironic detachment and use of mordant humor have prompted critics to label her an existentialist or nihilist, and despite her association with Southern gothic writers like Erskine Caldwell and Carson McCullers, O'Connor is lauded for her singularity of moral purpose and her uniquely powerful style.

BIOGRAPHICAL INFORMATION

O'Connor was born in Savannah, Georgia, the only child of Regina Cline and Edward Francis O'Connor Jr. Both her parents came from Catholic families that had lived in the South for generations. In the late 1930s her father developed disseminated lupus—an immunological disorder that causes the body to make antibodies against its own tissues—and the O'Connors moved to Milledgeville, which had been the home of the Cline family since the late 1880s. At that time lupus was untreatable and O'Connor's father died in 1941. Although she had attended parochial schools in Savannah, O'Connor enrolled in the progressive Peabody High School of Milledgeville, which she found disconcertingly eclectic. She graduated from Georgia State College for Women in Milledgeville with a degree in social science in 1945. A fellowship enabled her to attend the Writers' Workshop at the State University of Iowa, from which she earned a Master of Fine Arts degree in 1947 after completing six stories, including "The Geranium," which had appeared the previous year in the periodical *Accent.* After leaving Iowa she began work on her first novel at Yaddo, a writer's colony in Saratoga Springs, New York, and then in Connecticut, where she lived in the household of poet and translator Robert Fitzgerald. In December 1950, on her way home to Milledgeville for Christmas, she became seriously ill on the train and was hospitalized upon her arrival in Atlanta; she was diagnosed with lupus, the same illness that had killed her father nine years earlier. The recent discovery of cortisone had made the disease treatable, but it was still considered incurable. After several months, during which time O'Connor was in and out of the hospital, she and her mother moved to Andalusia, a dairy farm four miles from Milledgeville that Mrs. O'Connor had recently inherited. Accordingly, dairy farms, the capable and efficient women who run them, and their tenant help figure prominently in O'Connor's later stories. O'Connor spent the remaining fourteen years of her life at Andalusia, writing and raising various kinds of fowl, including peacocks.

During the first year after the outbreak of her illness, O'Connor continued to work on the final revisions of her novel, *Wise Blood,* which was published in 1952. Over the next few years O'Connor returned to writing short fiction. The stories composed between the summer of 1952 and 1955 were subsequently collected in *A Good Man Is Hard to Find* (1955). Although a softening of the bone in her hip caused her to rely on crutches, O'Connor frequently accepted invitations to speak at colleges and writers' conferences in the latter half of the 1950s and early 1960s. She took advantage of these opportunities not only to give perceptive talks on the nature of fiction but also to clarify her position as a writer "with Christian concerns." These talks, together with a number of essays on similar subjects, were edited by Sally and Robert Fitzgerald and published after O'Connor's death under the title *Mystery and Manners* (1969). Three of her later stories ("Greenleaf," "Everything That Rises Must Converge," and "Revelation") were awarded the prestigious O. Henry Award. She died of kidney failure triggered by lupus and the after-effects of abdominal surgery. Her second collection of stories, *Everything That Rises Must Converge,* was completed just before her death and published posthumously in 1965. In 1972 a comprehensive volume of her short fiction entitled *The Complete Stories* (1971) won the National Book Award for Fiction.

MAJOR WORKS OF SHORT FICTION

Mixing grotesque realism and absurd humor, O'Connor's short fiction examines the brutality and divinity of the human spirit against the backdrop of the American South. The stories in *A Good Man Is Hard to Find* are marked by their recurring depiction of salvation through disaster and the mysterious nature of faith. In "A Good Man Is Hard to Find," one of O'Connor's bleakest and most famous works, a stern grandmother takes her family on a drive to see an eerie antebellum mansion. As she guides her clan along abandoned country roads, her cat breaks free from a basket hidden under her seat, and the ensuing commotion causes the family car to be wrecked. They are subsequently rescued by The Misfit, an escaped convict who speaks like a twisted philosopher and commands his cohorts to shoot and kill the family one by one. Leaving only the grandmother alive, The Misfit engages her in a theological debate that culminates with the old woman making a rare statement of kindness, ultimately claiming The Misfit as one of her "babies." Repulsed by her words, he kills her, stating, "She would of been a good woman . . . if it had been somebody there to shoot her every minute of her life." The twelve-year-old heroine of "A Temple of the Holy Ghost" tries to understand her parochial school's assertion that her body is like the temple alluded to in the story's title. When her friends tell her about a hermaphrodite they saw at a sideshow, she comes to a profound—yet mysterious and troubling—epiphany regarding Christianity and the physical body. In "The Artificial Nigger," a naïve country boy named Nelson is taken to the city by his hardened grandfather, Mr. Head. Intent on showing Nelson the sinfulness and depravity of urban life, Mr. Head cautions his grandson about the city's African American population (there are no black people in their small, rural community). When the two find themselves lost in the African American section of town, Nelson accidentally knocks down an elderly woman and, faced with a startled crowd, Mr. Head denies knowing the boy. Although Nelson is hurt by his grandfather's denial, the two eventually reconcile while observing a lawn ornament cast in the image of a black man—a sight which prompts Mr. Head to exclaim with caustic irony, "They ain't got enough real ones here. They got to have an artificial one." Joy Hopewell, the protagonist of "Good Country People," is an intellectual spinster whose physical ailments (a heart condition and an artificial leg) force her to live at her mother's home. An avowed atheist and nihilist, Joy has given herself a new name, Hulga, which represents her antagonistic relationship with the world. Her façade of inner strength is soon torn when she is seduced by a sexually deviant bible salesman who viciously exposes the spurious nature of her belief system, completing his spiritual attack by stealing her artificial leg. A story of base betrayal, "The Life You Save May Be Your Own" concerns a drifter named Tom T. Shiftlet who marries a lonely and pathetic woman, Lucynell Crater, so that he can steal her car, leaving her stranded at a roadside café.

The social implications of theological concerns and the human capacity for both cruelty and kindness inform O'Connor's second collection, *Everything That Rises Must Converge.* Mrs. May, the protagonist of "Greenleaf," keeps her two grown sons financially and emotionally dependent on her because she cannot face her own mortality. She often taunts them, contrasting their unfulfilling lives with the success of the sons of her hired hand, Mr. Greenleaf. When Greenleaf's bull invades her yard, Mrs. May is fatally gored while trying to drive it away. An attack on modern liberalism, "The Lame Shall Enter First" is narrated by Rufus Johnson, a young fundamentalist who intellectually challenges a social worker named Sheppard while incarcerated in a reformatory. When Rufus is released, Sheppard takes him into the home that he shares with his young son, Norton. Sheppard's attempts to spiritually guide Rufus take the form of intense religious discussions in which Sheppard stresses his atheism and rejection of fundamentalism in favor of science and reason. The young man rebuffs such teachings and falls back into a life of crime. When Sheppard realizes that he has done more for Rufus than for his own son, he resolves to seek Norton's forgiveness, but discovers that his son has hanged himself. In "Parker's Back," Obadiah Elihue Parker is so strongly affected by a religious epiphany that he has the image of Christ's head tattooed on his back. When he is ridiculed by his friends and rejected by his wife, Sarah Ruth, he realizes the disruptive, yet redemptive, force of his spiritual beliefs. In "Revelation," a religious, highly judgmental woman reexamines her harsh and hypocritical attitude after being attacked by a college girl in a doctor's waiting room. The collection's final story, "Judgement Day" (sometimes rendered "Judgment Day"), tells of an elderly man who moves from his native Georgia to New York to live with his daughter. Lonely and missing his African American friend Coleman, the old man offers his friendship to an insensitive black neighbor who dismisses him. After the old man's death, his daughter initially ignores his wish to be buried in Georgia, only to reconsider and have his body moved, according to his instructions.

CRITICAL RECEPTION

Critics have consistently studied and admired O'Connor's stories since their initial publication, paying particular attention to their challenging and unabashed sense of religious conviction. The spiritually transcendent nature of suffering in O'Connor's short fiction has been likened to the philosophical ideas of Simone Weil, and the critical view of modern secularism evinced by *Everything That Rises Must Converge* has been compared to C. S. Lewis's worldview. Similarly, scholars have noted the espousal of St. Thomas Aquinas's theological contemplations in "Judgement Day" and have analyzed "The Lame Shall Enter First" as a reflection of theorist Hannah Arendt's emphasis on the value of faithful action and good works. Commentator Jeanne Perreault has interpreted Nelson's meeting of a large African American woman in "The Artificial Nigger" as an event conducive to a religious epiphany. Commentators also have illuminated biblical allusions in the text of "The Artificial Nigger," examining O'Connor's juxtaposition of religious and political references as applied to themes of spiritual transformation and social change. Additionally, they have identified the apocalyptic trope of the tornado as an agent of judgment in "Revelation" and "The Life You Save May Be Your Own," finding parallel symbolism in the works of such classic authors as William Butler Yeats and Dante. Reviewers have stressed the profound function of humor in O'Connor's stories, discussing this aspect of her fiction in light of philosopher Henri Bergson's theory of laughter and Mikhail Bakhtin's notion of the carnivalesque.

PRINCIPAL WORKS

Short Fiction

A Good Man Is Hard to Find, and Other Stories 1955; republished as *The Artificial Nigger, and Other Tales,* 1957
Everything That Rises Must Converge 1965
The Complete Stories 1971
**Collected Works* 1988

Other Major Works

Wise Blood (novel) 1952
The Violent Bear It Away (novel) 1960
Mystery and Manners: Occasional Prose (prose) 1969
The Habit of Being: Letters (letters) 1979
The Presence of Grace, and Other Book Reviews (criticism) 1983
Flannery O'Connor: Spiritual Writings (essays) 2003

*Includes *Wise Blood, A Good Man Is Hard to Find, The Violent Bear It Away, Everything That Rises Must Converge, Stories and Occasional Prose,* and *Letters.*

CRITICISM

Anne Elizabeth Carson (essay date fall 2001)

SOURCE: Carson, Anne Elizabeth. "'Break forth and wash the slime from this earth!': O'Connor's Apocalyptic Tornadoes." *Southern Quarterly* 40, no. 1 (fall 2001): 19-27.

[*In the following essay, Carson analyzes the apocalyptic function of tornado imagery in "Revelation," "The Life You Save May Be Your Own," and the novel* The Violent Bear It Away, *citing literary precedents for such symbolism in the works of Dante and William Butler Yeats.*]

The allegorical, metaphorical, and literal implications of the mighty, cataclysmic tornado resonate throughout artistic history. From William Blake's stunning depiction of a tornado-encircled God appearing to the wretched Job to Frank L. Baum's utilization of the ominous, whirlwind-driven chariot which brings young Dorothy to the beginning of her life-changing journey, the image has been for artists a means to occasion spiritual and emotional awakening. Thus, we must consider this particular symbol in all of its manifestations: meteorological, theological, and physical. Examine the prototypical shape of the structure, and we see a gigantic funnel, a helix spiraling toward infinity. We note the dizzying effects of the preternatural storm capable of lifting the human body, a tree, an entire edifice into oblivion. And we also recognize the apocalyptic potential of this phenomenon used, on occasion, by authors to rouse the soul and, as its shape suggests, to curtail and subsequently invert malign tendencies in some of the more incorrigible characters. One such writer, Flannery O'Connor, frequently accused of writing in the vein of the grotesque and macabre, deliberately adopts the symbol of the tornado in an effort to hasten the ethical and spiritual regeneration of the morally bankrupt figures she often creates. In one of the author's many letters to A, she bemoans this cynical world plagued by doubt, corruption, and emptiness: "if you live today you breathe in nihilism. In or out of the Church, it's the gas you breathe" (***Collected Works*** 949). By examining the use of tornado imagery in three of O'Connor's works, I intend to show that the appearance of the foreboding symbol is more than an arbitrary occurrence. Disillusioned and frustrated with an increasingly profligate society, O'Connor chastises her world with her own version of the formidable four horsemen. She checks sins of pride, vanity, and cruelty with punishments conjured by an imagination worthy of Dante. The tornado looms as an integral tool in her repertoire.

Many have sought to uncover the influences on Flannery O'Connor's life and writing. Her letters and occasional prose pieces offer the critic multitudinous possibilities, from Tielhard de Chardin to Nathaniel Hawthorne and Edgar Allen Poe. Perhaps the one person about whom she speaks most conclusively, however, is Dante Alighieri. In discussing the merits of the medieval Italian poet, O'Connor exclaims: "For my money Dante is about as great as you can get" (969). Quite possibly the intensity of his art attracted the southern author, or maybe it was his candor and courage when dealing with the incomprehensible—or just maybe it was his "tornado." No literary work transfigures the apparently simple structure of the tornado into a redemptive maze of horror and chaos like Dante's *Inferno.* His circles of Hell, each in its own potently graphic manner, combine to effect mental and psychological growth in Dante the pilgrim. Desperate to enter the final sphere, the paradisiacal realm, the pilgrim discovers that he must first traverse the vile funnel. Marianne Shapiro writes of the reciprocal and symmetrical relationship between Dante's Hell and his Heaven: "The pleasures of *Paradiso* are spiritual by stipulation, yet imaged in terms of a predominately circular, often dance-like motion whose invariance also relates it inversely to the underworld" (ix). Shapiro suggests that in order for a sojourner to eventually scale the divine summit he must first plunge into the rapturous counter-circles. Pictorially, whereas the path to the divine resembles an ethereal mountain, these counter-circles, the inverse structure, approximate a massively devastating tornado. Furthermore, throughout the text, readers encounter diverse symbols and symbolic punishments that duplicate, in miniature, the larger, infernal design, such as the literal tornado that envelops the lustful in Canto V, those whose spiraling penance reflects their intemperate, uncontrollable passions: "I reached a place where every light is muted, / which bellows like the sea beneath a tempest / when it is battered by opposing winds. / The hellish hurricane, which never rests, / drives on the spirits with its violence . . ." (5.28-32). The characters encased within this cyclonic system represent lost souls, who, when inhabiting the earthly realm, rejected virtuous protocol and, despite better judgment, cognitively digressed into sinful experiments. Dante the pilgrim is initially headed toward a commensurately precarious life, as he observes: "I found myself within a shadowed forest, / for I had lost the path that does not stray" (1.2-3). He finds that he must first atone prior to regaining the "true" course, expressly, that path toward God's light. And Dante the author's grand tornadic scheme will rigorously test the character's spiritual fortitude.

As evinced by the particularly ghastly and fantastic punishments doled out to those shades trudging through the various spheres of Hell and Purgatory, the medieval Dante seems to equate sinfulness and human corruption with physical deformity. Readers encounter the forlorn hypocrites eternally cloaked in suits of lead, the gluttonous of Purgatory emaciated and skeletal, and the envious whose eyes are sewn shut with wire. The contemptible human's punishment is to be disfigured, transmogrified so that he no longer appears to be of God's image. Similarly, Flannery O'Connor views man's transgressive nature as that which further alienates him from his divine provenance. Her sinful characters also emerge as deformed, often hideous creatures. Grotesqueness equals a withdrawal from God. In his study of O'Connor's religious convictions, David Eggenschwiler identifies the author's principal grievance with mankind. He explains that she laments man's "attempt to deny the essential self from which he has fallen and to substitute a more limited conception of what he is" (26); that is to say, society increasingly divorces itself from the doctrines and practices of Christianity, and in doing so, O'Connor believes, distorts all the more that inner soul which began with God, creating a wider, well nigh unbridgeable gulf between this life and the next. Human beings all have the potential, according to O'Connor, to unite spiritually with the Lord, but the modern world repeatedly rejects any such unification, causing the stringent southern Catholic to complain in a note to A: "Right now the whole world seems to be going through a dark night of the soul" (952).

But while the Catholic writer generates a number of malformed characters representative of man's rejection of and corresponding estrangement from his creator, she also, in many instances, situates herself as a redeemer. Not simply content to sketch pictures of utter human tragedy and irreversible doom, O'Connor, a firm believer in the regenerative power of grace, usually extends a sinking character a lifeline. Despite the pessimism and doubt of her letters, she regularly proves, through her fiction, that she harbors hope for the unanchored human spirit. Symbolically, via the sacramental acts of communion and baptism, the otherwise ill-fated character can reclaim his life and in the process renew his relationship with God. The good in mankind, O'Connor insists, is simply "under construction," not lost forever (qtd. in Fickett and Gilbert 87). Think of Harry/Bevel, a young boy rescued from the wicked atmosphere of the city and spiritually purified by the "River of Faith . . . the River of Life . . . the River of Love" (162). Or Mrs. Cope in **"A Circle in the Fire"** forced to endure a baptism by fire as her farm goes up in flames, as the holy "prophets . . . danc[e] in the . . . circle the angel had cleared for them" (251). Such fictional personae represent the author's faith, her feeling that at the core people are all "Temple[s] of the Holy Ghost." She desperately wants to believe that man can eventually be made to see the error of his ways and reconnect with his intrinsic holiness. Still, given the dismal state of the modern world, not everyone can be saved. One does meet with the irretrievable souls in O'Connor's body of work, those who completely forsake divine dicta, who are so deformed, so grotesque that not even the author can rescue them; they are destined only to suffer for their sins and die agonizing deaths.

* * *

In examining the actions and behavior of a number of O'Connor characters, it is easy to imagine several of the more dubious figures entrenched within the confines of Dante's funnel-shaped hell. Desirous to occasion the same revelatory transformations within her iniquitous characters that Dante induces within his condemned shades, O'Connor, in unmistakably apocalyptic overtones, inserts the image of the infernal tornado. It literally whirls into a character's life, heralding disaster and calamity; most importantly, it almost always signals a portentous reckoning. Perhaps no villain merits contempt more than Rayber, the apathetic schoolteacher, whom some critics view as the mortal incarnation of the Devil in *The Violent Bear It Away* (Scouten). Burdened with a deaf and mute child, whom he refers to as a "mistake of nature" (403), determined to eradicate all traces of the faith and zealotry of the elder Tarwater from his new charge, young Francis, Rayber leads an essentially insular existence. Speaking as though her pernicious character embodies a de facto symptom of a debased society, the author, in reference to the schoolteacher's mutilated ear, explains in a letter to John Hawkes: "I don't really know Rayber or have the ear for him" (1109). O'Connor throws up her hands in proverbial defeat and resigns herself to designing a Dantesque punishment for the modern-day nihilist, thereby hoping to instill the germ of good old-fashioned fear within her readers. Those who remain "deaf" to mankind, who negate the fellowship which as equal children of God yokes us together, in O'Connor's view, inevitably must suffer. At the moment of his "useless" son's ironic death, Rayber, situated in his room at the lodge, encounters Flannery O'Connor's sublimating tornado: "For a while he dozed and dreamed that he and Bishop were speeding away in the car, escaping safely from a lowering tornado-like cloud" (454). And yet escape is futile. Just as Virgil emerges as the embodiment of Dante's respective guide through the dark, twisting underworld, an ominous escort also arrives to convey Rayber to his implied journey: "When he [Rayber] awoke again, the moon . . . had lost its color. He sat up startled as if it were a face looking in on him, a pale messenger breathlessly arrived" (455). His tumble into a disposition-altering, tornado-configured inferno appears inevitable: "He waited expectantly. Then an instant before the cataclysm, he grabbed the metal box of his hearing aid as if he were clawing his heart" (455). In the *Divine Comedy,* Dante the vagrant soul awakens to the knowledge that he has in fact gone astray, in part because of the symbolic landscape extending before him: the *selva oscura* (shadowed forest) (1.2). O'Connor offers an unmistakable echo of this allegorical scenery: "he was headed for everything the old man had prepared him for . . . through the *black forest* toward a violent encounter with his fate" (456, emphasis added).

Rayber must ultimately recognize the travesty that is his life if he is ever to exist as a viable member of humankind. And indeed the author, ever championing the powers of God's grace, is reluctant to leave this character malingering about as merely an unsalvageable wretch. She must at least try. O'Connor intimates that the character will be subjected to some form of retribution, the consequence of which readers are left to envisage. Potentially, the only way that Rayber and similar characters can come to terms with the sinful nature of their personalities is when, as Ruthann Johansen suggests, a "ritual inversion" occurs. Johansen explains that such inversions "might humble the self-righteous, revive flagging faith, or even lead to conversion . . ." (20). After journeying through the infernal realm, Dante and his guide literally climb the body of Satan, occasioning the turnabout of the great funnel of hell. Following this inversion Dante notes that he and Virgil gradually "made [their] way back into the bright world" (34.134). His eyes were becoming clearer, increasingly able to see "those things of beauty Heaven bears" (34.137-38). The question remains, will the schoolteacher, in the wake of his tornadic encounter, emerge a regenerated soul? Or will he persist in his meaningless course? The same can be asked of Ruby Turpin, the self-satisfied protagonist of **"Revelation."** More so than in the case of Rayber, one can readily identify Mrs. Turpin's pivotal "moment of truth." Unable to endure the protagonist's self-inflating statements, the woman's insensate cries of "Thank you Jesus for making everything the way it is!" (644), Mary Grace, a girl who Mrs. Turpin inwardly notes has an "ugly," "blue" face with "acne" (635), hurls a book at Ruby's head. The result of this momentous debacle commemorates another literal and figurative inversion:

> All at once her vision narrowed and she saw everything as if it were happening in a small room far away, or as if she were looking at it through the wrong end of a telescope. . . . Magazines flew this way and that as the table turned over. The girl fell with a thud and Mrs. Turpin's vision suddenly reversed itself and she saw everything large instead of small.
>
> (644-45)

And again, the sinister insignia of this experience appears in the form of a tornado: "The dark protuberance over her eye looked like a miniature tornado cloud which might at any moment sweep across the horizon of her brow" (651). The funnel-shaped bruise displayed prominently on Mrs. Turpin's head memorializes the pain and humiliation that she causes Mary Grace, among others. O'Connor, however, not satisfied with just censuring the character's intolerable behavior with this waiting room incident, carries the *Inferno* analogy a step further. Directly prior to throwing her book at Ruby Turpin, Mary Grace offers the premonitory condemnation: "Go back to hell where you came from, you old wart hog" (646). The girl's pronouncement becomes an obsession, the effect of which has Mrs. Turpin anxiously reassessing the value of her life. She frantically wonders, "How am I a hog and me both?" (652), until finally her fate is decided: O'Connor sends her protagonist into the *third circle* of Hell:

> Then like a monumental statue coming to life, she bent her head slowly and gazed, as if through the very heart of mystery, down into the pig parlor at the hogs. They had settled all into one corner around the old sow who was grunting softly. A red glow suffused them. They appeared to pant with a secret life.
>
> (653)

The glassy eyes of the old sow now reflect her own image, not exactly the metaphoric windows, but, more appropriately, the mirrors to her soul. The "red glow," obviously symbolic, envelops the pigs as well as herself, insinuating a shared existence. Already cognizant of the loathsome fate that awaits, Mrs. Turpin recognizes a kindred spirit emanating from the hogs. She empathizes with the "secret life" perceivable within them, the life of a trapped, languid soul, struggling to stand aright, to raise itself from its own filth and muck, as she observes the sow "lying on her side grunting" (651). In the *Inferno* Dante interacts with a shade called Ciacco (Italian for pig), whom he first discovers lying upon his side howling beneath "heavy and accursed rain" (6.8), an image identical to the one O'Connor presents, as Ruby herself provides the "accursed rain" that showers her porcine "soul mates": "Mrs. Turpin stood on the side of the pen, holding the hose and pointing the stream of water at the hindquarters of any shoat . . ." (652).

The difference between Ruby Turpin's situation and that of Rayber lies in the author's attitude toward the characters' potential for rehabilitation. Whereas with Rayber the reader senses definite recidivistic tendencies or foresees no hope at all for spiritual modification—one of those deviants most likely condemned to suffer and die—O'Connor contrarily hints that Mrs. Turpin might genuinely be made to discern the error of her ways. At the story's end the author reveals:

> A visionary light settled in her eyes. She saw the streak as a vast swinging bridge extending upward from the earth through a field of living fire. Upon it a vast horde of souls were rumbling toward heaven. There were whole companies of people. . . . And bringing up the end of the procession was a tribe of people whom she recognized at once as those who, like herself and Claud, had a little of everything and the God-given wit to use it right. . . . They alone were on key. Yet she could see by their shocked and altered faces that even their virtues were being burned away. She lowered her hands and gripped the rail of the hog pen.
>
> (654)

Despite her initial conjecture that only those who replicate her own posture are "on key," Mrs. Turpin reluctantly begins to realize that those qualities which she considers "virtues" may not be thus. And in order to ascend the purgatorial ladder into heaven, she will first have to journey through a pig-laden, spiral-configured hell. Yet again, O'Connor utilizes the metaphorical construct of the dark, uncertain path through the wood: "At length she got down . . . and made her way on the darkening path to the house. In the wood around her the invisible cricket choruses had struck up, but what she heard were the voices of the souls climbing upward. . . ." (654).

The Dantean use of the tornado design does not embody the sole manifestation of this particular form. Defending her "Christian realism" in another letter to A, O'Connor comments, "I believe that there are many rough beasts now slouching toward Bethlehem to be born" (942); therein, she demonstrates her familiarity with the work of William Butler Yeats. Central among Yeats's private, personal symbols is the funnel-shaped gyre.[1] In "The 'Whirling Gyres' of History," Stuart Hirschberg argues:

> Both the "Great Year" and the reversing gyres of history form the conceptual basis for Yeats's grim prophecy of the violence and anarchy he feared would engulf

> the world within in the coming century. But, most importantly, these ideas allowed Yeats to supersede the naïve myth of progress fostered by nineteenth-century England with an ominous and tragically real vision of almost demonic corruption. . . .
>
> (305)

Through his gyres, the poet strives to illustrate a historical cycle that culminates in apocalyptic doom. But these shapes also indicate repetition of time, of life, and, by association, of the human soul. Once destroyed a wayward soul can be reincarnated and given what may optimistically be termed a "second chance." The poem that Yeats entitles simply "The Gyres" traces the destruction of a corrupt "modern" society and its subsequent resurrection. He begins with an apostrophe to "Old Rocky Face": "The gyres! The gyres! Old Rocky Face look forth; / Things thought too long can be no longer thought / For beauty dies of beauty. . . . And ancient lineaments are blotted out" (1-4). Yet even though death and devastation descend upon civilization, the metaphoric light glimmers at the end of the tunnel: "Out of the Cavern comes a voice / And all it knows is that one word 'Rejoice'" (15-16). And alas, "The workman, noble and saint, and all things run / On that unfashionable gyre again" (23-24). Striking a more sanguine note, Hirschberg, in a second article, argues that such gyres, despite their ominous connotation, also foretell a "sequence of regeneration"; they "emphasize the fact that a new cycle ('that unfashionable gyre') will bring forth living and vital personalities" ("Beyond Tragedy" 54). Doesn't O'Connor hope for the "regeneration" of Ruby Turpin's soul? And, anxious to efface the atheistic negativity infecting the world of her novel, that noxious energy which seems inherent to Rayber's character, Flannery O'Connor unveils a highly systematic and cyclic plan of retribution in *The Violent Bear It Away,* ultimately achieving an end comparable to that realized in Yeats's poem. The apocalyptic "tornado" and its "pale messenger" sweep in and eliminate the virulent factor from the scene. Consequently, young Tarwater, thus freed of the schoolteacher, does not hear a voice bellowing "Rejoice" from the hollow of a cave, but in its stead he hears a command: "GO WARN THE CHILDREN OF GOD OF THE TERRIBLE SPEED OF MERCY" (478).

While the spiritual and allegorical dimension of the tornado proves an effective tool for prompting an ethical metamorphosis, the value of the tornado's conventional facet cannot be ignored. In **"The Life You Save May Be Your Own,"** Tom T. Shiftlet must face both the symbolic and practical aspects of the dreaded tornado. His illusions about life and his misconceptions about his place in the world having been shattered (largely due to the vagabond boy's invective: "You go to the devil! . . . My old woman is a flea bag and yours is a stinking pole cat!" [183]), Shiftlet has no alternative but to face the horrifying spiral and, accordingly, to contend with the apocalyptic meaning attached to it. O'Connor's deliberate inclusion of the "devil" reference along with her depiction of the setting sun as a "reddening ball" (182), forecast a bleak future for the itinerant Mr. Shiftlet. Unlike Rayber and Mrs. Turpin, however, Shiftlet clashes with an actual tornado:

> A cloud, the exact color of the boy's hat and shaped like a turnip, had descended over the sun, and another, worse looking, crouched behind the car. Mr. Shiftlet felt that the rottenness of the world was about to engulf him. He raised his arm and let it fall again to his breast. "Oh Lord!" he prayed. "Break forth and wash the slime from this earth!"
>
> The turnip continued slowly to descend. After a few minutes there was a guffawing peal of thunder from behind and fantastic raindrops, like tin-can tops, crashed over the rear of Mr. Shiftlet's car. Very quickly he stepped on the gas and with his stump sticking out the window he raced the galloping shower into Mobile.
>
> (183)

One can plainly see that the theological dimension of this natural disaster looms largely over the scene. The image of the tornado descending "over the sun" quite overtly directs attention to the spiritual referent. But this passage, more than any other, allows the reader to envision a raging storm, the mammoth raindrops, the treacherous winds. Proffering not just a passing mention of the tornado as symbol, the author energetically draws the reader into the chaos of the explosive tempest. Shiftlet demands that the slime be eradicated from the world; ironically, it is he who will imminently be washed from the earth. Howling at the cosmos, his inept stump of an arm beating feebly against his chest, Shiftlet challenges, as the text denotes, both the "galloping storm" and God Himself. When one considers tornado as storm, this particular episode recalls another infamous scene in which the character, diminutive and pitiful beneath the awesomeness of Nature's fury, stumbles helplessly about beckoning for the rains to batter him harder, for the winds to attack him with greater ferocity:

> Blow winds, and crack your cheeks! Rage! blow!
> You cataracts and hurricanes, spout
> Till you have drench'd our steeples, drown'd the cocks!
>
> . . . . .
>
> Rumble thy bellyful! Spit, fire! spout rain!
>
> (*King Lear* 3.2. 1-14)

King Lear, at this point in the drama, arrives at the nadir of his mental and spiritual self—he has at last come to the City of Dis. The storm reproduces the character's personality as hitherto seen in the play: a raging despot who whirls in, conducts life-altering business, and then slowly begins to wane and weaken, until he is all but insignificant. Analogously, Mr. Shiftlet mirrors the storm that engulfs him; blowing into the lives of the Lucynell Craters, whisking the daughter away, provoking great commotion and change, and yet he has only to fade into inconsequentiality. Contrary to Lear on the heath, however, Shiftlet's storm, like his life, seems pathetic and even ridiculous. O'Connor delineates the looming tornado cloud not as magnificent or overpowering but as a turnip.

In yet another of her illustrious letters to A, O'Connor articulates: "I believe that the fiction writer's moral sense must coincide with his dramatic sense" (975). A flare for the dramatic is certainly something one ascribes to Flannery O'Connor. And in analyzing the above statement, reading audiences begin to understand more clearly the nature of her elaborate plots, her stories of near surreal violence, and her dramatic, retributive machines. She detests what she calls the "noxious gases of nihilism." She mourns the declining intrinsic worth of the human species. And yet, deep down she hopes that this species can ultimately be saved. Creations such as Rayber, Mrs. Turpin, and Mr. Shiftlet perhaps function as O'Connor's punching bags, as means to alleviate her pent-up anger and disquietude. The tornadic system offers a volatile, larger-than-life, yet compact (in its multi-dimensionality) method of contending with errant souls. As Dante and Yeats employ it, this shape functions as a harbinger of new beginnings, be they spiritual or historical. Dissatisfied with the skepticism and sorrow indigenous to her world, all Flannery O'Connor seems to be searching for are new beginnings.

Note

I would like to thank Linda Rohrer Paige. This essay would not have been possible without her guidance and wisdom.

1. Yeats's mystical prose work, *A Vision,* outlines the function, origin, and placement of gyres in his poetry. He explains, "I shall consider the gyre . . . for the sake of simplicity, as the whole of human life . . . and the contrasting cone . . . as the 'spiritual objective'" (210).

Works Cited

Alighieri, Dante. *The Divine Comedy: Inferno.* Trans. Allen Mandelbaum. New York: Bantam, 1980.

Eggenschwiler, David. *The Christian Humanism of Flannery O'Connor.* Detroit: Wayne State UP, 1972.

Fickett, Harold, and Douglas R. Gilbert. *Flannery O'Connor: Images of Grace.* Grand Rapids, MI: Eerdman's, 1986.

Gerald, Kelly S. "Thank God for the Shoe!: The Emblematic Shoe in O'Connor's Fiction." *Flannery O'Connor Bulletin* 23 (1994-95): 91-118.

Hirschberg, Stuart. "Beyond Tragedy: Yeats's View of History in 'The Gyres.'" *Research Studies* 42 (1974): 50-55.

———. "The Whirling Gyres of History." *Studies in Irish Literature* 68.1 (1979): 305-14.

Johansen, Ruthann. *The Narrative Secret of Flannery O'Connor.* Tuscaloosa: U of Alabama P, 1994.

O'Connor, Flannery. *Collected Works.* Ed. Sally Fitzgerald. New York: Library of America, 1988.

Scouten, Kenneth B. "The Schoolteacher as Devil in *The Violent Bear it Away.*" *Flannery O'Connor Bulletin* 12 (1983): 35-46.

Shakespeare, William. *King Lear. The Riverside Shakespeare.* Ed. G. Blakemore Evans. Boston: Houghton, 1974. 1249-1305.

Shapiro, Marianne. *Dante and the Knot of Body and Soul.* New York: St. Martin's, 1998.

Yeats, William Butler. *A Vision.* Rev. ed. New York: Macmillan, 1969.

———. "The Gyres." *The Poems: A New Edition.* Ed. Richard J. Finneran. New York: Macmillan, 1988. 321.

Jeffrey J. Folks (essay date spring 2003)

SOURCE: Folks, Jeffrey J. "Telos and Existence: Ethics in C. S. Lewis's Space Trilogy and Flannery O'Connor's *Everything That Rises Must Converge.*" *Southern Literary Journal* 35, no. 2 (spring 2003): 107-18.

[*In the following essay, Folks compares the treatment of modern secularism in* Everything That Rises Must Converge *with that in C. S. Lewis's novels, highlighting the model of contemplative living endorsed by both authors.*]

Within Western culture, narrative literature has always been the means by which people have understood the nature of the human condition and the shape of their lives. Through storytelling, as Alasdair MacIntyre explains in *After Virtue: A Study in Moral Theory,* readers or listeners gain a consciousness of their humanity and an understanding of their cultural traditions. The ethical value of literature lies in its ability to help readers consider, more than they otherwise might, the consequences of their choices and those of others. Most important, ethical reading focuses attention on the particular "shape" and telos of life; it encourages readers to imagine the bounded potential of human existence.

As Christian authors, C. S. Lewis and Flannery O'Connor wrote from within an antagonistic cultural context of twentieth-century secular humanism. Within this milieu, Lewis and O'Connor had to assume that many of their readers would, at the very least, respond skeptically to their reassertion of orthodox Christian dogma. In some cases, as in the harsh contemporary reviews of Lewis's work by liberal critics such as Q. D. Leavis or L. C. Knights, the reaction went far beyond skepticism: it reflected an uncompromising refusal to consider the role of spirituality in human existence. In his review of Lewis's *Rehabilitations,* for example, Knights wrote that Lewis "brings much needed support to those who wish to be confirmed in certain complacent attitudes" (92). Given the context of philosophical skepticism in which Lewis and O'Connor wrote, it is understandable that they would find it necessary to begin with fundamental matters, such as the ethical implications of the human condition of mortality and the value of the spiritual life over materialism or utilitarianism.

From within the Western tradition of classical-Christian thought, Lewis and O'Connor both viewed human nature and human society as innately corrupt, permeated with human selfishness, ignorance, and destructiveness, and both believed that within this earthly wasteland, human systems of ethics were ultimately ineffectual. Human society could approach an ethical condition only through the redemption of individuals. Since this moral revolution could not rely on collective action, both Lewis and O'Connor are skeptical concerning humanistic theories of ethics. From their point of view, humanistic approaches to ethics invariably devolve into self-interested action since they lack a point of moral reference outside of human nature (in this respect, Lewis and O'Connor write within the Aristotelian and Augustinian tradition in which, as MacIntyre points out in *Whose Justice? Which Rationality?,* an ethics of virtue is contrasted with the ethics of effectiveness). The very tendency of ethical philosophy to revert to moralistic discourse is the result of a human-centered philosophy in which power and ego always come to the fore and must be restrained by social pressure.

At this general level, Lewis and O'Connor are in complete agreement, and we should not discount the importance of how unusual they both were among modern writers in their unwavering defense of an orthodox Christian faith. If for no other reason, their works can be linked because they stood unflinchingly for the same set of beliefs and in opposition to the same intellectuals falsehoods.[1] On a more particular level, of course, some important differences of emphasis or methodology can be detected in their ethical positions. Lewis's valuation of humility (for example, the "duty" for a writer of "being derivative" rather than "original") contrasts with a more pronounced tension between self-effacement and self-assertion in O'Connor's writing. Lewis writes in "Christianity and Literature" that we are "mirrors" reflecting divine light: "'Originality' in the New Testament is quite plainly the prerogative of God alone; even within the triune being of God it seems to be confined to the Father. The duty and happiness of every other being is placed in being derivative, in reflecting like a mirror" (*Rehabilitations* 191). Lewis's emphasis on the "fatherly" nature of Christ's relationship to mankind has fundamental implications for his theory of ethics, as well as for his aesthetic theory, in which it counters the romantic conception of the "creative genius" and the value of originality in art. In terms of everyday conduct, it implies the need for modesty and self-restraint, and an appreciation of the limits of science and other forms of humanistic knowledge, key thematic elements in *Out of the Silent Planet, Perelandra,* and *That Hideous Strength.* "Our whole destiny seems to lie . . . in being as little as possible ourselves," Lewis writes (*Rehabilitations* 191).[2]

The destructive "originality" of proud romantic idealists is also stressed in several memorable stories in ***Everything That Rises Must Converge,*** including **"The Lame Shall Enter First," "The Enduring Chill,"** and the title story from the collection, yet O'Connor privileges other figures who undertake a vocation of "prophecy" that involves an unabashed assertion of self as an agent of divine will. Such a role, entailing the potential for martyrdom and sainthood, necessarily involves the temptation of pride, as Geoffrey Galt Harpham demonstrates convincingly in *The Ascetic Imperative in Culture and Criticism.*[3] As many critics have noted, O'Connor seems to be temperamentally committed to extreme forms of individualism and self-assertion,[4] and various sorts of violence are often connected with those moments in which her characters become receptive to grace. Recognition of the divine comes at radical moments of terror or death, a spectacular conception of moral transformation that differs from the moments of "testing" in Lewis's writing, for generally in these moments Lewis's characters are not redeemed from utter corruption but reconfirmed in the moral education that they have received in their upbringing. This does not imply that Lewis's Christianity was any less decisive than O'Connor's (as Dr. Ransom informs Jane Studdock, "there's no niche in the world for people that won't be either Pagan or Christian" [*Hideous* 315]), but it does reflect a different emphasis in the conception of ethical being. Unlike Lewis's protagonist in the space trilogy, who finds his instinctual tendency toward virtue confirmed in those segments of British society in which traditional "good sense" and moderation still prevail, O'Connor's prophetic characters are outcasts within the more thoroughly alienated and morally heedless society of postwar America. Certainly, Lewis's trilogy includes scenes of great violence, such as the carnage unleashed by Merlin in Chapter 16 ("Banquet at Belbury") of *That Hideous Strength,* yet the calm reserve and self-assurance of his protagonist is connected with Lewis's conception of the limited effectiveness of particular agents. By contrast, O'Connor's prophets shoulder the burden of their special knowledge and their role as agents of salvation (one notes the different physical aspect of these personae: Lewis's Dr. Ransom exhibits "mild, but strongly formidable glances" [*Perelandra* 22] while O'Connor's Rufus Johnson is "fierce" and "fanatic" in expression [***Works*** (***Collected Works***) 599]. In a letter to "A." of 28 August 1955, O'Connor admitted the severity of her temperament and connected in an interesting way to her youth (she was just thirty at the time, twenty-six years younger than Lewis): "I suppose the fullest writing comes from what has been accepted and experienced both and that I have just not got that far yet all the time. Conviction without experience makes for harshness" (***Works*** 949).

Another point of difference involves Lewis's Aristotelian conception of the "educated reader," one who has the experience, as he wrote in "High and Low Brows," to make possible a "spontaneous delight in excellence" (*Rehabilitations* 114). In Lewis's view, ethical understanding depends on one's upbringing within and in relation to the particular community from which one inherits values and tastes. Lewis's heroic figures are Christians whose faith is molded by a cultural tradition that includes classicism and medieval scholasticism and by the particular form that this tradition took in its historical development within Britain. O'Connor's characters find their basis for ethics more directly in the authority of scripture rather than in knowledge that is embodied within a particular culture. Because of her sense of the chasm between historical and spiritual existence, O'Connor employs her characters, often uneducated southern poor whites, in romance narratives in which there is a startling disconnection between the allegorical point of a character's action and its literal meaning: Rufus Johnson is at the same time a wise conduit of ethical knowledge and a malevolent criminal. As a Catholic author, O'Connor stands outside the local culture of southern fundamentalism that she employs as the primary matter for her fiction. As O'Connor wrote in "The Fiction Writer and His Country," "To know oneself is to know one's region. It is also to know the world, and it is also, paradoxically, a form of remoteness from that world" (***Works*** 806). Every Christian probably experiences some feeling of estrangement from temporal affairs, but not to the extent that O'Connor expresses. In Lewis's case, even with the travail of college politics, a long and difficult relationship with Mrs. Moore, his brother's alcoholism, and other burdens, he generally manifests a greater contentment with earthly existence. The beauty of nature and the common pleasures of eating and drinking are frequent themes in his writing.

These differences of disposition and emphasis might seem to separate Lewis and O'Connor were it not for the parallel role that these authors played, albeit within different literary contexts and periods, of reviving Christian narrative for a large audience of contemporary readers. Among mid twentieth-century British writers, no one was as important as Lewis in this work; among postwar American writers, O'Connor occupies the same position. Lewis and O'Connor devoted their lives to the task of preserving the Christian tradition, addressing their work to readers who were at risk of abandoning it as well as to those who were not. In the course of this defense, they asserted ethical principles that flew in the face of prevailing theories of ethics, for their conception required belief in a purposeful creation with both individual life and collective human history enacted within the bounds of a divine plan. From this perspective, human life is understood to be integral, meaningful, and purposeful so that, in terms of ethics, each moment of human life involves moral choice guided by an understanding of the end or telos of existence. The fact that ethical action involves choice also implies that while a true ethics cannot be conceived in relativist terms, neither can it be based on a simple set of fixed rules. Both Lewis and O'Connor understood that Christian ethics does not imply a prescriptive morality that would absolve human beings of moral choice: rather, the basis of their ethics lies in the transformative power of the religious experience itself as this experience leads the believer toward selfless and purposeful action.

In his opposition of natural versus legal justice, Aristotle pointed to a crucial distinction: some principles of justice are universal ("by nature"), varying little if at all from one society to another and reflecting an integral relationship between social and biological orders of existence; other matters of "positive" justice result from human legislation that varies from state to state. In Aristotle's view, the recognition of natural law is fundamental to human happiness since the constant deliberation of ends is a fatal impediment to moral action. Similarly, Lewis taught that fundamental ethical principles were universal and grounded in nature, reflecting the unchanging and natural structure of existence, and in *The Abolition of Man* he insisted that such first principles must be accepted as part of human nature: "It is no use trying to 'see through' first principles. . . . To 'see through' all things is the same as not to see" (48). Lewis's protagonist in the space trilogy, Professor Elwin Ransom, is a character who understands the dangers of thoroughgoing philosophical skepticism although he is also, at first, reluctant to commit his life fully to virtue. In a crucial passage in *Perelandra* at the point at which Ransom must decide to risk his life in opposing the seemingly invincible power of Weston, Lewis evokes the decisive moment of ethical choice, hinging on whether the individual will accept the truth that a single life is always of infinite value in the sight of God: "Either something or nothing must depend on individual choices. And if something, who could set bounds to it? A stone may determine the course of a river. He was that stone at this horrible moment which had become the centre of the whole universe" (142).[5] At the moment when he recognizes that his own resistance stands between God's love and his happiness, Ransom becomes an agent of moral action: he is instantly freed but also instantly bound by the necessity of moral choice.[6]

Rejecting natural virtue, Weston informs Ransom that good and evil "are only moments in the single, unique reality. The world leaps forward through great men and greatness always transcends mere moralism" (95).[7] The grandiose dream of freedom and power that Weston describes is, of course, a false promise: once we give up the distinction between good and evil, the world becomes infinitely small, not large. In the first two volumes of the space trilogy, Lewis demonstrates how Weston's ethical position evolves toward this point of Faustian arrogance. Initially the "great physicist" who appears to have his eyes closed to all of reality beyond scientific research, Weston becomes a dangerous fanatic whose extremism usurps all genuine devotion to science, as we see in his willingness to sacrifice life to his research. Weston's "solemn scientific idealism" (*Silent Planet* 30) at the beginning of the trilogy develops into a "fatal," death-oriented motive focused on power and ego. What Weston lacks from beginning to end is a sense of humility that would open his feelings toward the suffering of his fellow creatures, or even toward his own mortality. Lacking Ransom's curiosity and concern, Weston is incapable of looking and listening except in so far as he is gathering data for his experiments, and thus he misses both the beauty of the Malacandran and Perelandran landscapes and the virtues of their inhabitants, as well as the potential beauty and virtue of Earth and its people. Lewis's presentation of Weston is an implicit critique of the moral failing of science, and more broadly of all humanistic learning, when it is set up as self-sufficient, for by itself scientific experimentation can never arrive at first principles.

In his contrast of Ransom and Weston, Lewis conveys not only that the "pure" scientist is unfeeling and potentially brutal but also points up the impoverishment of his or her mental life: all of the new qualities of experience—aesthetic, linguistic, emotional, and intellectual—that Ransom enjoys on his journeys to Malacandra and Perelandra are lost on Weston, who never departs from his plan of imposing the rigid framework of experimental science on all of creation. Although Weston is not wanting in courage or intelligence, Lewis stresses the severe limitations of Weston's character that leave him morally unsound: his pride, his self-sufficiency, and his cynicism. Despite his capability as a scientist, Weston has "the mind of an animal," and his mind is filled with "fear and death and desire" (*Silent Planet* 134), as Oyarsa informs him. In response, Weston reveals that he believes that the advancement of human civilization justifies any action that would conventionally be termed "immoral," for as the servant of "Life" he feels justified in any act of violence or coercion. In fact, it is because he is a selfless true believer, full of "loyalty to humanity" (*Silent* 138), that Weston is especially dangerous (as Lewis implies in his conception of Weston, not Devine, as Ransom's primary antagonist in the first two volumes of the trilogy), for Weston's devotion to this one "good" encourages him to discard all other virtues.

In the final volume of the trilogy, Lewis reveals other types of ethical failing among Weston's associates, from the featureless determinism of Frost to the opportunistic cunning of Feverstone. In the evolution from Weston's devotion to experimental science to the Progressive Element at Edgestow College and the secretive authoritarian society at Belbury, Lewis provides a sense of the range and practical tendencies of modern secular ethics, and this evaluation finds a close parallel in O'Connor's treatment of ethics in ***Everything That Rises Must Converge.*** Like Weston, the character of Sheppard in **"The Lame Shall Enter First"** is blinded by his idolatry of science. As Richard Giannone points out, Sheppard "buys the telescope and microscope to instruct the two boys [his son Norton and his temporary ward, Rufus Johnson] about the enormous and minute aspects of the cosmos, in the belief that everything there is can be seen and everything that can be seen is explainable" (209). The ethical consequences of this materialistic philosophy—confusion, fear, and the loss of freedom—are made apparent in the course of O'Connor's story, for in this allegory of the soul's neglect we are forced to examine the radical condition of loss at the heart of genuine human love. Among the many forms of suffering that are present in O'Connor's fiction, the worst is the condition of spiritual torment resulting from the denial of God's love. To deny the worth of oneself and others and to ignore the worth of the created world is to reject the basis for loving communion, yet, as both

Lewis and O'Connor make clear, "love for others," in and of itself and without a basis in religious thought, is limited as an ethical and spiritual agent. Those characters in O'Connor's fiction, such as Sheppard, who "love deeply" while at the same time denying the need for grace are often seen to engage in a destructive and narcissistic form of "love." "The natural loves are not self-sufficient," Lewis writes in *The Four Loves*. "Something else, at first vaguely described as 'decency and common sense,' but later revealed as goodness, and finally as the whole Christian life in one particular relation, must come to the help of the mere feeling if the feeling is to be kept sweet" (116). Without knowledge of the foundation of love, the agonized sufferer is open to the worst sorts of misunderstanding, often taking the form of a travesty of religious belief.

Few characters in O'Connor's fiction understand this inadequacy better than Rufus Johnson, the lame young delinquent whom Sheppard is determined to "rescue" for society. Rufus knows that his physical handicap has nothing to do with his delinquency since, unlike his agnostic guardian who believes in an utterly deterministic universe, Rufus has made an ethical choice, albeit a choice of evil. One of the searing ironies of O'Connor's story is the fact that Sheppard's faith in scientific "progress" leads nowhere, for, like Weston's belief in experimental research as practically an end in itself, it is a misguided effort to substitute scientific method for a religious conception of telos. As Giannone puts it: "Neither heaven nor hell awaits the space age. Death no longer reveals human destiny" (205). Underlying his indifference toward his son Norton and his mistaken affection for Rufus Johnson is Sheppard's greater failure of love—his rejection of divine love in favor of a bleak, empty, and fruitless vision of a universe without telos.[8]

In her late story **"Revelation,"** O'Connor dramatizes an awakening of spiritual and moral understanding in a character who resists the gift of God's love and the acknowledgment of life's value that accompanies it. In much the same way that Lewis's narrative builds on metaphors of "size" to convey the scale of ethical consequences, O'Connor's story employs figures of size to express both the overblown self-assurance of humanistic philosophy and the true scale of plenitude following the experience of "revelation." Struggling to escape the imprisonment of her obese body and of her opinionated mind, Ruby Turpin's soul follows its natural path toward goodness and beauty. While Ruby may at first appear entirely obdurate—in John R. May's phrase, she "begrudges every inch of self she must yield to reevaluation" (115)—her closed-minded resistance to the truth is, on another level, testimony to her unconscious awareness of the daunting task of change that lies before her. Ruby's urgency to distinguish "the classes of people," an activity that has her focusing on the skin, the clothing, and the feet, but not on the soul, culminates in a Holocaust nightmare with the different classes "all crammed together in a box car, being ridden off to be put in a gas oven" (***Works*** 636). In the religious awakening that underlies Ruby's nightmare vision, her social biases are subsumed within an entirely different order of value. From an abstract, deathless world of self, in which petty social distinctions of the sort Ruby practices can have meaning, Ruby's midnight imagination transports her to the greater knowledge of a world that must end in death. Although she resists with every ounce of her reason, Ruby is compelled by her greater longing to open her heart to the worth of God's creation. Despite her self-centered resistance, Ruby possesses the "common sense," as Lewis might put it, to recognize the impoverishment of her own existence, based as it is on continual negation of the value of others.

The catalyst for Ruby's revelation is the attack on her by Mary Grace, the "ugly girl" whose smoldering and blazing eyes, looking "directly through" her, awaken Ruby to her own callousness and selfishness. As Mary Grace's act of hurling a copy of *Human Development* at her implies, Ruby's belittling defensiveness has its origin in a fear of or resistance to development, an unwillingness to acknowledge the spiritual and moral dimensions of which she, and all human beings, are capable. Ruby's denial of her potential is tied to fear of self-relinquishment: inordinately bound to her oversized physical self and to her grandiose if illusory social status, Ruby has closed herself off from the greater happiness of loving communion. Her hypocrisy and defensiveness are symptoms of a greater underlying malaise—the misguided belief in human self-sufficiency suggested by "the great empty drum of flesh" in which after Mary Grace's attack her troubled heart "swings from side to side" (***Works*** 645). The girl's charge that Ruby is a "wart hog from hell" is the decisive element in forcing Ruby to examine herself, as she finally exclaims to God: "How am I a hog and me both? How am I saved and from hell too?" (652). In her recognition of sin and death, Ruby begins to receive the "abysmal life-giving knowledge" (653) that will transform her vision. The story concludes with a joyful image of "souls climbing upward" (654), a vision of spiritual development that implies an ethical transformation as well, as Ruby's final account of the order of the procession of souls to heaven, with its restoration of justice and charity, makes clear. In its ending, **"Revelation"** provides O'Connor's most exact narrative embodiment of her understanding of the redemptive force of Christ's presence in the world. The ethical implication, in terms of

Ruby's new capacity to resist the temptation to "size up" her fellow humans, is a crucial aspect of O'Connor's story, comparable to what Scott Oury sees as the "key" to Lewis's thinking: "his attention and commitment to the value of somebody other than himself" (2).

At the end of *Perelandra,* Ransom, like Ruby Turpin, admits to having lived in "shadows and broken images" during his previous life on earth, and, in one of the most beautiful passages in the novel, he eloquently pleads to the King and Queen of Perelandra: "Take me for your son. We have been alone in my world for a great time" (205). In the "conversation" that follows, Ransom receives explicit teaching concerning the nature of existence, and in this teaching Lewis emphatically rejects modern ethical philosophy's collective diminishment of the individual and its devaluing of human life. As one of the unidentified "voices" tells Ransom: "It is not as in a city of the Darkened World where they say that each must live for all. In His city all things are made for each. When he died in the Wounded World He died not for men, but for each man" (217). The divine order that Lewis envisages, far from being a condition of moral rigidity, is a luxurious and sensuous realm of plenitude and joy. One of the ironies underlying Lewis's depiction of modern society is that, while it promises so much in the way of self-aggrandizement and liberated pleasure, it delivers so little. Indeed, the philosophy of secular humanism that promises a utopia of liberation and progress ends, in the view of Lewis and O'Connor, in suffering and death.

Aristotle, we should recall, began his study of ethics with the fundamental assertion that the "Good for Man" is "happiness," a condition of "living well and faring well" (I.4.5). By the end of Book Ten of *Nicomachean Ethics,* Aristotle leads us to understand that happiness consists not of pleasure, wealth, or power—the motives that Lewis explicitly rejects and that O'Connor satirizes in such stories as **"Revelation," "A View of the Woods,"** and **"Greenleaf"** in ***Everything That Rises Must Converge***—but of "the contemplative life" (X.7.263). As David Ross points out in his "Introduction" to the *Ethics,* contemplation in Aristotle's view is "the best activity of which we are capable. . . . It brings pleasures of wonderful purity and stability. . . . It is the life we ascribe to the gods" (xxii-xxiii).

In the writing of Lewis and O'Connor, a contemplative life of a similar order is the basis for a development of spiritual understanding that necessarily leads the believer, as witness or prophet, back into the troubled moral order of human society. The Aristotelian conception of telos, of life's purpose as at once contemplative and active, accords with the sort of ecstatic mission that Lewis and O'Connor envision for their fictional protagonists. It is precisely the sort of zealous joy, grounded in an embrace of divine love, which Lewis envisions in Ransom's conversation with the King and Queen at the conclusion of *Perelandra* and in Jane Studdock's anticipation of reunion with her husband at the conclusion of *That Hideous Strength.* In **"Revelation,"** O'Connor foresees the same joyful future for Ruby Turpin following her painful recognition of her own guilty and needful condition in relation to God's love. In the works of both writers, we are presented with characters whose ability to find happiness is contingent on their understanding of their need and willingness to accept divine grace. Finding the best way to live, Lewis and O'Connor knew, did indeed depend on the attainment of a contemplative relationship to God.

Notes

1. There is little indication of any direct influence of Lewis on O'Connor's work, but at the very end of her life Flannery O'Connor was reading a book that she "had tried to get hold of" for some time: C. S. Lewis's *Miracles* (Letter to Janet McKane [25 Feb. 1963] in O'Connor, *Works* 1178). Although O'Connor rarely mentioned Lewis in her letters or critical writing, it would seem from her seeking out his book in particular at this point that she had been familiar with his writing for some time.

2. In *The Great Divorce* (New York: Touchstone, 1996), Lewis comments on the corruption of the aesthetic sense in the artist who creates "for art's sake," for fame or riches, or for anything other than for the proper end of art: the glory of God. "Every poet and musician and artist, but for Grace, is drawn away from love of the thing he tells, to love of the telling till, down in Deep Hell, they cannot be interested in God at all but only in what they say about Him. For it doesn't stop at being interested in paint, you know. They sink lower—become interested in their own personalities and then in nothing but their own reputations" (80). The "love of the thing he tells"—for the Christian artist, the contemplation and celebration of the divine creation and plan—must be the constant focus of art, not the "paint" (read "technique" or, for the poststructuralist, "linguistic play") or the "reputation."

3. For a discussion of the relevance of Harpham's book to O'Connor's writing, see Robert H. Brinkmeyer, Jr., "Asceticism and the Imaginative Vision of Flannery O'Connor," *Flannery O'Connor: New Perspectives,* Ed. Sura Prasad Rath and Mary Neff Shaw (Athens: U of Georgia P, 1996), 169-182.

4. See Marshall Bruce Gentry, *Flannery O'Connor's Religion of the Grotesque* (Jackson: UP of Mississippi, 1986); Claire Katz, "Flannery O'Connor's Rage of Vision," *American Literature* 46 (1974): 54-67; and Edward Kessler, *Flannery O'Connor and the Language of Apocalypse* (Princeton: Princeton UP, 1986).

5. In a gross misreading of Lewis's fiction, David Holbrook interprets such decisive moments of moral action as mere "aggressiveness." See *The Skeleton in the Wardrobe: C. S. Lewis's Fantasies: A Phenomenological Study* (Lewisburg, PA: Bucknell UP, 1991), 19. Because he fails to acknowledge the consequences of relativism, Holbrook does not appear to understand the symbolic point of Ransom's "violent" resistance to Weston's diabolism. Holbrook's argument, which at one point refers to lying, deceit, greed, or selfishness of children as "very petty matters" (272), comes down to the question of whether *any* action can be defined as unqualified, objective evil. Holbrook's blanket assertion "that Lewis felt that to be human was a poor thing" (282) is of course partly true, but it ignores the larger framework of Christian belief within which human corruption is redeemed by divine love.

6. It is exactly this moment of freedom and commitment that O'Connor often conveys through the metaphor of "ice"—the "icy" sense of giving up one's limitation to self and embracing a purposeful but selfless role in creation.

7. In *Planets in Peril: A Critical Study of C. S. Lewis's Ransom Trilogy* (Amherst: U of Massachusetts P, 1992), David C. Downing provides an excellent summary of the "common traits" that Lewis's evil characters, such as Weston, share: "They set aside ordinary morality in favor of utility or in favor of some lofty, abstract goals for humanity; they disregard the sanctity of life, whether human or animal; they are 'progressive' and find little value in history, tradition, or the classics; they prefer the scientific, artificial, and industrial over the simple and the natural; they use language to conceal and distort reality, rather than to reveal it" (84).

8. Sheppard is a representative of moral relativism of a sort prevalent in the social sciences. One such real-life social scientist, Leonard W. Doob, characterizes his position of skepticism concerning objective ethical values in terms similar to those one might imagine for Sheppard. In *Slightly Beyond Skepticism: Social Science and the Search for Morality* (New Haven: Yale UP, 1987), Doob writes: "I am convinced that we cannot find a simple value or theory that is useful or applicable to all the different 'domains' in which moral judgments are passed. . . . All knowledge perforce, in short, is tentative; deviations and exceptions to almost all propositions is [sic] almost always to be anticipated" (8).

Works Cited

Aristotle. *The Nicomachean Ethics.* Trans. David Ross. Oxford and New York: Oxford UP, 1998.

Giannone, Richard. *Flannery O'Connor and the Mystery of Love.* New York: Fordham UP, 1999.

Knights, L. C. "Review of *Rehabilitations* by C. S. Lewis." *Scrutiny* 8 (1939): 88-92.

Lewis, C. S. *The Abolition of Man.* 1943. New York: Collins, 1978.

———. *The Four Loves.* 1960. New York: Harvest, 1991.

———. *Out of the Silent Planet.* 1943. New York: Scribner, 1996.

———. *Perelandra: A Novel.* 1944. New York: Macmillan, 1965.

———. *Rehabilitations and Other Essays.* London: Oxford UP, 1939.

———. *That Hideous Strength: A Modern Fairy-Tale for Grown-Ups.* 1945. New York: Scribner, 1996.

May, John R. *The Pruning Word: The Parables of Flannery O'Connor.* South Bend: U of Notre Dame P, 1976.

O'Connor, Flannery. *Collected Works.* New York: Library of America, 1988.

Oury, Scott. "'The Thing Itself': C. S. Lewis and the Value of Something Other." *The Longing for a Form.* Ed. Peter J. Schakel. Kent, OH: Kent State UP, 1977.

Ross, David. "Introduction." *The Nicomachean Ethics.* By Aristotle. Trans. David Ross. Oxford and New York: Oxford UP, 1998. v-xxiv.

Jeanne Perreault (essay date summer 2003)

SOURCE: Perreault, Jeanne. "The Body, the Critics, and 'The Artificial Nigger.'" *Mississippi Quarterly* 56, no. 3 (summer 2003): 389-410.

[*In the following essay, Perreault contends that the intimidating—yet maternal—physical presence of the black woman encountered by Nelson in "The Artificial Nigger" echoes O'Connor's prevailing concern with the unification of the body and the spirit.*]

Flannery O'Connor's stories provide some of the most penetrating dissections of white solipsism that American literature has to offer.[1] Of the many stories that include overt white perspectives on race, **"The Artificial Nigger"** is arguably the most complex and perplexing. Flannery O'Connor declared that **"The Artificial Nigger"** was her own "favourite story,"[2] and critics concurred, many seeing it as one of her "best" stories.[3] O'Connor does not explain why this story was her favorite; indeed, she had some trouble with it and had to write **"The Artificial Nigger"** "a good many times" (*Habit,* p. 78). Although she says that "it is the best thing I will ever write" (p. 209), O'Connor seems to puzzle over the story's resistance: "I have often had the experience of finding myself not as adequate to the situation as I thought I would be, but there turned out to be a great deal more to that story than just that" (pp. 100-101). The rather awkward phrasing of this comment suggests that her entanglement with this story lay not only or merely in her own limitations but in something unruly within the story itself. Most critical discussion of the story seems untroubled by such doubts, and few of the many published papers on it express discomfort with the happy reconciliation of Mr. Head with God and with his grandson, Nelson. O'Connor herself does not elaborate on what trouble in the story is "a great deal more" than her own inadequacy. Here, I want to suggest that **"The Artificial Nigger"** vexed O'Connor with a subtle contradiction: by attributing "body" to the "large colored woman" for the purpose of the spiritual development of the white boy,[4] O'Connor subverts her own deeply held belief in the necessity of unifying body and spirit for true spiritual integrity.

O'Connor sets the socio-political aspects of **"The Artificial Nigger"** alongside a discussion of her view that spiritual redemption requires redemption of the body. When she says "there is nothing that screams out the tragedy of the South like what my uncle calls 'nigger statuary'" (*Habit,* p. 101), she makes one of the few comments that demonstrate that she sees the South as tragic, and that the tragedy is specifically based in racial injustice. For O'Connor, social dynamics are metonymic of spirit and of body. Her observation of the "tragedy of the South" is not part of a conversation about a political or moral issue but rather is made in the context of a discussion of "Christ as God and man" (p. 100). For O'Connor salvation means that "flesh and spirit [are] united in peace" (p. 100). The mystery of the body (not designated black or white, male or female) is how it is to be united with spirit, not how it can be reconciled in social justice.[5] This concern for the embodied spirit is her obsession, apparent in her many stories in which the afflicted flesh is a precious and prized manifestation, the outward and visible sign of an inward, spiritual encounter.

Her Catholicism demands a reconciliation of spirit with body, but for O'Connor neither body nor spirit can be abstracted from its material, social condition. Repeatedly, O'Connor's characters confront that embodied materiality, leaving the reader with a collection of wooden legs, tattoos, club feet, and corpses, and very occasionally, as in **"The Artificial Nigger,"** a material object that produces the impression of reconciliation. But in **"The Artificial Nigger"** her representation of that inner and outer reconciliation is fraught with ambivalence. I believe that O'Connor's willingness to use "a large colored woman" (p. 262) to effect spiritual healing reproduces a white imaginary and makes the conclusion a representation of unredeemed failure.

Mr. Head must take Nelson to the city to teach him to be a white man and, rather than being an instrument of grace, the Negro statuary crystallizes the place of white maleness crucial to the "action of mercy" Mr. Head feels (p. 269).[6] O'Connor reiterates the profound displacement of body onto the figure of the black woman, and thus makes her the bearer of hope and possibility for the white characters. Part of the reason this story continues to fascinate is the contradiction that O'Connor settles on: racial prejudice is arbitrary and unnatural, yet the story positions that crucial black character primarily in terms of her spiritual usefulness to whites. Since body and spirit must be united for salvation to occur, displacing "body" onto the black woman and relegating the character to a mere function suggests she can provide the embodiment the white male characters lack.

O'Connor's literary and religious passion coheres in her commitment to the "resurrection of the body" as "the Essential" (*Habit,* p. 227), the bedrock of her faith. She argues that the "laws of the flesh" exist in their true form in the Christian mysteries: "The Virgin Birth, the Incarnation, the Resurrection" (p. 100).[7] She inverts a secular reading of the "laws of the flesh," which are commonly held to be the implacable ravages of time on the body, the fateful incursions of disease, or the brute fact of death. O'Connor insists that "Death, decay, destruction" are "the suspension" rather than the manifestation of the laws of the flesh (p. 100). Only because the unity of body and spirit has been disrupted (in the Fall of Man) are human beings subjected to suffering, and only through the reunification of flesh and body, as in the Christian mysteries, can they be saved. Examining the specific representations of the characters' bodies and the semiotic fields they inhabit and manifest shows the location and dislocation of O'Connor's hopes for the flesh. In **"The Artificial Nigger"** the *appearance* of flesh and spirit brought into peaceful unity is complete for the characters, while in fact Mr. Head fulfills his intention to ensure the divisions of body from body (black from white, male from female) that reassure him of his place in the world. The unity of white male only with white male excludes the possibility of spiritual integrity.

The country home, the city streets, and the bodies of the characters are thoroughly inscribed by Mr. Head with specific meanings that will determine for Nelson and himself their place in the universe. While Mr. Head is obsessed with fixing place, dividing light from dark, upper from lower, the story itself works against the secure places of his divisions. In contrast to the view that the statue he names an "artificial nigger" offers a moment of salvation, I see it as the element that finally cements Mr. Head's sure place in his desired world.[8] That statuary is of course created by white residents and used by them as one of the ways white consciousness articulates itself, which is exactly how Mr. Head uses it: Mr. Head has to take Nelson to the city in order to show him that he is white. Because the last African American had been "run out" of their county twelve years earlier (p. 252), Nelson is lacking in the essential training he needs to take his place as a white man. Some critics have looked at the issue of O'Connor's view of "Negroes" in order to examine her understanding of race.[9] Claire Kahane suggests that "by . . . universalizing their [black men's] victimhood, O'Connor . . . reaffirms a common equality, albeit an equality of human helplessness."[10] Kahane's argument reflects the general tenor of O'Connor's work. In this story, however, the black characters are fine and Mr. Head and Nelson in good cheer by the time they leave the city. For the reader the moment of coalescence of the statue, the old man, and the boy demonstrates not that there is "an equality of human helplessness" but that the white racist imagination that produces the statuary also grotesquely misshapes white people.[11]

The explicit lesson in white supremacy that is the point of Mr. Head's moral guidance has been traced by Maris G. Fiondella, who examines the linguistic structures and reads the sign systems (e.g., Mr. Head's constant reference to "niggers") that form around the presence of black people who can be used by Mr. Head to "usurp Nelson's viewpoint and make it into a duplicate of his own."[12] Fiondella warns that if "readers are to escape a similar fate, they must infer this process of signification and communication and separate themselves from it" (p. 124).[13] Those many readers who see in the conclusion of this story the same "action of mercy" that Mr. Head feels may well take this warning to heart: Mr. Head's viewpoint has become theirs.[14] O'Connor's irony catches readers where we least want to be caught, and Fiondella's reading of the black figures on the train may reveal such a moment. She suggests that all the black characters (or presences) seem "even to readers to be charged with a threatening sexuality" and that "descriptions must be made to yield up their virtual stereotypes, lest readers fall into identification with Mr. Head's viewpoint" (p. 125).[15] She goes on to describe certain aspects of the African Americans on the train, noting the man's stomach "which rode majestically," the jewellery, the bright color of his tie, and the spatial relation of the women who follow him. She suggests that these details are expressive of "the stereotype 'pimp'" (p. 125), but the word "pimp" does not come from O'Connor or Mr. Head.[16]

In addition to the ruby pin sitting on the yellow satin tie, O'Connor gives us other details, providing a kind of Rorschach image for our readings just as the scene makes many names for the man on the train available to Nelson (a "fat man," an "old man," a "tan man"); his grandfather, however, needs only one word, "nigger" (pp. 254-255). Fiondella's word "pimp" obscures alternate possibilities for these black figures—the dignified procession of these people, the "deliberate" movements of the man's walking stick, his "large brown eyes gazing over the heads of the passengers," or his "small white moustache and white crinkly hair"—nor does the low chatter of the young women who follow him suggest they are prostitutes, even though their voices are "throaty" (p. 255).[17] Fiondella does not mention other aspects of the group on the train and thus, I think, demonstrates what she is warning us all against and what in O'Connor is only too easy: the projection of one's own culturally encoded assumptions and selections, in this case those that sexualize blackness.

The later view from behind the curtain that separates the whites from the blacks in the dining car shows us "the tremendous Negro. He was speaking in a soft voice to the two women while he buttered a muffin. He had a heavy sad face and his neck bulged over his white collar on either side" (p. 256). The contrasts with the poverty and bleakness that the Heads live in are obvious. The clothing, the food (buttery dining car muffins vs. fatback for breakfast, a biscuit and a can of sardines in a paper sack for lunch), and the soft low voices of the blacks distinguish them in every way from the rural poverty of the Heads and show a marked class difference from Mr. Head's manners and aggressive/defensive posture. Mr Head cares for none of these distinctions. When Mr. Head is showing Nelson the elegant dining car, he is uninterested in the elegance of the room, the energy of the waiters, or the pleasant food being served. Ignoring the waiter who attempts to move them out of the doorway "with an airy wave of the arm as if he were brushing aside flies," Mr. Head directs Nelson's attention to only one aspect of the scene, the place set off for the black travellers. "'Look,' Mr. Head said. . . . 'They rope them off'" (p. 256). Three issues are of interest here: first, the black waiter is utterly contemptuous of the Heads and Mr. Head is indifferent to that attitude. Then, Mr. Head is blind to the multiple stimuli of the dining car that O'Connor frames almost as a vivid tableau of color and movement: he has eyes only for the place of the black group, and that is the only thing Nelson is required to look at. And, third, the fact of Jim Crow law is still in force. Mr. Head's lesson is reinforced by the social reality of their time and place.

Unlike his grandfather, whose obsessive categorization excludes most distinctions, Nelson still sees people. As well as seeing the various qualities of the man on the train, Nelson recognizes the store where "the Negro polished your shoes," and he deduces that they are lost when he observes "a colored man. Then another. Then another" (p. 260). The syntax emphasizes the cumulative effect of both the experience and the cognition as Nelson realizes they are in a black neighborhood. It is he who sees the "large colored woman" whom he asks for directions. I think that O'Connor is very careful here to avoid helping us place these black characters, and thus she forestalls or reveals the white readers' desire to "rope them off" with easy labeling. Critical commentary shows that this effort is not always successful. Despite the ordinariness that O'Connor insists upon and the fact that Nelson is surprised by "Negroes . . . going about their business just as if they had been white" (p. 262), preconceptions leak into interpretations. George Cheatham, for example, asserts that "the story's black people . . . all suffer" (p. 477) and says the story assigns "suffering and humility" to the black characters (p. 478). In fact, the African-American characters all enjoy greater material comforts than do Mr. Head and Nelson. "Humility" is not evident in the black waiter on the train, the well-off travelers, the people passing them in the black neighborhood, or the black woman to whom Nelson speaks. Moreover, the African Americans' economic or communal status is utterly irrelevant to Mr. Head's sense of himself. In his own eyes, he is superior simply and exclusively because of the color of his skin and his control over the primary signifier ("nigger") that expresses it.

Mr. Head and Nelson become wholly the seen, the marked presences in the black community, and while O'Connor does not describe the perceptions of the watchers, we feel the absoluteness of racial division when Mr. Head and Nelson feel that "black eyes in black faces were watching them from every direction" (p. 260). The assertion of double blackness of eyes and skin—when we have already been informed that skin color of African Americans varies from tan to brown to very black—suggests that the white characters' anxiety is creating this perception. The narrative notes more coolly that "neither looked at the Negroes who were passing, going about their business just as if they had been white, except that most of them stopped and eyed Mr. Head and Nelson" (p. 262).[18] Whiteness here is the measure of the ordinary, the unmarked condition that asserts the right to an unself-conscious place in the world. The whites do not look at the blacks but are themselves the object of surprise and curiosity.[19] To be in this position, the object rather than the agent of the gaze, makes the old man sweat and makes Nelson recall the white face of the "sneering ghost" who had looked at him from the train window (p. 262). That white face was measuring Nelson's adequacy, and it returns to haunt him in the moments when Nelson is not fulfilling the requirements of his proper place. As a ghostly mirror, it evokes the relentless demands of an externalized ideal that requires the interior self to fall into line with the visible surface, the white skin.

To be visible is to engage the world as and with a body, and to be embodied is to be subject to the demands of flesh. The excremental functions of the body are of central importance to these characters and to the text. As the story opens in the Heads' room, in the "only dark spot," young Nelson is curled into a fetal ball. O'Connor's narrative gives us the chamber pot, which has been "made snow-white in the moonlight" and "appeared to stand guard over him like a small personal angel" (p. 250). We must see the bleak comedy of a chamber pot transformed into a guardian angel and the sorry condition of anyone dependent upon such an angel. The pure whiteness of the chamber pot also belies its purpose and contents, surely a comment on the relation of interior (the condition of spirit) to exterior (the pure white surface).[20] It is not the snow-whiteness of the slop jar that guards Nelson but its relation to mere flesh.

Nelson must accept the most basic functions of the body if he is to be saved from the tyranny of Mr. Head's ideology. On the train, Mr. Head "particularly wanted the boy to see the toilet," examining carefully the plumbing as part of his design that everything should be understood hierarchically (p. 256), that is, brought into the terrain of the mind.[21] As Nelson begins to enjoy the city, to identify it as his source, Mr. Head, in a desperate attempt to reassert his hold, shows the boy the sewer, grasping the back of his coat while Nelson sticks his head in the sewer hole. Hearing gurgling, the boy draws back:

> Then Mr. Head explained the sewer system . . . how a man could slide into it and be sucked along down endless pitchblack tunnels. . . . He described it so well that Nelson was for some seconds shaken. He connected the sewer passages with the entrance to hell and understood for the first time how the world was put together in its lower parts.
>
> (p. 259)

The movement for Nelson is into mind—he has an ideological frame that links matters of spirit (ideas of hell) with the body but which require rejection of body. The lesson is a threat, but Nelson shrewdly judges that "you can stay away from the holes" (p. 259). His next comment demonstrates both his instinctive knowledge (that which Mr. Head is determined to correct) and his innocence about sex: "This is where I come from!" (p. 259). Nelson means, of course, the city, Atlanta, the great complex of buildings and peoples and even elaborate sewer systems; but the reader understands that he "comes from" the "lower parts," from "the holes"—as do we all. The narrative's recurring references to the association of Nelson's birth with the place of black people is one of Mr. Head's weapons against Nelson: "'Yes,' Mr. Head said, 'this is where you were born—right here with all these niggers'" (p. 260). The terrifying, mysterious, and unnamed power of female sexuality and maternity is thereby linked to blackness, and both are mystified by this conflation. The genuine mystery of human difference and sameness, however, is denied because Mr. Head imagines he can name it. Nelson's claiming of that urban and maternal source and his fantasy that he can "stay away" from the danger implicit there bring the issue of control over Nelson (that is, the future of white maleness) to the fore.

The only truly effective weapon Mr. Head has against Nelson's enthusiastic view of the city is the threat of abandonment. Each time Mr. Head asserts the threat of abandonment, Nelson becomes whiter: he looks to the "pale, ghost-like face" (p. 253) reflected in the train window and sees his dependency on his grandfather (p. 256); this ghost face returns "sneering" after his encounter with the black woman, and he takes hold of his grandfather's hand, "a sign of dependence he seldom showed" (p. 262). Mr. Head is "Pleased to see the boy turn white" when he threatens to leave Nelson alone (p. 261). The ordinary (to white-skinned people) reference to turning white in shock or dismay carries a metonymic here, as Nelson's racial identity gets foregrounded, to Mr. Head's satisfaction. It is when he watches the boy asleep on the hot street, again curled into a fetal posture, ready for rebirth, "his knees up under his chin," that Mr. Head conceives his special lesson to show Nelson how much he truly needs his grandfather. As he sleeps, Nelson is partially conscious of "black forms moving up from some dark part of him into the light" (p. 264). It is this potential consciousness Mr. Head must intercept if Nelson's allegiance to whiteness is to be wholly and irrevocably fixed. Mr. Head hides, then makes a great racket, waking Nelson in a panic. Nelson runs, crashing into a white woman who raises a huge fuss. At this point Mr. Head appears, then, frightened, denies that Nelson is his. When his plan appears to fail so profoundly and he is humiliated by his discovery of his own cowardice, Mr. Head himself feels that he is "wandering into a black strange place where nothing was like it had ever been before, a long old age without respect and an end that would be welcome because it would be the end" (p. 267).[22] Mr. Head does not fear the loss of love, nor does he imagine Nelson's fear and pain. After his denial of Nelson, Mr. Head is stricken with the enormity of his deed, but O'Connor gives us very carefully the egocentricism of his feelings. Fear, and his own "disgrace," not images of what Nelson might be feeling, dominate his mind. When he worries that "dark" will overtake them, "they would be beaten and robbed" in the city, the coding of color/race makes it possible to see that "leading the boy his doom" has much to do with making him available to the "dark." His assumption that he knows that God's justice would be visited upon the innocent Nelson is also a clue to his arrogance, and it parallels closely his assumption that he knows God's mercy. In fact, it suggests how much his God is like himself, punitive. When he trips over the water spigot, martyr-like he denies himself a drink of water though he has not had any since early morning. The text says, "Then he thought that Nelson would be thirsty and they would both drink and be brought together" (p. 266). Mr. Head thinks of the child's needs and decides to meet them only out of his own desperation. They are secondary to Mr. Head's desperation. Nelson sees through the ploy, as the reader must (p. 266). If Nelson will not reaffirm Mr. Head's place, his security, Mr. Head will be lost to himself.

Surrender to black femaleness (or female blackness) becomes imaginable even to Mr. Head, as he makes a profound association with the story's linking of embodiment (black tunnels) with excretion. Indeed, Mr. Head imagines himself as excreta: "The old man felt that if he saw a sewer entrance he would drop down into it and let himself be carried away" (p. 267). Lostness is figured as black, female, and strange; foundness must be familiar, male, and white. His whiteness is all he has, and it represents for him his whole means of self-knowledge. Place and position, indeed identity, and the value of life itself are entirely the gifts of white supremacy for this poor, ignorant, nasty, unloving, and cowardly man.[23]

The various white men he encounters give Mr. Head the opportunity either to ignore Nelson and spout his program of education or to reveal his weakness and ask for directions. When he sees a "fat man," whom we know is white as Mr. Head can identify the quality of fatness, he cries out, "Oh Gawd I'm lost! O hep me Gawd I'm lost" (p. 267). Since Mr. Head cries out "Oh Gawd," not when he is most isolated and vulnerable but when he sees another white man, we may wonder if he is actually *addressing* that man. Is the white male the highest entity Mr. Head can imagine? In any case, only another white man can affirm Mr. Head's link to his world. The white male characters need do nothing at all to support or re-enforce Mr. Head—the fact that they are there is sufficient. Mr. Head imagines that they share a world and a world view that is untouched by differences of class, locale, and so forth, and he has no hesitation whatsoever about addressing them, even in panic, although he will speak to no one else in the story. His dependency is so pronounced that when he cries out "Oh Gawd," O'Connor may well be suggesting that white men are indeed God to Mr. Head.

The representation of white women in the story is far different from that of white men. They are either dead, like Mr. Head's wife and Nelson's mother,[24] or dangerous. Mr. Head first notices he is lost (after Nelson realizes they have been walking in a circle by recognizing the black man), and the city becomes explicitly threatening to him when he glances into a window and sees "a woman lying on an iron bed, looking out, with a sheet pulled over her" (p. 260).[25] It is not the open invitation to sex that troubles Mr. Head but "Her knowing expression [that] shook him" (p. 260). What this white woman knows is that Mr. Head has a body, which is what links him to sexuality, thus to femaleness, and thus to the world in its lower parts, according to his hierarchy of value. The other white women in the story are punitive and vindictive, but not without some standards. The old woman Nelson has knocked down, who has been claiming a broken ankle, and the other women who were "milling around Nelson as if they might suddenly all dive on him at once and tear him to pieces" are so appalled by Mr. Head's denial of "his own image and likeness" that they draw away from both Heads (p. 265). Either absent, and thus abandoning, or present and degraded by prostitution, malevolent as harpies, or simply repelled and pitying, white women have nothing to offer the Heads in this story. That O'Connor shows white women as unmaternal and unloving, sexually or otherwise, reinforces my contention that the "large colored woman" (p. 262) is represented as the bearer of all nurturing, all embodiment.

O'Connor provides only one human source for the multiple connections that Nelson requires for his spiritual and human rescue: the "large colored woman." Mr. Head and Nelson struggle for position, each attempting to claim dominance, until the archetypal figure of the black woman threatens all that either Head has known and forces everything in the story into place. The central figure here is the extraordinary body of the black woman, who is drawn for us in a more sensual way than is any other O'Connor character. The presence and impact of the "large colored woman" offer insight into O'Connor's configuration of black femaleness.[26] However, few critics discuss extensively the significance of the black woman. To one she is merely a "rather large and domineering black woman" (Saunders, p. 110), to another, simply "the black woman" (Cheatham, p. 476), or more specifically, as the "artless" bearer of a "genuine feminine embrace" (Okeke-Ezigbo, pp. 376-377). Usually the large black woman is read (or under-read) as erotic and maternal, or over-read as a prostitute (Strickland, p. 456). In contrast, the white and the male are figured in the other space: the territory of the conscious mind, the head rather than the body, and by reproducing this commonplace of Western culture, O'Connor is re-inscribing it, re-enforcing its "natural" or inevitable appearance, and participating in its reproduction.[27]

I quote rather extensively to suggest another way of reading the passage than the one offered above. In response to Nelson's suggestion that Mr. Head ask one of the black people watching them the way back to the train station, Mr. Head says, "This is where you were born. . . . You can ast one yourself if you want to" (p. 261):

> Nelson was afraid of the colored men and he didn't want to be laughed at by the colored children. Up ahead he saw a large colored woman leaning in a doorway that opened onto the sidewalk. Her hair stood straight out from her head for about four inches all around and she was resting on bare brown feet that turned pink at the sides. She had on a pink dress that showed her exact shape. As they came abreast of her, she lazily lifted one hand to her head and her fingers disappeared into her hair.
>
> Nelson stopped. He felt his breath drawn up by the woman's dark eyes. "How do you get back to town?" he said in a voice that did not sound like his own.
>
> After a minute she said, "You in town now," in a rich low tone that made Nelson feel as if a cool spray had been turned on him.
>
> "How do you get back to the train?" he said in the same reed-like voice.
>
> "You can catch you a car," she said.
>
> (p. 262)

The least threatening of Nelson's alternatives, the black woman is outlined as Nelson sees her and as his vision makes him feel. She is holder of a gaze powerful enough to draw up Nelson's breath, and she is dispenser of elemental goodness, a "cool spray of water" to the parched boy. She also has the crucial knowledge that Nelson and Mr. Head require to find their way to the train station and to some salvation. Here, the black woman is in the position of agency, controlling the communication with the boy and clearly amused by the exchange. She plays with this moment, asserting the centrality of her place: "You in town now," she declares. Consistent with her resistance to representing African-American inferiority, O'Connor focuses the scene almost entirely upon Nelson's visual perception and his desire:

> He understood she was making fun of him but he was too paralyzed even to scowl. He stood drinking in every detail of her. His eyes travelled up from her great knees to her forehead and then made a triangular path from the glistening sweat on her neck down and across her tremendous bosom and over her bare arm back to where her fingers lay hidden in her hair. He suddenly wanted her to reach down and pick him up and draw him against her and then wanted to feel her breath on his face. He wanted to look down and down into her eyes while she held him tighter and tighter. He had never had such a feeling before. He felt as if he were reeling down through a pitchblack tunnel.
>
> (p. 262)

The narrative moves with his eyes traveling over her body, the adjectives underscoring her monumentality in his eyes.[28] She is utterly accessible to his gaze, and he wants to give himself to hers, to "look down and down into her eyes." The text traces the movement of Nelson's eyes and integrates the narrative tropes with the material sensations of the boy (he is thirsty: her voice is a cool spray of water; he drinks every detail of her). The reader necessarily cannot distinguish between the boy's perception (shaped by his desires, fantasies, and feelings) and what is really there.

Readers' responses to this encounter and its effects on Nelson suggest something of the power of O'Connor's narrative, for it does not seem possible to read/visualize that meeting without being drawn, like Nelson, into a figure that has been so deeply and powerfully figured in and by the white mind.[29] In her examination of "the mammy" in white women's novels, Diane Roberts notes that this figure "typifies the mythic Old South of benign slavery, grace and abundance,"[30] but unlike the sexually neutralized "mammy," this figure includes a sexual component referred to by various readers.[31] She is perceived by Nelson as "the seductive city come to life," argues Fiondella, who notes that O'Connor's "description . . . blends stereotypes of both 'mammy' and 'whore'" (p. 126). Some readers see in the black woman an invitation to miscegenation and therefore Nelson's recognition of his "common humanity with the Negro woman" (Shackelford, p. 81). In a different idiom, Kahane suggests a similar effect of the "kind of fusion to which Nelson almost succumbs," where "miscegenation is a living metaphor" of confusion, "blurring the distinction between black and white through sexuality, and obliterating the entire structure of defined power" (p. 190). Sadly, there is little evidence to support the belief that white men's sexual and/or infantile relationships with black women have confused power structures or increased white racists' capacity to recognize a "common humanity" with anyone.[32] Giannone, in his recent book, extends his discussion of the black woman: "[Nelson] feels a new excitement in her sparkling black flesh that gets him hopelessly lost in her sinews and fluids as he suckles at this terrifying mammary presence" (*Hermit,* p. 118). In this statement, Giannone makes some provocative additions to O'Connor's text. In O'Connor, the woman's skin is brown, her "sinews" not apparent, and her "fluids" are sweat or metaphors. The movement of Nelson's eyes up into the woman's face and down into her eyes takes us away from the oral sensory qualities of "suckling," which reduce the complexity of Nelson's possibly first experience of seeing and being seen. Giannone does seem to focus on the bosom of the woman, but, unlike O'Connor, he sees terror in Nelson's reaction. At least we assume he is referring to Nelson's reaction when he speaks of a "terrifying mammary presence." The "large colored woman" is reduced to maternal breast in Giannone's reading, and that breast is a "terrifying" organ. Although O'Connor's own words may seem to invite some aspects of that reading, "shock" is not necessarily terror, and maternity is far more than "mammary" allows:

> . . . I meant for her [the colored woman] in an almost physical way to suggest the mystery of existence to him—he not only has never seen a nigger but he didn't know any women and I felt that such a black mountain of maternity would give him the required shock to start those black forms moving up from his unconscious.
>
> (*Habit,* p. 78)

O'Connor sites the unconscious in spatial analogy to the sewer system of Atlanta and places the "black mountain of maternity" in his path only to give Nelson access to the necessary elements of his unconscious. The readers, like the narrative itself, enter a dynamic that suggests a deep entanglement in unconscious, gendered, and racialized assumptions.

The conflation of readers' eyes with Nelson's makes the black woman into a peculiar narrative presence. She has become wholly a canvas, both for the character and for the reader. Such a figure cannot exist for its own purposes—it is there for others. Lucinda H. MacKethan seems to be arguing a point similar to my own in her assertion that "the large black woman they meet . . . is the embodiment of the self-knowledge that Mr. Head, in his blindness, has avoided."[33] However, where MacKethan sees the woman as embodying "self-knowledge," I suggest that the presence of a very particular body and Nelson's response to it reveal what O'Connor has projected onto that figure. Connection with the black woman represents the possibility of (white not black) spiritual healing. And, yes, Mr. Head does avoid the possibility of healing. MacKethan goes on to argue that Nelson recognizes in himself "a bond with the woman" (p. 31); however, a "bond" usually requires that the other person's reality is recognized and respected. For Nelson, the image and his reaction are entirely based on his own need, his lack, his hungers. This absence of awareness is antithetical to the view that O'Connor is affirming a "common humanity" in this story. Only one character's humanity is significant here, and access to some measure of human wholeness—mind, spirit, and body—must be gained through another's. No one's humanity evolves in isolation. But to attribute to the black woman the properties that will humanize Nelson (and by extension whites) and to provide a black woman to represent the embodiment that Nelson needs, O'Connor assures the lack of integration, of wholeness in Nelson, Mr. Head, and the black character as well.

The simple color-coding of black and white makes some forms of the threat of body apparent: Mr. Head's project is to make Nelson "white"—which means to teach him to hate and fear and despise blackness—and "blackness" is elementally configured in the femaleness of sexuality, of birth, of tunnels and holes and consuming danger. The body, in Mr. Head and Nelson's world, is the sexual body, the excremental body, and the racialized ("black") body. It is all that is not head. But in O'Connor's world, without body, there can be no spirit, no nurturance, no love, and thus no salvation. Mr. Head's sure knowledge of the mind of God at the much-argued end of the story shows how grandiose his humility is. That O'Connor gives the last words to Nelson should have curtailed some of the celebratory affirmation of Mr. Head's revelation.[34] When Nelson says, "I'm glad I've went once, but I'll never go back again!" (p. 270), he repudiates where he actually does come from, a world that contains blacks and women of any race and, in the semiotics of the story, his own fleshly life. O'Connor's commitment to the Laws of the Flesh (the requirement of the body for the full affirmation of the spirit and the spirit for the body), Mr. Head's ongoing negation of embodiment, which would make him a body among others, makes his great revelation suspect.

A precise image from the moment of Mr. Head's betrayal of Nelson supports my view that the body is essential to O'Connor's sense of salvation: when Nelson, surrounded by the furious white women, sees Mr. Head, the boy springs toward his grandfather: "The child caught him around the hips and clung panting against him" (p. 265). We are made aware for the first time how small Nelson is, and in this scene he is positioned almost as though a birth were occurring. Flesh to flesh, the old man and the boy might have some defense against the white women and some born-again possibility of connection. Of course, Mr. Head, who feels (that is, imagines) the policeman (white male authority) at his back and "the women who were massed in their fury like a solid wall to block his escape" in front of him (p. 265), is unable to enter the world of flesh that would make love (in its larger senses) possible. He disclaims the boy and "felt Nelson's fingers fall out of his flesh" (p. 265). Despite their much-celebrated bonding by the end of the story, the man and the boy do not touch each other again. O'Connor's most incisive irony appears in Mr. Head's expression of complacent pride in his status as a "great sinner" and his confident takeover of God's place as judge and dispenser (to himself) of mercy. Mr. Head, so overwhelmed by the "true depravity" of his betrayal of the boy that he "judges himself with the thoroughness of God," believes he thoroughly understands God's mercy and feels ready at that moment to enter paradise (p. 270). O'Connor's excessive rhetoric here displaying Mr. Head's self-aggrandizement and spiritual arrogance ensures that Nelson's surrender to Mr. Head's space is marked by despair, not salvation.

In her study of the psychological paradigms of bigotry, Elisabeth Young-Bruehl identifies racism as a "hysterical prejudice," in which a group is appointed to "act out in the world forbidden sexual" impulses.[35] The women of the "lower" group are imagined as "either (and sometimes both) sexually lascivious or maternally bountiful, milk giving and care giving" (p. 34). The bracketing of the black female character as the representative of the "mystery of existence" through the maternal and sexual semiotic in which Nelson is swept up and the degree of the "cordoning off of their desires" that Mr. Head demands make these characters and this narrative both enactors of the hysterical prejudice that Young-Bruehl categorizes (p. 34). When Nelson encounters the black woman, he "felt as if he were reeling down through a pitchblack tunnel" (p. 262). These tunnels are reiterated by the sewer system of Atlanta, associated with female sexuality, and invoked by Mr. Head's terrified fantasy of being swept away in some parallel experience. For Nelson, the moment is full of possibility; for Mr. Head, only emptiness is imaginable.

By linking Young-Bruehl's analysis with this story, I mean not that O'Connor is to be judged a racist—Ralph C. Wood discusses this question with care and clarity—but that the habits of mind of a culture, habits of division, attribution, and self-deception that characterize our thinking about race, about sex, and about gender all find powerful and subtle voice in O'Connor's writing. Wood argues that her own, not fully conscious, integrity required O'Connor to keep the story's title in the face of John Crowe Ransom's editorial objections: O'Connor said that "to have sanitized the title would have robbed the story of its real power, the power to invert racist intention into anti-racist redemption" (*Habit,* p. 111). The "real power" of this story, for white readers at least, may be the peculiar, unconscious wish that "anti-racist redemption" could cost so little. For the Heads, nothing has changed. Observing that "the characters who stand most drastically in need of reconciliation are divided not by race but by will" (p. 111), Wood (and perhaps O'Connor herself, who continued to puzzle over this story) does not see that it is precisely *race* that finally reconciles them. Their will, not the "redemption *offered* by Negroes" [my emphasis] (p. 111), grounded in their common whiteness and maleness, *does* unite them. Katherine Prown does assert that the statuary represents "the signifier against which white identity is defined" (p. 73), yet Prown supports the conventional view that Mr. Head is correctly humbled and redemption is their lot. I share Wood's view that "[o]nly in overcoming the demonic urge to subject others to our own desires, [as] O'Connor shows, can there be hope for either families or races" (p. 111), but, unlike Wood, I see in O'Connor's narrative construction of the sexual, racial "other" a reiteration of the "urge to subject others to our own desires"—in this case our desire to make others the embodied repository of salvation or redemption. White readers may be able to recognize themselves in the Heads, and if that constitutes redemption, we may be hopeful.

In the logic of duality within which Mr Head lives and O'Connor writes, the black woman represents, offers, and, indeed, *is* body. By extension, spirituality, at least its potential, is contained in the figures of Mr. Head and Nelson. As critical commentary has shown, many readers find a unity of body and spirit and full humanity for all people articulated in **"The Artificial Nigger."** I argue, in contrast, that the Negro statuary that many critics, sharing Mr. Head's perspective, have seen as the catalyst for salvation is not that at all. Rather, Mr. Head's witty phrasing and Nelson's exact repetition—"An artificial nigger"—secures Mr. Head and Nelson in their knowledge of place and identity, isolated from the rest of the world in poverty of mind, body, and spirit. What is actually achieved in the celebrated end of **"The Artificial Nigger"** is a reiteration of the old, sad split between mind and body, male and female, black and white. In this story, we have the renewal of the idea that the female, the black are to function as a place for the body—in the mind or in reality, as threat or as promise—in the imaginary of white maleness. For the Heads, the "action of mercy" may well affirm their undivided connection with each other in their white male world, but that is no salvation.

Notes

1. The phrase "white solipsist" is from Adrienne Rich, herself an acute analyst of whiteness ("Toward a More Feminist Criticism," *Blood, Bread, and Poetry: Selected Prose, 1979-1985* [New York: Norton, 1986], p. 96).

2. Flannery O'Connor, *The Habit of Being: Letters,* ed. Sally Fitzgerald (New York: Farrar, Straus, Giroux, 1979), p. 101.

3. Ronald Schleifer, "Rural Gothic: The Stories of Flannery O'Connor," in *Critical Essays on Flannery O'Connor,* ed. Melvin J. Friedman and Beverly Lyon Clark (Boston: G. K. Hall, 1985), p. 165.

4. Flannery O'Connor, "The Artificial Nigger," in *The Complete Stories Of Flannery O'Connor* (New York: Farrar, Straus and Giroux, 1971), p. 262.

5. D. Dean Shackelford argues that O'Connor's "concern is for the salvation of the human race—red, yellow, black, and white. Without this salvation, social values are meaningless" ("The Black Outsider in O'Connor's Fiction," *Flannery O'Connor Bulletin,* 18 [1989], 89).

6. The plot is simple. Mr. Head, a rural poor white man takes his grandson, Nelson, whom he has raised alone since the boy's infancy, to visit the city. He is determined to "show him all it is to show" (p. 254). The two are ferociously competitive, and the primary site of their argument is Nelson's claim to have been born in the city, the grandfather's that Nelson has never seen a black person. Mr. Head consistently and obsessively repeats the word "nigger" in this context and throughout the story—an issue I will discuss below. The two get lost in the city and inadvertently wander into a black neighborhood. Nelson asks a black woman for directions and is deeply disturbed by his reactions to her and is mocked for them by his grandfather. After they make a wrong turn and cannot find the train station, Nelson falls asleep on the street, and Mr. Head, to teach him a firm lesson of dependence, hides. The boy wakens in a panic, runs wildly off, and knocks over an old white woman who screams that she will sue. Mr. Head, "the image and likeness" of the boy (p. 265), denies knowing him. The old man, attempting to make up with the bitterly resentful Nelson, affirms his place in the boy's world when they see

the wretched statue that gives the story its name: "they could feel it dissolving their differences like an action of mercy" (p. 269). Mr. Head secures their alliance with his quip, "They ain't got enough real ones here. They got to have an artificial one" (p. 269). The two, with relief, go home. Mr. Head, so overwhelmed by his newfound sense of his own helplessness and the "true depravity" of his betrayal of the boy that he "judges himself with the thoroughness of God," believes he understands God's mercy and feels ready at that moment to enter paradise (p. 270). Nelson, surrendering his earlier claim to have come from the city, in the last words of the story asserts, "I'm glad I've went once, but I'll never go back again!" (p. 270).

7. Readers may wish to contrast this with Richard Giannone's view that the movement of spiritual development in this story is toward an "invisible body" ("'The Artificial Nigger' and the Redemptive Quality of Suffering," *Flannery O'Connor Bulletin,* 12 [Autumn 1983], 7).

8. Some critics find themselves "discomfort[ed] while so many find such solace" in the reassurance of spiritual grace in this story (James Robert Saunders, "The Fallacies of Guidance and Light in Flannery O'Connor's 'The Artificial Nigger,'" *Journal of the Short Story in English,* 17 [August 1991], 105). Many critics seem to share or support O'Connor's view that suffering caused by whites can redeem whites. A scapegoat theology, however, requires a belief in a god that takes a willing victim as propitiation. Joseph Campbell observes that Christ, not only willing but joyful, insisted on dancing the evening before he was to be arrested (Joseph Campbell with Bill Moyers, *The Power of Myth* [New York: Doubleday, 1988], p. 136). I see no evidence to suggest that the pathetic statue or the very unpathetic black characters in this story are victims willing to be sacrificed for the spiritual good of whites. Readers wishing to pursue the argument that the statuary carries the spiritual weight of the scapegoat should see Richard Giannone, *Flannery O'Connor, Hermit Novelist* (Chicago: University of Illinois Press, 2000); Emeka Okeke-Ezigbo, "Three Artificial Blacks: A Re-examination of Flannery O'Connor's 'The Artificial Nigger,'" *College English Association Journal,* 27 (1984), 371-382; George Cheatham, "Jesus, O'Connor's Artificial Nigger," *Studies in Short Fiction,* 22 (Fall 1985), 475-479; Edward Strickland, "The Penitential Quest in 'The Artificial Nigger,'" *Studies in Short Fiction,* 25 (Fall 1988), 453-459; Katherine H. Burkman and J. Reid Meloy, "The Black Mirror: Joseph Conrad's 'The Nigger of the Narcissus' and Flannery O'Connor's 'The Artificial Nigger,'" *Midwest Quarterly,* 8 (Winter 1987), 230-247; and Ralph C. Wood, "Where Is the Voice Coming From? Flannery O'Connor on Race," *Flannery O'Connor Bulletin,* 22 (1993-94), 90-118, to list only a handful of the most recent (since 1984) discussions. Even those who disagree that Nelson and Mr. Head are saved, redeemed, etc., find in the statuary an icon "that may very well function as a vehicle for God's grace" (see W. F. Monroe, "Flannery O'Connor's Sacramental Icon," *South Central Review,* 1 [Winter 1984], 80).

9. All white critics will find Richard Dyer's discussions of whiteness useful. He notes, "most of the time white people speak of nothing but white people, it's just that we couch it in terms of 'people' in general" (*White* [New York: Routledge, 1997], p. 3).

10. "The Artificial Niggers," *Massachusetts Review,* 19 (1978), 184. Kahane's point here is that universalizing victimhood "destroys the political rationale for rebellion" (p. 184).

11. Susan Gubar, in her study of blackface in American culture, briefly mentions that the similarity of the Heads to the miserable statue is a form of blackface (*Racechanges: White Skin, Black Face in American Culture* [New York: Oxford University Press, 1997], p. 84).

12. "Augustine, The 'Letter,' and the Failure of Love in Flannery O'Connor's 'The Artificial Nigger,'" *Studies in Short Fiction,* 24 (Spring 1987), 124.

13. Simply by using conventions of metaphor or "ordinary" tropes, the reader or critic unfortunately demonstrates the ease of slippage into the simple binary (white/black: good/bad) that Mr. Head so rigorously affirms. W. F. Monroe, for example, making a cogent argument about the limitations of reason in relation to Mr. Head's "Pernicious bigotry" (p. 68), refers to Head's use of the word "nigger": "O'Connor has been scrupulous that her narrator avoid the use of the word, while the characters who refer to blacks as 'niggers' are marked by the darkness that they try to attribute to others" (p. 68). "Darkness" in this context can mean only negativity. In a discussion of race, white supremacy, and bigotry, to equate darkness with badness (of whatever sort that might be) without clarification of either the attribution or the content of the "dark" reinscribes the dichotomy of good/bad: light/dark. Giannone, too, in an argument referring forcefully to racist demons says of the evil within, ". . . a sudden external encounter can force a confrontation with one's dark self," and then "the dark woman has somehow sounded the dark of his heart" (*Hermit,* p. 119). When dark skin (matter) is blurred with the metaphor of a "dark heart" confusion of values is apparent.

14. Any critic who steps into a Flannery O'Connor story risks merging with the text. Elaine Scarry observes, "words in [literature] speak for us, objectifying not only forms of love or discomfort that seem beyond speech but perhaps above all the nature and significance of our own powers of invention" (*Resisting Representation* [New York: Oxford University Press, 1994], p. 71). The critic, she implies, constructs the reading, the argument, on the basis of his or her own desires and fears. These are mediated by the text and made accessible through it. The deep irony that pervades O'Connor's text seems almost inevitably to ensnare the reader, exposing rather mercilessly those desires.

15. This assertion suggests that all readers are white and that all white readers find sexuality (which must inhabit black bodies?) threatening, or that all African Americans are overdetermined as specifically sexual and therefore threatening. The black characters (the waiters on the train, for example) show that O'Connor does not share this view.

16. He has only a single, primary signifier, the word "nigger." The charge usually associated with the primary signifier, to demarcate self from other, here indicates to the white speaker an almost magical quality of difference. Fiondella notes that "[nigger] is an epithet taken from American racism that refers to a mental category and not to reality" (p. 125). The basic function of the epithet is to assert the primary value of the white speaker and reassure him of his secure place.

17. Katherine Hemple Prown says all the black characters in this story "are rendered in a dignified and sympathetic manner" (*Revising Flannery O'Connor: Southern Literary Culture and the Problem of Authorship* [Charlottesville: University Press of Virginia, 2001], p. 71).

18. See bell hooks's examination of the racialized gaze in *Black Looks: Race and Representation* (Boston: South End Press, 1992).

19. Okeke-Ezigbo argues that the inversion of position is so thorough that Mr. Head and Nelson are reduced to the "lowest level of nigger" (p. 379). This interesting discussion concludes with the unsupported (and, I believe, insupportable) assertion that Mr. Head has acquired "incipient scorn for those who still degrade the blacks" (p. 382).

20. Thanks to Jude Polsky for this observation.

21. Monroe discusses Mr. Head's "overconfidence in the rational mind" (p. 67), arguing that his reliance on his own knowledge at the conclusion of the story is "static, pat, and even hackneyed" (p. 76). Readers will remember, too, that a "head" is the toilet on a ship.

22. We note here that Mr. Head does not fear the afterlife. Hell does not exist for him and the "end" is the end.

23. One anonymous reader objected to this characterization of Mr. Head. I reconsidered his thoughts and actions, and was unable to find any instance in which Mr. Head was prosperous, well-informed, kind, loving, or courageous, so I let the line stand. Some critical discussions of this story have made much of the class markers—the household, speech, clothing, food, etc., of Mr. Head and Nelson. Mr. Head is called a "redneck," a "hick," and "bumpkin." I wonder if this kind of critical attention to those factors is part of some readers' wish to find ways to "other" Mr. Head, even while seeing in Mr. Head what they think Mr. Head has found in the "artificial Negro" statuary (p. 269)—the action of mercy that would separate them from Mr. Head's point of view. See, for example, Schleifer, p. 165, or Giannone, *Hermit,* p. 115.

24. O'Connor shows how unwelcome a place Mr. Head's home must be for a woman given that Nelson's mother runs off to the city when her mother dies, and then dies herself shortly after returning from the city with Nelson.

25. The reader knows this is a white woman because Mr. Head identifies her as a "woman" and registers her expression. Similarly, the "fierce-looking" cyclist must be white because he is not said to be black—that is, he is of the unracialized race. See Ruth Frankenberg's *White Women, Race Matters: The Social Construction of Whiteness* (Minneapolis: University of Minnesota Press, 1994) for a discussion of the unmarked condition of whiteness.

26. Readers should note Kahane's discussion of masks in this story.

27. Underscoring this point, Prown attributes agency to this character: "Assuming the role black women have traditionally played in relation to white southern men, the woman serves at once as an object of sexual desire and as a mammy figure" (p. 72).

28. Patricia Yaeger examines the "giant female body" as fundamentally transgressive of the "pleasant, undifferentiated, fragile body" that white Southern women have been expected to inhabit ("Beyond the Hummingbird: Southern Women Writers and the Southern Gargantua," in *Haunted Bodies: Gender and Southern Texts,* ed. Anne Goodwyn Jones and Susan V. Donaldson [Charlottesville: University Press of Virginia, 1997], p. 299). The ferocious white women that confront Mr. Head certainly challenge that delicate figure (indeed,

nowhere in O'Connor will we find her, black or white). That this giant woman is black makes her doubly outrageous.

29. Okeke-Ezigbo connects Nelson's desire with that of James Weldon Johnson's ex-colored man "on seeing a black mammy in Atlanta" (p. 377). He quotes Johnson: "She made me feel as though I should like to lay my head on her capacious bosom and go to sleep" (*The Autobiography of an Ex-Colored Man* [New York: Hill and Wang, 1960], p. 59). Johnson's comment suggests that the desire for a great mother may be general but does not explain why African-American women are so often the object of the infantile need.
30. *The Myth of Aunt Jemima: Representations of Race and Region* (New York: Routledge, 1994), p. 1.
31. Burkman and Meloy touch on this doubleness with their comment that "O'Connor has captured the young boy's regressive wish for mergence with the mother in its most frightening and gratifying aspects" (p. 242). They hint at but do not discuss the sexual elements of this desire. Nelson's wish to be drawn "up" into her arms and then to look "down" into her eyes indicates that he is positioned both as child looking up at and as lover looking down upon the woman.
32. It is beyond the scope of this paper to discuss the many excellent explorations of miscegenation, or, more specifically, the sexual exploitation of African-American women. Readers should be aware of the writing of Hazel Carby, Jean Yellin, Hortense Spillers, bell hooks, and Diane Roberts on this subject.
33. "Redeeming Blackness: Urban Allegories of O'Connor, Percy, and Toole," *Studies in the Literary Imagination,* 27 (Fall 1994), 31.
34. Louise Westling, seeking to reconcile secular and religious readings of O'Connor, argues that "we can at least metaphorically if not literally accept Mr. Head's lesson in humility" (*Sacred Groves and Ravaged Gardens: The Fiction of Eudora Welty, Carson McCullers, and Flannery O'Connor* [Athens: University of Georgia Press, 1985], p. 136). Richard Giannone's discussion of this story is entirely innocent of any awareness of O'Connor's irony and sees in Mr. Head a redemptive transformation that "changes his attitude toward himself, toward everyone, and toward God" (*Hermit,* p. 7). Mr. Head, however, does not so much change his "attitude" toward God as he acquires an attitude, one that assures him he knows God's attitude toward him. Readers of O'Connor should know that the moment characters feel secure in their knowledge of God and His views is the moment they are in most danger spiritually.
35. *The Anatomy of Prejudices* (Cambridge: Harvard University Press, 1996), p. 34.

Patricia Yaeger (essay date fall 2003)

SOURCE: Yaeger, Patricia. "Southern Orientalism: Flannery O'Connor's Cosmopolis." *Mississippi Quarterly* 56, no. 4 (fall 2003): 491-510.

[*In the following essay, Yaeger focuses on the exotic nature of tattooing in the short story "Parker's Back," underlining the confused orientalism intrinsic to O'Connor's depiction of an imperialist American society overwhelmed by references to disparate cultures.*]

And therefore I have sailed the seas and come
To the holy city of Byzantium.

—W. B. Yeats

In this essay I want to explore the weird connections among tattoo culture, Cold War imperialism, and Flannery O'Connor's funky love of the Southern vernacular. We will scratch the underbelly of O'Connor's passion for Christianity, a Western religion obsessed with the geography and myths of the Middle East (a way of life that is not only an epistemology in O'Connor's fiction but a formula for exoticism). We will ask whether an author as locally grounded and vernacularly driven as Flannery O'Connor can be described as cosmopolitan. If so, which brand of cosmopolitanism does she espouse? Is her sophisticated Christianity proof that she believes in the West's superiority, in the "higher" values held by Western elites, or can she be co-opted for new brands of cosmopolitanism propounded by theorists of global flows or diasporas who say that every "local" is globally inflected, who see fleeting mixtures of vernacular and multiworld cultures dispersed within any locale?

Within the fleeting locales of America, the multiverse of Christian kitsch has finally caught up with Flannery O'Connor. In an era in which tattoos are as common as tictacs and the Midwest can be hard to discriminate from the South, a local Presbyterian church sports a group of eye-catching posters that reach out to today's multi-pierced teens. One features a close-up of Christ's triple stigmata and decorates the wounds with this slogan: "Body piercing is nothing new to us. A lot of people have pierced body parts. But every single one of us has holes in our heart or soul. Jesus Christ suffered on the cross so you wouldn't have to suffer today." How do you sell Christianity to the cosmopolitan teens who come after Gen X? Another poster zeroes in on the fad for extreme sports. Underneath the likeness of a careening downhill skier we discover the sportiness of today's Christianity: "You fearlessly push yourself to all kinds of achievements. So why do you find church so formidable? After all, Jesus Christ knows something about extremes himself. And he's waiting to show you some truly awesome things." The final poster in this triptych offers the ultimate in empathic cool: a classic Sunday school portrait of the lonely figure kneeling at Gethsemane, accompanied by this earnest caption: "if you think your parents expect a lot, you're not alone."

These church posters grabbed my attention because they clarify the ways in which postmodern Christianity and Madison Avenue go hand in hand; they also made me think twice about my own high seriousness as I've tried to make sense of the relations among Christianity, "Orientalism," and Xtreme tattooing in **"Parker's Back,"** a story O'Connor finished in the last months of her life. The posters' loopy sales pitch reminds me of O'Connor's wild out-takes on Protestantism—her attempts to take Christianity to extremes and her irreverence for any form of cant or piety. As she writes to Maryat Lee: "That grasshopper you left in the cage . . . reminded me so much of the poor colored people in the jails that I let him out and fed him to a duck. I'm sure you'll understand."[1] O'Connor loves to shock. Her frank sadism in the grasshopper story suggests her ultra-conservatism in racial matters, but it also demonstrates the ways in which she refuses to domesticate any religious or political movement that comes her way.

This irreverence is an attitude the youth-group posters cannot muster. Each is a gem of kitsch showmanship; each tames its passionate subject. Xtreme sports aren't so dangerous, these Sunday School placards say, nor is body-piercing cutting edge; after all, Christ tried it first. In contrast, O'Connor's stories spin these body metaphors out of control. While triple-piercing may seem promisingly profane for millennial teenagers, for O'Connor, obsessive tattooing or body-piercing could lead to something more progressive: to mind-boggling, soul-penetrating, ethos-bending pain.

While these youth group posters use mod marketing techniques to flash past a series of themes that O'Connor treats with greater wit and comic seriousness, they also suggest a path into this essay. Why not be as cheeky about O'Connor's sacred texts as these posters are about Christian doctrine; why not take a few Xtra roads into her story? **"Parker's Back"** lashes out against easy truisms. Here O'Connor dallies with multi-national psychodrama when she explores an ex-sailor's stigmatized skin. She parodies fundamentalist Christian themes and revisits the church's Middle Eastern origins even as her words envelop the soft body of a Southern boy who joins the Navy—meeting, in a fashion both global and vernacular, the forces of global capitalism and the pressures of mid-twentieth-century American imperialism as they impinge on bodies in extremis.

Parker, a one-time sailor and ex-apple salesman, tries to win the affection of his mean-spirited wife by having the huge face of a Byzantine Christ tattooed on his back, the only portion of his limbs and torso that remains tattoo-free. The two-faced result is strange and erotic: O'Connor recreates Parker as both top and bottom, as all front and no back. His extra face terrifies his drinking buddies, who throw him into the street; it prompts his wife to beat him brutally. In a queer replay of the Christian passion, his astonishing, backwards face bleeds and swells. For all its rural and vernacular resourcefulness, **"Parker's Back"** is a *tour de force* of cosmopolitan story-telling; it provides a fascinating look at the suture between cultures we now call "East" and "West," as well as a commentary on the relation between local customs and international politics in the nineteen-fifties and sixties when O'Connor was writing her best fiction.

"Parker's Back" also defines an itinerary for examining the American academy's recent interest in new brands of cosmopolitanism that refute the self-congratulations of worldly intellectuals and expand our sense of what we mean by "the local": the ways every locale is globally cross-hatched. While most scholars use O'Connor's Southernness or Catholicism to explain the force of her craft, I will suggest that not only is her localism supra-national but it also asks us to reconsider a South that is distinctly unregional. A place riddled with the "foreign" experiences of poor Southern men who joined the Navy, this South is also obsessed with the Asiatic sources of Christian culture. What does it mean for the impoverished white man at the center of **"Parker's Back"** to stagger through Georgia with a Byzantine Christ on his back? Is it plausible that a Southern ex-sailor has "sailed the seas and come / To the Holy City of Byzantium"?

Despite assertions about her rootedness in place, O'Connor often blurs realms we expect her to separate. As she says in a letter to Maryat Lee:

> Lance's[2] pageant [for a local Civil War centennial] was such a smashing success that the Chamber of Commerce hopes to put it on during the season and make this another Wm'burg. The Civil War is just beginning to pay off its investment.
>
> I have bought 100 shares of Keystone B and 100 shares of Thrifimart & I feel like a bloody capitalist.
>
> (*Habit,* p. 432)

The South may be a local phenomenon, but it is shot through with expansive economic hopes and pretensions. The spiritual O'Connor sees herself as a "bloody capitalist"; in a modernizing Milledgeville the local Chamber of Commerce still wants to recoup its Civil War investments.

But if these profits are claimed by a local elite, their global impact can only be measured upon proletarian bodies. The blood on the back of the protagonist of **"Parker's Back"** suggests labor's difficulty in getting its fair share of extra-regional investments. For Parker is not only an artist of the extreme, a man whose body is covered with tattoos, but his sojourn in the Navy is quilted by U.S. imperialism; his skin is encrusted with the silty insignia of other nations. O'Connor insists that Parker's earliest tattoos bear the stamp of American militarism. On his "stubby reddish hand . . . emblazoned in red and blue was a tattooed eagle perched on a cannon."[3] His supernumerary tattoos reflect America's colonizing adventures: "I got most of my other ones in foreign parts," he tells his prickly, tattoo-hating wife-to-be; "These here I mostly got in the United States" (p. 512). How does one local body combine "other foreign parts" with "these here"? I want to use the insignia on Parker's front and back to advance our sense of how to decipher O'Connor's vernaculars as they connect with her cosmopolis, to reveal the ways in which local, national, and international preoccupations inflect her fictional world. Although O'Connor plays the role of Southern bumpkin, her fictions etch complex versions of an imperial political unconscious.

Caught in the thick of transnational conglomerates, serial commodification, outsourced oceans of labor, and witness to the trauma of state-sponsored terrorism and statelessness, contemporary academics share in a general frenzy to understand the ways in which the local and global intersect. Playing catch-up, scholars dissect the ghosts of colonialism, the costs of postcolonialism, and the explosion of global poverty and wealth. Newspapers light up with the planet's interconnections. In the summer of 2002, when huge forest fires raged in the once-more-wild U.S. West, the news on page two of the *New York Times* was just as frightening. Pakistani garment workers had to submit to massive layoffs when U.S. companies, worried about terrorism and a Pakistan-India war, began sending their representatives and their orders elsewhere. Since the United States rewarded Turkey for its assistance in the 1991 Persian Gulf war with a fifty-percent increase in textile quotas, Pakistan expected a similar boon for its risks in America's war against Afghanistan, but America only gave symbolic thanks; the U.S. government lowered its import quotas on leather gloves and hand-knotted carpets—consumer goods trivial to Pakistan's factory system. America's noblesse oblige is no minor matter: textile and garment factories account for sixty percent of Pakistan's industrial employment. As one laid-off worker protested, "America is like poison to me. . . . I'm still bitter about it. I felt they were our friends."[4]

What do Pakistan's textiles have to do with Flannery O'Connor—or she with them? If we want to find an analogue to Asian textile making in the annals of American literature, we could look to Hawthorne's Hester Prynne, whom Hawthorne accuses of a fulsome Orientalism. In addition to crafting Pearl's rich clothing and the voluptuousness of the scarlet letter itself, Hester bruises her fingers making garments for the poor:

> It is probable that there was an idea of penance in this mode of occupation, and that she offered up a real sacrifice of enjoyment, in devoting so many hours to such rude handiwork. She had in her nature a rich, voluptuous, Oriental characteristic, a taste for the gorgeously beautiful, which, save in the exquisite productions of her needle, found nothing else, in all the possibilities of her life, to exercise itself upon.[5]

Edward Said has taught us to read the assumptions behind Hawthorne's signs: "Orientalism was ultimately a political vision of reality whose structure promoted the difference between the familiar (Europe, the West, 'us') and the strange (the Orient, the East, 'them')."[6] In citing Hester's "orientalizing" strain, Hawthorne calls on a passel of stock responses: "The Oriental is irrational, depraved (fallen) childlike, 'different'; thus the European is rational, virtuous, mature, 'normal'" (Said, p. 40). Hawthorne asks the adulterous Hester with her needle, the spontaneous Hester in the forest, to call up these "easterly" associations; she is exotic, "fallen," "different," unlike her virtuous, Western, unadventurous peers.[7] O'Connor admired Hawthorne immensely; she praises the way his symbols deepen with each reading. And the marks on Parker's back call to mind the fondness for symbol as allegory that O'Connor shares with Melville and Ellison as well as with Hawthorne. In his obsessiveness, Parker, like Ahab, lives for a set of flagrant, body-searing symbols: the Byzantine Christ that adorns Parker's back flays him, body and soul, as does the scarlet "S" adorning Hester's front, Ahab's whale-carved leg, and the secret marks that scarify Dimmesdale's skin. But how far can we push this "oriental" connection? The shirts that come so quickly off O. E. Parker's back were probably made, in the years O'Connor's story was percolating, in a Southern textile mill—a thoroughly local production. With a pregnant wife, Parker has moved from an itinerant job as fruit hawker to the settled role of impoverished Southern farm worker. Still, if we look through the shirts on Parker's back to the marks that cover his body, we find an enduring dependence on the coverture of the East: many of Parker's tattoos were made in Japan. As he sits patiently in a Southern tattoo shop (receiving his Near Eastern emblem, the mosaic glossolalia of the Byzantine Jesus), "Parker felt no particular pain. In Japan he had had a tattoo of the Buddha done on his upper arm with ivory needles; in Burma, a little brown root of a man had made a peacock on each of his knees using thin pointed sticks, two feet long; amateurs had worked on him with pins and soot" (p. 523). Like Hester's scarlet letter, these figures set Parker apart and give his character an orientalist spin. The first tattooed man Parker sees at a sideshow is exotic, "different," out of the ordinary:

> The man, who was small and sturdy, moved about on the platform, flexing his muscles so that the arabesque of men and beasts and flowers on his skin appeared to have a subtle motion of its own. Parker was filled with emotion, lifted up as some people are when the flag passes. He was a boy whose mouth habitually hung open. He was heavy and earnest, as ordinary as a loaf of bread.
>
> (pp. 512-513)

O'Connor's insistence on the tattooed exotic constructs the usual orientalist binary. An "arabesque" is an ornate design of intertwined leaves and flowers: subtle geometries that create a powerful contrast to Parker's American dailiness—his inability to register, at least in O'Connor's similes, a thrill beyond the excitement of waving the flag. The flexed muscles of the tattoo artist create a contrast between "American" and "arabesque," a term derived from the Italian *arabesco,* "made or done in the Arabic fashion." To have "men and beasts and flowers on his skin" is to have an identity that travels East, beyond Merita or Wonder bread, the staff of the ordinary; it means venturing beyond the slouch of Parker's Southern vernacular. O'Connor scholars have mapped the religious portent of this rhapsodic body imagery quite eloquently. But I want to ask, instead, what happens when we consider the *world stage* these tattoos provoke and the ways they create a portal for Parker—and for the reader—into several Americas and at least two different "Orients," the "Near" East and the "Far" East, and two different histories, one close in time, the other far away. Parker's bodily geography recreates the East (in Said's words) as "a theatrical stage affixed to Europe" (p. 63); it also recreates the dynamics of Western colonization. His body offers a theater for U.S. policies of Pacific imperialism that continued to play themselves out during the Cold War.

If Orientalism is a delusional, pain-creating habit, a Western appropriation of the symbols, goods, and lands of vast numbers of non-Europeans, and if "European culture gained in strength and identity by setting itself off against the Orient as a sort of surrogate and even underground self" (Said, p. 3), then how does our analysis of this practice mobilize the complexities of O'Connor's most easternizing story? What we might call an "orientalist longing" re-emerges every time Parker's sense of his own exoticism starts to fade:

> Parker would be satisfied with each tattoo about a month, then something about it that had attracted him would wear off. Whenever a decent-sized mirror was available, he would get in front of it and study his overall look. The effect was not of one intricate arabesque of colors but of something haphazard and botched. A huge dissatisfaction would come over him and he would go off and find another tattooist and have another space filled up.
>
> (p. 514)

Parker's body fills up like a map of the world, as place after place that he visits becomes spatialized on his skin. Said's analysis invites us to see the ways in which the subliminal politics of this story could be said to replicate America's own story of conquest, its steady march from the Philippines toward Guam and Vietnam and finally into the Middle East, that source of all oil. But rather than reducing O'Connor's story to an old binary (an occidental world that uses its idea of the Orient for self-aggrandizement, for constructing a shadow self), I want to suggest another pattern in the carpet. Scholars have begun to explore alternate routes for reading global histories by touting a new brand of cosmopolitanism that reexamines the multiple influences that construct any vernacular. These new cosmopolitanists insist that we discover, in discrete locales, "mixtures of things believed to have been previously unmixed." Even though it would be easy to charge O'Connor with Orientalism, with using the East as a shadow figure to draw exoticism into her story in order to establish the otherness (or foreignness) for docile readers of her vision of Christianity, **"Parker's Back"** is more complicated: a weirdness best illustrated by way of a parable.

In a recent trip to Copenhagen, missing one train and waiting for another, I wandered into the Tivoli Gardens—Copenhagen's jewel of an amusement park. There, in the oh-so-Western heart of this city, I found what looked like another world: minarets with trembling rides attached, pagodas overlooking a sampan pond, walls encrusted with tilework as if from Arabian Nights, a giant tree clouded with pumpkin-sized Japanese lanterns: a potpourri of Orients scrambled together without rhyme or reason except to elicit desire and renewable pleasure; a site "irrational" and "childlike" that has now served for more than a century as foil and erotic underself to this occidental city.

"Ah, the guilty delights of Orientalism are all around me," I thought with scholarly pleasure. And then, in the midst of these musings, I opened my eyes to a sign etched in stone. In 1993, at Tivoli's one-hundred-fifty-year jubilee, the Hankyu corporation of Osaka, Japan, donated a monumental Japanese stone lantern and a small and beautifully maintained Japanese garden to Tivoli as a gesture of capitalist friendship between Japan and Denmark. And there it beckoned, between the sampan pond and Denmark's ideas of Arabia. What was I to make of Tivoli now? Its Islamic moons, its oasis with inflatable palm trees and leaping Burmese tigers suggest one source of nineteenth-century Europe's wealth and fantasmatic pleasure. But when the Japanese themselves embark on a conversation with these fantasies—what then? If globalization is a complex extension of colonialism, a mode of exporting inequality and a new hunger for Western trademarks throughout the planet, it meets an alternative plot-line in the idea of "cosmopolitanism": not the older form of this concept whereby urbane, elite Europeans and American expatriates show those mired in uncivil life a "higher set of values," but a more recent notion of cosmopolitanism asserting that the local is always globally inflected. "In port Parker wandered about comparing the run-down places he was in to Birmingham, Alabama. Everywhere he went he picked up more tattoos" (p. 514). Could Birmingham, Alabama, also be the Orient?

In the manifesto-like introduction to *Cosmopolitanism,* the editors argue for the creation of intellectual tools that will provide "new archives"—a fresh set of "quasi-objects" that can be "located at a series of intersections among cultures."[8] What happens if we look at **"Parker's Back"** as such an intersection? While Flannery O'Connor is busy writing a Christian parable about the overpowering cost of redemption, she is also fretting over relationships between global and local that now consume students of postcolonialism. How do we distinguish between the dangers of globalization, the costs of imperialism—and this phenomenon scholars have named the new "cosmopolitanism"—the attempt to create a more generative category that explores the ways in which localities are always globally striated?

While much can be gained by reading O'Connor's story through this lens, we will also encounter this paradigm's dangers. To make her fictional world into a global romance—to make her vernaculars too worldly—may not do justice to either O'Connor's story or scholarship on the new internationalism now underway. At the same time the connections between local and global, between provincial vernaculars and the swing of Parker's hybridized, mixed-up, minority-bred travels, provide a powerful frame for organizing O'Connor's last tale. Parker's tattoos are the gift of his early nomadism and his adherence to the rules of his class—the ways in which enlisted men (instead of naval officers) experienced the quiddities of American Empire. That is, tattoos were the provenance of the sailor class: a way to mark America's conquests on laboring men's conquered and conquering bodies. But even though these markers of American, class-based machismo are much admired in local bars, these tattoos fall off the map; they seem merely disreputable to fundamentalists like Parker's wife, Sarah. In fact, Parker's sense of being frustrated or misunderstood is heightened, as Sarah Gordon points out in her recent book on O'Connor, by the limitations, the parochialism, of his wife's unworldliness.[9] Although she has memorized the Bible, a script based on "eastern" stories that dominate the Christian "west" (and have also scattered the globe), Parker's wife remains untraveled, provincial, far more parochial than either Parker or the story's narrator, who has a good sense of the "Western" history carried on Parker's back in the form of a Byzantine Christ—that other East that blossoms in this story, making it a tale not only of the multivalent South but of the South as it encounters multiple orientations and Orients.

"Parker's Back" has always held a magnetic power for me; it feels so talismanic that I've been reluctant to write about it, in part because this tattoo-laden narrative dallies with the fantasy of what it would mean to have all one's stories written out in public, etched on one's skin. Peggy Phelan describes the ways in which, in Renaissance painting,

> skin suffers as it tries to contain the form of drama in which we love. Such dramas exceed the elasticity of skin; the skin cannot hold all we ask it to contain. Skin lacks the depth, the interiority, we want it to give us. If skin would give us this depth we might actually have proof that we do have such interiority, that the precarious feelings, dreams, phantasms, inner speech that we call subjectivity is real, that it can be embodied, enclosed in skin's own form. But this is precisely what skin, as surface covering, cannot offer us. Hence we suffer our skins and our skins suffer us.[10]

Skin is an important site of psychic disturbance in O'Connor's South. The tattooed body exists in an indeterminate zone—neither white nor black. It is a vehicle for registering both national and local phantasms: what is on the surface of Parker's skin also rages within. In contrast, the surface of his wife's face is "drawn as tight as the skin on an onion and her eyes were gray and sharp like the points of two icepicks" (p. 510): so tight that it leaves no space for interiority—no seepage—and yet her eyes threaten the flesh of anyone who comes into view (p. 524). Illegible, her body becomes a powerful container: "she was pregnant and pregnant women were not his favorite kind" (p. 510). Her flesh turns multiple; her hand becomes "a terrible bristly claw" (p. 511) when she punishes

Parker for cursing. She seems to change at will between a creature with scales and a hawk-eyed angel, depending on her mood. In contrast, something is always spilling out of Parker's multi-colored body—something like desire—that can only take the particular, local forms available to him in the tattoo parlors of the world. By making her protagonist a sailor and nomad, O'Connor brings together a potpourri of sign systems. What I love about this story is the everyday confusion these sign-systems promulgate when taken together. How do we think simultaneously about Southern race and class systems (the ease with which Parker's employer can threaten to replace him with a black man in order to keep Parker low wage), about protestant fundamentalism, about sideshows focused on exhibitionists (who have been recklessly tattooed by wild "Indians"), about a sailor stigmatized in the Garbo-esque ports of Asia and about an owl-headed tattoo artist whose work is so powerful that it makes Parker an immediate outcast when the story takes its weird, wild swing from the working-class South toward another location—toward not only the Holy Land of the burning bush but the universe of Constantinople, a land Muslims and Christians fought over for centuries. Does it matter that, in the 1960s, while O'Connor was writing her story, this religious conflict murmured at home, in America, as African Americans revisited their own Muslim heritage?[11] As O'Connor writes to Maryat Lee:

> About the Negroes, the kind I don't like is the philosophizing prophesying pontificating kind. . . . King I don't think is the age's great saint but he's at least doing what he can do & has to do. Don't know anything about Ossie Davis except you like him but you probably like them all. My question is usually, would this person be endurable if white? If Baldwin were white nobody would stand him a minute. I prefer Cassius Clay . . . Cassius is too good for the Moslems.
>
> (*Habit,* p. 580; O'Connor's ellipsis)

The battle of Istanbul versus Constantinople rages speechlessly on Parker's pagan-singed body and sings out in O'Connor's letters. Here a "Moslem" vies with Christians like King for moral and narrative authority: "Cassius Clay says he don't like all this talk about hate. Says, a tiger come in the room with you you gonna either run or shoot him. That don't mean you hate the tiger. It just means you know you and him can't make out. Did you see Cassius interviewed by Eric Sevareid on CBS? Worth seeing" (*Habit,* p. 571). Parker, of course, has "a tiger and a panther on each shoulder" as well as "Elizabeth II and Philip over where his stomach and liver were respectively." Although Parker "did not care much what the subject was so long as it was colorful" (p. 514), all this rich, ambiguous history is at play across his body, as well as the question of how class, race, and religion play themselves out in the local worldliness of O'Connor's story.

If we can define the new "cosmopolitanism" as a set of scholarly convictions insisting that, when we follow the multiple story-lines intersecting at any place or moment of history to their multiple sources, we catch glimpses of a "minoritarian modernity," a mode of looking at the world "across time and space" and "outside the box of European intellectual history" to "see how people have thought and acted beyond the local" (*Cosmopolitanism,* p. 10), tattooing is a powerful place to explore this beyond. It was practiced as a minor art form in Europe for centuries but became newly popular with Western exploration and colonization of the South Seas. In fact, "tattoo" is a word, as well as a craft, appropriated from Tahiti that O'Connor literalizes by sending Parker to Asia. This is the first site where Said's ideas about Orientalism become complicated by the drama of class. While Orientalist fantasies were profitable for the high bourgeoisie, the dominant class of world occupiers and travelers did not bring every tag-end of the Orient home. They left remnants like tattoos to be adopted by sailors, working men, vagabonds, global riff-raff. The tattoo becomes, for this class of men, a mark of travel—of having been elsewhere, just as, in the Early Modern period many pilgrims to the Holy Land had themselves marked or stigmatized with what we now call a "tattoo" to prove that they had seen Jerusalem. As he participates in this nomadic tattoo culture, is O. E. Parker an "Orientalist"? Or, do we see, in his obsession with tattooing, the meeting of several vernaculars, a stalwart hybridity where a traditional Asiatic cultural practice becomes, in America, a way of hyper-sexualizing the lower-class male body by expanding its claims to territorialize others?

Tattooing came to public prominence in America as a sideshow or fairway practice in the nineteenth and early twentieth centuries—another portal for popular fantasies about Asians and Native Americans. Almost every tattoo spectacle, from P. T. Barnum's inky men to those who were self-employed, touted a fantastic biography. If, according to sideshow legend, one tattooed man was "taken captive by Maoris in New Zealand . . . and forcibly tattooed" in order to be adopted, another was known as "The Tattooed Man of Burma" or "The Turk," while still others transposed this story to the "Wild West" and described acts of forcible tattooing perpetrated by American Indians (who would have had to appropriate a bizarre range of predictable Western symbols in order to explain the deeply conventional references plastered all over these Barnum and Bailey bodies).[12] As Parker's wife says,

"All that there . . . is no better than what a fool Indian would do" (p. 515).

Before pursuing the ways that sideshow imperialism pervades **"Parker's Back,"** I want to examine O'Connor's own refusal to be a "cosmopolitan" in the traditional sense of pretending to be a cultural elite, one who tries to spread Western values to less fortunate non-elites. O'Connor, of course, claims to be solely in favor of the local, to have little truck with worldly pretensions. A letter written July 4, 1963, makes fun of Euro-highbrow culture. "Katherine Anne sent me a review out of *L'Express* of *Les braves gens ne Whateveritis* [the French edition of ***A Good Man Is Hard To Find***]. It seems to be favorable but not sensible except it says I live on a vast estate among many beasts" (*Habit,* p. 528). O'Connor is at her most hilarious when she is pillorying intellectual or high cultural pretensions. She describes a TV interview in which an "arty young man" from "the museum in Boston" chats with Chagall. After a long and involved question designed to show off the young man's keen erudition, O'Connor delights in Chagall's ironic insistence that "his greatest influence was his mother. It took the poor young man an instant or two to get his bearings after that." But then O'Connor goes on to show—immodestly—her own erudition: "Rouault doesn't come out very well in this does he? And when Chagall speaks of 'the Spaniard' does he mean Picasso do you suppose? You see the Jewish sensitivity very well in this" (*Habit,* p. 531). Although she plays the role that many of her narrators play in making fun of self-importance or affectation, although her constant mantra is to chant and enchant us with her conviction that "the writer's check of himself is local where place still has meaning," this local is piebald and variegated (*Habit,* p. 495). She tells John Hawkes that her city of choice is New Orleans—where she delights in a nightclub called "Baby Green's Evening in Paris," a place "which I might some day like to investigate" (*Habit,* p. 500). Just as the South and Baby Green's version of Europe come together in her letters, so O'Connor makes fun of *Esquire* as "littry" (*Habit,* p. 504), but later shows the reach of her reading: "I am reading *Eichmann in Jerusalem*. . . . Anything is credible after such a period of history. I've always been haunted by the boxcars, but they were actually the least of it. And old Hannah is as sharp as they come" (*Habit,* p. 539).

O'Connor's critique of local boosterism shows her astute grasp of the trajectories of Southern capital. Ackbar Abbas has argued that "'preservation' and 'heritage' do not act as brakes against development: in some strange way, they further a developmental agenda. The problem of cosmopolitanism today still remains how we are to negotiate the transnational space that global capital produces."[13] In letters from the period in which **"Parker's Back"** was percolating (it was published posthumously in *Esquire*), we hear a similar critique from O'Connor about the marriage of heritage-boosting and capitalism in local Georgia pageantry:

> We have been vigorously celebrating Secession here—parade, pageant, pilgrimages, etc. I sat over the hole in the upholstery in the living-room sofa and shook the hands of all and sundry. . . . Everybody is falling around now trying to get the copyright out of [Lance Phillips], so they can make this thing like the Paul Green business in North Carolina. He is holding out for a rising percentage of the net profits, which is certainly what he should get. They spent $1000 for fireworks and $600 for floats, and would not pay him but $200 for the pageant.
>
> (*Habit,* p. 431-432)[14]

Her analysis of the trajectory of capital and the national aspirations of the local merchant class gets interrupted by a description of the "antics" of the African Americans who work for her family, as if they were a costly form of local color who flew right to her kitchen from "Amos 'n Andy" ("Louise recently stuck an icepick in Shot but otherwise we go on our peaceful way around here" [*Habit,* p. 432]). And yet O'Connor infuses her descriptions of the boosterism and localism around with her with a sense of her Georgia community's desire to use provincialism to go global—and to begin by attracting a national audience, like the one visiting "Unto These Hills." She recognizes the local as a prime site of exploitation and "place" as a complex site of profit. Despite her asseverations, we can call O'Connor "cosmopolitan" in the old-fashioned sense of the word, suggesting that she owns knowledge that is "native" to Western elites. But she is also interested in the second form of "cosmopolitan practices," in "mixtures of things believed to have been previously unmixed" (*Cosmopolitanism,* p. 12).

Let's think about the mixture that is Parker's body. In *The Communist Manifesto* Marx argues that "the need of a constantly expanding market for its goods chases the bourgeoisie over the whole surface of the globe. It must nestle everywhere, settle everywhere, establish connections everywhere."[15] To make this happen, the bourgeoisie exploits not only native peoples but its own proletariat or working class. Parker's skin offers a lonely parody of the way the West's bourgeoisie settled and nestled in every crevice it could find: a fact brought home when British royalty settle over Parker's heart and liver, respectively. Is it any wonder he goes AWOL?

> After one of his furloughs, he didn't go back to the navy but remained away without official leave, drunk,

> in a rooming house in a city he did not know. His dissatisfaction, from being chronic and latent, had suddenly become acute and raged in him. It was as if the panther and the lion and the serpents and the eagles and the hawks had penetrated his skin and lived inside him in a raging warfare.
>
> (p. 514)

Parker carries out the white man's burden, but he also carries that burden on his body; he *is* that burden, and also the means of implementing it. He cannot escape from this knowledge because it has gone inside him, and yet, he is not an elite, someone capable of discoursing about "this raging warfare." Instead of "O. E. D.," his initials are "O. E. P.," and sure enough, the liquid of his "words seemed to leave his mouth like wraiths and to evaporate at once as if he had never uttered them" (p. 525). A word-empty product of America's capital-driven conquest of the Pacific as well as its South, a cipher of U.S. dependence on the Near East for its theophanies, the O. E. Parker who is in love with tattoos is no longer the yokel whose heart rises when the flag passes. Instead of red, white, and blue, his body shines with "red and blue and ivory and saffron squares," white turning into ivory, that expensive good imported from Asia and Africa, and saffron, a spice that moved along the silk road, bringing wealth and color to those who traded or pilfered it from elsewhere.

And yet the best, most Easternizing moments are still to come. Covered with the frightening mosaic energy of the Byzantine Christ, Parker is uncertain who he is. Transported back in time eight hundred years, he is at once crusader and pagan: "Parker fell back against the door as if he had been pinned there by a lance" (p. 528). He abandons his Western for his Near Eastern name:

> "Who's there, I ast you?"
>
> Parker bent down and put his mouth near the stuffed keyhole. "Obadiah," he whispered and all at once he felt the light pouring through him, turning his spider web soul into a perfect arabesque of colors, a garden of trees and birds and beasts. "Obadiah Elihue!" he whispered.
>
> (p. 528)

Sarah cannot recognize the epic drama Parker is part of: the weight of East/West history on his back, the freight of imperialism covering the rest of him and Christian imperatives tearing him up inside. "I might have known you was off after putting some more trash on yourself" (p. 529).

Western culture is made out of this trashing, as is the institutional history of Christianity. Ignoring the vast of this history, it simply seems doomed to repeat itself as large welts form on the face of the tattooed Christ and O. E. Parker is lost, once again, in someone else's body. O'Connor's story—with its tale of fragile, embodied suffering—may carry the weight of Christian parable. But it is also written by a dying woman whose own history is at her back and whose regional history is compounded of many regions. "But at my back I always hear, / Time's winged chariot hurrying near."[16] What this chariot carries is not only mortality but the epic history of the East as it has mingled with and been mangled by the West—and the ways this mingling created, for O'Connor, an amazing cosmopolis as well as an Orient Express: a quick route for making her final short story into a clamorous American epic.

Conclusion

The method of this essay resembles the mathematical sublime: everything connected by "'and' and 'and.'" But this model of the sublime has also been the method of U.S. imperialism as the U.S. collects islands, bases, and dictators at whim to redefine the nation's changing economic needs. I have argued that **"Parker's Back"** refracts the trauma of living in a multiply inflected Cold War world—so replete with composite histories that it becomes impossible to make a smooth orientalist map of the many Easts that pop up in O'Connor's story: the "East" of the Cold War Pacific, the "East" of Old Testament prophecy as it has been grafted onto a fundamentalist South, the "East" of Byzantium (an antique version of beleaguered Christian ideals in conflict with other religions), and perhaps even the "East" of the Holocaust: of a Jewish world that calls out in scripture and reappears in the preoccupations of a postwar Israel. What I'm reaching toward in this analysis is a notion of American literature that is not so much coherently orientalist as it is confused; there are so many "Orients" and imperialisms to choose from, and none of them can be mapped neatly onto one another. Thus O'Connor's brief "epic" is something ambivalent as well as magnificent. Instead of arguing that O'Connor is politically progressive in creating these cross-global allusions, I'm suggesting that her writing is driven wild—or sent far afield—as it brushes against the bizarre political facts of Western imperialism: predatory acts supported by the ideologies of Manifest Destiny and WhiteMan'sBurden combined with the prophetic strains of Near Eastern stories. Culture is indeed a game of the in-between, of moves neither cosmopolitan nor local but so heterogeneous that the mind refuses to heap them together. Nevertheless O'Connor settles these paradoxa on the surface of one man's body; her story offers an intriguing experiment in moving this body too rapidly through incommensurable spaces (as the Pacific skims the parochial South) and incommensurable times (as the Old Testament temporality of the burning bush and the epochal time of Byzantium skirmish with "modernity").

To see how O'Connor both recreates and helps us sift through these transpositions, let's examine another set of visual sutures that travel even farther afield: the porcelain portrait heads created by the Beijing-born, Australian-based sculptor Ah Xian. In an art that teeters boldly between East and West, Ah Xian takes the bust (a form fixated on the surplus nobility of the individual) and laminates this occidental convention with traditional Chinese porcelain designs: dragons, floating landscapes, fat babies, floral arabesques, copulating couples. The result is beautiful and frightening. Butterfly wings smother one man's eyes while flowers stop his mouth; dragons, birds, and waterfalls beat wild tattoos or float serene cloud patterns over the brows and lips of another. Like the Byzantine Christ on Parker's back, the effect is dehumanizing, but it is also painfully, rhapsodically descriptive of the ways bodies are encrusted by culture, both made and limited by ideologies that striate our skins. If traditional porcelain patterns represent the "transcendent" beauty of Chinese form as ecstasy *and* as a cruel limit to vision, the suture between these patterns and the cogito that malingers in the Cartesian bust suggests the bewildering predicament of transculturation. As Grace Glueck writes in the *New York Times,*

> In every case, the potent cultural symbols of an earlier China appear like birthmarks—at once an ornament and a blemish—on contemporary faces from China and the Chinese diaspora in the West, evoking questions. What does "Chinese" mean in a global context? Is it intrinsic or cosmetic, something you inescapably are or something you choose to be? Is appropriation of art of the past a way to connect to that past, or to gain distance from it? Does it create a new Orientalism giving the West the Asia it thinks it knows and wants? Or is it a signal that an increasingly insular contemporary Western art is having less and less relevance for artists with strong formative roots elsewhere?[17]

These questions suggest the undecideability of the new cosmopolitanism. Ackbar Abbas says that "cosmopolitanism has been seen as an ability to acquit oneself, to behave well, under difficult cultural situations by juggling with multiple perspectives—even when these perspectives were forced upon us or adopted in indifference." But how can bodies behave well when they are blinded by the very cultural patterns that direct individual seeing? These porcelain busts ask: what does it mean to be swathed in incommensurable cultures? Does it help our common predicament to suggest that every culture is incommensurable and juggles too many perspectives? By exposing the fact that other cosmoi inhere in the local (or is it that other loci inhere in the cosmopolis?), Ah Xian unhinges both Asian and occidental self-certainty; he asks us to feel ideology as a multiple force that laps up people's skins. And yet, as Bryan Jay Woolf argues in his book on Vermeer: "What ideology produces is not space and time, but a notion of space and time as universal and constant, as foundation for the solidity and rectitude and believability of the projects of the nation-state; this notion is essential to the world-historical success of colonialism."[18] O'Connor's story and Ah Xian's sculptures set these coordinates spinning. Bodies become vehicles in transit from one culture to another—sites of overwriting that refuse this wily foundationalism.

At the beginning of O'Connor's story, Parker's tattoos seem to support this foundationalism; he is tragic twin to the Marx Brothers' beloved Lydia, a "Tattooed Lady" whose torso offers a quick trot through occidental history:

> Oh Lydia, oh Lydia, say, have you met Lydia?
> Lydia, the Tattooed Lady.
> She has eyes that folks adore so
> And a torso even more so.
>
> Lydia, oh Lydia, that encyclo-pidia.
> Oh Lydia The Queen of Tattoo.
> On her back is the Battle of Waterloo.
> Beside it, the Wreck of the Hesperus too.
> And proudly above waves the red, white, and blue.
> You can learn a lot from Lydia![19]

Again, the nonce body becomes epic; once again U.S. imperialism reigns supreme. If print capitalism is the begetter of a new world order in which state bureaucracies are supported by communities made out of novels, newspapers, television, and the World Wide Web, O'Connor, like the Marx Brothers, stumbles across a way of making this world order strange by Hebraizing rather than Hellenizing. Or does she blend both? In **"Parker's Back,"** the print culture of the Bible becomes newly "oriental" as Parker finds his Byzantine tattoo by reading its pattern book from left to right, like Hebrew scripture, and the tattoo's exoticism calls up for readers—what?—the Suez crisis (1956), the movie *Exodus* (1961), the concentration camp tattoo? The vernacular body becomes pastiche, a motley crew, a painful node where "for a dime you can see Kankakee or Paree / Or Washington crossing The Delaware." If we learn a lot from Lydia or Parker or Ah Xian, it is because their bodies open up the possibilities of a "minoritarian modernity" while encapsulating the sheer impossibility of operating within the space of global capital when so much is already written upon our backs.

Notes

1. Flannery O'Connor, *The Habit of Being,* ed. Sally Fitzgerald (New York: Farrar, Straus, and Giroux, 1979), p. 592.

2. Lance Phillips, author of Milledgeville's Secession pageant, is identified by O'Connor, in a letter to Ashley Brown, as "the Englishman whose house we went to for tea" (*Habit,* p. 431).

3. Flannery O'Connor, "Parker's Back," in *The Complete Stories* (New York: Farrar, Straus, and Giroux, 1979), p. 512.

4. Keith Bradsher, "Pakistanis Fume as Clothing Sales to U.S. Tumble," *New York Times,* June 23, 2002, p. 3

5. Nathaniel Hawthorne, *The Scarlet Letter: A Romance* (Indianapolis: Bobbs-Merrill Company, 1962), pp. 80-81. My thanks to Jee Yoon Lee and Sara Blair for this comparison.

6. *Orientalism* (New York: Vintage, 1978), p. 43.

7. Her "orientalist" associations are more fully explored in Bharati Mukherjee's *The Holder of the World* (New York: Ballentine Books, 1994), in which Hester travels to India and becomes known as "the Salem Bibi" before her long sojourn in America.

8. Carol Breckenridge, Sheldon Pollock, Homi K. Bhabha, and Dipesh Chakrabarty, eds., *Cosmopolitanism* (Durham: Duke University Press, 2002), pp. 9-13. For a dissenting view, see Timothy Brennan, *At Home in the World: Cosmopolitanism Now* (Cambridge: Harvard University Press, 1997).

9. Sarah Gordon, *Flannery O'Connor: The Obedient Imagination* (Athens: University of Georgia Press, 2000). Gordon explains that while "Parker's tattooed body surely demonstrates the fullness and unity of creation, Sarah R[uth]'s disapproval of the tattoo suggests her disapproval of the world and its flesh" (p. 250). Gordon sees Sarah as someone who falls into the Manichaean heresy, while Parker approaches the childlike stance of spiritual awakening.

10. *Mourning Sex* (New York: Routledge, 1997), p. 41.

11. See Melani McAlister, *Epic Encounters: Culture, Media, and U.S. Interests in the Middle East, 1945-2000* (Berkeley: University of California Press, 2001), pp. 84-124.

12. Stephen Oettermann, "On Display: Tattooed Entertainers in America and Germany," in *Written on the Body: The Tattoo in European and American History,* ed. Jane Caplan (London: Reaktion Books, 2000), pp. 198, 200.

13. "Cosmopolitan De-scriptions: Shanghai and Hong Kong," in *Cosmopolitanism,* p. 224.

14. O'Connor distances herself from facile regional identification: "On the 20th & 21st, we have to go in town for the house opening in connection with celebrating the Civil War. I sure am sick of the Civil War" (*Habit,* p. 426). She also parodied local desire to make Milledgeville the next Williamsburg—or Hollywood: "Lance Phillips is going to write the Secession Pageant. The returns are going to a Youth Center. And Susan Hayward of Hollywood California and Carrollton Georgia is going to come and hep [sic] us celebrate—January the 20th" (*Habit,* p. 418).

15. In *Karl Marx: Selected Writings,* ed. David McLellan (London: Oxford University Press, 1977), p. 224.

16. Andrew Marvell, "To His Coy Mistress," in *The Selected Poetry of Marvell,* ed. Frank Kermode (New York: Signet, 1967), p. 76.

17. "Art in Review," *New York Times,* November 8, 2002, p. B35.

18. *Vermeer and the Invention of Seeing* (Chicago: University of Chicago Press, 2001), p. 229.

19. E. Y. Harbourg, "Lydia the Tattooed Lady" (music by Harold Arlen), from *A Night at the Circus* <http://www.whyaduck.com/info/movies/scenes/lydia.htm.

Thomas F. Haddox (essay date summer 2004)

SOURCE: Haddox, Thomas F. "'Something Haphazard and Botched': Flannery O'Connor's Critique of the Visual in 'Parker's Back.'" *Mississippi Quarterly* 57, no. 3 (summer 2004): 407-21.

[*In the following essay, Haddox claims that "Parker's Back" offers "a sustained critique of the rigidly rationalistic definition of vision associated with the Enlightenment" and notes a feminist subtext conveyed through the character of Sarah Ruth.*]

"Parker's Back," the last short story that Flannery O'Connor published during her lifetime, occupies a unique position in her career, not just by virtue of its belatedness but also for the relative gentleness of its ending. Gone are the shocking deaths, annihilating epiphanies, and portentous descents of divine grace that characterize so many of O'Connor's final paragraphs. We do, to be sure, find Obadiah Elihue Parker, sensualist and collector of tattoos, getting thrashed with a broom by Sarah Ruth, his "Straight Gospel" wife, because he has just added an image of Jesus to his back. But not only is this violence small potatoes in O'Connor's fictional world, it neither provokes nor constitutes a religious awakening. The story ends with Parker "leaning against the tree, crying like a baby."[1] Even if we wish to read this ending as religious allegory, seeing in it allusions to crucifixion and rebirth, there is no sign here that Parker is aware of anything more than Sarah Ruth's displeasure. Instead, there is the evocation (for this reader at least) of a feeling rarely found in O'Connor: sympathy.

Many readings of this story, beginning with the critical tradition established by O'Connor and by Caroline Gordon, have considered it a particularly apt illustration of Catholic sacramentalism, in which Parker's tattoos function as a fumbling and largely unconscious attempt to apprehend the reality of the Incarnation.[2] Sarah Gordon, for instance, calls the story a "parable of obedience" in which Parker, having been reduced to tears by the consequences of his search for Christ in the world, finally reveals both his own need "for spiritual guidance and direction that only 'Mother Church' can provide" and O'Connor's turn toward "a moving acceptance of this world" and a comedic "celebration of divine love."[3] In other words, the sympathy that we may feel for Parker at the end, although unlike O'Connor's usual effects, points toward a more authentically Catholic understanding of grace than she had previously depicted.[4] In a very different vein, Katherine Hemple Prown rejects any claims to sympathy or even grace that Parker may have and discerns in Sarah Ruth's assault on Parker a nascent feminism. Prown traces this change in O'Connor's career to the waning influence of Caroline Gordon on her work and suggests that in **"Parker's Back"** O'Connor was able for the first and last time to present a woman "powerful enough to defy God and deny the male protagonist his claim to salvation."[5]

What interests me about these two readings is that while Gordon and Prown have drawn very different conclusions about **"Parker's Back,"** they have taken as their common starting point the anomalous nature of the story—above all, its atypical ending—and have attempted to account for its difference. In this essay, however, I will argue that neither kind of reading sufficiently emphasizes what makes **"Parker's Back"** distinct in O'Connor's oeuvre—not just its incarnational emphasis on the body or its strong female character but its examination of the connections between vision and subject formation.[6] The story presents a sustained critique of the rigidly rationalistic definition of vision associated with the Enlightenment and thus participates in what Martin Jay has called the "antiocularcentric," anti-Enlightenment project of much twentieth-century Western thought that questions our ability to know and master the world through observation.[7] Moreover, this critique of Enlightenment visuality (and of the human subject associated with it) allows us to reconcile Gordon's and Prown's readings, for O'Connor's antiocular stance has affinities both with certain tendencies in Catholicism and with certain kinds of feminism. In this way, we can account for both our sympathy for Parker and our desire to affirm Sarah Ruth for triumphing over him.

The body of thought that most closely resembles O'Connor's antiocularcentrism in **"Parker's Back"** is associated with twentieth-century France. In *Downcast Eyes: The Denigration of Vision in Twentieth-Century French Thought,* Martin Jay notes that despite France's reputation as a center of Enlightenment thinking since the time of Descartes, a range of influential twentieth-century French intellectuals, from Bataille to Lacan to Levinas, has cast the utmost suspicion on this Enlightenment heritage, seeing it as the wellspring of the nightmares of modernity. Of particular interest to Jay is the dethroning of the visual: from its hallowed place in the Enlightenment—a place that he traces back to the Greeks' privileging of vision over the other bodily senses—vision itself and the regime of clarity, empiricism, and reason that it once signified have been subject to attack (pp. 14-33). As Jay's survey points out, antiocular critique has taken a variety of forms, and distinguishing among them can be difficult. Some strands merely point to the inadequacies of vision, suggesting that although the eye promises mastery and transparency, it is just as likely to mislead us, presenting us with seductive images instead of the truth. Other antiocular critiques acquire a more oppositional aspect, pitting, as Jay says, "the body against the eye" and advancing the claims of other sense—particularly those of touch—against a hegemonic scopic regime. Paradoxically, some antiocular critics use visual excess and the grotesque to advance their critique, proffering images that resist the Enlightenment attempts to delimit and classify them. In this way, even movements in the visual arts such as Cubism can figure as antiocular because they reject Cartesian perspectivalism and frustrate the viewer's attempt to master the work of art (or, in some cases, even the attempt to see the work of art as a coherent whole) (p. 192).[8] What ties together all these strands of antiocularism is not necessarily opposition to vision *per se* but to vision as both metaphor and method of the Enlightenment project.

That O'Connor participates in antiocular critique—and, in fact, engages several of the strands that Jay identifies—may be initially surprising, given her consistent use of visual metaphors for the writer's task in her essays and letters. Her recommendation that aspiring writers focus on "[a]nything that helps you to see, anything that makes you look," her defense of the grotesque in visual terms ("to the hard of hearing you shout, and for the almost-blind you draw large and startling figures"), and her affirmation of Joseph Conrad's claim that the artist's job is to "render the highest possible justice to the visible universe" are all well known.[9] And yet it is also clear that O'Connor's "vision," throughout her career, has little in common with Enlightenment ocularcentrism. In *Wise Blood,* perhaps the most obvious example of O'Connor's antiocularism, Hazel Motes decides to blind himself—an event that, according to many readings of the novel, decisively shows that Motes is now moving toward the Christian truth from which he has hitherto fled. When Motes's landlady, Mrs. Flood, expresses surprise at his blinding and his other acts of self-mortification, he tells her, "You can't see" and suggests that his own "vision" has improved since his blinding: "If there's no bottom in your eyes, they hold more."[10] Only through violence against the eye does Hazel finally attain the truth he has been seeking.

The antiocularism in *Wise Blood,* however, is straightforward and even schematic—Motes's blinding is contrasted neatly with Asa Hawks's failure to blind himself (and subsequent attempt to pretend that he did). In **"Parker's Back,"** O'Connor deepens her critique considerably, drawing on several forms of antiocularism at once. While *Wise Blood* focuses squarely on the question of whether Motes will come to accept Jesus—and uses antiocularism exclusively in reference to this question—**"Parker's Back"** engages a broader frame of reference, showing how Enlightenment vision is not implicated just in the rejection of Christianity but also in the formation of the human subject. Through the use of Parker's tattoos, the story's central symbol, O'Connor suggests that the attempt to fashion a sense of selfhood and agency from visual spectacle ultimately fails—that the attempt to master the visual world all too quickly collapses into enslavement to images, which proliferate beyond our ability to make sense of them.

Parker's passion for tattoos goes back to a day at the fair when he was fourteen, when he saw a man covered with tattoos from head to foot:

> Parker was filled with emotion, lifted up as some people are when the flag passes. He was a boy whose mouth habitually hung open. He was heavy and earnest, as ordinary as a loaf of bread. When the show was over, he had remained standing on the bench, staring where the tattooed man had been, until the tent was almost empty.
>
> Parker had never before felt the least motion of wonder in himself. Until he saw the man at the fair, it did not enter his head that there was anything out of the ordinary about the fact that he existed. Even then it did not enter his head, but a peculiar unease settled in him. It was as if a blind boy had been turned so gently in a different direction that he did not know his destination had been changed.
>
> (p. 513)

Parker's lack of self-consciousness—his inability to reflect on his own existence—is aptly suggested by his open mouth, as if, in psychoanalytic terms, he is fixated at the oral stage and having difficulty separating from the polymorphous pleasures of infancy. The encounter with the tattooed man, however, changes everything, even if these changes manifest themselves only gradually and without his being fully aware of them. He begins to add tattoos to his body, admiring each one obsessively in the mirror, and this embrace of the visual translates into specifically masculine power: he also joins the navy, begins to drink and fight, and pursues women, who, he discovers, often find the tattoos attractive. This encounter with the visual, in other words, plunges Parker both into mature self-consciousness and into a potentially violent pursuit of power, and implicitly provokes the question of whether self-knowledge, long a guiding ideal of the Enlightenment, and a desire to dominate are mutually implicated or the same. Parker, we might say, becomes a child of the Enlightenment at this moment, realizing how his own visual self-fashioning can be made to serve his interests and to proclaim a vaunting sense of autonomy.

Yet at the same time, we are meant to see that this awakening in his life is an illusion: if he was "a blind child" before seeing the man with the tattoos, he is still blind afterwards; he has only been turned in a different direction. Parker's slow discovery of "wonder" in himself that the tattoos provoke is less a celebration of the body in itself—as sacramental readings of the story have emphasized—than a realization that bodies, as visual spectacles, can become sources of power. There are two related problems here. First, Parker desires the tattoos because he has seen them possessed by another. That is to say, his desire is always mediated, always directed toward the plenitude that the tattooed man seems to possess instead of toward the tattoos themselves. As René Girard puts it, "The impulse toward the object is ultimately an impulse toward the mediator."[11] No matter how carefully he imitates the tattooed man, Parker can never believe himself in possession of this fullness of power, precisely because his own desire for the tattoos was not "original"—and therefore can never be an expression of his own power and agency. In Girard's words, "he no longer chooses the objects of his own desire" (p. 1): a visual encounter has made him subject to the power and desires of another—and thus made him vulnerable to dissatisfaction and envy. Accordingly, he goes on adding tattoos, but he "would be satisfied with each tattoo about a month, then something about it that had attracted him would wear off" (p. 514). By the time he marries Sarah Ruth, he has covered the entire front of his body with tattoos, and yet, when he looks in the mirror, he sees not the unified splendor and power that the tattooed man had revealed to him but "something haphazard and botched" (p. 514). The dissatisfaction that he used to feel only after each new tattoo lost its novelty has become "general" (p. 514). Moreover, Parker seems to intuit that he has enslaved himself by pursuing the visual—hence the threat that he perceives in other people's eyes, from Sarah Ruth's, "gray and sharp like the points of two icepicks" (p. 510), to the "all-demanding eyes" (p. 522) of the tattoo of Jesus on his back—"eyes to be obeyed" (p. 527).

Even without the mediation of the tattooed man and the enslavement that it implies, however, a second problem centers on Parker's desire to admire himself in the mirror. Like Jacques Lacan's infant at the mirror stage, who misreads in his reflection a unified, coherent self that does not correspond to the reality of his uncoordinated and helpless body, Parker seeks not merely a sense of power and control but a confirmation of his own unified selfhood.[12] He wants to keep all of his tattoos on the front of his body so that he can view all of them at once. The "haphazard and botched" appearance of the tattoos results from their heterogeneity—from the difficulty of assimilating them all into the single "intricate arabesque of colors" (p. 514) that he desires. When Parker runs out of space and is forced to place the image of Jesus on his back, he can no longer see his reflection all at once—and can only see it at all if he stands between two mirrors. This disrupts not only the unity of aesthetic effect but also Parker's own sense of self: he is now split into two images, just as the Lacanian subject is "split," divided against itself, and incoherent. As Parker recognizes long before his dissatisfaction drives him to this desperate step, being forced to see this split by standing between two mirrors would be "a good way to make an idiot of himself" (p. 518). Parker's quest for visual power produces not the geometric forms, noble proportions, and aesthetic unity of classical art—the Greek model of the visual that Jay situates as the fountainhead of Western ocularcentrism—but excess and fragmentation. By showing that neither the act of looking in a mirror nor engaging in the visual spectacle proves ultimately satisfying, O'Connor engages two strands of antiocular critique at once: she points to the seductive and illusive nature of vision on the one hand and to its potential for producing active misery and even violence on the other.

We can now begin to account for Parker's attraction to Sarah Ruth and for the alternative that she represents. On the one hand, he fears her, and he associates this fear with her eyes. At their first meeting, when he tries to attract her attention by feigning an injury to his hand and cursing loudly, he experiences both the failure of his own vision and a threat from hers, imagining the latter as an instrument of divine vengeance: "Parker's vision was so blurred that for an instant he thought he had been attacked by some creature from above, a giant hawk-eyed angel wielding a hoary weapon" (pp. 511-512). And yet even though Sarah's initial violence results from Parker's cursing, it soon becomes clear that the power of her eyes flows precisely from her hostility to visual spectacle: she is not "taken in" by the tattoos and wages war against them, considering them idolatrous. Parker's attempts to make her desire the tattoos, culminating in the image of Jesus, therefore constitute a battle for supremacy: if he can put her in thrall to the same world of images that snared him, he can confirm his dominance over her.

At the height of his malaise, Parker experiences a vision of the kind that one expects to find at the end of an O'Connor story instead of in the middle. While operating a tractor, he observes the sun making strange movements, and in his confusion he crashes into a tree. The religious resonances of this experience are clear enough: in the words of Richard Giannone, Parker's "shoes and the tree and the tractor burst into a Mosaic theophany so intense that Parker feels the fiery breath of the burning tree on his face" (p. 221). There are also obvious parallels with other depictions of the sun as a symbol of the divine presence in O'Connor's work, such as in **"Greenleaf."** Giannone reads this experience as the second major turning point in Parker's life: "His quest for excitation [that had begun at the fair] ends, as it began, with a vision" (p. 221). And to be sure, this claim seems supported by the text: after suffering his experience, Parker "only knew that there had been a great change in his life, a leap forward into a worse unknown, and that there was nothing he could do about it" (p. 521). Here, then, must be the inevitable religious epiphany, the sign that if Parker has not yet been redeemed, he is at least demonstrably on the right path.

I would argue, however, that Parker's response to this "vision" shows at least as much continuity with his earlier self as rupture. Indeed, the hallucination holds out a tantalizing promise of visual power, only to revoke it and turn it into a threat, just as Parker's earlier encounter with the "giant hawk-eyed angel" of Sarah Ruth had. Parker imagines that "[t]he sun . . . began to switch regularly from in front to behind him, but he appeared to see it in both places as if he had eyes in the back of his head. All at once he saw the tree reaching out to grab him" (p. 520). For a moment, Parker seems to possess the sense of power and unified selfhood that he has been pursuing. If he can see both behind him and in front of him, then he can proceed with further tattoos on his back without disrupting the unity of his self-image—and thus heal his divided consciousness. This moment, however, is just as fleeting as his earlier intimations of power, and it immediately transforms into an attack against him. Moreover, even though afterwards he feels compelled to add the tattoo of Jesus, he had been considering such a step for some time—he already believed that "Sarah Ruth would not be able to resist" a tattoo of a religious subject (p. 519). And when he returns to Sarah Ruth, he does so not because he wants to communicate the religious truth he has discovered but because "she would at least be pleased. It seemed to him that, all along, that was what he wanted, to please her" (p. 527). Perhaps the most significant change in Parker is that whereas his earlier flaunting of the tattoos had been a conscious effort to make Sarah Ruth submit to him, he now considers the possibility that he has wanted to please her. Whether this marks a genuine change or a rationalization of his continuing desire to dominate, however, remains unclear. Surely the peremptory way he directs her attention to the tattoo—"Look at this and then I don't want to hear no more out of you" (p. 529)—suggests that he struggles for supremacy over her until the end.

In contrast to Parker's tormented ocularcentrism, Sarah Ruth's faith both challenges the hegemony of the eye and presents an alternative to it in its openness to other senses. To be sure, most readings of her character stress the distance between her faith and the sacramental dogmas of Catholicism, which necessarily affirm the intermingling of flesh and spirit. (Indeed, in perhaps the most extreme expression of Sarah Ruth's rejection of sacramentalism, she marries Parker in a civil ceremony because she finds even churches themselves idolatrous [p. 518]—which might suggest that for her God has nothing to do with the inescapably fleshly nature of marriage.) This emphasis on "spirit," however, takes an unusual form: while her hostility toward vision is unrelenting (and while, true to form, she adheres to familiar fundamentalist prohibitions against drinking, smoking, and other obvious pleasures), she displays a certain affinity with hearing, touch, and taste. Sarah Gordon's claim that Sarah Ruth "does not find pleasure in the physical" (*Obedient Imagination,* pp. 248-249) is overstated, for Sarah Ruth proves capable of some bodily pleasures. We can see her privileging of hearing over vision in the "Straight Gospel" nature of her faith itself, which stresses the preaching of God's message and the necessity of listening to it,[13] and we can see her appreciation of bodily delights in Parker's interactions with her. When Parker first comes courting her, bringing a bushel of apples (in a reversal of the familiar Garden of Eden story), she eats eagerly, "chew[ing] the apple slowly but with a kind of relish of concentration" (p. 516), and this unabashed "relish" is enough to make Parker uncomfortable: "Hungry people made Parker nervous" (p. 515). If the apples represent Parker's "tree of knowledge," a sign of his desire to tempt her into a world of visual spectacle and futile Enlightenment mastery, then the fact that she fails to succumb and experiences the apple only as a sensual delight can only be unsettling. She also seems to enjoy sex, though only when she does not have to see the tattoos: "Except in total darkness, she preferred Parker dressed and with his sleeves rolled down" (p. 519). Even Parker suspects that she enjoys sensual pleasure, considering the possibility that "she actually liked everything she said she didn't" (p. 510). If we observe that her hostility is less toward pleasure itself than toward the visual experiences that usually accompany it, Parker's hypothesis becomes less odd.

If we take Sarah Ruth, then, as a critic of ocularcentrism, we can perhaps align her with certain feminist theorists who also reject the primacy of the visual and affirm instead the tactile—Luce Irigaray, for instance. If, as Irigaray argues, "Woman takes pleasure more from touching than from looking, and her entry into a dominant scopic economy signifies, again, her consignment to passivity," then Sarah Ruth's rejection of the visual—including, for instance, her refusal to wear makeup and thus become a potential object of male desire—can be seen as an affirmation of an alternate sexuality and epistemology.[14] This assertion may seem counterintuitive, given the prominence of the female body in Irigaray's thought and Sarah Ruth's preference for "spirit": certainly we see no autoerotic meditations on Sarah Ruth's labia, or anything like a celebration of menstrual blood, milk, tears, or other manifestations of what Irigaray calls "an economy of *flow*" (p. 148). And yet, I would maintain that she in some sense "feminizes" Parker if her affirmation of "spirit" opposes not body but vision, and that her victory over him consists largely of the fact that she forces him into a world of tactility and even of "flow."

The first hint of Sarah Ruth's victory over Parker occurs at their first meeting. I have already alluded to Parker's fear of her eyes, but what is perhaps more revealing in this incident is the threat that her touch poses to him. When she reaches out to examine his supposedly injured hand, Parker finds himself "jolted back to life by her touch." Immediately after this moment, he looks "more closely at her" and concludes, "I don't want nothing to do with this one" (p. 512). Sarah Ruth's touch, though "life-giving," is also obscurely threatening, since his immediate response is to reassert the power of the visual and to conclude that he does not want her. But of course the most obvious example of Sarah Ruth's "touch" occurs not as a sensual caress but as her attack on the new tattoo, still tender and sore. The final moment of the novel takes on a new significance in light of Irigaray's theory: Parker leans against a tree, "crying like a baby" (p. 530). This crying suggests both the blurring of vision and a regression to earlier phases of subjectivity. Painful though it has been for him, Sarah Ruth has succeeded in bringing him into an "economy of flow"—and in destroying his last vestige of belief in the self-affirming power of the visual. Perhaps the title **"Parker's Back,"** then, also signifies as "Parker has returned"—to the self that he abandoned at the age of fourteen.[15]

Between these two instances of Sarah Ruth's touch, there is the turning point in the struggle between Parker and Sarah Ruth, which occurs when she refuses to open the door for him until he identifies himself by his full name. Theologically grounded readings of the story point to this as the moment of conversion, in which Parker finally accepts the meaning of his full name (Obadiah means "servant of God"; Elihue means "my God is he") and feels himself to be, in Giannone's words, "the visible dwelling of glory" (p. 229). And indeed, what follows this moment is unusually heavy-handed for O'Connor: "[A]ll at once he felt the light pouring through him, turning his spider web soul into a perfect arabesque of colors, a garden of trees and birds and beasts" (p. 528). Just as striking, however, is the way this moment revises the symbol of the tattoos. The "perfect arabesque" that Parker sought as a visual spectacle on his body has been achieved at last, but only because it has become invisible: the soul is now perfected, but the body remains as "haphazard and botched" as ever to the eye—and indeed becomes more so, as Sarah Ruth's broom raises welts on the face of Jesus. The link here between submission to God and the renunciation of a visible aesthetic pleasure for an invisible one is particularly clear. Although even after this moment Parker continues, feebly, to struggle against Sarah Ruth—"Look at this and then I don't want to hear no more out of you" (p. 529)—his capitulation to her and his renunciation of the visible now become inevitable.

Whatever the assimilability of **"Parker's Back"** to Irigaray's antiocular feminism, O'Connor would not, of course, wish to see her work interpreted through such a resolutely secular lens.[16] I would suggest, however, that we can bring O'Connor's Catholicism and Irigaray together precisely in the critique of the Enlightenment that both share. Parker may be in pursuit of Enlightenment autonomy through the visual, but instead of an autonomous and aesthetically unified self, he gets a fragmented, excessive, and submissive self quite at home in what Camille Paglia has called "Italian pagan Catholicism," with its sacraments, its overpowering visual excess, and its tendency toward an aesthetic of decadence.[17] In other words, I am suggesting that in Parker O'Connor invokes not the "rationalist" model of Catholicism that she clearly admired (for instance, the work of Aquinas, which has its own affinities with the Enlightenment) but something more akin to the sensuous, mystical, and even forthrightly irrational Catholicism of a figure such as Joris-Karl Huysmans, with its emphasis on submission.

Other critics have, to be sure, noted the overt irrationalism of O'Connor's vision. One of the first was Joyce Carol Oates, who famously argued, "There is no patience in O'Connor for a systematic, refined, rational acceptance of God; and of the gradual transformation of apocalyptic religious experience into dogma, she is strangely silent."[18] Indeed, it is precisely in this embrace of the immediate, the experiential, and the irrational that O'Connor departs in some ways from orthodox Catholic positions. The most recent official catechism of the Catholic Church, for instance, reaffirms that "there can never be any real discrepancy between faith and reason" because "the same God who reveals mysteries and infuses faith has bestowed the light of reason on the human mind."[19] Indeed, the same document defines sin not just as an offense against God but also as "an offense against reason, truth, and right conscience" (p. 505). The discrepancy between O'Connor's letters, with their detailed discussion of Catholic theology and their apparent endorsement of both reason and faith, and O'Connor's fiction, with its frequent rejection of reason, thus points to a fundamental tension in her work. (Indeed, one's interpretation of O'Connor's indebtedness to Teilhard de Chardin—long a focus of investigation—depends largely on whether one sees Teilhard primarily as a rationalist seeking to reconcile his Catholic faith with the science of evolution or as a mystic whose emphasis on "convergence" and evolution of consciousness is at bottom a rejection or transcendence of reason.)[20]

But if O'Connor's irrationalism departs from orthodox Catholicism, it dovetails nicely with Sarah Ruth's "Straight Gospel" emphasis on the spirit, which is also pitted against Enlightenment claims to mastery. Both are in the service of breaking down the solitary, autonomous (and usually masculine) ego, and reconstituting from its dissolution a more fluid self, subject, perhaps, to the love and grace of God but also freed from the agonies of mediated desire and envy. Parker suffers a double whammy, impelled by the power of visual excess on the one hand and the ferocity of Sarah Ruth's antiocularism on the other, but the two conspire together to rid him of his Enlightenment delusion of mastery. Indeed, it may well be that his encounter with the tattooed man functions as a fortunate fall—and that once he has fallen the only way out is through this double path of excess and renunciation.

By conjoining the iconoclastic, antiocular "Straight Gospel" of Sarah Ruth with an aesthetic of the grotesque—a display of visual excess that records both suffering and the pleasures of irrationality—O'Connor wages in **"Parker's Back"** a war against Enlightenment visuality and against the human subject that emerges from it. We may not wish to follow her into her particular construction of an irrational, florid, and visually overpowering Catholicism, but we should attend to the surprising, double-pronged nature of her attack, with its paradoxically antiocularcentric aesthetic of the grotesque on the one hand and its privileging of other bodily senses on the other. The distance between Milledgeville, Georgia, and the Left Bank is far less than we tend to think. For those of us who have become dissatisfied both with the piety of traditional readings of O'Connor and with predictable attempts to recuperate her work for a politically correct (and pedestrian) secular humanism, attention to O'Connor's antiocularcentrism, her fierce critique of the Enlightenment, and her surprising affinities with the thought of twentieth-century France offers valuable new points for departure.

Notes

1. Flannery O'Connor, "Parker's Back," in *The Complete Stories* (New York: Farrar, Straus, and Giroux, 1971), p. 530.
2. See Flannery O'Connor, *The Habit of Being* (New York: Farrar, Straus, and Giroux, 1979). In a letter of 17 July 1964 to Betty Hester, known to most readers as O'Connor's anonymous friend "A," O'Connor mentions that Caroline Gordon had praised her for "succeed[ing] in dramatizing a heresy" in "Parker's Back" (p. 593). O'Connor then clarified what Gordon had meant in a follow-up letter of 25 July: "No Caroline didn't mean the tattoos were the heresy. Sarah Ruth was the heretic—the notion that you can worship in pure spirit" (p. 594). These passages provide the kernel of all "sacramental" readings of the story, holding up Parker's delight in the flesh—including the tattoos—against Sarah Ruth's Manichean equation of God with spirit. For a particularly strong reading of this kind, see Richard Giannone, *Flannery O'Connor and the Mystery of Love* (Urbana: University of Illinois Press, 1989), pp. 221-231.
3. Sarah Gordon, *Flannery O'Connor: The Obedient Imagination* (Athens: University of Georgia Press, 2000), pp. 248, 251.
4. Some critics have suggested that despite O'Connor's explicit repudiation of Manicheanism, she sometimes expressed clear Manichean tendencies in her fiction. See, for instance, Frederick Asals, *Flannery O'Connor: The Imagination of Extremity* (Athens: University of Georgia Press, 1982), p. 58. Sarah Gordon seems to acknowledge the plausibility of such claims, noting that while "*Wise Blood* and other early works stand accused" of Manicheanism, "Parker's Back" presents "O'Connor's most clearly Catholic narrative" precisely because of its friendliness toward the physical world (p. 251).
5. Katherine Hemple Prown, *Revising Flannery O'Connor: Southern Literary Culture and the Problem of Female Authorship* (Charlottesville: University Press of Virginia, 2001), p. 106. Prown's larger argument—that Caroline Gordon played a significant and deplorable role in directing O'Connor away from the "female-sexed voice that governed her fictional landscape" (p. 7) in her earliest works and toward "masculinist forms and conventions" (p. 161)—is based on a comparison of O'Connor's manuscripts with her published work. Though Prown's book is often persuasive, I am uneasy with the essentialist implications of the phrase "female-sexed voice," which seems to be presumed as a given that can only be distorted or suppressed—not a construction in its own right. Moreover, Prown's reading has strong affinities with first-wave feminism, which, ever since Mary Wollstonecraft, is easily assimilable to an Enlightenment paradigm. As I hope that my argument shows, O'Connor's stance in "Parker's Back" is, surprisingly, closer to that of "second wave" feminisms, with their explicit critique of the Enlightenment.
6. In "The Being of Illness: The Language of Being Ill," Sue Walker anticipates my argument here, touching briefly on the significance of vision in "Parker's Back." Walker states that "O'Connor's postmodern representation of Parker subverts the dominant scopic view and revisions the anamorphic tradition that allows the spectator/viewer/reader to reform a distorted picture into one that incorporates faith" (*Flannery O'Connor Bulletin,* 25 [1996-97], 50). Aside from this brief reference, however, she does not delve further into what makes O'Connor's representation "postmodern." Nor, as I hope to show, does O'Connor's antiocularism necessarily mandate faith, even if it can incorporate it.
7. *Downcast Eyes: The Denigration of Vision in Twentieth-Century French Thought* (Berkeley: University of California Press, 1993), p. 16.
8. We might consider as an example of the first kind of antiocular critique (which emphasizes the deceptions of the eye) Jacques Lacan's account of the mirror stage, in which the infant sees in his re-

flection an image of unity that does not correspond to the reality of its inchoate self, brimming with desires that do not cohere into a whole. We might consider as an extreme example of the second kind of critique (that is, body against the eye) Georges Bataille's 1927 pornographic novel *The Story of the Eye,* trans. Joachim Neugroschel (San Francisco: City Lights, 1987), in which a woman seduces a priest, then strangles him, then enucleates his eye and places it in her vagina. Finally, the paradoxical use of vision against itself might be best seen in the work of an artist such as Marcel Duchamp, both in his Cubist phase (for instance, in *Nude Descending a Staircase*) and his later, more conceptual works such as *Etant donnés.* For a discussion of Duchamp as antiocular, see Jay, pp. 161-170.

9. Flannery O'Connor, "The Nature and Aim of Fiction," in *Mystery and Manners: Occasional Prose,* ed. Sally and Robert Fitzgerald (New York: Farrar, Straus, and Giroux, 1969), p. 84; Flannery O'Connor, "The Fiction Writer and His Country," in *Mystery and Manners,* p. 34; Joseph Conrad, preface to *The Nigger of the Narcissus,* qtd. in Flannery O'Connor, "The Nature and Aim of Fiction," in *Mystery and Manners,* p. 80.
10. Flannery O'Connor, *Wise Blood* (New York: Farrar, Straus, and Giroux, 1952), p. 222. In *Flannery O'Connor's Religion of the Grotesque* (Jackson: University Press of Mississippi, 1985), Marshall Bruce Gentry, in his reading of *Wise Blood,* emphasizes its antiocularism in terms very close to those of Jay, speaking of "Hazel's war between the eye (or 'I') and the body . . . [in which] the body . . . wins" (p. 133).
11. *Deceit, Desire, and the Novel: Self and Other in Literary Structure,* trans. Yvonne Freccero (Baltimore: Johns Hopkins University Press, 1965), p. 10.
12. See Jacques Lacan, "The Mirror Stage as Formative of the Function of the I," in *Écrits: A Selection,* trans. Alan Sheridan (New York: Norton, 1977), pp. 1-7.
13. Jay's contrast between an ocularcentric Greek culture and an audiocentric Jewish culture is perhaps relevant here: "If the Jews could begin their most heartfelt prayer, 'Hear, O Israel,' the Greek philosophers were in effect urging, 'See, O Hellas'" (p. 33). Like many fundamentalist Christian denominations that promote iconoclasm, Sarah Ruth's "Straight Gospel" faith displays an obvious attraction to the God of the Old Testament, whose Word has not become flesh.
14. Luce Irigaray, *This Sex Which Is Not One,* trans. Catherine Porter with Carolyn Burke (Ithaca: Cornell University Press, 1985), p. 26.
15. In "An Encounter with O'Connor and 'Parker's Back'" (*Flannery O'Connor Bulletin,* 24 [1995-96], 104-118), Alfred Corn has also proposed a reading of the title as "Parker Has Returned," but he interprets this phrase in a more overtly theological sense—as Parker having returned to God, in response to the tattoo of Jesus telling him to "GO BACK" (p. 115).
16. Ted R. Spivey, in *Flannery O'Connor: The Woman, the Thinker, the Visionary* (Macon, Georgia: Mercer University Press, 1995), maintains that not enough attention has been paid to O'Connor as a "secular intellectual" and social critic, despite the fact that she was conversant with a wide range of social thought beyond the theologians whom she so often mentioned in her letters (p. 7). I would agree that O'Connor needs to be brought into dialogue with secular intellectuals, even with those whom she violently rejected, but I am not arguing here for any kind of direct influence of Lacan or other secular French thinkers on her work. The similarities between her thought and theirs are, rather, a matter of confluence.
17. According to Paglia's characterization of Italian Catholicism in *Sexual Personae: Art and Decadence from Nefertiti to Emily Dickinson* (New York: Vintage, 1991), "A sense of the mystic and uncanny has pervaded Italian culture for thousands of years, a pagan hieraticism flowering again in Catholicism, with its polychrome statues of martyred saints, its holy elbows and jawbones sealed in altarstones, and its mummified corpses on illuminated display" (p. 127).
18. *New Heaven, New Earth: The Visionary Experience in Literature* (New York: Vanguard, 1974), p. 176.
19. *Catechism of the Catholic Church* (New York: Image Doubleday, 1994), p. 49.
20. For a representative reading of Teilhard's influence on "Parker's Back," see Karl-Heinz Westarp, "Teilhard de Chardin's Impact on Flannery O'Connor: A Reading of 'Parker's Back,'" *Flannery O'Connor Bulletin,* 12 (Autumn 1983), 93-113.

Denise T. Askin (essay date fall 2004)

SOURCE: Askin, Denise T. "Anagogical Vision and Comedic Form in Flannery O'Connor: The Reasonable Use of the Unreasonable." *Renascence* 57, no. 1 (fall 2004): 47-62.

[*In the following essay, Askin observes the blending of seriousness and humor in O'Connor's stories, tracing the progression from rationality to transcendent irrationality in her comedic works.*]

Flannery O'Connor warns in *Mystery and Manners* that unless the scholar can "apprehend the form, he will never apprehend anything else about the work, except what is extrinsic to it as literature" (129). Her creative instincts drew her to comedy, a mode that served her anagogical purposes well. The congruity of comedy with Christian belief has been widely discussed by theologians, philosophers and literary critics.[1] O'Connor scholars have addressed her "comic vision" from a theological perspective (Wood), her use of irony (Schloss) and her affinity for the grotesque (Gentry) as ways of approaching her comedic art. On the one hand, O'Connor uses comedy as an artistic strategy to dispatch moral tyranny and complacency, and to embody the sacred through a kind of faithful profanation. But, like Mark Twain, she is also employing in comedy an eminently rational form to purge a contemporary art corrupted by the demon of sentimentality. In doing so, she is working within a formal comedic tradition that extends back from Mikhail Bakhtin's medieval carnival to Aristotle's *Poetics.*

I would like to complement the discussion of O'Connor's "comic vision" by looking at the forms she employs in its service.[2] To situate O'Connor in the comedic tradition we need to examine the formal aspects of her art: paradigmatic pairing of *alazon* and *eiron,* comic deflation and resolution through plot structure, timing, unmasking devices, characterization, and language. O'Connor uses classic comedic elements (traditionally the enemies of sentiment and egocentricity), and she "customizes" them for her anagogical purposes by truncating the conventional comic plot resolution, and shifting modes at the ends of her works. Her story **"Greenleaf"** serves to illustrate the anagogical and formal aspects of O'Connor's comedic style.

* * *

O'Connor gives unrivaled priority in her essays to the function of "seeing." She advocates anything that will activate the writer's obligation to "stare" at things, a species of "stupidity" she says the fiction writer cannot do without (*Mystery and Manners* 77, 84, 91, 177; *The Habit of Being* 115). This stupidity, of course, is her term for the gradual and complex process of sacramental beholding that she calls the prophetic vision, or "getting the point" (*Mystery and Manners* 77). When stared at thus relentlessly, the concrete thing yields its "point," that is, its extensions of meaning. The prophetic writer sees the extensions of near (or visible) things, and sees "far" (or invisible) things close up. The extensions of the near lead to the "invisible" sphere of the divine (mystery). Conversely, the distance between the "far" things of the spirit and the visible world diminishes. This is what O'Connor calls the anagogical dimension of her art, akin to what Paul Ricoeur might call an "excess of signification" (55).

In the service of this anagogical function, O'Connor looks to make the concrete image do "double time," (*Mystery and Manners* 96), to "suggest both the world and eternity" (*Mystery and Manners* 111). In her comic grotesque, she seeks a single "image that will connect or combine or embody two points; one is a point in the concrete, and the other is a point not visible to the naked eye . . . but just as real" (*Mystery and Manners* 42). The anagogical vision sees "different levels of reality in one image or one situation" (*Mystery and Manners* 72). Neither a dogmatist nor a moralist, O'Connor was in the business of *seeing* and trying to make others see what is there but is invisible to the secular eye. How is it then, with this serious artistic agenda, that O'Connor chose comedy as her vehicle?

First of all, it is necessary to dispel the idea that there is an inherent conflict between seriousness and comedy, or between a vision of the sacred and an affinity for the incongruous. A host of writers from Kierkegaard through Reinhold Niebuhr have found in comedy's focus on the concrete, its movement from constraint to freedom, and its *anamnesis*—its recall of our fully embodied humanity (Lynch 98)—to be vitally attuned to the Christian perspective. Kierkegaard makes the claim that "the more thoroughly and substantially a human being exists, the more he will discover the comical . . . [T]he religious man, most of all [must] discover the comical" (qtd. in Hyers 10-11). The unifying theme of these writers is that comedy embraces the finiteness and incongruity of human existence, an essential perspective for a religion based on Incarnation. Insofar as it is a recognition of the incongruity of human existence, Reinhold Niebuhr claims that comedy is more profound than any philosophy which "seeks to devour incongruity in reason" (qtd. in Hyers 148). Conrad Hyers's claim that comedy is "closer to the deep springs of religion than tragedy" (233), is taken up by Nathan A. Scott, Jr.:

> . . . it is the function of comedy to enliven our sense of the human actuality, to put us in touch with the Whole Truth—particularly when, in the pursuit of some false and abstract image of ourselves, we have become embarrassed by the limitations of our creatureliness and undertaken . . . flight into the realm of pure idea. . . . [T]he comic imagination, it seems to me, summarizes an important part of the Christian testimony about the meaning of life.
>
> (Hyers 73)

One writer who had a notable influence on Flannery O'Connor's aesthetic theory was William Lynch, the Jesuit scholar whose essays on the Christian imagination and on comedy she had read approvingly in *Christ and Apollo.* He argues the supreme appropriateness of comedy for an incarnational and sacramental view of reality because of its fidelity to the finite "concrete," a word O'Connor herself used like a mantra in her essays. He argues that the shock of seeing the radical congruity between the comic figure and the divine, between the earth and Christ "with all the logic omitted" (109) is the distinctive province of comedy. Lynch concludes that comedy is the right vehicle for an incarnational vision:

> The "mud in man" is nothing to be ashamed of. It can produce . . . the face of God. . . . To recall this, to recall this incredible relation between mud and God, is, in its own distant, adumbrating way, the function of comedy.
>
> (109)

Clearly there is a strong tradition connecting comedy to the sacred in Christian thought that ratifies the delight O'Connor took in developing her eloquent incongruities. Comedy was second nature to O'Connor. Like the child in **"The Temple of the Holy Ghost,"** O'Connor figuratively rolled on the floor in laughter at the incongruities so remorselessly present to her in daily life. "The basis of the way I see," she wrote to John Hawkes, "is comic regardless of what I do with it . . ." (*The Habit of Being* 400). What she does with the comic, I would argue, is to make it the medium of the anagogical.

* * *

The journey toward God, O'Connor claimed, is often impeded by emotion, particularly when it leads one to skip the process of redemption "in its concrete reality" in order to arrive at a "mock state of innocence, which strongly suggests its opposite" (*Mystery and Manners* 148). "A mind cleared of false emotion and false sentiment and egocentricity," O'Connor says, "is going to have at least those roadblocks removed from its path" (*Mystery and Manners* 84). Her animus against emotion amounted to a virtual campaign against sentimentality and sappy compassion. She was dogged by readers who wanted to feel compassion for her cripples and idiots while she wanted "intellectual and moral judgments . . . [to] have ascendancy over feeling" (*Mystery and Manners* 43). She levels her aim at pious readers and writers, people "afflicted with sensibility" (*Mystery and Manners* 84), who produce and reward "soggy, formless" literature (*Mystery and Manners* 31). In "The Church and the Fiction Writer" she goes so far as to link sentimentality in art with obscenity and pornography (*Mystery and Manners* 147-48), both guilty of the Manichean tendency to separate nature and grace. She skewers romanticism, as did Mark Twain, by deflating falsified language and pious clichés at every turn. Like Moliere and Ben Jonson before her, O'Connor cannot resist unmasking the mock state of virtue. It is easy to see why she was so fond of the comedic mode. Comedy detests nothing more than the character that forgets his humanity (Lynch 29) in all its incongruousness.

In opposition to the romanticism and sentimentality responsible for "pious [literary] trash," comedy is the quintessentially rational form. It activates the intellect while numbing the emotions. Horace Walpole gave us the memorable dictum that life is a comedy to those who think and a tragedy to those who feel. In the same vein, Henri Bergson makes his classic claim that comedy is incompatible with emotion, that it is an appeal to intelligence, pure and simple. Comedy demands of the audience a "momentary anaesthesia of the heart" (64). O'Connor's tribe of morons, backwoods prophets, razor-tongued children, ironhanded widows, and ugly-spirited intellectuals, then, is depicted in a manner that does not elicit our sympathy or compassion. It calls for judgment. Their deformities are ludicrous, a species of the "ugly" that Aristotle sees as the proper sphere of comedy.

When O'Connor claims that her art is "a reasonable use of the unreasonable" (*Mystery and Manners* 109), she uses the term "reason" in a specifically Thomistic sense. If art is, as St. Thomas says, "reason in the making" (*Mystery and Manners* 82), O'Connor marshals her irrational materials in such a way that an underlying *logos* emerges. "The artist uses his reason to discover an answering reason in everything he sees. For him, to be reasonable is to find, in the object, in the situation, in the sequence, the spirit which makes it itself" (*Mystery and Manners* 82). She points us not to a rhetorical formulation but to the form of the work itself, a form that makes manifest the all-surrounding order of existence. If comedy, through its ordering of the unreasonable, allows the underlying reason to emerge, it becomes a fitting vehicle for the anagogical vision.

* * *

Northrop Frye locates the genre of comedy in the "mythos of spring." Comedy celebrates fertility by reenacting the death of the old order, typically characterized by irrational law and excessive constraints, and the rebirth of a society free to follow the impulses of love and harmony. As Aristotle tells us in the *Poetics,* comedy originated in the fertility processions in honor of Dionysus, and many modern theorists still see "eros" as the motivating force of the genre. Mikhail Bakhtin identifies the prototypical comic movement as one of liberation (Averintsev 80) from whatever obstacles impede the life force. In "new comedy" or romantic comedy, the impediment to true love or to change may be blocking characters (such as tyrannical fathers), oppressive laws, or mistaken identities. The resolution of the conflict brings about the required reversals and transformation of society. In Aristophanic, or satiric comedy, the tradition O'Connor appropriates, intruders or imposters threaten to destroy an already vulnerable society. The action requires that the characters be unmasked (deflated) and either absorbed into or expelled from a society that is ultimately saved from destruction, but does not necessarily undergo a transformation.

The action of comedy, varied as individual instances may be, does have a discernible structure. It moves toward freedom, typically liberation from blocking characters and social obstacles. Its characteristic elements include 1) the unmasking of false characters, 2) the *cognitio,* or recognition scene, 3) reversal, and 4) restoration of harmony. If the central movement of the plot is toward freedom, the central movement of the character is from *pistis* to *gnosis,* from opinion/illusion to knowledge/reality. Comic action typically concludes with restored harmony (usually united lovers) and a glimpse of an ideal society. In its satiric forms, comedy accomplishes its end by revealing the deformity of the existing social order and by overturning it, becoming in the process a potentially subversive genre.

The comic plot is typically quite complicated, often involving a disproportionate effort for an inconsequential result. Episodic and irrational on the surface, the comic plot turns on its own brand of inevitability. Blocking characters are outwitted by their own cleverness, led by their own vices into traps, or caught out by characters they had dismissed as marginal and powerless. Traps snap shut with a kind of ironic precision that suggests an underlying order and justice. Obvious juxtaposition of opposing scenes, coupled with clockwork timing give an impression of the victory of plot over character.

Comic characters are stereotypical (the senex, the crafty servant, the domineering parent, and the like) drawn in caricature or cartoon-like exaggeration. Comic characters are "worse" than the average, according to Aristotle. They are "ridiculous," that is, a species of "the ugly," and their language is low-class. Two conventional structures of the genre include doubling of characters (eg. twins, identical disguises, mirror images), and pairing characters with their opposites or foils (tall and short, smart and dumb, Quixote and Sancho Panza). These patterns build complexity and create balance, respectively. A combination of passages from the *Tractatus Coislinius* and the *Nicomachean Ethics* reveals that Aristotle named the oppositional comic characters by their defining tropisms: the *alazons,* or imposters; the *eirons,* or self-deprecators; the *bomolochoi* (buffoons), the characters with too much wit; and the *agroikos* (boors), those with too little (Rath 252).

As Sura Rath points out, the "contest of the *eiron* and *alazon* forms the basis of comic action" (252). The *alazon* inflates his self-image and is typically in a position of power or privilege when the comic action begins. The *eiron,* by contrast, appears to be less than he is. Often the *eiron* is a subtle, ironic dialectician like Plato's Socrates (Foulke 600) who may withdraw temporarily from the action, only to surface at a critical moment in the plot and deflate the *alazon* (Rath 256), thereby bringing about the comic reversal. In contrast to the overstatement of the *alazon,* the *eiron*'s most powerful weapon is Meisosis, or understatement (Bedford 177).

If Aristotle provides a generic structure of comic polarities, Henri Bergson provides the classic exposition of comic modality. His formulation of the comic as "the mechanical encrusted on the living" (92) defines the elements of comedic plotting and characterization. Humans are laughable, he says, "in exact proportion as they remind us of machines" (79). The comedic character is repetitive, robotic, fixated, and predictable. The language of the comic character: 1) contains "ready-made formulas and stereotypical phrases uttered automatically" (133) and 2) it takes the material element of a metaphor literally (135)—two favorite O'Connor devices.[3]

If the mythos of spring is the key to the comic action, Bergson shows how that concept is dramatized in the comedy itself. The *élan vital,* what I will call the life force, is what gives flexibility, adaptability, and grace to the human. Whatever constrains the *élan vital,* therefore, distorts the human comically. This is manifested in the character's rigidity of person, thought, and action. From this perspective, "a flexible vice may not be as easy to ridicule as a rigid virtue" (Bergson 137). The comic character is not only rigid but predictable, and this is the key to comic plotting. Predictability builds anticipation and provides the gears for the comic plot. And for all this, the comic character is utterly lacking in self-knowledge. "A comic character," says Bergson, "is generally comic in proportion to his ignorance of himself. The comic person is unconscious" (71). The comedic plot thus moves the character toward an encounter with the self, or as William Lynch would put it, with one's indestructible "rock-bottom being" (100), usually at the expense of the character's ego.

It is worth noting how closely Flannery O'Connor's Christian anthropology dovetails with the comic polarities of *alazon* and *eiron.* It is "usually some form of self-inflation," she says, that impedes spiritual growth. "This may be the pride of the reformer or the theorist, or it may only be that simple-minded self-appreciation which uses its own sincerity as a standard of truth" (*Mystery and Manners* 82). By contrast, self-knowledge brings humility because "to know oneself is, above all, to know what one lacks" (*Mystery and Manners* 35). Not only is it comic justice for the *eiron* to deflate the *alazon,* therefore, but for O'Connor it is a necessary part of the action of grace. As Fr. Finn of Purgatory warns the pseudo-intellectual *alazon* in **"The Enduring Chill,"** "the Holy Ghost will not come until you see yourself as you are" (345). And how, in fact, are her characters? Lacking in grace—both figuratively and literally.

* * *

O'Connor's graceless characters are both quintessentially comic and perfectly anagogical. A good Thomist, O'Connor defines evil as the absence of grace. It makes sense, then, that her characters are distorted to the degree that they lack grace, her anagogical equivalent of Bergson's *élan vital.* If grace is, as she says, what gives life to the soul (*Mystery and Manners* 204), her rigid "grotesques" serve to define that grace precisely by showing the effects of its absence. According to Bergson, comic portraiture captures "a tendency (bias, fixation) imperceptible to others and renders it visible to all eyes" (77). One way of doing this is to "call attention to the physical in a person, when it is the moral side that is concerned." This technique of characterization, which O'Connor employed relentlessly, is what she calls "distortion." It saved O'Connor from an artistic fate she feared worse than death—having to depict grace by means of piety and virtue.[4]

O'Connor's 1956 story **"Greenleaf"** illustrates how these comedic structures play out in her fiction. The mythos of spring dominates the story, and not only because the protagonist, Mrs. May (representing the old order) exclaims "spring is here" just before being killed (ritually?) in the center of a green meadow. The carnivalesque scene that opens the story establishes the mythos. An outlaw bull, adorned by a wreath of foliage (recalling the sacrificial carnival ox of the Middle Ages with ribbon-bedecked horns, described by Bakhtin in *Rabelais and His World* [202-203]), appears in the night and invades the dreams of Mrs. May. The bull is fecundity personified. His unbridled freedom of movement and flouting of all artificial constraints threaten both the (mechanized) "breeding *schedule*" (emphasis added) of Mrs. May's herd and the vulnerable order of *her* universe.

The story moves from illusion to reality, underscored by the materialized metaphor of "seeing the light" that concludes it: "she had the look of a person whose sight has been suddenly restored but who finds the light unbearable" (306). The plot yields a glimpse of the new order in the harmonious modern farm of the thriving Greenleaf boys. The archetypal freedom from obstructing constraint is symbolically achieved by the death of the widow and the consequent lifting of her "iron hand." But it is *her* freedom, not that of society that is at issue.

"Greenleaf" is patterned on archetypal inflation and deflation, a rhythm that builds momentum as the willful protagonist is stunned by degrees, until being deflated verbally by the *eiron,* and then physically by the bull, the intractable life force she has tried to destroy. The first two paragraphs establish the pattern of inflation and deflation. The bull is endowed by its creator/narrator with a romantic, deific aura: "the bull, silvered in the moonlight . . . like some patient god come to woo her" (286). This aura is deflated unceremoniously by Mrs. May's debasing label: "Some nigger's scrub bull" (286). Two adorned heads, the bull's and Mrs. May's—the latter's sprouting green curlers over a face masked in egg white paste—confront each other in the moonlight, preparing for the comic *agon.*

The comic action is appropriately trifling—the effort to catch and dispatch an intrusive bull—and the plot prototypically forces a disproportionate expenditure of energy on Mrs. May's part. Her relentless imaginary dialogues with Mr. Greenleaf, coupled with her physical chasing after Greenleaf and his sons, her responding like a jack-in-the-box to the barbs from her own sons, and her efforts to uphold an illusory order, exhaust her by the final scene, and accomplish nothing. She is face to face with the bull once more.

The central *agon* is between the widow and her detested hired hands, the Greenleaf family, to whose twin sons the bull belongs. Comic polarities abound. Mrs. May, thin, brittle, industrious, rigid, and unbelieving, is countered by Mrs. Greenleaf, "large and loose," obscenely sprawled in the dirt shouting "Jesus, stab me in the heart" (291). Mrs. May's sons are mechanized opposites: they "never had the same reaction to anything." They are opposed to the two Greenleaf boys who are like "one man in two skins" (299)—a bit of comedic doubling that helps to intensify the ironies. The Greenleaf boys marry well, get themselves educated, and run a model farm. Mrs. May's sons are the obligatory comedic stereotypes, "a business type" and an "intellectual," united only in their life-denying habits. The Greenleafs, like their bull, are offensively fertile. The Greenleaf boys produce three children apiece, while Mrs. May's sons remain sterile emotionally and physically. This contrast underscores the archetypal comedic mythos of life force versus the constraining forces of the old order. The surface action is farcical—Mrs. May as blocking character tries to impose rigid control over the Greenleaf bull—but the farce is a mimesis of the underlying movement: Mrs. May's effort to block the forces of change that will allow the Greenleaf trash to become "society" (292), and herself to accept grace.

Mrs. May is a good Bergsonian machine. She is near-sighted, she rules her world with an "iron hand," her back is as "stiff as a rake handle," her voice is "brittle," and her "screech" is "habitual." Similarly, her rigid social categories ("trash," "nice," "shiftless") all familiar distinctions in the O'Connor universe, lead her to try to impose her will on the intractable worlds, material and human, around her. Her arbitrarily timed movements reveal her affinity with the mechanical as opposed to the spontaneous, even in the heat of vengeance: "she waited until exactly eleven o'clock" (302); "she decided to wait exactly ten minutes by her watch" (304). Her fixed ideas make her reactions thoroughly predictable, and easily manipulated by her sons: "what did you start her off for?" (300). The plot mechanism, in fact, turns on her very predictability, her reacting on cue to each carefully planted stimulus.

One example serves to illustrate this comic mechanism. We know that one of Mrs. May's chief mortifications in life is that her son Schofield is a "policy man"; he sells insurance to Negroes instead of selling "nice" insurance. It is a constant source of agony for her and therefore a source of mirth for him. Her fixation about propriety sets the comedic trap. When Mrs. May visits the Greenleaf farm, she tries to assert her illusion of social superiority by pulling rank on the Negro boy who works for the Greenleaf twins. After her rude and transparent belittling of him, to which he seems impervious, he "looked at her suddenly with a gleam of recognition. 'Is you my policy man's mother?' he asked" (298). The question is the perfect deflator because it derives its effect from Mrs. May's own fixation. The scene is deliciously deflating, but the recognition that takes place is the child's and the reader's, not the protagonist's. It takes more than that to bring about Mrs. May's *cognitio*—if indeed it ever occurs.

Mrs. May is not only the *senex,* the opposer of the new order; she is also the *alazon,* inflating her fantasies of control, victimization, and moral superiority. She announces that she will not die until she is "good and ready" (295) and she even schemes to extend her "will" beyond the grave. Mrs. May labors under the illusion that she "handles" Mr. Greenleaf by keeping her "foot on his neck" (294), and that she can discern the moral deficiencies of others.

In a fantasized last judgment scene, Mrs. May finds herself, unlike the Greenleafs, to be worthy: "I've worked and not wallowed" (305). Her hopes for salvation are based on her own hard work. O'Connor takes an artistic risk by countering Mrs. May's egocentricity with Mr. Greenleaf's "I thank *Gawd* for ever-thang" (298) drawled in "Greenleaf English" to take the hex of piety off it. His grammar is worse, but his theology is better than Mrs. May's. Most egregiously of all, Mrs. May believes she speaks for God when she tells the wallowing prayer-healer, Mrs. Greenleaf, that "Jesus would be ashamed" of her and that he'd be happier if she would go home and wash her children's clothes (291). She recoils fastidiously from the filth and religious excess of Mrs. Greenleaf's ritual, literally refusing to accept the "mud in man" that William Lynch reminds us can produce the face of God.

In *Flannery O'Connor's Religious Imagination,* George Kilcourse cites "egocentric autonomy," a term he borrows from the theologian Roger Haight, as the besetting O'Connor sin (243). It is manifested in Mrs. May when she looks out her windows and sees only herself reflected: "When she looked out any window in her house, she saw the reflection of her own character" (295). Mrs. May has, in fact, taken the place of God in her own myopic universe. Until she encounters her own "rock-bottom being," she will never encounter God. Clearly this is an *alazon* awaiting both comic and anagogical comeuppance.

In a sense, Mrs. May is right when she laments that everything is against her. Each contact she has with reality can bring down her house of cards. To that extent, every character is an assistant *eiron.* But Mr. Greenleaf functions as the quintessential *eiron* in the work. In contrast to Mrs. May's energetic and frantic pace, he moves in slow motion and obliquely, as if on the perimeter of an invisible circle. With his "dark crafty face," his "fox colored eyes" and his habitual understatement, he is a shrewd match for his employer. Meiosis is his mode of speech. In answering the ad for his job, he writes merely "have two sons," but he appears on the scene with wife and five daughters as well. When Mrs. May asks him who owns the bull, his evasive answer, "it must be somebody's bull" (288), is taken by her as a sign of his idiocy. In fact it is a brilliant countermove. His seeming deficiency is the cover under which he positions himself to deflate the *alazon.*

Mr. Greenleaf's signature action is procrastination, a kind of evasive passive resistance that thwarts the force of Mrs. May's will. He seems startlingly out of character, therefore, when like clockwork he appears at her door precisely at the moment that her sons have broken into a violent brawl. As Mrs. May "stiffens" to conceal this reality from the *eiron* at her door, her dialogue bulges with inflation: she is the wounded victim of ingratitude, unfairly treated because she is a lone woman. This blatant imposture triggers the *eiron* to throw off his disguise and puncture her pretense: "Quick as a snake striking, Mr. Greenleaf said, 'You got two boys'" (302). This deflation threatens her at her core. From this point, it is a straight path to the concluding scene.

It is Mr. Greenleaf who exposes the mechanism of the final comedic trap. He tells Mrs. May (and thereby alerts the reader) that the bull (an enemy of the mechanical) "don't like cars and trucks" (296). Mrs. May, relentless in her determination to bend Mr. Greenleaf to her will and make him shoot the bull, predictably starts the engine of her car and drives to the center of the field. O'Connor here creates a comic suspense rivaling Chaucer's in "The Miller's Tale." Mrs. May honks the horn and then sits down on the bumper of the car to wait, thereby maddening and summoning the bull, a deliciously predictable result. It is her own will to power, of course, that springs the comic trap. But her resulting death comes as a shock to the reader, nonetheless.

Mrs. May's journey toward her final encounter with the Greenleaf bull, a seemingly definitive but ultimately ambiguous *cognitio* scene, leads naturally to the question of how O'Connor typically treats the comedic plot drive toward freedom and recognition. Frye argues that the conventional comedic plot moves toward freedom—an individual's freedom from the bonds of a restrictive society, or a society's freedom from bonds imposed on it by "humorous" characters (that is, people in some kind of "mental bondage" like the humours of Ben Jonson). The freedom toward which O'Connor's plots move, however, needs some clarification. Her protagonists are "humours" as Frye describes the type:

> helplessly driven by ruling passions, neurotic compulsions, social rituals, and selfishness. . . . [They are] people who do not fully know what they are doing, who are slaves to a predictable self-imposed pattern of behavior. What we call the moral norm is, then, not morality but *deliverance* from moral bondage.
>
> ("Argument" 237, emphasis added)

It is easy to trace society's deliverance from moral bondage in *Volpone* or *Tartuffe*; and it is easy to trace the deliverance of the individual from society's moral bondage in, for instance, *A School For Scandal.* But while O'Connor's humours characters and morally depleted societies are recognizably part of the comedic tradition, O'Connor's movement toward freedom is not. She exposes societies for their deformities, but she does not "free" them at the conclusion of the story. O'Connor subjects her characters to shocking confrontations with reality, but her plots often lead them only to the threshold of freedom.

Ruby Turpin's vision of the motley hallelujah procession at the end of **"Revelation"** and the silent communion of the grandfather and grandson at the end of **"The Artificial Nigger"** are relatively rare instances of comedic resolution in O'Connor's plots. The concluding scene in **"Revelation"** depicts a transformed society *and* an un-illusioned individual, both freed from familiar forms of moral bondage. In some extreme cases, such as those of the doomed characters Thomas (**"The Comforts of Home"**), or Mr. Fortune (**"A View of the Woods"**), O'Connor does employ comedic devices to serve satiric/ironic ends, but she omits the comedic deliverance to freedom. More commonly, however, the locus of freedom in O'Connor's fiction is in the deliverance of neither society nor the individual character. Rather, it lies in the formal pattern itself that exposes the tawdriness of clichéd virtue, the demonic aspect of conventional mores, the perversion of grace in "respectable" people, and the seductive rationalizations of "intellectuals."

If, as O'Connor claims, the kind of freedom she values is the "mind cleared of false emotion and false sentiment and egocentricity," then it is possible to trace its lineaments or at least its potential in the Grandmother, Hulga, Parker, Tanner, Mrs. Cope, or even Julian and his mother; but their deliverance is by no means certain. In the final analysis, then, it is the reader who "apprehend[s] the form" that can experience the comedic liberation from illusion. As Frye puts it, "illusion is whatever is fixed or definable, and reality is best understood as its negative: whatever reality is, it's not *that*" (Frye, *Anatomy of Criticism* 169-170).

O'Connor's revelations overturn the worlds of her characters without giving definitive formulation to what is revealed. This comedic way of negation suits O'Connor's anagogical design. A foundational claim of apophatic theology is that anything one says about God must also be seen as not absolute. O'Connor's emphasis on "seeing the form" points to the importance of seeing "the unspeakable or ineffable relationships that constitute the form, the interstices" (Noyalis 1). Characters such as Parker's wife need to live within clear, delineated certainty, but they are, in fact, "wineskins that cannot receive the new, non-delineated, ambiguous awareness of the mystery found only among things, never apart from things" (Noyalis 2). O'Connor's patterns negate the world's certainties—science, knowledge, hard work, cleanliness, respectability, even formulations of doctrine—("whatever reality is, it's not *that*"). Her comedic forms *may* deliver her characters, but *can* deliver her readers to apprehend her own brand of "freedom"—the encounter with mystery.

* * *

For better or worse, the generic classification of comedy has traditionally hinged on the ending of the work. Dante entitled his opus magnus a comedy because it began in hell and ended in paradise. Byron stated baldly that tragedies end in death; comedies in marriage. One need not have read much of Flannery O'Connor to realize that her endings do not fit the comedic paradigm. She described the reaction to her reading of **"A Good Man Is Hard to Find."** The listeners roared with laughter for the first half, and sat in stunned silence for the second half. The trajectory of her plots consistently departs from the comedic contract with the audience, the serene expectation of a happy ending. O'Connor appropriates the comedic paradigm as we have seen, in developing plot, character, and mode in her stories. She distances the action comedically, barring emotion and engaging the intellect. But her typical outcome leaves Julian's mother dead on the sidewalk, Hulga without a leg to stand on, Mrs. Cope watching fire consume her farm, Parker weeping, Bevel drowned, Mary Fortune and her grandfather dead, and Mrs. May gored by a bull.

O'Connor's endings move from the horizontal axis to a vertical one, catapulting the action into a different sphere. She opens a door to another dimension, but bars entry to the reader. Her endings occur before we can see the effects of grace, before we can see whether the characters have, in fact, achieved the self-knowledge and undergone the reversal they have been offered. They are unmasked, deflated, and reduced to their rock-bottom humanity, but then led offstage—or rather, left dead on stage. O'Connor's laughter is, in the final analysis, transitional.[5] It drops away at the end. The transparent mode of comedy shifts to dense symbolism, even ambiguity. The concluding tableaus are stunning and disorienting to readers expecting the restored harmony and festive reconciliation of comedy. The horizontal interplay of *alazon* and *eiron* is subsumed by an overarching irony. O'Connor is not interested in getting her characters to change their ways, a moral (or "tropological") message she scorned to indulge. Her interest is in their encounter with grace, or the offer of participation in the divine life, something quite different from mere good behavior. O'Connor therefore frustrates the facile comedic resolution and demands instead the hard work of anagogical interpretation.

What we see in O'Connor's design, then, is an appropriation of classic comedic devices and structures that she employs in a truncated plot design. She reveals the ridiculous element of her characters, unmasks their pretensions, and shatters their facades. But then, instead of reforming or reconciling her comic characters in the obligatory happy ending, she shoves them into a stark encounter with the ultimate in the form of death or defeat. This shift in mode suggests an encounter with mystery, the appropriate response to which is silence. The locus of resolution is more difficult to determine than in conventional comedy. O'Connor's is thus a hybrid form, arousing, like absurd theater, contradictory responses in an audience trained to respond to a recognizable comedic tradition (Leyburn 644). Her ironic endings have the flavor of the ludicrous about them, but they open into mystery. Resolution appears to be offstage, found on the level of anagogical interpretation.

Traditional comedy is marked by circularity. By connecting the mythos of spring with the genre of comedy, Frye emphasizes the cyclic structure of comedic action. The comedic plot and its resolution replicate the seasonal circularity of the death of the old god/order succeeded by the birth of the new order/resurrection in new life and fertility. The resolution brings lovers together, and restores the harmony of the community. Both the perennial cycle of nature and comedic endings are therefore comfortably predictable. O'Connor's plots, however, are linear, not cyclic. Their conclusions, rather than coming full circle to restored harmony, remain open-ended. Her characters are free to say "no" with their last breath.

Although O'Connor begins her comedic stories with the rational apprehension of the irrational (the distinguishing mode of the comic genre), she moves at last to the suprarational—to the mystery that transcends reason. And that is where she leaves her readers—with a concrete tableau that carries an excess of signification. Traditional comedic endings distribute justice and arrive at festive, if improbable, reconciliations based on the speedy reversal of blocking characters. But O'Connor leaves the reader to struggle for "the point"—the extensions of meaning—the hard way, by staring very hard at the concrete image until it yields its anagogical secret.

Notes

1. For a useful collection of essays by Peter Berger, Nathan Scott, Barry Ulanov, Reinhold Niebuhr and others on the relationship between Christianity and the comic tradition, see Conrad Hyers. See also William Lynch, *Christ and Apollo,* and Mikhail Bakhtin, *Rabelais and His World.*
2. A number of critics have addressed formal elements in O'Connor's comedy. Sura Rath outlines the comic polarities in *Wise Blood,* basing his

analysis on the interplay among the paired stereotypes identified by Aristotle. Kathleen Feeley gives an overview of O'Connor's comedic strategies, and Clinton Trowbridge addresses imagery.

3. See Trowbridge on O'Connor's technique of literalizing metaphors.

4. "The modes of good," O'Connor wrote in "A Memoir of Mary Ann," "have to be satisfied with a cliché or a smoothing-down that will soften their real look" (*Mystery and Manners* 226).

5. See Averintsev for a discussion of the transitional nature of laughter in the theory of Bakhtin.

Works Cited

Averintsev, Sergei. "Bakhtin, Laughter, and Christian Culture." *Bakhtin and Religion: A Feeling for Faith.* Eds. Susan M. Felch and Paul J. Contino. Evanston: Northwestern UP, 2001. 70-95.

Bakhtin, Mikhail. *Rabelais and His World.* Trans. Helene Iswolsky. Bloomington: Indiana UP, 1984.

Berger, Peter L. "Christian Faith and the Social Comedy." *Holy Laughter: Essays on Religion in the Comic Perspective.* New York: Seabury, 1969. 123-134.

Bergson, Henri. "Laughter." *Comedy.* Ed. Wylie Sypher. New York: Doubleday, 1956. 61-146.

Currie, Sheldon. "Freaks and Folks: Comic Imagery in the Fiction of Flannery O'Connor." *The Antigonish Review* 62-63 (1985): 133-142.

Feeley, Kathleen, S.S.N.D. "'Mine is a Comic Art . . .' Flannery O'Connor." *Realist of Distances: Flannery O'Connor Revisited.* Aarhus, Denmark: Aarhus UP, 1987. 66-72.

Foulke, Robert and Paul Smith, eds. *Anatomy of Literature.* New York: Harcourt, 1972.

Frye, Northrop. *Anatomy of Criticism.* Princeton: Princeton UP, 1957).

———. "The Argument of Comedy." *Comedy: Plays, Theory, and Criticism.* Ed. Marvin Felheim. New York: Harcourt, 1962.

———. "The Mythos of Spring: Comedy." *Comedy: Meaning and Form.* Ed. Robert W. Corrigan. San Francisco: Chandler, 1965.

Gentry, Marshall Bruce. *Flannery O'Connor's Religion of the Grotesque.* Jackson: UP of Mississippi, 1986.

Hyers, M. Conrad, ed. "The Dialectic of the Sacred and the Comic." *Holy Laughter: Essays on Religion in the Comic Perspective.* New York: Seabury, 1969. 208-241.

———. *Holy Laughter: Essays on Religion in the Comic Perspective.* New York: Seabury, 1969.

Kilcourse, George A., Jr. *Flannery O'Connor's Religious Imagination: A World with Everything Off Balance.* Mahwah: Paulist, 2001.

Leyburn, Ellen Douglass. "Comedy and Tragedy Transposed." *Types of Drama: Plays and Essays.* Ed. Sylvan Barnet, Morton Burman, and William Burto. Boston: Little Brown, 1972. 643-647.

Lynch, William F., S.J. "Comedy." *Christ and Apollo: The Dimensions of the Literary Imagination.* New York: Sheed and Ward, 1960. 91-113.

Murfin, Ross and Supryia M. Ray. *The Bedford Glossary of Critical and Literary Terms.* Boston: Bedford/ St. Martin's, 1998.

Niebuhr, Reinhold. "Humour and Faith." *Holy Laughter: Essays on Religion in the Comic Perspective.* New York: Seabury, 1969. 134-150.

Noyalis, Walter J. "Parker's Back: The Apophatic and the Analogical Imagination." Unpublished manuscript.

O'Connor, Flannery. "The Enduring Chill." *Three.* New York: Signet, 1983. 327-351.

———. "Greenleaf." *Three.* New York: Signet, 1983. 286-307.

———. *The Habit of Being.* Ed. Sally Fitzgerald. New York: Random, 1979.

———. *Mystery and Manners.* Eds. Sally and Robert Fitzgerald. New York: Farrar, 1969.

———. *Three.* New York: Signet, 1983.

Rath, Sura Prasad. "Comic Polarities in Flannery O'Connor's *Wise Blood.*" *Studies in Short Fiction* 21.3 (1984): 251-258.

Ricoeur, Paul. *Interpretation Theory: Discourse and the Surplus of Meaning.* Fort Worth: Texas Christian UP, 1976.

Schloss, Carol. *Flannery O'Connor's Dark Comedies: The Limits of Inference.* Baton Rouge: Louisiana State UP, 1980.

Scott, Nathan, Jr. "The Bias of Comedy and the Narrow Escape into Faith." *Holy Laughter: Essays on Religion in the Comic Perspective.* New York: Seabury, 1969. 45-75.

Trowbridge, Clinton W. "The Comic Sense of Flannery O'Connor: Literalist of the Imagination." *The Flannery O'Connor Bulletin* 12 (1983): 77-92.

Ulanov, Barry. "The Rhetoric of Christian Comedy." *Holy Laughter: Essays on Religion in the Comic Perspective.* New York: Seabury, 1969. 103-123.

Wood, Ralph C. *The Comedy of Redemption: Christian Faith and Comic Vision in Four American Novelists.* Notre Dame: U of Notre Dame P, 1988.

J. P. Steed (essay date spring 2005)

SOURCE: Steed, J. P. "'Through Our Laughter We Are Involved': Bergsonian Humor in Flannery O'Connor's Fiction." *Midwest Quarterly* 46, no. 3 (spring 2005): 299-313.

[*In the following essay, Steed applies philosopher Henri Bergson's theory of laughter to "Good Country People" and "A Good Man Is Hard to Find," stressing the inflexibility of O'Connor's humorous characters.*]

In his film *Manhattan* (1979), Woody Allen's character, Isaac Davis, complains about the poor quality of the TV sitcom that he writes, exclaiming, "It's worse than not insightful: it's not funny!" The implication here, of course, is that being funny is better and more important than being insightful. This sentiment may seem to run counter to conventional wisdom (and indeed it is this incongruity that lends the exclamation its touch of humor), but upon further examination it seems to have merit—after all, to be funny requires insight, and that which is funny often provides insight; thus, being funny encompasses and surpasses being merely insightful. Moreover, according to Jewish proverbial wisdom, the presence of humor means the presence of understanding and self-criticism. And this seems to be a primary function of humor: to provide and provoke self-examination, self-understanding, self-criticism. Don't we laugh hardest at—and appreciate most—those books, movies, and comedians that are able to most deftly, most *insightfully* expose our faults, foibles, and failures? Recognizing this, then, the question becomes one of direction. Once humor has exposed our faults and we are faced with examining and criticizing them, what do we do? Where do we go? And does the humor itself, after exposing these faults, suggest any solutions?

Flannery O'Connor is an author whose use of humor has attracted a great deal of scholarly attention. In her study of O'Connor's fiction, for example, Dorothy Walters notes that the "thrust of tragic intention against comic implication is of major importance." Walters observes that O'Connor asks, perhaps even forces, the reader to "recognize that the world is peopled by figures essentially laughable in their basic makeup and ludicrous in their typical life response." "Our initial reaction," Walters continues, "may be a superior grin at the spectacle of a world teeming with inanity. But, through our laughter, we are involved; and we are led to reflect upon the most serious questions touching the human experience" (25). In other words, O'Connor's humor is insightful, and provokes self-examination and self-criticism.

Walters's succinct and astute assessment aligns the source and function of O'Connor's humor squarely with the philosophy of Henri Bergson; and indeed, Walters mentions Bergson twice in her study, though only briefly and somewhat superficially. Bergson's theories of laughter and humor have much in common with a long tradition of superiority theories—theories of humor that state, in essence, that laughter is condescending, we laugh at what is beneath us. But what sets Bergson's theory apart is his insistence that laughter serves a distinctly social function as a potential *remedy* for undesirable human traits. That is to say, while superiority theories of humor generally see laughter's function as primarily derisive—the response of a "superior" subject to an object's perceived inferiority—Bergson insists that the function is, more properly, *corrective* in nature. The distinction here is subtle but crucial: the former sees laughter as essentially alienating, while the latter sees it as essentially assimilating. As Walker attests, when O'Connor makes us laugh at a character's stubborn and foolish pride, "we are involved." Our laughter is turned inward, so that we are not merely deriding that pride, alienating it as something outside and away from ourselves; rather, we are shifting in our seats, making internal adjustments that, in effect, are assimilating. And perhaps this is why so many of those who write about O'Connor's humor have a tendency to characterize it as satirical—because satire has as its essential quality the provocation of uneasiness in the reader, urging some sort of reform.

In this essay I will expand on this interpretation of Bergson's philosophy of humor and demonstrate more thoroughly its relevance to O'Connor's fiction, focusing on two of her stories in particular: **"Good Country People"** and **"A Good Man Is Hard to Find."** Miles Orvell claims that "what is most difficult to define" in O'Connor's fiction is her "peculiar blend of comic violence and mysterious shock" (54), and indeed most of those who have written on O'Connor's fiction have commented on this "peculiar blend" of violence and humor. It is, at least in part, the goal of this essay to examine this mixture and to define it, finally, as a result of O'Connor's distinctively Bergsonian humor.

I.

The principal trait of the Bergsonian comic figure is inflexibility, a certain "mechanical inelasticity" that surfaces "just when one would expect to find the wide-awake adaptability and the living pliableness of a human being" (Bergson, 120-21). According to Bergson, life is a continuous process of becoming. But the rational mind divides this process into discrete states of being, treating new objects and experiences as repetitions of familiar concepts, so that life is transformed into a succession of these states of being rather than a fluid, continuous, and irreversible flow. This approach is helpful in many respects: for example, I am thankful that I do not have to treat every encounter with a locked door as a new experience—I can rely on the familiar concept of unlocking the door with a key, to gain access to what is behind it. But, for Bergson, a sensitiveness to the uniqueness of objects and experiences, a certain flexibility or contextual awareness, is essential to free, well-adapted human behavior. And the comic figure is the figure that displays a lack of this flexibility. Thus, if I approach a door while holding a key in my hand, only to discover that the door has no lock, it will be my frantic search for a place to insert the unnecessary key, and my inability to gain access without completing the ritual, that will transform me into the observer's object of laughter.

But this example, it must be made clear, though it may fit within a broad interpretation of Bergson's theory, is not properly what I am referring to when I speak of Bergsonian humor. Where Bergson's philosophy distinguishes itself from traditional superiority theories is not only in its specificity of the source of the source of laughter as the presence of inflexibility, but also in its insistence on the essentially social function of that laughter. In Bergsonian humor, "the comic demands something like a momentary anesthesia of the heart. Its appeal is to the intelligence, pure and simple" (Bergson 118). For Bergson, laughter, or humor, is not a feeling or an emotion; it is an intellectual response. More pointedly—and perhaps more significantly—it is a social, contextual response. The intelligence which responds to the comic

> must always remain in touch with other intelligences. . . . You would hardly appreciate the comic if you felt yourself isolated from others. Laughter appears to stand in need of an echo. . . . Our laughter is always the laughter of a group. . . . However spontaneous it seems, laughter always implies a kind of secret freemasonry, or even complicity, with other laughers, real or imaginary. How often has it been said that the fuller the theatre, the more uncontrolled the laughter of the audience! On the other hand, how often has the remark been made that many comic effects are incapable of translation from one language to another, because they refer to the customs and ideas of a particular social group!
>
> (119)

This complicity with other laughers constitutes the social nature of humor, but while this assertion, concerning the social *nature* of humor, might hold true in any (even every) philosophy of humor, Bergson continues: "To understand laughter, we must put it back into its natural environment, which is society, and above all must we determine the utility of its function, which is a social one" (119). This social *function* of laughter, concludes Bergson, is to remove the inflexibility which is its object, through humiliation and ridicule. That is, its function is to promote freedom and adaptability—a sense of the process of becoming—over the too-rational and too-inflexible insistence on a state or states of being.

"There are vices," writes Bergson, "into which the soul plunges deeply with all its pregnant potency." "The vice," he continues, "capable of making us comic is . . . that which . . . lends us its own rigidity instead of borrowing from us our flexibility" (123). In other words, if a character in a story exhibits a vice, such as greed, which elicits the extension of our flexibility—that is, if the character's flaws draw out our sympathies then that character becomes to some degree a tragic figure. But the character that imposes his or her rigidity on us, that elicits an intellectual rather than an emotional response, is the comic figure. And our response to the imposition of that rigidity, signified by derisive laughter (there is, presumably, no other kind), is an attempt to throw it off—and attempt to avoid or to *correct* it.

My example of the door without a lock, then, might be said to fit within a broad interpretation of this philosophy, as my rigidity in looking for the absent lock becomes the object of laughter and that laughter functions as a corrective to my rigidity (i.e. you laugh because you are convinced you would not behave this way; you would correct my behavior). But I submit that this is too broad and simplistic an application of Bergson's philosophy, precisely because the behavior is too easily corrected. The fact is, the observer laughs at my inflexibility, but that inflexibility makes no serious imposition on the observer; the observer feels no real threat of my inflexibility being or becoming his or her own. Thus, the behavior I am exhibiting is in no real need of correction, and the laughter it elicits can have no real social function.

True Bergsonian humor, then—that which does have a real social function—is that humor which has as its source or object a certain inflexibility, and which also has as its purpose and its function the correction of that inflexibility. This corrective function necessitates the recognition of the presence, or at least the real threat of the presence, of inflexibility within the individual observer, or at least within the group of laughers with which the individual is complicit. Otherwise there is nothing to correct. As a result, true Bergsonian humor will most likely produce a sense of uneasiness in the observer, as it attempts to provoke the observer into correcting his or her behavior. Moreover, because Bergsonian humor has society as its natural environment; because the laughter associated with it is the laughter of a perceived or real group of intelligences; and because the function of the group's laughter is to correct an inflexibility that is perceived as present within its ranks, effecting a sort of conformity in behavior, we might say that Bergsonian humor—unlike other forms, modes and theories of superiority humor—is assimilating in nature, rather than alienating. The missing door lock scenario, because it provokes no real change in the observer, is in fact an instance of a more traditional superiority humor because it alienates the object (me and my absurd inflexibility) rather than provoking assimilationist changes within the group of laughers.

If we modify the example, however, it can easily become Bergsonian. A ready-made modification is Gary Larson's *Far Side* cartoon wherein a student at a school for the gifted is depicted as leaning heavily on a door that is clearly marked with the word "pull." Like my example of the door with the missing lock, this scenario also has inflexibility as its source of laughter. But Larson's scenario is far more capable of provoking the recognition of inflexibility within the observer. Few of us will entertain the notion that we are stupid enough to look for a lock when there isn't one, but most of us are capable of recognizing that, despite our sometimes even exceptional intelligence, we often, through a certain inflexibility, fail to apply that intelligence. (We've all pushed on the 'pull' door.) Bergsonian humor has as its purpose the correction of that inflexibility; it is, at its essence, socially persuasive; which is to say, finally, that it is essentially satirical. This is not to say that satire is, conversely, essentially Bergsonian, however. Satire and Bergsonian humor share the same general purpose—to be socially persuasive—but satire does not limit its sources or objects of humor to manifestations of inflexibility, nor does it limit its primary function to the correction of that inflexibility. In other words, Bergsonian humor is essentially satirical, but it is merely a branch, or a particular mode, of satire.

II.

It is this satirical bent, this intent to persuade, that is the fundamental link between Flannery O'Connor's use of humor and Bergson's philosophy. O'Connor, after all, "displays a remarkable unity of purpose and consistency of theme" in her fiction (Walters, 35), and that purpose is founded in her Catholic convictions, so that "her aim is persuasion concerning religious matters" (Burt, 138). O'Connor's work is principally about redemption and its various forms, and O'Connor herself attests to this, and to the fact that persuasion toward redemption of the reader and of society is her aim. She asserts that "[r]edemption is meaningless unless there is cause for it in the actual life we live." And she continues:

> The novelist with Christian concerns will find in modern life distortions which are repugnant to him, and his problem will be to make these appear as distortions to an audience which is used to seeing them as natural; and he may well be forced to take ever more violent means to get his vision across to this hostile audience.
>
> (*Mystery,* 33-34)

This focused effort to persuade, to enact some social reform, permeates O'Connor's fiction and explains why so many readers have identified it as, in some way or another, satirical; for its humor elicits from the reader a distinctly uncomfortable laugh (i.e. "we are involved"?). What distinguishes her humor as Bergsonian, however, is this, coupled with the fact that the object of the reader's laughter can so often be identified as inflexibility. For O'Connor, the Christian writer who is promoting and provoking redemption, inflexibility is anathema. Christian redemption can only occur with a change of heart, and change can only occur within a flexible process of becoming. Moreover, Bergson notes that inflexibility results in "a mind always thinking of what it has just done and never of that it is doing," creating a certain absentmindedness (ergo, "a comic character is generally comic in proportion to his ignorance of himself") (122-23), and this lack of self-awareness is likewise antithetical to the epiphany or the revelation that is needed for redemption. Thus, the butt of O'Connor's corrective humor is the inflexible, the self-unaware. As Frederick Asals observes, "O'Connor's people are among the least introspective in modern fiction, with minds at once so unaware and so absurdly assured that they have refused to acknowledge any deeper self"—and in words remarkably in tune with the present argument, Asals continues to note that "her protagonists are incapable of the flexibility of development" (93). O'Connor herself, again, attests to this presence of inflexibility in her fiction, and in fact claims it as essential to any story. "When you write stories," she says, "you have to . . . start exactly there—showing how some specific folks *will* do, *will* do in spite of everything" (*Mystery,* 90, emphasis O'Connor's).

In **"Good Country People,"** for example, it is primarily Hulga who *will* do in spite of everything, whose inflexibility and lack of self-awareness are the object of our laughter. Convinced unswervingly of her intellectual superiority, she stomps around the house like a toddler in a perpetual pout; and though she is thirty-two years old and hardly condescends to speak to her mother, everything she does is calculated to get her mother's attention. Furthermore, Hulga is fixated on the belief that "everything is nothing," that evil doesn't exist, and she sets out to educate a Bible salesman in that regard. Then, along the way, she decides to seduce him. This she *will* do, in spite of her extreme unattractiveness, in spite of the fact that the man, Manley Pointer, is a Bible salesman and supposedly religiously devoted—in short, in spite of everything.

Clearly, Hulga is possessed of the most common of vices explored in O'Connor's fiction—namely, an excessive, inflexible, ignorant, and foolish pride. And as the object of our uneasy laughter, this pride, this inflexibility and its spawned lack of self-awareness, is corrected and a redemption of some kind is finally achieved.

Inflexibility as a theme in the story, and as a primary source of humor, is introduced in the story's opening sentence: "Besides the neutral expression that she wore when she was alone, Mrs. Freeman had two others, forward and reverse, that she used for all her human dealings"; and only a few lines later we are told that "Mrs. Freeman could never be brought to admit herself wrong on any point" (***Good Man*** [***A Good Man Is Hard to Find***], 169). Mrs. Hopewell's inflexibility is then introduced, through her loyal use of and reliance on cliches, and as we learn that she still thinks of her daughter, Joy/Hulga, "as a child though she was thirty-two years old and highly educated" (170). Thus it only takes a few sentences to establish the women as comic figures, and the rigidity of their daily routine as a comic situation.

Significantly, it is the break in this daily routine—the introduction of variance into this mechanical life—that is the heart of the story, as Manley Pointer knocks on the Hopewells' door one afternoon. Mrs. Hopewell's inflexibility is highlighted, during the exchange, as she assesses Manley not with the contextual sensitivity of an individual aware of life as a continuous flow of new experience, but with a rigid insistence on some previously decided upon state of being: despite the salesman's interruption of her dinner, and despite his transparent flattery and "aw shucks" demeanor, and despite the fact that "Mrs. Hopewell never liked to be taken for a fool" (178), she welcomes him, trusts him, even admires him. In spite of everything, she displays an alarming lack of awareness by buying in to Manley's salesmanship: "'Why!' she cried, 'good country people are the salt of the earth!'" (179).

Manley's appearance, then, at once provides the opportunity for the portrayal of inflexibility, in Mrs. Hopewell and later in Hulga, as well as the potential remedy for it, as he disrupts the women's daily routine and, later, reveals to Hulga her unanticipated ignorance. The latter, occurring in the barn during Manley and Hulga's "picnic," is an example of, as Walters puts it, "the archetypal encounter of innocence with experience" (64), only, in a reversal of expectations, it is the supposedly intellectually superior Hulga who, despite her plans to educate and seduce, is revealed to be the ignorant, foolish innocent who is seduced. Manley reveals himself to be deceptive, mean, and worldly, and this revelation exposes Hulga's absentmindedness. In other words, like many of O'Connor's stories, **"Good Country People"** is the story of foolish pride overthrown—a feat that is, in part, accomplished through the use of Bergsonian humor. It is important to note, too, that this humor is created both *in* the story and *by* the story. Examples of the employment of Bergsonian humor *in* the story, ironically, at times involve Hulga as its employer. For instance, when Mrs. Freeman is talking about her girls, Glynese and Carramae, and specifically about Carramae's wedding, she says, "'Lyman said it sure felt sacred to him. She said he said he wouldn't take five hundred dollars for being married by a preacher,'" and Hulga responds by asking, "'How much would he take?'" (183). Hulga's query is dry, but though no laughter is observed in the characters, it is clear that Hulga is amused by her own question, and when we laugh as readers, we are laughing *with* Hulga. Half a page later, this time talking about Glynese's marital situation, Mrs. Freeman tells the others that Glynese "said she would rather marry a man with only a '36 Plymouth who would be married by a preacher," and Hulga, this time, asks, "what if he had a '32 Plymouth" (183). Again, the reader laughs *with* Hulga. The humor is created *in* the story and has as its source the rigidity of Hulga's literal interpretations of Mrs. Freeman's statements; but its object is also Mrs. Freeman's and her daughters' inflexibility with regard to marital matters and social propriety. This inflexibility is recognized by Hulga, and she tries to correct it with her Bergsonian wisecracks, but it is only underscored by Mrs. Freeman's utter lack of self-awareness, as she fails to recognize herself as the butt of Hulga's humor and continues on with her stories unabashedly.

The irony, of course, is that Hulga recognizes this inflexibility in others but remains unaware of it in herself; and in fact we are told early on that this stubborn lack of self-awareness is self-imposed. O'Connor makes this clear when she describes how Hulga, at times, "would stare just a little to the side of her, her eyes icy blue, with the look of someone who has achieved blindness by an act of will and means to keep it" (171). Images of blindness are omnipresent in the story. And much of the humor created *by* the story has as its object not only the inflexibilities of Mrs. Freeman and Mrs. Hopewell, but also Hulga's inflexibility and lack of self-awareness, which is revealed in bits and pieces as the story progresses. The laughter created *in* the story, then, from the examples above, is the laughter of a group consisting of (at least) the reader and Hulga; she laughs at inflexibility and we laugh with her. Meanwhile, the laughter created *by* the story, which gradually zeroes in on Hulga as its primary source, and which has her inflexibilities as its primary object, is the laughter of an imagined group, *at* Hulga instead of *with* her. We, as readers, assume that other readers, or at least the author herself, will find Hulga's inflexibility as ridiculous as we do; and indeed, we rely on this group complicity for our laughter. In this way, our laughter is assimilationist in nature: Hulga's willful ignorance, her foolish pride, are deemed undesirable traits, recognized as vices, and we attempt to correct them with our laughter as a united (albeit imagined) group of laughers.

What makes this humor Bergsonian in nature is, in part, the gradual revelation of Manley's deception. As Manley slowly reveals Hulga's folly, he also reveals our own—as we, as readers, have been likewise taken in by Manley's con. In other words, we are involved. The inflexibility and lack of self-awareness that we perceive in Hulga, we also perceive in ourselves, or at least within our imagined group. Thus, as our laughter increases, so does our uneasiness, and the Bergsonian effect of the humor crescendoes. The culmination of our discomfort comes at the end of the story, when Mrs. Freeman and Mrs. Hopewell watch Manley running off and they comment on how "simple" he is (195-96), and we realize as we laugh that the blindness, the inflexibility, has not yet been corrected but persists, so that our laughter is overshadowed by our uneasiness.

And it is this last revelation which finally gives O'Connor's humor its distinctly Bergsonian cast—for the revelation is, in effect, created *by* the story and not *in* the story itself. That is to say, while Hulga does receive a kind of revelation *in* the story, as her blindness is revealed to her, it is the revelation that is created *by* the story, *for the reader,* that is the focus of the fiction, and of the humor it employs. In effect, O'Connor reveals to us, as readers, the real presence, or at least the real threat of the presence, of inflexibility, of blindness or a lack of self-awareness in ourselves, or at least within our group of laughers; thus our laughter is uncomfortable and we are, as O'Connor hopes and intends for us to be, provoked or persuaded toward reform—in effect, toward an assimilation of and to O'Connor's sense of morality or reality. Through her use of Bergsonian humor, O'Connor strives to move society toward her version, or her vision, of redemption.

This reader-revelation is replicated in what is arguably O'Connor's finest, and certainly her most famous, story, **"A Good Man Is Hard to Find."** Like Hulga, the grandmother becomes the comic figure, whose inflexibility is exhibited in her selfishness, her self-absorption, and, again, in a lack of self-awareness. And, as in the previous story, a crescendo builds. The severity and extent of the grandmother's ignorance and rigidity is gradually revealed, until at last it is revealed fully *in* the story, to the grandmother herself—this time not by a small-time swindler like Manley Pointer, but by a serial killer who calls himself "the Misfit."

As with **"Good Country People,"** the presence of inflexibility in **"A Good Man Is Hard to Find"** is introduced in the opening sentences: "The grandmother didn't want to go to Florida. She wanted to visit some of her connections in east Tennessee and she was seizing at every chance to change Bailey's mind" (9). And again, in the end the laughter that is provoked by this inflexibility is overshadowed by uneasiness. This time, however, the revelation that occurs *in* the story coincides with the revelation created *by* the story, for the reader. That is, the reader shares the revelatory experience with the grandmother, whose inflexibility is recognized in an epiphany. The grandmother exclaims, "Why you're one of my babies. You're one of my own children!" and this exclamation follows on the heels of the Misfit's own confession of rigidity: he cannot believe in Jesus because he wasn't there to witness his miracles (29). The grandmother may not be capable of articulating this moment as a recognition of her inflexibility, but as readers we have a wider perspective. We have seen the grandmother's stubbornness and we recognize the Misfit's rigidity; thus, when the grandmother makes her exclamation, what is, for her, perhaps an emotional or spiritual recognition of that which connects them is, for us, a connection that we can articulate intellectually. It is the reflection of rigidity—as though the grandmother were looking into a mirror as she looks into "the man's face twisted close to her own" (29)—that triggers the unarticulated recognition, in the grandmother, that the Misfit's rigidity is the natural offspring of her own. And this revelation is simultaneous for the reader, who recognizes the presence, or the real threat of the presence, of his or her own inflexibilities, and thus experiences a climax of uneasiness.

With this revelation, then, comes a cessation of self-unawareness, and suddenly the grandmother is transformed, according to Bergson's definitions, from comic figure to tragic figure, as she no longer imposes her inflexibility onto us, but now demands our sympathies. But that this change, this correction, has been accomplished in part through humor and laughter is reasserted by the Misfit's comment that the grandmother "would have been a good woman . . . if it had been somebody there to shoot her every minute of her life" (29). There is no single passage in all of O'Connor's fiction more exemplary of Bergsonian humor than this, as our shock and uneasiness are at their peak, yet we are still moved to laughter. Here, we share our laughter with two groups: first, with the Misfit himself (as we shared laughter, previously, with

Hulga), the object of our laughter being the stubbornness of the grandmother, who refused to achieve any flexibility or self-awareness save on the point of death. And second, we return to our imagined camaraderie with other readers or the author, as we laugh at the Misfit's own rigidity—his own inability to turn from evil, for there he stands, quipping cleverly about the grandmother's failures, when he himself has failed to change, to modify or to correct his behavior, and he is utterly unaware of it. Thus we, as readers who are aware, laugh at his absentmindedness while still shaken with unease over the consequences of it, and the very real threat that such potential for rigidity exists in us all.

This recognition of inflexibility, and the reform that O'Connor hopes it will provoke, are, again, the redemption of society that O'Connor is after. And she pursues this redemption by any means necessary. She writes:

> St. Cyril of Jerusalem . . . wrote: "The dragon sits by the side of the road, watching those who pass. Beware lest he devour you. We go to the Father of Souls, but it is necessary to pass by the dragon." No matter what form the dragon may take, it is of this mysterious passage past him, or into his jaws, that stories of any depth will always be concerned to tell. . . .
>
> (*Mystery,* 35)

For O'Connor, clearly, the dragon is often represented by a confrontation with evil—in these stories, men like Manley Pointer and the Misfit. And violence often accompanies this confrontation. But humor can also be violent, and can be one of the forms this dragon takes, a refiner's fire through which the individual must pass, the laughter that is produced functioning as a corrective to the flaws and vices that are deemed undesirable. The "peculiar blend of comic violence and mysterious shock" in O'Connor's fiction, as described by Orvell, then, can be successfully defined as Bergsonian humor—which is to say that, by recognizing the humor in O'Connor's fiction as chiefly Bergsonian, we are able to reconcile and explain the coexistence of humor and horror. The "comic violence" that takes place *in* the story is combined with the "mysterious shock" created *by* the story, which we experience as readers, as we recognize the presence, or the real threat of the presence, of those flaws and vices within ourselves. In this way, through the use of a specifically Bergsonian humor, O'Connor pursues the correction of societal rigidity, promoting and provoking reform and a sense of becoming. She *involves* us, as, in effect, she pursues the assimilation of society into her distinctly Christian world.

Bibliography

Asals, Frederick. "The Double." *Flannery O'Connor.* Ed. Harold Bloom. New York: Chelsea House, 1986. 93-109.

Bergson, Henri. "Laughter: An Essay on the Meaning of the Comic." Tr. Cloudesley Brereton and Fred Rothwell. *The Philosophy of Laughter and Humor.* Ed. John Morreall. Albany, New York: State University of New York Press, 1987. 117-26.

Burt, John. "What You Can't Talk About." *Flannery O'Connor.* Ed. Harold Bloom. 125-43.

O'Connor, Flannery. *A Good Man Is Hard to Find.* New York: Harcourt, Brace & World, 1955.

———. *Mystery and Manners.* Eds. Sally and Robert Fitzgerald. New York: Farrar, Straus & Giroux, 1969.

Orvell, Miles. *Invisible Parade: The Fiction of Flannery O'Connor.* Philadelphia: Temple University Press, 1972.

Spacks, Patricia Meyer. "Some Reflections on Satire." *Genre,* 1 (1968), 13-20.

Walters, Dorothy. *Flannery O'Connor.* Boston: Twayne, 1973.

Mark Bosco (essay date spring 2005)

SOURCE: Bosco, Mark. "Consenting to Love: Autobiographical Roots of 'Good Country People.'" *Southern Review* 41, no. 2 (spring 2005): 283-95.

[*In the following essay, Bosco draws autobiographical parallels between O'Connor and the character of Hulga in "Good Country People," suggesting that the character Manley Pointer is based on Erik Langkjaer, a man whom the author dated just prior to writing the story.*]

> What would you make out about me just from reading **"Good Country People"**? Plenty, but not the whole story.
>
> —Flannery O'Connor, *The Habit of Being*

The year 2004 marked the fortieth anniversary of Flannery O'Connor's death from kidney failure brought on from her years of fighting the effects of lupus, in mid-century a debilitating disease and difficult to survive. The intervening time since her death has seen an explosion of critical and popular enthusiasm for her work, so much so that in 1988 she achieved canonical status in American arts and letters with the publication of her ***Collected Works*** by the Library of America. In the fall of 2003 an international symposium, the fifth of its kind, was held in O'Connor's hometown of Milledgeville, Georgia. It brought together over two hundred scholars and enthusiasts, including novelists, poets, and other artists who have acknowledged O'Connor's influence on their work.

Readers have been fascinated by this very private woman's stories, as well as by her life. Much of what is known about O'Connor's personal life is revealed in Sally Fitzgerald's award-winning edition of the writer's letters to friends and admirers, *The Habit of Being* (1979). These letters reveal the intelligence, wit, and religious sensibility of a writer proud of both her southern heritage and her Roman Catholic faith. Arranged chronologically, the letters give a sense of O'Connor's personal development as an artist and offer insight into her personality. What they do not provide, however, is an account of romantic interest in her life. Many critics have assumed that her physical condition, compromised after the onset of lupus in her twenties, precluded her forming—even hoping to form—deep attachments with men.

"Good Country People" (1955), one of O'Connor's most successful and most anthologized stories, centers on the maimed Joy Hopewell, fitted with a wooden leg as the result of a childhood accident. She has officially changed her name to Hulga to reflect the ugliness she feels about life and to spite her mother. Hulga, who has a doctorate in philosophy and displays a disdain for her mother's southern, Christian manners, lives as an aloof recluse on the family farm. One day she has an encounter with a disarming Bible salesman named Manley Pointer, a rustic Lothario who is attracted to this lonely intellectual, in part because he senses an unspoken kinship between her exotic beliefs and his own charlatanism. Surprised by Hulga's declaration of her atheism, he reckons that she is a woman who has thrown off the Bible-belt conventions of the South. They share a brief kiss on a walk in the country, a walk that ends in a secluded loft in a barn. Once there, Manley Pointer continues his amorous maneuvers and seems chagrined when Hulga resists. He asks her to take off her artificial leg to prove that she loves him, and she guardedly agrees. But when Hulga quickly discovers that Manley professed a naïve Christian faith just to get his way with her, he malevolently grabs her wooden leg, stuffs it into his suitcase, and leaves her stranded in the loft. With a sense of brutal revelation, she watches from the window the charlatan's "blue figure struggling successfully over the green speckled lake."

How art mediates life is a question of general interest in postmodern culture, and **"Good Country People"** has often made O'Connor fans wonder whether there is any connection between the author's own life and the creation of this story. Parallels abound between O'Connor's history and Hulga's: O'Connor was incapacitated by lupus, which forced her to leave the intellectual and cultural reaches of New York City and return to the South; there she was cared for by her mother on their family farm. A close reading of O'Connor's collected letters reveals in the writer's personality a bit of Hulga's ornery side. O'Connor comes through as a very complex woman who, with great intelligence, is aware of her own vices and virtues. Given these connections between O'Connor and Hulga, it's reasonable to wonder if someone in O'Connor's life served as the basis for the character of Manley Pointer in **"Good Country People."**

Several letters in *The Habit of Being* provide hints of O'Connor's emotional involvement with at least one man in her life. The most striking is her assertion in 1955 to Elizabeth Hester (known simply as "A" in the published correspondence) that she "used to go with" the nephew of Helene Iswolsky, a Dane named Erik Langkjaer. Another strong statement about experience with love is found in another letter to Hester dated August 24, 1956, and concerns the motivation for **"Good Country People."** O'Connor's letter responded to Hester's declaration that the character of Joy/Hulga seems very autobiographical, as if there were indeed an ugly, "Hulga" part of the author exposed in the story. O'Connor was most insistent in her response:

> Where do you get the idea that Hulga's need to worship comes to flower in **"GCP"** [**"Good Country People"**]? Or that she never had any faith at any time, or never loved anybody before? . . . Nothing comes to flower here except her realization in the end that she ain't so smart. It's not said that she had never had any faith, but it is implied that her fine education has got rid of it for her, that purity has been overridden by pride of intellect through her fine education. Further, it's not said that she has never loved anybody, only that she's never been kissed by anybody, a very different thing. And of course I've thrown you off myself by informing you that Hulga is like me . . . but you cannot read a story from what you get from a letter. . . . That my stories scream to you that I have never consented to be in love with anyone is merely to prove that they are screaming an historical inaccuracy. I have God help me consented to this frequently.

With all due respect to O'Connor's own caveat against "reading a story from what you get from a letter," O'Connor's unpublished correspondence with Erik Langkjaer shows that the creation of **"Good Country People"** follows on the heels of her last, powerful experience of romance. Her letters, in particular, reveal that this unrequited love was a likely source of inspiration for this story.

What is already known publicly of Erik Langkjaer in connection with Flannery O'Connor was derived first from four obscure references in *The Habit of Being.*

Additionally, O'Connor's biographers, Sally Fitzgerald and more recently Jean Cash, have brought to light further information about the relationship. Langkjaer worked as a college textbook salesman for Harcourt, Brace and traveled throughout the South during the 1952-1954 academic school terms. Danish on his father's side and Russian on his mother's, Langkjaer had graduated from Princeton and finished two years of graduate studies in philosophy at Fordham University before he decided to begin a career in publishing. Cash quotes Helen Greene, O'Connor's former history professor at Georgia College in Milledgeville, who is said to have introduced Mr. Langkjaer to O'Connor: "Flannery took him all over the county. I think she really liked him a lot . . . [but] he wasn't Roman Catholic." He visited her frequently, driving one hundred miles or so out of his way on weekends in order to spend time with O'Connor at Andalusia, the family's farm. To her consternation, however, he decided to return to Denmark, and in the course of the next year she began corresponding with him. In April 1955 he wrote O'Connor announcing his engagement to a Danish woman. Though it was a painful revelation for O'Connor, she continued corresponding with him. Her last letter to him is dated February 26, 1958.

In a 1997 article in *The Georgia Review,* Sally Fitzgerald focused on the significance of this friendship in the development of O'Connor's vocation as a writer. She mentions the importance of the Langkjaer relationship to O'Connor's emotional life, "the last, and most seriously painful, instance in which the old pattern of unrequited love was to reappear." Having located Langkjaer in Denmark, Fitzgerald interviewed him for her biography of O'Connor; Langkjaer, in turn, shared with her the twelve letters that O'Connor had sent him after he departed from the South. Fitzgerald noted a qualitative difference in these letters, which reveal a depth of feeling seen nowhere else in O'Connor's correspondence. She quotes a handwritten postscript in one such letter to Langkjaer as indicative of O'Connor's feelings for the young Dane: "I think that if you were here, we could talk for about a million years." The poignancy of this revelation lies in its timing, for her letter to Langkjaer was sent shortly before the arrival of his own letter to her announcing his engagement to marry. O'Connor, Fitzgerald notes, instantly withdrew into her customary reserve, and the letters sent to Langkjaer thenceforward were warm but very correct in their southern manners.

Sally Fitzgerald's death in 2000 has delayed the publication of her book-length biography of O'Connor; no doubt, our understanding of the relationship will be improved if and when the biography is published. In an attempt to set the record straight in the meantime and offer his own perspective on their relationship, Mr. Langkjaer made available to me his letters from Flannery O'Connor as well as the unpublished transcript of an interview he did in 1998 at Convergence Productions, London, with his friend Christopher O'Hare, also a friend of Fitzgerald's.[1] O'Connor's letters and the extended interview reveal how **"Good Country People"** is in part a creative response to her pain and distress following Langkjaer's departure from America and her life.

Erik Langkjaer was quite taken with O'Connor after his first visit to Andalusia in the summer of 1953, and he went to Milledgeville as frequently as possible on weekends. They often spoke about faith and religion, for Langkjaer admitted that he had the "luggage" of Catholicism without being a Catholic. His mother and grandmother had both converted from Russian orthodoxy to Catholicism, and he had been influenced by the convert Helene Iswolsky, especially during his recent studies in Fordham: Iswolsky, whom he referred to as his aunt, was a Fordham professor and the cousin of Langkjaer's Russian grandmother. She intermittently wrote and edited a Catholic publication called *The Third Hour* and contributed essays to Dorothy Day's *Catholic Worker* newspaper. O'Connor began a subscription to both publications soon after Langkjaer's initial visit. While studying philosophy, Langkjaer had also become familiar with Fr. William Lynch, a Fordham Jesuit whose articles in the journal *Thought* concerned the religious imagination of writers. Lynch would come to have a profound effect on O'Connor's own understanding of her art.

In his interview with O'Hare, Langkjaer recalls particulars of his year-long association with O'Connor:

> We did speak about faith, Flannery and I, an awful lot. . . . I think she found it extremely difficult to understand how anyone could live without faith. When I told her, soon after we met, that I was somewhere between being a watered down Lutheran and an agnostic, she saw this maybe as a challenge to her faith. . . . I will say that I, that we, grew fond of each other. . . . And I did sense that she was very anxious to have me visit, and we talked about many things, my background in Denmark, my coming to the U.S., my studies there, my meeting various people that she got interested in hearing about, and so all of this gave us something to talk about in addition to her own feelings about her writings or her mother, or whatnot. Then she would be very happy to have me take her for a ride, as this was her chance to get away from her home, and we drove through the countryside.

Langkjaer returned to Denmark in June 1954 mainly because he felt homesick and wanted to try resettling in his native country, but also (he told Fitzgerald in their first meeting in 1980) because he realized that O'Connor had fallen "mildly in love with him and that, although he liked and admired her, he was simply not in love with her." Soon after he left, O'Connor began writing him letters. They are filled with a high degree of affection, and expressive exclamation points punctuate the discourse. She wrote six letters prior to receiving Langkjaer's announcement of his upcoming marriage. The following quotations, chronologically arranged from these first letters, highlight an emotional side that is rarely seen in O'Connor's other correspondence.

> June 13, 1954
>
> . . . your aunt [Helene Iswolsky] for some reason sent me two copies of the *Third Hour* so I reckon I got my money's worth, having read you in EACH copy. Of course, I think you are better than WH Auden and Bishop John of San Francisco combined, but then I'm not exactly your objective critic any longer. . . . I haven't seen any dirt roads since you left & I miss you.
>
> August 20, 1954
>
> I got your letter and I like so much hearing from you! . . . Everything you are seeing and doing sound very rich and strange to me!
>
> October 17, 1954
>
> You are wonderful and wildly original and I would probably think you even more so if I didn't still hope you will come back from that awful place. . . . Did I tell you I call my baby peachicken Brother in public and Erik in private?
>
> January 4, 1955
>
> I have about decided that everybody must be a displaced person too, even if he had a place to be. You wonder how anybody can be happy in his home as long as there is one person without one. I never thought of this so much until I began to know you and your situation and I will never quite have a home again on account of it. . . . Write me because I want so much to hear. [handwritten postscript:] I feel like if you were here we could talk about a million years without stopping.
>
> January 9, 1955 [a handwritten postcard]
>
> Write me an unintelligible post card please so I will have an excuse to write you a letter. My mother don't think it is proper for me to send mail when I don't receive it.

Then in April 1955, O'Connor received Langkjaer's letter regarding his engagement. The six letters that O'Connor wrote following this surprise announcement show her pulling back, friendly and witty, but unrevealing of her emotions. On May 23, 1955, in her first letter to Langkjaer after his announcement—and the only piece of their correspondence that has been published—O'Connor ends the first paragraph by stating, "We are glad that you plan to return South and we want you to let us help you make your wife at home in this part of the country. Consider us your people here because that is what we consider ourselves." After the announcement of his engagement, O'Connor's letters shift from the personal "I" to the familial "we"; with southern propriety—and distance—she chooses to speak socially in conjunction with her mother, Mrs. Regina Cline O'Connor.

The engagement announcement was so unexpected that it left O'Connor in shock. Fitzgerald, in a separate interview with Christopher O'Hare shortly before her death, commented on the depth of O'Connor's emotional crisis on hearing this news. She recounts confronting Mrs. O'Connor on her silence about this significant moment in her daughter's life:

> Flannery's mother had never mentioned Erik Langkjaer to me but when I found out about him and met him I asked her why she hadn't told me and she was very reticent. Mrs. O'Connor seemed to feel that there was no reason, except that one didn't talk about such things. But we were old friends and I was able to push her a little bit, and I said, "but did she suffer, Regina, did she suffer over this?" And she looked down, and against her customary reserve, she was able to say yes, she did, and it was terrible.

In addition, the news of the engagement caused O'Connor to see the possibilities of her future in a profoundly new way. At thirty she was still a young woman but chronically ill. Though she was not yet on crutches when she met Langkjaer, they had become part of her life by the time she wrote her first letter to him. Later that year she claimed to Elizabeth Hester, "I have never been anywhere but sick. In a sense sickness is a place more instructive than a long trip to Europe, and it's always a place where there is no company, where nobody can follow." It seems significant that O'Connor's understanding of the determinant role illness had taken in her life clarified after her passionate friendship with Erik Langkjaer ended.

"Good Country People" was written by O'Connor while the fateful letters were still in transit, and she quickly had it added to her forthcoming volume of stories, ***A Good Man Is Hard to Find*** (1955). On February 26, 1955, a few months before the book was published, O'Connor wrote to her editor, Robert Giroux: "I have just written a story called **'Good Country People'** that Allen [Tate] and Caroline [Gordon] both say is the best thing I have written and should be in this collection." She also informed Sally and Robert Fitzgerald on April 1, "I wrote a very hot story at the last minute called **'Good Country People.'**" And she told Elizabeth Hester a year later, "I wrote **"GCP"** in about four days, the shortest I have ever written anything in, just sat down and wrote it."

Just how "hot" this story was in the aftermath of her bitter disappointment with Langkjaer is evident in the many significant parallels between the O'Connor-

Langkjaer relationship, on one hand, and the imaginative portrayal of Joy/Hulga Hopewell and Manley Pointer, on the other. Though Langkjaer admits that the tone of the story strays far from that of his relationship with O'Connor, there is a level of correspondence that suggests that O'Connor may have drawn on her own recent experience in imagining this story. Like Manley Pointer, Langkjaer was at that time a traveling salesman, in his own way a "displaced" person with no fixed abode. In the story, Manley tells Mrs. Hopewell that he is from "out in the country around Willohobie, not even from a place, just from near a place." And in the O'Hare interview Langkjaer discloses that O'Connor had often thought of him in the same terms: "she felt that I was very much like a displaced person, a displaced person as a character in one of her short stories, that I was the child of divorced parents, that I had come to the U.S., that I was now traveling somewhat rootlessly in the South, and that I had all these religious concerns and problems."

More interestingly, Langkjaer carried around what he called his "bible," a term that Harcourt, Brace used to describe the folder containing the tables of contents that would be presented to professors whom he visited throughout the South. On his sojourns to the O'Connor farm the two of them would often joke about his being a Bible salesman. Langkjaer remarks, "It amused her very much that something that was not a bible should have been called a bible." Manley Pointer's "profession" is a clear instance of O'Connor's creatively deploying a memory, though turning it to a darkly ironic use. Manley's "bible" is definitely something else: merely a covered box containing his pornographic playing cards, flask of whiskey, and his blue box of condoms.

A final obvious comparison between O'Connor's experience with Langkjaer and Hulga's with the Bible salesman that can be drawn concerns the manner by which each was courted and then suddenly dropped: just as Langkjaer initiated the car outings with O'Connor in order to spend some time out from under the watchful eye of Mrs. O'Connor, so Manley takes the same initiative in the story, inviting Joy/Hulga to take a picnic with him the following day. And with similar suddenness, Langkjaer departs from O'Connor's life quite dramatically across the ocean for Denmark, while Manley is seen departing "over the green speckled lake."

Yet by far the most striking revelation of O'Connor's artistic use of her own recent experience comes during the moment in the story when Manley Pointer kisses Joy/Hulga at the edge of the wood. O'Connor describes Hulga's reaction in a famous passage from the story:

> The kiss, which had more pressure than feeling behind it, produced that extra surge of adrenalin in the girl that enables one to carry a packed trunk out of a burning house, but in her, the power went at once to her brain. Even before he released her, her mind, clear and detached and ironic anyway, was regarding him from a great distance, with amusement but with pity. She had never been kissed before and she was pleased to discover that it was an unexceptional experience and all a matter of the mind's control. Some people might enjoy drain water if they were told it was vodka. When the boy, looking expectant but uncertain, pushed her gently away, she turned and walked on, saying nothing as if such business, for her, were common enough.

It is a brilliant piece of descriptive writing that has the feel of genuine experience, revealing a complex and clumsy reaction to a kiss.

Though O'Connor the artist was quick to deny an autobiographical basis for the kissing scene in her letter to Elizabeth Hester, it is fair to question if this kiss represents anything other than O'Connor's own experience. For his part, Langkjaer provides a frankly detailed and deeply moving account of a similar kiss with O'Connor. It occurred on his last visit to Andalusia, fifty years ago, not long before his decision to leave for Denmark. Langkjaer recalls that he had invited O'Connor for a ride in the countryside and she accepted. He describes what ensued as if it took place yesterday.

> As we drove along I parked the car and I may not have been in love, but I was very much aware that she was a woman, and so I felt that I'd like to kiss her, which I did, and I mean it wasn't as if I caught her by surprise. She had been surprised that I suggested the kiss, but she was certainly prepared to accept it. Now as it happened, as our lips touched I had a feeling that her mouth lacked a resilience, it was as if she had no real muscle tension in her mouth, a result being that my own lips touched her teeth rather than her lips, and this I must admit gave me an unhappy feeling of a sort of *memento mori,* and so the kissing stopped. And shortly after that two people turned up from a parked car nearby, poked their heads in as, you know, probably someone is apt to do to find out what's going on in another parked car where they see a man and a woman, and I don't know that there was much of an exchange of any sort, but they withdrew hastily, and Flannery found this rather enjoyable. . . . I was not by any means a Don Juan, but in my late twenties I had of course kissed other girls, and there had been this firm response, which was totally lacking in Flannery. So it's true that I had a feeling of kissing a skeleton, and in that sense it was a shocking, a shocking experience, and it was something that reminded me of her being gravely ill.

Langkjaer is uncertain whether O'Connor realized that the kiss had not been a success, but his memory of it stresses how the reality of her illness overwhelmed his own attraction to her in that moment.

But it is O'Connor's experience that is artistically reworked in the story. The supposedly detached and ironic Hulga, whose "mind . . . never stopped or lost itself for a second to her feelings," is at the same time passionately kissing Manley "as if she were trying to draw all the breath out of him." She is enraptured by the moment—certainly filled with more "Joy" than "Hulga" for the first time in the story. It moves her to surrender her wooden limb to this amorous imposter. It is fair to wonder if such a rush of adrenaline was part of O'Connor's feelings for Langkjaer, and if the car rides, and this fateful kiss, were calculated risks that she too was taking. Joy/Hulga's illusion of herself as a seducing nihilist is undercut by Manley's deception and flight from her; so, too, is O'Connor's illusion of romance shaken by Langkjaer's departure for Denmark.

Langkjaer himself provides evidence to corroborate how closely drawn Joy/Hulga is to O'Connor. If he was not completely sure at the time that O'Connor had fallen in love with him, he nonetheless sensed the strong feelings she had for him and knew that they shared intimate conversations. Langkjaer reads the following line from Hulga's point of view as a very personal declaration by O'Connor about her feelings for him: "This boy, with an instinct that came from beyond wisdom, had touched the truth about her. . . . It was like surrendering to him completely. It was like losing her own life and finding it again, miraculously, in his." Hulga surrenders the emotionally cautious, reticent, perhaps "wooden" part of her that was so essential to her sense of identity, and in its place discovers in her feelings for him the "Joy" part of herself, a more complex and emotionally engaged person. Langkjaer sees O'Connor in the same light: proud of her intellectual and artistic sense of herself, but cautiously willing to surrender her emotions and cede to a passionate moment. O'Connor's letters to Langkjaer illustrate this same kind of emotional yielding; despite the young Dane's absence, they make it painfully clear how much hope O'Connor had placed in his return to her and the South.

Though it would be wrong to argue from the evidence that **"Good Country People"** is simply autobiography, writing the story clearly served as a creative channel for O'Connor to come to terms with these decisive movements in her inner life. But if one reads the trajectory of the story as an imaginative literary negotiation of the real-life association, then one has to contend with the imperfect congruence between Manley Pointer's spiteful final act toward Hulga and O'Connor's presumed judgment of her last rendezvous with Langkjaer. The story presents such disappointment as a devilish betrayal. When Hulga is first asked to show the Bible salesman her wooden leg, she utters a sharp cry because "no one ever touched it but her. She took care of it as someone else would his soul, in private and almost with her own eyes turned away." Yet, she does allow him to take off the leg, and in consequence, she feels exposed. As Manley places it out of her reach and kisses her again, Hulga vacillates between a romantic vision of running away with him and the acute fear of her now defenseless state. The story hinges on whether Manley will accept the leg with the right intention, the one that Joy/Hulga deeply hopes for and desires. Only after he divulges the tawdry items from his valise is it clear that her leg is to be yet another one of his sexual trophies, like the glass eye of a previous conquest about whom he boasts.

Langkjaer himself wonders whether O'Connor actually thought of herself as a trophy, another feather in a young man's cap. In the interview he ponders:

> Flannery may have felt that I was, that she was, in a sense, another trophy, or to put it maybe even more starkly, a kind of another scalp. Of course this wasn't at all the way that I saw the relationship. But in the story he gets the leg from the Hulga part of Joy and she feels that in surrendering this leg voluntarily that in the end she has really given herself completely to the Bible salesman. . . . Nonetheless, she must have felt this, she must have felt not that I took advantage of her, but that in some sense, in some ultimate sense she was not being treated any differently than the girls I had met previously.

Langkjaer claims that the depth of her feeling for him—and the degree of exposure she felt—was not at all clear to him at that time because she was such a reticent person. Many years after her death, Langkjaer remembers being startled on first reading in *The Habit of Being* O'Connor's claim to Betty Hester that she had "gone with" him: "I must say, to my own surprise I read that she felt that she had gone steady with me, that she felt that strongly about our relationship." He then began rereading O'Connor's twenty-five-year-old letters in this new light, and it became clear to him that when O'Connor started writing him shortly after his return to Denmark, she had, in effect, given herself to him:

> I did recognize of course the fact that she wanted to see me and she encouraged me to visit her as often as possible, the fact that she wanted to go on these rides, the fact that she surrendered herself sufficiently enough to allow me to kiss her. I realized of course that she had become very fond of me, else she wouldn't have done that otherwise, especially as she was "a good Catholic"; but still I didn't realize at the time how much it all meant to her, and I only discovered this through the subsequent correspondence.

Upon reading **"Good Country People"** after it was published in ***A Good Man Is Hard to Find,*** Langkjaer wrote O'Connor a letter, offering his own assessment of the story and the perceptible autobiographical references in it, asking specifically if she identified her Bible salesman with him. He expressed shock that she might have perceived his actions as deceptive in the way Manley Pointer is deceptive with Hulga. O'Connor's eighth letter to him is her reply, both an admonishment and a word of assurance:

> April 29, 1956
>
> I am highly taken with the thought of your seeing yourself as the Bible salesman. Dear boy, remove this delusion from your head at once. And if you think the story is also my spiritual autobiography, remove that one too. As a matter of fact, I wrote that one not too long after your departure and wanted to send you a copy but decided that the better part of tact would be to desist. Your contribution to it was largely in the matter of properties. Never let it be said that I don't make the most of experience and information, no matter how meager. But as to the main pattern of that story, it is one of deceit which is something I certainly never connect with you.

On this point, real life and art diverge, for O'Connor assured Langkjaer that if he was a source for the story, in no way did she feel that he had anything to do with deception. Langkjaer remembers discussing with Sally Fitzgerald the timing of the story's creation. Fitzgerald told him that when O'Connor claimed in her letter that she had composed the story "not too long after" his departure, it was to make sure that he understood that it was written long before she had learned of his engagement and was not in any way a settling of scores. However elastic the term "not too long after" might be, the story was actually written in February 1955, more than half a year after Langkjaer had left. That O'Connor did in fact intentionally withhold the story from him—while she had sent numerous others for him to read—points to her perhaps uneasy awareness of the extent to which it was rooted in her feelings for him.

Writing a story more autobiographical than autobiography, with **"Good Country People"** O'Connor wrestled her way out of an emotional, even artistic crisis. Fitzgerald claimed that the concluded liason with Langkjaer "forced [O'Connor] to face the inescapable likelihood that her destiny was not to include any bond of human love closer than that of friendship." Indeed, after Langkjaer moved out of the South and thus out of her life, it would seem O'Connor reconciled herself both to the physical restrictions caused by lupus and to the interpersonal limitations imposed by social perceptions of the disease—both burdens having been perhaps greater then than they would be today. She came likewise to see that her proper calling was to be single and single-mindedly focused on her craft. O'Connor took great pleasure in writing the story: a creative way to come to terms with the romantic upheavals she had felt and the ability to see beyond her own disappointment. Langkjaer concurs, for he thinks that O'Connor discovered that her unspoken and unrealized hope for romance was very much her own wooden leg: "her sense of rejection broke her heart but in hindsight she benefited from it. That was her own wooden leg . . . she had a sense that this was her final chance. And she accepted it as her destiny, as one has to when one has a limitation." In consenting to love Langkjaer and seeing that love not returned, O'Connor hung onto this metaphorical "wooden leg" for the second and last time. But Langkjaer ends his interview noting, "Looking back I feel sorry that things did not work out the way she had wanted them to. That we might have had a meeting of minds, but not a meeting of hearts."

Note

1. Selections from O'Connor's six letters to Erik Langkjaer are used with his permission. Dr. Robert Mann of the Flannery O'Connor Foundation has given permission to quote from her unpublished letters. The 1998 interview with Mr. Langkjaer, conducted by Christopher O'Hare for Convergence Productions, is quoted with permission of Mr. Langkjaer and Mr. O'Hare. A separate interview with Sally Fitzgerald by Mr. O'Hare is also quoted here with permission. Finally, I acknowledge my gratitude to Erik Langkjaer for his assistance with drafts of this paper, verifying the historical accuracy of the information and offering points of clarification.

Vikki Bell (essay date spring 2005)

SOURCE: Bell, Vikki. "On the Critique of Secular Ethics: An Essay with Flannery O'Connor and Hannah Arendt." *Theory, Culture & Society* 22, no. 2 (spring 2005): 1-27.

[*In the following essay, Bell studies "The Lame Shall Enter First" in terms of O'Connor's position on secular morality, and speculates that political theorist Hannah Arendt would have concurred with O'Connor's interpretation of doubt as a strengthening aspect of faith.*]

> What then becomes of this category [ethics] if we claim to suppress or mask its religious character, all the while preserving the abstract arrangement of its apparent constitution ('recognition of the other', etc.)? The answer is obvious: a dog's dinner [*de la bouille pour les chats*].
>
> (Badiou, 2001: 23)

> In the absence of this faith now, we govern by tenderness. It is a tenderness which, long since cut off from the person of Christ, is wrapped in theory. When ten-

> derness is detached from the source of tenderness, its logical outcome is terror. It ends in forced labour camps and in the fumes of the gas chamber.
>
> (O'Connor, 1969: 227)

I

From the relative seclusion of her home in Milledgeville, Georgia—where she was forced to retreat by the lupus that would claim her life at the age of 39—the Southern novelist Flannery O'Connor (1925-64) followed the controversy surrounding the publication of Hannah Arendt's *Eichmann in Jerusalem* (letter dated 22 June 1963, in 1979: 526). On 14 September 1963 she wrote:

> I'm reading *Eichmann in Jerusalem* which Tom [Stritch] sent me. Anything is credible after such a period in history. I've always been haunted by the box cars, but they were actually the least of it. And old Hannah's as sharp as they come.
>
> (1979: 539)

One suspects that O'Connor's admiration of Arendt was due not only to the sharpness of the theorist's intellect but also to her capacity to be cutting in critique. Certainly Arendt's coverage of the Eichmann trial was a cutting down to size of this smug, self-important man, and O'Connor would surely have enjoyed Arendt's wit as she exposed him as a fool. For O'Connor—known for stories profoundly rooted in her Catholic faith that, without exception, turned on the inevitability of the revelatory 'action of grace'—was herself a formidable critic. And since her telling of the undoing of the flawed characters in her stories made their various moments of revelation both funny and shockingly violent, one can imagine her delight in Arendt's assertions that Eichmann 'illustrated how the horrible can be not only ludicrous but outright funny' (1984: 49), and that while Eichmann was perhaps not a 'monster', 'it was difficult indeed not to suspect that he was a clown' (1984: 54). Not infrequently O'Connor would pen her own 'clowns' only to dramatize their downfall.

But there is surely more to be said about this intriguing admiration for the work of Hannah Arendt evidenced in O'Connor's letters. First, it prompts one to reconsider the political context of O'Connor's work, so downplayed in the secondary criticism with its intensive focus on her religiosity. If the 'box cars' so haunted her, can their ghostly trace be detected in her fiction? And, second, it prompts one to consider whether the admiration would have been reciprocated: how would Arendt have responded to O'Connor's writings?[1] The relationship is triangulated by Eric Voegelin, who figured in the articulation of both women's responses to 'the secular'. O'Connor was an admirer of Voegelin, agreeing enthusiastically with his highly influential critique which railed against secularism in all its versions—in the guise of all those other 'isms' and most notably Communism—which he argued had led humankind astray. The Cold War fears of the period are an important political context within which to understand both Voegelin and O'Connor's work. Read in this way, O'Connor's literary interventions were never 'merely' literary, nor were they simply 'Catholic'. For her part, Arendt was less taken with Voegelin's views, and was dismissive in response to his 1953 review of her *Origins of Totalitarianism* (Arendt, 1953/1994). This is not to say that Arendt did not respect this fellow scholar, and she readily agreed to co-edit a special journal to celebrate his 60th birthday in 1961.[2] But Arendt questioned the central division that animated Voegelin—as it did O'Connor—between those who retained their 'love of being through love of divine Being as the source of its order' (Voegelin, quoted in Sandoz, 1997: ix) and those who had 'obliterated' the transcendent origin of being, placing the order of being as 'essentially under man's control' (Voegelin, 1997: 35).

These explorations would be little more than historical ruminations were it not for the resonance they have with recent re-invigoration of scholarly debate around the (im)possibility of ethics without God. Of late, the possibility of a 'secular ethics' has been placed in question, even under attack. The attack presented in Alain Badiou's (2001) *Ethics: An Essay on Radical Evil* is, in Barthes' sense,[3] a *cutting* critique in which the loftiest of aims—that is, the search for an ethics rooted in the love of human, *only* human, alterity—collides with the most scathing of pronouncements: a dog's dinner. Badiou presents a critique of dominant ethics discourses, not only those founded in 'human rights' but also the dominant alternative discourse founded in, as he disdainfully puts it, 'recognition of the other, etc.' He deflates those who seek to pronounce upon questions of response and responsibility from within the secular materialist traditions of cultural critique by reclassifying their task as a rehearsal of those perspectives to which they had believed themselves opposed. The trace of God remains, he argues, in the contemporary pursuit of 'the ethical', as in the Levinasian ethics of the face-to-face, where the face of the other simultaneously summons an absolute alterity. Thus, and despite their differences, Badiou joins with Derrida[4] insofar as both ask theorists of the ethical to 'admit' the trace of religion and, in the latter's case, to admit that the repeated figuring of an ideal future as one that privileges alterity means that this work's ultimate concern is disjuncture, writ small and writ large, such that it always returns one to mystery, to the reassertion of a relationship of wonder with other existents and with human existence itself. It is this reassertion that, as Derrida would say, may 'just as well' bear the name religion.

For Badiou, such a critique opens the space into which he is able to reassert the importance of truths, by which he means not Truth but the truths to which one holds, to which one is subjectively faithful. While contemporary 'anti-philosophy' pretends a form of materialism in its assertion that there are only bodies and language, it cannot simply be 'done with Platonism' (2003: 128). Badiou's 'Platonism' means that for him there is more than bodies and multitudes. And ethics is precisely about the subjective fidelity to a truth 'particular to but unlimited by the contents of the situation in which it comes to exist' (Hallward, 2001: ix). Truths are singular in location and occasion, but universal in their 'address' and import (2001: ix). Hence the lie of those who would attempt to be done with truths while espousing human rights or an 'ethics of the other' that set up certain Truths across all situations. These are the targets of Badiou's scorn, for it is they who reassert something akin to religion while considering themselves 'beyond' it. The rhetorical brilliance of Badiou's text—its shaming, mocking, 'redistributing'—makes the formulation of a dissenting response a formidable task. But to simply sign up to this cutting critique is to perform a remarkable *volte face.* If Derrida's 'just as well' is admitted, doesn't one renege on the very possibility of 'secular ethics' and its critical project, what Edward Said (2000) termed 'secular criticism'? The finesse of the unsettling Badiou effects makes him an important figure in present philosophical debates, once again challenging post-structuralist cultural theorists, *inter alia,* to reconsider their chosen path. Here, by returning to O'Connor and Arendt as an earlier instance of just such a debate, I mean to present such a reconsideration.

Through a reading of one of O'Connor's short stories **'The Lame Shall Enter First'** (1965), which directly turns on the question of secular ethics, and through the exploration of both the enjoyment of narrative 'cuts' that O'Connor displays in that story, as well as the conceit of 'secondary' criticism that either insists on identification with the author or else proceeds by sociological contextualization, I suggest that recognizing narrative as a form of social critique that is also an *intervention* rather than merely an illustration (of either her personal belief or her socio-historical context) is important in the formulation of a response. As such it is entirely appropriate to consider O'Connor on the same terrain as Arendt. That is, she can be approached not merely as a fictional writer to be contextualized within socio-political events, but also as a writer making interventions into the political theoretical world that was more obviously Hannah Arendt's domain.

While O'Connor's admiration of Arendt is documented, the latter's possible response to O'Connor's project remains necessarily speculative. In speculating on Arendt's possible response to the protagonist in **'The Lame Shall Enter First'** (1965), I argue that reading Arendt's work for the 'answer' to this speculation takes us to a, if not the, crux of the matter: how to understand the relationship between goodness and action. From Arendt's thought, formed within the political and religious context of the 1950s she shared with O'Connor, one can begin to draw out a response to the provocations at stake here. Ultimately, by following Arendt's responses both to Voegelin and to questions of religiosity more generally, one can form an Arendtian 'defence' of secular ethics that remains relevant to our contemporary debates.

II

In this section I want to discuss one of O'Connor's short stories—**'The Lame Shall Enter First'** (1965)—because of its explicit foregrounding of questions concerning what might be termed secular morality. The story is one of the longest of O'Connor's short stories, one that bears a strong affinity with the second of her two novels, *The Violent Bear it Away,* written as it was from the latter's rejected remnants, and rewritten—painstakingly, her letters suggest, and never to her complete satisfaction (1979: 460, 464, 475) over a period of some nine months during 1961-2. **'The Lame Shall Enter First'** was published in 1962, and again as part of the collection ***Everything That Rises Must Converge*** after O'Connor's death in 1964. The story illustrates O'Connor's characterization of unbelievers and 'intelleckuals',[5] those who reject faith. The central character, Sheppard, is a 'do-gooder' who rejects Christianity. The story turns on Sheppard's relationship with his son and with another boy to whom he has offered a home.

I use this story as the basis of a reading of the criticism of O'Connor, in order to see how different critical responses to O'Connor involve different critical strategies on the part of her readers. It is only recently that literary criticism has dared to criticize O'Connor's narrative strategies in 'defence' of her characters, an interesting if somewhat peculiar manoeuvre that in the critique ultimately seems to imply a passivity on the part of the reader. It is more recently still that the secondary criticism has criticized O'Connor herself on the basis of her downplaying of the inter-human aspects of her story in order to elevate the spiritual; indeed, to criticize O'Connor's own ethical stance by reading her work *against* her. I want to pursue the path implied in this later strategy in order to suggest that O'Connor can and should be read within a more overtly political context in which her political fears loom as large as her religious faith. The argument is not that her concerns are 'really' political, masquerading as religious. Rather, while the narrative displays O'Connor's faith, it is also and as much about O'Connor's politics, specifically: her sympathies for Voegelin's thesis; the 'revelations' that were emerging about the atrocities of the Nazi regime; and the contemporary US context in which Cold War ideologies were entwined with domestic fears.

The central character, who in O'Connor's deliberately curt[6] rendition 'thought he was good and was doing good when he wasn't' (1979: 490) is the widower, Sheppard, who works during the week as the city's recreational Director and on Saturdays at the reformatory 'receiving nothing for it but the satisfaction of knowing that he was helping boys no one else cared about' (1965: 145-6). His attitude to the world is thoroughly materialistic, anchored in a trust in scientific rationality to explain its ways and wonders. He is, however, a man of high principles and a moralist. His morality, the one he tries to pass on to his son, is that of an altruistic humanist, based in the confrontation of present inequities.

In the opening scene, Sheppard tries to convince his 10-year-old son, Norton, that he is better off than the young boy Rufus Johnson whom Sheppard has invited to come and stay with them since his release from the reformatory. His assessment of his son's comparative advantage operates only at the level of material situation; the boy's emotional life, and in particular his grief for his dead mother, is ignored by Sheppard's assessment:

> 'You have a healthy body . . . a good home. You've never been taught anything but the truth. Your daddy gives you everything you need and want. You don't have a grandfather who beats you. And your mother is not in the state penitentiary.'
>
> The child pushed his plate away. Sheppard groaned aloud.
>
> A knot of flesh appeared below the boy's suddenly distorted mouth. . . . 'If she was in the penitentiary' he began in a racking bellow, 'I could go seeeeee her.'
>
> (1965: 146)

Sheppard responds to his son's grief with admonishment, advising him to turn outside himself, and with generalized platitudes about 'helping other people'. He judges himself well: 'Do you see me just sitting around thinking about my troubles?' (1965: 147).

It is Sheppard's parenting of Norton that reveals O'Connor's judgement of him: Norton may have cake but it is stale; the boy may still have a father who provides for him but his grief for his mother is denied as indeed Sheppard denies his own. He sees neither the emotional needs of his child nor his own irreplaceable role in the child's life, using his son to further his own plan to prove himself a good person. To Sheppard, his own child is materially advantaged and intellectually average; Norton will be 'a banker. No, worse. He would operate a small loan company' (1965: 143). By contrast, he judges Rufus as materially disadvantaged, emotionally needy and intellectually promising. His judgement, however, is woefully askew. For although, as in so many of O'Connor's stories, Rufus enters the family home seemingly the one in need, he quickly emerges as an incarnation of evil. At least this is how O'Connor would have us read him. The afternoon he arrives the rain 'slashed against the window panes and rattled in the gutters'; Rufus appears 'like an irate drenched crow. His look went through the child [Norton] like a pin and paralysed him' (1965: 153). The visitor sets about his invasion of Norton's deepest and most personal emotions, insulting both his father's good intentions by mimicking Sheppard ('yaketty yaketty yak . . . and never says a thing' [1965: 155]) and, most painfully, the boy's dead mother. Rufus blithely crosses the line between the profane and the sacred, entering the shrine in the home, the faintly scented bedroom that had been Norton's mother's. Rufus combs his hair with her comb, and rummages in her clothes, forcing the 'stricken' Norton to watch as he fastens her corset around his waist and dances around the room singing rock and roll.

Sheppard is determined to pursue 'the good' and this makes him oblivious to the clues O'Connor gives the reader as to Rufus's evil. Despite the resistance and ridicule that his efforts meet, Sheppard persists, believing his intervention will eventually be rewarded with Rufus's gratitude and his own sense of satisfied pride in the difference he will have made for the boy. When Rufus refuses the new shoe that Sheppard had ordered for the boy's ill-formed foot, Sheppard comforts himself by understanding Rufus's response through the lens of psychology, another subject of O'Connor's disdain: 'something he had been was threatened and he was facing himself and his possibilities for the first time' (1965: 177). Sheppard wants to give the boy a new life, while Rufus is set upon ensnaring Sheppard.

O'Connor said of this story that she wanted people to be sure where the devil was in it. Certainly Rufus's dialogue is stark. When Sheppard tries to engender a fascination in the stars and the moon by buying a telescope and enthusing 'you boys could go to the moon' (1965: 163), Rufus replies: 'I ain't going to the moon and get there alive . . . and when I die I'm going to hell' (1965: 164). Later in the story he argues with Sheppard: 'Satan has you in his power. . . . Not only me. You' (1965: 184).

Sheppard tries to employ 'gentle ridicule' as a means of responding to Rufus's description of hell by answering 'nobody has given any reliable evidence there's a hell' (1965: 164). But ridicule is powerless here and, as one commentator would have it, Norton's 'boundaries of yearning' are gradually expanded[7] as Rufus works on the son, explaining to him, whispering like Iago in his ear, replying to his unanswered emotional needs. He undermines Sheppard's materialist belief, his secular ethics and his parenting, suggesting to Norton that there is a higher authority. While Sheppard attempts to maintain his paternal authority, to use his counselling training and to be endlessly patient, hoping to give Rufus 'security' and to 'save' (1965: 188) him from his material disadvantage, Rufus scoffs at Sheppard's modelling himself on Christ—just as Badiou scoffs at the contemporary ethicist—hissing to Norton: 'How do you stand it? . . . He thinks he's Jesus Christ!' (1965: 161).

Rufus teaches Norton that ultimately judgement occurs only at one's death. The young boy's initial fear is that his mother may be in the dreadful place that Rufus describes, where 'the dead are judged and the wicked are damned. They weep and gnash their teeth while they burn . . . and it's everlasting darkness' (1965: 164). But the idea that his mother might be 'saved' offers to Norton the possibility that Sheppard had had to deny him, lest he bring the boy up 'on a lie' (1965: 165). That is, the possibility that he might be reunited with her in Heaven.

O'Connor's negative judgement of Sheppard is evident throughout the story. Sheppard is portrayed by O'Connor as a fool who attempts to fight with the devil, who believes in his own powers to effect change but who must ultimately confront 'the failure of his own compassion' (1965: 181). While he finds this failure numbing, he is to face a much deeper blow. Sheppard places his quest to help Rufus above his paternal love for Norton. He fails to appreciate the impact that Rufus has on his son, and he fails adequately to challenge the power that works on the child. Rufus has the club-foot, but it is Norton who is 'lame'. Indeed, the first time the word is used in the story it is with reference to Norton, who answers his father 'lamely'. Later it is he who takes the 'hobbled step' (1965: 164) toward Sheppard to ask if his mother is in hell: 'Is she there?' It is Norton who has been chosen; and it is he who will 'enter first'.

Sheppard's attempt to interest Rufus in astronomy, to help him 'reach for the stars', backfires and instead it is Norton who begins to spend his time looking at the night sky searching for his beloved mother. Towards the end of the story, Norton thinks he has seen her: '"She's there!" he cried, not turning around from the telescope. "She waved at me!"' (1965: 186). Norton tries to show his father but Sheppard's attention is on Rufus, who has gone missing again, only to reappear escorted by two police officers who have arrested him for burglary. After they have taken Rufus away Sheppard tries to comfort himself in his 'failure' to help Johnson, but, as he slowly repeats his secular mantra, he is confronted with his revelation:

> 'I have nothing to reproach myself with' he repeated. His voice sounded dry and harsh. 'I did more for him than I did for my own child.' He was swept with a sudden panic. He heard the boy's jubilant voice. 'Satan has you in his power.'
>
> 'I have nothing to reproach myself with,' he began again. 'I did more for him than I did for my own child.' He heard his voice as if it were the voice of his accuser. He repeated the sentence silently.
>
> Slowly his face drained of colour.
>
> (1965: 189)

A visceral reaction accompanies the realization that dawns on him; he had 'stuffed his own emptiness with good works like a glutton. He had ignored his own child to feed his vision of himself. He saw the clear-eyed Devil, the sounder of hearts, leering at him from the eyes of Johnson' (1965: 190). Sheppard's heart constricts and he is breathless, 'paralysed, aghast' (1965: 190). When his child's image appears to him, he experiences 'agonising love' and rushes to find his son, 'to kiss him, to tell him that he loved him'. The child's bed is empty. He climbs the attic stairs and

> . . . at the top reeled back like a man on the edge of a pit. The tripod had fallen and the telescope lay on the floor. A few feet over from it, the child hung in the jungle of shadows, just below the beam from which he had launched his flight into space.
>
> (1965: 190)

O'Connor's portrayal and narrative 'punishment' of Sheppard is uncompromising. Even on his own terms, O'Connor repeatedly implies, Sheppard's desire to do good is streaked through with a desire to reflect well upon himself. There is an obvious calculation in Sheppard's ethics. He chooses to help the boy whose IQ test indicates he is already intelligent; he offers help and gifts while imagining the pride that he will feel in the future; and he admits defeat in a way that reveals his personal stake in Rufus's transformation. More than this hypocrisy, however, O'Connor judges Sheppard because he is, as Rufus accuses him, an atheist who 'thinks he's God' (1965: 187). While attempting to pursue a plan according to his own design, Sheppard is exposed to the vice beneath his virtues. He undergoes a 'shock of recognition [that] demolishes the fabricated vision' of himself, and according to this reading, he emerges with the possibility of a new integrity in which he might truly see that to which he is called: not a virtue according to his own image and likeness but, in the words of one critic, a 'shattering sacrifice that plunders whatever is not genuine love' (Giannone, 2000: 205). It is the harshest of lessons.

O'Connor's traditional critics tend to support this literary shattering of secular do-gooders because they accept the violent power of the love of God. As Giannone wrote in his earlier (1989) study of O'Connor, divine love is one that '*cuts and burns* to prepare for the glory to come' (quoted in Gordon, 2000: 131). The telescope and the microscope enhance the possibilities for literal vision, as scientific discoveries and possibilities of space travel were doing all around O'Connor at the time she was writing, but these pursuits of scientific knowledge are unable to help Sheppard to see what is unfolding before his eyes. Giannone asserts: 'Being able to recognise what is true and from God or what is false and from Satan is the habit of being that protects one's other habits from disintegrating into ends in themselves' (2000: 217). Sheppard attempts to see the natural world through the lens of rationality, and human relations through that of psychology. He cannot recognize, but neither will he escape, God.

O'Connor believed the novelist's task was to provoke 'a renewed sense of mystery' (1969: 184). Through the crafted portrayal of the untidy realities of 'weakened' life,[8] she argued, Catholic writers should promote their faith by showing 'mystery as it is incarnated in human life' (1969: 176). The writer has to both show the concrete and 'make the concrete work double time' (1969: 98) to allow the human action to show the action of God's grace. It is clear that, in this way, O'Connor regarded her fiction as a *weapon* 'in a world that is unprepared and unwilling to see the meaning of life' (1969: 185). She argued: 'This frequently means that [the fiction writer] may resort to violent literary means to get his vision across to a hostile audience, and the images and actions he creates may seem distorted and exaggerated to the Catholic mind' (1969: 185). Indeed, the action of grace as it is depicted in O'Connor's fiction is frequently shocking and violent, as she explained: 'I have found that violence is strangely capable of returning my characters to reality and preparing them to accept their moment of grace' (1969: 112). One commentator, Desmond, asserts that O'Connor's use of violence is a response to the spectre of 'human closure to metaphysical reality'. According to his interpretation, one influenced by a reading of Voegelin, O'Connor wanted to show through her fiction that this closure was:

> . . . a deformation of being and at the same time to reveal the possibility of breakthrough to a higher, more complex level of consciousness. Such a revelation would at least open her characters—if only in defeat—to the possibility of self-transcendence and a more authentic personality rooted in the divine. In the stories . . . *violence becomes the means of disrupting closure* in order to create these possibilities, for a world of possibility is a world governed by the mystery of being that she so forcefully reveals to the reader.
>
> (Desmond, quoted in Gordon, 2000, emphasis added)

However, by reading O'Connor's textual violence as illustrative of the depth of her faith and her explicit concerns for what she understood as the dangerous secularization of the Christian world, these critics read O'Connor without attention to the active pleasure exhibited in her penning of the narrative that punishes Sheppard. To the critic unattuned to the divine, this use of the narrator's privilege can appear all too human. A less theological reading might justifiably interpret O'Connor's literature as *sadistic,* inviting the readers into an enjoyment of the narrative punishments she metes out to her characters. Just as Nietzsche had found the pleasure of punishment at the heart of Christian morality, so Patricia Yaeger writes: 'there is no place the reader can feel safe, except in identification with the narrator's sadism and in the frequent upheavals of laughter that punctuate the text's discomforts with such bizarre gaiety' (1996: 195).[9] As Yaeger's thesis would suggest, throughout the story O'Connor is preparing the reader for Sheppard's eventual cutting, a revelatory cutting perhaps, but one that is also, more mundanely, a cutting down to size. So while O'Connor's narrative mimics the blow that she believes divine love can deliver, and in her stories will deliver, she is also presenting a critique of the secular world around her, a scolding that she invites us to accompany her in delivering. Indeed, the reader is invited to join her as she speaks through the character of Rufus. By judging Sheppard for his resistance to an individual's duty to further 'the divine plan for all creation' (Giannone, 2000: 131), she is aligning herself with Rufus: 'I'll admit the devil's voice is my own in this one', she wrote to John Hawkes,[10] an admission to which I shall return.

This reading insists that **'The Lame . . .'** [**"The Lame Shall Enter First"**] be read as *O'Connor*'s story. It is not, in that sense, divine love at work here. The invitation to identify with O'Connor, and to read Sheppard with her as an unseeing clown, is a literary strategy O'Connor employs masterfully. It is a strategy designed by O'Connor, and one designed, moreover, from within an understanding of the historical present. This is of utmost relevance to her portrayal of Sheppard.

As would Badiou, O'Connor repeatedly suggested that even Sheppard's 'secularism' is shaped by religious belief. His ethical sense is a (per)version of Christian heritage. She portrays him as a type who, as she categorizes it elsewhere, 'can neither believe nor contain himself in unbelief and who searches desperately, feeling about in all experience for the lost God' (1969: 159). That is, he has attempted to emerge out of a spiritual age, to dismiss the Bible as 'for cowards, people who are afraid to stand on their own feet and figure things out for themselves' (1965: 184), but he remains deeply and inevitably marked by it. Her present was, O'Connor believed, an unbelieving age where one 'breathes in nihlism' (1979: 97) but, nonetheless, one which was 'markedly and lopsidedly spiritual' (1969: 159). Sheppard's use of language reflects O'Connor's belief, as stated in one of her talks, that even secular outlooks could not escape the religious societies from which they have emerged:

> The Judaeo-Christian tradition has formed us in the west; we are bound to it by ties which may often be invisible, but which are there nevertheless. It has even formed the shape of our secularism; it has formed the shape of modern atheism.
>
> (1969: 155)[11]

Most clearly, when faced with Rufus's description of hell, Sheppard's mode of comforting his son is marked by the trace of a denied spirituality: '"Listen," Sheppard said quickly and pulled the child to him, "your mother's spirit lives on in other people and it'll live on in you if you're good and generous like she was"' (1965: 165).[12]

Sheppard's ethics led him to govern through what O'Connor termed 'tenderness'. Propelled by theory rather than faith, his tenderness is depicted by O'Connor as too weak to confront evil in the world as it is incarnated in the body of Rufus. This is a dramatization of O'Connor's strongest belief and strongest fear. Such was the strength of her conviction on this matter that, in one halting and oft-quoted comment, O'Connor offers a formulation that links secularism—and specifically its attempt to replace faith with forms of 'tenderness'—causally with Nazism:

> In the absence of this faith now, we govern by tenderness. It is a tenderness which, long since cut off from the person of Christ, is wrapped in theory. When tenderness is detached from the source of tenderness, its logical outcome is terror. It ends in forced labour camps and in the fumes of the gas chamber.
>
> (1969: 227)

As I have indicated, O'Connor's convictions were close to those of Eric Voegelin, whose works she praised; her 1958 review of Voegelin's *Israel and Revelation* (1956) called it a 'monumental study' in which Voegelin presents history as 'a journey away from civilizations by a people which has taken the "leap into being" and has accepted existence under God' (Getz, 1980: 143). O'Connor shared Voegelin's concerns about the unbelieving world that sought to replace faith with the quest for knowledge, thinking that 'the mysteries of life will eventually fall before the mind of man' (1969: 158). In one of her letters (to Betty Hester), O'Connor explained why her short stories appeared bleak and 'negative'. They had to be, she wrote, because of the nihilistic 'gas' within and against which she wrote:

> Another reason for the negative appearance: if you live today you breathe in nihilism. In or out of the Church, it's the gas you breathe. . . . With such a current to write against, the result almost has to be negative. It does well just to be.
>
> (To 'A' 28 August 1955, in O'Connor, 1979: 97)

The argument that I am developing here—that O'Connor's political imagination is as important a context for understanding her literary portrayal of Sheppard as her religious belief—is one that both agrees with and detracts slightly from the compelling analysis recently put forward by Sarah Gordon (2000).

III

Although Yaeger's critique usefully indicates the need for an awareness of the literary strategies employed by the writer herself, her reading of O'Connor still implies, as does the traditional theological reading, an obligation to identify in order to 'feel safe' within the world O'Connor paints. In a different vein, Sarah Gordon has suggested that readers of O'Connor need not be bound by explanations offered by the author herself, nor by those offered through traditional readings of her fiction. Indeed, despite the obvious 'truths' of these readings, 'like Tarwater's "congregation" on some anonymous street, we as readers of O'Connor's fiction may very well not feel a sense of connection—much less communion—with her stringently prophetic fiction' (2000: 219). Gordon's reading opens up the possibility that we might read **'The Lame Shall Enter First'** not only *without* identifying with the narrator but that we might even read it *against* O'Connor.

Reading *The Violent Bear it Away,* the novel from whose remnants **'The Lame Shall Enter First'** was crafted, Gordon highlights the desert of human love in the novel, the lack of 'delight in human exchange and community'. While O'Connor finds divine incarnation in the angelic or the afflicted child, or in the natural world, she never does so in a romantic relationship or that of a parent and child. In O'Connor's fiction 'human engagement is valuable only insofar as it directs the soul to salvation' (Gordon, 2000: 222). Gordon argues that this steady focus might be challenged by Sheppard's tale read as one of 'an innocent life lost by reason of [Sheppard's] inability to see the actual human face of his child before him' (2000: 233). For while Sheppard is punished for having his mind set on high-minded principles in his pursuit of the good, O'Connor's vision might be regarded likewise. That is, O'Connor's focus is set above the inter-human, only ever concerning the relationship between solitary (predominantly masculine) figures and God. O'Connor's need to tell the story as one of Sheppard's mistaken pursuit of secular morality serves to concentrate her narrative on his myopia while revealing, to the critical reader, her own.

Gordon ventures to suggest that in **'The Lame Shall Enter First'** O'Connor is inadvertently giving a warning to herself. For all her attention to manners, conventions and locale, O'Connor's own beliefs keep the eyes of her fiction steadily on the horizon, 'on last things, on human choice under the aspect of eternity'. Thus Gordon challenges any reading that only affirms O'Connor's own faith, without paying attention to what she chooses to ignore or, more fairly perhaps, under-emphasize. For while it is true that interhuman questions of socio-political community are muted in her fiction, her reference points were clearly in the world. This observation of the world is what gives authenticity to the action in her fiction. So, while muted, in **'The Lame Shall Enter First'** the social and political preoccupations of her geopolitical time are apparent, acting as indices of the society within which the story's action takes place, of a South where faith was entangled with the politics of sex and 'race', of religious, geographic and ideological divisions.

The hatred of abstraction that O'Connor dramatizes in Sheppard's character, and especially in his relationship to Norton, is one that reverberates with her political context, in which the Northern States were considered to be encroaching on the South, bringing ways of being that were secular, intellectualized and ultimately dangerous to the traditional ways of the South. In Tate's 1936 essay 'Religion and the Old South', with which O'Connor was familiar, Tate asserts that the northern industrialist has succeeded in 'making a society out of abstractions' and proposes that the southerner may 'take hold of his tradition' only 'by violence'.[13] Moreover, at this time tense North-South relations were figured not simply as a struggle on these terms, but also became figured as a struggle against the implications of secular political ideologies: communism and anti-Americanism. The North, and especially the urban North, was understood much as Voegelin implies, as a hotbed of ethical corruption, a breeding ground and hiding place for communism. It is unsurprising, then, that in **'The Lame . . .'** Sheppard's intentions are socialistic in broad sweep (Bacon, 1993). That the telescope and the stars feature so prominently reflects the 1950s Cold War culture, in which the exploration of space was a political drama fuelled by earthly rivalry. The optimism surrounding the exploration of space was accompanied by intense fear that attacks would come from above. The sky had become a source of deep fear, such that people's fears came to be repeatedly depicted as attacks that came from the sky to obliterate American life (Bacon, 1993).[14]

Even changing sexual mores and political struggles around race relations indicative of the soon-to-emerge civil rights movement make their shadowy appearance in the story, although, again, without having any real purchase on the action. They appear as casual references to the inter-human issues animating the political scene at the time. Rufus's dance in Norton's mother's bedroom—described by one commentator as 'an obscenely hermaphroditic phantom of his mother' (Giannone, 2000: 219)—has Rufus singing rock and roll, implying an association between the devil and 'youth culture', thus alluding to a contemporary culture anxious that sexual propriety and the clarity of gender roles were under threat from rebellious youth. Moreover, O'Connor has Rufus insult Leola the cook, calling her 'Aunt Jemima', reminding the reader of the exploitation that Sheppard unquestioningly tolerates on a daily basis.[15]

In these ways O'Connor references socio-political dynamics of the time but here, as in her *oeuvre* as a whole, they remain mere contexts. When Rufus combs his hair with Norton's mother's hairbrush he sweeps it, O'Connor tells us flatly, 'to the side, Hitler fashion' (1965: 157). Indeed, her cutting judgement of Sheppard's secular ethics takes precedence to such an extent that one can wonder, with Sarah Gordon, at the harshness of O'Connor's punishment of him. Surely the events of the Second World War deserved O'Connor's judgement more than Sheppard's plodding but well-intentioned ethical outlook? But even Nazism is merely a detail and cannot turn O'Connor from God to the inter-human aspects of the 'turbulent times'[16] in which she wrote.

But as we have seen in the preceding section, this is not simply, as Gordon would argue, a *refusal* to engage in the implications of inter-human community, a *reduction* of the socio-political contexts to one drama, that between belief and secular ethics. That Nazism is so subordinated *is precisely O'Connor's response* to the changes that were surrounding her, in the South and in the world. For her, the socio-political context in which the full horrors of Nazism were becoming apparent and in which Cold War ideology and its associated fears raged, *was* this same drama. The battle between belief and secular ethics was key to understanding all that had gone awry in the world, including the events precipitating the Second World War. One cannot 'win' an argument with O'Connor by the socio-historical contextualization of her narratives, therefore, because for her these contexts remain muted *in order* to concentrate on what she believed, in line with Voegelin's thesis, was the principal question: the world's loss of faith. It is 'worse' than Gordon portrays it, therefore, because O'Connor doesn't merely mute the socio-political contexts and inter-human aspects of her stories; her convictions were such that she would have wished to have actively translated those dimensions into the battle between faith and non-faith. If she was 'haunted' by the boxcars, she transformed that image into the portrayal of a character whose good intentions were leading him dangerously astray, whose life should be made into a fable warning of the dangers of following an ethics without God. **'The Lame . . .'** should be read, therefore, not merely as an illustration of O'Connor's belief, nor even as an illustration of her lack of attention to the socio-political and inter-human, but as both of these *and* also, as a *political* intervention on O'Connor's part.[17]

As such, it is possible to consider O'Connor on the same terrain as Hannah Arendt, whose arguments concerning faith, the loss of faith and politics are more conventionally understood as interventions. Arendt's writing may also, it is argued below, offer some subtle reflections on questions raised here that to a certain extent enable a reading of the debate surrounding 'secular ethics'.

IV

Let me return to the speculative question concerning Arendt's response to O'Connor. How, one wonders, would Arendt have responded to O'Connor's 'clown', the story of the 'self-regarding do-gooder'[18] Sheppard?

Certainly Arendt would have found O'Connor's textual punishment of Sheppard a harsh but unsurprising twist from a devotee of Eric Voegelin. Voegelin's thesis was that the 'essence of modernity' had its roots in heretical anti-Christian Gnosticism that was alienated from the real world and rebelled against the divine ground of being. For him 'modern' philosophy had lost its sense of the divine Being and sought the transformation of the world through the atheistic deification of Man (Sandoz, 1997). His argument put fascism and communism together, as did Arendt's concept of totalitarianism in a different sense, but it also sought to argue their equivalence with other modern movements such as positivism, Freudianism, existentialism, utopianism. These were indicative of the decline of faith and the rise of schools of thought that put man at the centre of the world order. Voegelin's critical review (1953) of her *The Origins of Totalitarianism* gave Arendt the opportunity to articulate her opposition to his central thesis, especially as it attempted to account for National Socialism (see 1994 'Reply to Voegelin').[19] In his review, Voegelin admired Arendt's book, but criticized her methodological habit of presenting the events of which she wrote in too fatalistic a manner. The story of Western disintegration, he believed, was not a fatal sequence. It arose not only due to the breakdown of institutions and modes of conduct, but also from the *spiritual* disease of agnosticism. For him totalitarianism was 'an immanentist creed movement' so that if one considered, as one should, 'the rise of immanentist sectarianism since the high Middle Ages . . . [then] the totalitarian movements would not be simply revolutionary movements of functionally dislocated people, but immanentist creed movements in which medieval heresies have come to their fruition' (1953, quoted in Cooper, 1999: 136).

One might suppose that Arendt's opposition to Voegelin's—and hence to O'Connor's—view that an 'immanentist heresy' associated with a loss of faith was threatening the world, would make her more sympathetic to Sheppard than to the judgement O'Connor passes on him. However, there is little about Sheppard that Arendt would obviously admire. Arendt, for her own reasons, would join O'Connor in a critique of the ethical stance implied by such a figure.

First, there is a sense in which Arendt would *also* regard Sheppard, despite himself, as a religious figure whose interventions in the world will falter. This is so exactly because Sheppard attempts to pursue 'the good'. As Arendt explains in *The Human Condition* (1959), the pursuit of 'the good' is always going to fail. In contrast to the model of action that Arendt is developing, goodness tends toward its own end. Whereas action proper is a sign of the human ability to begin, to—as it were—'open up' to the world, good works are 'eschatological' (see Gottlieb, 2003: 157). Wherever goodness is perceived, even by the actor him or herself, it is no longer goodness. It may arise out of solidarity or duty, but goodness as such has a 'curious negative quality' that means the pursuit of the good cancels itself out; goodness has 'an essentially non-human, superhuman quality', making 'the lover of goodness an essentially *religious* figure' (Arendt, 1959: 68, emphasis added). Indeed, teases Arendt, even Jesus taught no man can be good: 'Why callest thou me good? None is good, save one, that is, God' (Arendt, 1959: 66 quoting Luke 8: 19).[20] The same thought occurs in Matthew, Arendt continues in a footnote, where 'Jesus warns against piety. Piety "cannot appear unto men" but only unto God, who "seeth in secret"' (1959: 321, fn. 85). Arendt goes so far as to suggest that 'the whole life story of Jesus seems to testify how love for goodness arises out of the insight that no man can be good' (1959: 66). Sheppard's confidence in his own attempt to do good, his own awareness of his 'good deed' and his self-congratulatory attitude in relation to Rufus Johnson, would all suggest that Sheppard would be a target for Arendt's criticism. For Arendt, goodness has a paradoxical 'ruinous quality' (1959: 68) that, as Susannah Gottlieb has astutely observed, associates it with her messianic vision of 'the ruin to which the world would succumb were it not for the redemptive power of action' (2003: 157).

Second, having no 'outward phenomenal manifestation' (1959: 66), 'good works' have a 'worldlessness' that differentiates them from action; goodness lacks the capacity to *appear* in the world. Goodness as an activity can *never* appear in public without destroying its essential quality: 'The moment a good work becomes known and public, it loses its specific character of goodness, of being done for nothing but goodness' sake' (1959: 66). Thus Sheppard's pursuit of the good necessarily entails a retreat from the shared world. Sheppard's literal bringing home of Rufus—into the 'private' sphere—is different from action 'proper', which is orientated to the shared, public world, the space of appearance. For Arendt, goodness in its purity does not belong—indeed, cannot exist—within the public realm. But Sheppard attempts to pursue 'goodness' and to make his private sphere operate as if it were a public space. All that is associated with the private realm—particularity, affection and love—is demoted in this house where even the need to mourn the mother is ignored. The attempt to make the home operate in this way leads to problems that Arendt would associate with the attempt to make goodness appear in public.

In *On Revolution* (1963b), Arendt discussed the inability of goodness to appear, and to found political institutions, in relation to Melville's *Billy Budd.* She read the story as a commentary on the 'men of the French Revolution' (1963b: 77) who had proposed that 'man is good in a state of nature and becomes wicked in society' (1963b: 78). Billy Budd is a foundling, the 'natural man' who comes from outside society such that the story explores this reversal of the notion of original sin upon which the French Revolution was built. In the place of original sin, Budd personifies original goodness. But, argues Arendt, Melville's story dramatizes the violence which goodness harbours, precisely *because* it is part of '"natural" nature' (1963b: 78). When natural nature confronts wickedness—'nature's depravity'—it does not attempt to persuade, for it has no conception of temptation and is thus ignorant of the argumentative reasoning processes by which temptation is warded off (1963b: 82). Instead of persuasion, it acts violently. Budd murders the man who bore false witness against him, eliminating wickedness (1963b: 78) and displaying the violence by which goodness confronts evil. Herein lies the problem with goodness; that is, that the good man 'because he encountered evil', and because he must confront and eliminate it, becomes a wrong-doer himself (1963b: 79). Billy Budd shows that goodness is not capable of founding institutions because it is 'incapable of learning the arts of persuading and arguing' (1963b: 82); it is not weak but strong, perhaps more so than wickedness, and strikes with 'elementary violence' (1963b: 83). Institutions cannot be founded on goodness; they cannot respond to things outside the world, 'whether angels or devils' (1963b: 79), which is why Arendt reads Melville as arguing that any absolute will spell 'doom to everyone when it is introduced into the political realm' (1963b: 79). Sheppard's story might be read likewise as a doomed attempt to follow the path of goodness; he is attempting to give to the world, but his attempt to do so means he withdraws from it. In the course of events his pursuit of the good encounters evil and, although by a more indirect route than Billy Budd, Sheppard causes the death of pure goodness in the figure of Norton.[21]

In place of and in contrast to goodness, Arendt would of course offer her understanding of the term 'action'. Action doesn't transcend the world; it doesn't seek an otherworldly salvation. Rather, it testifies to the *human* capacity to begin in which it is ontologically rooted. Never one to allow the terms of religious discourse to 'belong' to religion alone, Arendt grants action a 'miraculous' quality, meaning that the potential to appear is rooted in the appearance of human beings in the world, in natality, which one can only witness and at which one can only marvel. Indeed, the public realm may be what inspires men to dare the extraordinary and insofar as it does 'all things are safe' (1959: 184) because action 'redeems' the world by interrupting the automatic quality of life; it intervenes for the sake of the world.[22] Unlike goodness, action is orientated to the public realm and the common world. Unlike goodness, action requires a shared space of appearance in which plurality is preserved.

Third, Arendt might well have considered Sheppard's story an example of unresponsiveness to the world. For while Sheppard's pursuit of good does not make him an evil man—'the sad fact is that most evil is done by people who never made up their minds to be or do evil or good' (Arendt, 1977)[23]—it does make him both naive and impotent. Sheppard's pursuit of the good approaches has an almost automatic quality that makes him fatefully unresponsive to events and people around him. In this he displays an attenuated sense of reality, the critique of which underlies the Arendtian project (Curtis, 1999). He is in danger, for all the this-worldliness with which the term 'secular' is associated, of becoming unresponsive to his immediate inter-human world. In the story this is played out most poignantly in Sheppard's unresponsiveness to his son, Norton, whose requests for comfort are refused or dismissed as Sheppard prioritizes his 'good works' project: Rufus. Further, it is apparent in Sheppard's failure to respond adequately to the power of the terms of Rufus's discourse on the younger boy's imagination. His response to Rufus's invocation of hell, for example, is articulated in the terms of 'scientific rationality'. Sheppard attempts to remove Norton's fear that his mother might be suffering in hell with the comment that 'there is no reliable evidence' for the existence of hell, as if the language of scientific method ('evidence', 'reliability') were all that is required to counter Rufus's deployment of these terms.[24] Sheppard fails to appreciate that Rufus's words are not merely based in faith (if they are at all), but are part of Rufus's intervention between father and son. Whatever Rufus's true beliefs, in this instance the notion of hell is deployed by Rufus as part of a power play, and not as part of an innocent debate between faith and non-faith. Sheppard's naivety about Rufus forces him to argue in terms inadequate to the task, just as Arendt argued there was a tendency to set up the debate about 'secularism' on the terms of faith, which gave the advantage to the latter. Speaking at a conference in 1953, Arendt objected to the way in which the conference rubric displayed an assumption common to arguments such as Voegelin's, that not only oppose secular outlooks in the name of faith but also seek to drag secular outlooks onto the terrain of faith regarding them as perverse forms of faith (in Arendt, 1994).[25]

As this suggests, however much Arendt would criticize the figure of Sheppard, she would nevertheless disagree with O'Connor, as she did with Voegelin, that the faults of Sheppard and his ilk were to be explained in terms of loss of faith.

Arendt argued forcefully that it was not faith and its loss that characterized the present era, but the events that made *doubt* central to all modern life. Here Arendt is referring principally to Galileo's demonstrations, registered most clearly at the philosophical level by Descartes, where Being and Appearance 'part company forever' (1959: 250). Descartes' doubt had resolved itself into a treatise on method, and it is this tradition of thought that lends Sheppard his discourse of rationality and evidence. But Sheppard mistakenly understands his own 'modern' attitude as succeeding Christian faith, as both coming after and as superior to Christianity, to such an extent that he fails to recognize that his response to historical events coexists with other responses to doubt, including those who had taken Kierkegaard's leap into faith, because they are both attempts to resolve the doubt that pervades the modern world. Indeed, the fact that Norton can find through that most modern of scientific inventions—the telescope[26]—confirmation that his mother was 'up there' waving to him, highlights the sense in which, while modern instruments can magnify and improve the sense-perception that had been put into doubt, they cannot of themselves relieve that doubt. Nor can they persuade a believer into non-belief, let alone confirm the necessity of so doing. Indeed, as Arendt asserts, modern science emerges from and requires doubt; doubt is the condition of possibility of all modern science.

But equally, insofar as it exists in this world, in this same present with its same history, so too does *faith* 'include' doubt. Without some place for doubt, one might say, faith becomes a refusal to dwell in this present world; not because belief has to shade into doubt, but because it has to be understood as a *response* to doubt. Arendt makes the argument in her reply to Voegelin by reference to Dostoevsky's *The Idiot.* The reference is employed in order to suggest that doubt is carried into 'authentic faith':

> Modern belief, which has leapt from doubt into belief, and modern atheism, which has leapt from doubt into non-belief, have this in common: both are grounded in modern spiritual secularism and have evaded its inherent perplexities by a violent resolution once and for all. Indeed, it may be that the leap into belief has done more to undermine authentic faith than the usually trite arguments of professional enlighteners or the vulgar arguments of professional atheists. The leap from doubt into belief could not but carry doubt into belief, so that religious life itself began to assume that curious tension between atheistic blasphemous doubt and belief as we know it from the great psychological masterpieces of Dostoevsky.
>
> (1953/1994: 369)

Later, in *The Human Condition,* she refers instead to Kierkegaard:

> No one perhaps explored its [Cartesian doubt's] true dimensions more honestly than Kierkegaard when he leaped—not from reason as he thought, but from doubt—into belief, thereby carrying doubt into the very heart of modern religion.
>
> (1959: 250-1)

In this way Arendt's manoeuvre makes symmetrical Sheppard's and O'Connor's 'mistake'. Again, one can read Sheppard with and 'against' O'Connor insofar as they both deny the condition of doubt that is 'the human condition' by resolving it in one direction: both attempt to 'still' the tension that arises between their different modes of living in the world. One might say that a stance such as O'Connor's risks the denial of modernity and its implications, while that exemplified in the character Sheppard risks the denial of alternative responses to modernity.

Sheppard's tragedy, then, is that he allows doubt its centrality within his belief system too late. Belatedly, because thinking, 'though it may be the most solitary of activities, is never altogether without a partner and without company' (Arendt, 1959: 67), it is in Sheppard's reflection upon his actions that he recognizes—even experiences—plurality. He recognizes that his actions might legitimately be understood not as the pursuit of goodness but in an opposing fashion: baldly stated, not goodness but neglect. This 'revelation' comes when he allows Rufus's words—'Satan has you in his power'—to enter his considerations. But his experience is a revelation that we do not have to understand as coming from God, as O'Connor would have us do; the words he recalls are after all *Rufus*'s words, not the words of God. Rufus's accusation becomes part of Sheppard's thought process. It is an existential experience of the 'two in oneness' of thought that allows him to reflect critically on his actions in the world. This admission of plurality leads to the acknowledgement of the partiality of his convictions and dislodges his previous unthinking assessment of himself as engaged in the pursuit of 'good'.

It is tempting to make a similar manoeuvre with regard to O'Connor in that, although she always asserted her faith in the strongest and most uncompromising of terms, there are times when she admitted of doubt—such as in her letter to Alfred Corn (Cash, 2002: 247), where it is significant that she reveals that it was the existence of other religions that once gave her (brief) pause, and where to comfort him she reaches for the prayer of St Peter 'Lord, I believe. Help my unbelief' (Cash, 2002: 247), or in her letters to her friend 'A' (now known to be Betty Hester), where she shows support for her friend's troubled relationship to Catholicism (although she admits elsewhere—in a letter to Cecil Dawkins—that she found it difficult to remain patient with Hester), or in her long friendship with atheist Maryat Lee. There is, however, little point in making O'Connor less religious (nor for that matter, as some have done, Arendt more Christian [see Bernauer, 1987]) because it is the story itself that leads us in such a direction.

The point is more the necessity of recognizing one's 'leap' as a leap and, consequently, of maintaining the ability to imagine oneself otherwise, the capacity for 'inner' plurality (Curtis, 1999: 63). It is in this respect that Arendt's work can be regarded as a forerunner of a contemporary political theorist such as William Connolly (2000), *inter alios,* in whose work the religious/secular distinction is refused.[27] Being open to plurality can, as Connolly's reading of Deleuze suggests, open us to the hilarity of having any faith at all, and to the potential—actual—clown in all of us, believers and non-believers alike. Perhaps one only need recall O'Connor's awareness that 'I'm the devil in this one' to get a glimpse of the moments in which such a movement potentially resides. Ultimately it is from this, 'the "naked fact of plurality", and not from any ethical code, that all action must spring' (Curtis, 1999).

V

Unsurprisingly perhaps, this discussion of O'Connor and Arendt does not enable one to provide definitive 'answers' to the numerous and varied questions raised in contemporary work on the (im)possibility of secular ethics. It does, however, potentially recast some of the lines of the debate in interesting, generative ways.

The discussion of O'Connor adds weight to the observation, made by Talal Asad (2003) among others, that it is wrong to presume that the 'religious motive' for arguments or actions can be easily discerned. For while there is of course plenty of evidence for O'Connor's 'religiosity' in her fiction writing, as well as in her lectures and letters, her depiction of a non-believer such as Sheppard as a foolish man whose fate is to lose his only son is not in any obvious way motivated by 'religion'. It is certainly contextualized by O'Connor's understanding of how the loss of faith operated in the social and political realm, but as such it is as political a comment, one motivated by socio-political issues of her time, as it is religious. Indeed, the two are entwined for O'Connor as the infamous 'gas chambers' comment suggests. To argue that O'Connor's work should be regarded as political intervention is not to escape the religious therefore, but to place 'the religious' in the world and as a response to the world.

O'Connor's admiration for Arendt is in part what gives us licence to make this manoeuvre in a re-reading of **'The Lame Shall Enter First'**. Not only because her admiration illustrates the interest that O'Connor herself had in political configurations of the changing world in which she lived—to the extent of being 'haunted'—but also because in reading O'Connor alongside Arendt one is obliged to question how a figure such as Sheppard—weak, ineffectual, pathetic—comes to represent non-belief?[28] One suspects that this also happens in contemporary debates around ethics wherever the 'secular figure' is metaphorically stripped of his or her convictions revealing the 'true' motivations underlying them. With the 'perversion' of faith exposed, the ethical project in which s/he was engaged is revealed as a wrong-headed calamity: a dog's dinner. Arendt offers the opportunity to dismiss this recurring figure as incorrectly drawn in opposition to a 'religious' figure. Her reconfiguration of the oppositions that continue to structure much debate emerges as important and fruitful.

In imagining Arendt's response to Sheppard it becomes clear that Arendt would also have her own critique to level, one that has little to do with his lack of religious belief. In fact, Arendt's arguments in *The Human Condition* provide something of a rejoinder to Derrida's well-known suggestion that, given the conditions of undecidability in which the decision is taken, with any decision one is asked to act like a 'knight of faith', insofar as her arguments lead one to notice how, likewise, those who act from a position of faith do so within a context of undecidability, that is, of doubt. This doubt is shared, in other words, by all who dwell in modernity, where modernity is characterized qualitatively by the events that have established doubt as procedurally integral to contemporary life. Arendt references Dostoevsky, but the modernity of which she speaks is also philosophical and scientific, governing the processes by which rational method has sought to contend with necessary doubt. It is, furthermore, institutionalized in the 'secularization' process within which political institutions have developed. Importantly, she argues, both believers and non-believers are obliged to respond to events in their shared history: both 'leap'.[29]

It is the possibility of recognizing that shared history that provides the glimmer of hope for a shared present and future. Although for Arendt, the world needed to be 'saved', there was no implication that this meant that humankind should appeal to a transcendent Being. It would be saved only if actors within it orientated themselves toward the public realm, the world shared in common with others. If, in expressing her hope in the human capacity for beginning, founded in natality, she returns us to mystery and wonder (the 'miraculous'), it is tenuous to read this as a simple smuggling back in of religion. Rather, Arendt was pointing to the evidence that humankind has shown a remarkable capacity to 'begin anew', to act. The contribution of this discussion has been to highlight the sense in which that action both emerges from and takes place within conditions of doubt. Moreover, the recognition of these common conditions, the sharing of a present formed in relation to this common past, together with the recognition that we will continue to leap in different directions, can only be enabling insofar as these acknowledgements underscore the simultaneous commonality and the plurality of human lives. The world is saved from ruin not by the articulation of any faith or secular-based ethical code upon which all must agree, but by action that serves—not by its results but in its very performance[30]—as the sign of this human capacity to use and to preserve their being-in-common.

Lest this sound platitudinous, verging on as 'vague and soppy and sentimental' a note as that struck by the versions of weak Christianity that so riled O'Connor, it is worth recalling that, just as there was a certain amount of friction between Arendt and Voegelin, so certainly would there have been between Arendt and O'Connor. Voegelin depicted Arendt's work as a version of the 'immanentist heresy' against which he pitted his own; Arendt was by no means sentimental in her reply. To allow the events of the Second World War to be understood within a 'secularization thesis' was anathema to Arendt. In her response to his 1953 review of *The Origins of Totalitarianism,* she dealt, *inter alia,* with his objection to her description of the Nazi concentration camps as 'hell on earth'. She argued that this description was both accurate and objective:

> When I used the image of Hell, I did not mean this allegorically but literally: it seems rather obvious that men who have lost their faith in Paradise will not be able to establish it on earth; but it is not so certain that those who have lost their belief in Hell as a place of the hereafter may not be willing and able to establish on earth exact imitations of what people used to believe about Hell. In this sense I think that a description of the camps as Hell on earth is more 'objective', that is, more adequate to their essence than statements of a purely sociological or psychological nature.
>
> (Arendt, 1953/1994: 404)

In her defence of her book, as in her defence of the need to preserve commonality and plurality, Arendt moved with an assured clarity and, it can be said, with a capacity to be 'cutting' that would have rivalled O'Connor's narrative twists. To accept Arendt's depiction of the necessity of 'action' in order to preserve the world is also to accept the need to enter the public realm boldly, for the political realm requires the capacity to cut, to redistribute language, to reconfigure the configurations of others. And such a task is especially pressing in situations in which those configurations entail or amount to a politics based on the suppression of plurality and the denial of doubt.

Notes

I would like to record my thanks to the Department of Sociology at Goldsmiths College for a term's sabbatical leave and to the Arts and Humanities Research Board who funded an extension of that leave for a further term. During that period I was visiting scholar at the Department of Sociology, Yale University and at the Department of Rhetoric at University of California at Berkeley. My gratitude to both institutions for receiving me and to participants in the seminars I presented there.

1. This will inevitably be a speculative discussion since there is no record of this question having been asked of Arendt.
2. Arendt's own contribution to the special issue, 'Action and "The Pursuit of Happiness"' (1962), became part of *On Revolution* (1963b).
3. 'Sade: the pleasure of reading him clearly proceeds from certain breaks (or certain collisions). . . . As textual theory has it: the language is redistributed. Now, *such redistribution is always achieved by cutting*' (Barthes, 1975: 6).
4. Most clearly exemplified in the work of Derrida, this is a turn I understand, with de Vries (1999), not as a reassertion of theological truths, but a consideration of their trace. Derrida's 'adieu' captures what he regards as the aporetic nature of the dismissal of, the a-dieu to, mystery in the name of secular knowledge that attempts to cut away absolute alterity to leave existence free of all religious overtones. For Derrida, the dismissal that tries to bid farewell to God—this continual refutation of religious truth claims itself reaffirming religion's 'ever provisional survival' (de Vries, 1999: 4)—seems always to re-orientate itself to some horizon of gathering which reinstates an ultimate ethical witness. Repeatedly, conceptions of gathering are articulated that involve response and responsibility to the other, giving oneself 'back to and up to the other. To every other and the utterly other' (Derrida, 2002). Others too have argued that attempts to reach for an ideal secular community based upon transparent relationships will always run the risk of violating the distance among singularities that is at the heart of existential humanism, such that those projects inheriting its concerns tend to reinstate some notion of mystery or wonder.
5. This despite the fact that, as her biographer Jean Cash points out (2002: 169), she was an intellectual herself as her reading of Voegelin alone illustrates.
6. She is being deliberately curt because she is replying to the 'mis-reading' of Cecil Dawkins, who had found Freud in her portrayal of Sheppard (O'Connor, 1979: 490).
7. By Rufus's warped versions of 'the Truth' (Giannone, 2000).
8. The writer should not promote a version of the good but reveal the ultimate reality in a world where—'as a result of the Fall'—that reality had been weakened in human beings.
9. Asked to encompass the distance between the disparities in O'Connor's fiction—the distance between 'sadistic diction' and the 'numinous diction of spiritual excess', 'the mundane and the spiritual, the high and the low, the pornographic and the biblical'—the reader is torturously stretched as on a rack (Yaeger, 1996: 196).
10. After the latter had written that, to his mind, the devil's voice in O'Connor's stories was always her own, a thesis she denied but found amusing.
11. Her argument was clearly influenced by her reading of Voegelin.
12. Underlining the point, O'Connor has Sheppard exclaim 'Oh my God!' twice (1965: 164, 168), pray 'God give me strength' (1965: 182) and three times describe himself as trying to 'save' Rufus (1965: 180).
13. Moreover, to be a Catholic at this time gave one a particular relationship to the majority Protestant South (see Bacon, 1993).
14. As we know from Cash's (2002) biography, O'Connor had had her brush with McCarthyism while at Yadoo.
15. We do not get to hear O'Connor's views on this relationship, as Leola remains a mere context incidental to the story, as if she were there simply to allow the children to eat in the story without having to depict Sheppard putting his care into cooking. Instead he serves it up to them, ready prepared, like his words of advice. Although, curiously, there seems to have been a scene that O'Connor cut from the story—as Norton, with no apparent motivation to lie, tells his father 'he danced with Leola' a scene the story does not describe.
16. The phrase is Arendt's.
17. See Bewes (forthcoming) for a different take on this same subject. Bewes makes the argument that O'Connor's 'metaphysical' impulses cannot be written out of her fiction, nor can they be said to define it; indeed, Bewes argues for a reading of O'Connor in terms of a Deleuzian immanence, such that 'there is nothing transcendental, as such, in O'Connor's stories'. Our response to the text shouldn't be thought of as 'interpretation', he argues, situated across a divide from the literary nature of the text, such that, for example, its lack of social commentary might become a criticism of the fictional text. Nor should the text be approached as if it were unable to refer to its own 'literary' nature; there are moments in O'Connor's

stories when Bewes argues that they do just this. Correlatively, the politics of the text is not to be approached in terms of O'Connor's representation of events, but operates, Bewes argues, on the plane within which we encounter it.

18. As Robert Fitzgerald called him in the introduction to the collection *Everything that Rises Must Converge* (1965).

19. This said, Arendt also recognized Voegelin's stature; as noted above, she accepted an invitation to co-edit a journal to celebrate his work on the occasion of his 60th birthday.

20. Arendt's surprising use of Jesus to support her argument that those who aim for goodness disconnect themselves from the world is indicative of her reading of Christianity generally. Simultaneously she seeks to argue that 'unworldliness' is a characteristic of Christianity—and this was also part of her critique of institutionalized Christianity (Bernauer, 1987)—while suggesting that it may even have been cautioned against by Jesus himself. Jesus appears in Arendt's texts as a quotable authority and only that. This is an important point here, for it displays the sense in which Arendt would wrest from Christianity the terms that it would seek to regard as belonging within its discourse.

21. Here one can see why Arendt's thoughts on goodness can lead to a conservative individualism. If one shouldn't attempt to pursue the good as an absolute, what room is there to judge one's own interventions and those of others? How can Arendt advocate the role of principles while disallowing a role for 'goodness'? The problematic qualities of her critique of 'goodness' as the foundation of social institutions have been pointed out in the secondary literature, as indeed have the conservative qualities of her version of democracy.

22. Somewhat surprisingly, Arendt's praise of human action is *also* praise of something 'unworldly' (1959: 95). Action is unworldly insofar as it has to be actualized; it has to be accompanied by speech (1959: 158) for speech materializes and memorializes the new things that shine forth so that they might be remembered: 'without the human artifice to house them, human affairs would be as floating, as futile and vain, as the wandering of nomad tribes' (1959: 183). So while Arendt insists that authentic action's full meaning is in the performance itself, it nevertheless loses its non-teleological aspect as soon as any product results. Political action has to be memorable (Kateb, 2000: 133), but when it is remembered through human speech it enters the world of fabrication. Action, like goodness, is also inevitably ruined. This ruination of action is necessary if the fleeting nature of action is not to pass 'as if it had never been' (Arendt, 1959: 95). But, as Gottlieb (2003) points out, the pessimism to which this thought might lead is refused by Arendt as strongly as she refuses the optimism that leads to complacency and inaction. For although action will pass into the world of fabrication, action begins from elsewhere, from a perspective which has to trust the world as a place fit for action and speech, as a place fit for human appearance.

23. Likewise, religiosity is not be blamed for the world's ills: 'the pious resignation to God's will seems like a pocket knife compared with atomic weapons' (1994: 380).

24. This is also Arendt's point about forgiveness; see 'What is Authority?' in *Between Past and Future* (1963a).

25. Second, Arendt sought to distinguish her argument from the equally unsatisfactory accounts of the social scientists who, she believed, mistook the world as composed of 'functions', so that religion and communism become equated as 'ideologies' which function to anaesthetize and control the population.

26. Arendt gives the telescope a privileged position in her arguments in *The Human Conditon* (1959).

27. Talal Asad also argues that the distinction is unhelpful, not least because, although the notion of 'the secular' works through a series of recurring oppositions, its meaning shifts and changes over history. 'The secular' is neither 'singular in origin nor stable in identity' (2003: 25).

28. As it does in other of O'Connor's works. In *The Violent Bear it Away,* as in 'Good Country People', the non-believer and 'intelleckuals' alike tend to receive this same treatment.

29. Leaping into faith with its ultimates provides no more assurance against political catastrophes than does leaping into non-belief or scientific method. As Arendt argued in the 1972 seminar transcribed in Hill (1979), totalitarianism cannot be avoided by any given set of values; those who are convinced of their values become attached to the support they provide, rather than the values themselves, such that the 'bannister' can be exchanged for a different set of values. She comments: 'I do not believe that we can stabilize the situation in which we have been since the seventeenth century in any final way' (Hill, 1979: 314).

30. 'Action does not have an "end" because the end (telos) . . . lies in the activity itself: "action has no end"' (1959: 209).

References

Arendt, Hannah (1953/1994) 'A Reply [to Voegelin's Review]', in *Essays in Understanding 1930-54,* edited by Jerome Kohn. New York: Harcourt Brace Jovanovich. (First published in *Review of Politics* 15.)

———. (1959) *The Human Condition.* New York: Doubleday and Co.

———. (1962) 'Action and "The Pursuit of Happiness"', *Politische Ordung und Menschliche Existenz: Festgabe für Eric Voegelin.* Munich: Beck.

———. (1963a) *Between Past and Future: Six Exercises in Political Thought.* New York: Meridian.

———. (1963b) *On Revolution.* London: Faber and Faber.

———. (1973) *On the Origins of Totalitarianism.* New York: Harcourt Brace. (First published 1951).

———. (1977) *Life of the Mind.* New York: Harcourt Brace Jovanovich.

———. (1984) *Eichmann in Jerusalem: A Report on the Banality of Evil.* New York: Penguin Books. (First published 1963.)

———. (1994) *Essays in Understanding 1930-54,* edited by Jerome Kohn. New York: Harcourt Brace Jovanovich.

Asad, Talal (2003) *Formations of the Secular: Christianity, Islam, Modernity.* Stanford, CA: Stanford University Press.

Bacon, Jon Lance (1993) *Flannery O'Connor and Cold War Culture.* Cambridge: Cambridge University Press.

Badiou, Alain (2001) *Ethics: An Essay on Radical Evil.* London: Verso.

———. (2003) 'Beyond Formalisation: An Interview', interview by Peter Hallward, trans. Bruno Bosteels and Alberto Toscano, *Angelaki: Journal of the Theoretical Humanities* 8(2): 111-36.

Barthes, Roland (1975) *The Pleasure of the Text,* trans. Richard Miller. New York: Hill and Wang.

Bernauer, James (1987) 'The Faith of Hannah Arendt: *Amor Mundi* and its Critique—Assimilation of Religious Experience', in *Amor Mundi: Explorations in the Faith and Thought of Hannah Arendt.* Boston, MA: Martinus Nijhoff Publishers.

Bewes, Timothy (forthcoming) 'What is a Literary Landscape? Flannery O'Connor, W. G. Sebald and the Metaphysics of Form', *Differences.*

Cash, Jean (2002) *Flannery O'Connor: A Life.* Knoxville: University of Tennessee Press.

Connolly, William (2000) 'Refashioning the Secular' in J. Butler, J. Guillory and K. Thomas (eds) *What's Left of Theory?* New York: Routledge.

Cooper, Barry (1999) *Eric Voegelin and the Foundations of Modern Political Science.* Columbia and London: University of Missouri Press.

Curtis, Kimberley (1999) *Our Sense of the Real: Aesthetic Experience and Arendtian Politics.* Ithaca, NY: Cornell University Press.

Derrida, Jacques (1995) *The Gift of Death,* trans. David Wills. Chicago, IL: University of Chicago Press.

———. (2002) 'Faith and Knowledge: The Two Sources of "Religion" at the Limits of Reason Alone', in *Jacques Derrida: Acts of Religion,* edited by Gil Anidjar. London: Routledge. (First published 1996.)

De Vries, Hent (1999) *Philosophy and the Turn to Religion.* Baltimore, MD: Johns Hopkins University Press.

Dostoevsky, Fyodor (2002) *The Idiot.* New York: Everyman's Library/Knopf. (First published 1868.)

Getz, Lorine M. (1980) *Flannery O'Connor: Her Life, Library and Book Reviews.* New York: Edwin Mellon Press.

Giannone, Richard (1989) *Flannery O'Connor and the Mystery of Love.* Urbana: University of Illinois Press.

———. (2000) *Flannery O'Connor: Hermit Novelist.* Urbana and Chicago: University of Illinois Press.

Gordon, Sarah (2000) *Flannery O'Connor: The Obedient Imagination.* Athens: University of Georgia Press.

Gottlieb, Susannah Young-ah (2003) *Regions of Sorrow: Anxiety and Messianism in Hannah Arendt and W. H. Auden.* Stanford, CA: Stanford University Press.

Hallward, Peter (2001) 'Translator's Introduction', in Alain Badiou, *Ethics: An Essay on Radical Evil.* London: Verso.

Hill, Melvyn A. (1979) *Hannah Arendt: The Recovery of the Public World.* New York: St Martin's Press.

Kateb, George (2000) 'Political Action: Its Nature and Advantages', in Dana Villa (ed.) *The Cambridge Companion to Hannah Arendt.* Cambridge: Cambridge University Press.

Melville, Herman (1997) *Billy Budd, Sailor, and Selected Tales.* Oxford: Oxford University Press.

O'Connor, Flannery (1960) *The Violent Bear it Away.* New York: Farrar, Straus and Giroux.

———. (1965) 'The Lame Shall Enter First', in *Everything that Rises Must Converge.* New York: Farrar, Straus and Giroux. (First published 1962.)

———. (1969) *Mystery and Manners: Occasional Prose,* selected and edited by Sally and Robert Fitzgerald. New York: Farrar, Straus and Giroux.

———. (1979) *The Habit of Being.* New York: Farrar, Straus and Giroux.

———. (1980) 'Good Country People', in *A Good Man is Hard to Find and Other Stories.* London: The Women's Press. (First published 1955.)

Said, Edward (2000) 'Secular Criticism', in Moustafa Bayoumi and Andrew Rubin (eds) *The Edward Said Reader.* London: Granta. (First published 1983.)

Sandoz, Ellis (1997) 'Introduction', in Eric Voegelin, *Science, Politics and Gnosticism.* Washington, DC: Regnery Publishing.

Voegelin, Eric (1953) 'The Origins of Totalitarianism: Review of Hannah Arendt, *The Origins of Totalitarianism*', and 'Concluding Remark', *Review of Politics* 15: 68-76 and 84-5.

———. (1956) *Israel and Revelation.* Baton Rouge: Louisiana State University Press.

———. (1997) *Science, Politics and Gnosticism.* Washington, DC: Regnery Publishing. (First published 1968.)

Yaeger, Patricia (1996) 'Flannery O'Connor and the Aesthetics of Torture', in Sura Rath and Mary Neff Shaw (eds) *Flannery O'Connor: New Perspectives.* Athens: University of Georgia Press.

Rodney Stenning Edgecombe (essay date fall 2005)

SOURCE: Edgecombe, Rodney Stenning. "O'Connor's 'A Good Man Is Hard to Find.'" *Explicator* 64, no. 1 (fall 2005): 56-8.

[*In the following essay, Edgecombe discusses allusions to William Shakespeare's* King Lear *and Robert Browning's "Childe Roland to the Dark Tower Came" in "A Good Man Is Hard to Find."*]

To avoid the melodramatic extravagance associated with *The Castle of Otranto* and its successors, many twentieth-century practitioners of the gothic embedded its statutory horrors in a matrix of ordinariness. Flannery O'Connor's short fiction bears witness to this tendency when, en route to their massacre by an escaped convict, the family in **"A Good Man Is Hard to Find"** stops at a filling station to drink Coca-Cola and eat sandwiches. They are traveling to Toombsboro, a fact of the Georgia landscape onto which she has laughingly imposed an allegorical value, just as, a century before, Thomas Hood had turned the gazetteer data of Babbacombe Bay (in Devon) and Port Natal (in South Africa) into a parable about the inequalities of birth:

> And one little craft is cast away,
> In its very first trip in Babbicome Bay
> While another rides safe at Port Natal.
>
> (565)

The gas station is itself a metaphor for O'Connor's domestication of the gothic, filling a medieval form (a tower) with the données of an unremarkable mid-century culture:

> They stopped at The Tower for barbecued sandwiches. The Tower was a part stucco and part wood filling station and dance hall set in a clearing outside of Timothy. A fat man named Red Sammy Butts ran it and there were signs stuck here and there on the building and for miles up and down the highway saying, TRY RED SAMMY'S FAMOUS BARBECUE. NONE LIKE FAMOUS RED SAMMY'S! RED SAM! THE FAT BOY WITH THE HAPPY LAUGH! A VETERAN! RED SAMMY'S YOUR MAN!
>
> (120-21)

Hal Blythe and Charlie Sweet have drawn parallels between the pilgrimage in Chaucer's *Canterbury Tales* and the antipilgrimage of the doomed family, finding a "contrast between medieval characters, frames, settings and motifs and their modern-day counterparts" (50), but O'Connor also alludes to Edgar's ballad fragment in *King Lear,* linked in turn with homely British folklore—a blueprint in itself for the mock-heroic transitions in the story:

> Child Rowland to the dark tower came,
> His word was still: Fie, foh, and fum,
> I smell the blood of a British man.
>
> (3.2.186-88)

The allusion to *King Lear* doesn't stop there, but also bounces forward to Browning's "Childe Roland to the Dark Tower Came," a congested Symbolist allegory that might or might not equate the dark tower with hell on earth:

> What in the midst lay but the Tower itself?
> The round squat turret, blind as the fool's heart,
> Built of brown stone, without a counterpart
> In the whole world.
>
> (132)

And then, a faint penumbral presence behind the Browning, there is the death of Roland in Alfred de Vigny's poem "Le Cor," the merest hint of the massacre to come in the woods of Georgia, which, being "tall and dark and deep" (125), are themselves a palimpsest of Robert Frost's "dark and deep" (145) forest of thanatos in "Stopping by Woods on a Snowy Evening": "Roncevaux! Roncevaux! dans ta sombre vallée / L'ombre du grand Roland n'est donc pas consolée" (19). As if to bring this murmurous chain of references full circle, O'Connor also evokes the traditional medieval topos of the hell-mouth when she describes the woods in which the family dies as gaping "like a dark open mouth" (127).

Red Sammy, the humdrum mechanic who presides over The Tower, no doubt owes his name to a florid complexion or to the red Irish heritage of the old

South, but his name also evokes the fancy dress cliché for the devil, a scarlet body stocking derived, no doubt, from nineteenth-century stagings of Gounod's *Faust.* We should likewise recall that Zamiel is the demon in Weber's opera *Der Freischütz,* presiding over the celebrated "Wolf's Glen" scene, "with an owl, a terrifying woodland landscape, [and] a chorus of invisible spirits" (Jacobs and Sadie 91-92). It is significant, therefore, that The Tower should stand "in a clearing outside of Timothy" and that a monkey (an emblem of lust) should be chained to a chinaberry tree, for, as Gertrude Sill points out, "When Satan appears as an ape bound in chains, he is the personification of evil being conquered by good" (16). Red Sammy's name at the same time evokes the figure of Uncle Sam, conjured out of the United States circa 1812. Because he plasters his screamingly capitalized billboards all over the highway, he represents the impact of the commercial North on the agrarian South, the spirit of capitalism demonized with precisely the same color that capitalism itself was demonizing its communist antitype in the postbellum years.

The grandmother is the exemplar of all the moral and social deficiencies of the old South, and she tries to freeze its racial and social inequalities in a pictorial frame, recalling the way in which the proponents of the Picturesque embellished their landscapes with laboring peasants: "'Little niggers in the country don't have things like we do. If I could paint, I'd paint that picture,' she said" (119). But there is one redemptive quality lodged amid her bigotry and manipulations—her responsiveness to the Georgia countryside: "She pointed out interesting details of the scenery: Stone Mountain; the blue granite that in some places came up to both sides of the highway; the brilliant red clay banks slightly streaked with purple; and the various crops that made rows of green lace-work on the ground" (119). It is to the specifics of her regionalist attachment that Red Sammy's billboards stand opposed—advocating a consumer culture in which everything is flattened into two-dimensional icons, and blotting out the landscape in the pursuit of profit. Because another southern "lady," the wife of L. B. Johnson, eventually re-disclosed the beauties that Sammy's billboards had obscured, the grandmother's imprimatur seems especially ironic—a near-allegory for the seduction of the South by the energy of what Blake had called the "dark Satanic mills" (491):

> "Because you're a good man!" the grandmother said at once. "Yes'm, I suppose so," Red Sam said as if he were struck with this answer.
>
> (122)

Works Cited

Blake, William. *The Complete Poems.* Ed. W. H. Stevenson. London: Longman, 1989.

Blythe, Hal, and Charlie Sweet. "O'Connor's 'A Good Man Is Hard to Find.'" *Explicator* 55.1 (1996): 49-51.

Browning, Robert. *Browning.* Selected by W. E. Williams. Harmondsworth: Penguin, 1955.

De Vigny, Alfred. "Le Cor." *The Penguin Book of French Verse: The Nineteenth Century.* Ed. Anthony Hartley. Harmondsworth: Penguin, 1957. 19.

Frost, Robert. *Selected Poems.* Introd. C. Day Lewis. Harmondsworth: Penguin, 1955.

Hood, Thomas. *The Complete Poetical Works of Thomas Hood.* Ed. Walter Jerrold. London: Oxford UP, 1906.

Jacobs, Arthur, and Stanley Sadie. *The Pan Book of Opera.* London: Pan, 1964.

O'Connor, Flannery. *The Complete Stories.* New York: Farrar, 1971.

Shakespeare, William. *King Lear.* Ed. Kenneth Muir. London: Methuen, 1964.

Sill, Gertrude Grace. *A Handbook of Symbols in Christian Art.* New York: Collier, 1975.

John Roos (essay date fall 2005)

SOURCE: Roos, John. "Thomistic Risings in 'Judgement Day.'" *Perspectives on Political Science* 34, no. 4 (fall 2005): 188-92.

[*In the following essay, Roos illustrates the influence of Thomas Aquinas's theological perspectives on "Judgement Day," highlighting O'Connor's concept of grace, as well as political and social concerns evidenced in the story.*]

That Flannery O'Connor was profoundly influenced by the vision of Thomas Aquinas has been discussed often in O'Connor criticism. But most of that attention has been paid to Aquinas as seer of theological truth and analyst of matters of revelation and grace. This has led many researchers who desire to concentrate on nontheological themes, such as political and social vision, to abandon Aquinas as a source of insight into O'Connor's art. Thus, for example, Bacon's book on O'Connor and cold war culture proceeds without any mention of Aquinas, nature, or natural law.[1] Yet that approach, by assuming that Aquinas was only a source of her explicitly theological themes, ignores the way in which Aquinas may have influenced her reflections on social and political things. Certainly any reflection on Aquinas will eventually lead to grace and God. But on the way there, as it were, O'Connor encountered in Aquinas, and then explored in her own art, a complex vision of the natural goods of humans and their associations in families and communities.

"Judgement Day," the main focus of our investigation, occurs in her posthumously published volume of stories for which she chose the title ***Everything That Rises Must Converge.***[2] O'Connor attributed the inspiration for the title to Teilhard De Chardin, the Jesuit paleontologist, whose *Phenomenon of Man* she greatly admired.[3] Throughout this work, Chardin talks of evolution, especially the evolution of human consciousness, as a rising and a converging that may converge in the Omega point of God. In his epilogue, Chardin says:

> If Omega were only a remote and ideal focus destined to emerge at the end of time from the convergence of terrestrial consciousness, nothing could make it known to us in anticipation of this convergence. At the present time no other energy of a personal nature could be detected on earth save that represented by the sum of human persons.
>
> If, on the other hand, Omega is, as we have admitted, already in existence and operative at the very core of the thinking mass, then it would seem inevitable that its existence should be manifested to us here and now through some traces.[4]

Let us juxtapose this with a quote from Aquinas, taken from *Summa Contra Gentiles,* with which O'Connor was familiar.

> Things distinct in their nature do not converge into one order, unless they be brought together by one controller. Now the universe is composed of things distinct from one another and of contrary natures; and yet they all converge into one order, with some things acting on others, and some helping or directing others. Therefore there must be one ordainer and governor of the universe.[5]

Chardin, forbidden to publish his work by the Vatican, went to great lengths to avoid being charged with distorting Church teaching, and in the body of his text he makes no reference to any of the Church fathers or doctors, or in fact to any scriptural text. Yet it would be hard to imagine a Jesuit in 1938 not being familiar with this text of Aquinas. It is even more unlikely that O'Connor would not have been aware of the parallel. For O'Connor, the theme of rising and converging comes from two sources, Aquinas and Chardin.

Now, one might ask, does this not immediately propel us out of the world as we all know it and into the special revelation of Christian grace through which the Divine governance works? Chardin, who begins his theory of evolutionary ascent far before Christ's birth, suggests not. Well, what of Aquinas?

In the *Summa Theologica,* Aquinas maintains a double voice. One voice, that of the grand narrative, tells undeniably what he takes to be the whole story. But within the whole story, there are parts that can be approached without the presuppositions of the grand narrative, that is, a personal creator. The structure of the *Summa* lays out for us the whole story and its parts. Aquinas begins with creation, wherein all things proceed from God. He then turns to the movement of creatures back to God, especially humans. Aquinas believes that a full return to God requires supernatural grace. But in the First Part of the Second Part he says that the intrinsic principles of human acts are habit and virtue.[6] He then moves to the extrinsic principle of human acts leading to good. He says: "But the extrinsic principle moving to good is God, who both instructs us by means of His Law, and assists us by His Grace."[7] At Question 90, Aquinas explains the kinds of law and finds the Eternal, the Divine, the natural, and the human. The Eternal law is the mind of God and encompasses all modes of governance. The Divine law, both Old and New Testament, is a special revelation to those with the theological virtue of faith. But Aquinas also teaches that we, as rational creatures, have a special share in the governance of creation, and this is the natural law, which he defines as "the rational creature's participation of the Eternal law."[8]

Now, unlike many interpretations, some still powerfully current today, Aquinas himself did not teach that this natural law was fully and completely displayed in us. He felt that the only universally known part of the natural law was certain simple first principles, what could be called "traces" in Chardin's terms. Because O'Connor was a careful reader of Aquinas, she would have turned to those passages in which he describes more fully these simple first principles. In various places, Aquinas speaks of these first principles as seeds, or beginnings, or murmurings at good and evil. For example, he says, "in man's reason there are to be found naturally present certain naturally known principles of both knowledge and action, which are the seeds of intellectual and moral virtues."[9] In Aquinas, O'Connor finds the claim, the hypothesis if you will, that all of us contain certain beginnings, fragile inclinations and capacities that, if listened to, will lead to a rising, and with grace, to a convergence.

To a Christian believer, then, the whole story, both for O'Connor and Aquinas, may be available. But for the non-Christian, how is this understandable? After all, there are only a handful of characters in O'Connor's writing who one suspects are in a full state of grace. And certainly O'Connor did not suppose that all, or most, or even many of her readers would bring to bear the full resources of a faith in Christian revelation.

Aquinas, facing the same problem, argues that although the final terminus of the natural law will lead to the need for the grace of revelation, the natural law, understood as the beginnings or seeds, was available to all of us. And these beginnings or seeds were subject to growth and decline, rising and falling. So Aquinas says that from these beginnings some things follow quickly and are grasped by most people, whereas others follow only with great difficulty and for only a few.[10] And, similarly, risings can be lost because all but the seeds can be abolished from the human heart by corrupt societies.[11] Aquinas thought that in corrupt societies coercion would be necessary to restrain vice. But coercion affects only our behavior, not our hearts. For the natural law to develop essentially, it has to be understood, arrived at by reason, and grasped as a principle per se. Hence, reason directed to the common good, rather than coercion, is the core of his teaching of politics.

In **"Judgement Day,"** one is at first glance tempted to think of Locke rather than Aquinas as the beginning of O'Connor's artistic investigation. Rather than rising and converging from the murmurings of natural law, one finds instead the clash of competing individual wills more associated with Locke's construal of free, rational individuals in the state of nature. For Locke, there is only one natural inclination, and that is to calculate how to preserve one's self, including one's life, liberty, and estate. Rather than appealing to any rising, Locke appeals to the lowest common denominator of self-interest. Locke builds his theories of property, family, slavery, and ultimately political society on the basis of solitary individuals' pursuit of their own interests and engagement in contracts to better achieve their private ends. The rule of impersonal law, supported by the desire of individuals attracted by the promise of secure acquisition of unlimited wealth, is enough to entice individuals to leave the state of nature and enter the acquisitive society.[12]

Locke is the quintessential American liberal theorist, and one finds elements of Locke or at least Lockean themes throughout **"Judgement Day."** The motives of Tanner's family are built on obligation and duty, not love. The daughter cares for Tanner, but her duty, as in Locke's notion, is in proportion to previously received benefits, so the daughter feels able to break the promise to Tanner, who has no inheritance. This rationale works similarly with property: Locke says that after the introduction of money, one has a right to unlimited acquisition of property. So it is with a Lockean sense of right that we see the Doctor taking possession of his land.

> If that nigger had owned the whole world except for one runty rutted pea field and he acquired it, he would walk across that way, beating the weeds aside, his thick neck swelled, his stomach a throne for his gold watch and chain.[13]

Locke suggests that commerce can transform the world if one knows how to pursue one's self-interest. Hence, the Doctor says, "Everything pays if you know how to make it" (252). Just as Tilman in **"View of the Woods"** offers all the benefits of an acquisitive society in his general store, so the Doctor was "everything to the niggers—druggist and undertaker and general counsel and real estate man" (251). Tanner and Parrum attempt to exercise their Lockean rights by claiming the right to acquire property from the commons by mixing their labor with it. The land for their shack is vacant, and Tanner "thinks it was too sorry for anyone to buy" (250). The land is described as full of weeds and Johnson grass. But in Locke's rationale, money changes all of this. Money allows for the unlimited acquisition of property, and hence it allows inequality and removes the original right to the commons.

Tanner realizes his mistake when he replies to the Doctor: "This shack ain't in your property. Only on it, by my mistake" (251). Tanner retains his right to free and equal use of his labor (he is not obliged to work for the Doctor), but he cannot lay claim to the land. Tanner's interpretation of his relationship to Parrum is Lockean. At one level, he believes that he has conquered Parrum in their encounter at the saw mill by his use of superior reason. And hence he says that Parrum was "paroled" to him for the last thirty years (250). This corresponds to Locke's saying that it is rational for the conquered to make a contract for their life by serving the conqueror.

The Doctor understands best the logic of such a polity. The Actor asserts his rational right to be considered free and equal. He wants Tanner to quit invading the "fence" around his private pursuit of liberty and equality. He wants to be left alone. Government is portrayed as being the umpire in this society, employing coercion where necessary. Hence, Tanner knows that he cannot fight the government, and government does help with acquisition by sending a check once in a while. Tanner's daughter understands the rules of the game. Although privately a violent racist, she understands the rules of the public contract quite clearly. When Tanner tries to befriend the black actor, she says:

> You keep away from them. Don't you go over there trying to get friendly with him. They ain't the same around here and I don't want any trouble with niggers, you hear me? If you have to live next to them, you just mind your business and they'll mind theirs. That's the way people were meant to get along in this world. Everybody can get along if they just mind their business.
>
> (260-61)

From this perspective, there appears to be little rising. Tanner is a racist. The Lockean vision of free and equal individuals has the advantage in that it is at least enforceable; one can use the coercive power of the state to force individuals to be rational contract partners who treat each other as legally equal, so that they can get on with taking care of their business. But there is no horizon other than individuals' solitary pursuit of that which they desire. Mr. Fortune, in **"View of the Woods,"** is the prototype of the American Lockean individual. When his independence is threatened by Mary Fortune's intervention in his right to dispose of his property as he sees fit, murder seems to be the logical outcome. Perceiving his right to liberty as being infringed, he exercises the right of punishment, which Locke places squarely in the hands of each individual in the state of nature. But in **"View of the Woods,"** Mary Fortune has some resources available to her to resist this vast, lonely, acquisitive enterprise in which everything is a means to someone's ends. For Mary Fortune, the woods murmur of another alternative. She finds "traces" of some other dimension of nature in that view.

But what of **"Judgement Day"**? At Question 94, Aquinas talks of three inclinations we have from nature, ranging from lower to higher. This passage is at the heart of Aquinas's teaching on natural goods, and it would have been read time and again by O'Connor. The first inclination is self-preservation, which we share with all beings that desire their own continuation. Second is that of procreation and raising of the young, which we share with other animals. It is the third order of inclination that is most important because it concerns our specifically human rational dimension. Aquinas writes:

> Thirdly, there is in man an inclination to good, according to the nature of his reason, which nature is proper to him: thus man has a natural inclination to know the truth about God, and to live in society: and in this respect, whatever pertains to this inclination belongs to the natural law; for instance to shun ignorance, to avoid offending those with whom one has to live, and other such things regarding the above inclinations.[14]

This is not to suggest that O'Connor simply aimed at enshrining Aquinas in fictive artifice. Quite the opposite—her enterprise was much more radical. Let us imagine O'Connor sitting at her desk at Andalusia, reading these lines over and over again. And wondering if she had encountered them in her own time and place. And wondering what it would be like if Aquinas were right, and then exploring in her stories the consequences of living out such inclinations. To take one example, in *Wise Blood* O'Connor once commented on certain readers of Hazel Motes:

> For them, Hazel Motes' integrity lies in his trying with such vigor to get rid of the ragged figure who moves from tree to tree in the back of his mind. For the author, his integrity lies in his not being able to.[15]

Wise Blood is a story that investigates what it would be like, in a society that no longer knows much about God, to try with the least of resources to listen doggedly to a natural instinct to know the truth about God. A similar dynamic is at work in **"Judgement Day."**

Tanner is a racist, as well as an individualist. As we reconstruct his life, we see a man who asserts his needs and his sense of superiority over everyone. And yet, as death approaches, there is something that tugs at him, and that is to return home. Well, what is home? Home is where he lived with Parrum. He thought that home was the piece of land that the Doctor took. But now, having experienced the solitary life of New York, he knows that it would be better to live poorly with Parrum than live in isolation with his daughter. In the relating of his earlier life, O'Connor directs us to two moments in which Tanner's heart and mind rise. The first moment occurs in the saw mill. Despite his solipsistic racism, which is encouraged by his society, in his confrontation with Parrum he hears but does not understand fully the murmur of his natural instincts toward justice. O'Connor describes the scene in terms of mystery, normally associated in the criticism with the presence of grace. But one must remember that for Aquinas grace is of two kinds: the full experience of the grace of conversion and the grace of encountering God as available partially and preliminarily in created nature. The mystery here is the stirring of Tanner's natural instincts to live according to reason rather than brute prejudice. "His own pen knife moved, directed solely by some intruding intelligence that worked in his hands" (254). Similarly, Parrum "watched as if he saw an invisible power working on the wood" (254).

For both of them, the spectacles become, in different degrees, the occasion of their affirmation of their common humanity. Parrum's grasp is the fullest, for when he looks through the glasses he sees a man whose whiteness or blackness is an accident and not a defining characteristic. For Tanner, the murmur or seed, the natural instinct, is there, but he neither fully comprehends nor affirms it or its consequences.

> The Negro reached for the glasses. He attached the bows carefully behind his ears and looked forth. He peered this way and that with exaggerated solemnity. And then he looked directly at Tanner and grinned, or grimaced. Tanner could not tell which, but he had an instant's sensation of seeing before him a negative image of himself, as if clownishness and captivity had been their common lot. The vision failed him before he could decipher it.
>
> (255)

Despite his society, his upbringing, his prejudices, Tanner grasps a glimpse of his common humanity with Parrum. As Robert Fitzgerald once said, this signals a rising, but only the slightest.[16]

But what follows from this glimpse? For the next thirty years, Parrum and Tanner live together in their own little city. As in Aquinas's description of similar situations, although both characters are driven by self-preservation and were each tempted to kill the other, they both decide to live together in society. Aquinas does not mean that this type of contract is only for the ends of material cooperation, although that is present too. For Aquinas, to live in society means quintessentially to talk, to converse together. The Latin for "live together" is *conversari,* which variously means dwell together, converse together, and be together in conversation.[17] For Aquinas, only by dwelling together in this sense can we rise and discern the true goods that hold us together. It is this that makes real politics for Aquinas; not simply coercion, but an association of friendship.[18]

How do Parrum and Tanner live together for these years? Little is said explicitly, but O'Connor gives us one small clue. In the scene in which the daughter steps out of the cabin, "The daughter stepped back on the porch. There were the bottoms of two cane chairs tilted against the clapboard, but she declined to take a seat" (249). Tanner and Parrum did many things together, and many of them were still marred by Tanner's blind racism. Tanner would claim to lead and patronizingly explain things to Parrum. Tanner would sleep on the bed, Parrum like a dog on the floor. But there must have been hints, tastes, partial instantiations, some analogue of a real and just human association. Think for a moment. There would be the two of them together, sitting on the porch, each in his own cane chair, conversing together, watching the sun set over the tree line.

And from this Tanner does rise, but he is not finally able to fully comprehend this association. The second moment of grace encountered through natural inclinations comes when Tanner realizes Aquinas's corollary regarding the instinct to dwell together in friendship with one's fellow humans. Aquinas says that one ought not to offend those one dwells with. When the daughter visits Tanner and finds him living with Parrum, she screams at Tanner, ignoring the presence of Parrum.

> If you don't have any pride I have and I know my duty and I was raised to do it. My mother raised me to do it if you didn't. She was from plain people but not the kind that likes to settle in with niggers.
>
> (250)

Parrum slouches out, "a doubled up shadow which Tanner just caught sight of gliding away" (250). For Tanner, at this point there is some rising, because he realizes that his friend Parrum has been hurt, offended. Tanner realizes that "She had shamed him" (250). Instinctively, inchoately, he knows that this is wrong, and his heart cries out against it.[19] He shouts loudly his defense of Parrum "so they both could hear him" (250). At this moment, Tanner and Parrum are like Huck Finn and Jim. Huck rises at least partially to his affirmation of a natural right of Jim as a human. Huck instinctively realizes Jim's humanity when Jim tells him of his shame at striking his deaf daughter because she did not shut the door. Huck listens to his natural murmurings and decides that somehow he must be faithful to Jim. Tanner tries, but he defends Parrum not for his value as a human, but for his instrumentality, as one who is useful for doing work and who "ain't a bad nigger" (250). The next day, the betrayal becomes complete. When his racist pride is faced with the challenge of being a "nigger's nigger," Tanner leaves, and in doing so he leaves his friend of thirty years behind, offended, shamed, and alone.

The story's apparent concentration on Tanner gives us little indication of the story from Parrum's view. But pause for a moment to see another source of rising. Parrum at the saw mill mysteriously chooses not to fight and kill Tanner. He then recognizes through the spectacles that Tanner is a human, like him. He understands, of course, the injustice of Tanner's racist hierarchy in their polity. But perhaps he knows more than Tanner that in his response to his daughter, Tanner was imperfectly trying to defend the friendship they had for thirty years.

How must Parrum have felt when Tanner left? And yet he is capable of what to me is the most gracious moment in the whole story. One recent critic claims that Tanner keeps in touch with Parrum by postcard.[20] But it is not Tanner who writes first. Parrum, who cannot write, asks Hooten from the railroad station to write his message for him: "This is Coleman—X—How you Boss" (259). Parrum still cares enough to take the initiative to communicate with Tanner, to try to keep alive their conversation of thirty years.

Tanner is again touched and begins to long for home. But, again, he cannot decipher his murmurings adequately. He latches on to the Actor, hoping here to find something of the friendship that he had with Parrum. But, still unaware of the way in which their friendship had been marred and deformed by his patronizing manner and assumption of superiority, he can only offend the black actor with whom he now has to live. As he awaits the chance to sneak away to the train yard and head for home, Tanner is still unable to decipher adequately the realization he had begun to have back at the saw mill. O'Connor tells us, as she describes him waiting to go: "A few snow flakes drifted past the window, but they were too thin and scattered for his failing vision" (245).

Tanner's thoughts increasingly turn to judgment. Because he has never fully acknowledged the real goods of human moral association, he, like too many secularists and Christians alike, grasps at coercion as the sole motivator of human moral order rather than friendship and dwelling together. When he learns of his daughter's plans to bury him in New York, his appeal is not one of humble and loving request, but of threat and self-righteous judgment. "He began to shake, his hands, his head, his feet. 'Bury me here and burn in hell'" (248).

And even as he imagines his own death, he is the center of attention, springing out of the coffin and crying "Judgement Day. Judgement Day," calling Parrum and Hooten the fools, when of course he is the one that is in for the surprise.

The temporal world of contending individuals gives him his judgment, as he sits in the stocks, a justice administered by the Doctor. But as was said before, both in Aquinas and O'Connor, the grace of natural inclinations eventually leads to the grace of revelation. Many critics have commented on the ambivalence we feel about the story. Because this was one of O'Connor's last stories, one wonders what it says about her vision of Judgment. I will mention only a few things for reflection. The title of this story suggests, of course, a pairing with **"Revelation."**[21] Both of them offer alternatives to the monolithic "fire and brimstone" reading of the Book of Apocalypse, an approach that is prevalent in American Christianity. At least in this reader's mind, **"Revelation"** tells us that the final coming will transcend justice and include mercy and cleansing, not just wrathful punishment. Like Ruby Turpin, Tanner will need to have his so-called virtues burned away, but in the end perhaps he too will be clean for the first time.

Ironically, O'Connor uses Tanner himself to indicate the three alternatives of the final judgment. Tanner rails at his daughter about the approach of Judgment Day, when the sheep will be separated from goats. He gives three possible meanings to what distinguishes the sheep from the goats. Two are legalistic: breakers of promises and those who dishonored their parents would be distinguished from God's sheep. The third distinction is not legalistic and not clear to Tanner, but I suggest it is clear to O'Connor: "Them that did the best they could with what they had, from them that didn't." Tanner, despite his failure to rise fully, may have done enough with what he had to merit a cleansing and mercy rather than damnation.

The reading given here to **"Judgement Day"** is parallel to a reading I have given to **"Revelation,"**[22] **"View of the Woods,"**[23] and **"The Displaced Person."**[24] This reading looks to Aquinas as the beginning point for an artistic exploration of natural human goods and inclinations and places it in opposition to our peculiarly American form of Lockean liberal materialism. If it is helpful, we may need to revisit some of the dichotomies that have risen in O'Connor scholarship. We may need to revisit the concept of grace, because Aquinas and, I believe, O'Connor speak of grace in a double voice, the grace of nature and the grace of that which transcends nature. And we may need to revisit the idea that her universal concerns are not related to her historical, political, and cultural concerns. We may have to take another look at the assumption that original sin means that all politics is on account of sin and, hence, fundamentally a matter of coercion. And we may have to explore more diligently the possibility that O'Connor does have something to tell us regarding our particular, historical American place in the flux of rising and converging. On the American question of race, **"Judgement Day"** seems to suggest that Tanner is wrong, that we cannot have friendship without equality. But it also suggests that equality and coercion will not allow for flourishing without friendship. Those two cane-bottom chairs are still terribly empty in American society, and we have not together found a way to fill them.

Notes

1. John Lance Bacon, *Flannery O'Connor and Cold War Culture* (New York: Cambridge University Press, 1993).

2. Flannery O'Connor, "Judgement Day," in *Everything That Rises Must Converge* (New York: Farrar, Straus, and Giroux, 1990).

3. Flannery O'Connor, *The Habit of Being* (New York: Vintage, 1980), 449.

4. Pierre Teilhard De Chardin, *The Phenomenon of Man* (London: Collins, 1959), 291.

5. Thomas Aquinas, *Summa Contra Gentiles* bk. 3, chap. 64, in *Basic Writings of Thomas Aquinas,* ed. Anton Pegis, 114 (New York: Random House, 1945). All references to Aquinas are to the Pegis edition unless otherwise noted.

6. Ibid., *Summa Theologica* 1-2, Prologue, Q. 49.

7. Ibid., Q. 90.

8. Ibid., Q. 91, art. 3, I ans. that.

9. Ibid., 1-2I, Q. 63, art. 1, I ans. that. See also 1-2, Q. 51, art. 1, I ans. that, and I, Q. 79, art. 12, I ans. that. At the latter point he says about *synderesis,* the natural habit whereby we know these beginnings or seeds, "synderesis is said to incline to good and to murmur at evil."

10. Ibid., 1-2, Q. 94, art. 4, I ans. that.
11. Ibid., art. 6, I ans. that.
12. For a fuller account of Locke's thought, and how it enters O'Connor's fiction, see John Roos, "The Political in Flannery O'Connor: A Reading of 'A View of the Woods,'" *Studies in Short Fiction* 29, no. 2 (Spring 1992): 161-79.
13. O'Connor, "Judgement Day," 250. Hereafter page numbers will be given in the text.
14. Aquinas, *Summa Theologica* I-II, Q. 94, Art. 2, I ans. that.
15. Flannery O'Connor, *Mystery and Manners* (New York: Farrar, Straus, and Giroux, 1969), 115.
16. Robert Fitzgerald, introduction to *Everything That Rises Must Converge,* xxx.
17. In the Latin text of Aquinas, the phrase "needs to live with" is *conversari,* which is the infinitive of the deponent verb *conversor* (*Summa Theologica,* Q. 94, art. 2, I ans. that. [Rome: Marietti, 1950]). Various meanings given by Forecellini's Lexicon include the following: to be about or along with anything; to live with, haunt, frequent; to live or converse with, keep company with, associate with.
18. The significance of the idea of conversations in Aquinas was in part suggested by Alasdair MacIntyre.
19. Bacon misreads this section when he interprets Tanner's shout as only about Tanner's being ashamed in front of his daughter. But the context seems to indicate that Tanner is concerned with the shame of Parrum, not just himself. Hence he shouts loudly enough for both to hear, which makes no sense if he is only concerned with his own shame in front of his daughter. See Bacon, *Flannery O'Connor and Cold War Culture,* 109.
20. Ibid., 106.
21. Flannery O'Connor, "Revelation," in *Everything That Rises Must Converge,* 191-218.
22. John Roos, "Flannery O'Connor and the Limits of Justice," in *Poets, Princes, and Private Citizens: Literary Alternatives to Postmodern Politics,* ed. Joseph Knippenberg and Peter Lawler, 143-68 (Lanham, MD: Rowman and Littlefield, 1996). See also John Roos, "Politics and the Limits of Justice in Flannery O'Connor," Conference on Southern Women Writers, Berry College, April 9, 1994.
23. Roos, "Politics and the Limits."
24. Ibid., "Flannery O'Connor and Natural Law: A Reading of 'The Displaced Person,'" Northeast Political Science Association, November 13, 1992.

Lucas E. Morel (essay date fall 2005)

SOURCE: Morel, Lucas E. "Bound for Glory: The Gospel of Racial Reconciliation in Flannery O'Connor's 'The Artificial Nigger.'" *Perspectives on Political Science* 34, no. 4 (fall 2005): 202-10.

[*In the following essay, Morel notes biblical references in "The Artificial Nigger," characterizing the scene in which Mr. Head and Nelson ponder the lawn ornament as an instance of momentary, yet meaningful, spiritual grace.*]

> The world is charged with the grandeur of God.
>
> —Gerard Manley Hopkins

> Jesus answered and said unto him, 'Verily, verily, I say unto thee, Except a man be born again, he cannot see the kingdom of God.'
>
> —John 3:3

> The loveliest lynchee was our Lord.
>
> —Gwendolyn Brooks, "The Chicago Defender Sends a Man to Little Rock"

> I believe that God's love for us is so great that He does not wait until we are purified to such a great extent before He allows us to receive Him.
>
> —Flannery O'Connor, "Letter to Dr. T. R. Spivey" (April 9, 1960)

Flannery O'Connor, a southern writer of deep Catholic convictions, once wrote that the subject of her work was "the action of grace in territory held largely by the devil" (*Mystery and Manners,* 118).[1] In the case of American history, the devil was in the details of black slavery and its legacy—a segregated South. O'Connor's short story **"The Artificial Nigger"** (1955)[2] uses a racist depiction of black Americans—a Negro lawn jockey of sorts—to illustrate how natural means become charged with God's glory to accomplish divine ends.[3] Her Christian portrayal of the human condition, a portrayal that confronts the freedom that gives rise to racial prejudice,[4] calls for an interpretation that conveys the spiritual principles and political lessons of a work that O'Connor called "my favorite and probably the best thing I'll ever write" (*Habit of Being,* 209). To borrow from Jesse Jackson, O'Connor "keeps hope alive" with stories that challenge the (post)modern world to look beyond itself to improve the human condition.

O'Connor writes that "there is nothing that screams out the tragedy of the South like what my uncle calls 'nigger statuary'" (*HB,* 101). Written in 1955, just as the modern Civil Rights movement began picking up steam, **"The Artificial Nigger"** shows how racial prejudice is born and nurtured in the pride and insecurity of human beings, and how the grace of God might come to liberate white southerners through their black neighbors. O'Connor transforms a commonplace totem of white prejudice against blacks, a plaster caricature of a Negro, into a symbol of Christ's redeeming death on the cross. She even alludes to the Madonna in the form of a black woman standing in a doorway, complete with a halo of hair that "stood straight out from her head for about four inches all around."[5] Talk about "Black is Beautiful"! These and many other references to the Bible, coupled with ubiquitous reminders of the segregated South, make for a dramatic juxtaposition of American religion and politics.

In **"The Artificial Nigger,"** a white, southern bigot (Mr. Head) takes his grandson (Nelson) on a train ride to the city to show him its vices and to teach him to be content with life in the country—which, of course, is free of Negroes. What gives the story its peculiar twist, not to mention its provocative title, is the visitors' miraculous encounter with a Negro statue. After losing their way in the city, they find themselves meandering about the black part of town. The grandfather, "hungry himself and beginning to be thirsty" (261; cf. Matthew 5:6), is now desperate to get back to the train station in time for the trip home. But in keeping with "the moral mission" (250) of the trip, Mr. Head attempts to show Nelson his youthful ignorance and therefore his necessary dependence on him: he hides while Nelson takes a nap on the sidewalk. The lesson succeeds in a way that inadvertently leads Mr. Head to betray Nelson. Now estranged from his grandson, Mr. Head eventually gets directed back to the white, but curiously lifeless, section of town. There, he and Nelson chance upon a plaster, Negro figure. The "artificial nigger" mysteriously dissolves the tension between them and enables Mr. Head, in particular, to experience the grace of God in a new and profound way.

O'Connor conveys her hopefulness in the area of civil rights, the "good news" of a racial reconciliation borne of individual reconciliation with God, in at least two ways: (1) through the ironic statements of her main characters, but especially of Mr. Head; and (2) through her use of color, especially black, to suggest an inversion of conventional associations of good and bad with white and black, respectively. The irony of the story suggests a providential or God-infused truth that runs counter to the intention of the speaker. Both what is said and how it is delivered suggest another power and hence intention at work besides that of the speaker. Simply put, one sees the Holy Spirit manifested in the speech of Mr. Head and Nelson. As for the use of color, like Ralph Ellison in *Invisible Man,*[6] O'Connor uses black and white in an unconventional way: for example, black, typically indicative of the obscure, sinister, and evil, now connotes truth, guidance, and enlightenment—in short, the path to God, at least for the particular situation of Mr. Head and Nelson. The color white, however, now signifies something bad, lifeless, desolate, or impotent.[7]

In **"The Artificial Nigger,"** O'Connor teaches the reader about opportunities for spiritual transformation that are missed by the main characters, Mr. Head and his grandson Nelson, because of their pride and self-justification, which manifest themselves most clearly in racial bigotry. The kingdom of God presents itself to them in the black characters of the story, who, although strangers to them by locale (residents of the city as opposed to the country) and race (owing to southern segregation), are fellow sojourners as coresidents of a modern America on the brink of racial integration.

When asked why she became a writer, Flannery O'Connor replied, "I write because I write well." But the self-described "hillbilly Thomist" (*HB,* 81) surprised even herself in composing **"The Artificial Nigger"**: "I think it's one of the best stories I've written, and this because there is a good deal more in it than I understand myself" (*HB,* 140). Her southern version of one "pilgrim's progress" invites a spiritual interpretation that also suggests the political implications of what O'Connor called "the redemptive quality of the Negro's suffering for us all" (*HB,* 78).[8]

Storyline and Commentary

Nelson sleeps "underneath the shadow of the window," the "only dark spot" in a room otherwise ruled over by Mr. Head's imperial presence—a presence so austere his clothes take on the stature of subordinate soldiers and even the moon(light) hesitates to enter. This indicates Nelson's need for enlightenment, which is what Mr. Head is set on providing by the imminent trip to the city—"the moral mission of the coming day" (250). Unbeknownst to Mr. Head, the train they will board for Atlanta will liken unto the fabled train "bound for glory"—that is, heaven or the kingdom of God—in American musical folklore.[9] Nelson sleeps in a fetal position, foreshadowing his rebirth at the close of the story. Physically and intellectually he is immature, perhaps even stunted, given his rearing by the proud and clearly limited Mr. Head.

Besides his own moral probity (noted above), just what are Mr. Head's credentials for acting as a "suitable guide for the young" (249)? He asks the impertinent grandson, "Have you ever . . . seen me lost?" and Nelson responds, "It's nowhere around here to get lost at." Precisely. This is just what needs to happen for the two of them to find their way to God. They do not know their lostness, and O'Connor is as determined as God the Father to communicate this fact to them through a material world they do not fully understand but that will have its way with them before their intended journey is completed. The Negroes they confront along the way will play a key role in offering God's truth to them, a truth they repeatedly deny or miss—through their repeated disparagement of, and separation from, Negroes—but eventually will see and accept when faced with the enigmatic Negro statue that gives O'Connor's short story its title. The reader learns later that Mr. Head and his fellow whites had run out the last black resident of their community, which suggests at least one reason for Mr. Head's inability to discover his lostness: namely, no black witness of his fallibility, a human imperfection only in part attributable to his insistent racism.

Mr. Head responds to Nelson's crack about their backwoods home as "nowhere . . . to get lost at" with a deliberate prophecy of the day's events: "The day is going to come . . . when you'll find you ain't as smart as you think you are." That makes two of them! Mr. Head in his own pride seeks to teach his grandson that "he had no cause for pride merely because he had been born in the city" (251). As O'Connor renders it, the proud teaching the proud likens unto the blind leading the blind. And as Mr. Head falls asleep the previous night pondering a trip he had conceived "for the most part in moral terms," he will prove to be smarter than even he perceived himself to be by taking a trip that will show both of them their limitations. But at the end of the day, literally, both will discover that they are not as smart as they think they are.

They "expected his head to grow," so Nelson would take his trip to the city in a new suit of clothes complete with a gray hat "a size large." Coupled with the grandfather's name, "Mr. Head," one cannot help but think of the New Testament exhortation that "knowledge puffs up, but love builds up" (1 Cor. 8:1). Knowledge has puffed up both characters, as their conversation indicates a battle of wit and struggle for interpersonal superiority. For example, O'Connor describes Nelson looking "ancient, as if he knew everything already" (251), and introduces Mr. Head with eyes containing the "look of composure and of ancient wisdom as if they belonged to one of the great guides of men," likening him to Dante's Virgil and the angel Raphael who came to earth to assist Tobias (250).[10] If Mr. Head had his druthers, knowledge would continue to puff up Nelson—but only through Mr. Head's teaching.

The reader is given to understand that Mr. Head, as head of the family, was so oppressive in his headship that he outlived not only his wife but also his daughter. The daughter runs away on her mother's death, unwilling to live with Mr. Head by herself, only to return after she gives birth—apparently out of wedlock—to Nelson. Her stay with her father lasts only a year, when "one morning, without getting out of bed, she died," which is how Mr. Head ends up with Nelson, "the year-old child."

O'Connor depicts the verbal sparring between Mr. Head and Nelson as a competition in self-justification. The depiction of a grandfather who should know better and a grandson who cannot is comic. When Nelson is shown his inexperience and insufficiency by having it pointed out that he has never seen "a nigger" after he "made a face as if he could handle a nigger" (252), Nelson changes the subject by pointing out that he had gotten up earlier than the grandfather. This one-upmanship constitutes their relationship, as the now ten-year-old Nelson vies against the sixty-year-old for his place in the world.

Returning to the subject of Nelson's knowledge of Negroes while an infant in Atlanta, Mr. Head states: "If you seen one you didn't know what he was," adding, "A six-month-old child don't know a nigger from anybody else." Of course, a "nigger" is precisely something that one would not recognize insofar as it is an artifice, a xenophobic label attached to the stereotype conjured up by an admixture of narrow experience and personal, as well as social, insecurity about people of a different race. In this sense, O'Connor introduces the reader early in the story to the idea of an artificial or fake Negro, signified by the word "nigger." Mr. Head is more right than he knows when he asserts that a six-month-old child "don't know a nigger from anybody else" because the concept of nigger has to be learned. It is a convention that takes on meaning within a given social context: in this case, the segregation of the American South representing and enacting the myth of white supremacy that has cast a pernicious shadow over American history. As racial prejudice is not innate but must be learned, Mr. Head unwittingly declares the unstated premise of his effort to school Nelson in nigger-spotting. It does not come automatically; it must be taught by those who know. The idea of "nigger" as an artifice, or an "artificial nigger," has now been planted by O'Connor. The balance of the story will show how that concept ultimately takes material form as a Negro statue, a physical manifestation of the unclean spirit that haunts Mr. Head, as it does a goodly portion of O'Connor's southern stomping grounds.

A black fuel tank (a positive symbol of power) contrasts with the train tracks that "looked white and fragile" (a negative symbol of conveyance) under "the useless morning moon," the latter duly intimidated by the imperious self-sufficiency Mr. Head exhibits at the outset of the story. Mr. Head's moral self-sufficiency not only produces the inefficacy of the morning moon but also results in passing trains that "emerge from a tunnel of trees and, hit for a second by the cold sky, vanish terrified into the woods again." Just as the biblical account of the fall finds Adam and Eve hiding from God "amongst the trees of the garden," (Gen. 3:8), so too O'Connor has these passing trains dart back into the woods in the face of a "cold sky," leaving Mr. Head and Nelson standing unashamedly out in the open. Their pose is accented by the cold—read, empty—sky, which finds them sufficient unto themselves with no God around (as there is no sun around), for none is needed or invited for the moral mission of the day.

As the two arrive at the spot where the train will pick them up, they show the extent to which they have prepared for the trip by their own efforts. They get to the junction "some time before the train was due to arrive," with lunch in hand—"some biscuits and a can of sardines," reminiscent of the loaves and fishes the Bible records Jesus multiplying for the sake of a hungry crowd of thousands. Nevertheless, although Mr. Head had made special arrangements for a train to stop for them, he secretly fears it will not actually stop and will lead to his grand humiliation before Nelson, who would quickly comment, "I never thought no train was going to stop for you." Despite a physical environment that from the story's outset appears intimidated in the presence of the grandfather, Mr. Head internally fears a disruption of his command of the outward elements of his life. The Eden of Mr. Head's existence, one suspects, awaits disruption.

O'Connor reinforces the pride of the two sojourners by relating their conviction to "ignore the train if it passed them" (253). Mr. Head is the more wary of the two, as he would suffer the greater embarrassment if the train (which was supposed to stop for them) were to pass them "slowly." That the train was in some sense "bound for glory," as in the title of the folk song, O'Connor indicates in her description of its arrival and departure. The second coach came to a stop "exactly where they were standing," with the conductor on the coach's step "as if he expected them." By adding that the conductor "did not look as if it mattered one way or the other to him if they got on or not," O'Connor shows that this trip to bountiful will happen by their choice. Apparently, no one is forced into heaven, but God certainly will take advantage of Mr. Head's intention to make of the trip a "moral mission." In addition, the train "took only a fraction of a second" to board them and be on its way, as if it was heaven-sent for a mission that could not brook delay.

The conductor also possessed "the face of an ancient bloated bulldog." Could this be an allusion to Francis Thompson's poem, "The Hound of Heaven"?[11] O'Connor wrote that her stories featured protagonists reluctant to accept the overtures of grace. As she put it, "All my stories are about the action of grace on a character who is not very willing to support it" (*HB*, 275). This jibes with God as the "hound of heaven" in pursuit of an elusive and reticent creation, populated by folks who resist God's initiative. Mr. Head and Nelson find themselves time and again resisting God's call until their own insufficiency creates the conditions for God's grace to find its way to their accepting hearts.

Nelson's first lesson comes when a "procession" of three "coffee-colored" individuals stride into their car, presumably from their inferior accommodations in a car for Negroes (254-55). Think, "And when the saints, come marching in . . ." This provides Mr. Head with his first formal lesson for Nelson in identifying a "nigger." It backfires in a way that indicates the problem with using skin color as a marker for good or bad: namely, coffee as a color is neither black nor white and hence is a poor set-up for Mr. Head's instruction in the South's racial caste. Nelson fails his test by not calling the man who leads the "procession" a "nigger." Repeated questioning from the grandfather elicits "a man," a "fat man," and an "old man" from Nelson (255). Nelson blames his failure on his grandfather's faulty teaching: "You said they were black. . . . You never said they were tan. How do you expect me to know anything when you don't tell me right?" The student can only be as good as his teacher. The humiliation of Nelson, however, is complete: "He felt that the Negro had deliberately walked down the aisle in order to make a fool of him and he hated him with a fierce raw fresh hate" (255-56). Nelson begins to sense his own limitations, which suggests why later in the trip he is more willing than his grandfather to ask for help—in the form of directions back to the depot—from a black person.

The lesson in racial discrimination, however, has taken hold. Nelson proves he is a quick study when the grandfather takes him to the dining car. There they see three "very black Negroes" serving breakfast, one of whom approaches to seat them. Learning that they had eaten before they boarded the train, the waiter dismisses them "with an airy wave of the arm as if he were brushing aside flies" (256). As O'Connor puts it, "Neither Nelson nor Mr. Head moved a fraction of an inch." Like grandfather, like grandson. Nelson cannot mistake that this waiter, "very black," falls under the category of "nigger," and so Nelson the pupil acts just like Mr. Head the teacher by not responding to the waiter's command to "Stan' aside then please." The notion of white supremacy has taken hold of Nelson. In fact, on seeing the coffee-colored Negro and his party, again, now eating breakfast, Mr. Head calls attention to the segregated seating—"They rope them off"—a matter-of-fact observation that may inadvertently allude to lynching.

Their trip to the dining car ends in a victory for Mr. Head (and Nelson by association) when the waiter prevents them from entering the kitchen with the statement: "Passengers are NOT allowed in the kitchen!" (257). Mr. Head shouts back, "And there's good reason for that because the cockroaches would run the passengers out!" This elicits laughter from the travelers as Mr. Head and Nelson grin on their way out. Nelson "felt a sudden keen pride" in his grandfather, which leads the ten-year-old to a humbling but comforting conclusion: "[T]he old man would be his only support in the strange place they were approaching. He would be entirely alone in the world if he were ever lost from his grandfather. A terrible excitement shook him and he wanted to take hold of Mr. Head's coat and hold on like a child."

This feeling of ownership and belonging will magnify the betrayal that comes later in the story. If Mr. Head only knew what was going through his grandson's mind. He could have turned back then and there—mission accomplished.

Finding no one to talk to when they return to their seats, Mr. Head decides to announce the names on the buildings they pass. All but one have "Dixie" or "Southern" in their names.[12] The reader is reminded of the region's history of racial strife with names like "Southern Maid Flour," "Southern Belle Cotton Products," and "Southern Mammy Cane Syrup." Nelson is embarrassed by his grandfather's bombast over building signs, and tells him to "Hush up!" The contest of wills has begun again.

When the conductor announces, "Firstoppppppmry,"—that is, "First stop, Emory,"—Nelson jumps from his seat out of fright as well as eagerness to get into the city. Mr. Head sits him back down and explains that the next stop will situate them at the heart of the town, not its edge. In his pride, the grandfather does not disclose that he made the same mistake when he first traveled to the city. Once more, Nelson realizes his dependence on his grandfather: "Nelson sat back down, very pale. For the first time in his life, he understood that his grandfather was indispensable to him." Nelson's pride and trust in his grandfather will lead him to trust the grandfather's apparent knowledge in other areas: namely, what to think about Negroes.

After exiting the train station, Mr. Head points out "where you walked in and sat on a chair with your feet upon two rests and let a Negro polish your shoes" (258). He turns the mundane act of shoe polishing into a lesson on color caste. The narrator has Mr. Head describe the procedure as one in which the Negro has to gain permission to polish your shoes, not one in which you enlist his services. The subservience is emphasized, further entrenching the color line in young Nelson's mind.

They look into the entrances but never enter any of the buildings. As the teacher, Mr. Head does not reveal that he had once "got lost" in a large building and only got out "after many people had insulted him." Once bitten, twice shy, Mr. Head could not afford to stumble before his student. Risk-averse, insecure, and therefore all the more likely to seek security and pride in putting down others, especially those whom society deems inferior, Mr. Head finds strength and security in numbers—namely, white supremacy—instead of humility before the Creator of all humanity.

They chance on a weighing machine, and each pluck a penny into it to see what it would tell them. Reminiscent of the scene from the book of Daniel (5:27), where King Nebuchadnezzar reads the writing on the wall that tells him he has been weighed and found wanting, Mr. Head and Nelson discover their weight to be overestimated. As for their respective fortunes, Mr. Head finds that his ticket confirms his own self-assessment ("You are upright and brave and all your friends admire you" [259]), whereas Nelson's ticket says "You have a great destiny ahead of you but beware of dark women." He dismisses this, as he "did not know any women," unaware that he would soon be faced with a woman that would test the significance of the novelty ticket.

To the grandfather's dismay, Nelson is thrilled with his visit to the city. So Mr. Head decides to give him a close-up view of the sewer system, explaining how "a man could slide into it and be sucked along down endless pitchblack tunnels." Nelson associates the "endless pitch black tunnels" (259) of the city's sewer system with "the entrance to hell" but concludes that one can "stay away from the holes." Nelson remains fascinated with the city, exclaiming, "This is where I come from!"

After circling around back to the station, Mr. Head leads his nephew in a different direction.[13] When the grandfather inadvertently takes them through a dilapidated black neighborhood, Nelson follows the racist script by observing, "Niggers live in these houses" (260). Mr. Head announces, "We didn't come to look at niggers." Well, yes and no, for Mr. Head has consistently pointed out the black aspects of the city as a good reason for staying away from the city. This suggests a counterconclusion: perhaps they should have come to look at black folk! What would have happened if they came not only to look at black folk but also to have a conversation with them? In other words, what might happen if they saw blacks not as the dreaded, mysterious, and sinister "other" but as fellow human beings, citizens, and potential friends?

Now lost in what Mr. Head and Nelson no doubt considered the wrong side of town, "they continued to see Negroes everywhere" and stepped up their pace to find their way out of the black neighborhood. "Black eyes in black faces were watching them from every direction." O'Connor presents the two sojourners with a proverbial "cloud of witnesses," with "colored men," "colored women," and "colored children" all around.[14] They soon passed "rows of stores with colored customers in them," but Mr. Head found no reason to stop at the entrances of any of these establishments. This would show blacks not only as servants in society but also as those who were served: namely, black buyers as well as sellers. This fact is only implied by the presence of the coffee-colored travelers on the train, whom O'Connor shows as dressed and eating better than Mr. Head and Nelson. Mr. Head was content at the time to ride as a passenger in the white car, a ride interrupted by the more affluent Negroes walking up to the dining car from their segregated quarters at the rear of the train.

To Nelson's consternation, Mr. Head turns the table on Nelson's earlier proclamation, "I was born here!," with the statement: "Yes, this is where you were born—right here with all these niggers." He reinforces the previously established point that Negroes are America's untouchables, a class of people one should avoid. Not one to be outdone if he can help it, Nelson retorts, "I think you done got us lost" (261). Instead of accepting Mr. Head's association of Nelson with the black part of town (which would emphasize Nelson's flaw as a native of a city that includes Negroes), Nelson points out for the first time that they are lost and, more to the point, that it is Mr. Head's fault. This puts the ball back in Mr. Head's court, as the two continue the verbal contest set in motion at the beginning of the story. Of course, Mr. Head cannot admit the truth of Nelson's observation and therefore tries to turn Nelson's observation into a rationalization for stopping: "You're just tired of walking."

They then discover that they left their lunch on the train. O'Connor describes Mr. Head, now, as "hungry himself and beginning to be thirsty." This allusion to Matthew 5:6 ("Blessed are those who hunger and thirst for righteousness, for they will be filled") suggests the spiritual import of their sojourn into what they presume to be the wrong part of town. O'Connor's providential rendering of what Mr. Head intended as a "moral mission" for his grandson becomes more pronounced. As their tour through the city becomes an extended one, their resources begin to fall away one by one. The lesson God intends for the grandfather will only take effect as Mr. Head gradually comes to the end of his own resourcefulness. Hunger, thirst, and sweat bear down on the two and leave them open to God's wisdom.

Nevertheless, Mr. Head has not given up yet. In reply to Nelson's "muttering under his breath, 'First you lost the sack and then you lost the way,'" Mr. Head "growl[ed] from time to time, 'Anybody wants to be from this nigger heaven can be from it!'" Here Mr. Head, as O'Connor has shown us before, says more than he knows. The black part of town is precisely the "heaven" or province of saints that O'Connor believes Mr. Head should look to for spiritual transformation. The fact that it is a "nigger heaven" reemphasizes her belief that Mr. Head needs to see blacks in a different light. The "cloud of witnesses" through which they are passing represent the kingdom of heaven in his midst. He just cannot see it as such because of his racial bigotry. He would do well, we infer, to follow Jesus' earliest admonition: "Repent, for the kingdom of heaven is at hand" (Matthew 4:17). The "nigger heaven" from which Mr. Head wants so quickly to flee is actually the kingdom of heaven for those who have eyes to see—namely, those not already blinded by the presumption of white supremacy.[15]

Nelson, desirous of passing the day-long test that is Mr. Head's journey into the city, has not yet fully imbibed Mr. Head's bigotry. It is therefore no surprise that it is Nelson who suggests that they ask for directions from the Negroes who are watching them pass through: "Whyn't you ast one of these niggers the way?"[16] If any sentence can summarize O'Connor's prescription for Mr. Head, it is this statement of Nelson's. Having run off the Negroes of his Georgia backwoods community a few years before Nelson's birth,[17] Mr. Head is not about to seek help from—that is, admit weakness or insufficiency before—a class of individuals he has desperately tried to keep beneath him. His stature as a white man, albeit a poor one from the hills of Georgia, depends on maintaining his position on a southern totem pole that insists on blacks holding the bottom position.[18]

Mr. Head replies sarcastically, "This is where you were born. You can ast one yourself if you want to." One suspects that if it were not for Nelson's earlier, proud insistence that he was born in the city, Mr. Head would not have suggested this to his grandson. So far they have had as little contact as possible with Negroes—just enough to teach that the difference in skin color makes all the difference for where Nelson should spend the rest of his life. Given Nelson's admission of lostness, the need to "ast one of these niggers the way," Mr. Head invites Nelson to follow his own advice and ask one of his putative homeboys, to use the modern vernacular, the way back to the station.

Nelson decides to ask for directions but must do so with minimal damage to his own self-esteem, for he "was afraid of the colored men and he didn't want to be laughed at by the colored children." He sees "a large colored woman leaning in a doorway," what O'Connor called in a letter "a black mountain of maternity" (*HB,* 78). O'Connor turns the stereotype of the black mammy into the Mother of God, a black Madonna, complete with an Afro that "stood straight out from her head for about four inches all around," giving the effect of a real-world halo. The impact of this maternal figure on Nelson, orphaned at the age of one but now an adolescent who inwardly yearns for a mother figure to supply the lack of Mr. Head, is mesmerizing enough that he forgets the weighing machine's warning to "beware of dark women" (259). Nelson "felt his breath drawn up by the woman's dark eyes" and, "in a voice that did not sound like his own," asks, "How do you get back to town?" His simple but urgent question appears called forth by the woman's mere presence, an indication that Nelson's pride cannot be overcome without the help of some outside influence.

Moreover, that it "did not sound like his own" is O'Connor's way of infusing the mundane with the supernatural. The spiritual import of this encounter is reinforced by references to the trinity ("His eyes . . . made a triangular path") and perhaps the pietà ("He suddenly wanted her to reach down and pick him up and draw him against her").

The fact that he asks how to get "back to town," insofar as it implies that the black section of town is irrelevant, reflects his grandfather's segregationist outlook and reinforces their inability to see the kingdom of God before them. They could not see the kingdom of God right in front of them, for, as Jesus says in John 3:3, "Except a man be born again, he cannot see the kingdom of God." Standing in the heart of Atlanta but surrounded by blacks, Nelson and Mr. Head see the black part of town as a separate and less desirable locale. O'Connor thereby illustrates the obstacle that still confronts them on their trip to glory.

After waiting a minute for Nelson's question to sink in, the woman replies playfully with a truth Nelson was unable to see because of the lessons in racism taught him earlier that day by the grandfather: "You in town now." Nelson feels "as if a cool spray had been turned on him" (262), which represents something of a baptism for the humbled and accepting youngster. This epiphany is broken when Nelson, who "would have collapsed at her feet," is rudely pulled away by the grandfather, who snorts, "You act like you don't have any sense." Shamed by his grandfather for deigning to ask directions from a black woman,[19] Nelson leaves with Mr. Head and owns his dependence on his grandfather by holding his hand.

With whites now in view, Mr. Head leads them down the trolley tracks he hopes are headed to the station. When Nelson asks, "How you know you ain't following the tracks in the wrong direction?" Mr. Head answers matter-of-factly, "All these people are white" (263). Again, O'Connor indicates how color dictates for Mr. Head the right way to go, which, in their immediate case, is based on a bigoted presumption. They had already been told the right way, but because the source was black, the help was rejected. Moreover, although they are now in the white—or as they see it, "right"—part of town, the neighborhood betrays little sign of life.

Exhausted by the morning's events, Nelson sits down and shortly collapses in a heap on the hot pavement. This gives his grandfather a perverse idea: he decides to hide around a corner, so when Nelson wakes up he will have to realize his utter dependence on his grandfather. Mr. Head perches himself, fittingly, on "a covered garbage can" (264), literally affirming his poor white trash identity. He had only a few minutes earlier derided Nelson for "grinning like a chim-pan-zee" (263), but now he finds himself, as the narrator describes it, "hunched like an old monkey on the garbage can lid," waiting for Nelson to "wake up alone." For his part, Nelson slept uneasily as "black forms mov[ed] up from some dark part of him into the light." What now appears sinister will later turn out to be a blessing to Nelson.

Impatient and worried about getting back to the station in time to return home, Mr. Head kicked the trash can he was sitting on and startles Nelson to his feet. After running a few blocks "like a wild maddened pony," Nelson knocks down an elderly woman with groceries and they fall to the ground. Mr. Head watches for a moment, "crouched behind a trash box," but then "[s]omething forced Mr. Head from behind the trash box and forward" (265). Again the reader witnesses some outside force move a character, indicating man's inability to do the right thing without help from outside or above. Alas, with the woman screaming for the police, the grandfather denies any relation to Nelson, who had "caught him around the hips and clung panting against him." The betrayal, clear to all present, causes Nelson to let go of his grandfather, who leaves Nelson behind and walks away alone seeing "nothing but a hollow tunnel that had once been the street."[20]

Nelson eventually begins following his grandfather twenty paces behind. When Mr. Head steals a glance behind him, "he saw two small eyes piercing into his back like pitchfork prongs" (266). The narrator comments: "The boy was not of a forgiving nature but this was the first time he had ever had anything to forgive." There is no mistaking O'Connor's intent: the devil is present in Nelson's vengeful stare at his grandfather. For now, Nelson rejects the option of forgiveness and turns his back on his grandfather when Mr. Head offers to get them "a Co' Cola somewheres." When Nelson disdains to drink from a water spigot from which his grandfather drank, Mr. Head despairs for his own life. Dante's *Inferno* looms large as Mr. Head "lost all hope" (266-67), feeling "the boy's steady hate."

As O'Connor presents the tale, Nelson was in a worse place, for "his mind had frozen around his grandfather's treachery as if he were trying to preserve it intact to present at the final judgment." The biblical admonition "forgive, and ye shall be forgiven" (Luke 6:37) found no place in Nelson's heart. At least his grandfather was now feeling bad for getting them lost and afraid his own pride would lead them to a nightfall mugging. Mr. Head "could not stand to think that his sins would be visited upon Nelson and that even now, he was leading the boy to his doom." But Nelson felt no desire to reconcile with his grandfather. Always one made to feel his inadequacy by his grandfather, Nelson sensed his power over him by denying Mr. Head what he needed and now desired most. But this sense of power was not absolute, for "he felt, from some remote place inside himself, a black mysterious form reach up as if it would melt his frozen vision in one hot grasp." Nelson's desire to freeze his grandfather's betrayal for the day of judgment is a sign of spiritual poverty. This makes the "black mysterious form" a grace unto Nelson.

They continue walking, separated physically and emotionally, and find themselves in "an elegant suburban section" where "everything was entirely deserted" (267). Unlike the black part of town, which teemed with life, this affluent neighborhood was filled with "big white houses" that looked like so many icebergs and not even a dog in sight.[21] At last Mr. Head sees a man walking two bulldogs and proceeds to wave his arms "like someone shipwrecked on a desert island." Worn out in body and spirit, Mr. Head finally asks for help in a cry that amounts to a confession of the true condition of his soul: "I'm lost! . . . I'm lost and can't find my way and me and this boy have got to catch this train and I can't find the station. Oh Gawd I'm lost! Oh hep me Gawd I'm lost!"

His request for help brings new life and hope into Mr. Head, who listens to the man give him directions "as if he were slowly returning from the dead" (268). When he tells Nelson, "We're going to get home," the grandson is described as "merely there, a small figure, waiting. Home was nothing to him." The grandfather is crushed—his hopeful resurrection short lived: "He felt he knew now . . . what man would be like without salvation." But he then chances on "the plaster figure of a Negro." The figure and its miserable condition—"pitched forward at an unsteady angle" with a "chipped eye" and holding "a piece of brown watermelon"—are so arresting that Mr. Head, with Nelson a short distance away, stops in his tracks and breathes, "An artificial nigger!" Nelson repeats the statement "in Mr. Head's exact tone," indicating his desire to be an apt pupil, once more, and therewith signify his submission to his grandfather despite the earlier betrayal. In short, Nelson shows he has forgiven the treachery he had hoped to hold on to until Judgment Day. By forgiving Mr. Head, a sign of God's grace extended through Nelson to his grandfather, Nelson becomes humble in a way rarely exhibited hitherto.

In addition, with them staring at the statue "with their necks forward at almost the same angle," and the statue already observed to be "about Nelson's size," their physical identification with the statue foreshadows the reconciliation soon to take place. Pride has kept them from learning from real Negroes, so God now uses the next best thing—a fake Negro transfigured into a crucifix. Providence took an object that bigoted whites have used to degrade black people and turned it to His own purposes. Gleaning from the story in Genesis of Joseph's forgiveness of his brothers, O'Connor wrote elsewhere that "God can make any indifferent thing, as well as evil itself, an instrument for good."[22]

Mr. Head and his grandson had spent much of the day running into black people, and Nelson in particular received one lesson after another on how to spot them (so as to avoid them). So, when they finally see one that is not real—something they have never seen or heard of—for no white man would want to make a model or copy of a despised class of people, let alone place it on his front lawn—they are stupefied. All they can do at first is give a pat description of the statue that reflects their bigotry.

The narrator observes: "They stood gazing at the artificial Negro as if they were faced with some great mystery, some monument to another's victory that brought them together in their common defeat. They could both feel it dissolving their differences like an action of mercy" (269).[23] This was the first time Mr. Head felt what mercy was like, because, as the narrator puts it, "he had been too good to deserve any." As for Nelson, he looked at his grandfather with eyes that "seemed to implore him to explain once and for all the mystery of existence." Trying to appear wise to his grandson, all Mr. Head could come up with is: "They ain't got enough real ones here. They got to have an artificial one."

This attempt at wisdom was more like a wisecrack,[24] but it does the trick. Nelson nods in agreement, then says, "Let's go home before we get ourselves lost again." Humbled by his encounter with the strange statue, and no longer excusing his being lost by blaming it on the grandfather, Nelson decides it is time to go home and assumes at least part of the responsibility for getting lost. Once again, O'Connor invests the scene with spiritual import through physical manifestations suggesting the presence of the Holy Spirit. Mr. Head "heard himself" utter the ironic wisecrack; Nelson nods in agreement "with a strange shivering about his mouth." Divine assistance is needed again to overcome personal pride and self-sufficiency.

The train arrived "just as they reached the station," as if God brought it right on time. The providential lesson about mercy is over; they are now free to return home. Even the moon, which began the story practically cowering before Mr. Head's self-sufficiency, is "restored to its full splendor." Stepping off the train, they behold an Edenic scene, resplendent with light, indicative of the duly chastened Mr. Head, who in his silence now emits no false light. He feels God's mercy a second time, but "no words in the world . . . could name it." Ashamed he possesses so little of the mercy that washed over his pride, "He stood appalled, judging himself with the thoroughness of God." The grandfather gives up trying to justify himself in the presence of God's grace. With Nelson reconciled to his grandfather (albeit still somewhat wary), the narrator notes that the train "glided past them and disappeared like a frightened serpent into the woods" (270). The devil, in other words, has left them for now.

O'Connor's stories often end with the seed of faith planted, the offering of grace presented, but leave the full flowering for the reader's imagination and consideration. This is what she meant by viewing stories not as problems to be solved—or as O'Connor put it, "a frog in a bottle"[25]—but as "experienced meaning" (*MM,* 96). Instead of presenting abstract statements, she wrote stories in which the mystery of life was preserved but suggested in the concrete experiences of her characters.

Her mode of writing was not to start with a theme or statement, per se, but with a character, and then write of his or her encounter with the divine and see how it worked itself out.[26] For example, if one were to begin with a Mr. Head figure, just how would God's grace work its way into his life, given the sixty years he already has behind him, especially on the subject of race? Answer: Give the devil his due, and man's own resistance to change, demonstrate the mountain of southern experience that has to be climbed, before divine intervention has its way with him. The southern Catholic writer lives in a region "struggling, in both good ways and bad, to preserve its identity." Its devotion to tradition has both faults and merits that complicate the search for progress on the civil rights front. And so O'Connor begins by depicting the "absence" of grace (*MM,* 204), a moon cowering in the presence of Mr. Head, intimidated by his self-sufficiency and moral hubris, and ends with a return to the beginning, but with both scene and characters transformed by the day's events.

In a letter to Andrew Lytle, *Sewanee Review* editor and an early teacher of O'Connor, she wrote: "There is a moment of grace in most of the stories, or a moment where it is offered, and is usually rejected" (*HB,* 373). This seems to be the operative mode in the gradual education of Mr. Head and Nelson. When the black woman in the doorway speaks to Nelson about how to get back to town, Mr. Head is too embarrassed to receive this help, coming as it does from a black person. His way back to the train depot does not come until repeated attempts fail. His awareness of his own spiritual need, as well, comes only after he is confronted with the enigmatic figure of the artificial Negro. The real ones he has faced in their trip to town never appeared to him as worth his while, except as object lessons for Nelson on what or whom to avoid.

The fact that neither Mr. Head nor Nelson comes to befriend any blacks as a result of their encounter with the Negro statue would seem to argue against an optimistic political interpretation. However, O'Connor liked to end her stories before the fruit of a character's "conversion" became a complete harvest. As she put it, "All my stories are about the action of grace on a character who is not very willing to support it."[27] Given later stories in which she implies a cautious approach to the Civil Rights movement—see **"The Enduring Chill"** (1958) and **"Everything That Rises Must Converge"** (1961)[28]—the gradual process of Mr. Head's spiritual rebirth suggests that any social or political reformation would take shape slowly, as well. Mr. Head's insistent bigotry derives, in part, from living in a region with a "history of defeat and violation" (*MM,* 209).

Aside from the reconciliation of the grandfather and Nelson, the effects or fruit of their encounter with the Negro statue remain to be seen, but what her story makes clear is that God's grace and mercy have taken root. And from a right beginning, we can expect a right end. As the Bible teaches, "every good tree bringeth forth good fruit" (Matthew 7:17). This fruit or harvest does not interest O'Connor as much as the tree that is its source. She chose to focus on getting the right tree, presuming that the results will speak for themselves as the reader ponders the implications of her story.[29] After all, as a Catholic, O'Connor is in for the long haul when it comes to God's sanctifying work in people. She wrote, "all good stories are about conversion" (*HB,* 275), and in **"The Artificial Nigger,"** O'Connor lets us see one front and center. O'Connor sees conversion as a gradual sanctification, as seen in the aftermath of Head's encounter with the artificial Negro (*HB,* 430).[30] Also, she noted that "in us the good is something under construction" (*MM,* 226). Simply put, grace works even through hypocritical people (*HB,* 389). O'Connor's "gradualism" is a result of her conviction that federal government intervention on civil rights forced southerners out of their virtues as well as their vices (*MM,* 28-29). Without manners to mend the social breech, what was there left to maintain civil society? The pace of grace may be slow, but it is ineluctable.

Notes

This article was prepared for delivery at the 2004 Annual Meeting of the American Political Science Association, September 2-5, 2004. Copyright by the American Political Science Association.

1. Quotations from Flannery O'Connor's works are cited in the text with the following abbreviations: *HB: The Habit of Being: Letters of Flannery O'Connor,* ed. Sally Fitzgerald (New York: Farrar, Straus and Giroux, 1979, 1988); *MM: Mystery and Manners: Occasional Prose,* ed. Sally Fitzgerald and Robert Fitzgerald (New York: Farrar, Straus and Giroux, 1961).

2. Quotations from Flannery O'Connor's "The Artificial Nigger" will be noted in the text by page number only and are cited from Flannery O'Connor, *The Complete Short Stories,* introd. Robert Giroux (New York: Farrar, Straus and Giroux, 1994).

3. O'Connor referred to this as "grace through nature" (*MM,* 153).

4. O'Connor saw evil as the necessary result of our freedom (*MM,* 157; see also 167).

5. I note all subsequent citations parenthetically in the text by page number and display emphases from the original unless otherwise noted.

6. Ralph Ellison, *Invisible Man* (New York: Random House, 1952; reprint, New York: Vintage Books, 1995).

7. "It was the whiteness of the whale that above all things appalled me." Herman Melville, *Moby Dick, or The Whale* (Berkeley: University of California Press, 1979; Arion Press, 1971; orig. 1851), chap. 42, 189.

8. See also O'Connor's statement that "what individuals have to suffer for the common good" is "a mystery, and part of the suffering of Christ" (*HB,* 543). In a January 12, 1955, letter to her editor, John Ransom, she wrote that the statue was intended "to give a sense of the mysterious suffering of that race to Mr. Head and Nelson, . . . a kind of redemptive suffering which acts on them without their taking it in as such." *Flannery O'Connor Bulletin* 23 (1994-95): 181.

9. What follows is the text to the folk spiritual, "This Train is Bound for Glory":

   This train is bound for glory, this train.
   This train is bound for glory, this train.
   This train is bound for glory,
   Don't carry nothin but the righteous and the holy,
   This train is bound for glory, this train.
   This train don't carry no gamblers, this train.
   This train don't carry no gamblers, this train.
   This train don't carry no gamblers,
   No hypocrites, no midnight ramblers,
   This train is bound for glory, this train.
   This train is bound for speed now, this train.
   . . . Fastest train you ever did see now
   This train don't carry no rustlers, this train,
   . . . Side-street walkers, or two bit hustlers
   This train is solid black now this train,
   . . . Where it carry you, you don't come back now
   This train don't carry white or black now, this train,
   . . . Everybody ride it is treated alike now.

10. A few weeks before she died, O'Connor sent a copy of a prayer to St. Raphael to a friend (*HB,* 592-93).

11. O'Connor was familiar with the poetry of Gerard Manley Hopkins and mentioned "The Hound of Heaven" in a letter as a poem she "wouldn't impound" as a model of religious poetry (*HB,* 554). From a hospital a day before she was allowed to go home after a month's stay, O'Connor wrote, "I like Hopkins . . . particularly a sonnet beginning[:] Margaret, are you grieving / Over Goldengrove unleaving? . . ." (*HB,* 586). See also *HB,* 112, 164, 476-77, and 517. Alternatively, the bulldog of a conductor coupled with the two bulldogs walked by the man who gives Mr. Head directions may add up to the three-headed Cerberus found in Canto 6 of Dante's *Inferno.* Cf. *HB,* 536: "prim diabolical dogs."

12. The one exception, "Patty's Peanut Butter," might be an allusion to George Washington Carver, the famous black agriculturalist and peanut innovator. O'Connor's father owned the Dixie Realty and Dixie Construction Company in Savannah, Georgia.

13. Cf. Dante's *Inferno,* which journeys "from first to second circle" to "smaller space and greater pain" (Canto 5, xx). Their trip takes them to the smaller space and greater pain of Atlanta's poor black neighborhood.

14. Hebrews 12:1 begins: "Wherefore seeing we also are compassed about with so great a cloud of witnesses . . ." Cf. O'Connor's description of a peacock's plume: "The eyes in the tail stand for the eyes of the Church. I have a flock of about thirty so I am surrounded" (*HB,* 509).

15. It is unclear whether or not O'Connor was aware of the novel titled *Nigger Heaven,* written by Carl Van Vechten (Urbana: University of Illinois Press, Octagon Books, 1973; orig. 1926). It portrayed Harlem as a "nigger heaven" of sorts, much to the dismay of black critics. The term "nigger heaven" was used in the black vernacular as a reference to the segregated seating area in the back, upper reaches of a theater—what today would be referred to as the peanut gallery. Van Vechten was a white patron of Langston Hughes and Zora Neal Hurston. O'Connor's depiction of a "nigger heaven" differs from Van Vechten's by charging her narrative with Christian elements, one of which gives the story its title, and by distancing her narrator from the racist perspective of her protagonist.

16. Cf. John 14:6: "Jesus saith unto him, 'I am the way, the truth, and the life; no man cometh unto the Father, but by me.'"

17. In a letter to fellow writer Cecil Dawkins, O'Connor notes how "most mountain people are hostile" to Negroes: "In Georgia the sun doesn't set on a Negro in a mountain county. The people run them out" (*HB,* 298).

18. References to a racial caste system are commonplace in O'Connor's short stories: for example, see "Everything that Rises Must Converge" and "Revelation."

19. The grandfather later comments, "And standing their grinning like a chim-pan-zee while a nigger woman gives you direction. Great gawd!" (263).

20. Earlier Mr. Head had shown Nelson the sewer system of downtown Atlanta, which he described as "full of rats" and a place where "a man could slide into it and be sucked along down endless pitchblack tunnels" (259). When his betrayal of Nelson appears to divide them forever, Mr. Head "felt that if he saw a sewer entrance he would drop down into it and let himself be carried away; and he could imagine the boy standing by, watching with only a slight interest, while he disappeared" (267).

21. Cf. Dante's *Inferno,* Cantos 31 and 32, which features a lake of ice.

22. Lest anyone assume this authority for himself, O'Connor adds, "but I submit that to do this is the business of God and not of any human being" (*MM,* 174). Genesis 50:20 reads: "But as for you, ye thought evil against me; but God meant it unto good, to bring to pass, as it is this day, to save much people alive."

23. Cf. Col. 2:13-15: "And you being dead in your sins and the uncircumcision of your flesh, hath he quickened together with him, having forgiven you all trespasses; blotting out the handwriting of ordinances that was against us, which was contrary to us, and took it out of the way, nailing it to the cross; and having spoiled principalities and powers, he made a show of them openly, triumphing over them in it."

24. Cf. Mr. Head's earlier joke on the train, which drew great laughter from the travelers and much pride from Nelson in his grandfather (257).

25. *HB,* 505. Regarding one student who asked her about the "enlightenment" she was supposed to get from one of O'Connor's stories, O'Connor commented that "she didn't want to enjoy them, she just wanted to figure them out" (*MM,* 107). We hasten to add that O'Connor insisted that a good story must communicate meaning by concrete details rather than conveying abstract themes: "The novelist makes his statements by selection, and if he is any good, he selects every word for a reason, every detail for a reason, every incident for a reason, and arranges them in a certain time-sequence for a reason" (*MM,* 75).

26. On another occasion, O'Connor said that she followed the "redemption" of her characters through their lives (*HB,* 536).

27. *HB,* 275; see also *HB,* 389, on grace using "as its medium the imperfect, purely human, and even the hypocritical."

28. On the "topical as poison," see O'Connor's "Letter to 'A,'" *HB,* 537, and Sarah Gordon, "Maryat and Julian and the 'Not So Bloodless Revolution,'" *Flannery O'Connor Bulletin* 21 (1992): 25-36.

29. In the same way, the reader is meant to ponder the result of The Misfit's shooting of the grandmother in "A Good Man is Hard to Find."

30. She also observed, "Ideal Christianity doesn't exist, because anything the human being touches, even Christian truth, he deforms slightly in his own image" (*HB,* 516).

L. Lamar Nisly (essay date fall 2006)

SOURCE: Nisly, L. Lamar. "Wingless Chickens or Catholics from the Bayou: Conceptions of Audience in O'Connor and Gautreaux." *Christianity and Literature* 56, no. 1 (fall 2006): 63-85.

[*In the following essay, Nisly contrasts the relationship between reader and text in works by O'Connor and Louisianan author Tim Gautreaux, focusing on "A Good Man Is Hard to Find" and "Welding with Children," respectively.*]

The critical receptions of Flannery O'Connor and Tim Gautreaux are at very different points, with O'Connor's stories clearly seen as canonical and Gautreaux still in the midst of his writing career. Yet they also have obvious connections, as Gautreaux, who lives in southern Louisiana, makes apparent in interviews:

> Well, naturally an influence on just about everybody writing in the South was Flannery O'Connor. She's probably the country's premier short story writer. If you analyze her stories you see she was working with tragedy, and humor, and irony. And putting all of these elements together in a technically perfect way. . . . Also, you know, she was Catholic, and I can relate to that because I'm Catholic.
>
> (Gautreaux, Hebert-Leiter interview 3)

More succinctly, he writes, "When I feel I'm losing my sense of humor, or that I'm becoming sentimental, I read an O'Connor story and her prose adjusts my perceptions" ("Behind the Great Stories" 1). Gautreaux's stated appreciation of O'Connor rings true when one reads his fiction, for particularly in his stories, his mix of humor and serious intent calls to mind O'Connor's best fiction.

Yet even though the two authors do share essential commonalities, a salient difference emerges within their fiction: *their sense of audience.* As I will explain, O'Connor presents a very clear vision of her audience—her "hostile audience," as she says in many of her essays—that she imagines herself addressing. It is an audience with a secular perspective that is uncomprehending and likely antagonistic to her Catholic vision, an audience prone to be confused and put off by her fiction. In contrast, Gautreaux has a very different conception of his audience. Gautreaux describes his audience in terms that sound warm, friendly, companionable. He imagines a broad range of readers, all of whom can connect with what he is writing. I argue that because of these divergent understandings of audience, O'Connor and Gautreaux develop strikingly different tones in their fiction, particularly through their treatment of characters. Finally, as I will show by analyzing **"A Good Man Is Hard To Find,"** O'Connor's prophetic stance to her unbelieving audience leads her, at times, to create characters as acted parables, characters who perform disturbing actions so that O'Connor can confront her reader. In contrast, "Welding with Children" reveals that Gautreaux's "audience as companion" position allows him to present an early crisis in the story and then guide his character to embrace the moral position he knew all along was right.

In his highly influential book *The Rhetoric of Fiction,* first published in 1961, Wayne Booth argues that critics have assumed for too long that "True artists . . . take no thought of their readers. They write for themselves" (89). Booth insists, to the contrary, that the audience always plays a role in literature: "nothing the writer does can be finally understood in isolation from his effort to make it all accessible to someone else—his peers, himself as imagined reader, his audience" (397). Booth in particular stresses the importance that shared beliefs play in this interaction between writer and reader, insisting that "literature is radically dependent on the concurrence of beliefs of authors and readers" (140). Yet Booth remains primarily concerned about the way a text creates a reader, considering the way the implied author addresses the implied or postulated audience (422).

Peter Rabinowitz creates a more complicated analysis of readers, working to sort out the various levels of audience addressed by an author. Rabinowitz argues that there are the actual, authorial, and narrative audiences. The actual audience "consists of the flesh-and-blood people who read the book. This is the audience that booksellers are most concerned with—but it happens to be the audience over which an author has no guaranteed control" (*Before Reading* 20). In contrast,

> Both the authorial and narrative audiences are abstractions, but they are abstractions in radically different senses. The authorial audience is a hypothetical construction of what the author expects his or her readers to be like; the narrative audience, on the other hand, is an imaginative creation by the author—something he or she hopes to convince the readers to pretend to become.
>
> ("Where" 23)

Of most interest for my purposes is Rabinowitz's authorial audience; no writer can know with certainty who will make up his or her actual audience, but "no author can make any rhetorical decisions (conscious or unconscious) without relying on prior assumptions about precisely what values, experiences, habits, and familiarity with artistic conventions his or her readers will bring to the text" ("Where" 5). While Rabinowitz acknowledges the role of the author in constructing the authorial audience, his primary concern is the role of readers in taking on the characteristics of the authorial audience, for "To the extent that we do not, our reading experience will be more or less seriously flawed" ("Where" 5). He particularly notes that no authorial audience is pristine, free from presuppositions; instead, "you need to ask what sort of *corrupted* reader this particular author wrote for: what were that reader's beliefs, engagements, commitments, prejudices, and stampedings of pity and terror?" (*Before Reading* 26). Rabinowitz presents a compelling case that authors envision a particular, "corrupted" audience as they are writing.

Wingless Chickens

Certainly Rabinowitz's argument rings true for O'Connor, as becomes clear in her letters and essays. She writes in her first letter to Elizabeth Hester, who became an extremely important correspondent (identified in *The Habit of Being* only as "A"),

> the moral sense has been bred out of certain sections of the population, like wings have been bred off certain chickens to produce more white meat on them. This is a generation of wingless chickens, which I suppose is what Nietzsche meant when he said God was dead.
>
> (*Habit* 90)

O'Connor is very aware of these "wingless chickens," for she sees herself as writing her fiction for them. As she further explains in her next letter to Hester,

> One of the awful things about writing when you are a Christian is that for you the ultimate reality is the Incarnation, the present reality is the Incarnation, and nobody believes in the Incarnation; that is, nobody in your audience. My audience are the people who think God is dead. At least these are the people I am conscious of writing for.
>
> (*Habit* 92)

In response to her perceived hostile audience, O'Connor embraces a stance as prophet in her writing, a position she makes clear in letters, essays, and interviews. Insisting that she has "to push as hard as the age that pushes against" her (*Habit* 229), she explains that the fiction writer should be characterized with "prophetic vision," a "realism which does not hesitate to distort appearances in order to show a hidden truth" (*Mystery* 179). O'Connor intends for her fiction to confront and persuade her readers, to convince them that they should turn from a modern skepticism of belief to an encounter with the Divine. Her Catholic outlook so directs her understanding of life that she feels compelled, as one of her literary group colleagues explains, "to hurl protests, as loud and vehement as she could make them, against the two-fold assumption that 'God is dead,' and 'Man is God'; i.e., modern man is now beyond the God of the Bible, and he doesn't need the God of orthodox Christianity" (Kirkland 160).

As she speaks about her audience, O'Connor makes clear for whom she is writing—and who is outside of her focus. O'Connor explicitly rejects writing for a Catholic audience, joking that the audience is too small (*Conversations* 14). However, apart from this practical consideration, I believe she also feels compelled to speak to a secular audience as a means of spreading the good news of the gospel. In one of her most famous statements about her audience, O'Connor provides a vision of a hulking reader unable to understand her fiction. Yet she asserts,

> I know that I must never let him affect my vision, must never let him gain control over my thinking, must never listen to his demands unless they accord with my conscience; yet I feel I must make him see what I have to show, even if my means of making him see have to be extreme.
>
> (qtd. in Feeley 45)

Particularly striking in this quotation is O'Connor's evident fear that her audience cannot comprehend her writing coupled with her own belief that she must only write what grows out of her faith. At the same time, the last phrases indicate that O'Connor is willing to pursue even "extreme" approaches to communicate her message.

Because O'Connor is so aware of writing for an unbelieving audience, she recognizes that her fiction is directly affected by her sense of her audience, particularly lamenting what is not understood by her audience:

> The problem of the novelist who wishes to write about a man's encounter with this God is how he shall make the experience—which is both natural and supernatural—understandable, and credible, to his reader. In any age this would be a problem, but in our own, it is a well-nigh insurmountable one. Today's audience is one in which religious feeling has become, if not atrophied, at least vaporous and sentimental.
>
> (*Mystery* 161)

Attempting to communicate with her audience, then, leads O'Connor to her shocking approach. The fiction that she writes is a response to this unbelieving world, a rejoinder that O'Connor insists on writing even if it is not understood. As Robert Brinkmeyer explains, "That her fiction was often misunderstood and occasionally viciously attacked in reviews reinforced O'Connor's view that she stood far outside the intellectual establishment" (11). Nevertheless, she continued to forge ahead, for, as she insists, "You have to push as hard as the age that pushes against you" (*Habit* 229).

Although O'Connor frequently alludes in her letters to her lecture tours being solely motivated by the need to pay bills, Jean Cash, in her biography, asserts that "O'Connor, by lecturing so widely, created her own pulpit, one from which she could and did use both clarity and humor to enlighten her listeners to the theological intention of her work" (263). Her willingness to "explain" her stories, as she frequently does in her letters and lectures, shows her intense desire for the reader to understand the theological dimensions of her stories.[1] Paul Giles is certainly correct that O'Connor's stories often have "potential ambiguity and excess of signification" which prevent them from "being mere diagrammatic expositions of Catholic principles" (362). Yet O'Connor keenly wants to communicate her core beliefs. She feels compelled to present to her unbelieving readers the "central Christian mystery: that [life] has, for all its horror, been found by God to be worth dying for" (*Mystery* 146). One way to describe her prophetic approach is to say that her message derives from her Catholic faith, but the directness of her method grows from fundamentalist preaching (Brinkmeyer 8). Because O'Connor believed so intensely her core convictions, she put on the mantle of prophet to reach her unbelieving audience.

Catholics from the Bayou

Unlike the collected essays and interviews available from O'Connor, Gautreaux's non-fiction materials are limited to a few brief essays and a series of uncollected—yet very helpful—interviews. From this material, though, it is readily apparent that Gautreaux's perception of his audience is radically different than O'Connor's sense of a hostile reader, as he seeks to appeal to a friendly audience.

Gautreaux was an English professor at Southeastern Louisiana University for thirty years until his retirement in 2002, yet he retains a strong affection for blue-collar, less formally educated people. As he often explains, Gautreaux comes from a blue-collar family; his father was a tugboat captain and his grandfather a steamboat engineer. Even in his self description, he downplays his career as an academic, describing himself as a retired schoolteacher rather than a writer because calling himself a writer "strikes me as being pretentious" (Gautreaux, Scanlan interview 4). Although he sees himself writing in the same Catholic tradition as Walker Percy, he explains, "I'm not a philosopher like Walker Percy. . . . I'm just a Catholic from the bayou. But it's one of the rhythms of life" (qtd. in Larson 2). Gautreaux's stories seem to appeal both to people within his Cajun culture, these Catholics from the Bayou, as well as those from outside southern Louisiana. Similarly, he also hopes to engage an audience that has a widely varied socio-economic and educational background:

> I pride myself in writing a "broad-spectrum" fiction, fiction that appeals to both intellectuals and blue-collar types. Many times I've heard stories of people who don't read short stories, or people who have technical jobs, who like my fiction. . . . My nephew, who installs wiring harnesses on oil rigs, was out on one last year, and he saw a man with his legs dangling over the Gulf, reading a paperback, and he walked up to see what he was reading, and it was my first collection of short stories. And I hear tales over and over about blue-collar types sitting around somewhere reading a Tim Gautreaux book. This is the crossover aspect, the broad-spectrum aspect, that I'm talking about, that I like about what I do.
>
> (Gautreaux, Kane interview 140)

Gautreaux imagines a very diverse audience, all of whom can connect with his tales.

Gautreaux's perception of audience seems clearly shaped by his experience growing up in southern Louisiana, for the shared values that Gautreaux encountered as a child have allowed him to imagine an audience that connects with many of his most firmly held beliefs. Themes of moral decisions and the possibility of grace have been ingrained in Gautreaux, allowing them to emerge naturally in his writing: "It comes from just living in Louisiana in the 1950s. Louisiana is one of those places that has a very strong spiritual presence, even though it's a place where people like to drink and fight" (Gautreaux, Meyering interview 8). He has experienced a solidity of common understandings, and his fiction reveals a conversation with a companion who shares similar beliefs. Gautreaux's goal is not to convert his reader since he already sees the reader as a companion along the way. Indeed, his understandings become clear when he speaks of his years of teaching modern poetry:

> After a while, I saw students struggling so hard to deal with *The Waste Land,* and I started to think, "Why am I making these people suffer so much?" It was so hard to deal with Eliot's early poems—the theme of which was, basically, life sucks—and my ultimate response was "What was your first clue?" . . . That's one of the reasons I like blue-collar people. With all their shortcomings and biases and pent-up angers, most of them understand the value of being good-natured and having a good time. You'd never catch a welder reading *The Waste Land,* thank God.
>
> (Gautreaux, Levasseur and Rabalais interview 31)

Thus, even though Gautreaux is not afraid to take on difficult subjects, his cordial relationship with his audience leads him to a gentler tone, a conversational approach with his readers. Unlike O'Connor, who feels compelled to confront her hostile audience, Gautreaux sees his audience as made up of fellow travelers. Gautreaux's imagined audience, it seems, consists of people who recognize the difficulties in life but, because of their Christian faith, do not see the world as finally brutal and hopeless. What he imagines his audience relating to are the moral questions that he finds compelling. These grounded questions are at the heart of Gautreaux's conception of his audience: "the business about value—what do you do with children, why do you do *anything* in life?—is always behind my fiction" (Gautreaux, Kane interview 135). Gautreaux's stories are not arguments about the right thing to do. Rather, they are tales that embody moral questions and dilemmas, pushing his readers toward decisions that, on some level, Gautreaux seems to believe, they already know are right.

Because of his conception of audience, Gautreaux's fiction embodies the values of Catholicism, community, and family. With a gentleness to his characters and frequently a deft use of humor, Gautreaux creates striking fiction that invites the reader into an individual's struggle with doing what is right. In this effort to choose the good, the character is often supported and confronted by a supportive community and extended family.

Characters in Acted Parables

In O'Connor's story **"Revelation,"** Ruby Turpin amuses herself by considering what type of person she would choose to be if she were not herself. If the reader of fiction were approached by the god of all literature and asked what fictive character he or she would like to become, a reasonable response might be, "Nobody from an O'Connor story!" Life tends to be difficult for O'Connor's characters, a fact often noted by O'Connor's critics. Martha Stephens complains, "what is oppressive about the O'Connor work as a whole, what is sometimes intolerable, is her stubborn refusal to see any good, any beauty or dignity or meaning, in ordinary human life on earth" (9). Joanne McMullen laments, "Impersonality in her treatment of character types forces O'Connor's audience away from any concern for the fates of her characters and often reduces to a ridiculing humor the vagaries of their souls" (21). Even more harshly—although eloquently—Laurence Enjolras insists, "we do not confront human beings; we encounter monsters who assail us either with their defects, with their impairments, or with their clownishness, caught as they are—fierce, violent, pathetic creatures—in the gruesome show of the puppet life through which they totter" (7).[2] In response to these critiques, other critics attempt to show that O'Connor loved some or all of her characters. For instance, Bill Oliver believes that O'Connor had sympathy for characters such as Mr. Head (**"The Artificial Nigger"**), Tanner (**"Judgment Day"**), Parker (**"Parker's Back"**), and the twelve-year-old girl (**"A Temple of the Holy Ghost"**) because, "despite their limitations, they have the capacity to respond with childlike wonder to the mystery of things. They differ radically from most of O'Connor's characters, who fear and try to suppress what they cannot grasp immediately through reason" (9). Sarah Gordon presents a somewhat different list:

> Surely one could argue that such strong and memorable characters as the grandmother, Mrs. McIntyre, and even General Sash, Hazel Motes, and the great-uncle and nephew Tarwater in a sense become lovable to us as readers through the extent to which we invest in their struggles and identify with them. We might surmise these characters were lovable to O'Connor in that sense as well.
>
> (227)

More broadly, Richard Giannone argues that love is at the core of all O'Connor fiction, with the surprising and violent endings reflecting "the overwhelming boldness of divine love invading human life" (*Love* 6).

Given the shock of O'Connor's treatment of her characters along with her explicitly enunciated theology, these wildly divergent responses should perhaps be expected. Characters are gored by a bull, shot by a son, blinded, drowned, raped, stuffed through a banister, wiped out on a family vacation, smashed against a rock, hanged in an attic, and driven over by a tractor. That list does not include the "milder" offenses, such as having a wooden leg stolen, being beaten by a broom, or having a woods burned. Yet my argument is that all of this discussion about whether or not O'Connor had compassion for her characters to some extent misses the point. Focusing on O'Connor's prophetic stance may help us know how to think about her characters.

It is important at the outset to insist that O'Connor was a writer not an allegorist, so her characters function as characters, not as representations. Sarah Fodor rightly points out that her characters "must be believable before they can stand for something else" (112). However, given her self-understood role as a prophet—what Giannone calls "a one-woman war against the age's moral blindness" (*Hermit* 6)—we may be led astray if we focus too heavily on the particulars of what happens to her characters. For I believe that, in the tradition of the Old Testament prophets, O'Connor was less concerned about her characters than she was about her *audience,* an audience, as we have seen, that she perceived as hostile to her message.[3]

O'Connor was certainly very familiar with the prophets, for she peppered her fiction with references to them and read books that focus on them. For instance, when Parker in **"Parker's Back"** is thrown out of the pool hall, "a calm descended on the pool hall as nerve shattering as if the long barn-like room were the ship from which Jonah had been cast into the sea" (***Collected Works*** 672). O. E. Parker's name, when he finally utters it, is also revealed to combine an Old Testament prophet's name, Obadiah, with Elihue, meaning "He is God." In **"The Lame Shall Enter First,"** Rufus Johnson chews up and swallows a page from the Bible and exclaims, "I've eaten it like Ezekiel and it was honey to my mouth!" (***Collected Works*** 628). *The Violent Bear It Away* contains several references to biblical prophets. At the moment that old Tarwater figures out that Rayber had written an article about him, "His eyeballs swerved from side to side as if he were pinned in a strait jacket again. Jonah, Ezekiel, Daniel, he was at that moment all of them—the swallowed, the lowered, the enclosed" (***Collected Works*** 378). Young Tarwater's arrival at Rayber's house sparks another prophetic reference, since "His whole body felt hollow as if he had been lifted like Habakkuk by the hair of his head, borne swiftly through the night and set down in the place of his mission" (***Collected Works*** 385). And as Tarwater drifts in and out of sleep while remembering his struggle to drown Bishop, "His pale face twitched and grimaced. He might have been Jonah clinging wildly to the whale's tongue" (***Collected Works*** 462).

Besides her own reading of the Bible, O'Connor's knowledge about the prophets was increased through books that she read to review. She praises J. C. Chaine's *God's Heralds* (1955) as an "invaluable aid in deepening appreciation of prophetic revelation and the conditions under which this was given to the world" (*Presence of Grace* 41). She is even more appreciative of Bruce Vawter's *The Conscience of Israel* (1961) for placing the prophets in their historical context. She notes, "In this setting alone it is possible to understand an Isaiah walking naked as a warning to Egypt, and [sic] Hosea agonizing over his prostitute wife or an Ezekiel baking his bread over dung to symbolize the destruction to come" (*Presence of Grace* 141).[4] Through these references and books that she read, it becomes clear that O'Connor was well familiar with the Old Testament prophets.

Indeed, O'Connor's comment about Vawter's study points toward the way that I understand O'Connor's characters: just as God had the prophets perform odd, even disturbing, actions as a way of communicating God's message to the Israelites, so O'Connor causes distressing outcomes for her characters as a means of reaching her hostile audience. The litany of Old Testament "acted parables," as Curt Kuhl identifies them, is as bizarre as it is lengthy. Besides his walking around naked and barefoot (Isa. 20:2-3), Isaiah is also directed to give his sons such odd names as "a remnant shall return" (Isa. 7:3, 8:3-4). Jeremiah must walk around wearing a yoke (Jer. 27:2) and is ordered to buy land when it appears that all is lost (Jer. 32:25). Ezekiel, the prophet with the longest list of acted parables, is directed in astonishing ways: to be tied hand and foot while unable to speak (Ezek. 3:25); to lie on his left side for 390 days and then on his right for 40 more days (Ezek. 4:4-6); to bake with human dung—although he receives an exemption to use animal dung (Ezek. 4:12-15); to shave, weigh, and burn his hair (Ezek. 5:1-2); to put aside any grieving for his dead wife (Ezek. 24:14, 18); to be unable to speak (Ezek. 33:22-3). Though Hosea's directions are not as numerous, his assignment is astonishing: to marry an unchaste woman, sometimes identified as a prostitute (Hos. 1:3). Even after she leaves him to chase other men, God directs Hosea to bring her back, although he is not to have sexual relations with her for a time (Hos. 3:1-3). In each of these instances, the word comes to the prophet to carry out this task, apparently with no concern for the prophet's own comfort, embarrassment, or welfare. What is foremost for God and the prophets is communicating a message from the divine to the people. As Kuhl dryly notes, "Ordinary standards of normality are not, of course, to be applied to a prophet . . ." (123). More substantively, E. W. Heaton explains,

> The prophets were violent, because they lived in a society where honesty and decency were being violated everyday. They could not profess a vocation from the Lord, the God of righteousness, and stand aloof when disgusting luxury was being purchased at the price of the blood of the defenceless poor.
>
> (60)

Following God's command and warning the people were foremost for the prophets, not a concern about the individual prophet's well-being. Nothing could come in the way of presenting the message as dramatically as possible, for "Prophets are first and foremost 'proclaimers'" (Sawyer 1).

To read O'Connor's fiction as prophetic utterances, then, changes the way we see the stories. They are realistic in a sense, since they are peopled with real, if odd, characters, typically in a rural Georgia setting. But they cannot be read as fully realistic because our focus, if we are considering them as prophetic speech, needs to be on the effect these characters and their outcomes have on the audience rather than any deep sympathy for the individual character. Seeing characters as taking part in an acted parable becomes perhaps most clear when we examine O'Connor's most shockingly famous story, **"A Good Man Is Hard to**

Find" (1953), a story that O'Connor often read aloud and one that many readers find compelling and disgusting, often all at the same time.[5] Indeed, in her comments about this story, O'Connor implies a reading such as I am suggesting, although she did not, of course, use the term "acted parable." In an introduction to her reading of this story, O'Connor tries to signal her audience how to understand her fiction: "in this story you should be on the lookout for such things as the action of grace in the Grandmother's soul, and not for the dead bodies" (*Mystery* 113). Similarly, in an interview response on the issue of brutality in her stories, O'Connor says,

> There really isn't much brutality. It always amuses me when people say "brutality." People keep referring to the brutality in the stories, but even **"A Good Man Is Hard to Find"** is, in a way, a comic, stylized thing. It is not naturalistic writing and so you can't really call it brutal.
>
> (*Conversations* 58)

Given the list of violent actions I mentioned earlier, O'Connor's response may initially seem somewhat disingenuous. Granted, it does appear to stretch credulity to say that there is no brutality in her fiction, but O'Connor's comment does helpfully point us away from fully naturalistic writing and toward a view of acted parables, with characters' action more important for its contribution to the total effect of the story rather than the outcome of an individual character.

"A Good Man Is Hard to Find" certainly performs O'Connor's common seduction of the reader with its comic ordinariness, as we become introduced to a bickering family preparing for a summer vacation. The humor of the pretentious grandmother's seeing herself as a lady, the familiar complaint of the father's seat kicked by the children in the backseat, the description of the redneck Red Sammy Butts's barbecue stand all draw in the audience and encourage us to lower our guard. The bizarre turn occurs when the grandmother's cat springs free from her basket, claws the father Bailey, and causes an accident. Shortly thereafter, the Misfit and his henchmen arrive on the scene, and the mood shifts from humorous to darkly disturbing. In small groups, the family is invited into the woods to be shot while the grandmother, hoping to distract him long enough to let her live, keeps up a running conversation with the Misfit. Finally, after a prolonged discussion about Jesus and the effect of his coming to earth, the grandmother suddenly reaches out her hand and touches the Misfit, exclaiming, "Why you're one of my babies. You're one of my own children!" (***Collected Works*** 152). In response, the Misfit shoots her.

Given the startling nature of this story, it is easy to become overwhelmed in the details of destruction. But just as the people of Israel were to remain focused on God's call to redemption rather than on Isaiah's nakedness or Ezekiel's sore side, reading O'Connor's stories as prophetic literature reminds us to focus on the effect on the reader rather than the harm done her characters. As such, the story works in at least two directions. First, the grandmother has been shown to operate entirely on the surface, being concerned about wearing proper clothing so that in case of an accident—which, of course, did occur—people would know she is a lady. But beyond her prattling chatter, the grandmother appears never to have deeply connected with others, never seen beyond whether or not someone has the proper upbringing to be a "good man"—nor ever realistically examined her own soul. Almost in spite of herself, in the midst of what is for her a meaningless conversation about the most important questions (in O'Connor's view) of how we respond to Christ's life and sacrificial death, the grandmother's "head cleared for an instant" and she acknowledges her deep kinship to the Misfit (***Collected Works*** 152). O'Connor uses this acknowledgement to show the centrality of a deep love and compassion for others, insisting that we must embrace their and our own sinfulness as part of our fallen humanness. The grandmother's revelation at the very end of her life leads to the Misfit's wonderful line, "She would have been a good woman if it had been somebody there to shoot her every minute of her life" (***Collected Works*** 153). Through the grandmother's change and violent death, O'Connor hopes to force the reader to examine his or her own soul as well.[6]

Part of the power of this story, of course, derives from the second punch that the ending packs, for O'Connor's acted parable includes not only the grandmother but also the Misfit. The Misfit has been shown to be a rationalist, insisting that he recognizes the potential impact of what Jesus claims to have done but, because of scant evidence, he cannot be certain of the truth of Christ's supposed actions. With his glasses, his professorial manner, and his carefully considered skepticism, one can almost imagine him with a coffee cup rather than a gun in his hand, lecturing to a group of college students. In what I trust is an aberration from professors, though, he informs the grandmother that he has determined that given the uncertainty of what is true, the only approach that makes sense is to "enjoy the few minutes you got left the best way you can—by killing somebody or burning down his house or doing some other meanness to him. No pleasure but meanness" (***Collected Works*** 152). After his encounter with the grandmother, when the Misfit's companions return from their murders, one of them says, "Some fun!" The Misfit responds, "It's no real pleasure in life" (***Collected Works*** 153). Though we are left with no narrative direction to know what will happen in the Misfit's life, it is clear from this response that the grandmother's action of graciously reaching out to him has affected his calm rejection of belief. Again, in seeing this gesture as part of an acted parable, we can see that the central issue is not exactly how the Misfit might eventually respond but rather how the audience is moved by the grandmother's sacramental act.[7] Will this astonishing gift of a recognized common humanity move the reader as it has unsettled the Misfit? Will the reader follow the Misfit's lead and move from a position of settled disbelief to being a seeker? If so, O'Connor's prophetic story will have found success.

Everything Worth Doing Hurts Like Hell

"Welding with Children," the title story in Gautreaux's second volume of stories, serves well as an example of his fiction, for it embodies many of Gautreaux's best attributes. Although Catholicism is sometimes overtly a part of his fiction, in this story none of the characters is Catholic—and, in fact, the only mention of Catholicism is a passing satiric comment that some Catholics contribute only a dollar each week, "but there's so many of them, and the church has so many services a weekend, the priests can run the place on volume like Wal-Mart" (15). Nevertheless, the story's humor, gentleness to characters, and distinctly moral tone serve as a delightful entrée into Gautreaux's fiction.

One of only a few first-person narratives in Gautreaux's oeuvre, Gautreaux explains the origin of the story:

> I was in Wal-Mart one day, in the compressed-air driven tools, sandpaper, Bondo, and auto paint aisle, when I heard a phlegm-filled smoker's voice float over the racks from the motor oil section. It was a middle-aged man talking to a friend he'd bumped into. He was complaining about his three daughters, who kept having children out of wedlock and then bringing them over to his house for him and his wife to take care of. The old guy had a great voice, southern, smart, and full of humor. But it was full of hurt too. His blue-collar salary was being eaten up by Cokes and diapers, and his blue-collar heart was smashed flat by children who were running their lives like a drunk runs a truck with bald tires downhill in a rainstorm.
>
> (*Best Stories* 289)

From that starting point, Gautreaux could have written a sad or bitter story—or his tale could have been a mere send-up of this unfortunate grandfather. Instead, Gautreaux has created a story with plenty of humor, but also a warmth and care for Bruton, this grandfather blessed with four squabbling grandchildren to watch.

To draw in the reader, Gautreaux infuses the story with some of the funniest lines written since O'Connor was at the height of fictional prowess. Bruton describes his brief experience as a student at Louisiana State University. He imagines that the Pakistani composition instructor sent their portfolios "back to Pakistan for his relatives to use as stove wood." In the chemistry class, with a professor who heated Campbell's soup over a Bunsen burner, he sat "way in the back." "Time or two, when I could see the blackboard off on the horizon, I almost got the hang of something, and I was glad of that" (3). His daughters drop off the grandchildren, Nu-Nu, Moonbeam, Tammynette, and Freddie, and his assignment is to weld his oldest daughter's bedrail.

> Now, what the hell you can do in bed that'll cause the end of a iron rail to break off is beyond me, but she can't afford another one on her burger-flipping salary, she said, so I got to fix it with four little kids hanging on my coveralls.
>
> (1)

With little for the children to do, they begin using an engine hanging from a tree as a swing: "Tammynette and Moonbeam gave the engine a long shove, got distracted by a yellow butterfly playing in a clump of pig-weed, and that nine-hundred pound V-8 kind of ironed them out on the backswing" (3-4). Bruton tries, amidst hilarious interruptions from the children, to talk to them about the Bible, a process that has little success because "the Bible was turning into one big adventure film" for them (10). Bruton appears at a loss to know how to deal with these four children who have been foisted upon him, particularly because he was not especially involved as a parent with his own children. Yet Gautreaux refuses to allow the humor to take over the story, instead using the comedy to invite the reader along for a closer consideration of Bruton and his difficult situation. As Liam Callanan writes in the *New York Times Book Review,* "Despite the laughter, the writing never entirely succumbs to the humor, and by the end Gautreaux is able to wrestle out a few moral lessons that even Tammynette can appreciate" (31). With his humor, Gautreaux creates a light tone, entices the reader, and creates space for a conversation about the deadly serious questions raised in the story.

These sober concerns circle around the prominent overlapping themes evident in much of Gautreaux's fiction. As often occurs, the larger community plays an important role. In two other stories in the *Welding with Children* collection, for instance, members of the community—almost against their own intentions—find themselves connecting with a vulnerable person: in "The Piano Tuner," Claude helps a lonely woman find work as a lounge pianist; in "Resistance," elderly Mr. Boudreaux assists the neglected girl next door with a science project. As a humorous twist on this theme in "Welding with Children," the impetus that moves Bruton to try to change is old Mr. Fordlyson's muttered comment of "bastardmobile" when Bruton arrives at the grocery store with his grandchildren in tow. Bruton later seeks out Mr. Fordlyson, recognizing that for all his nastiness, he has managed to raise his children well. The narrative provides clues that Fordlyson can provide needed wisdom for Bruton, for as he and his grandchildren are reading through the illustrated Bible, Moonbeam points out that Fordlyson looks like God (9). Bruton meets Fordlyson under a pecan tree called by the locals the "Tree of Knowledge," and Gautreaux insists on the Garden of Eden connection by Fordlyson's stopping Bruton from eating, with a command, "Don't eat that green pecan—it'll make you sick" (15). Fordlyson emphasizes a point typically important in Gautreaux's stories: the worth of children and the effort that relatives (commonly in his fiction, grandparents) must expend to help their children do what is right. Specifically, Fordlyson gives Bruton a list of duties:

> He pulled down one finger on his right hand with the forefinger of the left. "Go join the Methodists." Another finger went down and he told me, "Every Sunday, bring them children to church." A third finger, and he said, "And keep 'em with you as much as you can."
>
> I shook my head. "I already raised my kids."
>
> Fordlyson looked at me hard and didn't have to say what he was thinking. He glanced down at the ground between his smooth-toe lace-ups. "And clean up your yard."
>
> (16)

Though put in the mouth of an annoying character, this advice that Fordlyson gives connects to a core value that Gautreaux enunciates. He argues,

> You know, you don't give somebody values when they're fourteen or fifteen—you give them when they're two and three and four. Then when they're seven and they reach the age of reason, you've got to hit them real hard. [Others] would say, 'Well, I'll let my kids—when they grow up and when they're 21 they can decide whether or not they'll believe in God.' I think they're taking a gigantic risk. I don't particularly believe in that.
>
> (Gautreaux, Meyering interview 11)

This concern emerges in many of Gautreaux's stories, including "The Courtship of Merlin LeBlanc" and "Little Frogs in a Ditch" (both in *Same Place, Same Things*). It is just such an engaged parenting role that Bruton is beginning to embrace by the end of the story.

The moral choices characters make are central to Gautreaux's fiction. As Erin McGraw points out, he focuses on what O'Connor refers to as manners: "He writes about how people should act, and how people really do act. The gap is wide" (736). While they share common concern with what people do and how they behave, Gautreaux differs significantly from O'Connor in his treatment of his characters. Rather than O'Connor's prophetic model of using her characters to make a point with her readers, Gautreaux tends to be kinder to his characters, treating them with respect and allowing them to change within the course of a story. As Ed Piacentino points out, growing from his Catholic perspective, Gautreaux treats even his misfit characters sympathetically and with compassion (1). Again, to draw a specific comparison to O'Connor's **"A Good Man Is Hard to Find,"** Bruton, just like the grandmother, has a crisis that causes him to change, to enlarge his vision of his responsibility and connections. But rather than learning this insight at the end of a gun, Bruton's crisis occurs with hearing his car called a "bastardmobile," an incident that takes place on the story's fourth page. Bruton has the rest of the story to learn and begin to change in response to this crisis.

Bruton's transformation begins with an acknowledgement of his guilt and responsibility. "I started thinking about my four daughters. None of them has any religion to speak of. I thought they'd pick it up from their mamma, like I did from mine, but LaNelle always worked so much, she just had time to cook, clean, transport, and fuss" (*Welding* 7). Recognizing his mistakes but still immersed in a sense of helplessness, he says, "I guess a lot of what's wrong with my girls is my fault, but I don't know what I could've done different" (7). As he acknowledges the squalor of their lives, exemplified by the junk in his yard, "I formed a little fantasy about gathering all these kids into my Caprice and heading out northwest to start over, away from their mammas, TVs, mildew, their casino-mad grandmother, and Louisiana in general" (12). Yet, in a sign of his growing self-understanding, he "realized we couldn't drive away from ourselves. We couldn't escape in the bastardmobile" (12). One can almost hear echoes of the Harrison Ford character in the movie *Six Days, Seven Nights,* deriding the idea of people seeking to find happiness on a tropical paradise island: "It's an island, babe. If you don't bring it here, you won't find it here." Bruton accepts that whatever good will happen with his grandchildren will have to happen here, amidst the mess and distractions of their lives—but he decides that he can act to provide these children with more support than he gave their mothers.

Because she sees her audience as hostile, O'Connor's central point is to provide a shocking conclusion, hoping to jolt her readers into a confrontation with Christianity. Because he sees his audience as companions, Gautreaux follows his characters past their crisis, allowing his readers to experience changes that they themselves may need to make. Both approaches carry with them some risks, for O'Connor's readers may simply be put off by her extreme treatment of characters and turn away from her fiction. In contrast, Gautreaux's readers may too easily encounter Bruton's growth without feeling ethically challenged. Yet when most effective, each approach allows the author to connect with her or his imagined audience, pushing the reader to consider ultimate concerns.

In significant measure, Bruton does not need to experience a conversion, more a gentle nudge—or, perhaps more fittingly, a kick in the behind—to turn him back to what, on some level, he already knew he should do. Yet these changes, in Gautreaux's fiction or in life, are never cheap or easy. After Fordlyson offers his new four commandments, he smiles a mean smile and says, "Bruton, everything worth doing hurts like hell" (16). The final movement of the story shows Bruton embracing this pain and hard work. He cleans up his yard, hauling out "four derelict cars, six engines, four washing machines, ten broken lawn mowers, and two and one-quarter tons of scrap iron" (16). He cuts the grass, paints the shop and the house. He welcomes his grandchildren to stay at his house. As the story closes, Bruton and the children are planning to hang a tire swing from a tree and the youngest child has just said his first words:

> The baby brought me in focus, somebody's blue eyes looking at me hard. He blew spit over his tongue and cried out, "Da-da," and I put him on my knee, facing away toward the cool green branches of my biggest willow oak.
>
> (19)

Bruton has learned in the course of the story, has accepted that raising children is what he must do. The baby's gurgled words identifying him as a father suggest that he is taking on a role that he failed earlier with his own children, embracing the morally correct position that he needed to re-learn from his community. And Gautreaux makes this point quietly and with humor to his friendly audience.

Conclusion

O'Connor's focus on her audience seems to have served as a central driving force behind her writing. Frequently in her essays and her letters, she referred to her sense of her audience and her prophetic desire to influence them. In describing the role of a Hebrew prophet, Jewish theologian Abraham Heschel writes in 1962,

> To a person endowed with prophetic sight, everyone else appears blind; to a person whose ear perceives God's voice, everyone else appears deaf. No one is just; no knowing is strong enough, no trust complete enough. The prophet hates the approximate, he shuns the middle of the road. . . . Carried away by the challenge, the demand to straighten out man's ways, the prophet is strange, one-sided, an unbearable extremist.
>
> (16)

In the context of O'Connor's work, Heschel's words about the prophet have astonishing resonances. Certainly O'Connor's single-minded insistence that following Christ is the only possible antidote to her hostile audience's spiritual illness makes her seem to some an "unbearable extremist." She ardently resisted the reasonable, middle-of-the-road responses of the modern rationalism, seeing those analyses as simply a mask for unbelief. Perhaps even more striking is the resemblance between the first section of Heschel's comments and O'Connor's most famous description of her method, written in 1957:

> When you can assume that your audience holds the same beliefs you do, you can relax a little and use more normal means of talking to it; when you have to assume that it does not, then you have to make your vision apparent by shock—to the hard of hearing you shout, and for the almost-blind you draw large and startling figures
>
> (*Mystery* 34)

To the prophet O'Connor, her unbelieving audience appeared indeed deaf and blind, and she spent her writing career attempting to penetrate their limited understanding. For as a prophet, O'Connor could imagine no more important task for her fiction than to have it shock a reader into believing.

Gautreaux's view of his audience as companion leads him to a different tone and approach. Gautreaux's deep understanding of the people with whom he grew up and about whom he writes is made clear in a brief essay, "How Sweet It Was," that focuses on Louisiana's sugar mills. As he draws us into the web of connections that make up the community, he describes how the mill locomotive was also used to haul children to school and to Mass. Thus, Gautreaux explains, the old engineer says that when the railroad was shut down, "he felt as if a relative had died. His reaction was an emotional connection not with a machine but with the life the machine provided. Such was the mill community's relationship with the factory itself" (25). These kinds of profound relationships that Gautreaux formed when he was growing up seem to have fed into his sense of story writing and of audience. For in his fiction, his imagined audience is composed of people who share a common set of values, of a community that needs only to be called back to its best conception of itself. As such, Gautreaux's fiction does not have the prophetic ring of O'Connor's stories, for he is not trying to convert his readers. In this context, Wayne Booth's comment is instructive: "The reader whom the implied author writes to can be found as much in the text's silence as in its overt appeals. What the author felt no need to mention tells us who he thinks we'll be—or hopes we'll be" (423). Gautreaux feels no need to make a case for Catholic beliefs and values or the importance of community because they have become ingrained in him and, he assumes, in his audience, his companions on the journey.

Notes

1. O'Connor's willingness to speak about her stories is very different, for example, from her contemporary writer, Bernard Malamud, whose fiction she much admired. Malamud was reticent about seeming to explicate his writing, telling an interviewer, "You know one thing that I don't like about what we're doing is that I have begun to explain my fiction, and I don't like to do that" (*Conversations with Bernard Malamud* 143).
2. Katherine Hemple Prown views O'Connor as being especially negative toward female characters, citing as evidence that O'Connor said she admired only three characters, all male: Hazel Motes and both Tarwaters. Young girls could occasionally escape O'Connor's wrath, but for O'Connor, "ladyhood was a comical state at best, a perilous and cursed state at worse [sic]. Women who embraced it deserved their fate" (6). Christina Bieber Lake reasonably points out, in response to Prown, that few of O'Connor's characters—male or female—escape unharmed, so it seems difficult to draw conclusions about her views of women from her treatment of characters (121).
3. In focusing on O'Connor's desire to preach, Brinkmeyer notes that she is not as explicit as an evangelist, yet "her underlying strategies of shock and distortion are very similar to the evangelist's in terms of technique and intention" (7). Ralph Wood focuses on the connection between her tone and the Old Testament: "The narrative voice that speaks in her work is akin to the Old Testament in its unapologetic directness of approach to the reader" (81). The critic who most directly touches on my current point is John May:

   > O'Connor understood that the prophet interprets events in the light of the covenant, announcing God's judgment of the people's sins and His call to fidelity. An action or gesture of the prophet . . . often accompanies or replaces his words (e.g., Jeremiah's yoke and Isaiah's nakedness), a mode of prophetic symbolism that O'Connor frequently employed.
   >
   > (17)

   However, May does not explore this connection more fully.
4. Vawter writes, "The symbolic act, whether accompanied by words or not, is a dramatized prophecy. Jeremiah's yoke, Isaiah's nakedness, Ezekiel's dumbness, Hosea's marriage, are all symbolic acts" (51).
5. To offer just one example: One summer, I participated in a summer seminar focusing on the public theology of our students, with participants drawn from across the disciplines. As my contribution to the seminar's reading, I requested "A Good Man Is Hard To Find," since I see it as a form of public theology for O'Connor. Although the theology professor leading the seminar never spoke with me directly, I learned from another participant that she refused to have this story discussed because she was appalled by its gore.
6. When critics focus too fully on the characters as real people, they can be led to make odd assertions. For instance, Sally Fitzgerald finds this story to have a "happy ending," for the grandmother is in death child-like,

   > echoing the requisite for entering the cloudless kingdom of heaven, which was for Flannery O'Connor the only happy ending to be sought, or for that matter to be hoped for, by any of us. The grandmother has accepted the grace offered to her; she has passed the test of real charity and been transformed by her realization.
   >
   > (76)

   Fitzgerald's reading of the story is generally sound, but her insistence of seeing the positive impact of the story as a "happy ending" results from a misplaced need to evaluate how a *character* experienced the story rather than the reader.
7. O'Connor does offer some speculative hope about the Misfit:

   > I prefer to think that, however unlikely this may seem, the old lady's gesture, like the mustard-seed, will grow to be a great crow-filled tree in the Misfit's heart, and will be enough of a pain to him there to turn him into the prophet he was meant to become. But that's another story.
   >
   > (*Mystery* 112-13)

Works Cited

Booth, Wayne C. *The Rhetoric of Fiction.* Second ed. Chicago: U of Chicago P, 1983.

Brinkmeyer, Robert H., Jr. "A Closer Walk with Thee: Flannery O'Connor and Southern Fundamentalists." *The Southern Literary Journal* 18.2 (Spring 1986): 3-13.

Callanan, Liam. "La. Stories." *New York Times Book Review* 3 Oct. 1999: 31.

Cash, Jean. *Flannery O'Connor: A Life.* Knoxville: U of Tennessee P, 2000.

Enjolras, Laurence. *Flannery O'Connor's Characters.* New York: UP of America, 1998.

Feeley, Kathleen, S. S. N. D. *Flannery O'Connor: Voice of the Peacock.* New York: Fordham UP, 1982.

Fitzgerald, Sally. "Happy Endings." *Image* 16 (Summer 1997): 73-80.

Fodor, Sarah J. *"No Literary Orthodoxy": Flannery O'Connor and the New Critics.* Diss. U of Chicago, 1994.

Gautreaux, Tim. "Behind The Great Stories there are Great Sentences." *Boston Globe* 19 Oct. 1997: P4. NewsBank.

———. Contributors' Notes. *The Best American Short Stories 1998.* Ed. Garrison Keillor. New York: Houghton Mifflin, 1998.

———. "How Sweet It Was." *Preservation* May/June 2005: 24-25.

———. Interview with Christopher Scanlan. *Creative Loafing.* 9 May 2005. <http://charlotte.creativeloafing.com/2004-06-16/news_cover3.htmlprintout 1-4.

———. Interview with Darlene Meyering. Calvin College Festival of Faith & Writing. Grand Rapids, MI. 22 April 2004.

———. Interview with Jennifer Levasseur and Kevin Rabalais. *Mississippi Review* 27.3 (1999): 19-40.

———. Interview with Julie Kane. "A Postmodern Southern Moralist and Storyteller: Tim Gautreaux." *Voces de America, American Voices.* Ed. Laura P. Alonso Gallo. Cadiz, Spain: Aduana Vieja, 2004. 123-45.

———. Interview with Maria Hebert-Leiter. "An Interview with Tim Gautreaux." *The Carolina Quarterly* 57.2 (Summer 2005). Bluffton U Literature Resource Center. 18 Jan. 2006. printout 1-9.

———. *Same Place, Same Things.* New York: Picador USA, 1996.

———. *Welding with Children.* New York: Picador USA, 1999.

Giannone, Richard. *Flannery O'Connor and the Mystery of Love.* Urbana: U of Illinois P, 1989.

———. *Flannery O'Connor, Hermit Novelist.* Urbana: U of Illinois P, 2000.

Giles, Paul. *American Catholic Arts and Fiction: Culture, Ideology, Aesthetics.* Cambridge Studies in American Literature and Culture. New York: Cambridge UP, 1992.

Gordon, Sarah. *Flannery O'Connor: The Obedient Imagination.* Athens: U of Georgia P, 2000.

Heaton, E. W. *The Old Testament Prophets.* Atlanta: John Knox P, 1977.

Heschel, Abraham. *The Prophets.* New York: Harper & Row, 1962.

Kirkland, William. "Flannery O'Connor, the Person and the Writer." *The East-West Review* 3 (1967): 159-63.

Kuhl, Curt. *The Prophets of Israel.* Trans. Rudolf Ehrlich and J. P. Smith. Richmond, VA: John Knox, 1963.

Lake, Christina Bieber. *The Incarnational Art of Flannery O'Connor.* Macon: Mercer UP, 2005.

Larson, Susan. "The Writer Next Door." *Times-Picayune* 15 March 1998: E1. Lexis-Nexis Academic Universe. Bluffton U. 20 June 2001. printout 1-3.

Malamud, Bernard. *Conversations with Bernard Malamud.* Ed. Lawrence M. Lasher. Jackson: UP of Mississippi, 1991.

May, John R. *The Pruning Word: The Parables of Flannery O'Connor.* Notre Dame: U of Notre Dame P, 1976.

McGraw, Erin. "Authoritative Voice." Review. *Georgia Review* 54 (2000): 727-37.

McMullen, Joanne Halleran. *Writing against God: Language as Message in the Literature of Flannery O'Connor.* Macon: Mercer UP, 1996.

O'Connor, Flannery. *Collected Works.* New York: Library of America, 1988.

———. *Conversations with Flannery O'Connor.* Ed. Rosemary M. Magee. Jackson: UP of Mississippi, 1987.

———. *The Habit of Being.* Ed. Sally Fitzgerald. New York: Farrar, Straus and Giroux, 1979.

———. *Mystery and Manners.* Ed. Sally Fitzgerald. New York: Farrar, Straus and Giroux, 1961.

———. *The Presence of Grace and Other Book Reviews.* Comp. Leo J. Zuber. Ed. Cart W. Martin. Athens: U of Georgia P, 1983.

Oliver, Bill. "Flannery O'Connor's Compassion." *The Flannery O'Connor Bulletin* 15 (1986): 1-15.

Piacentino, Ed. "Second Chances: Patterns of Failure and Redemption in Tim Gautreaux's *Same Place, Same Things.*" *The Southern Literary Journal* 38.1 (Fall 2005). Bluffton U Literature Resource Center. 18 Jan. 2006. printout 1-12.

Prown, Katherine Hemple. *Revising Flannery O'Connor: Southern Literary Culture and the Problem of Female Authorship.* Charlottesville: UP of Virginia, 2001.

Rabinowitz, Peter J. *Before Reading: Narrative Conventions and the Politics of Interpretation.* Ithaca: Cornell UP, 1987.

———. "Where We Are When We Read." *Authorizing Readers: Resistance and Respect in the Teaching of Literature.* Peter J. Rabinowitz and Michael W. Smith. New York: Teachers College P, 1998. 1-28.

Sawyer, John F. A. *Prophecy and the Biblical Prophets.* New York: Oxford UP, 1993.

Stephens, Martha. *The Question of Flannery O'Connor.* Baton Rouge: Louisiana State UP, 1973.

Vawter, Bruce. *The Conscience of Israel: Pre-exilic Prophets and Prophecy.* New York: Sheed & Ward, 1961.

Wood, Ralph C. *Flannery O'Connor and the Christ-Haunted South.* Grand Rapids: Eerdmans, 2004.

Katherine Keil (essay date fall 2006)

SOURCE: Keil, Katherine. "O'Connor's 'A Good Man Is Hard to Find.'" *Explicator* 65, no. 1 (fall 2006): 44-7.

[*In the following essay, Keil comments on the subtle references to Samuel Taylor Coleridge's poem "The Rime of the Ancient Mariner" in "A Good Man Is Hard to Find."*]

Chaucer's *Canterbury Tales,* Shakespeare's *King Lear,* Browning's "Childe Roland to the Dark Tower Came," Frost's "Stopping by Woods on a Snowy Evening," Gounod's *Faust,* Weber's *Der Freischutz,* and Uncle Sam—according to Rodney Stenning Edgecombe, traces of all of these can be found in Flannery O'Connor's **"A Good Man Is Hard to Find."** Maybe so; however, look again and you will also find the deep shadowy presence of Samuel Taylor Coleridge's *Rime of the Ancient Mariner.* Lacking spiritual fulfillment, both Coleridge's sailor and O'Connor's grandmother journey through the desert of alienation and experience an epiphany that results in resurrection and rebirth.

The sailor in Coleridge's "The Rime of the Ancient Mariner" brings about his own alienation when he shoots the albatross. In killing this co-part of creation, he separates himself from the divine source from which life emanated. The sailor recognizes his foul transgression: "And I had done a hellish thing" (128). With that, he enters his spiritual desert. On the sea, surrounded by water, he laments his thirst, "Water, water, everywhere / Nor any drop to drink" (121-22). Suffering not from a literal thirst, but rather from a metaphorical longing for release from his alienated condition, he seeks divine intervention and tries unsuccessfully to pray:

> I looked to heaven, and tried to pray;
> But or ever a prayer had gusht,
> A wicked whisper came, and made
> My heart as dry as dust.
>
> (278-81)

Paralleling the sailor's condition is O'Connor's grandmother. She, too, is alienated from other members of creation. She is surrounded by people without any sign of intimate fellowship, just as the sailor is surrounded by water without being able to quench his thirst. After one of her many speeches, her son, "Bailey didn't [even] look up from his reading" (308), and after she addresses her daughter-in-law, we are told, "The children's mother didn't seem to hear her" (309). She is cut off and alone.

Just as the sailor shows his dispassion for creation in shooting the albatross, the grandmother shows her indifference for creation by selfishly manipulating and nagging to get her way on the family's vacation. She tells lies about a "secret panel" (312) to get her grandchildren to throw fits in the car to coerce Bailey into taking a side trip to a nonexistent house from her flawed memory. Her insistence on having her own way and sneaking Pitty Sing, her cat, into the car, despite her knowledge that Bailey would not allow this, directly causes the accident. Even as her family is killed by The Misfit and his men, she parleys for her own life saying, "You wouldn't shoot a lady, would you?" (315). Both the sailor and the grandmother lack a sense of other. The grandmother, too, longs for a divine connection and release from her "desert," her place of discontent. She recalls a "dirt road [that] was hilly [. . . with] sudden washes in it and sharp curves on dangerous embankments." She thinks about a "red depression with the dust-coated trees" (313): these words create an image that is devoid of peace and contentment. When brought face to face with The Misfit, the grandmother knows that "[h]is face was as familiar to her as if she had known him all her life but she could not recall who he was" (314). She is trying to remember and create a bond between herself and another creature, allowing her to break out of her alienation, but her escape cannot happen quite yet.

Both the sailor and the grandmother need to recognize their bond as members of creation. This epiphany happens for the sailor when, close to death, he finally opens his eyes and his consciousness to the grandeur of creation in his glimpse of the vibrant colored snakes. With their "flash of golden fire," he cries out in joy:

> O happy living things! No tongue
> Their beauty might declare:
> A spring of love gushed from my

heart,
And I blessed them unaware.

(282-86)

This sudden force of love is what Flannery O'Connor calls a "constraining love for the thing despised" (qtd. in Wyatt 67). The mariner is saved and brought into the fold of creation when he recognizes the beauty of even a wretched snake. His salvation is immediate, evidenced by his ability to pray—that is to connect again with the divine:

The self-same moment I could
pray;
And from my neck so free
The Albatross fell off, and sank
Like lead into the sea.

(287-91)

The grandmother, likewise, is brought salvation by a "wretched" creature—The Misfit. At the moment of her earthly death, she is awakened to their conjoinment in divine creation. We see this in her recognition of The Misfit as one of her own children: "Why, you're one of my babies. You're one of my own children!" (318). She experiences a gush of mother love that mirrors the sailor's cry of joy in the beauty of the snakes. She understands the wonder of and takes great joy in life itself, here envisioned in The Misfit. Elisabeth Piedmont-Martin refers to this as the grandmother's "moment of clarity," when she "recognizes his [The Misfit] twisted humanity as part of her own by calling him one of her children."

At first glance, it seems as if this immediate salvation and resurrection is cut short by the gunshot that kills her. However, the grandmother's epiphany, which leads to her rebirth and resurrection, is not one of an ongoing spiritually energized earthly life, as in the case of the sailor, but one of a Christian resurrection and eternal life. The Catholic Christian view teaches that grace alone saves and brings eternal reward; O'Connor herself claims that the grandmother receives this saving grace: "she [Grandmother] has been touched by the Grace that comes through him [The Misfit]" because she realizes "she is responsible for the man before her and joined to him by ties of kinship which have their roots deep in the mystery [. . .]" (qtd. in Piedmont-Martin). In fact, it is this "mystery" that the grandmother now understands.

The mystery solved, the sailor and the grandmother have achieved clarity of vision. They are able to recognize what was before them the whole time, demonstrating O'Connor's truism: "A good man *is* hard to find"—and sometimes a good allusion, too.

Works Cited

Coleridge, Samuel Taylor. *The Rime of the Ancient Mariner. English Romantic Poetry and Prose.* Ed. Russell Noyes. New York: Oxford UP, 1967. 392-400.

Edgecombe, Rodney Stenning. "O'Connor's 'A Good Man Is Hard to Find.'" *Explicator* 64.1 (Fall 2005): 68-70.

O'Connor, Flannery. "A Good Man Is Hard to Find." *Literature and the Writing Process.* 7th ed. Ed. Elizabeth McMahan, Susan X. Day, and Robert Funk. Upper Saddle River: Pearson Prentice Hall, 2005. 308-18.

Piedmont-Martin, Elisabeth. "An Overview of 'A Good Man Is Hard to Find.'" *Short Stories for Students.* Gale Research, 1997. Reproduced in Literature Resource Center. Galenet. Prescott Memorial Lib., Louisiana Tech U. 3 Apr. 2006 <http://galenet.galegroup.com/.

Wyatt, Bryan N. "The Domestic Dynamics of Flannery O'Connor: 'Everything That Rises Must Converge.'" *Twentieth Century Literature* 38.1 (Spring 1992): 66-89.

Ralph C. Wood (essay date spring 2007)

SOURCE: Wood, Ralph C. "'God May Strike You Thisaway': Flannery O'Connor and Simone Weil on Affliction and Joy." *Renascence* 59, no. 3 (spring 2007): 181-95.

[*In the following essay, Wood documents the acceptance of suffering as a means of transcending the horror and violence of the modern world in O'Connor's stories and philosopher Simone Weil's writings.*]

I have never been anywhere but sick.

—Flannery O'Connor in a letter to Betty Hester, 28 June 1956

It doesn't finally matter whether we get Faulkner right, for no one's salvation depends on it. But it matters absolutely whether we get O'Connor right.

—John Millis, personal conversation, December 1996

There is a persistent misgiving that Flannery O'Connor delighted in death, that she nurtured an incurable malignancy of the imagination, that a fundamental malevolence pervades her fiction, and thus that she reveled in the destruction of bodies if not also souls. The purpose of this paper is to demonstrate, exactly to the contrary, that—in both her personal life and her literary work—few other writers have enabled us to name so clearly the nature of both the violence that wracks our terror-stricken world and the grace that might redirect such violence to non-destructive ends.

* * *

Professor William Sessions' forthcoming biography will amply demonstrate that the young Mary Flannery O'Connor had an outsized ego. She did not like for others to cross her. She often conspired with her father against the domineering Regina Cline O'Connor. She had little patience for classmates whose wits were not as keen as hers. Nor could she abide the assurance of her schoolteacher nuns that guardian angels surrounded and protected her. Instead, she often flailed her fists at such ghostly familiars, shadowboxing at such invisible presences, in the conviction that she needed no such shielding. The young O'Connor was also defiant in her determination not to become the Southern belle that her mother desired, nor to conform to the conventional female expectations of her male-dominated society. When required to make a dress for a high school sewing class, for example, she brought one of her chickens to school, having first clothed it in the garment she had been told to make.

Even as an adult, O'Connor often chafed at the pusillanimity of small-town existence. Though immensely grateful that her imagination had been chastened by the limits of intimate life in rural Georgia—as it would not, if she had lived anonymously in the Deep North—O'Connor often found such provincialism irksome. A good deal of this abiding anger and frustration finds it way into her two most vivid fictional self-portraits: the eponymous Mary Grace of **"Revelation"** and, still more, in the joy-scorning, name-changing Hulga Hopewell of **"Good Country People."** O'Connor gives us other fictional versions of herself, of course, especially Sally Virginia Cope in **"A Circle in the Fire"** and the nameless girl in **"A Temple of the Holy Ghost."** Yet what remains most remarkable about these renderings of her own persona is the utter effacing of all self-pity. Instead, we find O'Connor exhibiting a steely-eyed honesty about these self-absorbed creatures whom she could easily have become.

I believe that we make a fundamental misprision of O'Connor's life and work, therefore, by characterizing it as mean in spirit and violent in implication. Only a wooden literalism of the interpretive faculty, a bankruptcy of the imagination, could prompt the counting of dead bodies in her work as if one were counting beans. No one is castrated in her fiction, as is Joe Christmas in the climactic scene of Faulkner's *Light in August.* No one is raped with a corncob, as is Temple Drake in *Sanctuary.* Not a single bed-wetting child is made to spend a sub-zero Russian night in an outdoor privy, weeping and pleading for mercy from "dear kind God," as in Dostoevsky's *The Brothers Karamazov.* And compared to the fiction of Cormac McCarthy, O'Connor's novels and stories are hardly sanguinary at all. So should it also be observed that almost no one in her work goes to death unwillingly. Only one major and one minor character face their final demise ungraciously—namely, the insufferable Mary Fortune Pitts in **"A View of the Woods"** and the spiteful June Star in **"A Good Man Is Hard to Find."** Instead, nearly all of O'Connor's dying characters validate her own witty saying: "A lot of people get killed in my stories, but nobody gets hurt."

O'Connor herself, by contrast, *did* "get hurt." And yet none of her interpreters has sufficiently addressed the violence that was done to *her.* Already as a teenager she was wracked with unaccountable pains in her legs. By the time she was working at Yaddo in 1948, Robert Lowell noticed that she was suffering from unidentifiable aches. Upon her return home from Connecticut at Christmas of 1950, she was deathly ill with lupus. And then she was to spend the last thirteen years of her life dying in Milledgeville. What I find most remarkable about both O'Connor's letters and her fiction is how *little* of her own pain appears there, how seldom she complains about the violence that she herself suffered. As I have sought to show elsewhere (*Christ-Haunted South* 212-16).

Flannery O'Connor refused to make her illness the central and defining event of her life. In a remarkable testament of faith, she handled her lupus rather as an inconvenient nuisance than as a terrible curse. Yet in the interstices of her letters and interviews, but especially her fiction, there are hints that Flannery O'Connor's personal suffering did require her to ask not one but two of the profoundest questions. This essay will seek to address them both. First, there is the question posed by both Job and the Psalmist: "Why do the wicked prosper? Why does God do such terrible violence to his faithful ones?" Then there is the cosmic question: "How might a proper response to such undeserved suffering offer a potential answer to the unprecedented violence of the late modern world?"

* * *

O'Connor's wry confession that she spent her mornings writing and her afternoons recovering has led most of us to assume that she was exhausted by the mental exactions of her craft alone. We have supposed that she spent her afternoons "po'ch sittin'" (as she called the splendid Southern art of whiling away the time) in order to refresh her depleted imagination. Too little have we acknowledged that she may have mastered her bodily misery only long enough to write for three hours. William Stuntz, a Harvard law professor who suffers from chronic back pain, explains that hope for a cure only worsens his suffering and thus that resignation to his torment becomes the only balm and salve. Strangely, he confesses, pain also serves to make his work "more satisfying, even though it's much harder to do . . . The feeling of accomplishment is indescribably powerful." Physical agony, Stuntz writes, also enables him to live in the present rather than the past or future: "Now, I have to concentrate harder to do anything, so I'm more focused on what I'm doing—not on what it might get me or what I should have done differently . . . Wanting and regretting take a lot of energy, and I don't have much energy to spare. So I do less of both [wanting and regretting] than in my earlier, healthier life" (Stuntz).

That Flannery O'Connor held out no great hope for the assuaging of her own physical pain was but a part, perhaps even the smallest part, of her suffering. Far more mysterious is her extreme reluctance to seek a miraculous cure for her illness. We know, of course, that she despised Catholic piety of the oleaginous kind. Yet her reluctance to take the baths at Lourdes remains surprising. When she finally relented, she confessed that she prayed more for the healing of her novel-in-progress (*The Violent Bear It Away*) than for the curing of her lupus. She also drolly declared that the *real* miracle of Lourdes is that so little disease is spread via those filthy, germ-laden waters. (Peter De Vries, the lapsed Calvinist novelist, depicts a healthy character who actually *contracts* an illness at Lourdes!) Yet something is at work here deeper by far than O'Connor's tough-minded refusal of all marvel-mongering. She was aware, I am convinced, that never in Christian tradition do believers seek miracles in order to *justify* or *vindicate* their faith: "I believe (and so should others) because I've been healed." Rather and always is the matter the other way around: Christians are *astonished* whenever miracles occur: "I believe no matter what, and this gift of healing is but 'God's importunate bonus.'"[1]

Flannery O'Connor may also have shared Dr. Thomas More's skepticism (in Walker Percy's *Love in the Ruins*) about taking his dying teenaged daughter Samantha to Lourdes. Since Samantha suffers from the same neuroblastoma that afflicts the young girl in *A Memoir of Mary Ann*—the girl who died *without* a miraculous answer to the prayers poured out on her behalf—I suspect that Percy created his character in her image. Tom More confesses, in one of the most riveting scenes in modern fiction, that he feared *not* a denial of a supernatural cure for his dying daughter; on the contrary, he dreaded that she might *indeed* be healed. For then, asks Tom More, what would he do with the rest of his life? How could he continue drinking and fornicating and leading a cynically self-indulgent existence? To receive such a blessing beyond all earthly blessings might be too great a miracle to bear. As a self-confessed "bad Catholic," More speaks darkly of his "delectation of tragedy," his "secret satisfaction" in Samantha's dying. "Is it possible," asks More, "to live without feasting on death" (Percy 374). Were such miraculous severities, we must ask, too overwhelming even for Flannery O'Connor?

This surely was O'Connor's own question as well. How could she prevent her illness from becoming her oxymoronic poisonous sustenance, making (as George Herbert says) "her purge her food" ("Affliction I" 51)? That O'Connor was no anti-modern made answers all the more difficult. She confessed to having been possessed "of the modern consciousness"—"unhistorical, solitary, and guilty" (*The Habit of Being: The Letters of Flannery O'Connor* 90)[2]. There seems little doubt that the chief accomplishment of modernity lies in the triumph of *techné*—the discovery that the world is ruled by both *necessity* and *chance*. Despite all the later qualifications put on the breakthrough insights of Galileo and Newton in the 17th century, most of us still believe that (so far as we humans can discern) every natural effect is the product of its antecedent causes, *necessarily* so. Yet these natural occurrences are not morally, much less mercifully ordered. As Darwin taught us to believe, events in the natural world collide with each other in often unpredictable ways, *chancily* so. O'Connor's lupus was no mystery, therefore, at least scientifically considered. She inherited it from her father. It was the violent result of random variations within the inexorable processes of the natural order, and it could be treated (albeit partially) by medications that controlled (while not curing) the causes that led to such dreadful, even deadly effects.

The victory of *techné* presents a drastic challenge to belief that the world is ruled by *logos*: i.e., the multi-millenary conviction that all things are ordered, if not by the just and good God whom Jews and Christians worship, then surely by the governing Reason which Plato and Aristotle honored. This brazen conflict was registered both spiritually and literally in Flannery O'Connor's bones. She was wracked with pains that were more than physical. So sharply did she discern the clash between ancient and modern ideas of nature that she became fascinated with the attempt of the Jesuit paleontologist and mystic, Teilhard de Chardin, to reconcile them. In the end, for reasons I have tried to trace elsewhere, O'Connor believed that Teilhard had failed ("Heterodoxy" 3-29).

* * *

The more pertinent comparison, I believe, is not with Teilhard but with Simone Weil[3] (1909-43), the French intellectual who came close to embracing Christianity but who finally refused baptism on the grounds that such religious consolation would spoil the authenticity of her faith. She died at age 34 from illnesses that were exacerbated by her prolonged fasts. O'Connor declared that Weil and Edith Stein were "the two 20th century women who interest me most" (*HB* 93). Their deeds, she remarked, "[overshadow] anything they may have written" (*HB* 98). O'Connor admitted that she found Weil "a trifle monstrous, but [with] the kind of monstrosity that interests me" (522). Thus does O'Connor make four times more epistolary references to Weil than to Stein. In the highest of tributes short of calling her a saint, O'Connor described Weil's life as an "almost perfect blending of the Comic and the Terrible" (*HB* 106).[4]

O'Connor leaves her readers to fathom what she means by this cryptic saying. I believe she is using the terms not in a Dantesque but a Kafkaesque sense. By the Terrible, she may refer to the *logos*-world in which everything is ordered to the will of God, but so obscurely that, given the fallen and finite condition of the world, we are made to walk by terrifying faith rather than comforting sight. By the Comic, she appears to have indicated the natural world as it is ruled by fickle chance and obdurate necessity, making it blithely blind to spiritual matters. For Weil, it is also a world made all the more sinister because it submits so readily to the human machinations and manipulations of *techné*.[5]

Simone Weil's redefined version of the contradiction between *techné* and *logos* became the virtual center of her thought. George Grant quotes her watchword: "As Plato says, an infinite distance separates the good from necessity—the essential contradiction in human life is that man, with a straining after good constituting his very being, is at the same time subject in his entire being, both in mind and in flesh, to a blind force, to a necessity completely indifferent to the good" (248). Weil called the experience of this infinite contradiction between the good and the necessary by the name *malheur,* a word usually translated "affliction" but also connoting "inevitability" and "doom" ("The Love of God" 117). Affliction means for Weil, as it does also for O'Connor, much more than physical suffering alone. *Malheur* is the encounter with all of those inexorable forces, both without and within, that make for oppression and evil, whether they take the form of war or disease, whether of human degradation or natural disaster:

> A blind mechanism, heedless of degrees of spiritual perfection, continually tosses men about and throws some of them at the very foot of the Cross. It rests with them to keep or not to keep their eyes turned toward God through all the jolting. It does not mean that God's providence is lacking. It is in his Providence that God has willed that necessity should be like a blind mechanism.
>
> If the mechanism were not blind there would not be any affliction. Affliction is anonymous before all things; it deprives its victims of their personality and makes them into things. It is indifferent; and it is the coldness of this indifference—a metallic coldness—that freezes all those it touches right to the depths of their souls. They will never find warmth again. They will never believe any more that they are anyone.
>
> ("The Love of God" 124-5)

In these strange and provocative sayings, it is difficult not to think of Franz Kafka on the one hand and Flannery O'Connor on the other. No wonder that the anonymous child in **"A Temple of the Holy Ghost"** would accept martyrdom only if they would "kill her quick." Affliction is not noble like martyrdom, Weil declares, but comic like the Cross. "Christ did not die like a martyr," she writes. "He died like a common criminal, confused with thieves, only a little more ridiculous. For affliction is ridiculous." That this nation's most eminent Christian artist did not hear the choruses of Palestrina as she lay dying but rather "Wooden boxes without topses, They were shoes for Clementine" (*HB* 578), is surely ridiculousness ratcheted to the highest degree. For all their many differences,[6] therefore, Weil and O'Connor are fundamentally agreed that evil serves to thrust us out of an otherwise bestial existence and into the anguishing (though also potentially joyful) contradiction of living in affliction before God. "The extreme affliction which overtakes human beings," writes Weil, "does not create human misery, it merely reveals [human misery]." "Evil," she declares in a staggering paradox, "is the form which God's mercy takes in this world."

In an important letter to Betty Hester, O'Connor makes similarly staggering claims. She seeks to answer the questions of the then-atheistic Hester concerning miracles, which appear to constitute a suspension of material processes and scientific laws. O'Connor suggests, in a passage remarkably redolent of Weil's claims, that we have understood these laws and processes exactly backward. "For me," she explains, "it is the virgin birth, the Incarnation, the resurrection which are the true laws of the flesh and the physical. Death, decay, destruction are the suspension of these laws." O'Connor then offers a drastic affirmation of the body as it is meant to transcend natural necessities, knowing well that her own *corpus* seemed to be at once her burden and her curse—her *malheur*:

> I am always astonished at the emphasis the Church puts on the body. It is not the soul that will rise but the body, glorified. I have always thought that purity was the most mysterious of the virtues, but it occurs to me that it would never have entered human consciousness to conceive of purity if we were not to look forward to a resurrection of the body, which will be flesh and spirit united in peace, in the way they were in Christ. The resurrection of the body seems to be the high point in the law of nature.
>
> (*HB* 100)

If "death, decay, and destruction" constitute the suspension of this natural law, then it follows that only by a gigantic act of divine mercy do they exist at all. A rightful embrace of their "comic" affliction—and thus a rightful affirmation of God's "terrible" mercy—thus become the means of living in accord with the true grain of the universe. No longer do we see ourselves as sufferers understood as passive victims, but sufferers understood as active agents.

The Archbishop of Canterbury, Rowan Williams, has discerned this terrifying pattern in O'Connor's fiction. It pushes "toward the limits of what is thinkable and 'acceptable,' let alone edifying," he explains. "She is always taking for granted," he adds, "that God is possible in the most grotesque and empty or cruel situations." Her aim, Williams insists, is to make the natural supernatural, to create "a recognisable world that is also utterly unexpected," a fictional milieu at once familiar and alien. Thus does she create "agents in fiction who embody excess of meaning and whose relations with each other and with the otherness of God are not limited by the visible, though inconceivable without the visible . . . [T]he infinite cannot be directly apprehended, so we must take appearance seriously . . . enough to read its concealments and stratagems" (Williams). Among its many hidden stratagems is the Cross. As an instrument for shameful death that has been transfigured into the true pattern of life, it makes havoc of ordinary life. Indeed, it discloses the terrible—the terror-striking—character of God himself. "A God who fails to generate desperate hunger and confused and uncompromising passion," writes the archbishop, "is no God at all." O'Connor's grotesque characters are who they are, he notes, because "God is as God is, not an agent within the universe, not a source of specialised religious consolation. If God is real, the person in touch with God is in danger, at any number of levels." To create such hunger and passion, Williams concludes, "is to risk creating in people a longing too painful to bear or a longing that will lead them to take such risks that it seems nakedly cruel to expose them to that hunger in the first place" (Williams).

Unlike both Rowan Williams and Flannery O'Connor, Simone Weil is exceedingly loath to find anything redemptive inherent in *malheur.* Hence her final refusal of baptism and the eucharist that would have followed from it. Thus did she also express her extreme envy of Christ, since he experienced the ultimate *malheur* of being utterly abandoned by God. Weil may thus have regarded her final refusal of food as a form of crucifixion, a denial of even the most basic worldly sustenance. For O'Connor, by contrast, Christians are meant to imitate rather than replicate Christ. We are his disciples and witnesses, feasting on rather than abstaining from his fractured body and streaming blood. Even so, I believe that there remains a deep kinship between O'Connor and Weil—as, for example, when O'Connor declares that "Evil not a problem to be solved but a mystery to be endured." For it is only by *suffering* the evil, enfolding the *malheur* within ourselves, that we will not turn it outward upon others in the destructiveness that is the essential characteristic of modernity.[7]

> Extreme affliction, which means physical pain, distress of soul, and social degradation, all at the same time, is a nail whose point is applied at the very center of the soul, whose head is all necessity spreading throughout space and time.
>
> Affliction is a marvel of divine technique. It is a simple and ingenious device which introduces into the soul of a finite creature the immensity of force, blind, brutal, and cold. The infinite distance separating God from the creature is entirely concentrated into one point to pierce the soul in its center.[8]
>
> ("The Love of God" 134-5)

* * *

I believe that Flannery O'Connor was thus pierced.[9] Because we have not yet dealt with this piercing, neither have we penetrated the abysmal depths nor ascended the sublime heights of her fiction and letters. O'Connor's protagonists consist largely of men and women who refuse such a piercing until the very end, if only because they couldn't withstand such affliction if it came earlier and was less than lethal. This, I contend, is the real violence at the core of O'Connor's work. As always, she speaks of such terrible things in a jaunty voice:

> Naw, I don't think life is a tragedy. Tragedy is something that can be explained by the professors. Life is the will of God and this cannot be defined by the professors; for which all thanksgiving. I think it is impossible to live and not to grieve but I am always suspicious of my own grief lest it be self-pity in sheeps [sic] clothing. And the worst thing is to grieve for the wrong reason, for the wrong loss. Altogether it is better to pray than to grieve; and it is greater to be joyful than to grieve. But it takes more grace to be joyful than any but the greatest have.
>
> (***Flannery O'Connor: Collected Works***[10] 928-29)

To declare that "life is the will of God" is to make the most radical of logocentric claims. It is to offer an unblinkered embrace of the affliction wrought by a mechanical world whose physical horrors have been worsened by the triumph of *techné.* As O'Connor declared in one of her letters: "if you believe in the divinity of Christ, you have to cherish the world at that same time that you struggle to endure it." Hence her even more instructive addendum: "This may explain the lack of bitterness in my stories" (*HB* 90). O'Connor presses home this same adamantine truth in her "Introduction" to *A Memoir of Mary Ann.* There she affirms *logos*-inspired clarity over visceral emotion: "If other ages felt less, they saw more, even though they saw with the blind, prophetical, unsentimental eye of acceptance, which is to say, of faith."

This rarely quoted statement precedes the often controverted claim that "When tenderness is detached from the source of tenderness, its logical outcome is terror. It ends in forced-labor camps and in the fumes of the gas chamber" (*Mystery and Manners* 227). O'Connor does not mean, as many have assumed, that Christ is the only source of unsentimental love, as if humanists were incapable of such love. Rather is Christ the fount of transcendent tenderness because he is also the spring of suffering precisely as Simone Weil defines it. He both embodies and demands the affliction that modernity is bent on denying. Though no Christian herself, Simone Weil nonetheless declared that "The extreme greatness of Christianity lies in the fact that it does not seek a supernatural cure for suffering, but a supernatural use of it." Ours is the Age of Ashes—of the Nazi ovens, of Hiroshima and Nagasaki and Dresden, of al-Qaeda's crumbled World Trade Center towers—all because we have sought to refuse affliction.[11]

Walter M. Miller, Jr. makes this case powerfully in *A Canticle for Leibowitz,* an apocalyptic novel about our world after it has already suffered a nuclear holocaust and is seeking to recover its life. There can be no recovery, argues Father Zerchi, so long as we indulge two deadly deviations from the past. The first, he says, is the idea that society alone determines whether an act is right or wrong. The second, he adds, is that pain constitutes the only evil. The real problem, as Zerchi discerns, is how to direct human life to ends which are just rather than expedient, ends which are not humanly devised and managed, ends which enable people to live for a higher good than the avoidance of pain, even agonizing pain. Such life entails affliction—the suffering which, as we have seen, produces pain that is moral and spiritual no less than bodily and physical. The desire to avoid such anguish, Zerchi confesses, makes us seek to create an affliction-free world. Failing to manufacture such a world of ease, our species turns bitter and destructive. The resulting ashes—whether in personal or political holocausts—are the products of what the dying Zerchi calls "the unreasoning fear of suffering. *Metus doloris.* Take it together with its positive equivalent, the craving for worldly security, for Eden, and you might have your 'root of evil' . . . To minimize suffering and to maximize security were natural and proper ends of society and Caesar. But then they became the only ends, somehow, the only basis of law—a perversion. Inevitably, then, in seeking only them, we found only their opposites: maximum suffering and minimum security" (Miller 330).

Ruby Turpin and Mrs. McIntyre and Mrs. Shortley seek refuge from what they perceive to be suffering. They do thus speak of the unwanted souls who are "left over," who are "too many," who ought thus to be ridden off in box cars to gas ovens or else sent back where they came from, and all for the same reason: Those "extras," as Mrs. McIntyre calls them, threaten to afflict their unafflicted lives. Unlike them, Hulga Hopewell is not a proto-Nazi, but she too nourishes fantasies of annihilation—even if only in her hilariously mistaken dream of seducing and destroying the faith of a faux-naïve country Bible salesman. Hulga is an annihilationist because she harbors what Nietzsche called *ressentiment*; she bitterly resents having been pierced at the center of her being. She is afflicted (as we have heard Weil saying) "with physical pain, distress of soul, and social degradation, all at the same time." That in the end Hulga was not slain but made at least to consider embracing her affliction may be one of the most hopeful signs in all of O'Connor's work. It may mean that Hulga has begun to make her way back toward the embrace of her true name: Joy.

* * *

All of the other creatures except man, argues Simone Weil, achieve beauty in their utter and necessary docility to God, a docility that she calls "obedience without knowledge" ("The Love of God" 130). Man is not such a docile creature. He alone can know and embrace the mystery that O'Connor described in saying that "Life is the will of God." Man acquires this knowledge, Weil teaches, through acts of attention.[12] These attentive acts, like the moral virtues, must be cultivated. Attention is acquired slowly and habitually. "As one has to learn to read or practice a trade," Weil declares, "so one must learn to feel in all things, first and almost solely, the obedience of the universe to God." "Whoever has finished his apprenticeship," she adds, "recognizes things and events, everywhere and always, as vibrations from the same divine and infinitely sweet word" ("The Love of God" 131).

This sweetness and this beauty are fierce, even rending and piercing. But by no other means than willingly embraced affliction does "the infinite love of God [come] to possess us. He comes at his own time. We have the power to consent to receive him or to refuse" (Weil, "The Love of God" 133). This consent brings joy no less than suffering. Weil describes them as "two equally precious gifts which must be savored to the full, each one in its purity, without trying to mix them." There is a strange quality of force and necessity present even in joy. That the Christ who makes his absolute consent to the will of God in Gethsemane and at Calvary could, in a certain sense, have done no other, is his necessary joy. He dies with a loud shout, as if his joy were forcibly pressed out of him. "In order that our being should one day become wholly sensitive in every part to this obedience that is the substance of matter, in order that a new sense should be formed in us to enable us to hear the universe as the vibration of the word of God, the transforming power of suffering and of joy are equally indispensable" ("The Love of God" 132).

In most cases, O'Connor's characters violently receive the afflicting truth about themselves only *in articulo mortis.* That so many of them find Life only in death has blinded many critics to the joyfulness of rightly embraced affliction—to that deeper and rarer thing that both Weil and O'Connor attest. A better guide in these matters, I believe, is to be found in one of G. K. Chesterton's earliest essays, "In Defence of Farce." There, Chesterton makes the surprising claim that, while "black and catastrophic" pain attracts the immature artist, "joy is a far more elusive and elvish matter, since it is our reason for existing, and a very feminine reason; it mingles with every breath we draw and every cup of tea we drink." Precisely because joy is elusive in its strangely invisible ubiquity—being neither pleasure nor delight, not even the fulfillment of transcendent desire, much less any relaxed life of "ease in Zion" (Amos 6:1)—joy requires an extraordinary mode of expression. "And of all the varied forms of the literature of joy," Chesterton concludes, "the form most truly worthy of moral reverence and artistic ambition is the form called 'farce'—or its wilder shape in pantomime" (124-5).

Few critics have noticed the pantomime character of O'Connor's most riveting and revealing scenes. The confrontation of The Misfit and the Grandmother, Manley Pointer's removing of Hulga Hopewell's leg, Bevel Summers' baptizing of Harry Ashfield, Tarwater's drowning of Bishop, the young hoodlums dancing like Daniel in the fiery furnace of Mrs. Cope's burning woods, Hazel Motes performing his awful *ascesis* at the end, Mrs. May whispering into the bull's ear as he buries his horns in her lap, Ruby Turpin trying to shout down God beside her hog pen, Mrs. McIntyre and Mr. Shortley and the two Negroes with eyes frozen in collusion as the tractor crushes Mr. Guizac, the early confrontation of Coleman and Tanner at the sawmill, and especially Nelson and Mr. Head standing before the Sambo Christ—surely these scenes all have the character of pantomime. There is japery here, something slapstick and buffoonish at work, almost a charade quality about them all—as if the deepest things cannot be said but only gestured and mimed. They are comic as Weil sees the Cross as comic. The only thing missing is a horse or cow played by two actors, one as the head and front legs, the other as the tail and back legs. No wonder that O'Connor, when describing Simone Weil's life as "a perfect blending of the Comic and the Terrible," described her own work in terms that are tantamount to farce and pantomime: "everything funny I have written is more terrible than it is funny, or only funny because it is terrible, or only terrible because it is funny" (*HB* 105).

Nowhere do the funny and the terrible come more fully into pantomime expression than in **"A Temple of the Holy Ghost."** There the little girl who had rather be a martyr than a saint has a dream vision of the hermaphrodite whom her cousins had seen at the fair. She imagines him as a preacher proclaiming the Good News of Affliction as his congregation responds with a steady litany of Amens. What enables this scene to accomplish more than the awakening of a brilliant but proud young girl to her own religious vocation is that the hermaphrodite has borne his affliction in the region that our late modern world regards as the ultimate defining center of human life: his sexuality. Not in spite of such deformity but precisely because of it does this contradictory creature embrace his suffering. Though he has due cause for regarding the cosmos as sheer mechanical necessity and absurd chance, he lives not as a bitter freak of nature but one who has consented to be afflicted by God.

Both Simone Weil and Flannery O'Connor regard such consent as the true means for overcoming the violence that is the terror of our time. To live at the intersection between the creation and its Creator, declares Weil, is to live at the juncture of the arms of the Cross ("The Love of God" 136). The hermaphrodite lives nowhere else. More remarkable still, he leads his people to live there as well: to embrace the inward ferocity of their own affliction so as to produce the lasting joy and that might yet prevent another Age of Ashes:

> God done this to me and I praise him.
>
> Amen. Amen.
>
> He could make you thisaway.
>
> Amen. Amen.
>
> But he has not.
>
> Amen. Amen.
>
> Raise yourself up. A temple of the Holy Ghost. You! You are God's temple, don't you know? Don't you know? God's spirit has a dwelling in you, don't you know?
>
> Amen. Amen.

If anybody desecrates the temple of God, God will bring him to ruin and if you laugh, He may strike you thisaway. A temple of God is a holy thing. Amen. Amen.

(***CW*** [***Collected Works***] 246)

Notes

1. The phrase is borrowed from a pivotal scene in Walker Percy's *The Moviegoer.* Having spied a black man entering a white Catholic church on Ash Wednesday—perhaps hoping to be seen as a cultured Negro making his way into the white man's business world—Binx Bolling asks whether the man may have emerged with the Gift he did not seek but was given nonetheless as "God's importunate bonus" (235). The root of the word "miracle" is the Latin mirari, "to wonder."

2. All future references to the letters will be indicated *HB.*

3. The only substantial treatment of O'Connor and Weil at the level of their comparative theological visions is to be found in John F. Desmond, "Flannery O'Connor and Simone Weil: A Question of Sympathy" 104-16.

4. If she "were to live long enough and develop as an artist to the proper extent," O'Connor added, "I would like to write a comic novel about [such] a woman [as Weil]—and what is more comic and terrible than the angular intellectual proud woman approaching God inch by inch with ground teeth"? (*HB* 106-7) [It is also worth noting that O'Connor refers to Weil nearly four times as often as to Edith Stein.]

5. Dwight MacDonald argues that Hiroshima and Nagasaki and Dresden were horrors actually worse than the Holocaust. For all that was undeniably demonic about it, the Holocaust was perpetrated by humans directly violating others humans—not by sanitized command officers ordering mile-high pilots to drop impersonal bombs on invisible targets.

6. The chief difference, perhaps, is to be found in their opposing ideas of creation and crucifixion. Weil understood creation as an act of divine self-limitation. Because God dwells in complete fullness and perfection of being, all things created (not merely plants and animals, but also worlds, even the cosmos itself) can exist only where God is not. Creation thus occurs only where God withdraws himself, where He is deliberately and willfully absent. Evil is thus no deviation or corruption of the good, as in the standard Augustinian account, but something inherent in the imperfect creation. Weil's attraction to the Albigenses, the heretical medieval sect that sought to live in liberation from bodily necessity, reveals her conviction that the flesh, though created by God, must be transcended.

   Such notions completely contradict O'Connor's orthodox Christian emphasis on the utter goodness of creation, especially of the bodily form which God himself assumes in the Incarnation. That Weil died as an anorexic may also exhibit her low regard for the body, though of course bodily deprivations have been central to Christian asceticism. St. Catherine of Genoa died after determining to subsist only on the Eucharist. Even so, Weil's drastic self-deprivation stands in stark contrast to O'Connor's declaration that the Eucharist was the center of human existence, that she fed on it daily whenever possible, and thus that she wanted to make her witness by living rather than dying. "Pray," she requested to a friend in one of her very last letters, "that the lupus don't finish me off too quick."

7. Individuals alone are incapable of such authentic suffering. It will require the church as a redemptive community to absorb such suffering, refusing to return evil for evil, especially in terror and warfare.

8. It may come as a surprise that, in his late novel with a pre-Christian setting, *Till We Have Faces,* C. S. Lewis has his protagonist make similar claims: "the Divine Nature wounds and perhaps destroys us merely by being what it is. We call it the wrath of the gods; as if the great cataract in Phars [a neighboring region] were angry with every fly it sweeps down in its green thunder." (284).

9. O'Connor bristled at any suggestion that she herself might have attained any sort of sanctity: "I haven't suffered to speak of in my life and I don't know any more about the redemption than anybody else does" (*HB* 536). On the other hand, she candidly confessed that, "There are some of us who have to pay for our faith every step of the way and who have to work it out dramatically [i.e., in artistic terms] what it would be like without it and if being without it would ultimately be possible or not" (*HB* 349-50).

10. Future references to this work will be indicated *CW.*

11. Roughly 180 million souls were taken by violent means, most of them by their own governments. Wendell Berry points out that we Americans have had our own Holocaust in our destruction of the Native Americans who first occupied this land. He quotes Bernard DeVoto: "The first belt-knife given by a European to an Indian was a portent as great as the cloud that mushroomed over Hiroshima . . .

Instantly the man of 6000 B.C. was bound fast to a way of life that had developed seven and a half millennia beyond his own. He began to live better and he began to die" (37).

12. "Attention consists of suspending our thought, leaving it detached, empty, and ready to be penetrated by the object; it means holding in our minds, within reach of this thought, but on a lower level and not in contact with it, the diverse knowledge we have acquired which we are forced to make use of . . . Above all our thought should be empty, waiting, not seeking anything, but ready to perceive in its naked truth the object that is to penetrate it." ("Reflections on the Right Use of School Studies with a View to the Love of God," 111-12.)

Works Cited

Berry, Wendell. "The Unsettling of America." *The Art of the Commonplace: The Agrarian Essays of Wendell Berry.* Ed. Norman Wirzba. Washington, D.C.: Shoemaker & Hoard, 2002.

Chesterton, G. K. "A Defence of Farce." *The Defendant.* London: J. M. Dent and Sons, 1940.

Desmond, John F. "Flannery O'Connor and Simone Weil: A Question of Sympathy," *Logos: A Journal of Catholic Thought and Culture* 8.1 (Winter 2005): 104-16.

Grant, George. "Introduction to Simone Weil." *The George Grant Reader.* Eds. William-Christian and Sheila Grant. Toronto: U of Toronto P, 1998.

Herbert, George. "Affliction I."

Lewis, C. S. *Till We Have Faces.* Grand Rapids: Eerdmans, 1966.

Miller, Walter M. *A Canticle for Leibowitz.* New York: Bantam, 1997.

O'Connor, Flannery. *Flannery O'Connor: Collected Works.* Ed. Sally Fitzgerald. New York: The Literary Classics of the United States, 1986.

———. *The Habit of Being: The Letters of Flannery O'Connor.* Sel. and ed. Sally Fitzgerald. New York: Farrar, Straus, & Giroux, 1979.

———. *Mystery and Manners: Occasional Prose.* Sel. and ed. Sally Fitzgerald. New York: Farrar, Straus, & Giroux, 1970.

Percy, Walker. *Love in the Ruins.* New York: Farrar, Straus & Giroux, 1971.

———. *The Moviegoer.* New York: Farrar, Straus & Giroux, 1967.

Stuntz, William J. "Suffering's Strange Lessons." *New Republic* online edition 11 Sept. 2006.

Weil, Simone. "The Love of God and Affliction." *Waiting for God.* Trans. Emma Craufurd. New York: Harper & Row, 1973.

———. "Reflections on the Right Use of School Studies with a View to the Love of God." *Waiting for God.* New York: Harper Torchbooks, 1973.

Williams, Rowan. "Grace Necessity and Imagination: Catholic Philosophy and the Twentieth Century Artist." The Clark Lectures. "Lecture 1: Modernism and the Scholastic Revival." Trinity College, Cambridge University, 10 Feb. 2005. <http://www.archbishopofcanterbury.org/sermons_speeches/050120a.html.

Wood, Ralph C. *Flannery O'Connor and the Christ-Haunted South.* Grand Rapids: Eerdmans, 2004.

———. "The Heterodoxy of Flannery O'Connor's Book Reviews." *Flannery O'Connor Bulletin* 5 (Autumn 1976): 3-29.

Denise T. Askin (essay date summer 2007)

SOURCE: Askin, Denise T. "Carnival in the 'Temple': Flannery O'Connor's Dialogic Parable of Artistic Vocation." *Christianity and Literature* 56, no. 4 (summer 2007): 555-72.

[In the following essay, Askin interprests the unnamed protagonist of "A Temple of the Holy Ghost" as loosely autobiographical and applies Mikhail Bakhtin's concept of the carnivalesque to underscore the function of humor as a catalyst for spiritual illumination and liberation in the story.]

Faced with a dreaded pilgrimage to Lourdes in 1958, Flannery O'Connor consoled herself by gleefully anticipating the conversations of her fellow pilgrims. They could not fail to be, as she put it, "professionally rewarding" (*The Habit of Being* 264). She considered her comedic art to be her vocation, and she tamed neither her tongue nor her wild imagination in pursuing it. She dismissed edifying fiction like Cardinal Spellman's *The Foundling* for "tidy[ing] up reality" (*HB* 177). Self-consciously religious fiction she called a "smoothing-down" (***Collected Works*** 830) that distorted reality and violated the demands of art. "Stories of pious children tend to be false," she wrote in her preface to **"A Memoir of Mary Ann"** (***CW*** [***Collected Works***] 822), and she peopled her fiction with impudent, even vicious, brats typically locked in mortal combat with domineering elders. O'Connor intended for her outrageous art to shock, perhaps even to scandalize her readers, but she repeatedly defended the comic mode as a fitting vehicle for prophetic vision. She went so far as to claim that she looked for the "will of God through the laws and limitations" of her own art (***CW*** 812). What God seems to have willed for O'Connor was an acid-tongued species of comic-prophetic writing that operates by unveiling human malice in unlikely characters, especially children.

Readers familiar with O'Connor's letters know the pleasure she took in portraying herself as a socially challenged curmudgeon known for her vernacular reductions of academic cant and her delight in the ludicrous aspects of her fellow humans. Her sole function at her mother's social gatherings, she said, was to cover the stain on the couch. In her letters she spoofed her significant theological learning by calling herself a "hillbilly Thomist" (*HB* 81), and she memorialized her social awkwardness among the artsy set at Mary McCarthy's sophisticated New York dinner party by telling the story of how gracelessly she blurted out her belief in transubstantiation: "Well, if it [the Eucharist]'s a symbol, to hell with it" (*HB* 125). The staunchly Catholic persona of the letters is nowhere to be found in her fiction, of course, but in the 1954 story, **"A Temple of the Holy Ghost,"** O'Connor makes a rare departure from custom. In the unnamed adolescent protagonist she traces, not very obliquely, the lineaments of the O'Connor of the letters. The story can be read, in fact, as a wry (if cartoon-like) portrait of the artist.

In **"A Temple of the Holy Ghost,"** O'Connor presents a twelve-year old "born Catholic" protagonist who is as acid-tongued and socially awkward as the O'Connor of the letters. O'Connor takes the artistic risk of creating a Catholic child protagonist (the only one in her canon) in a Catholic setting. The child can be read as a projection of O'Connor herself. The author admitted to Betty Hester that in some ways she was a perpetual twelve-year-old: "the things you have said about my being surprised to be over twelve, etc., have struck me as being quite comically accurate. When I was twelve I made up my mind absolutely that I would not get any older. I don't remember how I planned to stop it" (***CW*** 985). The child of the story is isolated from society, uninitiated into the mysteries of sexuality, smug (if immature) in her Catholicism, and proud of her (sophomoric) intellect. She replicates O'Connor's gaucherie in McCarthy's living room when she gracelessly blurts out a defense of the Eucharistic hymn, *Tantum Ergo*. "You dumb Church of God ox," (***CW*** 202) she shouts to the farm boy who cannot understand it. The prepubescent child has a precociously developed imagination that she uses to satirize the (supposed) fools around her. Surprisingly, by the end of the story, without suffering the scourge of O'Connor's signature ironic twists and violent epiphanies, the child is initiated—in a church setting—into the traditional Catholic mysteries of the Trinity and the Eucharist. While these biographical parallels are worth noting, what is significant from a literary perspective is that the protagonist—a prototype of the Catholic comedic artist—struggles with the edifying language of saints until she discovers the validity of her own comic voice. She is redeemed at last from the path of cynicism and bitterness, not by abandoning her laughter (a conventionally sappy ending that O'Connor would have scorned) but rather by uniting her comic perception to her apprehension of mystery.

Critics as perceptive as Richard Giannone have read **"A Temple of the Holy Ghost"** as a conventional humbling of the proud protagonist in the spirit of the desert fathers, when the child "prayerfully reflects . . . 'hep me not to talk like I do'" (Giannone 102). Christina Bieber Lake claims, more plausibly, that the child's imaginative experience with the "grotesque" hermaphrodite puts her in "a position of exceptional spiritual openness and potential fecundity" (137). O'Connor herself argued in 1955 that the conclusion reveals "the acceptance of what God wills for us, an acceptance of our individual circumstances" (*HB* 124). However, what O'Connor saw as God's will is neither a Hollywood plaster saint for her protagonist nor a parochial aesthetic for herself as writer. Through a complex interplay of contending voices, O'Connor allows the child's own comic discourse to emerge validated despite the efforts of authoritative language to suppress it. Rather than blunting the sharp edge of comic satire in the name of piety, O'Connor appropriates it as an unconventional weapon in the arsenal of grace. I will argue that the last laugh, in a story pervaded by laughter, is O'Connor's own sly endorsement of herself as comic-prophetic artist, the artist whose vocation is predicated on the inherent connection between the comic and the holy, between the carnival and the temple.

"A Temple of the Holy Ghost," can be a stumbling block even for experienced O'Connor readers because it has neither her paradigmatic plot nor her signature ironic ending.[1] Although there is relentless laughter in the first part of the narrative, the story stands out in O'Connor's corpus as singularly *un*comic. It seems rather to be a meditation on the springs (and pitfalls) of comedic vision. Further, the story is filled with pre-Vatican II Catholic "insider" references and allusions: Benediction; the monstrance; St. Scholastica, the brilliant sister of St. Benedict; St. Perpetua, the beautiful martyr in the arena with wild animals (who also had a prophetic vision of a kind of androgyny); St. Thomas, the "dumb-ox" Scholastic; the Stations of the Cross; the legendary medieval miracle of the bloody host; and the Latin office of Corpus Christi. In this story, a vintage nun tells her charges how to handle fresh boys; the child's convent-school cousins sing the *Tantum Ergo* in Latin; and the protagonist herself winds up in the convent chapel kneeling next to a nun and recognizing that she is in the "presence of God" (***CW*** 208). This is a rare and risky excursion for O'Connor into Catholic territory, and the precocious child with a sharp eye (and tongue) for the ridiculous bears a strong family resemblance to Mary Flannery herself. Moving from the protagonist's childish derision to her transcendent epiphany, the story traces the child's initiation into sacramental vision and O'Connor's vocation as a Catholic comedic artist.

The Jesuit scholar William Lynch, one of the formative influences on O'Connor's aesthetic, makes a forceful case for comedy as a fitting mode for the divine. He argues that comic vision is the enemy of rigid ideology, or as he calls it, the "univocal mind" (107). Comedy dispatches demonic abstract thinking that substitutes "phony faith for faith in the power of the vulgar and limited finite" (97). Comedy's descent into the concrete, with all its interstices and smells (95), makes it a genre well suited to the "scandal" of the Incarnation. Lynch argues that comedy serves as an antidote to angelism, the dualistic thinking that divorces the material from the spiritual. It combats pure intellectualism by depicting ludicrous human duality, insisting on images of "ugly human actuality" (98) as a path to God. The comic writer celebrates the mysterious union between the earth and Christ "with all the logic removed" (109). Lynch writes "[t]he mud in man . . . is nothing to be ashamed of. It can produce [. . .] the face of God" (109).

O'Connor appropriated Lynch's terminology in her letters and essays. In "The Nature and Aim of Fiction," she speaks of the "concrete details of life that make actual the mystery of our position on earth" (*Mystery and Manners* 68), and near the end of her life she wrote approvingly, "I agree with W. Lynch's general theory . . . in good fiction and drama you need to go through the concrete situation to some experience of mystery" (*HB* 520). She added, however, "I am no good at theory" (*HB* 520). The parade of freaks and marginal trash (to Ruby Turpin's eyes) that scandalizes Ruby in that raucous vision of heaven; the tattooed back of O. E. Parker that scandalizes his "Straight Gospel" wife; and the rogues' gallery of characters that scandalizes readers looking for recognizable expressions of religious faith are the fruit of O'Connor's vocation as a comic-prophetic writer. She makes Mrs. Greenleaf wallow in the mud shouting "Stab me in the heart, Jesus!" and Hazel Motes blind himself with lime and walk on penitential glass, and young Tarwater drown a "dim-witted child" named "Bishop" while murmuring the words of baptism. So outrageous are her inventions that John Hawkes saw her as a closet nihilist (as cited in Wood, *Comedy of Redemption* 97). But O'Connor challenges the reader to see beyond the surface to the prophetic dimension of her art. In O'Connor's lexicon, the word "prophetic" means "'seeing through' reality" (Magee 89), to extend the gaze "beyond the surface" (***CW*** 818) to the realm of divine life. To be true to this vocation, "[t]he prophet in [her] has to see the freak" (*MM* 82), and the artist must accept the validity of her own voice.

While Lynch provides a theoretical framework for O'Connor's literary vocation, Mikhail Bakhtin provides a technical framework that helps to reveal the intricacy of her art. The work of the Russian dialogic critic bears striking similarities to that of the American Jesuit Lynch. What Lynch calls the univocal mind, Bakhtin calls monologic discourse. While Lynch finds *univocal* or abstract, rigid thinking to be demonic in its exclusion of the finite, sacramental dimension of reality, Bakhtin finds *monologic* discourse, an expression of repressive authority (be it Soviet or other forms), to be tyrannical in its exclusion of the multiple voices of humanity. Both of these critics, approaching fiction from their different perspectives, find an antidote in similar literary forms. For Lynch it is comedy; for Bakhtin, it is the "carnivalesque." These forms give voice to the bodily, limited, phenomenological human condition. Lynch finds comic expression redemptive in its incarnational vision; Bakhtin finds in the carnivalesque a defense against and liberation from authoritative oppression.

Incarnation is central to the work of both Bakhtin and Lynch. Bakhtin saw all language as incarnate, the utterance of concrete persons. Further, Bakhtin's preference for "heteroglossia," a style that brings together "two 'languages,' two semantic and axiological belief systems" within a single syntactic unit (*Diologic Imagination* 304) can be traced to his orthodox roots. Bakhtin defines, according to Charles Lock, a "Chalcedonian, two-voiced, double-natured discourse" (98) that dispenses with clear markers between self-contained and singular voices, and especially in free indirect discourse, insists on "the incarnation of language" (111). Christ, he argues, is the paradigm for Bakhtin's *Dialogic Imagination*: "two natures, divine and human, in the one hypostasis of Christ . . . becomes the paradigm for the dialogical: two voices in the hypostasis of one word" (98).

Both Lynch and Bakhtin define the need for literary devices that can explode monologic discourse and revive sacred discourse through parody. Lynch argues that it is "ridiculous, in a Catholic world, to be afraid of the irreverent in so many secret places" (110). Bakhtin argues in the same vein that only through the "carnival spark" of "cheerful abuse" can calcified sacred language be liberated from "narrow-minded seriousness" and revived. The fiction writer, he says, is free to import discourses from other contexts and genres—such as poetry, song, newspaper articles, and prayer—and thereby activate a dialogue across social and ideological boundaries. This "incorporation of genres," and particularly the carnivalesque and parodic treatment of this imported discourse, serves an almost therapeutic role. It can bring language (often sacred discourse) back to life. The very "degradation" and "uncrowning" of the word, Bakhtin writes, bring about its renewal (*Rabelais and His World* 309).

What we see in **"A Temple of the Holy Ghost"** is not theory dressed in fiction, but rather a fictional exploration of the role of the comic artist in service of the divine mystery. The child protagonist's precocious imaginative life, rendered in free indirect discourse, outdistances the very limited lines allowed to her by polite society. For example, in response to the direct question, "how does a child like you know so much about these men [the Wilkins boys]?" she develops a rich Walter Mitty-esque fantasy about saving the Wilkins boys from Japanese suicide divers in the war. Her actual spoken response is limited to: "I've seen them around is all" (***CW*** 201). The story elevates the child's artistic/imaginative discourse above the diminished possibilities of ordinary discourse with the "morons" around her.

Above all, the child protagonist in **"A Temple of the Holy Ghost"** is endowed with a keen eye for the "mud" or freak in others. She is on the verge of becoming one of O'Connor's gallery of "curdled" intellectuals (Wood, *Flannery O'Connor and the Christ-Haunted South* 200). The child, whose outrageous laughter, sharp tongue, and fertile imagination seem to be in need of reform or suppression, penetrates mysteries no less daunting than the hypostatic union and a sacramental universe, and she does so by employing the very qualities she believes to be at odds with the holy.

The child lives in a world of freaks: "Cheat," the goofy farmer whose face is the color of the red clay roads he travels; Alonzo the odoriferous and obese taxi driver; the Wilkins boys, who sit "like monkeys" (***CW*** 201) on the porch fence. The child equates them with the dancing monkeys, the fat man, and the midget at the fair. The hermaphrodite is the freak that defies categorization, the one that activates the girl's hungry imagination. The child's eye for the freak, like O'Connor's grotesque art, is disconcerting. But if we consider the medieval folk tradition of the carnival, its licensed travesty of liturgy, its parody of sacred discourse, and its temporary replacement of the bishop by a boy/clown, we can situate O'Connor in a tradition that served, by its very excesses, to balance the church's formality and, as Bakhtin says, to renew its sacred discourse.

Both Lynch and Bakhtin identify the medieval Feast of Fools as the paradigm for the dialectic between the comic/carnivalesque and the sacred. As Lynch describes it, the "comic intrusion into the liturgy began with the singing of the Magnificat at vespers, with the words 'He hath put down the mighty from their seat and hath exalted the humble and the meek'" (108). With scripture intoning this ultimate comedic reversal, the carnival begins. Among the carnival travesties were mock sermons, reversals of class and gender roles, and clerics dressing in the clothing of women (Burke 182-89).

O'Connor develops the Feast of Fools motif from the outset: the visiting cousins doff their brown convent-school uniforms and don what can be seen as their "carnival" finery (red skirts, loud blouses, and lipstick). As brashly as carnival revelers, they perform an almost parodic rendition of the *Tantum Ergo* in the sacred language of Latin.

In a carnivalesque gesture, they literalize the trope of the "Temple." Sr. Perpetua has instructed them to fend off ungentlemanly behavior in an automobile by saying "Stop sir! I am a Temple of the Holy Ghost!" Calling themselves "Temple One" and "Temple Two," laughing uncontrollably with each utterance, the teenagers make sport of the sacred trope. Their parody reveals how diminished and calcified the sacred trope has become in the "official" discourse of the convent school.

But carnivalesque laughter, argues Bakhtin, uncrowns and debases the sacred language only to renew it. Because the child detests the mockery she witnesses, she is motivated to explore the trope of the **"Temple of the Holy Ghost"** that she accepts as a "present." The resulting transformation of the words **"Temple of the Holy Ghost"** closely conforms to a phenomenon described by Bakhtin in "Discourse in the Novel." He discusses the rare occurrence of unity between "authoritative discourse" and "internally persuasive discourse." Authoritative discourse "cannot be represented—it is only transmitted" and demands "unconditional allegiance" (*DI* 344). It is semantically inert, a relic, monologic. "Internally persuasive discourse—as opposed to one that is externally authoritative—is, as it is affirmed through assimilation, tightly interwoven with 'one's own word'" (345). In the sequence the child goes through in responding to the Temple trope, O'Connor portrays the process by which authoritative words become internally persuasive and restored to life. The phrase, **"A Temple of the Holy Ghost"** is, as Bakhtin writes about sacred discourse, "not so much interpreted . . . as it is further . . . developed, applied to new material, new conditions. . . . [I]n each of the new contexts that dialogize it, this discourse is able to reveal ever newer *ways to mean*" (*DI* 346, emphasis in original.) The child begins by appropriating the trope imaginatively, first for herself "I am a Temple of the Holy Ghost" (***CW*** 199), then for the pathetic Miss Kirby ("and she's a Temple of the Holy Ghost, too" (200), then for all humanity by having the hermaphrodite preach: "You are God's temple, don't you know?" (207). Finally, she sees the temple in the freak. The hermaphrodite in her dream-fantasy rejoices, "I am a temple of the Holy Ghost" (207). Her imagination endows the trope with "new ways to mean."

By means of carnivalesque travesty and materialization in the figure of the hermaphrodite, the trope is transformed from the static, diminished, official injunction against sexual misconduct. Authoritative discourse becomes internally persuasive, and the phrase emerges pregnant with meaning. Calling to mind the carnivalesque Feast of Fools, O'Connor introduces the language of the sacred, subjects it to parody, and finally reclaims the trope of the Temple of the Holy Ghost through an incongruous union of profane and sacred. The cousins, having fulfilled their carnivalesque roles, end their saturnalia, return to their brown uniforms, and disappear into the anonymous convent school choir singing the *Tantum Ergo* at Benediction. Order is restored, and the sacred discourse is renewed.

Just as the girls intrude into the child's world with their carnivalesque irreverence, so the hermaphrodite takes up the carnivalesque role in the child's imagination. As Susan Srigley reminds us in *Flannery O'Connor's Sacramental Art,* Thomas Aquinas viewed the imagination to be "the main receptor of the revelatory experience" (146). The carnival freak is a character made of words, never seen by the child, but given a voice by her imagination, nonetheless. Like a transdressing carnival participant giving a mock sermon, the hermaphrodite wears a blue dress and preaches like a revivalist in the circus tent. The hermaphrodite resides in her imagination, an "answer to a riddle that was more puzzling than the riddle itself" (***CW*** 206). The physical mystery of the two-gendered freak is the gateway to the true mystery of the Temple of the Holy Ghost, a mystery that must be grasped by the imagination. The freak's speech becomes, through the child's interpolation, a version of the *Magnificat.* She assigns new words to him: "God done this to me and I praise Him. . . . A temple of God is a holy thing. . . . I am a temple of the Holy Ghost" (207). Like the medieval Lord of Misrule who intrudes into Vespers during the *Magnificat,* the carnival freak intrudes into the ceremony of Benediction. At the elevation of the monstrance, it is this discourse of the freak that the child "hears."

In order to understand the power of this unifying epiphany, we need to consider the duality or "doubleness" that constitutes the story's structure. O'Connor employs binary opposition and comedic doubling as the pathway for the child's encounter with mystery. The entire story is contrapuntal. There are two Catholic girl cousins (Temple One and Temple Two), dressed identically, and matched with two Protestant farm boy brothers; these two character pairs engage in an antiphonal duel between two religious musical traditions ("I've Got a Friend in Jesus" and "The Old Rugged Cross" versus the *Tantum Ergo*). There are two sexes in the hermaphrodite, a creature the child at first imagines having two heads, like the androgyne in Plato's *Symposium* (his mythic image of the whole human). There are two warnings that God will strike the mocker by two marginal characters: the Negro cook and the carnival freak. There are two expositions (in carnival tent and convent chapel), two ivory circles (sun and host), two narrative versions of the hermaphrodite (the cousins' story and the child's dreamlike reverie), two "Amens" (the cousins' parodic ending of the *Tantum Ergo* and the carnival audience's reverent response to the hermaphrodite in the tent). The story pulsates with *two-ness.*

Enter the child with the comedic mean streak. From the first paragraph in the story, this two-ness affects her role: "[i]f only one of them [the cousins] had come, that one would have played with her, but since there were two of them, she was out of it, and watched them suspiciously from a distance" (***CW*** 197). The doubling forces the child to become a spectator, fostering both her derisive laughter and her creative imagination. As Lake remarks, the cousins are content "to live in a world of binaries defined by sexual desire" (136), but the child's ability to "see beyond the gender roles" leads her to "grasp profound spiritual concepts the girls only mock" (135).

Just as the hermaphrodite physically joins binary opposites, so the solitary child-as-artist brings together opposites throughout the story. She links the old farmer Cheat and the 250-pound Alonzo with the boy-crazy cousins, convulsing herself with laughter at the resulting incongruity. She matches the Catholic girls with the Protestant boys. She imagines martyrs wearing circus tights, and she imagines circus performers to be martyrs waiting for their tongues to be cut out. She unites the Temple of the Holy Ghost trope with the body of the hermaphrodite, seeing the *sacred* in the freak with "all the logic removed" (Lynch 109). Her quickened imagination introduces the words of the hermaphrodite at the elevation of the monstrance at Benediction, uniting profane and sacred. Finally, the child conflates the natural image of the sun, "like an elevated Host" (***CW*** 209) with the supernatural presence of God in the Eucharist.

Comedic doubling and binary opposition, then, become for the child a kind of bipolar, dialogic pathway to an overarching unity—an encounter with mystery. The mysterious joining of two sexes in one body is a parodic reflection of the hypostatic union defined by the Council of Chalcedon, a mystery of the true union of two full natures with neither of them compromised—the scandal of the God-made-man. O'Connor's protagonist is mystified by the concrete reality of the hermaphrodite's body, complete with a double set of genitalia. Ironically, it is this bodily manifestation of mystery that leads the child to encounter (using Lynch's phrase) "the face of God." All these connections conspire at the end to reveal the sacramental, or as Bakhtin would call it, the tropic nature of creation in the child's epiphanic vision of the sun. The intractable two-ness of the world reveals an underlying oneness. The incongruous realities of existence, then, become resolved in a new perception of congruence. Reality becomes eloquent of the sacred.

If the comic artist enjoys a double *vision,* O'Connor matches it with a *double-voiced style* in this story. O'Connor wages the battle for the comedic artist's vocation most definitively through language. As noted above, Bakhtin argues that dialogic narrative defends against the rigid reductionism of "authoritative" or monologic language. Three aspects of O'Connor's dialogic technique in this story—incorporated genres, the forging of a hybrid narrative discourse, and the contest with authoritative language—bring about the validation of the child's comedic voice.

O'Connor incorporates the genre of hymnody—both Catholic and Protestant—in a way that suggests Bakhtin's theory of uncrowning and renewing. Like Bakhtin's rebellion against the "official speech" of communism, O'Connor's parody suggests that for a secularized, desacralized discourse, the carnivalesque response can be renewing. When the "Church of God" Wilkins boys and the Catholic convent cousins engage in their musical duel, it would be a mistake to dismiss this exchange as a bit of vaudeville humor in the story. The scene "dialogizes" the narrative by introducing voices from vastly different discourses. In the process it mystifies those from other discourse traditions and excludes those who do not take pains to appropriate the discourse. "That must be Jew singing" (***CW*** 202) says the farm boy when he hears the Latin hymn. By placing the Latin words into the story with neither translation nor footnote, however, O'Connor also makes the words inaccessible even to the Catholic schoolgirls and presumably to much of O'Connor's pre-Vatican II Catholic readership who knew the hymn only by rote. In similar fashion, although she provides a couple of verses of "I've Got a Friend in Jesus," the narrator merely alludes to "The Old Rugged Cross" without providing the text, thereby excluding those unfamiliar with the Gospel tradition. By alienating or hiding these discourses, O'Connor continues the "in-joke" mode she established through her allusions. Only when the reader reclaims these incorporated genres, translating or supplying the texts, will the words reveal their web of connections with the central symbolism of the text.

Just as the cousins caricatured the phrase **"Temple of the Holy Ghost,"** they also make entertainment out of the words of the *Tantum Ergo.* Ironically, it is through their parody that the voice of Thomas Aquinas enters the dialogue, in the hymn commissioned by Pope Urban IV in 1264 for the newly-founded feast of Corpus Christi (Body of Christ). Thomas's hymn introduces references to the Eucharist (mysterious union of God and Man united mysteriously in the host) and to the equally mysterious union of three persons in the Trinity. In a different way, the narrator's allusion to "The Old Rugged Cross" taxes the reader to supply the missing discourse. Only then can its connections with the imagery of the child's inner life materialize. For example, the child is described as sometimes "think-[ing] of Christ on the long journey to Calvary, crushed three times under the rough cross" (***CW*** 205). Here O'Connor mixes the discourses of Protestant and Catholic traditions, because this is a distinctly "Catholic" meditation, based on the practice of the Stations of the Cross, not on Gospel accounts which make no mention of Christ's three falls.

The cross of the gospel song is "despised by the world," but also holds a "wondrous attraction"—language that can easily be applied to the child's meditation on the hermaphrodite. The cross of the gospel song is "stained with blood so divine" like the sun-host "drenched in blood" (***CW*** 209) at the end of the story. In the gospel song, the cross itself will be "exchanged some day" for a "crown"—echoing the crown of martyrdom to which the child aspires, but which she hopes to achieve without the tedious journey of the cross. The gospel hymn points to the child's task in the story: to trade her romanticized fantasy of quick martyrdom for the slow way of the rugged/rough cross.

The hidden discourses of both the *Tantum Ergo* and "The Old Rugged Cross," therefore, point to the mystery the child will encounter. These incorporated genres create a multi-voiced narrative, a chorus of voices all echoing the same mystery, and reaching a crescendo when, at the second singing of the *Tantum Ergo,* the mystery of the **"Temple of the Holy Ghost"** comes alive to the child in the words of the carnival freak.

The two key images of the story—the hermaphrodite (half man and half woman) and the host (Christ's body under the appearance of bread)—are supported by a series of subordinate hybrid forms that surround and amplify the mysterious unions of incarnation, Trinity, and Eucharist. The images include the gospel song that is "half like a love song and half like a hymn" (***CW*** 201), the child's dream of sainthood—half Hollywood and half hagiography,[2] and the hybrid discourse of the carnival freak—half *Magnificat* and half tent revival. Most significantly, O'Connor's hybrid narrative discourse works particularly well in this story to adumbrate the central theme.

The smooth discourse of the narrator is readily distinguished from the child's. Narrator: "the revolving searchlight . . . widened and shortened and wheeled in its arc" (***CW*** 204). The narrator's voice tends to be objective, "[t]he sound of the calliope coming from the window kept her awake and she remembered that she hadn't said her prayers and got up and knelt down and began them" (205). The child's own direct discourse, in stark contrast to the narrator's, is laced with childish epithets and colloquial grammar: "You big dumb Church of God ox!" (202), "I ain't eating with them" (202), "Those stupid idiots" (203).

While these two idioms are readily distinguished from one another, O'Connor introduces a strategic hybrid discourse. This form of "heteroglossia," according to Bakhtin, brings together two utterances, two speech manners, in a "double-accented, double-styled" construction (*DI* 304).[3] From the very first page, the child's "character zone," or field of action for a character's voice, (*DI* 316) infiltrates the narrator's discourse, blurring the distinction between the two. O'Connor develops double-voiced sentences that shift from narrator to child within one syntactic unit: "The child decided, after observing them for a few hours, that they were *practically morons and she was glad to think that they were only second cousins and she couldn't have inherited any of their stupidity*" (***CW*** 197, emphasis added). The sentence begins with the narrator's voice reporting the child's thoughts, but it ends by shifting to the child's language (italicized) through free indirect discourse. Throughout the story, the telltale idiom of the child erupts into the narrative, jostling the narrator's, and making the source of such claims as "the girls giggled *idiotically*" (202) ambiguous at best.

This extension of the child's character zone into the narrator's territory also leads to a struggle with "calcified" official language in the story. Just as Huck Finn's "conscience" (which speaks in the monologic, official language of society) nearly overrides the voice of his instinctive morality when he tries to pray, so too, the child's authentic voice in **"Temple"** [**"A Temple of the Holy Ghost"**] struggles for survival. Huck and the **"Temple"** child have much in common. Both are at a threshold age, innocent of sexual awakening, exempted from polite decorum, free to follow their wits (or wit), free to be ill-mannered, to "lie" creatively or to tell the truth crassly, to see through the falsified language of the grown-up world and properly name it as "flapdoodle" and "talky-talk" (Twain, 180, 187) or "twaddle" (**"Temple,"** ***CW*** 208). But Huck's voice—the triumph of Twain's work—is almost drowned out by the socially approved discourse of prayer. The problem is a real one for O'Connor, too, as she reveals in a 1956 letter to "A" regarding the language of novenas. "I hate to say most of these prayers written by saints-in-an-emotional-state. You feel you are wearing somebody else's finery and I can never describe my heart as 'burning' to the Lord (who knows better) without snickering" (*HB,* 145). By referring to the language of saints as "somebody else's finery," O'Connor points facetiously to the conflict between the discourse of others and authentic discourse in prayer. For the child in **"Temple,"** this struggle with authorized language leads at last to the validation of her own voice.

Two crucial moments in the story, the child's meditation on sainthood and her prayer in the chapel during Benediction, often serve as proof-texts for critical judgments about the nature of her development in the story. Looking at them from a dialogic perspective, we see an internal struggle between two kinds of discourse. When the child reflects on sainthood, she concludes that her "ugly" mode of speech disqualifies her from being a saint:

> she did not *steal* or *murder* but she was a born *liar* and *slothful* and she sassed her mother and was *deliberately* ugly, to almost everybody. She was eaten up also *with the sin of Pride, the worst one.* She made fun of the Baptist preacher who came to the school at commencement to give the devotional. She would pull down her mouth and hold her forehead as if she were in agony and groan, "Fawther, we thank Thee," exactly the way he did and *she had been told many times not to do it.* She could never be a saint, but she thought she could be a martyr if they killed her quick.
>
> (***CW*** 204, emphasis added)

The child's language of self-knowledge becomes self-accusation, rendered in free indirect discourse. The passage mixes the child's own idiom with the (italicized) language spoken in the confessional box, signaled by the use of a capital "P" for pride. This authoritative voice condemns the child's fertile inventiveness as "lies," labels her contempt for stupidity as "Pride," and ranks her sin at the top of the hierarchy. It requires that she suppress her outrageous language.

The child "has been told many times" not to do her comic parody of the minister, a send-up in the classic carnivalesque mode (and, interestingly, precisely the sort of mimicry that O'Connor herself delighted in throughout her life, as her letters attest). From the monologic perspective, the child's sassy, comic discourse is the enemy of sanctity, but this judgment smacks of angelism, the dualistic thinking that divorces the "vulgar concrete" from the holy. The only route to sainthood in the world of monologic discourse, the child concludes, is to leapfrog over concrete reality and its slow and often ludicrous journey, and to get herself killed "quick." Comical as the wording is, the passage reveals the child's voice to be in combat with a life-denying discourse. She must be liberated if she is to fulfill her comic vocation, and, more importantly, if she is to enter into an authentic dialogue with God.

The second passage deals precisely with that dialogue with God. It is easy to hear conventional piety in the child's prayer at Benediction: "hep me not to be so mean . . . [h]ep me not to talk like I do" (***CW*** 208). But we must remember that O'Connor believes that stories of pious children are usually "false." If we place the child's prayer in its linguistic context, we get a different result. Earlier in the story, the narrator had mocked the child's mechanical night prayers: "[s]he took a running start and went through to the other side of the Apostle's Creed" (205). Similarly, the narrator comments that her prayer at Benediction begins "mechanically" (208). Her rote recitation echoes the monologic catalogue of self-accusations. On the verge of renouncing her comedic role—"hep me not to talk like I do" (208)—the child is rescued by the unbidden voice of her imagination. The hermaphrodite intrudes as if in answer to her prayer: "I don't dispute hit. This is the way He wanted me to be" (209). Audaciously, O'Connor provides a vehicle for God's "voice" in the child's awakened imagination, turning her monologue into a dialogue. O'Connor described a similar dialogical process in her essay, "Catholic Novelists and Their Readers": "The Lord doesn't speak to the novelist as he did to his servant Moses, mouth to mouth. He speaks to him as he did to those two complainers, Aaron and Aaron's sister, Mary: through dreams and visions, [. . .] and by all the lesser and limited ways of the imagination" (*MM* 181). The child's acceptance of God's will, then, comes not from abstract angelism, but from its shocking opposite—from the discourse of the freak. Marshall Gentry reads the scene as a validation of the child's meanness (66), and Joanne McMullen sees it as evidence of her "non-redemption" (106), but it can be more convincingly read as the validation of her comic/satiric voice and vocation.

O'Connor provides a richly dialogic ending to the story, governing the exit scene by hybrid discourse: "[a]s they were leaving the convent door, the *big nun* swooped down on her mischievously and *nearly smothered her in the black habit, mashing the side of her face into the crucifix hitched onto her belt*" (***CW*** 209, emphasis added). The cheeky idiom of the child in "mashed" and "hitched" takes the hex off the potentially maudlin tableau. One could also argue that in this passage O'Connor cannot resist embedding the pun that the cross "makes an impression" on her. On the drive home, the child, like O'Connor on her pilgrimage to Lourdes, gathers professional (comic) material in the backseat of the taxi. Looking at Alonzo's ears, she sees them "pointed almost like a pig's" (209). After the epiphany, the comedic voice endures. No "pious" ending here.

Conclusion

In **"A Temple of the Holy Ghost"** O'Connor sets in motion a complex series of reverberations, a dialogic echo chamber that reenacts the tropic/sacramental nature of reality into which the child is initiated. Like a hall of mirrors at a country carnival, images of mysterious incarnation and containment correspond to this verbal echoing. The host of the Eucharist is God; God is three persons; the incarnate Christ unites God and humanity; the "temple" houses the Holy Ghost and therefore all three divine persons; the hermaphrodite is both male and female and is a temple of the Holy Ghost; the sun mirrors the host, and the host embodies the divine mysteries (Trinity, Incarnation); the "sign of the cross" signifies the God-made-man's suffering, naming all three persons of the Trinity. The concluding epiphany points to the metaphoric way of the cross that the child and the hermaphrodite (and by implication, all human beings) must travel. Waves of refracted and resonating meaning overtake the child; the world becomes eloquent of mystery—a mystery she can participate in without being a "saint." This dazzling array of reverberations can be read as O'Connor's approximation of sacramental vision, the spiritual illumination and liberation which the child—as uniter/artist—experiences at the end of the story.

As Bakhtin claims, carnivalesque laughter and dialogic narratives are liberating. Lynch, too, argues that the comic medium reminds us that "a thing need not step out of the human . . . to achieve the liberty of the children of God. The mud in man, the lowermost point in the subway, is nothing to be ashamed of" (109). The child in **"A Temple of the Holy Ghost"** is liberated to see the freak in herself as well as in Alonzo and the hermaphrodite, to see the freak as the temple of God, and even to see the freak in Christ in the Eucharist, Christ who was willing, as St. Paul tells the Philippians, "to assume the condition of a slave" (i.e.

a freak) for our salvation. The child is liberated, as well, to see her own outrageous voice as God's calling. The child's unifying vision can be seen as a gateway to what Susan Srigley calls O'Connor's "ethic of responsibility," the possibility of moving beyond "a life ordered solely by love of the self" (5). The isolated spectator-child with her "ugly" mean streak and sense of superiority becomes a creative unifier. She gives voice to a freak that is both mocked and mysterious, investing this "grotesque" character with prophetic utterance.

At the end of the story, the officials (preachers and police) with their univocal minds make an attempt to suppress the carnivalesque by shutting down the fair. The child is indeed silent in the last scene, but she is temporarily "shut up" more than permanently "shut down." The carnivalesque is alive in the child's comedic imagination, populated by the freaks and fat men, monkeys, farmers, and pigs she has the gift to see as both ludicrous and holy. O'Connor makes sure that the artistically risky sacramental image of the blood-drenched host in the sky[4] is followed by a vision of "a red clay road" (***CW*** 209) the very road on which travel old farmer Cheatam and his Negroes, not plaster saints. The child's comic imagination and voice are placed at last into the necessary dialogue with the sacred, and the comic artist is born.

Notes

1. The relationship between the mother and child in this story also departs from the O'Connor formula. The mother is neither domineering nor smugly complacent. Rather, she laughs (guardedly) at her daughter's rude jokes, speaks kindly to correct the child's insolent humor, and confides in the child about the horrors of the teenage visitors. This mother is so far from speaking in the clichéd discourse typically assigned to O'Connor's mother characters that she rescues the trope of the "Temple of the Holy Ghost" from the clutches of the cousins, validates it as true, and gifts her daughter with this metaphoric and mysterious "present."

2. There are striking parallels between the child's reveries about the hermaphrodite and the account of Perpetua's visions before her martyrdom. While awaiting death in the arena, Perpetua records a vision in which "all those who stood around said: Amen!" From this dream she learns, as does O'Connor's protagonist, that she "must suffer" (Musurillo, *Acts of the Christian Fathers*). In a later vision, Perpetua is called into an arena, surrounded by an "enormous crowd who watched in astonishment. . . . My clothes were stripped off, and suddenly I was a man." Perpetua becomes a woman (referred to as "her," and "daughter") in a man's body. When she dispatches her adversary in the dream, Perpetua writes "I began to walk in triumph towards the Gate of Life. Then I awoke." Her actual martyrdom proves difficult to accomplish, "as though . . . feared as she was by the unclean spirit, [she] could not be dispatched unless she herself were willing." At last she helps the gladiator to cut her throat. O'Connor's depiction of the child's martyrdom fantasy makes an interesting comparison: the lions will not maul her, and the Romans do not succeed in burning her, so "finding she was so hard to kill, they finally cut her throat." It seems to be hagiography more than Hollywood that informs the child's fantasies.

3. This dialogic form most closely approximates Bakhtin's understanding of the hypostatic union in Christ, according to Charles Lock in "Bakhtin and the Tropes of Orthodoxy."

4. McMullen argues that O'Connor gives the "commonly understood symbol" of the sun "uncharacteristic couplings" that disorient the reader. She cites the blood-drenched sun/host as a case in point (33). Other critics have seen the bloody host image as a symbol of martyrdom, of the cross, or even of the impending onset of the menses for the prepubescent protagonist. In fact, O'Connor is more likely alluding to a story that would have been familiar to pre-Vatican II Catholic school children: the story of Peter of Prague, the thirteenth-century priest whose doubts about transubstantiation were miraculously dispelled at Mass when, at the moment of the consecration, the host began to drip with blood. Partly in response to this miracle, Pope Urban IV instituted the Feast of Corpus Christi soon thereafter to honor Christ's presence in the Eucharist. Here we see another of O'Connor's "insider" allusions to the mystery celebrated by the *Tantum Ergo*.

Works Cited

Bakhtin, Mikhail. *The Dialogic Imagination: Four Essays*. Trans. Caryl Emerson and Michael Holmquist. Ed. Michael Holmquist. Austin: U of Texas P, 1981.

———. *Rabelais and His World.* Trans. Helene Iswolsky. Bloomington: Indiana UP, 1984.

Burke, Peter. *Popular Culture in Early Modern Europe.* New York: Harper & Row, 1978.

Gentry, Marshal Bruce. *Flannery O'Connor's Religion of the Grotesque.* Jackson: UP of Mississippi, 1986.

Giannone, Richard. *Flannery O'Connor: Hermit Novelist.* Urbana: U of Illinois P, 2000.

Lake, Christina Bieber. *The Incarnational Art of Flannery O'Connor.* Macon: Mercer UP, 2005.

Lynch, William F. "Comedy." *Christ and Apollo: The Dimensions of the Literary Imagination.* New York: Sheed and Ward, 1960. 91-113.

Lock, Charles. "Bakhtin and the Tropes of Orthodoxy." *Bakhtin and Religion: A Feeling for Faith.* Eds. Susan M. Felch and Paul J. Contino. Evanston: Northwestern UP, 2001. 97-119.

Magee, Rosemary M., ed. *Conversations with Flannery O'Connor.* Jackson: UP of Mississippi, 1987.

McMullen, Joanne Halleran. *Writing Against God: Language as Message in the Literature of Flannery O'Connor.* Macon: Mercer UP, 1996.

Herbert Musurillo, ed. *The Acts of the Christian Fathers.* New York: Oxford UP, 1972.

O'Connor, Flannery. *Collected Works.* Ed. Sally Fitzgerald. New York: Library of America, 1988.

———. *The Habit of Being.* Ed. Sally Fitzgerald. New York: Farrar, Straus and Giroux, 1979.

———. *Mystery and Manners: Occasional Prose.* Eds. Sally Fitzgerald and Robert Fitzgerald. New York: Farrar, Straus and Giroux, 1969.

Srigley, Susan. *Flannery O'Connor's Sacramental Art.* Notre Dame: U of Notre Dame P, 2004.

Twain, Mark. *The Adventures of Huckleberry Finn.* 1884. Ed. John Seelye. New York: Penguin. 1985.

Wood, Ralph C. *The Comedy of Redemption: Christian Faith and Comic Vision in Four American Novelists.* Notre Dame: U of Notre Dame P, 1988.

———. *Flannery O'Connor and the Christ-Haunted South.* Grand Rapids: Eerdmans, 2004.

FURTHER READING

Criticism

Coles, Robert. "Flannery O'Connor's Pilgrimage." *Logos* 6, no. 1 (winter 2003): 27-40.

Provides a biographical sketch of O'Connor.

Fallon, April D. "The Grotesque as Feminist Revision of the 'Southern Lady' in Carson McCullers's and Flannery O'Connor's Fiction." *Journal of Kentucky Studies* 23 (September 2006): 113-21.

Discusses the rebellion against gender roles in O'Connor's short fiction and that of Carson McCullers.

Hardy, Donald E. and David Durian. "The Stylistics of Syntactic Complements: Grammar and Seeing in Flannery O'Connor's Fiction." *Style* 34, no. 1 (spring 2000): 92-116.

Investigates the semantic connotations of the verb "see" in O'Connor's stories.

McGurl, Mark. "Understanding Iowa: Flannery O'Connor, B.A., M.F.A." *American Literary History* 19, no. 2 (summer 2007): 546-56.

Acknowledges O'Connor as the first major literary figure to emerge from an M.F.A. creative-writing program.

Additional coverage of O'Connor's life and career is contained in the following sources published by Gale: *American Writers*; *American Writers Retrospective Supplement*, Vol. 2; *Authors and Artists for Young Adults*, Vol. 7; *Beacham's Encyclopedia of Popular Fiction: Biography & Resources*, Vol. 3; *Beacham's Guide to Literature for Young Adults*, Vol. 16; *Concise Dictionary of American Literary Biography*, 1941-1968; *Contemporary Authors*, Vols. 1-4R; *Contemporary Authors New Revision Series*, Vols. 3, 41; *Contemporary Literary Criticism*, Vols. 1, 2, 3, 6, 10, 13, 15, 21, 66, 104; *Dictionary of Literary Biography*, Vols. 2, 152; *Dictionary of Literary Biography Documentary Series*, Vol. 12; *Dictionary of Literary Biography Yearbook*, 1980; *DISCovering Authors*; *DISCovering Authors: British Edition*; *DISCovering Authors: Canadian Edition*; *DISCovering Authors Modules: Most-Studied Authors* and *Novelists*; *DISCovering Authors 3.0*; *Encyclopedia of World Literature in the 20th Century*, Ed. 3; *Exploring Short Stories*; *Literature and Its Times*, Vol. 5; *Literature Resource Center*; *Major 20th-Century Writers*, Eds. 1, 2; *Major 21st-Century Writers*, eBook 2005; *Modern American Literature*, Ed. 5; *Modern American Women Writers*; *Novels for Students*, Vols. 3, 21; *Reference Guide to American Literature*, Ed. 4; *Reference Guide to Short Fiction*, Ed. 2; *Short Stories for Students*, Vols. 2, 7, 10, 19; *Short Story Criticism*, Vols. 1, 23, 61, 82; *Twayne's United States Authors*; *Twentieth-Century Literary Criticism*, Vol. 132; and *World Literature Criticism*, Vol. 4.

Edgar Allan Poe
1809-1849

American short story writer, poet, critic, nonfiction writer, and essayist.

The following entry provides an overview of Poe's short fiction. For additional information on his short fiction career, see *SSC,* Volumes 1 and 54; for discussion of the short story "The Fall of the House of Usher" (1839), see *SSC,* Volume 22; for discussion of the short story "The Tell-Tale Heart" (1843), see *SSC,* Volume 34; for discussion of the short story "The Cask of Amontillado" (1846), see *SSC,* Volume 35; for discussion of the short story "The Masque of the Red Death" (1842), see *SSC,* Volume 88.

INTRODUCTION

Poe's stature as a major author is primarily based on his intense and exquisitely crafted tales, and he is regarded by many critics as the architect of the modern short story. Both a romantic and a rationalist, Poe was influenced by the poetry of Lord Byron and Samuel Taylor Coleridge as well as German gothic writers Ludwig Tieck and E. T. A. Hoffmann. He was also an outspoken advocate of the aesthetic notion of "art for art's sake," and the unsettling imagery that dominates much of his fiction is presented in carefully arranged symbolic forms. He is credited with originating the first American detective story—a genre which suits Poe's thematic concerns by emphasizing the complementary psychological functions of intuition and logic. Fascinated with the world of dreams, trances, madness, and horror, Poe at the same time was interested in scientific analysis and sought in his short stories to draw realistic portraits of particular mental states in ways that would appeal to mass audiences.

BIOGRAPHICAL INFORMATION

Poe was born in Boston, Massachusetts, the son of professional actors David and Elizabeth Arnold Poe. By the time he was three, Poe, his older brother, and his younger sister had lost their mother to consumption; their father deserted the family. The children were split up, going to live in the homes of various families. Poe went to Richmond, Virginia, to the charitable home of John and Frances Allan, whose name Poe later took as his own middle name. The wealthy Allans treated him like an adopted son, saw to his education in private academies, and took him to England for a five-year stay. As Poe entered adolescence, however, he developed a troubled relationship with John Allan. Allan disapproved of his ward's literary inclinations and thought him surly and ungrateful. When, in 1826, Poe entered the newly opened University of Virginia, Allan's allowance was so meager that Poe turned to gambling to supplement his income. He had also begun drinking heavily, a vice that would plague him for the rest of his life. Within eight months he found himself badly in debt. Allan's refusal to help him led to total estrangement. In April 1827, Poe traveled to Boston, where he signed up for a five-year enlistment in the U.S. Army. That same year Poe published the poetry collection *Tamerlane* (1827) at his own expense, but it failed to attract notice. By January 1829, serving under the name of Edgar A. Perry, Poe rose to the highest noncommissioned rank in the army, sergeant major. He was reluctant to serve out the full enlistment, however, and he arranged to be discharged from the army on the understanding that he would seek an appointment at West Point. He thought such a move might bring about reconciliation with his guardian. Later that year *Al Araaf, Tamerlane, and Minor Poems* (1829) was published in Baltimore and received a highly favorable review from the novelist and critic John Neal. Armed with these new credentials, Poe visited Allan in Richmond, but another violent quarrel forced him to leave in May 1830. The West Point engagement came through the next month, but Poe did not last long as a cadet. Lacking Allan's permission to resign, he sought and received a dismissal for "gross neglect of duty" and "disobedience of orders." He moved to the home of his aunt, Maria Clemm, in 1831, and began publishing short stories in magazines. His first published story, "Metzengerstein," appeared in 1832. The following year he received a monetary prize for his story "MS. Found in a Bottle," and John Pendleton Kennedy got him a job with the *Southern Literary Messenger.*

In 1836 Poe married his thirteen-year-old cousin, Virginia Clemm, and moved to Richmond with his bride and mother-in-law. Excessive drinking cost him his job in 1837, but he had produced prolifically for the journal and had quintupled the magazine's circulation. Rejection in the face of such accomplishment left him in an extremely distressed state of mind. Poe subsequently moved with Virginia and her mother to New York, where he did hack work and managed to publish his novella *The Narrative of Arthur Gordon Pym of Nantucket* (1838). They then moved to Philadelphia, where Poe served as coeditor of *Burton's Gentleman's Magazine.* After contributing some of his most famous fiction (including "The Fall of the House of Usher") to its pages, he left to accept a position as literary editor for *Graham's Magazine.* His increased alcoholism and confrontational behavior, however, soon caused him to abandon this post. Although he continued to publish, Poe's deteriorating mental and physical state became greatly exacerbated when his wife began to show signs of consumption. Despite the popularity of his poetry collection *The Raven* (1845), he struggled to hold down steady work while his wife's illness became more severe. In 1847 Virginia died, but Poe managed to continue writing and publishing. He returned to Richmond in 1849, where he became engaged to a friend from his youth, Elmira Royster Shelton. Poe left for New York to bring his aunt back for the wedding, stopping off in Baltimore, Maryland, along the way. He was found in a stupor near a saloon, and died in a hospital four days later. The cause of and circumstances surrounding his death remain unknown. Poe was buried in the Westminster Presbyterian Cemetery in Baltimore.

MAJOR WORKS OF SHORT FICTION

Often narrated by an unnamed, first-person teller, Poe's stories display a psychological intensity that reflects the internal struggles of his characters. Such inner turmoil frequently manifests itself in the form of insanity, and Poe's short fiction details the violent consequences of giving oneself over to irrationality and madness. Poe avoided any hint of moralizing in these rather disturbing stories, believing that art's chief responsibility is the transmission of beauty. Set in a haunted mansion that seems to be a locus of sentient evil, "The Fall of the House of Usher" is the tale of twin siblings Roderick and Madeline, the last descendants of a cursed family. The struggle between the forces of life and death is paralleled in the story by the conflict of reason versus insanity; these tensions eventually cause the mansion to collapse in on itself, killing those inside. The title character of "William Wilson" is driven mad by the notion that he is being shadowed throughout his life by a mysterious double. At the end of the story, the narrator strikes his doppelgänger with a sword only to face a mirror image of his own body bleeding to death. Consisting entirely of an interior monologue, "The Tell-Tale Heart" is a psychological portrait of a mentally unbalanced individual who senselessly kills an elderly man and afterward continues to hear his victim's relentless heartbeat. An unbearable sense of remorse builds within the narrator's mind until he eventually confesses his crime to the police. Another tale of guilt and madness, "The Black Cat" focuses on an alcoholic who, increasingly drawn toward thoughts of violence, kills his beloved cat, Pluto. Immediately after this horrendous act, his house burns down. When he and his wife move to a new home, he finds himself being followed by another cat that bears a close resemblance to Pluto. The narrator begins to hate and fear the animal. When his wife tries to prevent him from killing the cat with an axe, he murders her instead. Although the narrator nearly gets away with the crime, the cat draws the attention of the police to the wall in which the wife's body is buried. The tension between madness and rationality is also at the center of "The System of Dr. Tarr and Professor Fether." Traveling through southern France, the narrator of the tale comes upon the insane asylum of M. Maillard, where a conflict is brewing between those in favor of the "soothing system"—in which patients are allowed to act out their delusions—and those supporting the "new" system of Professors Tarr and Fether, in which delusion is not tolerated. The narrator slowly discovers that the people posing as orderlies during his visit are actually those committed to the institution. The mental patients had recently overthrown the doctors, tarred and feathered them, and locked them in a basement prison. An odd hybrid of narrative and essay, "The Imp of the Perverse" consists of a condemned man's speculations on the "primitive impulse" that compels individuals to oppose their instinct for survival. The reader later learns that the narrator, after committing the perfect murder, was unable to prevent himself from compulsively confessing his crime to the police. "The Cask of Amontillado" is narrated by an Italian aristocrat, Montresor, who recounts the harrowing act of vengeance that he exacted upon his nemesis and fellow nobleman, Fortunato. Disguised as a jester, Montresor lures his foe into an underground chamber under the ruse of inspecting the quality of some recently purchased Amontillado wine. Once there, he chains Fortunato to a wall in a small alcove, and proceeds to seal it off with brick and mortar while his victim screams in terror.

Some of Poe's short fiction ponders the metaphysical aspects of death. The mortally ill title character of "The Facts in the Case of M. Valdemar" is hypnotized shortly before his projected time of death. He remains in a trance-like state for weeks, neither fully deceased nor fully alive, until his trance is broken and his body quickly decomposes. Vankirk, the hypnotized subject in "Mesmeric Revelation," continues to speak after physiological death, offering speculations on the mystical nature of the universe. In "A Tale of the Ragged Mountains," the sickly Augustus Bedloe remembers being killed in a city in the Orient, his description exactly duplicating the experience of Mr. Oldeb, a friend of Bedloe's physician, Dr. Templeton. Templeton, who shares a mesmeric connection with his patient, also notes the strong physical resemblance between Bedloe and his deceased acquaintance Oldeb. He soon realizes that Bedloe is inexplicably living the events of Oldeb's past concurrent with the doctor's recollection of those events. Later, the narrator of the story learns that Bedloe has died, remarking that the newspaper's misspelling of his name without the final "e" is "Oldeb" written backwards. The narrator of "Ligeia" is in mourning over the death of his wife, Ligeia, recollecting her deathbed proclamation that only a lack of will prevents a person from living forever. Later, the narrator moves to England and marries a woman whom he despises. After she dies mysteriously following their wedding night, the narrator is astounded to see her come back to life as Ligeia. In "The Masque of the Red Death," Prince Prospero seals himself and a thousand followers inside his abbey while a plague known as the Red Death ravages the Italian countryside. Life inside Prospero's compound consists of a series of festivities. At the last costume ball, a figure garbed like a victim of the plague appears, horrifying and enraging the spectators. Prospero dies in a confrontation with the stranger, who lacks a corporeal body beneath the macabre costume, and the revelers succumb to the Red Death.

Many of Poe's stories also display the author's acerbic wit. An absurdly humorous tale, "Loss of Breath" (originally titled "A Decided Loss") features a narrator who, after losing his breath while cursing at his wife, attempts to get along without the faculty of speech. During his subsequent attempts to regain his breath, the hero is beaten, accused of various crimes, hanged, partially dissected, and entombed—all while remaining conscious of his "sensations." A satirical look at war and technology, "The Man That Was Used Up" revolves around the narrator's efforts to uncover the mystery behind a war hero named Brevet Brigadier General John A. B. C. Smith. He eventually learns that the general, severely wounded in the Indian Wars, has had his entire body reconstructed via the wonders of technological innovation. Another of Poe's satires, "The Business Man" involves Peter Proffit, a man who applies his fastidious and serious-minded business habits to a series of lowly con schemes. "Mellonta Tauta" is about a balloon voyage across the Atlantic Ocean on April 1, 2848. The story functions as a satire on the Transcendentalists' ideas. "Some Words with a Mummy," on the other hand, parodies modern technological advances with its story of a garrulous mummy who is revitalized by the galvanic process of a doctor named Ponnonner.

While famous for his tales of the macabre, Poe is equally renowned for originating the detective story. "The Murders in the Rue Morgue" marks the first appearance of Poe's famous sleuth, C. Auguste Dupin, who served as a prototype for Arthur Conan Doyle's Sherlock Holmes and Agatha Christie's Hercule Poirot, among other fictional detectives. Investigating the violent murder of a mother and daughter, Dupin deduces that they were killed by an animal. He soon tracks down a sailor whose pet orangutan recently escaped with a straight razor and was seen entering the victims' apartment. Poe's tale introduced several devices now common in the mystery genre, including the brilliant detective, first-person narration by a close friend of the sleuth, and the announcement of the mystery's solution in advance of the reasoning behind it. Another tale of detection, "The Gold-Bug" follows the efforts of adventurer William Legrand and his servant, Jupiter, to unearth the treasure of Captain Kidd. In "The Man of the Crowd," the narrator boasts that he can classify by social stratum the people passing by a London café based on appearance or behavior. When he notices a seemingly unclassifiable man, the narrator follows him through the city streets, eventually concluding that the man is a master criminal.

CRITICAL RECEPTION

Although some critics have disparaged Poe's stories as sensationalistic or sophomoric, the vast majority have found in them a wellspring of material for scholarly investigation. In addition to conducting numerous analyses of literary style and technique, recent commentators have studied Poe's works in relation to ideas about psychology, technology, religion, and gender in nineteenth-century America. For instance, critics have cited the cultural fad of hypnosis during Poe's day as an influence in "A Tale of the Ragged Mountains," "Mesmeric Revelation," and "The Facts in the Case of M. Valdemar," interpreting the third tale as a bizarre allusion to the telegraph, a prominent example of electronic progress. Similarly, reviewers have perceived "The Man That Was Used Up" as a response, in part, to the potentially dehumanizing effects of technology, and have discussed "The Black Cat" in light of nineteenth-century scientific and religious thought, underscoring Poe's commentary on the inscrutability of the human will despite advances in human understanding. "The Black Cat" has also been examined as the inspiration for Joyce Carol Oates's story "The White Cat" with respect to Oates's comic subversion of Poe's male-dominated text. In other studies of gender and sexuality in Poe's short stories, scholars have inspected the homosexually suggestive conclusion of "Ligeia" with regard to the author's anxiety about femininity, and have uncovered the veiled misogyny of the character Dupin based on his identification with the murderous orangutan in "The Murders in the Rue Morgue." Supplementary readings of "The Murders in the Rue Morgue" have posited that the story speaks to the inevitability of urban decay on a global scale. Additionally, "The Murders in the Rue Morgue," "The Gold-Bug," and "The Fall of the House of Usher" have been scrutinized alongside Elias Canetti's treatise on mob psychology, *Crowds and Power.* Furthermore, "The Fall of the House of Usher" has been hailed as Poe's statement on the aesthetic importance of unifying romanticism and Enlightenment reasoning. Moreover, commentators have deemed "Loss of Breath" evidence of the author's narrowly defined notion of human physicality, and have focused on the act of "reading" the human body in "The Man of the Crowd." While Poe is most commonly identified with his evocation of the macabre and grotesque, many critics have extolled his short stories for the universality of their psychological insights, concurring with scholar Walter Shear's assessment that "[f]or all its extravagant moments, the essential drama of Edgar Allan Poe's fiction is that of the individual mind."

PRINCIPAL WORKS

Short Fiction

The Narrative of Arthur Gordon Pym of Nantucket 1838
Tales of the Grotesque and Arabesque. 2 vols. 1840
**The Prose Romances of Edgar A. Poe* 1843
Tales 1845
The Works of Edgar Allan Poe: Newly Collected and Edited, with a Memoir, Critical Introductions, and Notes. 10 vols. (short stories, poetry, prose, essays) 1894-95
The Complete Works of Edgar Allan Poe. 17 vols. (short stories, poetry, prose, esssays) 1902
Tales of Mystery and Imagination 1928
The Complete Tales and Poems of Edgar Allan Poe (short stories and poetry) 1938
The Complete Poems and Stories of Edgar Allan Poe. 2 vols. (short stories and poetry) 1946
Collected Works of Edgar Allan Poe. 3 vols. (short stories, poetry, prose, essays) 1969
The Short Fiction of Edgar Allan Poe 1976
Poetry and Tales (short stories and poetry) 1984
Tales of Horror and Suspense 2003

Other Major Works

Tamerlane, and Other Poems (poetry) 1827
Al Araaf, Tamerlane, and Minor Poems (poetry) 1829
The Raven, and Other Poems (poetry) 1845
Eureka: A Prose Poem (poetry) 1848
The Letters of Edgar Allan Poe. 2 vols. (letters) 1948
Poe's Poems and Essays (poetry and essays) 1955
Marginalia (nonfiction) 1981
Essays and Reviews (criticism) 1984

*Contains the short stories "The Murders in the Rue Morgue" and "The Man That Was Used Up."

CRITICISM

William Etter (essay date March 2003)

SOURCE: Etter, William. "'Tawdry Physical Affrightments': The Performance of Normalizing Visions of the Body in Edgar Allan Poe's 'Loss of Breath.'" *American Transcendental Quarterly* n.s. 17, no. 1 (March 2003): 5-22.

[*In the following essay, Etter suggests that "Loss of Breath" reinforces Poe's "rigid, normalized conceptions of the body," and also assesses Poe's depiction of Native Americans in the tale.*]

In response to a gift copy he received from the illustrator of a new Poe volume, William Butler Yeats complained, "Analyse the Pit and the Pendulum and you find an appeal to the nerves by tawdry physical affrightments, at least so it seems to me who am yet puzzled at the fame of such things" (77). Yet while the popularity of physical sensationalism in antebellum American literature, professional medical journals, magazines, and theater undoubtedly influenced the composition of Poe's fiction, this fiction opposed the mass cultural entertainment of Poe's day, entertainment in which extreme bodily violence, sensationalistic suspensions of physical reality, and hyperbolically physical performances abounded. Poe strove to construct prose works of finer taste and sophistication than those he believed he encountered in popular culture by exposing the crudeness and absurdity of the literary bodies commonly consumed by American readers.

Certainly, there are bizarre "physical affrightments" aplenty in Poe's own work: dismemberment, decapitation, violent medical intrusions on the body, and murder. Moreover, Poe's penchant for creating characters with abnormal bodies is evident in all phases of his career. The short-statured Pompey, Hugh Tarpaulin, and Bon-Bon appear in the comic and satiric tales of the 1830s while later, more horrific tales, such as **"Hop-Frog,"** feature protagonists with multiple physical abnormalities. These intriguing visions of extraordinary bodies for which Poe is so famous, however, ultimately are founded on a core vision of bodily normality that forms the ground for his critiques of antebellum popular culture. To diverge from established bounds of physical normality, or the presumed "natural" conditions of human bodily existence, is, in the context of Poe's short fiction, to be aesthetically vulgar, linguistically disruptive, and racially inferior. In satirizing antebellum popular literature and entertainment from this point of view, Poe simultaneously reinforced his culture's racist ideology. This essay considers how one early comic tale—**"Loss of Breath"**—demonstrates the profoundly conservative nature of Poe's vision of the body, a vision that insists upon the enforcement of rigid, normalized conceptions of the body, the transgression of which results in collapse into aesthetic, social, and political absurdity.

"Loss of Breath" (titled **"A Decided Loss"** when first published in November of 1832), depicts the misadventures of a narrator, appropriately named Mr. Lackobreath, who—while preparing to scream insults at his wife—suddenly loses the ability to breathe and must comically struggle to live as a body without "respiration" in a world where such a body is, of course, an impossibility. Structurally, the tale is quite odd. Its central conflict occurs in the opening paragraphs while the remainder of the text offers only a loosely plotted description of the trials and tribulations Lackobreath suffers as a physical "anomaly," ordeals which only render his body even more abnormal. While travelling in a cramped coach he is crushed by three men "of colossal dimensions," such that ultimately "all [his] limbs were dislocated and [his] head twisted on one side." They then hurl him from the coach, causing the "breaking of both [his] arms," and when they throw his trunk after him, they "fractured [his] skull." Lackobreath is soon picked up and, believed dead, sold to a surgeon who, he claims, "cut off my ears . . . made an incision in my stomach, and removed several of my viscera for private dissection" (67).[1] Poe's darkly slapstick humor becomes, in its excess, farcical.

While one might be inclined to read the tale as a comedic quest, an impaired man's odyssey to correct his physical deficiency, Lackobreath spends very little time actually searching for his lost breath and stumbles upon the resolution to his dilemma (bargaining with "Mr. Windenough" for some of his surplus breath) by accident. The tale's structure more logically resembles the medical case studies so prevalent in the popular and professional periodicals of Poe's day. Typically beginning with descriptions of a condition that deviates from "normality," the antebellum medical case study then depicted the course of this condition in the individual's life as the affliction unfolded of its own accord. In doing so, this genre presumed to expand readers' knowledge of the nature and "normal" operations of human bodies in general through discussion of a uniquely abnormal one. A popular, if frequently unreliable and sensational, format by which Americans of the 1830s and 1840s acquired information about, and encountered figurations of, the human body, the antebellum case study was the genre of choice for medical periodicals of the time, most of which appealed not to an established professional class of physicians (which did not yet exist in the United States) but to the expanding mass readership emerging out of the exploding publishing industry of the 1830s. By offering their readers sensational descriptions of medical abnormalities typically reprinted from English and French reports, these periodicals appealed to consumers with "tawdry physical affrightments."[2]

From 1830 to 1850 literally dozens of "medical journals" appeared in America's major cities, most for only a few months before folding. All bragged they provided the average American subscriber with the most current, reliable, and useful medical information, but even when earnest attempts were made to offer sound data the result was often a bizarre combination of the skeptical, sensational, rational, and shocking. In April 1837 the Philadelphia journal *The American Medical Intelligencer* took pains to question a "Case of Snake in the Stomach" which had "given rise to so many miraculous stories, in the public journals." Reputed cases of suspended animation, bizarre disfigurements, and hyperbolic deathbed agonies appeared in these very same journals. In January 1843, the *Medical News and Library,* a Philadelphia-based journal, ran its introductory volume with a "prospectus" stating that its primary purpose would be to combat medical fraud, but in this same introductory issue, this "reputable" journal reported the delightfully gruesome case of an amputated penis. Wildly vacillating in tone and content between earnest medical reporting and vulgar sensationalism, the medical case study as it appeared in antebellum America offered Poe irresistible fodder for satirizing the tastes of the reading public.

Critics like Thomas Mabbott have dismissed the odd juxtaposition of bizarre physical abnormality and deadpan humorous tone in Poe's **"Loss of Breath"** as evidence that the tale "cannot be called a success" and have shaken their heads at Poe wasting so much time revising a forgettable tale of "extravagancies" (51). These juxtapositions, however, offer crucial insight into the intersections of the body and humor in Poe's work and in antebellum literary and performing arts more generally, as well as Poe's belief in the power of the artist to influence cultural visions of the body. The central concern of Poe's comedic fiction is the healthiness of Americans' view of these bodies. Perhaps the long-standing critical uncertainty about how to place Poe's comic tales in relation to his other fiction derives in part from Poe's own anxiety of the body's instability in this respect in the context of antebellum America's reception of "tawdry physical affrightments." What exactly were the moral and aesthetic differences between depicting physical suffering for a serious purpose like disseminating medical information, and depicting physical suffering merely for a laugh, for the market, or for the delight of a bloodthirsty readership? If the same literary body could perform both sets of functions, then the "significance" of any given "body" was dependent upon authorial intention and skill in influencing its reception by a given readership rooted in a given historical context. A good deal of responsibility thus fell upon the artist to represent bodies in a manner conducive to the appreciation of good taste. The ongoing debate among Poe scholars about how to interpret the fact that Poe depicts bodies in horrifically damaged or perverse conditions in tales of comedy and terror alike testifies to the same context of literary production.[3]

Contrary to Mabbott and others' condemnation of the tale, **"Loss of Breath"** is actually a deft and creative negotiation of this authorial bind on the terrain of the abnormal body, critiquing the popularity of "tawdry physical affrightments" in antebellum America by turning such vulgar physical displays against the tasteless Lackobreath. The first-person narrator of **"Loss of Breath"** ultimately learns the harsh lesson that participation in crude entertainment and physical abnormality will be punished. In Lackobreath's case, this punishment is meted out via a succession of cruel and unusual physical abuse experienced in rapid succession once he ventures beyond the familiar confines of his home early in the tale. In their sensational excess Lackobreath's experiences satirize the tasteless delight antebellum American society at large took in reading about or witnessing bizarre physical excess and interpersonal violence.

Attention to the visions of the body offered as profoundly misanthropic popular entertainment in Poe's day helps us understand how **"Loss of Breath"** casts the disunity and incoherence of physical abnormality as aesthetically vulgar. The traveler Thomas Ashe, historian Henry Adams relates, cringed at the "American barbarism" of Southwestern brawling during this period and described witnessing "citizens . . . shout[ing] with joy" at the "tearing, biting" and eye-gouging common to such displays, much as Lackobreath is given "a thump on the right eye . . . a pull by the ear" and two broken arms by his boorish traveling companions (37-38; Mabbott 67). With respect to how Lackobreath's accidental jostling in a vehicle results in dislocated limbs and a twisted head, it is also important to note the titillating reports of disasters that killed or maimed large groups of Americans which appeared in antebellum periodicals. Newspapers from all regions widely covered such disasters, the most popular of which were those that caused excessive bodily damage: fires, explosions aboard steamboats, and railway accidents.

Stories of individual physical damage and suffering occupied no less of a place in antebellum periodicals. On the 2 January 1836 front page of the Philadelphia paper, the *Saturday Evening Post,* one encounters the shocking—and medically dubious—story of a priest who "in a fit of love" hugged the life out of his lover then attempted to conceal the crime by "cut[ting] the body into pieces, which he put into a sack. As he was carrying it away, the sack burst, and he was obliged to carry the members piece by piece" until apprehended, a story that begins with anti-Catholic hysteria yet concludes with an event that could be read as callous slapstick of the Lackobreath variety. In May of that same year the front page of this periodical offered the "SHOCKING SCENE" of a black man set afire by a vicious mob in St. Louis: "The shrieks and groans of the victim were loud and piercing, and to observe one limb after another drop into the fire was awful indeed." Poe's readers, therefore, regularly experienced the body as an injured spectacle, a veritable flaunting of abnormality produced by violent wounding. While the public clamored for bodies in pieces, however, Poe would only accept the body cohesive (and thus coherent), placing the injured body on display in his own tales to critique any such presentation as pandering to the demands of a vulgar American public.

The incongruities of antebellum texts, which offered shocking subjects for the purposes of entertainment and imagined the "tawdry" as both vulgar and titillating, are mirrored in the comedy of **"Loss of Breath"** as well as in the illogicality and incoherence of Lackobreath's own body. This body exhibits the conceptual frustration physical abnormality fosters, thereby also calling critical attention to the aesthetic crudeness of antebellum popular writing. Reacting initially to his disconcerting loss, Lackobreath is utterly shocked to discover he is now "alive, with the qualifications of the dead—dead, with the propensities of the living—an anomaly on the face of the earth" (63). He is an "impossibility," a body that takes in no oxygen and lives. Linguistically, the terms "alive," "dead," and "body" become so confusing and represent Lackobreath's condition so inadequately that they are stripped of meaning. Later in life Poe would represent this dilemma in terms no less scornful when he scoffs in his "prose poem" "Eureka" "That a tree can be both a tree and not a tree, is an idea which the angels, or the devils, may entertain, and which no doubt many an earthly Bedlamite, or Transcendentalist, *does*" (***Poetry and Tales*** 1268). Once the reader of **"Loss of Breath"** identifies such chaos as emerging out of the impossible breaching of the "natural" categories of life and death in a physiological context, the comedy of the tale begins to be generated. Poe would later explicitly outline this method of creating humor in an 1845 article for the *Broadway Journal* where he states, "When . . . Fantasy seeks . . . incongruous or antagonistical elements, . . . we laugh outright in recognizing Humor" (qtd. in ***Collected Works [Collected Works of Edgar Allan Poe]*** xix). The crucial term in this statement is "recognizing," for in coming to understand that "incongruity" has been produced by the imaginative "Fancy" of the author, the reader perceives that comedic truths and intellectual stability reside not in the suspension of such incongruity but in its rejection as mere absurdity in favor of the normalized, dualistic categories of Western philosophy and language.

Rosemarie Garland Thomson has referred to the process of figuring physical difference and disability in American culture and literature as the formulation of "rules about what bodies should be or do." These rules establish "a comparison of bodies that structures social relations and institutions" in order to render these physical entities meaningful (6). A case study of this process, **"Loss of Breath"** fosters demand for the restoration of consistent bodily limits in its depiction of the ridiculous misadventures of a body lacking the "genuine" qualities of a body. In a tale full of physical absurdities, Poe's imagination almost outstrips itself at the start when the narrator's initial search for his missing breath in a piece of household furniture turns up "only a set of false teeth, two pair of hips, an eye, and a bundle of *billets-doux* from Mr. Windenough to my wife" (64). This passage, left as it is without further explanation, is so weird as to appear meaningless. Critics of this tale typically either ignore the passage or focus their discussions on suggestions of Mrs. Lackobreath's infidelity to develop a psychoanalytic reading of the narrator's respiratory impotence.

Yet the significance of this part of the story lies precisely in its apparent meaninglessness. Far from serving as pieces of tangible, reliable evidence that the reader—and Lackobreath himself—can use to make sense of his unprecedented condition, the body parts he locates resist interpretation. The teeth are clearly "false," but the hips may or may not be, for as the citations of authentic medical sources in Poe's tale **"The Man That Was Used Up"** demonstrate, intricate prosthetics for a variety of body parts were available in nineteenth-century America (Varner 78). One may certainly understand why love-letters might be hidden away in a drawer, but the concealment of body parts—even "false" ones—eludes explanation. Even the descriptive language itself is unclear: does the phrase "two pair of hips" indicate enough hips for two people or only one? And why do Lackobreath and his wife—who seem to possess no other physical abnormalities—have these items in their possession? The playful nonsense of Lackobreath's discovery is aimed at highlighting Poe's assertion that a collection of body parts does not a "real body" make and that such bizarre, sensationalistic dismemberment is an absurd subject for a text.

Throughout Poe's short fiction, this view holds; only madmen and fetishists invest spiritual or intellectual meaning in body parts alone. Witness the narrator's insane obsession with his victim's eye, and later his heart, in **"The Tell-Tale Heart"** or the lover's hideous, rattling container of his dead beloved's pulled teeth in **"Berenice."** Significantly, the reader of **"Loss of Breath"** recognizes the meaninglessness of body parts when confronted with the fact that a disunified body, like an abnormal body journeying about aimlessly without a breath, is incoherent. The legibility of the body in this story corresponds directly to its legitimacy, to the recognition of "rules about what bodies should be or do," thus implicitly establishing a site of semantic stability in the "reality" of the "complete," and consequently "normal," body.

In Lackobreath's early struggles to find a means of functioning socially with his unusual, incomprehensible physical condition by making his body "legible," Poe constructs a pointed satire of one particular form of antebellum popular entertainment, melodrama. The earliest version of this story, **"A Decided Loss,"** emphasizes Lackobreath's theatricality even more profoundly than the later **"Loss of Breath."** After the protagonist discovers he has lost his breath, he strives immediately to find some means of achieving a voice to prevent his wife and closest acquaintances from learning the bizarre truth. Lackobreath fears he will be declared dead, a non-entity to everyone he knows. He realizes the negative social consequences of physical abnormality. The solution he hits upon to negotiate this dilemma is rooted entirely in the physically-excessive conventions of antebellum melodrama:

> I committed to memory the entire tragedies of Metamora and Miantinimoh. I had the acuteness to recollect that in the accentuation of these dramas, the tones of voice in which I found myself deficient, were totally unnecessary, and that the deepest guttural should reign monotonously throughout. . . . I found myself, in a few hours, as well qualified to quiz the Aborigines as

> their original representative himself. Thus armed at all points, I determined to make my wife believe that I was suddenly seized with a passion for the stage . . . folding my arms, working my knees, shuffling my feet, looking asquint, and showing my teeth, with the energy of the most accomplished and popular performer. To be sure they talked of confining me in a straight jacket—but good God! they never suspected me of having lost my breath.
>
> (55-56)

Though Lackobreath cannot use breath to form speech, he can use his muscles to do so, replacing "genuine" voice with bodily exertion. Designed solely to delude those around him, Lackobreath's performance is a hoax achieved by manipulating his abnormal body in such a way as to insert it into a recognizable cultural and rhetorical context. The well-known melodramatic context for the physicality of Lackobreath's performance allows his actions—"working my knees, shuffling my feet" (like the classic melodramatic villain)—to conceal the purpose of speaking in an unusually "guttural" manner and forces his audience to interpret him as he wishes to be interpreted. Yet the figure he cuts does not accurately reflect reality. In collusion with the extravagant melodramatic performers of his time, Lackobreath's presentation of his body enables a voice to enter society in a recognizable, yet false, way. However, this presentation is at best merely a hoax producing a sense of confusion or amusement in the viewer, and ultimately it is a failure. Lackobreath only hides the abnormality of his body temporarily; his performance cannot transform it into a normal body, a fact that becomes painfully evident when his body is continually misread as dead once he journeys beyond the protective confines of his own home.

In satirizing melodramas **"Loss of Breath"** highlights the ways in which the body was "read" in antebellum America in order to critique the response of the American masses to "physical affrightments." Transformed from an abrasive husband into an ever-present physicality via the salience of his abnormal physiological condition and the repeated injuries he sustains after he ventures into the world, Lackobreath's body becomes a spectacle for the characters with whom he interacts as well as for the reader. In this context Lackobreath's body seems to attain its greatest value. At one striking point in the story, Lackobreath is mistakenly identified as a mail-robber and publicly hanged. A consummate entertainer, Lackobreath puts on a masterful performance when the hangman drops him, relating triumphantly, "I did my best to give the crowd the worth of their trouble. My convulsions were said to be extraordinary. My spasms it would have been difficult to beat. The populace *encored.* Several gentlemen swooned" (69-70). The theatricality of this event would be familiar to those antebellum readers who attended melodramas as well as those who had ample opportunities to witness public executions throughout the 1830s and 1840s or, if they could not attend such functions, to buy one of the many cheap crime pamphlets of the period decorated with crude cover illustrations of hanging corpses.

Though Lackobreath had previously been mistaken for a corpse and a criminal, the *theatricality* of his hanging body renders it legible and satisfying for both performer (a narcissistic blowhard since the tale began) and viewers. Antebellum melodramatic actors, theater historian Bruce McConachie tells us, "worked within a highly conventional system of poses and gestures which physicalized states of emotion for the audience." Acting manuals of the period taught rigidly-delineated physical movements to correspond to, and thus convey, emotions like fear and anger, and personalities, like villainy. These movements were part of the pantheon of body language audiences typically witnessed on stage. "Overall," McConachie concludes, "melodramatic movement . . . presented to the audience 'an immediately translatable and unified "ritualized" physical expression'" (112-13). To communicate artistically, antebellum melodramatic actors put their bodies on display, and many did so to pandering, vulgar excess. "Straining muscles and [a] thunderous voice" were the trademarks of Edwin Forrest, one of the most famous melodramatic actors of 1830s America, who continually sought to "display the physical exertion sustaining his performance" in such "heroic" roles as Metamora (whom Lackobreath explicitly strives to portray), and Spartacus. For years Forrest even favored playing the latter character "bare-chested to show off his well-muscled body" (McConachie 114, 115).

In a classical sense, the oratorical performance of the actor—his "thunderous voice"—was intimately linked to his "physical exertion" because the author's embodied performance was itself symbolic, and the voice, presented as the actor engaged in his "'ritualized' physical expression," was an embodied one. These forms of expression could be taken to surprising, even ridiculous, lengths. Many actors actually injured themselves playing these roles, and Forrest, in particularly emotional scenes, even went so far as to mimic, in the words of one contemporary critic, "numerous seizures of a sort of histrionic asthma or shortness of breath" (qtd. in McConachie 114). Forrest's antics became so well known that even during the Civil War, decades after his reign as the king of melodramatic tragedy had ended, Louisa May Alcott would describe a mule cavorting on a Washington, D.C. street as "now and then falling, flat, and apparently dying *a la* Forrest: a gasp—a squirm—a flop, and so on, till the street was well blocked up," then "calmly regarding the excited crowd seemed to say—'A hit! a decided hit! for the stupidest of animals has bamboozled a dozen men'" (56-57).

It was precisely the hyperbolic quality of these melodramatic performances that prompted Poe in the late 1830s and early 1840s to criticize the "retrogradation" of American theater and to plead for new plays "with Feeling and Taste guided and controlled in every particular by . . . Common Sense," thus rendering the presentation "Natural" rather than extravagant (***Complete Works*** [***The Complete Works of Edgar Allan Poe***] XIII 37). Yet Poe's conception of good taste ran counter to that of the masses, for such performances as Forrest's were highly popular forms of entertainment in all regions of the antebellum United States. Forrest's performances were anything but "Natural" and guided by "Common Sense," yet when he played Spartacus in the tragedy *The Gladiator* in the early 1830s audiences, particularly those in the South, received it enthusiastically. It is within this context of physical rhetoric, embodied role-playing, the body as vehicle for mass entertainment, and visions of the body taken to extremes that Poe composes Lackobreath's own laughable performance in **"Loss of Breath."**

Poe converts melodramatic tragedy into a joke on the back of Lackobreath's abnormal body. In the short story the author transforms the figure of Edwin Forrest the actor, one of the most popular bodies-on-display in the 1830s, into the character of an abrasive, sexually disturbed, cuckolded husband while the excessive physicality of Forrest's performance—manifested in "seizures of a sort of histrionic asthma or shortness of breath"—is taken to an absurd extreme as a **"Loss of Breath"** entirely. Mirroring the melodramatic actors who produced tasteless mass entertainment with coarse physical display at its core, Lackobreath's body language compensates for a lack of "voice" or authentic intelligent expression. Forrest, like Lackobreath hanging from the gallows, used his body shamelessly, pandering to the crude tastes of his audience "to give the crowd the worth of their trouble," their indiscriminate patronage of vulgar entertainment (69). In the tale, the men of the crowd who observe Lackobreath's lowbrow acting participate in their own debasement by swooning, stereotypically degenerating from "gentlemen" to fainting women. Lackobreath's bizarre physical condition, along with his tasteless performance, transforms these audience members into abnormally-gendered freaks with no self-control.

Poe's ridicule of Lackobreath's virtually pornographic, and deliberately deceptive, display of the body to the masses indicates his conservative vision of the "normal" body. This body necessarily operates within its social context, but its owner does not allow it to be entirely determined by this context in its lowest common denominator. Lackobreath's freakishly breathless body becomes a grunting melodramatic jester, a "popular performer," initially believed by his wife and friends to be mad. The laughter generated in readers solidifies an ideology in which a distastefully managed body and an abnormal body are one in the same. In such laughter the tale strives to rescue Poe's readers from a descent into the maelstrom of tasteless popular entertainment that offers up the body for public consumption for profit or to pander for undeserved fame. Participating in the tale's humor, which ridicules this tasteless entertainment in the figure of Lackobreath, allows readers to attain a more critical view of this entertainment than that possessed by either Forrest's or Lackobreath's audiences.

Though Lackobreath's body corresponds to images of the wounded and performing body with which antebellum Americans would have been familiar, it remains fundamentally illegible, an unfortunate condition in the world of **"Loss of Breath,"** a tale which imagines physiological legibility to be an empowering effect of bodily normality. True, for the audience of Lackobreath's melodramatic performances, his gallivanting corpus temporarily assumes a textual and contextual comprehensibility, but for most of the tale this freakish body remains "an anomaly on the face of the earth" because it does the impossible, the unbelievable, and sustains life without breathing. In Poe's tale, however, a physical "anomaly" ultimately cannot sustain the pressure to function as a site of comprehensible reality, in spite of Lackobreath's attempt to regulate his unusual body's reception. The abnormality of his breathless condition causes, and in turn the comic superfluity of his physical injuries is caused by, the fact that this freakishness does not translate fully into the social realm. Lacking the genuine qualities of "normal" bodies, Lackobreath is unrecognizable as such to Americans outside of a strictly theatrical context. His breathless condition makes boorish coach companions and overly-curious surgeons misread his body as "dead" and gratuitously injure Lackobreath because of their misunderstanding. In **"A Decided Loss"** Poe includes an extensive description he later excised of the narrator's final journey from the gallows to the cemetery, depicting Lackobreath's lamenting that he is interred alive in a public tomb because "no one in the city appeared to identify my body" (79). Determined by scholars to be Philadelphia, though unnamed in the story, this city was not only the largest in the United States in Poe's time—enjoying honorary status as the birthplace of American independence, the Constitution, and therefore United States "citizenship"—it was also one of the largest producers of mass-market, literary, and medical periodicals as well as "a center for the comic theater" (Rourke 181). It would seem a city tailor-made for an actor like Lackobreath, but none of the residents knows him, most obviously because he has only recently arrived in their city, but primarily because he is unrecognizable as a living "body." A physically alien presence, he is also an alien in the United States, conceptually and politically.

Poe's vision of bodily "normality" hinges upon a certain conception of how the body normally appears to others. Thus, it comes as no surprise that he chooses to illustrate this concept, at least in part, by drawing from conventions and characters common to antebellum melodramatic productions. Bodies that do not enter the social realm in a manner imagined to be typical of all bodies cannot be "identified" as legitimate physicalities in the world of Poe's tale. They are not only ignored, abused, or punished as criminal, but, on a fundamental level of consciousness, they are not even perceived as real, living bodies. Apparently Lackobreath understands that fact even before embarking on his misadventures. By initially attempting to conceal his deviant respiration from his intimate social circle using the conventions of melodramatic acting, he struggles to cling to a modicum of social recognizability. In the United States in which Lackobreath lives, it is better to be thought mad than to be physically abnormal.

While disability theorists frequently emphasize the linguistic roots of the word "monster" in Latinate verbs meaning to "demonstrate" or "show," claiming that abnormality is typically valued only for its capacity to signify negative characteristics, **"Loss of Breath"** reveals how physical abnormality may be disparaged and feared precisely because of the way it disrupts conventional systems of representation. Lackobreath's "tawdry" performance is successful but only for a brief period of time. The artistic image of the freakish or grotesque in Poe's tales, Daniel Hoffman argues, ultimately "depends on a rationalistic view of experience as the norm against which the recorded monstrous defections can be measured," leading to "the exposure of the idiocy of the monstrous world" which reinforces normality in the face of an abnormality that can only appear absurdly irrational (206). It is this threat that the artist—whether the artist be Lackobreath or Poe himself—continually attempts to keep at bay by controlling the representations of abnormality.

"Loss of Breath" finally attempts to overcome these dilemmas by erasing physical abnormality entirely. The resolution of the tale comes when Lackobreath gets his breath back from Mr. Windenough (who himself is returned to a normal state by the corresponding reduction in his own superfluity of breath). In **"A Decided Loss,"** the means of resolution are different from those in the revised version **"Loss of Breath"**—Lackobreath's respiration is restored after an apothecary treats him with "the new Galvanic Battery" (a device frequently discussed in sensationalistic, popular antebellum medical journals)—but the result is identical. The tale concludes when the protagonist is "healed," rendered "normal," the only satisfactory resolution in the world of Poe's comic tales. Thus, the structure of the plot, in which a case study of a human freak ends with the full recovery of the individual, defuses the conceptual and social chaos created by a physically abnormal individual. Ultimately for Poe, textual coherence and the triumph of the tasteful artist's ability to compose a cohesive tale coincide in the achievement of the normalization of the body.

While Poe's depiction of Lackobreath's abnormal body satirizes the vulgar aesthetics of antebellum melodrama, and sensationalistic texts of the period in general, the description of Lackobreath's body and the laughable amateur stagecraft in which he engages is not ironic in its simultaneous normalization of bodies along racial lines. A particularly intriguing fact about the tale is that an examination of Poe's critique of Lackobreath as a tasteless artist helps illuminate and critique the tale's racist portrayal of Native Americans. To gain a voice, Lackobreath mimics the characters in *Metamora,* a melodrama about a heroic Native American protagonist (whom Edwin Forrest played in 1829), and *Miantinimoh,* a melodrama based on a James Fenimore Cooper novel, first produced in 1830. Poe undoubtedly selected this subject matter because Indian themes were an essential element of the violent frontier tales flooding American mass culture. In 1834 the *New-England Magazine* lamented: "Indian murder or speech is the heaviest drug in the market" (qtd. in Maddox 38-39). Like the minstrel show, which antebellum newspapers typically ridiculed as merely "absurd physical antics," mass cultural presentations of "the Injun" offered a venue in which non-white Americans could be depicted as themselves utterly tasteless (Lott 141).

The fact that the roles Lackobreath plays are two removes from "real" Indians contains the threat of slipping across racial boundaries from Anglo American to Native American. Forrest performs the part of an historically-based personage while Lackobreath plays the part of Forrest, complete with bizarre respiration, performing the native person. Though Poe ridicules antebellum melodrama, this art form's conventions of presenting historically-based figures as caricatures allows him to maintain these racial distinctions. Yet the humor of Poe's tale has more complex social purposes than simple racist degradation in the medium of artistic satire. Assuming the persona of the Native American, Lackobreath discovers, is surprisingly easy. In only "a few hours," he becomes as "well qualified to quiz the Aborigines as their original representative himself." Becoming an "Indian" is, in Lackobreath's view, equivalent to performing a role, and he attributes the ease with which he slips into this role to the pseudo-ethnological fact that "the tones of voice in which [Lackobreath] found [himself] deficient, were totally unnecessary" for the voice of an Indian (55).

White antebellum Americans would have understood Lackobreath's determination, for most of them assumed Native American speech was only what Richard Henry Dana called it in his popular 1840 autobiography *Two Years Before the Mast*: a "complete 'slabber'" (113). Having lost the element that would make him a complete human being, his breath, Lackobreath becomes the ideal candidate for the native's part because the native himself is inherently "deficient," lacking the full tonal range and rationality reflected in the Euro-American voice. Given conventional readings of this tale, like those expressed in Joan Dayan's *Fables of Mind: An Inquiry into Poe's Fiction,* which understand "breath" as referring to Lackobreath's soul via an implied pun on artistic "inspiration," the tale probably also suggests the Native American is spiritually and aesthetically, as well as physically, deficient.

Including a stereotyped native body in his tale, Poe codes this body as abnormal on two grounds. First, the non-white body is excessively physical, as emphasized by Lackobreath's guttural voice produced by sheer muscular effort as well as by the conflation of his body's social appearance with hyperbolically-physical melodrama. Second, the non-white body lacks a presumably "natural" element necessary to compose a "complete" person: the "breath" that produces life and the expanded range of normal (white) speech. That is, the Native American is imagined pejoratively as inherently physically disabled in **"Loss of Breath."** "Loss" or "shortness" of breath was indeed a marker of racial inferiority in antebellum America. In the South, proslavery physicians argued for decades that black laborers suffered from more respiratory problems than white laborers because, as their lungs were naturally of abnormally small capacity, they could not inhale quantities of air sufficient to maintain health. Blacks' supposed laziness was then attributed, at least in part, to this physiological deficiency which also clouded their minds and weakened their wills by restricting the flow of oxygen to the brain.[4]

"Loss of Breath"'s normalizing vision widens to its furthest expanse in Lackobreath's statement that he has transformed himself into a figure as "qualified . . . as their original representative" to epitomize native speech. Under this rationale, the white actor provides an accurate portrait of an entire group of non-white peoples. Written in an America still anxiously trying to fix racial categories, **"Loss of Breath"** shows Poe making a confused, but nonetheless earnest, attempt to stabilize these categories along axes of bodily normality and abnormality. Poe differentiates white from non-white peoples hierarchically by racializing socio-cultural adaptability and, by extension, artistic capacity. **"Loss of Breath"** depicts performative capabilities as marks of racial power. Forrest, upon whom Lackobreath is modeled, exhibited this power, according to an apocryphal story. Supposedly, the famous actor had proven the exceptional ability of a white man to make a "faithful drawing" of non-whites when, while walking to a blackface performance in Cincinnati, "an old Negro woman mistook him for a Negro whom she knew," unable, like those observing Lackobreath's Indian performance, to tell the player from the "original representative" (Rourke 79-80).

Parodies of romanticized, tragic melodramas became an especially popular form of theatrical amusement and further demonstrated white actors' ability to shift easily among the "roles" of various non-white races. After its successful run as a tragedy, *Metamora,* for instance, became a burlesqued *Metaroarer,* the Wampanoags became the "Pollywogs," and the title character killed a bear to the minstrel tune of "Ole Dan Tucker" (Rourke 123).[5] Like Forrest and minstrel performers, Lackobreath and his Euro-American body possess the capacity to assume entirely the "role" of a different race. Native Americans' inferiority to the white race is thus established in the assertion that their "bodies," that is, the role their bodies play in a social context, can be easily colonized by a white man playing within white artistic conventions that have themselves taken over the imaginary space of the "Indian" to become part of the "stock" of antebellum figures. Antebellum Americans typically denied this performative capacity to Native Americans, a denial that participated in racially-based normalization.

Many writers of this period shared Poe's views and suggested the figures of Native Americans were not only inherently susceptible to co-optation by white performers but also that Native Americans were inherently incapable of playing any other social role but that of a member of the "barbaric" culture into which they were born. The young travel narrator and historian Francis Parkman, writing in the summer of 1846, notes in the end papers of his journal: "An Indian's character is more rigid and inflexible than that of other savages. A Polynesian will become a good sailor, a good servant, or a good farmer. An Ind. is fit for nothing but his own mode of life" (440). "Each race of mankind," physician and apologist for slavery Josiah

Nott proclaimed, "has a certain degree of *pliability* of constitution . . . but there are limits to this *pliability*" and the white race possessed the greatest capacity for such manipulation (62). The performative capacities of white Americans testified to the racially-determined, unchangeable natures of non-white Americans, a view that was further solidified in the rigidly-delineated, stock caricatures of antebellum melodrama and popular culture.

As we have seen, in his construction of Lackobreath's character, Poe plays off stock portrayals of native peoples that had long been familiar to the American imagination. However, in the 1830s, when the front pages of major periodicals regularly referenced "Indian atrocities" committed on white emigrants to the frontier, violent clashes between United States soldiers and Southeastern tribes, and the forced removals of native peoples to the West, the author who depicted a Native American in his text was also confronting serious and immediate national affairs. By converting the revolutionary Metamora from a tragic character in antebellum drama to a character in a comic tale who lacks the basic human capacity for respiration (that is, giving this well-known character an abnormal body), Poe's narrative could help defuse the threats Native Americans were posing to United States expansion. On stage, a melodrama about a Native American hero might encourage a sympathetic response from an audience and prevent audience members from fully appreciating the very real threat native peoples posed to United States control of western territories. Poe's tale, however, takes control of these dangerous native figures by rendering their bodies abnormal and turning them into objects of comic pleasure for a white readership. In this respect Poe was writing from a position thoroughly within dominant antebellum aesthetic rules for the textual depiction of non-white races which demanded that fictional portrayals of these individuals must be vulgar in order to be accurate. In his famous critique of James Fenimore Cooper, Francis Parkman asserts Cooper's novels are flawed because they portray Indians as proud and noble savages. This portrait was at odds, Parkman implies, with the recent history of violent Native American resistance to imperialistic westward expansion which demonstrated these people were actually vicious, cowardly, and disgusting. In employing such commonplace vulgarities to satirize antebellum popular literature and entertainment, Poe was necessarily reinforcing the racist tenets of his culture.

In the 1830s and 1840s conceptions of Native Americans' (in)ability to play alternative social roles corresponded conveniently with, and undoubtedly was partially constructed by, the forced removals and military suppressions of peoples like the Choctaws and Chickasaws in the Southeast and peoples like the Arapahoes in the West. Proponents of these policies contended that native peoples would never be able to conform to the "settled" and "civilized" lifestyle of white Americans and therefore must be segregated from them. In his first historical work, *The Oregon Trail and The Conspiracy of Pontiac* (1851), Parkman summarizes this position concisely when he writes that Indians' "intractable, unchanging character leaves no other alternative than their gradual extinction" (732). The conservative bodily visions offered in **"Loss of Breath"** thus demonstrate that the "performativity" of race is not always a liberatory concept. Certainly, the capacity of individuals to perform roles typically considered to be entirely "outside" the bounds of their "natural" identities (non-white ethnicities "passing" for white, for instance), reveals the arbitrariness or the socio-ideological constructedness of categories society assumes to be "given," like race. But when performances are shaped by, and thus reinforce, conventional hegemonic categories, when performative capacity is granted or denied to particular peoples on the basis of presumed superiority or inferiority, or when the incapacity to perform roles is implicitly offered as evidence of racial determinism, such acts participate in, rather than resist, the project of normalization.

While Poe asserts ideals of artistic capabilities and aesthetic taste using the racial discourse of his time, he necessarily also participates in the antebellum construction of the racialized "normal" body via such ideals. **"Loss of Breath"** reveals notions of physical normality and notions of race being constituted simultaneously, each reinforcing the other. Poe's tale both legitimizes and excuses the enactment of violence against Native Americans in the project of federally-sanctioned removal even as it critiques the American public's "tawdry" delight in the physical violence so prevalent in the culture and popular media of the antebellum period.

Notes

1. Unless otherwise stated, references to Poe's work are taken from Thomas Ollive Mabbott's edition of the *Collected Works of Edgar Allan Poe.*

2. For detailed discussions of the rise of the print industry in antebellum America and the subsequent formation of a mass readership, consult Terence Whalen's *Edgar Allan Poe and the Masses: The Political Economy of Literature in Antebellum America* and Michael Allen's *Poe and the British Magazine Tradition.* For two astute discussions of the loosely regulated medical professions of the period, see Joan Burbick's *Healing the Republic: The Language of Health and the Culture of Nationalism in Nineteenth-Century America* and Cyn-

thia J. Davis's *Bodily and Narrative Forms: The Influence of Medicine on American Literature, 1845-1915.*

3. Classic examples of this critical conundrum remain Edward H. Davidson's *Poe: A Critical Study* and Daniel Hoffman's *Poe Poe Poe Poe Poe Poe Poe.* For what might very well be a cogent explanation of this issue, see Fyodor Dostoevski's "Three Tales of Edgar Poe."
4. The classic expression of this scientific fact is Dr. Samuel Cartwright's "Slavery in the Light of Ethnology" (1852), in E. N. Elliott's *Cotton is King, and Pro-Slavery Arguments.*
5. A conglomeration of precisely this sort appears in Poe's comic tale "The Man That Was Used Up," where the thick-headed narrator confuses "Man-Fred," the title of a performance some of his acquaintances have recently attended, with "Man-Friday." Constance Rourke informs us that romantic dramas were frequently "distorted" into popular entertainment in antebellum America in this manner. Burlesque pioneer William Mitchell, for instance, produced Byron's *Man-Fred* "in partial blackface, with a metaphysical Negro chimney-sweep for the hero" (120). The narrator in "The Man That Was Used Up" thus blends an African-American caricature with the most popular "native" of Anglo-American fiction.

Works Cited

Adams, Henry. *The United States in 1800.* 1889. Ithaca: Cornell UP, 1955.

Alcott, Louisa May. "Hospital Sketches." 1863. *Alternative Alcott.* Ed. Elaine Showalter. New Brunswick: Rutgers UP, 1988.

Allen, Michael. *Poe and the British Magazine Tradition.* New York: Oxford UP, 1969.

Burbick, Joan. *Healing the Republic: The Language of Health and the Culture of Nationalism in Nineteenth-Century America.* New York: Cambridge UP, 1994.

Dana, Richard Henry. *Two Years Before the Mast.* 1840. New York: Signet, 1964.

Davidson, Edward H. *Poe: A Critical Study.* Cambridge: Belknap, 1957.

Davis, Cynthia J. *Bodily and Narrative Forms: The Influence of Medicine on American Literature, 1845-1915.* Stanford: Stanford UP, 2000.

Dayan, Joan. *Fables of Mind: An Inquiry into Poe's Fiction.* New York: Oxford UP, 1987.

Dostoevski, Fyodor M. "Three Tales of Edgar Poe." 1861. Trans. Vladimir Astrov. *The Recognition of Edgar Allan Poe: Selected Criticism Since 1829.* Ed. Eric W. Carlson. Ann Arbor: U of Michigan P, 1966.

Elliott, E. N., ed. *Cotton is King, and Pro-Slavery Arguments.* 1860. Rpt. in New York: Negro UP, 1969.

Hoffman, Daniel. *Poe Poe Poe Poe Poe Poe Poe.* New York: Paragon, 1972.

Lott, Eric. *Love and Theft: Blackface Minstrelsy and the American Working Class.* New York: Oxford UP, 1993.

Maddox, Lucy. *Removals.* New York: Oxford UP, 1991.

McConachie, Bruce A. *Melodramatic Formation: American Theatre and Society, 1820-1870.* Iowa City: U of Iowa P, 1992.

Nott, Josiah. "Climates of the South in Their Relations to White Labor." Feb 1866. *The Cause of the South: Selections from De Bow's Review 1846-1867.* Ed. Paul F. Paskoff and Daniel J. Wilson. Baton Rouge: Louisiana State UP, 1982.

Parkman, Francis. *The Journals of Francis Parkman.* Ed. Mason Wade. Vol. II. New York: Harper and Brothers, 1947.

———. *The Oregon Trail and The Conspiracy of Pontiac.* 1851. New York: Literary Classics of the United States, 1991.

———. "The Works of James Fenimore Cooper." *The North American Review* 74 (Jan 1852): 147-61.

Poe, Edgar Allan. *Collected Works of Edgar Allan Poe.* Ed. Thomas Ollive Mabbott. 3 vols. Cambridge: Belknap, 1978.

———. *The Complete Works of Edgar Allan Poe.* Ed. James A. Harrison. 17 vols. New York: AMS, 1979.

———. *Poetry and Tales.* New York: Literary Classics of the United States, 1984.

Rourke, Constance. *American Humor: A Study of the National Character.* 1931. Tallahassee: Florida State UP, 1959.

Thomson, Rosemarie Garland. *Extraordinary Bodies: Figuring Physical Disability in American Culture and Literature.* New York: Columbia UP, 1997.

Varner, Cornelia. "Notes on Poe's Use of Contemporary Materials in Certain of His Stories." *The Journal of English and Germanic Philology* 32 (Jan 1933): 77-80.

Whalen, Terence. *Edgar Allan Poe and the Masses: The Political Economy of Literature in Antebellum America.* Princeton: Princeton UP, 1999.

Yeats, William Butler. "Letter to W. T. Horton." 1899. *The Recognition of Edgar Allan Poe: Selected Criticism Since 1829.* Ed. Eric W. Carlson. Ann Arbor: U of Michigan P, 1966.

Ed White (essay date summer 2003)

SOURCE: White, Ed. "The Ourang-Outang Situation." *College Literature* 30, no. 3 (summer 2003): 88-108.

[*In the following essay, White suggests a method for exploring the subtext of American slave rebellions in Poe's "The Murders in the Rue Morgue."*]

The interpretive premise of this essay is a simple one: the first American detective story, Edgar Allan Poe's 1841 **"The Murders in the Rue Morgue,"** is a response to American slave rebellions. But my primary concern in what follows will be with the *instructional* challenges this interpretation poses, for having become convinced of the pedagogical value of this reading while teaching Poe, I have struggled since with the difficulties of presenting it convincingly in the classroom.[1] I should stress from the start that these challenges do not strike me as idiosyncratic (to me, my students, Poe, or his story), but in fact illuminate a series of common questions about how we address "historical context" in the teaching of literature. And I want to go so far as to hypothesize that such pedagogical challenges as I describe here emerge from the contemporary academy's dominant theoretical tendencies, above all from what might loosely be called "Cultural Studies" approaches, in interpreting literature. In what follows, then, I will offer a brief and incomplete interpretation of Poe's story, contrasting it with what I take to be a sophisticated and representative contemporary interpretation. My goal will be to contrast two critical positions on the relationship between "Literature" and "History." I will then briefly outline a methodological framework that many readers may, at first glance, find hopelessly anachronistic—that of the Sartrean "situation." If readers can bear with this account of a by-gone philosophy of freedom, I hope to persuade them that a *situational* reading of Poe's story in fact takes us substantially beyond the old-fashioned conventions of today's "discourse analysis." I will conclude with some specific suggestions for teaching Poe, and some more general pedagogical ideas for teaching literature historically—and for teaching history literarily.

The Testing Ground

I begin with a nuanced and insightful analysis of Poe's story, that offered by Nancy A. Harrowitz, in her essay "Criminality and Poe's Orangutan: The Question of Race in Detection." Harrowitz begins her analysis citing Nietzsche's essay "Homer's Contest," which argued that cultural products fundamentally amount to an agon or contest "between savage impulses . . . and civilization": building on this premise, her account of the story will similarly focus on how Poe's story reveals "the agonistics of detective fiction as a budding genre," one that "invokes some specific historical tensions of America in the early 1840s." For starters, detective fiction emerges out of "the new phenomenon of larger urban areas that were undergoing a process of refinement and topographical categorization" (1997, 182). The development of "large uncontrolled urban areas" created "increasing anxiety" to which "the culture of criminology" and its fictional corollary—detective fiction—were responses (182-83). And specifically, *responses of control,* as classification attempts not only to categorize the criminal but to make clear the boundaries between the criminal and the citizen. Thus the story's odd construction of the orangutan, whose anthropomorphization gives him enough human qualities not only to commit the crime, but also, obversely, to draw certain qualities of cultural difference away from the normative populace. Thus linguistic foreignness, violent hypersexualization, and ultimately racial difference cohere around the figure of the orangutan, exemplifying "the conflict between our view of different civilizations and our desire to identify scapegoats" (188). In "transferring a cultural anxiety regarding the perceived murderous, monstrous capacities of 'foreigners'" onto the orangutan, Harrowitz proceeds to argue, Poe's text further demonstrates a corresponding displacement of racial anxiety and crisis onto the orangutan (190-91).

Such are the main claims of Harrowitz's essay, which concludes with the programmatic summation that **"The Murders in the Rue Morgue"** is a "paradigmatic" agonistic text on two basic counts (1997, 193). First, "it introduces some chilling concerns about difference and its perceived perniciousness that become a subtext in the genre of detection because of this genre's close affiliation with the development of criminology" (193). Secondly, "[b]y setting up duplicitous structures of understanding for the detective, which cover up the racial tensions . . . , the story unsettles the same epistemology of detection that it establishes as reliable and which has been adopted ever since as indispensable to the detective genre" (194). Given these two dynamics, she concludes, the story thus "*can function as a testing ground for theories* regarding race, sexuality, and the interactions of these two categories through a displacement of 'reason' onto xenophobia" (194; my emphasis).

Now the three points of this summation are revealing of a contemporary approach to historical criticism, and might be read initially as a *précis* of three related and influential theoretical projects:

1. First is what might be called the structural or Foucauldian point: that the text manifests certain dominant thought-systems operative at the moment of its

composition. These discourses, concerned primarily with the ordering and therefore construction of knowledge, ground the text's "concerns about difference." And the agon of the literary text is conflict between discourses (e.g., as in the Nietzschean clash "between savage impulses . . . and civilization").

2. Second is what might be called the deconstructive or Derridean point: that the text works to suppress its epistemological traces or conditions. The text "unsettles" the very norms of knowledge (here the methodological norms of detection) even as it constructs them. And through this process, the story "cover[s] up the racial tensions" even as it draws on them.

3. Third, drawing on and following from these two related critical projects, the text becomes a site of intersection and clashing, the "testing ground," within which we might trace the "interactions" (or negotiations, or articulations) of its constituent elements. This might be called the Cultural Studies point, drawing on Fredric Jameson's assessment that "[a]rticulation thus stands as the name of [its] central theoretical problem or conceptual core."

We can imagine how these three theoretical moorings might then be translated into pedagogical points for the historical study of Poe's story:

1. To situate **"Murders"** [**"The Murders in the Rue Morgue"**], we must map out the dominant discourses of the context in question (here, "America in the early 1840s"). These would be the related discourses of urbanization and criminology (including constructions of deviant sexuality, biological and racial difference, as well as emerging theories of scientific detection and criminology), most readily accessible in more "abstract" texts like Francis Galtons's "Eugenics" or *Finger Prints.*

2. We would then insist, as a transhistorical point, that cultures typically hide the conditions of their existence, by suppressing contradictions and tensions that cannot be admitted or acknowledged. This would bring us back to a close reading of the text to illustrate not only the "anxieties" of **"Murders"** or detective fiction in general, but American society as a whole.

3. From these two predicates, we would teach **"Murders"** as a kind of cultural laboratory in which we can track how competing, contradictory, and/or complementary discourses clash and combine. We have here illustrations of what happens when antebellum theories of sexuality come together with theories of race, and so forth.

Such a program will appear unobjectionable enough, even salutary, given its ambitious attempts to make the apparently secondary concerns of race, sexuality, and urban development central to the teaching of the story. Contrasted with a "traditional" focus (e.g., on Dionysian vs. Apollonian forms of thought, or on the formal conventions of the detective story), this would certainly seem a positive attempt to locate **"Murders"** historically, to capture some of the broad social and intellectual movements and tendencies of the period. But I would like to stress three historical elements missing from such an account, the absence of which, I hope to show, seriously limits the power of this kind of historical criticism.

1. Consistent with the contemporary critical repudiation of "hot history" or originary causes, specific historical *events* seem irrelevant to Harrowitz's account. She can speak in the passive voice or intransitively of the general emergence of broad epistemes, e.g., "the culture of criminology developing at the time" (1997, 183), but particular forms of *praxis,* even intellectual, are largely dismissed as manifestations of broader thought systems and anxieties. It is for this reason that Harrowitz writes of white discourses of racialization, but never speaks of the slave insurrection *per se*: the orangutan will be a *figure* around which coheres the discourses of sexualization, bestiality, and the like, but not an *agent* who, in Poe's society, might escape and kill white people.

2. Relatedly absent is the notion that Poe, *the author,* is doing something with this story. Telling here are Harrowitz's repeated references to the attitudes of Dupin: "Dupin entertains the possibility . . ." (1997, 180); "In the mind of Dupin, who is influenced by cultural attitudes and stereotypes . . ." (184); ". . . the creation of a subtext over which Dupin lacks vision or control" (189). These are not undergraduate instances of mistaking the character for the author, but are rather in the realm of the explicit rejection, à la Foucault, of the Author as a constructive agent: since Poe must be every bit as much a placeholder for the discourses of his time as Dupin is, there is no meaningful distinction to be made between them. This leads us to conclude that Poe's story manifests tendencies of the period, ruling out the possibility that Poe was working with the discourses of the moment intentionally to craft a specific insight.

3. Finally—and this too follows from the preceding silences—there is no sense that *readers* might be doing something in this story. In describing the story's nineteenth-century context, the implication is that antebellum readers would be attuned to the same anxieties and discourses that the story manifests; and in writing about readers today, the implication is that they must receive—passively—information about relevant thought systems of the past, and then be led—by the teacher-critic—through the intricacies of the sto-

ry's contradictions and suppressions. True, it is assumed that readers are, at some level, culturally processing these discourses: or, more accurately, that discourses are circulating through their subjectivities. But it is never considered that many readers (particularly American ones, black or white) will understand the story and take away a lesson intended by Poe.

The Situation

Harrowitz's "testing ground" approach is surely a common—and perhaps the dominant—approach to the problem of historical context: such and such discourses (or concerns, or beliefs, or issues) circulate at such and such a time, and our text in question is a conjunction (or articulation, or instantiation, or enactment). It may seem that we often teach this way as a kind of shorthand, because we don't have time to talk about context in detail. But Harrowitz's analysis, which is rich in detail and nuance, belies that excuse, and I think many teachers of literature will supplement a literary text with several texts illustrating a discursive context. The problem thus seems more fundamentally a theoretical one of how we approach context, and of how we have dismissed certain older problematics. For in stressing the *agency* of historical actors, author, and readers, many will automatically assume that I suffer from "agency panic," and am offering a regressive model for the reading of Poe's story, one that takes us back to hot history, celebration of the artist, and the like. Nor will it help my argument that the three elements I've outlined above are those most undergraduates find interesting and important (*What was going on at the time? What did Poe mean? My reaction to the story was. . . .*). So let me quickly reiterate that I find Harrowitz's analysis compelling, if incomplete, in the links she carefully traces between the racial, sexual, and xenophobic elements of the story, and her carefully argued skepticism toward the story's ostensible project of illumination. I do not at all want to rule out the "discursive" influences upon the story, nor do I mean to suggest complete aesthetic mastery on Poe's part, nor complete and sufficient understanding on the part of readers. But I do want to insist that the critical and pedagogical model Harrowitz's reading implies is incomplete and needs to be extended to account for the *praxis* of the work of art.

A model that moves in the right direction, the one I would like to outline here, is that offered in Jean-Paul Sartre's account of the *situation.* It is difficult to pin down Sartre's account of the situation, which was constantly being transformed from its extremely individualistic and voluntaristic rendering in *Being and Nothingness* to its later, more "materialist" formulations, explicit and implicit, in works like *Anti-Semite and Jew* (1948) and *Critique of Dialectical Reason* (1960).[2] For the purposes of this essay, however, I want to focus on the argument presented in *What is Literature?* (1948), written during that fruitful period in Sartre's career when he began to bring existentialism into dialogue with historical materialism. Sartre's goal in describing "being situated" was to provide a model for thinking about the interplay between determinants and agency; moving beyond the more naïve emphases on near-total freedom in his earlier writings, he now sought to explain specifically literary freedom *in terms of the limitations on freedom.* The first component of the writer's situation, then, would be the restrictions placed on the author (the authorial role, certain forms, possible content, material resources, etc.). These are not brute facts, things objectively "out there" in some simple sense: rather the author, in her writings, must "simultaneously enclose, specify, and surpass this situation, even explain it and set it up" (1988, 132-33).[3] Thus, to take the example of Racine, the "Jansenist ideology, the law of the three unities, and the rules of French prosody" do not construct seventeenth-century drama, save insofar as Racine must perceive them, take these into account, adapt and rework them. This is *not* an argument for the artist-as-genius creating literature from the whole cloth of her imagination, nor is it an argument for the total determination of the work by historical forces. Rather, it becomes an attempt to think "the limits of the demands" on the writer (133). In this respect, the model is both annoyingly and suggestively vague, providing little help in thinking about the specific play between givens and takens. Some of this uncertainty reflects the fact that the Sartrean situation is at once a descriptive *and* an evaluative or prescriptive model, in which the artist who resists the reification of her context as an inescapable absolute—that is, the artist more capable of seeing the context as something upon which she can work—is a *better* artist.

"What is Literature?" was and remains one of the most famous accounts of committed literature, and it is in this normative framing of the situation that the commitment of the artist is tested. But equally important for the essay is the more neglected and equally normative account of the reader's response to the author, which Sartre describes as "a pact of generosity," "a dialectical going-and-coming; when I read, I make demands; if my demands are met, what I am then reading provokes me to demand more of the author, which means to demand of the author that he demand more of me" (1988, 61-62). Such is Sartre's reworking of the idea of aesthetic pleasure (he calls it "aesthetic joy" instead): the artistic project undermines the "given" quality of the "horizon of our situation," becoming instead "a demand addressed to our freedom"

(64). The reader, drawn into the situation of givens and takens, comes to see herself "as *essential* to the totality of being"—that is, comes to see herself as a creator of the situation in her collaborative creation with the author (65). "[B]oth of us bear the responsibility" for the situation, as "the author's whole art is bent on obliging me to *create* what he [sic] discloses" (66-67). In this sense, the historical situation of the writer becomes part of the reader's literary-critical situation, in which *our* challenge is not simply to describe the writer's text or context, but rather to further construct it and, in doing so, to discern the limits she faced, misrecognized, and might have overcome.

Now in many respects the Sartrean situation is a far from original model for literary analysis, offering as it does another in a long series of attempts to account for the interplay between structure and agency. Besides simply reminding us of that interplay, however, the value of the situation seems to me to be twofold: first, in its emphasis that context is not some purely external series of determinants acting on the text, but involves the phenomenological construction and reworking of those determinants; and second, in its evaluative and interactive concern with the *readerly* (and thus critical) participation in the situation. So while Sartrean criticism has long been coded as old-fashioned and modern, inappropriate for our postmodern times, the situational model strikes me as well suited for taking us beyond poststructuralist accounts of discursive constructs. For Sartre's account of the situation not only accommodates an approach such as Harrowitz's, it in fact *demands* it in stressing the authorial construction of the situation from the cultural materials at hand. Where it surpasses this approach, however, is in insisting that the work of art is praxis akin to the slave insurrection, rather than a discursive instance or symptom. This model thus seems particularly important, as I have obviously been trying to suggest and as I hope to demonstrate, for thinking about historicist pedagogy. For it not only suggests a move beyond contextual framing, or some enumeration of historical factors acting on the text, toward some more dialectical approach in which writers assess *themselves* as historical products and try to respond accordingly; but in making reception part of context, it also demands participation, self-reflection, and evaluation from critical readers (like students) in making the text work historically.

An Invisible Agency

Poe's story arguably has three distinct narrative segments: the initial third, which introduces Dupin and the narrator and discusses "analysis"; the middle third, which describes the murders and the failed attempts to solve the crime; and the final third, in which the narrator is given the solution in the form of the orangutan. It is this last section which most obviously draws upon the charged nineteenth-century language of race, and in which the problem of slave violence, despite the story's Parisian displacement, enters most forcefully into the text. For here we have a humanoid captured in a distant land by sailors; brought to a metropolitan center for sale, but sequestered until healed of an injury in transit; holed up in a "closet" from which it spies upon the master shaving, thus learning the use of a razor; frightened by the master's whip into fleeing into the streets, where it finds two white women who are killed with brutal ferocity; ineptly hiding the bodies before fleeing again; and upon recapture, being sold once again. Given the loaded connotations of key terms of the narrative—"escaped," "master," "dreaded whip," "fugitive," "razor," and of course the "Ourang-Outang" itself—it would be nearly impossible to ignore the strong suggestions that the story is about slavery, and specifically about slave resistance. But asserting this simply begs a series of questions at the heart of my inquiry. If this reading is so obvious, why is an account of slave insurrections not more widely encountered in Poe criticism? What makes the connection at once clear and nearly inaccessible? And how might one convincingly teach this argument to students? I broach these questions in the classroom by writing the aforementioned words on the board and asking my students what they suggest. "Escaped," "master," "whip," "fugitive," "razor"—they always answer "slavery." I then ask them why, if these associations are so clear,[4] no one in our initial discussion of the story suggested that it was about slavery. What does it mean to *them* that the connection is obvious yet elusive?

I approach this problem by talking first about slave rebellions. Since I teach in Louisiana, I spend some time talking about the largest slave rebellion in U.S. history, the Deslondes Rebellion (c. 1811) and, closer to the moment of Poe's story, the spate of attempted actions that occurred in Louisiana in 1840 (in Avoyelles, Rapides, St. Landry, Lafayette, Iberville, Vermillion, and St. Martin parishes). To give some examples more proximate to Poe and his story, we discuss Nat Turner's Rebellion of 1831 (Poe was living in nearby Baltimore part of that year) and some of the reports of insurrections in Washington, D.C. in 1840. These are all discussed in Herbert Aptheker's celebrated *American Negro Slave Revolts* (1983).[5] But these actions are not the "key" to the story in the simple or naïve sense of providing relevant empirical data that consequently makes the story clear and understandable. In fact, such an approach would be downright detrimental, in suggesting that "events" are separate from "culture," or that Black slave actions are only significant as straightforward objects of allusion, or that there is a history of oppression and resistance out in the "real world" that might explain "what is going on at the time."

In fact, slave rebellions must be treated as *cultural* events of tremendous complexity—and specifically of a complexity illuminating for the literary production of the time. The greatest achievement of Aptheker's study is not his unprecedented cataloguing of slave resistance, but rather his insight into the cultural significance of these actions. In a two-fold thesis, he insists that the antebellum period was one of "widespread fear of servile rebellion" (1983, 18), and that our understanding of these rebellions is fundamentally shaped by "exaggeration, distortion, and censorship" (150). And while Aptheker does talk about some fabricated or magnified reports of slave actions (fostered for political or other motives), such cases are the *exception* to the rule of censorship: "it was a practice of the rulers of the South to censor news of slave unrest" (155). This is an important pedagogical point for explaining—in part—the contemporary neglect of slave rebellions. But more importantly, it explains a truly remarkable cultural milieu, the import of which remains unappreciated by cultural historians: slave-holding societies were at once cultures of (white) fear *and* censorship of the action feared. Newspapers, journals, and government bodies fairly consistently restricted information about slave resistance, for the obvious reason that the more you talk about it, the more likely it is to occur.

How might one illustrate this phenomenon in the classroom? One can discuss the sources found in Aptheker's study, which are typically nonpublic governmental documents, personal correspondence, or unusually terse journalistic reports. More illuminating, perhaps, is Thomas Gray's "Confessions of Nat Turner," which illustrates a remarkable fixation and celebration of Turner even in the act of demonizing and minimizing the action as an aberration. But I find particularly valuable the thematics of secret communication and racial codes found in Frederick Douglass's 1845 *Narrative of the Life of Frederick Douglass, An American Slave.* Douglass's discussion of slave secrecy, the coded meaning of spirituals, Northern naiveté in expecting straightforward communication with slaves, the covert practices of overseers like Covey, and the misguided openness of the abolitionists running the underground railroad—all of these lead to a complex sense of the racial code, and an insistence on a similar code to *fight* slavery. Thus Douglass's early condemnation of Covey as a man whose "*forte* consisted in his power to deceive" is not parried by a summons for open and straightforward communication as much as a call to terrorize the slaveholder and slavehunter.

> I would keep the merciless slaveholder profoundly ignorant of the means of flight adopted by the slave . . . [and] leave him to imagine himself surrounded by myriads of invisible tormentors, ever ready to snatch from his infernal grasp his trembling prey . . . let him feel that at every step he takes, in pursuit of the flying bondman, he is running the frightful risk of having his hot brains dashed out by an invisible agency.
>
> (Douglass 1994, 85)

"Invisible agency" powerfully conveys many of the dimensions of secrecy here—surveillance and management, covering up, playing dumb, covert planning, terrorizing and so forth.

A slave rebellion, then, is not a discrete event of so many slaves acting at this time and this place. *Culturally,* the slave rebellion includes the feigned ignorance, the defiance, and the planning of slaves, the suspicion, terror, and ignorance of whites, the rumors and secrets in circulation during and after the event, and the struggle to control the aftermath of information. Saying that **"Murders in the Rue Morgue"** is about slave rebellions means that it is about the orangutan's violence, yes, but also about the secrecy, the racial code, the overall hermeneutics surrounding slave insurrections. This should be apparent in a story that is so obviously about slave violence, yet which also never "gives away" its secret in any easy way. We might read Poe's story, then, as a white answer to the Douglass program: yes, we know about your invisible agency, but we have secrets of our own. **"Murders"** is about keeping the secret.

The Chantilly Method

What this means is that the parallels between orangutan and insurrectionary slave are important, but only *part* of the story. And we needn't gloss over the confusions this point raises for students, who will ask why a story about slave violence doesn't make its point more explicit. This is not a bad question—in fact, it's the *best* question to ask—and struggling with the pedagogical demands of an answer (once students are as equipped to answer as professors) can lead students (including teachers) to a more complex appreciation of the literary situation.

In my experience, the three most common ways in which students approach this problem are:

1. to assume we readers are simply not supposed to get it, because it's an inside "joke" for Poe;

2. to assume that the message is only for a select few readers, the "smart" ones who can make the connections; or

3. to assume that readers do get the message, but not necessarily in ways that they even understand (though they might).

I always insist on the latter position, in teaching Poe, and not out of some pedagogical commitment to equality. (T. S. Eliot's allusions aren't meant for everyone, for instance.) Rather, I argue that the association of "fugitive," "escaped," "whip," and "master" with slavery is not only *possible* for virtually anyone in the nineteenth century (not to mention the twentieth and twenty-first) but practically *unavoidable*. This point can be further made with reference to another Dupin tale, the famous **"Purloined Letter."** Almost everyone remembers the crucial lesson that the best place to hide something is out in the open, or, put differently, we often cannot find something right in front of us. Equally important to that story, though, is Dupin's mission—to get the letter so that *it may remain hidden*. Put another way, the story is about control of *the use of the secret*.

"Murders" itself makes a similar point, in the famous "Chantilly" passage. Strolling along, Dupin suddenly tells the narrator, "He is a very little fellow, that's true, and would do better for the *Théâtre des Variétés*." The narrator quickly agrees, noting that he "replied unwittingly, and not at first observing (so much had I been absorbed in reflection) the extraordinary manner in which the speaker had chimed in with my meditations" (Poe 1984, 402). The stunned narrator demands an explanation, and Dupin proceeds to reconstruct the narrator's "meditations" for the past fifteen minutes. A fruiterer bumps against the narrator, pushing him into a pile of paving-stones; the narrator slightly sprains his ankle and keeps his eyes to the ground, noticing overlapping and riveted blocks at a later point in the walk; this invites reflection upon "stereotomy" which in turn suggests "atomies, and thus . . . the theories of Epicurus;" this in turn calls to mind a discussion about cosmogony, which in turn prompts a look at the constellation Orion; Orion recalls a theater review in which an actor named Chantilly is panned; the narrator thinks about "the diminutive figure of Chantilly" and his critical "immolation," at which point Dupin finally utters his remark (403-04).

This passage at first seems a clever demonstration of Dupin's amazing analytical powers, akin to those thrilling moments when Sherlock Holmes figures out what Dr. Watson had for dinner three nights ago. But the passage takes on a different sense once the question of secret slave rebellions has been raised. For what is most striking about the Chantilly sequence is the way it parallels the pedagogical problem I've raised. The basic point of the Chantilly sequence concerns *not* Dupin's intelligence but the narrator's ignorance: *he does not even understand his own thought processes, the associations made in his imagination*. The passage could be unpacked further, for it surely seems fitting that a physical brush with a laborer might make one watch where one steps and to reflect upon the appropriate milieu for a "diminutive figure." The setting is likewise suggestive: the chain of associations unfolds during a walk "down a long dirty street, in the vicinity of the Palais Royal" (402), suggesting a contrast between the architecture of authority and our "long dirty" thought processes. But it is also worth examining the odd situation of this passage in the text, for as soon as Dupin gives his explanation, a new paragraph begins: "Not long after this, we were looking over an evening edition of the 'Gazette des Tribunaux' . . ." (404-05). Why this abrupt transition? Having considered the Chantilly passage, my students generally believe that the abrupt transition is analogous to that silent fifteen-minute walk: that there is a transition, a connection, but one that is not spoken. And this makes them pause and reflect on a truly disturbing revelation: like the narrator, *they may not understand their own reading processes, and the associations they make in their imaginations*.

The detective's subject, then, is not simply or even primarily *the crime*; it's the *process of thinking* about the crime. And this explication of the reading/thinking process may seem a departure from the question of historical context. Isn't the slave rebellion, according to my reading, the true "context"? And aren't we now talking about something else, i.e., the properly literary process of reading? Not at all. Because the slave rebellion, in the expanded sense outlined above, is a *hermeneutic* phenomenon (of secrecy and revelation, denial and insistence), the Chantilly passage must be read as Poe's methodological commentary on *how we think about context*. The invisible agency of the slave is matched by the invisible interpretation of the detective. This is how Poe has constructed his and our situation (slave violence) as we walk the long dirty streets. The context here is thus not an inside joke known only to Poe, just as the narrator's thought process is *not* at all reducible to Dupin's "*charlatanerie*" (1984, 403). Nor is the context for intellectual elites alone (Dupin, but not the narrator); we (like the narrator) can reconstruct it ourselves, if we think about how we constructed it the first time. The third interpretive option opens up, then, into two possibilities, in both of which we understand (to varying degrees) the context of the story. We either (a) understand the context implicitly, but without reflection, or (b) piece together our associations, as we've been instructed in the Chantilly passage.

I would not disagree with Harrowitz's philosophical and deconstructive point that knowledge typically effaces its traces or conditions of existence. But to assume that **"Murders"** is *only* concealing the conditions of detection is to jump the gun, to deny Poe's critical reflections on the phenomena of concealment. Not only is the Chantilly passage calling attention to, and inviting reflection upon, the ways in which whites suppress their understanding of slave resistance, but this point is made repeatedly throughout the introductory pages. For instance, like the Chantilly passage, the opening comparison of chess and cards—a potentially liberating passage for students who view literary analysis to be chess-like—invites a critical examination on the part of readers. Chess is the mathematical assessment of prescribed moves, and the greatest chess player "*may* be little more than the best player of chess" (Poe 1984, 398). Card games, on the other hand, require much more than knowledge of the rules of the game—namely, "a comprehension of *all* the sources whence legitimate advantage may be derived" (398). Poe's narrator goes on to stress that "[t]he necessary knowledge is that of *what* to observe," and the good card player does not "reject deductions from things external to the game," including the false clues constituted by "feint[s]" (399). Once again, the transition from these reflections to a more conventional plot—here, the introduction of the characters—is revealing: "The narrative which follows will appear to the reader somewhat in the light of a commentary upon the propositions just advanced" (400). The commentary on analysis is not simply a slight component of the story; rather, the story is an illustration of (racial) analysis, one in which the reader might test for herself the "necessary knowledge" of "*what* to observe."

Achilles and the Sirens

Poe announces this challenge again and again in his text, but initially in his opening epigraph from Sir Thomas Browne: "What song the Syrens sang, or what name Achilles assumed when he hid himself among women, although puzzling questions, are not beyond *all* conjecture" (1984, 397). And a similar reminder comes in the very last line of the story, in which Dupin mocks the Police Prefect for "the way he has '*de nier ce qui est, et d'expliquer ce qui n'est pas*'—of denying what is, and of explaining that which isn't" (431). In the middle of the story, too, we hear Dupin's critique of the celebrated Vidocq, who "impaired his vision by holding the object too close," thus "los[ing] sight of the matter as a whole" (412). Following the lesson of "The Philosophy of Composition," Dupin insists that, "as regards the more important knowledge, I do believe that she is invariably superficial," adding that we need to seek truth in the valleys, not in the "heavenly bodies" (412). Taken together, these tips suggest some guidelines for finding the "truth": we must be clear about the illusions that make perception difficult (figuring out the Sirens' song); we must seek out Achilles' disguise and see through it; we must explain what is (the slave action) and deny that which is not (the lies, silences, and feints of the story); we must achieve some distance and not hold our object too close; we must look "down" and not "up," focusing on the quotidian valleys and not the exceptional celestial bodies. We *are* invited, in other words, to make sense of the story, and, with the Chantilly passage, we're given numerous methodological pointers.

These methodological pointers apply to what we've determined so far: in connecting the orangutan with the resistant slave, we have partly found out the disguise of Achilles and identified the misleading song of the (police) Sirens; we have not denied that which is, nor tried to explain that which is not; and we have not held our object too close, nor focused on the celestial. Like the narrator in the midst of Dupin's explanation, "a vague and half-formed conception of the meaning of Dupin [has] flitted over [our] mind[s]," and we seem "upon the brink of remembrance" (Poe 1984, 421). But only on the brink: we have yet to determine why Poe has gone to all this trouble to hide the slave rebel, why he constructed *this* particular situation—a detective story set in Paris—to explain slave resistance. This problem is not beyond *all* conjecture, and while, in concluding, I do not aim to provide comprehensive "answers" to Poe's story, I do want to outline some of the connections my students and I have made along the way to a better understanding of **"Murders."** I should stress that understanding this story is, for me, an on-going process: making some claims about historical context does not bring interpretation to a screeching halt, nor does it leave us with the less interesting, "purely literary" problems. Rather, determining the context as a problem posed by Poe actually *opens up* the process of interpretation, *linking* the historical with the more literary dimensions of the story. My classroom approach has been to throw out questions about the story's details: Why are the murder victims two women living alone? Why is one thrown into a courtyard, the other jammed up a chimney? Why is the setting a sealed room? Why is the story set in Paris? Why is the broken nail important for the solution? Why are we given information about Dupin's lifestyle? And so forth. I do not assume there are interpretive "solutions" to all of these questions, but I do invite my students to think about approaching the story with the Chantilly method—the method of examining and foregrounding associational, connotative, and sometimes not-quite-conscious responses. I offer here some of their hypotheses to illustrate the way in which we've approached "context" in the classroom.

Dupin and the Narrator

We are told that they "live together . . . in a retired and desolate portion" of the city, where their "seclusion was perfect" and "no visitors" were admitted. "We existed within ourselves alone," declares the narrator, who also stresses how the two are "enamored of the Night for her own sake." The two "closed all the massy shutters of our old building" until they could venture out in the night. Within the relationship, the narrator gives himself "up to [Dupin's] wild whims with a perfect *abandon*"—imitating Dupin and his lifestyle. Dupin further declares that he can see into the "windows" of most men's bosoms (Poe 1984, 401).

Does the Chantilly method offer us any insights here? My students have noted numerous narrative and descriptive parallels between Dupin/Narrator and the two L'Espanaye women. These women "lived an exceedingly retired life"—with no servants and almost no visitors—in the upper stories of a large house in the Rue Morgue; their bodies are found in "a large back chamber" in which all the windows are sealed. Madame L'Espanaye reportedly "told fortunes for a living" (Poe 1984, 406-07). It is hard not to see some implicit parallels being established here: the predictive detective and the fortune-teller[6]; the reclusive lifestyle of the two pairs, right down to the closed windows, and nighttime lifestyle; the clear subordination within the couples. There may, too, be parallels with another character pair, the sailor and the orangutan, who likewise lodge in an upper-story apartment so as "not to attract . . . the unpleasant curiosity of . . . neighbors" (428). They too are night prowlers, they too display a relationship of subordination and imitation; they too live in a dwelling of locked rooms (428-29).

The parallels are not perfect, but they do seem significant, suggestive enough to trigger some tacit associations for readers. Why are they in the story? One answer suggested by my students is that Poe explicitly seeks to show the identity of the perpetrators, victims, and preventers of slave violence, meaning specifically the careless slave-abusers, the targets of slave violence, and those seeking to prevent the violence. It's as if Dupin and the narrator are trying to solve their *own* potential murders, since the crime they encounter is in a setting much like that in which they live. And in confronting the sailor about his brutal killing subordinate, there may be a further commentary on the naiveté of the narrator, whose blindness and ignorance are (from Poe's perspective) the enabling white corollaries of slave violence. In terms of the constructed *situation,* then, the parallels implicitly play on the nature and ubiquity of white fear of slave violence (*it could happen to me*) via associations stressing parallels between victims, negligent slaveholders, and observers (*each could be the other*). The horrifying logical conclusion (to whites) suggested by these parallels, then, is that they might be responsible for their own deaths. And this observation in turn offers an approach to the puzzle of the sealed room, suggesting that white southerners seal themselves up with their dangers, *or* that seclusion does not provide security, *or* that windows (of houses or of bosoms) are less barriers than passageways to be entered even when they appear closed.

Setting and Motive

Why is the story set in Paris? Does the Paris setting become significant at any point in the story? It does, arguably in a negative way, when Dupin considers the language of the "criminal" after hearing earwitness testimonies. The Spaniard hears an Englishman, the Italian hears a Russian, and so on, in a series of testimony *ruling out* "the five great divisions of Europe" (Poe 1984, 416). In other words, the Parisian setting gives us a cosmopolitan crowd that, together, rules out the possibility that the criminal is *white.* One of the most interesting moments of the story follows this conclusion, when Dupin notes, "You will say that it might have been the voice of an Asiatic—of an African. Neither Asiatics nor Africans abound in Paris; but, without denying the inference, I will now merely call your attention to three points . . ." (416). He goes on to talk about qualities of the orangutan's voice, but it is this dismissal of the African that is notable, and that needs to be compared with Dupin's earlier critique of the police, who "have fallen into the gross but common error of confounding the unusual with the abstruse" (414). "In investigations such as we are now pursuing," he insists, "it should not be so much asked 'what has occurred,' as 'what has occurred that has never occurred before'" (414). In other words, the good detective, the truly analytical thinker, does not confine herself to probabilities, but must consider the improbable as necessary. It is this kind of reasoning which leads Dupin to assume that the window nail *must* be broken (419), that the criminal *must* be a nonhuman (421-23).

Yet when we juxtapose these comments about Dupin's ostensible method with the manner in which he rules out the possibility of an African or Asiatic criminal, we find a tremendous inconsistency in a story that devotes so much attention to the proper analytical method. For now Dupin, "*without denying the inference,*" *does* deny the inference in practice! What allows him to skip over the African possibility? In his explanation to the narrator, the insistence that the criminal is an orangutan hinges on the "*excessively outré*" nature of the crime (Poe 1984, 422), which combines "an agility astounding, a strength superhuman, a ferocity brutal, a butchery without motive, a *grotesquerie* in horror absolutely alien from humanity, and a voice foreign in tone to the ears of men of many nations, and devoid of all distinct or intelligible syllabification" (423). (Note that, again, Dupin does not rule out *all* humans when he speaks of "men of *many* nations.") The narrator consequently concludes that the criminal must be a "madman," at which point Dupin produces the animal-like hair of the orangutan.

What we witness, in Dupin's analysis of the crime, is a clash between two lines of explanation, a linguistic one (raised by Dupin, and then dismissed without an explicit denial) suggesting that the criminal must be an African/Asiatic, the other insisting that the criminal must be an animal because no human could be *motivated* to commit such a ghastly crime. These two lines of reasoning clash because the former explanation (of a non-white criminal) is never laid to rest. For consistency's sake, Dupin should argue as follows: the linguistic misperception means that the criminal must be African, Asiatic, or animal; but *then,* the inhuman motivation of the crime rules out any African/Asiatic criminal, leaving only the animal as a possibility. In short, the missing step in Dupin's reasoning is this: *an African or Asiatic could never be motivated to kill so outrageously.* And this is exactly the analytical step that Poe will not articulate *because he knows the contrary*—that yes, there *are* motives for outrageous killing on the part of Africans. A close reading of the text, of Dupin's method of reasoning and then its actual practice, thus reveals this significant gap surrounding *motive,* a gap with which he calls attention (albeit indirectly) to the truth an apologist for slavery can never mention: one rational and predictable response to the brutality of slavery is a correspondingly outrageous violence. In Dupin's own terms, the motive for slave violence might be the story's purloined letter (sitting out in the open, yet hidden; and something to be retrieved in order to keep it hidden) or, to keep to the expressions of **"Murders in the Rue Morgue,"** the motive to kill whites might be the big picture, that which *is,* while the distraction from this motive might constitute the Sirens' song, or that which is *not.*

To return to the question of setting, then, Paris is important not because it is a simple feint (i.e., Poe puts the story in a non-slave setting to *hide* slavery), but because it is a feint which calls attention to the feint: when juxtaposed with Dupin's reasoning, it foregrounds the Great White Secret about slave violence, *that it makes sense*! In other words, "Paris," as a cosmopolitan setting of world peoples, calls attention to the specific denial about "Africans" and thus invites readers to be complicit in the secret of the story. Were the setting, say, "Richmond" or "Charleston," the associations might be so obvious as to prevent, paradoxically, an honest admission about slavery and slave violence. And here we have another important lesson about historical context, for Poe's construction of the situation of slave violence need not rely upon a correlational verisimilitude (e.g., setting the first detective story in Richmond or Charleston), but may instead proceed via a contrasting process (e.g., using a setting in which one may speak openly about Africans *and* then hide the secret). Reflecting on Poe's construction of the Parisian locale—a setting remarkably consistent with the hermeneutics of secrecy surrounding slave rebellions—allows us to find connections between, in this case, setting and motive.

Conclusions

My students have formulated other insightful interpretations about the story (about why one woman is thrown out the window while the other is put up the chimney, about the reasoning behind the sailor's response to Dupin's ad, about windows and shutters, about the narrator's fantasy of two Dupins, etc.) too numerous to summarize here. They all elaborate a basic hypothesis about Poe's story and his project, namely that *the first American detective story is about Black resistance to slavery and the white racial code that aims to deny and combat it.* But my point in this essay has been to stress how such an interpretation is possible only through a situational approach to historical context that allows for some consideration of creative historical agency. In the hopes that some readers have found these interpretive speculations suggestive and illuminating, opening up new dimensions to Poe's story, I would like to conclude by reiterating some general conclusions about the situational approach to historical context.

Historical Agency

The shift in emphasis from a "hot history" of events to a discursive history aims, among other things, to challenge the naïve voluntarism of great deeds and great actors of the past. By contrast, discursive history stresses the cultural parameters within which history unfolds, and this is a salutary emphasis. What is needed, however, is some mediation between these two views of history, some sense of the conflicts and options that remain *within* these cultural constraints. For *contexts are not fixed realities, but involve antagonisms, problems, and choices.* This is an important reminder for teachers of literature who, in attempting to offer context, may inadvertently present history as an iron cage, and texts as reflections or instances of the times. Harrowitz very usefully stresses white discourses of racialization, criminalization, urbanization, and so forth, but her approach, when carried over to the classroom, makes **"Murders in the Rue Morgue"** little more than a manifestation of cultural tendencies of the time. In this respect, literary historians need to think more about slave *agency,* praxis undertaken in conditions of extreme constraints. Texts, as projects of cultural praxis, are likewise attempts to transform the world (even if that means transforming our understanding), often in response to the more materialized but equally "cultural" actions around them. Slaves planned, studied, and organized, responding to the restrictions and limits in which they lived in an attempt to overcome them; and Poe's story, similarly, was an attempt to respond to the antagonisms and problems these slave actions posed. Teaching historical context, then, means identifying the praxis of the moment to which the text is likewise responding.

Authorial Agency

The "death of the author" announced a repudiation of the belief in the brilliant creative genius who constructed whole worlds from her imagination. By contrast, the reconstructed author has become more of a site or place-holder through which discourses circulate, and it matters little if we speak of "Poe," "Dupin," or **"Murders in the Rue Morgue,"** for these sites largely overlap. Again, we need a mediating position from which to think about authors engaged in the praxis of their literary work. We needn't elevate the author to some special status to grant her the same (qualified) agency that we observe outside literature. How then does the author act? Here we need to think about the cultural patterns the author encounters. There are no historical contexts or events removed from culture: contexts always imply patterns of interpreting, modes of perceiving, the conflicts, problems, and choices. While the author cannot, through words, engage in direct acts (such as hunting down slaves or killing slaveholders), she may attempt to transform our ways of understanding these acts. In other words, writers engage historical context not as supplemental data but as the horizon in which to address (to play with, challenge, reinforce, subvert, etc.) our perceptions of context. Context is not the background, or the secret, of **"Murders in the Rue Morgue,"** it's the problem of the story itself: in the antagonistic context of slavery and slave resistance, people tend to respond in certain ways that create further problems. . . . Poe *is* creating something of a "testing ground," but it is not the accidental testing ground in which discourses clash agonistically, unbeknownst to Poe or his less informed readers. It is a testing ground for our perceptions, considering ways in which they might be changed to detect and suppress, more effectively, the slave violence threatening whites. We needn't declare the author's praxis a success, nor are we obliged to agree with it, but we should recognize it as the intervention it is.

Classroom Agency

With a more dynamic and constructive account of context and authorial agency, we can invite students to participate in the literary project. This means breaking away from the view that students are passive observers who need us to clarify context, although it does not mean that we have to abandon the project of teaching students better—meaning, more fruitful—ways to read. What we must attempt is a pedagogical method that acknowledges readers' participation—and therefore readers' abilities—in the agency of the text. The pedagogical pattern outlined above is one in which my students and I think about the cultural patterns and conflicts of a historical context, and then the method for perceiving context implicit in the text, before finally taking up the project of the text together. When we talk about Jonathan Edwards' "Sinners in the Hands of an Angry God," for instance, we talk about the context of revivalism not as a fact but as an antagonistic context. We then try to think about Edwards' project in his sermon, but we can only do this by considering their reactions to this sermon, and how their participation is supposed to make the text work. Stressing the necessary participation of readers in historical context thus means promoting more self-aware readers and, hopefully, historical agents.

Notes

1. I would like to thank my students in English 270 at Cornell University, English 150 at Connecticut College, and English 3070 at Louisiana State University. I have also benefited from discussing this story with many, many colleagues, among whom I would particularly like to thank Rick Moreland, Michael Drexler, Judi Kemerait, Gerry Kennedy, and Jim Holstun.

2. Flynn carefully tracks the development of the "situation" concept (1984, 1997). I draw heavily on his explications in what follows. Flynn is particularly appreciative of the ways in which the ambiguities of Sartre's writings are as much strengths as weaknesses.

   For those interested in theoretical genealogies, it is worth noting that Sartre's understanding of the situation comes from early Heidegger (*Being and Time*'s treatment of situatedness) whereas the "discursive" approach outlined above is more closely tied to the later Heidegger, and his growing (postwar) emphasis upon the "destinal."

3. Fredric Jameson's *The Political Unconscious,* as some readers will recognize, offers one expansion and refinement of the Sartrean situation in his outline of the three horizons for literary analysis, similarly insisting that the situation must be un-

derstood as constituting its context: "The symbolic act therefore begins by generating and producing its own context in the same moment of emergence in which it steps back from it, taking its measure with a view toward its own project of transformation" (1981, 81).

4. And taking for granted, of course, that these are *significant* terms in the story's solution.
5. See Aptheker, (1983, 32-36, 98, 333, 293-324). Aptheker insists that 1840 was an important year for actions, rumors, and fears, while the "remainder of the forties were relatively quiet years" (336).
6. There are possible parallels implicit in the names here as well. Dupin's name suggests *duperie* or trickery of some kind, while L'Espanaye may suggest spying (*espionner*); the narrator, of course, has no name, while the younger woman is in name the junior version of her mother.

Works Cited

Aptheker, Herbert. 1983. *American Negro Slave Revolts.* 5th ed. New York: International Publishers.

Douglass, Frederick. 1994. *Autobiographies.* Ed. Henry Louis Gates, Jr. New York: Library of America.

Flynn, Thomas R. 1984. *Sartre and Marxist Existentialism: The Test Case of Collective Responsibility.* Chicago: University of Chicago Press.

———. 1997. *Sartre, Foucault, and Historical Reason.* 2 vols. Vol. 1: *Toward an Existentialist Theory of History.* Chicago: University of Chicago Press.

Harrowitz, Nancy A. 1997. "Criminality and Poe's Orangutan: The Question of Race in Detection." In *Agonistics: Arenas of Creative Contest,* ed. Janet Lungstrum and Elizabeth Sauer. Albany: State University of New York Press.

Jameson, Fredric. 1981. *The Political Unconscious: Narrative as a Socially Symbolic Act.* Ithaca: Cornell University Press.

Jameson, Fredric. 1995. "On *Cultural Studies.*" In *The Identity in Question,* ed. John Rajchman. New York: Routledge.

Poe, Edgar Allan. 1984. *Poetry and Tales.* Ed. Patrick F. Quinn. New York: Library of America.

Sartre, Jean-Paul. 1988. *"What Is Literature?" and Other Essays.* Trans. Bernard Frechtman, Jeffrey Mehlman, and John MacCombie. Cambridge: Harvard University Press.

John H. Timmerman (essay date summer 2003)

SOURCE: Timmerman, John H. "House of Mirrors: Edgar Allan Poe's 'The Fall of the House of Usher.'" *Papers on Language & Literature* 39, no. 3 (summer 2003): 227-44.

[*In the following essay, Timmerman describes Poe's attempt to unify Enlightenment thinking with romanticism in "The Fall of the House of Usher," and observes similar concerns with cosmic unity in the prose poem* Eureka.]

"The Fall of the House of Usher" is among those few stories that seem to elicit nearly as many critical interpretations as it has readers. More recent critical appraisals of the story have largely followed two directions: a reappraisal of the genre of the story as a Gothic romance[1] and a close attention to Madeline Usher as a type of Poe's other female characters.[2] But the tale presents the reader a multiplicity of problems that set it aside from Poe's other stories. Madeline is as enigmatic as a new language and as difficult to construe. While debates about Lady Ligeia have filled the pages of many journals, it is not hard to understand why.[3] Her contrarian social role, her purely gothic resurrection, and her defiant antithesis in character to Rowena sharpen her person from the start. But Madeline? This sylph-like creature, so attenuated and frail, seems to slip through the story like vapor, all the more mysterious for that and for her incredible power displayed in the conclusion.

Similarly, while the story is certainly Gothic in nature, here, too, we find exceptions and qualifications. In the majority of Poe's Gothic tales the narrative point of view is first person, and, significantly, the reader is also placed inside the mind of this leading character-narrator who is only a step away from insanity. In **"Usher"** [**"The Fall of the House of Usher"**] we also have a creeping horror and the mental disintegration of the principal persona, but the story is in fact narrated by an outside visitor (also representing the reader) who wants to find a way out of the horror. The only problem with this narrator is that, even having been given ample signs and warnings (as happens to Fortunato in **"The Cask of Amontillado"**), he is too inept to put the clues together. Poe has designed this deliberately, of course, for the reader is far more deductive than the narrator but has to wait for him to reach the extreme limit of safety before fleeing. However dull the narrator's mental processing, it is altogether better than being trapped in insanity.

One of the more penetrating of these studies of Gothic traits is G. R. Thompson's analysis of **"The Fall of the House of Usher"** in his *Poe's Fiction.* Thompson addresses the variations Poe creates with the Gothic tale by structuring a conflict between reason and irrationality. Particularly successful is his analysis of the decayed House mirroring Usher's mind so that "The sinking of the house into the reflecting pool dramatizes the sinking of the rational part of the mind, which has unsuccessfully attempted to maintain some contact with a stable structure of reality outside the self, into the nothingness within" (90). The analysis provides a lucid discussion of the process of that disintegration, of the dream-like qualities of Madeline as the devolution of the subconscious, and of the narrator's final infection by "Usher's hysteria." What Thompson does not explore, however, is an accounting for the loss of reason and what conclusion the reader may infer by the storm-struck house crumbling into the murky tarn.

To explore such issues, one must investigate beyond the confines of the tale proper, even beyond its generic home as a Gothic romance. The tale yields its full meaning as we turn to areas much overlooked in the study of this work; first, the influence of Poe's cosmology as set forth in other works but nonetheless pertinent, by his own telling, to his art; and, second, the historical context of his time when the effects of Enlightenment thinking of the prior century had not yet fully yielded (for Poe, at least) to the new spirit of Romanticism. The latter point in particular is crucial for an historicist appraisal of the story and of Poe, for it becomes evident that Poe did not reject Enlightenment thinking, that he was in fact suspicious of the newer Romanticism, and that at best he hoped for a tenuous harmony between the two. Keeping in mind such premises, we can observe the theory for unity, symmetry, and harmony emerging from *Eureka,* the aesthetic principles of the theory in his essays, and the application of those principles in a study of the conflict between Romanticism and Enlightenment in **"The Fall of the House of Usher."**

The casual treatment of Poe's cosmology no doubt springs from the conception that this is but one more entertaining hoax from the master trickster, somewhat akin to the elaborate architecture of "The Raven" described in "Philosophy of Composition." Undeniably, however, even Poe's most wildly Gothic romances, his most mysterious tales of ratiocination, and virtually all his poems, spring from some "idea" of order, a principle that this world can try to twist and break but can never quite succeed. Basically, his cosmology rests upon the philosophical principle that the very apprehension of disorder assumes an agency of order. Those familiar with the works of Aristotle will recognize the argument immediately. The essentials of Poe's cosmology reside in his essay *Eureka,* and there, too, he relies upon Aristotelian premises.

Since the work is less familiar to contemporary readers, I preface a discussion of it with a brief chronology. In 1843 Poe published the "Prospectus of *The Stylus,*" the literary magazine he hoped to launch in July of that year. In late 1847, he had completed the lecture "The Cosmogony of the Universe"[4] that would be the introduction to *Eureka,* but also a lecture (nearly two hours long) that he could use to raise funds for *The Stylus.* The lecture had limited use. The only event we are certain of was an appearance on January 17, 1848, at Society Library where only 60 people showed up, most of them journalists. Poe finally prevailed upon Putnam to publish the work, asking for a print run of 50,000 copies and receiving instead a run of 500. It appeared in early July 1848.[5]

There appeared to be good reason for caution. The narrative guise of the learned scholar adopted for the lengthy third section absolutely confounds the casual—or even the very literate—reader.[6] Elsewhere, the narrator moves from humble observer to snide satirist. In addition to the shifting narrative poses, the work itself is simply such a strange miscellany of facts and thoughts and extrapolations that it is nearly impossible to find an orderly, fruitful, and singular thesis emerging in it. Every issue seems to lead to an ever-widening gyre of new questions. Admitting that, however, the work still constitutes Poe's fundamental cosmological view, and it does remain central to understanding his aesthetic principles. That essential element of *Eureka,* at least, may be rather clearly and conveniently summarized.

Preceding all existence is a deity functioning like Aristotle's Prime Mover. Humanity, and all physical nature, exists because this Prime Mover willed it to exist. Poe states that "'In the beginning' we can admit—indeed, we can comprehend, but one *First Cause,* the truly ultimate *Principle,* the Volition of God" (237).[7] We have then, a fairly traditional view of God's creation *ex nihilo,* that is, he willed all things into being out of nothing more than his will. As with Aristotle (and also the Judeo-Christian tradition) God is that being beyond which one can go no further.

But here Poe throws some of his own twists into the proposition. If the creator being is that ultimate first cause, it must represent unity. All the created order is individuated; necessarily, therefore, its source is not chaos but unity. Poe speaks of this as "Irradiation from Unity"—the primary creative act. Moreover, "This primary act itself is to be considered as *continuous volition*" (237). This is to say that God's creative impulse continues through the creative order, including humanity, that he has willed into being.

We arrive at the old religious and philosophical conundrum. If willed into being by God, and out of nothing, then what constitutes both our individuation yet also our unity with this God? Judaism provides the earliest answer with the story of the Edenic fall, where because of an act of transgression the unity was partially severed and, according to the Kabbalistic myth of "God in Exile," God withdrew into mystery. Nonetheless, as God's creation, humanity was still *mindful* of God. Plato provides the first coherent philosophical accounting in the western world with his concept of the Ideal Forms being transmuted by the earthly stuff of humanity. Only humanity, however, possessed the quality of mind to apprehend the ideal.

Poe, on the other hand, insists upon an ongoing volitional act of God apprehended by intuition. The idea led to his notorious concept in "The Poetic Principle" that the task of the poet is "to apprehend the supernal loveliness" (*Essays* 77) of God's order and that the best way to do so is through sadness. Poe reflects "that (how or why we know not) this certain taint of sadness is inseparably connected with all the higher manifestations of true Beauty" (*Essays* 81). This leads Poe, then, to the idea that the most sad thing, and therefore the most beautiful, is the death of a beautiful woman. The result is a body of work littered with female corpses.

It remains difficult, even for the most earnest reader, to take "The Poetic Principle" altogether seriously. Yet, herein lie many of Poe's seminal ideas and aesthetic principles. Many of those ideas, moreover, relate directly to the cosmology of *Eureka.* One has to remember that Poe desires to startle the reader into an awareness of the divinity within, for, he insists, we are all part and particle of the divine.[8] Necessarily so, since God willed all things into being out of nothing. What then are we but particles of the divine itself? Therefore in all created order there resides what Edward Wagenknecht called "the Shadow of Beauty."[9] Poe describes it as such: "An immortal instinct, deep within the spirit of man, is thus, plainly, a sense of the beautiful" (***Complete Works*** [***The Complete Works of Edgar Allan Poe***] 14: 273). Therefore, Poe concludes that, since we are willed into being *ex nihilo,* since we are thereby part and particle of the divine, and since the ongoing volition of the divine rests among its creation as a shadow of beauty, symmetry that mirrors this unity of the universe is the paramount aesthetic quality of the work. Poe argues that the sense of the symmetrical "is the poetical essence of the *Universal—of the Universe* which, in the supremeness of its symmetry, is but the most sublime of poems. Now symmetry and consistency are convertible terms; thus poetry and truth are one" (***Complete Works*** 16: 302).

Poe takes the issue one step further, however. If indeed all things are willed into being *ex nihilo,* then not only all humanity but also all matter is part and parcel with God. Such a view Poe expresses as his infamous "sentience theory" in **"The Fall of the House of Usher."**[10] In particular the theory exerts itself twice. When Usher reveals that he has not left the mansion in many years, he describes the effect that the "mere form and substance" of the mansion has had upon him: "An effect which the *physique* of the gray walls and turrets, and of the dim tarn into which they all looked down, had, at length, brought upon the *morale* of his existence" (**"Usher"** 403).[11] Later, after Usher's rhapsody of creative expressions, the narrator and Usher fall into a conversation on "the sentience of all vegetable things" (408). Remembering Usher's description of this, the narrator describes the preternatural interconnectedness of mansion and family, and concludes, in Usher's terms, that "The result was discoverable . . . in that silent, yet importunate and terrible influence which for centuries had moulded the destinies of his family, and which made *him* what I now saw him—what he was" (408).[12]

Careful readers of Poe will quickly understand that this use of a mental landscape is nothing new to Poe. It appears most prominently, perhaps, in the poetry. In "Ulalume" for example, the weird and otherworldly geographical landscape is nothing more than an objectification of the narrator's own mind. But so too it appears repeatedly in the short stories, particularly in the descriptions of the ornate and convoluted furnishings of a room (**"Ligeia," "Masque of the Red Death"**) that mirror the mind of the narrator. In no other work, however, has Poe structured this sentience, or interconnectedness, between the physical world and the mental/psychological world more powerfully and tellingly than in **"The Fall of the House of Usher."**[13]

On the basis of his cosmological and aesthetic theories, Poe thereby constructs his architecture of mirrors to prop the movement of the story. Several studies have probed the pattern of mirror images, usually relating them to the rationality/irrationality of Usher or the physical/psychological tension between him and Madeline. Indeed, it falls beyond the space or provision of this essay to list them all, but in order to demonstrate the functions of pairing and splitting that the mirror images provide, a few central patterns may be noted.

The most evident, but eerily complex, of course, is the House of Usher itself. Roderick himself tells the narrator that over the centuries the mansion and the family had been so bonded as to become identified as one. Moreover, the diminishment of the Usher family, through years of inbreeding to this one lonely brother and sister, precisely parallels the physical collapse of the house, standing far apart from civilization as it does in some distant, lonely tract of country. The pairing between Roderick and the mansion is sustained in the careful detailing of descriptions, as the narrator observes first the one, then the other, and discerns unnerving similarities.

Although paired in matters of neglect and in physical description, both the Ushers and the mansion are undergoing a simultaneous process of splitting. The house is rent by a zigzag fissure that threatens its stability. In his letter to the narrator, Roderick admits to "mental disorder" that threatens his stability.[14] Similarly, the brother and sister are paired—not only by heritage but also by being fraternal twins. They, too, however, are simultaneously splitting apart, Madeline into her mysterious cataleptic trance and Roderick into an irrationally surrealistic world of frenzied artmaking.

Many other mirror images accumulate in the story. The house is mirrored by its image in the tarn and collapses beneath its waters at the close. Roderick's painting of the underground burial vault—at which the narrator marvels "If ever mortal painted an idea, that mortal was Roderick Usher"—preternaturally and prophetically mirrors Madeline's escape from the vault. The light with no apparent source in the painting may be referenced to Lady Ligeia's exclamation on the Conqueror Worm. "O Divine Father," Ligeia exclaims in a line that could be taken from *Eureka,* "Are we not part and parcel in Thee? Who—who knoweth the mysteries of the will with its vigor? Man doth not yield himself to the angels, *nor unto death utterly,* save only through the weakness of his feeble will" (**"Ligeia"** 319). Surprisingly with her glacial, ghostly demeanor prior to her entombment, Madeline possesses just such a will also.

"The Haunted Palace" provides another artistic mirror image. The work precisely traces the devolution of the House of Usher from a palace governed in orderly fashion by "Thought's Dominion" to a den of disorder in which demons flicker about like bats—except that these demons are in Usher's mind. An interesting submotif of the poem is the transition from spirits moving "To a Lute's well-tuned law" to forms moving fantastically "to a discordant melody." With the demise of some structured order, artforms rampage into dissonance and cacophony.

This process of devolution forms the centering thesis of Gillian Brown's innovative study, "The Poetics of Extinction." Drawing upon Charles Lyell's *Principles of Geology* (1830-1833), in which he argues the diminishment and passing of "organic beings" over vast periods of time, Brown finds a model for the disintegration of both the House and lineage of Usher. The value of the essay resides in Brown's crisp demonstration of the relationship between the devolution of environment and humanity, predicated on Lyell's theory. As we have seen, moreover, that close interconnectedness between the physical and psychological, the external environment and the internal mind, is amply supported by *Eureka,* as well as by Poe's essays and art. Nonetheless one questions to what end this devolution exists in the fiction. Is it simply that all things pass away? Nothing could be further from Poe's writings, with their tenacious, almost frenzied grip upon the great mind that endures, as *Eureka* has it. Beyond anything Poe sought the physical incarnation of Hippocrates's incantation in his *Aphorisms: Ars longa, vita brevis.* To complete the careful construction of the story into an imaginative architecture that endures, however, one final set of mirror images bears scrutiny.

In order to create something of a mental theater that draws out the suspense of the story, Poe constructed a conflation of such images at the ending. To put Roderick's mind at ease, the narrator reads to him from "Mad Trist" by Sir Launcelot Canning.[15] Every step of Ethelred to force the entrance to the hermit's dwelling has its mirror in Madeline's clangorous escape from the dungeon. Meanwhile, a storm descends upon and envelops the mansion, mirroring the swirling collapse of Usher's rationality. Here, too, in the mirror of the storm and Roderick's mind, we find a clear use of the sentience theory.

Yet, the reader somehow feels dissatisfied if only construing the story as a clever construction of Poe's cosmology in his sentience theory. However carefully structured, the pairings and splittings of the mirror images point suggestively to a larger pattern than mere aesthetic architecture. Many directions to this larger significance have been offered.[16] It may be profitable, however, to relate the story to a larger conflict that Poe had been struggling with for some time: how to balance Romantic passion with Enlightenment order. By virtue of his work in the Gothic tale itself, many readers are quick to place him without qualification in the Romantic camp. But it is a conflict that Poe had struggled with previously that does, in fact, inhabit *Eureka* and comes to bear most forcefully in **"The Fall of the House of Usher."**

Although literary scholars generally date the Enlightenment era from 1660 (as a departure from the Renaissance) to 1798 (with the publication of Lyrical Ballads), all acknowledge the artificiality of such dating. All such periods consist of attitudes, ideas, and cultural dynamics that precede and postdate the era. Benjamin Franklin's fervid belief in perfectibility of self[17] gave way to romantic dissolution in order to feel life more passionately. Moreover, one could convincingly argue that the conflict between Enlightenment, with its heroic grandiosity of the mind, and Romanticism, with all its disheveled passions, continue in full force. Perhaps the conflict was only more heightened at Poe's particular point in literary history.

The Enlightenment presupposed the primacy of human reason, the ethical template of formal order, and the lifestyle of staid decorum. It may be argued that Poe's short stories eclipse reason by the supernatural, disrupt ethical values by gothic disorder, and blast decorum by the weird and grotesque. The argument would be wrong, for Poe sought nothing less than the delicate symbiosis between the two—and the key quality of symbiosis is in the mutual benefit one to another.

That Poe had struggled with the national literary shift from Enlightenment to Romantic thinking is evident long before 1839.[18] And while many of the early nineteenth-century writers embraced Romanticism passionately as the full outlet for an intuitive, imaginative, and story-driven art, Poe was by far more reserved. In his "1836 Letter to B_____" Poe refers to the Lake Poets in quite derogatory terms: "As I am speaking of poetry, it will not be amiss to touch slightly upon the most singular heresy in its modern history—the heresy of what is called very foolishly, the Lake School" (*Essays* 6-7). The heresy of which Poe speaks, specifically in reference to Wordsworth, is that didactic poetry is seen as the most pleasurable. While admiring Coleridge's great learning, despite all that learning Poe is quick to point out his "liability to err." As for Wordsworth, "I have no faith in him" (*Essays* 8). Truly, the "Letter to B_____" ends in a gnarled fist of contradictions (of Coleridge, Poe says he cannot "speak but with reverence"), and his attempt to define poetry is, in his own words, a "long rigamarole." But shot through the essay resides the governing belief that intellect and passion work together in art.

Such also became the central argument of "The Philosophy of Composition," a much better known, much clearer, but not necessarily more credible work. Here Poe lays his famous rational grid upon the composition of a poem of irrationality—"The Raven." For example, he states his (predetermined) scheme for rhythm and meter: "The former is trochaic—The latter is octometer acatalectic, alternating with heptameter catalectic repeated in the refrain of the fifth verse, and terminating with a tetrameter catalectic" (*Essays* 21). Poe's "The Rationale of Verse," moreover, might well be called one of the preeminent Enlightenment documents of the Romantic era. Surely, there were poets of Poe's time who followed fairly rigid verse forms, yet none of them that I am aware of would likely ever claim such an ornate, intellectual concept prior to the poem's composition. The fact is all the more telling in that the elegy, "The Raven," corresponds in many ways with **"The Fall of the House of Usher,"** the singular exception being that in the former we are placed inside the disintegrating mind of the narrator while in the latter the narrator gives us some objective distance from the disintegration.

While "The Raven" remains one of the best known works in the western tradition generally, a second of Poe's elegies, "Ulalume," is perhaps of more critical importance to understanding the balancing act Poe was attempting between the Enlightenment and the Romantic. Upon a casual reading the poem seems archetypally romantic. We find the narrator wandering a strange landscape that ultimately is a mirror to his inner torment, if not his mind itself (his companion is Psyche). Similarly the time is more of a psychic state rather than the announced month of October with its withering and sere leaves. Into the groaning realms, he walks with Psyche his soul. Why? To what end? To discover the full meaning of the event for which they had traveled here the year prior.

The heightened, fantastic elements of the poem intensify throughout. The lonely season, the "dank tarn of Auber" (line 6), the unsettled and threatening landscape—all the essentials of the Gothic are here. Furthermore, supernatural figures enter—the ghouls who feed on the dead but also heavenly figures. The quarter moon rises, like twin horns hung in the sky. With it appears the figure of Astarte, Phoenician goddess of fertility and passion whose symbol is the twin horns of the bull. She is the consummate romantic figure, representing the outpouring of creative passion. The narrator observes that "She is warmer than Dian" (39), a reference to the Roman goddess of chastity and order. Strangely, and in spite of Psyche's caution to fly, the narrator trusts Astarte to lead him to the truth. Essentially, we have the old Appollinian-Dionysian conflict between order and impulse played out with two female goddesses—appropriate to the elegy for Virginia. In this case, and with the maddening desire to confront whatever lies at the end of his journey, the narrator insists,

> Ah, we safely may trust to its gleaming,
> And be sure it will lead us aright—
> We surely may trust to its gleaming
> That cannot but guide us aright. . . .
>
> (67-70)

Astarte, the goddess of passion, the fuel for the romantic flame, does in this poem lead him to the burning encounter with the fact of Ulalume's death. In this poem, Poe appears to recognize the enormous creative potential in romantic passion; yet, he remains wary of it, cautions that once unleashed it has the capacity to consume someone entirely.

This tension is similar to that which Poe takes to **"The Fall of the House of Usher."** Few other authors struggled as powerfully with that tension and with maintaining a balance between the analytic intelligence and the creative fancy. The possible exception is Nathaniel Hawthorne, whose "Rappaccini's Daughter" can very profitably be read as a clash between the coldly analytic Enlightenment man (Rappaccini) and the Romantic man (Baglioni). In **"The Fall of the House of Usher"** one notices the conflict already in the first paragraph, a masterpiece of prose poetry. The narrator possesses the initial rational distance from the scene, reporting to the reader what he sees and feels as he approaches the mansion. The organic form with which he reports his findings, however, allows the reader intuitively to grasp the sense of insufferable gloom. In the initial sentence, heavy, sinking, *o* and *u* vowels droop like sullen rain. The pacing of the sentences, with relatively brief, stumbling phrases in very long, heavy sentences, enhance the effect.[19]

The carefully ordered architectural grid Poe places upon the story, including the escalation of mirror images, is similar to the (purportedly) careful ordering of his poems. In this story, however, the balance between Enlightenment and Romantic itself is situated at the heart of the story. Roderick himself is emblematic of Romantic passion, while Madeline is emblematic of Enlightenment. Their genesis, as fraternal twins, is unified—a perfectly mirrored complementarity—but the story unveils their splitting to mutual destruction.

This way of viewing the relationship between brother and sister is not customary, to be sure. The common view is that the narrator, coming from outside the palace of horrors, represents rational order. An example of this view appears in Jack Voller's study of the sublime in Poe's tale, in which he states that "The narrator is associated with the rescuing force of reason. . . . Although he strikes few readers as cheerful, the narrator is suited to his task . . ." (29). Yet, it is hard to find the narrator exercising anything like a force of reason. In the main, his role is limited to some musing observations, a rather slow study in horror, and a hopeless inefficiency to do much of anything about the divisive destruction of the tenants of the House, which seems to be precisely Poe's point. When Romantic passion and Enlightenment order divide, their mutual destruction is assured.

Madeline therefore becomes abstracted to little more than a mental evanescence—Enlightenment at its extreme, out of touch with reality. When the narrator first sees her passing in the distance, he is filled with unaccountable dread, so otherworldly she appears. She is, Roderick discloses, simply wasting away of some illness with no known etiology. At the very same time, Roderick diverges in the opposite direction. While Madeline disappears into a vaporific mist, Roderick flames into an unrestricted creative power, full of unrestrained, raw passion. He becomes the fiery polar to Madeline's cold abstraction. The narrator describes his successive days with Usher and his artmaking thus: "An excited and highly distempered ideality threw a sulphurous luster over all" (**"Usher"** 405). Usher thereby enters a creative mania, churning out songs, paintings, and poems against the coming dark.

That is precisely the point Poe makes in this tale. When split apart, as they are here, Enlightenment thinking becomes all cold, analytic, and detached; Romanticism, on the other hand, blazes into a self-consuming passion. Aesthetically and ideally they ought to be mirrors to each other, working in a complementary fashion to serve art. When split from each other, they become mutually self-destructive. Preternaturally charged with his Romantic instincts, Roderick hears, above the storm, the approaching footsteps of Madeline. She enters, falls upon her brother, and together they die. The splitting pairs have conjoined once again, but tragically this time. The separation had gone to the extreme, disrupting the sentient balance, destroying both. As the narrator flees, the house itself parallels the act of Roderick and Madeline, first splitting apart along the zigzag fissure and then collapsing together into the tarn.

If *Eureka* teaches us the design of unity, and the essays teach us Poe's efforts to integrate intellectual order into his aesthetics, then it may be fairly said that **"The Fall of the House of Usher"** is a cautionary tale, warning of a way Poe would not have artists go. While he did exult in the freedoms of the Romantic imagination, he was also highly suspicious of it. He needed, and called for, the orderliness of design inherited from the Enlightenment to contain that imagination. Without that synchronous working, as **"The Fall of the House of Usher"** demonstrates, both are doomed.

Notes

1. Perhaps the most helpful study of this sort is Gary E. Tombleson's "Poe's 'The Fall of the House of Usher' as Archetypal Gothic: Literary and Architectural Analogs of Cosmic Unity" (*Nineteenth-Century Contexts* 12.2 [1988]: 83-106). Tombleson locates the place of the story—both its traditional and innovative elements—within the tradition dating to Walpole's *The Castle of Otranto, A Gothic Story* (1764). Also helpful is Stephen Dougherty's "Dreaming the Races: Biology and National Fantasy in 'The Fall of the House of Usher'" (*Henry Street* 7.1 [Spring 1988]: 17-39). Of particular interest, and with a revealing twist on interpreting the story, is Mark Kinkead-Weekes' "Reflections On, and In, 'The Fall of the

House of Usher.'" Kinkead-Weekes argues that the story is "not merely Gothick, but rather a 'Gothick' which at every turn signals a consciousness of its own operation" (17). This pattern includes, furthermore, an awareness of the writer of the Gothic.

2. See, for example, Cynthia S. Jordan's "Poe's Re-Vision: The Recovery of the Second Story" (*American Literature* 59.1 [Mar. 1987]: 1-19). Jordan sets forth the ways by which Poe differs from Hawthorne and pays close attention to such stories as "Berenice," "Morella," and "Ligeia," in addition to "The Fall of the House of Usher." In "'Sympathies of a Scarcely Intelligible Nature': The Brother-Sister Bond in Poe's 'The Fall of the House of Usher'" (*Studies in Short Fiction* 30 [1993]: 387-396), Leila S. May discusses the issue of the female persona with an interesting twist, arguing that the story represents Poe's vision of social destruction with the breakup of family structures in mid-19th century. That the relationship between Roderick and Madeline is aberrant goes without saying, but May provides insufficient evidence of a social meltdown at this time or support for Poe's holding this view.

3. It is nearly impossible to keep track of all the articles and dissenting opinions that "Ligeia" has engendered. In Poe's mind, at least, the story was his best to date. To Philip Pendleton Cooke he wrote, "'Ligeia' may be called my *best* tale" (9 August 1846 *Letters* 2: 329). Readers don't always agree with authors on such matters. The story is, nonetheless, a fascinating document for Poe's revision process. In *The Collected Works of Edgar Allan Poe,* volume 2, Thomas Mabbott discusses these at some length.

4. Technically, a "cosmogony," the term Poe uses, is concerned with the origins and the evolution of the universe. A "cosmology," the more fitting term here, deals with the universe in total relativity—from the origin to the acts and consequences of all life in the universe. As we will see, Poe's theory clearly points in the latter direction.

5. For helpful discussion of the relationship between the lecture and *Eureka* see Burton R. Pollin's "Contemporary Reviews of *Eureka*: A Checklist" (*Poe as Literary Cosmologer: Studies on "Eureka"—A Symposium.* Hartford, CT: Transcendental Books, 1975. 26-30) in addition to standard biographies.

6. Frederick Conner demonstrates the plethora of contradictions and fallacies in the third section in his "Poe's *Eureka*" (*Cosmic Optimism: A Study of the Interpretation of Evolution by American Poets from Emerson to Robinson.* New York: Octagon, 1973. 67-91).

7. Quotations from *Eureka* are from volume 16 of the Harrison edition of *The Complete Works.* Page numbers refer to this volume. More recently, Richard P. Benton has edited a new edition of *Eureka* with line numbers, a compendium essay, and a bibliographic guide (Hartford, CT: Transcendental Books, 1973). The text is quite difficult to find, however, while the Harrison edition is in nearly every library.

8. Poe made this point in a number of places, perhaps most forcefully in his 2 July 1844 letter to James Russell Lowell: "But to all we attach the notion of a constitution of particles—atomic composition. For this reason only we think spirit different; for spirit, we say, is unparticled, and therefore is not matter. . . . The unparticled matter, permeating and impelling all things, is God. Its activity is the thought of God—which creates. Man, and other thinking beings, are individualizations of the unparticled matter" (*Letters* 1: 257). Humanity is a part or extension of God. Since it is the nature of God to create, humanity's closest affinity to the Deity lies in its creativity. To express its godliness humanity must create in its own unique, but divine, method.

9. Wagenknecht puts it as such: "For though the Shadow of Beauty may float unseen among us, we can never make much contact with it in human experience unless it can somehow be made to impregnate the stuff of human life . . ." (151). It is precisely the task of the poet to make that "impregnation."

10. One should not be deterred from spotting similarities in cosmology by the fact that *Eureka* was published nearly a decade (1848) later than "The Fall of the House of Usher," which first appeared in *Burton's Gentleman's Magazine,* September 1839. The fundamental beliefs pulled together in *Eureka* were ones that Poe had been developing in part for years and in *Eureka* tried to systematize as a whole.

11. All quotations from "The Fall of the House of Usher" and "Ligeia" are from volume 2 of Mabbott's authoritative edition and will be cited as "Usher" and "Ligeia."

12. In his "Sentience and the False Deja Vu in 'The Fall of the House of Usher,'" John Lammers makes a distinction critical to understanding Poe. Sentience, he points out, is a matter of shared awareness:

> Since the word "sentience" can mean "feeling with awareness" or "feeling without awareness," since everyone believes that plants at least have "feeling without awareness," and since Usher's theory is unusual because only four writers in the

history of the world have agreed with him, then the meaning of "sentience" here must be the unusual one—"feeling with awareness or consciousness." In short, Usher believes that all vegetation has a mind.

(21)

This view comports precisely with the "volitional" act of creation appearing in *Eureka.* For another discussion of sentience, see David L. Coss's "Art and Sentience in 'The Fall of the House of Usher'" (*Pleiades* 14.1 [1991]: 93-106).

13. For a consideration of the disintegrating mind of Usher, see G. R. Thompson's *Poe's Fiction,* 87-97. Thompson's views have been contested by many. See, for example, Patrick F. Quinn's "A Misreading of Poe's 'The Fall of the House of Usher'" (*Critical Essays on Edgar Allan Poe.* Ed. Eric W. Carlson. Boston: G. K. Hall, 1987. 153-59). In a study of "Ligeia" and "The Fall of the House of Usher," Ronald Bieganowski observes that "Reflected images double the intensity of beauty" (186).
14. Earliest published forms of the story use the term "pitiable mental idiosyncrasy" here. See *s*2: 398. For a lengthier discussion of the house and the "divided mind," see Jack G. Voller's "The Power of Terror: Burke and Kant in the House of Usher."
15. In an unusual twist on Poe's notorious ending, Kinkead-Weekes views it as an ironic, comedic scene in which the affected superiority of the narrator is destroyed (30-31).
16. Several of these different interpretations explore the conflict between the natural and the supernatural, such as E. Arthur Robinson's "Order and Sentience in 'The Fall of the House of Usher'" (*PMLA* 76.1 [Mar. 1961]: 68-81) and David Ketterer's *The Rationale of Deception in Poe* (Baton Rouge: Louisiana State UP, 1979). Several studies explore the subconscious or the conflict between image and reality in the story. Representative here are Sam Girgus's "Poe and the Transcendent Self" (*The Law of the Heart.* Austin: U of Texas P, 1979. 24-36) and Leonard W. Engel's "The Journey from Reason to Madness: Edgar Allan Poe's 'The Fall of the House of Usher'" (*Essays in Arts and Sciences* 14 [1985]: 23-31).
17. "It was about this time I conceived the bold and arduous project of arriving at moral perfection. I wished to live without committing any fault at any time. . . . As I knew, or thought I knew, what was right and wrong, I did not see why I might not always do the one and avoid the other" (Franklin 1384).
18. For a more detailed analysis of Poe's relation with the English Romantics and the part they played in his aesthetics, see my article, "Edgar Allan Poe: Artist, Aesthetician, Legend" (*South Dakota Review* 10.2 [Spring 1972]: 60-70).
19. For linguists with an interest in quantitative rhetoric, the first paragraph is a treasure trove. Just dealing with the baseline figures, the first four sentences are 60, 22, 32, and 81 words in length, for an average of 49, an extraordinary average. But the proliferation of short phrases and clauses works as interior counterpart.

Works Cited

Bieganowski, Ronald. "The Self-Consuming Narrator in Poe's 'Ligeia' and 'Usher.'" *American Literature* 60.2 (May 1988): 175-87.

Brown, Gillian. "The Poetics of Extinction." *The American Face of Edgar Allan Poe.* Ed. Shawn Rosenheim and Stephen Rachman. Baltimore: Johns Hopkins UP, 1995. 330-44.

Franklin, Benjamin. *The Autobiography.* New York: The Library of America, 1987.

Kinkead-Weekes, Mark. "Reflections On, and In, 'The Fall of the House of Usher.'" *Edgar Allan Poe: The Design of Order.* Ed. A. Robert Lee. London: Vision Press, 1987: 17-35.

Lammers, John. "Sentience and the False Deja Vu in 'The Fall of the House of Usher.'" *Publications of the Arkansas Philological Association* 22.1 (Spring 1996): 19-41.

Poe, Edgar Allan. *Collected Works of Edgar Allan Poe.* Ed. Thomas Ollive Mabbott. 3 vols. Cambridge: Belknap Press of Harvard U, 1969-.

———. *The Complete Works of Edgar Allan Poe.* Ed. James Harrison. 17 vols. New York: T. Y. Crowell, 1902.

———. *Essays and Reviews.* Ed. B. R. Thompson. New York: Modern Library, 1984.

———. *The Letters of Edgar Allan Poe.* 2 vols. Ed. John Ward Ostram. Cambridge, MA: Harvard UP, 1948.

Thompson, G. R. *Poe's Fiction: Romantic Irony in the Gothic Tales.* Madison: U of Wisconsin P, 1973.

Voller, Jack G. "The Power of Terror: Burke and Kant in 'The House of Usher.'" *Poe Studies* 21.2 (1988): 27-35.

Wagenknecht, Edward. *Edgar Allan Poe: The Man Behind the Legend.* New York: Oxford UP, 1963.

Joseph Stark (essay date spring 2004)

SOURCE: Stark, Joseph. "Motive and Meaning: The Mystery of the Will in Poe's 'The Black Cat.'" *Mississippi Quarterly* 57, no. 2 (spring 2004): 255-63.

[*In the following essay, Stark evaluates theological and scientific implications in "The Black Cat," asserting that the murderous narrator's lack of motivation calls into question assumptions regarding the human will and moral responsibility.*]

Edgar Allan Poe's **"The Black Cat"** presents the reader with a troubled tale of homicide, presumably given "to place before the world, plainly, succinctly, and without comment, a series of mere household events."[1] This baiting language of the narrator given in the first paragraph has provoked numerous critical speculations on the "natural causes and effects" of the story, with particularly plentiful psychological examinations of the narrator and author.[2] Such contemporary analyses, however, may simply miss the point of the text, or better, indicate in their very strivings to provide answers that *no sufficiently clear cause* for the narrator's murder of his wife and the cat may be found in the text. Indeed, when seen in its historical context, this conclusion, with all its troubling implications, posed significant challenges to increasingly influential scientific thought as well as to shifting evangelical theology. In other words, by depicting a motiveless murderer whose actions cannot be sufficiently explained, Poe "place[d] before the world . . . without comment" difficulties in both scientific and religious thought and ironically upheld the mysterious nature of the human will in a time dominated by intellectual rationalism.

In "'The Murders of the Rue Morgue': Edgar Allan Poe's Evolutionary Reverie,"[3] Lawrence Frank highlights some of the pressing scientific questions of Poe's day. As he explains, Poe's detective stories come in the context of an America dominated by "a resurgent evangelicalism and conservative Natural Theology" but increasingly challenged by "a positivist science that was to have its nineteenth-century culmination in Charles Darwin's *Origin of Species* (1859)." Frank's thesis significantly exemplifies how Poe's time, especially during the writing of these short stories (**"Rue Morgue" ["The Murders in the Rue Morgue"]** in 1841 and **"The Black Cat"** in 1843) was a tumultuous period in which religious tenets were both clashing and coalescing with more naturalistic convictions. In particular, the increasingly popular, but oft criticized, nebular hypothesis of creation suggested how the cooling of heated gas could form the stars and solar system apart from divine intervention. Though some theologians incorporated this theory into their theism, many saw it as an atheistic challenge to Christian orthodoxy concerning the origin of the universe (pp. 173-174). Moreover, **"The Rue Morgue"** itself portrayed the connection being made between irrational animals like the Ourang-Outang and supposedly rational humanity. As with Darwin's *Origin of Species,* combining observations about the Ourang-Outang's similarities to humans with the nebular hypothesis led to the troubling conclusion that the universe (and hence, all humanity) may be motiveless, irrational, and physically determined (pp. 178-183).[4]

Not only does Poe's time reflect increasing concern with naturalism and its implicit determinism, but it also entailed an intriguing shift in evangelical theology. Though the 1830s and 1840s in America were a significant time for Protestants (part of what Mark A. Noll calls the "Protestant Century"),[5] the Reformed doctrines of the previous century were in significant decline. Even among purported Calvinists like Nathaniel Taylor, an heir of Jonathan Edwards's theology, traditional doctrines such as that of human depravity had been reworked sufficiently to lack resemblance to the teachings of their historic forebears. Taylor, for instance, argued that "sinfulness arises from sinful acts rather than from a sinful nature inherited from Adam" (Noll, p. 233). This view of human nature, by implication, ascribed greater freedom to the will by denying that the inherited disposition of depravity necessarily led one to sinful actions. Similarly, the revivalist Charles Grandison Finney denied the miraculous nature of revivals and advocated "the *right* use of the appropriate means" in bringing about conversions.[6] In so doing, he emphasized the power of the human will to overcome sin irrespective of any unique work of God. More traditional Calvinists like Archibald Alexander and Charles Hodge remained as active voices in American Protestantism, but in general, evangelicals ascribed greater power to the human will than their theological forefathers of the prior century (Noll, p. 233).

When we combine this religious context with Frank's observations about the scientific developments of the day, we discover that, in some ways, Protestant theology and scientific theories of human origin were intersecting as they crossed paths on different trajectories. Evangelicals emphasized the power of the human will to overcome sin and crime (culminating perhaps most dramatically in Finney's belief in perfectionism), while scientific examination narrowed the gap between the rational human and irrational animal, and thereby posited a kind of naturalistic determinism.

Our limited knowledge of Poe's religious convictions and interests makes it difficult to establish how clearly invested he was in Protestant theology and its debates on the issue, but there are signs of such interest, especially in the scientific aspects of the debate. In particular, his interest in physical determinism and the mysteries of the will are clear. The irrationality of "perverseness" forms the heart of **"Imp of the Perverse,"** as the narrator inexplicably murders only to inexplicably confess his murder.[7] This confession, indeed, is opened with a discussion of phrenology, the study of how personality relates to the size of the skull (pp. 283-284). Of greater interest, however, may be his curious essay "Instinct vs. Reason—A Black Cat," in which he discusses the mysterious line between the seeming instinct of an animal and the reason of a human. Such instinct, he comments, "is referable only to the spirit of the Deity itself, acting *directly,* and through no corporal organ, upon the volition of the animal."[8] Seen in the context of works which challenge human reason, such a statement indicates how Poe concerned himself with the mysterious relationship between divine providence and human volition. Moreover, he showed familiarity with Protestant writings on natural theology, specifically the Bridgewater Treatises, a series of essays in defense of Christianity. Notes in Poe's hand are contained in a copy of the first volume in the series *On the Power, Wisdom, and Goodness of God, as Manifested in the Adaptation of External Nature to the Moral and Intellectual Constitution of Man,* by Scotch Calvinist Thomas Chalmer.[9] Additionally, he wrote a critique of Peter Roget's treatise on physiology.[10] When combined with what Poe considered his most important work, *Eureka: The Material and Spiritual Universe,* a natural and theological treatise of his own, all of these links at least indicate some investment in the subject of science and religion and their relationship to nineteenth-century discussions of the will ("Poe and Religion").

In view of the historical context, we can now turn to one of the most troubling and puzzling aspects of **"The Black Cat,"** the question of motive. Numerous critics have taken this puzzle as an invitation to discern the narrator's motive, with a wide range of suggestions from pride[11] to repression of childhood peer abuse for effeminate qualities (Piacentino). Admittedly, the text encourages such analysis in the first paragraph when the narrator writes:

> Hereafter, perhaps, some intellect may be found which will reduce my phantasm to the common-place—some intellect, more calm, more logical, and far less excitable than my own, which will perceive, in the circumstances I detail with awe, nothing more than an ordinary succession of very natural causes and effects.
>
> (p. 230)

With this invitation, Poe the critic has ingeniously invited every critic since him to prove himself or herself an "intellect more calm [and] more logical." The ingenuity of such critics, however, better makes the story's point than the solutions they offer. These critics rightly divine that the narrator of the tale (or perhaps, better, Poe) has littered the story with "telltale clues" that disclose the text's secret.[12] The striking aspect of the story, however, is that there are so many clues. In fact, the diversity of the clues is one of the problems in the text, for they give rise to a variety of explanations. The most prominent of clues and explanations brings us quickly back to the theological context referred to above, for the most straight-forward reading of the text indicates that the cause for this aberrant behavior is the answer of the early 1700s: human depravity. The narrator makes this point quite clearly soon after he begins his first assault on the cat: "I am not more sure that my soul lives, than I am that perverseness is one of the primitive impulses of the human heart—one of the indivisible faculties, or sentiments, which give direction to the character of Man" (p. 232). His description of this perversity, in fact, could nearly be taken directly from Augustine's *Confessions* (a significant influence upon Reformed doctrine). As Augustine stole the pears solely for the joy of sinning, the narrator likewise claims to have killed the cat simply "because [he] knew that in so doing [he] was committing a sin" (p. 232). In this respect, the account accords well with orthodox Calvinism but contradicts the views of Nathaniel Taylor on the impotence of the human will. A person's choice to sin does not precede the existence of perversity; rather, the "spirit of PERVERSENESS" already in the heart causes the person to sin. Hence, in essence, the narrator offers a very traditional theological solution to the problem of motive; he assigns it to the perversity of the human heart.

Such a solution, however, fails to acknowledge the unreliability of the story's narrator as well as the insufficiency of the answer. Not only, for instance, is the narrator a confessed murderer, but his story also evidences a certain delusional paranoia. The narrator may be lying, as Susan Amper argues (cf. Piacentino, p. 5), or is simply insane. Regardless, we must take his testimony with a grain of salt. When he blames his crime on human depravity, we are skeptical of this solution, simply because he offers it. Having said this, we need not dismiss the idea outright to make the point. Even in the narrator's explanation of his perversity, he admits of a troubling mystery. Not only does philosophy fail to account for this possibility, but he himself offers no ultimate explanation for the cause *behind* the perversity. Hence, both in our skepticism and possible acceptance of the narrator's position, we find ourselves without a thorough explanatory cause.

Other potential motives arise in the text, but none of these satisfy either. The most obvious next culprit is his alcoholism. Again, one difficulty with this solution is that the narrator himself puts it forward as a possibility. He suggests that the original change in his character is due to the "instrumentality of the Fiend Intemperance" (p. 231). Moreover, this solution remains problematic for other reasons as well. For one, it still fails to account for what drove him into alcoholism in the first place. Was this simply an addiction begun at a young age, or was the narrator trying to hide some deeper troubles? No solution is immediately apparent. More insightful, however, is the observation that only one of his offenses occurs during a moment of drunkenness. As T. J. Matheson notes, the two murders (of cat and wife) occurred while he was sober. Only the gouging out of the cat's eye happened while he was drunk (qtd. in Piacentino, footnote 9). Hence, though alcohol may have been a contributing factor to his crime it cannot be described as the ultimate cause.

A psychological reading of the text, such as Ed Piacentino's, supplies a third explanation of motive, while also exposing the dangers such analysis bears. As with other critics, Piacentino takes the story as an invitation to solve the problem of motive within the text. He provides a solution by discerning the psychobiography of the narrator evidenced in the narration. Through his careful scrutiny, he infers that the narrator had a troubled childhood for his "tenderness of heart," a quality which his peers must have labeled effeminate. As he grew older, the narrator rejected this fault, even to the degree of assaulting his former affections (and representations of those affections, viz the cat!) until, in "the culmination of deep-seated and suppressed anxieties," he killed his wife (p. 5). Even as Piacentino completes his article, the difficulties with this reading become apparent. Two sentences bear this out. Piacentino writes, "The narrator's motive for this cruel and violent crime is, as I see it, psychologically plausible" and "[Considering] **'The Black Cat'** as the psychobiography of a demented narrator provides the key to discovering *plausible meaning and explanation* for brutal murder *when seemingly none exists*" (p. 7; italics mine). The qualifications Piacentino adds here are rather significant. While he sufficiently explains the plausibility of his solution, he fails to make it necessarily probable. Indeed, Piacentino's insistence upon this solution, even as he qualifies it, may indicate more about our longings as readers than about the evidence of the text. This longing, which at times looks like a grasping after the straws of Poe's multiple hints, indeed seems to be part of the game of the text. The narrator invites us to use our logic and discern "the ordinary succession of very natural causes and effects," when in reality no such succession can be found.

Moreover, in his psychobiographical reading, Piacentino demonstrates the pitfalls into which such an examination can lead us. Earlier in the article he writes, "When anxiety and frustration threaten a person's security and self-esteem, as in the case of Poe's narrator, such a combination of repression-displacement—though probably not to the extreme the narrator carries it—may be regarded as a *predictable* natural reaction" (p. 5, italics mine). Again, we see that Piacentino offers a significant qualifier to his thesis ("though probably not to the extreme the narrator carries it"). More striking, however, is his boldness. In essence, he argues that some childhood criticism led the narrator spontaneously to put an axe in his wife's head and then calls this act a "predictable natural reaction." Of course, anything might be deemed "predictable" in retrospect, but the idea that someone who was mocked as a child would "predictably" murder his wife is either frightening or laughable. Indeed, this statement itself plays most directly into the problematic conclusion towards which Poe baits his readers: all things can be explained by simple cause and effect. If such a conclusion is true, then all human actions have an irrational determinism at their core, indistinct from the behavior of the Ourang-Outang in **"The Rue Morgue."**

A more accurate solution may be what Piacentino and Amper so eagerly want to avoid: there is *no clear* explanation for the murderer's motive. The significance of this possibility is brought out rather vividly by John Cleman's intriguing article on "Edgar Allan Poe and the Insanity Defense." As Cleman makes clear, fervid debate was brewing in the 1840s in England and America over the legitimacy of the insanity defense for accused murderers. Significant to our purposes was how such debates centered around "a strongly deterministic view of human nature" and the problem of human culpability.[13] Strikingly, during a Philadelphia case in 1843, the time and place in which Poe was writing, lawyer Peter A. Browne focused his insanity defense of Sydney Mercer (accused of murdering his sister's seducer) on the question of "whether or not the accused was 'incapable of exercising free will'" (Cleman, p. 629). The primary determinant of this, according to the defense, was whether or not one was "motiveless" in one's impulse to kill (p. 629). Cleman suggests, then, that **"The Tell-Tale Heart," "The Black Cat,"** and **"The Imp of the Perverse"** all represent forms of insanity defenses which ironically undermine the logic of that defense. In **"The Black Cat,"** the means of undermining an insanity defense is essentially to show that the narrator's claim to being subject to "perverseness" is little different from the medical defense of one's temporary insanity. As Cleman puts it, the narrator's use of "perverseness" to defend his actions, like those of the medical authorities, "is presented as a logical, 'philosophical' explanation that voids overtly immoral acts of their moral implications" (pp. 636-637). In this respect, Poe parallels Calvinist doctrine (from a detractor's perspective) with the insanity defense; the narrator suggests his culpability is minimized if the cause comes from spiritually wrought depravity, just as phrenologists and defense lawyers minimized culpability if the cause was physically wrought depravity.

Poe, however, still offers no alternative explanation. In other words, even as his text may be seen as an indirect criticism of Calvinism through his more direct criticism of the insanity defense, no clear explanation is given for motive. We are still unable to explain why the narrator killed his wife. This seems the more interesting aspect of the piece, for, in essence, Poe demonstrates the complexities of the theological, philosophical, and even medical debates of his time. To the phrenologists and lawyers seeking to defend murderers through the insanity defense, he raises the question of how moral culpability can be dismissed simply because one appears "motiveless." To the revivalists and moderated Calvinists, on the other hand, he brings the question of how one might truly change from behavior which one hates. After all, even as his depravity continues, the narrator seems unable to turn away from the evil he knows he is perpetuating and recognizes as evil. He questions, in other words, the freedom of his will. In this sense, the text is radically ambivalent. It explores the issues of moral responsibility and the inexplicability of human evil but supplies no solution.

The "moral" of Poe's tale, then, may be more a statement on the insufficiency of human reason than the nature of the human will. Richard C. Frushell describes how the narrator "points up the disparity which exists between his puny rational attempts (his tale) to give form to extremely complex, shifting states of mind which precede or form life and death actions and the actual cause for such actions" (p. 44). Rationalistic and theological explanations, in other words, fail to account sufficiently for the horror of the event. Indeed, critical attempts to account for the crime may do more to prove this point than the story itself. Every investigative attempt to get to the heart of the narrator's crime operates solely within the realm of "plausibility" but cannot prove probable or conclusive. In this respect, Poe's work indicates the difficulty of the human condition, not only in our inexplicable propensity towards evil (in the case of the narrator), but also in our finitude. No one, it may be inferred, is so distinct from either the murderous tendencies of the narrator or from his inability adequately to explain such tendencies. In this regard, **"The Black Cat"** shows the limitations of both the human will as well as human accounts of the will.

Notes

1. Edgar Allan Poe, "The Black Cat," in *Selected Tales,* ed. David Van Leer (New York: Oxford University Press, 1998), p. 230.

2. See Ed Piacentino, "Poe's 'The Black Cat' as Psychobiography," *Studies in Short Fiction,* 35 (Spring 1998), 154n1.

3. *Nineteenth-Century Literature,* 50 (September 1995), 168-188.

4. I should add that Frank's thesis with regard to "The Rue Morgue" strikingly complements my thesis concerning "The Black Cat." Frank similarly demonstrates how the Ourang-Outang's irrationality became a statement on the implications of prevailing scientific thought. As he writes, "In the figure of C. Auguste Dupin, Poe depicted the individual as a creature of history who must reconstruct the past even as he comes upon the fact of the contingency of certain events, without any reassuring knowledge of the future. It becomes a harrowing vision, centered upon the presence of the Ourang-Outang with its seemingly motiveless frenzy, introducing the terror of a history secularized and devoid of design" (p. 187).

5. *A History of Christianity in the United States and Canada* (Grand Rapids, Michigan: William B. Eerdmans Publishing Co., 1992), p. 163.

6. "What a Revival of Religion Is," in *The American Intellectual Tradition,* 2nd ed., ed. David A. Hollinger and Charles Capper (New York: Oxford University Press, 1993), I, 195.

7. Edgar Allan Poe, "The Imp of the Perverse," in *Selected Tales,* pp. 283-288.

8. Edgar Allan Poe, "Instinct vs. Reason—A Black Cat," *Alexander's Weekly Messenger,* January 29, 1840, p. 2, cols. 6-7, rpt. December 12, 1998, *Edgar Allan Poe Society of Baltimore* online, August 8, 2003 <http://www.eapoe.org/works/essays/ivrbcata.htm.

9. "Poe and Religion," *Edgar Allan Poe Society of Baltimore* online, January 8, 2000, August 8, 2003 <http://www.eapoe.org/geninfo/poerelig.htm.

10. Edgar Allan Poe, "Roget's Physiology," *Southern Literary Messenger,* February 1836, p. 180, rpt. August 20, 1999, *Edgar Allan Poe Society of Baltimore* online, August 8, 2003 <http://www.eapoe.org/works/criticsm/slm36021.htm.

11. Richard C. Frushell, "'An Incarnate Night-Mare': Moral Grotesquerie in 'The Black Cat,'" *Poe Studies,* 5 (1972), 43-44.

12. Susan Amper, "The Untold Story: The Lying Narrator in 'The Black Cat,'" *Studies in Short Fiction,* 29 (Fall 1992), 475. Piacentino makes the same point (p. 5).

13. "Irresistible Impulses: Edgar Allan Poe and the Insanity Defense," *American Literature,* 63 (December 1991), 625.

Marita Nadal (essay date summer 2004)

SOURCE: Nadal, Marita. "Variations on the Grotesque: From Poe's 'The Black Cat' to Oates's 'The White Cat.'" *Mississippi Quarterly* 57, no. 3 (summer 2004): 455-71.

[*In the following essay, Nadal contrasts the treatment of the female in "The Black Cat" with that in Joyce Carol Oates's "The White Cat," noting the comic subversion of Poe's grotesqueries in Oates's story.*]

In her "Afterword" to *Haunted: Tales of the Grotesque* (1994), Joyce Carol Oates discusses the concept of the grotesque, pointing out its allure, variety, and pervasiveness in art throughout the centuries. Significantly, she refers to Poe's influence on the literature of the grotesque, "so universal as to be incalculable. Who has *not* been influenced by Poe?" she remarks.[1] Taking Poe's and Oates's concepts of the grotesque as a point of departure, I intend to analyze "The White Cat" (1987), included in Oates's *Haunted,* as a postmodern and parodic rewriting of Poe's classic **"The Black Cat"** (1843), showing that although Oates preserves the domestic atmosphere of Poe's tale and its central motif—the uncanny repetition of the cat—she reverses the characteristics of the original story and thereby produces an unexpected and parodic dénouement that undermines "the effect" intended by Poe's tale. In consequence, although the two tales mirror each other in more ways than one, their use of the grotesque is far from similar.

Significantly, both Poe and Oates approach the concept of the grotesque in a vague and comprehensive way. Thus, in his preface to his ***Tales of the Grotesque and Arabesque*** (1839), Poe writes: "The epithets 'Grotesque' and 'Arabesque' will be found to indicate with sufficient precision the prevalent tenor of the tales here published."[2] Using this sentence by way of explanation, he avoids the definition of the terms, remarking only that his stories are "phantasy pieces." As several Poe critics have pointed out, the distinction between both terms as applied to Poe's work is far from clear. For example, Kenneth Silverman notes that although historically these words refer to different types of decoration, the grotesque, "combining plant, animal, and human motifs, [the arabesque] using only flowers and calligraphy," in Poe's time the terms "were often confounded and used synonymously." Silverman concludes that critic Geoffrey Harpham's definition of the grotesque, a "transcategorical hybrid" mixing the normal and the abnormal, the archaic and the modern, condenses the features of both.[3]

Michael Davitt Bell, in contrast, though reacting against those who distinguish between two types of Poe's tales according to the characteristics implied by these terms, provides a sort of classification based on the clues interspersed in Poe's writing. In Bell's view, the grotesque "implies fanciful humor, burlesque exaggeration, caricature, and, above all, distortion," whereas the arabesque, as connected with the artistic style it describes, points to abstraction and vagueness. As Bell puts it, referring to Poe's indefinite use of the term, "the arabesque attains to 'ideality,' because, quite simply, it doesn't 'mean' anything" (pp. 104-105). Perhaps it is Poe's pragmatic approach to fiction that provides the best clues for the analysis of his work. Let us recall the well-known passage in a letter to Thomas White, the editor of the *Southern Literary Messenger,* in which Poe sums up his formula for successful Gothic writing:

> The history of all Magazines shows plainly that those which have attained celebrity were indebted for it to articles *similar in nature to Berenice*. . . . I say similar in *nature*. You ask me in what does this nature consist? In the ludicrous heightened into the grotesque: the fearful coloured into the horrible: the witty exaggerated into the burlesque: the singular wrought out into the strange and mystical. . . . To be appreciated you must be *read,* and these are invariably sought after with avidity.[4]

As can be observed, both the grotesque and the arabesque are mixed up in Poe's writing. If, on the one hand, the ludicrous is unambiguously associated with the grotesque, and if, on the other hand, the burlesque and the horrible are also related to it, the singular and the fearful can be linked to both the grotesque ("strange") and the arabesque ("strange and mystical"). No doubt, Poe was more concerned with "unity of effect" than with clear-cut classifications. In all cases it is excess that sets his formula in motion and pervades his composition practice. As we are going to see, **"The Black Cat"** epitomizes the sensational and successful effect of Poe's complex technique.

In her "Afterword," Oates wonders about the meaning of the grotesque, noting that "[t]he arts of the grotesque are so various as to resist definition" (p. 303). For her, the grotesque is an all-encompassing category that accommodates a wide variety of artistic works in painting, literature, and film from different periods: from *Beowulf* to Stephen King and Anne Rice, from Goya to Bacon. However, despite the comprehensiveness of the concept and the possible variations in style, Oates remarks that not all ghost stories belong to the genre of the grotesque; thus, Victorian ghost stories, much of Henry James's Gothic fiction as well as that by Edith Wharton, for instance, are too "nice," "too ladylike," "too genteel to qualify" (p. 304). In Oates's view, the grotesque "always possesses a blunt *physicality* that no amount of epistemological exegesis can exorcise. One might define it, in fact, as the very antithesis of 'nice'" (p. 304). Although in my opinion Oates's concept of the grotesque is too wide—it includes even Irving's "Rip Van Winkle"—her comments are useful for this analysis. Thus, whereas Poe's tale proves to be full of horror and excess, Oates's appears "genteel" and even "ladylike" in comparison; however, its nature originates in the manipulation of Poe's formula, except that the ingredients are used in different doses, and some extra elements are added to the whole. Hence its subtle but disturbing grotesqueness.

As is well known, **"The Black Cat"** portrays a first-person narrator-protagonist who makes a written confession of his crimes on the eve of his execution on the gallows. His "wild" but "homely narrative"[5] includes in succession drunkenness, the victimization of two cats, and the murder of his own wife. Interestingly, this accumulation of horrors proves to be a source of both fear and laughter. Just as the fearful turns into the horrible when Pluto, the first cat, is brutally abused and sacrificed (remember the narrator's sadistic extraction of Pluto's eye and his later hanging of the pet) before the wife similarly suffers an unmotivated, violent death (her husband buries an axe in her brain in a paroxysm of rage), so there are several details that point to Poe's exploitation of the ludicrous and that undermine the apparent solemnity of the narrator's confession. We could now recall the narrator's ridiculous explanation of the apparition of a gigantic cat, with a rope around its neck, as a "*bas relief*" graven on the only remaining wall of his burnt house. The narrator jumps to the conclusion that some witness of the fire must have removed the hanged cat from the tree and thrown it through an open window into his chamber: "This had probably been done with the view of arousing me from sleep," he adds. The fire and the "ammonia from the carcass" had completed the work, apparently (p. 1391). Is this not "singular," "strange," and "grotesque" at the same time?

On the other hand, it is worth recalling the way in which the murder of the wife is narrated. Although the first blow of the axe is intended for the cat, the wife's interference provokes the change of target: it seems that the narrator does not care which one is his victim. Last but not least, the final paragraph of the tale is full of ambiguous undertones: whereas the description of the wife's corpse, "greatly decayed and clotted with gore," evokes horror and disgust, the "erect" position of the body, as if ready for inspection, which the sitting figure of the ubiquitous and devilish cat presides over "with red extended mouth and solitary eye of fire" (p. 1396), constitutes a mixture of the serious and the comic, which points to the essence of the grotesque.

Undoubtedly, **"The Black Cat"** is a masterpiece, and as such it has brought about a high number of interpretations which study the text from a variety of perspectives. Critics have focused, among other things, on the literal uncanniness of the tale: how Poe, with his "wild" and "homely" narrative, anticipates Freud's essay "The Uncanny," published many years later (1919). Apart from this homelike/unhomelike quality, Poe's tale includes other elements described by Freud in his essay: for example, the phenomenon of repetition (the wall of the burnt house, the walls of the chimney in the cellar where the wife is buried; the cat on the head of the barrel, on the head of the wife; two hangings—that of Pluto and that of the narrator—and two reproductions of it—on the bas relief and on the cat's chest), which in turn contains the figure of the double, "the uncanny harbinger of death"[6] embodied in the mysterious duplication of the cat, which extend to the wife, given the progressive assimilation between the former and the latter. On the other hand, Poe's inclusion of blinding evokes castration, which in turn suggests the notion of the wife as castrated (as a surrogate of the cat) and also castrating, since it is thanks to the cat's voice that the wife takes vengeance on her husband, if only after death.[7]

Critics have also discussed the pun between "eye" and "I"—which Poe explores in other tales such as **"Ligeia"** (1838) and **"The Tell-Tale Heart"** (1843)—stating that in fact the fixation with the other's organ of sight is just a case of projection that, especially in **"The Black Cat"** and **"The Tell-Tale Heart,"** conceals a problem of displaced violence through which "desire for death translates into aggression."[8] Thus, the desire to die is replaced by the desire to kill. However, this death instinct emerges as a confessional urge, which in turn reflects a compulsion to exhibit intellectual superiority. Similarly, criticism of **"The Black Cat"** has focused on the mental degeneration of the narrator—his descent into alcoholism and his theorization and practice of perverseness, both of which are reflected in his frantic discourse. As Auerbach notes, the narrator of this tale "falls victim to his own seductive reasoning," showing that analysis "creates more mysteries than it tends to solve when it turns inward upon itself."[9]

More recently, criticism has tended to study **"The Black Cat"**—and all of Poe's work—in the light of its sociohistorical context. Thus, it has been pointed out that this tale echoes contemporary sensationalist fiction, parodies the temperance confessional, and critiques the growing acceptance of the insanity defense in antebellum courtrooms.[10] Joan Dayan emphasizes "Poe's racialized Gothicism" and approaches this tale as a portrayal of the "rare and special" relationship between slave and master, and between man and wife, based on the law of property.[11] Following Dayan's analysis, Ginsberg concentrates on "the peculiar psychopolitics of the master/slave relationship" (p. 99), discussing the antebellum free white male's right to absolute power over family, slaves, and pets and highlighting the dangers of dependency: **"The Black Cat"** exemplifies domestic tyranny and its confusion of persons and pets, and pits black against white and thus reproduces and critiques the cultural work of the American Gothic.

These cultural and racial notions have also been discussed from the African-American perspective. In *Playing in the Dark* (1992), Toni Morrison tackles the issues of blackness and whiteness, emphasizing the centrality of the black presence in the concept of Americanness and in American literature. Significantly, Morrison argues that "No early American writer is more important to the concept of American Africanism than Poe,"[12] and in her view, no image is more telling than the enigmatic white vision that emerges from the mist at the end of ***The Narrative of Arthur Gordon Pym*** [***The Narrative of Arthur Gordon Pym of Nantucket***] (1838). Morrison observes that since these figures of impenetrable whiteness recur in American literature almost always in conjunction with representations of black, they "seem to function as both antidote for and meditation on the shadow that is companion to this whiteness—a dark and abiding presence that moves the hearts and texts of American literature with fear and longing" (p. 33).

In fact, **"The Black Cat"** plays with whiteness and its shadow in such a way that both colors cease to be reliable signifiers of racial difference, as Leland S. Person has remarked.[13] Thus, although this tale links the cat's blackness with fear and the powers of darkness—remember the allusion to black cats as "witches in disguise" (p. 1389), the cat's name Pluto (the Roman god of the dead and the ruler of the underworld), and the progressive demonization of the pet—it also undermines black essentialism, most evident in the literal "amalgamation" of black and white made visible in the "splotch of white" (p. 1392) on the cat's chest, which in its suggestion of the gallows both encapsulates the hanging of the cat (by the narrator) and the execution of the latter (through the cat's intervention), thus white on black links white guilt and black revenge.

The preceding summary of interpretations provides a point of departure for the analysis of Oates's "The White Cat" since this story takes **"The Black Cat"** as its main intertext, although it explores its issues in a more playful, less impressive tone. As Oates has confessed, talking about literary masters, "I am a shameless hero-worshiper. . . . I very early in life latched onto spiritual, intellectual, visionary fathers, all kinds. . . ." And also: "It's a lot of fun to reimagine these famous old stories. . . . There's no question of anyone writing stories as good as those, so in a way one is free to try almost anything."[14] Like other stories by Oates published in an earlier collection (*Marriages and Infidelities,* 1972), "The White Cat" suggests a marriage with several infidelities.

To begin with, Oates starts her tale by copying the title of Poe's story but with a slight change: black turns into white. Needless to say, this choice of color—which ties in with and enlarges Poe's black cat's splotch of white—allows Oates to explore further Poe's deconstruction of color symbolism. If traditionally the color white has been taken to symbolize purity and innocence, this cat, beautiful and capricious, smart and devious, is far from embodying the good qualities that whiteness seems to convey. In fact, Oates's handling of white brings to mind Melville's *Moby-Dick* (1851): in "The Whiteness of the Whale," Ishmael, though recognizing the positive attributes of this color, emphasizes its negative aspects, which evoke terror, blankness, and annihilation:

> But not yet have we solved the incantation of this whiteness, and learned why it appeals with such power to the soul; and more strange and far more portentous—why, as we have seen, it is at once the most meaning symbol of spiritual things, nay, the very veil of the Christian's Deity; and yet should be as it is, the intensifying agent in things the most appalling to mankind.
>
> Is it that by its indefiniteness it shadows forth the heartless voids and immensities of the universe, and thus stabs us from behind with the thought of annihilation, when beholding the white depths of the milky way? Or is it, that as in essence whiteness is not so much a color as the visible absence of color; and at the same time the concrete of all colors; is it for these reasons that there is such a dumb blankness, full of meaning, in a white landscape of snows—a colorless, all-color of atheism from which we shrink?[15]

Similarly, the cat's name, Miranda (from Latin meaning "to be admired"), points to the beautiful and pure heroine of the same name in Shakespeare's *The Tempest* (1611), which reinforces the intertextual and parodic nature of Oates's tale. Thus, the gender of the cat is also changed, but Oates plays with its ambiguous identity through her characters. When the male protagonist is asked about the cat's gender, "[t]he question lodged deep in him as if it were a riddle: *Is it a male or a female*? 'Female, of course,' Mr. Muir said pleasantly. 'Its name after all is Miranda'" (p. 75). With this careless, illogical answer, Oates suggests the protagonist's confusion between cause and effect, which again takes the reader back to Poe's narrator-protagonist, asking for "some intellect more calm, more logical, and far less excitable" than his own to perceive in his story "nothing more than an ordinary succession of very natural causes and effects" (pp. 1388-1389).

"The White Cat" features an external, third-person narrator, who focalizes events from the male character's perspective and who has access only to his mind. This restricted point of view, which recalls that recurrently used by Henry James—another literary master for Oates—preserves the subjectivity of the situation and foregrounds the unreliability of the protagonist's perceptions; however, it greatly diminishes the power of his personality: deprived of the agency of voice, and with a tendency to observation rather than action (p. 82), this character is progressively reduced to a passive role; he will be absolutely and literally passive at the end of the narrative. Oates replaces the confessional but otherwise barren quality of Poe's text with a calculated variety of elements: whereas in Poe's tale, as in many others by him, the narrator-protagonist lacks a name, physical features, and ancestors and betrays a precarious identity, Oates's male character shows the opposite features: he has a name, Julius Muir, and, as the narrator explains, "[h]e knew who he was, who his ancestors were" and "[b]eing of old American stock, he was susceptible to none of the fashionable tugs and sways of 'identity'" (p. 72).

As could be expected, Oates combines contrasts and similarities with Poe's intertext and also with his work as a whole. For example, Julius Muir, like many of Poe's protagonists, is solitary, introverted, imaginative, and wealthy—"a gentleman of independent means" (p. 72)—cultivated, "[f]luent in several languages" (p. 73), like Morella and Ligeia, and an art collector: in short, a present-day version of Roderick Usher. It is no coincidence that an antiquarian book dealer should offer Muir a rare edition of the *Directorium Inquisitorium* and a Gothic copy of Machiavelli's *Belfagor,* titles included in Usher's collection and which in both tales point to the situation and fate of the two characters.[16] On the other hand, the name of Julius Muir is related both to Poe's work and to the events in Oates's story: whereas "Julius" evokes an unfinished travel narrative by Poe, "The Journal of Julius Rodman"—Muir dislikes traveling—"Muir" echoes both the walls in which Poe's fictional wife and cat are immured and also Julius's literal and metaphorical immurement in his own body. Significantly, his face is described as *lapidary* (p. 72, Oates's emphasis).

Apart from these more or less overt intertextual connections, Oates's protagonist could also be related to that of John Fowles's *The Collector* (1963), Frederick Clegg, a collector of butterflies and young women, one of whom, Miranda, becomes the main focus and victim of the novel. Once more, Oates reverses the intertextual plot, since her Miranda, despite Muir's recurrent, and frequently ridiculous, attempts to kill her, becomes his victimizer. In contrast with the more horrific weapons used by Poe's protagonist—a pen-knife, a rope, an axe—Muir starts choosing more sophisticated tools: first, mice poison[17] and then his elegant English-built car. However, both prove useless against the apparently preternatural creature. In the end, even his attempt to strangle the cat with his own hands ends up in failure, which foregrounds the ineffectual personality of this character, especially if compared to Poe's more impressive fictional figure.

Similarly, Oates transforms the eye/I relationship in **"The Black Cat"**: whereas Poe's narrator removes one of Pluto's eyes with a pen-knife, Muir stands in wonder of Miranda's enigmatic eyes, for, among other things, "they had the mysterious capacity to flare up, as if at will" (p. 77). No doubt, Oates is evoking here Poe's **"Ligeia,"** a tale in which the narrator keeps recalling the mysterious eyes of his beloved lady and her return after death out of power of will. Thus, the long paragraphs devoted to the description of Miranda's eyes parody both of Poe's tales, since on the one hand, cruelty to the organs of sight becomes fascination, and, on the other, the eyes of a female cat have come to replace those of a beautiful, ethereal lady in the mind of the male protagonist.

In any case, it is through the character of the wife that Oates most reverses the original plot. Whereas Poe reduces the narrator's wife to an unnamed shadow, a figure who is never allowed to speak in her own voice, Oates turns her into the central and most powerful character of the tale, and, in keeping with this feature, emphasizes the assimilation between wife and cat, a kind of identification that for Muir will become sheer confusion: "*Alissa*? or, no, *Miranda*—which?" (p. 95). In fact, Alissa can be approached as the parodic reversal of **"The Black Cat"** wife, but again Oates takes elements from other sources: thus, Alissa is "a minor but well-regarded actress" (p. 75), and her first marriage, contracted at nineteen to another actor, was a failure. These data bring to mind the name and life of Poe's mother, Eliza, similarly a minor actress, who at nineteen married another actor and whose marriage was also unfortunate.[18] On the other hand, the reference to the "diminished sort" of marriage between Alissa and Julius, in which "[m]arital relations had all but ceased" (p. 82), recalls the relationship between Poe himself and his cousin-wife, Virginia, allegedly platonic according to many critics and biographers.

However, it is the transgressive—and triumphant—nature of Alissa's personality that provides the forceful, disquieting touch to Oates's grotesque in this tale:

while Julius is portrayed as a devoted and loving husband, Alissa is depicted as capricious, selfish, and even adulterous. Significantly, the narrative juxtaposes the different activities of husband and wife in a subtle but humorous way; while Julius is suffering from a sudden and uncontrollable proliferation of cats after one of his frequent nightmares: the cat on his chest, on the carpet, in the shrubbery, on the roof—even on his lips—Alissa is having fun and company in the adjoining room, as the narrator-focalizer suggests:

> It was not so very late, scarcely 1:00 a.m. The undertone Mr. Muir heard was Alissa's voice, punctuated now and then by her light, silvery laughter. One might almost think there was someone in the bedroom with her—but of course she was merely having a late-night telephone conversation, very likely with Alban—they would be chatting companionably, with an innocent sort of malice, about their co-actors and -actresses, mutual friends and acquaintances. Alissa's balcony opened out onto the same side of the house that Mr. Muir's did, which accounted for her voice (or *was* it voices? Mr. Muir listened, bemused) carrying so clearly. No light irradiated from her room; she must have been having her telephone conversation in the dark.
>
> (pp. 88-89)

As can be observed, Oates's play with whiteness reaches Alissa's friend/lover, who in the light of the etymological meaning of his name (*Alban* derives from Latin *albus, alba, album*: white) can be taken as a human male prolongation of the elusive cat. On the other hand, the ambiguity implicit in this passage pervades most of Oates's tale and complicates her handling of the grotesque: just as adultery is suggested but never made explicit, so the main events of the story always appear filtered and therefore blurred by Muir's consciousness. We could recall the lack of consistency between cause and effect in the following examples: although Muir is convinced he has killed Miranda with his car, he cannot find any sign of his crime on the car fender or on the tires: "No proof! No proof!" (p. 84), he exclaims happily, but it seems there is no death, either, since the cat reappears at night.[19] Absurdly enough, Muir concludes that the run-over cat "must have been another cat" (p. 85). On a later occasion, after his attempt to strangle Miranda with his own hands, the cat shows "no sign of their recent struggle" (p. 92), while Alissa fails to notice his "lacerated hands and face" (p. 92)—indications, once more, of the hypothetical nature of the encounter.

In keeping with this uncertain atmosphere, the ending of "The White Cat" oscillates between the real and the unreal, the realm of desire and that of crude fact. After Muir's last failed attempt to get rid of Miranda, he undergoes another humiliating experience: when Alissa returns unexpectedly from New York—the narrative suggests that her sudden decision to quit the "professional stage" has to do with the end of a love affair—Muir realizes that she has come home, but not "to *him*" (pp. 92-93). Despite his supplications and expensive presents, she remains inaccessible, a fact which makes Muir a prey to despair. His attitude is really ludicrous, clearly contrasting with the misogyny and aggressiveness of Poe's narrator: "[Muir] lay alone in his solitary bed, amidst the tangled bedclothes, weeping hoarsely"; on top of that, his sleep is haunted by the white cat and her "hideous smothering weight" (p. 93). As in Poe's tale, the cat has become for Muir an all-powerful creature, the personification of the devil.

After a disquieting apparition of the cat,[20] upon which Muir enigmatically "realized what she was" (p. 93)—an ambiguous allusion that most likely points to Muir's overlapping of wife and cat, since the eyes of both seem to have turned brighter and smaller—he suffers a terrible accident with his car. The narrator describes it in italics, from Muir's point of view: according to this description, Muir is driving the car with Alissa—dressed in black—silent at her side. Out of spite, and after announcing his intentions and motivations to his wife ("It will be better this way, my dear wife. . . . Even if you love no other man, it is painfully clear that you do not love me" [p. 93]), he starts to drive faster, provoking the crash: the car spins in the air, drops down the hillside, and finally bursts into flame. According to this passage, it is apparent that Muir has planned both his wife's death and his own.

However, things seem to have turned out quite differently: in the following paragraph—no longer in italics—Muir appears seated in a wheelchair, blind and totally paralyzed: "Blind, yet not wholly blind: for he could see (indeed, could not *not* see) washes of white, gradations of white, astonishing subtleties of white like rivulets in a stream perpetually breaking and falling about his head, not distinguished by any form or outline or vulgar suggestion of an object in space . . ." (p. 94). The narrator adds that Muir has had a number of operations, and one more has been suggested in order to restore "his ability to move some of the toes on his left foot." As the narrator remarks, "Had he the capacity to laugh he would have laughed, but perhaps his dignified silence was preferable" (p. 95). Needless to say, this situation is really tragicomic, and openly reverses the terrifying plot of **"The Black Cat"**: if in Poe's story the protagonist is at least able to kill his wife—even if only by mistake—in Oates's he proves incapable of taking his own life, let alone those of the wife and the cat. As Alissa tells him, "How lucky you were, Julius, that another car came along! Why, you might have *died*!" (p. 95).

In order to account for this unexpected situation, the narrator offers a retrospective version of the accident, very close to the previous one, except for the introductory sentence: "It seemed that Julius Muir had been driving alone . . ." (p. 95). Significantly, this clarification—Muir's driving unaccompanied—provides the narrative with one more parodic touch, but at the same time, the use of "seemed" emphasizes the uncertainty that characterizes Oates's story. That forms part of her use of the grotesque: in postmodern fashion, she plays with the boundaries between the real and the unreal. This technique is reflected in the description of Muir's unreliable memory and fragmented consciousness: "So the story of how Julius had come to this place, his final resting place, this place of milk-white peace, emerged, in fragments shattered and haphazard as those of a smashed windshield" (p. 95).

In any case, Oates does not lose sight of the intertext, if only to subvert it: note that Muir's blindness parodies Poe's narrator's blinding of the cat; in Freudian terms, he has brought about his own castration, which in this case is more than symbolic: his paralyzed body is the proof of his absolute powerlessness. Unlike **"The Black Cat"** protagonist, he is a victimizer without a victim; in fact, he is his only victim. Oates closes the narrative by making the dénouement more than ludicrous, that is, grotesque in Poe's gradation: the white cat becomes the object of Muir's desire, whose warm physicality has come to make up for the wife's unfulfilled marital duties:

> He lived for those days when, waking from a doze, he would feel a certain furry, warm weight lowered into his lap—"Julius, dear, someone very special has come to visit"—soft, yet surprisingly heavy; heated, yet not disagreeably so; initially a bit restless (as a cat must circle fussily about, trying to determine the ideal position before she settles herself down), yet within a few minutes quite wonderfully relaxed, kneading her claws gently against his limbs and purring as she drifted into a companionable sleep. He would have liked to see, beyond the shimmering watery whiteness of his vision, her particular whiteness; certainly he would have liked to feel once again the softness, the astonishing silkiness, of that fur. But he could hear the deep-throated melodic purring. He could feel, to a degree, her warmly pulsing weight, the wonder of her mysterious *livingness* against his—for which he was infinitely grateful.
>
> "My love!"
>
> (p. 96)

Obviously, this placid, amorous image of the female cat sleeping on the man's lap constitutes an absolute reversal of the ending of Poe's tale, in which the male "hideous beast" appears sitting on the dead woman's head. Apart from this, the "strange" and "burlesque" dénouement of "The White Cat" triggers a number of reflections: for example, the recurrent allusion to Muir's visions of whiteness suggests the triumph of his antagonist, the white cat; on the other hand, the indefiniteness of these white forms—"washes of white, gradations of white, astonishing subtleties of white like rivulets in a stream" (p. 94)—points to Poe's conception and practice of the arabesque: something so lofty and abstruse that it hardly means anything. Likewise, the "milky" and "watery" invasion of whiteness at the end of the tale cannot but evoke the milky hue of the landscape—white waters, white creatures and birds, white impressive figure—at the close of Poe's ***The Narrative of Arthur Gordon Pym.*** If Toni Morrison approaches ***Pym*** [***The Narrative of Arthur Gordon Pym of Nantucket***] as one of the first examples in U.S. literature of the symbolic opposition blackness/whiteness, Oates reproduces the tradition—the blackness in her tale is represented not only by Alissa's black dress but also by Muir's blindness—but departs from it through her parodic detachment and playful tone. Significantly, the blankness suggested by the color white, or "absence of color" (Melville, p. 206), and by this ending as a whole, epitomizes "the gap between signification and reference," the absence of a coherently meaningful symbolic, regarded as typical of the American Gothic.[21]

What looks clear in Oates's tale, however, is the absolute triumph of the female, represented both by the wife and the cat herself, who prove superior to the male character and his silly, futile efforts to get rid of them; in contrast, the female in Poe's tale takes her vengeance only after death and through the cat, a male creature. But the superiority of the female in Oates's story goes beyond mere contrast with the marginal role of the woman in **"The Black Cat"** when we recall the transgressive behavior of Muir's wife: ironically, her lovelessness and suggested adultery are rewarded rather than punished. In this respect, "The White Cat" recalls Luis Buñuel's *Belle de Jour* (1966). In this film—considered the highest expression of surrealism in the history of cinema[22]—the wealthy female protagonist, Séverine, combines her boring life as a wife with her peculiar entertainment as a prostitute in a Paris brothel; the film's dénouement, playing with the real and the unreal, shows Séverine's loving husband with dark glasses, paralyzed and seated in a wheelchair as a consequence of his being shot by one of his wife's lovers. I do not know if Oates had *Belle de Jour* in mind when writing her tale, but the works share a similar postmodern, irreverent tone; significantly, Buñuel's film is also a recreation of a previous text, Joseph Kessel's *Belle de Jour* (1929).

On the other hand, Oates's treatment of the female can be taken not only as a reversal of Poe's tale but also as a departure from the recurrent characteristics of her fiction: as has been pointed out, many of her women characters are afraid of and victimized by men.[23] In "The White Cat," though, it is the man who suffers the haunting, which points not only to Oates's manipulation of Gothic conventions but also to her adoption of a pseudo-feminist, vindictive, and playful role, which is also evident in another tale of the same volume, "The Premonition."

Thus, in its peculiar and varied ways, "The White Cat" makes use of the characteristics of the grotesque: it is a "transcategorical hybrid," mixing the normal and the abnormal, the comic and the burlesque, in which distortion and exaggeration are part of its "unity of effect." On the other hand, Oates's tale is to a great extent faithful to Poe's formula for sensationalist writing: the ludicrous is heightened into the grotesque, the witty into the burlesque, and the singular into the strange and mystical. The fearful, however, has not been colored into the horrible: that is the reason why "The White Cat" may appear "genteel" and even "nice" as compared to **"The Black Cat"**: its parodic quality provides the additional distortion that subverts Poe's formula—here the fearful turns into the comic[24] rather than the horrible—and even Oates's defining feature, the blunt physicality of the grotesque, is undermined—and partly replaced—by the contrived *bizarreries*[25] of postmodern academic writing.

Consequently, although "The White Cat" incorporates into its narrative most of the elements on which criticism of **"The Black Cat"** has focused (the concept of the uncanny—including the phenomenon of repetition, the figure of the double and blinding as castration—the pun eye/I, sadism and the death drive, domestic relationships, confusion of persons and pets, and blackness versus whiteness), the inclusive, multivalent nature of the parodic mode puts the text "under erasure"[26] and points to a proliferation of meanings; thus, "The White Cat" is at once a fiction and a fiction about fictions; its critical distance works both towards the imitated text and towards the world, and, finally, its playful tone disrupts the implications of its own transgressiveness. In this way, "The White Cat"—an amusette especially intended for academic readers—evokes, for example, the solemn, metaphysical whiteness of *Moby-Dick,* the abstruse mystifications of ***Pym***'s white visions, Buñuel's irreverent surrealism, the distortions of the mock feminist tale, and, last but not least, the Gothic grotesqueries of **"The Black Cat."**[27]

Notes

1. New York: Plume, 1995, p. 305.
2. Qtd. in Michael Davitt Bell, "Imagination, Spirit, and the Language of Romance: Edgar Allan Poe," in *The Development of American Romance: The Sacrifice of Relation* (Chicago: University of Chicago Press, 1980), p. 104.
3. *Edgar Allan Poe: Mournful and Never-ending Remembrance* (1991; rpt. London: Weidenfeld, 1993), p. 153.
4. Qtd. in Vincent Buranelli, *Edgar Allan Poe* (Boston: Twayne, 1977), pp. 25-26.
5. Edgar Allan Poe, "The Black Cat," in *The Norton Anthology of American Literature,* 2nd ed., ed. Nina Baym et al. (New York: Norton, 1985), I, 1388.
6. Sigmund Freud, "The Uncanny," in *Art and Literature, Penguin Freud Library* (Harmondsworth: Penguin, 1985), XIV, 357.
7. Cf. Marie Bonaparte, *The Life and Works of Edgar Allan Poe: A Psycho-Analytic Interpretation* (1933; London: Imago, 1949), and Daniel Hoffman, *Poe, Poe, Poe, Poe, Poe, Poe, Poe* (1972; New York: Paragon House, 1990).
8. J. Gerald Kennedy, *Poe, Death, and the Life of Writing* (New Haven: Yale University Press, 1987), p. 137.
9. Jonathan Auerbach, "Disfiguring the Perfect Plot: Doubling and Self-Betrayal in Poe," in *The Romance of Failure: First-Person Fictions of Poe, Hawthorne, and James* (New York: Oxford University Press, 1989), p. 39.
10. Lesley Ginsberg, "Slavery and the Gothic Horror of Poe's 'The Black Cat,'" in *American Gothic: New Interventions in a National Narrative,* ed. Robert K. Martin and Eric Savoy (Iowa City: University of Iowa Press, 1998), p. 99.
11. "Amorous Bondage: Poe, Ladies, and Slaves," in *The American Face of Edgar Allan Poe,* ed. Shawn Rosenheim and Stephen Rachman (Baltimore: Johns Hopkins University Press, 1995), pp. 192, 207.
12. *Playing in the Dark: Whiteness and the Literary Imagination* (1992; London: Picador, 1993), p. 32. Significantly, this statement has been taken as a point of departure by editors J. Gerald Kennedy and Liliane Weissberg in their recent book *Romancing the Shadow: Poe and Race* (New York: Oxford University Press, 2001).
13. "Poe's Philosophy of Amalgamation: Reading Racism in the Tales," in *Romancing the Shadow: Poe and Race,* ed. J. Gerald Kennedy and L. Weissberg (New York: Oxford University Press, 2001).
14. Qtd. in Monica Loeb, *Literary Marriages* (New York: Peter Lang, 2001), pp. 13, 17.
15. Herman Melville, *Moby-Dick; or, The Whale* (Norwalk, Connecticut: Easton Press, 1977), p. 206.

16. *The Directorium,* by Nicholas Eymeric de Gerone, who was Inquisitor-General for Castile in 1356, records procedures for torturing heretics. In *Belfagor*—spelled *Belphegor* in "The Fall of the House of Usher" (1839)—a demon comes to earth to prove that women damn men to hell.
17. Cf. William Faulkner's "A Rose for Emily" (1930): in this short story, the protagonist gets rid of her victim by means of "poison [f]or rats" (in *Selected Short Stories of William Faulkner* [New York: Modern Library, 1993], p. 54). Significantly, Oates highlights this tale as "a supreme example" of the grotesque in her "Afterword" (p. 304).
18. Like the fictional Alissa, Eliza Poe got married on two occasions: at fifteen she married a character actor named Charles Hopkins, who died three years later (1805). At the age of nineteen, she married David Poe, Jr., a young actor and dancer who, after accumulating "money problems, parental disapproval, drinking habits, bad reviews, a more successful wife, and children to support" (Silverman, p. 7), abandoned his family in 1809.
19. Ironically, these exclamations echo the proud and triumphant words of Poe's narrator to the police in the cellar of his house: "this is a very well constructed house. . . . [T]hese walls are solidly put together" (p. 1395). However, the utterances of both protagonists only highlight their erroneous assumptions.
20. The pet is no longer called Miranda but "the white cat" or "the creature," a defamiliarization strategy also present in "The Black Cat."
21. Eric Savoy, "The Face of the Tenant: A Theory of American Gothic," in *American Gothic: New Interventions in a National Narrative,* pp. 3-19.
22. Agustín Sánchez Vidal, *Luis Buñuel: Obra cinematográfica* (Madrid: Ediciones J.C., 1984), p. 310.
23. Mary Allen, "The Terrified Women of Joyce Carol Oates," in *Joyce Carol Oates: Modern Critical Views,* ed. Harold Bloom (New York: Chelsea House, 1987), pp. 61-82.
24. In fact, "The White Cat" might well be analyzed in the light of what Avril Horner and Sue Zlosnik describe as "Comic Gothic": "narrative texts that, while exhibiting recognisable Gothic characteristics, have been considered amusing rather than terrifying in their effect." They employ "parody and burlesque," but "darker aspects" are also included ("Comic Gothic," in *A Companion to the Gothic,* ed. David Punter [Oxford: Blackwell, 2001], p. 242).
25. Poe's term used by Signora Psyche Zenobia, the narrator and main character in "How to Write a Blackwood Article" (1838).
26. Simon Dentith, *Parody* (London: Routledge, 2000), pp. 15-16.
27. The research carried out for the writing of this paper was financed by the Spanish Ministry of Science and Technology and by the European Regional Development Fund (MCyT and FEDER, Departamento Técnico de Humanidades y Ciencias Sociales: ref. no. BFF2001-1775).

Elena V. Baraban (essay date fall 2004)

SOURCE: Baraban, Elena V. "The Motive for Murder in 'The Cask of Amontillado' by Edgar Allan Poe." *Rocky Mountain Review* 58, no. 2 (fall 2004): 47-62.

[*In the following essay, Baraban examines the reason for Montresor's murder of Fortunato in "The Cask of Amontillado," suggesting that Fortunato "is being punished for his arrogance and for insulting someone who is equal or superior to him."*]

Edgar Allan Poe's **"The Cask of Amontillado"** (1846) has never failed to puzzle its readers. The story is a confession of a man who committed a horrible crime half a century ago. Montresor lures Fortunato into the family vaults under the pretext that he needs Fortunato's opinion of the newly acquired Amontillado wine. In a remote niche of the crypt, Montresor fetters Fortunato to the wall and then bricks him in. The reader is perplexed by a seeming absence of the motive for this crime. Unable to find a logical explanation of Montresor's hatred for Fortunato, most commentators conclude that Montresor is insane. Such interpretation, however, seems to make certain details in the elaborate structure of the story unnecessary and this, in turn, goes against Poe's approach to composition.

In the essay "The Philosophy of Composition," written in the same year as **"The Cask of Amontillado,"** Poe demonstrates that there are no details in his works that appear due to accident or intuition, and that his work proceeds "to its completion with the precision and rigid consequence of a mathematical problem" (166). While such an approach to creative writing has earned Poe an antipathetic reputation of the first "technocrat of art" from Theodore Adorno (193), it would find support with Russian Formalists. The Formalists' view of the form "as the totality of the work's various components" and their interest in analyzing the form by identifying the functions of the text's various components (Todorov 10-11) match Poe's ideas about writing. Indeed, **"The Cask of Amontillado"** could be among the Formalists' favorite texts, for the details in this story are like pieces of a mosaic, each of which serves the purpose of completing the whole. My hypothesis is that the story contains all the information necessary for finding an explanation for Montresor's heinous deed.

Although the subject matter of Poe's story is a murder, **"The Cask of Amontillado"** is not a tale of detection, for there is no investigation of Montresor's crime.[1] The criminal himself explains how he committed the murder. Despite this explanation, **"The Cask of Amontillado"** is a mystery, for at its heart lies an intriguing question: "Why did he do it?" This question is different from the "Who's done it?" of a classical mystery, as the latter presents crime as a logical puzzle solved by a detective thanks to his intellect (Rahn 49-50). Nonetheless, in the absence of the figure of a detective, the central question of Poe's story compels the reader to perform an intellectual act of detection himself. Moreover, this question requires that the reader reverse the process of solving the mystery. Whereas a detective begins his investigation with defining motives for the crime, the reader of **"The Cask of Amontillado"** should decipher the circumstances described by Montresor in order to determine the motive for his murder of Fortunato.

Far from being a mediocre murderer, Montresor elaborates a sophisticated philosophy of revenge: "I must not only punish, but punish with impunity. A wrong is unredressed when retribution overtakes its redresser. It is equally unredressed when the avenger fails to make himself felt as such to him who has done the wrong" (848). A successful realization of this plan is questioned in criticism. G. R. Thompson, for example, argues that Montresor has failed to accomplish a perfect murder: "Montresor, rather than having successfully taken his revenge 'with impunity' . . . has instead suffered a fifty-years' ravage of conscience" (13-14). David Halliburton also gives a didactic reading of the tale: "If the walls erected by Poe's masons (**'The Black Cat,' 'The Cask of Amontillado'**) are material, they are also existential: to take up mortar and trowel is to victimize the other, and through this process to bring about the victimization of oneself" (263).[2] According to Thompson, Montresor's words in the opening of the story, "you, who so well know the nature of my soul" (848), are probably addressed to Montresor's confessor, "for if Montresor has murdered Fortunato fifty years before,[3] he must now be some seventy to eighty years of age" (13-14).[4] Thompson uses the fact that Montresor's narration is actually a confession made on his deathbed to support the argument about Montresor's troubled conscience.

Without questioning the interpretation of Montresor's narration as taking place at his deathbed, I would still ask if the fact of this belated confession gives us sufficient ground to assume that Montresor has suffered pangs of conscience for fifty years. Following J. Gerald Kennedy, Scott Peeples quotes Montresor in support of the argument about Montresor's bad conscience: "Fifty years later, he still remembers his heart's 'growing sick—on account of the dampness of the catacombs,' but his heartsickness likely arises from empathy with the man he is leaving to die amid that dampness" (150). The quoted phrase, however, can hardly be used as evidence of the character's empathy towards his victim. In fact, it is one of the numerous instances of irony in Poe's text. Charles May notes in this regard, "Even if our hypothesis that Montresor tells the story as a final confession . . . is correct, the tone or manner of his telling makes it clear that he has not atoned, for he enjoys himself in the telling too much—as much, in fact, as he did when he committed the crime itself" (81). Indeed, the dash in the middle of the sentence—"My heart grew sick—on account of the dampness of the catacombs"—indicates a pause. When Montresor pronounces the first part of the phrase, the reader may believe that Montresor begins to feel sorry for the poor Fortunato. But when the narrator concludes that his heart is growing sick "on account of the dampness of the catacombs," it becomes clear that Montresor feels satisfaction about his monstrous deed even after fifty years. The narrator is perfectly aware of the effect the second part of his sentence produces on his listener (even if the whole narration is Montresor's last confession and his listener is a priest). It destroys any hope in Montresor's humanity and highlights once again that Montresor feels no guilt regarding the murder. A bit earlier in the text, Montresor recollects how, after laying the fourth tier of the masonry, he stepped back to listen to "the furious vibrations of the chain" produced by his poor victim: "The noise lasted for several minutes, during which, that I might hearken to it with the more satisfaction, I ceased my labors and sat down upon the bones. When at last the clanking subsided, I resumed the trowel" (853). Poe's character then is anything but Raskolnikov, the hero of Dostoevsky's *Crime and Punishment,* who confesses the murder he has committed because he is unable to overcome the excruciating feeling of guilt. Unlike Raskolnikov, Montresor is perfectly calm and rational in his account. He never expresses pity for his enemy or feels remorse for what he did. In the essay "Forms of Time and Chronotope in the Novel," Mikhail Bakhtin describes Montresor's tone as "calm, matter-of-fact, and dry" (200). This pitiless tone is partly responsible for the feeling of horror that seizes the reader at the end of the story. Indeed, while most contemporary detective fiction serves a didactic purpose by showing how criminals are caught, **"The Cask of Amontillado"** depicts a man who has successfully committed a premeditated murder and escapes punishment. Not only does Montresor feel no guilt, but he perceives his murder of Fortunato as a successful act of vengeance and punishment rather than crime.[5] Montresor presents himself as a person who had the right to condemn Fortunato to death; he planned his murder as an act of execution. Why did Montresor "punish" Fortunato?

For many, **"The Cask of Amontillado"** seems to start in the middle of Montresor's account: "The thousand injuries of Fortunato I had borne as I best could; but when he ventured upon insult, I vowed revenge" (848). J. R. Hammond argues that Montresor's revenge was caused by the thousand injuries he had received from Fortunato (89). Edward Wagenknecht makes a similar argument when he writes, "Poe carefully avoids specifying the 'thousand injuries' that [Montresor] has suffered, and there is an absolute concentration upon the psychological effect" (161). These interpretations are untenable, for Poe clearly contrasts injuries and insult in his story: the cause of Montresor's revenge was "insult," not "injuries." The narrator, however, never specifies the nature of this insult and thus puzzles Poe's commentators further (Hoffman 223). In the words of May, "The reader has no way of knowing what these 'thousand injuries' and the mysterious insult are and thus can make no judgment about whether Montresor's revenge is justifiable" (79). But is the reader indeed deprived of the possibility of judging whether the wrong done by Fortunato could warrant "capital punishment"?

Poe's intriguing silence about the nature of the insult that made Montresor murder Fortunato has given rise to explanations of Montresor's deed through insanity. Richard M. Fletcher, for example, maintains that Montresor's actions are irrational and that therefore he is mad (167). Other critics share this view. In an annotation to **"The Cask of Amontillado,"** Stephen Peithman writes, "If there is any doubt that Montresor is mad, consider how he echoes Fortunato scream for scream, shrieking even louder than his victim" (174). In turn, Edward Hutchins Davidson writes,

> We never know what has made him hate Fortunato nor are we aware that he has ever laid out any plan to effect his revenge. . . . There is nothing intellectual here; everything is mad and improvisatory—and Montresor succeeds just so far as he is able to adapt himself to a mad, improvisatory world.
>
> (201-202)

Stuart Levine considers Montresor mad since he "murders because of an unnamed insult" (72). In Levine's opinion, "**'The Cask'** [**"The Cask of Amontillado"**] has no passage to tell the reader that the narrator is mad; the entire story does that" (80). Levine is certainly right in observing that there is no textual evidence of Montresor's insanity. Therefore, one may add, there is no reason to assume it.

The argument about Montresor's insanity rests upon the presupposition that insults ought to be differentiated and that only some of them are offensive enough to call for murder while others may be handled in a more civilized manner. The story, however, suggests a different interpretation of Montresor's action. A significant detail in Montresor's narration is the absence of an article in front of the word "insult." This absence implies that the nature of the insult need not be named at all, because this "insult" is semantically contrasted with the "injuries" that Fortunato had done to Montresor. While "injuries" presuppose rivalry of socially equal enemies, "insult" involves contempt: that is, treating the other as a socially inferior person. To insult is, by definition, "to exult proudly or contemptuously; to boast, brag, vaunt, glory, triumph, esp. in an insolent or scornful way; to assail with offensively dishonoring or contemptuous speech or action; to treat with scornful abuse or offensive disrespect" (*OED,* VII: 1057). Fortunato's disrespect of Montresor, regardless of the form it takes, is a sufficient basis for Montresor's vengeance. It follows then that the story does not start from the middle and that Montresor is not mad. Rather than implying the protagonist's insanity, the first paragraph of the story delineates the conflict between the characters as arising from their social roles.[6] A number of onomastic and semantic characteristics of the text indicate that **"The Cask of Amontillado"** is a story about the characters' power relations and their social status.[7]

Hammond maintains that both characters "lead socially active lives" (221-222). This reading, however, contradicts a notable detail of the story: Fortunato can remember neither the coat of arms nor the motto of the Montresors. The display of family insignia was an indispensable part in the life of a socially prominent nobleman. Since a rich and powerful man such as Fortunato cannot remember the Montresors' insignia, it is logical to assume that Montresor was not an active participant in the life of local aristocracy. Montresor's inability to recognize a secret sign of the freemasons made by Fortunato and the latter's remark, "Then you are not of the brotherhood" (851), also imply that Montresor is probably a bit of a recluse.[8] Fortunato is definitely more powerful than Montresor who admits to this himself: "He [Fortunato] was a man to be respected and even feared" (848). Montresor's other remark, "You are happy, as once I was. You are a man to be missed" (852), provides further grounds to believe that Montresor is no longer as rich and socially conspicuous as he used to be.

Although not as wealthy and powerful as his enemy, Montresor probably has a better aristocratic lineage than Fortunato. The catacombs of the Montresors are extensive and their vastness genuinely impresses Fortunato. In the catacombs, surrounded by the remains of Montresor's ancestors, Fortunato realizes how powerful this family used to be. The protagonist's name, "Mon-tresor" (my treasure) is a metaphor, for Montresor's noble ancestry is indeed his treasure.[9] Such assumption is all the more legitimate, since the word "treasure" usually refers to hidden riches and in Poe's tale, the hiding place is the catacombs underneath Montresor's palazzo. Furthermore, if Montresor has a better aristocratic lineage than Fortunato, the following lines become apprehensible: "Fortunato possessed himself of my arm. . . . I suffered him to hurry me to my palazzo" (849). It is not accidental that Montresor uses the verbs "to possess" and "to suffer" to describe his sensations. He "suffered" when his offender virtually led him to his palazzo because etiquette does not allow minor aristocracy the liberty of touching someone of more noble origin. At that point, however, Fortunato does not even remember that the Montresors "were a great and numerous family" (850). He is a *Fortunato,* someone who becomes rich and prominent by chance (Fortune), rather than through personal virtue. The name of this character may derive from Fortunatus, "a hero of a popular European tale" who receives from Fortune a purse which can never be emptied and who is enabled to indulge his every whim (Barnhart 1603). The fortuitous ground of Fortunato's social standing is uncovered in the course of Montresor's sophisticated revenge.[10]

Being a descendant of a powerful aristocratic family, Montresor could not possibly let Fortunato insult him with impunity. The Montresors' motto is "*Nemo me impune lacessit*" ("No one insults me with impunity"), and therefore, for Montresor, punishing his offender is a matter of honor, a matter of fulfilling his duty before his noble ancestry.[11] A description of the Montresors' coat of arms also provides a clue for uncovering the motive for Montresor's crime. "A huge human foot d'or, in a field azure; the foot crushes a serpent rampant whose fangs are imbedded in the heel" (Poe 851), which is the Montresors' coat of arms, is a *mise-en-abyme,* for the protagonist destroys Fortunato, who metaphorically represents the serpent that has dared to attack Montresor. Fortunato may use his power to "injure" Montresor, but since he comes from a less prominent family, he has no right to insult Montresor.[12] In other words, the conflict between the two characters arises from the sensation of incongruity between their current social standing and their right to prominence by virtue of their origin.

Although at first glance it appears Montresor acknowledges Fortunato's capability to distinguish fine wines, a careful textual reading uncovers how Montresor actually impugns Fortunato's ability, further revealing Montresor's sense of aristocratic superiority. Montresor exposes Fortunato's inadequacy in every possible way:

> He had a weak point—this Fortunato—although in other regards he was a man to be respected and even feared. He prided himself on his connoisseurship in wine. Few Italians have the true virtuoso spirit. For the most part their enthusiasm is adopted to suit the time and opportunity—to practice imposture upon the British and Austrian *millionaires.* In painting and in gemmary Fortunato, like his countrymen, was a quack—but in the matter of old wines he was sincere. In this respect I did not differ from him materially: I was skillful in the Italian vintages myself, and bought largely whenever I could.
>
> (848)

From this passage, we learn that while consciously practicing imposture upon tourists in matters of painting and gemmary, Fortunato genuinely considers himself knowledgeable in vintages. Montresor, however, does not share this opinion: he thinks that Fortunato's "connoisseurship in wine" is a delusion and thus calls it his "weak point." This passage is significant for understanding why Fortunato, who prides himself on his ability to distinguish vintages, says that Luchesi "cannot tell Amontillado from Sherry" (849). Burton R. Pollin interprets this passage as Poe's error: "Even if Poe had not made the error about the Spanish origin of amontillado, I fear that he would have found it difficult to differentiate between sherry and amontillado, everywhere defined as 'pale dry sherry'" (36). Rather than considering Fortunato's words, "Luchesi cannot tell Amontillado from Sherry" (849), as the author's error, it is crucial to view them as a subtle means of characterization of Fortunato as unworthy of his reputation of a connoisseur in wine. Apparently, Fortunato does not know that Amontillado is a sherry.[13] The reader can actually hear the mistake, which is otherwise unheard in a dialogue—namely, that Fortunato capitalizes the word "sherry" and uses it as a proper name rather than a generic term for several varieties of wine. Fortunato's mistake conveys his ignorance and arrogance.[14]

The seeming absence of the motive for Montresor's crime and its atrocity raise the question about the time of action in **"The Cask of Amontillado."** Some critics tend to read the story as a tale set in the Middle Ages or Renaissance. The carnival and the description of the family catacombs, also used as a wine cellar, would seem to strengthen such view. Nonetheless, two details in the story suggest that the action in **"The**

Cask of Amontillado" takes place in the eighteenth or nineteenth century. Montresor wears a roquelaire, a cloak named after the Duke of Roquelaure (1656-1738). Roquelaire was a popular piece of clothing during the eighteenth century and the early part of the nineteenth (*OED,* XIV: 100), which means that the story is set no earlier than the eighteenth century but no later than the first half of the nineteenth century. Another detail that indicates the eighteenth or nineteenth century as the time of action in **"The Cask of Amontillado"** is a reference to wealthy tourists that visited the town.[15] Montresor calls them "British and Austrian *millionaires*" (848). A new class of *nouvaux riches,* of whom Fortunato was probably one, became socially prominent in the eighteenth and nineteenth centuries. In the earlier period, no nobleman would think of exercising "imposture" upon the bourgeoisie. In his study of the cultural and historical backgrounds of Poe's story, Richard P. Benton argues that the crime described by Montresor takes place right before the French Revolution, at the end of the eighteenth century. Since the key point in Benton's article is that the setting of the tale is French, he argues for the dating of the story before the Revolution because "both aristocratic privileges and the carnival had been abolished in France by 1796" (20). Although Benton's argument regarding the French setting of the story is debatable,[16] his interpretation of the conflict between Montresor, "a proud but relatively impoverished" aristocrat, and "the upstart Fortunato" is convincing (19). It is definitely a conflict that reflects social tensions of the capitalist period.

It seems that Montresor chose for his revenge "one evening during the supreme madness of the carnival season" (848) because his servants were not at home and because Fortunato was already exhilarated with wine[17] and was an easy prey for Montresor. The carnival setting is also important because the traditional carnival symbolism helps Montresor undermine Fortunato's position.[18] The "madness of the carnival season" (848) in Poe's story is "supreme" because carnival is not simply a temporary substitution of normal order by chaos, but its inversion. In *Rabelais and His World,* Bakhtin notes that during carnival festivities "the world [is] permitted to emerge from the official routine" (90). Jokes, excessive eating, drinking, and merry-making are tributes to "the honor of the time" (848). During carnival, identities are destabilized and traditional social hierarchy and etiquette collapse; the poor may be elected carnival kings, bishops, and popes, whereas representatives of the upper classes may disguise themselves as peasants, servants, or fools. It is not surprising then that Fortunato, a man of wealth and influence, is wearing a costume of a fool during the carnival: "He had on a tight-fitting parti-striped dress, and his head was surmounted by the conical cap and bells" (848). Fortunato's carnival identity is a significant detail in the story, for Montresor's plan is to make a fool of his enemy, to ensure Fortunato's engagement in "a tragic farce."[19] Hence, Montresor's sarcastic comment about Fortunato's looks: "How remarkably well you are looking to-day!" (848). Further, Montresor makes another pun about Fortunato's "foolish" looks: "And yet some fools will have it that his [Luchesi's] taste is a match of your own" (849). Having chosen the role of a fool, Fortunato becomes socially inferior to Montresor who is wearing a black silk mask and a *roquelaire,* a costume that makes him resemble an executioner.

Space symbolism in **"The Cask of Amontillado"** also serves the purpose of undermining Fortunato's social role. The action takes place in Montresor's palazzo, a space that is new to Fortunato. Fortunato's poor physical condition highlights his inadequacy. In a hostile space of Montresor's family catacombs,[20] the victim's gait becomes "unsteady," his coughing becomes longer, and he has to lean upon Montresor's arm (850-851).

For a long time, Fortunato does not notice that Montresor's words and actions have double meaning. Fortunato says that he will not die "of a cough," and the cunning Montresor agrees: "True—true" (852). "Producing a trowel from beneath the folds" of his cloak (851), Montresor mocks Fortunato's membership in the Order of Masons. Fortunato also misreads the double meaning of the word "Amontillado." Slowly making his way through the crypt, the foolish victim sees several signs testifying to a special meaning of "Amontillado." By making Fortunato try De Grâve, Poe "no doubt means a pun on the word 'grave'" (Peithman 171).[21] The whole imagery of the crypt suggests that the word "Amontillado" is a metaphor and evokes the meaning of the root of this word—*mons, montis.*[22] The walls of the crypt "had been lined with human remains, piled to the wall overhead. . . . Three sides of this interior crypt were still ornamented in this manner. From the fourth the bones had been thrown down, and lay promiscuously upon the earth, forming at one point a mound of some size" (Poe 852). A mound of some size would be *monticula* or, by extension, *montilla.* Already fettered to the wall of the niche, Fortunato still does not understand the metaphoric meaning of the word "Amontillado." In the best tradition of fairy-tales, the culmination comes at midnight:

> Now there came from out the niche a low laugh that erected the hairs upon my head. It was succeeded by a sad voice, which I had difficulty in recognizing as that of the noble Fortunato. The voice said—

> "Ha! ha! ha!—he! he!—a very good joke indeed—an excellent jest. We will have many a rich laugh about it at the palazzo—he! he! he!—over our wine—he! he! he!" The Amontillado! I said. "He! he! he!—he! he! he!—yes, the Amontillado."
>
> (853-854)

Critics have interpreted this passage in a number of ways. According to Levine, "Fortunato tries to laugh off the entire affair as a prank" (85-86). Since the character is not actually laughing but is simply *saying* "Ha! ha! ha!" in a "low" and "sad" voice, the scene produces the effect of horror. In addition to interpreting the scene as Fortunato's futile attempt to present Montresor's actions as a joke, critics maintain that Fortunato's laughter and his incessant repetition of the word "Amontillado" give Montresor ground to believe that his victim finally realizes that "Amontillado" is a pun. Charles W. Steele makes an informed argument in favor of the metaphoric meaning of "Amontillado":

> Rendered in English, the term means "Montilla-fied" wine. No other meaning does have relevance. . . . The Italian past participles *ammonticchiato* and *ammonticellato,* signifying "collected or formed into little heaps" are from two derivative forms of the verb *ammontare* (to heap up; Spanish: *amontonar*; past part. *amontonado*). The *ch* (k) and the *c* (ch as in chill) of the Italian past participles positioned as they are in their respective words and spoken rapidly would both approach our *j*. The *ll* of *amontillado* (variously like the *li* of *million* and the *y* of *yes*) when pronounced emphatically gives roughly the same result. Thus an apparent identity of sound exists for the untrained ear. (As Poe was taught Italian and Spanish at the same time in 1826 at Charlottesville by Professor Blaettermann, a German, it is quite possible that he was not an expert on pronunciation.)
>
> The implication of Montresor's pun may be understood as the pile of bricks he hastily threw to wall in Fortunato. As the climax of the story is reached, he causes his victim to repeat the word amontillado . . . a final time, as if to assure himself that his subtle and superior wit has been fully appreciated.
>
> (43)

According to Steele, Montresor gets an impression that Fortunato is able to understand the meaning of "Amontillado." If, as Kennedy writes, "for Montresor the drink has been from the outset a secret, figurative reference to death itself and in promising a taste of Amontillado, he has . . . been speaking of Fortunato's destruction" (141), the only way Fortunato may understand Montresor's pun is through devising associations between the name of the wine and Italian words. The name of the wine looks like the past participle of the Spanish verb *amontinallar.* Amontillado, thus, would mean "collected in a pile," "gathered in a mount," or "piled at the mountain." Although in modern Spanish there is no verb *amontinallar* (instead, there is the verb *amontonar*), in Old Spanish there was the verb *amontijar.* This means that it may not be necessary to explain similarities in the pronunciation of related Italian and Spanish verbs. Similarities in Romance languages allow us to believe that regardless of whether Fortunato knew Spanish, in the end of the story, he might realize that he himself is to become amontillado—a pile of bones gathered in a mount in Montresor's crypt.[23]

Whether Fortunato actually understands the reason behind Montresor's terrible vengeance—namely, that he is being punished for his arrogance and for insulting someone who is equal or superior to him—does not impede a successful completion of Montresor's plan. Montresor "punishes" Fortunato "with impunity" and escapes retribution. Moreover, in accordance with his plan, Montresor does not murder Fortunato secretly, but stages a spectacle of execution so that the victim knows who kills him.[24] If Fortunato does not understand why Montresor has decided to kill him, he may believe Montresor is a madman. Typically, some scholars who argue that Montresor is insane turn to the last scene in the story. John Rea, for example, maintains that Montresor's action is "perversity, not revenge. If he had cared about revenge, instead of echoing Fortunato, his last words would have been something about the insult that he says Fortunato has given him" (qtd. in Peithman 174). A careful examination of Montresor's last words, however, provides additional evidence in support of the thesis that the motive for Montresor's murder of Fortunato has been vengeance. The very last words in the story are, "Against the new masonry I re-erected the old rampart of bones. For the half of a century no mortal has disturbed them. *In pace requiescat*!" The sentence "*In pace requiescat*!" ("May he rest in peace") refers to Fortunato. The phrase is used in the Requiem Mass and during Last Rites, when, having listened to a dying person's confession, a priest forgives his/her sins. If Montresor's narration is his last confession, he should look forward to being forgiven and to hearing "*In pace requiescas*!" ("May your soul rest in peace") from his priest. Instead, Montresor maliciously subverts his role as a repentant sinner when he says "*In pace requiescat*!" in regard with Fortunato. Not only does he deprive the poor man of a Catholic's right to the last confession, he is arrogant enough to abuse the formulaic expression used by priests to absolve dying sinners. The fact that Montresor uses this expression for finally pardoning Fortunato highlights his conviction that he has merely avenged himself for the wrong that Fortunato afflicted upon him fifty years ago.

Notes

I would like to thank Steven Taubeneck for discussing portions of this article with me. My special thanks go to the anonymous reviewers of this work whose insightful comments have led to significant improvements of both form and content.

1. Edgar Allan Poe has long enjoyed the reputation of the founder of contemporary detective fiction. In three of his short stories, the detective Chevalier C. Auguste Dupin is the central character. See John Walsh (5, 82) on Poe's role in the development of modern detective fiction.

2. Other scholars who argue that Montresor has failed to commit the perfect crime because he has suffered the pangs of remorse are Thomas Pribek, Walter Stepp, J. Gerald Kennedy, Charles May, and Scott Peeples. Writing a few years after Thompson, Kennedy argues that Montresor's feeling of guilt overtakes his retribution (141-143). Peeples discusses Kennedy's interpretation in detail and supports his reading of "The Cask of Amontillado" (148).

3. This is clear from Montresor's words, "For the half of a century no mortal has disturbed them [the bones]" (854).

4. Peeples agrees with the interpretation of the tale as a deathbed confession (150). William H. Shurr also discusses Thompson's hypothesis regarding Montresor's audience in "The Cask of Amontillado." In support of this hypothesis, Shurr quotes Benjamin Franklin's tale published a few years before Poe's story. In the tale, a Frenchman whose name is Montresor is very ill. His confessor believes Montresor may die soon and suggests he "makes his peace with God." Shurr argues that Franklin's tale is one of the sources for the story by Poe (28-29).

5. The significance of the vengeance theme in "The Cask of Amontillado" cannot be overlooked. David S. Reynolds maintains that the story has biographical resonance with Poe's life: it "reflects Poe's hatred of two prominent New York literary figures, the author Thomas Dunn English and the newspaper editor Hiram Fuller" (93). Reynolds refers to earlier biographical studies of the story by Francis P. Demond and Marie Bonaparte: see Demond (137-146) and Bonaparte (505-506).

6. Much criticism focuses on Poe's use of symbols that enhance psychological portrayal of his characters. In the last decade, however, more studies have explored the immediate historical and social context of Poe's work: e.g., the reading of Poe's "House of Usher" by Leila S. May (387-396).

7. Some commentators suggest that the conflict between Montresor and Fortunato may be part of their blood feud. Such reading, however, cannot account for the fact that Fortunato willingly agrees to go to Montresor's residence to taste wine and talks with Montresor as if they were friends.

8. See a detailed discussion of the Freemasonic elements of Poe's story by Peter J. Sorensen (45-47); cf. Reynolds (99-100).

9. On the origins of the name Montresor, see E. Bruce Kirkham (23).

10. Graham St. John Stott provides a reading of the name "Fortunato" and of Poe's whole story in the light of the interpretation of God and virtue in Calvinism: "Fortunato means fortunate, wealthy, happy, or more generally, because of its derivation from the verb *fortunare,* blessed by the goddess *fortuna,* or random fate. Naturally, to embrace fortuna was unthinkable in the Reformed tradition. Fate was not random" (86). Montresor, according to Stott, is God's agent; he punishes Fortunato for representing ungodly ideas and qualities, the opposite of providence.

11. The motto of the Montresor family may also be translated as "Let no one have insulted me with impunity." Typically, the motto refers to "insult," not "injuries." The Latin verb "lacessere" means to "provoke," "ill-treat," "challenge," "harass," and "bully"; Latin equivalents for the verb "to injure" are "nocere" and "laedere."

12. Commentators have provided insightful interpretations of the Montresors' coat of arms including those who view the Montresors as represented by the serpent and those who argue that it is impossible to decide if the Montresor family is represented by the foot or by the snake. The latter interpretation is used in support of the argument that Poe's story is an exploration in the "circularity of revenge" (Kennedy 143). Peeples writes in this regard, "The Montresor family could be represented by the foot, which crushes its enemies, or the snake, which sinks its fangs into the heel of its adversary. . . . In either case, both the foot and the snake are injured, perhaps fatally (if the snake is poisonous); neither wins" (150). In Peeples' interpretation, the emphasis is on injuries. By contrast, if the Montresors' motto is to be taken into account ("No one insults me with impunity"), the emphasis in interpreting the coat of arms should be on retaliation.

13. Other principal types of sherry are Montilla, Manzanilla, Fino, and Vino de Pasto (Simon 483).

14. Burton R. Pollin refers to several sources on *Amontillado*: "For evidence that the name *amontillado* was applied to a fine, dry sherry in the 1840's see Richard Ford, *Gatherings from Spain* (London, 1906), chap. xiv, which concerns the production of sherry wines; the book dates from

1846, being revised from *The Handbook for Travellers in Spain* (London, 1845)" (Pollin 240-241). Pollin also refers to the book by Walter James: *Wine: A Brief Encyclopedia* (New York, 1960): 8.

15. A popular tourist destination, Italy attracted many international tourists from across Europe and North America throughout the nineteenth century especially during carnivals. The last chapters of *Smoke* (1867) by Ivan Turgenev are set during the carnival in Venice in the second half of the nineteenth century.

16. Although Montresor is a French name, the story is set in Italy. This is clear from the sentences, "He prided himself on his connoisseurship in wine. Few Italians have the true virtuoso spirit" (848). Other details that also testify to an Italian setting are "palazzo," "Italian vintages," and Italian names of Fortunato and Luchesi. These details help to counter the argument by Burton R. Pollin, Stanley J. Kozikowski, and Richard P. Benton, who maintain that the setting of the tale may be French. See Pollin (31-35), Kozikowski (269-277), and Benton (19-25).

17. Several commentators interpret the story as a tale about the evils of excessive drinking. Pollin mentions "self-destructive drunkenness" (25) as the basic idea that Poe borrowed from Hugo. According to Arthur Hobson Quinn, Fortunato's "craving for the wine has led him to his doom" (500). Jeffrey Meyers presents a similar argument: "There is a considerable amount of drinking in Poe's stories. He usually describes its negative effects, with a moral disapproval that suggests he shared contemporary attitudes and was passing judgment on his own disreputable behavior. In one story a victim is lured by the offer of fine Sherry and then permanently sealed up in a catacomb filled with Amontillado" (87). It is hard to believe that Fortunato, a wealthy and powerful man, would be "lured" by the offer of alcohol from his less powerful countryman. Fortunato follows Montresor in order to show his connoisseurship of wines.

18. In "Forms of Time and Chronotope in the Novel," Mikhail Bakhtin discusses the difference between the use of carnival imagery during the Renaissance and by authors of the later period (such as Poe). In "The Cask of Amontillado," the tropes of carnival are no longer used for asserting the "all-encompassing whole of triumphant life"; rather, they create "the denuded, sterile, and, therefore, oppressive contrasts" (199-200). Since Poe's characters, one a representative of the old aristocracy and the other a new "aristocrat," are most likely class enemies of the capitalist period, perception of the carnival by Poe's protagonist who feels himself as an outsider among the rising bourgeoisie cannot be the same as the carnival consciousness in Rabelais' *Gargantua and Pantagruel* (1532-1552), which Bakhtin discusses in *Rabelais and His World.*

19. A fool was always an important character in carnival performances. Fortunato, however, was not "engaged," and this gave Montresor a chance to arrange a special "performance" for the *unlucky* fool.

20. Used in the story in its original sense, the word "catacombs" refers to a subterranean cemetery of galleries with recesses for tombs.

21. Reynolds also notes that De Grâve is a pun that points to Fortunato's fate (97).

22. *Ad + montis* may mean "towards a mount."

23. The title of Poe's story may be read as a metaphor. One of the readers of this paper has drawn my attention to the fact that the word "cask" may be interpreted as part of the pun that points out to Fortunato's death. According to *OED,* in the past the word "cask" could mean "casket." In turn, in the nineteenth-century America the word "casket" began to be used in the meaning of "coffin" (*OED,* 941). If the word "cask" in Poe's story is to be associated with a coffin and if Amontillado is a pun on Fortunato's terrible death, then the title "The Cask of Amontillado" may in fact stand for "The Casket of Fortunato."

24. The mask that Montresor is wearing highlights the association of the murder with execution. Executioners used to wear masks so that relatives or friends of the condemned could not find them.

Works Cited

Adorno, Theodor. *Aesthetic Theory.* Trans. C. Lenhardt. London: Routledge and Kegan Paul, 1984.

Bakhtin, Mikhail. "Forms of Time and Chronotope in the Novel." *The Dialogic Imagination.* By Mikhail Bakhtin. Trans. Caryl Emerson and Michael Holquist. Austin: University of Texas Press, 1996. 84-259.

———. *Rabelais and His World.* Trans. Helene Iswolsky. Bloomington: Indiana University Press, 1984.

Barnhart, Clarence L., ed. *The New Century Cyclopedia of Names.* New York: Appleton-Century-Crofts, Inc., 1954.

Benton, Richard P. "Poe's 'The Cask of Amontillado': Its Cultural and Historical Backgrounds." *Poe Studies* 29.1 (June 1996): 19-27.

Bonaparte, Marie. *The Life and Works of Edgar Allan Poe: A Psycho-Analytic Interpretation.* London: Hogarth, 1971.

Davidson, Edward Hutchins. *Poe, A Critical Study.* Cambridge: Harvard University Press, 1957.

Demond, Francis P. "'The Cask of Amontillado' and the War of the Literati." *Modern Language Quarterly* 15 (1954): 137-146.

Fletcher, Richard M. *The Stylistic Development of Edgar Allan Poe.* The Hague: Mouton, 1973.

Halliburton, David. *Edgar Allan Poe: A Phenomenological View.* Princeton: Princeton University Press, 1973.

Hammond, J. R. *An Edgar Allan Poe Companion: A Guide to the Short Stories, Romances, and Essays.* London: Macmillan, 1981.

Hoffman, Daniel. *Poe Poe Poe Poe Poe Poe Poe.* Garden City, NY: Doubleday, 1972.

Kennedy, J. Gerald. *Poe, Death, and the Life of Writing.* New Haven: Yale University Press, 1987.

Kirkham, E. Bruce. "Poe's 'Cask of Amontillado' and John Montresor." *Poe Studies* 20.1 (June 1987): 23.

Kozikowski, Stanley J. "A Reconsideration of Poe's 'The Cask of Amontillado.'" *American Transcendental Quarterly* 49 (Summer 1978): 269-280.

Levine, Stuart. *Edgar Poe: Seer and Craftsman.* Deland, FL: Everett/Edwards, 1972.

May, Charles. *Edgar Allan Poe: A Study of the Short Fiction.* Boston: Twayne, 1991.

May, Leila S. "Sympathies of a Scarcely Intelligible Nature: The Brother-Sister Bond in Poe's 'Fall of the House of Usher.'" *Studies in Short Fiction* 30 (1993): 387-396.

Meyers, Jeffrey. *Edgar Allan Poe: His Life and Legacy.* New York: Charles Scribner's Sons, 1992.

The Oxford English Dictionary. 2nd ed. Ed. J. A. Simpson and E. S. C. Weiner. Oxford: Clarendon Press, 1989.

Peeples, Scott. *Edgar Allan Poe Revisited.* New York: Twayne, 1998.

Peithman, Stephen. "The Cask of Amontillado." *The Annotated Tales of Edgar Allan Poe.* Ed. Stephen Peithman. Garden City, NY: Doubleday and Co., Inc., 1981. 168-174.

Poe, Edgar Allan. "The Cask of Amontillado." *Poetry and Tales.* By Edgar Allan Poe. New York: The Library of America, 1984. 848-854.

———. "The Philosophy of Composition." *Poe's Poetry and Essays.* Introduction by Andrew Lang. New York: E. P. Dutton and Co., Inc., 1955. 163-177.

Pollin, Burton R. "*Notre-Dame de Paris* in Two of the Tales." *Discoveries in Poe.* Notre Dame: University of Notre Dame Press, 1970. 24-38.

Pribek, Thomas. "The Serpent and the Heel." *Poe Studies* 20.1 (June 1987): 22-23.

Quinn, Arthur Hobson. *Edgar Allan Poe: A Critical Biography.* London: Appleton Century Co., 1992.

Rahn, B. J. "Seeley Regester: America's First Detective Novelist." *The Sleuth and the Scholar: Origins, Evolution, and Current Trends in Detective Fiction.* Ed. Barbara A. Rader and Howard G. Zattler. Contributions to the Study of Popular Culture Series. No. 19. New York: Greenwood Press, 1988. 47-61.

Reynolds, David S. "Poe's Art of Transformation: 'The Cask of Amontillado' in Its Cultural Context." *New Essays on Poe's Major Tales.* Ed. Kenneth Silverman. New York: Cambridge University Press, 1993. 93-113.

Shurr, William H. "Montresor's Audience in 'The Cask of Amontillado.'" *Poe Studies* 10.1 (June 1977): 28-29.

Simon, Andre Louis. "Sherry." *Chambers's Encyclopaedia.* New Revised Edition. Vol. XII. Oxford: Pergamon Press, 1966. 482-483.

Sorensen, Peter J. "William Morgan, Freemasonry, and 'The Cask of Amontillado.'" *Poe Studies* 22.2 (December 1989): 45-47.

Steele, Charles W. "Poe's 'The Cask of Amontillado.'" *Explicator* 18.7 (April 1960): 43.

Stepp, Walter. "The Ironic Double in Poe's 'Cask of Amontillado.'" *Studies in Short Fiction* 13 (1976): 447-453.

Stott, Graham St. John. "Poe's 'The Cask of Amontillado.'" *Explicator* 62.2 (Winter 2004): 85-89.

Thompson, G. R. *Poe's Fiction: Romantic Irony in the Gothic Tales.* Madison: University of Wisconsin Press, 1973.

Todorov, Tzvetan. "Some Approaches to Russian Formalism." *Russian Formalism: A Collection of Articles and Texts in Translation.* Ed. Stephen Bann and John E. Bowlt. New York: Barnes & Noble Books, 1973. 6-19.

Wagenknecht, Edward. *Edgar Allan Poe: The Man Behind the Legend.* New York: Oxford University Press, 1963.

Walsh, John. *Poe the Detective: The Curious Circumstances Behind "The Mystery of Marie Roget."* New Brunswick: Rutgers University Press, 1968.

James Berkley (essay date 2004)

SOURCE: Berkley, James. "Post-Human Mimesis and the Debunked Machine: Reading Environmental Appropriation in Poe's 'Maelzel's Chess-Player' and 'The Man That Was Used Up.'" *Comparative Literature Studies* 41, no. 3 (2004): 356-76.

[*In the following essay, Berkley outlines the concept of technological dehumanization in the short story "The*

Man That Was Used Up" and in Poe's essay "Maelzel's Chess-Player," highlighting the aesthetic notion of the sublime in both works.]

The cultural and academic debates about the status of the human subject in an increasingly technological world may seem to have cooled slightly since the *fin-de-siècle* ferment of the 1990s, a time when 1980s hypotheses about cyberspace, cyborgs, and non-human intelligence could seem to be increasingly on the verge of realization.[1] Nonetheless, in these first years of the twenty-first century, it has come to be increasingly accepted that, in some meaningful way, we are now in fact living in the age of the "post-human" subject. This acceptance hardly implies unanimity, for there are still major disagreements about just what this might mean: for example, would the term "post-human" serve mostly to describe a dominant ideological configuration, or does it instead describe a realm of practical possibility and lived experience in technologically advanced, late-capitalist societies? And in either of these cases, would this post-human condition be something to be welcomed as liberating and enlightening, or to be defended against as dangerous and illusion-fostering?

These are some of the issues that N. Katherine Hayles took on in her 1999 study, *How We Became Posthuman.* There, Hayles examined the rise of the post-human view of subjectivity and embodiment as a successor to the bounded and centered subject of liberal humanism, a formation that the intellectual historian C. B. Macpherson had analyzed through the rubric of "possessive individualism." In Hayles's view, the emergence of the post-human subject had replaced the liberal emphasis upon possessive individualism with the centrality of information and computation: the result was a new subject seen to be "seamlessly articulated with intelligent machines" (34). As she wrote, this post-human subject typically presented itself as an "amalgam, a collection of heterogeneous components, a material-informational entity whose boundaries under[went] continuous construction and reconstruction" (3). This successor vision of subjectivity hence implied a quite different relationship between organism and environment than had the subject of liberal humanism. In Hayles's words again, the "posthuman future of humanity" tended to be invoked in terms that "implied not only a coupling with intelligent machines, but a coupling so intense and multifaceted that it [was] no longer possible to distinguish meaningfully between the biological organism and the information circuits in which the organism is enmeshed" (35).

In this essay, I would like to use Hayles's observations about the status of environmental relatedness in the post-human subject as a starting point for a rather different kind of analysis than the one she has offered in *How We Became Posthuman.* For one, I would like to turn back to the pre-cybernetic era of the nineteenth century to examine a particular version of post-human subjectivity—and with it, an overturning of the subject of liberal humanism—that we can already see at work in the writings of Edgar Allan Poe, an author whose influence upon multiple streams of nineteenth- and twentieth-century aesthetics, from decadence to science fiction, has played a major role in determining the contours of the contemporary imagination of the post-human subject. To be sure, examining such a "prehistory of the post-human" is a task that has already been occupying many critics: perhaps the most fitting example in this context is the recent work of Klaus Benesch, whose *Romantic Cyborgs* offers to read authors of the American Renaissance, and Poe specifically, as dedicated to investigating "imaginary zones of contact between the human and the technological" in the context of a rapidly modernizing society (26).[2]

In taking up a similar cause, my own emphasis will lie on how this coupling between subjects and technological environments is in itself a primary determinant of the "post-ness" of the post-human subject. That is, as Hayles's own work has suggested at certain junctures, the post-human condition we see in Poe's oeuvre is not simply a matter of temporal or historical succession, the passage from one "epoch" of subjectivity to another, but also a matter of spatiotemporal relations between subjects and environments that get played out simultaneously in narrative and phenomenological form. This will lead me to connect Poe's vision of post-human subjectivity with two topics in Western intellectual history that we might see as re-emerging in new ways in the post-human imagination from the nineteenth century down to our own day: these are mimesis and the sublime, both of which entail a relationship between self and alterity that, like the post-human, offer the possibility of transcending the conventional limits of the individualized human subject. What is peculiar in Poe's case, and what will animate much of my discussion here, is how this vision of transcendent post-humanism comes to be powerfully tied to a logic of what I shall term "mimetic debunking," whereby an original site of post-human transcendence situated within a textual space is exposed so that its wonder can be appropriated and rearticulated at the level of the narration itself.

Sublimity, Mimesis, and Poe-etic Usurpation

Before turning to Poe directly, and in particular to two of his texts that reflect most compellingly upon post-human embodiment—his 1836 essay "Maelzel's

Chess-Player" and his 1839 tale **"The Man That Was Used Up"**—I would like to offer some additional background on the intellectual contexts that inform this analysis. If we take a "long view" of Western discourses of subjectivity and embodiment, contemporary ideas of post-human subjectivity might be seen as emerging from a complex prehistory that joins a variety of sites where the centered, self-contained individual of Western humanism opens onto its broader environment, and where the processes that accomplish this tend to reveal a characteristic mixture of transcendence and anxiety. As Hayles herself notes in *How We Became Posthuman,* the "shift from the human to the posthuman both evokes terror and excites pleasure" (4). Yet this of course, as Hayles is likely aware, is the same affective profile that has long been associated with the sublime, from the first-century-A.D. treatise of Longinus down to Romantic reformulations of the sublime in eighteenth-century authors such as Burke and Kant. In Burke's 1757 *Philosophical Enquiry into the Origin of Our Ideas of the Sublime and Beautiful,* for example, Burke located the sublime in the peculiar admixture of "terror" and "delight" that occurs in the face of potentially annihilating experiences from whose violence we are spared.

If the discourses of the sublime typically invoke intense forms of relation between subjects and environments—we might think here of Percy Shelley's 1816 poem on the awesome power of Mont Blanc, with its "everlasting universe of things" that "flow through the mind"—one of the rhetorical hallmarks of the sublime has also been its association with the transcendence of the human. It is thus appropriate that, at nearly the same time, Mary Shelley composed a fiction that set the transcendence-seeking Victor Frankenstein and his post-human creature in this same alpine environment, one seen as simultaneously overwhelming and uplifting. Indeed, long before the Romantics, Longinus's *On the Sublime* (in Greek, *Peri Hypsos* or "On Height") had argued that the sublime was powered by a "passion for all that is greater [or] more divine than ourselves," and that this passion essentially worked to transport the soul "above the human" (147). To introduce the concept of the Romantic sublime, one of the best modern-day commentators on the issues even began on this very topic: "The essential claim of the sublime," wrote Thomas Weiskel, "is that man can, in feeling and in speech, transcend the human" (3). Below, I want to take up the question of how Poe's handling of technological wonder served to realign discourses of the sublime so as to contemplate technical environments as opposed to strictly natural or rhetorical ones: in texts such as "Maelzel's Chess-Player" and **"The Man That Was Used Up,"** the sublime thus becomes reconfigured as an encounter with technical alterity as opposed to a more conventional encounter with natural or textual alterity. Of course, to posit such a thing as a "technological sublime"[3] is not exactly a new idea: whether articulated in just these terms or not, variants of this idea are present in much writing about nascent cyberculture and post-human embodiment. But my own claim is somewhat more specific, for in Poe and in many of his descendents, the relationship between post-human subjectivity and the sublime is bound up with another site in Western philosophy and aesthetics that has probed the connections between humanness, environmentality, and transcendence. As I have suggested above, this site can be found in discourses of imitation and mimesis.

"Becoming post-human," in other words, can also be seen as a function of mimetic behavior, of the imitative dynamics between individuals and their environments that have occupied critical thinkers from Plato down to the twentieth-century Frankfurt School, dynamics that have been revisited in new ways by contemporary theorists of subject-forming performativity such as Judith Butler.[4] In his famous 1933 essay "On the Mimetic Faculty," Walter Benjamin asked whether modernity encouraged the disappearance of the human power for generating and recognizing "similarities" or instead was working to ensure this faculty's "transformation": if children typically "play[ed] at being [. . .] a windmill [or] a train," Benjamin speculated, then perhaps some residue of this faculty could be awakened in adults by modern life itself, and perhaps even in liberating and revolutionary ways (333). But Benjamin's hypotheses in "On the Mimetic Faculty" deserve to be seen as part of a long tradition of anthropological speculation about the role of mimetic behavior. Indeed, one way of viewing the history of mimesis in Western society is in terms of the ambivalence that has long surrounded attempts to understand the place of imitation in human subjectivity: does mimesis create human subjects, or does it instead in some important sense work to *un*-make them? Plato's warnings against hyperbolic and otherwise unpoliced imitation in his *Republic* were in many ways directed against mimesis's destructive and post-humanizing tendencies: in the viewpoint he there places in the mouth of Socrates, there existed a slippery slope from literary imitation to the wanton and chaos-producing mimicry of "thunder, the noises of winds, hailstorms, axels and pulleys, the voices of trumpets [. . .] even the sounds of dogs, sheep, and birds."[5] (Indeed, Plato's position, which already begins to raise the question of humans imitating their technical world, is perhaps the most famous and influential argument about the "bad" side of post-human mimesis.) On the other hand, Aristotle's *Poetics* held up imitation as a quintessentially human trait, one that not only defined the human species as such but that also underwrote the "delight" experienced in aesthetic activity and contemplation.

The conventional opposition that is drawn between Plato's and Aristotle's views of mimetic behavior can appear to provide two basic alternatives: Plato depicts a dangerous post-humanizing mimesis that must be shunned in favor of individuality and rational intellection, and Aristotle depicts an aesthetic mimesis that, against Plato, is practically equated with the human itself. Yet in a manner that has a certain resonance with the approach of modern theorists such as Benjamin and Butler, I would propose that we might see discourses of the sublime as providing a fascinating "third way" with regard to the anthropological status of mimesis. For beginning with Longinus, pre-Kantian accounts of the sublime often propose a mimetic relationship between self and environment as a pathway to post-human transcendence, not in the destructive form envisioned by Plato but in the form of a pleasure that is at once cognitive and embodied, and that is likewise simultaneously existential and aesthetic.[6]

Longinus's *On the Sublime,* for example, exchanged Plato's anxieties over mimetic dehumanization for an enthusiastic theory of mimetic *ekstasis* that has much in common with the rhetoric of post-human transcendence achieved through the human organism's willing subjection to alterity. In Longinus's elusively nonlinear and citational account, if the sublime "entrances" and "transports" the subject by "exerting [an] irresistible force and mastery," it is because the experience of an overwhelming exterior force can be converted into an internal force, and hence into a source of outward expression and "vaunting joy" (107). As the critic Neil Hertz has written, the Longinian sublime is essentially powered by such hidden "transfers of power" between author and reader, precursor and poet, the outside world and the sensing body (6).[7] But we can also see these transfers as a form of mimetic appropriation: if our response to the sublime is one of "proud exaltation," this, as Longinus notes, is because we typically feel "as if we [ourselves] had produced what we heard" (107). The sublime arises, that is, when a passive reception of an exterior force can be, through a kind of conversion or "turning" that we might liken to performative interpellation, experienced as an active articulation of force from within the subject.[8]

From this perspective, both the experience and the articulation of the sublime occur as a kind of strategic, ambivalently submissive mimesis: an overwhelming alterity is encountered, experienced potentially as violence, yet finally mimicked in a performative (and identificatory) re-articulation of subjective mastery—albeit a mastery that is always complexly bound up with an initial, self-abandoning subjection *to* authority.[9] For the critic Jonathan Lamb, the mimetic power dynamics celebrated in *On the Sublime* can thus work to destabilize previously existing orders of aesthetics and politics as much as to affirm them: they are part of what Lamb calls the Longinian "practice of mastery," a set of rhetorical and behavioral strategies whose primary motif he identifies as *usurpation.* "The Longinian sublime," he writes, "is a description of techniques of usurpation that perpetually overflow into paralogical performance," and its central maneuver is hence akin to "converting the servitude of reading into the mastery of writing" (Lamb 551, 553).[10]

So what does all this have to do with Poe, and with Poe's vision of post-human transcendence? Poe, I would claim, presents these Longinian "transfers of power" between organisms and their technical environments—as well as between authors and their textual environments—in such a way as to bring together mimesis, sublimity, and post-human subjectivity into a dense conceptual nexus. In both the non-fictional "Maelzel's Chess-Player" and the fictional **"The Man That Was Used Up,"** two texts that authors such as Benesch have singled out as crucial examples of Poe's imagination of human-machine hybridity, we see similar techniques of mimetic "usurpation." In each, Poe depicts the encounter with post-human technicity—in one case a fraudulent, human-inhabited automaton passing itself off as a machine, in another a fraudulent, prosthesis-enabled cyborg passing itself off as a human—as a story of debunking and mimetic reappropriation that allows the site of post-human wonder to be shuttled from one location to another. Following Lamb, we might say that in each, a passive or "readerly" account of post-human mimesis finds itself transformed into an active or "writerly" one. Tracing these dynamics of mimetic debunking can help to join Poe's investment in "the cultural logic of the hoax"[11] to issues in aesthetic theory; at the same time, they can also allow us to see the ways in which Poe viewed the technological world—and indeed, the technological sublime—through a lens of mimesis, debunking, and appropriation. For finally, in both "Maelzel's Chess-Player" and **"The Man That Was Used Up,"** Poe articulates a notion of the technological sublime, and of post-human subjectivity more generally, that is not static but dynamic, as the wondrous power of the mimetic device is mimetically "translated" into the wondrous power of the mimetic author and the mimetic text.

It should be relatively uncontroversial today to claim Poe as one of the first modern authors of the post-human condition, a claim that one might even derive from Theodor Adorno's description of Poe, along with

Baudelaire, as one of literature's "first technocrats" (133). Indeed, Adorno viewed the technocratic aesthetics that Poe and Baudelaire bequeathed to the twentieth century as grounded in an ambivalent form of mimetic behavior that was directed toward modernity itself. In his *Aesthetic Theory,* Adorno explained this as a paradoxical, last-ditch strategy of the artist trying to cope with a world of increasing rationalization and commodification: "Modern works," he wrote, "relinquish themselves mimetically to reification, their principle of death" (133). The simultaneous debunking and assimilation seen in "Maelzel's Chess-Player" and **"The Man That Was Used Up"** can be seen as stemming from just such a mimetic "relinquishing" to reification. Coming to artistic maturity in the 1830s and 1840s, Poe is perhaps the first great author of reification and mechanical reproduction, and certainly among the first of our modern masters who used his aesthetics to reflect upon the influence of a rapidly changing, technologically mediated lifeworld upon the human subject.[12]

How then do these 1830s texts by Poe invoke the post-human subject, and how does the post-human conjunction of bodies and machines in these texts relate to mimetic behavior? "Maelzel's Chess-Player" and **"The Man That Was Used Up,"** we should first note, present us with curiously analogous scenarios: in each, the transcendent authority of a bodily, cyborg-like "other" in the cultural landscape is debunked yet simultaneously appropriated, mimetically "taken up" both by the narrating subject and by the text itself. The theme of the post-human figures in these texts on a multiplicity of levels, but the element I wish to stress here is the thoroughly mimetic character of Poe's vision of the post-human. On the one hand, both "Maelzel's Chess-Player" and **"The Man That Was Used Up"** show Poe depicting worlds in which hybrid forms of post-human subjectivity have been constituted through the use of imitation to produce technical wonders: in an important sense, the authoritative technological objects in these texts have themselves been built up through processes of imitation. Yet beyond this, the mimetic basis of technical wonder in these texts finds itself re-enacted through the texts' own (and the narrators' own) appropriation of these forms of wondrous authority, a process that yields aesthetic "meta-imitations" that could be said to reveal a *mise-en-abyme* of technological mimesis itself. If, in Benesch's apt formulation, Poe sought to "redefine authorship under conditions of modern technology," suggesting that the artist must "adapt to these new conditions [rather than] resist them," these texts tend to frame this adaptation through strategies of assimilative mimesis (104).

These dynamics are perhaps best understood if we see them as bound up with the mimetic, appropriative logic that we saw above emerging from the traditional aesthetics of the sublime. Re-reading aesthetic theory through technological object relations, Poe envisions scenarios in which the sublime authority of the technological object—of machines that are already based on a kind of performative, sublime mimesis—ends up being taken over, usurped as it were, by the authority of narrating agents and texts.

The Turk and the General: Technical Wonder between Sublimity and Hoax

It will be helpful to review some details from these texts before undertaking an analysis of how post-human mimesis functions within them. "Maelzel's Chess-Player" is Poe's curious 1836 essay that, on the surface at least, claims merely to debunk an astounding chess-playing "automaton" that toured Europe and America during the late eighteenth and early nineteenth centuries—a robotic, larger than life-sized, turbaned "Turk" seated at a machine-filled cabinet that thrilled audiences with its expert playing.[13] **"The Man That Was Used Up,"** meanwhile, is the equally curious, burlesque-style 1839 fiction that debunks technological wonder in a rather different direction: here, an increasingly exasperated narrator tracks down the mysterious and legendary General John A. B. C. Smith of the "Kickapoo and Bugaboo Indian Campaigns," finally exposing him as, essentially, a cyborg who has been rebuilt out of prosthetic commodities.

That these are both tales of debunking should be clear enough—debunking being a favored mode of Poe's for a complex of reasons that complicate any easy boundaries between the psychological, the pathological, and the aesthetic.[14] But if all debunking involves a certain (partly fantasized) relationship to authority, these scenarios bear this out in a very specific sense: both texts hinge upon a simultaneously embodied and textual response to the emergence of *technological authority,* to both its threats and its pleasures. Both revolve, that is, around the narrating agency's confrontation with technological assemblages of seemingly unlimited and inexplicable power, a confrontation in which the wondrousness of a seemingly all-powerful, sublime object is obsessively researched and ultimately dispelled. In their epistemological compulsion to demystify, these texts thus form part of the late-1830s genesis of Poe's later detective stories.[15] But we also need to go somewhat further: in each case, this dynamic does not end with mere debunking; instead, each text hinges upon a "sublime transfer" that is enacted through the power of mimesis. That is, while each of these wondrous objects is exposed as a kind of mimetic fraud, the erstwhile authority of the fraudulent object is ultimately "incorporated" into the text's narrative voice and, more "generally," into the authority of a text that has been reconceived as a technical device in its own right.

This is, I think, a strategy that we can see as characteristic of Poe's post-human object relations—and for Poe, as Stephen Rachman has pointed out, object relations always include textual relations as well.[16] In what follows, I wish to lay out how these dynamics work in these two texts in detail, and how we might see them as grounded in the aesthetic logic of the sublime as it comes down from Longinus to Romanticism—a logic that Poe himself appropriates, radicalizes, and literalizes in his treatment of technological wonder. To do this, however, we should perhaps start with the texts' primary objects themselves before turning to the larger dynamic at hand.

Who exactly are the Turk and the General? Or, perhaps more fittingly, *what* are they? The objects of investigation in these texts can be profitably viewed in terms of two indigenous—and to some extent, competing—logics of the American nineteenth century. On the one hand, they participate in the rhetorical tradition that Leo Marx identified as that of the "technological sublime," as seen in discourses that celebrated the awe-inspiring wonder of technological achievement and progress in mid-nineteenth century society. On the other hand, they are also bound up with a logic that throws the status of the sublime technological object into question: this is a logic that Jonathan Elmer, in adapting from Neil Harris's work on P. T. Barnum, has analyzed as that of the "Barnumesque object."[17] On the surface, the technological sublime is the more straightforward of these: writers such as Leo Marx and David Nye have analyzed it as the ecstatic human response to nineteenth-century technological progress, a response where the wonder previously reserved for the natural world found itself transferred to emerging objects of the technological landscape, such as railroads, bridges, or electricity.[18] The Barnumesque object, however, is, to draw on Elmer's juxtaposition of Poe and P. T. Barnum, inherently more ambivalent and volatile: as part of what Elmer has described as Poe's "cultural logic of the hoax," the Barnumesque object is exactly *not* what it pretends to be—its pleasure is wrapped up in the very possibility of its deceptiveness, and in the promise that its inner workings might be revealed. The Barnumesque object, in other words, always carries suspended within it the possibility of its own exposure as fraud. In Elmer's subtle analysis, this possibility is shown to be bound up with a masochistic pleasure at being the "dupe" of authoritative objects and discourses, a pleasure that nonetheless manages to paradoxically underwrite the formation of the democratic subject within mass culture (187).

Of course, what is perhaps most striking in "Maelzel's Chess-Player" and **"The Man That Was Used Up,"** is how these texts are ostensibly—at their most superficial level—about *not* being duped at all. Instead, they are fundamentally tales of exposure, in which a sublime object in the contemporary environment is first reduced to the status of a Barnumesque object, and in which this Barnumesque object is in turn fully stripped of its power to deceive. Where duping reenters the picture, however, is when we realize that the sublime authority (as well as the sublime mimesis) of the technological object never really goes away: instead, it finds itself re-located in the narration itself, which usurps these Barnumesque qualities and subjects the text's reader to a secondary and more subtle form of hoaxing—and, I might add, to a secondary form of subjection to authority, now embodied in textual form. As we shall see, both texts achieve this transfer of power through forms of mimicry: in them, the post-human condition of sublime technological mimesis becomes mimetically contagious, and this contagiousness is exploited so as to strategically shift the site of post-human wonder from one location to another.

How might such shifts, such transfers, be understood as inherent to the technological sublime? If this seems initially hard to conceive, it is perhaps because writing on the sublime in nineteenth-century America, and particularly on the so-called technological sublime, can sometimes present a reified picture of what the sublime is, and even of how a writer such as Poe conceived it. To be sure, the sublime is frequently about "wondrous objects," but in the aesthetic tradition in which Poe was schooled, and whose contours we have briefly examined above, the sublime is more accurately about object *relations* between a living body and its environment.[19]

From all evidence, Poe was well-read in both Longinus and Burke, and this kind of usurping, assimilating, identification is everywhere present in his texts when he tackles the question of the sublime—often to the point of usurping the words of Burke and Longinus himself. In his 1836 essay on Defoe's *Robinson Crusoe,* for example, Poe performatively echoes the phrasing of Longinus's *On the Sublime* when he notes that the pleasure of reading *Crusoe* is such that "we close the book, and are quite satisfied that we could have written as well ourselves!"[20] Likewise, in his essays of the later 1830s and the mid-1840s (the era of the so-called "Longfellow War"), Poe began to treat appropriation and plagiarism as the natural results of sublime aesthetic rapture: since the poetic consciousness longs to assimilate external beauty into the self, as Poe claimed in his exchange with the pseudonymous "Outis" in 1845, this can go so far as to make plagiarism the ultimate form of aesthetic receptivity. (He would thus hold that "the liability to accidents of [plagiaristic] character is in the direct ration of the poetic sentiment—of the susceptibility to the poetic impression," and that "all literary history demonstrates that, for the most frequent and palpable plagiarisms, we must search the works of the most eminent poets.")[21] The poetic sentiment itself (a concept closely aligned with, if not always equivalent to, the sublime in Poe's writings, and often grounded in a Longinian rhetoric of the "elevation of the soul") thus becomes recast as a mediating transfer of authorship, and as a transfer of power from one locus to another.[22]

Miming the Master: Reading Poe's Techno-Textual Environments[23]

On one level, "Maelzel's Chess-Player" and **"The Man That Was Used Up"** hold up uncanny mirror images to one another. In the first text, the ostensible automaton's machinic sublimity is debunked as a merely human deception; in the second, the ostensibly human sublimity of General John A. B. C. Smith is debunked as a machinic, cyborgian deception. The underlying logics pervading the texts, however, are roughly the same, and are articulated in similar ways from the very beginning of each. Both texts thus begin by dwelling upon the wondrousness of their primary objects. In "Maelzel," we are told that "no exhibition of the kind has ever elicited so general attention as the Chess-Player of Maelzel"; the essay's narrator establishes the automaton as an "object of intense curiosity" that has everywhere led "men of mechanical genius" to pronounce it "beyond comparison, the most astonishing of the inventions of mankind" (Poe 6). (I purposively say "narrator" here and not simply Poe himself, for there is an element of narrative performativity even in the voice of what poses as simple journalistic investigation.) In **"The Man That Was Used Up,"** the text likewise begins with the wonder that emanates from a sublime human object, in a set of idealized, Petrarchan descriptions that seem something of a burlesque upon Poe's earlier 1838 tale **"Ligeia."**[24] Beginning with the admission that he "cannot just now remember when or where I first made the acquaintance of that truly fine-looking fellow, Brevet Brigadier General John A. B. C. Smith," the narrator goes on to catalog the General's astounding qualities:

> There was something as it were, remarkable—yes, remarkable—although this is but a feeble term to express my full meaning—about the entire individuality of the personage in question. He was, perhaps, six feet in height, and of a presence singularly commanding. There was an air distingué pervading the whole man, which spoke of high breeding, and hinted at high birth.
>
> (378)

This sort of description soon moves into a parodic and fetishistic enumeration of the sublime parts that make up the General's body: his whiskers, his teeth, his *tibula* and *os femoris,* and so forth. (Significantly, the narrator reinforces the uncanniness of the General's appearance by noting in him the same "rectangular" comportment that the Poe of "Maelzel" saw as giving away the deception of the chess-playing automaton [380].) Of course, the General's sublime construction ultimately turns out to be both more and less than the sum of its parts: after a lengthy and frustrating investigation, the narrator finally encounters the General "en toilette" and shockingly discovers that he is essentially a bundle of commodities, a "man of parts"—his entire body having been physically "used up" in the Indian wars, he must daily reconstruct his sublime presence using devices bought from Philadelphia purveyors of the prosthetic.

These texts' debunking encounters with post-human sublimity are enacted in two apparently different ways that are nonetheless structurally similar. "Maelzel's Chess-Player" achieves this primarily by becoming a veiled meditation on plagiarism, one of Poe's favorite themes. In a sense of course, an automaton already is a plagiarism: definitionally, it is a mechanical imitation of life, and such a defining of automata recurs frequently throughout the "Maelzel" essay. Poe's charge, however, might be summed up as the claim that the automaton is really a *plagiarized automaton*: while passing itself off as a "real imitation," it is actually a fake one. (As the text's narrating voice insists repeatedly throughout the essay, the Turk cannot be a "pure machine," and must thus be "regulated by *mind,* and by nothing else" [11].) But beyond this central claim, themes of imitation, plagiarism, and mimicry also circulate throughout the essay in some surprising ways. In fact, it has long been known that several paragraphs of this essay are *themselves* plagiaristic in nature: in them, Poe essentially purloins materials from Sir David Brewster's highly popular *Letters on Natural Magic: As Addressed to Sir Walter Scott,* a book of wonders that contained an entire section on automatons, and that contained a lengthy discussion—along with a more quotidian debunking—of the Chess-playing Turk. Thus, from an early point in the essay, Poe's discussion of mimetic wonder is essentially enacting its own imitation of an authoritative textual precursor.

As much as Poe's detractors have tended to oversimplify matters in this arena, it is important not to simply judge such plagiarism as a quirk or a moral lapse on Poe's part. For the second half of the "Maelzel" essay—comprised of a more rigorous, itself quite mechanically "rectangular" deduction of the Turk's status as hoax—continues to show how deeply plagiaristic behavior is really the key issue here. In an earlier essay, John Tresch has hinted at the mimetic plagiarism of mechanicity that underwrites the whole essay, noting that "Poe's claim to originality in 'Maelzel' is, paradoxically, the unveiling of the human agent inside the automaton in a mechanical fashion" (288). Yet this is perhaps not so much paradox as it is simply mimesis at work; indeed, performative transfers of both behavioral and cognitive states are what furnish the organizing logic for the essay's second half. Increasingly, these are put in terms of what we might call the *plagiarism of gesture,* and in terms of forms of embodied mimetic behavior that—evidenced particularly in the Turk's odd comportment—become central to outwitting both the automaton and its inventor. (It is on this front that "Maelzel" most strongly reveals itself as the prototype of Dupin's analytical techniques in the detective tales.)

Two separate realms of gesture are shown at work in this second half: belonging respectively to the narrator-investigator and the Turk-automaton, they are essentially locked in combat with one another as are players in a chess match. On the one hand, the narrator proposes that, to solve the riddle of the automaton, he must essentially "think his way into the machine"—into the corporeal being of the object and, by extension, into the mind of its inventor. But such a project of detection also leads to a particularly thorny question regarding the gestures performed by the Turk: namely, what is the difference between *true* machineness (always already a question of mimetic performativity when it comes to automata) and the mere imitative *performance* of machineness? Here, the narrator-investigator adopts a form of analysis that is equal parts phenomenology and the psychology of deception, telling us that the awkward, "rectangular" deportment of the automaton cannot simply be the result of a lack of technical means on the part of its creator, who has created other automata with "wondrous exactitude" and perfectly "natural" styles of embodied behavior (28-29). Instead, he claims, it must be attributed to an even higher level of artifice—that is, to an intentionally deceptive *performance* of rectangular "mechanicity" adopted by a human being that literally inhabits the machine.

Yet we would be wrong to say that this debunking of the automaton's status as wondrous imitation serves to fully dispel sublime theatricality from this text. On the one hand, the post-human performance of the amazing Turk—and equally, of its human "ghost in the machine"—are revealed to be mimetic frauds. On the other hand, however, through Poe's mimetic strategies of plagiarism and technological appropriation—both linked to the "rectangular" style of deduction and propositional logic that overtakes the text's second section—"Maelzel's Chess-Player" (that is, the essay) essentially takes up and usurps the sublime theatricality that had previously belonged to Maelzel's Chess-Player (the device that is already mimetically cited in the essay's title). The true model for this mimetic theatricality may in fact be the ersatz automaton's human inhabitant, whom Poe's narrator-investigator accuses of impersonating mechanicity from within the cramped quarters of a technical cabinet otherwise filled with "wheels, pinions, [and] levers" (14). By the end of the essay, the only performativity left intact—a plagiaristic performativity that is close to the logic of transfer within the Longinian sublime—is the one that belongs to the text itself and its authorial voice, which have been reconfigured as sublime assemblages of plagiarism, assimilation, and mimetic behavior in their own right.

If we turn now to **"The Man That Was Used Up,"** we can see some of these same dynamics in place even despite the general inversion between the texts I noted above. The major thematics, however, also undergo a shift in this text: instead of "Maelzel's Chess-Player's" stress on the sublime, post-human performativity of plagiaristic assimilation, **"The Man That Was Used Up"** speaks to a different aspect of post-human mimesis, one grounded instead in logics of citation and prosthesis. Anyone who reads this tale becomes quickly keyed in to its bizarrely patterned narrative structure: as the narrator sets out through the public spaces of genteel society to learn more about the illustrious (and again, mysteriously "rectangular" General), each in a series of conversations is interrupted at the precise moment his interlocutor utters the word "man." At the very moment that an interlocutor says, "General John A. B. C. Smith, why he's the man [. . .]," the word "man" is picked up in an interrupting non-sequitur that bursts into the conversation and ruins all efforts to acquire positive knowledge about the General. This happens first in an encounter with the General himself, who bursts in with the expression "Man alive! How do ye do?"—ironic given what we shall later learn of the General—and who immediately proceeds to go off on a long tangent about the "immense influence" of the "rapid march of mechanical invention" in the modern world, visible in the wonders he sees "springing up [. . .] about us and [. . .] around us" like "grasshoppers," in "contrivances" that are drawing the world together from "London to Timbuctoo" (382). It is worth pausing over the General's highly phenomenological conception of modern space, presented as something that surrounds and encloses the lived—or in this case, only "partly"-lived—body. Yet this pattern of interruption happens again and again as the narrator's frustration mounts: at church, at a theater, at an evening soirée—each moment of potential knowledge and disclosure is, at the very mention of the word "man," interrupted by some extraneous burst of discourse, which recycles this word "man" but prevents any knowledge of the General to come forth.

In *Reading at the Social Limit,* Jonathan Elmer has read this pattern of repetition as pointing to the ideological construction of the very idea of "man" in mid-nineteenth-century America's so-called "culture of publicity": in his view, what this tale ultimately exposes is a view of America's post-Jacksonian democratic man as himself built out of these very patterns of repetition and circulation.[25] This is an undeniably authoritative reading; if it has a weakness, however, it is perhaps in the way that it rather too quickly passes over the specifically technological nature of the General as object, and the questions of modern embodiment that this nature raises. For indeed, the interrogation of "man" in this text ends up bringing together issues of prosthesis and mimesis, sublimity and citation, in a manner that makes it impossible to separate the history of socio-political mimesis from either the history of technology or the history of the body's accommodation to (or perhaps, colonization by) the technical world.

Poe's unveiling of post-human mimesis in this tale as simultaneously social, technological, and corporeal—and ultimately, aesthetic and textual as well—is structured through the text's "general" movement from public to private space. It is perhaps no surprise that all the public spaces depicted in the main portion of the tale are essentially spaces of ritualistic mimetic behavior (the church, the theater, the evening soiree, and so forth), or that interpersonal communication in at least one of these spaces is referred to using the verb "to telegraph."[26] Yet when the narrator is finally granted access to *private* space, to the space of the General's bedroom, we begin to see these secrets of mimesis in their literally "undressed" state, as the narrator witnesses the performative constitution of the General's erstwhile sublime body. Led into the General's chamber by Pompey—the so-described "negro valet" whose social abjection provides still another dimension to Poe's account of technological abjection—the narrator first sees only a vague puddle, but then sees this puddle undergo an astounding transformation: in the narrator's words, it was "performing, upon the floor, some inexplicable evolution, very analogous to the drawing on of a stocking" (387). This "analogous" performance turns out to be, of course, the literal self-fashioning of the General, as he is handed his prosthetic body parts one by one to take on his recognizable, everyday form. In a sense, the General's awe-inspiring figure has been literally constituted out of a sublime appropriation of the wonders "springing up around him" in the technological environment. That this appropriative self-making of the sublime body is enabled by the violent "using up" of the body in a war of native-American colonization is, I think, exactly the point: in the General's fictional encounter with the dispossessed Native Americans, the ambivalent violence of colonial confrontation is transferred from the fraught site of race and ethnicity to the emerging site of technology and the human.

This act of narrative witnessing at the end of **"The Man That Was Used Up"** becomes the moment of revelation and debunking, figured conventionally as the moment of sublime shock: the exposed wonder of the General's artificially assembled body must in turn be assimilated by the narrator, who—true to parodied gothic conventions of the sublime—screams in terror and then collapses into awestruck silence. But post-human theatricality is, once again, contagious: in the final passages of the tale, it is the narrator himself who becomes the locus of mimesis and citation, as he absorbs the tale's general logic of iterability, performance, and prosthesis.[27] First stammering a few repeated phrases of ineffable shock—"What could I say to this? What could I?"—the narrator soon begins parroting back the words of the General in his "general" state of astonishment (387). As the General recounts his story of corporeal destruction and rebuilding—listing, for example, the best stores in Philadelphia to acquire particular artificial body parts—the narrator can only throw back isolated words and phrases of this discourse in a kind of mechanical echolalia that linguistically reenacts the General's "rectangular" and wholly discrete embodiment along with its origins in bodily violence: "Bosom! Scratch! Butt end! Ram down!! My eye!!" (388).

With the General's prosthetic composition exposed and assimilated, the final sentences of the tale can now finally complete the transfer of power and legitimacy from sublime object to narrator and, more pointedly, to the text itself, a transfer that might be seen as the "point" of this tale poised somewhere between science-fiction, horror, and social satire. In particular, the debunking and transfer of the General's sublime authority reveals the transfer of a "generalized" mimetic competency to a more anonymous post-human subject. With the General revealed as a mimetic fraud, the final sentence—completing the phrase that has been in suspension for the entire tale—fully absorbs the General's logic of prosthesis and citationality, a logic that has otherwise been circulating throughout the whole text: "It was evident [. . .] It was a clear case. Brevet Brigadier General John A. B. C. Smith was the man—was *the man that was used up*" (389).

Part of the humour in this ending comes from the double meaning of the idiomatic expression "used up," which in the nineteenth century could mean not only "to expend" or "to exhaust" (its normal meaning today), but also "to debunk" or "to critique."[28] The General's "used up" human body—located in a distinctly human regime of scarcity and singularity—thus contrasts with his post-human, post-scarcity body of replaceable and commodified parts, a body which nonetheless demands to be "used up" as akin to an emperor without clothes. But of course, to participate in idiomatic language, as the narrator finally does here, is also to engage in a kind of mimetic "using up" of discourse, a form of interaction that reveals a post-scarcity—and, in a respect, post-human—logic of circulation and iterability within language itself.[29] It is significant, I think, that we get these final words of the tale following a dash and in italics, both of which emphasize language's ability to circulate mimetically in forms that are curiously detachable, even prosthetic, with regard to individual agency. As I have stressed throughout this essay, however, this mimetic and assimilative logic of post-human "using up" is also closely linked to the aesthetic dynamics of the sublime: in both of these tales, the encounter with the sublimely mimetic technological object entails not so much the "exhausting" of sublime authority as a form of mimetic transfer that is characteristic of the sublime itself—"using up" becomes rethought as "*taking up,*" as a theatricalized act of incorporation that radicalizes and materializes what has always been present in the sublime's strategic interplay of environmental alterity and post-human transcendence. Guided by this logic, the wondrous authority of mimetic "others" in the technological environment finds itself, through the very power of mimesis, digested into Poe's investigating bodies and, simultaneously, into his own textual practice.

Notes

1. This essay is drawn from work conducted for a dissertation completed in 2003 at UCLA, entitled "Post-Human Mimesis and the Aesthetics of the Technical Milieu." I would like to thank N. Katherine Hayles, Vincent Pecora, Emily Apter, and Kenneth Reinhard for their guidance with this project, as well as my co-panelists and audience members at the "Poe and Textual Authority" session of the 2002 International Edgar Allan Poe Conference for their comments on an earlier presentation of this material.

2. I did not have the opportunity to read Benesch's provocative book until after the initial drafting of this essay. Nonetheless, I wish to acknowledge the complimentary analysis that Benesch's chapter on Poe provides on the topics addressed below, as well as the central role he also accords "Maelzel's Chess-Player" and "The Man That Was Used Up" within Poe's treatment of technology, authorship, and human embodiment. See Benesch, *Romantic Cyborgs,* 97-127.

3. On the "technological sublime," see the further discussion below and in note 31.

4. A suggestively similar idea is put forward in Benesch's introduction to *Romantic Cyborgs*: "Apart from their historic and cultural specificity," he writes, "cyborgs [. . .] bring to the fore the mimetic processes that are at work in the formation of the subject" (*Romantic Cyborgs,* 30). While Benesch does not foreground the topic of mimesis in his discussion of Poe, his recourse to the theoretical work of figures such as Lacan and Michael Taussig in this introduction has many points of contact with my own perspective.

5. Allan Bloom, tr. and ed., *The Republic of Plato* (NY: Basic Books, 1968) 75.

6. I stress the pre-Kantian sublime here because of the way that Kant, in *The Critique of Judgement,* eliminated some of the mimetic and corporeal elements of Longinus's and Burke's accounts by reading the sublime in terms of a supersensible identification with the power of reason.

7. See Neil Hertz, "A Reading of Longinus," in *The End of the Line: Essays on Psychoanalysis and the Sublime* (NY: Columbia University Press, 1985) 6. My reading of the sublime in this essay is indebted to Hertz's discussion of Longinus, as well as to the work of Thomas Weiskel in *The Romantic Sublime.*

8. The concept of the sublime "turn" is introduced by Neil Hertz in "A Reading of Longinus." As I suggest above, this "turning" might profitably be related to the kind of "turning" or "hailing" described by Louis Althusser as a fundamental aspect of subjectification and ideological interpellation.

9. This logic of alterity, mimesis, and transcendence can also be viewed in the terms offered by the cultural anthropologist Michael Taussig, in his work *Mimesis and Alterity: A Particular History of the Senses* (NY: Routledge, 1993). Despite its controversial and at times uncritical celebration of mimetic behavior, Taussig's work nonetheless sheds light on the continuities between post-human mimesis and post-colonial mimesis as strategies of both artistic practice and embodied subjectivity. Homi Bhabha's work on colonial mimesis is also relevant in this context; see for example Bhabha, "Of Mimicry and Man," in *The Location of Culture* (NY: Routledge, 1994).

10. My reading here has been shaped by Thomas Weiskel's attempt to trace the psychoanalytic dynamics of the Romantic sublime, which he reads

as a multi-stage Oedipal drama of desire, terror, and identification. See Weiskel, *The Romantic Sublime,* esp. pp. 83-106.

11. Jonathan Elmer's reading of this "cultural logic of the hoax" is discussed below. See Jonathan Elmer, *Reading at the Social Limit: Affect, Mass Culture, and Edgar Allan Poe* (Stanford, CA: Stanford UP, 1995) 174-223.

12. A general survey of Poe's investments in the science and technology of his day can be found in Harold Beaver's introduction to his specialized edited volume of Poe's tales. See Harold Beaver, ed., *The Science Fiction of Edgar Allan Poe* (NY: Penguin Books, 1976) vi-xxi. See also Clarke Olney, "Edgar Allan Poe—Science Fiction Pioneer," *Georgia Review* 12 (Winter 1958) 416-421. In more recent work, in addition to Benesch, see John Limon, *The Place of Fiction in the Time of Science* (Cambridge: Cambridge University Press, 1991), as well as Shawn Rosenheim, *The Cryptographic Imagination: Secret Writing from Edgar Poe to the Internet* (Baltimore, MD: Johns Hopkins University Press, 1997), esp. 89-111.

13. A useful recent account of the history of the chess-playing automaton, including discussion of Poe's essay, can be found in Tom Standage, *The Turk: The Life and Times of the Famous Eighteenth-Century Chess-Playing Machine* (NY: Walker and Company, 2002). An insightful early treatment of Poe's essay in the critical literature can be found in W. K. Wimsatt, "Poe and the Chess Automaton" in *American Literature* 2 (May 1939): 138-151.

14. For a discussion of Poe's oeuvre, including the Maelzel essay, that invokes some similar issues of debunking, plagiarism, and the sublime, see Tresch. I find myself in agreement with much of Tresch's insightful essay; my aim here is to push his conclusions somewhat further by showing how Poe's investments in automata, plagiarism, and sublimity can be structurally unified through the concept of assimilative mimesis. See also the discussion of "Maelzel" in Benesch, *Romantic Cyborgs,* 109-116.

15. The connection between the Maelzel essay and the later detective stories has been noted by critics throughout the twentieth century. For a brief overview of this critical reception (which goes on to note the ways Poe erred in the details of his solution), see Standage, *The Turk,* 181-183.

16. In Rachman's formulation, the "problem of other minds" in Poe's oeuvre is always paralleled by a "problem of other texts." See Stephen Rachman, "Es lässt sich nicht schreiben: Plagiarism and 'The Man of the Crowd,'" in Rachman and Shawn Rosenheim, eds., *The American Face of Edgar Allan Poe* (Baltimore: Johns Hopkins University Press, 1995), p. 62.

17. See Elmer, 182-192.

18. See Leo Marx, *The Machine in the Garden: Technology and the Pastoral Idea in America* (London: Oxford UP, 1964); David E. Nye, *American Technological Sublime* (Cambridge, MA: MIT Press, 1994). For treatments of a technologically inflected sublime that have a more contemporary focus, see for example Joseph Tabbi, *Postmodern Sublime: Technology and American Writing from Mailer to Cyberpunk* (Ithaca, NY: Cornell University Press, 1996); Fredric Jameson, *Postmodernism, or the Cultural Logic of Late Capitalism* (Durham, NC: Duke University Press, 1992) 34-35.

19. Poe's familiarity with Burke's *Enquiry* is well established; his familiarity with Longinus's treatise would seem incontrovertible both from his own aesthetic writings (see below), as well as the multiple allusions contained in the satirical "How to Write a Blackwood's Article." For a general discussion of Poe's treatment of the sublime, see Kent Ljungquist, *The Grand and the Fair: Poe's Landscape Aesthetics and the Pictorial Tradition* (Potomac, MD: Scripta Humanistica, 1984) 47-88.

20. Poe, *Southern Literary Messenger* (January 1836): 77.

21. Poe, *Complete Works,* vol. 12:104 (originally in *Broadway Journal,* April 5, 1845). Poe found many opportunities to make this claim, almost to the point of self-dramatizingly (and paradoxically) plagiarizing himself. Poe thus recapitulated elements of this text almost verbatim in his discussion of James Aldrich in *Godey's Lady's Book,* May 1846. See Poe, "The Literati of New York City," in Poe, *The Complete Works,* vol. 15:62. On another occasion he writes: "Keen sensibility of appreciation—that is to say, the poetic *sentiment* . . . leads almost inevitably to imitation" and that "all great poets have [thus] been gross imitators." See Poe, *Marginalia* (Charlottesville, VA: University Press of Virginia, 1981) 109 (April 1846).

22. The Longinian echoes are particularly clear in a text such as the late "The Poetic Principle," where Poe writes that the Poetic Principle is "strictly and simply, the Human Aspiration for Supernal Beauty" and that "the manifestation of the Principle is always found in an elevating excitement of the Soul." See Poe, "The Poetic Principle," in *Complete Works,* vol. 14:290.

23. The title of this section is appropriated from Mary Kelly's essay on gender and masquerade, "Miming the Master: Boy-Things, Bad Girls, and Femmes Vitales," a chapter in her *Imaging Desire* (Cambridge, MA: MIT Press, 1996) 203-230.

24. Shawn Rosenheim notes this "comic-Petrarchan admiration" of the General in *The Cryptographic Imagination,* 101.

25. Elmer, *Reading at the Social Limit,* 47-56.

26. Upon encountering "Tabitha T." at church, Poe's narrator explains alliteratively, the pair "telegraphed a few signals, and then commenced, *sotto voce,* a brisk tête-à-tête." As Shawn Rosenheim has pointed out, Samuel Morse's first public experiments with the electrical telegraph had begun in 1837, although Poe's use of the word could also be seen simply in light of the semaphoric systems of communication that had been introduced in France in the 1790s, for which the term telegraph was originally coined. See Rosenheim, *The Cryptographic Imagination,* esp. 91-93, 227 n. 23.

27. Benesch follows a similar line of argument when he reads the "plagiarist strategies" revealed in Poe's tale in terms of what he calls "the technologizing of discourse," a tendency that "turns the topical dominance of technology in antebellum discourse into [the text's] structural modus operandi." "In an environment of ever-proliferating texts," he notes, "the writer's work appears to be just as 'artificially' constructed [. . .] as the body and historical renown of General John A. B. C. Smith. While tackling an area supposedly foreign to the writing profession, Poe's enigmatic story, once more, only reflects the modern production of literary texts." See Benesch, 126.

28. Critics have often speculated that Poe's General John A. B. C. Smith may be a stand-in for an actual political figure of the day, most notably Martin Van Buren (the target of a presidential campaign jingle that contained the phrase "used up.") In his introduction to the tale in the *Collected Works,* Mabbott reviews such theories with skepticism, noting the currency of the expression in Poe's writing and in nineteenth-century American English more widely. See Mabbott, Introduction to "The Man That Was Used Up," *Collected Works,* vol. 2:377.

29. In this sense, "The Man That Was Used Up"'s parodic account of post-human embodiment and textuality can be seen as anticipating elements of post-structuralist theories of language and meaning, particularly as articulated by Jacques Derrida. On an especially curious note, it is worth recalling that a central text in Derrida's account of the disseminative iterability inherent to language is "Limited Inc a b c," an extended essay which aims to "use up" (i.e., debunk) John Searle, the contemporary American "General" of speech-act theory and ordinary language who had responded critically to Derrida's "Signature, Event, Context." See the texts collected in Jacques Derrida, *Limited Inc,* ed. and trans. Samuel Weber (Evanston, IL: Northwestern University Press, 1988).

Works Cited

Adorno, Theodor. *Aesthetic Theory.* Tr. and ed., Robert Hullot-Kentor. Minneapolis: U of Minnesota Press, 1997.

Benesch, Klaus. *Romantic Cyborgs: Authorship and Technology in the American Renaissance.* Amherst, MA: University of Massachusetts Press, 2002.

Benjamin, Walter. "On the Mimetic Faculty," in *Reflections: Essays, Aphorisms, Autobiographical Writings,* ed. Peter Demetz. NY: Schocken, 1978: 333-336.

Burke, Edmund. *A Philosophical Enquiry into the Origin of Our Ideas of the Sublime and Beautiful, and Other Pre-Revolutionary Writings.* Ed. David Womersley. NY: Penguin, 1999.

Elmer, Jonathan. *Reading at the Social Limit: Affect, Mass Culture, and Edgar Allan Poe.* Stanford, CA: Stanford UP, 1995.

Hayles, N. Katherine. *How We Became Posthuman: Virtual Bodies in Cybernetics, Literature, and Informatics.* Chicago: University of Chicago Press, 1999.

Lamb, Jonathan. "Longinus, the Dialectic, and the Practice of Mastery." *ELH* 60.3 (1993): 545-567.

Longinus. *On the Sublime,* in *Classical Literary Criticism,* tr. and ed. T. S. Dorsch. NY: Penguin, 1965: 97-158.

Poe, Edgar Allan. "Maelzel's Chess-Player," in *The Complete Works of Edgar Allan Poe,* ed. James A. Harrison, vol. 14. NY: AMS Press, 1965: 6-37.

———. "The Man That Was Used Up." Ed Thomas Ollive Mabbott. *Collected Works,* vol. 2. Cambridge, MA: Harvard University Press, 1969: 376-392.

Tresch, John. "'The Potent Magic of Verisimilitude': Edgar Allan Poe within the Mechanical Age." *British Journal for the History of Science* 30.3 (1997): 275-290.

Weiskel, Thomas. *The Romantic Sublime: Studies in the Structure and Psychology of Transcendence.* Baltimore, MD: Johns Hopkins University Press, 1976.

Philip D. Beidler (essay date spring 2005)

SOURCE: Beidler, Philip D. "Mythopoetic Justice: Democracy and the Death of Edgar Allan Poe." *Midwest Quarterly* 46, no. 3 (spring 2005): 252-67.

[*In the following essay, Beidler documents the thinly veiled contempt for democratic values and practices in many of Poe's stories, while noting the ironic possibility that Poe may have died while being exploited for the purposes of election fraud.*]

After more than 150 years, the strange death of Edgar Allan Poe continues to attract the kind of attention worthy of a tale of mystery and imagination by Poe himself. Discovered in the streets of Baltimore on Election Day, October 7, 1849, in a combined state of exhaustion and alcoholic stupor, did he simply meet his end, as asserted by contemporary detractors, as a form of drunken just desserts? Or, as the more charitable were prompt to suggest, was there an underlying physical cause: epilepsy, perhaps, or brain fever? Recent medical readings of the evidence have pointed to diabetic hypoglycemia and even hydrophobia, the consequence of being bitten by a rabid animal. Alternatively, interpreters of a detective bent have postulated extreme physical ill treatment: a series of beatings or some fatal blow to the head. One of these, John Evangelist Walsh, has now gone further to posit a murder scenario where, on a northward journey to complete arrangements for his marriage to Elmira Royster of Richmond, Poe is pursued and waylaid by that lady's brothers, forcibly made to ingest whiskey, and thereby launched on what turns out to be a fatal binge.

One can hardly fault the speculation; indeed one can hardly resist it when the mysterious circumstances in question and the complex of events surrounding them involve the demise of a writer who himself had made a career asserting the essentially mythopoeic character of existence in nineteenth-century America—the essential reciprocity, in a world largely void of the traditional markers of cultural identity, of myth and reality, imagination and experience, art and life. Poe, mourning the death of his beloved Virginia, undertakes a set of increasingly frantic and hallucinatory peregrinations, revisiting the locales of his luckless career. Leaving New York one last time, he sets out for Richmond. Along the way he becomes convinced that he is being pursued by shadowy assassins.

In Baltimore, he reverses course, returning to Philadelphia, where a drunken spree lands him in prison. In a humiliating legal spin on the literary-cultural celebrity he has so long coveted, he is released by a judge who recognizes him as "Poe, the poet" and resumes his southward progress. In Richmond, he alternates between decorous social intercourse and visible binge drinking. Persuaded that he may be able to marry Elmira Royster, a sweetheart torn from him during his youth, he makes a great show of joining the Sons of Temperance and undertakes a headlong return journey to New York to settle outstanding business and to fetch Virginia's mother back with him for the ceremonies. He never gets there. Possibly again going as far north as Philadelphia this time and then reversing course for Baltimore, he gets off the train in that city, the place of his paternal ancestry. He then disappears for a week before he is discovered in the street outside a tavern doubling as a "crib" for repeat voters. Taken to a hospital, he lives for four days, where his last communications with the world comprise a series of oracular, melancholy utterances, some of them with seemingly literary connections to his own mysterious texts.

The whole business is all almost too Edgar Allan Poe-like to be true. It is Poe's last gothic tale of terror: the great exegete of American existential and aesthetic loneliness vanishes into one of his own nightmare worlds of self-creating and self-annihilating reflexivities. Alternatively, it is his last great tale of detection: afoot in some master final conjuration of plot, simple and odd, the ghost of Poe awaits the Dupin who will accomplish the great unriddling, find the obvious, single thing, there for all the eye to see, that will set everything in place.

As importantly, however, at its obdurate circumstantial core—Poe, discovered dead drunk, or nearly so, in front of a tavern notorious as a collecting point for derelicts herded from polling place to polling place to cast fraudulent multiple votes—it also becomes the realization, I would propose, of a single political nightmare that Poe had been fabulating with increasing obsessiveness in the last decade of his life: the vision of sottish, addled, irrational *homo democraticus* in general and of tumultuous, anarchic nineteenth-century American participatory democracy in particular.

Two of Poe's most visible anti-democratic satires of the period, although omitted now from most anthologies, remain fairly well known. In **"The Man That Was Used Up"** (1839), the latest backwoods military upstart elevated to the status of popular political demigod is revealed to be a disembodied collection of prostheses. In **"The System of Doctor Tarr and Professor Fether"** (1842), an American student of dementia visits a French model institution where the inmates have literally taken over the asylum.

Some mention of what might be called the antidemocratic mythopathy in Poe's satires—comparable to that found, for instance, in such acerbic fables of egalitarian excess as Irving's "Legend of Sleepy Hollow" or Hawthorne's "My Kinsman, Major Molineux"—has been made by commentators, most notably Daniel Hoffman. What distinguishes it from the work of contemporaries, however, is the compounded violence *and* virulence of the literary grotesquerie. In the first case, the symbology is that of mutilation and dismemberment. In the second, it is that of madness and incarceration. The composite effect suggests a totality of loathing, a uniform, pathological contempt.

Were one to attempt a current entitling spin on **"The Man That Was Used Up,"** it might be re-styled as *Fear and Loathing on the Campaign Trail, 1839.* In fact, the vernacular title stems from a political slogan trailed through the narrative as a running joke. The narrator, styling himself a kind of roving election correspondent in search of the inside story on the popular military candidate, Brevet Brigadier General John A. B. C. Smith, hero of the Bugaboo and Kickapoo Wars, repeatedly arrives on scenes of conversation about the latter in which one speaker begins promisingly by saying "He's the man . . ." only to have the sentence completed by another's non-sequitur.

Deciding to interview the luminary in person in his chambers, the narrator at length supplies the punch line with a vengeance. The disembodied reification of a violent colloquialism—"I'll use you up!"—that has come down through backwoods generations as a threat of being whipped to flinders, Smith is a man who literally has been flogged to physical nothingness. To wit: having sacrificed his body parts on the altar of the republic in a series of Indian conquests, he himself is revealed only to exist as formless protoplasm reconstructed from the ground up out of artificial body parts—even down to his sonorous vocal apparatus (***Complete Stories*** [***Complete Stories and Poems of Edgar Allan Poe***], 356-57). The man of the hour or man of the moment, he is in fact, the man who has been used up.

To be sure, even today it all reads nicely for an age of media candidates all properly concocted by handlers and focus groups, their appearances reduced to slogans and sound bites. While admiring such prescience, however, one too easily misses the bite of the contemporary political humor. As a violent historical creation "Smith" is clearly that stock figure of early American humor, the frontier *miles gloriosus,* Nimrod Wildfire, the Lion of the West, now literally resurrected *and* reconstructed out of political spare parts into the latest canebrake Napoleon.

Further, given the subtitling of the story as "A Tale of the Bugaboo and Kickapoo Wars," the bloodthirsty populist picture could not be more complete. "Smith's" exalted brigadier generalship is a "brevet"—a temporary field promotion, likely a militia rank, in that era most frequently conferred by politicians, on condition of conquering native peoples, in hope of some eventual quid pro quo. His imposing initials confer an equally dubious genealogy, the alphabet as American pedigree.

"Smith" speaks for itself, the great man as democratic everyman. And finally, of course, there is the ground of heroism itself: the various wars of Indian removal and extermination that in the early decades of the century became the launching pads for innumerable political careers. The prototype of the figure was, to be sure, Jackson himself, by no coincidence, in 1836, at the end of his presidency, having completed his martial triumphs of the early decades of the century with the last of the great Indian removals east of the Mississippi.

There was also, however, General Winfield Scott, more recently in the limelight for his campaigns against the Seminoles and his military supervision of the final Creek and Cherokee removals, including the notorious Trail of Tears. And in fact, in the election of 1840, which the story most likely concerns, Scott was at least initially advanced as a prospective presidential candidate.

These are both good guesses. But there are two better. The first was the military hero as Indian fighter who turned out to be the election's actual man-on-horseback nominee. That was William Henry Harrison, a well-born Whig Virginian who, for campaign purposes styling himself a log-cabin populist, must have seemed to Poe a particularly noxious amalgam of class traitor and political sellout. The victor of an Indian battle years earlier at Tippecanoe Creek in Indiana, he managed to resurrect its memory long enough to engineer a rallying cry—"Tippecanoe and Tyler Too"—ingeniously marrying his decades-old martial feat with the name of his running mate. The other was, of course, the Democratic incumbent and Jackson's anointed successor, the oily, diminutive, decidedly un-Jacksonian Martin Van Buren, the Red Fox of Kinderhook, the Little Magician, the ultimate politician as protean midget. The Whigs, it turns out, had some memorable words for him as well. "Van, Van," they went, "He's a used up man" (Lynch, 453).

Thus, in Poe's complex play on contemporary political sloganeering, we arrive at the core of political loathing lodged at the heart of his satire. "Tippecanoe and Tyler Too!" "Van, Van, He's a Used Up Man!" Here is the political flaying not of one politician but two, of the political process at large, of the whole ghoulish, grotesque masquerade of man-making that passes for electoral ritual in participatory American democracy. To be a candidate for office in America, Poe tells us, is to be the man of the hour; and to be the man of the hour is to be, inevitably, a candidate for the title, **"The Man Who Was Used Up."**

A later story, **"The System of Doctor Tarr and Professor Fether"** (1842), is displaced to France. The title, however, makes a precise assignment of more localized political geography and practice. The "system" for treating mental illness it describes, as imaged in the phony, inflated titles borne by the American originators it purports to honor, is no system at all. The grand project of "Tarr" and "Fether," and dreamed up, as it turns out, by a rebellious lunatic, is organized insanity, the logic of the smooth-talking leader of the demented mob. So the particular institutional setting is distinctly "American" as well; it is an asylum that has been taken over by the inmates.

Again, the narrator is a somewhat dim-witted roving observer, in this case something of a parody of the friend of Roderick Usher, continually persuading himself that everything is normal despite frequent naggings of unease and suspicion. The inmates, cast into the role of keepers, seem most nervously sane. The keepers, cast by the inmates into the dungeons, constantly protest that it is they who are sane and the others mad. It is altogether a model asylum. The overthrow, it turns out, has been made possible by a permissive treatment of madness, invented by the Americans of the title, called the "system of soothing"—itself a mocking reference to the "moral treatment" asylum method instituted by the English reformer William Tuke and his French counterpart Philippe Pinel—in which lunatics are granted the "apparent freedom" of walking around in normal clothes as if they were in their right mind (***Complete Stories,*** 293).

The ringleader, one Maillard, elected head lunatic, treats the narrator to a dinner—an opulent banquet of grandees in ill-fitting borrowed aristocratic dress complete with dissonant orchestra. It is a lavish feast, full of opulence and plenitude, but with "very little taste in the arrangements" (296). Conversation among guests runs to tales of favorite lunatics, who think they are chickens, teapots, and the like.

One, "Bouffon Le Grand," fancies himself with two heads, one of Cicero, the other a composite of Demosthenes and Lord Broughton, in honor of his passion for oratory (298-99). Meanwhile, Maillard extols the new philosophy of "soothing." The product of "a better system of government," he calls it, a "lunatic government" (303). As the narratives continue, the behavior of the guests becomes increasingly erratic.

Apace, Maillard, a vain, voluble popinjay, becomes so boastful of his own schemes that he can't help spilling the story that is really being played out under his orchestration, even as the counterrevolution occurs and the imprisoned storm upward from the dungeons. He is last seen hiding under the buffet.

Meanwhile, the general upheaval brings the final triumph of anarchy, a frenzy of dancing on the tables to the mad playing and singing of "Yankee Doodle" (304). A "perfect army of what I took to be Chimpanzees, Ourang-Outangs, or big black baboons" (304), the narrator tells us, rushes in to restore order. He himself receives a serious beating and is imprisoned for more than a month until things are sorted out. Only then is the full plot revealed. Maillard, as it happens, was actually the keeper of the asylum until he himself went insane, thence conniving with the inmates to overthrow their guards. It has also been those latter, in their own tar and feathers, whom he has mistaken for apes.

As a fable of mob politics, American-style, it is again all beautifully circular and complete. As at Jackson's inauguration, the democratic rabble take over the mansion, a mob breaking furniture and throwing crockery and drunkenly dancing on the tables. Yet when the counterrevolution occurs, it seems mainly a mob of avenging semi-anthropoids, with the innocent narrator among those violently assaulted and imprisoned. It has all been very confusing, he says. Further, he concludes, in his opinion at least, at the particular Maison de Sante in question, the contest of systems remains very much in the balance. "The 'soothing system,' with important modifications," he says, "has been resumed at the chateau; yet I cannot help agreeing with Monsieur Maillard, that his own 'treatment' was a very capital one of its kind. As he justly observed, it was 'simple—neat—and gave no trouble at all—not the least'" (305). A good American to the end, he would seem to cast his vote in a given instance for whatever set of inmates happens at the moment to be running the asylum.

As to Poe's most vicious critiques of democracy, democratic man, and democratic process at large, however, one looks to the far more explicit content of what might be called the mouthpiece or ventriloquist sketches, all clustered in the latter part of the 1840s. Here, the mode is that of Cooper, the bitterness and acerbity of whose anti-democratic politics Poe's most closely resembled. Yet in contrast to the elitist japery of Cooper's traveling bachelor in *Notions of the Americans,* for instance—itself modeled on that in a host of popular works of the era by literary travelers from abroad come to dissect and caricature the follies of the great democratic experiment—what distinguishes the anti-democratic comment in comparable works by Poe such as **"Mellonta Tauta"** or **"Some Words with a Mummy"** is their sheer essayistic blatancy. In both cases, Poe's correspondents travel in time; and in both cases such journeys supply the barest pretexts for fulminating expressions of a political contempt so profound that it appears simply apropos of nothing. Transmitted across the ages from future or past, the message to history is virtually identical. Democracy is the dominion of King Mob.

"Mellonta Tauta," published in 1848, is set in the year 2848. (The title, roughly translated, allegedly means "it shall come to pass.") The speaker in the tale is Pundita, with a pundit's views on a variety of matters. Since she is a Poe narrator on a fantastic balloon voyage through time and space, these include metaphysics, astronomy, and celestial navigation. Closer to home, however, she also provides some distinctly time-bound remarks on a political phenomenon of a thousand years earlier, now mercifully consigned to ancient history, called participatory democracy. She is astounded, she tells us, to hear from her husband Pundit "that they ancient Americans *governed themselves*!" (***Complete Stories,*** 379). She goes on:

> —did anyone ever hear of such an absurdity?—that they existed in a sort of every man-for-himself confederacy, after the fashion of the "prairie dogs" that we read of in fable. He says that they started with the queerest idea conceivable, viz.: that all men are born free and equal—this in the very teeth of the laws of *gradation* so visibly impressed upon all things both in the moral and physical universe. Everyman 'voted,' as they called it—that is to say, meddled with public affairs—until, at length, it was discovered that what is everybody's business is nobody's, and that the "Republic" (so the absurd thing was called) was without a government at all.
>
> (379)

This notion in turn led to the equally "startling discovery that universal suffrage gave opportunity for fraudulent schemes," called at the time popular elections, "by means of which any desired number of votes might at any time be polled, without the possibility of prevention or even detection, by any party which should be merely villainous enough not to be ashamed of the fraud." Further, "a little reflection upon this discovery sufficed to render evident the consequences, which were that rascality *must* predominate—in a word, that a republican government *could* never be anything but a rascally one" (379).

Reform, however, was balked, when "the matter was put to an abrupt issue by a fellow by the name of *Mob,* who took everything into his own hands and set up a despotism, in comparison with which those of the fabulous Zeros and Hellofagabaluses were respectable and delectable." Rumored of foreign origins, "this Mob," we are told further, "is said to have been the most odious of all men that ever incumbered the heart. He was a giant in stature—insolent, rapacious, filthy; had the gall of a bullock, with the heart of a hyena and the brains of a peacock" (379).

Fortunately, his own chaotic energies insured his eventual self-extinction. Still, the speaker notes from her position of future enlightenment, "he had his uses, as everything has, however vile, and taught mankind a lesson which to this day it is in no danger of forgetting—never to run contrary to the natural analogies." And, as for the "Republicanism" that spawned him, she concludes, "no analogy could be found for it upon the face of the earth—unless we except the case of the 'prairie dogs,' an exception which seems to demonstrate, if anything, that democracy is a very admirable form of government for dogs" (379).

Compare a similarly extended passage from **"Some Words with a Mummy,"** published in the *American Whig Review* of 1845. The titular character is an ancient Egyptian, Count Allmistakeo. Resurrected by a friend of the narrator, one Dr. Ponnonner, after several millennia of sleep, he discourses on myth, metaphysics, art, and architecture. Finally he turns to the historical folly of a certain form of experimental government tried during his time. "Thirteen Egyptian provinces," he recalls bemusedly, "determined all at once to be free, and to set a magnificent example to the rest of mankind. They assembled their wise men, and concocted the most ingenious constitution it is possible to conceive. For a while they managed remarkably well; only their habit of bragging was prodigious. The thing ended, however, in the consolidation of the thirteen states, with some fifteen or twenty others, in the most odious and insupportable despotism that was ever heard of on the face of the earth."

The narrator goes on:

> I asked what was the name of the usurping tyrant.
>
> As well as the Count could recollect, it was *Mob.*
>
> (***Complete Stories,*** 461)

So it goes with Poe's voyagers throughout history. Whether scathingly uttered by the futuristic Pundita of **"Mellonta Tauta,"** or by the back-from-the-dead titular informant of **"Some Words with a Mummy,"** it is all the same with participatory electoral democracy. In fact, the commentaries are virtually word-for-word in their bitter identicalities of phrasing and sentiment. Pursued throughout time and space by the politics of the age, Poe turns about only to confront near the end of his life a despised democratic present. It was as if he could not find enough venues toward the end to register this vision of political apocalypse. History was indeed for Poe a nightmare from which he could not awake. And the nightmare was the omnipresent specter of nineteenth-century American mobocracy.

Do such texts make Poe anything more than an *occasional* political allegorist or barely-disguised anti-democratic editorialist? Certainly one can point elsewhere to a fascination with images of anarchy and mob violence. In his well-known review of Longstreet's *Georgia Sketches,* Poe put himself on record as a partisan of the Southwestern Whig humorists of the era, themselves well-known and applauded for their grotesque, violent depictions of the backwoods bully, the buffoon, the Jacksonian rabble. In a similar southern-frontier vein, the mutineers launching the travails of the titular character in ***The Narrative of Arthur Gordon Pym*** [***The Narrative of Arthur Gordon Pym of Nantucket***] include a bloodthirsty Negro and a dim, suggestible half-breed.

Again, the obsessiveness of the content becomes markedly pronounced in works of the 1840s. A political reading of **"The Masque of the Red Death"** suggests that the plague, the contagion threatening at any moment to break down the doors of the castle, may be the Terror. The western geography suggests so. Likewise does the name of the monarch of the western realm, Prince Prospero. Correlatively, in **"The Imp of the Perverse,"** the condemned murderer madman, one of Poe's frequent hyper-cerebral and aestheticized manipulations of the popular press formula of the likeable criminal, transmogrifies before our eyes into the ultimate man of the crowd. Another of Poe's aristocrats of the intellect, preening, disdainful, smugly arrogant and safe among the throng of lesser mortals with his secret knowledge of the perfect crime, he gradually breaks down, descending back into madness precisely as he recounts at length how he has blurted out the confession of his crime after being hunted down and nearly lynched—by a mob attracted by his odd behavior.

Even in works of a primarily aesthetic orientation, such politically-nourished intellectual elitism had always been the core emotion of Poe's persona. The poetic dreamer of "Sonnet—To Science," complaining of his being awakened from an aesthetic afternoon's nap under the tamarind tree, easily became the dark aphorist of the *Marginalia,* decrying the inevitable link between superior genius and popular misunderstanding. (Entries from 1849, the year of his death, include, "The nose of a mob is its imagination. By this, at any time, it can be quietly led" [193]; and, "In drawing a line of distinction between people and a mob, we find that a people aroused to action are a mob; and that a mob, trying to think, subside into a people" [195].) During two decades before the public eye, Poe, the self-proclaimed apostle of supernal, sublimely non-political and non-utilitarian imagination flaunted his aestheticism in a cash-and-carry democracy, all the while eking out its professional literary artist's pittance against page-filling and meeting editorial deadlines.

In a land where the homely charms of democratic art were supposed to mildly instruct and uplift, Beauty—and its cognate Taste—were part of a signature vocabulary brandished by Edgar Poe against his popularly beloved three-name poet-contemporaries—the Henry Wadsworth Longfellow, William Cullen Bryant, and John Greenleaf Whittier—in all the perverse glee with which Richard Nixon used the trademark double V-for-Victory sign in crowds of anti-war protestors. Beauty in a land where art was supposed to popularly instruct and uplift was a barely disguised term for political contempt.

So too, the formula phrase "the heresy of the didactic," erected a blasphemous religion of art against the popular politics of poetry as a celebration of civic virtue and domestic piety. Finding genuine popular celebrity *as a poet* near the end with "The Raven," he even then made box-office success the occasion for making his audience sit through an insulting tutorial on an aestheticism beyond their lumpish concerns for usable meanings and morals.

"The Philosophy of Composition" promises an inside look at the mysteries of the creative process while simultaneously unwriting and demystifying the poem back down to a collocation of technical cheap tricks—the literary equivalent of prostheses. Like the other lecture of the era, "The Poetic Principle," with which it is virtually interchangeable, or the recycled aesthetico-political harangue—suggestively, probably again, as Daniel Hoffman speculates, by "Pundita"—that begins *Eureka,* it is at once a valedictory stump speech on art and a last bitter hoax on the mob, the tasteless, unreasoning rabble to whom he had been beholden throughout his life for his meager living and reputation. Aesthetic defiance, grounded in profoundly political contempt, conquers history itself, the belief that outside the present age, timeless genius will yet prevail.

"*I care not whether my work be read now or by posterity. I can afford to wait a century for readers when God himself has waited six thousand years for an observer. I triumph. I have stolen the golden secret of the Egyptians. I will indulge my sacred fury.*" So asserts

"Pundita" in Eureka, writing again from the future, by way of a quote from Kepler, writing from the past (*Selected Prose,* 495). Here, as elsewhere, on the basis of his relentless distancing and projecting of a theory of creative genius into a cosmic aestheticism, Poe is frequently cited among his nineteenth-century American contemporaries as a uniquely apolitical writer. In fact, on the basis of such stratagems, he has been thus characterized by such recent commentators as Jonathan Elmer and Terence Whalen within two major books devoted to his career in relation to mass culture and the popular literary marketplace. And within the context of arguments so framed, the assertion is correct. As with his critical evenhandedness in refusing to kowtow to a text because it was British, or puff one because it was American, Poe, while deeply attuned to the commercial politics of literary production, does *not* in fact seem to have been notably a political partisan, nor political in the sense that, aside from the occasional satirical reference, he addressed major party figures and issues, Whig or Democrat. What he surely did possess, at the deepest springs of his art and his personality, was a profound contempt for democracy as a concept, social or aesthetic. Accordingly, at the topical political level, his works swirl with a pathological anti-egalitarianism. At the very least—in such an Irving-like work as **"The Unparalleled Adventures of Hans Pfall,"** for instance—politics is hot air, flatulence, windy chaos; in **"Von Kempeln's Discovery,"** a send-up of the California Gold Rush, it also comprehends herd behavior and money-lust; most frequently, it promises a Hawthornean descent into a netherworld fueled by rum and riot, mindless mob frenzy.

Accounts of Poe's death now at last give us occasion, I think, to rethink just how much, politically, in life and death alike, he was of that turbulent democratic world, and that world of him. Indeed, in 1851, just two years after the fatal episode in Baltimore, the popular artist George Caleb Bingham would produce one of the best known genre paintings of the era: "The County Election." And if already styled in frontier nostalgia, it also carried a contemporary political bite. The scene is all hubbub and bustle, a small town literally mobbed by voters. One man, corpulent, genial, obviously sated with drink while motioning for more, sits facing us, the tipsy beneficiary of the custom of "treating,"—enjoying a limitless free liquor supply, often provided by political candidates for several weeks in advance of an election (Lender, 54-55). Another, too drunk to stand without help, is being dragged to the polling place. Another, sitting on a bench, drunkenly nurses a broken head. A banner above the door proclaims, "The Will of the People the Supreme Law." To update the cultural connection, Poe, it also turns out, could easily have explained to me why, as recently as twenty years ago, in my hometown of Tuscaloosa, Alabama, it was illegal to sell beer, wine, or liquor on election day. Nor would the historic interest of the conversation have been diminished by the fact that the town in question, the seat of the state university *and* the state hospital for the insane, had also once, in its days as the old frontier capital, flourished as one of the literary epicenters of Southwestern Humor, including service as the fictional site of some the most celebrated episodes in the career of the rapscallionish hero of Johnson Jones Hooper's 1845 *Adventures of Captain Simon Suggs,* itself a roistering, vicious parody of Jacksonian campaign biography. There, well into the twentieth century, the custom of election-day treating had continued, including the usual Democratic party roundup of drunkards and derelicts as repeat voters. Indeed, even Prohibition had done little to forestall the anarchic ritual of subsidized election-day drunkenness, and only with passage of specific statutes did a righteous legislature attempt to assure the public of its desire to free the ballot box from the dominion of that twin-headed monster Demon Rum and King Mob.

It was the final playing out of a political theater of the absurd that Edgar Poe would have understood. It may have been the final act of the political drama that he saw in his last moments on earth. Comatosely selling his vote repeatedly for the price of a drink on election day in the city of his aristocratic forebears, Poe, the ultimate anti-democratic mythopath, had met with the ultimate form of mythopoeic justice. Alcohol was the fatal agent; and a rough-and-tumble nineteenth-century American election was the fatal occasion. Democracy, in a word, was the death of him.

Bibliography

Elmer, Jonathan. *Reading at the Social Limit: Affect, Mass Culture, and Edgar Allan Poe.* Stanford: Stanford University Press, 1995.

Hawthorne, Nathaniel. *The Snow-Image and Uncollected Tales.* Columbus: Ohio State University Press, 1974.

Hoffman, Daniel. *Poe Poe Poe Poe Poe Poe Poe.* New York: Doubleday, 1972.

Irving, Washington. *History, Tales, and Sketches.* New York: Library of America, 1983.

Lender, Mark Edward, and James Kirby Martin. *Drinking in America: A History.* New York: Free Press, 1982.

Lynch, Denis Tilden. *An Epoch and a Man: Martin Van Buren and His Times.* New York: Liveright, 1929.

Peeples, Scott. "Life Writing/Death Writing: Biographical Versions of Poe's Final Hours." *Biography,* 18/4 (1995), 328-38.

Poe, Edgar Allan. *Complete Stories and Poems of Edgar Allan Poe.* Garden City, New York: Doubleday, 1966.

———. *Edgar Allan Poe: Selected Prose, Poetry, and Eureka.* San Francisco: Rinehart, 1950.

———. *Marginalia.* Charlottesville: University Press of Virginia, 1981.

Walsh, John Evangelist. *Midnight Dreary: The Mysterious Death of Edgar Allan Poe.* New York: St. Martins, 2000.

Whalen, Terence. *Edgar Allan Poe and the Masses.* Princeton: Princeton University Press, 1999.

Jeffrey J. Folks (essay date spring 2005)

SOURCE: Folks, Jeffrey J. "Edgar Allan Poe and Elias Canetti: Illuminating the Sources of Terror." *Southern Literary Journal* 37, no. 2 (spring 2005): 1-16.

[*In the following essay, Folks discusses "The Gold-Bug," "The Fall of the House of Usher," and "The Murders in the Rue Morgue" in light of* Crowds and Power, *Elias Canetti's tract on crowd psychology and behavior.*]

In *The Torch in My Ear,* the second volume of his four-volume autobiography, Elias Canetti recounts an episode from his university days in which he passed an uneasy morning in chemistry laboratory with a fellow student, Eva Reichmann: "I talked about a book I had started reading the day before: Poe's tales. She didn't know them, and I told her about one, **'The Tell-Tale Heart,'** which had really terrified me. . . . I tried to free myself of this terror by repeating the story to her" (191). In seeking to dispel the terror generated by reading Poe's tale, Canetti turns to another human being and attempts to relieve his uneasiness by communicating his frightening experience to her as they seek to analyze his fears. In its approach of uncovering and dispelling the sources of terror in human relations, the episode points toward the long and distinguished career that Canetti would enjoy, not as a chemist but as novelist, playwright, literary critic, autobiographer, and, most importantly, as author of *Crowds and Power,* the most authoritative and original of modern treatises on crowd psychology.[1]

It is hardly coincidental that Canetti should have been struck so forcefully by the writing of Edgar Allan Poe, for there is a remarkable sense in Poe's tales of a writer who anticipated many of Canetti's insights. The fact that literature is, among other things, the record of instinctual crowd behavior was apparent to Canetti at a very early point in his life, and the affinity that Canetti perceived between his and Poe's interests is connected with a life-long effort to explain and to ameliorate the destructive potential of mass behavior. In Canetti's mind, the Holocaust was the culmination of a long history of unfaced and unresolved fear. This history, characterized by increasingly tyrannical forms of control, involved precisely those psychological terrors that Poe focused on: the sense that the world was increasingly dominated by accidental forces beyond comprehension and, in response, the rise of increasingly authoritarian conceptions of history and social order. As a result, the central focus for both writers was nothing less than the fear of annihilation.

Elias Canetti's classic work, *Crowds and Power,* is a detailed analysis of the patterns of crowd behavior and of the ways in which individuals relate psychologically to crowds. Canetti begins his analysis with a classification of different crowd types under such headings as crowd flight, prohibition, and doubling. A second major section of the work analyzes the existence of the pack, a smaller and more primitive unit that anticipated the development of the crowd in civilization. Canetti then turns to the effects of the crowd in human history, with particular emphasis on the violence of the Holocaust. He studies the primitive human instincts that anticipate modern power, and he traces the rise of what he terms the "survivor," the paranoiac leader obsessed with absolute command of others. Canetti follows this analysis of the survivor with a more detailed examination of the workings of power, carefully analyzing the ways in which commands are issued and received. He also studies transformation of crowd types and psychological identification with these types. Canetti, finally, concludes with a dissection of power and an analysis of the tendency toward paranoia in rulers.

In Canetti's sympathetic reading of Poe, he intuitively focuses on the terrifying elements of fear and isolation that Poe projects. Poe's writing evinces a profound psychological intuition concerning the instinct for power underlying social relationships, particularly those relationships involving postures of dominance or victimization. In one of Poe's most popular tales, **"The Gold-Bug,"** the protagonist is an isolated gentleman who, like many of Poe's main characters, dreams of restoring himself to wealth and social prominence. A crucial element of **"The Gold-Bug,"** of course, is the motif of hidden treasure, a psychological fixation with which Canetti deals at considerable length. The idea of hidden treasure contains a peculiar tension between "the splendour it should radiate and the secrecy which is its protection" (*Crowds* 89). Inherent in the concept is "the lust of counting," the universal passion for increase, and particularly irresistible is the hope of the discovery of buried treasure, a sudden windfall that can occur at any moment to anyone. The concept of buried treasure is particularly appealing to the paranoid personality, for the sudden expansion of control over units of money can be extended figuratively to control over units of men as well, a form of self-increase that confirms the paranoiac's desire for invulnerability.

"The Gold-Bug" begins by introducing William Legrand, a member of an ancient family that had "once been wealthy" (560). According to Canetti, the most intolerable situation is to be reduced in wealth or power, for a person identifies with his or her units of wealth (*Crowds* 90).[2] Legrand has withdrawn from New Orleans and taken up residence at Sullivan's Island, near Charleston, South Carolina. Here, following Canetti's crowd symbolism, he lives surrounded by the element of sand, whose innumerable units he now rules in place of coins or men. The island is largely unpopulated, and trees, which for Canetti symbolize human beings, are practically non-existent. Thus, Legrand, literally and figuratively, reigns as nearly the only human inhabitant. Living at the remote end of the island, Legrand experiences alternating states of enthusiasm and melancholy that are characteristic of the paranoiac. Significantly, Legrand's chief amusements are shooting and fishing, both forms of seizing and grasping, and even his less predatory hobby, collecting seashells, involves amassing units. His collection, one that "might have been envied by a Swammerdamm" (561), is described in the grandiose terms of the paranoiac.

The story's setting and its very donnée underline the isolation of its protagonist from society and his fantasy of unlimited power. Legrand's only companion on the island is an ancient and much abused servant, a sort of court jester whom Legrand has "permitted" to live and on whom, we assume, he has mockingly conferred the title of "Jupiter" (though Jupiter views *himself* as the supervisor and guardian of the unstable Legrand).[3] Jupiter possesses peculiar insight into the personality of his master, and his comment that "Massa were bit somewhere bout the head by dat goole-bug" recognizes that a form of mental illness underlies Legrand's obsession with treasure, though it does not appreciate the particular nature of this illness (565).

At the beginning, it is fitting that Legrand should be pictured in a mood of enthusiasm that is only partially explained by his discovery earlier that day of the gold-bug, a species of scarabaeus "which he believed to be totally new" (561). The gold-bug ties together two key elements of paranoia that already dominate Legrand's personality: the desire for sudden wealth and the control over life and death. A good deal of menacing repartee takes place between the narrator, who sees the drawing of the gold-bug as only a death's head or skull, and Legrand, who insists that the drawing represents an insect with antennae. Noticing that the document contains a drawing on the obverse, Legrand grows violently red and then excessively pale, the result of his alternating moods of aggression and passivity. At this point, presumably, Legrand has not yet grasped that the drawing is a treasure map; significantly, it is not the passion for treasure itself which arouses Legrand but the *secrecy* of the writing. As Canetti notes, the tyrant always fears secrecy on the part of others, and in a paranoid condition the ruler exhibits a mania "for finding causal relations" (*Crowds* 452) that would unmask and explain the actions of those around him. The prototypical situation of the paranoiac is that he feels surrounded by a crowd of enemies, and "what occupies him most . . . are his acts of recognition" (*Crowds* 456).

Only later does Legrand explain to the narrator his "method" in deciphering the parchment. The salient point, however, is not the matter of ratiocination, Poe's clever attempt to awe the popular reader with secret codes and tricks of decipherment, but rather the psychological response of Legrand to the existence of secrecy itself: that is, the narrative crux of this scene is not the decoding but the compulsion to decode. As Legrand admits, the coincidence of the discovery of a skull figure drawn directly beneath his own sketch of the scarabaeus caused his mind to "establish a connection—a sequence of cause and effect—and, being unable to do so [to suffer] a species of temporary paralysis" (120). There could be no more accurate description of the reaction of the paranoiac to circumstances over which he initially lacks control. The immediate response to the uncontrollable situation is, as in the case study of Daniel Paul Schreber that Canetti analyzes, paralysis (*Crowds* 458-60). When subsequently Legrand establishes the sequence of cause and effect, the rational connection of events that lead him to the discovery of treasure, his mind erupts in a euphoric sense of victory. Focusing on the providential "necessity" of his discovery, Legrand emphasizes the "very extraordinary" series of accidents and coincidences that led him to unravel the mystery, including the intervention of his dog "Wolf" that indirectly "causes" the narrator to hold the map before the fire while he caresses the dog with his other hand.

The search for treasure leads Legrand and his companions from the island to the mainland, a setting where Legrand no longer exercises habitual control. Symbolically, and literally as well, the mainland is more densely populated than the island. On the mainland the searchers come upon a densely wooded, almost inaccessible hill, the forest suggesting an opposing army that Legrand sets out to conquer. For Canetti, another symbolic suggestion of the forest is divinity. The key to the location of the treasure is an enormously tall tulip tree, whose foliage rises above the forest, symbolizing God, to whom the paranoiac often stands in special relation by virtue of the sense that God is "speaking" to him. The psychological effect of entering a forest is a sense of awe. Looking up at the sheltering canopy of the trees "is a preparation for being in church, the standing before God" (*Crowds* 84). Poe conveys this feeling toward the forest in his description of the "general majesty" of the tulip tree.

Following directions that he has deciphered from the parchment, Legrand sends Jupiter to the seventh limb of the tree, on the end of which he discovers a skull nailed to the branch. Legrand directs Jupiter to drop the gold-bug through the left eye socket of the skull, and he marks the spot where the gold-bug strikes the ground. Following the directions on the parchment, the group moves fifty feet from the site of the gold-bug, with Jupiter clearing the forest with a scythe. There the men set to work, digging a hole somewhat more than four feet in diameter and two feet in depth. Finding nothing, Legrand is struck with the "bitterest disappointment" (576) until he realizes that Jupiter must have dropped the gold-bug through the *right* rather than the *left* eye socket, a mistake that results in a significant miscalculation. The group now digs a circle "somewhat larger than the former" attempt, in other words about the size of a human grave, where they discover two complete skeletons lying atop the treasure. Significantly, after two trips hauling the treasure back to their hut, the party leaves the holes unfilled, suggesting a further use. The treasure itself is first estimated at $450,000 in coin and an enormous value in jewels, but these early estimates rapidly increase, a detail that concurs with Canetti's finding that the authoritarian individual tends to exaggerate the amount of his or her possessions, skipping madly to greater and greater figures.

One of the significant points in the search for treasure is Legrand's identification of the white spot on the limb of the tulip tree as a human skull—perhaps the remains of a sacrificial victim. As Canetti points out, in premodern societies it is the head of the ritual victim that must be collected and that carries his spirit and strength. One assumes that Captain Kidd has performed a human sacrifice and nailed the skull of the victim to the limb of the tree that represents God, and this not just for the practical purpose of marking his treasure but for the psychic increase of power that human sacrifice always enacts. What is remarkable in Poe's story is that neither Legrand nor Jupiter, nor for that matter the narrator, comments on the peculiarity of a skull nailed to the limb of a tree: each is participating in the ritual events from within the same compelling instinctual logic. After all, in many societies it is considered an honor to be selected as the sacrificial victim of the king.

Legrand's pretense of madness, his "grandiloquence," his odd behavior of swinging the gold-bug by a string as the group sets off in search of treasure, and his insistence on letting the gold-bug rather than a bullet fall through the eye-socket are all manifestations of an obsession with power. Legrand explains his odd behavior as a form of pique, his annoyance at the narrator's suspicions concerning his sanity, but he adds that he "resolved to punish [the narrator] quietly, in my own way, by a little bit of sober mystification" (595). Despite its apparent facetiousness, Legrand is acting in deadly earnest. He is outraged by the narrator's betrayal, and he resolves to punish the "traitor." Positioned at the end of the story, this suggestion of punishment carries particular weight, for the next question is what to make of the skeletons found in the hole. Like so many of Poe's madmen, Legrand obscures his ghastly motives with a display of civilized humor. In mock disbelief he protests that "it is dreadful to believe in such atrocity as my suggestion would imply" (595), the fact that Captain Kidd has had his two assistants dig their own graves and then "thought it expedient to remove all participants in his secret" (595-596). It would seem that Legrand identifies with Captain Kidd throughout the story, and the coincidence that he has two helpers just as Captain Kidd had points toward the horror of the next and final sentence. Here Legrand, savoring his own mental superiority and perhaps pondering his next move, speculates on how many blows would have been necessary for Captain Kidd to kill his victims. As he states, "perhaps a couple of blows with a mattock were sufficient . . . perhaps it required a dozen. Who shall tell?" (596). Who, indeed, but Legrand himself?[4]

"The Gold-Bug" takes us well into Poe's understanding of the personality of the survivor, but others stories in ***Tales of the Grotesque and Arabesque*** offer a more subtle reworking of Canetti's theme. The character of Roderick Usher resembles that of Legrand in certain respects, but the situation in **"The Fall of the House of Usher"** traces the protagonist's relationship to both a human and a microscopic crowd. Like Legrand, Usher suffers excessive mood swings between despair and euphoria, and his nervous disease is characterized by an acute sensitivity to the external world. He feels excessively threatened by "rays" of sunlight, and in this respect Roderick's painting of a rectangular vault with smooth white walls is most revealing. Though admitting no light, neither natural nor artificial, the vault is flooded with "intense rays" that "bathe the whole in a ghastly inappropriate splendor" (325). A similar sensation of being attacked by rays is characteristic of Canetti's case study of Daniel Paul Schreber. The paranoiac seeks to detect threatening crowds everywhere, on the microscopic as well as on the human scale.

Roderick's large luminous eye, attentive to watching and unmasking others, is another gauge of his fear. The suggestion of extraordinary intellectual capacity in the "inordinate expansion above the regions of the temple" and the further suggestion of a superhuman quality in the face's "Arabesque expression," which the narrator cannot connect with "any idea of simple humanity," imply Roderick's intellectual separation from the rest of mankind (321). As Canetti points out, perhaps the most common symptom of paranoia is a defensiveness regarding physical space. In the case of the Ushers, the family has gradually merged its identity with the house itself, symptom of the "nervous illness" that, as Roderick admits, has been passed down through generations from father to son, but the imminent collapse of the house is in its way merely a reflection of the instability of megalomania. Even the exterior is under siege, covered with a minute fungi, a gathering of an insidious and hostile crowd of the sort that the paranoiac would be most concerned with.

For the paranoiac, as Canetti shows, "greatness and persecution are intimately connected and both are expressed through his body" (461). Critical to Roderick, as to all rulers, are those who attend his physical health. While the point in this tale is largely underdeveloped, the relevance of physicians in many of Poe's stories is clarified by an understanding of the paranoiac's interest in the secret functions of the body. Since the most secret events, those to which even the greatest rulers are not privy, take place within the human body itself, the physician or the shaman, those who possess special insight into the workings of the body, are both necessary and dangerous. The ruler must align himself with the shaman, for the shaman can perceive what the ruler cannot. The immediate usefulness of the physician is to ensure the ruler's health, but, with the possession of specialized knowledge and access to poisons, the physician may also be a potential traitor. Canetti points out the similarity between the ruler and the physician: "It is only a step from the primitive medicine man to the paranoiac, and from both of them to the despot of history" (292): thus, the frequency with which doctors linger around the thrones of Poe's protagonists, and the sense that they are "in" on the secret. It goes without saying that such physicians are normally exempt from the death sentence that falls on everyone else.

In all monarchial societies, the health of the king is uppermost, but in **"Usher"** [**"The Fall of the House of Usher"**] both the mental and physical health of Roderick, the figurative "ruler" of the narrative, is in serious doubt from the beginning. In the cases of African kingship that Canetti analyzes, one method employed to secure the king's well-being is the practice of imitation on the part of his subjects: doubling the person and actions of the ruler guarantees his survival and increased potency. Since the metaphorical role of the narrator in **"Usher"** is to serve as something of an attendant at Roderick's court, he comes to play the role of a subject and his actions are increasingly devoted to repeating the interests and concerns of his "king." Despite his protests that he barely knew Usher in his adult life, he feels compelled as if by command to join Usher when he receives what he calls "a very singular summons" (318). One senses that the purpose of the summons is, in part, to gain support from the narrator and thus to prolong Usher's existence.

Like Canetti's prototypal paranoiac, Usher exists largely through language, though his interests in music and painting are also great. As the narrator points out, books "for years, had formed no small portion of the mental existence of the invalid" (328). Included in his collection are a number of works of European mysticism and Gothicism, but more interesting are the *Directorium Inquisitorium,* a peculiar volume dealing with African satyrs and oegipans by Pomponius Mela, and, the chief delight of Usher, the manual of a "forgotten church" (328). These obscure volumes hint at a repression of heresy, an opposition to change of any sort, and an obsessive attachment to ritual—all of which are aspects of control.

Roderick conveys the impression that he is a virtuoso in all of the arts that he touches. No other human can approach his level of ability, whether in music, painting, or poetry, yet the poem that we have from him, "The Haunted Palace," exhibits a striking sense of vulnerability. Within the stately palace of the poem is a throne where a ruler sits. Surrounding the ruler is "a troop of Echoes whose sweet duty / Was but to sing / In voices of surpassing beauty, / The wit and wisdom of their king" (326). The monarch, however, is assailed by an ambiguous crowd of "evil things," sorrows that Poe does not identify. The last stanza presents the state of the palace after the ruler's defeat and execution: now it is inhabited by "vast forms" who move to "discordant melody" rather than to the "stately music" of the former king, and rushing out from the door is "a hideous throng," laughing but not smiling (326). The forms that have defeated and executed the king are both innumerable and vast, and clearly the survivor cannot imagine himself overthrown except by a numerous and powerful crowd such as this. Also, the execution of the king takes place not without a peculiar sense of malice, for the throngs that rush out "forever"—apparently the masses who were once controlled by the ruler and who served as echoes to his song—are now liberated from his control and are enjoying their retribution. Their malicious laughter torments him.

In Roderick's case, the ruler's suspicion of hostile crowds extends not merely to human beings but to all existence, since he believes in the sentience not only of all vegetable things, but also of inorganic matter. The gray stones of the house begin to take on a sentience suggested to Roderick by the "order of their arrangement, as well as in that of the many fungi that overspread them, and of the decayed trees which stood around," and the doubling of the image in the waters of the tarn only adds to its quality of sentience (327). This description repeats several of Canetti's key crowd symbols: the stones arrange themselves in regiments; the trees though decayed suggest a potentially hostile army; and the numbers of each of these multitudes is doubled in the tarn.

The central action of the tale, the premature burial of Madeline and her escape from the tomb, may be related to Canetti's discussion of the ruler's imposition of the death sentence and to the violation of ancient burial rites. Consciously or not, Roderick imposes a death sentence of a sort on the individual who is closest to him and who therefore shares in his secrets and his history, indeed in his conception. It should not be surprising that Roderick wishes to survive his twin sister when one considers that her intimate knowledge of her brother makes her a rival to his existence and that, given his declining health, Madeline stands to succeed him. Canetti points out the peculiar relationship between kings and their successors: when the succession is hereditary, "both father and son have every reason to hate each other" (*Crowds* 243). Significantly, Roderick has no children; in this regard, he has deliberately avoided creating rivals, thus safeguarding his own rule but also ensuring the end of the family succession. As Canetti writes, "the intensest feeling for power is that found in a ruler who *wants no son*" (245).

With the premature burial of Madeline, however, Roderick violates the most universal of human rituals concerning the treatment of the dying and of burial itself. Among the aborigines that Canetti has studied, so long as death has not yet occurred the lamenting relatives surround the dying in an effort to support that member of the pack, but, as soon as death takes place, the lamenting pack transforms itself, shifting from support to a fearful discarding of the corpse. After death, every trace of the deceased's existence is eliminated. The tribal village itself is removed from the place of death for fear that the soul of the ancestor will linger. In lamenting their dead, aborigines continue the lament in their new camp, even to the point of wounding themselves as a sign of the sincerity of their grief. Canetti writes that "there is much anger in this self-mutilation, anger at impotence in the face of death. It is as though they were punishing themselves for death, as though the individual wanted to exhibit the mutilation through loss of the whole group by the mutilation of his own body" (106-107).

Canetti's analysis of these rituals is based on the universal fear of the dead. To the premodern mind it is obvious that the dead are envious of the living and wish to take revenge upon them. The elaborate rituals whereby the dead are mourned and sent on their journey with everything they will need in the next world are designed to avoid a wrathful response, yet the attitude of the living to the dead is equivocal: the death of one of their number weakens their group, but they also feel "a kind of satisfaction in their own survival," though this must not be admitted lest it arouse the anger of the dead (*Crowds* 263). The living must call on the soul of the dead to return so that they may convince him that they did not wish his death. They attempt to prove that the deceased was treated well in life, and the last wishes of the dead are carried out carefully. Behind all of this is "the unshakable conviction that the dead man must hate them for having survived him" (*Crowds* 263). The development of ancestor cults in countries such as Japan may be explained as a protective system by which people have learned how to propitiate the dead. Sacrifices and invocations are performed, and the dead person's memory is treated with consideration. In return for this care, the ancestor assumes a benevolent interest in his descendants. Thus, in these societies a mutually beneficial connection may be maintained between the dead and the living. Yet this orderly form of propitiation is the exception.

In Poe's tale, the effect of Roderick's violation of ritual is catastrophic. It is as though he wishes to bring destruction upon himself through the instrumentality of the vengeance of the dead. There is the suggestion that, consciously or not, Madeline cooperates in this murder-suicide, for when she is placed in the tomb not only is there a faint blush on her face but a "suspiciously lingering smile" (329). Haunted by the knowledge of what he has done, Roderick seeks solace in precisely the wrong place: in his collection of Gothic books that focus almost exclusively on the relationship of the living to the dead. As the narrator takes up the *Mad Trist of Sir Lancelot Canning,* he reads the tale of Ethelred, a knight who slays a dragon. As he approaches to grasp the brazen shield, it falls at his feet on the silver floor. The key elements of the story are reproduced by the sounds of Madeline's struggle to force her way from the coffin and the vault. At this point Roderick admits his lingering suspicion that he has placed the living Madeline in the tomb, and he reveals his primitive sense of fear of the dead as he cries: "Is she not hurrying to upbraid me for my haste" (335).

The story ends with the narrator fleeing in terror as the wild light of "the full setting and blood-red moon" (335) shines through the newly opened crack running from the roof to the base of the house. As the house splits apart, the moon's full shape appears, a visual echo of Roderick's enormous eye. As the house sinks, there is a long tumultuous shouting "like the voice of a thousand waters" (336), a crowd of shouts that proclaims the victory of the dead over the living as well as the biblical phrase associated with the voice of God—in this case, a god with whom the protagonist cannot align himself. We are left with the narrator fleeing from the scene but pursued by rays, just as Roderick had earlier felt threatened by rays. A blood-red eye now stares at the narrator, the sole survivor of the scene, for the narrator now inherits Usher's burden, including the secret of the Usher family history. He is Roderick Usher's successor, the new object of "attack" burdened with a "throng" of voices.

Like the narrator at the end of **"Usher,"** the protagonist of **"The Masque of the Red Death"** flees the site of cataclysm—in this case, an epidemic.[5] Transporting a thousand members of his court with him to a series of chambers resembling a burial vault, Prospero intends to guarantee his own survival, not that of his subjects. The court is necessary only as an echo to Prospero's rule: he summons a "thousand" (a number, Canetti points out, indicative of a stage toward the ultimate goal of the ruler—to survive "millions" and ultimately "all") to join him in "deep seclusion" within one of his castellated abbeys (485). Here the group finds apparent security, but a question remains as to why the group must engage in revelry at a time when masses of their countrymen are dying. Why should Prospero entertain his friends at a magnificent masked ball, if not to celebrate his own survival over the dead who lie without the abbey?

The scene of the revels suggests the paranoiac's familiar compulsion to control space. Prospero carefully selects the color and decoration of each of seven rooms, ranging from the eastern blue room, through purple, green, orange, white, violet, and finally the western black room that is fitted with window panes of scarlet and the light of a fire projecting its rays—another instance of the image of a hostile microscopic crowd that haunts the survivor's mind. Though each room is lighted by a tripod bearing a brazier of fire, the horrifying rays in the west room must pass through blood-tinted panes of glass. Also in the west room, a gigantic "clock of ebony" suggests another crowd—that of hours, minutes, and even seconds—hostile to one who values his own survival above all (487). When the clock strikes the hour, all activity ceases: the orchestra is silenced and the dancers are paralyzed by the clock's reminder of a greater power than that of Prospero, a fact that the narrator makes explicit by converting the hour into three thousand and six hundred seconds.[6]

Like the Roman emperors whom Canetti recounts, Prospero directs every detail of his fete: his guiding taste controls the celebration, combining elements of the "beautiful," the "wanton," the "bizarre," the "terrible," and much that "might have excited disgust" (487-488). This explicit comment invites consideration. Poe's list of Prospero's concerns suggests the aspiration of the paranoiac toward "enlargement" and control, as does the "multitude of dreams" that stalk to and fro among the seven chambers (488). Are these actual impersonators of dreams, masked and sent through the room at Prospero's command to mystify and thus control the guests, or are they insubstantial forms that the narrator only senses? In either case, they are powerful enough to control the orchestra, which plays as an "echo" of their moods, much as the crowd echoes Prospero.

Prospero's instinctive reaction to the masked figure is that of the paranoiac confronted by a rival whose masking appears to mock the secrecy that all rulers take on. The masked figure further offends the crowd, striking it with a sort of blow as he "impersonates" the Red Death. Poe writes, "There are chords in the heart of the most reckless which cannot be touched without emotion. Even with the utterly lost, to whom life and death are both jest, there are matters of which no jest can be made" (489). The figure, dressed in black shrouds, wears the mask of a "stiffened corpse," and his form is dabbled with blood to suggest the Red Death (489). The figure passes unimpeded within a yard of Prospero, as if to violate the ruler's space, then makes his way "with the same solemn and measured step" through each of the chambers until he stands on the threshold of the last (490). At this point Prospero, either recovering from his cowardice or embracing his doom, rushes, dagger drawn, at the masked figure. As he approaches his rival, Prospero drops his dagger and falls dead to the carpet.

Why is it that at this moment the crowd recovers its courage? Perhaps it is not so much that it wishes to rescue its endangered leader as that it senses the sudden relaxation of Prospero's authority. With "the wild courage of despair" the group rushes into the last apartment and seizes the insubstantial figure, its black attire and mask falling to the ground (490). The crowd not only realizes that it is in the presence of the Red Death: perhaps more important, the victim that it seeks in exchange for its own murdered king slips beyond the crowd's vengeance. The body of the enemy, the most important object to the vengeance pack, has evaded its grasp. The crowd's terror lies not simply in its awareness that its members are in the presence of a contagious disease; it also results from their failure to secure the body of the enemy which might assure their own increase. The fundamental instinct of grasping, seizing, and incorporating (their intention of "slaying death" and "cannibalizing" it) has been frustrated (490). Poe uses a familiar simile to characterize the figure of the Red Death: he has come "like a thief in the night" (490). Indeed, in Canetti's terms, the figure is a "thief" depriving the crowd of the victim's body that is its right.

In a broader sense, **"The Masque of the Red Death"** speaks of what is most threatening to the crowd, the threat to the group's own survival that it attaches to any threat to the figure of its king. The equation of increase with survival explains the central role of "Prospero" (his very name suggesting increase) in throwing a revel at the very time when death surrounds his group of followers. The consumption of food and drink, and the vitality of dance, are mimetic acts designed to preserve the entire court and enlarge its numbers. Equally striking is the fact that, in contrast to the thousand courtiers, the Red Death appears as a single and isolated individual. If the crowd of courtiers possesses strength by virtue of their numbers, the Red Death enjoys greater power by virtue of his "density" and by the absolute secrecy that solitude enables. The masked figure paralyzes the court when he first appears; he proves daunting even to Prospero because of his singleness and density. After all, to the primordial human imagination, the most fearful crowds are the invisible crowds of spirits, and it is these that the pestilence mimics.

The significance of the ebony clock, which forms its own dense crowd of "seconds" resembling the Red Death's crowd of bacilli, is reiterated in the final paragraph, which stresses the gradual ("clock-like") but steady and complete annihilation of the revelers. With the death of the last of these, the clock stops and the flames of the tripods expire. The tripods are ritual hearths on which burnt offerings could be made, but they are also the only source of vital light in the rooms and (as fire) elemental crowd symbols that Prospero employs to invite increase. The extinction of the tripods, coming at the end of the tale, marks the complete victory of the Red Death over Prospero's crowd. As Poe writes in the final passage: "Darkness and decay and the Red Death have illimitable dominion over all" (490).

Poe's stories reveal an author focused on the destructive effects of social isolation and victimization, and on the consequent responses of paranoia and schizophrenia. In his fiction Poe was well aware of the destructive potential of instinctual responses underlying human social relationships. In all human contacts, as Canetti demonstrates, there exists a pervasive fear of exclusion and victimization in response to which humans seek security through the seizing of power, yet this response too often perpetuates the cycle of domination and victimization. An obsession with power leads to the rise of what Canetti calls "the survivor," the tyrannical personality that attempts to secure its survival at the expense of others. For Poe, as for Canetti, only a clear understanding of the instinctive nature of power offers any real hope of transforming human relationships into a healthy form of interaction and of breaking the cycle of fear and repression that governs so much of human existence.

Notes

1. Further evidence exists of the impact of Poe's imagination on Canetti. During the first days of his acquaintance with the woman who would later become his wife, Canetti was introduced to "The Raven." When Vera (Venetia Roubner-Calderou) read the poem aloud, "the bird flew into my nerves; I began to twitch in the rhythm of the poem" (*Torch* 158).

2. Although a similar "reduction in wealth"—that accompanying his alienation from his guardian, John Allan—was a central fact of Poe's early life, the stories that I examine in this essay must be read as cautionary tales, not projections of Poe's personality. The practice of reading Poe's tales as a reflection of his fall from southern aristocracy, the status that he lost with his separation from the Allan family, can be traced to Jay B. Hubbell in *The South in American Literature* (see 535-536), a reading which is repeated by Robert D. Jacobs in *Poe: Journalist and Critic* (1969) and later in Richard Gray's essay on Poe in *Writing the South: Ideas of an American Region* (Cambridge UP, 1989). According to Jacobs, Poe viewed himself as "a suffering, sensitive aristocrat in a democratic shopkeeper's world" (15), yet, as Jacobs admits, after he became editor of Burton's *Gentleman's Magazine* the maturing Poe "assumed that it was the duty of the critic to educate the public taste" (227). Thus, despite his posturing of aristocracy, in his day-to-day existence Poe was almost totally engaged in the popular literary marketplace.

Though he was not always comfortable with this role, Poe spent his professional life writing for and editing mass-circulation magazines and newspapers. As Jacobs admits: "In spite of his often expressed contempt for the standards of the mob, Poe never quite relinquished the neoclassic notion that universality of appeal was one of the tests of art" (259). In the mid-1840s, "the first principle of his current criticism" was "that an artist should make a conscious effort to achieve universality of appeal" (Jacobs 361).

3. Legrand's frequent man-handling, striking, and seizing of Jupiter can be understood, in terms of Canetti's theory, as the release of primitive instincts of aggression. The origin of the instinct toward power, according to Canetti, can be located in the elemental act of seizing and grasping, the act of the predator at the moment of first touching and then securing its prey. The instinct of the human hand to grasp and hold and then to incorporate the prey is so fundamental to both animal nature that it is normally unconscious in humans. The innumerable ways in which humans mimic this activity, if enumerated, would comprise much of human social existence, from the common handshake, to the "bear hug," to the act of "devouring" another with one's eyes. In "The Gold Bug," Legrand frequently employs his hands in moments of passion to grasp, to strike, to embrace, and to hold in place, behavior which is an instinctual response to his fear of extinction.

4. The discovery of Captain Kidd's treasure takes place at night. Of course there are practical reasons for a night expedition, and one can imagine that Legrand takes pleasure in secrecy for its own sake, but, as in "The Tell-Tale Heart" and other stories of midnight mayhem, another reason is suggested by Canetti's analysis of "mana," the spirit of a slain man that enters the body of his killer. For this mana to be acquired by the slayer, the killing must take place at night, "for by day the victim will see his murderer, and will then be much too angry to enter his body" (*Crowds* 252).

5. Canetti groups epidemics with other phenomena which produce a "heap of corpses": battle, for example, and mass suicide. One result of contagion is the altered psychology of those people who do recover. Those miraculous survivors feel that they have become invulnerable, and they often demonstrate this by aiding the sick and dying. Canetti points to the example in Thucidydes' description of the plague in Athens, where those who recovered felt that they might never die of any disease.

6. As Geoffrey Harpham stresses in a valuable reading of "The Masque of the Red Death," the structure of Poe's art itself reveals a profound anxiety concerning survival. As Harpham writes: "Poe's imagination and art flourished at the margin, for only there could he interpose a fiction between himself and a fate impossible to confront directly" (118). Prospero's flight from the plague involves a self-effacement, reducing life to the abstract form of arabesque decoration and the mechanical enumeration of time. Prospero, like many of Poe's characters, seeks "the serenity of pure appearance and impersonality" (120), but he is unsuccessful because he carries with him to his retreat the hidden bacterial source of his destruction. Yet Poe was all too conscious of the futility of Prospero's flight, and much of his art is, as Harpham suggests, self-parodic, "exposing his art, the only means he had of attaining unity, for the ragbag parody of real creation that it was" (120).

Works Cited

Canetti, Elias. *Crowds and Power.* Trans. Carol Stewart. New York: Farrar Straus and Giroux, 1984.

———. *The Torch in My Ear.* Trans. Joachim Neugroschel. New York: Farrar Straus and Giroux, 1992.

Harpham, Geoffrey Galt. *On the Grotesque: Strategies of Contradiction in Art and Literature.* Princeton: Princeton UP, 1982.

Jacobs, Robert D. *Poe: Journalist and Critic.* Lexington: UP of Kentucky, 1969.

Poe, Edgar Allan. *Poetry and Tales.* New York: Library of America, 1984.

Adam Frank (essay date fall 2005)

SOURCE: Frank, Adam. "Valdemar's Tongue, Poe's Telegraphy." *ELH* 72, no. 3 (fall 2005): 635-62.

[*In the following essay, Frank ponders the impact of the mid-nineteenth-century phenomena of mesmerism and telegraphic communication on three of Poe's stories—"The Facts in the Case of M. Valdemar," "A Tale of the Ragged Mountains," and "Mesmeric Revelation."*]

Poe's **"The Facts in the Case of M. Valdemar"** caused a stir when it first appeared in American magazines in December 1845; many readers were willing to believe the tale's first-person scientific account of a mesmeric experiment in deferring death which ends with an instantaneously putrefying body. While Poe did not seem actively interested in perpetrating **"Valdemar" ["The Facts in the Case of M. Valdemar"]** as a hoax, he played with his readers' desires to know whether it was true—"It does not become *us,* of course, to offer one word on the point at issue. . . .

We leave it to speak for itself."[1] This is Poe's sly joke, for precisely what the tale does through its most startling device, Valdemar's vibrating tongue, is speak for itself to utter into circulation the last, echoing word, a grotesque metacommunication: "I am dead." As Poe put it several years later in a pseudonymous self-review, **"Valdemar"** "perhaps made a greater 'sensation' than anything else he has written," and it has continued to surprise and attract readers: Poe's main twentieth-century editor Thomas Mabbott introduces **"Valdemar"** as a "repulsive masterpiece"; Jonathan Elmer, in his reading of the story, labels its climax "one of the most powerfully effective moments in all of Poe"; and the tale has been taken up by Barthes and Derrida.[2]

This essay reads Valdemar's tongue and its impossible utterances as figures for electromagnetic telegraphy and its unlikely communications, and takes up **"Valdemar"** in the context of Poe's other writing on mesmerism of the mid-1840s to unfold perceptions and experiences of this ambient technology.[3] In part this essay tests a reading method that begins from an observation: at moments when some writers experience shifts in authorial status, their writing and poetics become particularly attentive to whatever publication means, and whatever publication means will be crucially informed by emerging technologies of reproduction or mediums of communication—not only print but also, in the mid-nineteenth-century, photography, telegraphy, and others, whether these are conceived as rival or competing media for print, or simply as newly available and making possible distinctive perceptual experiences.[4] Between 1843 and 1846 (and especially from the fall of 1844 to the fall of the next year), Poe reached the highpoint of his career, gaining new fame and infamy, and this moment coincides with his extensive treatment of mesmerism in the three tales and several entries in *Marginalia* that form my main texts in what follows: **"A Tale of the Ragged Mountains," "Mesmeric Revelation,"** and **"Valdemar."**[5] Mesmerism offered Poe a way to theorize what a medium for writing could be or do at the moment when just such a new medium was visibly, and audibly, emerging, and he is especially drawn to think through these questions at a moment of transition in his own status as author (or medium).

Poe's writing makes audible a peculiar experience: Morse's telegraph offered its perceivers both code—dot and dash inscriptions on paper, in the early version of a recording telegraph—and a kind of sound and movement. The quiet, tap-tap sound, consistently cast as a voice that utters in the absence of the body that is its source, was distinct from other experiences of sound communication without visible sound source, such as thunder, cannon or gunfire, or yells and yodels, all of which depend on sound volume, spatial configuration, and sound wave propagation in the medium of air. Electromagnetic telegraphy communicated coded language by way of electrical signals propagated in the medium of wires and electricity, and its force, I'll suggest here, lay both in its binary code and in an extension in indexicality which enabled much faster transmission than previous writing or communication at a distance. The strangeness of telegraphic experience for we later users of telephones and CD players is in offering to perception a "voice" that, unlike these later audio technologies, is heard as already code or writing coming from an operator's fingers and coordinated to the movement of the telegraph key or armature.

This movement was repeatedly figured in nineteenth-century writing as the "clattering tongue" of the telegraph, and if I read Valdemar's tongue as an early figure for this machine, my aim is to attend to Poe's writing as it estranges this figure to render telegraphy's acoustic experiences as a manipulative, violent touch. Poe's few explicit references to telegraphy make clear that he understood the technology in the specifically graphic terms of his manipulative poetics and theory of writer-reader relations. For example, consider this brief section of the *Marginalia* (November 1844) referring to the device that had six months earlier become a subject of reporting in the newspapers and magazines Poe read, edited, and contributed to:

> How many good books suffer neglect through the inefficiency of their beginnings! It is far better that we commence irregularly—immethodically—than that we fail to arrest attention; but the two points, method and pungency, may always be combined. At all risks, let there be a few vivid sentences *imprimis,* by way of the electric bell to the telegraph.
>
> (1322)

Unlike what would rapidly become the standard idealization—the telegraph would be said over and over again to "annihilate space and time"—Poe uses the device as a doubled figure for a "vivid" or arresting writing. Like the bell that signals a communication about to come through the wire, the pun *imprimis* (which condenses the meaning "in the first place" with a word that sounds like impression) directs a reader's attention specifically to writing. Poe's advice to begin irregularly or immethodically oddly contrasts with the attention-getting efficiency of this device, as if the telegraphic bell here signals less the efficiency of the new communications medium and more some new risks that accompany it—the risks of the "vividness" of Poe's preferred sentences or the startling "pungency" he proposes as a method. All Poe's references to this technology address a figure (specifically an acoustic figure) for his graphic poetics of effect or a theory of writing's force.

Poe's writing contrasts with those contemporary treatments that registered telegraphy's effects with an idealizing, breathless exhilaration that emphasized experiences of simultaneity. Consider this report published in the *New York Herald* on the occasion of an early telegraph line (often described as the first) being tested between Washington, D.C. and Baltimore:

> Professor Morse's telegraph is not only an era in the transmission of intelligence, but it has originated in the mind an entirely new class of ideas, a new species of consciousness. Never before was any one conscious that he knew with certainty what events were at that moment passing in a distant city—40, 100, or 500 miles off. For example, it is now precisely 11 o'clock. The telegraph announces as follows:—
>
> "11 o'clock—Senator Walker is *now* replying to Mr. Butler upon the adoption of the 'two-third' rule."
>
> It requires no small intellectual effort to realize that this is a fact that *now is,* and not one that *has been.* Baltimore is 40 miles from Washington. It is a most wonderful achievement in the arts.[6]

The reporter casts this experience as originating a form of certainty: Senator Walker is now replying to Butler, or rather, Walker is "*now*" replying, as the reporter tries to emphasize with print convention the new experience of simultaneity. If I insist that this fact cannot be known with any more certainty than any other statement—the telegrapher sending the message could be lying or wrong, or the operator receiving the message could be misunderstanding the communication—I still do not mean to detract from the reporter's distinctive experience, which is an experience of writing: "[t]he telegraph announces," that is, the reporter is listening to someone or something writing at this moment.

Contrast the reporter's experience with that of a reader of this report who encounters the phrase "11 o'clock—Senator Walker is *now* replying to Mr. Butler"; this reader has no need for telegraphic technology to have some sense of the scene in question, and indeed must be aware of the total lack of simultaneity: "it is now precisely 11 o'clock," with the accompanying technology of ink on paper and the present tense, insists that it is not precisely 11 o'clock at all; it is any time but 11 o'clock, the 11 o'clock in question; and this any-time-but-now permits the now to be signified. This is Derrida's point in *Speech and Phenomena* where he cites Valdemar's impossible utterance in the context of his critique of Husserl's elaborations of phenomenological presence: "The statement 'I am alive' is accompanied by my being dead, and its possibility requires the possibility that I be dead; and conversely. This is not an extraordinary tale by Poe but the ordinary story of language" (97). But what difference does it make that this moment from Poe which assists Derrida in specifying a basic structure of language is both generally or ordinarily graphic and quite specifically telegraphic?

"[T]his is a fact that *now is*": if there is a new species of consciousness that accompanies electromagnetic telegraphy, it emerges from how aural telegraphic experience makes "this" and "now" and "fact" go together as writing. Electromagnetic telegraphy's signs are symbolic, but also indexical signs which do not in the first place refer (to some content, "the fact") but only insist (on some moment) or declare. For the reporter, however, telegraphic experience coordinates indexicality, simultaneity, and truthful representation to reconfigure a form of "liveness" that already belongs to writing but becomes differently embedded in the perception of sound as a guarantee of antifigurative certainty. This reconfigured form of liveness—call it telegraphic sensationalism—is part of C. S. Peirce's definition of the index: "The index asserts nothing; it only says 'There!' It takes hold of our eyes, as it were, and forcibly directs them to a particular object, and there it stops." Peirce's speaking sign has particular physiological powers that he casts in these terms:

> [T]he *index* . . . like a pointing finger, exercises a real physiological *force* over the attention, like the power of a mesmerizer, and directs it to an object of sense. . . . A blinding flash of lightning forces my attention and directs it to a certain moment of time with an emphatic "Now!" Directly following it, I may judge that there will be a terrific peal of thunder, and if it does not come I acknowledge an error. One instant of time is, in itself, exactly like any other instant, one point of space like any other point; nevertheless dates and positions can be approximately distinguished.[7]

Blindness, electricity, and mesmeric power—a power cast as the directing force of utterance—in an experience of simultaneity, a homogenization of space and time, and a control over a reader's or listener's attention: Peirce theorizes the index within a discourse of telegraphic sensationalism, a modern (often nationalizing) discourse that coordinates utterance with temporal collapse and physiologized powers over attention and emotion cast as mesmeric.[8] Perceptions of telegraphy may be crucial to Peirce's theoretical elaborations, and via Poe as well as Peirce, to Derrida's.

I turn to Poe's writings on mesmerism to articulate the relations between the new technology's acoustic and graphic nature and accompanying fantasies of emotional manipulation. Mesmerism offered Poe and his contemporaries a medium at once spiritual and material in which an individual's sensations or feelings could be imagined to be connected to those of others and to larger social networks. Electromagnetic telegraphy literalized these social networks of feeling, elaborating a physiologized social body comprised of wires and electricity, keys and armatures. Poe's writings on mesmerism theorize this physiologized field as it offers access to potentially shared sensations, especially via a (male) reader's body and its potential for being de-differentiated from the body of the writer. His tales of mesmerism stage scene after scene of writing, each more unlikely, controlling, and dangerous for both writer and reader than the last; they depict not scenes of individualizing mastery but scenes of control's excess or loss of control for everyone involved.

Poe's mesmeric poetics depict at an early moment of its emergence the phenomenon that Jonathan Sterne calls telegraphic intimacy, the investment of sound telegraphy "with the possibility of a depth of feeling and communication that was hitherto reserved for face-to-face and written interaction."[9] Besides **"Valdemar,"** the most startling instance of telegraphic intimacy I have encountered is a passage from Robert W. Chambers's 1932 *Whistling Cat,* a very late addition to the subgenre of telegraph romance that became popular after the Civil War. Two-thirds of the way through the book the narrator Juan and his partner Iris, Union Army telegraph operators, are trapped behind a group of Southern militia who have downed a communications wire, and Iris uses the two ends of the cut wire to send for help. Juan worries that they cannot receive any message in return since they don't have an armature or key to read with, but resourceful Iris shows Juan what to do:

> "Hold them that way," she said to me. . . . "Try not to hurt me, darling—" And again she thrust out her tongue and I gently pressed the two ends of the wire into it.
>
> Instantly the electric pulsations gave to her tongue a vibratory movement like a telegraph armature. I could read the involuntary oscillations of her little pink tongue as easily as I could have read my own magnet.[10]

This over-the-top staging of the graphic quality of electromagnetic telegraphy offers a sadomasochistic love scene between Juan and Iris; but there is also a third person, the distant (and gender unknown) operator who remotely controls Iris while Juan assists and watches. A magnet, a distant finger, a little pink body-part out of control: I think the specific vividness of this scene comes from how it condenses or de-differentiates various body parts and devices, and maps their movements onto a network of communication and control in which organic nerves and inorganic wires are not only analogized but made to be functionally continuous. And the specific function is writing: a hand at a distance produces coded or symbolic utterance without any physical interiority—no breath coming from lungs through vocal chords shaped by lips and mouth, but rather an electrical transmission, read visually as if the tongue were part of a writing machine, which it is. Such perceptions of telegraphic writing are only very tenuously perceptions of any individual's "voice"; but they are, in the first instances, perceptions of a vibratory, and most often acoustic, phenomenon. Jay Clayton has suggested that telegraphy's acoustics have made it less easily assimilable to grand narratives of modernity's "scopic regime": "By consolidating the sensory effects of the signal, sound technology appears to intensify rather than abstract," thereby bringing listeners into embodied, close, and potentially queer contact.[11] Poe's mesmeric poetics do intensify along acoustic lines, bringing readers into extremely close contact with the writer and writing instruments. But whether the particular forms of embodiment that accompany electromagnetic telegraphy make it any less assimilable to modernity remains unclear to me.[12] Poe's mesmeric poetics are central to that other frustratingly large and unwieldy periodizing term, not "modernity" but "mass culture." The following pages explore part of the technological basis for "mass culture," the specific perceptual experiences of telegraphy and its (anti)figurative elaborations.

* * *

In the early 1840s *magnetism* named an eclectic variety of phenomena. The magnetism long associated with the attractive and repulsive forces of certain materials such as iron and amber had recently been shown to interact with electric current. Experimenters in the 1820s and 1830s had determined that an electric current produced magnetic effects and vice versa, and this work (especially that of Michael Faraday in England and Joseph Henry in the U.S.) permitted new approaches to the old problem of communicating "intelligence," especially military intelligence, at a distance.[13] But magnetism, as animal magnetism, also connoted the theory and practice of the eighteenth-century Viennese physician Franz Anton Mesmer, whose startling cures and crises scandalized Vienna and then Paris in the 1770s and 1780s.[14] Mesmerism reemerged in the United States and England in the late 1830s and 1840s with theories of the unified nature of electrical, magnetic, and nervous phenomena. These overlapping meanings and unifying theories help to explain why mesmerism plays a minor but curious role in all the standard narratives of the invention of telegraphy in the United States.[15] In these mostly heroic and individualizing narratives, mesmerism appears just after Morse finally succeeds (in February 1843) in having a bill brought to Congress to appropriate thirty thousand dollars to construct a telegraph line between Washington and Baltimore. The bill is almost defeated when a speaker "moved that one-half of the appropriation be expended in making experiments with mesmerism"; one of Morse's supporters appeals to the chair to rule out this amendment as in bad faith, and the chair replies: "'It would require a scientific analysis to determine how far the magnetism of mesmerism was analogous to that to be employed in telegraphs.' ('Laughter.')"[16]

This scientific analysis was being pursued, at least in England. Alison Winter's cultural history of Victorian mesmerism shows both that the investigators of electrical and mesmeric phenomena overlapped, and how this overlap contributed to understandings of the social. Winter tracks changes in the meaning of "consensus" from the coordinated action of different body parts in a single physiology (as in coughing and blinking) to a description of a social body, and locates this physiologizing of the social body, among other places, in the responses to sensation fiction. Readers especially of Wilkie Collins's *The Woman in White* (1859-1860) described their responses in terms of reflex acts, their "rapt" attention a "direct physiological response that was prior to, and perhaps in many cases more powerful than, self-conscious thought."[17] Reflex physiology attempted to explain not only how a reader could physically experience something that was represented in the narrative (in Margaret Oliphant's famous review, a touch on the shoulder) but also how reading sensational material could be communal: reflexes might vary among individuals, and these differences were greater at higher levels of organization; but at the lower physiological levels at which Collins's writing was said to operate, reading sensation novels could be a collective activity.[18] The idea that "mass culture" as group sensation operates at the level of the lowest common denominator appears to have one theoretical basis in this mid-nineteenth-century theory of reading in terms of sense-physiology.[19]

The physiologizing of the social body made consistent use of reciprocal, literalizing analogies between telegraph wires and human or animal nerves.[20] Poe uses such analogies in a review of the popular Swiss Bell-ringers act; the bell-ringers, Poe suggests, are actually automata operating according to the same principles as the electromagnetic telegraph, principles which explain both the performers' remarkable precision and also their ability "to *electrify* their hearers" (1120) (here is another instance of the sound of a telegraphically produced bell that thrills a public). Electrified publics appeared often, especially in U.S. journalistic and other mid-century writing on the technology, as for example in the memoirs of J. G. Bennett, one of the most successful early publishers of American tabloid journalism. These memoirs typify the idealizing mid-century discourse on telegraphy: "the Magnetic Telegraph, which radiates intellectual light like the sun itself, or, as a network, spread from city to city, transmits its subtle fires, vitalized by thought, from one end of the country to the other, as it were uniting into the same day's life and sympathies, and virtually narrowing more than a million square miles into a cognizable span." This national-theological discourse of the "electrical sublime" idealizes national unity, sympathy, and the powers of the press for creating consensus, as in this citation of Bennett's depiction of telegraphy's powers: "The whole nation is impressed with the same idea at the same moment. One feeling and one impulse are thus created and maintained from the centre of the land to its uttermost extremities."[21]

While this fantasy of centralized national control invokes a kind of physiologized national body, whose center—or competing centers, New York and Washington, D.C.—controls its extremities through nerve-like telegraph wires, the work of creating and maintaining feeling takes place in the paragraph that immediately follows this, through the simple means of depicting Bennett's face and body: "In this foreshadowing of the future importance of the Magnetic Telegraph, Mr. Bennett displayed that same enthusiasm which is natural to his disposition when he perceives the certainty of an event of public interest. At such a time his face is swiftly crimsoned with excitement—he breaks forth into a few swift words of exclamation—walks a few steps away and reflects, lest he should be deceived by his own fancy—becomes convinced that he is not in error, and it may be, dictates an article, or writes it with his own hands, to stamp his thought upon the public mind."[22] A reader is given Bennett's passion and reflexivity, his sincere enthusiasm tempered by thoughtful reflection, in a generic depiction of mid-century sentimental masculinity. As much as it is about creating national unity and creating or regulating a public mind, the promise of telegraphic sensationalism (or sentimentalism, which may come to the same thing here) is made good by the supposed guarantee of transmission of feeling or affect, from a closely observed face to dictation or writing coming from a properly individuated tongue or hands. In print this transmission of feeling over a network of sympathy relies on the careful depiction of faces and bodies, and many of Poe's prose romances (including the tales of mesmerism) offer stark and idiosyncratic versions of such depiction.

In mid-nineteenth discourse the relation between mesmerism and sympathy is close: mesmeric or magnetic fluid is the stuff of the network of sympathy, and Poe radically condenses this fluid within his theory of mesmeric sensation.[23] Where Bennett's more sentimentalizing telegraphic network insists on properly individuated and assigned body parts, Poe's more sensationalizing mesmeric methods of gaining access to readerly sympathies take advantage of the problem of properly individuating and assigning body parts within a field of mesmeric fluid; and body parts which fail to be properly individuated can become particularly vital or telling, indeed they become points of powerful communication. Poe describes the conditions for such bodily non-individuation in **"Mesmeric Revelation"** (August 1844), published a little more than a year before **"Valdemar."** This "essay," as Poe liked to call it, largely consists of a philosophico-theological dialogue between P—and a mesmerized consumptive, Vankirk, who once entranced transmits his knowledge of the material substratum of the universe. He explains that there is no immateriality, only gradations of matter, with the final gradation being the "ultimate, or unparticled matter," "a matter as much more rare than the ether, as this ether is more rare than the metal" (1034). This unparticled matter permits man to have "two bodies—the rudimental and the complete" or "ultimate." The former experiences ordinary sensation, communicated by way of "vibrations," say, from a "luminous body" to the retina to the optic nerve to the brain; that is, Vankirk understands ordinary sensation to work by way of associationist theories of the vibratory action of the nerves as well as sense-physiology's doctrine of specific nerve energies. The "ultimate body," however, gives one access to "unorganized" sensation much more directly.

> [I]n the ultimate, unorganized life, the external world reaches the whole body, (which is of a substance having affinity to brain, as I have said,) with no other intervention than that of an infinitely rarer ether than even the luminiferous; and to this ether—in unison with it—the whole body vibrates, setting in motion the unparticled matter which permeates it.
>
> (1037-38)

The "ultimate body" is all unparticled matter, but we only feel unorganized sensation when the rudimentary body dies or exists in a state that resembles death—between sleep and waking, the mesmeric state. Mesmerism, for Poe, is a method for gaining access to "unorganized" sensation: he is after the "ultimate body."

Given that the "unparticled matter, not only permeates all things but impels all things—and thus *is* all things within itself" (1033), it remains far from clear how any object or body, in its "whole" or "ultimate" form, can be individuated or distinguished from any other. But this problem turns out to be productive for Poe's poetics, as can be gathered from the *Marginalia* for March 1846, where he revisits mesmerism as a method of gaining access to particular sensations. "I do not believe that any thought, properly so called, is out of the reach of language," asserts Poe against transcendentalizing theories of the inexpressible; yet the subject of this short piece is "a class of fancies, of exquisite delicacy, which are *not* thoughts, and to which, *as yet,* I have found it absolutely impossible to adapt language."[24] His search for a method of gaining written access to such fancies leads Poe once again to the mesmeric state.

> I am aware of these "fancies" only when I am upon the very brink of sleep, with the consciousness that I am so. I have satisfied myself that this condition exists but for an inappreciable *point* of time—yet it is crowded with these "shadows of shadows"; and for absolute *thought* there is demanded time's *endurance.*
>
> (1383)

In the somnambulistic state Poe can open out this point of time and put words to what he calls these "psychal impressions" (a term Vankirk uses as well) (1384). These are no ordinary impressions; accompanying them is a "pleasurable ecstasy," a feeling-state that Poe analyzes in terms of a "delight [that] has, as its element, but *the absoluteness of novelty*" (1383). This physiologized novelty—"It is as if the five senses were supplanted by five myriad others alien to mortality"—is what he's after, and motivates his efforts at self-control. Poe writes that he can "prevent the lapse from *the point* of which I speak—the point of blending between wakefulness and sleep" and, waking himself up, "*transfer the point itself into the realm of Memory*; convey its impressions, or more properly their recollections, to a situation where (although still for a very brief period) I can survey them with the eye of analysis" (1384). In **"Valdemar,"** Poe's mesmerist-narrator/writer will attempt to open up this point of time in the experiment to defer Valdemar's death, and there we encounter similar transactions between time, writing, and memory. Here Poe's solitary mesmeric efforts give him access to a social space of shared fancy:

> I am not to be understood as supposing that the fancies, or psychal impressions, to which I allude, are confined to my individual self—are not, in a word, common to all mankind—for on this point it is quite impossible that I should form an opinion—but nothing can be more certain than that even a partial record of the impressions would startle the universal intellect of mankind, by the *supremeness of the novelty* of the material employed, and of its consequent suggestions. In a word—should I ever write a paper on this topic, the world will be compelled to acknowledge that, at last, I have done an original thing.
>
> (1384-85)

"In a word," the mesmeric method may have more to do with Poe's intense desire for successful written material than with anything else. The psychal space, at once Poe's own and shared by "all mankind"—which, if tapped through mesmerism, guarantees compelling writing ("an original thing")—sounds remarkably like the space of Vankirk's ultimate body.

Originality and novelty continue to appear as key terms for Poe's mesmeric poetics. He returns and complicates these terms in his second Hawthorne review (published in *Godey's Magazine and Lady's Book* for November 1847), written, according to Michael Allen, when he was "exultant" about **"Valdemar"**'s success.[25] Here Poe spins out a theory of originality and popularity that lets him mark his difference from Hawthorne, "the example, *par excellence,* in this country, of the privately-admired and publicly-unappreciated man of genius."[26] Poe disagrees with the conventional critical explanation of Hawthorne, the one that accepts the cliche that a very original writer necessarily fails as a popular one, and he exults in these "facts" and "truths": "But the simple truth is, that the writer who aims at impressing the people, is *always* wrong when he fails in forcing that people to receive the impression"; "It is, in fact, the excitable, undisciplined childlike popular mind which most keenly feels the original. . . . The fact is, that if Mr. Hawthorne were really original, he could not fail of making himself felt by the public." Poe's embrace of the mass market casts true originality in these terms:

> This true or commendable originality, however, implies not the uniform, but the continuous peculiarity—a peculiarity springing from ever-active vigor of fancy—better still if from ever-present force of imagination, giving its own hue, its own character to everything it touches, and, especially, *self impelled to touch everything.*[27]

Poe reaches out and touches someone, everyone, everything, a force which emerges from that space of supreme novelty Poe describes in the *Marginalia.* But this novelty is only apparent, as he further specifies his manipulative touch in an interesting gloss on "true originality":

> But the true originality—true in respect of its purposes—is that which, in bringing out the half-formed, the reluctant, or the unexpressed fancies of mankind, or in exciting the more delicate pulses of the heart's passion, or in giving birth to some universal sentiment or instinct in embryo, thus combines with the pleasurable effect of *apparent* novelty, a real egoistic delight. The reader, in the case first supposed, (that of the absolute novelty,) is excited, but embarrassed, disturbed, in some degree even pained at his own want of perception, at his own folly in not having hit upon the idea. In the second case, his pleasure is doubled. He is filled with an intrinsic and extrinsic delight. He feels and intensely enjoys the seeming novelty of the thought, enjoys it as really novel, as absolutely original with the writer—*and* himself. They two, he fancies, have, alone of all men, thought thus. They two have, together, created this thing. Henceforward there is a bond of sympathy between them, a sympathy which irradiates every subsequent page of the book.[28]

"True originality" passes through a set of disjunctive phrases, sets itself up in two cases, and concludes as a series of doubles: "pleasure is doubled," the "real egoistic delight" turns out to be both "intrinsic and extrinsic," the novelty shared "with the writer—*and* himself," and the repetitions of "They two" and "sympathy." Elmer reads this passage to suggest that "Poe's sympathy . . . creates a unity . . . a single, mass reading public," but if so it is a unity that is structured not as a mass but as a potentially infinitely iterable series of readers, "subsequent" as the pages of a book, each of whom doubles the writer.[29] Poe decomposes "true originality" to guide the erotics of writing for publication: in imagining his "self impelled to touch everything," to coax only "*apparent[ly]* novel" serial pleasures, Poe makes a familiar male body the mesmeric space of fancy shared by readers and writer.

This male body appears in Poe's first tale of mesmerism, **"A Tale of the Ragged Mountains,"** a baroque story initially published in *Godey's Magazine and Lady's Book* for April 1844. The tale offers an opportunity to track some aspects of Poe's poetics as I have been unfolding them in the last few pages: a mesmeric scene of writing, an accompanying manipulative control over a male body, and the opening up of a point of time with fatal results. As well, a less condensed and more legible version of the figure that appears as Valdemar's tongue appears in this tale, which will permit me to locate the new graphic technology in this scene of writing. The tale begins with the narrator's detailed attention to the mysterious neuralgic Augustus Bedloe's face and body:

> He was singularly tall and thin. He stooped much. His limbs were exceedingly long and emaciated. His forehead was broad and low. His complexion was absolutely bloodless. His mouth was large and flexible, and his teeth were more wildly uneven, although sound, than I had ever before seen teeth in a human head. The expression of his smile, however, was by no means unpleasing, as might be supposed; but it had no variation whatever. It was one of profound melancholy—of a phaseless and unceasing gloom. His eyes were abnormally large, and round like those of a cat. The pupils, too, upon any accession or diminution of light, underwent contraction or dilation, just such as is observed in the feline tribe. In moments of excitement the orbs grew bright to a degree almost inconceivable; seeming to emit luminous rays, not of a reflected, but of an intrinsic lustre, as does a candle or the sun; yet their ordinary condition was so totally vapid, filmy and dull, as to convey the idea of the eyes of a long-interred corpse.
>
> (940)

This moon-eyed Bedloe resembles a typical Poe beloved, all big eyes and bloodless complexion, skinny, melancholy, and intense. Entranced, like Berenice (whose "lifeless and lustreless" eyes and commanding teeth fix the narrator's attention in that tale), melancholy and (it will turn out) reincarnated like Morella, and feline like the black cat: here are Poe's unlucky beloveds all rolled up into one, and his specialty too is returning from the dead.[30] Like Poe's heterosexual romances, this tale and **"Valdemar"** feature struggles of will, episodes of violence, possession, and revenge. The main difference is that the erotics of this romance reside in Bedloe's "singular" body, which resembles that other sensitized mesmeric subject, "M. Valdemar . . . particularly noticeable for the extreme spareness of his person—his lower limbs much resembling those of John Randolph" (1234). Bedloe is singular, except that he resembles M. Valdemar, who in turn resembles John Randolph, the "cadaverous Virginia statesman" (1243) (as Poe's editor Mabbott puts it)—in this context, the "spareness of [Valdemar's] person" seems a pun, for these subjects are all spares for one another.

The tale is largely comprised of Bedloe's description of his strange experiences wandering through the Ragged Mountains of Virginia. Bedloe is reminiscent of Charles Brockden Brown's sleepwalkers for whom the altered magnetic state of romance animates the American ground as inexhaustible source for writing. Bedloe finds himself looking down upon "an Eastern-looking city, such as we read of in the Arabian Tales. . . . I could perceive its every nook and corner, as if delineated on a map," and what he sees is graphic, dense, and detailed: "The streets seemed innumerable, and crossed each other irregularly in all directions, but were rather long winding alleys than streets, and absolutely swarmed with inhabitants." The description that follows, in the mode of what Poe terms arabesque, depicts "wildly picturesque" houses, "a wilderness of balconies, of verandahs, of minarets," "bazaars abounded" with "rich wares," and so on (945). This is at once orientalist fantasy and a description of the American ground as inexhaustible resource: the ground, delineated by crossing streets, alleys, and the river, is already a map or writing.

Bedloe's experience turns out to be a hallucination guided entirely by the writing of his physician-mesmerist, Doctor Templeton: "[A]t the very period in which you fancied these things amid the hills, I was engaged in detailing them upon paper here at home" (949). This, at its most literal, is Poe's theory or fantasy of the mesmeric relation between writer and reader: Templeton transmits detailed impressions from his pen and Bedloe receives them right in the temple. When Bedloe sets out on his wanderings and follows "the windings of a pass" new to him, imagining that the secluded spot was "absolutely virgin" and he the first human to tread on that terrain—"the very first and sole adventurer who had ever penetrated its recesses" (942-43)—we can hear what Derrida describes as breaching or path-making, the "excessively sinuous" (943) path that will be Dr. Templeton's presumably cursive script on the "freshly written" (949) manuscripts he produces that day.

Writing means getting into Bedloe's brain. We are given a number of reasons for Bedloe's peculiar susceptibility to Templeton's writing. For one, there's the "very distinct and strongly marked *rapport,* or magnetic relation" (941) that had developed between them that seems to be the explanation for how Bedloe could receive Templeton's transmission. But then there's a strange duplication of faces and names: Templeton writes of seeing his friend Mr. Oldeb killed by a poison arrow at "the insurrection of Cheyte Sing" (949) in Benares in 1780, and Bedloe's and Oldeb's names are almost perfect converses; Templeton also shows Bedloe and our narrator a watercolor portrait of Oldeb which exactly resembles Bedloe, of whom readers have received a detailed description. The continuities between these two are both graphic and photographic: Poe had already written about an uncannily accurate portrait in **"The Oval Portrait,"** and the "miraculous accuracy" (948) of Oldeb's picture, especially if (anachronistically to the tale's setting, but not writing) a daguerreotype would invert Oldeb's image, as the name "Bedloe" inverts "Oldeb." Both graphic image and name make redundant Templeton's agentive, writerly control, for Bedloe's experiences seem to be already determined by the graphic nature of Bedloe as Oldeb reincarnated.

Templeton's redundant writerly control turns out to have fatal consequences for Bedloe. In his hallucinations, Bedloe is suddenly motivated to join some men in partly British uniforms battling the inhabitants of the city. He relives Oldeb's foolhardy rush to combat the crowd, is set upon by spears and arrows, and dies when one of the arrows hits him: "They resembled in some respects the writhing creese of the Malay. They were made to imitate the body of a creeping serpent, and were long and black, with a poisoned barb. One of them struck me upon the right temple" (947). A week after these hallucinations, our narrator reads an item in a Charlottesville newspaper announcing "the death of AUGUSTUS BEDLO" (note the missing "e") from an accidental application to his temple of a poisonous leech which closely resembles the proper medicinal leech (949). Templeton, it would appear, has unintentionally killed Bedloe twice, for the report concludes with this note:

> N.B. The poisonous sangsue of Charlottesville may always be distinguished from the medicinal leech by its

> blackness, and especially by its writhing or vermicular motions, which very nearly resemble those of a snake.
>
> (950)

Poe gives us an always distinguishable (except this time) black leech in an iterated series: black leech, black arrow, black snake, writhing creese. This iterated figure turns up in its most powerful version as Valdemar's tongue, at once extended and creased.

In addition to this iterated figure and the careful description of Bedloe's face and body, I want to take one other thing from this tale back to a reading of **"Valdemar,"** its insistent emphasis on sound: a drumbeat first indicates to Bedloe that he is in some altered magnetic state, or beginning to hallucinate what will turn out to be Templeton's writing; and soon after, "there came a wild rattling or jingling sound, as if of a bunch of large keys" (943). Recall the narrator's particular attention to Bedloe's teeth: "more wildly uneven, although sound, than I had ever before seen teeth in a human head." Bedloe's sound teeth assonate with the creeses and leeches, those agents of his and Oldeb's death, and with the keys which initiate Templeton's transmission. If his eyes are photographic, his teeth are telegraphic: the typographical error which takes away the silent "e" in Bedloe's name—the narrator worries over this error at the end of the tale—both indexes the graphic continuity between the identity of Bedlo/Oldeb, and summons the point of time so central to Poe's poetics of "psychal impressions," the "e," that is, the single dot of Morse's code.

Like **"Ragged Mountains" ["A Tale of the Ragged Mountains"]**, **"Valdemar"** offers an allegory of writer-reader relations in the environment of the new graphic technology. But where the earlier tale poses this relation as one of unidirectional (though unintentional and unpredictable) control, **"Valdemar"** does something different. Valdemar, the subject of the mesmeric experiment, is himself a writer, specifically a translator who can serve well as a medium. He has published Polish translations of Rabelais and Schiller "under the *nom de plume* of Issachar Marx"; that is, Valdemar is a link to European political theory, and in Meredith McGill's terms, a figure for Poe's "creative embrace of America's cultural secondarity." McGill summarizes a crucial aspect of Poe's manipulative poetics: "Poe's association of authorial control with duplicity defines authorship not as origination but as manipulation, a practice defined by interruption, inconsistency, and uncertainty, not mastery."[31] Mesmerism, for Poe, names this form of duplicitous authorial control; it may connote mastery, but in practice it operates via interruption, inconsistency, and uncertainty, figuring the manipulation of a social body that is undecideably writer's and reader's. This manipulative agency begins on the side of the mesmerist-narrator in **"Valdemar"** but does not remain there: in this tale agency is transferred to Valdemar, or more specifically, to Valdemar's tongue. Like Templeton's pen and the leech that kills Bedloe, Valdemar's tongue is the point of mesmeric access to the ultimate body of readerly sensation, and while such access is necessarily by way of print for Poe the magazinist, print's possibilities become imbued with perceptions of telegraphic communication.

Much is at stake, then, in the narrator P—'s desire for mesmeric control over Valdemar's body, which is cast as a struggle for control over writing and, particularly, style. The narrator's distinctive style, an officious first-person narration, almost entirely avoids figurative language in favor of a facts-in-the-case insistence on strict timekeeping and medical terminology. This trumped up style echoes that of contemporary publications that aimed to make mesmerism legitimate as a scientific subject in the 1840s.[32] But it solicits sensation from the opening paragraph, in which the doctor-mesmerist introduces himself, hyper-defended and overexposed before a voracious, unbelieving public:

> Of course I shall not pretend to consider it any matter for wonder, that the extraordinary case of M. Valdemar has excited discussion. It would have been a miracle had it not—especially under the circumstances. Through the desire of all parties concerned, to keep the affair from the public, at least for the present, or until we had further opportunities for investigation—through our endeavors to effect this—a garbled or exaggerated account made its way into society, and became the source of many unpleasant misrepresentations, and, very naturally, of a great deal of disbelief.
>
> It is now necessary that I give the *facts*—as far as I comprehend them myself.
>
> (1233)

"To announce a truth is to stipulate the existence of an enigma," writes Roland Barthes, and when the narrator repeats this stipulation (the extraordinary case, the circumstances, the affair, the account, the facts), he builds up the "garbled or exaggerated account" that is both the tale itself and its pretext.[33]

Valdemar's writing in a direct, stoic note contrasts with the narrator's officious style and makes clear the urgency of the experiment: "My dear P—, You may as well come *now*. D—and F—are agreed that I cannot hold out beyond tomorrow midnight; and I think they have hit the time very nearly." When P—arrives Valdemar is still strong enough to be "occupied in penciling memoranda in a pocket-book," but the narrator immediately begins to draw the agency of writing away when he "press[es] Valdemar's hand" and "postpone[s] operations" for more than twenty-four hours, as if to weaken him further. This perverse deferral accompanies P—'s narrative style: he defers for want of "more reliable witnesses" than the nurses in attendance and only continues with the experiment when a medical student shows up. The presence of this student permits the transfer of Valdemar's writing agency to P—, for "it is from [the student's] memoranda that what I now have to relate is, for the most part, either condensed or copied *verbatim*" (1235-36).

The tale literalizes the interruption, uncertainty, and inconsistency that comprise Poe's understanding of manipulation in descriptions of the mesmerist's attempts to control Valdemar's limbs. Eventually these succeed, but P—excitedly misreads this success as mastery over Valdemar's psychic state. He asks Valdemar the same question over and over again ("do you still sleep?") until the mesmeric operation begins to backfire.

> While I spoke, there came a marked change over the countenance of the sleep-waker. The eyes rolled themselves slowly open, the pupils disappearing upwardly; the skin generally assumed a cadaverous hue, resembling not so much parchment as white paper; and the circular hectic spots which, hitherto, had been strongly defined in the centre of each cheek, *went out* at once. I use this expression, because the suddenness of their departure put me in mind of nothing so much as the extinguishment of a candle by a puff of the breath. The upper lip, at the same time, writhed itself away from the teeth, which it had previously covered completely; while the lower jaw fell with an audible jerk, leaving the mouth widely extended, and disclosing in full view the swollen and blackened tongue. I presume that no member of the party then present had been unaccustomed to death-bed horrors; but so hideous beyond conception was the appearance of M. Valdemar at this moment, that there was a general shrinking back from the region of the bed.
>
> (1239)

As sudden here as Valdemar's apparent death is P—'s awareness of writing: he interrupts the scientifico-legal style to become reflexive in his choice of words. We get drawn through emphasis and reflexivity to the more or less banal analogy of death as the extinguishing of a candle, but this misdirects our attention from the tale's first instance of the figurative, the preceding analogy of Valdemar's skin to white paper.

The presence of the figurative, and the specific figure of white paper, marks the change in both **"Valdemar"** and Valdemar: it brings Valdemar further along his passionate trajectory from someone who writes to writing surface, and its concealment brings us closer to what Neil Hertz would call the sublime turn in the story, "the point where the near-fatal stress of passion can be thought of as turning into—as indistinguishable from—the energy that is constituting the poem."[34] Valdemar seems to have become Locke's perfect passive receptor, the mind as white paper. But it is not Valdemar's mind—interior, private, nonmaterial—that is likened to white paper, it is the skin of his face; and Valdemar is an old, dead or dying man rather than a newborn blank slate. Poe's Valdemar, Locke's epistemological subject turned inside out, is able not just to be impressed or imprinted upon but to impress upon others.[35] And he has brought along his own instrument for this sensational effect: Valdemar's "swollen and blackened tongue," so exposed and disclosed against his "white paper" skin, displaces the previous figure by making it the ground in this picture. The figure of white paper becomes concealed as a ground is concealed, in plain sight.

This reversal of figure and ground prepares the way for the next long passage, in which Valdemar's disgusting face forces P—'s writing to shuttle back and forth between the figurative and the inexpressible. The narrator once again becomes reflexive about his writing, and tries to guide a reader.

> There was no longer the faintest sign of vitality in M. Valdemar; and concluding him to be dead, we were consigning him to the charge of the nurses, when a strong vibratory movement was observable in his tongue. This continued for perhaps a minute. At the expiration of this period, there issued from the distended and motionless jaws a voice—such as it would be madness in me to attempt describing. There are, indeed, two or three epithets which might be considered as applicable to it in part; I might say, for example, that the sound was harsh, and broken, and hollow; but the hideous whole is indescribable, for the simple reason that no similar sounds have ever jarred upon the ear of humanity. There were two particulars, nevertheless, which I thought then, and still think, might fairly be stated as characteristic of the intonation—as well adapted to convey some idea of its unearthly peculiarity. In the first place, the voice seemed to reach our ears—at least mine—from a vast distance, or from some deep cavern within the earth. In the second place, it impressed me (I fear, indeed, that it will be impossible to make myself comprehended) as gelatinous or glutinous matters impress the sense of touch.
>
> I have spoken both of "sound" and "voice." I mean to say that the sound was one of distinct—of even wonderfully, thrillingly distinct—syllabification. M. Valdemar *spoke*—obviously in reply to the question I had propounded to him a few minutes before. I had asked him, it will be remembered, if he still slept. He now said:
>
> "Yes;—no;—I *have been* sleeping—and now—now—*I am dead.*"
>
> (1240)

This amazing passage enacts the disintegration and figurative reconstitution that Hertz calls the sublime turn: the disintegration of P—'s writing in shuttling between the figurative and the inexpressible, and the reconstitution of a different writing in Valdemar's impossible utterance. What has been transferred is agency of expression or writing itself, from the mesmerist to Valdemar's tongue: this tongue gives forth utterance that does not have its source in the controlled body that is uttering. The vibrating movement of the tongue aims to make accessible the shared psychic space of the "ultimate body" in Poe's poetics (to recall the terms of **"Mesmeric Revelation"**) by way of the broken and hollow telegraphic voice or sound heard as if "from a vast distance." The narrator's uncertainty over whether to describe this utterance as "voice" or "sound" registers the particularity of perceptions of Morse's device, and the "thrillingly distinct syllabification" both radically exaggerates his own antifigurative style and describes the telegraphic transmission's precision and tap-tap distinctness.

The telegraphic effect of Valdemar's tongue is cast as much more powerful than the mesmerist's, perverse and unavoidable. "No person present even affected to deny, or attempted to repress, the unutterable, shuddering horror which these few words, thus uttered, were so well calculated to convey" (1240): here, again, Poe makes acoustic experience available through poetic devices, as the half-rhyme unutterable/shuddering maps the sensation of shuddering onto the movement of the tongue and those who are listening to its utterances. "Mr L—I (the student) swooned. The nurses immediately left the chamber, and could not be induced to return. My own impressions I would not pretend to render intelligible to the reader" (1240-41): Valdemar's stuttering utterance communicates its effects like a tuning fork struck against the page, as if the stop-start form of the words and punctuation (a semi-colon followed by a dash), emphasis and repetition ("Yes;—no;—I *have been* sleeping—and now—now—*I am dead*"), makes the tongue, its words, and the swooning persons continuous, part of a single sensational medium; and aims to make a reader's tongue shudder too, or perhaps laugh, for who is doing the calculating here?

My point is not to insist, once again, on Poe the master of manipulation. Poe's writing, I am suggesting, is itself a medium that registers the "indescribable" perceptions of telegraphic communication, perceptions both of writing in general and of how telegraphic writing appears to make contact: by way of a "thrilling" consensus of bodily movement. If this tale registers the thrill of telegraphic perception figuratively (the primary figure of Valdemar's tongue) and formally (in terms of verbal technique), it also does so affectively: Valdemar's utterance is framed by the overly legible expression of disgust (upper lip up, mouth distended, tongue out), and some of the forceful effects of this tale come from this blatant depiction of a disgusted and disgusting face. Other moments in the tale evoke disgust: when the narrator struggles to describe the feeling of the sound coming from Valdemar's tongue as "gelatinous or glutinous," he makes the voice continuous with the substance that later flows from Valdemar's eyes, a "profuse outflowing of a yellowish ichor . . . of a pungent and highly offensive odor" (1242). This in turn reappears as the substance of putrefaction with which the tale leaves us at the end when, after seven months of suspended animation, the narrator finally decides to end the experiment and bring Valdemar out of his trance.

> As I rapidly made the mesmeric passes, amid ejaculations of "dead! dead!" absolutely *bursting* from the tongue and not from the lips of the sufferer, his whole frame at once—within the space of a single minute, or even less, shrunk—crumbled—absolutely *rotted* away beneath my hands. Upon the bed, before that whole company, there lay a nearly liquid mass of loathsome—of detestable putridity.
>
> (1242-43)

The temporal collapse and the collapse of Valdemar's "frame" are both mapped onto the collapse of the frame of the tale, the tongue's telegraphic emissions bringing everything to a revolting climax.

But why would the force of the new graphic technology be framed specifically by disgust? Are we to conclude that, for Poe, telegraphy is disgusting? I think there are a number of other, more interesting reasons for the presence of this particular affect. First, quite simply, disgust is the only affect that gives you an outstretched tongue; the literalization of a telegraphic "voice" as emerging from a tongue/stylus may, in part, accidentally be disgusting (that is, contingent of the evolution of the human face and this particular expression). As well, disgust lets Poe make fun of us: to tone down the thrill of the conclusion of the tale, think of it as a kind of Bronx cheer. Poe's mockery may make more sense if one considers the role of disgust in the dynamics of what Silvan Tomkins calls decontamination scripts, scripts or affect theories that organize perception around some impurity; disgust motivates attempts to expel the impurity.[36] The narrator's facts-in-the-case, antifigurative style can be understood as governed by a decontamination script, one that tries to purify itself of figurative language: the struggle between the narrator and Valdemar, a struggle over style, is more specifically over figure, and it is just after the first figure of Valdemar's "white paper" skin appears that Valdemar's expression changes to that of disgust. Poe's Bronx cheer at the end concludes what would then be a broad joke, a burlesque of the antifigurative style and its desire for a purified control. The more the mesmerist-narrator tries to control Valdemar's limbs (his figure), the more Valdemar responds by exaggerated figurations, impossible utterances and, eventually, his exploding body. The decontamination script offered by this tale would not be about the "impurity" of the new graphic technology, but rather what this technology has already begun to serve as a figure for: antifiguration, the coordination of "this" and "fact" and "now" that idealizes the technology within the discourse of telegraphic sensationalism. What Poe's tale lets us read in his twisted version of this discourse is, in part, the decontamination script that guides the tendency to use telegraphy to figure precisely the goal of vanishing mediation and producing transparency, what will become generic movements toward varieties of realism.[37] Poe's writing insists not on telegraphy as antifigurative but on telegraphy as (from the start) an overdetermined figure for, precisely, effective or manipulative writing, writing that may conceal the figurative but can never do without it.

This could be one conclusion of my essay: that Poe's writing is a joke on the antifigurative style that the new technology will come to stand for, the changes in how writing can be imagined to make contact. But I want to offer a more positive conclusion as well. Winfried Menninghaus's book on disgust offers a number of possible answers to the question of why disgust frames perceptions of telegraphy in Poe's tale. Disgust, he shows, plays a particular role in defining the field of eighteenth-century (German) aesthetics: in its association with the proximity of the "lower senses" of touch, smell, and taste, disgust short circuits reflection and prevents the experience of aesthetic illusion; disgust becomes the defining limit for Enlightenment aesthetics, especially in rules for depicting the beautiful human form as exemplified by classical sculpture. In nineteenth-century European literature disgust comes to play a different role, in part because music (rather than sculpture) becomes the ideal of the poetic: "with just that art possessing the weakest link to the disgust-sensation coming to dominate the post-1800 stage of aesthetic reflection, the older disgust-taboo loses a considerable amount of its powers of distinction."[38] Poe's tale insists on the possibilities of auditory disgust, or to put this differently: disgust foregrounds the indexicality of telegraphic communication by coordinating sound (as well as sight, in depictions of Valdemar's voice and face) to a forceful touch. The force of this touch emerges in part from the role of disgust in the "poetry of putrefaction" (Baudelaire is Menninghaus's primary example): "as an organic process, 'putrefaction' is a(n) (ironic) figure of defiguration that, starting with the advent of Romanticism, is repeatedly used in the description of libidinous desire, vice, and the historical signature of the passions in general."[39] For Poe's poetics of manipulation, Valdemar's putrefaction can represent a (fully and formally self-ironized) manipulation of the passions in general: the stuff of Valdemar's body is the stuff of sympathy, affect, or sensation itself, a much less refined version than what Vankirk describes in **"Mesmeric Revelation."**

Derrida's reading of Valdemar's utterance as it insists on the requirement of absence for signification remains more than ever to the point here. What I hope to have done is to open out this point to a variety of experiences of presence, and especially to affective presence in print as taking on the (acoustic, indexical) forces of other graphic means. Valdemar's utterance, as well as his disgusting face and putrefying body, frames perceptions of telegraphy as they raised the stakes of the liveness/deadness of writing. These stakes are political insofar as the control of body parts, thinking, and feeling of people at a distance through the operations of writing creates the imagined possibility of a social body's consensus through the powerful force of a mass medium. If these stakes belong more properly to the "liveness" of radio or television than to that of electromagnetic telegraphy (never quite a mass medium), part of what this essay shows is how the groundwork for this configuration was laid in the mid-nineteenth-century discourse of telegraphic sensationalism and the mesmeric powers granted to the indexicality of the new technology. Poe's writing acutely registers and theorizes such perceptions in the terms of his primary poetic problem, the control of his readers' sensations or feelings, staged in the form of a repetitive manipulation.

Notes

1. From Poe's introduction to the tale in the *Broadway Journal,* 20 December 1845. Reprinted in *Edgar Allan Poe: Tales and Sketches,* ed. Thomas Ollive Mabbott, vol. 2 (Chicago: Univ. of Illinois Press, 2000), 1230. Unless otherwise specified, all references to Poe are to this volume and are cited parenthetically by page number.

2. Poe, "A Reviewer Reviewed," in *The Collected Works of Edgar Allan Poe,* ed. Mabbott, vol. 3 (Cambridge: Harvard Univ. Press, Belknap Press, 1978), 1377; Mabbott, in *Tales and Sketches,* 1228; Jonathan Elmer, *Reading at the Social Limit: Affect, Mass Culture, and Edgar Allan Poe* (Stanford: Stanford Univ. Press, 1995), 123; Roland Barthes, "Textual Analysis of a Tale of Poe," in *On Signs,* ed. Marshall Blonsky (Baltimore: The Johns Hopkins Univ. Press, 1985), 84-97; Jacques Derrida, *Speech and Phenomena* (Evanston: Northwestern Univ. Press, 1973), 1 and 96-97. Gregory Whitehead mentions "Valde-

mar" in the context of a literary prehistory of radio art in "Out of the Dark: Notes on the Nobodies of Radio Art," in *Wireless Imagination: Sound, Radio, and the Avant-garde,* ed. Douglas Kahn and Whitehead (Cambridge: The MIT Press, 1992), 253-63.

3. See Christopher Johnson, "Ambient Technologies, Uncanny Signs," *Oxford Literary Review* 21 (1999): 117-34. Johnson defines ambient technologies by contrast with invisible ones which have become "more or less unconsciously assimilated into everyday practice and behaviour"; "'ambient' technology . . . would refer to 'new' technologies that have not yet undergone such assimilation and as such retain a degree of visibility. This visibility would relate not only to the immediate, empirical instances of when, where and how new technologies are used, but also to their *revealing* function, that is, how they permit modes of experience, conceptualization, and representation hitherto unimagined" (132 n. 2). My interest here in audibility rather than visibility will make revelation less to the point than selective or directed attention. For a different treatment of Poe and telegraphic writing see Shawn Rosenheim, *The Cryptographic Imagination: Secret Writing from Edgar Poe to the Internet* (Baltimore: The Johns Hopkins Univ. Press, 1997), 87-111.

4. I am seeking here to contribute to the growing body of critical work on media change, for example as collected in *Rethinking Media Change: The Aesthetics of Transition,* ed. David Thorburn and Henry Jenkins (Cambridge: The MIT Press, 2003). For another essay that practices this particular reading method see my "Emily Dickinson and Photography," *Emily Dickinson Journal* 10 (2001): 1-21.

5. In October 1844, not long after moving to New York, Poe took up a position at the *Evening Mirror,* and the beginning of the next year saw the publication of "The Raven" and Poe's sudden rise to fame: his entry into New York literary society; the publication of *Tales* (Wiley and Putnam, 1845) and *The Raven and Other Poems* (Wiley and Putnam, 1845); his contributions to the *Broadway Journal,* of which he then became editor and proprietor; the "Little Longfellow War" that took place between January and August; and his scandalous reading of a "juvenile poem" at the Boston Lyceum. See Meredith McGill on this moment in Poe's career and the conditions of literary production in relation to the Young America movement of literary nationalism in "Poe, Literary Nationalism, and Authorial Identity" in *American Literature and the Culture of Reprinting, 1834-1853* (Philadelphia: Univ. of Pennsylvania Press, 2003).

6. James G. Bennett's *New York Herald,* 30 May 1844.

7. C. S. Peirce, *The Essential Peirce: Selected Philosophical Writings,* ed. Nathan Houser and Christian Kloesel, 2 vols. (Bloomington: Indiana Univ. Press, 1992), 1:226, 232.

8. Peirce worked for about thirty years with the U.S. Coast Survey and would have been familiar with the Survey's early use of the electromagnetic telegraph to determine longitude. See Carlene E. Stephens, "The Impact of the Telegraph on Public Time in the United States, 1844-1893," *IEEE Technology and Society Magazine* 8 (March 1989): 4-10.

9. Jonathan Sterne, *The Audible Past: Cultural Origins of Sound Reproduction* (Durham: Duke Univ. Press, 2003), 153.

10. Robert W. Chambers, *Whistling Cat* (New York: A. L. Burt & Co., 1932), 287. The telegraph romance subgenre begins in the 1870s and addresses, among other things, the role of women telegraphers in the labor force. See Thomas C. Jepsen, "Women Telegraphers in Literature and Cinema," in *My Sisters Telegraphic: Women in the Telegraph Office, 1846-1950* (Athens: Ohio Univ. Press, 2000).

11. Jay Clayton, "The Voice in the Machine: Hazlitt, Hardy, James," in *Language Machines: Technologies of Literary and Cultural Production* (New York: Routledge, 1997), 223. Clayton has suggested that, in its nineteenth-century literary treatments, telegraphy is associated with a specifically female homoerotics, and the scene in *Whistling Cat* could be read queerly as primarily between a distant woman operator and Iris. The tapping fingers and vibrating tongues which are constitutive of telegraphic intimacy and sexuality, especially in North America, emerge in part from the specificity of Morse's device: unlike Cooke's and Wheatstone's telegraph in England which operated with needles pointing to letters of the alphabet, Morse's telegraph was both more abstracted from everyday language (via its binary or digital dot-dash code) and more connected to specific body parts. The telegraph sounder or key, in giving a distant finger's movement and clicking sound, permitted a faster operation of sending and receiving than recording and needle telegraphs, eventually enabling Morse's device to displace its competitors. After the first decade or so operators did away with the automatic recording stylus of Morse's earlier machines and learned to send and receive based on sound. Operators learned to distinguish each others' sending rhythms, forming competitive subcultures around speed of transmission and reception;

stories of rivalries, friendships, and romances developing over the telegraph wires are a staple of telegraph lore. One might say that telegraphy became sexy because operators could have (manual, digital) style. See *Lightning Flashes and Electric Dashes: A Volume of Choice Telegraphic Literature, Humor, Fun, Wit and Wisdom,* compiled by W. J. Johnson (New York: W. J. Johnson, 1877), and Katherine Stubbs, "Telegraphy's Corporeal Fictions," in *New Media, 1740-1915,* ed. Lisa Gitelman and Geoffrey B. Pingree (Cambridge: The MIT Press, 2003) 91-111.

12. Clayton's claims may be contrasted with those of James Carey, who practically makes telegraphy into modernity's cause in opening up the field of telegraphy's effects in relation to monopoly capitalism, business practices, religious discourse, common sense, perceptions of time, and language. His claim that the telegraph "can stand metaphorically for all the innovations that ushered in the modern phase of history" strikes me as a desire to engage in genetic explanation; rather, it would make more sense to think of genetic explanation and the notion of code as source (of history, of life) as both emerging, at least in part, with electromagnetic telegraphy. Carey, "Technology and Ideology: The Case of the Telegraph," in *Communication as Culture: Essays on Media and Society* (New York: Routledge, 1992), 203. See also Evelyn Fox Keller, "The Body of a New Machine: Situating the Organism Between Telegraphs and Computers," in *Refiguring Life: Metaphors of Twentieth-Century Biology* (Columbia Univ. Press, 1995).

13. Telegraphic forms that predate the electromagnetic varieties that emerged in the 1830s and 1840s are optical: smoke signals, warning fires, naval semaphore systems, and the Chappé brothers' optical telegraph system in France.

14. The best social and cultural histories of mesmerism I have read are Robert Darnton, *Mesmerism and the End of the Enlightenment in France* (New York: Schocken Books, 1970), and Alison Winter, *Mesmerized: Powers of Mind in Victorian Britain* (Chicago: The Univ. of Chicago Press, 1998). On the relations between human automata and idealizations of social order, see Simon Schaffer, "Enlightened Automata," in *The Sciences in Enlightened Europe,* ed. William Clark, Jan Golinski, and Schaffer (Chicago: The Univ. of Chicago Press, 1999). On mesmerism and romantic poetics see Nigel Leask, "Shelley's 'Magnetic Ladies': Romantic Mesmerism and the Politics of the Body," in *Beyond Romanticism: New Approaches to Texts and Contexts, 1780-1832,* ed. Stephen Copley and John Whale (New York: Routledge, 1992). For an essay that offers to explain the ubiquitous presence of Benjamin Franklin in American Spiritualist séances of the 1840s and 1850s and argues that this cultural moment can best be understood in relation to technological innovations of the day and especially telegraphy, see Werner Sollors, "Dr. Benjamin Franklin's Celestial Telegraph, or Indian Blessings to Gas-lit American Drawing Rooms," *American Quarterly* 35 (1983): 459-80.

15. See Alfred Vail, *The American Electromagnetic Telegraph* (Philadelphia: Lea & Blanchard, 1845); James Reid, *The Telegraph in America* (New York: John Polhemus, 1886); Carleton Mabee, *The American Leonardo: The Life of Samuel F. B. Morse* (New York: Knopf, 1943); Lewis Coe, *The Telegraph* (Jefferson, NC: McFarland & Company, 1993); and Tom Standage, *The Victorian Internet* (London: Weidenfeld & Nicolson, 1998).

16. Quoted in Nathan Sargent, *Public Men and Events,* 2 vols. (Philadelphia: J. B. Lippincott & Co., 1875), 2:194. For a report of the debate in Congress, see Mabee, 256-58.

17. Winter, 324.

18. See Margaret Oliphant, "Sensation Novels," *Blackwood's Magazine* (May 1862): 572-73.

19. D. A. Miller's reading of Collins would imply the queerness of group sensation. Miller shows how sensation consists first in a male reader catching nervousness from the woman in white: "Every reader is consequently implied to be a version or extension of the Woman in White, a fact that entails particularly interesting consequences when the reader is—as the text explicitly assumes he is—male." Miller reads this in relation to the inversion model of male homosexuality and the homophobic defense against it. For Poe, sensation does not appear to be gendered in quite the same way, for nervousness is not made available in or as the body of a woman, an identification with which is then both enacted and disavowed. Miller, *The Novel and the Police* (Berkeley: Univ. of California Press, 1988), 153-54.

20. See Laura Otis, "The Other End of the Wire: Uncertainties of Organic and Telegraphic Communication," *Configurations* 9 (2001): 181-206; and "The Metaphoric Circuit: Organic and Technological Communication in the Nineteenth Century," *Journal of the History of Ideas* 63 (2002): 105-28.

21. [Isaac C. Pray?], *Memoirs of James Gordon Bennett and His Times* (New York: Stringer & Townshend, 1855), 342, 364. On the "electrical sublime," see Carey. For the racial logic that accompanies discourse on telegraphy as a mid-

19th century national unifier, see Paul Gilmore's "The Telegraph in Black and White," *ELH* 69 (2002): 805-33.

22. *Memoirs of James Gordon Bennett,* 364-65.

23. In *Reading at the Social Limit* Elmer addresses sympathy as sentimentalism's "liquid principle" and reads Poe's sensationalism in his tales of mesmerism as revising the conventions of the sentimental. In "Valdemar" and "Mesmeric Revelation" Elmer notes that Poe rewrites the generically sentimental scene of a character on his deathbed "dying of the disease of choice in nineteenth-century sentimentalism—consumption . . . delivering his last communications and visions of the world to come" (115). By contrast with Little Eva's visions of the afterworld, Poe's sensationalism gives us Valdemar's overly literal utterances and his disgusting body. Elmer reads a moment towards the end of "Valdemar" when the narrator observes a substance emerging from Valdemar's eyes as possibly "the most grotesque revision of sentimentalism in all of Poe's work, the tears which figure and confirm the precious moment of connection—those 'sacred drops of humanity,' to recall Rowson's phrase—become . . . revoltingly opaque" (122).

    All of Poe's mesmeric writings are located at or within what Elmer calls the "social limit" indexed by "the ambivalence of affect, the unavoidable experience of being taken out of oneself into another, an unmasterable affection by the otherness internal to the self" (14). By mapping this internal limit onto a limit "internal to the discursive sociality of mass democratic society." Elmer offers a powerful way to read "Poe's ostensibly psychological tales and poems, in their very focus on representational and psychic division attending the individual—and despite their frequent lack of reference to contemporary conditions—[as] in fact profoundly responsive to social reality" (19-20). The social limit offers a solution to the problem of reading "romance" in American Studies as this names a kind of disconnection to the social, to the symbolic, and an accompanying compensatory embodiment. Informed by Elmer's work, my reading of Poe in this essay nevertheless attempts to move away from the reification "mass culture" and its accompanying genre/gender configurations and toward sexuality, specific affects, and how perception is reciprocally shaped by emerging technologies and mediums.

24. Poe, *Edgar Allan Poe: Essays and Reviews* (New York: Literary Classics of the United States, 1984), 1383.

25. Michael Allen, *Poe and the British Magazine Tradition* (Oxford: Oxford Univ. Press, 1969), 150. For Poe's second Hawthorne review, see *Essays and Reviews,* 577-88.

26. Poe, *Essays and Reviews,* 578.

27. Poe, *Essays and Reviews,* 583, 579.

28. Poe, *Essays and Reviews,* 581.

29. Elmer, 118.

30. Poe, vol. 1 of *Tales and Sketches,* 215.

31. Meredith McGill, *American Literature and the Culture of Reprinting, 1834-1853* (Philadelphia: Univ. of Pennsylvania Press, 2003), 152, 186.

32. For examples, see Chauncey Hare Townshend, *Facts in Mesmerism, with Reasons for a Dispassionate Inquiry into It* (New York: Harper & Brothers, 1841), and John Elliotson, *Numerous Cases of Surgical Operation without Pain in the Mesmeric State* (Philadelphia: Lea and Blanchard, 1843).

33. Barthes, 84. It would be possible to describe the narrator's style using terms from Anthony Wilden's work on analog and digital communication: Poe's techniques of interruption, negation, and avoidance of figure are digital techniques for the creation of the analog effects of deferral and anticipation. This redescription would permit a return to the use that Barthes and Derrida make of Poe's tale as it invites a critique of presence, the self-presence that phenomenological perception locates in or as speech or voice, and which writing as difference, iteration, and supplement deconstructs. Poe's digital techniques make salient both writing in general and Morse's digital telegraphic code in particular. See Wilden, "Analog and Digital Communication," in *System and Structure: Essays in Communication and Exchange* (London: Tavistock Publications, 1972).

34. Neil Hertz, "A Reading of Longinus," in *The End of the Line: Essays on Psychoanalysis and the Sublime* (New York: Columbia Univ. Press, 1985), 5. Hertz reads Longinus to describe aspects of sublime turning, both in poetic texts and in texts that make more historical truth-claims than do poems, as would the case study here. In these latter, not only must passion shift to poetic action, as in poetic texts, but in addition, this figurative action must be concealed; what must be concealed is "the figurativeness of every instance of the figurative": "It is when a literary text provides us with a powerful apprehension of this phenomenon [oscillation between two poles] that we are drawn to characterize it as 'sublime'" (18-19). The tongue becomes the tale's transfer point from passion to poetic, figurative action, enacting the "vibratory activity of sublime turning" (17) in which movement the figurative language of the "facts in the case" is concealed.

35. See Joan Dayan, *Fables of Mind: An Inquiry into Poe's Fiction* (Oxford: Oxford Univ. Press, 1987).

36. See Silvan Tomkins, *Affect Imagery Consciousness,* 4 vols. (New York: Springer Publishing Company, 1991), 3:348-76; and "Revisions in Script Theory—1990," in *Exploring Affect: The Selected Writings of Silvan S. Tomkins,* ed. E. Virginia Demos (Cambridge: Cambridge Univ. Press, 1995).

37. See Richard Menke, "Telegraphic Realism: Henry James's *In the Cage,*" *PMLA* 115 (2000): 975-90. Menke explores how, for realist writers like Dickens, Thackeray, and Gaskell, "the figure of electric telegraphy helps crystallize the assumptions and evasions of Victorian realism, its claims to transmit a domain of shared meaning neutrally." Menke shows how Henry James's *In the Cage* treats telegraphy rather differently at the end of the century, and argues that James "literalizes and estranges a metaphor that had occasionally provided Victorian writers with a powerful technological analogue, and even a kind of working model, for Victorian realism" (976).

38. Winfried Menninghaus, *Disgust: The Theory and History of a Strong Sensation* (Albany: State Univ. of New York Press, 2003), 107, 122.

39. Menninghaus, 141.

Walter Shear (essay date spring 2006)

SOURCE: Shear, Walter. "Poe's Fiction: The Hypnotic Magic of the Senses." *Midwest Quarterly* 47, no. 3 (spring 2006): 276-89.

[*In the following essay, Shear concentrates on the relationship between sensory experience and the material world in Poe's short fiction.*]

For all its extravagant moments, the essential drama of Edgar Allan Poe's fiction is that of the individual mind, orchestrated and ordered by the life of the senses. While the disciplined minds of his characters tend to regard their immediate environment as a problem to be solved, the mind as sensibility is essentially a reactor voraciously transforming and absorbing sensuous data into experience, creating in the process a character whose very impetuosity makes him dramatically convincing.

In his more intense stories Poe confines his protagonists to enclosed spaces or hostile environments (the fatal quarantine in **"The Masque of the Red Death,"** the bizarre chamber in **"Ligeia,"** Pym's claustrophobic confinement in ***The Narrative of Arthur Gordon Pym*** [***The Narrative of Arthur Gordon Pym of Nantucket***], etc.), a practice that encourages a kind of blindered attentiveness on the part of enclosed characters. In such isolation the characters are intensely alone. Indeed the keen appreciation of another's humanity, the feeling of having a socially meaningful relationship to the world which might provide some comfortable assurance for facing the problem of life—all this is almost totally absent in Poe's entire fictional canon. Instead the characters find themselves strangely isolated, facing a world that is almost fiendishly physical, one whose material nature they will come to regard as their chief obstacle. Indeed most of Poe's dramas center on this meeting of material and bodily limits. Poe was one of those nineteenth-century thinkers who tried to use contemporary science to imagine the transcending of material bounds, but scientific thinking itself grounded him in materialism.

In fiction Poe's answer to the problem involved an examination of the role the senses played in defining and limiting human nature. He focused on environmental interaction on many levels. While the rhetorical surface of many of the stories seems a superficial agitation of recalcitrant immediacies, Poe's larger view of mental activity is evinced in the example of Dupin reading the mind of his companion in **"The Murders in the Rue Morgue"**: "You stepped on one of the loose fragments. . . . You kept your eyes upon the ground. . . . I saw you were still thinking of the stones. . . . I could not doubt that you murmured the word 'stereotomy'" (***Tales*** [***Poetry and Tales***], 403-4). An incredible anticipation of modern stream of consciousness, Dupin's reading (however improbable) reveals a reflective dimension absent in the other stories with their anxious rush to purely sense-induced conclusions. This study will attempt its own mind reading, specifically, looking at a narrator's deployment of sensuous materials for hints of broader meaning dimensions.

In one of the less intense moments of **"MS. Found in a Bottle,"** the narrator notes, "While musing upon the singularity of my fate, I unwittingly daubed with a tar-brush the edges of a neatly-folded studding-sail which lay near me on a barrel. The studding-sail is now bent upon the ship, and the thoughtless touches of the brush are spread out into the word DISCOVERY" (***Tales,*** 195). This signal of meaning has a curious history. As pointed out by Selma B. Brady, the narrator's act is paralleled in a book Poe knew very well, David Brewster's *Letters on Natural Magic.* The passage cited is Brewster's account of a seemingly preternatural instance, that of a Swede (Peter Heaman) intuiting his own fate through an identical action, using a tar brush on a sail and surprising himself to see that he had daubed out a gallows with a headless man underneath.

Heaman tells his companions, "You may depend upon it that something will happen;" later he is executed (*Letters,* 29). The incident is merely one of many anecdotes featuring amazing sensory phenomena, each of which is explained by Brewster as a form of natural illusion (or delusion) of the senses.

That Poe was fascinated by the illustrations is further evidenced by the remarkable likeness between another of Brewster's anecdotes and the ending of ***The Narrative of Arthur Gordon Pym.*** In ***Pym*** [***The Narrative of Arthur Gordon Pym of Nantucket***] the title character, drifting on an ocean which gives off a "luminous glare," is suddenly confronted by "a shrouded human figure, very far larger in its proportions than any dweller among men. And the hue of the skin of the figure was of the perfect whiteness of the snow" (***Tales,*** 1179). With this vision Poe's work ends abruptly. In Brewster's account Dr. A. P. Buchan looking out at the ocean on a foggy morning is surprised to see himself and a companion reflected and elevated in the air. Just as he was skeptical about Heaman's experience, regarding it as a delusion of the senses, Brewster analyzes Buchan's vision with a rather metaphoric debunking: "when, in the midst of solitude, and in situations where the mind is undisturbed by sublunary cares, we see our image delineated in the air, and mimicking in gigantic perspective the tiny movements of humanity . . . when such varied and striking phantoms are also seen by all around us and therefore take the character of real phenomena of nature, our impressions of supernatural agency can only be removed by a distinct and satisfactory knowledge of the causes which gave them birth" (*Letters,* 140). What this suggests about ***Pym*** remains unclear but it begins to suggest how problematic sensuous material could become for Poe.

In key particulars, **"MS."** [**"MS. Found in a Bottle"**] echoes Brewster's skepticism, though more cruelly. The would-be transcender crying "I shall never—I know I shall never—be satisfied with regard to the nature of my conceptions. . . . A new sense—a new entity is added to my soul," is at the end abruptly plunged into the bowels of the earth (***Tales,*** 195). The broader significance of Brewster's empirical analyses for Poe's fiction, however, is much more far-reaching. Instead of treating sensation as fact (or fictional fact), Poe could regard it as perception or even, as Brewster's comment on the state of mind suggests, as symptom. Such a perspective would add a whole new structure of meaning to the experiential narrative by making the mind itself the essential subject matter and centering questions of meaning on the whole idea of spectral material. By making the drama of the mind such an intensely personal experience, Poe's fiction could push the senses into defining not only a subjective uniqueness but also into examining the ambiguous relationship of that experience to the material world in which the experience occurs.

In his discussion of plotting Poe spoke approvingly of a "reciprocity between cause and effect" so that "we cannot distinctly see . . . whether . . . one depends from any other, or upholds it" (*Essays,* 1316). Rather than abandoning these basics of rational orientation (cause and effect), Poe creates his rhetorical unity by making them part of the desperation of the isolated mind. Indeed, as the history of Poe criticism has suggested, the meanings which arise out of a character's interpretation often suggest their own sly alternatives for making sense of the senses. For example, **"Metzengerstein"** and **"A Tale of the Ragged Mountains"** both use what seem to be instances of metempsychosis to raise the issue of whether the idea entertained is an attribution of an interpreting character or the dramatization of a marvelous belief come to pass. In **"A Tale"** [**"A Tale of the Ragged Mountains"**] the first-person narrator declines to be explicit in endorsing the supernatural event, but his selection of material—the cadaverous appearance of Bedloe, the vividness of the Benares vision, the re-experiencing of Oldeb's death, and the final implicit suggestion of an occult connection—all lead a reader to conclude that Oldeb has, however briefly, inhabited the body of Bedloe. Challenging the supernatural view, Sidney E. Lind has argued it is Dr. Templeton who believes in metempsychosis and it is his belief that has infected the others. Since Templeton had been treating Bedloe with mesmerism (to the extent that there was an almost occult relationship between the two), the apparent glimpse of a previous existence is really a trance resulting from Templeton's hypnotic hold on his patient—though one might concede that the weight of spectral material (here an entire city and the experience of death) would require an extremely intense hypnotic state.

"Metzengerstein," the earliest articulation of the soul migration theme, has also been the subject of critical disagreement. Its issue centers about the internal, unspoken assumption of the major character, Baron Metzengerstein. The easiest case to make is, oddly, the deception interpretation. The Baron obviously knows the motto wherein the rider over the horse is parallel with the mortality of Metzengerstein over the immortality of Berliftzing; there is more than a hint that he has set the fires currently burning in the stables of the Castle Berliftzing so he might well be feeling some guilt; he is alone with his thoughts staring at the horse in the tapestry whose eyes seem to have "an energetic and human expression." "The longer he gazed, the more absorbing became the spell" (***Tales,*** 137). When the servants bring the strange, unaccounted for horse with WVB initialed on its forehead, what can he conclude but that the soul of the dead Berliftzing has passed into the horse he sees before him? Readers can put the Baron's extraordinary mental stress together with the warning at the story's opening—"Of the doctrines themselves . . . of their falsity, or of their probability . . . I say nothing;" "points in the Hungarian superstition were fast verging to absurdity"—and regard the supposed supernatural event as self-delusion (***Tales,*** 134). By contrast, a reading which accepts the fantastic at face value would see the Baron's state of mind as sharpened insight, would tend to emphasize narrative cause and effect (the death of Berliftzing and the sudden appearance of horse) as independent of the Baron's thought processes, and would call attention to the seemingly supernatural altering of the horse's position on the tapestry with, again, the "human" expression and the strangely missing piece of tapestry. Responding to those who argue that its absurdity places the story among Poe's hoaxes, Benjamin Fisher has contended that the story should be taken seriously as a tale of soul transmigration simply because the gothic elements are for the period typical indications of supernatural forces at work. The psychological dimension, however, creates another context, one which regards events not as supernatural effects but as worldly causes.

Although Poe's familiarity with Brewster might seem to privilege an empirical skepticism in these stories, it is the sensational supernatural that probably still attracts most readers and both readings contain their respective pleasures, the implications of the alternatives, however, beyond simple choice, go deeper into Poe's creative world. Cause and effect there are less the meaning cement of the material world signaled through the senses than a mode of thought that could be rather loosely applied to any sensory experience, a manner of meaning whose propensity is to generate more than one reading of a situation.

This complexity of meaning is clearer in those stories which systematically frame the senses as experience capacities. **"The Pit and the Pendulum"** structures by enfolding experience into history. Here the supernatural is contained in an allegorical frame that isolates the senses as symptoms of an earthly state, presumably the conceptualization of the Inquisition. Although Poe was curtly dismissive of allegory's tendency to sap dramatic effect "if allegory ever establishes a fact, it is by dint of overturning a fiction"—he here forestalls that problem by pushing the allegory into the background and subtly concealing it from his narrator (*Essays,* 582). As a man imprisoned by the Inquisition and subject to their diabolic tortures, the narrator is too immediately occupied to think about broader meanings. The external frame is both definite and surprisingly dramatic as a bare-bones pattern of meaning: it envisions the imprisonment of the soul-self, subject to the keen scythe of time, doomed by the encroachments of a constricting space, and threatened by a yawning, ever-present pit ("typical of hell"). Indeed, if one regards the design's machinery as the embodiment of a macabre vision of life that the Inquisition seeks to imprint on the prisoner's psyche, somewhat in the manner of the writing on the body in Kafka's "In the Penal Colony," the allegorical dimension begins to be totally absorbed into the fiction. Regardless of what lurks in the background, the narrator's account of his resourcefulness is fittingly the central focus and his ability to utilize his senses so keenly and with such discipline makes him seem heroic rather than naïve. Often too dismissive—"I had little object—certainly no hope—in these researches"—he shows himself the intrepid explorer as he paces off the circumference of his cell (50 yards), cleverly uses the rats to cut his bonds, and while lucky in avoiding the pit, still has the presence of mind to plumb its depths with a stone. Going beyond the mechanics of dimensions, he inspects the texture of the place as well: "It was a wall, seemingly of stone masonry—very smooth, slimy, and cold"; at the edge of the pit, "my forehead seemed bathed in a clammy vapor, and the peculiar smell of decayed fungus arose to my nostrils"; the pendulum is "[l]ike a razor also . . . seemed massy and heavy . . . appended to a weighty rod of brass, and the whole hissed as it swung through the air" (***Tales,*** 495, 496, 499). It is perhaps appropriate that part of his rescue should be facilitated by the rats who, despite the disgust they arouse, seem here to act as natural fellow creatures trapped in the same design. An additional frame of meaning is also proffered by the presence of skepticism in the narration's beginning and ending: the presumed heresy that is the narrator's crime and the secular French army serving as his rescuer. In this instance the earthly reminders reinforce the image of the narrator as conqueror of his assigned, constricted space and thus trump the Inquisition's attempt to create a broader reading with its own machinery; the prison machinery is not an effect caused by an abstract idea but simply a physical cause of suffering.

A framing also serves to illuminate meaning in **"The Fall of the House of Usher."** Using the first-person narrator as observer-reporter rather than experiencer lets the telling center on Roderick and his particular symptoms, chief among them being a systematic derangement of the senses: "the most insipid food was alone endurable; he could wear only garments of a certain texture; the odors of all flowers were oppressive; his eyes were tortured by even a faint light; and there were peculiar sounds and these from stringed instruments, which did not inspire him with horror" (*Tales,* 322). These signs that his world is not merely closed but enclosing defy the notion of some redemptive harmony in the romantic sensibility's relation to its environment. As indicated in the epigraph ("Son coeur est un luth suspendu; / Sitot qu'on le touche il resonne") the aeolian harp, that signature image of the Romantic movement, is being transformed from passive instrument to physical vulnerability by a world that insists on its physicality. In this story of the sensitive artist at the end of his tether, Roderick is in the process of being overwhelmed with an influx of senses that seem to have a life of their own. Reversing the claim that a finer sensibility leads to a transformation of the material world through spiritual transcendence, Roderick presents a theory of animistic "sentience," claiming that a capacity of feeling in the surroundings has displaced and sapped his own capacities. In short, he no longer sees himself as creative cause but as an effect: "the gradual certain condensation of an atmosphere . . . about the waters and walls . . . made him what I now saw him—what he was" (*Tales,* 328). His artistic work, the poem "The Haunted Palace" and the picture of a long rectangular vault below the earth (the latter so reminiscent of the buried soul and the closed world about the senses suggested in **"The Pit and the Pendulum"**) both seem attempts to get outside, as it were, by encapsulating his fate. And in the entombment of Madeline, the soul source of his creative drive, Roderick seeks to repress and bury the torturing sensitivity and once again gain control of his emotions. As he indicates, what he fears is not the world but his tortuous reaction to it: "I dread the events of the future, not in themselves, but in their results. I shudder at the thought of any, even the most trivial, incident, which may operate upon this intolerable agitation of soul" (*Tales,* 322).

To this, the unimaginative narrator is steadfastly noncommital, though by bits and pieces he makes clear he will have none of it. In his reading Roderick is basically a hysterical hypochondriac, possessed of a mind "from which darkness . . . poured forth upon all objects of the moral and physical universe" (*Tales,* 324). For him, Roderick is the cause, not an effect. Many of the narrator's initial remarks call attention to an esthetic reluctance in the landscape: instead of a sense of the sublime, my "feeling was unrelieved by any of that half-pleasurable, because poetic, sentiment with which the mind usually receives even the sternest images of the desolate or terrible"; instead of a feeling of the senses veiling nature's holy secrets, there is "the hideous dropping off of the veil"; and instead of any pleasure from holding the mirror up to nature, the narrator's glimpse into the tarn produces a "shudder" at "the remodeled and inverted images of the gray sedge, and the ghastly tree-stems, and the vacant and eye-like windows" (*Tales,* 317, 318). The narrator's conventional taste fails to see any relation between these obdurate denials of traditional paths to artistic vibrance and Roderick's increasingly subjective agony. One whose sensibility functions at a conveniently low wattage, the narrator finds no meaning in these sensuous experiences beyond feeling depressed. Nor is there for him anything suggestively symbolic in the burial of Madeline; though the mere sight of her earlier had left him feeling dazed, stupefied, it now makes perfect practical sense as he explains in detail that her basic value would be her material body and the real danger that of grave robbers.

The return of Madeline, the specter figure now embodying the self-destructive impulses of the sensibility, is an explosive violence that accuses Roderick of both moral and artistic failure. Yet the guilt is curiously shared. Heralded by Roderick's sense-keyed response to the "Mad Trist," the pitch of the narrative crescendos with Roderick's own indictments: "We have put her living in the tomb."; "Madman! I tell you that she now stands without the door!" With these last words he challenges everything we have been told by the narrator: though both were guilty of denying her life, the narrator, not Roderick, is the true madman because he would ask nothing of the world but that it be. Roderick may be destroyed for his belief in the senses' power to mold and unify the world into forms of the beautiful, but the question of who is the real madman remains entwined in the natural and supernatural strains of the melodramatic ending. As Usher implies, without the cohesive potency the sensibility represents, his physical environment must collapse into the fragments of materialism (which literally occurs). In death Roderick seems to take the whole setting with him. The narrator's last glimpse is plain sensuous ferocity, the romantic moon gone mad: "the entire orb of the satellite burst at once upon my sight" (*Tales,* 335).

The senses, however, could be more dangerous than any delusion or constriction. Much in the manner of the mesmeric suggestion, the senses in several of Poe's psychological stories—**"William Wilson," "The Black Cat,"** and **"The Tell-Tale Heart"**—are structured as invading forces formulating a provocative frame of uncertainty for the narrators' sensibilities. In these stories the mind is not merely subject to its inherent fallibilities, it is in danger of being literally possessed by personal soul daemons that announce themselves preternaturally through the senses and work to impel the mind to betray the self. So dynamic is the ambiguity of cause and effect in these tales that even as the threatening animism in the environment becomes an increasing danger, it is undercut by a spectral aura that insinuates an intimate alliance between the internal and the external, between a perverse morality and self-destruction.

"William Wilson" on the surface is the moral tale of a spoiled selfish cad who refuses to heed his conscience, but in the telling it becomes an intense struggle on the part of the narrator to preserve his being from a psychic intruder. Since conscience, arguably an effect of character, is consistently in the story taking the part of a cause (of psychic distress, and perhaps perversely, behavior), these two incompatible readings begin to create a third. As an Other, the conscience-double is both distanced and familiar, qualities emphasized by its fiendish ubiquity, by its sinister whispering, personally mocking voice, and through a relentless objectifying of the negative features of the narrator. In a scene in which the narrator invades the other's bedroom, the uncanny power of the double as externalized image conveys the instability that taunts the impulse toward a literal resolution: "a numbness, an iciness of feeling pervaded my frame. My breast heaved, my knees tottered, my whole spirit became possessed with an objectless yet intolerable horror. . . . Were these the lineaments of William Wilson? I saw, indeed, they were his, but I shook as if with a fit of ague in fancying they were not. What was there about them to confound me in this manner" (***Tales,*** 347)? How can one relate to a self-image that is so defiantly detached from one's inherent being? It is as if the narrator had said, "I am a stranger to myself, to my own body."

However much this narrator might confess his sins to the reader, it is strangely the conscience figure with his objectifying powers and "singular, low, hissing utterance" who comes to seem the evil presence and though the story seems finally to settle for the irony of the mind turning against itself, the persistence of such a smarmy self-indictment and the alien nature of the apparent moral standard stake out a meaning between the literal and the moral allegory. Like the other stories in this vein, **"William Wilson"** moves bizarrely toward a moral denouement which the narrator not only regards with total incredulity but which his entire narration has attempted to belie.

In **"The Black Cat"** and **"The Tell-Tale Heart,"** self-hatred displays many of the same identifications of external and internal as in **"Wilson"** [**"William Wilson"**]. In both the stories the sense object—the evil eye and beating heart in **"Heart"** [**"The Tell-Tale Heart"**] and the sight of the cat in **"Cat"** [**"The Black Cat"**]—ignite a hatred which progressively and intensely becomes more internally directed. In both the bizarre identifications with the victims grow to magnified sensuous apparitions. Hearing from the old man "the low stifled sound that arises from the bottom of the soul . . . overcharged with awe," the **"Heart"** narrator says, "I knew the sound well . . . it welled up from my own bosom, . . . the terrors which distracted me" (***Tales,*** 556). At the end a similar "low, dull, quick sound" which he associates with the old man's beating heart and which he alone hears becomes his hysteria-inducing compulsion to confess. The **"Black Cat"** narrator hangs the cat "with tears streaming from my eyes . . . hung it because I knew that it had loved me" and because in killing the cat he is doing violence to himself, committing a sin that "would . . . jeopardize my immortal soul" (***Tales,*** 599). The next day, after a fire, he sees upon a wall the image of a gigantic cat with a rope around its neck. It is an image reprised in the fur of cat number two where it seems so hideous and ghastly, the narrator thinks of himself as "a brute beast." In a final effort to rid themselves of their sensuous fetters both narrators futilely attempt to bury and wall up their sense demons, but the senses will not be silenced.

In **"The Murders in the Rue Morgue"** one of Dupin's major rhetorical tasks is to tame sense details such as these, though here the incredible violence of the crime (the young woman's body jammed up the chimney and her mother's head nearly severed) makes the effort extremely challenging. Significantly the detective's most explicit distancing is a critique of police methodology which derives again (as I have shown elsewhere) from Brewster. Vidocq, Dupin declares, "impaired his vision by holding the object too close" (***Tales,*** 412).

> To look at a star by glances—to view it in a side-long way, by turning toward it the exterior portions of the retina . . . is to behold the star distinctly—is to have the best appreciation of its lustre—a lustre which grows dim just as in proportion as we turn our vision fully upon it.
>
> (***Tales,*** 412)

Emphasis on controlled, unemotional perception creates the basic shape of detective fiction where the agony of murder is transformed into a puzzle for the intellect. Although the fatal locked room of **"Murders"** [**"The Murders in the Rue Morgue"**] is the formulation once again of the enclosed space so typical of other stories (here defining not only the tale's puzzle but setting in motion that subgenre of mystery fiction, the closed-room enigma), now it is others who are confined and the reader is not called upon to imagine their torment. Instead of a scene of horror, the room is reduced to the idea of the crime. While the violent invasion through the window suggests some parallels with other stories, here all is in the past and requires only the ordering of reasoned justice, a pattern in which details become clues that analyzed produce that clear and convincing formulation, cause and effect.

Poe's other successful detective story, **"The Purloined Letter,"** is more concise as a story and even more abstract in its presentation of feeling. It intellectualizes the harmful effects of the crucial cause, the letter, as "the robber's knowledge of the loser's knowledge of the robber" (***Tales,*** 682). And the document is further abstracted and hooded by being hidden in plain sight so that it is there but not there until sensibly discerned. So intellectualized are the sensory elements in this story that each twist of the plot involves a contest of sense deceptions. To counter D___'s cleverness in disguising the letter, Dupin not only substitutes his own facsimile but employs a theatrical ruse complete with gun fire thereby invading his opponent's mind and seizing by stealth the man's picture of reality. What should be an effect, the result of D___'s evil machinations, will now become a cause reacting negatively upon him, his lack of possession the effect.

In providing a systematic framework for an analysis of the senses Poe's treatment of affective consciousness begins to absorb human subjectivity into the objectivity of process. A parallel impulse can be discerned in Poe's technological hoaxes, which manage for all their foolery to suggest that hopes for transcending human limitations would find technological innovation a promising path. In this respect the work anticipates later writing such as the case study and the technical report as well as the detective story. Poe's popularity, however, will always be tied to the intensity with which he broods on the fate of the body in a material world. For all their melodrama the stories are less concerned with the doom of the protagonist than with the physical meaning of that fate.

Bibliography

Brewster, David. *Letters on Natural Magic Addressed to Sir Walter Scott.* New York: J. J. Harper, 1832.

Brody, Selma. "Poe's Use of Brewster's *Letters on Natural Magic.*" *English Language Notes,* 27 (1989), 50-54.

Fisher, Benjamin. "Poe's 'Metzengerstein': Not a Hoax." *American Literature,* 42 (January 1971), 487-91.

Lind, Sidney E. "Poe and Mesmerism," *PMLA,* 62 (1947), 1077-94.

Poe, Edgar Allan. *Essays and Reviews.* New York: Library of America, 1984.

———. *Poetry and Tales.* New York: Library of America, 1984.

Shear, Walter. "Poe's Use of an Idea on Perception." *American Notes & Queries,* 21 (1984), 134-36.

Joseph Church (essay date June 2006)

SOURCE: Church, Joseph. "'To Make Venus Vanish': Misogyny as Motive in Poe's 'Murders in the Rue Morgue.'" *American Transcendental Quarterly* n.s. 20, no. 2 (June 2006): 407-18.

[*In the following essay, Church alleges that the uncanny facility with which Dupin solves the case in "The Murders in the Rue Morgue" suggests an identification between the detective and the orangutan that exposes his distrustful attitude toward women.*]

Despite his otherwise unconventional ways, in his personal life Edgar Allan Poe held the most conventional early nineteenth-century views about the subordinate place of woman in man's world. As Ernest Marchand concludes, "in all matters touching women, sex, marriage, 'morals,' no more conventional-minded man than Poe ever lived" (35). Poe makes explicit his assumptions about women's subservience in his remarks about their proper education:

> The business of female education with us, is not to qualify a woman to be head of a literary *coterie,* nor to figure in the journal of a traveling coxcomb. We prepare her, as a wife, to make the home of a good, and wise, and great man, the happiest place to him on earth. We prepare her, as a mother, to form her son to walk in his father's steps, and in turn, to take his place among the good and wise and great. . . . Her praise is found in the happiness of her husband, and in the virtues and honors of her son. Her name is too sacred to be profaned by public breath. She is only seen by that dim doubtful light, which, like "the majesty of darkness," so much enhances true dignity.
>
> (***Complete Works*** [***The Complete Works of Edgar Allan Poe***] 8:14-15)

In his writings as critic and journalist, Poe assails powerfully intellectual women who esteem the "head" and ignore his orthodox strictures: according to Burton R. Pollin, Poe routinely mocks the "successful, professional woman," and thus derides Margaret Fuller, for example, as "absurd," a victim of a "fine phrenzy" (49-50). Ashby Bland Crowder observes in "Poe's Criticism of Women Writers" that Poe considered female writers in America "at best a mediocre lot" (111) and quotes his complaint that "'literary women . . . are a heartless, unnatural, venomous, dishonorable set, with no guiding principle but inordinate self-esteem'" (118 n26). In his own poetry and fiction, as readers have long noted, Poe often depicts the suppression or annihilation of women who because of overpowering beauty, intellect, or wealth depart from the conventional and threaten man's superior position. As Eliza Richards succinctly puts it, "Poe's male characters enact violent revenge on women because of their enthralling power" (10). Reviling signs of her autonomy,

Poe understands woman as essentially subordinate to man, in Margaret Fuller's proto-Sartrean terms, "*for man*" (19). He reviles the autonomous woman in this world. Of course at times Poe idealizes some women, but he always requires that they lose their lives to serve an interest of man. In "Poe on Women: Recent Perspectives," Michael J. S. Williams helpfully details these interests and calls attention to Joseph Moldenhauer's representative argument that Poe's protagonists typically "'murder their beloved and lovely women . . . in order to further their perfection as *objets de virtu*'" (34). Addressing Poe's own psychological maneuvering, many critics, such as Marie Bonaparte, Elisabeth Bronfen, J. Gerald Kennedy, and Diane Long Hoeveler, convincingly argue that his hostile dramatizations in fact allegorize his efforts to subordinate elements of his psyche associated with woman—all that to him stands over against intellect and reason, above all, emotion, sensuality, the body—and that his psychological and social attitudes, bordering on misogyny, thus reinforce one another.[1]

Recently, however, some have attempted to show Poe as actually enlightened about the plight of woman in the nineteenth century. In *Aesthetic Headaches: Women and a Masculine Poetics in Poe, Melville, and Hawthorne,* Leland S. Person, Jr., asserts that Poe challenges the premises of "conventional masculinity by demonstrating its weakness or impotence in the presence of strong women" (175). In "Poe's Women: A Feminist Poe?" Joan Dayan, after describing his several idealizations of dead women, asks, "But what are we to do with Poe's bleeding, raped, decapitated, dead, and resurrected women, brutalized, buried, cemented in cellars, and stuffed up chimneys?" She answers, "Poe is after nothing less than an exhumation of the lived, but disavowed or suppressed experiences of women in his society . . . he lays bare the mechanics of cultural control in the Anglo-American experience" (10). And in *Second Stories: The Politics of Language, Form, and Gender in Early American Fictions,* Cynthia S. Jordan sees in Poe's work an "evolving feminist ethos, a growing awareness and renunciation of death-dealing, male-authored fictions" (150-51). Jordan, concentrating on his narratives of detection in her essay "Poe's Re-Vision: The Recovery of the Second Story," writes, "In the Dupin tales . . . in which the task of solving crimes against women calls for a detective with an awareness that other men lack, the androgynous Dupin becomes virtually a feminist critic. In Dupin, Poe created a new caretaker of social and political order, and Dupin fulfills these responsibilities by going beyond the imaginative limits of the male storytellers around him and recovering the second story—'the woman's story'—which has previously gone untold" (5).

I believe these conclusions mistaken. Far from working as a "feminist critic" to disclose the gendered "mechanics of cultural control" and to tell woman's untold story, Poe and his avatars such as Dupin work to punish and silence womankind in the world and its correlatives in the mind that threaten a masculinist ontology. We discern this unambiguous enterprise of suppression in a closer examination of Dupin's part in **"The Murders in the Rue Morgue."** Although less-sanguine commentators than Person, Dayan, and Jordan have called attention to the psychological hostility toward women in the tale, none has adequately set forth the extent of its misogyny. Bonaparte ultimately reduces the story's murder of two women to a fantasy of a Freudian "primal scene" (445). Terry J. Martin views the deaths through the lens of Dupin's "lack of mental proportion," his intellectual one-sidedness, that sets him in severe opposition to women generally; hence, Martin holds that the tale's murdered mother, whose "head is severed from her body, . . . vividly portrays Dupin's failure to integrate thought and feeling" (41-42). And in "The Psychology of 'The Murders in the Rue Morgue,'" J. A. Leo Lemay envisions the attacks on the women as primarily symbolizing the deleterious consequence of modern humankind's sexual repression. Lemay clarifies some of the psychological machinations, especially the unconscious doubling, in the story, but he deplorably errs when he claims that the women bring their murders upon themselves: "by their deliberate suppression of sexuality, by their denial of the body, [they] have created the monster who kills them" (186).

Most know the events in **"Murders in the Rue Morgue"**: the brutal and evidently motiveless deaths of a Parisian mother and daughter have baffled the police until the brilliant Auguste Dupin solves the crimes by deducing and demonstrating that a sailor's escaped orangutan has carried out the carnage. Often overlooked, however, is the tale's leaving the women's deaths strangely unpunished. The man mistakenly arrested for the murders, the bank clerk Le Bon, of course gains instant release. The orangutan, a blameless creature, obtains a new home along the Seine in the Jardin des Plantes. And the sailor, although indirectly involved, proves guiltless, as Dupin insists from the first: "'Cognizant . . . of the murder'" although "'he was innocent of all participation in the bloody transactions'" (148). The sailor even gets a "very large sum" (154) from the Jardin for the animal. Women murdered, men rewarded and going free (the orangutan is a male; the name itself Malaysian for "man of the woods")—one suspects the likelihood of misogyny. Indeed, a closer reading of **"The Murders in the Rue Morgue"** reveals not only an intense ambivalence toward women in the tale but also Dupin's and the narrator's (and by extension Poe's) own misogynistic satisfaction in the deaths of the mother and daughter. In fact Poe's self-disclosing narrative depicts both Dupin's and the narrator's identifying with the sailor and his orangutan and their bloody deeds. Representing the author's interests, the men's aims differ only superficially in their object: Dupin would attack woman primarily in the world, the narrator in the psyche.

Although Lemay reaches a different conclusion, he makes a convincing argument that "the sailor and the orangutan are a double for Dupin. That also means, of course, that they are doubles for one another; and since Dupin is a double for the narrator, all four characters are symbolic doubles" (170). A risk of seeing too much doubling, however, is the loss of responsibility for action (no one is responsible for an act). Lemay goes on to argue that the two women also function as doubles of the four males: "all three sets of characters are symbolic doubles" (171). He claims that, combined, the six equal one genuine being in Poe's mind: the "implied final unity of the three couples—Dupin and the narrator, Madame and Mademoiselle L'Espanaye, and the sailor and the orangutan—suggests the proper ingredients of what, in Poe's vision, constitutes an achieved unified life" (173). But this conflation re-eliminates the women as such and makes investigation and ascription of responsibility for their murder futile.

Poe's great "analyst" (117), Dupin, prefers an all-male world of the intellect—he lives hermetically with the narrator ("We existed within ourselves alone" [121])—and in this realm where "mind struggles with mind" (119), he exults in and excels at competitively establishing his mental superiority over other men. Poe's protagonist rises superior because together with his great reasoning powers he possesses a "*truly* imaginative" (120) sensibility, an "ingenuity" that derives from his whole being, as it were, head and body both. He deems this imaginative acumen a male power, for when he bests the superficially rational Prefect of Police, he mocks the unimaginative man as castrated: "'I am satisfied at having defeated him in his own castle . . . the Prefect is somewhat too cunning to be profound. In his wisdom is no *stamen.* It is all head and no body, like the pictures of the Goddess Laverna'" (155). Dupin's attraction to events in the Rue Morgue involves more, however, than his competition with the Prefect: given his biases, and those of his creator, he must see in the circumstances of these two women, and modern women generally, their possession of new powers—intellectual, material, and sexual—and therein must experience an excruciating affront to man's, but above all, his own superiority.

In his satirical criticism Poe often attacks intellectual women, the so-called bluestockings, as, for example, in "Fifty Suggestions," where he writes, "When we think very *ill* of a woman, and wish to *blacken* her character, we merely call her 'a *blue*-stocking'" (***Complete Works,*** 14:170). One notes the menace in his emphasized "black" and "blue." In **"Murders in the Rue Morgue"** he symbolizes the women's doomed association with intellect by having them, like Dupin and the narrator, reside on the top floor of their building, and, then, as Lemay suggests, allegorizing man's reasoning powers vanquishing woman's "mind" (171). Instructively, Poe locates meaningful, rational discourse in the two men and limits the two women to "'shrieks'" and "'screams'" (129). In the tale the often insolvent Poe also takes aim at woman's material wealth. His Dupin could take no joy in learning that the mother and her daughter "have money" (128) and own the large house in which they have lived. Dupin himself leads a materially impoverished life. Of an "illustrious family" (120) now reduced to penury, he exists frugally on a "small remnant of his patrimony" (121), a son forced in modern times to subsist on the resources of a fallen father. Again, given his masculinist philosophy, he must hold that these women, a mother and daughter and thus matrilineal, wrongly possess wealth and power and a future properly belonging to men, to fathers and sons patrilineally. Poe's tale in fact mocks the legitimacy of Madame L'Espanaye's wealth by several times repeating the rumor that she "'told fortunes for a living'" (128), thus contrasting her fraudulent use of the mind to gain "fortunes" with Dupin's virtuous reasoning. And it is to the point that the women not only receive a large sum of money from the bank (delivered by Le Bon) just before their murder but also receive that sum in testicle-like sacks: the daughter "'took from [Le Bon's] hands one of the bags, while the old lady relieved him of the other'" (130), as if the arrogant women have appropriated phallic power. From the standpoint of Dupin their illegitimate affluence and its attendant powers warrant a punishing attack.

Dupin also loathes these women because he could scarcely countenance their evident indifference if not antipathy toward men. One such as he must expect that women subordinate themselves to man, but in this case he finds the mother and daughter self-reliant. In this tale Madame L'Espanaye has no husband, her daughter no father, and, we learn, some years earlier the mother had summarily expelled their one male tenant for an "'abuse of the premises'" (128). In short, the women apparently consider themselves superior to and satisfied without men: as their laundress recalls, the "'old lady and her daughter seemed on good terms—very affectionate towards each other'" (128).

This affection between the two obliquely hints at homoerotic values, women who have one another and need no man, and accordingly, in Poe's prejudicial handling, their family name—L'Espanaye—resonantly betokens "Lesbian." Lemay, too, notes this similarity (174), but he then works his way into a disturbing contradiction when he argues that although the women likely exist as lesbians they enact a "deliberate suppression of sexuality, by their denial of the body" (186). How is it that lesbianism and sexuality exclude one another? Yet he uses this argument to claim that the murderous orangutan symbolizes a kind of "return of the repressed," retribution for the women's fear of eros, their "continual suppression of the body and sex" (186). Lemay concludes, "The psychological level of the story suggests that a man's penis is the bludgeoning instrument of death. Not, to be sure, a real penis—but such a one as might exist in the imagination of a severely repressed female neurotic" (186). In a woman's mind? or in a man's? Poe's?

On the face of it Dupin himself shows no interest in eros, but he must assume that desirous man—made desirous by woman—succeeds with and subordinates her when and where he pleases. The story anatomically symbolizes this mastery when it has the gendarme remembering his "'endeavoring to gain admittance'" to the "'gateway'" of the "'screaming'" (128-29) women: "'Forced it open, at length with a bayonet. . . . Had but little difficulty in getting it open, on account of its being a double or folding gate. . . . The shrieks were continued until the gate was forced—then suddenly ceased'" (129). However, if women provoke but will not satisfy desire—as the L'Espanayes evidently will not (this mother, prima facie sexual, needs no man)—they stand superior to men. A portion of the tale's epigraph, taken from Browne's *Urn-Burial,* reads, "What song the Syrens sang . . . although puzzling questions, are not beyond all conjecture," indicating Poe's interest in probing and mastering the debilitating temptation of women. When Dupin observes, "'it is possible to make even Venus herself vanish from the firmament by a scrutiny too sustained, too concentrated, or too direct'" (134), he ostensibly praises indirect means of analysis, but he leaves in place the idea that "direct" action, of the sort the orangutan takes, will make Venus vanish. Indeed, the animal does seek to make the mother and daughter disappear, throwing one out the window, shoving the other up the chimney. Insofar as Dupin identifies with the sailor and his "beast" (152), he himself has resorted, however symbolically, to direct action, signifying in this case his frustration with more cerebral stratagems.

"The Murders in the Rue Morgue" carefully associates Dupin's avatars—the sailor and his male animal—with man's physical, sexual conquest of women. An hour before the murders, the mariner has been on a "sailor's frolic" (152) in Paris; in the meantime, the orangutan has broken free and, with the returning sailor in pursuit, found the mother and daughter "in their nightclothes" (153). In Borneo the sailor had "passed into the interior on an excursion of pleasure" where he captures and takes "exclusive possession" of the orangutan, a creature of "intractable ferocity" (152). The imagery implies that his taking sexual pleasure has brought to life an interior beast, one now requiring reconfinement because too-insistently demanding expression. On the night of the frolic in Paris, the sailor secludes the animal but returns to find "the beast occupying his own bed-room, into which it had broken from a closet adjoining, where it had been, as was thought, securely confined. Razor in hand, and fully lathered, it was sitting before a looking-glass, attempting the operation of shaving, in which it had no doubt previously watched its master" (152). In this strange scene it appears as if the orangutan, shaving in the bedroom, grooms himself for his own frolic. Tellingly, he then makes his way to the dwelling of two women who scorn men: in an explosion of sexual symbolism he kills them, again, as if in punishment for their power, here not in material wealth (he leaves the gold lying on the floor), but in sexual autonomy.

While its master looks through the window to get at the "interior" (153) not of Borneo but woman's dwelling, he witnesses in voyeuristic "anxiety" (153) the beast let loose. The animal mounts a sexual psychodrama, attacking the women, rifling their drawers (implying underclothes), and hurling their bedding to the floor. With his phallus/razor he sets out to shave Madame L'Espanaye, "flourishing the razor about her face, in imitation of the motions of a barber" (153). In his "The Psychology of 'The Murders in the Rue Morgue,'" Lemay views this scene as a symbolic rendering of a woman's own self-destruction. He notes that the figure of an imitative monkey's wielding a razor and cutting its own throat has a long tradition in humorous broadside ballads, insists on the woman's being a "severely repressed neurotic" (186), and preposterously concludes that "Madame L'Espanaye psychologically and symbolically decapitated herself . . . the orangutan's shaving is thus a splendid analogue for the murders" (184). But the episode in fact signifies Poe's misogyny, for in the brutal shaving he depicts the animal's now treating the resisting woman as if she were a counterfeit man. The tale thus mocks and punishes the women for aspiring to be men when they should be sexually subservient, just as it punishes them for appropriating man's treasured sack when they should be materially subordinate. When the animal sees blood (and all that would imply for eros), he uses the razor to decapitate the mother, signifying that, unlike man, she cannot possess both body and head. In further symbolical castrations he shatters "all the bones of the right leg and arm" (132), and, turning to the daughter, chokes her in such a way that her "tongue [is] partially bitten through" (132)—an image of self-castration forced upon her—enragedly punches her abdomen/womb (a "large bruise was discovered upon the pit of the stomach" [132]), and finally thrusts her feet-first up the chimney. In her reading of this scene, Bonaparte emphasizes the maternal character of the room and argues that the chimney represents the mother's "vagina" (454), her "inner genital region" (455), but given Poe's misogyny we have to see the chimney as phallic and the daughter's inverted position an image of her being mockingly reborn via man.

As we should expect, Dupin tries to exculpate this ravage, blaming the women's screams for having "had the effect of changing the probably pacific purposes of the Ourang-Outang into those of wrath. . . . The sight of blood inflamed its anger into phrenzy" (154). Such palliation, here only halfheartedly advanced (how can "probably pacific purposes" exist in a beast of "intractable ferocity"?), recurs more emphatically throughout **"Murders in the Rue Morgue."** For example, Poe's protagonist tentatively hypothesizes that the mother "could have first destroyed the daughter, and afterward have committed suicide" (137). He rejects this solution for obvious reasons, noting that he speaks "'of this point chiefly for the sake of method'" (137), but importantly he leaves the possibility openly declared: that the women killed themselves (no men responsible), a conclusion Lemay lamentably subtilizes when he argues that "Psychologically, the L'Espanayes cut off their own heads" (186). To the extent that an ultimately blameless animal carries out Dupin's interests, it is not surprising to hear the tale speculate that in hurling the mother from the room and hiding the daughter in the chimney even the beast may have been "conscious of having deserved punishment" and thus "desirous of concealing its bloody deeds" (154). But the insistence on qualified innocence receives its greatest emphasis in Dupin's repeatedly asserting the sailor's innocent part in the women's death. He has good reason to do so if he sees in the man and animal his own culpable hostility toward women. We hear Dupin's self-referential and self-exculpating identification with the animal's owner when he declares to him, "'I perfectly well know that you are innocent of the atrocities in the Rue Morgue. It will not do, however, to deny that you are in some measure implicated in them. From what I have already said, you must know that I have had means of information about this matter—means of which you could never have dreamed. . . . You have done nothing which you could have avoided—nothing, certainly, which renders you culpable'" (151). These "means of information," beyond the obvious reference to Dupin's acumen, I take to signify an identification, one heard when the Parisian Dupin confides, "'A Frenchman was cognizant of the murder'" (148), one speaking French "'of a Parisian origin'" (150).

Further evincing this identification is the uncanny way in which Dupin, reflecting upon the evidence, rapidly reconstructs the murders, even specifying the type of animal and the nationality of its master. Of course Poe's hero takes pride in drawing inferences and seeing into the thinking of others—says the narrator, "He boasted to me . . . that most men wore windows in their bosoms" (122)—but in this case he demonstrates an almost preternatural identification with the sailor. When he places a public notice directed to the attention of that man, Dupin not only readily envisions but bizarrely ventriloquizes his response: "'He will reason thus:—I am innocent; I am poor; my Ourang-Outang is of great value. . . . Should [the police] even trace the animal, it would be impossible to prove me cognizant of the murder, or to implicate me in guilt on account of that cognizance. Above all, *I am known*'" (149). The emphasized words hint at self-disclosure, perspicacious Dupin's awareness that in the sailor's and orangutan's actions he sees his own interests. It is suggestive that he confides to the creature's master, "'I almost envy you the possession of him; a remarkably fine, and no doubt a very valuable animal. . . . I shall be sorry to part with him'" (150). Dupin's name itself hints at doubling and division (duplicate, duplicity, duping), and early on the narrator wonders if his companion in fact possesses a "Bi-Part Soul": "I amused myself with the fancy of a double Dupin," perhaps the product of a "diseased intelligence" (122). In this characterization of Dupin Poe self-reflexively hints at his own anxieties concerning a "diseased" mind, and represents that worry in the story's central clue, the nail that only appears to secure the women's window: this nail seems like any other, just as a human might seem like his or her fellows, but in fact, Usher-like, it possesses an invisible "'fissure'" in its "'head portion'" (141).

Working to eliminate such anxieties at their source, Poe's tale emphasizes the initially baffling lack of motive for the murders—"'The police are confounded by the seeming absence of motive . . . that startling absence of motive in a murder so singularly atrocious as this'" (136, 145)—and then has Dupin's revelations dispose of the question entirely (apart from involving the blamelessly instinctual behavior of an animal). As Martin observes, "Dupin goes so far as to deny the idea of motive altogether. . . . The overall effect of his analysis is thus to negate all moral responsibility for the murders and utterly diminish their significance" (40). Yet Dupin's own misogynistic interests go far toward explaining if not the immediate reasons for, then at the least the man's satisfactions in, the deaths of women who have intellectual, material, and sexual power. Significant is the fact that Dupin shows neither sympathy for the victims nor interest in involving himself in this apparently "insoluble mystery" until he learns that "Le Bon had been arrested and imprisoned" for the murders. The narrator observes, "It was only after the announcement" of Le Bon's incarceration that the analyst "seemed suddenly interested in the progress of this affair" (133). Dupin has a personal connection to the bank clerk ("'Le Bon once rendered me a service for which I am not ungrateful'" [134]), and now motivated to acquit this wrongly accused good man (Le Bon) and all men, including himself, Poe's analyst quickly resolves the crimes, makes pointless the question of motives, and thus releases all the men from responsibility. In effect the murders no longer count as criminal acts; the women's deaths go unpunished.

But what specific satisfaction has the narrator gained from the deaths of these women? Events in the tale suggest that the narrator has come to doubt his own masculinity, fears that he increasingly occupies woman's assumed position of subordination viz. his companion, and consequently identifies himself with the "powerful man" (132), i.e., the orangutan, who destroys and rids the dwelling (psyche) of woman. The tale's epigraph includes an unusual reference to Achilles: "What song the Syrens sang, or what name Achilles assumed when he hid himself among women, although puzzling questions, are not beyond *all* conjecture" (117). Poe's narrator, troubled at what he takes to be womanly attitudes arising within, fantasizes himself an Achilles among women, in other words, a powerful man merely and necessarily in the temporary guise of a woman. The man has come to Paris in the spring upon a brief visit when he meets and finds himself instantly captivated by Dupin. The narrator confesses, "I felt my soul enkindled within me by the wild fervor, and the vivid freshness of his imagination. . . . I felt the society of such a man would be to me a treasure beyond price; and this feeling I frankly confided to him" (121). Indeed, he yields himself to Dupin's every "freak of fancy": "into all his [*bizarreries*] I quietly fell; giving myself up to his wild whims with a perfect *abandon*" (122, Poe's italics). Clearly he has subordinated himself to the more masterful Frenchman, and in the symbolism of this tale has accepted the woman's position.[2] In a way the hyper-competitive Dupin, cheerful castrator of the Prefect, permits no other relation.

On an evening just before the murders the two men have been walking when Dupin suddenly enacts upon the narrator one of his preternatural feats of mind-reading. "He boasted to me . . . that most men wore windows in their bosoms," the narrator has said, but now it is his turn to be penetrated by an analyst who demonstrates "intimate knowledge" (122) of the man's inner world. Part of what Dupin discloses involves the narrator's thinking about "Epicurus" (125) and by association sensual pleasure, but the content is less important than the fact that Dupin can enter the interior of the narrator but the latter cannot do the same with his companion. The narrator finds himself in the passive/receptive position. And on that same evening the narrator gets knocked to the ground by a passerby but remains unable to assert an objection: he tells how a "fruiterer, carrying upon his head a large basket of apples, had nearly thrown me down" (124); Dupin firmly corrects him, saying the fruiterer in fact "'thrust you upon a pile of paving-stones. . . . [You] slipped, slightly strained your ankle, appeared vexed or sulky, muttered a few words . . . then proceeded in silence'" (124-25). Immediately following the narrator's being knocked down and penetrated, the two companions become engrossed in—"arrested" (126) by—the newspaper's account of the murdered women. Given Dupin's investment in these events, we can now surmise that in them the narrator gains from Dupin's penetrating attention being diverted, identifies with a lethally "powerful man," and symbolizes the annihilation of woman within his psyche. He would make Venus vanish within himself.

Poe suggests that Dupin himself risks and resists association with internal femininity. Poe's analyst triumphs in his interpretations because of reason and imagination, but in his metaphysics he must link the latter, with its endless variability, to woman as such. Thus he has the problem of how to be powerfully imaginative without being a woman. **"Murders in the Rue Morgue"** evasively addresses this dilemma and consequent anxiety by identifying Dupin with the orangutan and then tentatively associating the animal with androgyny. People at the scene of the murders recall having heard strange articulations: "'Could not be sure whether it was the voice of a man or of a woman'"; "'Could not be sure if it was a man's voice. It might have been a woman's'"; "'Was sure that the shrill voice was that of a man'" (129); "'Might have been a woman's voice'" (130). Poe's protagonist, too, when aroused, expresses himself in a shrill voice ("his voice . . . rose into a treble" [122]). As Jordan approvingly deduces, Dupin himself herein evinces an androgyny ("crossing gender boundaries"), especially "when he recounts the experience of a female victim" (15). But for men in Poe's work this uncertainty about gender in fact signals both in the mind and in the world a danger not a desideratum. When in the tale it is demonstrated with certainty that the perpetrator is in fact a blameless wild beast with the strength of a "very powerful man" (132)—indeed, explicitly a "He" (150)—all the men obtain deliverance, the women unrequited annihilation. And insofar as Poe represents his interests in those of these men, he convicts himself of a blameworthy misogyny.

Notes

1. See Elisabeth Bronfen's *Over Her Dead Body: Death, Femininity and the Aesthetic,* J. Gerald Kennedy's "Poe, 'Ligeia' and the Problem of Dying Women," and Diane Long Hoeveler's "The Hidden God and the Abjected Woman in 'The Fall of the House of Usher.'"

2. See J. A. Leo Lemay's detailed argument for the "homosexual romance" (172) between Dupin and the narrator. It is also telling that Poe's narrator appears drawn to the "not unprepossessing" (150) sailor. He confides, "I pitied him from the bottom of my heart" (151), but expresses no such compassion for the brutalized women.

Works Cited

Bonaparte, Marie. *The Life and Works of Edgar Allan Poe: A Psycho-Analytic Interpretation.* New York: Humanities, 1971.

Crowder, Ashby Bland. "Poe's Criticism of Women Writers." *University of Mississippi Studies in English* 3 (1982): 102-19.

Dayan, Joan. "Poe's Women: A Feminist Poe?" *Poe Studies* 26:1-2 (1993): 1-12.

Fuller, Margaret. *Woman in the Nineteenth-Century and Other Writings.* Oxford: Oxford UP, 1994.

Jordan, Cynthia S. *Second Stories: The Politics of Language, Form, and Gender in Early American Fictions.* Chapel Hill: U of North Carolina P, 1989.

———. "Poe's Re-Vision: The Recovery of the Second Story." *American Literature* 59:1 (1987): 1-19.

Lemay, J. A. Leo. "The Psychology of 'The Murders in the Rue Morgue.'" *American Literature* 54:2 (1982): 165-88.

Marchand, Ernest. "Poe as Social Critic." *American Literature* 6 (1934): 28-43.

Martin, Terry J. "Detection, Imagination, and the Introduction to 'The Murders in the Rue Morgue.'" *Modern Language Studies* 19:4 (1989): 31-45.

Moldenhauer, Joseph. "Murder as a Fine Art: Basic Connections between Poe's Aesthetics, Psychology, and Moral Vision." *PMLA* 83 (1968): 284-97.

Person, Leland S., Jr. *Aesthetic Headaches: Women and a Masculine Poetics in Poe, Melville, and Hawthorne.* Athens, GA: U of Georgia P, 1988.

Poe, Edgar Allan. *The Complete Works of Edgar Allan Poe.* 17 vols. Ed. James A. Harrison. New York: AMS, 1965.

———. "The Murders in the Rue Morgue." *Tales of Horror and Suspense.* Mineola, NY: Dover, 2003.

Pollin, Burton R. "Poe on Margaret Fuller in 1845: An Unknown Caricature and Lampoon." *Women & Literature* 5:1 (1977): 47-50.

Richards, Eliza. "Women's Place in Poe Studies." *Poe Studies* 33:1-2 (2000): 10-14.

Williams, Michael J. S. "Poe on Women: Recent Perspectives." *Poe Studies* 26:1-2 (1993): 34-40.

Paul Woolf (essay date fall 2006)

SOURCE: Woolf, Paul. "Prostitutes, Paris, and Poe: The Sexual Economy of Edgar Allan Poe's 'The Murders in the Rue Morgue.'" *Clues* 25, no. 1 (fall 2006): 6-19.

[*In the following essay, Woolf appraises the symbolic significance of the Palais Royal—a hub of Parisian commerce and prostitution—to "The Murders in the Rue Morgue." Woolf further maintains that the story presents a fatalistic view of urban life in general.*]

Today, the vast Palais Royal is one of central Paris's most popular tourist attractions. At the start of literature's first detective story, Edgar Allan Poe's **"The Murders in the Rue Morgue"** (1841), the first demonstration of detective ability takes place within the shadow of this great building.

The story's unnamed narrator and its hero, Auguste Dupin, take one of their customary nocturnal walks "amid the wild lights and shadows of the populous city," seeking "that infinity of mental excitement" only to be found in the modern metropolis (Poe, ***Tales*** [***Tales of Mystery and Imagination***] 415).[1] "We were strolling one night down a long dirty street, in the vicinity of the Palais Royal," the narrator says. "Being both, apparently, occupied with thought, neither of us had spoken a syllable for fifteen minutes at least" (416). At this point, Dupin speaks and, to the narrator's astonishment, reveals that he has been mind-reading—following perfectly his companion's train of thought during this quarter hour of silence. He recounts every step in a long series of thoughts that runs from street paving to astronomy to a theater performance. Dupin explains his method: not telepathy, but a display of what the narrator calls "analytical power" (413), consisting of intense observation and attention to detail, an apparently infallible understanding of the human psyche, an "illimitable" education (417), and a rigorous application of deductive logic.

The scene lays out the techniques that Dupin will use as he goes on to investigate and solve the terrible crime at the heart of **"The Murders in the Rue Morgue"**—the brutal murder and mutilation of a mother and daughter in the bedroom of their home. The police are without "the shadow of a clue" as to how, why, and by whom these murders were committed (425). Dupin alone is able to work out that the culprit is, famously, a razor-wielding orangutan, escaped from its owner, a French sailor.

Stories of criminals and detectives were, of course, a feature of newspapers and novels long before Poe, but it was in his three stories about Dupin—what he called "tales of ratiocination" (Brand 104)—that the literary genre that we recognize today as detective fiction first emerged. Poe established its fundamental formulaic elements: recurring central characters and a story structure that follows the process of detection: the introduction of the detective, the statement of an apparently insoluble problem, the investigation, and finally the detective's revelatory explanation of events. **"The Murders in the Rue Morgue"** has thus been described as "the founding text" of detective fiction (Nickerson 6).

Historians of detective fiction agree that the genre's rise to prominence in America and Europe during the nineteenth century was intrinsically connected to the rapid, unprecedented growth of cities. Urban crimes provided the source material, and the ever-increasing urban population offered an audience eager to consume stories that reflected its paranoia about the dangers of city life. In the proliferation of new periodicals, the urban publishing industry supplied the ideal vehicle for an episodic, popular literary form. The conventional critical view is that detective fiction achieved its enormous, enduring popularity because it put forward accounts of the new urban experience that were ultimately comforting for its largely city-dwelling audience. Intended primarily for a bourgeois, conservative readership, early detective fiction, according to the argument, offered a reassuring perspective of urban life, in which through the application of scientific reasoning—"ratiocination"—the detective renders the city knowable, its mysteries solvable, its relentlessly multiplying lower classes and immigrant populations controllable, its criminals able to be captured.[2]

In a 1998 article, Philip Howell restates this outlook succinctly: "The force of the anxieties raised by the modern city is absorbed and repelled by the reassurance that the city can through description be known and by knowledge be controlled. This ideological claim to know the city seems to enter into the formal structure of detective fiction" (360). Certainly, such an "ideological claim" seems subtly present when Dupin tracks his companion's thoughts at the beginning of **"The Murders in the Rue Morgue."** This first demonstration of Dupin's "analytical power" (413) is staged, notably, in an exterior, public space rather than in either of the interior, private spaces in which we have previously encountered him: the "obscure library" where the narrator and Dupin first meet and the "grotesque mansion" where they live (414). We are invited to notice the connection between the duo's pedestrian movement along the city's streets and the process of detection, between the material geography of the metropolis and Dupin's "analytical" methods of investigation. Indeed, the narrator later describes that intellectual process in terms of walking through physical space:

> There are few persons who have not [. . .] amused themselves in retracing the *steps* by which particular conclusions of their own minds have been attained [. . .] he who attempts it for the first time is astonished by the apparently illimitable *distance* and incoherence between the starting-point and the goal.
>
> (417; emphasis added)

Dupin reinforces the association between a person's inner thoughts and his or her physical progress through the city streets when he uses the same word a few paragraphs later: "'I had correctly followed your *steps*'" (418; emphasis added). It is as if Dupin can chart the sequences of a person's thoughts and simultaneously their actions in and movements through the city: that, theoretically, to know one is to know the other. In this sense, Dupin's detective ability is presented both as mastery of other individuals' thought processes and of the "topography" of the city.

Howell goes on to show how today's detective stories often resist this kind of "ideological claim"—that it is possible for the city and its myriad individuals to be comprehended and controlled—and represent the city instead as an unknowable, irredeemably dangerous place. I want to suggest here that in **"The Murders in the Rue Morgue,"** the very "founding text" of detective fiction, Poe too ultimately depicts the city as beyond control. Dupin may be able to trace a person's "'steps,'" literal and figurative, but such acts of intellectual brilliance do not necessarily bring order to the modern metropolis. Poe portrays an urban milieu that is characterized by a symbiotic relationship between rampant commercialism and commercialized sexual pleasure. This relationship is, as much as any murderous orangutan, responsible for the atrocious killing of the two women. Poe's vision of urban life is not entirely pessimistic; after all, through the narrator, he evinces a sense of being energized by the city. Nonetheless, in my reading, Poe wants to draw attention to dangers unleashed by the city's expanding capitalist economy and its burgeoning commercial sex industry. Significantly, these dangers are not dispelled by the seemingly successful conclusion of Dupin's investigation. Poe's inclusion of the Palais Royal at the start of **"The Murders in the Rue Morgue"** gives our first clue to this understanding of the story.

I have never seen an analysis of the tale that more than mentions in passing the presence of the Palais. However, as the first named and first real building in the story, it might, not unreasonably, be expected to carry some symbolic value. Certainly, the history of the building chimes with the tale in interesting ways. Constructed in the 1630s by Louis XIV, the Palais was a royal residence until 1789, when it became "the birthplace, the propaganda-centre and the barometer of revolution" where "radicals [. . .] declaimed speeches [. . .] paraded heads on pikes and organised the attack on the Bastille" (Mansel 42). In 1830, the Palais was again "the focus of riots and demonstrations" (Mansel 290). Critics have proffered numerous reasons that Poe selected Paris as the location for his three narratives of crime, disorder, and detection, among them the city's unrivaled notoriety during the early and mid-1800s as a place of rampant criminality (Kalifa 178-79), its "generally sinister atmosphere" (Méral 11), and its then very recent history of social turmoil (Irwin 340-56; Miller 327-30). Scholars have long suggested that Poe set the stories in Paris specifically to conjure up images of the bloody revolutions of 1789 and 1830 in the minds of his readers. The specific reference to the Palais is perhaps a pointer to such an interpretation. In solving the mystery of the murders, argue scholars such as John Irwin and Elise Lemire, Dupin, a "young gentleman of an excellent—indeed of an illustrious family" (414), symbolically reverses the effects of the French Revolution. Understanding the uncontrollable orangutan as a figure for the revolutionary mob, they see Dupin reasserting aristocratic authority over a city terrified by a lower class uprising (Irwin 340-56; Lemire 177-204).

Such readings contend that Poe projects onto Paris his anxieties about American cities—specifically, about the frequent working-class riots that during the 1830s troubled Philadelphia and New York, the cities in which Poe lived while writing his detective stories. Through Dupin, Poe, who considered himself something of an aristocrat, fantasizes about restoring order to American cities.[3]

For me, however, it is more than its role in Paris's history of riots and revolutions that gives the Palais Royal significance in **"The Murders in the Rue Morgue."** Poe never visited France but was a true Francophile, a keen reader about the country, with an expert's grasp of the complexities of postrevolutionary Parisian culture and politics (Irwin 340-43). Almost certainly, Poe would have known the two things for which the Palais was internationally renowned in the mid-nineteenth century: sex and shopping.

After 1789, the Palais was transformed. The once royal palace now housed "the most celebrated concentration of shops, cafes, casinos and brothels in the world." It became known as "the capital of Paris," "the rendezvous of Europe" and "the most salient point of the world." A "typical cross-section of the Palais [. . .] contained a restaurant in the basement; a shop on the ground floor; a café on the first; a brothel on the second floor; and rooms for single people, frequently prostitutes, in the attics" (Mansel 42). Joachim Schlör adds, "The clientele of the shops and promenades [. . .] proved a strong attraction for prostitutes . . . its arcades were once *the* prostitutes' catwalk [. . .] their provocative presence is mentioned in every contemporary guide" (Schlör 27, 37; emphasis in original). An English travelogue of 1815 rhapsodized: "All the senses are aroused, all the passions are excited and a general intoxication of pleasure may be said to prevail in this enclosure of luxury; it is the centre of trade, the meeting place of rogues and swindlers, the abode of idleness and festivity; it is the Palais-Royal" (qtd. in Mansel 42).[4] The luxury shops of the Palais attracted a wealthy clientele to its arcades. This clientele, in turn, attracted prostitutes. These prostitutes then became a feature of the tourist literature that advertised Paris to the world. The brothels helped to bring sex-seeking visitors to the Palais and these visitors, in turn, became potential customers for its shops. Commercial and sexual activity formed a reciprocal relationship; they fed from each other in a "virtuous" circle of the market economy. Unsurprisingly, the Palais was a "volatile" place where crime was rife and disputed deals between prostitutes and clients led to frequent outbursts of fighting (Harsin 141). In its promenades crowded with shoppers, prostitutes, men looking for sex, and "rogues and swindlers" hoping to prey on them all, the Palais nurtured a strange and dangerous ecosystem.

Significantly, prostitution in nineteenth-century France was a legalized trade, subject to intense regulation by the Parisian authorities and taxed by the state. Prostitution played an officially recognized and profitable part in Paris's then rapidly enlarging urban economy.[5] In the American cultural imagination, Paris was consequently considered to be the world capital of sexual immorality, with the Palais at its heart.[6]

The 1815 guidebook summed up the Palais as "this temple of merchandise and sin." Nathaniel Willis, the popular travel writer and a friend of Poe's, echoed the phrase when he described the Palais for the American audience in his best-selling book *Pencillings by the Way* (1832). He called it "a public haunt [. . .] of pleasure and merchandise" (qtd. in Mabbott 570).[7] Poe, who probably read *Pencillings,* would surely have known that when Willis used the word *pleasure,* he referred among other things to prostitution. As **"The Murders in the Rue Morgue"** was first published in *Graham's Magazine,* a middle-to-highbrow periodical with an educated audience,[8] I would suggest that, given the widespread notoriety of the Palais that was disseminated in books such as Willis's, Poe could depend on readers of the story also making an immediate mental association. Poe's reference to the Palais would, if only subliminally, have inserted into his readers' minds the idea of prostitution.

Just two sentences after mentioning the Palais, Dupin and the narrator discuss at length a certain performance at a Parisian theater (416). In antebellum American cities, the theater was intimately connected to the sex trade with, controversially, the galleries of public theaters always reserved for prostitutes, who, according to theater owners, attracted theatergoers (Burrows and Wallace 484). Having raised the thought of prostitution in readers' minds by mention of the Palais, Poe ensured that thought did not get away by reinforcing it with talk of the theater.

If anything was associated with prostitution more than theaters in nineteenth-century America, however, it was sailors. Historically, the dockyard areas of U.S. cities were red-light districts. By the 1830s, prostitution had spread geographically across cities such as New York and Philadelphia, but the docks and shipyards remained among the busiest and most notorious sites for the sex trade (Burrows and Wallace 484; Hobson; Hill). As Valerie Burton and Lisa Norling have demonstrated, nineteenth-century sailors were commonly believed to be inveterate users of prostitutes. Anyone familiar with Herman Melville's 1849 novel *Redburn* will recognize the popular image of the sailor who spends his shore leave drunkenly indulging in sexual "depravity" (Melville 202).

In **"The Murders in the Rue Morgue,"** it is, of course, a sailor who brings the murderous orangutan into Paris. This sailor is the nineteenth century's stereotype of the seaman, "tall, stout and muscular-looking" with a sunburned, mustachioed face and uncouth manner (440). Like the Palais Royal, the mere presence of a sailor in the narrative might have suggested to Poe's original readers that this was, on some level, a story involving prostitution. Poe goes further, though; he makes matters more explicit. It is on voyage to Borneo during "an excursion of pleasure" on land that the sailor "captured the Ourang-Outang," bringing the animal back to Paris to sell (441). Notably, it is when he returns "home from some sailors' frolic on the night, or rather in the morning of the murder" that he discovers the "ferocious" animal has escaped from its "closet" and is in possession of the razor with which it later kills the two women (442). I am confident that the audience of *Graham's* would have understood phrases such as "excursion of pleasure" and "sailors' frolic" to indicate sexual activity. I think it would have been clear to them that it is because the sailor seeks sex in Borneo that he first encounters the orangutan, and because he is out visiting prostitutes in Paris that the killer ape is able to escape into the streets and commit murder.

Poe, then, identifies prostitution as a key factor in the murders, but he also implicates the wider capitalist system. The sailor captures the orangutan to sell it, and does eventually receive for it "a very large sum" (444). The sailor recognizes that the orangutan has an exchange value in the urban market economy, and his desire to capitalize on that value is at the root of the bloodshed and fear depicted in the story. Just as in the Palais, where a "volatile" mix of commerce and prostitution begets criminality and violence, so with the sailor, it is a combination of sexual desire and profit-making that generates danger.

It should not be surprising if Poe did indeed, in writing a tale about the dangers of contemporaneous urban life, put prostitution center stage. More than street crime or rioting, prostitution became the focal point of America's anxieties about urbanization in the mid-nineteenth century.[9] It was known as the great social evil and provoked constant public debate (Hill 17). This was a boom period for the sex industry. By the 1830s, there were more than two hundred brothels and ten thousand prostitutes in New York alone (Burrows and Wallace 484; Hill 18). In the United States, there was awareness of prostitution's officially recognized place in Parisian society, with proposals regularly put forward—and promptly rejected—to follow the French model and legalize the sex trade, so that it could be better regulated by public authorities (Hill 136-39).

Fears about the connection between commercial sex and moral decline reached a peak in 1836 when the murder of prostitute Helen Jewett by a client, and subsequent high-profile trial, became front-page news. It would prove to be a crime, like the Jack the Ripper murders, that would live in the public memory for decades (Hill 9-16). Jewett was killed with an ax blow to the head, and Poe could have been invoking this murder when in **"The Murders in the Rue Morgue,"** the head of one victim, Madame L'Espanaye, bears wounds from a sharp instrument. Poe was perhaps planting a red herring here, suggesting to his readers that the murder of Madame L'Espanaye was, like that of Jewett, the killing of a prostitute by a disgruntled lover. After all, a neighbor of Madame L'Espanaye asserts that the murdered woman "'told fortunes for a living,'" and *fortune-teller* was sometimes used in the 1800s as a euphemism for *prostitute* (Lemay 173-74).

If we want further evidence that Poe had prostitution on his mind when writing his "tales of ratiocination," we might look to his second Dupin story, **"The Mystery of Marie Rogêt"** (1842-43). Here, too, Poe raises the issue of prostitution and its symbiotic relationship with other forms of urban commerce and inserts it into a story of vicious murder. Famously, Poe based his tale on a real-life murder, the unsolved killing in New York in 1841 of Mary Rogers.[10] Although there was "no evidence that Rogers was a prostitute," many New York press stories insinuated that she was (Srebnick 51). Poe reproduces several such newspaper reports in his tale, giving the publications invented French titles but otherwise almost exactly maintaining the original texts. He reinforces suggestions that Mary was a prostitute in his description of the fictional Marie's job. She was employed for "her great beauty" by a "perfumer" whose shop, significantly, is "in the basement of the Palais Royal, and whose custom lay chiefly among the adventurers infesting that neighbourhood." "His rooms," the narrative explains, "soon became notorious through the charms of the sprightly *grisette*" (447; emphasis in original). At the very least, Marie's sex appeal is what makes her employer's business a success. It is also what makes her vulnerable; Dupin eventually blames her grisly murder on a "'young naval officer much noted for his debaucheries,'" who, Dupin believes, had a sexual relationship with Marie (474). In each of his first two "tales of ratiocination," then, Poe implies the interconnectedness of sex, commerce, and violence as characteristic of the capitalist city.

In the Paris of **"The Murders in the Rue Morgue,"** all personal interaction, whether sexual or otherwise, is conditioned by economics. After the murders of Madame and Mademoiselle L'Espanaye, the first newspaper report is based on interviews with the women's neighbors. They are named and then identified by their jobs: laundress, tobacconist, gendarme, silversmith, restaurateur, banker, clerk, tailor, undertaker, and confectioner (420-24). There is no suggestion of friendship or intimacy between the L'Espanayes and their neighbors; the only firm details that they can offer about Madame L'Espanaye pertain to her participation in commercial exchanges, mostly ones that involve themselves. The laundress "'deposes that she has known the deceased for three years, having washed for them during that period [. . .] They were excellent pay'" (420). The tobacconist says that he "'has been in the habit of selling small quantities of tobacco and snuff to Madame and Mademoiselle L'Espanaye for nearly four years'" and that Madame L'Espanaye had once been a professional landlady (420-21). The banker states, according to a newspaper account read by Dupin: "'Madame L'Espanaye [. . . h]ad opened an account with his banking house in the spring of the year—(eight years previously). Made frequent deposits in small sums. Had checked for nothing until the third day before her death, when she took out in person the sum of 4000 francs'" (422). In the city, it seems, one is defined primarily by the services and products that one buys and sells and by one's financial status. Poe anticipates urban theorists such as Engels, Simmel, and Benjamin in suggesting that under capitalism, and especially in the city, all human relationships become commodified.[11]

Dupin is no exception to such commodification. Like the L'Espanayes and their neighbors, he too is defined by his financial existence. The first details by which we know Dupin are not, for instance, to do with his appearance (about which we find out almost nothing) but his bank balance: a "young gentleman" of an "illustrious family" now "reduced to [. . .] poverty," who has "creditors," "a small remnant of his patrimony" and who exercises "rigorous economy" (414). Dupin is only rescued from "poverty" by the narrator who, we are told, rents and furnishes a secluded mansion for the two of them to live in (414).

Readings of **"The Murders in the Rue Morgue"** that argue that Dupin, in solving the crime, restores order to the terrorized city are troubling. Dupin may provide the answer to the mystery of who killed the L'Espanayes, but he, in fact, does nothing to make the city safer. He does not put his time and his enormous brainpower into finding and securing the homicidal orangutan, which continues to roam free; he, instead, merely revels in uncovering its role in the killings, showing off to the narrator about the cleverness of his investigation and stagily duping the sailor (427-41). What is more, Poe's Dupin utterly absolves the sailor—the orangutan's greedy, irresponsible owner—of all culpability for bringing the animal into Paris and then allowing it to escape while he is on his "sailors' frolic." Dupin is uncharacteristically repetitive when he announces, "[Y]ou are innocent of the atrocities in the Rue Morgue," using six different phrases in one passage to affirm the sailor's guiltlessness (441). Dupin permits the sailor to go free to recapture and sell the orangutan, as he had always intended, and Poe seems insistent that we notice this. In other words, Poe draws attention to the fact that Dupin does nothing to interrupt, regulate, or even punish the economic and sexual activities that bring disorder to the city. He just solves the puzzle.

Dupin states that his primary motivation for investigating the case is to exercise his intellectual powers (426). With that goal achieved, his interest ends. But one can discern a more secretive motive. Both Leo Lemay and Graham Robb (254-60) have argued that Dupin and the unnamed, presumably male narrator are more than friends, but are lovers. One could offer a plausible reading of the story that takes this a step further and interprets the relationship as one of homosexual prostitution. Here, our narrator is effectively a sex tourist in Paris, a city, as Michael Sibalis describes, that decriminalized homosexuality in 1789 and that was known for homosexual as well as heterosexual prostitution. The narrator pays for the "treasure" of Dupin's company when he bankrolls their shared home. Such a reading would argue that Dupin—once impoverished, now a kept man—is as dependent on the city's sexual commerce as the prostitutes of the Palais, and does nothing to interfere with it because it provides him too with a good living.

However, something more seems to be going on that invokes Howell's statement about the "ideological claim" of detective fiction—to show the city to be both knowable and controllable—and to the Palais Royal and Dupin's opening display of detective brilliance in its shadow. First, however, it is useful to look at Poe's claims regarding detective fiction during the writing of **"The Mystery of Marie Rogêt."** The history of the tale's composition has been the subject of much critical discussion, with Walsh's *Poe the Detective* (1968) and Daniel Stashower's *The Beautiful Cigar Girl* (2006) dedicated to recounting Poe's investigative work into the Mary Rogers case. The first two installments of **"Rogêt" ["The Mystery of Marie Rogêt"]** were published in late 1842, when the real-life Rogers murder was still a mystery to police and press alike. Poe, at this stage, declared himself confident that his narrative would actually reveal Rogers's killer and would point to useful extratextual truths about crime and detection, telling a potential publisher:

> [. . .] I believe not only have I demonstrated the fallacy of the general idea—that the girl was the victim of a gang of ruffians—but have *indicated the assassin* in a manner which will give renewed impetus to investigation. My main object, nevertheless, as you will readily understand, is an analysis of the true principles which should direct inquiry in similar cases.
>
> (*Letters* 112-13; emphasis in original)

However, at this point, new information came to light in the Rogers case that forced Poe to reconsider his planned ending. Poe delayed the third and final installment until later in 1843, ostensibly to allow him to conduct further research and amend the draft version of the story's finale. Before the last installment, Poe had laid the groundwork for Dupin's revelation that the "young naval officer" committed the murder. The new evidence, however, strongly suggested that Rogers's death was the result of a botched abortion. Poe left the conclusion more open ended to incorporate the possibility that the abortion was behind the tragedy. Poe made further amendments before the story was republished in 1845, discounting the idea that the deaths of Mary and Marie are analogous:

> [. . . L]et it not for a moment be supposed that [. . .] it is my covert design to hint at an extension of the parallel [between Mary and Marie], or even to suggest that the measures adopted in Paris for the discovery of the assassin of a *grisette,* or measures founded in any similar ratiocination, would produce any similar result.
>
> (492; emphasis in original)

Dana Brand has argued persuasively that Poe never seriously believed that Dupin's "method" could solve real crimes and that Poe's assertion that his tale constituted "an analysis of the true principles which should direct inquiries in similar cases"—in other words, that detective fiction could somehow solve real crimes—was, in truth, no more than a ploy to sell the story. Poe himself had said of the stories, "'[P]eople think them more ingenious than they are—on account of their method and their air of method'" and had asked of **"The Murders in the Rue Morgue,"** "'[W]here is the ingenuity of unraveling a web which you yourself (the author) have woven for the express purpose of unraveling?'" (qtd. in Brand 104). Brand adds, "Poe understood the methods of the detective story to be a hoax, an air of method, just as the flaneurs who wrote for the magazines presumably did not believe that they could actually read a person's entire history at a glance" (104). I believe that the Dupin stories slyly acknowledge that they are, in this sense, a "hoax." And it is here that the Palais Royal again becomes important.

As I have shown, the Palais is included at the start of **"The Murders in the Rue Morgue"** because, with its heady, flammable cocktail of sex and commerce, it is, to some extent, a microcosm of the whole of Paris itself, in turn, the epitome of the modern city as Poe envisages it. As Poe knew from his experiences living in Baltimore, Philadelphia, Richmond, and New York, American cities were quickly becoming, or perceived to be becoming, just like Paris, that is, hotbeds of "sin and merchandise." Indeed, just a few years after **"The Murders in the Rue Morgue,"** Poe's friend Nathaniel Willis referred to the "imminent Paris-ification of New

York" in a magazine article (qtd. in Brand 76). At first glance, Poe seems to show that Paris—and, by extension, American cities—can be known, their mysteries solved, by the application of scientific reasoning such as Dupin's. After all, Dupin's first act of detection involves demonstrating mastery of the streets around the Palais, the very epicenter and embodiment of urban evils.

However, although Poe begins his story with a sense of geographical verisimilitude, placing Dupin and the narrator next to the Palais, the Paris of **"The Murders in the Rue Morgue"** soon becomes a semi-imaginary place as the narrative progresses. The Palais is one of only a handful of real locations named in the tale.[12] Otherwise, as William Henry Smith noted in an 1847 review, Poe demonstrates "a disregard for accuracy" in his depiction of the French capital (Walker 221-22).[13] "There is no want of streets and passages," Smith observes, "but no Parisian would find them, or find them in the juxtaposition he has placed them." Poe "misname[s]" or simply invents many of the streets that he mentions in the tale. Even the Rue Morgue itself is a fabrication.[14] Smith finds it "a surprise, that one so partial to detail should not have more frequently profited by the help which a common guide-book, with its map, might have given him." Of course, Poe—an expert on Paris and a writer usually methodically consistent in his use of references[15]—could easily have made his story topographically accurate if he had so wished. Instead, he uses real streets and buildings, such as the Palais, to draw us into believing that his is a truthful depiction of Paris. By using some genuine place-names in the stories, Poe invites the reader to compare Dupin's city to the real Paris, as Smith seems to have done. But readers who sit with a map of Paris open alongside the book containing Poe's detective stories will be frustrated if they attempt to follow the movements of the fictional characters along the "real" streets. They will soon find themselves searching for imaginary avenues and wondering why two streets that are supposed to adjoin are, on the actual map, miles apart. We learn to trust Dupin's methods in a scene in which the process of detection is systematically built into these city streets, in which the "steps" involved in tracking a person's thoughts are the same as the "steps" that one takes as one moves through the city. It is as if, by following on a map the narrator and Dupin's walk, one can also follow the twists and turns of Dupin's detective work, as if the secret of solving crimes is simply a matter of plotting a route on a map. However, Poe then asks us to notice that the appearance of geographically rearranged and fictional streets undermines the story's apparent topographical verisimilitude. Dupin's "analytical" process of detection may be imbedded into those streets, but if we cannot trust (the narrator's description of) the street layout, should we also distrust Dupin's detective work, given that even as we are learning to trust his intellectual process, we are being told that it exists only in a nonexistent city? It is, Poe seems teasingly to be telling us, as much a work of fiction as is his Paris; it is a "hoax," and we would get as lost in trying to solve a crime by following Dupin's intellectual reasoning as we would in trying to navigate Paris by following the story's "mapping" of the city.[16]

I would suggest, then, that Poe asks us instead to recognize this Paris as an unrealistic city. Only in unrealistic cities do crimes occur as fantastical as an escaped Borneo orangutan murdering a mother and daughter with a stolen shaving razor. And only in unrealistic places can a brilliant man single-handedly solve such "outré" crimes, as Dupin calls them (427). What Dupin cannot do is tackle the real problems of modern urban life—problems that Poe's readers would have identified through his references to the Palais Royal, theaters and sailors. In the story, Dupin both literally and figuratively walks away from the Palais and into a world of fiction. Poe asks us to understand that Dupin's ability to solve urban crime exists only on a fictional plane. One might legitimately argue that in **"The Murders in the Rue Morgue,"** Poe moves from describing Paris authentically and toward a more imaginary version of the city for precisely the opposite reason: It is because he wants to make this city function as a symbol of all cities, and to show that Dupin's methods are as applicable in New York and Philadelphia as in the French capital, that he must avoid leading readers to believe this is a story solely about the actual Paris. However, when Dupin makes no effort to recapture the orangutan and goes out of his way to declare the sailor innocent of all responsibility, Poe draws our attention to the fact that the real problems of modern urban life have been untouched by his hero's investigation. Even Dupin, with his incredible "analytical power" and astonishing detective logic, can do nothing to regulate the real city. Far from instigating the "ideological claim" of detective fiction that Howell describes, to demonstrate the modern city to be knowable and controllable, Poe instead makes us aware that, although a genius may be able to solve a bizarre crime in a semifictional city in a work of literature, there are much more powerful forces still operating unchecked in the real city: sex and money.

Notes

1. Unless otherwise stated, all page references refer to Poe, *Tales of Mystery and Imagination.*

2. For "traditional" accounts, see Symons and Knight. See Brand (64-105) for a more recent overview of this theme in detective fiction and its criticism.

3. See Miller for a fuller account of Poe as an urban writer. Godden, meanwhile, traces the impact of rioting in New York and Philadelphia on Poe's fiction.

4. Citation originally from Deterville.

5. See Harsin for a detailed account of prostitution in nineteenth-century Paris.

6. See Méral for an examination of Paris in the American mind. For more on U.S. writers' interest in the perceived disorder of European cities, see Bender 8-70; Boyer 131; Srebnick 8-9. It should be noted that by the time Poe wrote "The Murders in the Rue Morgue," the Palais was in decline, dealt a severe blow by the forced closure of its gambling salons in 1836 (Benjamin 494; Schlör 56). Notably, Poe seems to set the story in the early 1830s, when the Palais was still central to Parisian nightlife (Irwin 342-43; Mabbott 573). One might argue that, in public perception at least, Paris became even more dangerous after 1836, with the activities associated with the Palais—sex and violence in particular—no longer contained in one area. See Kalifa on the development of the "criminal topography" of the city.

7. Nathaniel Parker Willis, *Pencillings by the Way* (1832), Letter ix, qtd. in Mabbott 570. Mabbott cites no further publication details for Willis's book. Information on Poe's relationship with Willis may be found in Thomas and Jackson 220-21 and 471.

8. For discussions of *Graham's* and Poe's relationship with his audience, see Silverman, esp. 162-174, and Whalen 63-95.

9. See Hobson and Hill for accounts of prostitution in nineteenth-century U.S. cities.

10. For information on Poe's use of the Rogers case, see Saltz; Srebnick 109-33; Walsh; and Stashower.

11. Notably, the Palais Royal is central to Benjamin's thinking about the significance of urban prostitution (489-515).

12. There are four real buildings named—the Palais, the *Théâtre des Variétés,* the Jardin des Plantes, and "the *bureau* of the Prefect of Police" (444; emphasis in original). These are, perhaps significantly, arranged in two pairs, with the Palais and the theater mentioned within a few lines of each other at the start and the Jardin and the Police office both mentioned near the end.

13. The review was originally published in *Blackwood's* (November 1847): 582-87.

14. In his notes on the story, Mabbott confirms that there was no Rue Morgue in Paris in 1841, a fact ascertained easily by reference to commonly available, contemporary guidebooks. Mabbott also notes several such invented streets in the story: for instance, the Rue Dubourg, in which Dupin pretends that he has housed the captured orangutan (569, 574).

15. See Irwin for a portrait of Poe's careful, systematic use of references.

16. "The Purloined Letter," the third Dupin story, is skeptical about the trustworthiness of maps themselves. Dupin describes "'a game of puzzles [. . .] played upon a map'" in which the map misleads participants, concealing as much as revealing information about the city (508).

Works Cited

Bender, Thomas. *Toward an Urban Vision: Ideas and Institutions in Nineteenth-Century America.* Lexington: UP of Kentucky, 1975.

Benjamin, Walter. *The Arcades Project.* Trans. Howard Eiland and Kevin McLaughlin. Cambridge: Harvard UP, 2004.

Boyer, Paul. *Urban Masses and Moral Order in America.* Cambridge: Harvard UP, 1978.

Brand, Dana. *The Spectator and the City in Nineteenth-Century American Literature.* Cambridge, Eng.: Cambridge UP, 1991.

Burrows, Edwin G., and Mike Wallace. *Gotham: A History of New York to 1898.* Oxford: Oxford UP, 1999.

Burton, Valerie. "'As I wuz a-rolling down the Highway one morn': Fictions of the 19th-Century English Sailortown." *Fictions of the Sea: Critical Perspectives on the Ocean in British Literature and Culture.* Ed. Bernhard Klein. Aldershot, Eng.: Ashgate, 2002. 141-56.

Deterville, H. *Le Palais Royal, ou les Filles en Bonne Fortune. . . .* Paris: ca. 1815.

Godden, Richard. "Edgar Allan Poe and the Detection of Riot." *Literature and History* 8 (1982): 206-31.

Harsin, Jill. *Policing Prostitution in Nineteenth-Century Paris.* Princeton: Princeton UP, 1985.

Hill, Marilynn Wood. *Their Sisters' Keepers: Prostitution in New York City, 1830-1870.* Berkeley: U of California P, 1993.

Hobson, Barbara Meil. *Uneasy Virtue: The Politics of Prostitution and the American Reform Tradition.* New York: Basic, 1987.

Howell, Philip. "Crime and the City Solution: Crime Fiction, Urban Knowledge, and Radical Geography." *Antipode* 30.4 (1998): 357-78.

Irwin, John T. *The Mystery to a Solution: Poe, Borges, and the Analytic Detective Story.* Baltimore: Johns Hopkins UP, 1994.

Kalifa, Dominique. "Crime Scenes: Criminal Topography and Social Imaginary in Nineteenth-Century Paris." *French Historical Studies* 27.1 (Winter 2004): 175-94.

Knight, Stephen. *Form and Ideology in Crime Fiction.* London: Macmillan, 1980.

Lemay, J. A. Leo. "The Psychology of 'The Murders in the Rue Morgue.'" *American Literature* 54.2 (1982): 165-88.

Lemire, Elise. "'The Murders in the Rue Morgue': Amalgamation Discourses and Race Riots of 1838 in Poe's Philadelphia." *Romancing the Shadow: Poe and Race.* Ed. J. Gerald Kennedy and Lillian Westberg. Oxford: Oxford UP, 2001. 177-204.

Mabbott, Thomas Ollive, ed. *Tales and Stories.* Cambridge: Harvard UP, 1978. Vol. 2 of the *Collected Works of Edgar Allan Poe.*

Mansel, Philip. *Paris between Empires, 1814-1852.* London: Murray, 2001.

Melville, Herman. *Redburn.* 1849. Ed. Harold Beaver. London: Penguin, 1976.

Méral, Jean. *Paris in American Literature.* Trans. Laurette Long. Chapel Hill: U of North Carolina P, 1989.

Miller, Linda Patterson. "The Writer in the Crowd: Poe's Urban Vision." *American Transcendental Quarterly* 44 (1979): 325-39.

Nickerson, Catherine Ross. *The Web of Iniquity: Early Detective Fiction by American Women.* Durham: Duke UP, 1998.

Norling, Lisa. "The Sentimentalization of American Seafaring: The Case of the New England Whalefishery, 1790-1870." *Jack Tar in History: Essays in the History of Maritime Life and Labour.* Ed. Colin Howell and Richard J. Twomey. Fredericton, Can.: Acadiensis, 1991. 164-78.

Poe, Edgar Allan. *Letters.* Ed. James A. Harrison. Introd. Floyd Stowall. 2nd ed. New York: AMI, 1969. Vol. 17 of *The Complete Works of Edgar Allan Poe.*

———. *Tales of Mystery and Imagination.* Ed. Graham Clarke. London: Everyman, 1993.

Robb, Graham. *Strangers: Homosexual Love in the 19th Century.* London: Picador, 2003.

Saltz, Laura. "'(Horrible to Relate!)': Recovering the Body of Marie Rogêt." *The American Face of Edgar Allan Poe.* Ed. Shawn Rosenheim and Stephen Rachman. Baltimore: Johns Hopkins UP, 1995. 237-67.

Schlör, Joachim. *Nights in the Big City: Paris, Berlin, London 1840-1930.* Trans. Pierre Gottfried Imhof and Dafydd Rees Roberts. London: Reaktion, 1998.

Sibalis, Michael D. "Paris." *Queer Sites: Gay Urban Histories since 1600.* Ed. David Higgs. London: Routledge, 1999. 10-37.

Silverman, Kenneth. *Edgar A. Poe: Mournful and Never-Ending Remembrance.* New York: Harper, 1992.

Srebnick, Amy Gilman. *The Mysterious Death of Mary Rogers: Sex and Culture in Nineteenth-Century New York.* Oxford: Oxford UP, 1995.

Stashower, Daniel. *The Beautiful Cigar Girl: Mary Rogers, Edgar Allan Poe, and the Invention of Murder.* New York: Dutton, 2006.

Symons, Julian. *Bloody Murder: From the Detective Story to the Crime Novel—A History.* London: Faber, 1972.

Thomas, Dwight, and David K. Jackson, comps. *The Poe Log: A Documentary Life of Edgar Allan Poe 1809-1849.* Boston: Hall, 1987.

Walker, I. M., ed. *Edgar Allan Poe: The Critical Heritage.* New York: Routledge, 1986.

Walsh, John. *Poe the Detective: The Curious Circumstances behind "The Mystery of Marie Rogêt."* New Brunswick: Rutgers UP, 1968.

Whalen, Terence. "Poe and the American Publishing Industry." *A Historical Guide to Edgar Allan Poe.* Ed. J. Gerald Kennedy. Oxford: Oxford UP, 2001. 63-95.

Valerie Rohy (essay date 2006)

SOURCE: Rohy, Valerie. "Ahistorical." *GLQ* 12, no. 1 (2006): 61-83.

[*In the following essay, Rohy discusses the suggestion of lesbian sex at the conclusion of "Ligeia" and speculates about how this anachronistic reading of a culturally dated text affects "queer theory's temporal concerns."*]

> They are always *there,* specters, even if they do not exist, even if they are no longer, even if they are not yet.
>
> —Jacques Derrida, *Specters of Marx*

Along the way to its gothic conclusion, **"Ligeia"** (1838) produces one of the strangest bedroom scenes in American literature. In the tale that Poe declared "undoubtedly the best story I have written," a nameless narrator endures the loss of his first wife, Ligeia, and the death of her hapless replacement, Rowena, before witnessing an impossible revival.[1] As he watches at her deathbed, Rowena's shrouded form stirs, rouses, and relapses into a lifeless state as "time after time, until near the period of the gray dawn, this hideous drama of revivification was repeated."[2] Recounting the various acts of this drama, the impatient narrator would "hurry to a conclusion" (233), but Poe takes his time. The cycle of "alarming recurrence" that began with Rowena's illness ends only when, the narrator reports, "the thing that was enshrouded advanced boldly and palpably into the middle of the apartment" (230, 233), in so doing revealing that the body has become Ligeia's.

This last indelible image of Ligeia rising from Rowena's deathbed cannot, however, match the spectacle that we do not see directly. Proving that there were *two* women in that bed, Poe's conclusion retroactively reveals a queer intimacy. Now we see why, as Rowena strained for life, "each agony wore the aspect of a struggle with some invisible foe" (233), if not why that foe got rather more than friendly. Ligeia bends Rowena's body to her will in a corporeal exchange whose rhythms of excitation and exhaustion can hardly be understood outside the realm of the sexual.[3] Attentive to the symptoms of Rowena's arousal, the narrator reports: "There was now a partial glow upon the forehead and upon the cheek and throat; a perceptible warmth pervaded the whole frame" (232). The "warmth," the "glow," the flush, the sighs, the "tremor," and the "pulsation" announce an event, he says, of "unspeakable horrors"—a moment of intercourse between two women who share one body (232). Prefiguring later tropes of lesbian sexuality, their relation appears as a predatory form of occult possession, companion of arcane horrors and half-seen monsters.[4]

There needs no ghost come from the grave, though the odds of that are good, to tell us that a Poe story is perverse. But the apparition of queer sexuality in **"Ligeia"** raises the epistemological stakes in a text already consumed by not knowing. From its first line, "I cannot, for my soul, remember" (222), to its ending, regarded as a "mystery" (232) by Poe's narrator and generations of skeptical readers, **"Ligeia"** is about uncertainty. As if forgetting were the precondition of remembering, the labor of narration begins under the sign of lack, founded on that "I cannot." In life, Ligeia is as obscure as the apparition she will become; after years spent studying her "expression," the narrator finds himself unable to "define that sentiment, or analyze, or even steadily view it" (224). In death, she returns in "wild visions," as "shadow-like" as the scene of resurrection that the narrator will insist he "distinctly saw" but also "might have dreamed" (231-33). Like the spectacle of that return, the text's queer effects resist empirical proof. As Ligeia's spirit enters her body, Rowena sighs and stirs, but what does that mean? The scene seems sexual, but *it cannot be.* It shows a weird intimacy between women, but *surely we are imagining it.* It is impossible—and yet, as the narrator wonders at Rowena's revival, "Why, *why* should I doubt it?" (233). Is lesbian sexuality more implausible than Poe's gothic plot, more preposterous than metempsychosis and the resurrection of the dead?

In historical terms, perhaps it is. Despite the appearance of sapphic love in nineteenth-century French novels—Balzac's *Girl with the Golden Eyes* and Théophile Gautier's *Mademoiselle de Maupin* were both published three years before **"Ligeia"**—in 1838 the lesbian had been neither named as such nor conceptualized as "a personage, a past, a case history."[5] Poe's tale comes nearly half a century before the first mentions of female homosexuality in American medical journals and much longer before scholarly notions of queer theory and queer desire.[6] How then can we know that the eerie frisson of **"Ligeia"** is not a backward projection of contemporary concerns? What can protect the reader from the careless assumption of "an ahistorical, or transhistorical, homosexuality"?[7] What indeed, since the uncanny return, the temporal reversal, and all that is dismissed as ahistorical in much recent criticism are precisely what makes Poe's text so queer. I mean to take such historical questions seriously, not to avoid charges of anachronism but to meet them, by examining the anachronism that operates in **"Ligeia"** and in queer literary history. Poe's lesbian effect is an optical illusion, visible only from one historical vantage point, but just the same it hangs before our eyes. Turning to **"Ligeia,"** I want to hold that angle of vision, neither denying nor confirming what it seems to show, because my subject is not, finally, the truth value of the lesbian effect in Poe's tale but the angle of vision itself. Such a reading cannot speak to history, but it can speak to historicism. A historically "illegitimate" approach may suggest how **"Ligeia"** anticipates and proleptically answers questions about historical illegitimacy—may suggest, that is, how its anachronistic narrative structure and its invitation to a certain backward glance address queer theory's temporal concerns.

How can the text's perversity be so elusive and so obvious? Nothing could be less mysterious than the "mysteries of the will" described in Poe's epigraph. Woman, as they say, will have her will, and Ligeia is all will, all appetite (222). That this desire, purportedly a lust for life, must signify as sexual needs no witness but Will Shakespeare, whose sonnets turn on the bawdy pun: "will" as wish or purpose, as male or female genitals, as carnal desire. In the words of sonnet 135, Ligeia has "*Will* to boot, and *Will* in overplus"; she is nothing if not too much.[8] The double double entendre of the epigraph, "the will therein lieth, which dieth not" (222), sets Ligeia's body and desire against the narrative closure conventionally found in death and consummation. Although her return cannot last—the narrator tells us early on that she "is no more" (222)—she is always excessive, always so much more. Her "gigantic volition" renders Ligeia "more than womanly" (225, 226), and in the old phallic sense of *will* it can hardly do anything else. But she need not be so well endowed to overstep the narrow bounds of nineteenth-century feminine propriety, for she is a woman of "immense," "astounding" learning—with an intellect, the narrator says, "such as I have never known in woman" (225)—and exempt from the law of the father, unmarked by a "paternal name" (222).

Both more and less than womanly, Ligeia makes a mockery of motherhood. While Rowena's rhythm of climax and collapse evokes sexual intercourse, this sequence of spasmodic "struggle" followed by "terrific relapse" also conjures labor and childbirth (233). In an 1839 letter to Poe, Philip P. Cooke took the hint, remarking on the image of Ligeia's spirit "quickening *the body of the Lady Rowena.*"[9] That "quickening" registers a grotesque pregnancy, in which Ligeia is both the child born out of Rowena's body and the paternal agent of insemination. Changing the deathbed to a ghastly parody of the childbed, Ligeia mimes birth in the service of death and of an impossible, still more deathly life: this woman giving birth to herself delivers not the future but the past. Small wonder that Ligeia has a vexed relation to heterosexual love, even by the generous standards of Poe's oeuvre. The narrator, for his part, explains that his wife's will to live reflects only her "idolatry" for him: "In Ligeia's more than womanly abandonment to a love, alas! all unmerited, all unworthily bestowed, I at length, recognized the principle of her longing, with so wildly earnest a desire, for the life which was now fleeing so rapidly away" (226). This tangled passage credits Ligeia's vitality to her heterosexual devotion; it claims that her eventual return from the dead bespeaks a normal love, however abnormal its proportions. Her conjugal bond, the narrator argues, forms the governing premise of her lust for life, the premise that her will to live merely imitates or allegorizes. Yet predicting the final moment when a revived Ligeia will cast off her veil, "shrinking from [his] touch" (233), he admits that her love for him is at best a dim echo of her "eager vehemence of desire for life—*but* for life" (226).

If the perversity of Poe's bedroom scene seems gratuitous, an accidental side effect of the "real" narrative, that apparent insignificance recalls the narrative function of lesbian sexuality. In the heterosexual plot whose favorite end is reproduction, female homosexuality is at best irrelevant (a meaningless by-product of the plot) and at worst obstructive (a detour that delays or obviates its conclusion). Regarded as endlessly unproductive, it cannot be an end in itself. Ligeia may have her reasons to claim Rowena's body, but the effect of lesbian eros born of their encounter becomes the obscene waste material of a story that in the end has no use for it. In fact, the shadow of queer enjoyment in **"Ligeia"** misdirects the plot at the moment of its most crucial turn. Peter Brooks has argued that delay, deviance and bad object choice belong to the middle of narrative structures, where they work to delay closure.[10] Such heteronormative conventions, Judith Roof writes, reduce sexual deviance to useless foreplay, a time of lingering "in the field of pleasure that constitutes part of the narrative's 'détour.'"[11] In Brooks's view, this detour serves narrative closure by deferring it and thus rendering the postponed conclusion more satisfying. But this is so only when the narrative obstacle, like a youthful delinquency or infatuation, cedes its place in due time to proper ends. The hetero narrative, Paul Morrison suggests, resists "any teleology that is simply for pleasure, any sexual economy in which pleasure does not work toward its own effacement."[12] Like the "gigantic" will that drives it, the lesbian effect of Poe's text exists "simply for pleasure," detached from narrative aims. To go on in defiance of sexual norms is to go back; desires that cannot die signal a malignant cycle of return. If in the wake of the AIDS crisis straight culture has figured gay male sexuality as a lively death wish, Poe represents Ligeia's desire as a morbid life wish.

As plainly as **"Ligeia"** bears the hallmarks of deviance, the collocation of these terms with each other and with lesbian desire, not to say lesbian identity, belongs to the twentieth century. Such rare qualities would not have signified in 1838 what they might have meant a half century later, when sexology found female masculinity symptomatic of sexual inversion, or still later, when the refusal of motherhood joined the diagnostic rubric. Early-nineteenth-century American culture would have judged as deviant any woman whose appetites so far exceeded heterosexual ends, but not until the twentieth century were reproductive status and gender identity taken as expressions or determinants of object choice and sexual identity.[13] A lesbian reading of **"Ligeia"** cannot then make Ligeia a lesbian, nor can a queer reading make her queer, since history precludes any trace of desire that in 1838 would answer to those more modern names. Instead, a backward, "ahistorical" approach offers an occasion to revisit the time lines of queer literary history: the straight-arrow rhetoric against anachronism, the turn back toward retrospection and queer temporality, the Victorian association of sexual deviance with temporal deviance, and contemporary queer accounts of identification, anachronism, and alterity. Directing our eyes to anamorphic images—forms intelligible only when viewed aslant—**"Ligeia"** offers an allegory of its own reading, including the queer reading structured by temporal obliquity. Seen from the wrong time, Poe's story confronts the modern reader with an instance of *historical* anamorphosis, and with it a refracted view of the strategic anachronism through which queer theory has lately adjusted the angle of its gaze on the past.

Always Historicize?

The queer past was overdetermined from the first, not least by the reparative impulse of "making up lost time," from whose pathos the most rigorous historicism is not exempt.[14] Inspired by visions of those silenced in former ages, queer scholars sought to discover loves, in the words of one landmark book, "hidden from history."[15] As Michel Foucault has argued, however, the past's continuity with the present cannot be assumed. Attentive to historical alterity, the dangers of metanarrative, and the disjunction between an earlier register of homosexual acts and a modern rubric of gay identity, queer criticism has largely translated Foucault in a cautionary tone.[16] It warns against the hasty assumption of commonalities between present and past same-sex desires and refuses as "ahistorical" or "anachronistic" readings that would project modern concepts back in time. In this logic, historicism, now broadly cognate with social constructionism, becomes the hallmark of progressive politics. Hailed as the universal defense against universalism, historicism promises respect for difference, particularity, and pluralism where the ahistorical would impose tyrannical conformity.

To grasp the influence of this argument, one need only track the recurrence of the words *ahistorical* and *anachronistic* in the queer criticism of the past fifteen years. The rise of historicist methodologies in queer literary studies in the 1990s brought a set of apotropaic gestures—the perfunctory nod to historical cautions, the pointed aside on a rival's anachronism, the dutiful apology for an unavoidable retroversion—that by now have been honed and condensed to a stylized, almost *purely* gestural form. Where the ahistorical is concerned, distinguished scholars from widely different critical positions seem to share a common language. When Eve Kosofsky Sedgwick notes that the "modern view of lesbians and gay men as a distinctive minority population is of course importantly anachronistic in relation to earlier writing," we are asked to remember something that *of course* everyone already knows (and to remember that we already know it), because, however well-known, this important point must endlessly be acknowledged.[17] Writing in 1996, Bonnie Zimmerman blames queer theory for the distortion of lesbian experience and "the appalling misrepresentation and ahistorical construction of the past twenty years."[18] Reviewing anthologies of gay male literature, George Haggerty remarks on "the danger of misreading the past" by positing an "ahistorical homophobia," but he notes that he too has been accused of "reading the past in terms of the present."[19] Even in a book that outlines an unconventional historiography of "perverse presentism," Judith Halberstam complains that Lillian Faderman "relentlessly imposes contemporary understandings of lesbian desire on a text in which lesbian identity cannot be imagined as such."[20]

From this point of view, the dangers of anachronistic projection might be personified in Poe's narrator, who in his yearning for the past abandons fact for "the suggestion of a vivid imagination" and allows his "labors" to take "a coloring from [his] dreams" (231, 228). But what else might **"Ligeia"** tell us about history and retrospection? What makes anachronism so "appalling" and "relentless" a threat? And how might queer theory interpret the desire and disgust underlying notions of the ahistorical? Such questions do not deny the value of queer literary history, nor do they presume that all accounts of the past can be equally credible. Rather, they speak to the critical discourse in which something called historicism is defended as the sole ethical possibility and something called the ahistorical is denounced by a shaming rhetoric whose vehemence seems at times to outstrip its object. Queer reading requires attention to historical specificity, but it does not demand a defense of an authentic past against the violation of backwardness.

It is worth noting the tendency, in that defensive effort, to treat *ahistorical* and *anachronistic* as synonymous and thus to obscure the difference between a neglect of history and a violation of chronology. When *ahistoricism* becomes another word for *anachronism,* the lack of engagement with the past becomes indistinguishable from the guilty overcathexis that clings too closely to it; an overinvestment in history mirrors an indifference to it; and, by implication, the improper treatment of history is tantamount to the outright rejection of it.[21] Rightly or wrongly, the anachronistic use of contemporary terms is now first among the intellectual offenses designated as ahistorical. Naming the scholarly fault of retrospective projection, it marks the guilty party as old-fashioned, decked out in the trappings of the scholarly past. Anachronism is anachronistic, out of step with the times, a throwback to the essentialism that, like those other styles of the 1970s and 1980s, we can't quite admit we ever liked. In the twenty-first century, we are told, the history that will be—the history of "an emerging futurity"—is not anachronistic but properly sequential.[22] The discontinuous, genealogical history held up as a shield against progressivism has become a mark of progress, relegating "transhistorical" thinking, like a primitive belief—or like literary close reading—to the pages of the history whose lessons it has failed to learn.[23]

Here the rhetoric against anachronism begins to sound like the theories that have historically labeled homosexuality regressive and premature, belated and derivative—in short, out of order. Annamarie Jagose outlines the ways in which "regulatory technologies of sequence," enforcing the rule of linear progression, accommodate the "drive to secure heterosexuality as chronology's triumph."[24] This temporal discipline governs the phobic myths that variously deem homosexuality a form of regression, a violation of narrative form, a case of arrested development, a threat to futurity, and a "bad copy" of heterosexual love. While straight culture at its own convenience finds homosexuality primitive or derivative, too early or too late, it is the old idea of queer retrogression that most clearly echoes in the complaint against scholarly anachronism. In the nineteenth century, sexologists such as Richard von Krafft-Ebing drew on post-Darwinian theories of primitivism and arrested development extant in scientific racism to represent homosexuality as an atavistic sign of evolutionary and individual regression.[25] In *Three Essays on the Theory of Sexuality* Freud too mapped a developmental trajectory in which inversion appears as a kind of atavism, ineluctably bound to the past. Taking homosexuality as evidence of "a predominance of archaic constitutions and primitive psychical mechanisms," he attributes inversion to childhood, the historical past, and early evolutionary stages.[26] That notion extends far beyond psychoanalysis: as Guy Hocquenghem explains, heteronormative society, its sexual time lines measured by the sovereign goal of reproduction, deems homosexuality "a regressive neurosis, totally drawn towards the past."[27] From Victorian sexology to right-wing radio, homosexuality has been made to figure the corruption of history, the retroactions of anachronism and arrested development, and all that violates the developmental chronology we might call *straight time.*

Despite its complicity in the diagnosis of homosexual backwardness, psychoanalysis—no stranger to charges of ahistoricism—also sought to acknowledge the central place of retrospective processes in both private and public anamnesis. Where psychic formations are concerned, Freud insists that time runs no straight course and that cause may lie far from effect. In processes of *Nachträglichkeit,* uncanny returns of the repressed, screen memories, and the persistence of memory that Freud compares to impressions on a "mystic writing-pad," the past recurs in the present, and the present invents the past.[28] The Oedipus complex, for example, must be approached through belated reconstructions of early childhood: "Whenever someone gives an account of a past event, even if he is a historian, we must take into account what he unintentionally puts back into the past from the present or from some intermediate time, thus falsifying his picture of it."[29] Going back in memory, we build a history that anticipates what is to come, a history that will in time forget its own retrospective construction and assume the naturalized status of linear temporality. Although retrospection here implies a "falsifying" projection "back into the past," for Freud memory is nothing but falsification—that is, nothing but representation. Because anachronism structures all psychic life, the ahistorical—like the propensity for homosexual attraction—is typical, not exceptional. Freud's understanding that the normal is pathological and the pathological is normal may be his greatest and most humane insight: everyone fails at development, everyone is subject to sexual perversity, everyone falls back in time. Under these circumstances, straight hegemony must represent anachronism as deviance in order to displace the burden of the ahistorical onto others—queers and people of color, each differently stigmatized as "primitive"—and to claim for itself the role of truth, not falsification, the path of progress, not regression.

Although no one now denies that historiography's backward glance colors the past with traces of the present, that reminder changes the case against scholarly anachronism. When compelled by an ethical imperative to read the past *on its own terms,* the practice of historical criticism is impossible *on its own terms.* Historical alterity is, after all, a recent invention; the conviction that past ages are noncontinuous with modernity is a hallmark of modernity.[30] To apply such theories retroactively to texts whose own view of time more nearly matches what is now called continuism can only in the most paradoxical sense constitute a "respectful" acknowledgment of the texts' historicity. In "Song of Myself" Walt Whitman declares that "these are really the thoughts of all men in all ages and lands" and imagines the poet's subjectivity extending across time and space: "Here or henceforward it is all the same to me, I accept Time absolutely."[31] Whitman's dream of universal connection among "all men in all ages" may indeed be a product of his age, but the theory that would protect Whitman's age from contamination by the present imposes, in that prophylactic effort, a contemporary notion of the past's fragile specificity.

The Whitman example suggests not that we should be more truly historical but that there is no truly historical historicism. As its canniest practitioners acknowledge, historicism is always to some degree ahistorical—or rather, anachronistic. A screen memory of the public sphere, historiography cannot cease to transfer ideas of the present to the past. And if historiography without anachronism is impossible, then resistance to anachronism is resistance not to the other of historicism but to an abject aspect of its own methodology, a projected image of its own atavism. The impossibility of a "true" historicism, however, does not undermine charges of anachronism but ensures their effective performance. This rhetoric has no outside; it interpellates everyone as a guilty subject of temporal self-governance and measures all against a standard that none can meet. Perhaps that is why Haggerty styles himself at once the cop and the criminal of historicism, why Sedgwick must "of course" insist on something that, even in 1990, everyone already knew. The charge of anachronism recurs endlessly because no one is ever innocent of it. In this respect the historical argument mirrors the fundamental logic of sexual discipline, in which no one's hetero credentials are ultimately above suspicion and in which, under the threat of an ineradicable perversity, to be heterosexual is always to be policed by one's vulnerability to being seen otherwise.[32] Faced with its own uncertainty, straight culture seeks a categorical distinction from the deviance whose backwardness might oppose reproductive futurity. Although in the queer historicist version of this logic it is not the future that must be rescued but the past, the same pathos of untenable boundaries informs each—whether the counterfactual, hegemonic fantasy of straight families' vulnerability to the predations of homosexuality or queer theorists' defense of a hard-won history.

It may seem that a properly historical queer theory is the one anodyne for doctrines of primitivism and regression that devalue gay and lesbian desires, or that undoing hurtful theories of queer anachronism means rejecting anachronism as such. Indeed, with greater awareness of its own not-knowing, the critique of anachronism might serve as a reminder that, to revise Sedgwick's axiom, we can't know in advance what the past will turn out to have been.[33] But when the insistence on historicism is, first and foremost, an effort to put the past first and foremost, it mimes the heteronormative demand for proper sexual sequencing. Construing retroaction as abomination, it upholds the illusion of a true, unidirectional history, whose effect of veracity and realism is in fact sustained by the very retroaction it condemns. Resistance to phobic definitions of homosexuality as anachronistic does not require the same temporal logic that has sustained such diagnoses; instead, resistance might mean a turn away from the discipline of straight time, away from the notions of historical propriety that, like notions of sexual propriety, function as regulatory fictions.

The Last Shall Be First

While objections to the ahistorical continue in queer criticism, they are increasingly joined by discussions of "queer time." Revisiting anachronism, scholars seek to open a space for temporal variation in queer methodologies by recognizing the fictional status of linear time and the fact of our retrospective investment in the past.[34] With a few exceptions—Terry Castle's claim that the lesbian "is not a recent invention" explicitly opposes the queer theory epitomized, in her view, by Foucault and Judith Butler—the majority take their cue from poststructuralist theory.[35] In "The History That Will Be," Jonathan Goldberg borrows from Derrida to trace the proleptic and analeptic effects inherent in historiography. Even empire-building metanarratives include temporal distortion: origins are retroactively constructed, and events unfold in the future perfect, anticipating their own significance (as Whitman says to a historian, "I project the history of the future"). Queer reading, accordingly, might "open the historical text to its multiples" by noting the double temporality that determines "the relation between the writing of history as prediction and as retrospection."[36]

With the goal of rereading queer history, other scholars have stressed the power of identification, desire, and affective attachment to forge connections across time. In their introduction to *Premodern Sexualities* Louise Fradenburg and Carla Freccero question the past's categorical alterity and the assumption that only an armature of alienation can prevent its contamination by present scholars. They do not defend anachronism—indeed, they caution against "transhistoricist nostalgia"—but by inviting queer critics to acknowledge identificatory and pleasurable links with the past, their essay functions as an apologia for any work whose historical cathexes caused it to be dismissed as "transhistorical."[37] No less than critical intimacy with the past, the violation of the chronological rule of law has changed from a scholarly blunder to a strategic possibility. In *Getting Medieval* Carolyn Dinshaw imagines tactile, erotic, affective connections across time as the bases of a new historiography, reclaiming transhistorical reading as a "queer historical impulse" distinct from simple identification with the past.[38] As Dinshaw explains in a later essay, "Since I am trying to explore unconventional temporal possibilities in history writing, I do not tremble at the very concept of anachronism but rather want to investigate its potential productivity." Toward that end, her study seeks "to demonstrate the simultaneous copresence of different chronologies in any moment."[39]

Anachronism becomes, in the work of many scholars, both an object and a method of inquiry, a means to investigate the knotting and redoubling of time that Goldberg observes in history. Though wary of endorsing the ahistorical, Halberstam offers in "perverse presentism" a compromise formation that would avoid backward projection but allow the latitude to "apply insights from the present to conundrums of the past."[40] In *How to Do the History of Homosexuality* David M. Halperin proposes alternative temporal models to supplement the notion of historical alterity, addressing such difficulties as the implicit narrative of progress toward modern Western sexuality and the denial of identifications between present and past.[41] And in *The Renaissance of Lesbianism* Valerie Traub offers a cogent account of "strategic anachronism" and "strategic historicism"—tactics that might, by admitting the reader's implication in connections across history, "keep open the question of the relationship of present identities to past cultural formations—assuming neither that we will find in the past a mirror image of ourselves nor that the past is so utterly alien that we will find nothing usable in its fragmentary traces."[42] If, as Freud would have it, a backward element haunts every historical effort, then anachronism represents not a foreign threat or a radical alternative to queer historicism but an inherent aspect of it. As queer theory has turned back to the question of temporality, it has discovered in itself the ageless anachronism whose other name is literariness.

Queer theories of retrospection speak to **"Ligeia"** because the text so pointedly anticipates them. Structured by hysteron proteron, the rhetorical effect of temporal inversion, the narrative advances backward. In "The Philosophy of Composition," an essay that opens by pointing out Dickens's "backwards" writing, Poe says that his own poem "The Raven" "may be said to have its beginning—at the end."[43] The same might be said of **"Ligeia."** Counting back from its sensational denouement, the narrative trades on inversions of chronology, retracing Ligeia's monstrous journey from death to life. Poe may allude to conventional emplotment in the narrator's fantasy of his wife's learning as a "delicious vista . . . down whose long, gorgeous, and all untrodden path, I might at length pass onward to the goal" (225), but the story's own course is nothing of the kind. Ligeia's death obstructs that straight and narrow road to knowledge, leading both narrator and text to the less productive pleasures of regression and return. In place of progress "onward," the narrator gets "a circle of analogies" that circle back in time: "My memory flew back" (224, 229). Against the teleological path of human life from birth to death, the text moves from death to birth. Ligeia "is no more" at the tale's beginning, but she lives at the end: her will bequeaths to the future the unending persistence of the past.

Fulfilling all too literally the biblical promise, **"Ligeia"** ensures that the last shall be first for its reader. We must enter into the text's anachronism, placing the end of the story in relation to the later moment of its beginning and understanding its beginning as an effect of its earlier end. The meaning of Ligeia's will stays veiled until it is materialized in her macabre return, and, like the meaning of that insatiable will, the lesbian effect appears *après coup.* Only later do we learn what must have happened in the "bed of death" and solve the puzzle of the moment when "she who had been dead once again stirred" (231, 233). Only in retrospect, when we learn that a second woman has been with Rowena all along, does that deathbed present a different sort of bedroom scene. Regarded in hindsight, the encounter between Ligeia and Rowena leaves a ghostly afterimage. This backward logic enacts in narrative terms Freud's notion of deferred action or *Nachträglichkeit,* the process through which a past moment belatedly assumes significance. In this fractured temporality, an event may "occur" long after its actual date, and the work of memory may re-create the past it pretends merely to recall. Patricia White suggests that the deferred action of *Nachträglichkeit* offers one model for the contemporary viewing of lesbian figures in the cinema of the past. What White neatly terms "retrospectatorship" mimics the psychic process whereby "an unconscious 'scene' becomes meaningful in retrospect, [when] it is opened onto and transformed by experience in the present."[44] Where lesbian representation is concerned, she argues, this act of historical retrospection is not an error but a strategic practice, resisting the allegation of presentism that would construe all "reading back" as illegitimate "reading into."[45]

Retrospectatorship could then describe our reading of **"Ligeia,"** a text that yields its most arresting visions after the fact. But the story itself offers another model for this backward glance. Its temporal illusions can be read as a form of anamorphosis, the optical effect in which a meaningless blot assumes its true form when observed from a certain oblique angle. As Stephen Greenblatt notes in his reading of Hans Holbein's *Ambassadors,* the painting's anamorphic image appears in proper perspective as an "unreadable blur," but becomes meaningful through the "radical abandonment of what we take to be 'normal' vision."[46] Poe's own example of anamorphosis concerns the outré furnishings of the home to which the narrator brings Rowena.

Here the tapestries, "changeable in aspect," produce a "phantasmagoric effect," appearing "Arabesque only when regarded from a single point of view": "To one entering the room, they bore the appearance of simple monstrosities; but upon a farther advance, this appearance gradually departed; and, step by step, as the visitor moved his station in the chamber, he saw himself surrounded by an endless succession of the ghastly forms which belong to the superstition of the Norman" (229). In a curious cultural shift, the patterns look Eastern or European according to the visitor's position. The tapestries' "appearance," "aspect," and "forms" respond to the observer's line of sight, just as their meaning depends on their relation to a spectator—or a reader. After all, what better purpose for this long, seemingly gratuitous excursus on interior decorating than a lesson in how to read **"Ligeia"**? (Scholars who identify **"Ligeia"** as orientalist are thus following Poe's directions: the text, like the draperies it depicts, reveals its "arabesque" patterns to a single vantage point.)[47] And like the "ghastly forms" of the bridal chamber, the text's lesbian effect appears from the right angle—that is, from the wrong angle. Its phantasmagoric forms invisible to the straight gaze, **"Ligeia"** reserves its clearest visions for those who look aslant.

While Poe's account of anamorphosis presumes a viewer who enters and advances, Jacques Lacan tells a story of withdrawal and retrogression. His own discussion of *The Ambassadors* includes instructions to the viewer who would discover the painting's secret: "Begin by walking out of the room in which no doubt it has long held your attention. It is then that, turning around as you leave—as the author of the *Anamorphoses* describes it—you apprehend in this form . . . What? A skull."[48] The anamorphic form appears through a lapse of attention; it is unintelligible when sought directly. Only in hindsight can one recognize the death's-head, emblem of the gaping hole in symbolic reality and the intolerable lack around which our own subjectivity is structured. This revelation turns on a turn: it is when "turning around as you leave" that you see the skull for what it is. Lacan explains that "the secret of the picture is given at the moment when, moving slightly away, little by little, to the left, then turning around, we see what the magical floating object signifies" (92). The physical turn that exposes the secret of *The Ambassadors* becomes in **"Ligeia"** another sort of return, which turns back the clock to confront a *historical* anamorphosis. Only when we regard the scene of Rowena's revival from the moment of Ligeia's reappearance can Ligeia's will appear morbid and the "unspeakable horrors of that night" (232) seem distinctly queer. Like the past events whose temporal displacement Freud's theory of *Nachträglichkeit* seeks to explain, the perverse effects of the text appear when observed from the wrong time, through the specific obliquity of belatedness.

Viewing the 1838 text from the twenty-first century, we find our own retrospectatorship already inscribed in Poe's tale. Traub's "strategic anachronism" and White's "retrospectatorship" can apply to **"Ligeia,"** but **"Ligeia,"** with its own instructions for reading aslant, applies no less to them. The text calls for a historical version of the "anamorphic reading" that, as Slavoj Žižek writes, reveals through a shift in perspective the trauma or scandal that symbolization otherwise occludes.[49] That critical practice of "looking awry" cannot, of course, provide the sole key to Poe's meaning.[50] In *The Ambassadors,* the memento mori may, as Lacan argues, explain the unsightly blot that "looks roughly like fried eggs," but in **"Ligeia"** queer sexuality resolves no mysteries.[51] The notion of anamorphic reading would untether meaning from intent, whether Holbein's or Poe's, and foreground instead the relational and the contingent. Although it cannot uncover the secret of the text, it would make visible a textual shading not available to the direct gaze, an anamorphic afterimage visible to those who turn back in narrative sequence and historical time. As Henry Abelove suggests, questioning the necessity for close focus, "Sometimes the best way to apprehend an object may be to look away from it."[52]

Memento Mori

As an impossible, anticipatory response to the queer theory of our time, Poe's invitation to look awry is also an encounter with alterity. Both sides of the critical debate have largely presumed that anachronism contravenes historical alterity, that ahistorical methods shore up contemporary identities by affording readers opportunities for sentimental investment and narcissistic reflection. Traub notes that scholarly anachronism is often impelled by the search for a "useable past" in which the present finds the reassurance of "personal affirmation, homo life support," and Halperin guardedly acknowledges the "queer project of identifying with and reclaiming non-heteronormative figures from the past."[53] All fantasy and identification across time may be anachronistic, but not all anachronism must serve these ends. Despite the identificatory lure of Ligeia's "immense" learning for the queer scholar, she cannot be a lesbian, and for more than historical reasons. We cannot say that she loves Rowena, only that she uses her. She does not want to *have* Rowena (even when, as they say, she wants her body); she wants to *be* Rowena (to be in her place, replacing her replacement). Rowena is not an end in herself but a means to an end—that is, in Poe's own endgame, a means for Ligeia to avoid ending. What she wills is her own will's power, and what she desires is desire itself.

However queer Ligeia's turn from heterosexuality, then, queerer still is her refusal of object choice as such; however appalling her return from death, more appalling is the will that drives it, traversing "the field of a pure and empty want."[54] Ligeia's meeting with Rowena produces the somatic signs of arousal without the armature of object choice usually mistaken for sexuality tout court; it shows something like lesbian sexuality stripped of anything like same-sex attraction. What is sex between women who don't really want each other? One answer: a straight fantasy. Indeed, Poe's bedroom scene, structured by the voyeuristic presence of its male observer, resembles mass-marketed lesbian tableaux. As a corporeal event without affect or interiority, it evokes the pornographic dream of a lesbianism manifested in acts, not identities, and conveniently dissociable from the "real," ultimately heterosexual status of the actors. In this sense, the scene would merely describe Poe's desire, saying nothing about the true love of the fictional Ligeia or the factual experience of American women in 1838. But there is another answer to the question—what is sex between women who don't really want each other?—and it is lesbianism. The idea, of course, is absurd, if not dangerously dehumanizing, countering as it does the liberal rhetoric of subjectivity, interiority, and personal fulfillment that anchors gay rights arguments in the public sphere. That is exactly why it should be pursued.

In fact, the spectral lesbian effect of **"Ligeia"** makes visible what such well-intentioned arguments tend to repress or romanticize. Poe's fantasy reflects reality despite itself. The perversity of Ligeia's will, which spurns the promise of satisfaction in favor of "the reproduction of desire as such," is the perversity of all desire.[55] That Ligeia does not really want Rowena but something else in no way negates the sexual valence of the scene, for as Lacan reminds us, sexual desire is always the desire for something else.[56] The object of desire, whatever it may be, is never more than contingent. When an oblique gaze reveals in **"Ligeia"** a ghostly figure, the counterpart of Holbein's memento mori, what returns there is the blind, meaningless insistence of desire beyond any object. Oriented only toward its own continuance, Ligeia's will enacts the sheer force of desire's quest to sustain itself, a quest in which the object, hetero or homo, must be secondary and substitutive. The object is an effect and not a cause of desire, never adequate to satisfy the will that persists, like the leering skull of *The Ambassadors,* beneath and beyond what passes as desire's accomplishment.

Although the discovery of Holbein's secret in *The Ambassadors* is not without its pleasures—ask any student who has failed to see it when the picture made the rounds—that secret entails a traumatic return of the repressed. As Lacan suggests, the skull that stares back at us from the picture is more than a reminder of mortality; it expresses the radical incompleteness of human subjectivity, whether named as castration or as the displacements of the signifying chain. The image we cannot see directly is an image of what we *must* not see, what we eternally *try* not to see. In **"Ligeia"** as well, the anamorphic blot conceals not a love letter but a death's-head, not the life-affirming confirmation of any lesbian reality but the presence of a lack we strive endlessly to deny. Poe's camp-gothic aesthetic effectively disguises the true horror of the story—what could be less frightening than how obviously it intends to frighten, how thickly its lurid colors are applied? Yet **"Ligeia"** is a horror story, not because it shows love between women but because it doesn't. The text's real monstrosity is not its reanimation of the dead, or even its hint of necrolesbianism, but the objectless, grimly instinctual dimension of desire to whose existence both testify.

When Poe's narrator struggles to understand "the principle of her longing," the essence of Ligeia's desire "but for life," by deciphering the greater principle of which that desire is an emblem or an effect, he fails because the answer is *nothing.* Ligeia's will refers to nothing, signifies nothing, seeks nothing except its own persistence. Accepting no conclusion and knowing no satisfaction, it describes the aspect of desire that is most drivelike and inhuman. Lee Edelman contends that heteronormative society compels queers to embody the future-negating energies of the death drive: "As the name for a force of mechanistic compulsion whose formal excess supersedes any end toward which it might seem to be aimed, the death drive refuses identity or the absolute privilege of any goal. Such a goal, such an end, could never be 'it'; achieved, it could never satisfy."[57] Ligeia's will "for life" cannot constitute a death drive in any literal sense—but then, the death drive is never literal. This relentless, mechanical lust, this desire as unconcerned with the narrator as Rowena, this will whose repetitive rhythms exceed anything we might imagine as its object—*this* is the death's-head in **"Ligeia."** This is the skull that grins obscenely from the anamorphic spot, as a reminder of what we cannot see because we daily take pains not to see it: the endless, ultimately objectless energy of desire. There is nothing distinctly queer about this, but everything queer about its legibility in a society that must deny the impossibility of desire's satisfaction in order to defend the aims of heteronormative reproduction. Only in the form of the monster, the grotesque, and the pervert can straight society recognize the perfectly ordinary but intolerable logic of sexuality as such.

Queer communities, however, are no less reluctant to confront this image. Long after essentialist notions of sexual identity have been dismantled, the authenticity of object choice and the possibility of sexual satisfaction remain central to queer culture. Fantasies of a simple, sentimentalized homosexuality—whether in the coming-out story's happy ending or in the politically expedient discourse of gay familialism—must refuse to recognize the anamorphic blot whose message is not death itself but the deathly insatiability of desire. This, then, is the alterity of the present, the difference that haunts the now of queer theory. In *Specters of Marx* Derrida notes that while ghostly figures indicate an uncanny return, this temporal violation does not befall a historically innocent moment. The ghost is no anomaly, but a strange reminder of what Derrida calls the "non-contemporaneity of present time with itself (this radical untimeliness or this anachrony on the basis of which we are trying here to *think the ghost*)."[58] If, as some historians would have it, the past is always other to the present, the present is no less other to itself.

Rather than impose a narrative of continuous time or render the past identical to the present, then, an anamorphic reading of **"Ligeia"** can bring into focus the anachrony of the present. The case against scholarly anachronism assumes that historical criticism maintains a rigorous awareness of alterity, while ahistorical reading offers identification's guilty pleasures and a comforting, if phantasmatic, sense of the familiar. In **"Ligeia"** the opposite is true. Reading anachronistically, going temporally awry, we find a certain lesbian effect, but that effect unsettles what today's queer discourse takes for granted about sexuality. In place of any reassuring reflection of modern sexual identity or sustaining identification, Poe's story shows a ghostly figure, its own memento mori, in which returns the alienating force of sexuality as such. The anachronism named as ahistorical is not bound, in other words, to an essentially conservative work of identification and self-affirmation; it need not project cherished values backward or repeat what we already know. Instead, the critical engagement with historical anamorphosis can open our own queer moment to alterity, serving the "denaturalization of the present" promised by Halberstam's theory of perverse presentism.[59]

When, like Lacan standing before *The Ambassadors,* we turn back to look once more at **"Ligeia,"** whose every contour we think we know, the text produces, in place of Holbein's death's-head, an anamorphic lesbian image. Both in that specter of queer sexuality and in the ways that it eludes our grasp, the text confronts us with alterity—the alterity not only of history but also of our own desire. Reading **"Ligeia"** from the wrong angle, we may catch a backward glimpse of the discourses that, in Poe's time and our own, braid together narrative, developmental, and historical time lines: the retrospectatorship of recent queer theory, the normative construction of homosexuality as regressive in nineteenth-century rhetoric, and the scholarly effort to defend literary history against perverse anachronism. At the same time, the phantasmagoric effects of **"Ligeia"** hold out the possibility of readings that, informed by psychoanalysis and by "queer historical impulses," might recognize, aslant and at a distance, the queer figures that still burn in our field of vision.

Notes

For their helpful comments on versions of this essay, I thank Annamarie Jagose, Ann Cvetkovich, and the editorial readers at *GLQ*; the junior faculty writing group at Bowling Green State University's Institute for the Study of Culture and Society; the members of the University of Vermont English department; and especially Matthew Bell, Lee Edelman, Jane Gallop, Erin Labbie, Eithne Luibhéid, and Jonathan Mulrooney.

1. Poe's remark on "Ligeia" appears in Arthur Hobson Quinn, *Edgar Allan Poe: A Critical Biography* (New York: Appleton-Century, 1941), 496.

2. Edgar Allan Poe, *The Complete Poems and Stories,* 2 vols. (New York: Knopf, 1951), 1:231-33. All quotations from "Ligeia" are cited by page number in this edition.

3. Other readings that discuss lesbianism in "Ligeia" are Ralph J. Poole, "Body/Rituals: The (Homo)erotics of Death in Elizabeth Stuart Phelps, Rose Terry Cooke, and Edgar Allan Poe," in *Soft Canons: American Women Writers and Masculine Tradition,* ed. Karen L. Kilcup (Iowa City: University of Iowa Press, 1999), 239-61; and Camille Paglia, *Sexual Personae: Art and Decadence from Nefertiti to Emily Dickinson* (New Haven: Yale University Press, 1990), 338-39.

4. See Andrea Weiss, *Vampires and Violets: Lesbians in Film* (New York: Penguin, 1993), 85; and Patricia White, *Uninvited: Classical Hollywood Cinema and Lesbian Representability* (Bloomington: Indiana University Press, 1999), 63.

5. Michel Foucault, *The History of Sexuality,* trans. Robert Hurley, vol. 1 (New York: Vintage, 1990), 43. On Balzac and Gautier see Lillian Faderman,

Surpassing the Love of Men: Romantic Friendship and Love between Women from the Renaissance to the Present (New York: Morrow, 1981), 264-68.

6. Carroll Smith-Rosenberg, *Disorderly Conduct: Visions of Gender in Victorian America* (New York: Knopf, 1985), 272.

7. Estelle B. Freedman, "The Historical Construction of Homosexuality in the US," *Socialist Review* 25 (1995): 31.

8. *The Riverside Shakespeare,* ed. G. Blakemore Evans (Boston: Houghton Mifflin, 1974), 1774. On Shakespeare's notion of *will* see Joel Fineman, *Shakespeare's Perjured Eye: The Invention of Poetic Subjectivity in the Sonnets* (Berkeley: University of California Press, 1986), 26-28, 292-93.

9. Quoted in I. M. Walker, ed., *Edgar Allan Poe: The Critical Heritage* (New York: Routledge and Kegan Paul, 1986), 112.

10. Peter Brooks, *Reading for the Plot: Design and Intention in Narrative* (New York: Knopf, 1984), 98-100.

11. Judith Roof, *Come as You Are: Sexuality and Narrative* (New York: Columbia University Press, 1996), 36.

12. Paul Morrison, *The Explanation for Everything: Essays on Sexual Subjectivity* (New York: New York University Press, 2001), 62.

13. Judith Halberstam contests the conflation of gender identity and expression with sexual object choice in *Female Masculinity* (Durham: Duke University Press, 1998), 45-73.

14. Laura Doan and Sarah Waters, "Making Up Lost Time: Contemporary Lesbian Writing and the Invention of History," in *Territories of Desire in Queer Culture: Refiguring Contemporary Boundaries,* ed. David Alderson and Linda Anderson (Manchester: Manchester University Press, 2000), 13. On issues in queer history and historiography see also Susan McCabe, "To Be and To Have: The Rise of Queer Historicism," *GLQ* 11 (2005): 119-34; Annamarie Jagose, *Inconsequence: Lesbian Representation and the Logic of Sexual Sequences* (Ithaca: Cornell University Press, 2002), 8-24; Lisa Duggan, "The Discipline Problem: Queer Theory Meets Lesbian and Gay History," *GLQ* 2 (1995): 179-91; and Jennifer Terry, "Theorizing Deviant Historiography," *differences* 3, no. 2 (1991): 55-74.

15. See Martin Bauml Duberman, Martha Vicinus, and George Chauncey Jr., eds., *Hidden from History: Reclaiming the Gay and Lesbian Past* (New York: New American Library, 1989); and Foucault, *History of Sexuality,* 42-44.

16. I have no quarrel with the notion of historical alterity; indeed, I will suggest that anachronism is most valuable precisely when it stages an uncomfortable confrontation with alterity. However, the common conflation of historicism, social constructionism, and the notion of alterity, like the conflation of the ahistorical and the anachronistic, produces a Manichaean scheme in which any unorthodox reading of temporality can be accused of stupidly positing a past identical to the present.

17. Eve Kosofsky Sedgwick, *Epistemology of the Closet* (Berkeley: University of California Press, 1990), 51. As Sedgwick notes in a later essay, historicism often seems to appreciate the contingency of everything except itself. I borrow a phrase from her epigrammatic reading of Fredric Jameson's injunction: "*Always* historicize? What could have less to do with historicizing than the commanding, atemporal adverb 'always'?" ("Paranoid Reading and Reparative Reading; or, You're So Paranoid, You Probably Think This Introduction Is about You," in *Novel Gazing: Queer Readings in Fiction,* ed. Eve Kosofsky Sedgwick [Durham: Duke University Press, 1997], 5).

18. Bonnie Zimmerman, "Placing Lesbians," in *The New Lesbian Studies: Into the Twenty-first Century,* ed. Bonnie Zimmerman and Toni A. H. McNaron (New York: Feminist Press at the City University of New York, 1996), 274. Sue-Ellen Case similarly charges queer theory with the promotion of "revisionist history" and the "mis-remembering of lesbian feminism" ("Toward a Butch-Feminist Retro-Future," in *Cross-Purposes: Lesbians, Feminists, and the Limits of Alliance,* ed. Dana Heller [Bloomington: Indiana University Press, 1997], 210-11).

19. George Haggerty, "The Gay Canon," *American Literary History* 12 (2000): 287-88, 292.

20. Halberstam, *Female Masculinity,* 50, 62.

21. The conflation can have troubling effects, as Lisa L. Moore suggests: "This caution against anachronism has most often taken the form of an ahistorical prohibition against reading sex between women in history" (*Dangerous Intimacies: Toward a Sapphic History of the British Novel* [Durham: Duke University Press, 1997], 11).

22. Valerie Traub, "The Rewards of Lesbian History," *Feminist Studies* 25 (1999): 392. This view is not universal; those lesbian scholars, like Zimmerman, who attribute ahistoricism to queer theory tend to regard both as new and unwelcome developments that threaten established lesbian history.

23. Louise Fradenburg and Carla Freccero, "Introduction: Caxton, Foucault, and the Pleasures of His-

tory," in *Premodern Sexualities,* ed. Louise Fradenburg and Carla Freccero (New York: Routledge, 1996), xv.

24. Jagose, *Inconsequence,* 102, 112. Jagose's acceptance of the argument against the ahistorical—she questions any reading that "finds the modern category of 'lesbian' anachronistically written across preceding sexual systems of female eroticism" (10)—is the one troubling thread in a masterful discussion of sequence and temporality in heteronormative discourses. While she frames the critique of historical anachronism as a counter to homophobic discourses of lesbian atemporality, I see that critique of anachronism as an extension and a reflection of the temporal model on which homophobic rhetoric is founded.
25. Jennifer Terry, *An American Obsession: Science, Medicine, and Homosexuality in Modern Society* (Chicago: University of Chicago Press, 1999), 30-39.
26. Sigmund Freud, *Three Essays on the Theory of Sexuality* (1905), in *The Standard Edition of the Complete Psychological Works,* ed. and trans. James Strachey, 24 vols. (London: Hogarth, 1953-74), 7:146.
27. Guy Hocquenghem, *Homosexual Desire,* trans. Daniella Dangoor (Durham: Duke University Press, 1993), 108.
28. Sigmund Freud, "A Note upon the Mystic Writing-Pad," in *Standard Edition,* 19: 227-32.
29. Sigmund Freud, *Introductory Lectures on Psychoanalysis* (1916), in *Standard Edition,* 16:336.
30. In Terry Eagleton's formulation, "The belief that our beliefs are bound up with a historical form of life is itself a belief bound up with a historical form of life" ("The Estate Agent," *London Review of Books,* March 2, 2000, 10; see also Fradenburg and Freccero, "Introduction," xv).
31. Walt Whitman, *Leaves of Grass,* ed. Harold W. Blodgett and Sculley Bradley (New York: New York University Press, 1965), 45, 51. Freedman contrasts a "respectful" deference to the past with the error of "ahistorical" approaches ("Historical Construction of Homosexuality," 31).
32. See Eve Kosofsky Sedgwick, *Between Men: English Literature and Male Homosocial Desire* (New York: Columbia University Press, 1985), 88-89; and Morrison, *Explanation for Everything,* 5.
33. Sedgwick, *Epistemology of the Closet,* 27.
34. Judith Halberstam traces a "queer sense of temporality" through an archive of lived experiences, subcultural communities, and representational practices in her book *In a Queer Time and Place: Transgender Bodies, Subcultural Lives* (New York: New York University Press, 2005), 187. On this experiential sense of queer time see also Stephen M. Barber and David L. Clark, "Queer Moments: The Performative Temporalities of Eve Sedgwick," in *Regarding Sedgwick: Essays on Queer Culture and Critical Theory,* ed. Stephen M. Barber and David L. Clark (New York: Routledge, 2002), 1-53. Other significant work seeks to revalue formerly disavowed identifications with the past: see Elizabeth Freeman, "Packing History, Count(er)ing Generations," *New Literary History* 31 (2000): 727-44; and Heather K. Love, "'Spoiled Identity': Stephen Gordon's Loneliness and the Difficulties of Queer History," *GLQ* 7 (2001): 487-519. Projects that address queer history in terms less directly concerned with anachronism include Scott Bravmann, *Queer Fictions of the Past: History, Culture, and Difference* (New York: Cambridge University Press, 1997); and Christopher Nealon, *Foundlings: Lesbian and Gay Historical Emotion before Stonewall* (Durham: Duke University Press, 2001).
35. Terry Castle, *The Apparitional Lesbian: Female Homosexuality and Modern Culture* (New York: Columbia University Press, 1993), 8.
36. Whitman, *Leaves of Grass,* 4; Jonathan Goldberg, "The History That Will Be," *GLQ* 1 (1995): 385-403; see also Goldberg, introduction to *Queering the Renaissance* (Durham: Duke University Press, 1994), 1-14.
37. Fradenburg and Freccero, "Introduction," xvii-xix.
38. Carolyn Dinshaw, *Getting Medieval: Sexualities and Communities, Pre- and Postmodern* (Durham: Duke University Press, 1999), 1, 34.
39. Carolyn Dinshaw, "Got Medieval?" *Journal of the History of Sexuality* 10 (2001): 209.
40. Halberstam, *Female Masculinity,* 52-53.
41. David M. Halperin, *How to Do the History of Homosexuality* (Chicago: University of Chicago Press, 2002), 13-18.
42. Valerie Traub, *The Renaissance of Lesbianism in Early Modern England* (New York: Cambridge University Press, 2002), 16, 28, 32. A willingness to reevaluate presentism and anachronism also informs Madhavi Menon, "Queer Time" (paper presented at the annual meeting of the Modern Language Association, Philadelphia, December 2004); and Gregory Tomso, "Reading Queerly: A Presen-

tist's Confession," *Romanticism and Contemporary Culture,* February 2002, www.rc.umd.edu/praxis/contemporary/tomso/tomso.html.

43. Poe, *Complete Poems and Stories,* 2:983. On inverted chronology in and around "Ligeia" see also Elisabeth Bronfen, *Over Her Dead Body: Death, Femininity, and the Aesthetic* (New York: Routledge, 1992), 336.

44. Patricia White, "Hollywood Lesbians," interview by Annamarie Jagose, *Genders* 32 (2000), www.genders.org/g32/g32_jagose.html. White develops her theory of retrospectatorship in *Uninvited,* 196-205. *Nachträglichkeit* also figures in Brett Farmer's theory of gay spectatorship and fantasy (*Spectacular Passions: Cinema, Fantasy, Gay Male Spectatorships* [Durham: Duke University Press, 2000], 55-56, 71-73).

45. White, *Uninvited,* 15.

46. Stephen Greenblatt, *Renaissance Self-Fashioning: From More to Shakespeare* (Chicago: University of Chicago Press, 1980), 18-19.

47. See, e.g., Malini Johar Schueller, "Harems, Orientalist Subversions, and the Crisis of Nationalism: The Case of Edgar Allan Poe and 'Ligeia,'" *Criticism* 37 (1995): 601-23.

48. Jacques Lacan, *The Four Fundamental Concepts of Psycho-analysis,* ed. Jacques-Alain Miller, trans. Alan Sheridan (New York: Norton, 1981), 88.

49. Slavoj Žižek, *The Plague of Fantasies* (New York: Verso, 1997), 75.

50. Slavoj Žižek, *Looking Awry: An Introduction to Jacques Lacan through Popular Culture* (Cambridge, MA: MIT Press, 1992), 11.

51. When you look at *The Ambassadors,* Lacan explains, "you will see an enigmatic form stretched out on the ground. It looks roughly like fried eggs. If you place yourself at a certain angle from which the painting itself disappears in all its relief by reason of the converging lines of its perspective, you will see a death's head appear, the sign of the classic theme of *vanitas*" (*The Seminar of Jacques Lacan: Book VII,* ed. Jacques-Alain Miller, trans. Dennis Porter [New York: Norton, 1992], 135).

52. Henry Abelove, *Deep Gossip* (Minneapolis: University of Minnesota Press, 2003), 88.

53. Traub, *Renaissance of Lesbianism,* 27: Halperin, *How to Do the History of Homosexuality,* 16.

54. Jacques Lacan, *Feminine Sexuality: Jacques Lacan and the Ecole Freudienne,* ed. Juliet Mitchell and Jacqueline Rose, trans. Jacqueline Rose (New York: Norton, 1982), 131.

55. Žižek, *Looking Awry,* 7.

56. Jacques Lacan, *Ecrits: A Selection,* trans. Alan Sheridan (New York: Norton, 1977), 167.

57. Lee Edelman, *No Future: Queer Theory and the Death Drive* (Durham: Duke University Press, 2004), 22.

58. Jacques Derrida, *Specters of Marx: The State of the Debt, the Work of Mourning, and the New International,* trans. Peggy Kamuf (New York: Routledge, 1994), 25. For Castle, ghosts figure the homophobic repression of real, embodied lesbian life (*Apparitional Lesbian,* 2-8). But as Mandy Merck suggests in an astute response to Castle, the defense of embodiment against such specters may mean "the veritable petrification of the subject and its desires" ("The Queer Spirit of the Age," in *Literature and the Contemporary: Fictions and Theories of the Present,* ed. Roger Luckhurst and Peter Marks [Harlow: Longman, 1999], 209).

59. Halberstam, *Female Masculinity,* 53.

Yonjae Jung (essay date winter 2007)

SOURCE: Jung, Yonjae. "Poe's 'William Wilson.'" *Explicator* 65, no. 2 (winter 2007): 82-5.

[In the following essay, Jung applies Jacques Lacan's theory of "the Father's Law" to the protagonist's psychological distress in "William Wilson."]

The theme of doubleness is one of the recurrent subjects in Poe's oeuvre and is given its most formal expression in **"William Wilson."** In the story, the first-person narrator, William Wilson, meets a strange boy who is his manifest double at Dr. Bransby's academy. They have the same name, the same birthday, the same height, the same features, similar voices, and equal strengths. They always wear the same clothes, and they also share the same dates of admission to and removal from the school. Wherever William Wilson goes, he is pursued by the second Wilson. At Dr. Bransby's school, Eton, Oxford, throughout Europe, and finally in Rome, the second Wilson appears at every critical moment to thwart and expose the first Wilson's increasingly evil deeds. In an attempt to analyze and make sense of his life, the narrator reconstructs his story about the annoying presence of a mysterious double. The first Wilson tells the singular story with a great regret: in the opening paragraphs, Wilson, reprimanding himself, speaks of his "years of unspeakable misery" and of an "unpardonable crime" (426); he even describes himself as an "outcast of all outcasts most abandoned" (426). Unfortunately, though, Wilson does not seem to understand the specific cause of his extraordinary past, nor exactly what his real crime is: "I would fain have them believe that I have been, in some measure, the slave of circumstances beyond human control [. . .]. Have I not indeed been living in a dream? And am I not now dying a victim to the horror and the mystery of the wildest of all sublunary visions?" (427). In this article, by using the Lacanian concept of foreclosure, I intend to examine the true nature and significance of Wilson's enigmatic "unpardonable crime."

Much of the earlier criticism tends to see the first Wilson as the innocent victim of the destructive superego. In defense of the narrator, Eric Carlson argues that Wilson has not committed any atrocious crime at all: he is "a helpless victim of some strange 'fatality' that has left him a miserable and disgraced outcast," rather than "the real perpetrator of an unpardonable crime" (36). In a similar vein, Tracy Ware claims that Wilson's crimes are "youthful caprices," "profligacy of Eton," and "a series of intrigues at various points in continental Europe and Egypt" (45). At first glance, indeed, the narrator's crimes, for the most part, are mildly mischievous acts: dishonest gambling, collegiate dissipation, and attempted sexual liaison. But, what has not been considered is Wilson's usurpation of the lawful authority, or the radical abolition of what Lacan called "the Father's Law." In Lacan's formulation, for the child to become a true subject, he must take over the symbolic function of the father through the resolution of the Oedipus complex. Without the strong paternal image or *imago,* the subject will have difficulty in internalizing the Law of the Father that allows him to enter the Symbolic order. If the figure of the father is felt to be absent or fails to hold the symbolic position assigned to him, it results in psychological chaos and catastrophe. Lacan designates this mechanism "foreclosure." In his 1956 paper "On the Rejection of a Primordial Signifier," Lacan poses the rhetorical question, "What is at issue when I speak of *Verwerfung* (foreclosure)? At issue is the rejection of a primordial signifier into the outer shadows, a signifier that will henceforth be missing at this level. Here you have the fundamental mechanism that I posit as being at the basis of paranoia" (150). "Foreclosure" refers to the process of complete exclusion of a certain key signifier, and this mechanism is "determined by the failure of the fundamental symbolic operation at the structural moment of the installation of the Name-of-the-Father and hence by the failure to enter into the symbolic" (Hecq 75). In Poe's **"William Wilson,"** the narrator's foreclosure of the Name-of-the-Father is suggested in the description of his childhood. Looking back on his childhood, Wilson boasts that he was rebellious and that his weak parents could not restrain his obstinate willfulness:

> I grew self-willed, addicted to the wildest caprices, and a prey to the most ungovernable passions. Weak-minded, and beset with constitutional infirmities akin to my own, my parents could do but little to check the evil propensities which distinguished me. Some feeble and ill-directed efforts resulted in complete failure on their part, and, of course, in total triumph on mine. Thenceforward my voice was a household law; and at an age when few children have abandoned their leading-strings, I was left to the guidance of my own will.
>
> (427)

Wilson usurped the place of the father, and by doing so he lost the source of his own name and his family identity. Moreover, Wilson's repugnance toward his real name, which is closely connected with his father's name, is further proof that he has failed to introject the Name-of-the-Father. In the story, Wilson repeatedly emphasizes his strong dislike for his own name: "I had always felt aversion to my uncourtly patronymic, and its very common, if not plebeian, praenomen [. . .]; and When [. . .] a second Wilson came also to the academy, I felt angry with him for bearing the name, and doubly disgusted with the name because a stranger bore it, who would be the cause of its twofold repetition" (434). He expresses shame for having such a patronymic and calls the "words" of his real name "venom in my ears" (434). The new, fictional name of the narrator (which is often analyzed as "Will-I-am Will's son") also unmistakably signifies his transgressive desire to deny his father's lawful authority and substitute himself as originator or namegiver in place of his father. In Freud's formulation, the successful Oedipal resolution, which is believed to produce the superego, makes the subject susceptible to all "the influences of those who have stepped into the place of parents—educators, teachers, people chosen as ideal models" ("The Dissection" 64). In grammar school, Wilson encounters a powerful paternal figure, the Reverend Dr. Bransby, who is both the principal of the school and pastor of the local church. As a result of the total foreclosure, however, Wilson never comes to understand Dr. Bransby's significant function as the father-surrogate, the figure of the Symbolic Law. For Wilson, Dr. Bransby appears to be nothing but an incomprehensible "gigantic paradox" (429).

The previous reading of **"William Wilson,"** which identified the second Wilson with the Freudian superego, is based on the assumption that the protagonist's internalization of the castrating father's prohibiting law is already accomplished. In contrast to the dominant critical view, Poe's confessional narrative reveals that the narrator, even in the earliest stage of his childhood, established himself as an authority figure, "a household law," revolting against the father's law. Because his "weak-minded" parents failed to govern his "evil propensities," Wilson became "the master of [. . . his] own actions" (427). Wilson seeks to exercise "a supreme and unqualified despotism," defying "the laws" and eluding "the vigilance of the institution" (431, 438). Wilson becomes trapped forever in the detrimental imaginary structure when he forecloses what Lacan calls "the paternal metaphor," or the Name-of-the-Father, embodied in the figure of the father. As I have attempted to show, Lacan's theory of foreclosure can account for Wilson's mysterious "unpardonable crime," which lies at the heart of his dreadful misery.

Works Cited

Carlson, Eric W. "'William Wilson': The Double as Primal Self." *Topic* 16 (1976): 35-40.

Freud, Sigmund. "The Dissection of the Psychical Personality." *The Standard Edition of the Complete Psychological Works of Sigmund Freud.* Ed. and trans. James Strachey et al. Vol. 22. London: Hogarth, 1964. 57-80.

Hecq, Dominique. "Foreclosure." *A Compendium of Lacanian Terms.* Ed. Huguette Glowinski, Zita Marks, and Sara Murphy. London: Free Association Books, 2001. 71-75.

Lacan, Jacques. "On the Rejection of a Primordial Signifier." *The Seminar of Jacques Lacan, Book III: The Psychoses 1955-1956.* Ed. Jacques-Alain Miller. Trans. Russell Grigg. New York: Norton, 1993. 143-57.

Poe, Edgar Allan. *Collected Works of Edgar Allan Poe.* Ed. Thomas Ollive Mabbot. Cambridge: Belknap, 1978.

Ware, Tracy. "The Two Stories of 'William Wilson.'" *Studies in Short Fiction* 26 (1989): 43-48.

FURTHER READING

Criticism

Behling, Laura L. "Replacing the Patient: The Fiction of Prosthetics in Medical Practice." *Journal of Medical Humanities* 26, no. 1 (spring 2005): 53-66.

Contrasts the prosthetic wholeness in "The Man That Was Used Up" with social fragmentation caused by modern technology.

Beuka, Robert A. "The Jacksonian Man of Parts: Dismemberment, Manhood, and Race in 'The Man That Was Used Up.'" *Edgar Allan Poe Review* 3, no. 1 (spring 2002): 27-44.

Views "The Man That Was Used Up" as a satire of Andrew Jackson's political ethos.

Cody, David. "'What a tricke wee'le serve him': A Possible Source for Poe's 'The Cask of Amontillado.'" *ANQ* 17, no. 1 (winter 2004): 36-9.

Underlines the likely influence of Sir Nicholas L'Estrange's anecdote "Merry Jests and Passages" on "The Cask of Amontillado."

Coviello, Peter. "Poe in Love: Pedophilia, Morbidity, and the Logic of Slavery." *ELH* 70, no. 3 (fall 2003): 875-901.

Studies the problematic symbol of the child in Poe's work.

Duquette, Elizabeth. "Accounting for Value in 'The Business Man.'" *Studies in American Fiction* 35, no. 1 (spring 2007): 3-20.

Investigates the attribution of numerical value to abstract concepts in "The Business Man," suggesting that the story is a parody of the philosophy of Benjamin Franklin.

Hayes, Kevin J. "Visual Culture and the Word in Edgar Allan Poe's 'The Man of the Crowd.'" *Nineteenth-Century Literature* 56, no. 4 (March 2002): 445-65.

Explores the act of "reading" a person based upon physical appearances in "The Man of the Crowd" and comments on the story's allusion to the sixteenth-century prayer book *Hortulus Animae.*

Renza, Louis A. "Never More in Poe's Tell-Tale American Tale." *Edgar Allan Poe Review* 4, no. 2 (fall 2003): 22-40.

Studies the use of voyeurism, ocular imagery, narrative incommunicability, and societal allegory in "The Tell-Tale Heart."

Weinstock, Jeffrey Andrew. "The Crowd within: Poe's Impossible Alone." *Edgar Allan Poe Review* 7, no. 2 (fall 2006): 50-64.

Explores solitude in "The Man of the Crowd," "Alone," and "To M—."

Zimmerman, Brett. "Frantic Forensic Oratory: Poe's 'The Tell-Tale Heart.'" *Style* 35, no. 1 (spring 2001): 34-49.

Traces the oratorical and rhetorical qualities of "The Tell-Tale Heart," contending that the narrator's well-structured appeal to the reader ultimately fails because of his lack of moral grounding and his demonstration of his mental illness.

Additional coverage of Poe's life and career is contained in the following sources published by Gale: *American Writers*; *American Writers: The Classics,* Vol. 1; *American Writers Retrospective Supplement,* Vol. 2; *Authors and Artists for Young Adults,* Vol. 14; *Beacham's Encyclopedia of Popular Fiction: Biography & Resources,* Vol. 3; *Beacham's Guide to Literature for Young Adults,* Vols. 5, 11; *Concise Dictionary of American Literary Biography,* 1640-1865; *Dictionary of Literary Biography,* Vols. 3, 59, 73, 74, 248, 254; *DISCovering Authors*; *DISCovering Authors: British Edition*; *DISCovering Authors: Canadian Edition*; *DISCovering Authors Modules: Most-Studied Authors* and *Poets*; *DISCovering Authors 3.0*; *Exploring Poetry*; *Exploring Short Stories*; *Gothic Literature: A Gale Critical Companion,* Ed. 3; *Literary Movements for Students,* Vol. 1; *Literature and Its Times,* Vol. 2; *Literature and Its Times Supplement,* Ed. 1:1; *Literature Resource Center*; *Mystery and Suspense Writers*; *Nineteenth-Century Literature Criticism,* Vols. 1, 16, 55, 78, 94, 97, 117; *Poetry Criticism,* Vols. 1, 54; *Poetry for Students,* Vols. 1, 3, 9; *Poets: American and British*; *Reference Guide to American Literature,* Ed. 4; *Reference Guide to Short Fiction,* Ed. 2; *St. James Guide to Crime & Mystery Writers,* Vol. 4; *St. James Guide to Horror, Ghost & Gothic Writers*; *St. James Guide to Science Fiction Writers,* Ed. 4; *Science Fiction, Fantasy, and Horror Writers*; *Science Fiction Writers,* Eds. 1, 2; *Short Stories for Students,* Vols. 2, 4, 7, 8, 16; *Short Story Criticism,* Vols. 1, 22, 34, 35, 54, 88; *Something about the Author,* Vol. 23; *Supernatural Fiction Writers*; *Twayne's United States Authors*; *World Literature Criticism,* Vol. 4; *World Poets*; and *Writers for Young Adults.*

Eudora Welty
1909-2001

(Full name Eudora Alice Welty; also wrote under the pseudonym Michael Ravenna) American short story writer, novelist, essayist, critic, and autobiographer.

The following entry provides an overview of Welty's short fiction. For additional information on her short fiction career, see *SSC,* Volumes 1 and 51; for discussion of the short story "A Worn Path" (1940), see *SSC,* Volume 27.

INTRODUCTION

Welty is hailed as a chronicler of the American South whose short stories reflect the language, history, and customs of this regional culture, yet simultaneously address universal themes. Frequently compared to William Faulkner, Flannery O'Connor, and Katherine Anne Porter for her distinctively Southern aesthetic, Welty has also been linked with such modernist authors as James Joyce and Virginia Woolf for her ability to render a complex fictional world through a network of mythological symbols and allusions. In contrast to many works of modern American fiction which emphasize alienation and the failure of love, Welty's stories show how tolerance and generosity allow people to accept each other's shortcomings and adapt to change, no matter how troublesome or painful. Welty is acknowledged for her uniquely comic vision, one that affirms the sustaining power of community and family life as well as the need for solitude.

BIOGRAPHICAL INFORMATION

Welty was born in Jackson, Mississippi, to Mary Chestina Andrews, a former teacher, and Christian Webb Welty, the president of an insurance company. After attending a public high school in Jackson, Welty went to Columbus to attend the Mississippi State College for Women, where she contributed drawings, prose, and poetry to student publications. From there she transferred to the University of Wisconsin, from which she graduated two years later with a degree in English. After college she studied advertising for a year at the Columbia University School of Business in New York City—an attempt on her part to find a means of practical employment. Entering the job market in 1931 at the height of the Depression, she returned to Jackson. That same year her father died, creating a heavy burden on her and her family. She was able to find part-time work in radio and the newspaper industry, and began to focus on writing stories. By 1933 she had found a job as a publicity agent and photographer for the State Office of the Works Progress Administration. This position required her to travel for three years around the eighty-two counties of Mississippi doing feature stories on local projects, meeting and conversing with many different types of people, and photographing her experiences on the road. While her photographs were received with enthusiasm by various publications and during private showings, her short stories were widely rejected. Undaunted, she continued writing and trying to publish her work. Her first literary success came in 1936 with the appearance of "Death of a Traveling Salesman" in *Manuscript.* The subsequent publication of her stories in such prestigious periodicals as the *Southern Review* and the *Atlantic Monthly* led to her first collection of short fiction, *A Curtain of Green* (1941). She took first prize in the O. Henry Awards in 1942 and 1943 (for "The Wide Net" and "Livvie Is Back," respectively), and her novella *The Ponder Heart* (1954) received the William Dean Howells Medal of the Academy of Arts and Letters. In 1972 Welty won the Gold Medal from the National Institute of Arts and Letters, and garnered the Pulitzer Prize the following year for her novel *The Optimist's Daughter* (1972). The Presidential Medal of Freedom was bestowed upon her in 1980. In 1998 she became the first living writer to have a commemoration of works published by the Library of America. She died of pneumonia at her home in Jackson in 2001.

MAJOR WORKS OF SHORT FICTION

Marked by a subtle, lyrical narrative style, Welty's work typically explores the intricacies of the interior life and the small heroisms of ordinary people. Rather than simply relating a series of events, her stories convey her characters' experiences in a specific moment in time, always acknowledging the ambiguous nature of reality. Through the use of traditional symbols and mythical allusions, Welty links the particular with the general and the mundane with the metaphysical. *A Curtain of Green* introduces Welty's enigmatic vision of the South and recounts the personal revelations of its inhabitants. Ruby Fisher, the young and unfaithful wife in "A Piece of News," chances on a newspaper story in which a girl with the same name is shot in the leg by her husband. Although Ruby knows that her husband, Clyde, would never commit such a deed, she romanticizes the possibilities of such a situation, imagining herself dressed in a new nightgown with a remorseful Clyde hovering over her as she dies. "Petrified Man" deals with a common Welty motif, the traveling freak show. Gossip among women in a beauty parlor reveals that one of the exhibits might be a notorious local rapist. The distasteful dialogue between the beautician and her client highlights the self-absorption, envy, and material obsession of the story's principal characters. The semiautobiographical story "A Memory" revolves around the daydreams of a young, artistically inclined girl as she visits the beach and observes the behavior of a group of vulgar bathers. In "A Visit of Charity," Marian, a fourteen-year-old Campfire Girl, is obliged to make a visit to a nursing home to collect points. Her experience with two feeble and embittered elderly women terrifies her, but her fear slowly turns to empathy before she flees the institution in a fit of uncontrollable emotion. One of Welty's most famous stories, "A Worn Path" concerns the arduous journey of an elderly black woman, Phoenix Jackson, as she makes her way to town to retrieve medicine for her ailing grandson. Along the way she comes across a sadistic white hunter from whom she steals a nickel that she later uses to buy her grandson a paper windmill. The grandmother's pilgrimage is read as an allegory of the difficult road to equality from the perspective of a freed slave.

The stories in *The Wide Net* (1943) are set in the region along the Natchez Trace—the five-hundred-mile trail covering the territory between Natchez, Mississippi, and Nashville, Tennessee—which was traveled by traders, pioneers, and Indians from the 1790s through the early decades of the nineteenth century. "First Love" is the story of Joel Mayes, whose parents disappear on the Natchez Trace, swallowed up by the wilderness or perhaps captured by Indians. The boy is so traumatized by the loss of his parents that he becomes a deaf-mute; he eventually finds a place in Natchez as the boot boy at an inn for travelers. One of those travelers is Aaron Burr, the Revolutionary War hero who served as the third Vice President of the United States and was later charged with treason for allegedly attempting to form his own republic in the Southwest. Joel identifies with Burr and comes to an understanding about his own identity by observing the stately and enigmatic man. In "The Winds," the violence of an equinoctial storm symbolizes the transition of a girl from adolescence to maturity. "At the Landing" deals with a young woman's coming-of-age in a more oblique manner. Jenny Lockhart lives under the strict rule of her grandfather until he dies and a flood destroys her house, at which point she takes up with another domineering man, Billy Floyd. When Floyd rapes her, she returns to her ruined home and compulsively cleans the mud from the debris.

The Golden Apples (1949) marks an advancement in Welty's experimental style. It consists of stories written and published individually in various journals over a period of about two years, then revised by the author, arranged in loosely chronological order, and published as a short-story cycle that may be read as though it were a novel. Allusions to classical Greek mythology and works of literature, including the poetry of William Butler Yeats and Sir James Frazer's *Golden Bough,* are densely interwoven in the collection, heightening its artistic unity. Covering a time span of forty years, this volume focuses on families in the delta town of Morgana. The lives and destinies of the characters flow together and apart as the town's inhabitants and wanderers search for the "golden apples" of fulfillment through love or art. The stories are told from different narrative vantage points. The first, "Shower of Gold," is a dramatic monologue in which garrulous Katie Rainey familiarizes the reader with Morgana life. She relates the story of King MacLain's amorous career; his wife Snowdie's patience and the town's shocked, but admiring, response to it; and a Halloween trick played on him by his mischievous twin sons. "June Recital" makes use of multiple points of view, juxtaposing various kinds of innocence against experience. It introduces a German music teacher, Miss Eckhart, and her attempt to pass on her musical passion and talent to the one gifted student in Morgana, Katie's daughter Virgie. The girl rejects her gift and the discipline required to express it in favor of the instant gratification of sex. "Sir Rabbit" deals with the rape of a girl, Mattie Will, by King MacLain, while "Moon Lake" is the story of three young girls—Jinny Stark, Nina Carmichael, and Easter (an orphan who is one of King MacLain's illegitimate children)—who explore the mysteries of life and death, self-protection, and sexuality while at summer camp. The denouement centers on the rescue of Easter by a nearby Boy Scout during an incident of near drowning. "Music from Spain" tells of Eugene MacLain—one of King and Snowdie's twins—whose marriage has failed, perhaps due to his lack of a sustained relationship with his perennially absent father. Eugene travels to San Francisco, where he meets a mysterious and beautiful Spanish musician. Eugene's brother, Randall, whose similar despair is the subject of "The Whole World Knows," is now the mayor of Morgana but none the happier for it. The final story, "The Wanderers," finds Virgie

Rainey, now a woman of forty, a detached participant in her mother's funeral rites. Now an adult, she finally receives the gift and meaning of Miss Eckhart's music through a mature understanding of humanity.

The mysterious aspects of sexual and familial relationships take center stage in *The Bride of the Innisfallen* (1955). Another reworking of classical mythology, "Circe" is a retelling, from Circe's perspective, of Homer's episode by the same name in the *Odyssey.* "The Bride of the Innisfallen" relays the thoughts and impressions of a young American wife as she travels through County Cork, Ireland, while fleeing from her husband. Set during the Depression, "Ladies in Spring" involves a day in the life of a Mississippi boy named Dewey. When he and his father go into the woods for a fishing sojourn, they come across a woman, Opal Purcell, who mysteriously calls for Dewey's father through the trees. In "Kin," Dicey Hastings and her cousin Kate visit their senile Uncle Felix while his home is being rented out to a photographer. This encounter inspires in Dicey and Kate an appreciation of their youth as well as an understanding of their mortality. Featuring two main characters who reveal little about their lives or emotions, "No Place for You, My Love" details the abortive relationship between a married man and an adulteress as they travel south of New Orleans to the Gulf of Mexico on a blistering afternoon.

CRITICAL RECEPTION

Welty is widely recognized as a leading voice in American short fiction. Her collection *The Golden Apples,* in particular, has received a steady stream of critical attention over the years. For example, scholars have lauded Welty's depiction of the complicated bond between mother and daughter in this volume, and have examined Virgie Rainey's personal transformation from a mythological standpoint. Also, reviewers have compared the portrayal of the female artist in *The Golden Apples* with that in Virginia Woolf's *Mrs. Dalloway.* They have studied the impact of culturally defined gender roles in such stories as "June Recital," identifying this work as one that challenges the restrictions of the short-story format. Another of the collection's celebrated tales, "Music from Spain," has been cited as an example of Welty's inventive use of descriptive prose to suggest the inner development of her characters. As commentator Matt Huculak elucidated in his analysis of the story's setting, "Welty deliberately remains faithful to the actual 'place' of San Francisco. . . . She uses real street names, and her characters move in such a way that one can plot their paths along a map. Welty's *external* attention and fidelity to actual place-names in San Francisco permits her to play with and manipulate time in order to reveal the expansion of self and *internal* time and place movements of her protagonist, Eugene MacLain." Additionally, critics have investigated the relationship between Welty's short fiction and her photography, especially as it pertains to the stories in *The Bride of the Innisfallen,* and have detected recurring instances of cinematic stylization in her work. Subtextual considerations of civil rights and Christianity have been identified in "A Worn Path," while an underlying autobiographical element has been exposed throughout her short-fiction oeuvre. Moreover, scholars have underscored Welty's insights into the nature and limits of human knowledge, commenting on epistemological overtones in her writing as they apply to the interplay between reader and text. Overall, Welty is remembered for the unconventional, impressionistic style of short fiction through which she projected a transcendent vision of human experience.

PRINCIPAL WORKS

Short Fiction

A Curtain of Green 1941
The Robber Bridegroom 1942
The Wide Net, and Other Stories 1943
The Golden Apples 1949
The Ponder Heart 1954
The Bride of the Innisfallen, and Other Stories 1955
Thirteen Stories 1965
The Collected Stories of Eudora Welty 1980
Stories, Essays, & Memoir 1998

Other Major Works

Delta Wedding (novel) 1946
Losing Battles (novel) 1970
One Time, One Place: Mississippi in the Depression; A Snapshot Album (nonfiction) 1971
The Optimist's Daughter (novel) 1972
The Eye of the Story: Selected Essays and Reviews (essays and criticism) 1978
One Writer's Beginnings (autobiography) 1984
Eudora Welty: Photographs (nonfiction) 1989
A Writer's Eye: Collected Book Reviews (criticism) 1994

CRITICISM

Leslie A. Kaplansky (essay date fall 1996)

SOURCE: Kaplansky, Leslie A. "Cinematic Rhythms in the Short Fiction of Eudora Welty." *Studies in Short Fiction* 33, no. 4 (fall 1996): 579-89.

[*In the following essay, Kaplansky surveys Welty's use of cinematic techniques in her short fiction, claiming that this aspect of the author's writing results in an inventive evocation of time and space.*]

> This little clicking contraption with the revolving handle will make a revolution in our life—in the life of writers . . . We shall have to adapt ourselves to the shadowy screen and to the cold machine. A new form of writing will be necessary . . . But, I rather like it.
>
> Tolstoy (1908)

At the same time that Eudora Welty, born in 1909, was learning to process literature by reading and being read to as a young child in Mississippi, she was also being initiated into the world of a burgeoning new art form, the cinema; as she explains in *One Writer's Beginnings*:

> All children in those small-town, unhurried days had a vast inner life going on in the movies. Whole families attended together in the evenings, at least once a week, and children were allowed to go without chaperone in the long summer afternoons. . . .
>
> (36)

Given such memories, it is not surprising that we should find reflections of this same film culture in a number of Welty's stories: Stella-Rondo's "marvelous blonde child" is aptly named Shirley T; the ladies of Leota's beauty parlor read *Screen Secrets*; and Wilbur Morrison wields power over his children in **"June Recital"** by threatening to withhold picture show money. Moreover, note the similes Welty uses, again in **"June Recital,"** to convey Loch's and Cassie's perceptions: from his window, Loch sees the Maclain porch hanging "like a cliff in a serial at the bijou" (***CS*** [***The Collected Stories of Eudora Welty***] 275) and Cassie views her father opening his morning paper "like Douglas Fairbanks opening big gates" (***CS*** 295). Clearly, Welty grounds these characters in a world in which "all children had a vast inner life going on in the movies."

Of course, Miss Welty would attest to the fact that being a "constant moviegoer" (qtd. in Ferris 169) has inspired her writing in this way. Whereas Alfred Appel, Jr. finds one of the sources of Miss Welty's comedy to be "a revival in spirit, if not in form, of the most ancient sources of comedy, the Dionysiac revels" (60), Welty suggests a more immediate association with cinema: "In devotion to Buster Keaton, Charlie Chaplin, Ben Blue, and the Keystone Kops. . . . My sense of making fictional comedy undoubtedly caught its first spark from the antic pantomime of the silent screen . . ." (*One Writer's Beginnings* 36). In fact, we need only look to **"June Recital"** to see this notion played out:

> Upstairs, the sailor and Virgie Rainey were running in circles around the room, each time jumping with outstretched arms over the broken bed. . . . They went around and around like the policeman and Charlie Chaplin, both intending to fall down.
>
> (***CS*** 282)

Welty would also likely accept the argument posited by Ruth Weston that Welty's childhood encounter with *The Cabinet of Doctor Caligari*[1] influenced her creation of "a landscape of gothic terror in **'First Love'** . . . images of suffering, entrapment, and death in the unusual cold . . ." (34).

The presence of these film allusions in her stories attests to Welty's engaged involvement with film *culture,* to be sure. But I would argue that her work reveals a formal association with film as well—one that centers on her use of various cinematic *techniques* that, learned from her experience as a moviegoer, afforded Welty new ways of experiencing "stories" and, in turn, inspired new ways of writing them. Welty herself concludes that a significant relationship exists between the techniques of film making and her work as a short story writer—a "kinship" that affects her almost intuitively, as she explains:

> [Film] can do all the things you do as a short story writer to bring out what you are trying to do. And I think as a short story writer I feel that I must have absorbed things. I've been a constant filmgoer all my life. I must have absorbed some of the lessons which have come in handy. I don't mean anything I can put my finger on. I never think of it. But it's just like the way of folklore, these things come into your mind, and you learn from them without really knowing.
>
> (qtd. in Ferris 169)

Of course, it is important here to point out that, as a newfound art form to this century, film was itself subject to many influences—from photography, painting and theater, and most certainly from literature. And so, because film and short stories do share characteristics and are, in many ways interdependent, it is often difficult to determine just where a certain "shared" technique originated; as Welty says, it is hard to know "who thought of it first." Still, there are certain techniques that are specifically (idiomatically) cinematic, such as the accelerated montage Hitchcock[2] used in the famous shower scene in *Psycho* (a scene conceived according to his notion of "pure cinema," adopted from Pudovkin's montage theories[3]). Simply, that scene could not have been realized in any other media but film. In addition, film has reformulated certain techniques that, though originally borrowed from other sources, are now considered primarily cinematic; for example, an effect such as slow-motion may have existed in prose before the advent of film, but not until film took up its use did it emerge as a truly recognizable and important *convention.* In order to avoid engaging in a what-came-first debate (no doubt a daunting dilemma), I will thus limit my specific discussion of Welty's cinematic techniques to those particular to or more conventionally associated with cinema and will avoid examining those techniques that may be more reasonably traced back to earlier origins than cinema, such as references to *mise en scène* (about which Welty undoubtedly learned more from her experience as a painter and photographer than from the cinema) or narrative devices as easily learned from Dickens' work as from D. W. Griffith's. In short, I will demonstrate that by drawing upon those uniquely cinematic techniques that "elide," "compound," and "exaggerate," as she says, Welty is able to exploit what we may call a "cinematic rhythm" in her stories (while at the same time remaining powerfully and expressively visual).[4]

Indeed, that Welty assumes "kinship" between narrative film and the short story is quite logical—after all, they are both short, or as she says, both "have only a set space or time to prove themselves" (149). Thus, if we accept the notion that brevity has formal and stylistic implications for the short story (one of the less contentious arguments among critics), then we may assume the same holds true for film. Of particular interest in this study is that both forms tend to express meaning through the "rhythms" of scenes or sequences (the interplay of fast and slow pacing, methods of transition, the building and relaxing of tension)—as opposed to "the rhythm in the novel," which E. K. Brown defines as a system of "strong repetition" and "artful, pleasing, or powerful variation" by which readers can make sense of the mass of information contained (and easily forgotten) in the long form of the novel (8). Simply, as Allan Pasco explains, with a short form whose anity of effect is experienced in one sitting, readers (and I would add, by extension, film viewers) have less need—and tolerance—for such repetition (125). What is more, as Charles May argues, the novel is "more conceptually created and considered," whereas short stories (and, again I would add, film) are more "directly and emotionally encountered" (133)—in large part, I would suggest, because of the expressiveness of their rhythms. Indeed, in the case of film, directors are often able to exploit the pacing of a scene (in a typical suspense thriller, for example) so effectively that this rhythm becomes the scene's most salient feature, even capable of producing a visceral response in the viewer.

Clearly, the rhythms in Welty's stories are meant to be equally expressive as those of a film, as Alfred Appel suggests when he identifies the "rhythm of style [that] controls tone" in a number of her stories (109). For example, he attributes the humor of **"Why I Live at the P.O."** to its "glancing rhythms of the short sentences"; the "pathos" of **"Death of a Traveling Salesman"** to sentence rhythms "slackened, sluggish, seeming to rise and fall with the fluctuations of Bowman's failing heart"; and the "sonorous" quality of **"A Still Moment"** to its "measured pace and balance" (109). But one of Welty's most pronounced and characteristic manipulations of rhythm is her verbal equivalent of filmic slow-motion—a specific cinematic rhythm used to heighten a profound moment of (subjective) revelation.[5] One such moment can be found in **"A Curtain of Green,"** in which Mrs. Larkin remembers her husband's death:

> In the freedom of gaily turning her head, a motion she was now forced by memory to repeat as she hoed the ground, she could see again the tree that was going to fall. There had been no warning. But there was the enormous tree, the fragrant chinaberry tree, suddenly tilting, dark and slow like a cloud, leaning down to her husband. From her place on the front porch she had spoken in a soft voice to him, never so intimate as at that moment, "you can't be hurt."
>
> (***CS*** 109)

Alfred Appel appropriately reads the scene as one in which: "*slow motion effects* dramatize Mrs. Larkin's refusal to accept the terrible fact of [her husband's] death, the verbs keeping the tree in mid-air another instant, prolonging that moment when she tried to will him life" (106; emphasis added). He also finds in **"Death of a Traveling Salesman"** a similar instance in which "passages are rendered in the manner of a slow-motion picture, where everything is deliberately felt . . ." (116). However, I detect an even more striking instance of cinematic slow-motion—a rhythm of exaggeration—in **"A Worn Path."** In the story, Phoenix moves slowly but steadily throughout her journey, even as she encounters various difficulties along the way: she catches her dress on a thorny bush, is forced to surmount a log laid across her path, and is frightened by a scarecrow. Thus, each of these experiences occupies equal weight in the story; Welty gives no greater emphasis to any one of them, and so the rhythm of Phoenix's journey (and Welty's story) remains steady. Indeed, even when Phoenix is knocked over by a dog and left lying helplessly in a ditch, Welty does surprisingly little to interrupt the steady flow of the story. The episode is described without flourish:

> A black dog with a lolling tongue came up out of the weeds by the ditch. She was meditating, and not ready, and when he came at her she only hit him a little with her cane. Over she went in the ditch, like a little puff of milkweed.
>
> (***CS*** 145)

We see that Phoenix is unfazed by this event (she simply daydreams there in the ditch until she is rescued), as she is unfazed by the other mishaps because, as the title suggests, she is accustomed to her trip on the "worn path." What she is unaccustomed to, however, is seeing "with her own eyes a flashing nickel fall out of [her rescuer's] pocket" (***CS*** 145), and it is at this instant that the steady rhythm of the story is interrupted. The scene begins with short, declarative statements: "Phoenix heard the dogs fighting, and heard the man running and throwing sticks. She even heard a gunshot" (***CS*** 146). Then, as Phoenix is overcome by the surprising impulse to "steal" the coin, the rhythm of the scene changes: in addition to the direct mention that the movement is "slow," Welty draws out her sentences (made longer with layers of modifiers and with repetition) to emphasize this moment and render it—as it would be treated in film—in slow-motion:

> But she was *slowly* bending *forward* by that time, *further and further forward,* the lids stretched down over her eyes, as if she were doing this in her sleep. Her chin was lowered almost to her knees. The yellow palm of her hand came out from the fold of her apron. Her fingers slid *down and along* the ground under the piece of money with the grace and care they would have in lifting an egg from under a setting hen. Then she *slowly* straightened up, she stood erect, and the nickel was in her apron pocket.
>
> (***CS*** 146; emphasis added)

Then suddenly, with short, crisp statements, Welty abruptly returns the scene to "real" time: "A bird flew overhead. Her lips moved. 'God watching me the whole time. I come to stealing'" (***CS*** 146).

Such a moment, in which Phoenix interrupts her journey to "steal" the coin (which we later come to understand will be used to buy her grandson's Christmas present) reveals a bit of her "mystery" (a term indispensable to a discussion of Welty). And, as Charles May argues, these moments are essential to modern short stories, because "the short story, by its very shortness, cannot deal with the denseness of detail and the duration of time typical of the novel . . ." and so it must focus on "the revelatory break-up of the rhythm of everyday reality" (200). Here then, Welty achieves emphasis for this provocative moment by rendering it in slow-motion, an exaggerated effect that readers can easily recognize and "process" as we read the passage.

Just as slow motion contributes to a scene's *internal* rhythm (the movement within a "frame"), film editing creates *external* rhythm—that which links shots or scenes ("elides" or "compounds") and manipulates fictional time and space, a prerequisite of storyness, according to John Gerlach: "Stories, like all complete, satisfying forms such as essays and poems, exhibit point—point enacted not as the stasis of metaphor or reflection [what he would classify as a sketch] but under the *illusion of space and time*" (84; emphasis added). I would thus argue that much of Welty's success in exploiting time and space in her stories can be traced to her use of rhythms of cinematic editing (considered by many theorists, most notably Pudovkin, to be the foundation of film art).

Cinematic rhythms that "elide," for example, help Welty achieve compression—a feature necessary to all short forms (both films and stories alike). One such rhythm, "cutting to continuity," is an editing technique by which an action or movement is rendered fluidly in a scene without being shown in its entirety. For instance, in a scene in which a man crosses a room to answer the telephone, the scene might open with a shot of him beginning his movement across the room, quickly followed by a second shot of him, now from a different angle, finishing his movement across the room and answering the call. Thus, the middle section of the man's walk is eliminated, condensing the time of the action without the viewer sensing the jump in chronological time (as one would with a "jump cut"). Clearly, in **"A Worn Path,"** Welty relies on this rhythm of compression to begin the story: she uses the same sequence of perspectives (establishing shot—to medium shot—to close up) that is conventionally used to condense time in the opening of a film. The first lines begin:

> It was December—a bright frozen day in the early morning. Far out in the country there was an old Negro woman with her head tied in a red rag, coming along the path through the pinewoods.
>
> (***CS*** 142)

Here, the descriptions—Phoenix is a woman, "old . . . Negro," wearing a "red rag"—are all features distinguished from a distance. Next, Welty describes the woman's gait, now observed from medium range, then she brings Phoenix into close-up and describes her eyes and skin and cheeks, "illuminated by a yellow burning under the dark" (***CS*** 142). Thus, Welty fluidly condenses the duration of Phoenix's movement on the path (without providing authorial narration to mark her progress) so that the character appears both from afar and dramatically close, though only a short interval of real (reading) time has elapsed.

Another editing rhythm, the Hollywood style of "classical cutting" (advanced by D. W. Griffith) expands upon the principles of "cutting to continuity," whereby a sequence of shots is edited according to a scene's dramatic or emotional focus rather than by its physical action alone.[6] For example, if that same scene of a man crossing a room to answer a phone were re-edited according to the conventions of "classical cutting," the scene might begin with a full shot of the man reading a newspaper. Upon hearing the phone ring, we might then see him in close up, looking up from his paper in the direction of the phone. Next, we might see a shot of him rising from his chair, followed by a shot of him finishing his movement by picking up the receiver. Thus, part of the man's movement has been eliminated in favor of showing the cause-effect relationship that exists in the scene—the phone call compels the man's action—a dramatic logic that we can understand without having observed his physical action in its entirety. Welty "edits" the World Cafe scene in **"Powerhouse"** according to such a rhythm of "classical cutting." As she begins the scene, Powerhouse and his band enter the cafe:

> Valentine patters over and holds open a screen door warped like a sea shell, bitter in the wet, and they walk in, stained darker with the rain and leaving footprints. Inside, sheltered dry smells stand like screens around a table covered with a red-checkered cloth, in the center of which flies hang on to an obelisk-shaped ketchup bottle.
>
> (***CS*** 135)

Welty continues her description of the interior of the cafe for several more lines, then she "cuts" away to a quick reaction "shot"—the suspended line: "A waitress watches" (***CS*** 136). Welty then returns to the original focus of the scene with a "shot" of Powerhouse—only this time, apparently, he is already seated at a table and calls the waitress to him: "Come here, living statue, and get all this big order of beer we fixing to give. . . . Where are you going to find enough beer to put out on this here table?" (***CS*** 136). Of course, we never "see" Powerhouse as he moves to the table (Welty does not provide the details of his physical action). And yet, the construction of the scene still seems logical to us, because Welty has guided us through it according to its *dramatic logic*—the performance-to-response structure that informs the story as a whole. In so doing, she has also been able to condense time—all in keeping with the rhythm of classical cutting.

Unlike editing techniques that seem to adhere to temporal logic (even as they unobtrusively compress or expand time), certain editing techniques skew logical (realistic) time and space in order to blur the distinction between dream and reality and between present and past—particularly the "match cut."[7] Through this editing technique, "two shots are linked by visual, aural, or metaphorical parallelism" (Monaco 416), and thus, it is an ideal technique for Welty to use in **"A Memory"** in order to portray "mystery"—what Austin M. Wright calls "a sign of recalcitrance at the level of the fictional world" (119). In this story, a girl lies on a beach remembering an encounter with a boy whom she loves, and while contemplating this memory, she does not "notice how . . . bathers got there, so close to [her]" (***CS*** 77). Of course, the girl suggests that she may have been asleep while the scene transformed, but even she does not seem to be convinced by this explanation; she "would not care to say which was more real—the dream [she made] blossom at will, or the sight of the bathers," and so, she presents them "only as simultaneous" (***CS*** 77). Accordingly, this episode lacks temporal logic; Welty does not provide a clear connection between the moment the girl lies alone on the beach and the moment the bathers appear, de facto, in the girl's view. But through the use of a match cut, Welty can join the two scenes into one seamless, "simultaneous" sequence, and in so doing, can provocatively suggest that the grotesque bathers somehow and at some time "mysteriously appeared" on the scene.

Welty again uses a cinematic "match cut" in **"June Recital."** However, in this instance, the link is aural rather than visual, and its rhythm is not meant to create "mystery" but to contribute to the story's "unity of effect" (by integrating the perceptions of Cassie and Loch, through whose distinct points of view the story is told). The match cut occurs at the end of the first section, controlled by Loch's point of view, in which he "hangs still as a folded bat" in the tree outside his bedroom window (a vantage point from which he can better observe the curious activities going on inside the house next door). As he hangs there, he hears "the old woman . . . [play a] tune," a sound upon which Welty then "cuts" to Cassie, who is "in her bedroom when she [hears] the gentle opening, the little phrase . . ." of "Für Elise" (***CS*** 285). For Cassie, the tune carries vivid associations that, in turn, trigger a series of memories of Miss Eckhart and Virgie Rainie (memories that guide the next section of the story). And so, by using this fluid cinematic rhythm (which "compounds"), Welty is able to affirm the simultaneity of her characters' disparate experiences and, in turn, to control the "unity of effect" of the story—as varied as its two controlling points of view may be.

"June Recital," in fact, draws on a number of such cinematic transitions that similarly contribute to a "unity of effect." Among them, a quick fade-in-from-black allows Welty again to move smoothly between sections—this time, from the second section (in which Cassie's perceptions control the scene as she stands in her window singing) to the third (in which Loch regains control of point of view). At this instance, "after a moment of blackness, upside down, Loch open[s] his eyes" (***CS*** 316). Thus, in exploiting cinematic rhythms—those that contribute to a story's continuity—Welty guides her readers through the complexities of the varying perspectives of **"June Recital."**

Lacking this "frame" of cinematic technique, Welty's critics often fail to account for the simultaneous presence of visual and rhythmic impulses in Welty's work (a simultaneity implicitly considered in this study). An example of the limitations of such criticism is Barbara McKenzie's account of the analogies between the "way of seeing represented in [Welty's] photographs" and her "prose style":

> The opening paragraphs of **"The Key"** recreate verbally the inclusiveness and disorderly truth of a snapshot. The yellow light . . . shines indiscriminately on the passengers who sit silently. . . . And *then the focus shifts* to Ellie and Albert Morgan and settles there, *elaborating* on their clothes and suitcases . . . and *then attention moves* to a young man. . . .
>
> (392-93; emphasis added)

However, in commenting on the ways in which Welty's prose is photographic, McKenzie fails to account for the strong sense of movement in the passage. Recognizing Welty's proclivity for employing cinematic techniques to heighten the expressive effects of her short fiction, we can readily see that the passage is not a static snapshot, but is a motion picture, moving about the living scene as it records it, roving and then lingering on small revelations. It is a scene successfully rendered by the use of internally rhythmic pans, tilts, close-ups and long-shots (as we see consistently employed throughout Welty's stories), unlike the failed attempt by the girl in **"A Memory"** to control her vision of the world by squaring it between the frame of her fingers, like a *still* painting.

Welty once said that she would have liked to write an original screenplay (qtd. in Keith 149). However, I would argue that she has, indeed, accomplished something far more interesting; that is, in taking advantage of the techniques of the cinema—a powerful and evocative medium—Welty has been able to write *cinematic stories* (the perfect synthesis of the two media). In so doing, I believe she has insured her reputation as a technical and stylistic master of the short story.

Notes

1. Welty remembers her experience with the film vividly: "*The Cabinet of Dr. Caligari* turned up by some strange fluke in place of the Saturday western on the screen of the Istrione Theatre. . . . I learned 'somnambulist' in terror, a word I still never hear or read without seeing again Conrad Veidt in black tights and bangs, making his way at night alongside a high leaning wall with eyes closed, one arm reaching high, seeing with his fingers" (*One Writer's Beginnings* 36-37). She similarly remembers: "'Jeopardy' I got to know from *Drums of Jeopardy* with Alice Brady, who was wearing a leopard skin, a verbal connection I shall never forget" (36). Ironically, this latter recollection is not entirely accurate—Brady never appeared in *Drums of Jeopardy,* though she did appear in *The Leopardess* in 1923 (which may have been the film Welty remembers). Still, despite this error, the importance that Welty confers upon these memories does not change.
2. Welty greatly admires Hitchcock's films, and said that "he had something you could learn" as a short story writer (qtd. in Ferris 170). Hitchcock, it seems, shared Welty's belief in the affinity between short stories and cinema: "the nearest art form to the motion picture is . . . the short story" (qtd. in Beja 59).
3. Among Pudovkin's theories is the notion that the way in which a film scene is constructed can "work upon the emotions." For example, "a series of pictures, rapidly alternating pieces, creat[es] a *stirring scenario editing-construction.*" Thus, editing is in actual fact a "compulsory and deliberate guidance of the thoughts and associations of the spectator" (69-71).
4. This simultaneous presence of Welty's visual and rhythmic impulses is subtly suggested in Daniel Burke's analysis of "Powerhouse," in which he says both that "Welty attempts to echo features of the music itself, especially as she develops an elaborate parallel between the improvisational brilliance of the jazz and of Powerhouse's own storytelling. . . . through the *rapid tempo* and exclamatory excitement of [her] writing" (165, 170; emphasis added), and that Welty's "imagery is dominantly visual" (165). Of course, Welty herself speaks about writing in terms of an author's "perspective, the line of vision, the frame of vision" (*One Writer's Beginnings* 87)—language that she clearly borrows from her days as a photographer and painter; however, she also explains that in addition to having a "visual mind," she also writes "by ear": "I see everything I write, but I have to hear the words when they're put down" (qtd. in Kuehl 85).

5. Appel does not comment further on Welty's use of this cinematic technique, but this brief mention is significant because it comprises perhaps the only other remarking (however incidental) on the subject.
6. This method of cutting, then, may or may not result in compression, because the temporal framework depends on the emotional or dramatic needs of the scene (which may, in fact, require that the scene be drawn out rather than condensed).
7. A famous example of a match cut, James Monaco explains, occurs at the end of *North by Northwest*: Cary Grant pulls Eva Marie Saint up the cliff of Mt. Rushmore—then match cut—we suddenly see him pull her up a Pullman bunk on their train ride home (416).

Works Cited

Appel, Alfred, Jr. *A Season of Dreams: The Fiction of Eudora Welty.* Baton Rouge: Louisiana State UP, 1965.

Beja, Morris. *Film and Literature.* New York: Longman, 1979.

Brown, E. K. *Rhythm in the Novel.* Toronto: U of Toronto P, 1950.

Burke, Daniel. *Beyond Interpretation: Studies in the Modern Short Story.* Troy, New York: Whitston, 1991.

Ferris, Bill. "A Visit With Eudora Welty: Summer 1975 and 1976." Prenshaw 154-71.

Gerlach, John. "The Margins of Narrative: The Very Short Story, the Prose Poem, and the Lyric." Lohafer and Clarey 74-84.

Keith, Don Lee. "Eudora Welty: 'I Worry Over My Stories.'" Prenshaw 141-53.

Kuehl, Linda. "The Art of Fiction XLVII: Eudora Welty." Prenshaw 74-91.

Lohafer, Susan, and Jo Ellyn Clarey, eds. *Short Story Theory at a Crossroads.* Baton Rouge: Louisiana State UP, 1989.

McKenzie, Barbara. "The Eye of Time: The Photographs of Eudora Welty." *Eudora Welty: Critical Essays.* Ed. Peggy Whitman Prenshaw. Jackson: UP of Mississippi, 1979. 386-400.

May, Charles E. "The Nature of Knowledge in Short Fiction." May, *New Short Story Theories* 131-217.

———, ed. *The New Short Story Theories.* Athens, Ohio: Ohio UP, 1994.

Pasco, Allan H. "On Defining Short Stories." May, *New Short Story Theories* 114-30.

Prenshaw, Peggy Whitman, ed. *Conversations with Eudora Welty.* Jackson: UP of Mississippi, 1984.

Pudovkin, Vsevolod I. "On Editing." *Film Theory and Criticism.* Ed. Gerald Mast and Marshall Cohen. New York: Oxford UP, 1974. 67-74.

Welty, Eudora. *The Collected Stories of Eudora Welty.* New York: Harcourt Brace Jovanovich, 1980.

———. *One Writer's Beginnings.* Cambridge, Massachusetts: Harvard UP, 1984.

Weston, Ruth D. *Gothic Traditions and Narrative Techniques in the Fiction of Eudora Welty.* Baton Rouge: Louisiana State UP, 1994.

Wright, Austin M. "On Defining the Short Story: The Genre Question." Lohafer and Clarey 46-53.

Harriet Pollack (essay date summer 1997)

SOURCE: Pollack, Harriet. "Photographic Convention and Story Composition: Eudora Welty's Use of Detail, Plot, Genre, and Expectation from 'A Worn Path' through *The Bride of the Innisfallen.*" *South Central Review* 14, no. 2 (summer 1997): 15-34.

[*In the following essay, Pollack investigates the relationship between Welty's stories and her photographs, emphasizing the involvement of the reader in the plotless structure of* The Bride of the Innisfallen.]

My first habit when reading Welty is to watch for effects that could surprise—to watch for obstructions of expectations—believing that Welty's play with readers' conventional expectations is often a location of meaning. My first assumption in this essay is that Welty uses details in ways that sometimes provoke surprise, and my central assertion is that she uses detail as plot, a composition more familiar in photography than in earlier short stories. To develop my argument, I will discuss the reception of detail and the idea of plot in the early **"A Worn Path"** before the more obviously risk-taking **"No Place for You, My Love"** and **"The Bride of the Innisfallen."** I intend to evoke parallels between Welty's story compositions and the compositional tendencies of photography throughout.

Readers have at times objected to Welty's plotlessness as obstructive of meaning and found her use of detail inundating rather than illuminating. Diana Trilling's early remarks in the *Nation* (1943) faulted Welty's stories for developing "technical virtuosity" rather than conventionally meaningful narrative. She accused Welty of writing "a book of ballets, not of stories" and read the stories as staying "with their narrative no more than a dance, say, stays with its argument."[1] Trilling's remarks are representative of a particular reaction to finding Welty's fiction not what was expected. John Fleischauer's responses in "The Focus of Mystery: Eudora Welty's Prose Style" (1973) are similar; he speaks of "vagueness contrasting with or containing delightful and colloquial concentrations of detail," arguing that "the vagueness, or sketchiness, or selection of detail is so pronounced . . . as to lead to complaints" while readers look for "a steady progress of action."[2] Teachers of Welty's fiction sometimes find similar responses in classrooms of new Welty readers. Of all Welty's collections, ***The Bride of the Innisfallen*** receives the most criticism of this sort in responses commenting on density of detail and "plotlessness." Her earliest stories are different from these later ones, but I will argue that many early stories are nevertheless connected to the technique she expands in the later volume.

Welty's use of detail is linked to her work with photography in as much as photography presents one notion of composition as the framing of chance details. Reception, in that case, is to see those details closely. That principle of photographic composition has little to do either with our most conventional ideas regarding short story plots or with our most conventional strategies for interpreting them (both of which emphasize notions of "no detail not contributing to a unity"[3]). In the sort of photographic composition I have in mind, revelation and meaning are related to details that may be random and that are not in themselves portentous but become interesting once they are framed—as they are in Welty's photograph, "Town in a Store Window, Canton."[4] There, the details of the town skyline, its everyday buildings, useful fencing, imposing trees, and the cloudless Mississippi sky itself, are all framed by the items for sale in the small-town store window—lanterns, clocks, tins, scales, a mailbox, belts, a life preserver—as well as by the window's shredding shade. The town store window's two views are informed by one another. The backdrop of the town wavers behind the window's miscellaneous display and gives random items of hardware an imaginative life that they would not have in themselves. The image recalls the night light from Marmion in *Delta Wedding* on which the back-lighted Great Fire wavered behind and imaginatively lit the London skyline. In "Town in a Store Window, Canton," two pictures are caught in a single frame—the observers' and the world's. Seeing double is again brought into focus, and its statements made visible by the camera's fixing frame.

Roland Barthes points out that "in an initial period, Photography . . . [photographed] the notable, but soon, by a familiar reversal, it decrees notable whatever it photographs."[5] Photographic framing causes details—which otherwise might not even have been seen—to signify. With the development of photography as an art form came a new aesthetic. In Susan Sontag's words from *On Photography*: "what is beautiful became just what the eye can't (or doesn't) see."[6] By definition and by contrast, painting, photography's predecessor, could frame no expression, detail, or signifier valuable by virtue of its not previously having been "seen" to signify. Photography extends artistic convention and composition by privileging the framed—the random, accidental, signifying detail, and the reverie it evokes. Barthes writes that photography "induces us, vaguely, to think. . . . Ultimately, Photography is subversive not when it frightens, repels, or even stigmatizes, but when it is *pensive,* when it thinks."[7] He describes how, as a reader of photographs, he looks in the photographic frame. "A 'detail' attracts me. I feel that its mere presence changes my reading, that I am looking at a new photograph."[8] He develops the example of looking at a James Van Der Zee family portrait of a man and two women (*Family Portrait, 1926*). The grouping suggests to Barthes "respectability, family life, conformism, Sunday best, an effort of social advancement."[9] But the strapped pumps worn by one of the two women—signifiers which, if we had seen them in person, might not have spoken—utter something that only comes clear in this speaking photo: something about the position of this middle-aged woman who may be a daughter in the family. Her adult Mary Janes convey some conflicted message—between a discordant effort for girlish femininity and a sanctioned effort to remain the family daughter even after youth has been overgrown. The expressiveness of those shoes may or may not have been in the photographer's anticipated composition, but there it is in the spectator's photo. Photography's relationship to the details it frames (such as those shoes) can be understood through a remark Welty herself made about the sculptor José de Creeft's work with specific stones: "This is almost to say that the material is making the sculpture as he, simultaneously, is learning and working from it."[10]

Welty's use of details belongs to a world where this sort of detailed seeing is understood. In discussing Welty's use of details, I am not describing writing with "natural symbols"—that is, writing with details or gestures that should be read as symbolic, physical emblems of an abstract idea. I mean to suggest how these details open without being "symbols."

Framing is the common topic between Welty's photographic composition of detail and her own accounts of her beginnings as a writer who, during travel, simultaneously "became aware of the outside world" and also of her own imaginative, "introspective way into becoming a part of it."[11] In *One Writer's Beginnings,* Welty describes what could be called her early, traveling, potentially photographic vision—developing before she ever carried a camera. Sitting with her father, she glimpsed the flying countryside from train windows, a frame resembling both a camera's frame and the painterly compositional frame described in **"A Memory,"** her portrait of the artist as a young girl. Fleeting details expanded in imagination:

> I dreamed over what I could see . . . as well as over what I couldn't. . . . A house back at its distance at night showing a light from an open doorway, the morning faces of the children who stopped still in what they were doing, perhaps picking blackberries or wild plums, and watched us go by. . . . For now, and for a long while to come, I was proceeding in fantasy.

In the train window *frame* that gave them importance, physical details were seen, focused, and unpacked in reverie. Moreover, Welty explicitly connects the effects of these trips to her idea of plot:

> The trips . . . were stories. . . . When I did begin to write, the short story was a shape that had already formed itself and stood waiting in the back of my mind.[12]

Her association of the shape of the story with the shape of a trip, and of plot with the heightened observation of detail, is literally realized in the stories that I bring together below. They are all traveling stories in which observation replaces action.

Eventually the camera became her augmentative tool; Welty's WPA work, which took her around Mississippi with camera-in-hand, required her to make her traveling vision actually photographic. The connection between her travel, her photographs, and her stories is convincing; anyone who plays the provocative game of matching her photographs to specific moments in her stories and essays can spot organic relationships between them.[13] The courthouse in **"The Wanderers,"** the Natchez Trace in **"A Still Moment"** and other stories, the houseboat and knife throwers of **"At the Landing,"** the bottle trees in **"Livvie,"** Ida M'Toy, a pageant of birds, and John David's Boy from **"Some Notes on River Country"**: there are photographs of all these and more. Even more interesting than this relationship is the one between her story compositions and her claim to have recognized her narrative goal while working with the camera. In the preface to her photo album, *One Time, One Place,* she tells what photography taught her about fiction:

> I learned quickly enough when to click the shutter, but what I was becoming aware of more slowly was a story-writer's truth: the thing to wait on, to reach there in time for is the moment in which people reveal themselves. You have to be ready, in yourself; you have to know the moment when you see it. The human face and the human body are eloquent in themselves and stubborn and wayward, and a snapshot is a moment's glimpse (as a story may be a long look, a growing contemplation) into what never stops moving, never ceases to express for itself something of our common feeling. Every feeling waits upon its gesture.[14]

Welty's frequent, resonant use of the word "exposure" informs her conception of plot. Elsewhere I have written at some length about the importance of this word in her comments and criticism, borrowed repeatedly from her photographer's vocabulary,[15] of her longing for perfect fictional exposure, her need for "exposure to the world,"[16] and yet her "terrible sense of exposure"[17] felt as she risks yielding her complex and experimental fiction to her reader. The relationship between this anxiety for and about exposure and her stylistic experimentation—which obstructs readers with too conventional expectations and in a sense selects for an understanding reader—is generally strategic. It is not surprising then that plot in her work, like the art of photography itself, emphasizes disclosure, exposure of what—had it not been framed and snapped by a click of finger and shutter—would have gone unseen. Sontag describes photography as peeling away "the dry wrappers of habitual seeing" and creating a "habit of seeing . . . charmed by the insignificant detail, addicted to incongruity," a perception that magnifies "tiny details," however arbitrarily seeming, to disclose "by proper focusing, infinite layers of significance."[18]

"A Worn Path," a short story usually thought of as readily accessible that nevertheless holds some surprises for readers, is a good laboratory in which to examine Welty's use of detail and plot. Welty's essay "Is Phoenix Jackson's Grandson Really Dead?" testifies to the author's astonishment at readers' reactions and at finding readers rewriting the story by asking their "unrivaled favorite" question.[19] She finds them implicitly expressing surprise that she is not writing a "better" story—that is, one with a more conventional plot. She writes, "It is not the question itself that has struck me as much as the idea, almost without exception implied in the asking, that for Phoenix's grandson to be dead would somehow make the story 'better.'"[20] Welty's effort to clarify is perplexed, impatient, self-assertive:

> To the question "Is the grandson really dead?" I could reply that it doesn't make any difference. . . . But my best answer would be: "Phoenix is alive."[21]

To help her inquiring readers, she describes the origin of her story in "its key image," a figure seen against a landscape:

> One day I saw a solitary old woman like Phoenix. She was walking; I saw her at a middle distance, in a winter country landscape, and watched her slowly make

> her way across my line of vision. That sight of her made me write her story. . . . I brought her up close enough, by imagination, to describe her face, make her present to the eyes, but the full-length figure moving across the winter fields was the indelible one.[22]

In this essay's start, Welty proposes to speak analytically, "tracing out . . . a meaning" for readers reaching for traditional plot,[23] but then, in this central passage, she instead repeats her habit of bringing details to her reader, describing the solitary old woman's exposure as if revealed in a camera's zooming lens.

Rather than discard the tension apparent between Welty's readers' question and her reply, I want to consider what causes readers to want to rewrite the story. What are readers finding unexpected and responding to by adding twists (and plots) that make the story more conventional? The situation comes clearer when Neil Isaacs in his 1963 article asks, "What makes this a story? It barely appears to fulfill even . . . generous criterion of 'turning a corner or at least a hair.'"[24] Calling the story "road literature," Isaacs goes on to discuss "some inherent weaknesses" in the form. "The story concerns the struggle to achieve a goal, the completion of the journey; and the story's beginning, middle, and end are the same as those of a road. The primary weakness of this structure is its susceptibility to too much middle."[25] This comment is another reaction to Welty's comfort with plotlessness and to her use of detail as plot.

"A Worn Path" presents the detail of Phoenix's journey along the Natchez Trace. The first two paragraphs deliver meticulous description:

> It was December—a bright frozen day in the early morning. Far out in the country there was an old Negro woman with her head tied in a red rag, coming along a path through the pinewoods. Her name was Phoenix Jackson. She was very old and she walked slowly in the dark pine shadows, moving a little from side to side in her steps, with the balanced heaviness and lightness of a pendulum in a grand-father clock. She carried a thin, small cane made from an umbrella, and with this she kept tapping the frozen earth in front of her. This made a grave and persistent noise in the still air, that seemed meditative like the chirping of a solitary bird.
>
> She wore a dark striped dress reaching down to her shoe tops, and an equally long apron of bleached sugar sacks, with a full pocket: all neat and tidy, but every time she took a step she might have fallen over her shoelaces, which dragged from her unlaced shoes. She looked straight ahead. Her eyes were blue with age. Her skin had a pattern all its own of numberless branching wrinkles and as though a whole little tree stood in the middle of her forehead, but a golden color ran underneath, and the two knobs of her cheeks were illumined by a yellow burning under the dark. Under the red rag her hair came down on her neck in the frailest of ringlets, still black, and with an odor like copper.[26]

These paragraphs, filled with description, are not unconventional. What is unexpected, however, is that they do not give way to dialogue or dramatic action. In the story that follows, the lengthy description continues. The building accumulation of this detailed description effects a reader's anticipation. Phoenix's monologue intermittently interrupts the story's narrative description, but does not deliver dramatic change; instead Phoenix speaks to herself about the details of the landscape and her progress. An oral quality develops: "On she went. . . ."[27] As if in a folk tale, we are invited to enter a ritual of repetition as Phoenix surmounts the small obstacles on the worn path.

The story's generous use of detail invites readers to try one of two reading strategies that are more or less inappropriate. Both involve the idea of "getting somewhere," in contrast to Welty's statement that "in the story, the path is the thing that matters."[28] The first method is to read its details as overly determined symbols in an allegory. Readers meeting all the quiet detail of Phoenix in the world frequently have responded as if Phoenix's trace were Young Goodman Brown's forest. Critical articles as well as students do this. The overwhelming majority of articles (written from 1960-80) on the story read it as allegory—mostly Christian allegory.[29] These readings find symbolic evocations of Christ, the Virgin Mary, Bunyan's Celestial City, the crown of thorns, the Stations of the Cross, and the like throughout the story. Such readings—the product of a dominant reading strategy in that specific time span—are also recognizably the product of readers' responses to the unexpected abundance of detail. These and other varied allegorical interpretations (calling up mythology other than Christian—the story of Kore, for example[30]) "decipher" that detail, making it "significant" in ways that contain and control it, and fix its unexpected openness.

The second reading strategy is to expect a dramatic shift or surprise twist—an action plot—to follow the quiet accumulation of detail. Roland Bartel, for example, in his 1977 article, "Life and Death in Eudora Welty's 'A Worn Path,'" risked the reading that already astonished and perturbed Welty—interpreting the story's attention to detail as a prelude to drama fulfilled by news of the grandson's death. After he suggests reasonably that we not allow "the obvious archetypal significance of [Phoenix Jackson's] name to overshadow the uniqueness of one of the most memorable women in short fiction," he suggests surprisingly that Phoenix's character "becomes unusually poignant if we consider seriously the possibility that her grandson is, in fact, dead."[31] Bartel interprets the story's attention to detail as a prelude to drama. In search of a plot to stress, he seeks the action twist that Welty disavowed in her 1974 essay. Other readings that seek plot regularly de-emphasize all the detail of the worn path in favor of interactions at the clinic. Still others turn away from the detail of the path by developing a moral drama in which Phoenix keeps, rather than returns, the hunter's dropped nickel.

My point here is that readers who are uncomfortable with Welty's "photographic" composition—a story framing details in a way to produce slow "exposure"—produce reading strategies that transform the story into a type more readily readable. But the details of this story in themselves expose neither a secret death, a secret allegory, nor a moral choice, but a *woman* whom we see in detail. The figure moving on the Trace is observant, clever, playful, and something of a trickster. Above all, she eludes the too-easy, reductive, dismissive, conventional interpretations imposed first by the white hunter who says, "I know you old colored people," and then by the white clinic nurse who marks her down as "charity" (145, 148). Both *think* they know her story without knowing her. Their automatic categorizing mirrors readings which too automatically categorize the story itself. More recent readings (since 1990) attend to the difference between the story and old plot structures. They read Phoenix as displacing literature's Dilsey characters—African-American characters too readily readable as embodiments of "service" and "charity"—or as displacing its marginalized Clyties—characters whose paths have been too obscured by Sutpen designs.[32]

I do not assert that **"A Worn Path"** is a very experimental story, although I think it is better not appropriated too simply nor too conventionally, that it is better read as a story that obstructs readers' expectations and displaces more conventional story formulas. Like a photograph, it heightens emphasis on subject as color, texture, light, and nuance—and on class and social structure—altering a more traditional emphasis on subject as event. Welty's use of detail as event in **"A Worn Path"** is full of risks; it is also an indication of things to come, particularly in **"No Place for You, My Love"** and **"The Bride of the Innisfallen"** where details are used even less conventionally. Details are instead given more attention and more elaborate development than the characters who live among them and who, in a sense, are overmatched by them.

Early response received these stories with phrases that rejected Welty's use of detail: "top-heavy, overburdened by a mass of detail . . . obscure, undecipherable,"[33] "less plot than ever before,"[34] "virtually plotless," and "unnecessarily indirect and self-consciously elliptical . . . not so much a story as a highly specialized, highly private game."[35] Descriptions and details of place are spoken of as usurping "the vitality that ought to belong to the characters";[36] "revelatory moments" are described as submerged "beneath the attenuated surface of the prose, elusive or out of sight."[37] Characters are described as being viewed "from a distance," and "the weighty burden of communication [as falling] fully on the telling external gesture."[38]

Articles which followed those early ones in rescue, next aggressively read the stories' details as coherent. In those readings, details are all brought into unified focus. For example, Noel Polk, in his discussion of **"The Bride" ["The Bride of the Innisfallen"]** in "Water, Wanderings, and Weddings: Love in Eudora Welty," explains that "everything . . . centers around things that come between husbands and wives."[39] Michael Kreyling's chapter, "Rhythm in Stillness: *The Bride of The Innisfallen,*"[40] similarly uncovers an elusive pattern and coherence in the stories. This second group of arguments strategically writes over readers' experiences of searching for plot amid detail and displaces this uncertain seeking with coherence and, to quote Kreyling's book title, the achievement of order.

What I want to show is that early observation about detail overwhelming character was fair and accurate, even while the companion conclusion that Welty had relinquished coherence and meaning was premature and inaccurate. These stories do lock the reader's attention on arresting but seemingly irrelevant detail. Characters are overwhelmed by place while readers are denied a secure, stable point of view from which to order the fictional world they encounter.

These stories are experimental in that they are more pictorial than dramatic. They blend the short story with a habit specific to American visual arts and to photography in particular. Critical remarks that passages seem "starkly concrete,"[41] overly-detailed, and "though good in themselves . . . [ultimately] irrelevant,"[42] resemble early criticisms of the details in daguerreotypes, once criticized for "depicting the merest surface" in comparison to paintings' "more summed-up statements."[43] A daguerreotype, in contrast to a painting, captured the random detail, expression or gesture as well as the intended ones. But as Hawthorne's character Holgrave—one of photography's first defenders—argues in *The House of Seven Gables,* photographs can bring out a "secret character . . . no painter would [venture] upon, even if he detected it."[44] Framing inconsequential gestures and inconsistent details, photography can give us time to see their significance.

It is perhaps ironic that the frustrations characterized precisely in reviews of ***The Bride* [*The Bride of the Innisfallen*]** circumscribe and so identify the nature of Welty's experimentation. Early critical objections that characters are overwhelmed by a sea of surrounding details are a brief step from recognition that, in their development, these characters are given "the barest means to contend with" the expanse around them.[45] There is a spatial presentation sometimes apparent in Welty's own photographs, in American photography in general, and art critic John MacCoubrey suggests that it pervades American art from the colonial period through the modern. On American canvases he argues, the "figures . . . do not command . . . space, but live tentatively within it." Further, "[t]hey . . . are not given an easy mastery of the space they occupy. Rather, they stand in a tentative relation to it, without any illusion of command over it."[46]

Welty's photograph, *Hamlet, Rodney,*[47] is one of the sort in which figures are given "the barest means to contend with" the space around them;[48] among others are *Union Square, New York,*[49] and *The Mattress Factory/Jackson/1930s.*[50] The last of these is an especially beautiful photograph, filled with repeating shapes and textures such as the recurring lines in the mattress ticking and the wood. The dark space of a workroom is relieved by two small windows and a door opening onto the bright outdoors. Three figures escape the workspace obliquely: in rest. A story is locked in the faces of its two women who look away from work and work space, out the door. The figures of the women are not at the photograph's center—the mattress and space of the workroom dominate. Instead of being central, the figures of the women are cornered by their workspace, and they are drawn to its liminal aperture: the door to another space—one they do not enter. In other Welty photographs, additional figures are also pushed off center by space. In *Home/Jackson/1930s,* for example,[51] the day's gleaming laundry competes with four children for centrality, in part because the children's stares lead us out of the frame toward an unknown horizon or event. The shifting angles of the porch further destabilize the image, and the steps led us out of the frame. Similarly in another porch scene, *With a Dog/Utica,*[52] the relaxed, satisfying comfort of a boy with his dog is compressed into a corner, all but over-balanced by the utility of the screen door, the drying laundry, and carefully stored, serviceable pots and cans. But of all of Welty's provoking uncentered images, my personal favorite is her droll *Too Far To Walk It/Star/1930s*[53] where the ground tilts precariously to run out of the photograph, an untamed chicken threatens to walk into its central space, and a tiny mysterious figure, hard-to-see, is in the back brush. Its annoyed dominant figure, arms akimbo, petulant face pursed with a look between frustration, despair, and contempt, situates her vexed body in a way that clearly discovers her desire as far, far outside of the picture frame. Her body leads a viewer's eye hastily out of the photograph. The space of the photo, the place where its subjects don't want to be, has pushed its figures into a corner. My point about these remarkable uncentered photographs is that their spatial presentations repeatedly suggest the size of the life around the figure—that is, circumstances—large, impinging circumstances.

In *Chopping in the Field,*[54] a woman bent in work, back turned towards us, pushes through the air a fragile, slender hoe that is falling onto an empty field. I compare this figure with the windswept woman who appears on the horizon of Winslow Homer's *The West Wind,* a stormy canvas not dominated by the woman's presence any more than by a dark bush blowing at its center. Both of these figures—central and yet dwarfed—are analogous to the characters of **"No Place for You, My Love"** who stand against an expansive Southern backdrop, "a strange land . . . [that] whether water-covered, grown with jungle, or robbed entirely of water and trees . . . had the same loneliness" (479). The figures are all spatially overmatched. Here I do not mean to suggest that Welty's photographs are not people-centered, as Louise Westling, Suzanne Marrs, and Reynolds Price have observed her published photos to be.[55] But I suggest that in photography as in some American painting, space and its random details often crowd into the focus with people, a composition with which Welty the photographer was familiar and used.

I want to emphasize that as readers travel the road in **"No Place for You, My Love,"** where "dead snakes [stretch] across the concrete like markers—inlaid mosaic bands, dry as feathers, which their tires licked at intervals" (471), their experience of character is to a very great degree subordinated to the apparently designless description of place. The passage cited below is in this sense more representative of the story than any narrative summary, although the segment is one in which character is rather more predominant than elsewhere. Kreyling names it as the story's center, calling the "woman's questions about the man's marriage . . . its moment of risk."[56]

> They moved on into an open plot beyond, of violent-green grass, spread before the green-and-white frame church with worked flower beds around it, flowerless poinsettias growing up to the windowsills. Beyond was a house, and left on the doorstep of the house a fresh-caught catfish the size of a baby—a fish wearing whiskers and bleeding. On a clothesline in the yard, a priest's black gown on a hanger hung airing, swaying at man's height, in a vague, trainlike, lady-like sweep along an evening breath that might otherwise have seemed imaginary from the unseen, felt river.
>
> With the motor cut off, with the raging of the insects about them, they sat looking out at the green and white and black and red and pink as they leaned against the sides of the car.

> "What is your wife like?" she asked. His right hand came up and spread—iron, wooden, manicured. She lifted her eyes to his face. He looked at her like that hand.
>
> Then he lit a cigarette, and the portrait, and the right-hand testimonial it made, were blown away. She smiled, herself as unaffected as by some stage performance; and he was annoyed in the cemetery. They did not risk going on to her husband—if she had one.
>
> Under the supporting posts of the priest's house, where a boat was, solid ground ended and palmettos and water hyacinths could not wait to begin; suddenly the rays of the sun, from behind the car, reached that lowness and struck the flowers. The priest came out onto the porch in his underwear, stared at the car a moment as if he wondered what time it was, then collected his robe off the line and his fish off the doorstep and returned inside. Vespers was next for him.
>
> (472-73)

Here as elsewhere the characters are overwhelmed by the detail of the scene around them—seemingly unfocused detail creating an expanse that de-centers the characters. The catfish and the priest are presented without an obviously determined purpose. One reader has told me that the catfish recalls William Wallace's spring dance with a catfish on his belt in one of the renewing moments of **"The Wide Net"** and so evokes a sort of rebirth that is just missed in the pages that follow; another reader has suggested that the priest evokes a possibility of miraculous resurrection, another sort of rebirth. The priest may be associated with the sacrament of marriage. Here, where a husband avoids speaking of his wife, the priest is exposed in his underwear. His vestments—daily wear, now off duty as our characters are—sway in a "lady-like sweep"; they dance in the hot air. But without a reader's construction (reverie), these details have minimal meaning in relation to this man and woman, more blurred than sharply focused by their surroundings.

Yet oddly the focus may be precisely in this blurring. The details that crowd into this story's frame, suggesting objects and events torn from a continuing, unfocusing life, are unexpected. Even the attentive, familiar, skilled reader who, like Kreyling, listens for the story's repeating rhythms, must contend with those many details that appear in distractingly clear focus. In this modernist short story as in a photograph that emphasizes a stray object recorded by chance in a scene, or a modern painting that intercepts a line that runs off the canvas, Welty's technique conveys a disorder not ordered, an external reality that her characters will not shape to yield a more coherent unity. **"No Place for You"** [**"No Place for You, My Love"**] is the detailed portrait of a space which an action might have dominated but did not. The chance objects and events which exist in that space intensify our sense of the characters' drifting interaction and of the beckoning relationship that "rises like a human and drops back between them."[57] Their resources for asserting themselves over the circumstances of their lives, in this setting on this day at least, are minimal; their surroundings (unnamed circumstances and histories, as well as the details of this landscape) overshadow and limit them as in a photograph that places a figure against a large landscape.

In **"The Bride of the Innisfallen,"** Welty again amasses strikingly sharp, seemingly designless details: for example, the gold pin seen on a woman's hat "in the shape of a pair of links, like those you are supposed to separate in amateur-magician acts" (497).[58] The story records the conversation between passengers on a night train from London, which connects with *The Innisfallen,* a boat bound for Cork. For some thirty pages readers observe the passengers and follow their detailed—seemingly accidental—conversation, looking for some thematic focus. "On they went" (499),[59] the narrator tells us here, echoing the similar line in **"A Worn Path."** For a while we do even without a sense of central figures, as in a type of photograph—Welty's *Political Speech, Political Speaking,* or *The Store,* for example[60]—group scenes in which a viewer looks for a focal center.

It is not until the characters board *The Innisfallen* that the narrative, without remark, gradually rests to focus clearly on one perceiving consciousness. Only when we leave the other characters behind at the customs post in Cork are we absolutely certain that the narrative settles on the quiet American woman. Noel Polk shows how the details focus on a conjugal emphasis long before the bride in white appears on *The Innisfallen*: the young pregnant women traveling with Victor, a little boy who has been to a wedding, the lovers, the conversations—one about a pair of married ghosts, Lord and Lady Beagle, and another about a parrot whose death was perhaps caused by his owner's jealous wife. But to see this focus before the reader finds the American's centrality is unlikely. Until the reader discovers both her point of view and her dilemma, the focusing lens which connects details to her situation is not available. A skilled reader may, as Kreyling does, discover and pursue the story's emphases on brides, on marital relationships, on coming and going from loved ones, on journey. But the connectedness of these themes to character is most available when a reader settles into the viewpoint of the American woman with three pages left to the story. Yet by the time we move into her mind we are rather surprised to find ourselves there. This is because we have moved toward her from such a great distance. The narrative has resembled a film of the woman recorded by a camera initially held at a far range; the film, therefore, is at first filled with all the extraneous characters and details that approach her space. Then the camera moves in on her until suddenly it shares the spot where she stands and looks out from her perspective on the scene.

This thirty-six page story which tunnels toward meaning in its final three pages is, therefore, quite different in reading than in summary analysis. In the reading process, even if beguiled by the train conversations, readers may struggle with a growing anxiety that they have failed to find the key to interpretation, overlooking some obvious focus. Because of Welty's narrative technique, readers become—like the characters themselves—strangers traveling, looking for, as Sontag says of those who travel with a camera, a "device that will help [them] to take possession of space in which [they] are insecure."[61] Our insecurity is the product of Welty's detailed narrative, once described by Chester E. Eisinger as "made up of fragments" and of encounters that "are chanceful."[62] Again, this chanceful randomness makes the story. We may expect a short story more committed to conventional order and meaning, one in which the young American wife would be the obvious focus of the narrative from its outset, one in which the reader could interpret immediately the other characters' remarks either by their effect on the girl or by their relevance to her plight. But Welty frustrates these expectations and leads us quietly to the precarious edge of a genre based routinely on notions of both artistic economy and the selective accumulation of meaningful detail.

Welty's experiment with detail in these stories, at second glance, merges into her multiple experiments with point of view. The speculating narrator and the shifting location of the narrative viewpoint are familiar to Welty readers. Here in **"The Bride,"** these combine with another technique of Welty's, also used in **"Powerhouse,"** for example, where the point of view without remark shifts from its position in the white audience at the dance hall to follow Powerhouse to the World Café in Negrotown during intermission. In these narratives, the movement is from a distant perspective to a privileged selective omniscience which keeps readers uncertain of their distance from the central character and, for the most part, working to move closer.

And we do move closer. These stories initially set us searching for a revelatory gesture that will bring us close, and they finish in our reverie. Yet it would be difficult to classify **"The Bride"** as either a character analysis or an interior drama, two more familiar "plotless" story types. Unlike these forms, Welty's fictions maintain the distance between reader and character by a narrative tendency to conjecture rather than to know. Her fictions may present a narrator's or community's speculations about a focal character (as in **"A Shower of Gold,"** or much less obviously, in **"Powerhouse"** and **"Old Mr. Marblehall"**). But these characters are rarely known in any simplifying sense. The effect suggests the difficulty of knowing others, while stimulating reveries give a speculative substance to unknowable mystery.

In her early stories Welty often allows the narrator, someone in the fiction, to stand between the reader and her story's characters (although some narrators are only obscurely apparent as in **"The Key," "Powerhouse,"** and **"Old Mr. Marblehall"** in comparison to such perfectly obvious cases as **"Why I Live at the P.O."**). But in these two later stories from ***The Bride,*** Welty eliminates the narrating character, while maintaining the distance between reader and characters. The result is fiction which involves the reader differently. The camera's eye technique makes the reader an observer who watches from a well-kept distance. The narrative seems a stranger to its strangers; it lacks facts about them. (Kreyling notes that the details of the American wife's marriage were pointedly revised away by Welty.[63]) The effect is like the impact of Edward Hopper's paintings (I am recalling *Night Windows* [1928], *Rooms for Tourists* [1945], and *Nighthawks* [1943] in particular) which view figures through closed windows. Our point of view is an onlooker's; we peer into a lighted room where strangers are sitting together. Is it for the sake of this effect that **"The Bride"** is not a first person or a more focused third person narrative, and that **"No Place for You"** is not the story of one of the two characters reacting to the other? We, like the characters, are not permitted to settle comfortably. We are outside as if with a camera's point of view.[64]

This technique transforms the reader into a wanderer exploring an unfamiliar territory. It causes us to use our minds as Welty, a shy young woman touring Mississippi when much of it was new to her, admittedly used the camera. We may overcome feelings of uncertainty by focusing on details that seem provocative, telling, the basis for an imaginative reverie. Like Welty's characters, we may be stimulated by the excitement of traveling an unfamiliar literary landscape, and may become unusually observant, developing a photoscopic vision that searches for a detail that will unfold. We may look harder, see more, and not knowing too much about what we see, we may fantasize more. We indulge in the sort of speculation that the characters on the London night train feel for other passengers. Like these characters who wonder about the red-haired boy with "queenly jowls" traveling with an English nurse, and who speculate on what they see (499), we speculate on them. Like the woman leaving the train compartment who flings the others a look that says, "Don't say a word, or start anything, fall into each other's arms, or fight, until I get back to you" (498), we don't want to miss any exposing gesture. And we are all strangers speculating on each other's stories. As characters approach one another, we approach them—through reverie.

Ultimately our movement from discovered obstruction to our own directed reverie is synonymous with Welty's plot in these stories. Abandoning expectations of what plot must be and yielding to suggestion, we discover these plots are like the performances of a knife thrower who "does not pierce but surrounds the living target" (as Welty said of Henry Green's fictional technique).[65] They resemble photographs and are, as Sontag describes photographs, "inexhaustible invitations to deduction, speculation, and fantasy," prompting us to think—or rather "intuit—what is beyond [the surface], what the reality must be if [the surface] looks this way."[66] Reading stories like **"No Place for You"** and **"The Bride,"** we repeat the steps Welty took in her kitchen darkroom—we review what was fortuitously recorded by the camera's unblinking eye; we select significant details from the camera's cropping of reality; focusing on these, we imagine their meaning. Along with Welty, who learned that what she needed to transform one more negative into a valuable print was not machinery but reverie, we convert detail into speculation. Welty's remark on what she learned about the effectiveness of oblique approaches in fiction from taking pictures is to the point: "Anything lighted up from the side, you know, shows things in a relief that you can't get with a direct beam of sun."[67] Her plots are our reveries, begun in her details.

Notes

1. Diana Trilling, "Fiction in Review," *Nation* 157 (2 October 1943) 386-87.
2. John F. Fleischauer, "The Focus of Mystery: Eudora Welty's Prose Style," *Southern Literary Journal* 5 (Spring 1973): 64-79.
3. Edgar Allan Poe, "Twice-Told Tales, by Nathaniel Hawthorne," in *The Centenary Poe,* ed. Montagu Slater (London: The Bodley Head, 1949), 470.
4. Eudora Welty, *Town in a Store Window, Canton* in *One Time, One Place* (New York: Random House, 1971), 52.
5. Roland Barthes, *Camera Lucida: Reflections On Photography,* trans. Richard Howard (New York: Hill and Wang, 1981), 34.
6. Susan Sontag, *On Photography* (New York: Dell Publishing Co., 1973), 91.
7. Barthes, 38.
8. Ibid., 42.
9. Ibid., 43
10. Eudora Welty, "José de Creeft," *Magazine of Art,* February 1944, 46.
11. Eudora Welty, *One Writer's Beginnings* (Cambridge: Harvard University Press, 1984), 75-76.
12. Ibid., 68.
13. Patti Carr Black, in an exhibition catalog called *Welty* (Jackson: Mississippi Department of Archives and History, 1977), did this well as she juxtaposed photographs with selected passages from Welty's writings.
14. Welty, *One Time, One Place,* 7-8.
15. Harriet Pollack, "Words Between Strangers: On Welty, Her Style, and Her Audience," in *Welty: A Life In Literature,* ed. Albert J. Devlin (Jackson: University Press of Mississippi, 1987), 54-81.
16. Welty, *One Time, One Place,* 8.
17. Linda Kuehl, "The Art of Fictions XLVII: Eudora Welty" (1972), in *Conversations with Eudora Welty,* ed. Peggy W. Prenshaw (Jackson: University Press of Mississippi, 1984), 76.
18. Sontag, 99, 159.
19. Eudora Welty, "Is Phoenix Jackson's Grandson Really Dead?," in *The Eye of The Story: Selected Essays and Reviews* (New York: Random House, 1970), 159.
20. Ibid., 160.
21. Ibid.
22. Ibid., 161.
23. Ibid.
24. Neil Isaacs, "Life for Phoenix," *Sewanee Review* 71 (January-March 1963) 75-76.
25. Ibid.
26. Eudora Welty, "A Worn Path," in *The Collected Stories of Eudora Welty* (New York: Harcourt Brace Jovanovich, 1980), 142; hereafter cited parenthetically in the text.
27. Ibid.
28. Welty, "Is Phoenix Jackson's Grandson Really Dead?" 162.
29. Isaacs, for example, asserts that the whole story is suggestive of a religious pilgrimage, and that the grandson is a "Christ-like child waiting for her" (81). Saralyn Daly continues this reading strategy

with Phoenix rising "from the grave-like ditch . . ." in resurrection and then having her shoes tied by a woman who is "more than the angel Isaacs indicates; her odor of roses is characteristic of the Blessed Virgin." "Natchez, 'the paved city,' at Christmas time" suggests "the Celestial City Bunyan's Christian sought" ("'A Worn Path' Retrod," *Studies in Short Fiction* [Winter 1964]: 133-39.) Sara Trefman reads "Phoenix and her grandson . . . as different aspects of the same entity[;] this single being is clearly a symbol of Christ" and details such as the thorns on the trace that "tear at her long, full skirt, thorns that do their 'appointed work'" are a part of the allegory ("Welty's 'A Worn Path,'" *Explicator* 24 [February 1966]: item 56). Marilyn Keys suggests that Phoenix's entire journey is an "[analog] to Passion Week, including several of the very familiar exercises of Christian piety, the Stations of the Cross" ("'A Worn Path': The Way of Dispossession," *Studies in Short Fiction* 16 [Fall 1979]: 354-56).

30. For example, Frank R. Ardolino varies the allegory and mythology, finding that "Phoenix, who effects the rebirth herself, her grandson, and the earth through her perennial healing journey, represents the Kore figure." In his reading, Phoenix, "the nature priestess," is described as "curing her grandson" and "[bringing] about the rebirth of the lost god" ("Life Out of Death: Ancient Myth and Ritual in Welty's 'A Worn Path,'" *Notes on Mississippi Writers* 9 [Spring 1976]: 1-9).

31. Roland Bartel, "Life and Death in Eudora Welty's 'A Worn Path,'" *Studies in Short Fiction* 14 (Summer 1977): 288-90.

32. For example, see Elaine Orr, "'Unsettling Every Definition of Otherness': Another Reading of Eudora Welty's 'A Worn Path,'" *South Atlantic Review* 57 (1992): 57-72; and Barbara Ladd, "'Too positive a shape not to be hurt': *Go Down Moses,* History and the Woman Artist in Eudora Welty's *The Golden Apples,*" in *Having Our Way: Women Rewriting Tradition in Twentieth-Century America,* ed. Harriet Pollack (Lewisburg, Penn.: Bucknell University Press, 1995), 79-103.

33. William Peden, "The Incomparable Welty," *Saturday Review,* 9 April 1955, 18.

34. Alfred Appel, *A Season of Dreams: The Fiction of Eudora Welty* (Baton Rouge: Louisiana State University Press, 1965), 243.

35. Peden, 18.

36. Thomas H. Carter, "Rhetoric and Southern Landscapes," *Accent* 15 (Autumn 1955): 293-97.

37. Appel, 243.

38. Ibid.

39. Noel Polk, "Water, Wanderings, and Weddings: Love in Eudora Welty," in *Eudora Welty: A Form of Thanks,* ed. Cleanth Brooks (Jackson: University Press of Mississippi, 1979), 112.

40. Michael Kreyling, *Eudora Welty: The Achievement of Order* (Baton Rouge: Louisiana State University Press, 1980), 118-39.

41. Robert Penn Warren, "The Love and Separateness in Miss Welty," *Kenyon Review* (September 1944): 258.

42. Fleischauer, 64.

43. Nathaniel Hawthorne, *The House of Seven Gables* (New York: W. W. Norton, 1967), 91.

44. Ibid.

45. John MacCoubrey, *American Tradition in Painting* (New York: Bazillier, 1963) 116.

46. Ibid., 116, 02.

47. Welty, *Hamlet, Rodney,* in *One Time, One Place,* 51.

48. MacCoubrey, 116.

49. Welty, *Union Square/New York,* in *Photographs* (Jackson: University Press of Mississippi, 1989) plate 153.

50. Welty, *The Mattress Factory Jackson/1930s,* in *Photographs,* plate 87.

51. Welty, *Home/Jackson/1930s,* in *Photographs,* plate 61.

52. Welty, *With a Dog, Utica,* in *One Time, One Place,* 33.

53. Welty, *Too Far to Walk It/Star/1930s,* in *Photographs,* plate 41.

54. Welty, *Chopping in the Field,* in *One Time, One Place,* 11.

55. I mean to distinguish between Welty's published photographs (those that were chosen for publication) and the photographs Welty chose to make—represented in the Welty Special Collection of The Mississippi Department of Archives and History. See, Louise Westling, "The Loving Observer of *One Time, One Place.*" *Mississippi Quarterly* 39 (Fall 1986): 587-604; Suzanne Marrs, "Images into Fiction: Teaching the Welty Photographs," (a paper presented at American Literature Association Meeting, Baltimore, 1995); and Reynolds Price, "The Only News," in Welty, *Photographs,* vii-xii.

In their articles on *One Time, One Place,* Westling and Barbara McKenzie ("The Eye of Time: The Photographs of Eudora Welty," in *Eudora Welty:*

Critical Essays, ed. Peggy Whitman Prenshaw [Jackson: University Press of Mississippi, 1979], 386-400) discuss Welty's indirect perspectives—what I discuss as the displacement of figures. Westling suggests that Welty's photos were taken from the side or back because Welty declined to be intrusive on her subjects as more voyeuristic photographers are; these photos were, in Welty's words, "snapped without the awareness of the subjects or with only their peripheral awareness" (183) This indirect quality may or may not display a planned compositional effect. My point is to see a connection between the prints that Welty developed and claimed in their frames and her ideas about what is possible in composition.

56. Kreyling, 123.

57. Welty, "How I Write," *Virginia Quarterly Review* 31 (Winter 1955): 247.

58. Like the experience of reading the story, the image may ultimately suggest complex tasks, puzzles, secrets to be discovered by the barely initiated, but it is also arrestingly and disconcertingly concrete—a puzzle itself.

59. I am referring back to the line from "A Worn Path": "On she went."

60. Welty, *Political Speech,* in *Photographs,* plate 62; *Politically Speaking,* in *One Time, One Place,* 66; and *The Store,* in *Photographs,* plate 25.

61. Sontag, 9.

62. Chester E. Eisinger, "Traditionalism and Modernism in Eudora Welty," in *Eudora Welty: Critical Essays,* 20-21.

63. Kreyling, 137.

64. This alienation delays and limits the reader's involvement with the fiction, and committing to this effect is taking another risk. Plotless works, Wayne Booth tells us, rely on a reader's "desire to discover the truth about the world of fiction" (Wayne Booth, *The Rhetoric of Fiction* [Chicago: University of Chicago Press, 1961], 125). The desire is usually based on curiosity about a character, situation, or—even better—some limited identification with a character.

    The mystery of character is usually central in Welty's fiction in the way that it is in "A Worn Path." Here too that mystery becomes central but gradually so. In these two stories, Welty risks distancing the characters so that identification is not the means through which readers first approach them; that distance yields a different relationship than the one readers have with Phoenix. Those readers expecting close identification sometimes find it difficult to be curious about these characters. The American woman's problem of feeling "too much joy" to share easily—not a common crisis, although not rare in Welty—may make her approach more difficult still. In reading these stories, it is necessary to extend to meet another, rather than to identify easily.

65. Eudora Welty, "Henry Green: Novelist of the Imagination," *Eye,* 22.

66. Sontag, 23.

67. Quoted in Charles T. Bunting, "'The Interior World': An Interview with Eudora Welty," in *Conversations,* 53.

Gail L. Mortimer (essay date summer 1997)

SOURCE: Mortimer, Gail L. "Memory, Despair, and Welty's MacLain Twins." *South Central Review* 14, no. 2 (summer 1997): 35-44.

[*In the following essay, Mortimer probes the nature of perception in* The Golden Apples *by focusing on the essence of difference and sameness embodied by the MacLain twins.*]

A narrative feature of Eudora Welty's fiction that has long been noted is her strategy of doubling or mirroring fictive characters and situations. While this phenomenon appears throughout her fiction, it is particularly evident in her short story sequence ***The Golden Apples*** and, within the collection, most explicitly in her characterization of the MacLain twins, Ran and Eugene. ***The Golden Apples,*** a series of seven related stories featuring residents of Morgana, Mississippi, set in the early decades of the twentieth century, is a text focusing primarily on several of the community's women. Only after presenting four stories contextualized through such feminine experiences as children's piano lessons and summer camp does Welty turn to male protagonists, Ran and Eugene, to create a counterpoint for the otherwise feminine milieu of her book. It is here that her doubling of character and incident becomes most prominent—and enigmatic.

We do not know whether Welty imagined the MacLain brothers as identical or fraternal twins; the text itself offers evidence for either interpretation. Yet while at least one critic insists on a reading of their stories that assumes they are identical twins,[1] I find there are differences between them that are at least as intriguing as the similarities. Moreover, I would like to suggest that through her characterizations of the brothers in their respective stories, Welty may be exploring, as she does elsewhere in this collection, deeper questions about the nature of perception itself and that among these questions is her concern with precisely the problem of perceiving difference and sameness, of making or not making distinctions, and of the discrimination *between* events or their synthesis. The strategy of doubling, then, serves her wider epistemological purpose by virtue of highlighting the characteristics the brothers do (or do not) share in their perception of the world around them.

Studies of early childhood development by object relations theorists and ego psychologists emphasize how we learn to perceive our experience in ways that constitute a personal style of knowing, expressing what Heinz Hartmann calls the "organizing function" of one's ego.[2] Our knowledge is acquired, that is, through our ego's habitual balancing of the need both to synthesize and to differentiate our experiences. Recognizing and remembering differences has much to do with how we locate the meaningful distinctions that direct our behavior. Equally important, though, is the role of *forgetting* distinctions among discrete events, of seeing similarities among them that may then serve as the basis for our reaching accurate conclusions about the nature of similar future events. Our formation of such generalizations enables us to sense continuity and similarity in ways that make up our individual patterns of thought and, beyond that, inform our behavior.[3] Psychoanalysts like Marion Milner tend to associate the habit of focusing on sameness with a developmental stage they call "primary process thinking" (similar in various respects to Lacan's Imaginary) in which perceptions are more or less fluid and pre-verbal.[4] On the other hand, an emphasis on the making of distinctions accompanies what is known as "secondary process thinking" (similar in ways to Lacan's Symbolic realm) involving a recognition of differences and separateness that accompanies more logical thinking and the formation of language. Milner and his peers emphasize that we do not simply grow out of one stage into the next, leaving the former behind. Rather, we continue to use both modes of thought, and it is the nature of the *interplay* between these processes that matters and that reveals our idiosyncratic styles of thinking. In other words, our habitual ways of remembering and forgetting distinctions among perceived phenomena offer insightful glimpses into our personalities and our styles of being in the world.

The stories of Ran and Eugene MacLain—**"The Whole World Knows"** and **"Music from Spain,"** respectively—exhibit a number of striking parallels that extend well beyond Welty's decision to make them twins. Both brothers have occupations that serve as images for the psychological entrapment they feel: Ran works behind a barred window as a bank teller; Eugene works behind one as well, as the repairer of watches. Both men are temporarily alienated from their wives; both wander away from their marriages and take a stranger along with them; both approach bodies of water that seem to signify the possibility of rebirth or renewal; and both back away from the precipice overlooking this water, as they do from the self-knowledge they might have achieved. As several critics have noted, both men resemble T. S. Eliot's J. Alfred Prufrock; they are ineffectual and troubled by a malaise that seems as much cultural as it is personal.

In describing their habits of thought, however, Welty implies distinct differences between them. Ran, as the title of his story indicates, is plagued with events his consciousness—and his community—will not let him forget. *His* whole world—the small town of Morgana, Mississippi—knows all about his wife's, Jinny Love's, affair with another man and closely observes his daily behavior in response to this crisis. We find him unable to dispel the excessive self-consciousness that the town's perpetual gossip keeps alive. Burdened with the details and constant reminders of his situation, as well as by townspeople like Miss Perdita Mayo, who regularly report to him what the town is saying about him "now" and what they expect him to do (or not to do) next, Ran is depicted as incapable of achieving any distance from or perspective on his problems. He appears unable to talk things out with his wife, who deliberately complicates his efforts at reconciliation by living with her mother, by keeping herself surrounded with friends so that he is never alone with her, and by refusing to acknowledge that anything is wrong between them. Left on his own, as she intends him to be, Ran, nevertheless, remains unable to generalize among events and thus learn from his past in order to secure a different future. Perceiving only the individual, discrete events contributing to his ongoing sense of futility and humiliation, Ran fails to synthesize. He cannot forget.

When our capacity to generalize does not function, the result may be an overloading of our memories. Ran's cognitive dilemma is echoed—and exaggerated to the point of parody—in the great Argentinean writer Jorge Luis Borges's well-known story, "Funes, the Memorious." The protagonist of Borges's tale, the eponymous Funes, carries around with him an extraordinary burden of superfluous details. He remembers each separate moment of his experience, every detail he observes, as utterly distinct from every other, so that his very thought processes have ceased to function in ways we would consider normal. The narrator explains, for example, that Funes had a hard time understanding "that the generic term *dog* embraced so many unlike specimens of differing sizes and forms; he was disturbed by the fact that a dog at three-fourteen (seen in profile) should have the same name as the dog at three-fifteen (seen from the front)."[5] He would see and remember "the many faces of a dead man during the course of a protracted wake. . . . [Funes] could continuously make out the tranquil advances of corruption, of caries, of fatigue. He noted the progress of death, of moisture."[6] The result is that Funes withdraws into a darkened room, where he lies looking at a blank wall in order to reduce the inevitable accumulation of impressions burdening his mind, yet even so, he dies shortly thereafter of pulmonary congestion. Borges's story and its conclusion show humorously and brilliantly how the act of forgetting—which we so often thoughtlessly deplore in ourselves—is crucially necessary to enable us to understand our world. As Borges's narrator tells us, "The truth is that we all live by leaving behind. . . . To think is to forget a difference, to generalize, to abstract."[7]

Since no one will let him forget what has happened and what continues to happen in his personal life—or so, at least, he believes—Ran MacLain shares a version of the same sort of "information overload" that Funes experiences. Ran does not move forward in his life or in his understanding of it because there are so many parts of the past that haunt him. His mother-in-law, Lizzie Stark, tells Ran that he started the trouble between himself and his wife, and that his wife's behavior since then—her affair with Woody Spights—is just her response to his originary transgression. Ran cannot understand how Jinny Love's behavior in hurting him and his in hurting her are related, and his failure to see the similarities in their behavior leaves him unable to contemplate the possibility of forgiveness. Moreover, because he has not learned from his experience with his wife, Ran is also unable to anticipate what will later happen with Maideen Sumrall, the country girl he has begun to spend time with in the hope of making Jinny Love jealous. And since Ran does not recognize the problem in understanding as his own, he ends by concluding that the women he knows are "cheats" because he can never forsee their reactions to his behavior.[8]

Ran's oblivion is largely a function of the clutter that prevents his seeing clearly or finding a perspective on the discrete facts of his experience. He plunges through the events of his life in a stupefied state. The first-person narrative in which his story is told gives special vividness to the portrayal of his numbness, his obsessive and at times nearly hallucinatory state of mind. Twice he believes he has attacked others in his rage. First, he pummels his wife's lover, Woody Spights, with a croquet mallet, beating "on him without stopping till every bone, all the way down to the numerous little bones in the foot, was cracked in two" (382). Then he shoots Jinny with his father's old pistol:

> Jinny looked at me and didn't mind. I minded. I fired point-blank at Jinny—more than once. It was close range. . . . I was watching Jinny and I saw her pouting childish breasts, excuses for breasts, sprung full of bright holes where my bullets had gone.
>
> (385)

But the reader of Welty's story, who until now has had little reason to doubt Ran's perceptions, is quickly brought back to the truth of things. Woody is standing up "with no sign of pain," "his blue eyes . . . just as unharmed" (382). And "Jinny didn't feel it. She threaded her needle" (385). Even Ran's mother notes his failure to deal with reality: "*Son, you're walking around in a dream*" (380).[9]

Like his father, King, Ran runs away when his marriage troubles him, for even growing up without a father has not taught him to see the futility and destructiveness of this response. Having learned nothing from the example his father set, Ran seems doomed to copy him. When toward the end of the story he learns the name of Maideen Sumrall's mother, Mattie Will, Ran recalls that he and his brother Eugene had once shared casual sex with Mattie Will as teenagers (an event recorded in **"Sir Rabbit,"** an earlier story in ***The Golden Apples***), and this becomes yet another detail to assimilate:

> And now I was told her mother's maiden name. God help me, the name Sojourner was laid on my head like the top teetering crown of a pile of things to remember. Not to forget, never to forget the name of Sojourner.
>
> (386)

The country girl Maideen, whom he eventually seduces in despair and callousness, just *might be* his own child.

Quite the opposite of his brother in this respect, Eugene MacLain, having escaped from Morgana, Mississippi, to San Francisco, finds that he cannot *remember* relevant facts. He doesn't make connections either, but Eugene's repeated forgetting leaves him perpetually vulnerable to surprise as new events occur for which he has not been able to prepare. Taking a day off from his job and his wife, Eugene wanders the city of San Francisco. Among his reveries on this day of playing hooky, Eugene finds himself longing "to see the world—there were places he longed for the sight of whose names he had forgotten" (399). On the previous evening at the concert, as he now recalls, Eugene had "felt a lapse of all knowledge of Emma as his wife, and of comprehending the future, in some visit to a vast present-time. The lapse must have endured for a solid minute or two . . ." (403). Eugene's forgetting of his wife is only the most recent symptom of his personal distress with his marriage. The day before, he had invited Emma to go on a holiday with him down the peninsula south of San Francisco, but he had forgotten that it was the anniversary of their daughter Fan's death, and his wife slammed the door in his face for his insensitivity and the disastrous timing of his invitation.

During his day in San Francisco, Eugene recognizes the guitarist he and Emma had heard the previous evening. Although he feels rather proud of himself for recognizing the artist "at this distance and from the back" (401), Welty's narrator notes repeatedly during the day they spend together that Eugene cannot remember the man's name (401, 402). Only at the very end of the story is he reminded—by Emma—that the artist is Bartolome Montalbano. When Welty's text finally discloses this name, we, her readers, are meant to remember the mythological significance associated with the Alban Mount in the ancient world. As I argue elsewhere,[10] if we know and recall that sacrifices took place on this mountain that provided for the renewal of a kingdom through the fertility of another vegetative cycle, we understand that Eugene might have initiated such a period of rebirth and renewal for himself had he chosen to act either as a hero or as a scapegoat figure. But Eugene misses his chance because he does not, himself, remember the relevant story. Like the final piece of a puzzle, though, Welty provides us with the clue that makes sense of Eugene's entire day of apparently random wandering. Eugene's excursion with the guitarist has given him opportunities he has failed to recognize and act on for changing the direction of his life.

Both of the MacLain brothers suffer from an indecisiveness that seems at its roots to be related to their mother's emotional primacy in their lives, her continuing motherly expectations. Whereas the community sees Snowdie as very nearly a saint because of her long-suffering patience with her husband King's repeated absences, the boys experience her as a benign but oppressive presence, as the conversations between Ran and Snowdie recorded in **"The Whole World Knows"** make clear:

> *Have you been out somewhere, son?*—Just to get a little air.—*I can tell you're all peaked. And you keep things from me, I don't understand. You're as bad as Eugene Hudson. Now I have two sons keeping things from me. . . . If you were back under my roof,* Mother said, *if Eugene hadn't gone away too. He's gone and you won't listen to anybody.*—It's too hot to sleep, Mother.—*I stayed awake by the telephone. The Lord never meant us all to separate. To go and be cut off. One from the other, off in some little room.*
>
> (375, 386; emphasis in original)

These conversations play back in Ran's mind like an insistent refrain throughout his story, even as he tries to replace them with a meaningful—but thoroughly imaginary—dialogue with his absent father. Snowdie repeatedly expresses her longing to be at the center of her sons' lives because, through the long neglect of her husband, she has discovered a loneliness that only they can alleviate. The sons, for their part, feel all of the guilt and self-consciousness of any child who has "let down" a martyred parent by choosing to live his or her own life. It is in their efforts to escape these feelings of entrapment that Ran and Eugene turn to "real familiar strangers" for company. Being with Maideen Sumrall, Ran decides, "was the next thing to being alone" (377). Although, in their own ways, they try to run away as their father had done, Ran and Eugene take their neurotic responses to their mother with them, projected *now* onto their wives. Ran's inability to forget and Eugene's inability to remember cogent details in their lives constitute variations on a single theme and result in a numbness that leaves them powerless to recognize and deal effectively with the causes of their despair.

* * *

The MacLain twins reveal close affinities with those twentieth-century prototypes of malaise and ineffectuality, J. Alfred Prufrock and William Faulkner's Quentin Compson;[11] all four characters are tortured alike by memories (and hence, anticipations) that ultimately paralyze them within their respective visions of the world. But whereas we find this type of cognitive uneasiness often in early twentieth-century literature, and particularly in modernist literature, within Welty's canon such troubled figures are decidedly rare. There are echoes of Ran and Eugene's despair in just a few figures—each of them male and each of them appearing only in Welty's early stories, collected in ***A Curtain of Green*** in 1941. The most important of these is Howard in **"Flowers for Marjorie"**; to a lesser degree we find hints of Ran and Eugene's particular forms of suffering in the characters Steve in **"Keela, the Outcast Indian Maiden"** and Tom Harris in **"The Hitch-Hikers."** Ran and Eugene, in fact, are the last such figures to appear in Welty's texts.

Howard, in **"Flowers for Marjorie,"** shares so many similarities to the dreamy blundering of Ran MacLain that he may have represented Welty's first attempt to create such a peculiarly tormented figure. Moreover, Howard is so plagued by his awareness of time's passing—like Quentin Compson in Faulkner's *The Sound and the Fury*—that his characterization may well express one of Welty's earliest impulses to address and respond to the fiction of her famous Mississippi neighbor. Howard's imagination taunts him with the unrelenting knowledge of his failure to find work and anticipates in brutal detail the starvation he and his wife now face, so that he can no longer believe in the possibility of altering their future. In terror and insanity, he kills Marjorie to stop time from progressing. Yet immediately after Marjorie's death, events begin to mock him at every turn with the lesson that change *can* happen: Howard wins playing a slot machine and is soon given the key to the city for being "'the ten millionth person to enter Radio City'" (104). Through his inability to generalize and to forget, Howard has generated his own passivity and hopelessness, and by being able to see nothing else, he has brought about his own doom. His numbness is palpable; a messenger boy runs into Howard with his bicycle, "but it never hurt at all" (102). Both Howard and Ran MacLain are victimized by the overwhelming details of their lives; they can envision no alternatives. The striking difference between them, of course, is that although Howard has seemed throughout his story to be in much the same sort of hallucinatory state we often see in Ran, Howard's murder of his wife proves to be all too real.

Two other figures in Welty's early stories resemble Ran and Eugene MacLain, respectively, in their mental habits: Steve in **"Keela"** [**"Keela, the Outcast Indian Maiden"**] and Tom Harris in **"The Hitch-Hikers."** While they do not as fully anticipate the characterizations of Ran and Eugene as does Howard in **"Flowers for Marjorie,"** their depictions offer an early example of how Welty associates failures of memory with the failure of relationships and with an isolation that pervades so many modernist texts. In **"Keela, the Outcast Indian Maiden,"** the protagonist Steve's motives for tracking down the club-footed black man, Little Lee Roy, are to eradicate the memories of his own complicity in Little Lee Roy's abuse in a sideshow. Steve can neither forget nor forgive his failure of compassion in cooperating with the exploitation of Little Lee Roy. As with Ran MacLain, Steve was so preoccupied with the details of his daily existence that it led him into a form of blindness; he simply did not see what was going on in front of him. That his companion Max does not now acknowledge the enormity of what happened is for Steve virtually an insult, and he knocks Max down with his fist: "'I had to do it,' said Steve. 'But I guess you don't understand. I had to hit you. First you didn't believe me, and then it didn't bother you'" (44). Steve's inability to forget makes him somewhat callous as well. Even now he does not know how to begin putting the past behind him. Even now he does not address Little Lee Roy directly, does not apologize, does not offer to make amends.

Tom Harris, a traveling salesman, is so utterly passive about the events in his life that he does not even remember people who once were significant in his life. He meets a girl named Carol at a party, and she has to remind him that they knew one another five years ago, that she had, in fact, been "crazy" about him then "and now too!" (73). Moreover, the reactions to Tom of Ruth, the woman who gives the party, make it clear that he has disappointed her as well, perhaps by taking her presence in his life for granted. Ruth's eyes are said to flash and glare at him, and she makes several ironic (even sarcastic) comments directed at Tom. When he arrives with a bottle of liquor, she cries "'He never forgets!'" (68). The conversation that follows, however, makes the reader suspect that he *always* does; the narrator notes that on this particular evening Ruth chooses not to accuse him of his usual failing, "carelessness or disregard of her feelings" (69). Tom thinks of himself as rootless, as not belonging to any "of these towns he passed through"; he is "free; helpless" (72). But his very dazed movement through life is part of the oblivion that keeps him from recognizing anyone else's feelings and, on the day of the story, any of the clues hinting of the violence to occur between the two hitch-hikers he has picked up.

In these characterizations, Welty participates in the visions of Faulkner and Eliot in that she sees such introspective paralysis, such tormented and flawed relationships with one's memory, as problems faced only by male characters, and only a few of them at that. Strikingly, none of her female characters exhibits anything approaching the despair at events revealed in these men. What might the decidedly temporary presence of such Prufrockian protagonists mean in terms of Welty's larger themes? Critics have noted that Welty turns from writing about isolated and alienated figures to the broader themes of family and community relationships with the appearance of *Delta Wedding* in 1946.[12] To some degree, at least, the disappearance of these brooding male protagonists may echo that shift in thematic emphasis. Their initial presence in her work, however, may also have been a response to her awareness of modernists' concerns with issues of time, memory, and a general preoccupation with the past.[13] We know from Rebecca Mark's powerful study, *The Dragon's Blood: Feminist Intertextuality in Eudora Welty's "The Golden Apples,"* just how much of Welty's work in the 1940's seems to have addressed and responded to various concerns of male modernists like Joyce and Faulkner.

Yet the vast majority of Welty's prose, the wider fictive world that she creates, reveals a markedly different attitude toward memories and the details that comprise them than what we see expressed by such characters as Ran and Eugene and their peers. Typically, Welty's texts—both the tenor of her language and the attitudes of her characters—express a positive pleasure in details, precisely the sort of details recalled through vivid memory. As Harriet Pollack suggests in a companion essay in this issue, Welty's fiction is full of apparently random detail, whose meaning comes to resemble that found in photographs which frame and thus foreground particulars we might otherwise have overlooked or considered irrelevant.[14] Welty's fictive world reveals a plenitude, and an exuberance about that plenitude, that implies a delight in the variety all around us, a sensual pleasure in texture, color, and the particularities of a given scene.

Welty's own memory appears to have equipped her with especially vivid recollections of the past and of the myriad sensory and emotional details that have made up her life and that continue to pervade her observations of the life around her. Welty's fiction affirms that her appreciation of the details of her world is part of a pleasure—utterly basic to the atmosphere of most of her stories—that permeates her vision. Welty is ultimately not at home with the sort of malaise that Ran, Eugene, Howard, Tom, and Steve all feel, or with the sort of ennui that destroys their perspective and kills hope in their lives. Unlike those male modernists who so powerfully chronicled their sense of cultural (and at times, personal) despair, Welty finds palpable satisfaction in the physical world around her, in the details and subtleties of daily life, and her fiction ultimately reflects, as a basic feature of her vision, the plenitude she finds around her and her joy in its discovery.

The distinct differences in tone and atmosphere between the texts of male modernists and those of Welty and other women writers of her time reflect in part a cultural phenomenon that scholars Paul Fussell, Sandra Gilbert, and Susan Gubar have described as a masculine crisis of confidence associated with the devastation of World War I.[15] In their masterful *No Man's Land: The Place of the Woman Writer in the Twentieth Century,* Gilbert and Gubar demonstrate that the post-World War I sense of loss and malaise so often featured in male texts of the period is frequently absent from women's texts, largely as a result of the strikingly divergent experiences of men and women of this era. In the men's absence overseas women often found themselves holding down jobs and taking on roles that left them feeling empowered, highly competent, confident for the first time in their own skills, relatively autonomous, even—paradoxically in such a troubled time—exhilarated by the possibilities they found in themselves and their capacities to deal with the vicissitudes of the work they had undertaken. Eudora Welty seems always to have felt sheer exhilaration about her writing; her sense of her own talents and her love for the possibilities of language have given her prose a vitality and vivid specificity that readers are aware of as they read her fiction. I suspect that the modernist theme she has incorporated into these early stories embodies her attempt to understand more fully the cultural sadness that haunts male modernist fiction, that sense that the individual (male) can scarcely hold his own, let alone be heroic or self-sufficient in the complex and enervating modern world. Welty does not experience the world this way, and she soon leaves this imaginative experiment behind, following her own vision of the world instead, a vision that is characterized by joy at the very intricacies and details of daily life that trouble the failed heroes of male modernist fiction.

Notes

1. Alison Pingree concludes that they are identical twins but at the cost, I think, of ignoring occasions in the novel when people have no trouble telling them apart (see "The Circles of Ran and Eugene MacLain: Welty's Twin Plots in *The Golden Apples,*" *The Significance of Sibling Relationships in Literature,* eds. JoAnna Stephens Mink and Janet Doubler Ward [Bowling Green, Ohio: Bowling Green State University Popular Press, 1993], 83-97). For example, in the first story of the collection, "Shower of Gold," a character, Plez, easily distinguishes between the two boys although they are dressed in costumes for Halloween and have masks over their faces. See Eudora Welty, *The Collected Stories of Eudora Welty* (New York: Harcourt Brace Jovanovich, 1980), 271. All further references to Welty's stories are to this edition and appear parenthetically in the text.
2. Quoted in Victor H. Rosen, "The Relevance of 'Style' to Certain Aspects of Defence and the Synthetic Function of the Ego," *International Journal of Psychoanalysis* 42 (1961): 447.
3. Learning to recognize such perceptual patterns in oneself is, of course, a major goal of psychotherapy.
4. For example, see Marion Milner, "Aspects of Symbolism in Comprehension of the Not-Self," *International Journal of Psychoanalysis* 33 (1952): 181-95, and Charles Rycroft, "Symbolism and Its Relationship to the Primary and Secondary Processes," *International Journal of Psychoanalysis* 37 (1956): 137-46.
5. Jorge Luis Borges, "Funes, the Memorious," *Ficciones,* ed. Anthony Kerrigan (New York: Grove Press, 1962), 114.
6. Ibid., 112-14.
7. Ibid., 113, 115.
8. We should note that the sort of generalization inherent in Ran's seeing the women in his life as "cheats" is hardly illuminating or helpful. It serves merely to deflect his thoughts away from his own responsibility in creating their behavior.

9. My thanks to David McWhirter for suggesting that the hallucinatory quality of Ran's interior monologue demonstrates his living "too much in the Imaginary"; emphasis in original.

10. I discuss this mythological allusion more fully in *Daughter of the Swan: Love and Knowledge in Eudora Welty's Fiction* (Athens: University of Georgia Press, 1994), 102-105. Welty's use of mythology to enhance the implications of her stories is just one example of her sense of the power of memory, and the importance of memory, in structuring what we know. In Welty's view, Eugene's failure of memory clearly circumscribes his life.

11. On correspondences between Prufrock and Eugene MacLain, see especially Michael Kreyling, *Eudora Welty's Achievement of Order* (Baton Rouge: Louisiana State University Press, 1980), 94-100. Quentin Compson and the MacLain brothers are discussed in Rebecca Mark, *The Dragon's Blood: Feminist Intertextuality in Eudora Welty's "The Golden Apples"* (Jackson: University Press of Mississippi, 1994), 146-151, and Mortimer, 99-100.

12. See, for example, Carol Manning, *With Ears Opening Like Morning Glories: Eudora Welty and the Love of Storytelling* (Westport, Conn.: Greenwood Press, 1985), 13-18. In 1946 Welty was also working on some of the stories that were to make up *The Golden Apples.*

13. Consider Herbert N. Schneidau's study, *Waking Giants: The Presence of the Past in Modernism* (New York: Oxford University Press, 1991), for an important reading of this dimension of literary modernism.

14. See Harriet Pollack's "Photographic Convention and Story Composition: Eudora Welty's Uses of Detail, Plot, Genre, and Expectation from 'A Worn Path' Through *The Bride of The Innisfallen*" in this issue, 15-35.

15. Paul Fussell, *The Great War and Modern Memory* (New York: Oxford University Press, 1975); and Sandra M. Gilbert and Susan Gubar, *No Man's Land: The Place of the Woman Writer in the Twentieth Century, Volume 2: Sexchanges* (New Haven: Yale University Press, 1989).

Dennis J. Sykes (essay date spring 1998)

SOURCE: Sykes, Dennis J. "Welty's 'The Worn Path.'" *Explicator* 56, no. 3 (spring 1998): 151-53.

[*In the following essay, Sykes comments on Phoenix Jackson's witnessing of the slow road to racial equality in "A Worn Path."*]

In the notes that accompany his epic poem "The Waste Land," T. S. Eliot says of the blind prophet Tiresias, "although a mere spectator and not indeed a 'character', [he] is yet the most important personage in the poem, uniting all the rest. What Tiresias *sees,* in fact, is the substance of the poem" (218). For Eliot, Tiresias serves as a medium through which characters can transform themselves, a character who links both past events and future occurrences. A similar character exists in Eudora Welty's short story **"The Worn Path."** Phoenix Jackson, herself a blind seer of sorts, reveals through a difficult pilgrimage many of the themes that Welty attempts to convey. As Tiresias witnesses the transformation of the merchant into the Phoenician sailor, so Phoenix Jackson witnesses the Southern black's transformation from slave to citizen. In Welty's **"The Worn Path,"** Phoenix Jackson's thoughts and perceptions, as well as her encounters with other characters, illustrate the theme of impending black equality and amalgamation in the South after the Civil War.

Phoenix's perseverance is soon noticeable, as she pleads with a higher being to "keep the big wild hogs out of my path. Don't let none of those come running in my direction. I got a long way" (142). This woman of one hundred years, nearly blind, and with a cane, struggles onward up the "worn path," toward the city to obtain medicine for her grandson. A parallel exists between the journey described and the plight of the Southern blacks after the Civil War. The Thirteenth Amendment made black people legally free, but their place in a society in which they were previously considered three-fifths of a person was certainly in question. Like Phoenix, they endured an endless struggle, if not against scurrying hogs, then against the thorny bush that "never want to let folks pass" (143).

At times, Welty is even more obvious with her imagery. As Phoenix climbs up the tiresome hill that the path traverses, she notes that it "seems like there is chains on my feet, time I get this far" (143). The unsettling reference to the bound slaves that Phoenix can recall from her long life is clear, yet she continues. While resting on a log, Phoenix has an almost hallucinatory vision: She envisions a boy offering her a piece of marble cake, a proposition, Phoenix says "that would be acceptable" (143). The vision of a slice of black and white cake appears to be a reference to the idea of integration in the South. But "when she went to take it there was just her own hand in the air" (143), an unattainable dream, a utopian fantasy, and Phoenix's struggle continues through the barbed wire and dead corn (144).

The quest for integration seems more hopeful as Phoenix walks out of the woods and into the brightly lit town that is her destination. Upon entering the medical building, Phoenix has an epiphany of sorts, for gazing at the wall, she notices "the document that had been stamped with the gold seal and framed in the gold frame, which matched the dream that was hung up in her head" (147). Phoenix dreams about the day when degrees hang on her grandson's bedroom wall, when blacks can go to college. As she is leaving the doctor's office, Phoenix, with only two nickels in her pocket, has promised to buy her grandson "a little windmill they sells, made out of paper. He going to find it hard to believe there is such a thing in the world" (149). Welty has created through Phoenix a modern Don Quixote. Her grandson's sparring with the windmills will be his quest for freedom, for equality in this new world that has been opened up for him.

The characters Phoenix encounters on this pilgrimage all represent attitudes of whites in the South after the war. Her first encounter is with a hunter who, after running off a black dog, remarks, "Well, I scared him off that time" (146). Welty uses the symbol of the white hunter scaring off the black dog to show the strength of Phoenix's dignity: "'Doesn't the gun scare you?' he said, pointing it at her. 'No, Sir, I seen plenty go off closer by, in my day'" (146). The hunter's attempt to instill fear in Phoenix, a fear she disposed of years ago as she came to terms with her plight in society, fails. The hunter's parting advice for Phoenix comes in the form of a threat: "But you take my advice and stay home, and nothing will happen to you" (146). Phoenix realizes that the importance of the trip far exceeds the possible harm that can be done to her brittle frame. The incident with the hunter symbolizes the resiliency of the black movement toward equality.

In the medical building, the attendant, upon seeing Phoenix, dismisses her with, "Charity case, I suppose" (147). When asked by the nurse about her grandson, Phoenix replies, "We is the only two left in the world. He suffer and it don't seem to put him back at all. He got a sweet look. He going to last" (148). The adoration of her grandson are the final words Phoenix speaks to another character in the book, a parting premonition that the struggle is going to last. Much like the incident with the hunter, Phoenix reiterates here that conflicts are just stones in the road, obstacles in the path.

Work Cited

Welty, Eudora. *The Collected Stories of Eudora Welty.* New York: Harcourt. 1980.

Stephen M. Fuller (essay date fall 1998)

SOURCE: Fuller, Stephen M. "Memory's Narrative Gossamer: Configurations of Desire in Eudora Welty's 'A Memory.'" *Studies in Short Fiction* 35, no. 4 (fall 1998): 331-37.

[*In the following essay, Fuller notes the complex interconnectedness of memories, dreams, and reality in "A Memory."*]

In her introduction to the first edition of ***A Curtain of Green,*** Katherine Anne Porter admits a preference for stories like **"A Memory,"** "where external act and internal voiceless life of the human imagination almost meet and mingle on the mysterious threshold between dream and waking, one reality refusing to admit or confirm the existence of the other, yet both conspiring toward the same end" (Welty 969). Considering waking and dreaming realities provides a way into reading **"A Memory"** because Welty uses the story to probe the texture and quality of and reciprocation between both states of mind. The story unfolds from the perspective of a first-person narrator who recalls her thoughts as they came to her on a summer morning in adolescence. Currents of desire swell in the young woman who lounges at a lakeside and ponders her inchoate love for a boy whom she has only brushed past on the stairs at school. Despite not knowing him and fearing his unknown, perhaps less than desirable, social standing, she loves him obsessively. This memory, however, yields to the overbearing and intruding presence of a family of bathers, who preoccupy her thoughts for the remainder of the story.

Memories abound in **"A Memory,"** overlapping, mingling, and bleeding into one another. The narrator's memory contains multiple memories. Welty's use of the indefinite article in the story's title suggests a single recollection; however, her narrative demonstrates that strands of memory cannot exist in isolation, and that they meet, elide, and merge with one another in a psychic reservoir where the "strands are all there: to the memory nothing is ever really lost" (933). **"A Memory"** encourages readers to separate and disentangle one memory from another, yet attempting to do so only tightens the bonds that ensure that each recollection remains contiguous with those memories surrounding it and positively not singular or discrete. For Welty, it seems that memory consists of a web of joining and linking connections and associations, which together form part of a larger entity. Late in her career, she still appears to hold to such an understanding when, in *One Writer's Beginnings,* she describes her mother's mind as a "mass of associations. Whatever happened would be forever paired for her with something that had happened before it, to one of us or to her. It became a private anniversary" (858). Moreover, in the conclusion to her memoir, she defines memory in terms that suggest that the tributaries of experience empty into a pool of remembrances:

> the greatest confluence of all is that which makes up the human memory—the individual human memory. . . . Here time, also, is subject to confluence. The memory is a living thing—it too is in transit. But during its moments, all that is remembered joins, and lives—the old and the young, the past and the present, the living and the dead.
>
> (948)

In **"A Memory,"** Welty exposes the gossamer of interconnected narratives that constitute a living memory. The narrator's first memory, her lounging at the lakeside, has another memory, the boy at school, nested inside. Further, a more primary, and, therefore, more disfigured and disguised recollection embeds itself within the nested memory. The initial remembrance of the lazy day at the lakeside, then, contains two interrelated reminiscences. Daydreaming about the boy at school triggers the most repressed and deeply rooted memory of the story: the narrator dreams of a family of bathers, who come to assume the position of her own family and who embody an oedipal scenario. The oedipal dream temporarily displaces the present desire for the schoolboy; however, ultimately, the two memories fuse together to form a single living narrative of love that accompanies and modifies rather than "destroy[s] the 'recovered dream'" (Lief 343).

Lounging at the lakeside forms the focus of the narrator's first memory. Welty depicts a pubescent girl who feels threatened by the seemingly unforgiving austerity of the external world, which she processes through the frame that she creates with her fingers. Through this viewfinder, sunlight, mirrored and concentrated by the lake's surface, glares threateningly and ominous "dark rounded oak trees" (Welty 92) surround her projection "like the engraved thunderclouds surrounding illustrations in the Bible." The severity of a Sunday school education tinges the play of childhood with anxiety. The girl's body demands its desires sated, but her Christian upbringing seems to militate against such sexual fulfillment. Satisfying her desire in the external world appears out of the question for this girl.

The first memory also yields information about the girl's relationship with her parents, who shield her from what "was not strictly coaxed into place" (92). This sheltering and repressive overprotection, however, intensifies the girl's obsession "with notions about concealment" (93). For example, she fantasizes about the boy at school who might live in a "slovenly and unpainted" house and whose parents might "be shabby—dishonest—crippled—dead" (94). The girl feels shameful about the hostilities she has for her parents, who kept things from her, and this hostility makes compulsive her desire for exposure: "from the smallest gesture of a stranger I would wrest what was to me a communication or a presentiment" (93). Gestures of strangers, such as the boy at school, thrill the girl who harbors yet resents her inherited middle-class proprieties.

The lakeside setting supplies an appropriate location for the flowering of the young girl's sexuality. She has spent the whole summer lounging, here, beyond her parents' control, and, having just finished swimming, she now rests spent and languid on the sand. Immersion in lakes or bodies of water in Welty often signals transformation or, at least, the potential for it. The girl seems to welcome her sexual awakening even if her parents "would have been badly concerned if they had guessed how frequently the weak and inferior and strangely turned examples of what was to come showed themselves to me" (92). She rejects her parents' warnings, though, and embraces the dark depths of the lake and all the unconscious desires and potential fulfillments that its deepness suggests.

The first memory's embracing of desire informs the narcissistic eroticism of the second, nested recollection. Perhaps fearing the social and familial repercussions of satisfying her desire without, the girl loves within, imaginatively. She recreates the brief encounter on the stairs with the boy at school, and the imaginative control she exerts over the action exalts her and heightens the sense of love she experiences. In her contact with the boy, she recognizes loving at once: "I was in love then for the first time: I had identified love at once" (93). This immediate recognition, however, suggests a love not experienced for the first time, but one familiar because of an earlier encounter since repressed. As we shall see, her love for the boy finds its provenance in her imagined liaison with her father. The desire generating both fantasies (for her father and the boy), however, remains "hopelessly unexpressed."

The nested memory shows the girl's megalomania; in psychoanalytic terms, she overvalues her thoughts. For her, reality and the mind's contrivance of it appear inseparable. In *Notes Upon a Case of Obsessional Neurosis,* Sigmund Freud explores such megalomania and theorizes that the overvaluation of thoughts in obsessional neurotics produces such a narcissistic affect (10: 153-249). Later, in *Totem and Taboo,* he uses the phrase "omnipotence of thought" to describe "the overvaluation of mental processes as compared with reality" (13: 87). In **"A Memory,"** the girl's compulsive fantasizing demonstrates her "omnipotence of thought" in operation. For example, she admits to "think[ing] endlessly" (Welty 93) on the scene at school until thoughts of her seduction come to replace the actual occurrence. For her, the brushing on the stairs simulates the light caressing and pressing associated with an actual sexual encounter. Perpetually rehearsing the brushing until "it would swell with a sudden and overwhelming beauty, like a rose forced into premature bloom for a great occasion," she fetishizes the imaginatively realized scene.

Welty emphasizes the girl's preoccupation with herself as a sexual object by describing the bloom of her love as "forced" and "premature." Bringing the rose to flower before its time demands considerable mental exertion. The bloom remains in the bud unless it blossoms over time or by coercion. This second memory, which embeds itself within the first, has the quality of a masturbatory fantasy, producible on demand. The girl's obsession with the scene on the stairs belies an essential narcissism of which overvaluation forms an "essential component" (Freud 13: 89). Her recollection of the brushing swells as a result of the girl's compulsion to bring the moment to an only imagined climax.

The second memory also negotiates the trauma associated with the girl's first period. Her repressive childhood leads her to find comfort in the dreary regularity of the school day and especially Latin class, the setting for what "was unforeseen, but at the same time dreaded" (Welty 93). While in class, the boy whom she "watched constantly" suddenly bends and bleeds from his nose: "I saw red—vermilion—blood flow over the handkerchief and his square-shaped hand; his nose had begun to bleed." His bleeding comes as a "tremendous shock" to the young girl who grows limp and faints. The boy's flooding blood suggests the girl's first and "unforeseen" menstruation, and, in the girl's mind, the beginning of her menstrual flow gets displaced by and associated with the story of the boy's bleeding in the schoolroom. Her sense of shock at the bleeding and her need to conceal this evidence of her sexual blooming forces the displacement.

In this schoolroom scene, Welty emphasizes the connection between the girl and the boy by describing the boy's hand as "square-shaped." In the first memory, the young girl's hands make "small [rectangular] frames" (92), too. Following the bleeding, she remembers the teacher (perhaps a screen for her mother) speaking "sharply in warning" (93). The traumatic moment of menstruation, followed by castigation, seemingly leaves an indelible mark on the storyteller's consciousness. Perhaps the narrator still fails to recognize her sexual potential and continues to feel the guilt of her teacher's/mother's reproach. The adult looks to the child within her for an explanation as to "why, ever since that day, I have been unable to bear the sight of blood?"

The narrator twice refers to the incident on the stairs as the lengthy tale of her love; she calls it "a very long story" (94) and a "long narrative" (97). Two principal recollections overlap to make the narrative of the storyteller's love: the scene on the stairs and the oedipal memory that it triggers in the dream of the bathers which follows. Welty clearly means to present both memory and dream as seamlessly connected to one another. She joins the remembered past and the present moment at the beach together by describing the children at the lakeside running "like a needle going in and out among my thoughts" (94). The stabbing needle and the "upthrust oak trees" link the present to the past and take on a phallic significance when considering the dream of the bathers who perform the oedipal drama. The needle and the oaks anticipate the dream's central presence—the father.

When Louise Westling writes that the girl's thoughts "about [the family's] untidy physical reality intertwine with her fantasies about the boy in her school who is the object of her first infatuation" (65), she accents Welty's intentional conflating of the real and the imagined. Welty's story disturbs the separation of the actual and the imagined when she writes, "I still would not care to say which was more real—the dream I could make blossom at will, or the sight of the bathers. I am presenting them, you see, only as simultaneous" (94). I suggest that the young girl dreams the family of bathers because their sudden and mysterious appearance surprises her: "I did not notice how the bathers got there, so close to me. Perhaps I actually fell asleep, and they came out then." The girl dreams up the family who materialize and manifest themselves in her imagination.

Other evidence further suggests that the young girl dreams the family. Welty writes that at the water's edge the "grown-up people" lie sprawled; however, earlier in the story, the narrator tells us that only children or older people occupy the park "since this was a weekday morning" (92). Should not the grown-ups be at work? Moreover, Welty describes the family curiously as "loud, squirming, ill-assorted" (94) and "thrown together only by the most confused accident." The chaotic disorder of this tableau closely resembles the organized confusion of a dream.

The dream does not present a harmonious family unit, however, but one riven by sibling hostilities and oedipal divisions. In this dream, the family figures as a displaced representation of the narrator's own kin, and it renders them in the most shocking detail, wholly antithetical to the picture of respectable, middle-class propriety we might have formed. For example, the elder brother asserts his dominance by persecuting the younger as his rival, and both brothers mock and show contempt for their father by encircling him and "pitching sand into the man's roughened hair" (96). The beach family knows little restraint and seems to relish ugliness; they squabble and insult each other and, in their bathing costumes, present a provocative yet repelling mise-en-scène. The depiction suggests the unacknowledged, repressed side of the narrator's family life.

The dream's trio of husband, wife, and child lie suggestively entangled "in leglike confusion" (95). In this oedipal triangle, the dreamer corresponds to the young girl lying at her father's feet, an indication of her servility and adoration, and she registers her hostility toward her mother through the derogatory description of her body: "She was unnaturally white and fatly aware, in a bathing suit which had no relation to the shape of her body. Fat hung upon her upper arms like an arrested earthslide on a hill." Westling notes the depiction of the woman who seemingly nears disintegration: "The woman's body is associated with enormous features on the landscape, but rather than providing a sense of solidity, it seems surrealistically fluid and ready to collapse" (65). The young girl fumes and wishes ruin on her mother; the narrator feels her rage explicitly, describing her anger as a "genie-like rage" (Welty 95) pent-up within, and, appropriately, the girl wears a "bright green bathing suit" which likely reflects her unconcealed jealousy of her mother.

The girl clearly disdains her mother and laughs hysterically when her father plays a joke on his wife by pouring sand down the front of her bathing costume, making a grotesque third breast that hung "brown and shapeless" (96). The daughter takes succor from her father's act of disfigurement because she still has a youthful "narrowed figure" (95), whereas her mother has a body marked by childbirth and age: "Her breasts hung heavy and widening like pears into her bathing suit." The girl leaps to her feet, her legs "jumping and tottering" (96) like a newborn foal and, energized by the slight, joins the game of chase with her brothers.

The young girl's dream, though for her really a nightmare, shames her, and its content disturbs her austere moral sense. Contrary to the narrator's sober and restrained descriptions of the boy at school, here, she notes the older brother as "greatly overgrown" (95) and bulging from his swimming costume. She attempts to blot out the family's "moans and their frantic squeals" (97) and "the fat impact of all their ugly bodies upon one another," but these powerful figments, which demonstrate the erotic at work in the family unit, persist. The man bather, who embodies a memory trace of the girl's first stirrings of desire for her father, overwhelms her "most inner dream, that of touching the wrist of the boy I loved on the stair." The oedipal fantasy, which has her father at its nucleus, displaces the pubertal fantasy of her schoolboy love, and the "heavy weight of sweetness" that she feels, and then surrenders to, comes attached to the memory of her father, masked as a bather. The nightmare's return to infancy exposes the potency of a first and unquenchable love that remains unfulfilled and haunts the narrator even as a woman.

When the girl finally emerges from her reverie the bathers have, like a dream, mysteriously dissipated. As she comes to consciousness, the dream continues to affect her, the sight of the "unfinished bulwark" making her feel victimized. The sand bulwarks had surrounded the bathers' bodies furnishing protection whereas now they stand breached, a powerful image of the girl's compromised psychic defense that produces Porter's double reality of dreams and waking life. Averting her eyes, the girl spies the weathered and "small worn white pavilion," and in pitying it, she pities herself and weeps.

In *One Writer's Beginning,* Welty writes that "Learning stamps you with its moments. Childhood's learning is made up of moments. It isn't steady. It's a pulse" (847). Stamped moments pulse in **"A Memory,"** too. A woman takes a backward glance at her girlhood and at the particular moments that have had crucial significance in bringing her to the present. This early story demonstrates the notion of memory that Welty would still maintain four decades later in *One Writer's Beginnings.* The narrator of **"A Memory"** recalls moments separated in time and location but brought into conjunction or confluence through the medium of a living transitory memory. The incident on the stairs, together with the dream it provokes, forms a central part of the long narrative of her love. In *Eudora Welty,* Ruth Vande Kieft notes that "This [squirming family] is the vision of reality which must be squared to the dream" (29). However, I suggest that the dream and the reality form part of a single thread in her love's history that comprises both memories spliced inseparably to one another.

Works Cited

Freud, Sigmund. *Notes Upon a Case of Obsessional Neurosis.* Strachey vol. 10.

———. *Totem and Taboo.* Strachey vol. 13.

Lief, Ruth Ann. "A Progression of Answers." *Studies in Short Fiction* 2 (1965): 343-50.

Strachey, James, ed. and trans. *The Complete Psychological Works of Sigmund Freud.* London: Hogarth Press and the Institute of Psychoanalysis, 1953-74. 24 vols.

Vande Kieft, Ruth M. *Eudora Welty.* New York: Twayne, 1962.

Welty, Eudora. *Stories, Essays, & Memoir.* Ed. Richard Ford and Michael Kreyling. New York: Library of America, 1998.

Westling, Louise Hutchings. *Eudora Welty.* Totowa, New Jersey: Barnes, 1989.

Helen Hurt Tiegreen (essay date 1999)

SOURCE: Tiegreen, Helen Hurt. "Mothers, Daughters, and *The Golden Apples.*" In *Southern Mothers: Fact and Fictions in Southern Women's Writing,* edited by Nagueyalti Warren and Sally Wolff, pp. 142-55. Baton Rouge: Louisiana State University Press, 1999.

[*In the following essay, Tiegreen views the mothers and daughters in* The Golden Apples *as figures struggling with the expectations of their community and the strain that this places on their relationships with one another.*]

> [In Morgana] nobody . . . was surprised at anything. . . . They only hoped to place [others], in their hour or their street or the name of their mothers' people. Then Morgana could hold them, and at last they were this and they were that.
>
> —Eudora Welty, ***The Golden Apples***

Eudora Welty's ***Golden Apples,*** a collection of stories which may also be read as a novel, revolves around the lives and activities of two generations of Morgana, Mississippi townspeople.[1] As in most small towns, everybody knows everybody else's business, and one can easily "place" kin and connections by the name of their "mothers' people." For this tale is primarily about women, although the beguiling and legendary King MacLain appears throughout from time to time, staying just long enough to produce twin sons and countless "orphans," as folklore has it. When the women aren't whispering about King, they are involved in the traditional southern woman's activities—cooking, child-rearing, sewing, gardening, nurturing, and participating. These everyday activities are the expectations, the requirements, the community imposes upon its women. What's more, they may even be imposed by women—by mothers upon their daughters. Sometimes the expectations are too great; they may stifle, overwhelm, or destroy the individual. Rarely do they leave her with time for herself, or even a vision for her life. As each daughter thus struggles to define herself in the shadow of her mother, all of Morgana watches to see how she fulfills her role.

In Morgana, not many mothers or daughters have a chance to pick up any of Atlanta's golden apples; rather, the destinies of most are predetermined. Daughters remain in the social caste of their mothers from their birth to her death or beyond. Those who try to break away, such as talented and spirited young Virgie Rainey, meet with community disapproval and gossip. Virgie spends half her life resisting the restraints placed upon her, and not until her mother dies does she break free. Others, such as Cassie Morrison, who becomes a spinster piano teacher and caregiver to her aging father, devote themselves to a life-time of martyrdom. Still others, such as Jinny Love Stark, who marries one of King MacLain's twins, emulate the parent in smug self-aggrandizement, both mother and daughter exercising control over others, sometimes in contest, in the absence of control over their own lives. These three daughters and their mothers represent the citizenry of Morgana—the plain country people, the better-educated civic leaders, and the controlling aristocracy—all of whom unite in everyday activities in this small southern community. The daughters, just as their mothers before them, are expected to provide continuity and conformity to the system.

* * *

Cassie Morrison and her mother are tragic victims of community expectations. Mrs. Morrison, the only female in the set of stories who at first appears to have no given name, not even in Welty's preliminary cast of characters, quietly puts a gun to her head one day and pulls the trigger. Everyone is surprised, to say the least; she had seemed light-hearted enough, relaxed, "flighty" almost. But apparently somewhere along the way Mrs. Morrison lost herself and her identity. She had done everything so well—wearing a pretty, flowery dress to Cassie's June recital, one that was "just right for a mother" (63), Cassie thought, so "right" that Cassie wished Mrs. Morrison had been there earlier when Jinny Love's mother had turned to inspect the other mothers. Perhaps to rebel against such inspection, Mrs. Morrison was always late, although two intriguing phrases here suggest a deeper interpretation of her constant tardiness: she was late, "perhaps because she lived so near," (a typical Welty phrase that insists upon the need for love *and* separateness) and because she could not arrive on time "to save her life" (63). This cliché takes on a more ominous tone in retrospect, as it foreshadows her ultimate choice between life and death. Mrs. Morrison is most poignantly depicted when she joins a "lackadaisical, fluttery kind of parade" of ladies en route to an afternoon Rook party: according to the narrative voice, she was "*absorbed* into their floating, transparent colors" (24, emphasis added).

Mrs. Morrison does her best to conform to Morgana society, but she cannot accommodate her dour husband, her son and daughter, and the men and women of the community without becoming spiritually absorbed into nothingness. The female population of Morgana shifts to accommodate and meet whatever expectations are present, and Mrs. Morrison never rebels against going with this flow. If she ever desires to do so, she is stymied by a lack of societal precedent to follow or a vision for individual power—the power to say no. Elaine Upton Pugh, referring to various dualities that exist in Morgana, suggests that "the female characters in ***The Golden Apples,*** on the whole, tend to accept contrarieties" with "little struggle for power." She notes that "the actions of the women are not so much directed toward conquering 'kingly power' as toward accommodating. . . . Sometimes the women's mode of acceptance is carried so far as to become self-destructive."[2]

Only in looking back do the clues to Mrs. Morrison's discomfort with Morgana's social expectations become significant, and her small habits and mannerisms expose her inner tensions. Although she seems relaxed at her daughter's recital, "not betraying [Cassie], after all," at its conclusion her yellow program, which appears to be folded nervously into a little hat (64), suggests her self-conscious isolation from the group of mothers. Similarly, she is excessively casual about a neighbor's exhibitionism and King MacLain's amorous pursuits, but her finger revealingly traces "a little pattern on the screen door" (81). All the while, she puts on the face that pleases her family and friends, the face of a gracious southern lady. Her laughter remains "soft and playful but not illuminating" (43) and belies her underlying stress. Though her husband does not like "for people not to be on the inside what their outward semblances led [one] to suppose" (82), subtle hints indicate that building inside Mrs. Morrison is a growing awareness of her lost dreams and a quiet revolution against such never-ending conformity. She complains to Cassie that a metronome is "an infernal machine" (40). "Mercy, you have to keep moving," she protests, yet she, like clockwork, keeps moving through each day, forgoing any possibility of developing her creative self. Cassie wonders if she could have played the piano. "Child, I could have *sung,*" she exclaims, and "she threw her hand from her, as though all music might as well now go jump off the bridge" (41). With this metaphorical language of suicide, Welty suggests that what Mrs. Morrison could have done creatively with her life weighs heavily upon her.

For survival, she in a sense removes her inner self from her surroundings; wistfully talking "to the wall," she tells her son, Loch, about the fanciful party plate served at the Rook party—"a swan made of a cream puff" with "whipped cream feathers, a pastry neck, green icing eyes." In her longing for creative expression, she "sigh[s] abruptly" (83). Young, adventurous Loch, bedridden with a fever all summer, hears "little waits in her voice" and sees her as "just a glimmer at the foot of his bed" (82). Mrs. Morrison is not an individual to her family or the community, but an enabler and presence. Franziska Gygax sees her as the "glimmering girl" or spiritual muse of whom Yeats speaks in "The Song of Wandering Aengus," a poem that runs through young Cassie's mind; Mrs. Morrison becomes only a "glimmer" in her own mind as well, for she exists solely for the gratification and inspiration of others.[3]

Mrs. Morrison's husband, a practical, no-nonsense newspaper editor, is apparently of no help to his wife in her plight. Cassie thinks that her mother's laughter is "like the morning light that came in the window each summer breakfast time around her father's long head, slowly [making] its solid silhouette where he sat against the day" (43). Her mother's early-morning gaiety, however, dissipates in the face of Mr. Morrison's moral uprightness. He sits "against the day" as the voice of a community that does not reward spontaneity. Further indications of Mrs. Morrison's despair emerge. Cassie reflects, for instance, that when her sensitive mother told bad news, "she wore a perfectly blank face and her voice was helpless and automatic, as if she repeated a lesson" (43). Mrs. Morrison's mechanical response protects her from railing against reality, for to whom in this community can she express herself? Loss of control is out of the question.

Life in Morgana ultimately asks too much of Mrs. Morrison. Although she can discreetly remove herself from the inane babble of political gatherings ("Cassie would try to stay in sight of her mother, but no matter how slightly she strayed . . . when she got back to their place her mother would be gone" [46]) or from Miss Eckhart's grief and pain at her sweetheart's burial (Cassie noticed she "had slipped away" [48]), she has no sanctuary from the day-to-day strain of living—and she finally removes herself from life itself. Her suicide reflects the utter loneliness of trying to please and care for everybody but herself, of meeting every social expectation this small southern town demands.

Cassie Morrison is as conscientious and as exquisitely sensitive as her mother. Moreover, she is as unable to seize control of her life and act on her desires as her ineffectual mother was. She cannot rebel against expectations, nor can she overcome her guilt over her mother's suicide. Unlike her mother, she perseveres, but only through the sacrifice of her womanhood to an ailing, childlike father and a restrictive community. Gygax observes that "Cassie . . . does not resemble the 'glimmering girl' [of Yeats's poem] so much as she reminds us of the [poet's] desire for fulfillment."[4] Unfulfilled, that desire cripples Cassie emotionally, but she feels bound by duty to her father, her mother's memory, and the town.

Even as a young girl, Cassie perceives the restrictions the town imposes upon women who do not conform, particularly upon women such as her music teacher,

Miss Eckhart (an "outsider") and Virgie Rainey, Cassie's unconventional friend. These restrictions are somehow more obvious when women are "different," she thinks. The fear of being different ultimately dominates her life. Although Cassie can sense the "terror and pain in an outsider," she perceives that it is "not so easy to be sorry about it in the people close to you" (46), and knows that "there could have been for Miss Eckhart a little opening wedge—a crack in the door" of acceptability among the townswomen. With rare self-knowledge, however, she admits that "if I had been the one to see it open . . . I might have slammed it tight for ever" (59). Just as her mother kept an expressionless face when relating bad news, Cassie, who "stared down at her . . . shoes" (48) during Miss Eckhart's bizarre display at Mr. Sissum's funeral, shields herself from the pain of others.

She finds her own solution in Miss Snowdie MacLain, King's wife, who, she thinks, stays kind "through always being far away in her heart" (56). This type of distancing is what her own mother attempted, unsuccessfully, for self-preservation. Cassie further perceives that her mother kept her taking piano lessons after the other mothers had abandoned the eccentric Miss Eckhart and she, the child, "had to make up for her mother's abhorrence [to Miss Eckhart], to keep her mother as kind as she really was" (56). Gail Mortimer suggests that Mrs. Morrison may have been jealous of Miss Eckhart's role as an artist, and for this reason kept Cassie taking lessons.[5] In any case, Cassie recognizes her mother "could not help but despise Miss Eckhart . . . [and] despised herself for despising" (56).

Teenaged Cassie, who even when tie-dyeing a scarf keeps "her gaze at a judicious distance from the colors she dipped in" (32), like her mother does not know what to do with her deepest, most passionate feelings, so she seals them off. Once, during a sudden rainstorm, she finds herself a captive audience to Miss Eckhart's rich and personal interpretation of a Beethoven sonata; Cassie stands, listening, in the back of the room "with her whole body averted as if to ward off blows. . . . She began to think of [other things]; . . . that was one way" to deal with the intensity of the music (50). Cassie has the temperament, determination, and commitment of the true artist, but she, like her mother, is too busy accommodating the community to find a proper outlet for her talents. Lacking the rebellious spirit of Virgie Rainey, she allows the community to determine her future by awarding her a music scholarship that should have gone to Virgie. Later recalling that "she had seemed to be favored and happy," Cassie now sees herself—"without even facing the mirror" as "pathetic—homeless-looking—horrible." In her insecurity, she sees "the gathering past [come] right up to her," engulfing her "like a wave." Anguished, she thinks that "next time it would be too high." At the apex of her penetrating self-realization, "the wave moved up, towered, and came drowning over her stuck-up head" (33). Now thoughts of Yeats's poem fill Cassie's mind and surround her, but she, again like her mother, continues to conceal her despair, settling for a kind of internal isolation as she surrenders to community expectations.

Plainly, Cassie is in a trap, and even as a teenager begins to separate herself from the actuality of life. She watches, through a window and "standing scared" (33), Miss Eckhart's fearful preparations for setting afire the abandoned house next door, "seeing [Miss Eckhart's] knowledge and torment beyond her reach" (68); later, on a hayride with her friends, she "let nobody touch even her hand" (84). Pitifully, she realizes she is experiencing abnormal inhibitions and, recalling the neighborhood exhibitionist, Mr. Voight, she acknowledges to herself that "without thinking, she could *be* Mr. Voight," a thought that was "more frightening still" (43).

Cassie is awash in loneliness. Like her mother, who "opened [Cassie's door] to come in, only to exclaim and not let herself be touched, and to go out leaving the smell of rose geranium" (32), once she reaches adulthood, her life is empty. A spinster, she devotes her time to teaching music in Morgana, caring for her demented father, and tending a floral shrine—a creation of her own—to her dead mother. Pathetically, this memorial saves her from guilt. A giant flower bed spelling out her mother's name, it occupies the front yard of the Morrison home. Cassie never utters the appellation she perpetuates in the front yard, referring to it only as "Mama's Name;" the reader doesn't know what that name is until Virgie Rainey, always the nonconformist, responds to Cassie's proud description of the shrine: "I guess it takes a lot of narcissus to spell Catherine" (239). "Two hundred and thirty-two bulbs!" is the quick and prideful response.

Cassie devotes herself to this memorial, feeding and separating bulbs, and daily directing her guilt into the soil. "You'll never get over it, never!" she tells Virgie (239), who, in contrast, finds release at her mother's death. But Cassie perseveres, facing "those yellow Schirmer [music] books: all the rest of her life" (56), admitting that no one ever plays her piano now except her students. Her final words in ***The Golden Apples*** are wistful and pitiable; she tells Virgie, "You'll go away like Loch. . . . A life of your own, away—I'm so glad for people like you and Loch, I am really" (240). Unlike Virgie and Loch, who have the courage to step out of the circle, Cassie remains in Morgana. One suspects that she, who will not "let herself be touched," will, like her mother, also "go out leaving [only] the smell of [flowers]."

* * *

Virgie Rainey's dilemma is quite different from Cassie's. She has abundant musical ability, requiring very little effort on her part; but because she does not get the town's music scholarship, her education ends and she begins playing piano at the picture show. Unrestrained and passionate, whether cavorting as a child, playing the piano (Virgie wouldn't play with the metronome), or confronting her early sexuality, Virgie is always a free spirit. Even a free spirit, however, can be forced into a life of thwarted dreams if the pressure is great enough, and Virgie's vitality may be partly in defiance of the expectations of the community.

In the first place, Virgie's mother, Katie, a hard-working, resourceful country woman who recalls carefully saving her bulb money so that she could afford to get married, has very little use for adventure. She is content to accept her lot in life and make the best of it. Proud of having a daughter—she feels superior to Snowdie MacLain who gave birth to twin boys, "being that lucky over Snowdie" (10)—she never quite adjusts to the fact that her daughter is of a different temperament than she. "Where's my girl? Have you seen my girl?" (205) she wants to call out in her old age, waiting by the road for Virgie to come home from work and do the chores Katie always did.

Virgie wants more than life as Katie Rainey's daughter offers her. Knowing that the Raineys are looked down upon in Morgana—"[Cassie] didn't go home from school with the Raineys" (39)—Virgie taunts the other children with her insouciance, drinking vanilla out of the bottle, for instance, "because she knew they called her mother Miss Ice Cream Rainey, for selling cones at speakings" (39). Virgie does all she can to create an "air of abandon" (38), including assuming characteristics that are antithetical to Katie Rainey's personality.

In Virgie's childhood, her manner was "so strangely endearing" that it "made even the Sunday School class think of her in terms of the future—she would go somewhere, somewhere away off . . . she'd be a missionary" (38). Unfortunately, the Morgana community denied Virgie a heroic future because of both her sex and her social status. Patricia Yaeger observes, "The Morgana community acts together, man and woman alike, to prevent *feminine* acts of Prometheanism: woman is not allowed to steal man's holy fire."[6] Perhaps Miss Lizzie Stark's mother, "old Mrs. Sad-Talking Morgan," says it best in her ironic commentary on the mores of Morgana: "'Virgie would be the first lady governor of Mississippi, that was where she would go.' It sounded worse than the infernal regions" (38).

In her teen and adult years, Virgie's sexual inhibitions bring shame to her mother; even though "[Katie] could feel little else coming to her from the outside world" (205) in her last feeble years, she could still "feel" the gossip. Likewise, Virgie suffers from the gossip about her family's poverty and country ways. She recalls after her mother's death that the only "drop [of anxiety that] spilled" (212) at a June recital was when she thought about everyone laughing at her mother's hat, for the way one's mother dressed for this annual event was every bit as important as the way the little girls themselves were dressed. Although she seemed on the surface not to care, Virgie does feel shame for her family. The Raineys' hard life is conspicuously apparent, although they somehow "scraped up" money for Virgie's piano lessons for awhile; later, everyone knew that Miss Eckhart gave them to her for free, since she was "gifted." The old piano the Raineys borrowed for her to practice on is torn up by goats, "something that could only happen at the Raineys'," the townspeople snicker. Clearly, both mother and daughter suffer from the whispers of this small town, although the whispers hurt them for different reasons. They both know that they, measured against a locally determined respectability, fit into the social structure only as Morgana has placed them, and Morgana has placed them quite low on the social ladder.

When Katie Rainey dies, Morgana rushes into the house of the dead to attend it properly. "Don't touch me" (212), Virgie says to those officious female mourners who, at her mother's wake, insist she view the body; "They were all people who had never touched her before who tried now to struggle with her" (213). One woman, overlooking the shortcomings of the many, delivers the piercing epithet to this independent daughter, who is now a middle-aged woman: "Your mama was too fine for you, Virgie, too fine. That was always the trouble between you" (213). But Virgie, beyond hurt now, endures this affront to her privacy. As the nonconformist who will not be crushed, she is what Welty calls "the answer to all the others."[7]

Later that day, Virgie walks to the river, steps out of her clothes, and swims in the restorative waters that had been her only solace in her youth. She floats, meditatively, feeling grains of sand, grass, and mud "that touch her and leave her, like suggestions and withdrawals of some bondage that might have been fear" (219). Now, with the years of oppression drawing to a close, churning memories and a rush of pent-up emotion surge to the surface. Before the townspeople return the next day, Virgie goes out to the yard and "attacks" (220) the high grass with her sewing scissors, "as though for a long time she had been extremely angry and had wept many tears" (221). The emotional release is almost palpable. Miss Eckhart, something of a surrogate mother to her, had once given Virgie her own butterfly pin, symbol of the creative artist, during her adolescence, but she had grown up in this house where "a child could slip through" (228), and in Morgana, where women know their place. Virgie has slipped through and does not find her place here. As the funeral party drives through the cemetery, the only tombstones Virgie notices are those of men; they are "like the repeating towers in the Vicksburg park" (230). She looks for Miss Eckhart's "squat, dark stone" but the outsider, in final escape, is not buried in this town that could never accept her.

After the funeral, Virgie gives away her mother's possessions and leaves Morgana forever. "Always wishing for a little more of what had just been" (220) of her good times, and not willing, like Cassie, to accept, martyrlike, what the community allots her, Virgie attempts to salvage what is left of her life. The waste is enormous, for Virgie has been a victim of Morgana's narrow expectations for a long time. Many years before, young Cassie had thought that "both Miss Eckhart and Virgie Rainey were human beings terribly at large, roaming on the face of the earth. And there were others of them—human beings, roaming, like lost beasts" (85). Mary Jane Hurst notes that Miss Eckhart's artistic bent alone "would be sufficient excuse for poetic madness, but . . . she is pushed to clinical insanity when her poetic nature cannot be verbalized and accepted."[8] Virgie Rainey, it seems, will not let that happen to her. Her spirit, perhaps stronger than Miss Eckhart's, protects her, but she waits almost too long. Finally, she recalls that one of King MacLain's twin sons, Eugene, who had gone far away from Morgana, had learned "that people don't have to be answered just because they want to know."

Virgie has wasted half her life and all of her musical gift in a frustrating blend of defiance and compliance. She did not choose the easy path. "There's nothing Virgie Rainey loves better than struggling against a real hard plaid" (207), Katie notes shortly before her death as she watches her daughter cut out a dress. She thinks "there should be [a simple line] down through every woman's body . . . making each of them a side to feel and know, and a side to stop it." Welty suggests that Virgie, however, will ultimately remain undaunted. All of her energies thus far have been directed toward resisting the dictates of society, and in Welty's vision there still seems to be hope for the adventurous girl who rode a boy's bicycle. Seymour Gross comments that Welty knows that "despite the world's substantial weight—its pain and sadness—human nature has an astonishing capacity for dancing free."[9]

* * *

This resiliency of the human spirit is perhaps tested most severely in the case of aristocracy. Jinny Love Stark, who was named for her maternal grandmother, could not have been named "anything else. Or anything better" (118). Her maternal ancestry is significant to the entire community; Morgana, after all, was named for her mother's people. Miss Lizzie Morgan Stark, her mother, owned all the woods around Morgana—Morgan's Woods—and she was "real important." When she attended the June recital, she always sat on the front row and turned around to "spot" each of the other mothers; she was "the most important mother there" (63). Furthermore, Miss Lizzie arrived daily at summer camp to "see how [it] was running" (129), and, as self-appointed community leader, she "takes charge" (8) at childbirth and "supervise[s] the house" of the dead too—except in the case of poor old Katie Rainey, when she "felt too weak" (210). Knowing that she cannot now befriend her longtime neighbor, whose house she had never entered except momentarily, she acknowledges their common bond as old women and sends a ham, her maid, and monogrammed napkins.

Jinny Love assumes the same role of authority with her young friends. She does not hesitate to give Cassie and Virgie a knowing "grown-up look" during Miss Eckhart's impassioned, impromptu piano performance, even though she is not as old as they are, and she, herself, acts as self-appointed page turner. (However inconsequentially, she turns pages for the wrong music). Young Jinny is "[Miss] Lizzie's own" (146) in her officious nature, demanding and self-centered.

Life so completely revolves around Jinny, in her perception, that she seems to forget that others are of any significance at all. For example, when she, her friend Nina Carmichael, and the orphan Easter slip away from summer camp for an adventure of their own, she says "Let's don't go back yet. . . . I don't think they've missed [me]" (117).[10] Even while the teenaged Loch Morrison resuscitates Easter after a swimming accident, Jinny stands obtrusively by with a towel, looking at the circle of spectators "until she caught their eye—as if the party was for *her*" (133).

That passage may also be prophetic of the time to come when Jinny and her mother will vie for the controlling position in Morgana. Miss Lizzie, who has arrived at camp to make her daily check, comes upon the dramatic scene at the lake. She stands in the center of the group of onlookers, "hugging the other little girls" to her (131), her gaze hardening on Jinny who stands center stage wiping the unconscious child's brow. Jinny, purposefully "catching her mother's eye" (133), continues to wipe, only "[stealing] brief rests," until finally she says, "I give up" (134) and moves from the front to her mother's side, relinquishing the dominant position to her mother. At this point, Miss Lizzie "[sinks] her fingers critically into the arms of the girls at her skirt" (134), and they, understanding, tiptoe away. The competition between Miss Lizzie and Jinny thus starts early.

Jinny Love marries the only man from Morgana who is suitable for someone of her position, King MacLain's son Ran, but she gives him a trying life, betraying him with unabashed adultery. Her mother, who "hated all men," deplores Jinny's behavior, but this daughter, like her mother, doesn't pay too much attention to anyone else's opinion, not even her mother's. Poor Ran, caught between a legendary absent father, a saucy, unfaithful wife, and a mother-in-law who blames him for letting the affair happen, struggles to maintain equilibrium in his first-person narration of **"The Whole World Knows,"** a story title that suggests what ***The Golden Apples*** encompasses. Eventually Jinny and Ran reunite, and Ran becomes mayor of Morgana, but the mature Jinny is "at odds in her womanhood" (225). Although she had seemed wise for her years as a child, she now "was in her thirties strangely childlike; was it old perversity or further tactics?" Welty asks (224). Gathering with her family for Katie Rainey's funeral, she, "grimacing out of the iron mask of the married lady," tells Virgie that she should marry now that her mother has died. Living in partnership with someone else is foreign to Jinny's nature, and "it appeared urgent with her to drive everybody, even Virgie for whom she cared nothing, into the state of marriage along with her" (225). Ever the controlling one, she even scans the room as if to find a suitable mate for Virgie. This humorous echo of the young, manipulative Jinny becomes strangely wrenching in view of her own limited life choices and wasted leadership abilities.

She is, however, the hope of Morgana's future, the survivor, the progenitor. Cassie never marries, remaining chaste for a lifetime of martyrdom; Virgie has several lovers, but remains single, finally leaving Morgana to find a better life for herself; but Jinny, spunky and irreverent, produces a son named King (about whom we know nothing) and a resilient and unscrupulous little girl who climbs through windows to view the dead and issue commands, who nonchalantly mashes the heads of lizards to make them cling to her ears. The child is also named Jinny, like her mother and grandmother and great-grandmother, too. She will, no doubt, someday direct society for the community of Morgana, where everything is changing, where woods are being cleared out and grass and shrubs are scorching, where nothing appears the same except "the Morgan sweet olive," her great-great-grandmother's tree (204). Significantly, the sweet olive is still blooming.

* * *

These, then, are the mothers and daughters of Morgana. Old Mrs. Eckhart and Miss Lotte Elisabeth Eckhart do not count in Morgana society, perhaps because they are outsiders. (Not knowing "the name of their mother's people," the community could not "place" them.) They neither conform nor provide continuity to the system, and they are included in nothing in Morgana. Sometimes young Cassie would watch them at night through her window next door, while Miss Eckhart patiently tended her invalid mother. One day old Mrs. Eckhart purposely broke a doll her daughter had received from her sweetheart—broke it across her lap. Another time she stared at her daughter's piano pupil until she made the little girl cry. Again she mocked her daughter, "*Danke schoen,*" when Miss Eckhart thanked Virgie Rainey for her performance—she knew her daughter loved Virgie. When the music ended, Miss Eckhart slapped her mother; the old lady still looked as though "she would scream at the whole world, at least at all the music in the world and wasn't that all right?" (54). Apparently Miss Eckhart's mother was jealous of all that her daughter loved, even though her daughter, whose "spirit drooped its head" (41), did not have much love in her life.

When Cassie wonders, "Should daughters *forgive* mothers (with mothers under their heel)?" (54), she poses a question that the women in ***The Golden Apples*** do not answer, but each gropingly resolves in her own way. Cassie digs away the guilt of her mother's suicide in floral tributes to her; Virgie springs free of this burden by finally escaping the restrictions placed on Morgana's women; spunky Jinny Love, as she tries to direct her friends into marriage too, perpetuates the mother-daughter relationship with her own offspring. The golden apples lie untasted in Morgana society.

Notes

1. Eudora Welty, *The Golden Apples* (New York: Harcourt, Brace, 1949), hereinafter cited parenthetically by page number in the text.
2. Elaine Upton Pugh, "The Duality of Morgana: The Making of Virgie's Vision, The Vision of *The Golden Apples,*" *Modern Fiction Studies* 28 (1982): 442.
3. Franziska Gygax, *Serious Daring from Within: Female Narrative Strategies in Eudora Welty's Novels* (New York: Greenwood Press, 1990), 45.

4. Ibid., 46.
5. Gail Mortimer, *Daughter of the Swan: Love and Knowledge in Eudora Welty's Fiction* (Athens: University of Georgia Press, 1994).
6. Patricia Yeager, "'Because a Fire Was in my Head': Eudora Welty and the Dialogic Imagination," *PMLA* 99 (1984): 968.
7. Eudora Welty, interview by Clyde White, in *More Conversations with Eudora Welty,* ed. Peggy Prenshaw (Jackson: University Press of Mississippi, 1996), 236.
8. Mary Jane Hurst, "Fire Imagery," *PMLA* 100 (1985): 237.
9. Seymour Gross, "Eudora Welty's Comic Imagination," in *The Comic Imagination in American Literature,* ed. Louis D. Rubin, Jr. (New Brunswick, N.J.: Rutgers University Press), 328.
10. In the first edition of *The Golden Apples* the text reads, "I don't think they've missed us." In *The Collected Stories of Eudora Welty* (New York: Harcourt Brace Jovanovich, 1980), the singular *me* replaces *us.*

Axel Nissen (essay date autumn 2000)

SOURCE: Nissen, Axel. "'Making the Jump': Eudora Welty and the Ethics of Narrative." *Journal of the Short Story in English,* no. 35 (autumn 2000): 55-68.

[*In the following essay, Nissen details aspects of otherness, love, and sentimentality in Welty's stories.*]

> [M]orality as shown through human relationships is the whole heart of fiction . . .
>
> (Welty, *Eye of the Story* 148)

Eudora Welty has never made a secret of the fact that the propelling force behind her writing is love. When, during the 1960s, she was accused of lacking social consciousness and a political agenda, she responded by saying simply: "I think we need to write with love. Not in self-defense, not in hate, not in the mood of instruction, not in rebuttal, in any kind of militance, or in apology, but with love" (*Eye of the Story* 156). A dozen years later, she stated in an interview: "I never write stories or novels with the object of criticizing people. I want the reader to understand the people, and people as individuals. I'm not condemning people at all and *never* have" (*Conversations* 202). Finally, in 1980, we find her saying this about her artistic purpose: "I have been told . . . that I seem to love all my characters. What I do in writing of any character is to try to enter into the mind, heart, and skin of a human being who is not myself. Whether this happens to be a man or a woman, old or young, with skin black or white, the primary challenge lies in making the jump itself. It is the act of a writer's imagination that I set most high" (***Collected Stories*** [***The Collected Stories of Eudora Welty***] xi).

Welty's choice of metaphors is no less striking in her essays than in her fiction and "making the jump" is one of her most intriguing ways of figuring her own artistic process. This essay is an attempt to elucidate what that metaphor means in practice. What does it mean for Eudora Welty to make the jump? How does she do it? What strategies does she employ for coming to terms with otherness? Further: What does it mean for Welty to write with love? How does she love something while at the same time bringing into being? How does she avoid sentimentality? How does she guide our judgement?

The short answer to these questions is, of course, form. It is through the form of her stories that Welty loves; it is narrative technique that allows her to enter into the minds, hearts, and skins of human beings who are not herself. Michael Kreyling writes in the conclusion to his monograph *Eudora Welty's Achievement of Order*: "In Welty's work the *how* is the *what.* Technique is its most fundamental aspect—its unique way of responding to the world and of expressing the impact of the world it meets—is what is given to the reader" (177).

Even after half a century of criticism, I feel we have work left to do in coming to terms with Welty's narrative technique, in understanding how the "how" becomes the "what." I have chosen to call the sum total of narrative techniques and stylistic devices that constitute Welty's love in practice, an "ethics of narrative." Herein lies an important distinction: The ethics *of* narrative is different from the ethics *in* narrative. In other words, every narrative has an ethics, but not every narrative is about ethics.[1] I intend that the term "ethics of narrative" be understood to mean the study of the ethical aspect of narrative form. I choose to call this aspect *ethical,* because any formal choice within a communicative situation is value-laden. What is said comes into focus through what is not said. How a character or event is narrated may be highlighted through comparison with the means that have not been chosen. Whether or not the author is making systematic and ethical claims in or through her story, she cannot avoid making claims through the story's form. Who is given voice? Who is silenced? Who is characterized directly, who indirectly? Who is the focalizer? Who is focalized? What events are elided? What events are described scenically? Whose minds may we enter and whose not? How are these depictions of consciousness structured? As far as these choices guide us in determining our attitude to the novel's characters and events, they are ethical choices.[2]

Based on the insights of poeticians of narrative such as Gérard Genette, Dorrit Cohn, Roger Fowler, and Boris Uspensky, I hope to indicate new ways of talking about the form of Welty's stories. I particularly want to focus on how Welty maintains her distance, while at the same time creating sympathy for her characters. As she herself has stated: "Getting my distance, a prerequisite of my understanding of human events, is the way I begin work" (*One Writer's Beginnings* 21). I will discuss Welty's manipulation of narrative voice and perspective; her use of irony; her attempt to engage the reader, through the use of obstructionism and defamiliarization; her figurative language; and the role of metanarrative, including mind-style and coloring. I hope to show that for Welty, love and separateness are as much a part of the creative process as they are a reality in the created world.

* * *

Welty has never been afraid of tackling alien experience; individuals, scenes, and situations far removed from her own life. Consider alone the varied cast of protagonists she sets before us in her first published collection, ***A Curtain of Green and Other Stories*** (1941): two poor young girls, who might be described as "simple-minded"; several middle-class matrons, spinsters, and roving bachelors; two deaf mutes; two mentally unbalanced ladies; an elderly, upper class, white man; several impoverished couples; two African American performers; an elderly African American woman; and two adolescent girls. With the exception of the character-narrator of **"A Memory,"** none of these figures can be said to have much in common with their creator, an unmarried, upper middle-class white woman of sound mind and body, writing about them during her late twenties and early thirties. In other words, in ***A Curtain of Green,*** we may observe Welty making some of her most daring jumps.

I have chosen as my exemplum the little discussed story entitled **"A Piece of News."** Published in the *Southern Review* in 1937 and included in ***A Curtain of Green*** four years later, it is among the briefest of Welty's stories, but nevertheless exhibits a narrative complexity and sophistication that makes it representative of Welty's short fiction to the extent that any single story by her may be called representative. It contains the emphasis on the detailed rendering of marginal characters, the lack of a conventional plot, and the dreamlike atmosphere that are typical of many of Welty's stories. **"A Piece of News"** is also paradigmatic in that it embodies both of Welty's central themes, as expressed by Granville Hicks: "the mystery of others and the mystery of self" and "the problem of what brings people together and what holds them apart" (72).

"What eye in the world did she feel looking in on her?" asks the narrator of **"A Piece of News"** (Welty, ***Collected Stories*** 13). This is one of the many direct and indirect questions raised by this deceptively simple narrative, depicting a scene from the life of a young country woman. The young woman is Ruby Fisher, willing of body and imagination, who comes home one day after an afternoon of infidelity and reads in the newspaper about a woman named Ruby Fisher having been shot in the leg by her husband. The rambling reverie that this reading sets off is the stuff of the story, as is what happens when dream meets reality, when Ruby is faced with the flesh-and-blood presence of her husband Clyde, rather than a romantic vision.

To tell Ruby Fisher's story, Welty has chosen a narrator from outside Ruby's backwoods world. The narrator immediately and irrevocably draws attention to her own disembodied presence by giving us a long scene where Ruby is entirely alone. No one sees her, no one hears her, but the narrator. The narrator has the power to interpret and to generalize about the myriad of actions Ruby performs, to speed up or slow down the telling of the tale, and to describe both people and things, often by comparing them with other things, directly through simile or implicitly through metaphor. We find the characteristically Weltyan similes; the simple and colloquial comparisons are taken from the same world as that of the story, as in the following example: "her hair began to slide out of its damp tangles and hung all displayed down her back *like a piece of bargain silk*" (12; italics mine). The modifier here is particularly apt, taking into account what we later learn about Ruby's extramarital activities. Her hair is like a piece of silk, but it (and metonymically) its owner are not expensive. Further, we find: "She did not merely look at it [the newspaper]—she watched it, as if it were unpredictable, like a young girl watching a baby" (12-13). This makes us wonder how old Ruby really is. Is she a young girl or just *like* one? Also, the reference to the baby raises the question of why there is no child for her to love.[3] Ruby's movements are twice likened to those of a cat and this forms an interesting contrast to her birdlike voice: "a small fluttering sound" (12). Significantly, figurative expressions are not used about her husband Clyde, who is simply described as being "steamy" and "wet."

Despite a certain homespun simplicity in its use of figurative language, there is something highly wrought about the surface of the story, which at times borders on the opaque. The narrator plays a vital and active role in the signifying process, watching Ruby with such care and attention that she comes to identify entirely with her needs. She describes Ruby's movements in an indirect, abstract language, that we in turn must interpret. This is the mode of "must have been" and "seemed," of "as if" and "as though." Boris Uspensky was the first to identify these forms of "operators." In his words: "The use of operators is a device which justifies the application of *verba sentiendi* to a character who has been consistently described from an external (estranged) point of view. We may call these operators 'words of estrangement'" (85). What these words of estrangement imply is that the narrator does not know if her conjectures are correct. They are connotators of restricted knowledge.

Uspensky has made a further observation on the type of narrative perspective Welty employs in **"A Piece of News"**:

> The external point of view, as a compositional device, draws its significance from its affiliation with the phenomenon of *ostranenie,* or estrangement. The essence of this phenomenon resides primarily in the use of a new or estranged viewpoint on a familiar thing, when the artist "does not refer to a thing by its name, but describes it as if it had been seen for the first time—and in the case of an event, as if it were happening for the first time."
>
> (131; quote from Victor B. Shlovsky's "Art as Device")[4]

Naturally, this effect of estrangement is closely allied with the use of words of estrangement and the following passage from the final scene is a good example:

> There was *some way* she began to move her arms that was mysteriously sweet and yet abrupt and tentative, a delicate and vulnerable manner, *as though* her breasts gave her pain. She made many unnecessary trips back and forth across the floor, circling Clyde where he sat in his steamy silence, a knife and fork in his fists.
>
> (15; italics mine)

In a delicate and ladylike manner the narrator is describing the sexual arousal Ruby experiences after her fantasy (Hollenbaugh 67). Ruby's feelings are not in themselves unusual, but through the indirection of her description the narrator takes the reader on a process of discovery.

In other passages, the narrator holds back information to postpone our understanding of the significance of an action or description. As a consequence, our understanding is affected to the extent that we sometimes feel the narrator is actively getting in the way of that understanding. We see this obstructionist device clearly at the point in the first scene when Ruby suddenly jumps to her feet and screams for her husband (13; italics mine throughout): "'You Clyde!' screamed Ruby Fisher at last, jumping to her feet. 'Where are you, Clyde Fisher?'" It is unclear whether the scream is one of fear, anger, or excitement. The narrator continues: "She ran straight to the door and pulled it open. A shudder of cold brushed over her in the heat, and she *seemed striped with anger* and bewilderment." The narrator is now willing to give a tentative explanation. Then: "There was a flash of lightning, and she stood waiting, as if she half thought that would bring him in, a gun leveled in his hand. She said nothing more and, backing against the door, pushed it closed with her hip. Her *anger* passed like a remote flare of elation." There is no longer any hedging, it *was* anger Ruby felt.

In her fine essay "Words Between Strangers," Harriet Pollack comments on this phenomenon: "Welty's style," she says, "urges a reader to attend the text, to be a reader responding to a writer. Her 'obstructions,' paradoxically, are a measure of her apprehension for successful interaction with her audience" (69). The narrator of **"A Piece of News"** is not going to make anything easy for us, and we must make an effort at understanding Ruby Fisher equal to her own.

In this connection, Ruby's monologue in the first half of the story is vital because it unites the two functions of metanarrative: The monologue has an *explanatory* function in that it allows us to understand the reality of Ruby's present existence, and a *thematic* function in that it is an index of her loneliness. Having observed Ruby's voice and movement in unison, the narrator (and the reader) are better equipped to interpret her body language and to gauge her moods later in the story. We do not need to enter her thoughts, because Ruby in her childlike way lets everything show.

Ruby's monologue has the peculiar quality that it is not related to us directly in the form of quoted speech, but indirectly in a mixture of the narrator's and Ruby's voice. Consider the following sample:

> Clyde would have to buy her a dress to bury her in. He would have to dig a deep hole behind the house, under the cedar, a grave. He would have to nail her up a pine coffin and lay her inside. Then he would have to carry her to the grave, lay her down and cover her up.
>
> (14-15)

If we did not know otherwise, we would think this was a summary of the thoughts going through her head. This is in fact a rather loose form of free indirect speech; what Dorrit Cohn calls *narrated monologue* (14 and passim). The narrator retains the content of Ruby's narrative, but the standardized language, third-person reference, and "future in the past" verb forms indicate the narrator's mediating presence. This is the narrator's way of creating a more dreamlike effect and of creating a distance to the character, a distance which is to a great extent ironic.

Ruby's monologue is a concentrated illustration of her "mind-style," a term coined by Roger Fowler to denote "any distinctive linguistic presentation of an individual mental self" (103). Ruby's mind-style is first and foremost distinguished by its simplicity and its lack of originality. This is reflected in the simple, repetitive sentence structure (e.g. "Clyde would have to buy her/dig her/nail her up/carry her"), and in the paired and often corny adjectives ("strange and terrible," "handsome and strong," "wild, shouting, and all distracted"). Her "soliloquy" reveals a penchant for melodrama and a longing for romance and its retelling in concentrated form serves to heighten its schoolgirl pathos.

If we look carefully we begin to notice other ironic touches, such as the following line in the middle of Ruby's fantasy: "She lay silently for a moment, composing her face into a look which would be *beautiful, desirable, and dead*" (14; italics mine). The comic effectiveness of this line is due to the bathetic alliteration of "desirable and dead" and the incongruity of the grouping of these three qualities together. A different type of ironic effect is created by the sack of coffee being marked "Sample" in red letters. Again the joke is on Ruby, who has sold herself for nothing.

Despite these distancing devices, the narrator is remarkably in tune with Ruby's feelings and the meanings of her actions. When Ruby is alone she is the object of the narrator's external focalization; the reader does not see anything from Ruby's perspective, spatially or cognitively. The narrator maintains her distance physically; she is only close enough to make out the fluttering sound of her voice in the emptiness of the room, and sometimes not even that: "'The pouring-down rain, the pouring-down rain'—was that what she was saying over and over, like a song?" (12). Sometimes she comes so close as to look *with* Ruby, usually at the rain outside: "She moved slightly, and her eyes turned toward the window. The white rain splashed down" (15).

From the beginning of the second scene, we notice a subtle change in the code of focalization. This is first signalled by Clyde's appearance out of nowhere, like the phantom-lover of Ruby's dream, come to wreak his vengeance. This change in focalization does not so much mean that we are now seeing Clyde consistently from Ruby's perspective, but rather that the narrator evinces a sympathetic willingness to see Clyde in the role of the wronged husband, driven by passion to murder his faithless wife. The narrator is *willing* Clyde to be what Ruby wants him to be. He is depicted as a large, wet, massive figure, growling for his supper and he even asks the crucial question: "Well, where have you been, anyway?" in a grumbling tone of voice (15). Yet the narrator cannot be untruthful, she cannot suppress the fact that Clyde, far from harming Ruby with the gun, only pokes her with it, that he has "a stunned, yet rather good-humored look of delay and patience in his face" (15), and that the question is asked not as a challenge, but with accustomed amusement: "He almost chuckled" (15). The ludicrousness of Ruby's hopes becomes painfully clear to us, while she herself is oblivious to the jarring discrepancy between fact and fancy and wanders about in a mood of heightened sensual pleasure.

In the climactic scene, right after Ruby has shown Clyde the newspaper notice, we again have a passage touched by Ruby's romantic fantasy, and not without elements of her melodramatic imagination:

> He looked up, his face *blank and bold.*
>
> But she drew herself in, still holding the empty plate, faced him *straightened and hard,* and they looked at each other. The moment *filled full* with their helplessness. Slowly they both flushed, as though with a double shame and a double pleasure. *It was as though Clyde might really have killed Ruby, and as though Ruby might really have been dead at his hand.* Rare and wavering, some possibility stood timidly like a stranger between them and made them *hang* their *heads.*
>
> (16; italics mine)

"Blank and bold" is a cliché taken right out of Ruby's idiom, and reminds us of her adolescent description of Clyde as "handsome and strong" (14). The pairs of adjectives seem inflated and trite and appear to belong to the same register as the "beautiful, desirable, and dead" of Ruby's monologue. What we are observing here is the phenomenon called "coloring," through which "the narrator's language reacts to the language and the structure of consciousness of the characters" (Fowler 78). The narrator has not adopted Ruby's visual perspective, but rather her mind-style. The passage is full of the type of "infinite significance" Ruby is longing for.

We are not allowed into Ruby's and Clyde's minds, yet we know the penultimate sentence in the quoted passage is based on a fantasy that is solely Ruby's. She has had a vision of how things once were and of how they might be, that Clyde has not. Thus I cannot agree with the critics who take this scene as evidence of how both Ruby *and* Clyde, for a brief moment, have a flash of insight and see each other in a new light. Ruth M. Vande Kieft writes that "For an instant they have had a vision of each other in alien fantasy roles—an experience which is pleasing, exciting, and rather frightening" (45). W. U. McDonald, Jr. observes that "the possibility of the fatal shooting exists in the minds of both of them for a moment before common sense again prevails" (233). More recently, Jan Nordby Gretlund has written that "There is a moment when husband and wife have a chance to bridge the gap between them," and "it works as a confirmation that Ruby and Clyde need to be able to go on together" (115, 116). Even Dawn Trouard, author of the most riveting reading of the story to date, writes of "an epiphanic moment . . . that takes into account the possibility of murder, death, agency, and consequence," though she adds in a footnote her suspicion that "the 'rare and wavering' possibility that rises up between Ruby and Clyde . . . is totally unassigned and indeterminate" (343, 353 n. 7).

What these critics forget is that the newspaper item is about a woman being shot *in the leg,* not being shot through the heart. Unless Clyde has extra sensory perception, there is no way his and Ruby's minds could meet at this point. Clyde can have no idea of what the newspaper item has triggered in Ruby's consciousness. To him it is all just an unconceivable mistake, which is cleared up to his complete satisfaction when he discovers the paper is from Tennessee. The only possibility that stands wavering between them, whether the narrator is willing to admit it or not, is the strong possibility that the couple is hopelessly mismatched and that they will never understand each other.

Through the great number of words of estrangement, conjectural descriptions, and tentative assertions, the narrator abdicates her right to the final word and leaves it up to the reader to interpret the signs in such a way that he or she feels is coherent with the depiction of the characters up to that point. There is no reason to believe that Clyde should suddenly experience a quantum leap of understanding and intuit the fantasy awakened in Ruby by the newspaper item. The reason why so many critics seem willing to believe that Ruby and Clyde experience a moment of mutual revelation and communion is that the *narrator* seems to want to believe it. As we have just seen, this belief is not logical. The narrator has allowed herself to be carried away by her love for Ruby.

* * *

In **"A Piece of News,"** defamiliarization and distance go hand in hand. In a story such as this, where an intellectual narrator tries to understand a semiliterate woman, there is bound to be distance on many planes. We have seen it on the spatial plane, where the narrator is an "invisible witness" who keeps her physical distance. We have seen it even more clearly on the linguistic plane, where we have the opportunity to distinguish the narrator's estranged, indirect voice from Ruby's plain, homegrown idiom, before the two merge. The narrator's figurative expressions also create a distance; they do not state what things *are,* just what they are like. We have also noted that Ruby's thoughts are never related to us, directly or indirectly. Yet morally and emotionally there is no distance. The closest the narrator ever comes to judging Ruby is her comment early on that Ruby "must have been lonesome and slow all her life, the way things would take her by surprise" (12). It is important for the reader to understand that Ruby cannot be judged by the standards we apply to normal, "rational" beings. On the emotional level, there is identification to the extent that the narrator begins to fantasize herself.

In her attempt to "come to terms" with the identity of a simple, even simple-minded young country woman through the minute observation of her every move, word, and gesture, the narrator of **"A Piece of News"** enacts a process of observation, understanding, and sympathy that we may call love. It is a measure of this love and the story's supreme irony, that the narrator is the only one to see Ruby as she wants and needs to be seen, on her own terms, however melodramatic they may seem to us. For Ruby is a performer—a performer without an audience. No matter what she may feel, there is no one watching Ruby Fisher.

"A Piece of News" is a vivid illustration of what Welty has described as her "continuing passion," her wish "not to point the finger in judgement but to part a curtain, that invisible shadow that falls between people, the veil of indifference to each other's presence, each other's wonder, each other's human plight" (*Eye of the Story* 355). In this and many other stories, we admire her daring in writing about people and parts of life which are far removed from her own personal experience. Yet, as Wayne Booth has pointed out: "It is not the degree of otherness that distinguishes fiction of the highest ethical kind but the depth of education it yields in *dealing with* the 'other'" (*Company We Keep* 199). In the words of Lynne Tirrell: "The experiences *most* worth having and the experiences recorded and perpetuated are not those of the characters within stories but rather those of the artist" (124). Ultimately, it is the form of Welty's story—its enactment of love—rather than any abstract moral principles we may want to draw from it, that constitutes its contribution to ethics in general and to the ethics of narrative in particular.

Notes

1. The last decade has seen a renewal of interest in the "ethics of fiction," in the ways in which narrative poses and attempts to answer questions about how best to live in the world. This interest has been shared by philosophers as well as literary critics. In her collection of essays, *Love's Knowledge,* the neo-Aristotelian philosopher and classicist Martha Nussbaum stresses the significance of literary texts in arguing for "a conception of ethical understanding that involves emotional as well as intellectual activity" (ix). Nussbaum is currently one of the most prominent promulgators of "philosophy through literature," in which "a theme that is also the object of philosophical deliberation is given literary interpretation in terms of an imaginary world artistically constructed" (Lamarque and Olsen 391). Among literary critics, on the other hand, we find the old-timer and formalist Wayne Booth, who suggests in *The Company We Keep* that "there are many legitimate paths open to anyone who decides to abandon, at least for a time, the notion that an interest in form precludes an interest in the ethical powers of form" (7).

   The emphasis on the significance of form has been a recurring aspect of the renewed interest in the ethical aspects of fiction. Booth emphasizes that a writer's "choice of devices and compositional strategies is from the beginning a choice of ethos, an invitation to one kind of ethical criticism" (*Company* 108). In Nussbaum's words: "Style itself makes its claims, expresses its own sense of what matters. Literary form is not separable from philosophical content, but is, itself, a part of content—an integral part, then, of the search for and the statement of truth" (3). Yet Nussbaum and other philosophers-turned-literary critics such as Hilary Putnam have been criticized for being too little concerned with "literature as a separate and independent practice defined by its own logic and its own constraints and conventions" (Lamarque and Olsen 397). Nussbaum herself admits that "[w]e need to pursue in much greater depth and detail the stylistic portion of my argument, saying a great deal more, in connection with many more authors and many different genres and styles, about the practical and human expressive content of structural choices at all levels of specificity" (186).

2. There are of course ethical dimensions to the narrative text that are not of a structural nature; first and foremost, the actions of the characters themselves. It is the discussion of the epistemological status of fictional events and their evaluation as a basis for ethical arguments—the ethics *in* narrative—that is at the center of much current work within the "ethics of fiction." In due time we may want to examine the ethics in Welty's stories, but we must always keep in mind that in a text there are no actions in themselves; all is language. Thus any evaluation of a narrative's ethical stance must begin with the analysis of the ethics of narrative representation in the work.

3. Peter Schmidt appears to have endowed Ruby with children when he describes her as "a vigilant mother" (35), but I can find no evidence in the story that she and Clyde have offspring.

4. Wayne Booth has also given an interesting description of this type of rhetoric in his *The Rhetoric of Fiction*: "Modern authors have often managed to give an acceptable air of objectivity while reaping all the benefits of commentary, simply by dealing largely with the appearances, the surfaces, while allowing themselves to comment freely, and sometimes in seemingly wild conjecture, on the meaning of those surfaces." He uses Faulkner's *Light in August* to exemplify this form of "conjectural description" and concludes: "This device may for some readers serve the general realistic demands—it is 'as if' the author really shared the human condition to the extent of not knowing for sure how to evaluate these events" (184).

Works Cited

Booth, Wayne C. *The Rhetoric of Fiction.* Harmondsworth: Penguin, 1987.

———. *The Company We Keep: An Ethics of Fiction.* Berkeley: U of California P, 1988.

Cohn, Dorrit. *Transparent Minds: Narrative Modes for Presenting Consciousness in Fiction.* Princeton, New Jersey: Princeton UP, 1978.

Fowler, Roger. *Linguistics and the Novel.* London: Methuen, 1977.

Gretlund, Jan Nordby. "The Terrible and the Marvellous: Eudora Welty's Chekov." *Eudora Welty: Eye of the Storyteller.* Ed. Dawn Trouard. Kent, Ohio and London: Kent State UP, 1989. 107-18.

Hicks, Granville. "Eudora Welty." *College English* 14 (1952): 69-76.

Hollenbaugh, Carol. "Ruby Fisher and Her Demon-Lover." *Notes on Mississippi Writers* 7 (1974): 63-68.

Kreyling, Michael. *Eudora Welty's Achievement of Order.* Baton Rouge: Louisiana State UP, 1980.

Lamarque, Peter and Stein Haugom Olsen. *Truth, Fiction, and Literature: A Philosophical Perspective.* Oxford: Clarendon, 1994.

McDonald, W. U., Jr. "Eudora Welty's Revisions of 'A Piece of News.'" *Studies in Short Fiction* 7 (1970): 232-47.

Nussbaum, Martha C. *Love's Knowledge: Essays on Philosophy and Literature.* New York and Oxford: Oxford UP, 1990.

Pollack, Harriet. "Words Between Strangers: On Welty, Her Style, and Her Audience." *Welty: A Life in Literature.* Ed. Albert J. Devlin. Jackson: UP of Mississippi, 1987. 55-81.

Schmidt, Peter. *The Heart of the Story: Eudora Welty's Short Fiction.* Jackson and London: UP of Mississippi, 1991.

Tirrell, Lynne. "Storytelling and Moral Agency." *The Journal of Aesthetics and Art Criticism* 48 (1990): 115-26.

Trouard, Dawn. "Diverting Swine: The Magical Relevancies of Eudora Welty's Ruby Fisher and Circe." *The Critical Response to Eudora Welty's Fiction.* Ed. Laurie Champion. Westport, Conn. and London: Greenwood, 1994. 335-55.

Uspensky, Boris. *A Poetics of Composition.* Trans. Valentina Zavarin and Susan Wittig. Berkeley: U of California P, 1973.

Vande Kieft, Ruth M. *Eudora Welty.* New York: Twayne, 1962.

Welty, Eudora. *The Collected Stories of Eudora Welty.* Harmondsworth: Penguin, 1983.

———. *One Writer's Beginnings.* Cambridge, Mass.: Harvard UP, 1984.

———. *Conversations with Eudora Welty.* Ed. Peggy Whitman Prenshaw. New York: Washington Square, 1985.

———. *The Eye of the Story: Selected Essays & Reviews.* New York: Vintage International, 1990.

Dean Bethea (essay date 2001)

SOURCE: Bethea, Dean. "Phoenix Has No Coat: Historicity, Eschatology, and Sins of Omission in Eudora Welty's 'A Worn Path.'" *International Fiction Review* 28, nos. 1 & 2 (2001): 32-41.

[*In the following essay, Bethea examines the Christian symbolism and sociohistorical perspective on race in "A Worn Path."*]

Unsurprisingly, Eudora Welty's short story **"A Worn Path"** has inspired many interpretations. Most critics, including Elaine Orr, James Walter, Peter Schmidt, and James Robert Saunders, assert the work as an optimistic depiction of its protagonist, Phoenix Jackson.[1] However, no previous study has discerned what I believe to be the work's primary purpose: to attack the debased Bible Belt Christianity that does not eradicate but instead accommodates racism through sins of both commission and omission. Even the many poststructuralist readings of **"A Worn Path"** have exhibited a shared, essentially formalist strategy: a tendency to divorce the "text" from the vitally important historical conditions and social relationships so carefully limned therein. But an understanding of the history from which the story's action emerges is required if we are to grasp Welty's larger concerns. Through the profound implications of its setting during the Christmas season in and around Natchez, Mississippi, in the twentieth century's early decades, and through its delineation of the protagonist's selflessness and courage, **"A Worn Path"** calls for the implementation of a theology that would make Phoenix's dangerous—and possibly fatal—journey unnecessary. In my view, Welty's primary intent is not to console, inspire, or edify her readers; nor does she want them merely to take heart from Phoenix's example. Rather, the story is a call to action against the "Christian" world that oppresses the protagonist. Phoenix's arduous, life-threatening trek is not solely reflective of the human spirit's capacity to triumph over circumstantial difficulties but revelatory of a society in which very different, patently unjust standards exist.

"A Worn Path" illuminates crucial distinctions between apocalyptic and ethical eschatology in Christian theology. Apocalyptic eschatology refers to the conventional belief that a last judgment will be meted out by a deus ex machina, and allows, indeed encourages, disinterest in and disdain for the events and realities of the mundane world. In contrast, ethical eschatology argues for an apocalypse in that quotidian realm, for an "end time" in the here and now achieved by humans who seek to transmogrify the mores of a corrupt social realm. This interpretation of apocalypse forms the basis of Liberation Theology, a phenomenon whose origins can be traced back to the Civil Rights Movement in the United States: "in the 1950s [Martin Luther King, Jr.] was the pioneer, the forerunner, of all the other liberation theologies that began only in the 1960s and 1970s."[2] If a Christian framework is to be imposed on **"A Worn Path"** at all, this radical eschatology seems the best choice, since it stems from the same racist experiences as those Phoenix endures. Attempting to read the story through the lens of a quietist eschatology recalls James H. Cone's cogent assertion that American theology has "failed miserably in relating its work to the oppressed in society by refusing to confront this nation with the evils of racism. . . . Most of the time American theology has simply remained silent, ignoring the condition of the victims of this racist society."[3] I wish to argue that Welty has sought at the fictional level what Cone demands at the theological: through the acute historical consciousness and moral vision that infuses **"A Worn Path,"** she confronts her nation with the lasting effects of its troubled history.

Readers of the story must decipher a subtle prose puzzle, one whose carefully chosen components—including tone, plot structure, setting, the juxtaposition of characters, the racist misinterpretations of Phoenix—only cohere when they are closely examined in light of the story's sociohistorical bases, revealing the rage churning beneath its deceptively placid surface. First, Welty filters her assault through her objective tone, a task she accomplishes perhaps too skillfully, as her concealed authorial presence may have fostered the consensual view of **"A Worn Path"** as a story concerned primarily with spiritual triumph. Second, the work's cunning structure invokes and apparently valorizes racist stereotypes while withholding crucial information until a final, revelatory reversal. Third, deep and furious irony is expressed through the title itself and its physical and seasonal settings. While the latter has been interpreted as an optimistic framework for the plot, this setting shows instead that the spiritual rebirth which the Christmas holiday symbolizes has not occurred in the heart of the so-called Bible Belt. Welty is also quite specific about where in the Bible Belt Phoenix is journeying to: Natchez—one of the South's most grandiose architectural gems and a bleak monument to the slave economy that built it. The setting's precise geography is thus complemented by its historical associations. The story's picaresque plot also augments Welty's fourth tactic, the juxtaposition of the other characters' material wealth and self-concern with Phoenix's poverty and selflessness, a contrast intensified by their interactions with, and misunderstanding of, her.

Taken together, these four components recall Christ's directive as stated in the Gospel of Matthew that "if anyone wants to sue you and take your coat, give your cloak as well. And if anyone forces you to go one mile, go also the second mile. Give to everyone who begs from you, and do not refuse anyone who wants to borrow from you."[4] Welty's careful description of her protagonist's clothing reveals that Phoenix has no coat, and despite the freezing weather, none of the several people she meets offer her one. It seems probable that Welty, a product of the Bible Belt herself, had this precise verse in mind when she wrote the story. Christ demands that humans give more than what is asked of them and indicts the passive acceptance of another's suffering as an active form of evil, as a sin of omission. Yet no one in the story offers to "walk" even a mere yard with Phoenix, neither on the specific and perilous trip at hand nor on the larger "journey" that is her life. All of the work's white characters, because they do nothing in any real sense to improve Phoenix's plight, are revealed through their apathy as active sinners by the standards of their espoused religion's namesake. Welty invites us to castigate them not merely for their racist actions, but also for their callous inaction. She also implies that if they will not help Phoenix even now, during Christianity's most sacred season, they certainly will not do so during "ordinary times" either. Finally, after examining these four primary issues, we can turn to the story's open-ended conclusion, which should strike us as ominous and foreboding that the road's end for Phoenix will be the complete loss of her faculties or simply death—a fate that the work implies is near at hand.

The exclusion of such important factors from interpretations of **"A Worn Path"** diminishes its powerful range of meanings and recalls Walter Benjamin's assertion that "nothing that has ever happened should be regarded as lost for history."[5] By pursuing what Benjamin calls the "fullness of the past" through the restoration of the story's historical and social contexts, we discern not a benign and bland Christian allegory, but instead an impassioned and comprehensive indictment of the American South and, by extension, of the larger republic to which it belongs.[6] Phoenix does not live "primarily" as "a text . . . beyond the boundaries drawn by her social superiors."[7] Nor does she exist merely "within the world created by her own interior monologue," but rather as an individual trapped within the very real boundaries of a historically defined, deeply racist society.[8] These boundaries create monumental barriers to her expressive love, barriers that would have been confronted only by an illiterate, impoverished, isolated, and elderly African-American woman in the Deep South.

"A Worn Path" inveigles readers by invoking and apparently endorsing a host of "Aunt Jemima" or "Mammy" stereotypes regarding Phoenix's appearance and behavior. This entrapment begins with the story's first two paragraphs: "Far out in the country there was an old Negro woman with her head tied in a red rag. . . . She wore a dark striped dress reaching down to her shoe tops, and an equally long apron of bleached sugar sacks, with a full pocket."[9] Her makeshift cane and clothing accord perfectly with racist clichés of the time, as do her untied shoes, which many mid-century readers would have seen as corroborative of their specious belief in African-Americans' "innate" laziness and lack of self-regard. More importantly, Welty indicates that her readers must be acutely aware not only of those details she mentions but also of those that she does not. We must notice that Phoenix has no coat, for this fact greatly magnifies the callousness of the white people she encounters, none of whom could have failed to remark her inadequate clothing, and none of whom bother to remedy it.

The invocation of racist stereotypes in describing Phoenix's appearance is immediately augmented by her behavior, as she begins conversing with both her surroundings and herself. In the next several paragraphs she continues to "talk loudly to herself" as well as to trees and to a thorn bush in which she becomes tangled, to a boy who brings her a slice of cake in a moment of hallucination, and then to a "ghost" that she finally realizes is only a scarecrow, around whom she subsequently dances a jig of relief (143). Phoenix's appearance is "comical," her behavior "childish" and "superstitious." Welty augments this apparent valorization of racist clichés by withholding the true reason for Phoenix's journey until the story's concluding paragraphs. Readers are tempted to agree with the white hunter Phoenix encounters who claims "I know you old colored people! Wouldn't miss going to town to see Santa Claus!" (145).

James Walter argues that "the red rag [Phoenix] wears on her head, then, is, in one perspective, her tiara, signifying her sovereignty over the creatures in her domain."[10] Similarly, Elaine Orr sees this passage as exemplifying a dominant concern with inscribing "contradictions" in the story: "For example, Welty describes her protagonist as 'neat and tidy' and yet Phoenix walks all the way to town with her shoes untied . . . but no careful reader will believe Phoenix could not tie her own shoes."[11] "Careful readers" ought to realize that Phoenix has untied laces not because she is lazy or unconcerned about her appearance but rather because her advanced age—the white hunter claims she "must be a hundred years old"—prevents her from tying them (146). That she is so wizened by time, yet so determined to complete her life-threatening quest, is a detail meant to deepen our admiration of and empathy for Phoenix. Walter's claim that the red rag she wears is a "tiara" signifying her dominance of a world that so clearly dominates her seems inaccurate, especially since such notions of sovereignty are quickly dismissed when she is knocked into a ditch by a dog and jeered at by the white hunter who discovers her there. The rag signifies the cause-and-effect relationship between Phoenix's indigence and her slave heritage: such scraps of fabric were the most common regalia of slave women in the South, the closest thing to a hat that they were often allowed, or could afford. Finally, her apron made of sugar sacks not only comments movingly on her privation but also alludes to the terrible legacy of the Jim Crow laws, which in many Southern towns prohibited most black men from wearing white shirts during the week and required all black women to wear aprons in public as humiliating signs of their continued oppression.

Neil Isaacs focuses on the symbolic dimensions of the Christmas setting, which for him inspires hope and provides a transcendental, timeless framework within which the text's specific details should be subsumed.[12] Yet the rebirth implied in Phoenix's name not only pertains to her repeated journeys in search of medicine, but also reveals the complete absence here of the spiritual rebirth that the Christmas holiday represents: the arrival of a new god, one whose love extends to all people regardless of skin color and whose main dictum to humanity is to love their neighbors as themselves. Phoenix's plight, and the indifference she faces, indicate that this spiritual rebirth has not occurred in her world. Welty's description as Phoenix first arrives in Natchez is deceptively innocuous: "Bells were ringing. Phoenix walked on. In the paved city it was Christmas time. There were red and green electric lights strung and crisscrossed everywhere and turned on in the daytime. . . . A lady came along in the crowd, carrying an armful of red-, green-, and silver-wrapped presents" (146-47). The spirit of Christmas, however, is nowhere to be found as Natchez exhibits all of the season's trappings but none of its true meanings. While the city can afford not only to pay for decorative lights but also to burn them in the daytime, Phoenix is forced to live in a primitive house so cold that her grandson awaits her return wrapped up in "a little patch quilt" (148). Moreover, the contrast between Phoenix's makeshift clothing and the woman who approaches her bearing an armful of gifts only deepens the scene's irony.

Having Phoenix arrive in Natchez sets a host of negative historical associations reverberating throughout the story. Mississippi's first capital, Natchez was once the apotheosis of the King Cotton, slave-built South, a territorial hub where by 1850 two-thirds of the nation's millionaires lived and where at least forty mansions had been erected by 1860.[13] Moreover, the town marked the southern terminus of the Natchez Trace, the Mississippi River route that provided cheap and quick transportation for cotton—and for the newly arrived slaves who would be shipped to regional plantations, making the Trace forever a "Trail of Tears" for all African-Americans. After 1812, the rapid expansion of the Cotton Empire in the Southwest made Natchez and Algiers, Louisiana, the busiest slave markets in the nation. Natchez records for an "unknown part of the year 1833" show that thirty-two nonresident slave traders made the then staggering sum of $238,879, a figure that does not include the earnings of resident slavers, who conducted a much greater portion of the sales. Natchez's thriving economy is further evidenced by the presence of the regional offices of Franklin, Armfield and Company, the nation's major slave-trading firm. Moreover, slave prices in the city quadrupled over the course of sixty years primarily because of the "increasing significance of chattel ownership as a symbol in the frenzied quest for status among the middle and upper class whites."[14]

Finally, unlike similarly magnificent cities in the eastern Deep South such as Savannah and Charleston, which had been long established before the cotton gin's invention in 1793 and the ensuing explosive rise of King Cotton, Mississippi as a whole and Natchez in particular owed their very existence—and certainly their wealth—to Whitney's technological innovation. Beginning with Mississippi, Alabama, and western Tennessee, and finally extending into northern Louisiana, Arkansas, and parts of Texas, the slave-based cotton industry itself impelled the westward expansion of the American South, as the demand for more and more suitable land drove new settlement. When Phoenix enters the streets of Natchez, we should be struck not only by the obvious contrast between her material poverty and the wealth that surrounds her, but as well by the deeper irony that she is walking through the midst of a material opulence she once labored to build, against her will. Her story is a living testament to the dismal origins of the city's spurious grandeur; her understanding of, connection to, and exclusion from the "splendors" of Natchez is immediate and personal, rendering the racist condescension the city's white residents subject her to even more intolerable and maddening.

If Phoenix is a symbolic figure, then she has arrived in a kind of "Anti-Bethlehem," a spiritual necropolis whose white denizens cling to the wreckage of an ideology that is the antithesis of the egalitarian and unifying philosophy attributed to Christ in the Gospels. In this city festooned with and illuminated by seasonal decorations, Phoenix is the only true "Christmas light," so to speak, but that small flame does nothing to mitigate the emotional darkness enveloping Natchez, as her experiences there will prove. Natchez, built largely through what Benjamin has labeled the "anonymous toil" of people like Phoenix, perfectly exemplifies his characterization of "cultural treasures" as composites of both barbarism and civilization.[15] Using the city as a setting deepens the necessity of examining the historical wreckage that **"A Worn Path"** subtly delineates and indicts.

The interactions between Phoenix and the story's other characters augment its setting's multiple ironies. The first person Phoenix encounters is a white hunter, who pulls her out of a ditch into which a dog has just knocked her. Isaacs asserts this man as "a Santa Claus figure himself (he carries a big sack over his shoulder, he is always laughing, he brings Phoenix a gift of a nickel)."[16] Similarly, Saunders asserts that "there is enough of an understanding between the hunter and the woman for him to be genuinely concerned; he had helped her off her back and shared a word or two."[17] Isaacs and Saunders fail to mention, however, that "Santa" finds the frail Phoenix in the ditch, that his initial laughter occurs when he sees her lying helpless, that this outburst is not followed by an apology, that his subsequent laughter is derisive of her, and that he refers to her by the racist term "Granny," which he would never use for an elderly woman if she were white. Moreover, Isaacs's "Santa" does not intend to give Phoenix a nickel but drops it just before claiming that he would give her a dime if he had any money. He then points his gun at her only to see if she will react in terror, which she does not. Finally, the hunter abandons Phoenix miles from town, without offering her a coat or helping her reach her destination.

Other important contrasts are created in this scene as well: the hunter, in addition to the money he claims not to have, carries a string of dead quail on his belt, an abundance of food that Phoenix is not likely to experience. His claim that he understands "colored people" only typifies the repellant thinking of those who equate racist stereotypes with knowledge. The hunter's reaction upon learning of her destination further reveals his complete misunderstanding of her: "Why that's too far! That's as far as I walk when I come out myself, and I get something for my trouble" (145). This encounter ends with his attempt to terrify Phoenix by threatening her with his gun. Phoenix believes he is aiming the rifle at her because she has been caught "stealing" his dropped nickel, although he does not realize that he has lost the coin. She has seen "plenty" of other African-Americans getting shot, at closer range and for less than the crime she believes she might have committed: stealing five cents (145). Her resigned tone evidences the absolute lack of both justice and safety for blacks in her world, as if being shot now would be the next "logical" consequence in a world founded on injustice.

The story's ironies continue in the apparently benign encounter between Phoenix and the white lady in Natchez. This scene initiates a series of important reversals of the racist stereotypes invoked earlier: Phoenix asks someone to tie her shoes as soon as she arrives in town. Far from being slovenly, she is quite concerned with her appearance, and has not tied her laces only because her aged fingers lack the dexterity to do so. The white woman must set her armload of presents down beside Phoenix's untied and worn shoes, after asking "What do you want, Grandma?," using, as did the hunter, the patronizing terminology sanctioned by a racist world (147). That Phoenix asks a favor of the "lady"—a title then reserved for white women—alludes again to Christ's commandment in Matthew, yet the woman, despite being confronted with an elderly, coatless woman on a day earlier described as "frozen," only grudgingly fulfills the request and then abandons her (142).

The next passage contains the story's crowning misinterpretation of Phoenix by the white people she meets. Having finally reached a doctor's office, she simply asserts "Here I be." The office attendant immediately assesses Phoenix, whom she calls "Grandma," as "a charity case" because she is elderly, black, and poorly dressed. Perhaps flustered by this snideness, Phoenix seems to forget temporarily why she has come, but the attendant's response is not concern but consternation: "'Are you deaf?' cried the attendant." Her shouts cause a nurse to come in, who reveals "that's just old Aunt Phoenix. . . . She doesn't come for herself—she has a little grandson. She makes these trips as regular as clockwork. She lives away back off the Old Natchez Trace" (147).

At this juncture Welty's carefully laid trap is sprung as she annihilates the racist stereotypes she seemed to endorse. In Phoenix's poignant recollection of the reason for her pilgrimage, we learn that we have not really "known" her at all and that she is the only truly humane character in the work: "I'm an old woman without an education. It was my memory fail me. My little grandson, he is just the same and I forgot it in the coming. . . . Every little while his throat begin to close up again, and he not able to swallow. He not get his breath. He not able to help himself. So the time come around and I go on another trip for the soothing medicine . . ." (148). Phoenix is uneducated, of course, because she was denied schooling due to her race. In the world depicted in the story, she and her grandson are the "only two left in the world" who care about each other. By the explicitly Christian standards invoked in the story, they are its "only two" truly humane characters. No one else exhibits more than a slightly vexed interest in them, a reality underscored by the nurse's two responses to Phoenix's speech: "'All right. The doctor said as long as you came to get it, you could have it. . . . But it's an obstinate case. . . .' The nurse was trying to hush her now. She brought her a bottle of medicine. 'Charity,' she said, making a check mark in a book" (148). The grudgingly donated medicine does not constitute charity in the sense demanded by Christ, an irony that is only deepened by the seasonal setting. Moreover, Phoenix's forgetfulness, coupled with her earlier hallucinations, augurs ominous developments. Rather than being a confident assertion, her claim that "I not going to forget him again, no, the whole enduring time" functions as a kind of desperate incantation, as a magic spell she wields against the increasing desperation of her plight and the inexorable advance of time. But people of her age and condition, especially those with no access to proper care, will not get better (148). When Phoenix does lose her grasp of reality, no one else in her world—as this scene makes abundantly clear—will step in to help her grandson.

And Phoenix's utter isolation in this deeply racist world is borne out by the story's most ironic passage: "'It's Christmas time, Grandma,' said the attendant. 'Could I give you a few pennies out of my purse?'" (148). This statement culminates Welty's incremental attack on the Bible Belt's self-serving definition of Christian duty: moral sanctity purchased for a few pennies, not through any real, substantive concern for other humans. Appropriately, even the typically unflappable protagonist approaches curtness in her response: "'Five pennies is a nickel,' Phoenix said stiffly" (149). Besides constituting a final reference to Christ's directive in Matthew, this passage is the crowning denouncement of the miserable inhumanity exemplified throughout the story. It is imperative to note that every white character—the hunter who terrifies her, the white lady, the snide attendant, and the dismissive nurse—is revealed as someone who views Phoenix through the dehumanizing perspective of racism.

Phoenix then combines her charitably acquired nickel with the one from the hunter, and instead of spending it on something for herself, she states her intention to buy her grandson a little paper windmill. We must remember that, despite her long journey to Natchez and the return trip she now faces, Phoenix has not eaten at all; her earlier hallucination of a boy offering her a piece of cake is just that, a dream of sustenance in an uncharitable world. This passage recalls the white woman and her armful of brightly wrapped presents, in stark contrast to Phoenix's grandson's reality, for whom a simple paper windmill promises to be an unexpected gift. Such an obvious allusion to the journey of the magi in the Gospels only intensifies Welty's ironic rendering of the South's racist Christianity. The story's final sentence also augments this anger, as Phoenix leaves the office: "Then her slow step began on the stairs, going down" (149). The participial phrase symbolizes a bleak future for her and her grandson—and for the society that perpetuates inhumanity. That symbolic foreshadowing is augmented by the conclusion's lack of closure, which impels readers to wonder if Phoenix, unfed, coatless, having already suffered a hallucination and a memory blackout, will be able to make the trip safely.

At this juncture the story's title demands further consideration: at one level **"A Worn Path"** stakes a claim for the deep humanity, fortitude, and courage of black women, the most oppressed of all the oppressed in the American South. At another level, the title is an indictment of the social world that causes Phoenix's suffering, a call to Welty's readers to exit the "worn path" of human relations constructed by a racist society, one in which an elderly woman must imperil her life to gain begrudged medical treatment for her grandson. Through this story, Welty attempts to make her readers relinquish the established road of social interaction, to break new ground in their treatment of each other, to effect at one level the kind of rebirth signified by the story's Christmas setting.

As the final work in ***A Curtain of Green and Other Stories,*** **"A Worn Path"** functions as a sort of last testament on the Southern world presented in that collection. The story is as radical an assault on racism for its time as Faulkner's story "The Bear." Both authors came, of course, from white Mississippi families and both deftly delineate the dimensions and lasting effects of the South's racist heritage, with Faulkner asserting the "mongrel" Sam Fathers as the true role model for Ike McCaslin, and Welty according the same status to Phoenix Jackson for all of her readers.

Notes

1. See Orr, "Unsettling Every Definition of Otherness: Another Reading of Eudora Welty's 'A Worn Path,'" *South Atlantic Review* 57 (1992); Walter, "Love's Habit of Vision in Welty's Phoenix Jackson," *Journal of the Short Story in English* 7 (1986): 78; Schmidt, *The Heart of the Story: Eudora Welty's Short Fiction* (Jackson: University Press of Mississippi, 1991); and Saunders, "'A Worn Path': The Eternal Quest of Welty's Phoenix Jackson," *Southern Literary Journal* 25 (1992): 71.
2. Alfred T. Hennelly, *Liberation Theologies: The Global Pursuit of Justice* (Mystic, CT: Twenty-Third Publications, 1995) 122.
3. James H. Cone, *A Black Theology of Liberation* (Philadelphia: Lippincott, 1970) 46.
4. *The New Oxford Annotated Bible: New Revised Standard Version* (New York: Oxford University Press, 1991) Matt. 5:40-42.
5. Walter Benjamin, *Illuminations,* ed. Hannah Arendt (New York: Harcourt Brace, 1968) 254.
6. Benjamin 254.
7. Orr 66.
8. Schmidt 39.
9. Eudora Welty, "A Worn Path," in *The Collected Stories of Eudora Welty* (New York: Harcourt Brace Jovanovich, 1980) 142. Subsequent references are to this edition and are cited parenthetically in the text.
10. Walter 82.
11. Orr 63.
12. Neil Isaacs, "Life for Phoenix," *Sewanne Review* 71 (1963): 40.
13. Clayton D. James, *Antebellum Natchez* (Baton Rouge: Louisiana State University Press, 1968) 144.
14. James 197-98.
15. Benjamin 256.
16. Isaacs 40.
17. Saunders 71.

Annette Trefzer (essay date summer 2002)

SOURCE: Trefzer, Annette. "Tracing the Natchez Trace: Native Americans and National Anxieties in Eudora Welty's 'First Love.'" *Mississippi Quarterly* 55, no. 3 (summer 2002): 419-40.

[*In the following essay, Trefzer links Welty's treatment of history and politics in "First Love" to the concept of the "linguistic trace" espoused by philosopher Jacques Derrida.*]

> Why, just to write about what might happen along some little road like the Natchez Trace—which reaches so far into the past and has been the trail for so many kinds of people—is enough to keep you busy for life.
>
> (Eudora Welty, 1942)

In the early 1940s, Eudora Welty was developing ideas for a series of stories on the Natchez Trace, stories she variously referred to as "the Natchez stories" or simply the "Natchez book."[1] Eight of these stories inspired by the Natchez Trace were published in 1943 in her second collection of short stories titled ***The Wide Net.*** This collection, strung together by the famous historical pathway named for local Indian populations, contains some of Welty's most explicitly "historical fiction." Her interest in local history began with her work as a publicity agent for the WPA in 1933 for which she traveled all over Mississippi collecting information, conducting interviews, and taking photographs on the side.[2] When the Federal Writers Project was published in 1938 as *Mississippi: A Guide to the Magnolia State,* three of her photographs were included. The *Guide,* a volume of impressive length, would have familiarized Welty with the history of her hometown and state, the Indian tribes in Mississippi, territorial acquisitions and Indian treaties, and with the historical significance of the Natchez Trace and its famous travelers. In the early 1940s, Welty was deeply immersed in reading and writing about the history of the Natchez Trace as material she used not only for her stories but also for the novella ***The Robber Bridegroom*** (1942). Considering Welty's interest in and use of local history, it seems all the more startling that she cautions us against reading her fiction historically. In a 1980 interview she declared: "I don't write historically or anything. Most of the things that I write about can be translated into personal relationships. I've never gone into such things as guilt over the Indians or—it just hasn't been my subject."[3] And yet, the Natchez Trace with its historical encounters and its origin in Indian history is at the center of her early work.

Perhaps as a result of Welty's own conviction that her writing shrinks away from the larger issues of Southern history and politics, historical traces in Welty's fiction are generally minimized. Michael Kreyling, for instance, argues that "even though the stories [of ***The Wide Net***] are grounded in the history and geography of the Natchez Trace, they take place—as fiction—in a state of heightened imaginative possibilities."[4] Reviewing ***The Wide Net*** in 1944, Robert Penn Warren also concluded that Welty has shifted her emphasis away from history and "very far in the direction of idea."[5] Because Welty is said to foreground "ideas," the "actual world" of politics and history appears to recede into the background. This understanding of Welty remains prevalent even with recent critics like Alexander Ritter, who argues that in order to foreground her thematic concerns with identity and individuality, Welty "withdraws to the back-country of the state of Mississippi in the 1920s and 30s"[6] and to Natchez as "a region altered to a provincial, narrowed, regressive locality. . . . [where] the world appears as if foreshortened because world history and global possibilities of the place are indiscernible" (p. 26). Welty's apparent flight from history and world politics is itself a political gesture in which Ritter perceives an essentially conservative "agrarian conception of society" (p. 26). But the fact that Welty often does not *explicitly* deal with social and political reality does not mean that she is not representing such a reality in her stories, or that she is not "historicizing" her fictional materials. Patricia Yaeger suggests that Welty might approach "History" differently from her male colleagues in Southern literature. Welty, Yaeger argues, catalogues histories that are "subsemantic, unspoken, out of use" and much like other Southern women writers, she weaves her politics into domestic scenes and female bodies.[7] Like Yaeger, I want to historicize and politicize Welty's fiction against traditional claims (Welty's own included) that her fiction shrinks away from the larger issues of Southern history and politics. But unlike Yaeger, who privileges stories that are not explicitly "historical," I want to focus on a story from the Natchez Trace series that uses historical personas and materials. Thus probing Welty's understanding of history, I argue that the understated nature of Welty's historical and political commentary does not make it less important, or "present," but that the "presence" history assumes in her writing is precisely over things that are left out.

Welty's denial of history is interesting particularly in conjunction with Mississippi's Indian heritage. When prompted about Faulkner's sense of "blood guilt about the Indians" by an interviewer who suggested that her own work lacks that aspect, Welty simply replies: "Well, it's not my theme" (Brans, p. 299). Why does Welty claim that "blood guilt" about the Indians is not her "theme"? Why should it be Faulkner's but not hers? For Welty, Faulkner's Indians are an integral part of the entire Yoknapatawpha saga. "Faulkner created an entire world: all the history of Mississippi and the Indians and everything. Mine was just an appropriate location."[8] Although Welty does not see her own writing as an attempt to write toward a panoramic view of history, her modesty should not mislead us into believing that her own fiction was not also rooted in the history of Mississippi and that the Indian characters she creates have no significance in her stories. On the contrary, Welty's Indian characters are central to the history she sketches, particularly in her early fiction.

A close look at **"First Love,"** the opening story of ***The Wide Net,*** reveals that Welty's fiction represents not so much a conservative rejection of local ethnographic and political materials as an artistic transformation of those materials. The fact that the larger political and historical meanings of the Natchez Trace are not immediately visible on the textual surfaces of her stories does not mean they are not there. I would like to suggest that what is "there" in Welty's Natchez Trace fiction is historical meaning precisely as a "trace." Borrowing Jacques Derrida's concept of the linguistic trace, we might see how Welty uses the history of the Natchez Trace to address questions that are, like Derrida's, profoundly philosophical and historical. Derrida argues that "sense"—historical, philosophical, or literary—is never simply present; "it is always engaged in the 'movement' of the 'trace,' that is in the order of signification."[9] Applied to Welty this means that the meaning of her story is never simply present but available only in the traces that the text might leave. This process of presencing (and absencing) is itself addressed in Welty's fictional method, particularly in her way of sketching a moment in the history of the Natchez Trace that famously obscures as much as it seems to reveal.

My project in this paper, then, is to trace a return journey into the kind of historical "truth" that Welty weaves into the opening story of ***The Wide Net.*** I want to argue that the Natchez Trace in **"First Love"** functions as a signifier with three different but related meanings: linguistic, historical, and political. As a linguistic concept, Welty, like Derrida, uses the "trace" to probe the manifestations of speech and truth in a philosophical and phenomenological context. If we understand Welty's concern with the language used to make sense of an event—any event—we recognize more readily that her choice of a deaf narrator in **"First Love"** is not aimed at concealing or distorting the truth about a historical incident or at simply romanticizing it, but at reflecting on the difficulties of telling the "truth" about any historical event. When Welty writes her Natchez Trace collection in the early 1940s, gone is the illusion that we can accurately describe political and social reality; gone is the illusion that literature is mimetic and that ethnographic and political details can be "correctly" described. Consistent reflection from the Western viewpoint is precisely what modernism begins to critique and what postmodernism more openly and radically attacks. If we take seriously Welty's concern with problems of representation and "linguistic traces," we might recognize that Welty is a modernist writer with a postmodern sensibility.[10] She uses this sensibility to question post-revolutionary American history at a time when the country is faced with difficult decisions about engaging in the international war theater of World War II. Traveling the Natchez Trace back to the early days of the nation, Welty reflects upon a topic of timely and continuing interest in the early 1940s: American nation-building. As a historical signifier, the "Trace" is for Welty an important symbol for nineteenth-century national history when the famous Natchez Trace was a vital link from the nation's capital to the Mississippi River town of Natchez and into the "territories." It was the Natchez Trace that made expansion and travel into the "Southwest" possible, after General Wilkinson gained permission from the Chickasaws and Choctaws to transform the path into a wagon road in 1801. The WPA Guide describes its stream of travelers: "Mail carriers, traders, boatmen, and supercargoes from New Orleans followed it north; an increasing stream of settlers afoot and on horseback traveled on it south to the new Eldorado of the lower Mississippi Valley."[11] As one of the most important North-South routes, the Natchez Trace grounds the lives of many characters traveling through American history and through Welty's fiction.[12] In **"First Love,"** the path leads us back to a contemporary of Thomas Jefferson, Aaron Burr, whose alleged plot was to secede from the Union and establish himself as the new leader of a Southwestern Republic. Traveling the Natchez Trace in order to reach his dreams of empire, Burr becomes a historical symbol for national expansion and U.S. colonial politics. But while the Natchez Trace in Welty's story points to the contest for territories and the American political and military presence in the wilderness, it also signifies an absence. Originally brought into being and used by Indian tribes, the Natchez Trace in **"First Love"** signifies the absence of Native Americans from the political events of 1807 that centered around nation-building and the expansionist politics of the United States at the cost of Native lands and lives. Reading the "Trace" as a political signifier in Welty's story will lead us back to the country's historical origins, origins grounded in acts of political exclusion and physical extermination which culminate a few years later in the traumatic removal of Native Americans from the East and Southeast. By exploring these related meanings of the figuration "trace," we will see that "tracing" is a method for Welty that simultaneously presences and absences history, a method that allows her to reflect on the fragility of language as the medium for the transmission of historical "truth."

* * *

In **"First Love,"** Welty weaves the historical episode of Aaron Burr's alleged conspiracy into a story centered around a young deaf boy's encounter with Burr. Joel Mayes, who is a boot-boy in an inn along the foot of the Natchez Trace, encounters Aaron Burr and his friend Harman Blennerhassett one evening as they search for shelter and privacy in Joel's room. Seemingly unaware of Joel's presence, they talk until morning and meet for many nights thereafter to discuss their plans. Joel, who is deaf and therefore does not understand the meaning of their words, is nevertheless fascinated by the men and their nightly visits. Waiting every night for them to return, he imagines that his room and his silent companionship might provide the safety and hospitality they are looking for, and from this new sense of self-importance he gains positive self-awareness. It is only after a few days that Joel learns from a public notice that Burr is wanted for treason and that his trial will be held in Washington, capital of the Mississippi Territory. Alerted to the true circumstances of Burr's nightly visits, Joel closely watches his friend and the town's reactions to his presence. He sneaks off to the river to see for himself the indicting evidence, the remains of Burr's flotilla; he watches as Burr and Blennerhassett gather in celebration on the last evening before the trial; he witnesses Burr's splendid performance at the trial, and he stands in the shadows as Burr makes his escape on horseback, followed by a posse.

Whether or not Burr was really guilty of treason remains unclear, not only in Welty's fictional account but in history books as well. As an ambitious young man seeking the office of the president of the United States, Aaron Burr ran for office against Thomas Jefferson in a tied election that was decided by the House of Representatives, which chose Jefferson as president and Burr as vice-president. After his four-year term in 1804, Burr failed to be re-nominated as vice-president and he also failed to win the governorship of New York State because of the forceful opposition of Alexander Hamilton, a sharp Federalist critic of Burr. After Burr killed Hamilton in the famous duel, he became involved in a scheme that made his political recovery hopeless. Scholars have not been able to determine the exact outlines of the so-called Burr conspiracy. Alexander DeConde summarizes three different scenarios: "Some contemporaries, as well as historians, believed that . . . Burr planned to detach Louisiana and states along the Mississippi from the Union and create a separate nation. His defenders said no; he merely wished to live in peace on lands he owned in the Territory of Orleans. Others . . . thought he wanted to raise an army to invade Texas and Mexico, an idea that appealed to the anti-Hispanic prejudices of Westerners."[13] The precise nature of Burr's political intentions remains shrouded in mystery, but his desire for conquest, whatever shape it took, was shared by many of his contemporaries. When Burr came to Natchez in 1807 to seek refuge and to launch his new adventure into the "territories," he had already been arrested twice on the charge of treason for seeking Western secession from the Union. Both times he was triumphantly released and evidently "his popularity mounted with what seemed to be persecution of him."[14] Welty focuses on this glamorous side of Burr while keeping his true political intentions veiled.

Welty's choice of making a deaf observer privy to Burr's nightly discussions with his confidant Blennerhassett seems to be an effective way for perpetuating his aura of mystique and avoiding disclosure. Almost all critics have commented on Joel as a narrative consciousness and most agree that the deaf narrator's limited perspective on the historical incidents in Natchez unfortunately reduces the story's social and political impact. The result of this narrative technique is that Welty appears to shrink the "political factum Aaron Burr to a romantic myth of subconscious self-experience of man" and that "reality becomes an integrated part of a visionary view of the world, which is experienced as mystery" by the adolescent narrator (Ritter, p. 24). This narrative strategy seems "unsettling" and has been characterized by Victor H. Thompson as an outright "problem of narration" created by the fact that the reader encounters two views of Burr simultaneously: Joel's private view and history's public view.[15] But while Thompson believes that Welty assigns private meaning to public history through Joel's limited consciousness, I think the opposite might be true. Welty's concern with Joel's perception draws attention not to a private world of symbols but to the very constructedness of public meaning. In other words, Welty's choice of a marginal character to report on the events of Aaron Burr's trial is not a romantic flight from historical reality as it may seem but a shrewd reflection on the ever-elusive nature of past events. Her concern with the construction of historical meaning, expressed through Joel's communication handicap, leads Welty to phenomenological speculations about how language makes meaning, speculations intricately linked with her message and revisionary view of "History." Looking at a particular historical moment through the eyes of a marginal adolescent observer who is detached from the world of speech estranges the events surrounding Burr's visit to Natchez and calls into question the very nature of historical reality as a construction of the past that is never fully available for knowledge. In the story's opening, Welty provides a comment on time and the elusive nature of the past:

> Whatever happened, it happened in extraordinary times, in a season of dreams, and in Natchez it was the bitterest winter of them all. The north wind struck one January night in 1807 with an insistent penetration, as if it followed the settlers down by their own course, screaming down the river bends to drive them further still. Afterwards there was the strange drugged fall of snow.[16]

"Whatever happened." This opening qualifier questions accepted certainties about knowledge and truth, and by casting its doubt over history it marks a crisis both in epistemology (what can be known) and ontology (what exists).[17] As if to counteract the stormy thrust of epistemological uncertainty, Welty anchors the location of her story securely in a specific narrative moment, a living present literally frozen. And yet, despite the freezing of time and space, neither the historical moment nor its meaning is ever simply present other than as a "trace" of something else.

Welty's representation of history as a net of elusive traces might be illuminated by Derrida's idea of the "trace." The concept of the trace, for Derrida, is central to a post-humanist theory of meaning as located in difference. Commenting on his choice of the term "trace," Derrida writes: "If words and concepts receive meaning only in sequences of differences, one can justify one's language, and one's choice of terms, only within a topic [an orientation in space] and an historical strategy" (p. 41). Looking back at the history of philosophy, Derrida critiques the understanding of meaning as presence and substitutes in its stead the idea of the "trace."[18] As a concept, the trace is neither an entity, nor an origin, nor the signified itself. "The trace is nothing, it is not an entity, it exceeds the question *What is?* and contingently makes it possible" (p. 47). The trace defies our search for origins as well, as Gayatri Spivak explains: "In our effort to define things, we look for origins. Every origin that we seem to locate refers us back to something anterior and contains the possibility of something posterior. There is, in other words, a trace of something else in seemingly self-contained origins."[19] When Derrida introduces the concept of the "trace," he refers to an idea of temporality that implicates the past and the future in the present moment:

> the living present springs forth out of its nonidentity with itself and from the possibility of a retentional trace. It is always already a trace. This trace cannot be thought out on the basis of a simple present whose life would be within itself; the self of the living present is primordially a trace.
>
> (p. 26)

Signification is always engaged in the "movement" of the trace, as Welty's own comments on time show; "time tells us nothing about itself except by the signals that it is passing."[20] The fiction writer may tamper with time by freezing or accelerating action, but she is incapable of capturing the present, or in other words presenting the present to itself. Welty's comments about the ephemeral quality of the present again evoke the Derridan understanding of time:

> It is by the ephemeral that our feeling is so strongly aroused for what endures, or strives to endure. One time compellingly calls up the other. Thus, the ephemeral, being alive only in the present moment, must be made to live in the novel as *now,* while it transpires, in the transpiring.
>
> (p. 168)

What exactly transpires in the frozen historical moment of **"First Love"**? By freezing the setting, Welty prepares the reader for a transformed understanding of reality and history characterized by a loss of proportion and a new narrative perspective: "Bands of travelers moved closer together, with intense caution, through the glassy tunnels of the Trace, for all proportion went away . . ." (p. 4). As Welty is negotiating the tunnels of her own textual "traces," she prepares the reader for the seemingly disproportionate perspective of the twelve-year-old deaf boy. His deafness is crucial because it allows Welty to link the character's ontological isolation (and her own interest in the mysteries of language, signification, and speech) with problems of historical transmission, trauma, and "truth." Thus composed of numerous interrelated layers of interest, the fabric of her story, as Welty characterizes it, is woven of interior and exterior realms of experience in which history, phenomenology, and psychology intersect to form a rich texture. Welty says, "Maybe that was the trouble with the story, everything (for me) carried the burden of being so many things at once" (Kreyling, *Author,* p. 58). But this multitude of meanings merges successfully in the figure of the "trace" which relates Welty's exploration of signification (the linguistic trace) to the historical location (the Natchez Trace) and to questions of political representation. It is for this reason that Welty renders Joel's speech visible. As a deaf boy, Joel cannot hear himself or others except under the special circumstances of this winter when the icy air makes invisible speech visible:

> He saw the breaths coming out of people's mouths, and his dark face, losing just now a little of its softness, showed its secret desire. It was marvelous to him when the infinite designs of speech became visible in formations on the air, and he watched with awe that changed to tenderness whenever people met and passed in the road with an exchange of words.
>
> (p. 5)

This physical and visible manifestation of speech becomes a central concern in this story. When Joel walked out in the cold, he "let his own breath out through his lips, pushed it into the air, and whatever word it was it took the shape of a tower. He was as pleased as if he had had a little conversation with someone" (p. 5). By seeing himself speak, Joel is able to (re)present himself in language to himself. The phallic "tower" of his breath signifies self-presence in language made visible; his silent phonemes literally present themselves to his gaze and in the process transform his understanding of his position in the world.

Joel learns what speech and silence mean to the world of hearing. When the settlers are hiding from the Indians in the cane brake off the Natchez Trace, Joel cries and makes a sound. The frontier guide, old man McCaleb, threatens to kill him with an axe in "a kind of ecstasy of protecting the silence they were keeping" (p. 7). In an instinctive reflex, Joel presses his mouth against the earth, comprehending for the first time "what silence means to other people" and feeling in this "speechless embrace" a "powerful, crushing unity" (p. 7). His learning experience here is not just of private importance as critics often assume. His story is not simply about his overcoming "the numbing effects of his private psychological and spiritual tragedies."[21] Nor is Joel a handicapped observer who simplifies the political and historical dimensions of the events to a "childish level of experience" (Ritter, p. 24). Far from providing us with a naive perspective, Joel's silent observations highlight the presence of other silent characters, the anonymous Indians, with whom his life is inextricably linked. Joel's experience of the "powerful crushing unity" therefore extends not only to the speaking settler community of Natchez and later on specifically to Aaron Burr, but to the silent Indians who are responsible for making him an orphan in the first place.

Joel's story, much like Burr's own, is about the American experience of settlement. As settlers who came from Virginia looking for new land and a new life, Joel and his parents are part of the American national epic of westward expansion marked by the violence of the encounter with Native American populations. Like his counterpart Aaron Burr, Joel represents the flotsam of this pioneer spirit and the promise of the American dream. Welty zooms in on the dreamlike quality of the frontier experience; she focuses on the dreams of the men who sleep in the little inn on their journey into the wilderness, on Joel's own difficulty in distinguishing between his dreams of Burr and the reality of his visit, and finally on Burr's own dreams. Recast as a dream of expansion and conquest, and symbolized by the boots of the westward travelers and pioneers, this American dream is rooted in personal trauma for Joel. On his way to Natchez, Joel loses his parents as they become separated from the group of travelers on the Trace and "vanished in the forest, were cut off from him, and in spite of his last backward look, dropped behind" (p. 6). The trauma of his loss and separation, deeply ingrained in Joel's memory, is repressed. Welty captures such repressed violence and terror in an appropriately Western image: "His memory could work like the slinging of a noose to catch a wild pony. It reached back and hung trembling over the very moment of terror in which he had become separated from his parents, and then it turned and started in the opposite direction, and it would have discerned some shape, but he would not let it, of the future" (pp. 12-13). Dreams of the future, the "arms bent on destination" that dragged him forward and away from the scene of loss and death, are necessary for the young nation's destiny and development. But for Joel as well as for Burr, conquest also involves leaving loved ones behind and the dream of conquest is never far from being a nightmare as colonial cultures succeed each other.

Welty carefully sketches such a colonial environment. When Burr enters Joel's room, "[e]verything in the room was conquest, all was a dream of delights and powers beyond its walls" (p. 15). Burr and Blennerhassett sit at Joel's table, carved with Spanish words of love, "for anyone to read who came knowing the language" (p. 9). Languages of colonial conquest, Spanish and American, mark Joel's room, signaling the West as a continuous process of colonial domination and as an ongoing contest for property, profit, and cultural dominance. Joel's environment is characterized by a climate of national expansionism, and Burr's "dream" becomes Joel's dream in the famous gesture Burr makes during his first visit to Joel's room, a gesture "like the signal to open some heavy gate or paddock" that opens Joel's mind and heart to larger panoramas of historical and personal significance. Burr's dream is also passed on through the pressure of his burning hand, which transmits his "wisdom" to Joel at the climax of the story and before Burr disappears from Joel's life. The fierce, possessive grip of Burr's hand is nevertheless that of a sleeper who is wildly dreaming and threatens to reveal himself in his dangerous dreams of conquest. When Joel grasps the hand of Burr, he shares the same cultural dream that uproots him and his parents in the first place and brings them to a violent confrontation with Indians. This memory of violence has to be repressed in order for America's belief in progress and expansion to succeed, and therefore Joel does not allow himself to remember or grieve for his parents until he stands on Liberty Road at the end of the story. Having lost Burr, the person who most fiercely embodies this dream, "Joel would never know now the true course, or the true outcome of any dream" (p. 33). With the dream of expansion cast in such uncertainty and eluding his grasp as Burr is riding off on Liberty Road, a shadow is cast as well over the American credo of "life, liberty and happiness." And it is only then, in the catharsis brought about by the recognition of loss, that Joel falls to the ground and weeps for his parents killed by the Indians.[22]

In fact, a careful reading reveals that Joel's perspective on the political events of 1807 is haunted by Indians, who are voiceless like himself, who live in a world deaf to their presence, and whose ghostly traces are deeply rooted in his unconscious. Indian traces appear five times in the story and in the signifier of the Natchez Trace itself. As a spacial signifier, the Natchez Trace is a meeting place between colonizer and colonized, a place that ultimately points to the disenfranchisement of Native American nations and towards white westward expansion and nation-building, whether in the form of the Lewis and Clark Expedition or in the form of Burr's treasonous "plot." The Indians first appear when Welty describes the time and setting of the story:

> The Indians could be heard from greater distances and in greater numbers than had been guessed, sending up placating but proud messages to the sun in continual

> ceremonies of dancing. The red percussion of their fires could be seen night and day by those waiting in the dark trance of the frozen town.
>
> (p. 4)

We encounter Native Americans here as a typically proud, fierce, dangerous but anonymous force. The description of drumming and dancing Indians serves the purpose of othering them, with the "red" of their fires marking their racial difference. Welty's failure to identify the Indians by tribe or affiliation indicates that they function merely as traces of an American past, and as a group of people who seem marginal to the current political events. By depicting the Indians as sun worshipers, Welty most likely alludes to the Natchez, who were famous for their sun worship and the perpetual fires they kept burning in their temples. As historical signifiers, the Natchez Indians do not mark the narrative present, however, but are a historical trace that takes us back to the French/Choctaw massacre of the Natchez in 1729, which left the tribe nearly extinct. Natchez survivors joined the Creek, Cherokee, and Chickasaw tribes and became assimilated, or they were sold into slavery by the French. Therefore, it is historically highly unlikely that Joel's parents were killed by "a band of Natchez," as Kreyling assumes.[23] The Natchez were believed to be practically extinct by this time in history, and at the time of the composition of this story they were already listed as an extinct native tribe. Welty's allusion to the Natchez therefore registers their sudden ghostly presence, which takes us back *and* forward in time to scenes of Indian slaughter. In the narrative present of 1807, when the settlers in Mississippi Territory were after all on Indian lands, U.S. territorial conquest involved not only negotiation with other European powers—a conflict foregrounded by the Burr case—but also negotiation with Native Americans who were systematically dispossessed of their homes, languages, cultures, and lives. This historical reality manifests itself as a trace in Welty's text that points backwards to attempts at their extinction in the past and forward to their removal from Mississippi in the 1830s. Accordingly, Indians file through Welty's text in metaphorical fashion:

> The Indians had then gone by, followed by an old woman—in solemn, single file, careless of the inflaming arrows they carried in their quivers, dangling in their hands a few strings of catfish. They passed in the length of an old woman's yawn.
>
> (p. 7)

The Indians are solemn figures followed by an old woman who symbolizes the nearness of death, connoting their own extinction. This passage seems to be Welty's elegy for the noble savages who live by their arrows, work with simple tools and eat from the rivers and forests. By recording the passing of a subsistence society to the advances of the settlers, Welty evokes nineteenth-century discourses of social Darwinism that were often used to justify colonialist enterprises. The Indians themselves are marked by "single files," "arrows," and "strings"—all signifying the linearity of their passing (through and away). Their brief appearances—in the length of a yawn—and immediate disappearance both from the settler's and the reader's view emphasize their temporality, immateriality, and ghostliness.

It is therefore not surprising that the next trace marking Indian presence in the text links them with the disembodied presence of ghosts. After the first mysterious nightly visit of Aaron Burr to Joel's room, Joel wakes up and "his first thought was of Indians, his next of ghosts, and then the vision of what had happened came back into his head" (p. 12). Joel is haunted by Indian ghosts who have found their way into his dreams and his unconscious. But this presencing of the repressed is not just Joel's individual nightmare; the ghostly return of Indian slaughter and dispossession is shared by the settlers of Natchez and the United States at large. If "haunting belongs to the structure of every hegemony," as Derrida asserts,[24] the haunting in Welty's text expresses a drama of national guilt. Because such guilt about conquest and extermination is repressed, it returns in the textual traces of Indian presence whose absence the settlers so desire.

The Indian traces manifest guilt and doubt perhaps also in Welty's own unconsciousness, returning us to her earlier insistence that she does not go "into such things as guilt over the Indians." But for the writer who occupies a space in the South that is marked by the traumatic removal of Chickasaws and Choctaws to Indian territory just one hundred years earlier, it is precisely such a denial that points to an important presence in the traces of her own fiction. Renee Bergland argues that "when ghostly Indian figures haunt the white American imagination, they serve as constant reminders of the fragility of national identity."[25] In writing about Burr's conspiracy, Welty presents a well-known public discourse about national unity and identity, one so familiar that its plot threatens to erase the underlying traces of Native American history. By alluding to the Indian presence in the story, however, Welty does more than create a historical backdrop; she presents the plot of American history in the local traces that remain. Welty was interested in local history and place names. In her review of George Stewart's book *Names on the Land,* written just three years after the publication of ***The Wide Net,*** Welty remarks that "the record of our place-names is of course the skeleton of our nation; in that array the intrinsic and underlying structure shows" (*Eye,* p. 182). She was particularly interested in the structures that pointed to Indian names: "the book deals constantly with Indians, of course, and manages to correct many an error about Indian names" (p. 187). In this discussion of Indian signifiers in the American landscape, Welty highlights the history of colonization which led to the obliteration of origins, and she explains that place names are often untraceable:

> Transference, translation and false etymology are the three ways in which a place name can be passed from language to language. . . . So the Indian names enduring as such are not the actual, original Indian names—they are what the French priests wrote down, what the Spanish thought they sounded like, what the English thought they undoubtedly meant, what the Dutch made sound as nearly Dutch as they could.
>
> (*Eye,* p. 187)

For Welty, Native American names are signifiers of a colonial history that opens up "panoramas of the nation at a given time" (p. 185). The linguistic displacement of Indian names in the mapping of American geography corresponds both to the physical removal of Indians (from the Southeast) and perhaps also to the psychic displacement of the Native American presence in Welty's imagination. In both external and internal landscapes, Native Americans function as traces—repressed, displaced, and silenced, traces that threaten the rationalist hegemony of the U.S. and hence the successful construction of national identity.

American national identity in 1807 was still very young (it was less than thirty years earlier that amidst calls for a revolutionary war with Great Britain the Declaration of Independence was adopted) and the boundaries of the new nation were ever changing and often ambiguous. Because national identity centered around issues of expansion and conquest, Welty uses Burr primarily as a symbol of American expansionism. In researching the Burr conspiracy, Welty may have encountered the historical study by Walter Flavius McCaleb (1903), who conspicuously shares his name with one of Welty's frontier characters. McCaleb, the historian, argues that

> the conspiracy of Aaron Burr was preeminently a revolutionary product, receiving its inspiration from that unprecedented period of upheaval which began with the Revolution of 1776, its compelling force from the character of the American pioneer, its license from the disturbed condition of affairs existing in the New World.[26]

In short, Burr's expansionist schemes were a product of American nationalist ideology and perhaps only one symptom in the drama of American expansionism, which was officially pursued by Thomas Jefferson in the Louisiana Purchase of 1803 and in the Lewis and Clark Expeditions from 1803 to 1806.[27] President Jefferson himself instructed his Indian agent to convince native tribes "of the justice and liberality we are determined to use towards them, and to attach them to us indissolubly" (qtd. in McCaleb, p. 12). Clearly, Burr is not the only expansionist who favored growth at the expense of other nations. During this time in history, armed intrusions into countries then at peace with the United States, so-called filibustering expeditions, were rather common (although most of them were unsuccessful).[28] Similar to earlier border skirmishes of English, French and Spanish colonists, such private forays into neighboring countries, particularly popular in the America of the early nineteenth century, grew out of the ideology of expansionism. Encouraged by the prerogative of Manifest Destiny, American filibusters, like Burr, had an interest in the acquisition of territory for political and personal financial gains. McCaleb argues that one must take into consideration the mind of the settlers in the territories when looking at the conspiracy. Emphasizing the West's fervent nationalism and its revolutionist disposition, McCaleb reminds us that "for years the West harbored the most devoted adherents for the Constitution *and* the most unscrupulous filibusters" (p. 13, emphasis mine).

Put into this socio-historical context, Burr's paradoxical activities (both for and against his own country) appear more representative of a general political climate and less the sign of a greedy man's personal character flaw, and this may be the reason why he is not depicted as a villain but as an ironically romanticized hero in Welty's story. Charles Nolan's study of Aaron Burr in the American literary imagination singles out Welty's depiction of Burr as an unusual portrait because "Welty is able to depict Burr as an object of adoration and a seducer at the same time, harmonizing these apparently antipodal poles by making the Colonel's seductiveness lie in what he is, a character of dazzling brilliance whose personal charm makes people cherish and want to support him."[29] But despite Burr's popularity, his filibustering enterprise with Harman Blennerhassett failed.

Welty's depiction of Burr's failure centers around the arrival of his sadly diminished flotilla in Natchez, which Joel witnesses.[30] And not surprisingly Indians appear also in the context of this event:

> Where Joel stood looking down upon them, the boats floated in clusters of three, as small as water-lilies on a still bayou. A canoe filled with crazily wrapped-up Indians passed at a little distance, and with severe open mouths the Indians all laughed.
>
> (p. 22)

Why are they laughing? At whom are they laughing? The Indian laughter here might be a comment on

Burr's miserable failure to dispossess native inhabitants of their lands. Their "severe" laughter signifies amusement and triumph but perhaps also anxiety and even terror. It is this laughter that haunts the American national consciousness and ultimately pollutes American attempts at seriously justifying rightful possession of the land. Bergland argues that "land ownership may be the source of the nation's deepest guilt" (p. 8), and I think it may also be the reason why traces of Indian presence undermine the official drama of Burr's "transgressions" in Welty's story.

In a final brilliant stroke, Welty even links Burr with Native American identities. As a fugitive traveler on the Trace, Burr disguises himself as an Indian to escape the posse sent after him. Welty here changes the historical record, which claims that Burr was disguised as a river boatman, although historians disagree on this aspect of Burr's adventure as well.[31] Dressed as an Indian, Burr represents a double figure of the nation in crisis: he is a "native son," first, because of his famous American ancestry and his role in shaping the political destiny of the nation, and second, because of his feathery disguise which symbolizes original native ownership of America and alliance with the Indians. Articulating this paradoxical double-bind, Burr's disguise—his dirty and ragged clothes, the "little cap of turkey feathers on his head," and his boot-black face—is part of a persistent tradition of Indian-masking in American culture. Philip Deloria reminds us that Indian disguise symbolizes the age-old American desire to "feel a natural affinity with the continent."[32] Indians, he argues, could best teach settlers such "aboriginal closeness." The tragic irony, however, is that in order to possess themselves of the land they called their own, the settlers tried to destroy the native inhabitants, their source of native identification. By destroying the Indians but preserving and adopting the very images that served for national identification, Indian-masking was (and is) an important means for creating an American national identity. Read in this context, it seems that Welty uses Burr's Indian disguise to articulate a crisis in American identity by drawing attention to the ironic gap between the "rightful" possession of land—Jefferson's and not Burr's—which is always at the same time the wrongful dispossession of the Native populations. Such a historical scenario, which centers around the political silencing of Native American voices in the national drama, is also symbolically reflected in Joel's deafness (the young settler's deafness) which represents the nation's inability to hear and listen to Native American interests and needs.

Read carefully for the textual traces of Native American presence, **"First Love"** takes on a decidedly socio-historical theme. By anchoring this theme in the specific location of the Natchez Trace, Welty chooses a historical place that perfectly embodies the epistemological struggle for historical truth. In 1934, the Department of Interior made a National Park out of the Natchez Trace and began paving it over and opening it for car travel. Along the route are marked sites where historical incidents occurred, many of them remnants of Indian days, such as pre-historic Indian mounds, the foundations of Chickasaw villages, sites of former council houses, territorial markers, travel stops, and camps that dot the parkway. As the trace was reconstructed, history was "preserved," but more so it was rewritten: the paved road which is the "Trace" today is not identical with the old "historical" pathway. So the Natchez Trace of 1934 captures a historical moment that never was and can never be repeated; only new non-identical traces can be created. As a historical location whose modern construction dates from Welty's time as a WPA agent, the Natchez Trace itself reveals the very constructedness of time and place, history and location. Welty writes that location "is not simply to be used by the writer—it is to be discovered" (*Eye,* p. 129). What Welty discovers on the Natchez Trace, I believe, is an anxiety around the Indian voices of the nation and the ultimate irony of American nation-building.

Notes

1. See Welty's correspondence with her agent Diarmuid Russell in Michael Kreylings's *Author and Agent: Eudora Welty and Diarmuid Russell* (New York: Farrar, Straus, Giroux, 1991). This source also includes a publication history of each of the stories in *The Wide Net.*
2. Welty speaks about her work for the WPA in an interview with Bill Ferris in *Conversations with Eudora Welty,* ed. Peggy Whitman Prenshaw (Jackson: University Press of Mississippi, 1984), p. 155.
3. Jo Brans, "Struggling Against the Plaid: An Interview with Eudora Welty," in *Conversations with Eudora Welty,* p. 299.
4. Michael Kreyling, *Eudora Welty's Achievement of Order* (Baton Rouge: Louisiana State University Press, 1980), p. 17.
5. "The Love and Separateness in Miss Welty," in *Critical Essays on Eudora Welty,* ed. Craig W. Turner and Lee Emling Harding (Boston: G. K. Hall & Co., 1989), p. 50.
6. Alexander Ritter, "Natchez in the Fiction of Three Centuries: Variants of Literary Regionalism in Chateaubriand, Sealsfeld and Welty," *Southern Quarterly,* 35 (Fall 1996), 25.
7. Patricia Yaeger, *Dirt and Desire: Reconstructing Southern Women's Writing, 1930-1990* (Chicago: University of Chicago Press, 2000), p. 157.

8. John Griffin Jones, "Eudora Welty," in *Conversations with Eudora Welty,* p. 333.
9. Peggy Kamuf, ed. *A Derrida Reader: Between the Blinds* (New York: Columbia University Press, 1991), p. 27.
10. Chester E. Eisinger discusses Welty's work as situated between the "traditional novel" and the modernist novel. But in characterizing Welty's affinity for modernism, he groups under the rubric "modernist" many characteristics which are even more pronounced in the work of postmodernists such as non-linear concepts of time and space, reality as illusion, uncertainties concerning identity, and the critique of ontology ("Traditionalism and Modernism in Eudora Welty," in *Eudora Welty: Thirteen Essays,* ed. Peggy Whitman Prenshaw [Jackson: University Press of Mississippi, 1983], p. 4).
11. *Mississippi: The WPA Guide to the Magnolia State.* Intro. Robert S. McElvaine (Jackson: University Press of Mississippi, 1988), p. 84.
12. These historical characters include, for instance, Lorenzo Dow, a Methodist minister; James Murrell, the infamous bandit; and John James Audubon, the well-known ornithologist and painter from "A Still Moment" (1942) and Mike Fink from *The Robber Bridegroom* (1942).
13. Alexander DeConde, *This Affair of Louisiana* (New York: Charles Scribner's Sons, 1976), p. 237.
14. Jonathan Daniels, *The Devil's Backbone: The Story of the Natchez Trace* (Gretna, Louisiana: Pelican Publishing Company, 1992), p. 164.
15. Victor H. Thompson, "Aaron Burr in Eudora Welty's 'First Love,'" *Notes on Mississippi Writers,* 8 (1976), 77.
16. Eudora Welty, *The Wide Net and Other Stories* (New York: Harcourt Brace, 1971), p. 3.
17. Robert Penn Warren, in a perceptive review of *The Wide Net,* remarks that the opening sentence begins "as though the author cannot be quite sure what did happen, cannot quite undertake to resolve the meaning of the recorded event, cannot, in fact, be too sure of recording all of the event" (p. 43). This "coyness" is more than the warning Warren takes it to be; it is a calculated effect that is thematically related to the meaning of the story. Granted it is difficult to distinguish "conscious" from "unconscious" effects in literature; but Welty's narrative framework, her choice of subject matter, and her creation of Joel as a filtering consciousness to mediate historical "truth" strongly point towards her intention to question history.
18. Derrida sees the trace as taking shape particularly in the works of Nietzsche and Freud. The deconstruction of presence that Derrida discovers in their work "accomplishes itself through the deconstruction of consciousness, and therefore through the irreducible notion of the trace (Spur)" (p. 42).
19. Gayatri Spivak, "Sex and History in *The Prelude,*" *Postcolonialist Readings of English Poetry,* ed. Richard Machin and Christopher Norris (Cambridge: Cambridge University Press, 1987), p. 194.
20. Eudora Welty, *The Eye of the Story* (New York: Vintage, 1990), p. 163.
21. St. George Tucker Arnold, "Eudora Welty's *First Love* and the Personalizing of Southern Regional History," *Journal of Regional Cultures,* 1 (1982), 97.
22. Suzanne Marrs argues that the only way Joel can move forward is by confronting his past. In this sense, Welty's story is a comment on the power of memory, and her choice of Liberty Road as a final setting is "an emblem of Joel's development and an ironic comment on Burr's" ("The Conclusion of Eudora Welty's 'First Love': Historical Backgrounds," *Notes on Mississippi Writers,* 13 [1981], 77).
23. Michael Kreyling, *Understanding Eudora Welty* (Columbia: University of South Carolina Press, 1999), p. 52.
24. Jacques Derrida, *Specters of Marx* (New York: Routledge, 1994), p. 37.
25. Renee L. Bergland, *The National Uncanny: Indian Ghosts and American Subjects* (Hanover, New Hampshire: Dartmouth College, 2000), p. 5.
26. Walter Flavius McCaleb, *The Aaron Burr Conspiracy* (New York: Dodd, Mead & Co., 1903), p. 1.
27. Lewis and Clark were scouting out new territories, apparently trying to curry favors from Indian tribes who were enlisted in the war against Spain. The Spanish clearly recognized the ulterior purpose of the expedition, which was ostensibly about the discovery of new territories but really designed to estrange the Indians from alliances with the Spanish. See McCaleb, p. 12.
28. Settlers were not always waiting for official decisions about new territories from Washington. For instance, two frontier men, Nathan and Samuel Kemper, and about thirty followers marched on Baton Rouge in June of 1804 with the intention of overthrowing the Spanish regime. The revolt was quickly crushed and the insurgents were forced to seek refuge in Mississippi Territory (DeConde, p. 220).

29. Charles J. Nolan, Jr., *Aaron Burr and the American Literary Imagination* (Westport, Connecticut: Greenwood Press, 1980), p. 112.

30. A good historical account of the flotilla incident is mentioned in Herbert S. Parmet and Marie B. Hecht (*Aaron Burr: Portrait of an Ambitious Man* [New York: Macmillan, 1967]). The purpose of this flotilla was apparently as unclear as Burr's plans. It is reported to have been composed of a total of "sixteen oars, eight flatboats, and six keels" (p. 269). Apparently no women and children were on the boats which, according to eyewitnesses, seem to have been loaded with boxes of muskets.

31. Parmet and Hecht write that Burr was disguised "as a riverboat man in an old blanket coat with a leather strap across from which dangled a tin cup and a scalping knife. A broken down white hat almost completely obscuring his face, completed his attire" (p. 282). Victor Thompson, who cites J. F. H. Claibourne's book as a historical source for Welty's image, believes that Burr was disguised as an Indian. Claibourne writes: "I cannot describe his dress; but from the description I have heard of it, it appeared to me to be that of an Indian country man carricatured [sic]" (qtd., p. 80).

32. Philip J. Deloria, *Playing Indian* (New Haven: Yale University Press, 1998), p. 5.

Carey Wall (essay date summer 2002)

SOURCE: Wall, Carey. "Ritual Technique and Renewal in Eudora Welty's 'Kin.'" *Southern Quarterly* 40, no. 4 (summer 2002): 39-52.

[*In the following essay, Wall studies the symbolic function of photography in the ritualistic family milieu of "Kin," highlighting the mixture of mockery and solemnity that informs the story.*]

Eudora Welty's **"Kin"** presents a condensed history of the passage of life through a particular place, Mingo, from the time a couple came into the wilderness to make a home here, to the development of a large extended family in the place, to the present in which most of the extended family have moved away and even those remaining in the nearby town find Mingo, only nine miles away, very remote, a place of life past. Welty validates place as a source of life; she says that where life has been, life remains (*Eye* 286). She shows that in **"Kin,"** for the collective action of **"Kin"** passes the flame of family life to the newly engaged, now visiting young woman Dicey, who will return to the North after the story's end full of the spirit of life that once infused Mingo.

"Kin" is full of rambunctious action; these kinfolks treat one another roughly, offending many readers and eliciting their scorn and their belief that Welty satirizes her characters.[1] According to the understanding bred by the social norms these readers bring to the story, this action could not be the way, certainly not the proper way, to pass on the torch of family life. It is the wedding in all its structure, keeping all participants in their proper places, surely, that performs that transmission. Not so. A ritual studies analysis of **"Kin,"** one based on anthropologist Victor Turner's demonstration that there are *two* modes of people's social interrelatedness, indicates that the rough mayhem of **"Kin"** (like that of many Welty stories), has not just a powerful but a vital role to play in the construction of ongoing life. A well-constructed wedding ceremony may indicate what family life ought to be; Welty's characters' actions in **"Kin"** shows what family life probably will be and fortifies Dicey Hastings for a life within the construction of family.

In the second mode of social groups' interrelatedness, Turner argues, groups set aside the confining, selective constructions of proper and good behavior according to the hierarchically marked "structure" that determines most of everyday life. They move into liminality, frequently by reversing structural norms and definitions. What structure calls bad behavior is called for (*From Ritual* 43), necessary for the fumigation, so to speak, of highly reductive prescriptions. Groups act to re-enter messy, chaotic, contestatory, full-powered life, in its myriad possible constructions, its riches of materials for people to construct to meet their needs. At exceptional moments, by trying out the elements of their culture in new combinations, groups bring some of the seemingly bizarre constructions of liminality back into social structure. At other times groups air their social constructions, so that when they inevitably return to social structure, it is basically unchanged but its members know what it is. Social structure suppresses the untidinesses of life and the powerful forces it tries to overmaster. Social structure causes forgetfulness, repression, dangerous ignorance, blockage of people's access to their creative unconscious. What groups' journeys into liminality and its reversal do for them is retrieve the materials of life that social structure shuts out. It renews life by bringing life up to people in its full dimensions. Liminal practices in the rituals to which I will compare the action of **"Kin"** serve to make adjustments between the norms of social structure and life's real forces.[2]

There is another necessity for people's disassembling old social relationships. People cannot leap or fly from one construction of human relationships—or status—to another. Just as in physical travel, they need bridges, psychological and spiritual bridges. The old has to be taken apart before the new can be formed (Turner, *From Ritual* 84). Persuasive, effective constructions and transitions have to be lived through, acted on. Words only accompany action. Ritual is action, enactment, symbolic and thus different from everyday "automatic" routine; ritual action constitutes thinking by doing.

Ritual is one of the storehouses of life-making. Neither its materials nor its meanings are firmly fixed; they cannot be fixed because the realm of realities that produce interpretations of axiomatic meanings fluctuates and materials at hand change. What ritual offers is a set of techniques for such things as the displacing of the everyday so that people temporarily cease thinking in everyday flat mode and shift into the capacity for symbolic, relational thought that connects materials of the present scene with the storehouse of vibrating, multifaceted symbols any acculturated person has in her or his creative unconscious as a legacy from millennia of generations of ancestors. Living ritual is inventive.[3]

* * *

Welty's own version of life's motion and people's generating it is condensed in Virgie Rainey's awareness, not new but surfaced by the occasion, in **"The Wanderers."** From the perspective of a moment of hope and despair, she formulates doubling:

> Virgie never saw it differently, never doubted that all the opposites on earth were close together, love close to hate, living to dying; but of them all, hope and despair were the closest blood—unrecognizable one from the other sometimes, making moments double upon themselves, and in the doubling, double again, amending but never taking back.
>
> (***Stories*** **[*The Collected Stories of Eudora Welty*]** 452-53)

Dying is close to living. Thus, in **"Kin"** the main characters come out of their various "death"-stamped conditions to resurrect the pulse of family life. Dicey emerges from her forgetting both the Milky Way and Mingo; Anne emerges from her condition as a parasitic, homeless relative; Ethel emerges momentarily from the dying she has chosen as a response to her husband's death; and Felix emerges from his dying old-man's lethargy to communicate with Dicey. They know that they should and can remember their family's life. That is, they know their obligation to life, from which their own lives derived. They act on their *deep* knowledge (Turner, *Dramas* 36, 239, 258; emphasis added), which prescribes, so to speak, ritual action, drama, performance.

"Life crisis," the movement of someone from any status in the sequence of life stages to another, starts the action in **"Kin."** Dicey brings her transition from unmarried girl to married woman to her relatives and to Mingo. Her journey generates many people's action because a life crisis arouses not just the central person on the move but also all those around that person (Turner, *Forest* 7). Dicey's readiness for marriage constitutes an opportunity for a family in crisis: will its life go on or go out? Ethel, Anne, Felix, and Kate all come together around charismatic Dicey to play their parts in connecting her with the rich old family life at Mingo. Anne pulls Dicey there; Ethel pushes Dicey there from her bed in town; once Dicey is there, Felix makes physical contact and communicates; and Kate goes along to reiterate obtuse social judgments, thereby reminding Dicey how inadequate and false they are.

In crisis, life shifts. Definitions and appropriateness shift to accommodate the now dominant need (Turner, *Dramas* 16). Maintaining life, as in passing the flame of a family's life so that that life may continue, requires illumination that ordinary social definitions of politeness and caring, for example, cannot provide. **"Kin"**'s action derives from the importance of preserving the quality of Uncle Felix's life, from that goal's taking precedence over being polite to him and not disturbing him in his dying days (in other words, simply accepting his death). Ordinary dispositions shift to the margins of less importance; crucial symbols dilate.[4] In performing ritual, real people and literary characters still perform acts motivated by social structure's (society's) definitions, but they deploy these acts for liminal and ritual ends, to resolve life crises. In other words, liminal redistribution of realities takes precedence over the social act of separating by defining, and even prejudicial acts driven by social definition are reversed in their effects, doubled.

In **"Kin"** the central symbols are elementary ones—the house and the street. Roberto Da Matta, analyzing Brazilian Carnival, identifies their domains and interplay. The house is an orderly place where people are taken in and secure. Rules make their lives orderly. Here people have a clear connection with family and an identity. In contrast, in the street one has no identity and is not safe from life's roughness. At the same time, however, the house can severely limit people's lives. Adventure, growth, and even morality—choices—belong to the street. Life flows when there is interaction between the house and the street (209-13, *passim*). People with the house and the street at hand need no more; they are richly endowed with instigating sources of action. *The actions of the characters of* **"Kin"** *reincorporate the street within the house, reconnect the two into the interplay people must maintain between them to produce rich, creative life.* Sister Anne, as well as Uncle Felix, knows this before Dicey learns it in the course of the story.

Sister Anne brings in the photography that plays a crucial part in the action. The photographer, his clients and the very explosive process itself (the light flashes suggest gunpowder) bring the street aggressively into Uncle Felix's house. But this invasion is beneficent. Photography is the "sweet cheat" that Dicey calls it just before she leaves Mingo; life moves, it cannot be fixed and preserved as people want it to and as photography seems to offer. Dicey has wanted life to be fixed, thus safe, too; it is that desire the action at Mingo persuades her to leave behind, so that she can face marriage and her life with an openness to what comes comparable to that of her ancestress Evelina when she came to the wilderness to make a life. Photography cheats but it also elicits a reverence for life that provides a context in which Uncle Felix can be displaced and for the moment depreciated and Dicey can learn without harm to him. In this context of crisis at Mingo, the photography session works like the saints' processions in the streets of Rio. Da Matta argues that a procession in which a saint (the statue of a saint) is taken out of the church and carried through the streets "is a moment in which the saint, being above everyone, overcomes the dichotomy of house and street, creating his or her own social domain" ("Carnival" 217). The photographing, the clients' desire for it and for the life it seems to capture and make permanent, transform the strangers' invasion of Uncle Felix's house into the place of a celebration of life. Dicey receives her communications from Uncle Felix *while the photographing is being performed, thus under the protection of its reverence for life.* Photography makes Mingo on this day a place where what at first looks like a wake for the dead turns out to be a moment of solemnity for life akin to the life Uncle Felix used to supervise and to center at Mingo. Life's irreverence—Anne's and the photography clients' disruption of Felix, Dicey, and Kate's ridiculing Sister Anne, Dicey's sassing Sister Anne—gets incorporated as subordinate in an encompassing, dominant love of life, and thus life is safe here.

Mingo is in fact highly charged for ritual action when Dicey visits her relatives. Da Matta, following Turner's primary lines of thought, points out that people make ritual not out of exotic things but out of the everyday. All it takes to transform the things of automatic everyday life into the quickened things of ritual is displacement (212-16). **"Kin"** compounds displacement. Dicey is displacing herself from her girlhood; Uncle Felix gets displaced from his slow, quiet dying and from his bedroom by the photography session; Sister Anne gets happily displaced into a hostess role from her status as a homeless, visiting, relative; the photography clients are displaced by the opportunity to get their photographs taken from their usual work-day chores; and the family once centered at Mingo is being displaced by Uncle Felix's impending death. By means of Anne's presence and Dicey's visit, the Mingo that has been forgotten (even by those, like Kate, who still visit it) comes alive again as the place of ritual.

For there was ritual at Mingo, in the Sunday gatherings of the clan there, in the placement of the ancestress Evelina's portrait on the wall, in the "home-place" epithet Mingo carried, in Uncle Felix's making everyone behave decorously, in his wife Beck's always giving everyone a nosegay of Mingo flowers as they left and bidding them to remember, in the generational sharing when Uncle Felix and Dicey as a small girl looked at his stereopticon slides together and Dicey realized that although the slides were so charged that they seemed to lay their pictures against her brain, there was more in them for Uncle Felix than she could fathom. On this day Mingo is sufficiently revived to nurture Dicey and thus to effect through her the continuation of this family's life. In these practices Felix and the others reinforced the decorum of family life, and Dicey's remembering these things gathers them into the knowledge of family life the day makes intense. The roughness she learns to accept will not displace the decorum; these opposites will cohabit with her family life.

The converged displacements send a ripple through everyone. Dicey gets engaged to be married and comes to visit her southern relatives to tell her news. The local small town newspaper, as small town newspapers always do, or did, carries news of the presence of this visitor from far away. Sister Anne goes into action. Without blatant announcements of day and time of day, Welty's text makes it probable that Sister Anne accepts the photographer's request to use Mingo's parlor because she has just read that Dicey is visiting. Without Dicey, despite her longing for company, she might respect the social law that gives Uncle Felix's dying more importance than her satisfying her own desire for company. But Dicey's visit, at this moment, in this context, pivots priorities.

In bringing her marriage to the time of Uncle Felix's dying, Dicey accepts her connection to her larger family. It is up to her relatives to show her the value of the integration of the house and the street, the site of marriage and family life that gives people room to develop.

Dicey's Aunt Ethel demonstrates how not to take marriage. She has incorporated her husband's life with her own so exclusively that when he dies, her active life finishes. Seventeen years a widow, she has been carrying Harlan's death and withering away with it. Now a bedridden invalid, she still speaks from the perspective she has chosen and thus makes fun of her antithesis, "Sister" Anne, that "lily of the field." On the occasion of this visit and the note that arrives from Anne at Mingo, Ethel knows that she must send Dicey to the homeplace and to this woman who has chosen the street as her site of allegiance. Ethel makes fun of Anne but also makes her interesting, a scapegrace who gets away with always being up to something. Her description entices the girls to go out to Mingo to check up on Anne.

Anne's competitiveness is at work when she accepts the photographer's request to use Mingo's parlor as a temporary studio. If Ethel can have company in town, so can Anne have company in the country. She may even be able to lure Ethel's company away from her by means of that note she sends. But the competitiveness she has honed in hierarchical society here serves another purpose. Anne tells the photographer that his day at Mingo had better come soon; that is, Felix may die at any moment. A photography session cannot displace a wake or intrude on an early period of mourning. That is the social structural reason. The other reason is that there may be very little time in which to draw Dicey together with a still living Felix, the man who was the center of the family life. As doubling occurs, the one reason tips or opens into the other effortlessly.

What Dicey perceives in her contact with Uncle Felix on this day is that he has been a man of the street as well as the man of the house whom she has known. Most particularly, in relation to her forthcoming marriage, she perceives that, married to Beck, he has had an affair of unknown dimensions with a woman named Daisy;[5] he has had an extramarital affair and yet the affair did not destroy the man of the house, who held together the extended family with his attention to and respect for family. Because she looked at his stereopticon slides of places in the world with him, Dicey has known of Uncle Felix's yearning for the world, the street. Unsurprisingly, slide views of the world have not been enough. Probably incited by the explosions of light by which the photographer is making his slides in the front of the house, Felix says "Hide" and speaks of killing; Kate suggests he may have served as a drummer boy in the Civil War. In whatever context, he has known the roughness of the street. In his mature years, sometime, according to Dicey's construction, he has taken the adventure of the street in the means available in this countryside, in a romantic affair. Clearly, Daisy meant a lot to him. These experiences in the street are what *he* remembers, what he requests now in the note he writes and hands to Dicey: "River—Daisy—Midnight—Please" (***Stories*** 561).

While Kate cannot hear what Uncle Felix's words reveal, she is too much her mother's daughter with her mother's rigid belief in fidelity, Dicey, with a little difficulty, embraces what she perceives. Dicey herself helps to stimulate Uncle Felix's communication when she holds her handkerchief with fragrant flowers tied in a corner under his nose. She does it, significantly, "without knowing I was going to do it" (***Stories*** 555). She has made this trip to her relatives to see Uncle Felix without consciously knowing it was he she was coming to see.[6] She is about to trust her life and happiness to a man, in marriage, and Uncle Felix is the married man she has known in whom she has greatest faith. She comes for a reconnection with him. In choosing to come, she shows she is set to take in stride what she effectively learns from him.

Sister Anne makes the connection possible. She does a great deal more than lure Dicey out to Mingo. She works hard at her dramatic ritual role on this day, but she carries off her work easily, with gusto, because she is so stimulated by company coming into the house and, especially, by the photographer's reality: "He's *itinerant*. . . . That's almost but not quite the same thing as a Gypsy" (***Stories*** 550, 552). All her life Anne has rejected an allegiance to the house: "she never cooked nor sewed nor cultivated her mind" (***Stories*** 544); she stood up some man who was going to marry her at the altar! It makes sense that a woman only a half-sister and constantly reminded about it has had to develop an antithetical allegiance to the street against the taunting, smug women of the house.

Immensely limited by her gender in the culture of her moment and place, *she* cannot travel as an itinerant, Sister Anne's traveling now consists of her moving from one relative's house into another when she is needed because the relative is sick or dying. And Anne loves life; she loves mixing with people. She does not need someone, Ethel has the magnitude wrong there. "Someone" posits the house; Anne needs the street, its whole raft of people. No wonder her excitement mounts and mounts on the day of the photographing until "she was in such a state of excitement and pride and suspense that she seemed to lose for the moment all ties with us or the house or any remembrance of where anything was and what it was for" (***Stories*** 558-59). She transcends for the moment the limitations of her unmarried woman's life. She is engaging in ritual travel of the sort Da Matta addresses; its aims are "blessings, cures, and signs of faith" (216).

Sister Anne knows how to make the most of her personal opportunity on this day, but taking personal pleasure does not prevent her from performing accurate work to bring Uncle Felix and Dicey into useful communication; she says she has always been able to be in two places at once. By bringing the photographer and his clients into the house, people who are strangers, Sister Anne brings the street into the house in much the same way, only more immediately and forcibly, as Uncle Felix brought it in with his stirring pictures of places in the world. By letting in all these people, she brings community and activity into Mingo, as Uncle Felix did when he opened its doors to the extended family. Coming to be photographed makes the people of this countryside a community of fellow voyagers through life. It is an appropriate community to come into Uncle Felix's house at this moment when he is about to make a major passage from life to death and when his personal self becomes less important than his self as a member of the human community (Durkheim 16-17). In this second self, Uncle Felix has been a man who knew how to organize life, accepting and promulgating its joys and managing its sorrows. This is the part of him that is transferable.

Sister Anne, knowing ritualist, assists communication between Uncle Felix and Dicey by rousing him out of the torpor of his dying. She does it by conventional ritual means, producing a lowering of status that breaks the old status and prepares for elevation to a new one (Turner, *Process* 95). She moves him from his bedroom, which is now his shrunken house, to the back room with a window to the west where odds and ends of old accumulations are stored; she puts him out of the house into the street. (Dicey says she never considered this room a serious part of the house.) And Kate sees immediately that Anne has had Uncle Felix put on "a nigger bed" (***Stories*** 553). From this position Uncle Felix is ready to rise spiritually, to communicate a crucial dimension of his former self when Dicey puts the flowers under his nose. That former self is the man he was when Dicey was a child, the man whom she needs to understand now more fully than she could then. Anne's excitement expressing a high engagement with life, the boxroom "street," the photographer's gunpowder reports and flashes of light, the low bed from which he must rise, the flower fragrance he associates with Daisy: all these lift Uncle Felix to awake, arouse himself, remember as Dicey has been remembering, and so to communicate more of who he was as a man to the bride-to-be.

Before she leaves Mingo, Dicey has a session with an ancestress who was once a bride as she faces the portrait of her great-grandmother. This confrontation reveals what lesson Dicey has absorbed from Uncle Felix's self-revelation, what understanding she confirms as she communes with Evelina. Dicey performs work here as Sister Anne does throughout the story (Turner, *From Ritual* 30, 31, 55); she surrenders her desire for life to hold still and be secure. She tells herself she is like Evelina—

> And still those eyes, all pupil, belonged to Evelina—I knew, because they saw out, as mine did; weren't warned, as mine weren't, and never shut before the end, as mine would not. I, her divided sister, knew who had felt the wildness of the world behind the ladies' view.
>
> (***Stories*** 561)

Dicey sees that the structural life of conventions cannot subdue complex reality. The itinerant painter of Evelina's time painted her face into a prepainted, irrelevant and irreverent (falsely romantic) backdrop, just as the people being photographed today find themselves posed not against Mingo's parlor but against the photographer's backdrop, and yet it does not matter a bit. Evelina's eyes come through in the painting, her own eyes, and they enable Dicey's communing with her.

When she tells herself her eyes, too, see out, Dicey is not bragging to herself; she is making a vow. She is committing herself to accept some dimension of the street's wildness in her life and marriage. She will not close herself off and wither away like Ethel. Commitment requires an effort, for like the people being photographed, trying to hold their lives still, Dicey and Evelina "were homesick for somewhere that was the same place" (***Stories*** 561). As the girls watch the photographer depart, Dicey still wants her life and marriage to be safe: "I felt the secret pang behind [the photographer]—. . . the helpless, asking cheat. I felt it more and more, too strongly" (***Stories*** 564). The ritual these people carry out on this day has to deal with this desire, so that it becomes manageable even when people feel it strongly.

Ritual mockery plays a part in these events. Mockery occurs in many rituals to counteract the awesome or awful, to maintain opposition and proportion. Here, set up to do this by Ethel, who has teased Anne from the time of their youth, Kate and Dicey ridicule Sister Anne. They spend much of their time at Mingo watching her as her excitement rises, leading to a climax in her preparations to be photographed looking younger and more romantic than she is, even exotic. The girls' mocking Anne keeps the visit to Mingo from becoming too awesome and frightening. For Dicey and Kate, the day offers a series of shocks that could freeze them into solemnity. At first sight of the people gathered at Mingo, they believe Uncle Felix has died. They know that Ethel is dying, too. It is a shock to find a big group of strangers in the house and another to find that Anne has violated decorum by having Uncle Felix moved to the boxroom. Anne herself, as a street-choosing opponent of the house, is shocking as well as funny. Uncle Felix's own aged, immobile person shocks Dicey, as does her perceiving that Uncle Felix had an extra-marital affair. Furthermore, an underlying sadness or desperation may be embedded in Mingo. Felix and his wife Beck lived in the ancestral home, but there is no indication that they had any children of their own. Beck's always giving people a nosegay of Mingo's flowers as they were leaving and bidding them remember suggests anxiety concerning the family's continuance.

The visiting photography clients set a mood of solemnity: "The solemnity on the porch was overpowering, even at this distance. It was serene, imperturbable, gratuitous" (***Stories*** 547). This solemnity, again, is important in bringing dignity to this day's proceedings. If Dicey's and Kate's ridiculing Sister Anne dominated the day, irreverence would sour the ritual proceedings. But at the same time, all of the shocks for Dicey and Kate might accumulate for Dicey into a solemnity akin to that of the photography clients' celebration of their lives but darker, frightening, a solemnity such as may have caused Ethel's withdrawal from the street. The performance Sister Anne puts on and their attention to it leavens the impact of the day's shocks perfectly. (Does Anne know she is being ridiculous, enticing the girls to mock her? Yes, with the ritual-performing part of her mind, she knows. Perhaps it is because she is going to put on this particular performance for them that she exacts a "reprisal-kiss" from Dicey when the girls arrive.)

Life at Mingo when Uncle Felix held it together was polite but not solemn. He shared his pictures of places in the world with the child Dicey in one kind of solemnity; they handed the slides between them silently, without conversation, as if that great world in the pictures were too awesome and aroused too much desire to be let into speech. But Uncle Felix did take off his Sunday coat after dinner (Dicey remembers his suspenders), and he let the Sunday children climb all over him. Life is motion; the motion of the family coming in, of people going into the street as well as taking pleasure and finding security in the house, makes for life's flowing. Dicey and Kate dissolve in laughter when they see the photographer rush out of the house, into his car and away. They imagine, possibly quite correctly, that Sister Anne has brought her fabulous day to one possible conclusion by trying to kiss the photographer. As their laughter grows, they laugh at everything, at the whole combination of everything: "Kate tried to say something new—to stop us disgracing ourselves and each other, our visit, our impending tragedy [Uncle Felix's death], Aunt Ethel [her impending death], everything" (***Stories*** 565). Their laughter carries them back to their early childhood, when they were safe in the intact family and when they were together. They are recovering an initial confidence in life.

* * *

Roughness, startling, seemingly inappropriate behavior that violates a scene of solemnities will occur wherever groups of people reverse social structure's divisive definitions (appropriate/inappropriate; good/bad; correct/shameful; and so on).

My examples at hand are Richard Schechner's analysis of the Arizona Yaqui Easter ritual, Waehma, and Don Handelman's analysis of the Palio of Siena. Waehma, Schechner argues, starts from the Yaquis' contemporary Catholicism, goes back through the deer dancer and the *pascolas* (who mock) to the spiritual content of their pre-conquest religion, and returns the ritual actors to good standing as contemporary Catholics. The Palio does something quite similar for the Sienese. The techniques of the Palio set aside for the time being the unified peace of the modern city. All the still-extant wards of the centuries before Siena's cityhood and Italy's nationhood compete fiercely through the extended festival practices and odd horseraces at their center, after which the Sienese carry out the measures that return them to new unity. The oxymoron of this last statement is intentional. There is no continuance without renewal.

Roughness abounds in Waehma; ritual beings from the mythical wild place and magical place assault and contest the Christian action. Schechner argues that Waehma allows the Yaquis to succeed in their "quintessential task": "to keep open a road between the everyday world and the *huya aniya,* the modern and the originary, the Catholic and the Yaqui, the 'civilized' and the idyllic wild" (111). He points out that for the contemporary Yaqui Catholic, "'the pre-Catholic, pre-civilization' worlds are not distant primeval truths encoded in myths and songs, but contingent actual energy sources" (111). Comparably, rough behavior abounds in the Palio; ordinarily peaceful and polite citizens take on ritual acts of attack (women, for instance, beat jockeys with their handbags). A further "roughness" lies in the Palio's doubling of the Virgin Mother, so that she is earthy as well as spiritual. The Palio as the Sienese have devised it and as Handelman sees it would seem to provide the Sienese means of accumulating their identity rather than merely moving into new presents by sloughing off pasts. The Sienese wards' organizations and still intense ritual practice indicate rich pasts of energy, pride, fidelity, obligations met, allegiance to tribe: still meaningful within that other set of demands that peace and unification require.

Three terms especially identify the effects of these rituals: incorporation, modeling, and testing. Handelman and Schechner both talk about ritual techniques that serve as safety measures; these allow incorporation of the old within the new without displacing the new, the modern or contemporary. For instance, towards the end of the ritual sequence, the Yaquis who fulfill their ritual obligation by playing the parts of Judas and the Pharisees burn the masks that give them that evil-from-a-Christian-perspective identity and rush into the church to be reidentified as good Catholics. The winner of a Palio race becomes a symbolic baby, giving new birth to the city as a unified whole. Using these sorts of safeties, the Yaquis and the Sienese can incorporate the contentious old within the contemporary.

At the same time, the originary and contestatory are timeless; they cannot be eliminated. The Yaquis do not burn all the year's Chapayeka masks; they keep two. They also at times conflate Jesus and Judas. The Yaqui "negotiate the complex, dynamic, living relationships among native American, Catholic, Spanish, Mexican and U.S. cultures" in their lives. Annually, they use Waehma ritual to model their multifaceted identities; in the ritual sequence these strains "repeatedly, and with shifting emphasis, play themselves out during Waehma" (97).

Modeling, as in ritual and ritualistic actions, is effective because it combines thought and action; it does not express thought, rather the action performs the thinking. Living ritual draws material from the creative unconscious up into symbolic action that effects conjunctions of opposites, incorporations, etc. In doing so, it bridges—keeps a road open between—everyday life, awake and in the world life, with the fountain of cultural understanding.

Moreover, taking social structures apart and playing with them before putting them back together, Handelman suggests, performs testing that we should not assume we can do without. The ritual is a means of its performers' achieving a total consciousness of the city:

> The self-testing by social entities of their own viability and validity is often overlooked but should not be disregarded. Qualities of coherence may be well-known, yet neither self-evident nor static, and thus require the repetitive experience of being so.
>
> (117)

Demonstration, modeling, participating in action: these heighten and convince.

"Kin"'s action is ritualistic, spontaneous rather than calendared, but full of ritual technique.[7] Fictions such as this one demonstrate that the transition from traditional life to "modernity" has not necessarily stripped people of ritual knowledge. The action displays the reversal in appropriateness that identifies liminality, the conjunction of solemnity and mockery, and the provision of safety in the purpose of the photographing. Just as Waehma tests and restores Yaqui identity and just as the Palio tests Siena's civic construction of wards and the unified city, **"Kin"** tests the family, and extended kinship, and shows the roughness that has to be incorporated and accepted for family to hold firm. The action of the day of Dicey and Kate's visit to Mingo models the roughness that has to be incorporated in family life and kinship if they are to function strongly because they are expressions of life's roughness.[8] Kinship makes a half-sister part of the family but allows her to be teased by full members. Life brings death, and lets that half-kinswoman invade the house of any dying member of the family. Kinship allows Sister Anne to give Dicey a reprisal-kiss for a long-lost cousin and more; "She took my face between her fingers and thumb and shook my cheeks. . . . She could do this because we were kin to each other" (***Stories*** 551). There is roughness in the girls' mocking Sister Anne and, on their way home, putting her down as "common." That roughness intensifies when, perhaps to retaliate for Anne's shaking her cheeks as well as to bring Ethel into the action, Dicey sasses Sister Anne, telling her that Ethel did not come today because she cannot stand Anne.

"Kin"'s penultimate action corresponds to the symbolic rebirth of Siena as a baby. When Dicey and Kate laugh and laugh together, they renew their childhood: "We had not laughed together that way since we were too little to know any better" (***Stories*** 565). And the last sentence implies the new family life that will emerge from Dicey's marriage: "I thought of my sweetheart, riding, and wondered if he were writing to me" (566). Ordinary family life strong enough to ride out the roughnesses is the renewed form for living comparable to the Yaquis' everyday Catholic life and Siena's citizens' unity.

But has the family really needed such pummeling? Yes. The family once located at Mingo has shrunk spiritually as well as physically. Now there are few family members in the area, and "sparing" is the family trait, in other words, denial, avoidance. **"Kin"**'s ritualistic action counteracts the deadening effects of denial, such as Kate's insistence that Uncle Felix must have been mistaken when he wrote "Daisy" instead of "Beck." Restored to its fullness, the family of Evelina, Felix, Sister Anne, and Dicey prepares for a return to women marrying and trusting their lives to the institution of the family.

* * *

Ritual studies illuminate ritual, and in ritual over the human millennia and in immensely varying cultures, groups of people have found ways of integrating solemnities and roughnesses, the smooth and the turbulent, the good and the bad. Ritual displays people's knowledge, inventiveness, creativity. Understanding ritual leads to reconception of the people about us and their potentialities. For literary criticism, ritual studies lead to another dimension of what Eudora Welty knew when she was working on the materials of her stories.

Notes

1. Diana Pingatore reports almost comprehensively on criticism of "Kin" to 1991. She omits Albert J. Devlin's discussion of the story in *Eudora Welty's Chronicle* and Patricia Spacks's brief mention in *Gossip.* Since 1991, Gail Mortimer and Carol Johnston have contributed to the commentary on this story. The theoretical background of the present interpretation of "Kin" can be found in compressed compass in chapter 5 of Victor Turner's *The Ritual Process* and chapter 6 of Turner's *Dramas, Fields, and Metaphors.* Turner says, "[A] major stumbling block in the development of sociological and anthropological theory has been the almost total identification of the social with the social structural" (*Dramas* 269).
2. This paragraph condenses and interprets Turner's many chapters on *liminality, communitas,* ritual, and "deep knowledge," which I take to be the largely unconscious (known as a concert pianist knows musical notes and all their combinations and fluctuations, which the pianist does not think about consciously as she or he plays) network of symbols speaking of home, origins, travel, freedom, and confinement, etc.
3. In his *Tradition,* Edward Shils speaks of the constant need for adjustment, change, to maintain meanings formerly defined. Durkheim says that ideas that have been held by many generations have more power and are more readily accessible than individual ideas (238). See Turner on "living ritual" (*From Ritual* 81).
4. Don Handelman discusses dilation as an effect of people's move into ritual action (122-23).
5. Welty critic Noel Polk insists that Felix's request that Daisy meet him at the river "could be a fantasy of his, a dream of youth or even a memory of his youth before he got married" (personal communication). In any case, Felix is revealing an allegiance in his life outside the family.
6. Dicey's unconscious but powerful intention to meet Uncle Felix (her remembering him gives evidence of this motivation) constitutes part of a pattern of such journeys for meetings in Welty's fiction. Bowman, in "Death of a Traveling Salesman," gets lost accidentally on purpose on roads he knows. Dying, he returns to a place that suggests his grandmother's. Similarly, Judge Moody in *Losing Battles* gets lost on hill roads he knows so that he can meet not with his consciously intended goal, Miss Julia Mortimer, but with the young man he needs to come to terms with, Jack Renfro.
7. Da Matta reiterates Turner's argument that meaning lies in process rather than in category when he says, "it is important for us to retain the concept of movement, process, and dislocation . . . rather than cling to the categorical term ritual. . . . This perspective permits us to see ritual as something that is created and no longer to see it simply as a finished and definitive type of social action" (214).
8. In Welty's *Delta Wedding,* Ellen tells Robbie, "There's a fight *in* us, already, I believe—*in* people on this earth, not between us. . . . It's part of being alive" (163).

Works Cited

Da Matta, Roberto. "Carnival in Multiple Planes." *Rite, Drama, Festival, Spectacle.* Ed. John J. MacAloon. Philadelphia: Institute for the Study of Human Issues, 1984. 208-40.

Devlin, Albert J. *Eudora Welty's Chronicle.* Jackson: UP of Mississippi, 1983. 158-74.

Durkheim, Emile. *The Elementary Forms of the Religious Life.* Trans. Joseph Ward Swain. Glencoe, IL: Free Press, n.d. [1912].

Handelman, Don. "The Palio of Siena." *Models and Mirrors: Towards an Anthropology of Public Events.* Cambridge: Cambridge UP, 1990. 116-35.

Johnston, Carol Ann. *Eudora Welty: A Study of the Short Fiction.* New York: Twayne, 1997. 196-98.

Mortimer, Gail. *Daughter of the Swan: Love and Knowledge in Eudora Welty's Fiction.* Athens: U of Georgia P, 1994. 78-83.

Pingatore, Diana R. *A Reader's Guide to the Short Stories of Eudora Welty.* New York: G. K. Hall, 1996. 374-85.

Polk, Noel. Personal communication to the author. 21 Mar. 2001.

Prenshaw, Peggy Whitman, ed. *Conversations with Eudora Welty.* Jackson: UP of Mississippi, 1984.

Schechner, Richard. "Waehma: Space, Time, Identity, and Theatre at New Pascua, Arizona." *The Future of Ritual.* London: Routledge, 1993. 94-130.

Shils, Edward. *Tradition.* Chicago: U of Chicago P, 1981.

Spacks, Patricia Meyer. *Gossip.* New York: Knopf, 1985. 248-58.

Turner, Victor. *Dramas, Fields, and Metaphors.* Ithaca: Cornell UP, 1974.

———. *The Forest of Symbols.* Ithaca: Cornell UP, 1967.

———. *From Ritual to Theatre.* New York: PAJ Publications, 1982.

———. *The Ritual Process.* Ithaca: Cornell UP, 1969.

Welty, Eudora. *Delta Wedding.* New York: Harcourt, 1945.

———. *The Collected Stories of Eudora Welty.* New York: Harcourt, 1980. 538-66.

———. *The Eye of the Story.* New York: Vintage, 1990.

———. "Kin." *Collected Stories.* 538-66.

———. "The Wanderers." *Collected Stories.* 542-53.

David J. Piwinski (essay date winter 2003)

SOURCE: Piwinski, David J. "Mistletoe in Eudora Welty's 'A Worn Path.'" *ANQ* 16, no. 1 (winter 2003): 40-2.

[*In the following essay, Piwinski discusses the allusion to Christianity signified by the mistletoe in "A Worn Path."*]

After struggling up a hill, extricating herself from a thorn bush, and crossing a log over a creek, Phoenix Jackson, the aged and infirm protagonist of Eudora Welty's short story **"A Worn Path,"** sits down on the banks of the creek for a rest:

> Up above her was a tree in a pearly cloud of mistletoe. She did not dare close her eyes, and when a little boy brought her a plate with a slice of marble-cake on it she spoke to him. "That would be acceptable," she said. But when she went to take it there was just her own hand in the air.
>
> (143)

Most explicators of this passage have focused on an interpretation of the little boy's gesture; for example, Roland Bartel suggests that Phoenix is having a vision of her grandson (290), while Neil D. Isaacs argues that the slice of cake is an allusion to the Christian rite of Communion (77). Only three critics, however, have attempted to explain the possible significance of the mistletoe above Phoenix's head. Isaacs sees this image as part of "a pattern to underline the idea of Christmas time" (76). Similarly, Alfred Appel, Jr., claims that the mistletoe relates to Phoenix's journey "as a kind of Christmas pageant or pilgrimage" (169). In tracing the story's allusions to the mythological phoenix and the regenerative power of the sun, Frank R. Ardolino points out that, as an evergreen, the mistletoe symbolizes immortality (3). While making valid points, these commentaries, however, do not fully explicate the allusive significance of this particular botanical image. The presence of mistletoe in this story, in addition to providing another Christmas image and a symbol of immortality, further supports the interpretation of Phoenix Jackson as Christ-like and, in alluding to the symbolic language of flowers and plants, reinforces Welty's portrait of Phoenix as the epitome of love-inspired fortitude.

Several critics (for example, Isaacs, Trefman, and Keys) have described Phoenix as a Christ-figure, but none of these commentators have noted that Christian legend has given mistletoe an alternative name, one whose etymology complements the story's other Christological allusions. According to this legend, mistletoe was once a strong tree that provided the wood from which Christ's cross was built. Because of its role in the Crucifixion, it underwent a metamorphosis from a sturdy tree to a parasitic shrub (Evans 735-36). It was thereby known throughout Europe by the Latin name *Lignum Sanctae Crucis* (Wood of the Holy Cross) and in France was called *l'herbe de la croix* (Huxley 1750). In a story that, according to Sara Trefman, "recalls the earlier journey of Christ up the hill of Calvary," Welty's reference to this shrub alternatively known as "Wood of the Holy Cross" provides an especially resonant allusion.

Phoenix Jackson also embodies the human qualities assigned to mistletoe in the language of flowers, which attaches symbolic meanings to flowers and plants. According to Ernst and Johanna Lehner, this ancient Persian system of botanical symbols was introduced into Europe early in the eighteenth century by Charles XII of Sweden after his return from exile in Turkey, where he had lived at the Ottoman court for five years (109). Lesley Gordon credits Lady Mary Wortley Montagu, wife of England's ambassador to Constantinople in 1716, for popularizing this Turkish floral symbolism in England (105). By the mid-1800s the language of flowers, according to Gordon, had become especially popular in England and America, with books such as Thomas Miller's *The Poetical Language of Flowers* (1847) and Sara Josepha Hale's *Flora's Interpreter* (1852) providing lovers with "a sort of floral Esperanto" (108). As a result of the publication of dozens of similar books in the second half of the nineteenth century, the assigning of human sentiments and messages to flowers and plants had become an entrenched part of Victorian popular culture. In these books, mistletoe, cited as an emblem of "Affection and Love," is said to convey the message, "I shall surmount all difficulties" (Lehner 121). Thus, the image of mistletoe in **"A Worn Path"** allusively complements Welty's characterization of Phoenix Jackson, for in her self-sacrificing devotion to her grandson, she embodies the love and affection signified by this plant, and her persistence in overcoming numerous difficulties on her journey epitomizes the mistletoe's message.

Works Cited

Appel, Alfred, Jr. *A Season of Dreams: The Fiction of Eudora Welty.* Baton Rouge: Louisiana State UP, 1965.

Ardolino, Frank R. "Life Out of Death: Myth and Ritual in Welty's 'A Worn Path.'" *Notes on Mississippi Writers* 9 (Spring 1976): 1-9.

Bartel, Roland. "Life and Death in Eudora Welty's 'A Worn Path.'" *Studies in Short Fiction* 14 (Summer 1977): 288-90.

Evans, Ivor H., ed. *Brewer's Dictionary of Phrase and Fable.* 14th ed. London: Cassell, 1990.

Gordon, Lesley. *Green Magic: Flowers, Plants, and Herbs in Lore and Legend.* New York: Viking, 1977.

Huxley, A. J. "Mistletoe." *Man, Myth and Magic: The Illustrated Encyclopedia of Mythology, Religion and the Unknown.* Ed. Richard Cavendish. New York: Cavendish, 1994.

Isaacs, Neil D. "Life for Phoenix." *Sewanee Review* 77 (January-March 1962): 75-81.

Keys, Marilynn. "'A Worn Path': The Way of Dispossession." *Studies in Short Fiction* 16 (Fall 1979): 354-56.

Lehner, Ernst, and Johanna Lehner. *Folklore and Symbolism of Flowers, Plants and Trees.* New York: Tudor, 1960.

Trefman, Sara. "Welty's 'A Worn Path.'" *Explicator* 24 (February 1966). Item 56.

Welty, Eudora. *The Collected Stories of Eudora Welty.* New York: Harcourt, 1980.

Carol Ann Johnston (essay date spring 2003)

SOURCE: Johnston, Carol Ann. "Sex and the Southern Girl: Eudora Welty's Critical Legacy." *Mississippi Quarterly* 56, no. 2 (spring 2003): 269-87.

[*In the following essay, Johnston contends that Welty "both records and interrogates cultural configurations of gender and sexuality" in "Petrified Man," "At the Landing," and "June Recital."*]

Legends about the South remain as powerful as the place itself. Whether or not a genteel Southern aristocracy has ever existed continues to be an issue for scholarly debate, yet the legend of such an antebellum South and of the South as a backward-looking region longing to rise up from the ashes of Sherman's pyrotechnics as an openly genteel, white supremacist nation looms powerfully in the minds of many readers and critics. These received images of the Old South, hanging around like a bad penny, present formidable obstacles for Southern writers who take the South as their subject. The new legend of the "sunbelt South" may have begun to chip away at these hegemonic myths, but for much of the twentieth century, Southern writers were allowed two topics: the myth of the Old South—"ladies'" stories detailing faded aristocracy, laced with extremely good manners—or the direct opposite of Southern gentility, manly stories about abject poverty and perverse depravation (see: William Faulkner). A writer working explicitly with neither topic, Eudora Welty finds her work more often than not caught awkwardly between these diametric subjects in critical discussions of her short fiction. In addition to its awkward relationship to historical myth, Welty also finds her work captive to a series of personal myths generated by her reticence about her private life, about a third of which she lived alone in her parents' house in Jackson, Mississippi. These personal myths, along with generic historical myths about the South, position Welty's work in peculiar zones: a zone of misapprehension because her stories do not conform to conventional historical subjects; and a zone of under-reading, because of misconstrued ideas about the narrowness and prudishness of Welty's personal vision.

In this essay, I consider several of Welty's stories apart from the standard historical and personal myths that have governed their reading. I find in these stories a writer offering up explicit discussions of sexuality, the kinds of sexual conversations that occur among women in the exclusive space of the beauty parlor, in **"Petrified Man,"** the legacy of boys educated in sexuality by women in **"At the Landing"** and **"June Recital,"** and a hopeful prophecy of how sexuality may be discussed and envisioned in **"The Wanderers."** Throughout these stories, Welty both records and interrogates cultural configurations of gender and sexuality.

Critics almost universally agree upon the technical brilliance of Welty's stories—they show her sharp ear for dialogue and gift for recognizing and capturing a dramatic scene, her profound uses of intertextuality. Yet, as the Georgia writer Alice Walker explains in a recent interview, the East Coast critical establishment is notorious for forcing writers into preconceived categories. Acknowledging the power of critics to build or destroy a literary reputation, Walker talks about the freedom she found in her work after moving from the East Coast:

> The east-coast critics are really afraid of the spirit. . . . I don't feel I've had a decent critic ever on the East Coast. There's also that feeling that they have the right to suggest what you should be doing. That's absurd. . . . People always want to keep you in a little box or they need to label you and fix you in time and location.[1]

Consistent with Walker's experience, many of Welty's critics in the popular press as well as in scholarly venues keep her in the "little box" of genteel antebellum Southern lady writer. Yet by neither interrogating nor allowing the subject of what women hear and observe into the canonical subjects that a Southern writer may address, critics can diminish Welty's literary achievement and can as well diminish what we can know about the South. In addition to the restricting power of Southern myth, the power of personal myth also can corrupt a clear reading of Welty's work. Though she has been vilified in some circles for doing so, Eudora Welty lived in her parents' house on Pinehurst Street in Jackson, Mississippi, for most of her life. She lived primarily on her own; when asked about marriage in the *New York Times* a few years ago, she answered that the subject "never came up,"[2] an ingenious way to fend off the *Times*'s implication: her solitary life in her parents' house suggests that she is a spinster incapable of finding a husband or living on her own away from home. Welty did spend a brief year due north of the Mason Dixon, studying business advertising at Columbia University, in Manhattan, which one critic has called her "true spiritual home,"[3] as if she somehow couldn't bring herself to move to New York even though she wished to. In the *de facto* chronicle of that "spiritual home," the *New Yorker,* Claudia Roth Pierpont argues recently that Welty has "entered the national pantheon as a kind of favorite literary aunt—a living exemplar of the best that a quaint and disappearing Southern society still has to offer."[4]

Besides her "lifestyle" being the object of scrutiny, Welty has also been taken to task by some for the way she has written about her home and her region: because readers see nothing blatantly anti-racist or feminist in her work, she is spanked for not attacking the evils of the slave-stained South. To further complicate reading Welty's work, as Jay Tolson summarizes, she is viewed "on the one hand, cuddly and dear, virtually a state monument . . . on the other hand, too difficult, too obscure, too literary."[5] On the one hand, a person who has spent most of her life in the same house in the same town with the same people cannot know anything about the wider world (and Welty's home in a Southern city shrinks the scope of her knowledge even further); and on the other hand, certainly one writing in such an hermetically sealed environment cannot but write hermetically, and thus inscrutably. Yet Eudora Welty has written clearly and sharply about her region, and assumptions about that region projected onto Welty and her work prevent some readers from reconciling a pre-conceived idea of Welty's work with what Welty writes. This complex reading problem threatens Welty's literary survival, even though her work arguably is the most sophisticated and penetrating of any writer of her generation.[6]

In her earliest stories, Welty's sophistication is both masked and embellished by her droll timing and unsexed sexual language. Welty seems to copy down exactly what she has heard, a complex deception that places trust in the reader to penetrate and unpack the multi-layered innuendo that comprises public conversation among Welty's women. "I'm not one-sided, I'm the same," Sister announces at the outset of **"Why I Live at the P.O.,"** a reference not to her personality but to the common belief that women have one breast larger than the other. While Sister's double talk is typical of the stories in ***A Curtain of Green,*** Welty's **"Petrified Man"** embodies the most outrageous example in the volume of Welty's ability to deploy her sly narrative tactics. **"Petrified Man"** takes place in a beauty parlor in a Mississippi town, specifically in the chair of the head beautician, Leota, who gossips with her customer, Mrs. Fletcher, intermittently throughout the story. Customers return weekly for a "shampoo and set," so the conversation in the story stretches over several appointments. Leota and her husband have taken in boarders, Mr. and Mrs. Pike. Mrs. Pike is in the employ of Fay's Milliners, and her three-year-old son Billy Pike lurks underfoot at the beauty shop during the entire story. Through "eavesdropping" on the gossip, we learn a great deal about what is going on, not just in the shop, or in the town, but, I would argue, in a much larger arena of the culture of Southern women.

"Petrified Man" depicts an exclusive Southern matriarchy; the only male present during the gossip sessions is the boy Billy Pike. The stereotypical South is a matriarchy, generally thought to be so because all Southern men were either killed or maimed during "the War Between the States." While it is true that Southern men did "grow back" after this rather abrupt and rude pruning by the Union army, their sensibilities were forever changed by the fact of the war and by the legacy of boy children being reared in female-dominated homes. Or at least this is a theory that has had currency among those who study the South.[7] Billy Pike's presence in this exclusive female space draws upon this stereotype—"only three years old and already just nuts about the beauty-parlor business"[8]—but we learn whether or not his place in the story is stereotypical only at the end of the story. In the final scene Billy makes himself a nuisance, rooting around in Leota's purse to get the stale peanuts rolling around among the hairnets, hairpins, and other paraphernalia. Since the seventeenth century, "purse" has been a slang term for a woman's uterus, and peanuts, of course, are seeds. An over-determined reading of the story would read this incident too strictly; this is one of many complex sexual references in the story, part serious representation, part subversive joke. This visual pun maintains the broadness of jazz songs of the period, such as "My Handyman Ain't Handy No More," in which the handyman just loves to clean his lover's front lawn:

> Sometimes he's up long before the dawn
> Busy trimmin' the rough edges off my front lawn
> Yeah that man is such a handy man
>
> Why you know he never has a single word to say
> No not while he's working hard
> And I wished that you could see the way
> He handles my front yard![9]

When Leota discovers Billy's meddling in her purse, Mrs. Fletcher immediately yanks him onto her lap, where Leota "paddl[es] him heartily with the brush" while his "angry but belittling screams" cause "ladies [to begin] to gather round to watch the paddling" (p. 28). Billy seems to experience humiliating domination within the matriarchal domain; he can live in this space but not on his terms: he cannot invade it.

Yet Billy strikes back, "kick[ing] both Leota and Mrs. Fletcher as hard as he [can]," escaping their clutches and "stomp[s] through the group of wild-haired ladies and [goes] out the door" (p. 28). His is literally the last word: "If you're so smart, why ain't you rich?" he asks Leota. This question, coming "out of the mouth of babes," represents a powerful challenge to Leota and her maternal authority. She has no answer to his question; Mrs. Pike has identified the Petrified Man as the serial rapist sought by the police, and earned a five-hundred-dollar reward for doing so. She found the evidence of the man's identity in a magazine of Leota's which Leota had placed in the room rented to the Pikes. Billy, with the last word, exposes Leota somewhat threateningly—she knows that he has heard and understood the jealous slurs she has uttered about his mother. While he received a literate sexual education in this most female of places, Billy nevertheless confounds the stereotype, for he certainly doesn't show signs of timidity or effeminacy, in spite of his public beating with the hairbrush, one of the instruments responsible for a woman's beauty in the shop.

The story also embraces a stereotype that extends beyond the South. Matriarchy clasps hands with gossip in **"Petrified Man"**; in fact the gossipy dialogue between Leota and Mrs. Fletcher dominates the story. This dialogic language may seem at first reading to be guileless and flat, and could cause one to wonder what, if anything, is remarkable about the story or, indeed, about the author. Welty discusses obliquely in an interview the language that she uses in such a story as **"Petrified Man,"** and why that language is important. When Hermione Lee quizzes Welty about the kinds of stories that she writes, Welty offers this incisive anecdote:

> I know when I was in William Faulkner's house a couple of times, I heard him and his cronies telling stories, and they were all men. But those would be the stories they would tell at hunting camp or out sailing. Or stories about crazy people in Oxford, Mississippi. Men know more stories, at least they did in those days, because they get out and live in the world more, and their stories are more adventurous and full of action.[10]

Perceiving that Welty might have the other side of the coin in mind as she links Southern male writers with "liv[ing] in the world more," the interviewer interjects at this point, "But it's women who make up the fabric of gossip, who know what's going on?" Welty agrees, "That's true—the gossip, the domestic kind. . . . I think women tell their kind of story to women and men tell theirs to men" (Lee, p. 121). Welty's depiction in this Faulkner anecdote of the "male" story and her placement of herself as a teller of women's stories illustrate both the understatement and the deflection of the self that characterize Welty's approach to Southern myth.

Welty always delivers a sanguine and wry truth when she discusses her work, though more often than not readers unfamiliar with the layers of Southern comportment insist upon a certain misprision about that wryness. A "naive" reading of her comments upholds the received critical view of Welty: Southern men in general just live larger lives and tell real stories; Southern women are restricted to the house, the beauty parlor, and the neighbor's yard, and can tell only stories that are mythical, and therefore trivial. Yet reading this anecdote with the knowledge that Welty understands that a certain kind of self-presentation can brilliantly project her good manners as well as maintain her privacy without hiding her critical acumen, is to see it as the harshest criticism: Faulkner and his drunk buddies make up or embellish stories about the abnormal (mythical) Mississippi, while Welty writes down what people talk about in normal (real) conversation in Jackson. This interpretation keeps fidelity with the multiple layers of Southern speech, and when we see Welty gouge Faulkner in this manner, we wonder how critics can refer to her as "a kind of favorite literary aunt." (Her other famous comment about Faulkner also maintains a lovely decorum while packing ironic heat: writing in proximity to Faulkner is like writing in the shadow of a mountain.)[11] In order to test the validity of a reading based upon Welty's belief in Southern manners as civility without lobotomy, let's assume that Welty writes as a Southerner, in a pithy and multilayered code that may be lost on listeners unfamiliar with the language, and that the dialogue in **"Petrified Man"** is in a language pitched to a Southern audience, not an unreasonable premise, since the characters and the location are Southern.[12] Here, too, is where we may deepen the Southern grasp of its own legend, while also allowing Welty's unforgiving genius for seeing and listening to inform our reading of her stories so that we may penetrate their quiet style. Welty's Southern ladies play both with and against type; most are not aristocratic, but even the most impoverished among them attempt to carry themselves in a manner that reflects Southern aristocracy, while remaining true to their individual wit and desire.

The initial layer below the surface of beauty shop gossip in Welty's story is a language of punning intimation. The most obvious of these puns places the absent presence of the story, "Mrs. Pike," under immediate suspicion. "Pike" alludes to the fish with the phallic snout lined with teeth. To drive the reference home, Leota assures Mrs. Fletcher that "Mrs. Pike ain't goin' to bite" her (p. 20), though throughout the story, the suggestion about just who Mrs. Pike might bite is strong. She represents matriarchy *in extremis*—Mrs. Pike, the man-eater. And then we have the Petrified Man himself, a "member" of a travelling freak show that Leota and Mrs. Pike visit. The triple punning Welty executes with his name will take considerable unpacking, extending until the surprising ending of the story: "they got this man, this petrified man, that ever'thing ever since he was nine years old, when it goes through his digestion, see, somehow Mrs. Pike says it goes to his joints and has been turning to stone" (p. 21). Other delights in the show set up the punning reference inherent in the **"Petrified Man"** tag. These include full-term unseparated twins in a jar. Leota and Mrs. Fletcher determine that such deformity is a result of incest and feel the need to assure each other that their husbands "aren't one speck of kin" to either of them, so no need for them to worry about birth defects. Along with the babies in a jar, the show features a group of pygmies, members of one of the characteristically short tribes of Africa. Leota's description of the pygmies, perhaps the richest veiled sexual language in the story, deserves to be quoted entirely:

> "They've got these pygmies down there, too, an' Mrs. Pike was just wild about 'em. You know, the teeniniest men in the universe? Well, honey, they can just rest back on their little bohunkus an' roll around an' you can't hardly tell if they're sittin' or standin'. . . . Just suppose it was your husband!"
>
> "Well, Mr. Fletcher is five foot nine and one half," said Mrs. Fletcher quickly.
>
> "Fred's five foot ten," said Leota, "but I tell him he's still a shrimp, account of I'm so tall. . . . Well, these pygmies are a kind of a dark brown. . . . Not bad lookin' for what they are, you know."
>
> (p. 21)

This brief dialogue contains several layers and references several controversial issues—not the least being "Is Welty a racist? If not, how come she is making fun of pygmies?" While this is an important issue, I would argue that the pygmies represent a coded sexual language, not a racist one. Images of pygmies circulating in the 1920s and 30s showed them wearing penis sheathes and little else. So when Leota talks about "teeniniest," "bohunkus," "just s'pose it was your husband!," "shrimp," and so forth, the question she raises about pygmies does not concern blackness, or even height, but rather the more interesting and taboo sexual subject of penis size. When we place this discussion cheek by jowl against the petrified man nuances, the question "What is so interesting (sexual) about a petrified man?" becomes less mystifying. Obviously, the issue is: does he have a petrified penis—a permanent erection? Should this reading seem a bit beyond the pale, consider the phenomenon of Serena de la Hay's sculpture *Willow Man* on the M5 motorway in Bridgwater, Somerset, a giant nude man woven out of steel and willow branches. According to a report on BBC radio, the majority of those stopping in town to ask about the sculpture are women, and the majority of those are asking if there are postcards of willow man's "bohunkus."

Beyond this punning sexual entendre, the story also presents the beauty parlor as a sexual space, one where women find multiple satisfaction. We expect the beauty shop experience to please, since it is a safe zone in which women may unabashedly pamper themselves. Leota's beauty shop extends the space beyond pampering, however; Leota's beauty shop experience is metaphorically a sexual experience. In the opening paragraphs of **"Petrified Man,"** as Mrs. Fletcher abruptly asks, "Who's Mrs. Pike?" our narrator tells us that "other customers . . . were being *gratified* in other booths" (***CS*** **[*The Collected Stories of Eudora Welty*]**, p. 17; emphasis mine). When Leota finishes her work on Mrs. Fletcher, she sends her off to one of the booths to be "gratified" as well—and her charge—with a wink and a nod—suggests a particular kind of gratification: "Now go git under the dryer. You can turn yourself on, can't you?" (that is, you can push your own button, can't you?). The conversation previous to this evocative question provides wonderful sexual context leading to this double reading of Leota's question. Mrs. Fletcher and Leota have been discussing how they met their husbands. We learn that Mrs. Pike has met Mr. Pike (where else?) on a train. Then Leota tells Mrs. Fletcher, (who has "with dignity" announced that she met her husband in a "rental library"): "Honey, me an' Fred, we met in a rumble seat eight months ago and we was practically on what you might call the way to the altar inside of a half an hour." With such a set-up, Leota's query "You can turn yourself on, can't you?" assumes a brilliant autoerotic shimmer (p. 23).

Returning to the beginning of this scene, after we've learned that Mrs. Pike is "cute" and has a "sharp eye out" (no pun intended?), the conversation circles around what seems to be a scalp disease: "Hair fallin'," Leota observes, and Mrs. Fletcher seems to be concerned: "Any dandruff in it?. . . . I couldn't of caught a thing like that from Mr. Fletcher, could I?" No dandruff and no "over-cooking" during her last perm, but Mrs. Fletcher has definitely "caught" something from Mr. Fletcher. Leota finally comes out with it; she has heard that Mrs. Fletcher is "P-R-E-G." Mrs. Fletcher is quite determined to hide her condition, for reasons not yet clear, but Leota persists: "How far gone are you?" (p. 18). The discussion of the pregnancy takes a surprising turn at this point, surprising if you believe that motherhood is a woman's highest calling and that marriages are happy havens of love (in other words, if you believe that Eudora Welty is a nice, genteel, Southern writer, as she is described by many of her critics). The bratty three-year-old Billy Pike pops off from under the sink, and Mrs. Fletcher, "unmollified," responds, "Well! I don't like children that much. . . . Well! I'm almost tempted not to have this one." With this remark she makes clear why she has wanted the pregnancy to be secret—so that she might not have to deliver the child at all.

Leota takes the news in stride. Indicating her belief that women are not in control of their bodies, Leota has intoned that pregnancy "just ain't our fault, the way I look at it" (p. 18). She continues, "Mr. Fletcher would beat you on the head if you didn't have it now. . . . after going this far" (p. 19). "Going far" and "far gone" are the euphemisms Leota has settled on to refer to sexual intercourse—probably related to that Americanism "going all the way" that everyone hears whispered in high-school hallways on Monday morning. With her response to Leota's commanding version of Mr. Fletcher, we see that Mrs. Fletcher does not share Leota's capitulation to men. She knows what to do when she doesn't want to "go all the way": "Mr. Fletcher can't do a thing with me. . . . If he so much as raises his voice against me, he knows good and well I'll have one of my sick headaches, and then I'm just not fit to live with" (p. 19). Within Welty's carefully constructed sexual framework, the comment takes on the added denotation of the stock phrase "Not tonight, honey, I have a headache."

The subject of control arises again in the story within a context that seems to epitomize the stereotypical Southern woman's complete obsession with her appearance. Mrs. Montjoy, a member of the "Trojan Garden Club" (we can't help but wonder what's hidden inside this particular Trojan), has come into the shop much further along in her pregnancy than Mrs. Fletcher. Leota narrates:

> Child, we was all plumb scared to death. There she was! Come for her shampoo an' set. Why, Mrs. Fletcher, in an hour an' twenty minutes she was alayin' up there in the Babtist Hospital with a seb'm-pound son. It was that close a shave. I declare, if I hadn't been so tired I would of drank up a bottle of gin that night.
>
> (p. 24)

Mrs. Fletcher's response to this last-minute coiffeur seems to reverse her attitude towards control of her own husband: "Her husband ought to could make her behave. . . . He ought to put his foot down." Likewise, Leota seems to switch sides as well: "Ha . . . A lot he could do. Maybe some women is soft" (p. 25). Mrs. Fletcher, however, immediately clarifies her position regarding how wives should handle husbands, and in doing so, offers an excellent template for reading the Southern lady in Welty's stories in general:

> Oh, you mistake me, I don't mean for her to get soft—far from it! Women have to stand up for themselves, or there's just no telling. But now you take me—I ask Mr. Fletcher's advice now and then, and he appreciates it, especially on something important, like is it time for a permanent—not that I've told him about the baby. He says, "Why dear, go ahead!" Just ask their advice.
>
> (p. 25)

Mrs. Fletcher develops for Leota a rubric for controlling while seeming to be controlled: let your husband advise you on appearance ("something important"), and you can take control of truly important issues. Leota doesn't quite get the subtle gradations of the pattern, but she seems too put out with her husband to give any strategy a try: "Huh! If I ever ast Fred's advice we'd be floatin' down the Yazoo River on a houseboat or somethin' by this time. . . . I'm sick of Fred" (p. 25).

Though Welty's dialogue initially may seem like inane small talk, the jumbled minutia one sees through the microscope of small-town living, with it Welty exposes the double, and sometimes triple, energy of women's conversation. Southern matriarchy has taken at least two twists in the story: Billy Pike defies his effeminate surroundings with a stereotypical male question about the relationship between money and brains. Further, though the Southern lady, Mrs. Fletcher, believes that she, not her husband, has control of her body; she will decide whether or not to keep her baby, and she decides whether or not to engage sexually with Mr. Fletcher.

The ending of the story reveals a deepening of the subject of power relationships between men and women. Once we become attuned to the sexual entendre of the beauty shop conversations, we first laugh, but as we follow the story that accompanies the banter, we become aware of the serious issues behind the humor. The ending of the story turns on the subject of sexual power and violence. The Petrified Man is identified by Mrs. Pike as the multiple rapist pictured in the "most wanted" criminal section of *Startling G-Man.* The aftershock of the ending sends us back into Welty's playful, punning language to re-examine its subtext. The myth of Welty's sheltered innocence is easily punctured when we look at the bald subjects of the story: a woman who is pregnant but unsure if she wants the child; Mrs. Fletcher's strategies for gaining control in marriage; a rapist on the run; and the serious unanswered questions of what happened to Mrs. Pike when she was living in Mr. Petrie's (the rapist's) house for six weeks in New Orleans. Mrs. Pike's noticeable absence in the beauty shop (even though Leota announces that she is a beautician), along with her teeth that can bite, takes on an added significance within such a serious context. The rapist's victim, since the tale of Philomel, typically is silenced by the crime. While Mrs. Pike understandably stays clear of the world of female sexuality created in the beauty shop, her protracted (and possibly violent) encounter with the Petrified Man neither cowers nor silences her. Mr. Pike tries to persuade her not to turn Mr. Petrie over to the police, but Mrs. Pike prevails and collects her five-hundred-dollar reward. Leota narrates: "Mr. Pike didn't want to do anything about it . . . said he kinda liked that ole bird. . . . But Mrs. Pike simply tole him he could just go to hell" (p. 27).

The playful yet somber subject of the story gives us unusual insight into Southern culture in the early twentieth century. You can, of course, draw your own conclusions, but I would suggest the following: from Welty we learn how Southern women discuss the central but taboo topics of female sexuality and of female powerlessness in the face of aggressive male sexuality. We learn how boys learn about female sexuality without sacrificing masculinity. The story seriously damages the myth of Welty as the naive Southern belle, and the sheltered Southern spinster completely ignorant of male sexual diversions, and completely disinterested in sex herself.

While I've used **"Petrified Man"** to represent Welty's earliest work, the legacy of the story is profound and deep in her later work. **"At the Landing,"** from her second collection of stories, ***The Wide Net*** (1943), depicts a vulnerable young girl who strikes out into the world at the death of her parenting grandfather. She is first "violated" by Billy Floyd, a local fisherman, and when she tries to find him, is gang-raped by his buddies:

> But after a certain length of time, the men that had been throwing knives at the tree by the last light put her inside a grounded houseboat. . . . One by one the men came in to her. . . . When she called out, she did not call any name; it was a cry with a rising sound, as if she said "Go Back," or asked a question, and then at the last protested.
>
> (*CS,* pp. 257-258)

The narration here takes on quite a different tone from that of the more popular and well-known stories in ***A Curtain of Green*** (if we base popularity upon appearances in anthologies), but readers seem to have as much difficulty with the layers beneath Welty's metaphorical writing as they do with those beneath her humorous writing. Few critics have written about the story as a rape, and in an essay on Welty's photographs, literary critic Louise H. Westling describes Welty as a photographer whose world is "largely sheltered from poverty and violence," and a writer whose fiction "rarely betrays any knowledge of the violent enforcement of white male authority."[13] The subject of **"At the Landing"** and in many of Welty's stories is "the violent enforcement of white male authority," a subject she addresses in her early career with humor, in her middle career with chilling metaphor, and in her later career with a dazzling combination of these techniques. **"Circe,"** from ***The Bride of the Innisfallen*** (1955), depicts the story of Odysseus and his men from Circe's point of view, humorously softening Homer's monstrous woman. Men become what they truly are when they drink her potion, and in Circe's house, one must pick up one's own things: "In the end it takes phenomenal neatness of housekeeping to put it through the heads of men that they are swine" (p. 531). Odysseus has been brought up well—he cleans up after himself—so he remains a man in the company of swine.

Likewise the legacy of boys' sexual education carries through Welty's work. The final scene of **"At the Landing"** shows sons throwing knives at tree trunks as their fathers rape the young girl, and as their mothers and grandmothers sit idly by, around a fire. While these boys follow the violent pattern set by their fathers, Loch Morrison, the boy at the core of Welty's interlinked stories ***The Golden Apples,*** lives almost exclusively among women; we witness his relationships with his sister Cassie and his mother, but his father rarely appears. In **"Moon Lake,"** he is the lone male in a summer camp for girls, where he is every bit the quintessential boy, using the lake when the girls are indoors, "div[ing] high off the crosspiece nailed up in the big oak. . . . He [goes] through the air rocking and jerking like an engine" (***CS,*** p. 342). As a Boy Scout, he saves a drowning girl's life:

> The Boy Scout reached in and gouged out her mouth with his hand, an unbelievable act. She did not alter. He lifted up, screwed his toes, and with a groan of his own fell upon her and drove up and down upon her, into her, gouging the heels of his hands into her ribs again and again.
>
> (***CS,*** p. 366)

A mother of one of the girls happens onto this scene, and believes that she is witnessing something other than "lifesaving": "But what's he doing to *her*? Stop that . . . Boy Scout? Why, he ought to be—he ought to be—" (***CS,*** pp. 366-367). Welty plays out the protracted scene in delicious visual language that blurs the lines between life-saving and life-giving. Whether or not Loch himself plays upon this visual pun is not clear; we do know that he knows a bit about sexual intercourse. During his long and unspecified illness[14] in **"June Recital,"** he is confined to his bedroom, with little more to amuse him than his father's telescope. He uses it to spy on the vacant house next door.

> Loch trained the telescope to the back and caught the sailor and the girl in the moment they jumped the ditch. They always came the back way, swinging hands and running low under the leaves. . . . Loch squinted; he was waiting for the day when the sailor took the figs. And see what the girl would hurry him into. . . . It was she that had showed the sailor the house to begin with, she that started him coming. They were rusty old fig trees but the figs were the little sweet blue. When they cracked open, their pink and golden flesh would show, their inside flowers, and golden bubbles of juice would hang, to touch your tongue to first.
>
> (***CS,*** pp. 277-278)

The glorious sexual image of the figs epitomizes Welty's expression and conception of sexuality throughout ***The Golden Apples.*** Expressively, the passage is very frank in its description of both male and female sexuality, while it avoids either the crude language of "blue balls" (giving us instead the vivid image, "the figs were the little sweet blue") or the Latinate medical terminology of "vagina" (offering, "when they [crack] open, their pink and golden flesh," which exquisitely evokes female sexuality, the hanging juice something "to touch your tongue to first"). Welty recognizes that no language exists between slang and medical terminology to describe sexual equipment; her solution here to create such a language by using a vivid description of figs is innovative and brilliant. Further, the figs show us metonymically her conception of sexuality: both male and female exist in the identical locus, the figs. "The girl" here is Virgie Rainey, star pupil of piano teacher Miss Eckhart. Virgie emerges at the end of the interlocking stories, along with Loch, as an escapee of Morgana and its fixed sexual and gender roles. In the final story, **"The Wanderers,"** Virgie prepares to leave Morgana, having buried her mother and all attachments to Morgana's vision as well. The final scene shows us a Virgie who has understood the level of her passion and the compulsion of male-defined society to squelch women's passionate thrusts. She meditates on a picture above Miss Eckhart's dictionary, of Perseus and the Medusa:

> Cutting off the Medusa's head was the heroic act, perhaps, that made visible a horror in life, that was at once the horror in love, Virgie thought—the separateness. She might have seen heroism prophetically when she was young and afraid of Miss Eckhart. She might be able to see it now prophetically, but she was never a prophet. Because Virgie saw things in their time, like hearing them—and perhaps because she must believe in the Medusa equally with Perseus—she saw the stroke of the sword in three moments, not one. In the three was the damnation—no, only the secret, unhurting because not caring in itself—beyond the beauty and the sword's stroke and the terror lay their existence in time—far out and endless, a constellation which the heart could read over many a night.
>
> (***CS,*** p. 460)

Because Virgie has broken Perseus's destruction of Medusa into three parts, she will be able to isolate the central part, the essence of Medusa as a living, penetrating, passionate woman, a vision apart from her destruction and from the heroism that Perseus earns throughout history for that destruction. Thus by dissecting the myth, Virgie is in the unique position potentially to revise it, moving the focus onto the beauty and necessity of a woman's passion, rather than upon its threat to and annihilation by male-dominated society. She moves beyond Miss Eckhart in this regard, the Miss Eckhart who possessed her own passion but was destroyed by it, because she could not understand the myth that bound her to male-defined expressions of passion.

Loch sees the beginnings of Virgie's seizing possession of her passion as he watches her seduction of the sailor—"it was she that started him coming"—and because the scene is related through Loch's eyes, Welty signals that Loch is on his way to comprehending a woman's initiation of sexual passion. If the fig-enhanced description of sailor and girl sneaking into a vacant house remains too metaphorical to suggest Loch's awakening sexuality, then Welty gives us, through Loch's telescope, a more explicit sexual scene to mull over:

> He moved his eye upstairs, up an inch on the telescope. There on a mattress delightfully bare—where he would love, himself, to lie, on a slant and naked, to let the little cottony tufts annoy him and to feel the mattress like billows bouncing beneath, and to eat pickles lying on his back—the sailor and the piano player lay and ate pickles out of an open sack between them. . . . Sometimes they held pickles stuck in their mouths like cigars, and turned to look at each other. Sometimes they lay just alike, their legs in an M and their hands joined between them, exactly like the paper dolls his sister used to cut out of folded newspaper. . . . And then, like the paper dolls sprung back together, they folded close—the real people. Like a big grasshopper lighting, all their legs and arms drew in to one small body, deadlike, with protective coloring. . . . He clasped the cool telescope to his side, and with his fingernail close its little eye.
>
> "Poor old Telescope," he said.
>
> (*CS,* pp. 281-282)

While explicit, because we see the scene through Loch's lens, the scene is boyish and delightful—the lovers remind him of the paper dolls he cut out with his sister Cassie, pulling apart and springing together. He relates intercourse to his everyday experience of watching insects "do it." Further, we see Loch here fantasizing a vision of sensuality that fits a feminine stereotype; he longs to feel the tufts of the mattress against his bare skin. Loch's delicate sense of his own body comes to the fore in **"Moon Lake"** as well; Nina and Jinny Love peer into his tent as he undresses after manfully saving Easter from drowning, and he "[stands] there studying and touching his case of sunburn in a Kress mirror like theirs" (*CS,* p. 373). Here Loch is caught in the feminine gaze of Nina and Jinny Love, and we might be tempted to believe in the power of that gaze to effeminize Loch's sense of his body as he looks in a mirror "like theirs." But Welty offers up an answer to that suspicion in the passage above from **"June Recital,"** where both Loch's gaze and his meditation upon his own body are just as gentle and tender. Loch's paean to his fading sexual innocence as he temporarily closes his eye on the subject shows Welty at the height of her power, the language describing his voyeurism rich with metaphor at once humorous and empathetic: the power of the male gaze tempered with the sensitivity of the female, a boy understanding sexuality in terms of the paper dolls he has made with his sister.

Welty's extraordinary powers of observation allow her both to render and to revise sexual and gender stereotypes. Depicting Southern society as it exists in the beauty parlor, the fishing party, the piano recital, and summer camp, Welty gives us a complex, nuanced society that in notable instances both understands and undermines easy stereotypes and assumptions. Southern society as Welty depicts it is as complex as society at large, yet like keen observers of Southern society before her, such as Kate Chopin, Welty cannot break the jam that has fixed female passion into an immovable and self-destructive force. Welty reveals in *One Writer's Beginnings* that she sees in herself more of Miss Eckhart than any of her other characters; yet unlike Miss Eckhart, Welty's passion does not send her to a mental institution.[15] Instead, Welty delivers a series of stories that if read seriously and with care can offer inventive solutions to issues of insidious stereotyping that demean all—male and female, Northerner and Southerner—alike.

The legend of the Old South begets the subjects of faded aristocracy and gentility, as well as the nasty flip sides of those coins. These subjects in turn serve to reinforce the legend that gives them life. Because she has seen and listened so well and with such constancy, Eudora Welty has a unique vantage point from which to report Southern life, "to know what's going on," and that is what her stories can tell us. The Polish poet Anna Swir has said that artists are the "antennae of society." If we agree that an artist's service to a society is to take in the incomprehensible waves surging through a culture and transmit them "loud and clear" to anyone who can and will receive them, then we must also believe that to lose a writer is to lose a translation of a culture. The conundrum with reading Welty, then, is profound and perhaps irreversible: received ideas about "the South" and about Southern women in the first half of the twentieth century prevent us from learning about the South and about Southern women in the first half of the twentieth century. We must ask the literary establishment to reread Welty's *oeuvre* with greater care and lesser bigotry. Hers is a precious music.[16]

Notes

1. Duncan Campbell, "A Long Walk to Freedom," *Observer* (London), 25 (February 2001), 3.
2. Nicholas Dawidoff, "Only the Typewriter Is Silent," *New York Times,* August 10, 1995, p. C1.
3. Jay Tolson makes this slip in what is otherwise a sensitive and well-argued essay about why reading Welty confounds some in the "lit biz" ("The Necessary Optimist," *Wilson Quarterly* [Winter 1999], 10 April 2001 <http://wwics.si.edu/OUTREACH/WQ/WQSELECT/WELTY.htm>).
4. "A Perfect Lady," *New Yorker,* October 5, 1998, p. 94. Pierpont uses hearsay evidence—Welty's con-

fession to Katherine Anne Porter about her virginity, and Porter's response—in order to read Welty's *oeuvre* as one briefly open and daring in terms of depictions of the hot-button issues of sexuality and race. Pierpont reads Welty with the sensitivity of Walker's typical East Coast critic.

5. P. 2. Tolson offers this observation in the service of his larger argument that Welty's literary reputation is in danger: "Last year [1999] was in many ways the best and worst of years for Eudora Welty. Not only did more than the usual number of tributes come her way, all richly deserved for a career of astonishing literary achievement; more pointedly, proof of her achievement . . . was brought together. . . . in the *Library of America* series, an honor tantamount to canonization. . . . But the year also had its lows. . . . Almost inexplicably, none of Welty's works appeared on a curiously assembled (but widely discussed) list of the 100 best English-language novels of the 20th century drawn up last summer by the board of the *Modern Library*. . . . [T]he slight seemed to hint at troubles ahead as far as Welty's literary reputation is concerned" (pp. 1-2).

6. Critics such as Patricia Yaeger and Danièle Pitavy-Souques have brilliantly placed Welty's work in the context of post-structuralist critical theory (see Patricia Yaeger, "'Because a Fire Was in My Head': Eudora Welty and the Dialogic Imagination," in *Welty: A Life in Literature* ed. Albert J. Devlin [Jackson: University Press of Mississippi, 1987], pp. 139-167; and "The Case of the Dangling Signifier: Phallic Imagery in Eudora Welty's 'Moon Lake,'" *Twentieth Century Literature,* 28 [Winter 1982], 431-452; and Danièle Pitavy-Souques, "Of Suffering and Joy: Aspects of Storytelling in Welty's Short Fiction" in *Eudora Welty: Eye of the Storyteller,* ed. Dawn Trouard [Kent, Ohio: Kent State University Press, 1989], pp. 142-150), but for many scholarly readers, such contextualization places Welty firmly into the "obscure" and "literary" category. The post-structuralist critique of binary categorical thinking could help erase the cuddly/difficult bifurcation, but many influential critical voices in Southern literary studies remain untrusting of critical theory. Other critics such as Rebecca Mark have located Welty's work convincingly within gender studies, finding that Welty's work in many ways transforms the traditional boundaries between genders into locations of exchange (see *The Dragon's Blood: Feminist Intertextuality in Eudora Welty's "The Golden Apples"* [Jackson: University Press of Mississippi, 1994]). Welty has attempted to inoculate her work against readings focused upon gender with her firm claims that she is not a feminist, and thus many readers shy away from gender issues in reading Welty.

7. I can only add to this debate that my father's favorite author is Jane Austen, because reading Austen reminds him of sitting in the kitchen listening to his aunts and mother gossip while his unemployed father was off doing something "in town."

8. Eudora Welty, *The Collected Stories* (New York: Harcourt Brace Jovanovich, 1980), p. 19.

9. Lyrics attributed to Bessie Smith ("My Handyman Ain't Handy No More," 12 April 2001 <http://www.geocities.com/BourbonStreet/Delta/2541/blhhumes.htm#My312>); first recorded in 1928 by Ethel Waters.

10. "Interview with Hermione Lee," in Carol Ann Johnston, *Eudora Welty: A Study of the Short Fiction* (New York: Twayne, 1997), p. 121.

11. Flannery O'Connor refers to the situation as being like "a mule and wagon stalled on the same tracks the Dixie Limited is roaring down" (*Mystery and Manners* [New York: Farrar, Straus and Giroux, 1979], p. 45), an even more damning comment than Welty's.

12. The dense code that comprises Southern middle-class language has its origin in the language of slaves, who spoke in code continually to mask their actions and feelings from their owners and overseers. The language of spirituals most readily illustrates the practice: "Swing low, sweet chariot, comin' for to carry me home" uses apocalyptic language of Protestantism to plea for freedom from slavery. As Benjamin Schwarz explains, "Without doubt the fundamental element of the temperament and culture of the South is that blacks and whites have lived there together for so long. Of all [W. J.] Cash's insights [in his *The Mind of the South*] into the Southern ethos, none was so penetrating—or, unfortunately, so underdeveloped—as his argument, scandalous for the time it was written, that blacks had a profound influence on whites in the South. . . . Nearly every distinctive aspect of Southern life . . . developed from the interchange of the two races" ("The Idea of the South," *Atlantic Monthly,* December 1997, p. 122).

13. "The Loving Observer of *One Time, One Place,*" in Devlin, pp. 168-187.

14. He is being treated for malaria.

15. "What I have put into [Miss Eckhart] is my passion for my own life work, my own art. Exposing yourself to risk is a truth Miss Eckhart and I had in common. What animates and possesses me is

what drives Miss Eckhart, the love of her art and the love of giving it, the desire to give it until there is no more left" (Cambridge: Harvard University Press, 1984, p. 101).

16. Thank you to Jacqueline Fear-Segal, Eric Homberger, and Adam Fairclough for inviting me to give lectures to students and faculty in English and American Studies at the University of East Anglia. The opportunity to write those lectures germinated my thoughts on Welty and sexuality, and sharp questions from my colleagues in EAS developed those thoughts significantly. Elizabeth Frost as always was a sensitive reader and listener; thanks to her and her colleagues and students at Fordham University for their keen attention to these ideas.

Suzan Harrison (essay date spring 2003)

SOURCE: Harrison, Suzan. "Playing with Fire: Women's Sexuality and Artistry in Virginia Woolf's *Mrs. Dalloway* and Eudora Welty's *The Golden Apples.*" *Mississippi Quarterly* 56, no. 2 (spring 2003): 289-313.

[*In the following essay, Harrison assesses the influence of Virginia Woolf's* Mrs. Dalloway *on the portrayal of the female artist in* The Golden Apples, *observing the link between creativity and sexuality in both works.*]

While the start of the twenty-first century finds us with a large, varied, and sophisticated body of criticism about Eudora Welty's fiction, essays, and photographs, there are still some surprising gaps in that criticism.[1] The recent publication of *Eudora Welty and Politics: Did the Writer Crusade?* moves toward filling in one of those gaps and recognizing the subtle yet pervasive political dimension of Welty's work, a dimension that has been overlooked by some readers, as Harriet Pollack observes in the introduction to that collection, because they fail to realize the degree to which women writers, and Welty in particular, have often approached "the public and historical through the private,"[2] and they have failed to notice the ways in which Welty's characteristic narrative strategies of obstruction, intertextual play with masculine texts, and indifference to authoritative Histories are in themselves highly political (pp. 4-5).

Another gap in Welty criticism, one this special issue of the *Mississippi Quarterly* calls on Welty scholars to question, has to do with sexuality in Welty's *oeuvre.* The answer to the question of why Welty scholars have not fully explored this significant dimension of Welty's work is complex and multifaceted. Perhaps there has been a reluctance to address sexuality in her work because of a tendency, particularly in the study of Southern fiction, to identify the work closely with the individual author, with his or her life and personality, despite the cautions first of New Criticism and then postmodernism, and despite the critical sophistication of Welty scholars. Eudora Welty is, after all, a living author (having turned ninety-two this year), and she has cultivated a public persona—that of the Southern lady—that may steer writers away from a consideration of sexuality in her works. Then again, the critical reticence about sexuality in her work may have something to do with our knowledge that Welty never married, or it may result from the widespread knowledge that Eudora Welty is a private person, carefully choosing what she will and will not reveal about her personal life.[3]

Of course, the topic of sexuality in Welty's work has not been entirely ignored. Writers like Patricia Yaeger and Rebecca Mark,[4] among others, have done much to map out the ways in which sexuality is figured in Welty's fiction. Much of the work on sexuality in Welty's fiction has, not surprisingly, focused on the stories in ***The Golden Apples.*** In addition to being some of Welty's most sensual writing, the stories in this collection include several explicit sexual encounters: Virgie Rainey and Kewpie Moffitt enjoy playful sex in the abandoned MacLain house in **"June Recital."** In **"Sir Rabbit,"** Mattie Will Sojourner engages in sex with King MacLain, the Zeus-like masculine fertility figure of the collection, a tryst that reminds her of an earlier sexual encounter with MacLain's twin sons, Ran and Eugene. Loch Morrison's life-saving technique in **"Moon Lake"** is, as Miss Lizzie Stark observes and numerous critics have noted, graphically sexualized.

By contrast, Virginia Woolf is a writer in whose work sexuality is, and has been for over two decades, a major critical concern, despite the fact that there are virtually no overtly described sexual encounters in her fiction. Scholars have explored sexuality in Woolf's writing as well as her biography and have devoted much attention to the relationship between the two. In particular, the relationships, for women, between sexuality and artistic creativity, between being a woman and being a writer, are central to Woolf's work. Her body of writing suggests multiple and complex responses to the question of what it means to be an artist and a woman. "There are," as Xaviere Gauthier points out, "women who write. . . . *In what ways does their writing call attention to the fact that they are women*?" she asks.[5] For Woolf, the answer to that question is intimately tied to sexuality, and in particular, as many writers have observed, to an erotic attraction between women.

"'Chloe liked Olivia. . . .' Do not start. Do not blush. Let us admit in the privacy of our own society that these things sometimes happen. Sometimes women do like women," writes Virginia Woolf in *A Room of One's Own,* as she tries to map out the imaginative landscape opening up before the woman writer in the 1930s.[6] What happens in fiction when Chloe likes Olivia? According to Woolf, "an immense change" (p. 86). We begin, she suggests, to fill in some of the gaps, some of the silences in fiction, and we open up new possibilities for women's imaginations and women's sexualities. We begin to articulate that which "has been left out, unattempted" (p. 86). Elizabeth Meese writes that Woolf's intention in this passage is precisely to free women's sexuality, creativity, and subjectivity from the limits imposed by a masculine economy:

> [Woolf] first places Chloe and Olivia in the laboratory, and then sees their differences (from one another, two women who are not waiting for men but for each other, an economy of difference not lack, not sameness; and their sufficiency, not waiting for a man to fulfill them, to fill them up, to plug up the w/hole so the body can be summed up).[7]

Chloe's liking Olivia, argues Woolf, will lead to a new form of creativity, "For if Chloe likes Olivia and Mary Carmichael knows how to express it she will light a torch in that vast chamber where nobody has yet been. It is all half lights and profound shadows like those serpentine caves where one goes with a candle" (p. 88). The language Woolf uses here to describe the creative discovery, the enlarging of imaginative possibility available to the writer who can conceive of and articulate the subtitles of relationships between women, relationships ignored or repressed by patriarchal culture, is similar to the language she uses to describe her own creative process in *Mrs. Dalloway,* a novel in which the female protagonist admits to often "yielding to the charm of a woman."[8] In her diary, Woolf describes her ability to imagine her characters' lives as creating caves: "How I dig out beautiful caves behind my characters: I think that gives exactly what I want; humanity, humour, depth. The idea is that the caves shall connect and each comes to daylight at the present moment."[9] Homoeroticism is thus allied with the particular type of creativity that marks Woolf's own imaginative approach to character.

The two works I examine in this essay are relatively early, yet pivotal considerations of female creativity and sexuality for each writer. *Mrs. Dalloway,* published in 1925, is considered by many to be Woolf's first successful modernist novel and marks the transition to her mature fiction; ***The Golden Apples,*** Welty's third collection of stories, was published in 1949, relatively early in her career, which began with the publication of her first story, **"Death of a Traveling Salesman,"** in 1936 and continued into the 1980s. In these works Welty and Woolf seem to be grappling with what it might mean to be a woman and an artist. At one moment the writers present us with a heady, exhilarating triumph of feminine creativity and then in the next moment undercut it or show its dangers. In both of these works, artistic vision is initiated by and closely allied with an erotic attraction to another woman. The homoerotic attraction takes the same form in each work: a girl or young woman, rather traditional and even shy or restrained, is attracted to another girl or young woman who represents freedom from restraint through her daring behavior and/or social status. In each case, this attraction calls forth an opening up, blossoming of the imagination and sparks a new creativity or artistic impulse. As Rachel Blau DuPlessis, writing about Woolf's novel *Orlando,* claims, "lesbianism is the unspoken contraband desire . . . that itself frees writing."[10] Both works displace conventional heterosexual attraction in order to center the woman as artist.

The influence of Virginia Woolf's writing on Eudora Welty's fiction has been profound and enriching; in particular, it has contributed to Welty's fictional consideration of female artistry and the possibilities of intertextuality as a vehicle for those subversive narrative strategies of obstruction, appropriation, rewriting, and decentering.[11] In addition to the intertextual relationship between *Mrs. Dalloway* and ***The Golden Apples,*** each text uses intertextuality as an important narrative strategy. Clarissa Dalloway quotes from both *Othello* and *Cymbeline* repeatedly throughout Woolf's novel. Numerous critics have noted the similarity of *Mrs. Dalloway* to James Joyce's *Ulysses,* which Woolf read in 1922 while writing *Mrs. Dalloway,* commenting unfavorably, "I finished Ulysses, & think it a mis-fire. Genius it has, I think; but of the inferior water. The book is diffuse. It is brackish. It is pretentious. It is underbred, not only in the obvious sense, but in the literary sense" (*Diary,* p. 199). Several years later, Woolf wrote of Joyce more positively in her essay "Modern Fiction," published in the same year as *Mrs. Dalloway,* calling him "spiritual" in contrast to earlier materialist writers, and praising his ability "to reveal the flickerings of that innermost flame which flashes its messages through the brain."[12]

As Rebecca Mark convincingly demonstrates, Joyce's *Ulysses* is one of the texts Welty makes use of in the intertextual tapestry of the story **"Music from Spain"** (pp. 175-229). ***The Golden Apples*** is, perhaps, Welty's most intertextual work, and as such has received a great deal of attention. Early criticism of the collection focused on Welty's intertextual use of classical mythology. Feminist approaches to the work's intertextuality include Patricia Yaeger's "'Because a Fire Was in My Head': Eudora Welty and the Dialogic Imagination" (1984), which explores Welty's intertextual conversation with the poetry of William Butler Yeats, arguing that Welty "simultaneously presents Yeats's language as a form of 'otherness' and expropriates this language to make it articulate her own point of view."[13] In "'Too Positive a Shape Not to Be Hurt': *Go Down, Moses,* History, and the Woman Artist in Eudora Welty's *The Golden Apples,*" Barbara Ladd reads Welty's text as a response to William Faulkner's collection of interrelated short stories in terms of both its form and its construction of the woman artist's relationship to history.[14] Rebecca Mark's *The Dragon's Blood* is the fullest study of ***The Golden Apples***'s intertextuality. Specifically, Mark examines Welty's play with *masculine* myths and texts, arguing that Welty uses intertextuality to critique "the Western heroic tradition" through "parodying, battling, and above all transforming the subtext of masculine superiority embedded in their texts" (p. 4).

Not only do Woolf and Welty engage in intertextual "play" with works of high modernism, but they also invoke various other kinds of play. Clarissa Dalloway's party is play in several senses of the word: it is entertainment, meant to create pleasure in its participants, and it involves a performance on Clarissa's part, as she plays the role of hostess. **"June Recital,"** the longest story in ***The Golden Apples,*** is also full of play, from piano playing to card playing to child's play to the performances of the recital itself. **"Moon Lake,"** set in a girl's summer camp, is also full of play. Of course, while play is central to these works, it is serious play, exploring the question of women and writing in the context of life and art, life and death.

In addition to their use of play and their serious consideration of the woman as artist, there are a number of other significant parallels between these two works, in particular between *Mrs. Dalloway* and **"June Recital,"** that suggest that reading Welty's text as a response to Woolf's can be illuminating. Each is set on a single day in mid-June in the early 1920s, and though World War I has ended, its shadow still haunts these narratives. The primary narrators in each—Clarissa Dalloway and Septimus Warren Smith in Woolf's work, and Cassie and Loch Morrison in Welty's story—are narrating the same or related events independently of one another. Clarissa and Septimus do not know each other and never actually meet in the course of the novel. Yet the same events, concerns, and images occupy their thoughts during the course of the day that shapes the novel. While Loch and Cassie do know each other, being brother and sister, they do not share their individual narratives, but each reacts in his or her own way to the stimuli from the supposedly vacant house next door. In each work, it is only in the mind of the reader that the interaction between the two narratives takes place and acquires meaning.

Playing upon the high modernist mixing of memory and desire, in both works events in the present of the narrative spark memories that take on significance in the course of each work. For Mrs. Dalloway, the beauty of the June morning, the excitement over her imminent party, and the removal of the doors for that party initiate her memory of a summer thirty years earlier at Bourton, her family's country home: "What a lark! What a plunge! For so it had always seemed to her, when, with a little squeak of the hinges, which she could hear now, she had burst open the French windows and plunged at Bourton into the open air" (p. 3). For Cassie Morrison, the opening phrase from "Für Elise" played on a piano nearby summons for her a memory of her piano teacher, Miss Eckhart, and the piano recitals from earlier Junes: "Like a wave, the gathering past came right up to her. Next time it would be too high. . . . Then the wave moved up, towered, and came drowning down over her stuck-up head."[15] Cassie reviews the history of her childhood friend Virgie Rainey, her "secret love, as well as her secret hate" (p. 292); Clarissa remembers a kiss from Sally Seton, "the most exquisite moment of her whole life" (p. 52).

This attraction of woman for woman in these works and the connection of that attraction to the artistic imagination not only suggests a critique of compulsory heterosexuality and the sacrifices it requires of women but also challenges the mainstream modernist construction of creative inspiration as requiring a male artist and a female muse. While both *Mrs. Dalloway* and ***The Golden Apples*** do concern themselves with the struggle of the woman artist to resist and redefine the culture's exclusion and silencing of her, they also question the possibility of sustaining this resistance in a culture that works to reinscribe them continually as victim or object. These are works that explore the pleasure and the costs of a woman's art. In both *Mrs. Dalloway* and ***The Golden Apples,*** female creativity runs the risk of madness, as, indeed, it did for Virginia Woolf herself.

Clarissa Dalloway identifies her attraction to Sally Seton as her first experience of "falling in love with women. Take Sally Seton; her relation in the old days with Sally Seton. Had not that, after all, been love?" (p. 48). What attracts Clarissa is not merely Sally's beauty, but her extravagance, courage, and rebellion, "that quality which, since she hadn't got it herself, she always envied—a sort of abandonment, as if she could say anything, do anything" (p. 48). Clarissa associates Sally with artistic practices and sees Sally's potential for creativity as growing directly out of her wildness and abandon:

> She ran down the passage to fetch her sponge bag without a stitch of clothing on her. . . . She stole a chicken from the larder because she was hungry in the night; she smoked cigars in her bedroom; she left a priceless book in the punt, but everybody adored her (except perhaps Papa). It was her warmth; her *vitality—she would paint, she would write*. . . . She accused Hugh Whitbread, of all people . . . of kissing her in the smokingroom to punish her for saying that women should have votes. Vulgar men did, she said. And Clarissa remembered having to persuade her not to denounce him at family prayers—which she was capable of doing with her daring, her recklessness, her melodramatic love of being the centre of everything and creating scenes. . . .
>
> (p. 276, emphasis added)

Sally Seton breaks rules and violates taboos, celebrating her own physicality, eating on the sly, and disregarding the "words of the father," leaving Papa's book out in the rain, and playfully appropriating a symbol of male power. (Sometimes, of course, a cigar is not just a cigar.) Even her flower arrangements break the rules of association: Sally mixes "hollyhocks, dahlias—all sorts of flowers that had never been seen together" (p. 50).

At her most rebellious, she kisses Clarissa; the references to flowers in the passage reinforce the alternative sexual possibilities suggested by her flower arrangements:

> Then came the most exquisite moment of [Clarissa's] whole life passing a stone urn with flowers in it. Sally stopped; picked a flower; kissed her on the lips. The whole world might have disappeared; there she was alone with Sally. And she felt that she had been given a present, wrapped up, and told just to keep it, not to look at it—a diamond, something infinitely precious, wrapped up, which as they walked (up and down, up and down), she uncovered, or the radiance burnt through, the revelation, the religious feeling!
>
> (pp. 52-53)

Elizabeth Meese describes feminine sexuality as the site of rebellion: "Women often play out resistance to [masculine] authority in sexual terms: as the appropriated objects of men, we seek to disturb the system of patriarchal control through acts of sexual defiance."[16] Sally's kiss destabilizes the triangular romantic plot between Clarissa, Richard Dalloway, and Peter Walsh, the traditional construction of masculine desire, and introduces a subversive form of female desire into the novel. This homoerotic desire is allied with the imagination and with revelation. The total effect of Clarissa's love for Sally is liberating and expanding: "Sally it was who made her feel, for the first time, how sheltered the life at Bourton was" (p. 48).

But the heterosexual imperative reasserts itself immediately after this kiss, when Peter Walsh, one of Clarissa's male suitors, and Joseph Breikopf intrude. "It was," recalls Clarissa, "like running one's face against a granite wall in the darkness! It was shocking; it was horrible!" (p. 53). Clarissa experiences the men's intrusion as a form of violence and loss but also as inevitable: "'Oh this horror!' she said to herself, as if she had known all along that something would interrupt, would embitter her moment of happiness" (p. 53). This is not, as Patricia Juliana Smith argues, an instance of "lesbian panic," "the disruptive action or reaction that occurs when a character—or, conceivably, an author—is either unable or unwilling to confront or reveal her own lesbianism or lesbian desire."[17] The reassertion of the heterosexual romance plot is represented as a social imperative that brings with it a loss of creativity and potential, but it does not result in Clarissa's denial of her erotic attraction to Sally or to women in general, an attraction she admits to and ponders several times in the novel. Both Clarissa and Sally marry, and when they meet at Clarissa's party later in the novel, Sally's loss of creative energy and sexual passion is tied, in Clarissa's thoughts, directly to her marriage. Sally's vitality and daring were "bound, Clarissa used to think, to end in some awful tragedy; her death; her martyrdom; instead of which she had married, quite unexpectedly, a bald man with a large buttonhole who owned, it was said, cotton mills at Manchester" (p. 277). Sally's story ends in marriage rather than death, but the result is still a form of loss and diminishment: "her voice was wrung of its old ravishing richness; her eyes not aglow as they used to be" (p. 276).

Smith argues that the courtship plot often involves, early on, an erotic attraction between the heroine and another woman, an attraction which must be repressed in service to the successful fulfillment of this type of plot—marriage: "The dangerous and even seductive 'masculine' woman makes the plot interesting . . . but she must be sacrificed lest she stand between the heroine and the economic security and social responsibility of the marriage bed" (p. 573). But Woolf's novel does not follow the traditional courtship plot. While Clarissa's attraction to Sally is indeed sacrificed for Clarissa's entry into the world of heterosexual marriage, *Mrs. Dalloway* works to questions the values of the courtship plot. Woolf's novel does not end with Clarissa's marriage; instead, the novel represents the doubts and questions Clarissa has, at fifty-two, about the wisdom and motives behind her choice, over thirty years earlier, to marry Richard Dalloway. Economic security and the responsibility of the marriage bed are called into doubt in Clarissa's musings and the novel's imagery.

For Clarissa, like Sally Seton, marriage is a loss of sorts, as a shrinking and reduction rather than expansion, as it is figured in the description of her bed:

"The sheets were clean, tight stretched in a broad white band from side to side. Narrower and narrower would her bed be. The candle was half burnt down and she had read deep in Baron Marbot's *Memoirs.* She had read late at night of the retreat from Moscow. . . . [S]he could not dispel a virginity preserved through childbirth which clung to her like a sheet" (pp. 45-46). These images of restriction, diminishment, sterility, and retreat are in direct contrast to the images of the erotically charged passage (which follows just a few lines later, as if to underscore the differences) describing Clarissa's experience of "sometimes yielding to the charm of a woman" (p. 46):

> It was a sudden revelation, a tinge like a blush which one tried to check and then, as it spread, one yielded to its expansion, and rushed to the farthest verge and there quivered and felt the world come closer, swollen with some astonishing significance, some pressure of rapture, which split its thin skin and gushed and poured with an extraordinary alleviation over the cracks and sores! Then, for that moment, she had an illumination; a match burning in a crocus; an inner meaning almost expressed.
>
> (p. 47)

Feminine sexuality and artistic vision—particularly the ability of the Woolfian artist to see into the heart of things—are yoked in the figure of the match burning in the crocus, a clitoral image of feminine eroticism and intimacy that is as expansive and passionate as Clarissa's bed is narrow and cold, and her bedside candle half burnt.

While homoerotic desire—figured here as a flame—is one way in which Woolf disrupts and challenges traditional gendered hierarchies, it is in the representation of the hostess as an artist that she calls into question the construction of the artist as male. The hostess is an artist in *Mrs. Dalloway,* and the party is art, a particularly modernist yet feminine or domestic form of art. Clarissa's memories of Sally Seton and her contemplation of her desire for women are part of her reflections on the day of her party. The images of the party and fire are yoked in Mrs. Dalloway's thoughts: "she, too, was going that very night to kindle and illuminate; to give her party" (p. 6). The flame of homoeroticism is translated here into a creative flame. The party is a highly orchestrated performance, framed by the theatrical opening left by the removal of the doors. It creates community out of disparity, conjures presence out of absence, as first Peter Walsh and then Sally Seton, now Lady Rosseter, appear, and it resolves the tensions between past and present, putting to rest Clarissa's ambivalence about her choice, thirty years earlier, to marry Richard Dalloway. J. J. Wilson describes Clarissa Dalloway's party in terms that connect it with Woolf's form of modernism: "The party has the potential for joining outer and inner experience, the individual with humanity, the instant with the constant, all goals of Virginia Woolf's art. Party-giving becomes an analogy for artistic creation, reflecting within the fictional realm the struggles and desires of the author."[18]

Through her representation of the artist as hostess, as creator of domestic illusions, Woolf creates what Genevieve Sanchis Morgan calls "a poetics of domesticity."[19] Like Mrs. Ramsay's dinner party and Lily Briscoe's artistic vision in *To the Lighthouse,* the party in *Mrs. Dalloway* is a transcendent triumph of order and human connection over the chaotic forces that separate and destroy meaning. "And it was an offering," thinks Clarissa Dalloway of her party, "to combine; to create; but to whom? An offering for the sake of an offering, perhaps" (p. 185). But the threat of dissolution, the risk of losing oneself in the performance, is always present. Artistic fire can be dangerous: "Why, after all, did she do these things?" wonders Clarissa. "Why seek pinnacles and stand drenched in fire? Might it consume her anyhow! burn her to cinders!" (pp. 254-255).

The power of the chaotic, destructive forces, the dark side of the artistic impulse, is represented most fully, however, in the character of Septimus, whose descent into a madness separates him from emotion, sensation, communion with the living, from his marriage. As Septimus looks at a motor car that may or may not carry the Queen, he thinks that "this gradual drawing together of everything to one centre before his eyes, as if some horror had come almost to the surface and was about to burst into flames, terrified him. The world wavered and quivered and threatened to burst into flames" (p. 21). Woolf claims that in her first version of the novel, "Septimus, who later is intended to be [Clarissa's] double, had no existence. . . . Mrs. Dalloway was originally to kill herself or perhaps merely to die at the end of the party" (Introduction to the Modern Library edition of *MD,* p. vi). When Woolf chose to separate the two characters, she split off the dangers of creativity into the character of Septimus, who commits suicide, in effect, for Clarissa. Woolf's novel thus elides the danger of female creativity that haunts the narrative.

But Septimus is not the central figure of the novel; in choosing Clarissa Dalloway's story over Septimus's, Woolf rejects the tortured, Joycean epic artist in favor of a feminine, domestic artistic vision. As Elizabeth Abel points out, "the potentially epic plot of the soldier returned from the war is demoted to the tragic subplot centering on Septimus Warren Smith. By echoing the structure of *Ulysses* in the narrative foreground of her text, Woolf revises a revision of the epic to accommodate the values and experience of women."[20] Woolf "novelizes" Joyce's novelization of Homer's epic, privileging the domestic plot over the quest plot, which Peter Walsh clearly thinks is more important, or the political plot favored by Mrs. Bruton, both of which are masculine plots in which women are subordinate.

The tension between the potentiality and dangers of creativity are momentarily resolved in the scene in which Clarissa leaves her party and stands alone at the window in another room. "She felt somehow very like him—the young man who had killed himself. She felt glad that he had done it; thrown it away. The clock was striking. The leaden circles dissolved in the air. He made her feel the beauty; made her feel the fun. But she must go back. She must assemble" (p. 284). The knowledge of Septimus's suicide and her momentary psychic identification with his refusal of the complications and confusion of the temporal and corporeal heightens Clarissa's pleasure in the success of her party and in her connection with her husband, Richard. "He made her feel the beauty; made her feel the fun" (p. 284), thinks Clarissa.

Were the novel to end at this point, it would offer a triumphant image of feminine creative power, of a woman's ability to appropriate the role of artist and to resist the cultural pressures to push her to the margins. But the closing scene raises questions about this affirmation of a woman as the triumphant creator of art. *Mrs. Dalloway* closes not with Clarissa's vision but with Peter Walsh's: "What is this terror? what is this ecstasy? he thought to himself. What is it that fills me with extraordinary excitement? It is Clarissa, he said. For there she was" (p. 296). In this final scene Clarissa herself, and not her creation, takes the position of art. She is figured, not as a creator but as an image, a projection of Peter Walsh's emotional state. She becomes, to use Laura Mulvey's terms, a "signifier for the male other" and "the bearer of meaning rather than the maker of meaning."[21] The last page of the novel thus calls into question the novel's representation of the female artist's ability to escape the binary system that labels her object rather than subject of art.

If we read ***The Golden Apples*** as a Weltian response to *Mrs. Dalloway,* we see that Welty is even more emphatic and direct about the dangers that artistry and creativity pose for women but potentially more hopeful about women's abilities to escape them. In several stories in ***The Golden Apples,*** we see the female imagination expanded by attraction to another girl or woman.[22] When freed from the constraints of conventional heterosexuality, female desire and eroticism become creative forces. As in Woolf's novel, the shutting down or silencing of this creative process coincides with an initiation into or return to heterosexuality and the repression of the homoerotic attraction. This sort of dynamic frames the opening story of the collection, **"Shower of Gold."** Mrs. Katie Rainey's narrating of the story is inspired by the sight of another woman: "That was Miss Snowdie MacLain" (p. 263), reads the first line. Although, as many have observed, Katie Rainey does speculate erotically about King MacLain—"With men like King, your thoughts are bottomless" (p. 274)—she tells the story of Snowdie, King MacLain's wife, of whom she says, "And I love Snowdie. I love her" (p. 267). Snowdie's differences, emblemized by her albino whiteness and her refusal to adopt conventional "feminine" behavior in response to being abandoned by her husband, draw Katie Rainey into her storytelling:

> She must have had her thoughts and they must have been one of two things. One that he was dead—then why did her face have the glow? It had a glow—and the other that he left her and meant it. And like people said, if she smiled *then,* she was clear out of reach. I didn't know if I liked the glow. Why didn't she rage and storm a little—to me, anyway, just Mrs. Rainey?
>
> (p. 266)

The end of Katie Rainey's storytelling is a silencing gesture brought on by the thought of her husband's reaction to her creativity: "What makes me say a thing like that? I wouldn't say it to my husband, you mind you forget it" (p. 274). The pattern established in this story—female imagination and artistry set into motion by attraction to another girl or woman who in some way defies or resists the culture's gender imperatives for women—can be seen in a variety of forms in the stories of ***The Golden Apples*** that follow **"Shower of Gold,"** particularly in **"June Recital"** and **"Moon Lake."** But in these stories, the eroticism of the relationships is often overlooked because the stories focus on adolescent girls who stand on the threshold of becoming women. Both **"June Recital"** and **"Moon Lake"** are coming-of-age stories in which homoeroticism opens the imagination and creative possibilities, while heterosexuality closes them.

In **"Moon Lake,"** Nina Charmichael (whose last name associates her with the fictional novelist of Woolf's *A Room of One's Own*) finds in the unlikely setting of a girls' summer camp that her imagination is set afire by her encounter with Easter, an orphan and, in Nina's mind, thereby exempt from the social conventions and restraints that govern the Morgana girls: "The reason orphans were the way they were lay first in nobody's watching them, Nina thought, for she felt obscurely like a trespasser. They, they were not answerable" (p. 352). Easter simply ignores the society's gender requirements, carrying a phallic knife, playing the boy's game of mumblety peg, and carrying on her neck "a ring of pure dirt" that fills Nina "with a feeling of elation" (p. 347). Like Sally Seton, Easter is a potential artist: "I'm going to be a singer," she announces (p. 358).

Her encounter with Easter opens Nina's imagination and heightens her sensory awareness: Easter's "indifference made Nina fall back and listen to the spring running with an endless sound and see how the July light like purple and yellow birds kept flickering under the trees when the wind blew" (p. 348). As a result, Nina begins to re-imagine herself as an artist, writing her name in the sand: "Nina, Nina, Nina. Writing, she could dream that her self might get away from her—that here in this faraway place she could tell her self, by name, to go or stay" (p. 355). Nina's discovery of the power of writing and her newly awakened desire for greater adventures, even dangerous ones, is followed by a highly erotic passage in which Welty uses the sensual imagery of pears as a sexually charged language in which to capture Nina's attraction to Easter:

> [Easter's] lolling head looked pale and featureless as a pear beyond the laughing face of Jinny Love. . . . Again [Nina] thought of a pear—not the everyday gritty kind that hung on the tree in the backyard, but the fine kind sold on trains and at high prices, each pear with a paper cone wrapping it alone—beautiful, symmetrical, clean pears with thin skins, with snow-white flesh so juicy and tender that to eat one baptized the whole face, and so delicate that while you urgently ate the first half, the second half was already beginning to turn brown. . . . It's not the flowers that are fleeting, Nina thought, it's the fruits—it's the time when things are ready that they don't stay. She even went through the rhyme, "Pear tree by the garden gate, How much longer must I wait?"—thinking it was the pears that asked it, not the picker.
>
> (pp. 355-356)

In this passage of sensual, lush orality, Welty articulates sexual desires of which Nina is only vaguely aware, desires that lead her to a new level of creative imagination: "The orphan! she thought exultantly. The other way to live. There were secret ways. She thought, Time's really short, I've been only thinking like the others. It's only interesting, only worthy, to try for the fiercest secrets. To slip into them all—to change. To change for a moment into Gertrude, into Mrs. Gruenwald, into Twosie—into a boy. To *have been* an orphan" (p. 361). Nina's imaginative act here, an act of transformation, of transgressing the boundaries of identity, even of sex, is markedly similar to Eudora Welty's description of her own imagination. In the introduction to ***The Collected Stories*** [***The Collected Stories of Eudora Welty***], Welty writes,

> I have been told, both in approval and accusation, that I seem to love all my characters. What I do in writing of any character is to try to enter into the mind, heart, and skin of a human being who is not myself. Whether this happens to be a man or a woman, old or young, with skin black or white, the primary challenge lies in making the jump itself. It is the act of a writer's imagination that I set most high.
>
> (p. xi)

The exultant, transformative creativity of **"Moon Lake"** is, however, interrupted and cut short by Easter's fall into heterosexuality. Early on in the story, we find that an awareness of heterosexuality and the dangers it poses has come sooner to Easter than to the Morgana girls: "Mr. Nesbitt, from the Bible Class, took Easter by the wrist and turned her around to him and looked just as hard at her front. She had started her breasts. What Easter did was to bite his right hand, his collection hand" (p. 347). Easter's refusal to be "collected" awakens a thrill of resistance in Nina. "It was wonderful," thinks Nina, "to have with them someone dangerous" (p. 347). But Easter's fall into Moon Lake becomes a sexual rite of passage from an adolescent homoeroticism to a mature and dangerous heterosexuality. Loch Morrison's life-saving process is described in terms that are both graphically sexual and violent: "He lifted up, screwed his toes, and with a groan of his own fell upon her and drove up and down upon her, into her, gouging the heels of his hands into her ribs again and again. . . . The children drew together. Life-saving was much worse than they had dreamed" (p. 366). Even worse, to the other girls, than the Loch's violence is Easter's passivity, "the carelessness of Easter's body" (p. 366). Hers is "a betrayed figure" (p. 371), and the betrayal in the story is the loss of autonomy, creativity, and even identity that follows the initiation to heterosexuality. Easter remains a passive figure throughout the remainder of the story, her voice robbed of inflection, her movements halting and clumsy.

For Nina, observing Easter's initiation, the process is "hard and cruel and, by something Nina felt inside her body, murderous" (p. 372). This killing off of feminine eroticism and creativity is signaled in the end of the story by the identification of the flame with masculinity. Loch Morrison's "candle . . . jumping a little now" is associated with "his little tickling thing hung on him like the last drop on the pitcher's lip" (p. 373). Watching him, Nina sees that his "Minnowy thing . . . matched his candle flame, naked as he was with that, he thought he shown forth too" (p. 374). Fire, the emblem of artistic creativity, is identified with the phallus in the closing scene of the story; Easter's fall from being the object of homoerotic desire to the victim of heterosexual "life-saving" is followed by a transfer of creative power from girl to boy.

"June Recital" offers a more complex and fuller treatment of female creativity and its relationship to sexuality. As in *Mrs. Dalloway,* in **"June Recital,"** the party becomes a trope for female artistic creation, and fire represents both the potentials and the dangers of feminine creativity. The consideration of women as artists is initiated in the story by the sound of the opening phrase of "Für Elise" played gently on the piano in the house next door to the Morrisons', a house that is referred to as vacant but which teems with life, both present and recalled, as the story progresses. When Cassie hears the musical phrase, she recalls several lines of a poem,

> Though I am old with wandering
> Though hollow lands and hilly lands,
> I will find out where she has gone. . . .
>
> (p. 287)

These lines are from William Butler Yeats's "The Song of the Wandering Aengus," a poem about the artist's discovery or creation of, loss of, and perpetual quest for his artistic inspiration in the figure of a "glimmering girl." The evocation of this poem introduces the image of fire representing creative imagination; the first two lines of the poem read, "I went out to the hazel wood / Because a fire was in my head."[23] One of Yeats's relatively early works, this poem presents a modernist vision of art that can "conjure presence out of absence, closure out of uncertainty, eroticism out of ennui" (Yaeger, "Because," pp. 959-960). In Yeats's poetic equation, the maker of meaning, the poet, is male, and the art that he creates, the projection of his imagination, is female. **"June Recital"** questions this equation in its exploration of women artists.

Music is a subversive force in **"June Recital."** It is a primarily feminine art, as it would have been in a small Southern town in the 1920s: most of the piano students are girls, and only one man in the town of Morgana attends the yearly piano recital. The first of three parties in the story, the remembered June recital is almost parodically feminine, "For the recital was, after all, a ceremony" (p. 310):

> In the studio decorated like the inside of a candy box, with "material" scalloping the mantel shelf and doilies placed under every moveable object, now thus made immovable, with streamers of white ribbons and nosegays of pink and white Maman Cochet roses and the last MacLain sweetpeas dividing and redividing the room, it was as hot as fire.
>
> (p. 312)

The description of Miss Eckhart—"her hair was as low on her forehead as Circe's, on the fourth grade wall feeding her swine" (p. 314)—suggests that men would be in danger in this setting. Like Mrs. Dalloway's party, the recital does momentarily unite its participants. For this one evening a year, Miss Eckhart, whose foreignness and art make her an outsider in Morgana, is a part of the community.

Within this story, music serves as a language of specifically female creativity and artistry, and, like Nina's vision of "the other way to live" (p. 361) and Welty's imaginative ability to enter into the hearts and minds of her characters, this artistry has the power to transform the artist and her audience. Playing the piano,

> Miss Eckhart assumed an entirely different face. Her skin flattened and drew across her cheeks, her lips changed. The face could have belonged to someone else—not even to a woman necessarily. It was the face a mountain could have, or what might be seen behind the veil of a waterfall. There in the rainy light it was a sightless face, one for music only.
>
> (pp. 300-301)

As in Woolf's novel, the art created by Miss Eckhart results in a modernist resolution of tensions and oppositions, erasing the boundaries of gender, social status, even species.

Virgie Rainey, Miss Eckhart's talented student, represents freedom from parental and social restraints. Welty's text celebrates Virgie's freedom and abandon that shock the town at Morgana's "public speakings": "Virgie let herself go completely, as anyone would like to do. . . . She never rested as long as the music played except at last to throw herself hard and panting on the ground, her open mouth smiling against the trampled clover" (p. 297). As a twelve-year-old, on the cusp between childhood and adolescence, Virgie Rainey is for Cassie Morrison "a secret love, as well as her secret hate" (p. 292). Cassie, the well-behaved, obedient daughter of Morgana's newspaper editor, is attracted to Virgie's "air of abandon" (p. 291). Like Sally Seton, Virgie is joyously rebellious; "full of the airs of wildness, she swayed and gave way to joys and tempers, her own and other people's with equal abandon" (p. 291). "Exciting as a gypsy would be" (p. 291), Virgie ignores Morgana's gender distinctions, riding a boy's bicycle and carrying her "sheets of advanced music rolled naked (girls usually had portfolios)" (p. 289).

Virgie's wildness is connected to her artistic talent as she refuses the discipline of the metronome, stomps on a piece of sheet music that keeps rolling up, and decorates Miss Eckhart with clover chains. The phrase from "Für Elise" awakens Cassie's memory of her "secret love"; it was Virgie's signature piece. The effect of this piece of music is to take Cassie out of herself, out of the present, and into an imaginative reconstruction and interpretation of the past. Her attraction to Virgie allows her an expanded, enhanced imagination and an understanding of people who are not like her. While Cassie "could never go for herself, never creep out on the shimmering bridge of the tree, or reach the dark magnet there that drew you inside," while "She could not see herself do an unknown thing" (p. 316), her desire for Virgie Rainey allows her to understand that "Both Miss Eckhart and Virgie Rainey were human beings terribly at large, roaming on the face of the earth. And there were others of them—human beings, roaming, like lost beasts" (p. 330).

As women artists, Miss Eckhart and Virgie Rainey are, as Cassie comes to understand, at odds with their community, outsiders and wanderers. Feminine creativity puts women at risk in a patriarchal setting. **"June Recital"** chronicles the restraint and suffering of the female artist. "Child," Mrs. Morrison tells her daughter, Cassie, "I could have *sung,*" and she "threw her hand from her, as though all music might as well now go jump off the bridge" (p. 293). But instead of singing, Mrs. Morrison expends her creative energy on sewing dresses for her daughter's piano recital, nursing her son through malaria, and attending women's card parties. The lavish artistry of the food at one of these parties is an expression of women's artistic talent given too narrow a scope:

> An orange scooped out and filled with orange juice, with the top put back on and decorated with icing leaves, a straw stuck in. A slice of pineapple with a heap of candied sweet potatoes on it, and a little handle of pastry. A cup made out of toast, filled with creamed chicken, fairly warm. A sweet peach pickle with flower petals around it of different-colored cream cheese. A swan made of a cream puff. He had whipped cream feathers, a pastry neck, green icing eyes. A pastry biscuit the size of a marble with a little date filling.
>
> (p. 328)

Mrs. Morrison sighs after describing these delights to her son. Throughout the story there are signs that she is restless, abstracted, not content with what Morgana has to offer her. In a later story, we find out that "After being so gay and flighty always, Cassie's mother went out of the room one morning and killed herself" (p. 449).

Not surprisingly, Virgie's musical talents are a subject of dissatisfaction and disbelief in Morgana because of her gender as well as her social class. When Mrs. Eckhart tells the town that Virgie "would be heard from in the world" (p. 302), Morgana scoffs. Despite Virgie's musical talent, "It was Cassie who was awarded the Presbyterian Church's music scholarship that year to go to college—not Virgie" (p. 306). Instead of going on to study music,

> Virgie Rainey had gone straight from taking music to playing the piano in the picture show. With her customary swiftness and lightness she had managed to skip an interval, some world-in-between where Cassie and Missie and Parnell were, all dyeing scarves. Virgie had gone direct into the world of power and emotion, which was beginning to seem even bigger than they had all thought.
>
> (pp. 302-303)

That "world of power and emotion" is also a world of heterosexuality; in the present setting of the story, Virgie enjoys sex with Kewpie Moffitt in the house next door to the Morrisons'. While Virgie does exercise control over her sexuality, it also corresponds to a diminishing of her art. Instead of playing Beethoven, Virgie plays popular songs at the Bijou, Morgana's movie theater. The loss of her art is signified for Cassie by the fact that Virgie plays "Für Elise" now only "for the advertisements; she played it moodily while the slide of the big white chicken on the watermelon-pink sky came on for Bowles' Gro., or the yellow horn on the streaky blue sky flashed on for the *Bugle*. . . . *Für Elise* never got finished anymore; it began, went a little way, and was interrupted by Virgie's own clamorous hand" (p. 303). Virgie's entry to the adult world of heterosexuality, the world of Valentino and "You've Got to See Mama Every Night," is marked by an interruption of her art.

Miss Eckhart will not accept and seems, in fact, oblivious to the role of woman in Morgana; she refuses to be confined by socially accepted narratives or defined in relation to a masculine center: "Missy Spights said that if Miss Eckhart had allowed herself to be called by her first name, then she would have been like other ladies. . . . Or if she had been married to anybody at all, just the awfullest man—like Miss Snowdie MacLain, that everybody could feel sorry for" (p. 308). Miss Eckhart's silence about her past marks another refusal to allow the town to write and control her narrative: "Where did Miss Eckhart come from, and where in the end did she go? In Morgana most destinies were known to everybody and seemed to go without saying" (p. 308). Because she does not fit in the town's script for women, Miss Eckhart is gradually erased and displaced until she is reduced to a safe, knowable text in the town's eyes, merely "old lady Eckhart hoeing peas out there on the County Farm" (p. 308).

On the day that marks the story's present, Miss Eckhart returns to the site of the previous June recitals and begins a re-enactment, another party scene in which Welty literalizes the dangers of feminine creativity. As Loch Morrison watches from the tree outside his room, Miss Eckhart enters the vacant house and begins to decorate: "As if she were giving a party that day, she was dressing up the parlor with ribbons of white stuff. It was newspaper. . . . She made ribbons of newspaper and was hanging them all over the parlor, starting with the piano, where she weighted down the ends with a statue" (p. 282). But unlike the preparation for earlier recitals—"Like a military operation," Mr. Morrison described it (p. 308)—this one seems haphazard. Using what she finds—old newspapers, woven matting from the floor, an old quilt, magnolia leaves, and her metronome—she prepares the recital room. Her decorating in this scene is a form of bricolage, which, as Geraldine Chouard demonstrates in her fine article "Sew to Speak: Text and Textile in Eudora Welty,"[24] is a favored artistic method of Welty's:

> The old woman was decorating the piano until it rayed out like a Christmas tree or a Maypole. Maypole ribbons of newspaper and tissue paper streamed and crossed each other from the piano to the chandelier and festooned again to the four corners of the room. . . . Soon everything seemed fanciful and beautiful enough to Loch; he thought she could stop. But the old woman kept on. This was only a part of something in her head. And in the splendor she fixed and pinned together she was all alone.
>
> (p. 383)

Miss Eckhart seeks to burn the site of her art from which she was banished, physically sent to the margins of Morgana and silenced. But in a literalized image from the second line of the Yeats poem, "Because a fire was in my head," Miss Eckhart succeeds only in setting fire to herself: "This time, the fire caught her own hair. The little short white frill turned to flame" (p. 322). Given no scope for expression of her artistry, Miss Eckhart's artistry turns inward and becomes a self-consuming fire, as does Septimus's in *Mrs. Dalloway.* Mrs. Eckhart's burning hair is the literal manifestation of Clarissa Dalloway's fear that her party "Might . . . consume her anyhow! burn her to cinders!" (p. 255)

On the level of plot, theme, and imagery, then, the representation of women as artists in Welty's stories is not as positive as Woolf's. Each triumph is undercut by a violent reinscription into an artistic economy in which a woman is either muse or victim. On the level of structure, however, the collection is such a marked transgression of literary forms and boundaries that it suggests alternative possibilities. ***The Golden Apples,*** a collection of interwoven stories, has spawned endless critical arguments over its "proper" generic identity. Welty refuses to call this work a novel, claiming that the stories

> have independent lives. They don't have to be connected, but I think by being connected there's something additional coming from them as a group with a meaning of its own. I've had students write to me and say, "I'm writing a thesis to prove that ***The Golden Apples*** is a novel. Please send me. . . ." They want me to support them. So I write back and say that it isn't a novel, I'm sorry.[25]

Welty's refusal to identify the collection as a novel disrupts and decenters the dominant literary paradigm of genre, while the work's structure fragments the linear progression of plot, the same sort of linearity and unity of plot to which Woolf objects in the essay "Modern Fiction" and which she self-consciously set out to avoid in *Mrs. Dalloway.* Taken as a whole, ***The Golden Apples*** is anything but univocal. Welty uses music and myth as disruptive voices that engage the dominant discourse in dialogue. Her use of Yeats's poem and the artistic paradigm it represents draws that perspective into a dialogue. Although their female artists do not succeed in escaping the ideologies that silence them, Woolf and Welty do escape, as their narratives actively question the ideology that yokes female artistry and female sexuality and labels both as dangerous.

Thus it appears that sexuality *is* political in the fiction of both Virginia Woolf and Eudora Welty, as these writers explore the potential of language to articulate feminine desire and pleasure, and as they represent and critique the social regulation and containment of both female sexual desire and female creativity. Both *Mrs. Dalloway* and ***The Golden Apples*** link sexuality and creativity, displacing heterosexual eroticism in order to foreground the woman as artist.

For Welty, as for Woolf, imagination and language itself are erotic. In her essay "A Sweet Devouring," Welty represents reading as an erotic, oral pleasure. "The pleasures of reading," she writes, are "like those of a Christmas cake, a sweet devouring."[26] She carries the metaphor of reading as oral pleasure throughout the piece, describing her desire to read as a "higher appetite and gratification" (p. 279), and writing of "gobbl[ing] up installment after installment" of a children's book (p. 282). "I was in love with books," she proclaims; "I loved the printed page" (p. 282). Her complex manipulation of intertextuality in ***The Golden Apples*** demonstrates that Welty's reading fed her imagination richly, productively, and even erotically. As Mark explains, "Welty's intertextuality is 'intersexuality,' precisely because her writing evokes an enlivening of metaphor, character, and symbol or an eroticization of the word" (p. 12).

In a 1972 *Paris Review* interview, Welty describes the excitement and enchantment she experienced in her first encounter with Woolf's fiction: "[Virginia Woolf] was the one who opened the door. When I read *To the Lighthouse,* I felt, Heavens what is this? I was so excited by the experience I couldn't sleep or eat. I've read it many times since."[27] The language Welty uses to describe her experience of rereading *To the Lighthouse* in 1981, in order to write a foreword to that novel, echoes the language of the enlivening and expanding of the imagination that characterizes both female creativity and female eroticism in ***The Golden Apples***:

> That feeling of discovery you get with such a novel is the most marvelous thing. A door has been opened. I've just now been trying to write about Virginia Woolf's novel *To the Lighthouse.* Harcourt Brace is getting out a new edition of three of her novels, and they're having a living woman writer to write a little foreword for each; just sort of what it means to you. So I'm doing the one that meant the most to me which was *To the Lighthouse.* I've been trying to describe that feeling you get when you come upon something. I came upon it absolutely cold and it just knocked me out. I've read it lots of times since, but I read it again in order to write this piece, and it did the same thing.[28]

In an often-quoted interview with Joanna Maclay, Welty uses a quotation by the novelist Henry Green to describe both herself as a reader and her imagined ideal reader: "Prose should be a long intimacy between strangers."[29] Eudora Welty's imaginative interaction with Virginia Woolf's fiction has been just this sort of interaction, this sort of intimacy. The two writers never met, and since Virginia Woolf committed suicide in 1941, the year that Welty's first collection of short stories was published, it is doubtful that Woolf ever read any of Welty's work. But Welty's reading of Woolf's work had a profound impact upon Welty, an impact upon her imagination that resembles the impact of Easter on Nina Carmichael's imagination or the impact of Virgie Rainey on Cassie Morrison's.

Notes

1. The original version of this paper was presented in December 1999 at the Centre de Recherché Intertextualities Littéraires et Artistiques, Universite de Sorbonne, Paris, France.
2. "Eudora Welty and Politics," in *Eudora Welty and Politics: Did the Writer Crusade?,* ed. Harriet Pollack and Suzanne Marrs (Baton Rouge: Louisiana State University Press, 2001), p. 3.
3. Welty's privacy has become in recent years a matter of scholarly discussion because of her refusal to authorize a biography and her request that her friends not cooperate with Ann Waldron on her unauthorized biography, *Eudora Welty: A Writer's Life* (New York: Doubleday, 1999). Ten years earlier, Welty's insistence on maintaining her privacy, her refusal even in her autobiographical work *One Writer's Beginnings* (Cambridge: Harvard University Press, 1984) to reveal much about her personal life or emotions came under fire from Carolyn Heilbrun in *Writing a Woman's Life* (New York: Norton, 1988).
4. See Patricia Yaeger, "The Case of the Dangling Signifier: Phallic Imagery in Eudora Welty's 'Moon Lake,'" *Twentieth Century Literature,* 28 (Winter 1982), 431-452; and Rebecca Mark, *The Dragon's Blood: Feminist Intertextuality in Eudora Welty's "The Golden Apples"* (Jackson: University Press of Mississippi, 1994).
5. Xaviere Gauthier, "Is There Such a Thing as Women's Writing?" in *New French Feminisms,* ed. Elaine Marks and Isabelle de Courtivron (New York: Schocken Books, 1980), p. 161.
6. New York: Harcourt, 1929, p. 86.
7. "When Virginia Looked at Vita, What Did She See; or, Lesbian: Feminist: Woman—What's the Differ(e/a)nce?" *Feminist Studies,* 18 (Spring 1992), 99-117, rpt. in *Feminisms: An Anthology of Literary Theory and Criticism,* revised edition, ed. Robyn R. Warhol and Diane Price Herndl (New Brunswick, New Jersey: Rutgers University Press, 1997), p. 478.
8. Virginia Woolf, *Mrs. Dalloway* (New York: Harcourt, 1925), p. 46.
9. *The Diary of Virginia Woolf, Volume Two, 1920-1924,* ed Anne Olivier Bell (New York: Harcourt, Brace, Jovanovich, 1978), p. 263.
10. *Writing Beyond the Ending: Narrative Strategies of Twentieth-Century Women Writers* (Bloomington: Indiana University Press, 1985), p. 63.
11. See Suzan Harrison, *Eudora Welty and Virginia Woolf: Gender, Genre and Influence* (Baton Rouge: Louisiana State University Press, 1997); and Louise Westling, *Sacred Groves and Ravaged Gardens: The Fiction of Eudora Welty, Carson McCullers, and Flannery O'Connor* (Athens: University of Georgia Press, 1985).
12. In *The Common Reader* (London: Harcourt, 1925), p. 151.
13. *PMLA,* 99 (October 1984), 959. Revised and reprinted in *Welty: A Life in Literature,* ed. Albert J. Devlin (Jackson: University Press of Mississippi, 1987), pp. 139-167.
14. *Bucknell Review,* 39 (1995), 79-103.
15. Eudora Welty, "June Recital," in *The Collected Stories of Eudora Welty* (New York: Harcourt, Brace, Jovanovich, 1980), p. 287.
16. *Crossing the Double-Cross: The Practice of Feminist Criticism* (Chapel Hill: University of North Carolina Press, 1986), p. 117.
17. "'And I Wondered If She Might Kiss Me': Lesbian Panic as Narrative Strategy in British Women's Fictions," *Modern Fiction Studies,* 41 (Fall-Winter 1995), 569.

18. Qtd. in Christopher Ames, *The Life of the Party: Festive Vision in Modern Fiction* (Athens: University of Georgia Press, 1991), pp. 105-106.
19. "The Hostess and the Seamstress: Virginia Woolf's Creation of a Domestic Modernism," in *Unmanning Modernism: Gendered Re-Readings,* ed. Elizabeth Jane Harrison and Shirley Peterson (Knoxville: University of Tennessee Press, 1997), p. 91.
20. "Narrative Structure(s) and Female Development: The Case of *Mrs. Dalloway,*" in *Virginia Woolf: A Collection of Critical Essays,* ed. Margaret Homans (Englewood Cliffs, New Jersey: Prentice-Hall, 1993), p. 97.
21. "Visual Pleasure and Narrative Cinema," in *Feminisms: An Anthology of Literary Theory and Criticism,* p. 433.
22. In "Music from Spain," Welty represents the expansion and transformation of the male imagination through homoerotic desire in Eugene MacLain's attraction for the Spaniard.
23. *The Poems of William Butler Yeats,* ed. Richard J. Finneran (New York: Macmillan, 1983), p. 59.
24. *South Atlantic Review,* 63 (1998), 7-26.
25. Charles T. Bunting, "'The Interior World': An Interview with Eudora Welty," in *Conversations with Eudora Welty,* ed. Peggy Whitman Prenshaw (Jackson: University Press of Mississippi, 1984), p. 43.
26. "A Sweet Devouring," in *The Eye of the Story: Selected Essays and Reviews* (New York: Random House, 1979), p. 281.
27. Linda Keuhl, "The Art of Fiction XLVII: Eudora Welty," *Paris Review,* 55 (Fall 1972), 75.
28. John Griffin Jones, "Eudora Welty," in *Conversations,* pp. 324-325.
29. "A Conversation with Eudora Welty," in *Conversations,* p. 282.

Rebecca Chalmers (essay date spring 2003)

SOURCE: Chalmers, Rebecca. "Untangling *The Wide Net*: Welty and Readership." *Southern Literary Journal* 35, no. 2 (spring 2003): 89-106.

[In the following essay, Chalmers suggests that "First Love" and "At the Landing" engage the reader in a difficult, yet rewarding, contemplation of textual meaning.]

Eudora Welty has written extensively about the responsibility that writers have to be mindful of and to establish connections with their readers. "At the other end of the writing is the reader," she says. "There is sure to be somewhere the reader, who is a user himself of imagination and thought, who knows, perhaps, as much about the need of communication as the writer" (106). She notes that "looking at short stories as readers and writers together should be a companionable thing" (85), a process in which both parties participate, a friendly dialogue in which the ultimate goal is textual understanding and meaning. But, declarations of affection for readers notwithstanding, Welty's fiction often belies her avowed closeness to readership and reveals instead an entirely different and problematic paradigm for discovery. To be sure, some of Welty's fiction might be said to offer a kind of companionable read, but much of her fiction challenges readers in peculiar and disturbing ways and imposes on them an obligation to make sense of the implications that reside in those texts. Perhaps more than other collections, ***The Wide Net*** contains stories that demand a genuinely difficult readerly commitment. These texts seem so experimental and vexing that, in the process to discover meaning, readers may well become the subject of the experiment. Indeed, the nature of the relationship between reader and text thematically connects the uneven and otherwise disparate pieces of the collection.

Welty's fiction often challenges readers to think about the ways of being that characters demonstrate while, at the same time, exploring the methods by which readers can apprehend texts: the ways of being and seeing that allow readers to engage with the texts and the specific level of being and seeing that Welty's texts themselves allow. On another level, these same stories present real obstacles to readers who unwittingly become the subject of an experiment on ways of knowing or understanding the texts, on how to determine what texts mean, on how we come to know what we know (as the stories in ***The Wide Net*** certainly do). Although the natural inclination of readers might be to involve themselves with a text, Welty's fiction often distances the reader/companion and provokes an examination of the extent to which readers are allowed to participate in the co-creative process. An exploration of the two stories which bound ***The Wide Net*** reveals Welty's thematic experimentation with the function of readership and her primer on the nature, obligation, and experience of readership. **"First Love,"** the collection's opening story, evidences this theme, one that resounds forcefully in the final story, **"At the Landing."** In both stories, while Welty presents fictional characters who act as models both of readership and of texts to be read, she imbues them with limitations or defects which condition not only their ability to read texts, but also our ability to apprehend meaning of the texts in which they appear. These stories particularly confront and vex readers—assault their senses, at times—and establish a significantly less-than-companionable relationship between text and audience.

Michael Kreyling notes that "the writing of the stories of ***The Wide Net*** had proven much more difficult, even alienating, than the writing of the earlier stories, which, Welty has said, went in a rush and were scarcely revised" (596). Welty's struggle with this collection may have something to do with the fact that, more than her earlier stories, these pieces explore what constitutes reality (for both the characters and for the readers of the texts), how human beings see and engage reality, and what kinds of confinements and restrictions control their gaze and cause their vision to be perverted in some way. By providing access to the consciousness of characters whose ability to see and to understand is necessarily restricted by the peculiar physical and emotional ailments that define their human condition, these texts unsettle and displace expectations of normalcy. Restricting the perspective of readers—as, for example, in the presentation of the deaf Joel Mayes as the only access to consciousness in **"First Love"**—significantly limits the amount of information available to readers. It forces them instead to wrestle with the altered perceptions presented through the consciousnesses of defective characters and to make sense of what happens in the stories within that limited context. The texts, then, distort reality and force readers to grapple with the distortion, a condition that, according to Wolfgang Iser, "depends for its effect on our conception of what is normal" (41) in the first place. But Welty's positioning of abnormal or damaged characters problematizes or potentially renders impossible the reader's ability to determine what constitutes normalcy for these characters. Iser notes that, in order for readers to make meaning of texts, "the distance between the story and the reader must at times be made to disappear" (37), but these texts interrupt that process by distancing the reader, by altering virtual perspective.

In the chapter on "Learning to See" in *One Writer's Beginnings,* Welty comments on the gradual nature of the development of vision and on the way that vision changes with a shift in geography—"crossing a river, crossing a county line, crossing a state line—especially crossing the line you couldn't see but knew was there" (44)—which rouses consciousness and causes us to "draw a breath and feel the difference" (44). Perhaps this is the experience the texts of this collection attempt to replicate as they cross back and forth between being and knowing, and seeing and understanding, in the reader's consciousness. Not only does ***The Wide Net*** force the reader into the marginal areas in the geography of perspective—between reality and imagination, between wakefulness and dreamlike sleeping, between fact and fiction, between reading a text and being read as text—but also it blurs the distinctions between the known and the unknown (or unknowable).

In "The Theory of Signs and the Role of the Reader," Umberto Eco suggests that, despite the number of ways in which a text can be read, it "is a lazy machinery which forces its possible readers to do a part of its textual work" and that the "semiotic strategies displayed by the text" are imposed by the author and must be recognized if readers are to do their work (36). Eco's statement expresses an expectation and an assumption that readers engage in such work by reading the signs that authors provide, although there is no guarantee that readers, in a general sense of that term, will be able to identify them. As Eco presents them, readers become what (in a response to Eco) Teresa de Lauretis calls "textual strategy" because they (and their responses to textual signs) are "already contemplated by the text, as a function of the text" (46).[1] The metaphorical "net" of Welty's title is the collection's first sign and suggests the entanglement that readers experience as they are snared in one place by a glimpse, a tease of information that promises a development that frequently does not materialize while, in other places, texts flood reader consciousness with images in an expressionistic deluge. Such shifts in the degree of access to information can disorient a reader who, according to Iser, "must be made to feel for himself the new meaning" of a text he is helping to create; in order "to do this he must actively participate in bringing out the meaning and this participation is an essential precondition for communication between the author and the reader" (30). Welty's manner of presentation—her insistence on limiting readers' access to consciousness while in other ways providing specific, detailed, and evocative images; her creation of dreamlike and occasionally surrealistic passages that are counterbalanced by starkly realistic events—provokes readers into an uneasy collaboration not immediately apparent to them but revealed in their struggle to create meaning. As Welty's style captures readers in its mystery—a term which Ruth Vande Kieft says must be defined as "the enigma of man's being, and his relation to the universe . . . what is concealed, secret, inviolable in human beings, putting up the barriers, making our meaning and identity puzzling to ourselves" (10)—the collaboration with author and text becomes, for readers, a genuine struggle to untangle the net that entraps them in the text: a nearly impossible act.

One of the first mysteries of ***The Wide Net*** is contained in the title **"First Love."** While it is true that the story does mention love once in connection with Joel Mayes, the protagonist and the eyes through which we read the story, it does so in terms of Joel's love for the characters (Burr, Blennerhassett, and Blennerhassett's wife) to whom he feels connected, but this connection does not seem to satisfy the promise of the title. What, then, is the first love to which Welty's title refers? More than anything else, this title and the story itself operate as a metaphor for Welty's own first love: reading. Welty says that "reading can teach us something, and it is endless, about *reading,* about meeting with art" (Welty 29). The italicized emphasis on *reading* demonstrates her belief that inherent in fiction lies "the possibility of a shared act of the imagination between its writer and its reader" (147), but one initiated by and, to a great extent, controlled by its writer. As **"First Love"** begins, the narrator comments on the unusual time "in a season of dreams" (153) and establishes fictional time and place as surrealist transparencies placed over realistic history and landscapes that like "the whole world . . . must be in a transfiguration" in which "all proportion went away" (153). The text signals that readers are crossing boundaries, entering new territory as they begin the story. When Joel Mayes is introduced as "a deaf boy twelve years old," and it becomes clear that Joel will provide the medium through which they can apprehend the meaning of the story, readers are doubly distanced from the text—by setting and by narrative consciousness. Because of his disability, Joel has been forced to become an interpreter of both the spoken language he cannot hear and its context. "It was marvelous to him when the infinite designs of speech became visible in formations on the air, and he watched with awe that changed to tenderness whenever people met and passed in the road with an exchange of words" (154). Joel, then, is a reader of texts who loves the reading process. Like Joel, readers have indirect access to the author's voice when they read; they cannot hear exact intonations and are left to interpret the author's textual signs. Just as Joel attempts to make sense of what happens around him, so, too, do readers work to discover meaning. But, despite the joys of reading, this is not easy work, as Joel's struggle indicates.

Joel's living situation indicates that his involvement (like the involvement of any reader) with the texts he reads is "a noncommital arrangement" (155) that allows him access to what happens but does not impel him to participate in the process of creation of meaning. He is allowed to stay at the Inn, at no charge, as long as he does the work: "He never paid them anything for his keep, and they never paid him anything for his work. Yet time passed, and he became a little part of the place where it passed over him" (155). In addition to narrating and interpreting events, Joel becomes a part of the text he reads. Iser notes that "the reader, in bringing about the virtual dimension, is actually entangled"—an apt word for this discussion—"in what he has produced" (43). And Joel literally sees texts everywhere. "The messages of love carved into [his candlestick] . . . in Spanish words" are illuminated when the candle is lit and "[come] out in black relief for anyone to read who came knowing the language" (156). Readers must, then, understand the language of the text in order to create a virtual reality they can access. Thus, Joel constructs texts mostly in the context of his everyday life/reality as a bootblack. "He had learned boots; under his hand they stood up and took a good shape. This was not a slave's work, or a child's either. It had dignity" (156), as does cocreation of texts, a shaping of reality. Some texts hold real surprises, like the unexpected "rattlesnake [that] had shoved its head from a boot as he stretched out his hand; but that was not likely to happen again in a thousand years" (156). As the bootblack, Joel lives in a solitary world of the reader, "alone in the way he liked to be" (156). For readers, Joel models readership and also defines the form or shape of **"First Love,"** a process which Iser identifies as basic "communication or as negotiation of insight" (57). With Joel, readers watch as text is recreated through reader interpretation; without Joel, the passages would be dark and curiously silent; no spoken dialogue exists anywhere in this story. Thus, the text itself turns the experience of co-creating text back onto the reader.

With Joel functioning as both text and reader and with Welty's audience in tow as the readers of both the story and the readers of the narrator as text, Welty complicates the process by introducing "a new adventure" into Joel's world, a new text which Joel opens and which readers of the story must read along with him. When it begins, "boots went completely out of [Joel's] head" (156); workaday chores are forgotten as the possibilities of exploration and interpretation of a different text present themselves. What follows is a wholly constructed fiction in which two unknown men who "were not of Natchez," not local, not familiar, and whose "names were not in the book" present themselves to be read. The appearance of two characters, "at some moment outside his knowledge or consent" (156-157), allow the experience of reading to descend into and take over Joel's consciousness. Joel gazes at these men "with the feasting the eyes do in secret" (157), a phrase that echoes Welty's comment about her own experience of reading: "The pleasures of reading itself—who doesn't remember?—were like those of a Christmas cake, a sweet devouring" (*One Writer's Beginnings* 281).

Before readers discover, along with Joel, who these characters are, the text outlines, in a particularly powerful passage, what a story should do and how readers should experience the discovery of a new text:

> To Joel it was like the first movement he had ever seen, as if the world had been up to that night inanimate. It was like the signal to open some heavy gate or paddock, and it did open to his complete astonishment upon a panorama in his own head, about which he knew first of all that he would never be able to speak—it was nothing but brightness, as full as the brightness on which he had opened his eyes. Inside his room was still another interior, this meeting upon which all the light was turned, and within that was one more mystery, all that was being said. . . . He had no idea of how long they had stayed when they got up and stretched their arms and walked out through the door, after blowing the candle out.
>
> (157)

In this reflection, the text discusses how character, plot, setting, and narration—the key elements of fiction—affect the relationship of the reader to the text, to make the text's work possible. Joel falls asleep while creating the text for the reader, forgetting his literal (as opposed to literary) work in the process. But, because of this experience, his life is altered; reading has made his senses acute. "All day long, everything in the passing moment and each little deed assumed the gravest importance" (157-158). As Iser defines it, Joel has assumed the reader's role: "he will leave behind his individual disposition for the duration of his reading. In this way, and in this way only, he will gain a positive and active insight into human nature" (56). Joel can barely contain his excitement at the mystery: "He waited for night. In his own room the candlestick now stood on the table covered with the wonder of having been touched by unknown hands in his absence and seen in his sleep" (158). And, when he returns to his boot work, the identities of the men quite suddenly come to him: "There was no one to inform him that the men were Aaron Burr and Harman Blennerhassett, but he knew. No one had pointed out to him any way that he might know which was which, but he knew that" (158). According to Lucinda H. MacKethan, Welty wants her readers to connect to the "vital images for fiction," but what she most cares about is "the way they are *seen,*" not the way they are heard:

> Eventually "our knowledge depends upon the living relationship between what we see going on and ourselves." "Insight," says Miss Welty, "doesn't happen often at the click of the moment, like a lucky snapshot, but comes in its own time and more slowly and from nowhere but within." It is through what she calls "the act of focusing" that place acquires the sense of identity that men can use to measure themselves and to endure. "The act of focusing itself," she says, "has beauty and meaning; it is the act that, continued in, turns into meditation, into poetry."
>
> (259)[2]

For Joel, the overwhelming "brightness" he feels at the acquisition of insight, of secret knowledge, "like part of his meditations" (158), marks his ability to see his own life in terms of its relationship to the texts he reads. Texts can, then, alter readers' apprehension of the conditions of their own lives. Like the story unfolding before Joel, secrets of reading are "endlessly complex." Conversations with texts are "never finished" because they can "never be all told." Readers and texts "always have to meet again" (158). So the possibilities for insight and discovery continue with each visit.

With their nightly visits and apparent unconcern with Joel's presence, Burr and Blennerhassett continue to create texts for him to read; vulnerability to the reader, then, does not keep the writer from the task of writing. Perhaps one of the protections for the writer is that the defect of the reader, represented by Joel's inability to hear/understand completely, is an asset which allows "a kind of hospitality" (158) to exist between writer and reader. This very limited "hospitality" may be what Welty has in mind for a "companionable" relationship between writer and reader. The writer "may [talk] in another language, in which there [is] nothing but evocation" (158); readers of texts, like Joel, "would allow Burr [the text] to take him with him wherever it was that he meant to go" (158). In engaging the writer, Joel has experienced the joy of immersion in text. And, when texts are not available, when Joel "[sees] nothing more than the dormant firelight stretched on the empty floor . . . he [has] a strange feeling of having been deserted and lost, not quite like anything he had ever felt in his life" (159-160). Once the relationship with literature is established, readers take on a protective posture; Joel says that "he might have been their [the characters' and also his text's] safety, for the way he sat up so still and looked at them at moments like a father at his playing children" (160), and finds himself, with new eyes, reading landscapes and all other texts as he does "the spell unfolding by night in his room" (160).

Joel gathers knowledge (in this case, about Burr's upcoming trial) "to himself by being, himself, everywhere," and "he [is] driven to know everything" (162), a condition that depends upon the author's ability to create the range of emotions we call suspense. In a suspense-driven section, Welty's narrative sends Joel out to determine what the soldiers are planning for the characters whose text has changed his life, but, at the end of his wandering, Joel recognizes that "all his walking about was no use. Where did people learn things? Where did they go to find them? How far?" (163). The answer would seem to be that people learn things from reading texts with which they have a relationship of some duration and intensity, that a mere wandering about and through texts, in an effort to collect data, will not yield the knowledge that arises from actual engagement. Indeed, in a discussion of Welty's childhood, Gail Mortimer comments on the literal texts and tools which provoked the author's early curiosity: "a dictionary and encyclopedias in the dining room to help answer questions raised during family dinner conversations" and the "telescope, magnifying glass, gyroscope, kaleidoscope" which her father kept "in a table in the library to 'instruct and fascinate' . . . and to introduce his children to the mysteries of the wider (and the smaller) world" (51).[3] But Mortimer notes:

> These objects may have conveyed to children the idea that knowledge was accessible and benign, the world ordered and meaningful. . . . Welty gradually realized that the sorts of information they revealed did not actually answer the kinds of questions she had begun to formulate about life. The dictionary and encyclopedia offered only facts; the instruments only data . . . the knowledge they offered did not illuminate the questions that truly concerned [Welty]: human motivations, communication, relationships, mystery, the allure of beauty around her, the functioning of memory and imagination. What had been offered to her as answers—fascinating though the data might be at times—was only part of the truth.
>
> (51)

Joel gains access to this kind of partial, fact-based truth when he is "given a notice to paste on the saloon mirror saying that the trial of Aaron Burr for treason would be held at the end of the month" (160) and when he walks through town in the role of observer, onlooker to the action, a role which sits in opposition to the role of participant in the action which he has come to know vis-à-vis the intimate connection he has established in the space he shares with Burr and Blennerhassett and the text which that connection has created.[4] But "works of art [texts] should be analyzed less from the point of view of representation than from that of suggestion" (Iser 58). The outside world, the literal language which provides data, cannot provide all the answers; interpretation is key to understanding.

When Blennerhassett's wife, who Joel thinks does not "[bother] to speak at all" (163), arrives with her fiddle, the instrument provides another text for Joel to read. And strange things happen: first, Joel is transported to another place and time, to Virginia where his mother had told him "the story of the Princess Labam" (163); then he realizes "that he had *heard* the sounds of her song, the only thing he had ever heard" (emphasis added) and that "he did not care to learn her purpose or to wonder any longer" about it (163). So not all texts, despite their obvious ability to connect to a reader's emotions, need to be plumbed for secrets. Some can simply please the eye or ear and transport readers to locations in their memories, or, like Joel's mother's story, they may evoke strong feelings which need only to be recognized and accepted for what they are.

On what Joel knows will be his last night with his companions, Burr stretches himself out, like an open book, "full length upon" the table, and Joel observes that the only real speech in the world is achieved in listening and that he will feel genuine sadness at the end of this story because, he notes, "nothing had been told":

> If love does a secret thing always, it is to reach backward, to a time that could not be known—for it makes a history of the sorrow and the dream it has contemplated in some instant of recognition. What Joel saw before him he had a terrible wish to speak out loud, but he would have had to find names for the places of the heart and the times for its shadowy and tragic events, and they seemed of great magnitude, heroic and terrible and splendid, like the legends of the mind. But for lack of a way to tell how much was known, the boundaries would lie between him and the others, all the others, until he died.
>
> (165)

The problem here is that Joel, in a state of "child-like supplication," cannot, like all readers, fully understand how to read texts. His limited experience allows him to understand something about the power behind the transmission of ideas—"the furious pressure of this man's dream" (165)—but he cannot translate these ideas into complete, readable texts of his own. The text poses the same problem for readers who feel a sense of loss at the completion of a story whose full meaning eludes them. If, as Welty comments, readers know "as much about the need of communication as the writer" (106), they become dissatisfied with insufficient resolution that displaces their companionship with the text. Like Joel, they may feel a jealous identification with and possession of the text, but they are unsure about what to make of it. "Joel would never know now the true course, or the true outcome of any dream: this was all he felt . . . he did not see how he could ever go back and still be the boot-boy at the Inn" because, even without fully understanding the story, the act of reading has changed him; his life has been so altered by the experience that he can no longer imagine it in terms of what he has come to know.

By the time readers arrive at **"At the Landing,"** they have traveled a circuitous route through the title story, **"The Wide Net,"** an exploration of the way in which husband and wife are trapped in the net of the text they create to define their lives; **"A Still Moment,"** in which three historical characters share a moment, but nothing more, and create individual texts that suit their needs and deny them the grace Welty suggests is possible in shared communication; **"Asphodel,"** an interestingly drawn story about how myth and legend are created and the power they have over readers; **"The Winds,"** a text that examines the connection between dreams and reality and ties it to a coming-of-age experience for a young woman; **"The Purple Hat,"** a curious story which forces readers to suspend their disbelief and to engage willingly in the process of storytelling; and **"Livvie,"** about a young woman whose ability to read the text of her own life is severely restricted by the condition of her marriage to an old man. In her presentation of such a widely disparate set of characters and situations, Welty indicates that no person's or event's significance to inform or to create readers is any more or less important than another's. What is important is that readers give themselves over to the task. "Both reading and writing are experiences—lifelong—in the course of which we who encounter words used in certain ways are persuaded by them to be brought mind and heart within the presence, the power, of the imagination. This we find to be above all the power to reveal, with nothing barred" (Welty 134). But readers must yield to the revelatory power of words and, "by yielding to what has been, by all [the writer's] available means, *suggested,* we are able to see for ourselves a certain distance beyond what is possible for him to say" (138). Readers can, in this yielding, Welty suggests, become co-creators of the text; but "of course [the writer] knew this would be so: he has been, and he is a *reader*" (142) who anticipates readers' willingness to submit to the text. In that context, the challenge that Welty presents her readers in the final story of the collection, **"At the Landing,"** a profoundly disturbing story on a number of levels, is even more difficult to understand. To an even greater degree than elsewhere in the collection, this text reveals in half-concealment and frustrates readers by denying them full access to information that might make clear (or clearer) the chilling and complex conclusion to the piece.

Jenny, the protagonist of this story, is a young woman (presumably adolescent, although no direct evidence of her age is presented) whose world has been severely restricted by the overbearingly protective grandfather with whom she lives. Like **"First Love," "At the Landing"** begins with a dream. Jenny is awakened by her actively dreaming, somnambulist grandfather on the night of his death as the old man predicts a flood he sees in his dream and then, as she tries to wake him, dies in her arms. With the grandfather's death, Jenny's life changes; she is free for the first time to make decisions for herself. But this situation creates an enormous problem for her because she has no idea about how to read the world or how the world might read her as text. Her grandfather has enforced externally the only control she has known, so she understands nothing about internal control. And the problem is further exacerbated by the fact that Jenny is shy and, with her mother dead, that she has no model for womanhood to which she can subscribe.

As Iser remarks, modern writers are challenged to create characters whose identities are lost in subjectivity: "Clearly the self needs a specific reality in order to take on a concrete form of its own, and when there is no such reality, its contours begin to blur" (122). Jenny's contours are totally blurred by the subjectivity of the text. Like her mother, Jenny longs to see things, to have some sense of how the world operates, but she has no teacher and no frame of reference through which to understand what she sees. Neither do readers of the text. Jenny is, intellectually and socially, a child, and she becomes a victim of her own inability to see, a condition that results from the repressive restrictions her grandfather has placed on her. Some of Welty's female characters, Susan Donaldson notes, often "find themselves in various forms of confinement and entrapment, and quite often their imprisonment is signified by the boundaries of the stories that enclose them and by the communities and readers who scrutinize them" (570).[5] This text forces readers into a kind of complicity in Jenny's entrapment and in their own entanglement in a story which challenges the power of vision to exact answers about troubling situations.

The repeated use of terms related to sight strongly suggests that this is a story about the way in which vision constructs meaning and identity. Almost immediately, in a small early section which introduces Billy Floyd, the wandering fisherman who moves "like a dreamer through the empty street and on through the trackless haze toward the river" (241), Welty twice uses the term "haze" to indicate blurred vision. Here, too, the river, which will soon flood, is said to be "beyond sight," and the grandfather and Jenny are acknowledged as "the people least seen in The Landing" (241). Little is known about any of these characters, but the view of the old ladies of The Landing is that "the grandfather was too old, and the girl was too shy of the world, and they were both too good . . . to come out, and so they stayed inside" (241). The town believes what it sees—"In the Landing, every person that moved was watched out of sight" (243)—and explores no other possibility to explain the behavior of Jenny or the grandfather. To some extent, readers of the text become inhabitants of the town who can understand only what they see.

The suggestion of incest in this family would explain the recurring silence in **"At the Landing."** But, no matter what the circumstances of Jenny's experience may be (and Welty does not explain them), she is trapped in her grandfather's house as her mother was trapped before her. And the house holds the secret of her mother's existence, a secret only hinted at, which would provide the half-concealed evidence that might explain Jenny's condition. On the night that the grandfather dies, the narrator notes that he "reached as if to lift an obstacle that he thought was stretched there—the bar that crossed the door in her mother's time" (240), a clear indication that he had made a prisoner of his own daughter while she was alive. Later, the narrator explains that the grandfather hates raving because it is "a force of Nature and so beneath notice or mention" (242), so Jenny knows that she must not rave. "And yet—even now, too late—if Jenny could plead . . . !" (242). This is a curious almost-sentence in that it contains the stifled longing to scream, to rave, that Jenny wants to exercise but which she realizes it is too late to do anything about because "in his daughter's first raving he rang a bell and told the cook to take her off and sit by her until she had done with it, but in the end she died of it" (242). So her mother's death results from "a daughter's frustration when her father turned jailer," as Harriet Pollack remarks (23). And only when she is given permission does Jenny "walk up there to visit the grave of her mother" (243).

Whether or not Jenny or her mother is a victim of incest, the girl and her readers are certainly made victims of the absent knowledge of her mother whom "Jenny could not plead for" (242). Why is Jenny "never to speak to Billy Floyd, by the order of her grandfather" (249), and what kind of connection exists between Jenny and Mag Lockhart, the albino woman whom Jenny observes with Billy? Jenny senses a connection—"she had felt whatever Mag had felt"—and imagines that she has had a vision of some kind. "She thought she could see herself, fleet as a mirror-image, rising up in a breath of astonished farewell and walking to the well of old Mag . . . stand on top, look about, and then go into the dark passage" (246). When the text reveals that "the stone on the grave of [Jenny's] mother [has] her married name of Lockhart cut into it," it provides no frame of reference for this information. Has Jenny imagined her mother's death in this vision? Has her mother thrown herself down a well? To whom was her mother married? Who is Jenny's father? Is Mag Lockhart Jenny's sister or half-sister? Is Billy Floyd, as the old ladies of The Landing think, "the bastard of one of the old checker-players" (255), or is he Jenny's mother's child or Jenny's grandfather's child or a child of an incestuous union between father and daughter? What are the secrets in these tangled family relationships? Readers are snared in this net of conflicting and confusing undeveloped storylines.

The text provides no answers—no reasons and certainly no excuses—for Jenny's behavior or for her grandfather's and, as Donaldson comments about reading another piece of Welty fiction, the reading process itself becomes "roughly akin to looking at an exhibit and being vaguely uneasy about the possibility of being on exhibit oneself" (574). The role of voyeur is reversed, and the gaze is turned on readers, who witness a spectacle of sorts that they do not know how to interpret. **"At the Landing"** could, in this respect, be compared to Faulkner's *The Sound and the Fury* and the use of Benjy, the idiot, as narrator. "The reader's attention is drawn," Iser says, "to the peculiar nature of this perception [the reality of an idiot] rather than his effect on the intersubjective world; indeed, this could only become the subject if he were seen in the context of normality" (137). But Jenny is not normal; her inability to ask questions, to communicate, to rage against her personal circumstances indicates an absence of self-identification. The tension created between the reader's awareness of this spare information about Jenny and her family and the questions that the information prompts forces the reader into the role of creator of text. Because vital information about the family to which the text alludes is obscured, the construction of meaning is left to the reader's imagination. What determines the reader's ability to construct meaning at all, though, is the control exerted by Welty's larger text, very much like the control that the grandfather exerts over both Jenny and her mother. Jenny is, like Joel Mayes, a reader of texts and a text herself; but, like the readers of Welty's text, Jenny's vision, despite her attempts to apprehend the world around her, is limited by her experience, by her inability to see clearly. In her grandfather's library, she "gaze[s] at the backs of the books without titles" (241), which serve as metaphor for Jenny's absent identity, particularly her self-identity. And the prisms at which Jenny looks but cannot bring herself to touch are the perfect metaphor for an enlightened but distorted vision of life; "it was like something in her vision that kept her from seeing" (249).

Jenny wants to catch Floyd "and [like the prisms] see him close, but not to touch him" (244). The passage that deals with Jenny and Floyd's first encounter is filled with terms about vision: "She wanted to watch him a while longer"; she "waited on him to see how long he could drink without lifting his face"; "she could see only the one arm flung out in the torn sleeve"; "she watched him in the woods"; "she would wait and see him come awake"; "Jenny could see to start with that no kiss had ever brought love tenderly enough from mouth to mouth" (244). While a certain loss of innocence results from such intense gazing, the text indicates that it is not through sight/vision that one learns; rather, it is in action, in touch. "When Jenny did touch Floyd, touch his sleeve, he started . . . He went alert in the field like a listening animal" (244). While readers' vision can become distorted by imagination, by earlier texts, by expectation, touch demonstrates actual experience that cannot always be fathomed or articulated. Jenny understands that "a fragile mystery [exists] in everyone and in herself" and that "the secrecy of life [is] the terror of it" (245). This mystery and secrecy refer to the essential human experience that cannot be recreated by vision or by text; it is far too illusory to be held captive and too delicate to avoid the damage caused by faulty or misdirected vision. Jenny is a misguided mystic whose quest for selfhood is lost to the gaze and control of other people's expectations of her. "She knew it was a challenge Floyd made with his hard look, and she lost to him" (249).

Colleen Warren's discussion of **"At the Landing"** argues for a reading of a less disempowered Jenny and says that the story presents

> a female vision of relationship which strives not for unity and possession but preservation of otherness, a philosophy of change which rejects predictability and stability and opens oneself to alterability and personal risk, and a definition of language which emphasizes not structure and "truth," but exchange, a flux of giving and receiving which is obviously compatible with the two prior values.
>
> (51)

Warren notes that "Jenny is seldom credited with having the capacity for change" (53), that Billy Floyd is most often identified as the character of change—because of his wandering fisherman role—but that, in fact, Floyd is static; he does not change from beginning to end of the text. She points to the passage in which Jenny contemplates Floyd's effect on her life (253-254); the passage ends with a comment about self-discovery: "She looked outward with the sense of rightful space and time within her, which must be traversed before she could be known at all. And what she would reveal in the end was not herself, but the way of the traveler" (254). Although Warren's argument provides a somewhat more palatable reading of Jenny's ability to reason, it does not answer the nagging question about what to do with the ending of the text. It seems more likely that this passage comments, once again, on the role of the creation of text, on the reader-traveler relationship to Jenny. Jenny does not reveal herself; readers are, in fact, more confused about who she is at the end of the story than they are earlier in the text, even "when [with] her eyes . . . opened and clear upon him, [Floyd] violated her" (251).

Jenny's life lacks a sense of purpose; "there was nothing in her life past or even now in the flood that would make anything to tell" (251). Her "dream of love" (252) is a false, misleading notion. Once Floyd rapes her, Jenny's consciousness is altered without her ever having realized any part of that dream. At the very least, the dream—and her ability to make sense of the experience—is confused and equally confusing for readers; what she experiences with Floyd, she misidentifies as "the shock of love" (253) because she does not know what else to call it. But how are readers to respond to this disturbing situation? Before the rape, despite all of her gazing at him, Jenny is unable to hold Floyd's gaze. As she creates a mental dialogue with him in which she imagines asking him to "have a little vision too, of all clumsiness fallen away," Floyd is looking "out over the landscape," away from her (249). When, after days without sleep during the flood, Jenny announces that she is sleepy and he puts her into his boat, she closes her eyes to the world and looks into "Floyd's shining eyes and [sees] how they held the whole flood, as the flood held its triumph in its whirlpools, and it was a vast and unsuspected thing" (250). Floyd becomes her world; he floods her sense of self and provides her with an identity, the enormity of which is as damaging as the literal flood; she is completely lost in this constructed identity. If readers are Floyds, who, Warren would argue, are not receptive to change and who can see Jenny only in the context of "taking freely of what was free" (251), then Jenny is symbolically raped every time she is misread. Perhaps it is the recognition of this response to Jenny, to this complicity in Jenny's victimization, and, ultimately, to the responsibility for reading even perplexing texts carefully that leaves readers in a state of bewildered revulsion at the close of the story.

After the rape, Jenny no longer wants to see anything: "She did not like to see faces, which were ugly, or flowers, which were beautiful and smelled sweet" (255). She relinquishes her job as reader because her ability to read has been compromised by experience, and she regresses. When floodwaters have receded, Jenny returns to her damaged home, which is described as "crouched like a child going backwards to the womb" (253), a condition that mimics Jenny's own journey, her attempt to identify herself. Like the books she finds, her "pages . . . have been opened and written on . . . by muddy fingers" (253); they and she are damaged beyond repair.

Before she leaves her home, Jenny examines "the amber beads they used to give her mother to play with" and comments on the reader's inability to see fully:

"She looked at the lump of amber, and looked through to its core. Nobody could ever know about the difference between the radiance that was the surface and the radiance that was inside. There were the two worlds. There was no way at all to put a finger on the center of light" (255). Amber becomes an apt metaphor for Jenny; she seems transparent but coreless and, as a result, unreadable. If readers can only construct meaning or assign identity in terms of what and how they can see, then Jenny's identity is caught in the net of her experience and in the net of the text; she reaches the point at which "vision and despair are the same thing" because, for her, there are no options in this context. When the fishermen "put her inside a grounded houseboat," it becomes another metaphor for Jenny's life, which is going nowhere. "The original smile now crossed Jenny's face, and hung there no matter what was done to her" (258).

This story demands that readers consider themselves in the context of their ability to see and to read what the text offers. When, at the end of the collection, the "old, bright-eyed woman who went and looked in the door, and crept up to the now meditating men outside," asks, "Is she asleep? Is she in a spell? Or is she dead?" (258), her questions suggest three approaches which readers can assume in response to texts: they can sleep through them, imagining that their expectations will be met as they have dreamed they will be; they can operate under the spell which the text casts and attempt to make sense of it in the act of surrendering to it; or they can have their senses assaulted and their expectations of the text killed off as they meet the challenge of reading and interpreting fiction with new eyes. Ruth Weston says that, in ***The Wide Net,*** Welty engages in "a poetics of surprise, perhaps for author and reader alike, at the creation that is coming into being on the page" (59). Readers of this collection bear a remarkable creative burden as they anticipate the surprise and find their surprise anticipated by a collection that explores what it means to be a Welty reader.

Notes

1. De Lauretis, in fact, further suggests that Eco's "definition of the reader . . . denies to the reader the possibility of intervening in the world, of changing the codes, of transforming the universe of signification" (46).
2. MacKethan's sources for the Welty citations are *One Time, One Place* (New York, 1971) and "Place in Fiction," *South Atlantic Quarterly* (January, 1956).
3. Mortimer's source for this information is *One Writer's Beginnings.*
4. MacKethan argues that Welty's "act of focusing" takes four shapes in terms of the characters she creates: "the Objects, the Insiders, the Outsiders, and the Seers or 'Onlookers'" (259) and that "relationships among the four types of characters . . . develop solidly within the places in which they are all fixed, temporarily or permanently, as their stories progress" (264).
5. Donaldson specifically focuses on Nancy in Faulkner's "That Evening Sun" and Clytie in Welty's *A Curtain of Green,* in the story by the same name.

Works Cited

De Lauretis, Teresa. "Response" *The Bulletin of the Midwest Modern Language Association* 14 (Spring 1981): 45-47.

Donaldson, Susan V. "Making a Spectacle: Welty, Faulkner, and Southern Gothic." *Mississippi Quarterly* 50 (Fall 1997): 567-584.

Eco, Umberto. "The Theory of Signs and the Role of the Reader." *The Bulletin of the Midwest Modern Language Association* 14 (Spring 1981): 35-45.

Iser, Wolfgang. *The Implied Reader: Patterns of Communication in Prose Fiction from Bunyan to Beckett.* Baltimore: The Johns Hopkins UP, 1974.

Kreyling, Michael. "History and Imagination: Writing 'The Winds.'" *Mississippi Quarterly* 50 (Fall 1997): 585-599.

MacKethan, Lucinda H. "To See Things in Their Time: The Act of Focus in Eudora Welty's Fiction." *American Literature* 50 (May 1978): 258-275.

Mortimer, Gail L. *Daughter of the Swan: Love and Knowledge in Eudora Welty's Fiction.* Athens: U of Georgia P, 1994.

Pollack, Harriet. "On Welty's Use of Allusion: Expectations and Their Revision in 'The Wide Net,' *The Robber Bridegroom* and 'At the Landing.'" *The Southern Quarterly* 29 (Fall 1990): 5-31.

Vande Kieft, Ruth M. Introduction. *Thirteen Stories by Eudora Welty.* New York: Harcourt Brace Jovanovich, 1977.

Warren, Colleen. "Revolutions of Change: Female Alterability in 'The Children' and 'At The Landing.'" *The Southern Quarterly* 35 (Fall 1997): 51-63.

Welty, Eudora. *The Collected Stories of Eudora Welty.* New York: Harcourt Brace Jovanovich, 1980.

———. *The Eye of the Story: Selected Essays and Reviews.* New York: Vintage, 1990.

———. *One Writer's Beginnings.* Cambridge: Harvard UP, 1984.

Donna Jarrell (essay date 2003)

SOURCE: Jarrell, Donna. "The Challenge of 'June Recital': Generic Considerations in the Structure of *The Golden Apples.*" In *Postmodern Approaches to the Short Story,* edited by Farhat Iftekharrudin, Joseph Boyden, Joseph Longo, and Mary Rohrberger, pp. 3-8. Westport, Conn.: Praeger, 2003.

[*In the following essay, Jarrell examines the narrative recounting of Miss Eckhart's life in "June Recital" as a "novel-like" digression within an otherwise clearly defined example of the short-story genre.*]

> A metronome was an infernal machine, Cassie's mother said when Cassie told on Virgie. 'Mercy, you have to keep moving, with that infernal machine. I want a song to *dip.*'
>
> (40-41)

The story **"June Recital,"** second of seven in Eudora Welty's 1949 work, ***The Golden Apples*** (18-85), is difficult to categorize generically. Its place in the collection of linked short stories has posed many questions of interpretation since its first appearance in *Harper's* in 1947. **"June Recital"** consumes nearly one-third of the 244-page volume and is nearly thirty pages longer than **"The Wanderers,"** its closest challenge. It is not simply proportion or length that creates problems in responses to **"June Recital."** Approximately midway, it digresses from a story about Loch and Cassie Morrison into an expansive history of Cassie's spinster piano teacher, Miss Eckhart, and her relationship with her student, Virgie Rainey. As Suzanne Hunter Brown discusses in "Discourse Analysis and the Short Story" (217-248), the "reader can . . . shift frames" to accommodate such a change in a story's direction (220). In the instance of **"June Recital,"** however, we are left with the challenge of reconciling what Hunter Brown would call "incompatibilities" in "selected frame[s]" (223).

A closer examination of **"June Recital"** will demonstrate that Welty has essentially embedded a "novel-like" story about Miss Eckhart within a "short story" about Cassie Morrison. I contend that Cassie's epiphany, her initiation, could be effected without this elaborate development of Miss Eckhart, found primarily from pages 42-67. Here, the story deviates from its established generic frame and *dips* into the past. Using Cassie as narrator, it develops Miss Eckhart into what Frank O'Connor has described in his book *The Lonely Voice* as a novel-protagonist, a character placed "in opposition to society . . . then . . . mastered by it" (21). Although this novel-like movement may not be essential for the success of **"June Recital"** as a short story, it establishes Miss Eckhart as an unforgettable character, and places her "story" at the center of the structure of the seven-story sequence. In what Ian Reid termed "intratextual" framing in his essay "Destabilizing Frames for Story" (299-310), this memory of Miss Eckhart's life-fable emphasizes the role of **"June Recital"** within the collection. It also helps us understand the fates of Cassie Morrison and Virgie Rainey as revealed in **"The Wanderers"** (Welty 203-244), the final story in ***The Golden Apples.***

"June Recital" opens recognizably as a short story: Loch Morrison, sick in bed with malaria, is using his father's telescope to view some surprising activities in the vacant house next door. Upstairs, he sees sixteen-year-old Virgie Rainey and her sailor-lover engage in an afternoon romp; downstairs, he watches a woman he presumes to be the sailor's mother busy herself scattering newspapers. He frames her actions as preparations for a party, but we understand her intention to burn down the house, at once identifying her as a "fallible" narrative center and beginning to recognize a plot beyond Loch's understanding.

At this point, the foundation for the short-story movement in **"June Recital"** is well laid. The reader has not only had the opportunity to draw on what Ian Reid would refer to as "circumtextual (or paratextual) markers" (301), such as the story's physical placement in a story collection, but also upon his personal "knowledge," or "extratextual frames" (307) to classify genre. Hunter Brown describes the process as "activat[ing] . . . a framework for meaning" (219). In other words, the reader facilitates comprehension of a text by sorting it into a particular category or schema early in the process.

As the **"June Recital"** continues, the point of view shifts from Loch to his sister Cassie, who is in her bedroom dyeing a scarf to wear on a hayride to Moon Lake that evening. Prompted by the signature theme of Beethoven's "Für Elise" coming from next door, she thinks about Virgie Rainey, whom she considers her "secret love, as well as her secret hate" (38). Virgie is a gifted musician, "full of the airs of wildness" who "sway[s] and gives way to joys and tempers" (38). This quality, along with her low social status, prevents her from securing approval and acceptance in Morgana.

Cassie also reflects on Miss Eckhart, a German immigrant, and the music teacher she and Virgie shared. Miss Eckhart used to live in the now derelict house, where she held an annual June piano recital. The reader soon realizes Miss Eckhart must be the old woman Loch has seen through his telescope in the downstairs of the house next door. She is not spreading the newspapers for her fire arbitrarily, but effecting a mockery of the way in which she decorated for each year's June recital.

Spontaneous and spirited, Virgie Rainey is the apparent antithesis of Miss Eckhart. A harsh, flat woman with rigid rules and a flyswatter she doesn't hesitate to crack across her students' hands, Miss Eckhart favors Virgie, who plays the piano with the genius and passion we suspect Miss Eckhart once expressed, but now represses. On this afternoon in June, Miss Eckhart's attempts to set a fire in her old studio are as awkward as her long-ago impromptu piano performance during a morning thunderstorm (49). In the last fifteen pages of the story, she manages to set her head on fire but is thwarted from igniting the house by two village men, Mr. Fatty Bowles and Old Man Moody, who afterwards guide her away without much dignity: "The old woman . . . held on her head some nameless kitchen rag; she had no purse . . . she wore shoes without stockings . . . [she] had fallen down and they had to hold her on her feet" (Welty 77-78).

As Miss Eckhart is led away, the disheveled Virgie flees the house with her sailor. The two women—the town's notorious misfits—pass each other on the street. Watching now, with her brother, Cassie expects Virgie to acknowledge Miss Eckhart, but Virgie disappoints her. Later that night, after her hayride, Cassie thinks of the incident: "Both Miss Eckhart and Virgie Rainey were human beings terribly at large, roaming on the face of the earth. And there were others of them, human beings, roaming like beasts" (Welty 85). Here is Cassie's moment of insight, where she appears to realize not every individual succeeds in finding a social niche—that our humanity, in and of itself, doesn't guarantee acceptance, and that many people will spend their lives as misfits. She experiences an epiphany, another signal to classify **"June Recital"** as a short story.

Yet at nearly eighty pages, her "story" is by no means physically short, and the digression that so elaborately details Miss Eckhart's life in Morgana is itself (33-67) as long or longer than several of the other stories collected here. There is no question that this allowance for Miss Eckhart's development places an unusual demand on the structure of **"June Recital."** However, by taking this *dip* into Miss Eckhart's life, the author also confuses the reader's expectations. The reader is prompted to change the "activated . . . framework for meaning" (Hunter Brown 219); a new schema is introduced, that of the novel.

Frank O'Connor observes that in the novel: "Time is [the author's] greatest asset; the chronological development of character or incident is essential" (21). In this dip into Miss Eckhart's past, we follow just such a paradigm. We are given an overview of the signature events in her life after her arrival in Morgana, sometimes in summary and sometimes in vivid vignette, and through these incidents we discover the complex character of Miss Eckhart.

We learn of her unconsummated affair with Mr. Sissum, Morgana's shoe salesman and cello player (44-49). Through Cassie's point of view, we watch Miss Eckhart allow Virgie to playfully, yet ceremoniously, adorn her with a floral wreath while she sits on a newspaper on the evening grass, listening to Mr. Sissum play the cello at the town political meetings (46). We hear Miss Eckhart's rare laughter from the delight she finds in Mr. Sissum's gift of a Billikin doll, a doll given away with every purchase of Billikin shoes by the department store where he works, a doll her mother spitefully breaks (47). We learn Miss Eckhart has pretty ankles for a large lady (44), and in a poignant moment, we see her public display of grief at Mr. Sissum's funeral after he has accidentally drowned. She "nods" her head at the people gathered at the cemetery, queerly, "increasing in urgency . . . the way she nod[s] at pupils to bring up their rhythm, helping out the metronome" (48). These incidents reveal both her passion and her repression. Others demonstrate her entrapment, her deprivation, and her victimization.

One day when Virgie is using Miss Eckhart's piano to rehearse her lesson, Miss Eckhart's mother "screams" at Virgie, "Danke schoen, danke schoen, danke schoen!" (54), mocking the phrase Miss Eckhart often uses to express her pleasure with Virgie after she completes playing a piece of music. In response, Miss Eckhart walks calmly across the room and slaps her invalid, perhaps demented mother on the face, then invites Virgie and Cassie to stay for dinner. They refuse. In this scene, we understand that Miss Eckhart accepts her present situation—the responsibility that she has to care for a disabled parent and the sacrifice of that which she loves. However, she will not allow her mother to suppress Virgie Rainey's gift, as we suspect her mother may have once done to her.

As a German immigrant during World War I, Miss Eckhart is indeed the victim of circumstance, but she is also a victim of a crime. After an attack by a deranged African-American man, and her subsequent lack of "shame" (Welty 51), she is ostracized by the community. In a classic case of "blaming the victim," Cassie suggests that it is this incident, "perhaps more than anything . . . that people could not forgive Miss Eckhart" (Welty 51). Eventually the mothers in the community, with the exception of Mrs. Morrison, will not allow their daughters to take lessons from Miss Eckhart. Before this time comes, however, she hosts an annual June recital, an elaborate occasion, where "all of her pupils . . . [partake] of the grace of Virgie Rainey" (67).

In this novel-like movement in the story, Miss Eckhart is a protagonist set in conflict with the community—a German in the United States, a yankee in the South, an old maid among families, an artist living in repression. Her conflicts are numerous and allow for a wide range of reader identification, which O'Connor also posits as novelistic (17). However, in the short-story movement, in which Cassie is the protagonist, Miss Eckhart's contribution is less that of a protagonist and more that of a catalyst. Her imprisonment—within the community and within herself—her alienation, and her relationship with Virgie Rainey are used to facilitate Cassie's epiphany. Surely she could have served in this capacity without appropriating such a disproportionate amount of story time and space.

The "incompatibilit[y]" in these two seeming movements (Hunter Brown 223)—"story" and "novel"—prompts us to take a closer look at the structure of **"June Recital."** If this elaborate digression into Miss Eckhart's life is not essential for the success of "June Recital" as a short story, why would Welty include this novel-like dip? In a letter quoted in *Katherine Anne Porter: A Life,* Porter refers to ***The Golden Apples*** as formally self-indulgent (311). I disagree. I believe the digression in **"June Recital"** is essential for the collective impact of these seven stories. Although the stories may have been published individually at one time (Harris 131), this fact does not preclude Welty from having had a broader picture in mind, if not from the outset of writing, certainly by some point in their creation. In fact, **"June Recital"** was originally published under the title **"Golden Apples"** in the September 1947 issue of *Harper's Bazaar,* where it already had both "movements"—with some difference in details.

The necessity for the reader to "shift frames" created by Welty's novel-like excursus into Miss Eckhart's past encourages the reader to "*reduce*" her life-fable into a familiar schema, enabling its storage in long-term memory (Hunter Brown 220; 217). "[A]ctive . . . as well as retrospective interpretation," writes Hunter Brown, "relies on memory" (223). This well-established memory of Miss Eckhart resonates throughout ***The Golden Apples*** and contributes to its overall cohesion, forming what Robert Luscher refers to in his essay "The Short Story Sequence: An Open Book" (148-167) as the "larger unifying strategies" (149). Ian Reid, in the essay mentioned earlier, discusses the links between stories in a sequence as "intratextual" framing (302). In this sequence, Miss Eckhart acts as what he terms "a part-for-whole-mirror" and provides a "proleptic framing" (302) of the fates of Cassie Morrison and Virgie Rainey as revealed in the final story **"The Wanderers."**

While Cassie is dyeing her scarf for the hayride and reflecting on Miss Eckhart and Virgie Rainey, we learn that she, rather than Virgie, has been awarded the town's musical scholarship (56). As a result, she resigns herself to a future in which she will take Miss Eckhart's place giving piano lessons in the community. What Cassie doesn't see, but what might be foreseen in the concluding page of the story, is her future as a full-blown version of Miss Eckhart. When Cassie comes home from her excursion to Moon Lake, she thinks about the incident with Miss Eckhart and Virgie Rainey that occurred that afternoon. She considers her behavior at the lake and is proud that she has allowed no one to touch her. Yet, as she sleeps, as her conscious guard is lowered, she dreams a Yeats poem—"all of it passed through her head, through her body" (85).[1] Through this symbolism of Cassie's emotion, we see the authenticity of her ambivalence toward Virgie Rainey (her "secret love . . . her secret hate") (Welty 38).

In the next two lines of the story, Cassie sits up in bed and recites the final line of the poem, the last words, "'*Because a fire was in my head.*'" Again, we have a symbolic representation of emotions, of passion. Cassie goes back to sleep, dreaming about a "grave, unappeased, and radiant face . . . the face that was in the poem" (Welty 85)—the face of her own repressed feelings and passion. One cannot be surprised then to learn in Welty's closing story, **"The Wanderers,"** that Cassie has become an old maid. She lives in her home among boarders, tending to the memory of her parents and giving piano lessons, an existence more than vaguely reminiscent of that of the tragic Miss Eckhart. Nor is it surprising that the untamable Virgie Rainey continues to defy the community's expectations and intends to leave Morgana now that her own mother has passed away.

In **"June Recital,"** Eudora Welty has written a short story about Cassie Morrison containing the novel-like narrative of Miss Eckhart. In the short story, Miss Eckhart and Virgie Rainey serve as catalysts for Cassie Morrison's epiphany. However, Miss Eckhart could serve the story in this capacity without such an expansive development. Cassie's epiphany is one of several cues encouraging the reader to classify **"June Recital"** as a short story, but the elaborate digression into Miss Eckhart's life encourages the reader to dip into a "novel" schema. These "incompatibilities" in "selected frame[s]" (Hunter Brown 223) have posed problems for readers and critics from the first publication of the story. Though Welty's dip isn't essential to the short-story movement, it helps the reader to frame ***The Golden Apples*** in its entirety and enables us to understand Cassie and Virgie's fate as revealed in **"The Wanderers."**

Note

1. This poem is Yeats' "The Song of Wandering Aengus." Its role in "June Recital" and *The Golden Apples* is discussed at length in Patricia S. Yaeger's essay, "'Because a Fire Was in My Head': Eudora Welty and the Dialogic Imagination," originally published in *PMLA,* 99 (October 1984), 955-973.

Works Cited

Givner, Joan. *Katherine Anne Porter: A Life.* New York: Simon & Schuster, 1982.

Harris, Wendell V. "The Thematic Unity of Welty's *The Golden Apples.*" *The Critical Response to Eudora Welty's Fiction.* Ed. Laurie Champion. Westport, Conn.: Greenwood Press, 1994. 131-134.

Hunter Brown, Suzanne. "Discourse Analysis and the Short Story." *Short Story Theory at a Crossroads.* Eds. Susan Lohafer and Jo Ellyn Clarey. Baton Rouge: Louisiana State University Press, 1989. 217-248.

Luscher, Robert M. "The Short Story Sequence: An Open Book." *Short Story Theory at a Crossroads.* Eds. Susan Lohafer and Jo Ellyn Clarey. Baton Rouge: Louisiana State University Press, 1989. 148-167.

O'Connor, Frank. *The Lonely Voice: A Study of the Short Story.* Cleveland: World, 1962.

Reid, Ian. "Destabilizing Frames for Story." *Short Story Theory at a Crossroads.* Eds. Susan Lohafer and Jo Ellyn Clarey. Baton Rouge: Louisiana State University Press, 1989. 299-310.

Welty, Eudora. *The Golden Apples.* New York: Harcourt, 1949.

Yaeger, Patricia M. "'Because a Fire Was in My Head': Eudora Welty and the Dialogic Imagination." *Mississippi Quarterly: The Journal of Southern Culture,* 39 (1986): 561-586.

Terry W. Thompson (essay date summer 2004)

SOURCE: Thompson, Terry W. "Welty's 'Petrified Man.'" *Explicator* 62, no. 4 (summer 2004): 228-31.

[*In the following essay, Thompson illuminates the reference to the mythological figure of Janus in "Petrified Man."*]

First published in ***A Curtain of Green and Other Stories*** (1941), **"Petrified Man"** is one of Eudora Welty's most frequently anthologized tales. Although roundly praised for its authentic sounding dialogue and its cutting humor, much has been made by critics of its many allusions to the myth of Medusa, a female being who could turn any man into stone with a single stunning glance. Lauren Berlant, for example, argues that "the Perseus-Medusa paradigm" in Welty's narrative deftly explores "the ways both people and texts deal with the conditions of sexual and class difference" (69). Robert G. Walker likewise sees the influence of the Medusa myth in this waggish tale of Southern women who spend much of their time having their hair painfully curled into long, snakelike tendrils while gossiping about their menfolk and each other in the shampoo-and-set female sanctuary of the local beauty parlor (10). In his article "Gorgons in Mississippi," Jeffrey Helterman also perceives subtle references in the text to women who can—by one form of manipulation or another—translate their men into cold and unthreatening stone (12). However, there is another important mythological allusion extant in the story, one that has rarely been mentioned in the critical canon.

When a tawdry "'travelin' freak show'" comes to the small town and rents the vacant storefront next to the beauty parlor for a few days, there are four main attractions in the modest exhibit to entice the locals into parting with their hard-earned nickels and dimes (Welty 20). First, there are the pygmies, "'the teeniest men in the universe,'" most probably black dwarves who have been hired to dress and play the part of authentic equatorial Africans (21). Second, there is the requisite gypsy fortuneteller, Lady Evangeline, who prattles on and on about the future but has no more Romany blood in her veins than does a fence post. Third, there is the petrified man; he provides the title for the piece as well as a clear Medusan allusion, but he is as much a fraud as the first two attractions because he is not ossified at all; he is merely in white-powdered disguise because he is wanted in California for a series of violent rapes. And finally—mentioned only briefly—there are the grotesque Siamese twins who are preserved in a jar of nebulous liquid and gawked at by the curious visitors to this tatty, third-rate sideshow.

This last exhibit is described in morbid, rapturous detail by one of the loquacious beauticians: "'Well, honey, they got these two twins in a bottle, see? Born joined plumb together—dead a course. [. . .] an' they had these two heads an' two faces. [. . .] this face looked this-a-way, and the other face looked that-a-way, over their shoulder, see'" (Welty 21). Although the conjoined twins—like the first three attractions—

are possibly Barnumesque fakes, they still provide a subtle allusion to the obscure myth of Janus, the two-headed Roman god of new beginnings, a minor male deity who represented the power of possibilities and for whom the month of January is named. By referencing the Janus myth, however obliquely, Welty adds two important undercurrents of feminine intrigue and beauty parlor politics to this tale. First, everyone in the beauty shop is duplicitous and has more than one face. And second, two possible futures—two alternate beginnings—are open to Mrs. Fletcher, the main character of the story.

According to Thomas Bulfinch, Janus was "the doorkeeper of heaven and patron of the beginning and end of things" (917). Edith Hamilton, the doyenne of twentieth-century classicists, says of this deity, he was "the god of good beginnings, which are sure to result in good endings," and in the center of his great temple in Rome stood "his statue with two faces" gazing stoically in opposite directions (45). This provides the origin of the term *two-faced,* meaning someone who is deceitful or unctuous, and almost every woman in the beauty shop, stylist and client alike, fits easily into this category. The beauticians, for example, all babble on about their customers behind their backs: "'Who is it you got in there, old Horse Face?'" (Welty 18). Their delight in cattiness and their skill at avoiding blame or censure for such spirited gossiping provide much of the story's humor.

As the narrative begins, the middle-aged Mrs. Fletcher, seated snugly in her usual chair, is worried about dandruff and hair loss. Leota, her beautician, casually tells her, "'you know what I heard in here yestiddy [. . .] that you was p-r-e-g, and lots of times that'll make your hair do awful funny, fall out and God knows what all'" (Welty 18). The stunned and temporarily speechless Mrs. Fletcher has been trying, by dressing in loose-fitting garments, to keep her condition a secret; even her husband does not know. When she discovers that a new customer at the beauty shop—the young and attractive Mrs. Pike—has surmised her condition and then spread the news around town, she is flummoxed with anger and indignation, fuming at the backstabbing nosiness of the beauty shop clientele: "'All I know is, whoever it is 'll be sorry some day,'" she hisses. "'Just let her wait!'" (19). Seething with outrage, she excoriates those two-faced women who smile warmly at "'you on the street'" but then slander and mock "'you behind your back'" (19); "'The nerve of some people!'" (20)

When, "in a discouraged way," she gazes into the beautician's mirror, Mrs. Fletcher bemoans her new condition: "'You can tell it when I'm sitting down, all right'" (Welty 23). However, because her pregnancy is not very far along, she still has the option of seeking an illegal abortion, although the operation is never mentioned by name: "'I don't like children that much. [. . .] I'm almost tempted not to have this one'" (19). In short, Mrs. Fletcher, worried about her expanding waistline, her falling hair, and her status in the community, has two Januslike options facing her: she can have the abortion and save herself the weight gain, the nausea, and the other assorted discomfort, or she can decide to have the baby—almost certain to be a boy—and face the challenge of another child in the family and all the headaches and demands that a boisterous, headstrong male child will bring.

Several men are mentioned in absentia during the course of the story—husbands, boyfriends, paramours, criminals—but only one male visits the inner sanctum of the lavender-trimmed beauty shop so redolent with the odors of perfumed cigarettes and henna packs, of hair dyes and curling fluids. He is a bratty and obnoxious three-year-old named Billy Boy; his mother frequently drops him off at the salon for gratis babysitting while she works in a hat store up the street. When at the shop, the incorrigible tyke is forever clawing into purses, eavesdropping on conversations, lurking under furniture, sassing the women, and, in general, making a total nuisance of himself. As the story comes to its resolution, Billy Boy is caught stealing stale peanuts from Leota's purse, so he scurries to escape just punishment for his trespass and larceny. However, Mrs. Fletcher, despite her condition, is too quick for him: "'I caught him! I caught him! [. . .] I'll hold him on my lap. You bad, bad boy, you!'" (28). As Billy Boy is vigorously paddled by a hairbrush-swinging Leota, Mrs. Fletcher—evidencing clearly that she has decided to continue her pregnancy to term and not have the illegal abortion—exclaims with delight, "'I guess I better learn how to spank little old bad boys'" (28). Given her two Januslike choices, she has chosen life; there will be a new beginning, a new child, for Mrs. Fletcher and her husband.

In Eudora Welty's **"Petrified Man,"** a middle-aged woman is stunned to discover that she is pregnant without planning it; then she is even more stunned when she learns that local gossip has suddenly and cruelly made her condition the subject of community dialogue. Thus, Mrs. Fletcher's two opposing alternatives have been rendered much more difficult as well as much more public. When the lone male interloper in the beauty shop suffers a thorough spanking by the women and when the new woman in town who first spread the gossip about her pregnancy abruptly leaves, the planets in Mrs. Fletcher's universe are once again aligned. In contrast to her frowning, brooding countenance at the beginning of the story, in the closing paragraph, she exhibits a "new fixed smile" (Welty

28). Reconciled, she is at peace; the beauty shop is once again her inviolate temple to the gods of cosmetology.

Works Cited

Berlant, Lauren. "Rewriting the Medusa: Eudora Welty's 'Petrified Man.'" *Studies in Short Fiction* 89.1 (1989): 59-70.

Bulfinch, Thomas. *Bulfinch's Mythology.* New York: Avenel, 1979.

Hamilton, Edith. *Mythology: Timeless Tales of Gods and Heroes.* New York: Mentor, 1969.

Helterman, Jeffrey. "Gorgons in Mississippi: Eudora Welty's 'Petrified Man.'" *Notes on Mississippi Writers* 7 (1974): 12-20.

Walker, Robert G. "Another Medusa Allusion in Welty's 'Petrified Man.'" *Notes on Contemporary Literature* 9.2 (1979): 10.

Welty, Eudora. "Petrified Man." *The Collected Stories of Eudora Welty.* New York: Harcourt Brace Jovanovich, 1980. 17-28.

Joseph Millichap (essay date fall 2005)

SOURCE: Millichap, Joseph. "Eudora Welty's Personal Epic: Autobiography, Art, and Classical Myth." *Southern Literary Journal* 38, no. 1 (fall 2005): 76-90.

[*In the following essay, Millichap interprets Welty's short fiction in light of the personal information disclosed in her autobiographical works, and addresses the classicism that runs throughout the author's oeuvre.*]

The importance of fairy tale, legend, and myth, especially many aspects of classical myth, to the creation and understanding of fiction by Eudora Welty has been long recognized and widely accepted. Many of her works have been read in mythical terms, in particular her short fiction cycle ***The Golden Apples*** (1949); yet only a few critical efforts have extended the perspectives of myth to her entire canon, and even fewer have considered Classicism as central to her overall accomplishments.[1] Welty's work is vital to the contemporary transformation of the twentieth-century American and southern literary pantheon, so earlier considerations of her classical connections focus on feminine, if not feminist, retellings of ancient narratives. Although recent readings of Welty's fiction by way of female myths reveal much of its subtle beauty and cultural complexity, more may be discovered by re-reading her canon within the full contexts of the Classicism that informed the origins, accomplishments, and traditions of the Southern Renaissance.[2]

Certainly, feminist readers are right to contrast Welty's use of the Classics with that of her more traditional male role models such as William Faulkner and Robert Penn Warren as well as with their modernist mentors such as T. S. Eliot and James Joyce. The classical intertextualities that form her fictions are employed more on the model of female modernists such as Virginia Woolf and Elizabeth Bowen, or, closer to home, Katherine Anne Porter and Caroline Gordon. Yet Welty's fictional canon might be read as her Modernist epic of the self, much in the terms that Alan Williamson applied to Allen Tate's poetic oeuvre by defining this contemporary variant of the epic tradition as "that particularly modern form which views historical material entirely through the glass of private sensibility, fragmenting it as a series of lyrics rather than presenting it as a whole, as narrative" (714). Lyrical narratives rather than poetic lyrics are the individual aspects of her personal vision, while her canon is united in a quest for fulfillment as a woman and as an artist. These two aspects of Welty's art share much with male and female precursors alike in her recreation of American, southern, and Mississippi history by autobiographical, artistic, and classical means.

Although Eudora Welty did not have the rigorous classical training of academic colleagues learned in Greek and Latin in the Southern Renaissance, such as Allen Tate and Robert Penn Warren, her formal and informal education in the Classics was still substantial. Her memoir, *One Writer's Beginnings* (1984), recalls her immersion in mythical material almost from the time she began to read; certainly it dated from the sixth or seventh birthday when doting parents presented her with *Every Child's Story Book,* a compilation of "fairy tales . . . myths and legends . . . [and] history" (*One Writer's Beginnings* 8). English lessons at Jefferson Davis School and later French and Latin classes at Jackson Central High School confirmed the young Eudora's love for words and stories. Her high school Latin was strong enough to excuse her from assignments in order to tutor her less proficient classmates (Waldron 11). The Classics were still the center of college preparation in the early 1920s, and Central High's honoraries were organized around classical themes; for example, the club book in Welty's senior year was *The Aeneid* (Waldron 12). English, French, and Latin were once more her favorite classes at nearby Mississippi State College for Women, where Welty studied for two years before transferring to complete a degree in English at the University of Wisconsin-Madison in 1929 with a creative thesis, now lost (Waldron 41).

Evidently, the writer returned often to her favorite books in all three literatures and languages, or in translations, to mark transitions in her career (Waldron 183). For example, after completing ***The Golden Apples,*** her book most fully structured by classical allusion, Welty reread Homer's *Odyssey* in preparation for her first trip to Europe in 1949 by way of Italy and the Mediterranean (Marrs 145). An interesting byproduct of her reading and her travel is her somewhat neglected later story, **"Circe,"** Welty's first in the group that would become ***The Bride of the Innisfallen*** in 1955 and her only effort to directly engage, incorporate, and rewrite mythical material. As almost every commentator on **"Circe"** has noted, the tale is an obvious retelling of the classical narrative from the woman's point-of-view, as Welty herself made clear in correspondence to her literary agent (Marrs 145). Those readers who consider the story more closely, especially those who compare its periodical publication as **"Put Me in the Sky"** in 1949 to its final form and title in the 1955 volume, become aware of much more in the final text of this "twice-told" tale. Among other things, some critics have discerned Welty's interests in and tentative answers to questions of time and mortality, magic and memory, as well as humanity and heroism.

"Circe" also raises interesting issues of art, of epic, and of autobiography in Welty's work. Although the powerful goddess probably existed as timeless archetype and as ancient myth long before Homer, her fateful encounter with Odysseus during the telling of his epic wanderings fixed her existence and identity for the Western artistic tradition by way of its primal narrative. When Joyce became the precursor novelist of the modernist century with *Ulysses*—his 1922 recreation of the *Odyssey*—he also fixed the literary context for fictive intertextual engagements with the ancient epics, just as T. S. Eliot became the precursor poet of the contemporary self epic by publishing *The Waste Land* in that same *anno mirabilis* of Modernism. Modern fictionists retelling Circe's story, whether Joyce or Welty, engage not just the myth but the epic—both the *Odyssey* and its genre—just as do the modernist poets, whether Eliot or Tate. Of course, modern adaptations of classical exempla exist in other areas of the American endeavor beyond literature, including art, architecture, music, philosophy, religion, politics, and psychology. Thus Welty's encounter with Homer involves her identity as a woman, as an artist, and as an American.

This reading of **"Circe"** is supported by its text and reinforced by Welty's revision of the initial text for its publication as an integral part of her final story collection. Despite the replication of all the sensational elements of Circe's power to transform men into animals, Welty is careful to underline the artistry integral within the sorcery. In fact, Circe becomes the prototype of the feminine artist in that her magical power derives from female creativity grounded in the domestic arts of weaving, of cooking, and even of cleaning. Circe opens her narration "Needle in air, I stopped what I was making"; she continues, "I left them thus and withdrew to make the broth"; and, after the porcine transformation, she concludes "With my wand seething in the air like a broom, I drove them all through the door" (***Collected Stories*** [***The Collected Stories of Eudora Welty***] 531). As she concludes: "In the end, it takes phenomenal neatness of housekeeping to put it through the heads of men that they are swine" (***Collected Stories*** 531).

Then Circe realizes that "One man was left," that "enchantment had met with a hero" (***Collected Stories*** 532). And Odysseus is not just the protagonist of his many epic adventures, but their narrator as well. "As though the hour brought a signal to the wanderer, he told me a story . . . of the monster with one eye—he had put out the eye he said" (***Collected Stories*** 532). This archetypal teller of tall tales becomes the prototype of the masculine artist, stringing his adventures like beads on the thread of his epic quest, of his voyaging. Circe reveals, "I had heard it all before . . . I didn't want his story, I wanted his secret" (***Collected Stories*** 533). This secret she desires so much has been variously identified by critics of Welty's tale depending on their reading of its themes—Odysseus's masculinity or his mortality, his heroism or his humanity. At some level the secret may also be his meaning. Circe does not want his story, not even his wanderings nor his adventures; she wants her own narrative and her own feminine meaning drawn from it. At Odysseus's embarking, Circe thinks that she could have a black ship as well, "if I were not tied to my island, as Cassiopeia must be to the sticks and stars of her heavenly chair" (***Collected Stories*** 537). So Circe will not follow him, though Telegonos, his son she now carries, will—and finally slay him. "That was the story" (***Collected Stories*** 537). And thus it becomes her story with her own meaning that enfolds her own creative identity as a goddess and a sorceress as well as a woman and an artist.

The autobiographical connections and historical contexts of Eudora Welty's **"Circe"** are oblique but meaningful, especially against the background of the author's personal and professional life during the years from 1949 and 1955 when the tale was transformed. In literary terms **"Circe"** might be read as a sort of coda to ***The Golden Apples*** as well as a prefiguring of ***The Bride of Innisfallen.*** As such, the tale marks a movement away from the Mississippi materials of the earlier fiction to the wider world of the new volume, and, more importantly, **"Circe"** confirms the complex mode and manner of the 1949 volume that might be denominated, after the example of Henry James, as Welty's "major phase" of tale-telling. These artistic developments existed in complicated relation to Welty's personal growth during these same years. Her literary successes supported travels at home and abroad that in turn not only provided the materials for her new stories but symbolized the same intellectual and emotional restlessness that helped form her new fictional methods. As Welty matured into her forties, she must have contemplated her choice of the single life devoted to her art, often a subject in her later fictions. Roles and opportunities for single women as well as for other marginalized groups in American culture were changing in these years, even in Jackson, Mississippi, where Welty still lived with her aging mother between her outward voyages, both literal and literary.

"Circe" thus forms an interesting and important lyric fragment in Eudora Welty's self epic. Approaching this story by means of its evolution also suggests just such a chronological pattern for consideration of her career and her canon within the perspective of Classicism, the Southern Renaissance, and the epic of the self. Indeed, Welty may be said to have grown up with these literary movements connected most closely in fiction with her fellow Mississippian, William Faulkner, in poetry with her first champion, Robert Penn Warren, and in criticism, with her early editor, Warren's colleague and collaborator, Cleanth Brooks. Brooks and Warren not only published her apprentice work in the *Southern Review,* but they helped determine the literary contexts that could appreciate Welty's subtle fictions in distinction from the ideological demands of the Depression decade. At the same time, Welty learned as much as or more from female mentors such as Ellen Glasgow, Caroline Gordon, and Katherine Anne Porter as she shaped the disparate materials of her first collection, ***A Curtain of Green and Other Stories*** (1941).

Classical references are present in Eudora Welty's earliest work, especially her most autobiographical fictions. In her first volume, the stories drawn most closely from her childhood personal experience are **"A Memory"** and **"A Visit of Charity."** In chronological terms, their relation proves complicated; though the protagonist seems more mature in the first selection, both girls must be about the same age. **"A Memory"** had appeared under that title in *Southern Review* (1937) while **"A Visit of Charity"** was published as **"The Visit"** in *Decision* (1941); but manuscript evidence indicates both were probably written at about the same time. Perhaps Welty placed **"A Memory"** at a pivotal point in the volume as a story of artistic vision and development, as at least one critic suggests from the consideration of textual revisions for the volume (Devlin 23). The revision of **"A Visit"** [**"A Visit of Charity"**], including its recast title, might suggest a somewhat more ironic piece that relieves the cluster of darker tales that conclude ***A Curtain of Green.***

In any case, several critics have paired the two stories, not just in their autobiographical subject matters but in their themes and meanings as stories of female initiation and feminine artistry. **"A Visit of Charity"** also has been discussed as one of Welty's many fictions informed by allusion to fairy tale, legend, and myth, often refracted through earlier literary representations of these primal materials. In this case, images of captivity and imprisonment coalesce with symbolic journeys to the after-life and/or the underworld. In particular, the myth of Persephone functions in this early story, as it does in at least a dozen of Welty's other texts. The author's comparison of herself as a young girl to Persephone in her personal essay, "The Little Store" (1975), reinforces the importance of this mythological figure to her own growth and to the development of her autobiographical characters. Trips to the neighborhood grocery marked nine-year-old Eudora's first forays into a world beyond the bright circle of her family, one like the family above the store "of life, or death . . . of pride and disgrace . . . of people coming to hurt one another, while others practiced for joy" (*The Eye of the Story* 334-335). On her brothers' dare, she returned by way of the storm sewer: "down there in the wet dark by myself, I could be Persephone entering my six-month sojourn underground" (*The Eye of the Story* 332).

Marian, the Campfire Girl on **"A Visit of Charity"** to the "Old Ladies Home," is "fourteen," perhaps a few years older than the would-be Persephone of "The Little Store," but she seems almost as much a part of Welty's youthful reality (***Collected Stories*** 113). Welty relates the story to her own expeditions to Jackson's Old Ladies Home on West Capitol Street: "I used to visit the old ladies. They scared me. I couldn't wait to leave" (Waldron 116). Mythical possibilities begin as the innocent arrives at the Old Ladies Home on an icy winter morning bearing a symbolic potted plant the nurse-receptionist identifies as "a nice *multiflora cineraria*" (***Collected Stories*** 113). Welty inherited her life-long love of plants and flowers from her mother, who presided over Jackson's Garden Lovers Club, and horticultural allusions in the author's work are both accurate and meaningful (Marrs 4-7). The winter-blooming *cineraria* would be a thoughtful seasonal gift for the old ladies at the home, while its etymology from the Latin *cinis* or "ash" will prove appropriate symbolically as Marian learns lessons not anticipated by the *Camp Fire Handbook* (1914).

Interestingly enough, in her autobiographical essay, "A Sweet Devouring" (1957), Welty uses literature of the Camp Fire movement to illustrate her early development as a serious reader. Again positing fairy tale, legend, and myth as the matrix of her growth, she discusses various aspects of what was considered the children's literature of the early twentieth century, whether "authorized" or popular (*The Eye of the Story* 279). Many of these volumes were Series Books: "*The Five Little Peppers* belonged, so did *The Wizard of Oz,* so did *The Little Colonel,* so did *The Green Fairy Book*" (*The Eye of the Story* 280). Eudora soon discovered the flaw in these works: "As long as they are keeping a series going . . . nothing can really happen" (*The Eye of the Story* 285). No thing, that is, involving the dark, hard, and inexorable revelations of real experience as in the sad history of the little store or the more arresting narratives such as compilations of fairy tale, legend, and myth. The two series of "The Camp Fire Girls," whether the paperback books sold at the Kress dime store where heroines Bessie and Zara inevitably escape the ineffectual villain or the authorized hardback volumes from the Carnegie Library where "teamwork" inescapably triumphs, were soon left behind when Welty discovered Mark Twain—"twenty-four volumes, not a series, and good all the way through" (*The Eye of the Story* 285).

Welty's autobiographical Camp Fire Girl, Marian, drifts through silent halls, "like the interior of a clock," conveyed by the nurse impatient to return to her reading of *Field and Stream,* into the dark, dank, and cold lair of two old ladies. Marian feels as if "caught in a robbers' cave, just before one is murdered" (***Collected Stories*** 114). When the "first robber" asks her, "Did you come to be our little girl for a while?" (***Collected Stories*** 114), allusions to fairy tale, legend, and myth abound. The classical epics are invoked as well, however; like Odysseus, Marian must make her dark journey into the underworld in order to learn her fate. Circe gave her departing guest his fateful itinerary in the *Odyssey*: "You must travel down / to the house of Death and the awesome one, Persephone, / there to consult Tiresias," (10:540-545). In Homer, Persephone allows the hero to consult with the shades, beginning with his own mother. Anticleia explains the condition of the dead: "the fire in all its fury burns the body down to ashes / . . . and the spirit, / rustling, flitters away . . . flown like a dream" (11:250-253). Indeed, Persephone then parades a grand array of famous women past Odysseus to figure for him lessons of death and life.

The pair of wraiths Marian consults in the crowded room of the Old Ladies Home likewise represent her possibilities as a woman in her modern world. Asked "Who—are—you?" Marian can only reply, "I'm a Camp Fire Girl" (***Collected Stories*** 115). Her answer recalls why she is there, to earn points toward some honor proffered by the society that sponsors her. The visitor begins to see these relationships when the first old woman reveals that she too "was a little girl like you . . . went to school and all" (***Collected Stories*** 116). The little potted flowers of youth are snatched away by the first "robber," who finds them pretty, while the second bleats "Stinkweeds . . . Ugly" (***Collected Stories*** 115-116). As the pair of crones disagree on every subject—flowers, visitors, religion, education, illness, medications—Marian begins to realize the twin possibilities open to her as a woman in her world. She can play along with society's expectations in hope of a cultural merit badge, like the first, passive-aggressive old lady, or she can rebel like the angry, bed-ridden old woman. In either case, the bright and hopeful young woman will become lonely and empty like them, literally penniless like many white spinsters and widows of Welty's youth in the early 1920s, much less the poor black women Welty knew in the late 1930s when the story was written.

Like **"A Visit of Charity," "A Memory,"** set in Jackson's Livingston Park with its "whites-only" pavilion and swimming beach, presents autobiographical reflections concerning the personal and cultural complexities of gender relations. **"A Memory"** has elicited greater critical attention than **"A Visit of Charity,"** at least in part because of its more extended treatment of artistic development. The unnamed autobiographical protagonist's perceptions of young and middle-aged women on the beach create insights into human and feminine limitations that parallel Marian's intuitions at the Old Ladies Home, but those in **"A Memory"** are literally framed by her growing artistic consciousness. The Classics are again elicited in the heroine's youthful crush on a boy from her high school Latin class that forms a contrasting vision to the harsher reality perceived at the park. Yet even this treasured recollection is punctuated by a disturbing memory of the boy's sudden and embarrassing nosebleed, a foretaste of adult life's bloody flux acutely meaningful to the probably pubescent protagonist.

These concerns with sexual and aesthetic development in young women continue into Welty's second volume of stories, ***The Wide Net*** (1943), especially in its most autobiographical selection, **"The Winds."** First published by *Harper's Bazaar* in 1942, the story had evolved from a much earlier and shorter version tentatively titled **"Beautiful Ohio,"** and it was revised even more for its place at the heart of Welty's second fiction collection (Marrs 71-72). The changes between the versions of **"The Winds"** demonstrate the subtle differences between **"A Visit of Charity"** and **"A Memory,"** between a direct representation of autobiographical experience through the characters' consciousness and a more complex reclaiming of it through layers of memory and perception. The recollection becomes a portrait of the protagonist not just as a developing young woman but as an evolving young artist. As such, the story exemplifies Welty's new directions in fiction that would be further developed in her first novel, *Delta Wedding* (1945), and in her short fiction cycle, ***The Golden Apples*** (1949).

In her later memoir, *One Writer's Beginnings,* Welty attributes to her parents the "strong meteorological sensibility" that would help structure her stories where "atmosphere took its influential role from the start" (4). As an example she added parenthetically, "I tried a tornado first, in a story called **'The Winds'**" (*One Writer's Beginnings* 4). In this story, Josie, the prepubescent protagonist, is awakened from a dreaming sleep on the screened porch by her parents who fear an equinoctial storm may spawn damaging, perhaps tornadic winds. The father's caution and the mother's bravado reflect the attitudes of Welty's parents as dramatized in her memoir. The description of Josie's house and neighborhood likewise suggests the Welty house on Congress Street in Jackson, where nine-year old Eudora lived in 1918, the story's chronological setting. Clearly, **"The Winds"** demonstrates the atmospheric pattern she outlines in her memoir: "Commotion in the weather and the inner feelings aroused by such a hovering disturbance emerged in connected form" (*One Writer's Beginnings* 4).

The inner feelings Welty evokes in **"The Winds"** involve personal and cultural anxiety about imminent disorder and alteration. The framing narrative employed here, Josie's slow awakening to the night of storms and then to the brighter morning following, clearly references her personal development from girlhood toward adolescence—as the tale's few critics all agree. Moreover, the filtering of cultural developments through Josie's emerging consciousness marks it as a story of artistic as well as female maturation. Criticism has only touched on the cultural significance of **"The Winds,"** however, in terms of meanings that may be fully developed through consideration of its geographical and chronological settings as well as its allusions to art, epic, and autobiography. As a fictionalized personal memoir, the story may be linked to "The Little Store" as well as to *One Writer's Beginnings,* and the connection with the Persephone myth that informs **"A Visit of Charity"** again proves valuable to interpretation—though here Demeter becomes more influential than her daughter.

Throughout her canon Welty identified her female characters and, by extension, herself with Persephone, so it proves interesting in biographical terms that her classically-minded high school classmates linked her with Demeter. Her 1925 yearbook was structured by Classic myths, and Eudora was identified in the "superlatives" as "Demeter," for "Most Dependable" (Waldron 13). Even as a high school girl, Welty showed the responsible, generous, and nurturing behavior that marked most of her adult life as care-giver for her friends and family, especially for her aging, infirm mother. Indeed, Demeter is a mother figure identified not just by her concern for Persephone confined in the Underworld but also by her central place in fertility myths as the goddess of agriculture in general and grain in particular. Although the Homeric Demeter was a composite of ancient deities, her complex persona as a feminine archetype emerges in the epics. Calypso's divine passion for Odysseus is compared to Demeter's lust for the mortal, Iasion, that was consummated in a thrice-plowed furrow and then was productive of Plutus, god of wealth and instigator of plutocracy or the rule of the wealthy.

Like the autobiographical persona of "The Little Store," pre-adolescent Josie in **"The Winds"** invokes Persephone through her confined home situation, yet at the same time she is identified with tripartite Demeter figures representing three stages of female development—her own mother, an adolescent near neighbor named Cornella, and the female cornetist heard by daughter, mother, and neighbor at a Chautauqua program. The mother is the most influential feminine image for Josie, and, like Eudora's mother Chestina Andrews Welty, this fictional surrogate is far removed from the stereotyped post-Victorian wife, despite her "verbena sachet" (***Collected Stories*** 209), "cretonne pillows" (***Collected Stories*** 210), and "wicker arabesques" (***Collected Stories*** 212). Like the Chestina Andrews remembered in *One Writer's Beginnings* (61), Josie's mother was raised on a farm and keeps her own "small tender Jersey" in the pasture for its milk (***Collected Stories*** 217). Moreover, she is unimpressed by the threat of the storms and argues with her husband about waking the children to move in from the sleeping porch (***Collected Stories*** 209).

Josie's romantic imagination wants a role model simultaneously further from and closer to her own home situation, one that she finds in her older neighbor, the significantly named Cornella. Although the teenager's given name is historically accurate, as even a passing glance at a Mississippi genealogy will demonstrate, it is more symbolically noteworthy. Impressed with the high school girl's "bright yellow, wonderfully silky and long" hair, Josie would "invoke Cornella" thus: "Thy name is Corn, and thou art like the ripe corn, beautiful Cornella" (***Collected Stories*** 214-216). Although several critics associate Cornella with other sexual blondes in Welty's novels such as Bonnie Dee

Peacock in ***The Ponder Heart*** or Wanda Fay Chisom in *The Optimist's Daughter,* she really recalls the nameless transient cast off by the Fairchild family in *Delta Wedding.* "Cornella was not even a daughter . . . she was only a niece or a cousin, there only by the frailest indulgence. She would come out with this frailty about her, come without a hat, without anything" (***Collected Stories*** 216).

Like Josie, Cornella is searching for an appropriate role model, in her case one unlike the older female relative who screeches from the upper window of the "double house" or rental duplex scorned by homeowners like Josie's parents. Both girls are confined by their homes, Persephone-like, and both long for the freedom of the night, the storm, and the darkened Lovers Lane evolved from what was once a local section of the romanticized but dangerous Natchez Trace. The girls' desires triangulate on the female cornetist at the Chautauqua program, another goddess figure. "She was draped heavily in white, shaded with blue, like a Queen, and she stood braced and looking upward like the figurehead on a Viking ship" (***Collected Stories*** 220). This feminine artist is associated, like Demeter, with natural wonders as well: "If morning-glories had come out of the horn instead of those sounds, Josie would not have felt a more astonished delight" (***Collected Stories*** 220). It was as if a "proclamation" had been made in the final note when the "lady trumpeter" released her "passion" for all in the audience to hear—particularly Cornella and Josie (***Collected Stories*** 220).

During the First World War, the chronological setting of **"The Winds,"** Jackson was a part of the Chautauqua circuit, and the changes in the world beyond Mississippi are represented by its program (*One Writer's Beginnings* 32, 86). In this regard, the female trumpeter proves important on several levels, including the fact that Chestina Andrews Welty played the instrument, a rare accomplishment for a woman of her era when girls would have been instructed in ones more gentle and genteel (*One Writer's Beginnings* 50). This autobiographical detail connects the performer with Josie's mother, just as her cornet recalls the oddly named "Corn/ella." The allusions to classical myth are mixed with ones to the American mythos as well. The lady trumpeter is part of an all-female trio, "one in red, one in white, and one in blue [playing] a piano, a coronet, and a violin," and set within a panoply of "vases" and "little bunches of flags on sticks" (***Collected Stories*** 219). The trumpet solo that excites the audience, particularly Josie and Cornella, is quite likely a patriotic air, transformed into a feminine anthem by this invocation of Lady Liberty as well as the Goddess Demeter, and signaling coming cultural changes in women's roles.

World War I created general transformations in Deep South states such as Mississippi, including the Southern Renaissance itself with its forward motion into Modernism and its simultaneous "backward glance" at Classicism. Some time after World War II, the transition between the Modern and the Post-Modern periods complicated the history of southern letters that provided the backdrop for Eudora Welty's literary development. Her first real novel, *Delta Wedding,* and her first real short-fiction cycle, ***The Golden Apples,*** demonstrate analogous developments for her canon in 1945 and 1949 respectively. Classical readings could well focus on the personal elements in **"June Recital"** and **"Moon Lake,"** the longest and richest elements in intertextual complexities of the stories in ***The Golden Apples,*** ones extending backward by way of W. B. Yeats' Modernist appropriation of ancient myth to the primal efforts of Homer, Virgil, and Ovid. Many critics have observed at length and in detail that both *Delta Wedding* and ***The Golden Apples*** are thick with classical allusions, however, and that both contain frequent autobiographical references as well. In my view, the personal connections in these transitional works are much like those in the later stories and novels, based more on imagined or observed rather than on remembered experience, even in works often considered autobiographical such as **"No Place for You My Love"** (1952) or *The Optimist's Daughter* (1969).

Until she returned to her youth in Jackson once more for *One Writer's Beginnings,* Eudora Welty did not recreate the sort of personalized writing discussed in the stories singled out above. This late memoir also recalls the personal essays alluded to earlier such as "The Little Store" and "A Sweet Devouring," texts that closely resemble and obliquely explicate short fictions such as **"A Visit of Charity"** and **"The Winds."** Although the final title indicates the memoir's origin as a "set of three lectures delivered at Harvard University in April, 1983, to inaugurate the William E. Massey lecture series," the final volume published by Harvard in 1984 extends far beyond the story of Welty as writer to become a personal history ranging as far back as her family roots in the Old and New Worlds (*One Writer's Beginnings* vii). If *One Writer's Beginnings* serves as a sort of coda to Welty's canon and career, as such it provides a summarizing perspective for her engagement with autobiography, epic art, and classical myth.

The book's tripartite sectional structure—"Listening," "Learning To See," and "Finding a Voice"—reflects this triple use of Classicism in Welty's work: the ancient myths are referenced, particularly in terms of astronomy; the ancient epics are discussed, mainly as language and as narrative; and the classical heritage of modern American and southern life is revealed, especially in terms of architecture. When her memoir opens with the house on North Congress Street in Jackson, Mississippi, where she was born in 1909, Welty defines her setting in terms of clocks that represent a sense of passing time as she looks back over seven decades to her earliest recalled experiences. Her father's love for "instruments" of knowledge includes not just chronometers, but kaleidoscopes, cameras, and telescopes—"with brass extensions, to find the moon and the Big Dipper after supper in our front yard" (*One Writer's Beginnings* 3). Even more important are the narratives explaining their mythic origins: "I could see the full constellations . . . and call their names; when I could read, I knew their myths" (*One Writer's Beginnings* 10). At college, she learned more, incarnating one of the "Three Graces" (*One Writer's Beginnings* 77). Then as a writer she created stories with a "shadowing of Greek mythological figures, gods and heroes that wander in various guises, at various times, in and out, emblems of their character's heady dreams" (*One Writer's Beginnings* 99).

In high school and again at college, Welty learned the deepest meaning of words by savoring their etymological roots in the ancient tongues themselves. "It took Latin to thrust me into a *bona fide* alliance with words in their true meaning" (*One Writer's Beginnings* 28, emphasis added). As a child she had discovered among the books passed down from her mother's Virginia patriarch "his leather-covered Latin dictionary and grammar" (*One Writer's Beginnings* 58). Later these delectable words are combined into sentences and stories such as Virgil's mighty anthem that opens the epic of Aeneas: "*Arma virumque cano* . . ." (*One Writer's Beginnings* 80, emphasis added). Of course, Welty's feminine epic of the self would sing women and the instruments of domestic creativity instead of "Arms and the man." Implied in the epic sweep of Aeneas's flight to transport the sacred fire from Troy to Rome is the whole history of classical culture and literature, the ultimate textual patrimony waiting to be transformed by modern writers, including women like Welty.

So Latin taught the young Eudora the laws of language, of "words upon words, words in continuation and in modification, and the beautiful, sober, accretion of a sentence" (*One Writer's Beginnings* 28). Yet even as a grammar school girl, she knew the cultural continuities of language and narrative. "I could see the achieved sentence finally standing there, as real, intact, and built to stay as the Mississippi State Capitol at the top of my street, where I could walk through it on my way to school and hear underfoot the echo of its marble floor, and over me the bell of its rotunda" (*One Writer's Beginnings* 28). The ante-bellum Mississippi building reiterated the classic style of the national capitol realizing in stone the Roman virtues of the early Republic. In Jackson, other classical references marked the commercial life: "The Lamar Life was in those days housed in a little one-story, four-columned Greek temple, next door to the Pythian Castle" (*One Writer's Beginnings* 34), and her father's greatest attainment was the thirteen-story expansion of the insurance company (*One Writer's Beginnings* 82).

Her father's final achievement occurred in 1925, as Welty prepared to move from high school to college, and from her sheltered home to the larger world. She quotes his dedicatory speech, but it concerns the more quotidian effects of the building on the company and the community (*One Writer's Beginnings* 83). Earlier, a younger Eudora had rediscovered her maternal grandfather's remarks at the dedication of a new courthouse in his native West Virginia. "The student turns with a sigh of relief from the crumbling pillars and columns of Athens and Alexandria to the symmetrical and colossal temples of the New World" (*One Writer's Beginnings* 47). Such is more the spirit of her summary of her father's great work. "The Lamar Life tower is overshadowed now, . . . but the building's grace and good proportion contrast tellingly with the overpowering, sometimes brutal, character of some of the structures that rise above it" (*One Writer's Beginnings* 83). If contemporary commercial temples prove more colossal than symmetrical, the classical balance, harmony, and order that persist in the present provides a better model.

The same might be said of American and southern culture generally, and of their literature in particular. *One Writer's Beginnings* stands as a final declaration of Eudora Welty's life-long commitment to the Classics and as a guide to her use of classical myth and literature in the creation of her own personal epic. Although Welty's artistic vision is focused by a quest for fulfillment as a woman and as a writer, her considerable achievement of her purpose is realized by rereading her canon within the contexts of the Classicism that informed the origins, triumphs, and traditions of the Southern Renaissance. Finally, it proves instructive to compare Welty's Classic accomplishments with those of other American and southern colleagues, whether female fictionists such as Ellen Glasgow, Caroline Gordon, and Katherine Anne Porter, or male forebears and contemporaries such as Allen Tate, Thomas Wolfe, and Robert Penn Warren, or even her fellow Mississippians William Faulkner, Tennessee Williams, and Walker Percy.

Notes

1. In my view, Robert L. Phillips' systematic reading in "A Structural Approach to Myth in the Fiction of Eudora Welty" comes closest to comprehensive

treatment of Welty's use of myth and fantasy; see Peggy W. Prenshaw, Ed. *Eudora Welty: Critical Essays* (Jackson: UP of Mississippi, 1979), 56-67. Many of Phillips' examples are classical in origin, and my reading of Welty's work is indebted to his concept of myth as a structuring device varying in terms of narration, point-of-view, and characterization. Another influential study in the same collection is Danielle Pitavy-Souques' "Technique as Myth: The Structure of *The Golden Apples*"; see 258-268. Although this reading is focused on a single volume, the book is Welty's most mythic effort, and Pitavy-Souques' intuition of mythical and especially classical intertextualities has influenced readers of this and other works in the Welty canon, particularly later feminist critics. Salient critical works concerned with particular Welty texts or with individual classical myths are referenced in the text and works cited.

2. The present essay forms part of my larger study of the Southern Renaissance and the classical tradition, one that will include both general considerations and individual readings of important writers within these contexts. Although these formulations have been considered generally in several of their most interesting aspects, no extended study is focused on or by them as yet. Most often considered to be a reinterpretation of cultural history in Dixie by Modernist literature, the Southern Renaissance is influenced as much by classical letters—especially by way of the traditions of Renaissance England and nineteenth-century Romanticism—in its formation, reception, and interpretation. However, I do not mean to imply an either/or dichotomy between Classicism and Romanticism, much less between Classicism and Modernism. Writers of the Southern Renaissance including Eudora Welty often presented Romantic characters, events, and themes ironically by way of classical analogues and intertexts in the Modernist manner of T. S. Eliot and James Joyce.

Works Cited

Devlin, Albert J. *Eudora Welty's Chronicle: A Story of Mississippi Life.* Jackson: UP of Mississippi, 1983.

Homer. *The Odyssey.* Trans. Robert Fagles. New York: Penguin, 1996.

Marrs, Suzanne. *One Writer's Imagination: The Fiction of Eudora Welty.* Baton Rouge: Louisiana State UP, 2002.

Waldron, Ann. *Eudora: A Writer's Life.* New York: Doubleday, 1998.

Welty, Eudora. *Collected Stories.* New York: Harcourt Brace, 1980.

———. *The Eye of the Story: Selected Essays and Reviews.* New York: Vintage Books, 1979.

———. *One Writer's Beginnings.* Cambridge: Harvard UP, 1984.

Williamson, Alan. "Allen Tate and the Personal Epic." *Southern Review* 12 (1976): 714-732.

Matt Huculak (essay date winter-spring 2005-06)

SOURCE: Huculak, Matt. "Song from San Francisco: Space, Time, and Character in Eudora Welty's 'Music from Spain.'" *Mississippi Quarterly* 59, nos. 1-2 (winter-spring 2005-06): 313-28.

[*In the following essay, Huculak maintains that Welty's specific and realistic depiction of San Francisco in "Music from Spain" allows her to assume an impressionistic time structure which, in turn, represents the internal growth of the protagonist.*]

> And walk among long dappled grass,
> And pluck till time and times are done
>
> —W. B. Yeats, "The Song of Wandering Aengus"

Eudora Welty considered time *and* place to be the "two bases of reference upon which the novel, in seeking to come to grips with human experience, must depend for its validity," and she notes that they "operate together, of course" ("Some Notes" 483). In ***"Music from Spain,"*** the sixth chapter in ***The Golden Apples,*** Welty explores the symbiotic relationship between time and place in a unique way since the setting of the story, San Francisco, is an identifiable, geographically mapped city that she contrasts with the fictional space of Morgana, Mississippi, the setting of her other chapters.[1] As Michael Kreyling notes, neither Welty nor her agent, Diarmuid Russell, was sure that "the San Francisco story" could be a "part of the Battle Hill [Morgana] collection" but in the end included it in ***The Golden Apples*** after it was published separately by the Levee Press in 1948 (141-44). Russell was suspicious that the San Francisco story was nothing more than "the 'lazy man's' exit" for Welty—since it had nothing to do with Morgana—and would disrupt the overall plot line of ***The Golden Apples***[2]; however, Welty addressed his concerns by saying, "I should have foreseen it would be part of the [stories], because what worried me about the leading character in all the work I'd done was his lack of any taproot" (Kreyling 141). That taproot is Eugene MacLain's history in Mississippi, which he has somehow branched out of by moving to San Francisco—a displacement that is never explained by the author. Rebecca Mark, in fact, believes that Welty's fictional foray outside of the South "alleviated the claustrophobic atmosphere of Morgana, Mississippi" (175).[3] The San Francisco setting, however, provides the reader with more than claustrophobic relief or mythic reference, for it allows Welty to play with the meanings of time and place as the two primary characters, Eugene MacLain and a mysterious Spanish musician, travel about the city. In fact, Welty deliberately remains faithful to the actual "place" of San Francisco, based on her personal experience there.[4] She uses real street names, and her characters move in such a way that one can plot their paths along a map.[5] Welty's *external* attention and fidelity to actual place-names in San Francisco permits her to play with and manipulate time in order to reveal the expansion of self and *internal* time and place movements of her protagonist, Eugene MacLain.

In "Some Notes on Time and Fiction," Welty argues that "time goes to make that most central device of all, the plot itself" (484). Though **"Music from Spain"** takes place over the course of a day, Eugene's internal timepiece does not conform chronologically to the twenty-four-hour clock. During this period, time seems to slow for Eugene, and at the climatic point in the novel he reaches a state of timelessness. Although Ann Ricketson Zahlan explores Welty's use of "adventurous California space-time to counterpoint the potentially oppressive harmonies of her fictional South" in tandem with M. M. Bakhtin's idea of "*chronoscope*" (57), she does not concentrate on Eugene's actual, "plottable" internal/external movements. Also, one need not go to Bakhtin for an explanation of Welty's use of time and place. Welty writes that the "[d]istortion of time is a deeply conscious part of any novel's conception, is an organic part of its dramatic procedure, and throughout the novel's course it matters continuously and increasingly, and exactly as the author gives it to us" ("Some Notes" 490). Welty's distortion of time in **"Music from Spain"** ultimately reveals the most meaningful psychological and emotional growth of any character in ***The Golden Apples***—in the city of San Francisco.

The geographic importance of San Francisco is emphasized by the lack of biographical detail for Eugene MacLain. The reader is not given a reason why the twin scion of King MacLain, the daunting patriarch of ***The Golden Apples,*** left his brother Ran and the state of Mississippi to move out west, nor does the reader know how Eugene meets his wife, Emma. The only "history" of Eugene is given through occasional flashbacks he has while walking through San Francisco.

The opposition Welty creates between Morgana and San Francisco is critical when we consider Eugene's movements through this actual place. Morgana is not only a fictional town, it is also replete with mythical characters. Mark also comments, "Whether we think of Morgana as alluding to Morgan Le Fay, the Celtic Goddess Morrigana, or the Fata Morgana [a mirage], the name has definite feminine origins. MacLain, however, means son of Lain and is masculine" (149). San Francisco is also a masculine city, perhaps even a hypermasculine one—its name is rooted in the patriarchal Christian tradition as the Spanish translation of Saint Francis, and it has a well-known historical tolerance of homosexuality, hinted at by Eugene's discovery of his own homosexual leanings in **"Music from Spain."** Thus, Welty juxtaposes a feminine mythological space with an actual masculinized one in which to place her characters. Indeed, the San Francisco in **"Music from Spain"** is steeped in mythology. Mark notes, "The literary and mythic allusions, and there are many—including the myth of Perseus . . . and above all James Joyce's *Ulysses*—set the modernist tradition against the backdrop of myth, folklore, and oral history" (175).

This study does not seek to challenge Mark's comprehensive mythological description of San Francisco; rather, it aims to broaden an understanding of the site of Welty's story by examining the actual, non-mythological aspects of the city that she carefully inserts into her plot like street signs. The insertion of specific details like the names of streets and cable-car lines and references to San Francisco landmarks allows Welty to call attention to space and time:

> Place, the accessible one, the inhabited one, has a blessed identity—a proper name, a human history, a visible character. Time is anonymous; when we give it a face, it's the same face the world over. While place is in itself as informing as an old gossip, time tells us nothing about itself except by the signals of its passing.
>
> ("Some Notes" 483)

With its history and character, San Francisco is Welty's "blessed identity" in **"Music from Spain."** Yet time is *not* anonymous in this story; it is a manifest force that Eugene—a watchmaker—actively tries to escape throughout the story. Thus, it is imperative that Welty find a way to "signal its passing" in the novel. She accomplishes this by faithfully revealing the San Francisco cityscape, which provides the signals of time's passing, like a *flâneur* ticking off every street name as he walks down a new avenue.

"Music from Spain" begins at the breakfast table when Eugene reaches across the table and slaps his wife, Emma, after she makes an innocent comment. That Eugene does not have "the least idea of why he did it" (182) begins the self-examination and self-questioning that propels Welty's story. Ironically, this slap wakes Eugene himself from deep passivity and shocks him into seeing the world and himself in a new way. As soon as he steps out of the house, he realizes, "The air, the street, a sea gull, all the same soft gray, were in the same degree visible and seemed to him suddenly as pure as his own breath was. The seagull like a swinging pearl came walking across *Jones Street* as if to join him" (183, emphasis mine). Welty carefully locates Eugene on Jones Street, an actual steep road in the eastern portion of San Francisco. This authentic street name becomes the first external marker of geographic time that Welty inserts into the story as Eugene enters the cityscape of his imagination—the two entities, character and city, become one at this point. As Peter Barta notes in *Peripatetics in the Novel,* "The slow, strolling movement about the city in the plot [of city novels] produces a uniquely close tie between the central human characters and their urban environment; together city and walker serve as city's protagonist" (xiii). When Eugene begins to walk down Jones Street towards his workplace on Market Street, he wonders whether he injured Emma; he concludes, "[I] couldn't have hurt Emma. There couldn't be a mark on her" (183). His walking and thinking seem dependent on each other. As he strolls, the reader is given more access into his conscious thoughts and his character's history. His recalling of Emma's reaction to a phone call in the middle of the night seems to suggest that Eugene suspects her of infidelity[6]: "[T]he rosy mole might be riding the pulse in her throat as it did long after the telephone rang late in the night and was the wrong number—'Why, it might have been a *thousand* things'" (184). Moreover, as Eugene walks, his internal thoughts become externalized and follow him like a shadow in his movement through the city:

> Why, in the name of all reason, had he struck Emma? His act—with that, proving it had been a part of him—slipped loose from him, turned around and looked at him in the form of a question. At *Sacramento Street* it skirted through traffic beside him in sudden dependency. . . . Down hill the eucalyptus trees seemed bigger in the fog than when the sun shone through them . . . he had the utterly strange and unamiable notion that he could hear their beating hearts. Walking down a very steep hill was an act of holding back; he had never seen it like that or particularly noticed himself reflected in these people's windows.
>
> (184, emphasis mine)

This life-changing question becomes a part of the cityscape's "skirt[ing] through traffic" and pushes Eugene forward and down past Sacramento Street. His thought that walking down a very steep hill is an "act of holding back"[7] suggests how cautiously he lives his life and that there is something about himself that he is trying to avoid. As Eugene becomes one with his surroundings and hears the heartbeats of the trees around him, he sees himself—both literally and figuratively—for the first time in the windows that line Jones Street.

Eugene as a character is moving through the dark, previously unexplored pathways of his soul, a movement precipitated by his reaction against Emma that morning, which is mirrored in his actual movement down the street. This plottable progression of character is reinforced shortly afterward when Eugene has another epiphany: "He clung to one small revelation: that today he was not able to take those watches apart. He had only reached California Street. He stood without moving at the brink of the great steepness, looking down" (187). Though Welty does not locate the cross street closest to Eugene's house, one deduces that it is just above Sacramento Street, if Eugene notes that he had only reached California Street, which is one block down from Sacramento. This is not just a pedantic observation. Eugene experiences profound character-changing thoughts in a very short geographical space. His present life, his worries, his thoughts are brought out and questioned in a two-block span. Moreover, Eugene's commitments to his wife, work, and time break down at California Street as he realizes that he can no longer repair or sustain clock time as a watch-repair person. Presumably, the watches will remain stopped, just as objective time has for Eugene. Thus, the expansive cityscape becomes the only marker of external progression and internal consciousness—or subjective time.

In "Some Notes on Time and Fiction," Welty writes, "Fiction does not hesitate to accelerate time, slow it down, project it forward or run it backward. . . . It can freeze action in the middle of its performance. It can expand a single moment like the skin of a balloon or bite off a life like a thread" (485). The first section of **"Music from Spain"** represents the deflated balloon—Eugene's consciousness—which will expand as he moves through the city. Welty divides **"Music from Spain"** into seven distinct sections, and the first three, before Eugene meets the Spaniard, are confined to two- and six-block increments—which form a semicircle. When Eugene meets the Spaniard, his time and consciousness expand in what Eugene calls a "vast present-time" (196). Thus, the latter portions of the story represent the explosion of space and time as the characters move through the city together. Welty uses this distortion of time as a metaphor for Eugene's expanding consciousness when he discovers his burgeoning sexual identity. On this subject, Welty writes, "Distortion of time is a deeply conscious part of any novel's conception, is an organic part of its dramatic procedure, and throughout the novel's course it matters continuously and increasingly, and exactly as the author gives it to us" ("Some Notes" 490).

In section 2, Welty immediately locates Eugene "below in Market Street" and calls attention to his "meticulous" work on watches (187-88). On Market, Eugene

> walked among crumbs and pigeons and crossed over the wide trashy street and when he looked to the right he could see, quite clearly just now, the twin brown-green peaks at the end of the view, the houses bright in their sides, while the lifted mass of blue and gray fog swayed as gently over them as a shade tree.
>
> (190)

Indeed, a person walking south down Jones Street would see Twin Peaks, an imposing San Francisco landmark at the end of Market Street to the west. Twin Peaks calls attention to Eugene's twin, Ran. Eugene notes that the peaks are "brown" and "green," perhaps a metaphor for the lives of both Ran and Eugene. Mark believes that Ran, in **"The Whole World Knows,"** is associated with Rain (Ran), thus conflating him with a fertility god (152). Since the hills are both brown and green, one might align Ran with the green color of the hills, as a fertility god, while Eugene represents the childless brownness of the peaks. I suggest that the green of the peaks represents Eugene's expanding self-awareness—for he is the one who left Morgana and became an exile, an action that stimulates his self-questioning, for being far away in San Francisco provides him the space for this exploration. Eugene notices, "The lift of the fog in the city, that daily act of revelation, brought him a longing now like that of vague times in the past, of long ago in Mississippi, to see the world" (190).

Fog is another San Francisco landmark of sorts, and its diurnal dissipation, the moment when sunlight breaks through the cold grayness of the day, is an apt metaphor for Eugene's own moment of light. Fog contracts time and space as well, for when it rolls in, it covers the sun; thus one cannot tell what time of day it is. Also, it creates limited visibility, drowning out cityscapes and the perception of distance. Mark writes that the mist "allows us to imagine that Eugene is indeed entering another dimension, a forgetful place beyond the structures of civilization, beyond buildings. This mist covers the modern constructions" (197); this is an essential movement for Eugene so that he can question societal norms in his discovery of self. When the fog lifts on his internal landscape, he can see the expansiveness and burgeoning of his life. He thinks,

> Now, too late, when the city opened out so softly in beauty and to such distances, it awoke a longing for that careless, patched land of Mississippi winter, trees in their rusty wrappers, slow-grown trees *taking their time,* the lost shambles of old cane, the winter swamp where his own twin brother, he supposed, still hunted. . . . where had the seasons gone?
>
> (191, emphasis mine)

Instead of measuring his life by the bullying hand of the watch, Eugene yearns for the days when time was measured by seasons and imagines his brother in the bucolic pursuit of hunting. This is an indication that he has entered the space of timelessness, where childhood is conflated with the present, where the hope of an expansive future, spread out like a city, is contained in a singular moment. This moment will expand further when Eugene meets the Spaniard in section three.

Section three, like the one before it, begins on Market Street. Eugene has sneaked past his place of work and does not seem to have a destination as he walks briskly down the street toward the bay. Welty writes, "Bright mist bathed this end of the street and hid the tower of the Ferry Building; but as he walked he saw, going ahead of him and in the same direction, a tall and distinct figure that he recognized" (193). Eugene sees this mysterious figure, the Spanish musician, and then saves him from walking out in front of a car. He lifts the Spaniard out of harm's way "like a big woman who turns graceful once she's on the dance floor" (194). Welty immediately feminizes the Spaniard with this metaphor—a crucial fact as Eugene begins to question his own sexuality. Shortly after the rescue, Eugene thinks back to the first time he had seen the Spaniard, in a concert hall the night before. While listening to his music, he "felt a lapse of all knowledge of Emma as his wife, and of comprehending the future, in some visit to a vast present-time. The lapse must have endured for a solid minute or two, and afterwards he could recollect it" (196). Thus, the Spaniard is not only feminized, but also conflated with Eugene's special moment, this vast present time, when all rules break down and consciousness enters an alternate space beyond the boundaries of heterosexual marriage.

In section four, Eugene and the Spaniard walk to Maiden Lane, just off Union Square in the city. The word "Maiden" further feminizes the relationship between these two men.[8] The two men step into a restaurant off Maiden Lane where Eugene experiences three critical realizations. First, while pondering the life of the Spaniard—since they cannot converse, sharing no common language—he thinks, he had "had speculations about a man on the stage exactly as if he had known he would meet him in closer fashion afterward. As if he had known that by morning he himself would have struck his wife that blow and found out something new, something entirely different about life" (201). While at the concert the night before, Eugene knew, fatefully, that the Spaniard would usher in a new phase of his life; by coupling this knowledge with the act of physical violence against his wife—against women—he has discovered something surprising about himself and his growing homosexual consciousness. Second, Eugene realizes that "the formidable artist [the Spaniard] was free. There was no one he loved, to tell him anything, to lay down the law" (201). Eugene yearns to be himself, beyond the social conventions of his time, a period that is not tolerant of homosexuality, particularly in Mississippi. This passage may also allude to the suffocating atmosphere of heterosexual marriage Eugene lives in with Emma, the phallic mother who enforces the conventions by "lay[ing] down the law" with Eugene. Thus, striking out at her is a physical reaction to the psychological constraints of heterosexuality.[9] Third, he thinks, "Suppose he, Eugene, found himself in San Francisco for only a day and a night, say, and not for the rest of his life? Suppose he was still in the process of leaving Mississippi—not stopped here, but simply an artist, touring through" (202). This is the first time that he identifies himself as an artist and not as a husband or watchmaker. Also, this is a prescient thought since Eugene will return to Mississippi, wifeless, to die of tuberculosis; however, this return will not be a tragedy, for he will experience his true self in San Francisco and bear that knowledge back to Morgana. During this lunch, images of Morgana rise and fade, like *fata morganas,* to haunt Eugene. He thinks of the "black" name of his father and of Miss Eckhart's piano lessons (202, 203); these images are distant enough that they do not paralyze him but allow him to ponder his past in his construction of the new present moment. The final, and most important, image that Eugene summons during this lunch is a picture in one of his father's books: "Eugene saw himself for a moment as the kneeling Man in the Wilderness in the engraving in his father's remnant geography book, who hacked once at the Traveler's Tree, opened his mouth, and the water came pouring in" (204). This life-giving image will be repeated by Eugene in section six, when his body will replicate the exact position of the wanderer who "drinks" from the tree; it foreshadows Eugene's sexual experience with the Spaniard.

When he and the Spaniard emerge from this lunch on Maiden Lane, Eugene's internal space changes, and he becomes a new person—his consciousness expands like Welty's metaphor of the skin of a balloon. They begin walking, "the Spaniard with spirit," and "the square shone" (208). This is most likely Union Square, a commercial and transportation center in the city near Maiden Lane. Indeed, Eugene has walked in a tightly bound circle up to this point; however, both he and the Spaniard will escape this enclosed space by heading west. Both characters walk up to a streetcar, probably the "C" streetcar according to the Master Plan of City and County of San Francisco Transit Existing Routes from 1944 (Kelly n.p.). That Welty has her characters use actual transportation routes in the city is important in understanding Eugene's expansion of consciousness. While sections one through four occur in a suffocatingly tight circle, in section five Eugene and the Spaniard cross the entire city in what seems like mere moments. Welty even inserts the progression of street names like Divisadero and a "numbered avenue not far, now, from the ocean" (209, 211). Indeed, the "C" streetcar ended at Thirty-third Street in the Richmond District, near the ocean (Kelly).[10] Eugene's sense of time and space have collapsed; he has truly entered a timeless state of being, with his Spaniard, outside of the *normal* expectations of these dimensions. Here, the city of San Francisco becomes a metaphor for this timelessness as they head west. Mark notes that

> [t]hese two travelers are now walking directly toward the setting sun, toward death,[11] allowing the sun to set and rise and to set again and rise again. It is interesting to note that the rebirth of the male is not a return of the feminine but a movement to a heightened awareness of, and willingness to accept, the full range of masculinity—both its projections and fantasies and its dreams and myths.
>
> (208)

Each man is entering a world of timelessness where the conventions and expectations of society no longer matter to these two future lovers. At this moment of Eugene's journey, he has a revealing, life-changing thought or what Mark calls the "dramatic transition" of the story (210). He thinks of his brother Ran, and experiences "all at once an emotion that visited him inexplicably at times—the overwhelming, secret tenderness toward his twin, Ran MacLain, whom he had not seen for half his life, that he might have felt toward a lover" (212). Eugene has his ultimate epiphany here when he recognizes the homosexual tendencies that he has felt since childhood—embodied in his passion for his twin brother, Ran. This realization of self and expansion of consciousness will allow him to experience a "true" sexual moment with the Spaniard when they reach Land's End.

At the beach, on the western edge of the city, Eugene sees the Spaniard as "a woman, a 'nude reclining,'" and while they walk together there "had evidently been, without their knowing it, a loss of the wish to go back" (218, 220). Then, an unmistakable moment happens between Eugene and the Spaniard:

> Eugene clung to the Spaniard now, almost as if he had waited for him a long time with longing, almost as if he loved him, and had found a lasting refuge. . . . Then a bullish roar opened out of [the Spaniard]. . . . Then within himself [Eugene] felt a strange sensation. . . . He had felt it before—always before when very tired, and always when lying in bed at night, with Emma asleep beside him. Something round would be

> in his mouth. But its size was the thing that was strange. It was as if he were trying to swallow a cherry but found he was only the size of the stem of the cherry. His mouth received and was explored by some immensity. It became more and more immense while he waited. . . . He seemed to have the world on his tongue. And it had no taste—only size. He held on to the Spaniard. . . . The fog flowed into his throat and made him laugh. . . . As he gasped, the sweet and the salt, the alyssum and the sea affected him as single scent. It lulled him slightly, blurring the moment. . . . He was without a burden in the world.
>
> (221-23)

Here, Eugene acts out the scene in his father's geography book of the kneeling Man in the Wilderness at the Wandering tree who, on his knees, opens his mouth and feels the water come pouring in (204). As Eugene performs fellatio on the Spaniard, his mouth, "explored by some immensity," feels the white fog flow into his throat and realizes his true self as a homosexual as he receives the life-giving "water" of the "tree."[12] At the moment of the Spaniard's climax, Eugene looks up and sees a boy and a girl, a heterosexual couple, and wonders, "Was that happiness?" (223).[13] For Eugene, the answer is a resounding "No," as he becomes conscious of his homosexuality. Mark calls this "Eugene's homecoming":

> This is . . . his discovery of his own body, his own sexuality, and his release from social convention. This is his return to his love, this big father man. Eugene has become . . . the Christ open-armed, the all-forgiving, the body in the moment of sexual orgasm. Eugene thinks, "My dear love comes," and the Spaniard makes a loud emotional cry.
>
> (225-26)

This is one rare moment of sexual tenderness in ***The Golden Apples.*** Most other sexual moments, ranging from those involving Miss Eckhart or Maideen, tend to be rapes or illicit encounters. Only Virgie Rainey, Eugene's childhood acquaintance, seems to have a similar tender moment with her sailor in **"June Recital"** (though the house is burning down while she makes love). Thus, at the edge of San Francisco with the great vastness of the ocean before him, Eugene undergoes his transformation, which has been foreshadowed in the butterfly imagery throughout the story, from a woman's tattoo to the Mariposa flower the Spaniard picks (191, 221).[14] However, like most good things, this experience must end.

In the relatively short section seven, Eugene and the Spaniard return to the city from Land's End. This passage also reveals Welty's notion of fiction and time: "[Time] can freeze an action in the middle of its performance. It can expand a single moment like the skin of a balloon or bite off a life like a thread" ("Some Notes" 485). After the rapid expansion of Eugene's consciousness, mirrored in his travels across San Francisco, the thread snaps in section seven when the whole story—and city—collapse back in upon themselves. The bottom line represents Eugene's deflating consciousness at the end of his voyage back to the point where he began: his kitchen on Jones Street. Welty does not even feature her protagonist in the last two paragraphs but instead gives them to Emma and her friend Mrs. Herring. In fact, it is Emma who identifies the Spaniard as "Bartolome Montalbino" at the end of the story while popping a grape into her mouth (228).[15] Mrs. Herring proclaims,

> A Spaniard? There was a Spaniard at early church this morning. . . . He was next to a woman and he was laughing with her out loud—bad taste, *we* thought. It was before service began, it's true. He laughed first and then slapped her leg, there in Peter and Paul directly in front of me home from my trip.
>
> (228-29)

In what may be the most enigmatic line in the story, Emma, still popping grapes into her mouth, says, "That would be him" (229). How does Emma know that it was this particular Spaniard in the church that morning; did she have an affair with him as well, and was it she that Mrs. Herring saw sitting next to the Spaniard? Welty is careful to conflate the color of the Spaniard's lips, which are grape-colored, with the grapes Emma enjoys at the end of **"Music from Spain."** Perhaps the initial slap at the beginning of the story stemmed from Emma's transgression of the night before—thus, it is possible that both Emma and Eugene enjoy the "fruit" of the Spaniard in this story. The section's ending, with Emma and Mrs. Herring, completely effaces Eugene from both time and the space of the kitchen on Jones Street—it is as if his journey happened in another geographic/psychic space all together. Where does this leave Eugene? Virgie Rainey's description of him in **"The Wanderers"** (for Eugene has truly become a wanderer, having tasted the water from the tree) is the only clue Welty gives the reader as to his fate.

The final chapter of ***The Golden Apples*** only fleetingly alludes to Eugene's transformation in San Francisco as Welty locates the reader back in Morgana, Mississippi, which becomes a small-town foil to the cosmopolitan San Francisco in the previous chapter. Here, Welty moves the narrative many years forward to the funeral of Mrs. Fate Rainey. Welty places Virgie Rainey in a privileged position as the book's final critical consciousness. In **"The Wanderers,"** Virgie leaves her mother's funeral, which has become nothing more than another inauthentic stage on which the other characters strut. The funeral becomes another occasion for acting, and Virgie knows it: "Always in a house of death, Virgie was thinking, all the stories come evident, show forth from the person, become a part of the public domain. Not the dead's story, but the living's" (238). Virgie suggests that the new mayor, Ran MacLain, Eugene's brother, has a sinister past and so is not the smiling politician who shakes everyone's hands but rather "the *bad* twin" who "had taken advantage of a country girl who had died a suicide": Ran, the man who "ruined" a girl (238, emphasis mine). Thus, Virgie's subtle praise of Eugene is all the more powerful when she passes the cemetery and thinks about the "other" twin:

> Here lay Eugene, the only MacLain man gone since her memory. . . . Eugene, for a long interval, *had lived in another part of the world, learning while he was away that people don't have to be answered just because they want to know.* His very wife was never known here, and he did not make it plain whether he had children somewhere now or had been childless. His wife did not even come to the funeral, although a telegram had been sent. A foreigner? "Why, she could even be a Dago and we wouldn't know it." . . . (he was never reconciled to his father . . . all he loved was Miss Snowdie and flowers) but he bothered no one.
>
> (273, emphasis mine)

This memory is a tightly packed enigma. Why does Virgie single out Eugene as the man who *learned* something while he was away? This passage suggests that she has veiled respect for Eugene's life, for he too is an exile, both physically in **"Music from Spain"** and figuratively upon his return as a man who keeps to himself and who does not participate in the staged machinations of Morgana, Mississippi. More importantly, it appears that he brings with him to Mississippi the profound sexual transformation he undergoes in San Francisco. His return is just as mysterious as his departure in that it remains unexplained. That Eugene has learned "people don't have to be answered" suggests he has attained some peace concerning the question mark—perhaps his homosexuality—which "skirted through traffic" in San Francisco in the first part of the chapter (184). He had to go there in order to become himself here.

The most revealing aspect of Virgie's commentary on Eugene is that of Eugene's "wife." When Eugene dies, a telegram is sent, perhaps from Emma.[16] The reader must fill in the blanks here and decide why Eugene separated from her and left San Francisco. Their separation must have been precipitated by a significant event, one that would have made their marriage irreconcilable. Eugene's homosexual epiphany could be such an event. Virgie makes it clear that no one in Morgana ever saw Eugene's wife, Emma, and that perhaps she was a "Dago." This word choice is significant, for Eugene calls the Spaniard a "Dago" in **"Music from Spain"** (215). The word is used only twice, each time referring to Eugene's lover—this in fact conflates Emma, his wife, with the Spaniard, who, indeed, was a "foreigner." Whatever Virgie means by these statements is overshadowed by the fact that Eugene is dead. His character has undergone the ultimate transformation of space and time by his complete corporeal disappearance from the text—the gravestone being the only "marker" of his passing through Morgana.

Ultimately, Eugene's story is tied to the city of San Francisco, known for its liberalness and homosexual history. In "Place in Fiction," Welty muses, "the more narrowly we can examine a fictional character, the greater his is likely to loom up. We must see him set to scale in his proper world to know his size . . . by confining character [place] defines it" (62). Eugene rises out of the narrow confines of his geographical past to make San Francisco his own in letting its boundaries help define him. **"Music from Spain"** could not have happened anywhere else. It is an homage to a man's discovery of his true self, emotions, and sexual orientation, as well as to the city of the Golden Gate. Axel Nissen notes that Welty "spent a substantial amount of time, particularly during her artistically formative years, surrounded by a loving circle of gay men" (211).[17] Welty treats Eugene's transformation and personal exploration with understanding, and she uses the city to further illustrate that transformation. As Nissen writes, "Welty is seeking not judgment but understanding both for herself and her readers. She is seeking understanding and reveling in the truly wonderful variety of human character and experience" (229). San Francisco allows a space for such understanding and variety in human experience for Eugene, a space Mississippi could not offer. Welty uses her own experience on the coast to open new spaces in which she allows her characters to thrive. Indeed, Diarmuid Russell had every reason to question the inclusion of **"Music from Spain"** in ***The Golden Apples,*** but what he did not realize at the time was Welty's genius in creating a counterpoint to Mississippi, which allowed Eugene to escape the living dirge of sexual confinement that Morgana promised. Eugene is the quiet hero of the text, a character who experiences an expansion of character and learns something about himself and love, something that separates him from every other male in his family. Perhaps Eugene is the only character in Welty's novel who actually plucks the golden apples of the sun, appropriately, in San Francisco, California.

Notes

1. Michael Kreyling writes that the story is "a sort of oblique diary of [Eudora Welty's] stay" in San Francisco (125).

2. Diarmuid Russell had good reason to be concerned; Welty wrote to him explaining, "I think *this* time I got it [the story] right—and the key is, you'd never guess, the little man in it is from Battle Hill and who he is is one of the MacLain twins—don't faint" (Kreyling 141).
3. Mark examines the mythic allusions in "Music from Spain" and points out in great detail the story's similarities with James Joyce's *Ulysses.*
4. Welty went to San Francisco on December 18, 1946, to visit her friend John Robinson and rented her own apartment there on January 4, 1947 (Marrs 151). "Music from Spain" was written between January and March 1947 in San Francisco.
5. An interactive map of Eugene's route is available at http://jmhuculak.googlepages.com
6. Infidelity is a leitmotiv throughout the entire work of *The Golden Apples,* particularly with the MacLain family.
7. The image of Eugene's walking down a large hill recalls Dante's walking down into the pits of hell—an image that is echoed in "The Whole World Knows," the antecedent chapter to "Music from Spain" about Eugene's brother Ran, and noted by Naoko Thornton when she observes that Ran walks down the "Dantean circles of the riverbank" (103). The striking similarities between "The Whole World Knows" and "Music from Spain" are myriad and deserve their own proper study, but, because of the limits of this essay, I will note only the most significant moments of verisimilitude in each.
8. In "The Whole World Knows," Ran runs away with a woman named "Maideen," with whom he too will have an affair. Mark notes that "The Whole World Knows" was the first story Welty wrote in *The Golden Apples* (146); however, the similarity between "Music from Spain" and "The Whole World Knows," particularly in this instance where the name Maiden/Maideen occurs in what will become a sexual context for each brother, suggests that Welty was thinking about this story as well and might have taken the name Maideen from the actual San Francisco street name. Moreover, Mark writes that that "Maideen is not some lost innocent country girl, but the maiden . . . the one who will awaken the consort's vital sexual potency" (153), much like the Spaniard, who will awaken Eugene's homosexual potency.
9. Mark argues that the slap is not against Emma's body but the "social construction called wife" (187).
10. Interestingly, the Richmond District is just above the Sunset District in San Francisco. Ran stays at "Sunset Oaks" (180) in Vicksburg when he has his sexual experience with Maideen. A visitor to the city could easily confuse the two districts since the western portion of the city is usually called "the Sunset"; of course, the sun sets over the western portion of the city.
11. Ran, at Sunset Oaks, also has a "death" experience when he contemplates suicide by shooting himself.
12. Ran also places a phallic symbol in his mouth: the revolver, which "clicks" but does not go off (181). Ran is denied the life-changing power of the phallus, while Eugene receives it.
13. When Ran has his imagined or real sexual experience with Maideen, he wonders, "Father, Eugene! What you went and found, was it better than this?" (181). Eugene can answer, "Yes."
14. *Mariposa* means "butterfly" in Spanish.
15. Eugene calls the Spaniard's lips "grape" colored while they are walking on the beach (215).
16. It is unclear whether the telegram is from Emma, or perhaps the Spaniard.
17. This would include John Robinson, who encouraged Welty to visit San Francisco in 1946-47 (Marrs 150).

Works Cited

Barta, Peter. *Bely, Joyce, and Döblin: Peripatetics in the City Novel.* Gainesville: UP of Florida, 1996.

Kelly, Greg. "Re: Streetcar Map." *E-mail to the Author.* 8 April 2004.

Kreyling, Michael. *Author and Agent: Eudora Welty and Diarmuid Russell.* New York: Farrar Straus Giroux, 1994.

Mark, Rebecca. *The Dragon's Blood: Feminist Intertextuality in Eudora Welty's* The Golden Apples. Jackson: UP of Mississippi, 1994.

Marrs, Suzanne. *Eudora Welty: A Biography.* New York: Harcourt, 2005.

Nissen, Axel. "Queer Welty, Camp Welty." *Mississippi Quarterly* 56.2 (2003): 209-230.

Thornton, Naoko Fuwa. *Strange Felicity: Eudora Welty's Subtexts on Fiction and Society.* London: Praeger, 2003.

Welty, Eudora. *The Golden Apples.* 1949. New York: Harcourt, 1975.

———. "Place in Fiction." *South Atlantic Quarterly* 55 (1956): 57-72.

———. "Some Notes on Time in Fiction." *Mississippi Quarterly* 26.4 (1973): 483-92.

Zahlan, Ann Ricketson. "'Out Where It's Gold and All That': California as Adventurous Exile in Eudora Welty's 'Music of Spain'" [sic]. *South Dakota Review* 35 (1997): 47-60.

Leverett Butts (essay date summer 2006)

SOURCE: Butts, Leverett. "One with the World: The Arthurian Myth Cycles in Welty's 'Ladies in Spring.'" *Eudora Welty Newsletter* 30, no. 2 (summer 2006): 10-17.

[*In the following essay, Butts explores the subtextual appropriation of the Holy Grail myth in "Ladies in Spring," drawing a parallel between Percival's role as Grail-keeper in the legend and Dewey's miraculous act of catching a fish in Welty's story.*]

> When we read such highly imaginative prose, infused with the learning of the great schools of mythology of the Middle Ages, we understand all over again that most great literature is doubled with mythology.
>
> (Goodrich, *King* 7)

> I've lived with mythology all my life. It is just as close to me as the landscape. It naturally occurs to me when I am writing fiction.
>
> (Welty, qtd. in Gretlund 224)

The abundance of myth and fairy-tale in Eudora Welty's fiction comes as no surprise to anyone even remotely familiar with her work. Her first novel, ***The Robber Bridegroom,*** for instance, is a retelling of the Grimm fairy-tale set on the Natchez Trace (Welty *Eye* 307). In her collection ***The Golden Apples,*** Welty used classic Greek, Roman, and Celtic myths "as freely as [she] would salt and pepper," retelling and rewriting the myths as they suited her needs for the stories (Jones 331).

Welty's short story **"Ladies in Spring,"** is no different in this respect. As Dewey Coker, the young protagonist of the story, walks to the river with his father, he feels as if "the world h[olds] perfectly still for moments at a time" (625-26). This sense of stillness gives the story a feeling of timelessness and places the tale firmly in the realm of myth rather than reality. However, few have chosen to write about this story. Margaret Bolsterli, however, has written a good introduction to the mythic qualities found in this deceptively simple story of a young boy fishing with his father. She claims **"Ladies in Spring"** as an "initiation story" dealing with Dewey's first steps into the adult world (69). She cites the significance of spring as a time of "rebirth" (70), the importance of the color black in rainmaking (71), and the equation of "fish" with "fertility" to illustrate the "combination of rights . . . unconscious . . . [and] conscious" that shepherd Dewey through his transition from child to adult (70-71).

With a reading of James Frazer's *The Golden Bough,* Bolsterli examines other symbols of fertility found in the story. Spring represents rebirth and fertility since it is the season of "yearly renewal" (Frazer 70). Frazer links rain to fertility, when he discusses the belief of some tribes that miscarriage prevents rain (243). He further points to the importance of the color black in rainmaking (Frazer 78). Bolsterli then points out the prevalence of black in the story (71): Miss Hattie the rainmaker, wears black, and Dewey's father, named "Blackie," is "the darkest Coker of the family" (**"Ladies"** [**"Ladies in Spring"**] 626, 633). To this I might add that the name Coker, meaning one who manufactures coke (a fuel derived from coal), also implies blackness.

With the obvious equation of "black" with "sin," it seems fairly clear that for Bolsterli, Dewey's transition is one from innocence to experience. Dewey is unaware that his father, Blackie, has been seeing another woman (possibly the rainmaker's daughter) and that the second fishing pole Blackie carries is not intended for Dewey, but for Blackie's girlfriend (**"Ladies"** 625). However, Bolsterli claims that Dewey's skipping school and his presence at his father's assignation makes him "as guilty as his father" despite the fact that he has understood none of what he has seen (72). Dewey's exposure, even without understanding, has been enough to initiate him into the "adult world of sex" (70).

What is surprising in Bolsterli's essay, though, is the absence of Arthurian myth. Admittedly, Welty relies primarily on local folklore, Irish fairy tales, and the Greco-Roman myths (Buckley 107). While she rarely employs the Arthurian cycle in her fiction, though, this is not to say that she never uses it.[1] For example, aspects of the Arthurian cycles show up at least twice in ***The Golden Apples*** collection. Take for example the town of Morgana, Mississippi. In an interview with John Griffin Jones, Welty claims that the name of her town "is sort of like the Fata Morgana, or sea mirage" (332). Welty chose the name of Morgana because "[e]verybody [in Morgana] was sort of trapped in their own dream world there" (332). "Fata Morgana" is the Italian name for Morgan Le Fay,[2] and in Arthurian myth, Morgan Le Fay is the Queen of the Faerie and Arthur's half-sister (Ashe and Lacy 380, 379-80). As queen of fairyland, she can alter a mortal's perception and trap him or her in dreams. For example, she appears to Arthur as his wife Guinevere in order to bear Mordred, Arthur's son who will one day destroy his kingdom (Goodrich, *King* 221).

Morgana is also the ruler of Avalon, the idyllic paradise to which Arthur is taken to be healed after his final battle (Ashe 13). It is often described as an enchanted dream-like realm where the Faerie watch over the affairs of mortals (Lupack 129-30). The name Avalon derives from the Welsh word meaning "apple"; another name for Avalon, in fact, is "The Isle of Apples" (Goodrich, *Merlin* 202). In addition to the Greek myths involving golden apples, then, the title of Welty's collection also refers to Arthur's dream-like island ruled over by a mistress of mirage and illusion.

Admittedly, Arthurian myth is rare in Welty, so ordinarily it should come as no surprise that Bolsterli does not discuss the Arthurian cycle when describing the mythic qualities of the story. However, on the very first page, Dewey debates going fishing with his father and missing his teacher, Miss Pruitt, read from *Excalibur,* presumably a novel or collection of Arthurian stories, named for his magical sword (Welty **"Ladies"** 625). *Excalibur* is mentioned again toward the end of the story when Dewey considers returning to school: "'I may can still go,' he said dreamily, '*Excalibur*—'" (635). It seems improbable that Welty would twice reference a particular mythic cycle in one of her stories without a thematic reason.

In "Textual Variants in 'Spring'/'Ladies in Spring,'" W. U. McDonald, Jr., points out the changes Welty made to her story between publishing it in *Sewanee Review* and adding it to ***The Bride of the Innisfallen*** collection and subsequently supports the idea of Welty's intentional use of the Arthurian mythos. While most of the changes were minor substitutions or variants, Welty made a significant change to Dewey's exclamation. Instead of "*Excalibur*—," Welty originally had Dewey exclaim, "Miss Pruitt—" (McDonald 5). If Welty made the conscious decision to add another clear reference to the Arthurian mythos, it seems reasonable to examine the story for more oblique references.

When discussing the mythological elements in Welty's fiction, one must keep in mind that there will rarely be a "one-to-one" correlation between the myth and Welty's work (Haller 313). As Welty herself explains:

> [E]quivalents like that are all apart from my intention. I use [myth] in the way I think life does. Life recalls them. These likenesses occur to you when you are living your life. They are plucked out of here and there because they seem to apply.
>
> (Jones 332)

Welty's practice of "mak[ing] free" with myths (Jones 324), of using only those aspects of a myth that "seem to apply" (332), is especially appropriate for the Arthurian myths since no two are ever exactly alike. In fact, most blatantly contradict each other. Where Malory identifies Mordred's mother as Arthur's other sister Morgawse (29), other legends claim she is Morgana. Where Malory claims that Arthur is Mordred's father (29), Tennyson says Mordred is simply Arthur's nephew (9). Some myths identify Avalon as Glastonbury Tor, others as the Isle of Man, and still others claim it never existed on the mortal plane. In **"Ladies in Spring,"** as in her other stories, Welty mixes and matches her myths to suit her need.

One of the first indirect references to the Arthurian cycle may be found in the very first sentence:

> The pair moved through the *gray* landscape as though *no one could see them*—dressed alike in *overalls* and *faded coats,* one big, one little, one black-headed, one tow-headed, father and son.
>
> (625, emphasis added)

The two figures are hidden by the color gray. Their faded coats and overalls (which must be just as faded) blend with gray landscape concealing them. Additionally the mix of their black and white hair implies gray, too. This seems almost a direct allusion to the Welsh bards who consider King Arthur "a hazy shadow wrapped . . . in the gray veil of concealment, staring out over the kingdom from the westward-facing cliff of Camelot" (Goodrich, *King* 3).

Further examples of Arthurian myth present themselves through the characters of **"Ladies in Spring."** For example, the Lady of the Lake appears briefly in the role of Miss Pruitt, Dewey's teacher. According to *Bulfinch's Mythology,* the Lady of the Lake offers Arthur the magical sword Excalibur (39). Similarly, Miss Pruitt offers Dewey stories from *Excalibur.* The other three ladies in Welty's story, Hattie Purcell, Opal Purcell, and Dewey's mother, could represent the three queens who take Arthur to Avalon and care for his wounds. Almost all the myths agree that the three queens are women, one old, one middle-aged, and one young, who are close to and care for Arthur (usually the three ladies are portrayed as Arthur's mother Igraine, his wife Guinevere, and his sister Morgan Le Fay). The three ladies in Welty's story fit the ages of the three queens. At least two of them, Hattie and Dewey's mother, act as Dewey's caretakers. Admittedly, Opal never openly reacts to Dewey; however, she exhibits many of Morgan Le Fay's characteristics.

More importantly, Blackie Coker, Dewey's father, whose name implies sin, clearly represents Arthur's father, Uther Pendragon. In his book, *King Arthur in Legend and History,* Richard Barber claims that "the name of Arthur's father, Uther, may be due to a misunderstanding of 'Arthur mab uthr,' Arthur the terrible, as Arthur son of Uther" (Barber 40). "Uther" then means "terrible." Misreading or not, this is an appropriate name for the father of the legendary Arthur. According to Thomas Malory, the fifteenth century author of *Le Morte Darthur,* before Arthur's birth, Uther Pendragon, a fierce warrior, invites his enemy, Gorlois, the Duke of Tintagel, to his castle to make peace. When Gorlois arrives with his wife Igraine, Uther "like[s] and love[s] this lady well . . . and desire[s] to lie by her" (Malory 3). To do this, he elicits the help of the magician, Merlin. Merlin alters Uther's appearance into that of Igraine's husband, so the king may sleep with her and father Arthur (5).

Like Uther, Blackie Coker participates in adultery. When he encounters Dewey outside the school, he attempts to send him away. "Scoot," he says, "Get on back in the schoolhouse. You been told" (625). However, even though he does not initially plan on taking his son fishing with him, he carries two poles. Clearly, then, Blackie intends to meet someone else at the river. Blackie's illicit affair becomes more obvious when the strange lady appears three times and beckons to him from across the river.

Further circumstantial evidence connects Dewey to King Arthur. Like Arthur, Dewey is the son of an adulterous father. Where the Lady of the Lake offers Arthur Excalibur, Dewey spends a large part of the morning and evening wanting to hear the stories of *Excalibur* from Miss Pruitt. More importantly, one thing all the Arthurian legends agree on is that Arthur was "an ideal leader who personified justice, . . . order, and harmony" (Goodrich, *King* 3). When Opal appears on their way back to Royal, Mississippi, Dewey gives her "his place" under the umbrella (632). He then "marche[s] ahead of them, still in step with his father, but out in the open rain" (632). Thus Dewey leads his company home and demonstrates his innate sense of fairness by giving up his dry place to a lady. He further demonstrates his generosity when he wishes he could give his fish to Miss Hattie (632), when he draws her a picture of his fish instead (636), and when he finally offers the fish to his mother (637).

Perhaps the most obvious allusion to Arthurian myth lies in the character of Miss Hattie Purcell and her resemblance to Merlin. Many myths ascribe to Merlin the power to affect the weather. For example, some writers credit Merlin with the presence of fog hiding Arthur's small army during his final battle (Boorman). Besides being the postmistress of Royal, Hattie is a self-proclaimed rainmaker. When she first appears in the story, her appearance is very much like that of a magician with her "black hat" and her long black winter coat hanging to her ankles (626). The umbrella she carries under her arm "like a rolling pin" could very well be a magic wand (626).

According to Bulfinch, Merlin "ha[s] the ability to transform himself into any shape he please[s]" (30). When Hattie begins her rainmaking vigil, she almost literally transforms herself into the land:

> Miss Hattie brought rain by sitting a vigil of the necessary duration beside the nearest body of water. . . . She made no more sound at it than a man fishing. But something about the way Miss Hattie's comfort shoes showed their tips below her skirt and carried a dust of the dry woods on them made her look as though she'd be there forever: longer than they would.
>
> (626)

Hattie also has the ability to disappear and reappear at will as evidenced by Dewey and Blackie's encounter with her disembodied voice as they run to escape the rain:

> "Trot under here!" called a pre-emptory voice.
>
> "Miss Hattie! Forgot she was anywhere near," said Dewey's father, falling back. "Now we got to be nice to *her.*"
>
> "Good evening Lavelle." . . .
>
> Something as big as a sail came out through the brambles.
>
> "Did you hear me?" said Miss Hattie—there she stood.
>
> (630)

Like her mother, Opal Purcell also represents a magical figure from Arthurian literature. Like Merlin, Morgan Le Fay has magical powers. Many legends claim that Morgan Le Fay was Merlin's last pupil (Goodrich, *Merlin* 21). As an aging rainmaker, it is conceivable that Hattie would be training Opal to take over her profession (this would also give Opal a legitimate reason for being in the woods when Blackie plans to be fishing).

However, there are less circumstantial connections between Opal and Morgan Le Fay. Fifteen years after the events of **"Ladies in Spring,"** it occurs to Dewey that Opal had "very likely been" the woman in the woods calling to his father (636). However, since young Dewey doesn't recognize Opal the four times he sees the woman, obviously her appearance is different from that of the familiar daughter of the postmistress. If the woman in the woods and Opal are one and the same, then Opal can, like Morgan Le Fay, alter her appearance. She also has the ability to ignore the laws of the physical world. When the strange woman appears for the fourth time in the rain, she is "in the distance behind them" (630). Almost immediately after that, Opal shows up on the side of the road "wait[ing] for them" (631).

It is also significant that Opal's doppelganger appears near the water. In Italian, Morgan Le Fay's name Fata Morgana is the term for a sea mirage (Ashe and Lacy 380). On the edge of the riverbank, Opal's face appears illuminated like "a lantern in nighttime" (627). Her face is "white and still as magic" when it stands behind a "trembling willow" (628), a tree often associated with witchcraft. When Dewey, Blackie, and Hattie walk home through the rain, the woman appears one more time "like a ghost" before she "disappears for good" into an orchard (630-31).

Welty, then, goes to great pains to include the Arthurian myths in her story. However, the question remains: To what end does she do this? If she picks and chooses her myths because they "seem to apply" (Jones 332), how do the Arthurian myths apply to **"Ladies in Spring"**?

Welty's use of Arthurian myth is fitting for a story set in rural Mississippi. Arthurian mythology was very popular in the antebellum South. Antebellum Southerners preferred to read popular romances such as Walter Scott's *Ivanhoe* and other tales of medieval knights in armor (Wimsatt 92). In fact, the stereotypical "Southern gentleman" was very heavily influenced by the knights of old and their code of chivalry (Page 5). Plantation owners often likened their economics to the feudalism of the Middle Ages (though not with the negative connotations implicit in feudalism today). Indeed, for the antebellum Southerner, the South represented a return to the golden age of chivalry (Eaton 319-20).

"Ladies in Spring," however, is set much later, after this "golden age" has fallen and the town of Royal is in the middle of a drought. It is a wasteland where crops are failing and many people are going hungry. Welty's story, then, bears a close resemblance to the Holy Grail myth of Arthurian legend. According to Geoffrey Ashe and Norris Lacy in *The Arthurian Handbook,* the wasteland is a

> [r]ecurrent feature of the Grail stories. The basic theme is that the country around the Grail Castle in Arthur's time has become barren because of an enchantment or sacrilege. . . . The state of the land is associated with the Grail-keeper's wound, which is usually of a sexual nature.
>
> (405)

The Grail-keeper, then, bears a strong connection to the land. If so, then one might assume that besides Merlin, Hattie Purcell represents the Grail-keeper due to her ability to become one with the land as she makes rain (626). Opal, though, can also become one with the land. She "disappears" into trees at least three times during the story: once with a willow tree (628), then with a bay tree (629), and finally with a pear tree (631). However, Blackie Coker serves as a better representation of the Grail-keeper than either of these two ladies.

In *Bulfinch's Mythology,* the Grail-keeper names himself King Pecheur (83). However, this is more a title than a name since "pêcheur" is French for "fisher" (83). Therefore, the Grail-keeper is the Fisher King, which is demonstrated when Percival first encounters him outside the Grail castle:

> At evening he came to a lake. There fishermen, whose domain these waters were, had cast their anchor. When they saw him ride up they were close enough inshore to hear quite well what he said. One man he saw in the boat whose apparel could not have been richer if all lands had been subject to him. Of this fisherman he made inquiry . . . [of] where he might find lodgings. . . .
>
> [T]he fisherman said, "I myself will be your host tonight."
>
> (Eschenbach 124)

Besides fisher, though, with a change of accent, pécheur also means "sinner" (83). When Percival next encounters the fisherman, he notices a horrible wound in his host's groin where he had been "struck through the two thighs" (Goodrich, *Holy* 80). According to Bulfinch, this wound is punishment for the King's lust:

> [A]t length one of those holy men to whom [the Grail's] guardianship had descended so far forgot the obligation of his sacred office as to look with unhallowed eye upon a young female pilgrim whose robe was accidentally loosened as she knelt before him. The sacred lance[3] instantly punished his frailty, spontaneously falling upon him and inflicting a deep wound.
>
> (85)

The primary characteristic of the Fisher King, then, is less his connection to the land and more the lust that has made him unworthy of his sacred calling.

Like the Fisher King, Blackie, the Royal fisher, gives in to lust, as evidenced by his affair with Opal. However, if the Fisher King's duty is to protect the Grail, what is Blackie's duty? While much of the Grail literature draws a link between the Grail, the Fisher King, and the land, it equally emphasizes the importance of the Grail family. Some sources describe this family as the Fisher Kings themselves, the descendants of Joseph of Arimathea whose job it is to guard the Grail (Gardner 178). Others believe the Grail family to be the actual descendants of King David and Jesus Christ (Baigent, Leigh, and Lincoln 419-20). Still others claim that both suppositions are correct, and the Grail Family is both the descendants of David and their protectors (Gardner 249). Whatever the case, the emphasis on family is evident.

Blackie's affair has caused him to give in to lust and neglect his duty towards his family. That his wife knows of Blackie's infidelity is at least implied by her violent reaction when Dewey offers her his fish, proof of his participation in his father's escapades:

> "Get away from me!" she shrieked. "You and your pa! Both of you get the sight of you clear away!" She struck with her little green switch, fanning drops of milk and light. "Get in the house. Oh! If I haven't had enough out of you!"
>
> (637)

Dewey, too, seems to understand his father's desertion, if only on a subconscious level since he takes on the role of family provider. When he returns from fishing, he asks his mother for the responsibility of the newborn calf (637), thus entering into the family business of running the farm. Additionally, he wishes he could give Miss Hattie the fish he caught (632), but clearly, he feels obligated to give it to his mother (637). He therefore puts on his family's table the food his father can't provide.

This assumption of the family duties ties Dewey to the character of Percival. Like Dewey, Percival's father abandoned his familial duties. According to legend, Percival's father left his family and never returned, having presumably died in battle (Troyes 414-19). As a result, his mother took her only son into the wilderness, futilely trying to protect him from his father's mistakes by working "hard to keep [him] from all knowledge / Of knighthood" (Troyes 409-10). Similarly, Mrs. Coker's reaction to Dewey's fish implies that she feels like she has failed to shield her son from his father's failings. However, in this, Mrs. Coker is quite mistaken, for instead of following in his father's steps, Dewey accepts the familial responsibility his father neglects.

Another resemblance between Percival's legend and Dewey's story lies in the setting. When Lancelot, an adulterous knight, tries to enter the Grail Chapel, a disembodied voice warns him. "[I]f thou enter," it says, "thou shalt regret it" (Malory 612). In Welty's story, a sign reading "Cross at Own Risk" stands before the bridge (627). According to Malory, the Grail Chapel is a chamber with "a table of silver" in the middle (612). Welty describes the bridge from which Dewey and his father fish as "a table in the water" (627). Though Bolsterli, in her essay on Welty's story, points out the similarity to an altar (71), by ignoring the Arthurian elements, she misses the significance. According to Malory, the Holy Grail sits upon the silver altar in the Grail Chapel (612). Upon the bridge, Welty's altar, sit Dewey and his father, a family. The Coker family, then, represents both the Grail and its guardians.

There are other similarities between Percival and Dewey. Where Blackie, the symbolic Fisher King of the story, is Dewey's father, Anfortas, the Fisher King in Wolfram von Eschenbach's *Parzival,* is Percival's uncle (444-45). During a Grail ceremony, Percival remains oblivious to the meaning of the proceedings (Eschenbach 127-32). Though Dewey participates (albeit passively) in his father's delinquency, he does not realize the implications of the strange woman's overtures. However, neither Percival's nor Dewey's ignorance keeps them from accepting their responsibilities.

Once Percival discovers the Grail, he becomes its new guardian, the new Fisher King. The title's significance though is altered. Unlike his uncle, Percival is pure. While "fisher" sometimes means "sinner," it now means "savior."[4] When Percival relieves Anfortas of the responsibility towards the Grail, his uncle is magically healed (Eschenbach 415). While we do not know what happens to Blackie, once Dewey assumes his familial responsibility and becomes a leader, the land is healed. As Dewey leads his company back to Royal, he notices his surroundings take on new colors in the rain: the Baptist church turns "red as a rose," the Methodist church gets "streaky," and even the citizens of Royal look "like the faces of new people" (632-33).

Finally, both Percival and Dewey are chosen for their duties by a higher power. Percival learns the only way to achieve the Grail is to be chosen by God: "[N]o one [can] ever fight his way to the Grail," a hermit tells him, "unless he has been summoned by God" (Eschenbach 408). Even though the river is dry, Dewey miraculously catches a fish (628), suggesting that a higher power has chosen him to pick up the responsibilities his father has shirked. When Percival takes over as the Grail-keeper, he takes part in the Grail mass, his consecration as Fisher King (Eschenbach 421). Dewey, too, undergoes a kind of anointing ceremony when he returns to town from the bridge: "In a sudden moment [Miss Hattie] . . . rubbed his head—just any old way—with something out of her purse; it might have been a dinner napkin" (634-35).

Welty's message is clear. The Arthurian allusions within this relatively simple story of a father and son's fishing trip point out the connections we share with our environment. Just as Anfortas's sin causes his country to suffer and Blackie's neglect of his familial responsibility causes his family to suffer, one person's irresponsible act can detrimentally affect innocents, too. Percival's relief of his uncle's duties and Dewey's assumption of his father's role, then, suggest that even though someone may not be responsible for a problem, sometimes he has to be responsible for the solution.

Notes

1. Indeed, as a child Welty read *Our Wonder World,* a children's encyclopedia, extensively. Volume V of *Our Wonder World, Every Child's Story Book* contains a ten-page section titled "Stories and Plays of Knights and Yeomen" (179-89). This section includes several Arthurian stories under the heading "King Arthur and the Table Round" and a play "The Knighting of Perceval."
2. Since legends vary on the spelling of Arthurian names, for the sake of convenience, I will use the most common spellings.
3. The Spear of Longinus, which pierced the side of Christ, usually appears alongside the Grail in most Grail legends.
4. Christ calls his disciples "fishers of men."

Works Cited

Ashe, Geoffrey. *The Discovery of King Arthur.* London: Guild, 1985.

Ashe, Geoffrey, and Norris J. Lacy. *The Arthurian Handbook.* New York: Garland, 1988.

Baigent, Michael, Richard Leigh, and Henry Lincoln. *The Holy Blood and the Holy Grail.* 1982. London: Corgi, 1983.

Barber, Richard. *King Arthur in Legend and History.* Cardinal ed. London: Cox & Wyman, 1973.

Bolsterli, Margaret. "Mythic Elements in Ladies in Spring." *Notes on Mississippi Writers* 6 (1974): 69-72.

Boorman, John. "Director's Commentary." *Excalibur.* Dir. John Boorman. DVD. Warner Brothers. 1981.

Buckley, William F. "'The Southern Imagination': An Interview with Eudora Welty and Walker Percy." *Firing Line.* Prod. by Southern Educational Communication Association. WMAA, Jackson. 12 December 1982. Rpt. in Prenshaw 92-114.

Bulfinch, Thomas. *The Illustrated Bulfinch's Mythology: The Age of Chivalry.* New York: Macmillan, 1997.

Eaton, Clement. *The Growth of Southern Civilization.* Torchbook ed. New York: Harper, 1963.

Eschenbach, Wolfram von. *Parzival.* Trans. Helen M. Mustard and Charles E. Passage. New York: Vintage, 1961.

Frazer, Sir James George. *The Golden Bough: A Study in Magic and Religion.* Abr. ed. New York: Macmillan, 1950.

Gardner, Laurence. *Bloodline of the Holy Grail.* Rockport: Element, 1996.

Goodrich, Norma Lorre. *The Holy Grail.* Perennial Library ed. New York: Harper and Row, 1992.

———. *King Arthur.* Perennial Library ed. New York: Harper and Row, 1986.

———. *Merlin.* Perennial Library ed. New York: Harper and Row, 1988.

Gretlund, Jan Nordby. "An Interview with Eudora Welty." *Southern Humanities Review* 14 (1980). Rpt. in Prenshaw 211-29.

Haller, Scot. "Creators on Creating: Eudora Welty." *Saturday Review* June 1981: 42-46. Rpt. in Prenshaw 308-15.

Jones, John Griffin. "Eudora Welty." *Mississippi Writers Talking, I.* Jackson: UP of M, 1982: 3-35. Rpt. in Prenshaw 316-41.

Lupack, Alan. "The Figure of King Arthur in America." *King Arthur's Modern Return.* Ed. Debra N. Mancoff. New York: Garland, 1998: 121-36.

Malory, Sir Thomas. *Le Morte Darthur.* Ed. R. M. Lumiansky. New York: Collier, 1986.

McDonald, W. U. "Textual Variants in 'Spring'/'Ladies in Spring.'" *The Eudora Welty Newsletter* 20.1 (1996): 4-6.

Our Wonder World. Vol. V. Chicago: Geo. L. Shuman & Co., 1914.

Page, Thomas Nelson. *The Old South: Essays Social and Political.* New York: Scribners, 1919.

Prenshaw, Peggy Whitman, ed. *Conversations with Eudora Welty.* 1984. Jackson: UP of Mississippi, 1998.

Tennyson, Alfred. *Idylls of the King.* Pathfinder ed. New York: Bantam, 1965.

Troyes, Chretien de. *Perceval: The Story of the Grail.* Trans. Burton Raffel. New Haven: Yale UP, 1999.

Welty, Eudora. *The Eye of the Story.* New York: Vintage, 1990.

———. "Ladies in Spring." *Stories, Essays, & Memoirs.* New York: Library of America, 1998. 625-38.

Wimsatt, Mary Ann. "Antebellum Fiction." *The History of Southern Literature.* Ed. Louis D. Rubin et al. Baton Rouge: Louisiana State UP, 1985. 92-107.

Jeffrey J. Folks (essay date fall 2006)

SOURCE: Folks, Jeffrey J. "The Fierce Humanity of Morgana: Welty's *The Golden Apples.*" *Southern Literary Journal* 39, no. 1 (fall 2006): 16-32.

[*In the following essay, Folks chronicles the transformative journey of Virgie Rainey in* The Golden Apples, *underlining the book's mythologically-colored and ritualistic acceptance of the tragedy of the human condition.*]

A sense of terror underlies the seemingly uneventful daily life of Morgana, Mississippi. Terror—surprisingly, perhaps, one of Eudora Welty's favorite words—governs much of the psychological existence of human beings in ***The Golden Apples,*** and Welty's central concern in the novel is the difficulty of comprehending its causes and dealing with its effects. The widespread sense of anxiety among the characters in Welty's writing can be traced to the fact that human society, as Welty comprehends it, would appear to be an illusory structure of polite discourse that barely conceals an underlying strata of violence. Beneath the genteel fabric of middle-class social interaction there lies a savage world of selfishness, spite, and ambition. Given the force of these primal motives, the conventional social rituals that are meant to contain them appear to be little more than hypocritical gestures. In light of Welty's depiction of the ineffectuality of human social rituals, it is not surprising that more profound values of truthfulness and creativity should be fundamental in her writing and that those who strongly assert these values should be among her major protagonists; yet among the many characters in ***The Golden Apples*** who are motivated by underlying primal fears, only two figures respond in a truly creative and self-conscious manner: Miss Lotte Elisabeth Eckhart and her pupil, Virgie Rainey.

Miss Eckhart's teaching, which amounts to far more than the conventional small-town schooling in one of the "feminine arts," attempts nothing less than to awaken in her pupils an awareness of the momentous importance of their lives within a world of opportunity and risk. As one learns in **"June Recital,"** the most important occasion for enacting this knowledge is through the annual piano recital that Miss Eckhart organizes for her students. Like Prospero in Shakespeare's *The Tempest,* or like another, less appealing character of the same name in Poe's "The Masque of the Red Death," Miss Eckhart controls every detail of her fête, including the costuming. She insists that, like a bridal gown, the recital dress must be new and cannot be displayed prior to recital night, and even that it rarely be worn again, "certainly not to another recital" (68). Although Miss Eckhart "disregarded her own rules" (72) in regard to recital dresses, she displays a quality of glamour and a surprising sensuality in her previously worn gowns. As she intends, the recital marks the passage not only into summer but into everything that summer's ripeness connotes. Welty writes that "Miss Eckhart pushed herself to quite another level of life for it. A blushing sensitivity sprang up in her every year like a flower of the season" (70).

Certainly Miss Eckhart's powers as a teacher involve an element of the magical. After the concert, Miss Eckhart goes about with her foreign-sounding cake, her "kuchen," insisting that the girls eat it "to the last crumb." "A decoration of slipping flower garlands and rowdy babies" (75) revealed on the empty plate points to the rebellious and uncontrolled potential of the occasion, and the girls under her charge surrender themselves to Miss Eckhart's direction as they sense its significance. Even for the cautious Cassie Morrison, Miss Eckhart's recitals were the highlight of her year, especially the recital performance at age thirteen of Virgie Rainey, wearing a white "Swiss dress" with a red satin band in her hair and a red sash in front. The life-affirming and sensuous implications of Virgie's performance are suggested by Welty's description of the sweat running down Virgie's face, a salty elixir of life that "she licked . . . in with her tongue" (74).

Unfortunately, in reward for her heroic effort to introduce her students to life's mysteries, Miss Eckhart is condemned by the better society of Morgana to live forever in the role of a pariah. As Suzanne Marrs points out, "the community fears Miss Eckhart because she seems to accept the unusual, the extraordinary, the terrifying aspects of life and does not try to hide from them" (121). Only in the case of Virgie Rainey can Miss Eckhart be said to have succeeded in passing down her prophetic knowledge of the inseparability of life's splendor and cruelty, for, as Miss Eckhart understands all too well, it is at the primal level of love and fear that the heroic struggle for life is enacted. Although Virgie tells us in **"The Wanderers"** that she "had hated" Miss Eckhart (260)—perhaps, as Thomas L. McHaney suggests, because Virgie is "the unsatisfied wanderer" (618)—the two are linked by their sense of both being outsiders within the community of Morgana. As the narrator tells us through the consciousness of Cassie Morrison, they were "deliberately terrible . . . no one could touch them now" (96). Cassie, who seems to register everything around her without entering life deeply herself, thinks of the Yeats poem and the line "Because a fire was in my head" and of the terrible beauty that Yeats implies. Miss Eckhart, this outcast of Morgana, is eventually condemned by the town to be sent away: in the state's care, she is beyond either gratitude or rescue, at large and roaming like a lost beast, but still "deliberately terrible."

Among several mythological associations, Miss Eckhart resembles the figure of the enchantress Circe, who also lived a solitary life in a remote land of magical transformation. In both the Greek and Slavic languages (both of which are associated with Circe), Circe's name connotes "heart," and it is the extent to which Miss Eckhart responds with her heart that makes possible her creation of beauty and that also produces truth, a recognition of the terror that those with less truthful hearts hide from themselves. The terror of Miss Eckhart's life is hinted at in the German compound of "eck" ("corner," "edge," or figuratively "awkward") and "hart" ("hard" or "severe"), and she and Virgie are linked not only as those who feel with their hearts but also as those who are destined to live a difficult and marginal existence. They will both fail in the ordinary activities of life because of their refusal to compromise. Pursuing only the golden apples, with all the pain and sacrifice that this entails, they scorn the commonplace fruits with which society rewards their peers. This failure, however, is also a means of survival, springing as it does from Virgie's "wildness," which admits no separation from life, and from Miss Eckhart's uncompromising love. Paradoxically, it is in this dangerous lure of freedom, the wanderer's lust for adventure beyond Morgana's provincial society, that Miss Eckhart becomes the artist with whom Welty most identifies.

In **"The Wanderers,"** a denouement to the collection narrating the death and funeral of Virgie Rainey's mother, Virgie demonstrates that she shares Miss Eckhart's resistance to participation in the town's ritualized society. At Katie Rainey's funeral, the unsettledness of the natural order is incongruous with the "dignity" of the funeral ritual from which Virgie withholds herself. The little "crumbs" and "clods" run down into the grave; the "tumbling activity and promptitude of the elements" that cause the cornucopias of flower to tip over also upset the human assumption of stable social order. As J. A. Bryant, Jr. stresses, for the townspeople a funeral is "one of several rituals by which they periodically assert their continuity" (312), but at the wake for her mother Virgie withholds herself from the crowd of mourners who attempt to force her to view her mother's body. The crowd's "touch" is especially offensive to Virgie, because it is through grasping and seizing that they wish to direct her grief into conventional channels and to incorporate her into the communal way of life. Hands are pulling and reaching out to her, smoothing her down and shoving her forward, but they are instinctively resisted. "Even their hands showing sorrow for a body that did not fall, giving back to hands what was broken, to pick up, smooth again. For people's very touch anticipated the falling of the body, the one, the single and watchful body" (241-242). However innocuous they may appear, the social rituals of Morgana are the means by which the group exercises control over the individual, a degree of control that often results in madness or even death. As Marrs notes in connection with **"The Whole World Knows,"** "perhaps the most difficult aspect of life in [the southern small town] is the veneer of politeness that covers and obscures the most heartfelt emotions" (113). Although Marrs somewhat inexplicably localizes this failing to southern small towns (the "veneer of politeness" plays a similar role in nearly all complex societies), she is certainly correct in pointing to the element of coercion that underlies social rituals.

With justification, Welty can write that the touch "anticipated" the falling of the body. As the twentieth-century philosopher Elias Canetti demonstrates in *Crowds and Power,* the touch is the initial stage of seizure and incorporation leading to the fall of the prey before the predator, even if this predation, within the genteel society of Morgana, takes the form of ostensibly innocent social rituals. In Canetti's discussion of "seizing and incorporation" he asserts that "there is nothing about us which is more strongly primitive" than our resistance to touch (203). According to Canetti, the activity of predation is "doubled" in human consciousness because of man's awareness of his own potential victimization. What is feared most in this activity is the "first touching": "the design of one body on another becomes concrete from the moment of touching. . . . It contains the oldest terrors; we dream of it, we imagine it, and civilized life is nothing but a sustained effort to avoid it" (204).

Beyond this first touching, the next stage is the act of seizure, the closing of fingers upon the prey. The urge to go beyond simple killing, the urge actually to "crush" the prey, results from the predator's contempt for that which he has killed. Humans betray their primordial desire to crush in the habitual killing of insects or the "finger exercise" of crushing plants. (A more extreme gesture suggesting extinction is grinding, involving use of the teeth.) Canetti notes, for example, the remarkable respect accorded a strong grip in social relations, a gesture connected with the ability to seize prey. The respect for the lion, "one of the great seizers," is something that kings aspire to (*Crowds* 206). The inverse psychological effect of this predatory nature is the awareness of man's own vulnerability, his role as prey, and therefore arises the revulsion at subjecting oneself to the seizure of others. "Every man, even the least, seeks to prevent anyone else coming too near him. Every form of social life established among men expresses itself in distances which allay the ceaseless fear of being seized and caught" (*Crowds* 207).

Beyond seizing the next step in power is incorporation. Canetti stresses the frightful symbolism of the teeth and the way in which the smoothness and order of the teeth have entered the symbolism of power. The social configuration of power itself is imitative of qualities of the teeth and of the mouth, "a strait place, the prototype of all prisons" (209). The human imagination has always been preoccupied with the stages of seizure and incorporation; the very process by which food is assimilated has always been known and anxiously represented in literature and art. Evidence of this knowledge is the manner in which humans hide their excrement, according to Canetti, and the shame universally attached to it, for excrement is the residue of "blood guilt" and the process of digestion that is set into motion by the daily murder of other life.

In the final section of ***The Golden Apples,*** Virgie clearly understands that this merciless process of incorporation extends beyond animal life to all of nature. In Morgana, the heavily loaded logging trucks haul the forest life to mill, evidence of the predatory relationship of human life toward the natural world. The county seat of MacLain, seven miles from Morgana, is a pleasing town, and yet Virgie is aware of the callousness of having turned Virgil MacLain's deer park into a row of stores, a theater, and a cemetery, a process described as "a cataract of the eye over what was once transparent and bright" (273). Because of her knowledge, a perception that is essentially political because it unmasks decisions driven by money and power, Virgie is increasingly isolated from the community of Morgana.

Still, even as her perspective is increasingly alienated from the town's social rituals, Virgie is deeply moved by Morgana's transcendent beauty and the mystery of creation embodied in its life. After the guests have departed following her mother's funeral, Virgie looks out over the "shimmering world" at the end of September. In this crucial section of the narrative, Virgie reveals to us that her vision has widened to include a realm of life coterminous with yet distant from Morgana as she has known it. During her swim past the old MacLain place, in a section of water still lit by the late afternoon sun, Virgie reveals that it is "like walking into sky," and she experiences a perception of matter as translucent. Everything, including the river, herself, and the sky, are "vessels which the sun filled" (248). The sand, shells, grass, and mud of the river are "like suggestions and withdrawals of some bondage that might have been dear" (248), a dismemberment and loss that "might" have been cherished but which she has chosen to reject or which it has happened that she has rejected. She is only a little "dappled" by memory, a slight agitation like that of the mild September wind on the water's surface. Careless, she allows herself to flow with the river, merging her body with the water and closing her eyes. She trembles at the passing of a fish or snake across her knees. Floating in the middle of the river that is almost without current, she feels suspended as she would be in "felicity." Only the appearance of a magical cloud, like some messenger from Zeus, prompts her to pull herself from the river and return home. The next day Virgie wakes early enough to see the morning star, and Venus watches her work of cutting the overgrown grass with domestic sewing shears, an act that is both leisurely and fierce. In an incisive description of grief that captures the mourner's anger and loss, Welty writes that it was "as though for a long time she had been extremely angry and had wept many tears" (250). Finally, Virgie can permit herself to forego the cutting of her mother's overgrown grass, this furious but indispensable gesture of release having done its work.

Like Miss Eckhart, Virgie comes to recognize and accept the fact that human existence is invariably tragic. Virgie's return home from Memphis at seventeen after the death of her father and of her brother in the First World War had made her more aware of oppositions, of coming from city to small town, but also of opposites coming together, and particularly aware that "hope and despair were the closest blood" (265). The image that Welty uses to describe Virgie's early vision of tragedy is that tableau in which Virgie is suspended in air as she jumps from the high step of the train that brings her home; she is once again in flight but this time a flight that involves return. As Welty writes: "in that interim between train and home, she walked and ran looking about her in a kind of glory, by the back way" (265). Virgie's "back way" to glory, as it turns out, is the only way, for it is a glory unknown to Jinny Love or Cassie or even to Ran or Eugene MacLain.

On the night of her mother's funeral, Virgie is troubled by the arrival of an old lady, a stranger who brings a flower from her night-blooming cereus. Like Virgie, the cereus will "endure the night" but wilt to the shape of a "wrung chicken's neck" in the day: that is, like Virgie the flower has in its nature both beauty and death, as well as a remarkable facility for expressing this paradox. The stranger speaks of hearing Virgie play the piano at the picture show and reawakens a memory of her past life as child and daughter and her former closeness to nature. Troubled, Virgie walks into the yard to her car where she keeps a pistol and a cache of cigarettes and begins smoking. In the night, Virgie is surrounded by the noise of barking dogs. The tension of this sequence, which culminates on the day of her mother's funeral, summons up for Virgie the distance of her childhood, the loss of the unique joy embodied in music, and the transience of life. Like Virgie, the cereus will shrivel in the daylight and can only bloom like a single pale soul surrounded by its darkness. All of these elements speak to Virgie's situation as one alone in her mother's house, isolated within the community, and increasingly separated from the natural world itself, but they also speak to her strength and triumph in living self-consciously and bravely.

By contrasting Virgie Rainey with Miss Eckhart and with other characters in ***The Golden Apples,*** Welty allows the reader to experience the painful heroism of her struggle for life. Among the characters with whom Virgie is closely compared is Easter, one of the orphan girls in **"Moon Lake."** To the girls from conventional homes, Easter embodies an imprudent power and an almost unbelievable ignorance of social propriety. On the other hand, the Morgana girls find that orphans such as Easter possess a knowledge of life well beyond their own experience, truly an Easter-like resurrection of life, and some at least sense the importance of acquiring this knowledge. The orphanage girls are pictured as socially isolated until befriended by Nina; it is not only their "dumb" quality of not speaking, as the Morgana girls do all too glibly, but also their knowledge that makes them "truly alone," though envied to some degree for their freedom from social restrictions. As Nina thought, "The reason orphans were the way they were lay first in nobody's watching them" (127).

The "unwatched" orphanage girls are "not answerable to a soul on earth. Nobody cared!" (127). Like Virgie Rainey, Easter carries a "pure" odor of sweat that links her with the physical level of nature and that suggests a kind of innocence. As with all of Welty's characters who move beyond the genteel limitations of Morgana, Easter reveals a frank openness regarding the physical level of existence. After Nina follows Easter on a shortcut to the lake, leaving Jinny Love behind temporarily, the two girls enter a dark, threatening swamp: "It was like being inside the chest of something that breathed and might turn over" (128). Being thus inside, incorporated within the body of a living creature, is among the most familiar of human myths: a motif associated with transformation. As with the biblical story of Jonah, the time spent inside the beast is a necessary stage on the way to a state in which the survivor of this incorporation assumes a greater power by miraculously emerging from the beast's maw. Entering the swamp, Nina and Easter partake of the vital but alarming power of the swamp, even as they are swallowed up by it.

At this point Easter prints her name as "Esther," thus establishing a further mythic lineage. Easter's life-giving qualities are suggested by her biblical namesake, the beautiful and exotic woman who marries King Ahasuerus, displacing his previous wife. Like the Old Testament Esther, Easter harbors a power of life and death as well as a sensuality that the more conventional young women of Morgana lack. Like the biblical figure, she is in essence a moon goddess who embodies both death and rebirth, and it may be that her feast replicates the celebration of the Egyptian moon goddess, Thoth. Also like Esther, who preserves herself and her people by disguise—not at first revealing herself as a Jew and then posing as the daughter of Mordecai—Easter engages in a form of deception that sustains life. Esther's tale speaks of primal fears of annihilation and of the need for self-preservation. By way of the two royal decrees, scripted by Haman and Mordecai, respectively, the narrative endorses a policy of survival in the face of ever-present threats. The feast of Purim, instituted at the end of the Book of Esther, ensures the timeless celebration of this determination to survive. In a similar manner, Welty's Easter/Esther refuses to accept the premature death sentence that life has issued her. She rises out of death just as Esther's people escape Haman's plans for their extermination.

But Welty's Esther is also Easter, a scapegoat who suffers her own crucifixion and resurrection. As an orphan, she is outside of the conventional family structure and excluded from the conventional social life of Morgana, yet in this way she is spared the restrictiveness of middle-class respectability. Her social existence is a form of absence, but also a kind of freedom. The lack and fullness that she, as an orphan, represents to the girls from conventional families raises troubling questions for them regarding the security of their own families and of the continuance of known social relationships altogether. Especially with her "drowning," Easter's unconventional existence and her presumed childhood death present the other girls with the specter of their own potential destruction. The knowledge that might be gained from Easter's "drowning," however, is redemptive rather than destructive, for it is a knowledge of the negative potentiality of the world of experience that is crucial for development of any sort of mature personality. Still, however much the implication of her misfortune insinuates itself into their consciousness, the impulse of the more fortunate girls is to deny the lesson that it presents to them and even to deny Easter's very existence. Jinny Love, the most limited of the Morgana girls, asserts that "Easter's just not a real name. It doesn't matter how she spells it, Nina, nobody ever had it. Not around here." To which Easter responds, "I have it" (133).

Upon the girls' arrival at Moon Lake, one senses that a process of transformation is underway. The lake's surface, where the girls have waded in the daylight, is broken by the splash of a devilishly frightening snake dropping from a tree limb into the Edenic waters. When Easter, without apparent forethought, leads the girls to a leaky boat, Nina, "taking a strange and heady initiative," pictures the three girls far out on the lake. Holding the boat back with her powerful hands, Nina envisions the image of a pear: a sensuous but fleeting delicacy, "beautiful, symmetrical, clean pears with thin skins, with snow-white flesh so juicy and tender that to eat one baptized the whole face, and so delicate that while you urgently ate the first half, the second half was already beginning to turn brown" (131). This headlong voyage toward experience figured in Nina's imagination, however, is halted by the rusty chain attaching the boat to the bank, forestalling the voyage into this terrible fruition. With a sense of relief and vindication, Jinny Love returns to her childish building of sandcastles.

The magical quality of the boat was its hesitation, its majestic slowness. In the boat one felt that the world seemed to drift and not merely the boat. All the world—the abundance of fireflies, the distant light of the stars, the luminous moon, the match that Easter strikes, and the sun that burns Jinny Love's pale skin—centers on the image of Moon Lake itself. The lake seems "to run like a river" in the moonlight; it is not a static body of water but a movement embodying change, its reputedly depthless sections carefully marked off from where the girls may swim. Snakes, both venomous and not, play in the lake, luminous with vital existence but mysterious and unfamiliar, and in this sense threatening. Sleeping by the luminous lake, this image of beauty and change, Nina lies awake imagining "the other way to live, the secret way of the orphan" (138).

Among the Morgana girls, Nina in particular is fascinated by Easter's quality of license. As Easter lies asleep on the cot, her hand hanging with palm upward, Nina stretches her arms opposite Easter's and, of itself, her hand seems to open. She lies there looking at her hand stretched out in the same receptive gesture toward the night as Easter's, and when Nina sleeps, she dreams that her hand is "helpless to the tearing teeth of wild beasts" (139). (Compare Cassie's "gloved hand" in adulthood, or Jinny Love, who shows off her diamond in **"The Wanderers."**) The relationship of the girls' hands toward the night, imagined as a giant or beast that the girls command to approach, reflects a primitive impulse to reach toward and close upon prey, but Nina's dream of her hand being torn while she sleeps connotes the risk, perhaps unknown to the imprudent Easter, of the danger of extending one's hand toward a larger or more violent predator than oneself.

Within this story, the consciousness of the human relationship as predator to prey (which may also be predator) is revealed only to Nina, and the potential violence that Nina glimpses is underlined by the scene in which Easter nearly drowns. After Loch Morrison pulls Easter from the lake, Loch and Miss Moody, with Jinny Love wonderfully "bearing an arm," carry Easter to a picnic table, a place of crucifixion and communion that "was itself still mostly tree" (143). (Here the group was preparing to eat watermelon.) Believing that Easter is dead, Nina faints while contemplating the outstretched arm that rests palm up in the gesture of the night before, and her body is placed head-to-toe alongside Easter's. Momentarily, as Nina awakens, she realizes the terror of her situation: lying next to the "dead" girl on the table, closely surrounded by a group of horrified onlookers, Nina is at that moment Easter's double. Both of them are the sacrificial host of life's communion. Realizing that Easter's freedom is a dangerous thing that can easily lead to destruction, Nina's impulse on waking is to revert to the security of "so much she loved at home" (150), and among the group Nina in particular "hates" Easter after she is "dead" since she so painfully dramatizes the possibility of her own extinction. Within this primordial psychic economy, the single loss bespeaks loss not only of the individual but of the group as a whole. There is also that most haunting fear of the human imagination, the prospect of the vengeance of the dead on the living: "Was there danger that Easter, turned in on herself, might call out to them after all, from the other side of it?" (150). Anxiously the group speculates that Easter's fall into the lake "bathed her so purely in blue for that long moment" (151), the same blue in which San Francisco is bathed as Eugene leads the Spaniard toward the western ocean, that she is irretrievably lost to the living. Welty's narrator stresses the group's primal urge to remove the corpse from threatening proximity to the living, yet just at the moment when the resented corpse has been cast off, Easter gasps, kicks Loch Morrison off the table, and sits up, resting her head on her knees. The rehearsal of future lament and burial rites, things belonging to the adult world, is cut short as, miraculously, Easter is called back to life.

Nina feels a sense of mystery has been released as well when the girls, at Nina's request, carry her body from the table; something hard, cruel and murderous is revealed. This mystery may refer to the dangerous freedom that Nina now admits, a risk more forbidding than the adventure imagined by the three silhouetted girls on Moon Lake. The actual moment of dropping through blue space, repeating the sense of levitation that Nina imagined in connection with the boat the night before, parallels the dangerous exhilaration of plunging into water. With its suggestion of a baptism, the lake surface now is darkened "like the water of a rimmed well" (155), an allusion to Esther at the well made explicit. The little device of Nina's cup, that leaky folding instrument that contrasts with Easter's less genteel but more efficient method of taking water with her palms, is also suggestive of a relationship to the waters of life: mediating between lake and drinker, Nina's cup is an emblem of the town girls' playful detachment from life. Ostensibly sanitizing, its actual function is as an object of display; it is a child's version of the more costly objects that adults acquire to separate themselves, literally and symbolically, from the fierce waters of life.

Moving from **"June Recital"** and **"Moon Lake"** to **"The Whole World Knows,"** Welty's reader better understands the worrying possibilities implied in the earlier stories. After his separation from Jinny, Ran MacLain runs off with Maideen Sumrall to Vicksburg, nineteen miles from Morgana. Elements of the landscape suggest a point of entry into a debased underworld: Vicksburg is located in a "tunnel" and the barge where they drink rum cokes is a place of emptiness and desperation. The river itself is full of reptiles, fishes, trash, uprooted trees, and man's "throw-aways" that, taken together, create an odor that overpowers Ran. The stars of Morgana appear distant and thin, and at the river the road ends suddenly without any apparent destination. An unexplained shot rings out, foreshadowing the ending of the story. Even in her drunken condition, Maideen realizes that they are "lost" in a way that, she assumes, one is "never lost" in Morgana.

Maideen's sense of loss is an accurate gauge of the risks involved in stepping completely outside one's inherited system of values. What she intuits, and what leads to her sudden death, is the impossibility of any human survival outside an inherited cultural tradition, for this separation involves not only the uncertainty or unease of alienation from familiar things: it is a rejection of the essential instinct for order, justice, and truth that gives meaning to human life. To step abruptly beyond all cultural traditions—even assuming that this would be possible—would alienate one not only from familiar society but from one's particular mode of rationality, isolating one not merely from a way of life but from any means of conceiving of a way of life. Like Richard Wright's "outsider," Damon Cross, a person outside all cultural tradition would face an unlimited number of possible choices and an infinite and constantly shifting basis of rationality in making those choices. He would not only be "lost" as Ran and Maideen are when they arrive at Sunset Oaks, but would be doomed within an underworld of indeterminacy and ambiguity.

It is exactly this destiny that awaits the lovers at Sunset Oaks, a desolate half-circle of whitewashed cabins symbolic of a bloodless underworld, complete with its keeper, a black child leaning on the gate prepared to ferry them across to their doom. Still, even this shabby, anonymous ruin seems not lifeless enough for Ran, who comments that the night is not dark enough (he especially dislikes August, the month of falling stars, because it is never completely dark). Though human self-contempt may pursue its doom to such a place as Sunset Oaks, nature cannot be silenced, and even here it speaks in the night of fruition and beauty. In contrast, Ran's rejection of Maideen, his horror of being touched, and his radical desire for complete isolation betray a human being utterly at odds with life. He tells us: "I got down in the bed and pointed the pistol at her, without much hope, the way I used to lie cherishing a dream in the morning, and she the way Jinny would come pull me out of it" (180).

In the dark cabin Ran confuses Maideen with Jinny, but it is not only Jinny and Maideen but all women that threaten the misguided selfhood that leads to his failed suicide attempt. Since intimacy requires commitment to a definite object of affection and affiliation, the touch that Ran shrinks from threatens to restrict his future to one definite purpose and meaning. It opens the possibility of new life, but it obligates Ran to be seen, to step into the light that he so dislikes, and to take on the risk of love. Paradoxically, to forestall the possibility of this kind of joy and the pain of its possible loss, Ran is willing to forfeit his life: death is preferable to his terrible anxiety over failure. When Ran awakens, however, he finds that Maideen has killed herself, "cheating" him in the same way that Jinny did by her adultery. He then calls on his father and brother: "What you went and found, was it better than this?" (181). The answer in both cases, I believe, is "no."

Both **"The Whole World Knows"** and **"Music from Spain"** involve a serious rupture of the conventional social restraints that, in Welty's view, mask but, as it turns out, also restrain a hidden world of ego and aggression. The latter story centers on the consequences of Eugene's slap to his wife, Emma, a year after the death of their daughter. Like his brother Ran, Eugene has been burdened by a painful self-consciousness, and he finds this burden has become intolerable since the death of Ran. Having left for work, Eugene commutes into downtown San Francisco but finds himself "shadowed" by his act of violence. The force of this shadowing implies that he lacks the strength to hold himself as an equal in society. Even in his marriage, Emma is indomitable; in the event of a quarrel, "she would be unfair, beg the question . . . she would cry" (184). In a Kafkaesque passage Welty describes how the timorous Eugene realizes that he could have hurt her more by not eating, but "he wouldn't have dared not to eat—under any circumstances" (185).

Then comes the startling revelation that the slap was "like kissing the cheek of the dead" (187). What does it mean to say that the violence of the slap is like "kissing the cheek of the dead"? What emotion is invested in that final gesture of kissing the corpse that lies unmoved like marble, unresponsive to our love? The relationship of Eugene and Emma is like that of the living to the dead, one marked on the part of the living by constant fear of the jealousy and retribution of the dead. Following the death of their child, Emma has become a corpse, and Eugene is "guilty" simply because he is alive.

Welty's portrayal of Eugene and Emma implies that violence underlies the everyday life of human beings in society, especially within the family, and in his brief holiday from domesticity Eugene experiences an epiphany concerning the ambiguous nature of social institutions such as marriage. As he wanders the streets of San Francisco, Eugene notices "that Market had through the years become a street of trusses, pads, braces, false bosoms, false teeth, and eyeglasses" (187). The groceries of the past have been replaced by stores that accommodate an aging population of symbolical corpses; the new establishments cater to a population that is a sort of "walking dead." In these new stores, body parts replace, prop up, or beautify the failing human anatomy. A health food store displays shark liver oil pellets for similar purposes. Mixed in with these "restorative" establishments are jewelry stores that sell gems and gold, a fact that Eugene feels should make a man "ashamed" (188). As Canetti points out, "justice begins with the recognition of the necessity of sharing" (*Crowds* 191). In these terms, jewelry is a kind of "booty" that the woman employs to display her status and power. Almost by definition, it is something that cannot be shared. Ironically, Eugene works as a watch repairman at a jewelry store that, he believes, is "more respectable than most of the jewelry stores" (189). His rationalization of his role in society, however, seems weak, given his "shame" at jewelry stores in general and his repressed need to rebel against a system in which jewelry performs a central symbolical function.

Eugene's entire life, in fact, is characterized by a sense of heedless flight away from all sources of control and authority. This flight has carried him as far away from Morgana as possible, to the very edge of the continent and to a culture antithetical to his own. In contrast with Morgana, San Francisco is depicted as an impersonal urban setting in which Eugene hopes to "dissolve" into the crowd. Nonetheless, Eugene harbors a masochistic desire to return, in imagination at least, to the place that he associates with his father's tyranny. Despite his flight from home, Eugene still wants to be the child receiving punishment, and he longs for the Mississippi winter that Welty describes as "patched" and "lost." Even when he was young, Eugene spoke in ways "strangely spitely or ambiguous," sarcastic toward King though loving toward his mother. Welty writes that "he bothered no one" (273), an ambiguous comment that is repeated and that sums up Welty's great misgivings concerning Eugene. He dies early, some time after his grandfather, Virgil, and he is buried anonymously; not even his wife attends his funeral.

Throughout his life, Eugene has been in flight from his father and yet controlled by King's distant authority. Eugene separates himself from Morgana more completely than does any other character in the novel, but he is perhaps more fully controlled by it than anyone else. In his encounter with the Spanish musician, Eugene's relationship to his father is projected onto a strange figure who summons up all facets of the filial relationship: Eugene's total submission; his erotic desire; his repressed violence; his inability to detach his own from his father's personality. As Welty writes, Eugene's relationship to the Spaniard represents a turning back toward the "great fatherly barrel of chest." While the Spaniard's animalistic nature, like that of King MacLain, is disturbing, Eugene is fascinated by the freedom and authority of this Perseus-like figure. As the afternoon sun declines and bathes the city in blue, the Spaniard as "conductor" looks toward the city and raises his hand in a gesture that duplicates Perseus's lifting of the Medusa head. At this point, Eugene thinks: "He looked wonderful with his arm raised." Like the blue of the lake on which Virgie Rainey senses herself floating, the blue light of San Francisco points toward an ecstatic but fiercely demanding freedom, its beauty so striking because of its admission of risk. As a passionate embrace of life and its dangers, the Spaniard's gesture seems "wonderful" to Eugene, but it suggests an act of courage that is beyond his power. Eugene, after all, is the watch repairman who feels compelled to "memorize" the city so that he will be able to "rebuild" it after the next earthquake. He is a fearful and self-protective individual, quite the opposite of his father and of the mysterious Spaniard.

In the important final section of the novel, **"The Wanderers,"** Virgie Rainey recalls the same gesture of impassioned triumph as it appeared in the dark painting of Perseus and the Medusa's head that was hung on Miss Eckhart's walls. Significantly, Virgie views "the heroic act" of cutting off the Medusa's head differently from Miss Eckhart: not as a "prophet" but "in their time, like hearing them" (275). The three moments in one that Virgie comprehends—"the beauty, and the sword stroke, and the terror"—contained the "damnation," the condition of the present, a moment like her apprehension of the stars that she focuses on so often and reads with her heart. No longer hating Miss Eckhart, Virgie realizes the immense value of the "gift" that her teacher has offered: a discovery of hate and love abiding together. Though she is not able to prophesy or teach what she knows, Virgie now understands the fierce rapture of existence that Miss Eckhart has taught her: the "beauty" of life; the "sword stroke" like the movement of a pendulum measuring time; the "terror" of realizing that great beauty and great loss abide together. With this realization, Virgie must now live within time, experiencing the full tragedy of the human condition but without passing on the burden of her pain to another.

Finally, standing in the rain under a chinaberry tree, Virgie is left "with her modesty seeming to spread out over the entire world" (277). In the company of an old beggar woman, the world beating in their ears, Virgie listens to the magical rhythm of rain. For J. A. Bryant, Jr., the significance of this scene is that "it brings [Virgie] to a recognition that wandering itself is fulfillment" (313). Certainly, as many critics have noted, Virgie is in some sense a wanderer like King MacLain, but in the end she must find her fulfillment in something more rewarding than wandering. She is not to be another King MacLain, nor another Eugene, nor even another Miss Eckhart. Finally, Virgie discovers a way of fulfillment that includes both the freedom of the wanderer and the security of home. One is left with a sense of integration but not into the community of Morgana, which Virgie is preparing to leave, nor merely into the impersonal wasteland that Eugene has so fruitlessly explored. It is an integration that includes the legacies of tradition and history and myth, yet preserves her particular selfhood distinct from that of others. In the end, more so than any other, Virgie is a character who can be described in terms of creative self-transformation.

Specifically, Virgie's power is what Elias Canetti describes as "circular" transformation. Like the example Canetti cites of Proteus, the Wise Old Man of the Sea in the *Odyssey,* Virgie's relationship to place is circular since it comprises a sort of flight that is nonetheless static. Virgie is hunted by her community and by its adherence to convention, yet Virgie's reaction to this pursuit is not *physical* flight. As Canetti points out, stressing the importance of remaining in one place, "Everything happens on one spot. Each transformation is an attempt to break out in another shape, in a different direction, as it were: but each is fruitless and ends where it begins" (*Crowds* 344-345).

In Canetti's words, transformation has the aim of "loosening of the grip." One of the most common means of transformation involves taking on the shape of a dead creature; the pursued hopes to be given up as dead and thus, having been mistaken for dead, to live. Given the hostile environment in which Virgie and all of humanity exist, one can understand the necessity of such a radical survival strategy. It is a strategy, however, that goes well beyond simple deception intended to throw a predator, whether animal or human, off the track. By its very nature, this mimicry of death awakens the human understanding to philosophical issues beyond mere physical gratification or even survival itself. For this reason Canetti notes the extent to which creative transformation involves an accompanying "transition from processes of an erotic to a religious nature" (*Crowds* 346). This ultimate transformation, a freedom that results from an enactment of death, inevitably leads one away from an impulsive vivacity—the "wildness" that characterized Virgie at the beginning—toward a more genuine vitality resulting from the passage from life to death and back. Like Perseus, Virgie Rainey will lift her arm in triumph, but she will do more: she will participate in life even as she appreciates the momentous nature of her performance; she will lift her arm in triumph even as she suffers the burden of the Medusa's head in her grasp.

Works Cited

Bryant, J. A., Jr. "Seeing Double in *The Golden Apples.*" *Sewanee Review* 82 (Spring 1974): 300-315.

Canetti, Elias. *Crowds and Power.* Trans. Carol Stewart. New York: Farrar Straus Giroux, 1984.

Marrs, Suzanne. *One Writer's Imagination: The Fiction of Eudora Welty.* Baton Rouge: Louisiana State UP, 2002.

McHaney, Thomas L. "Eudora Welty and the Multitudinous Golden Apples." *Mississippi Quarterly* 26 (Fall 1973): 589-624.

Welty, Eudora. *The Golden Apples.* 1947. New York: Harvest, n.d.

FURTHER READING

Criticism

Johnston, Carol Ann. "Eudora Welty: The Eye of Her Stories." In *Eudora Welty: A Study of the Short Fiction,* pp. 3-15. New York: Twayne Publishers, 1997.

Discusses Welty's stories in view of the author's essays on writing.

McWhirter, David. "Eudora Welty: 'A Real Familiar Stranger.'" *South Central Review* 14, no. 2 (summer 1997): 1-2.

Comments on the minimization of Welty in some literary circles.

Nissen, Axel. "Queer Welty, Camp Welty." *Mississippi Quarterly* 56, no. 2 (spring 2003): 209-29.

Contrasts *The Optimist's Daughter* with Susan Sontag's essay "Notes on Camp."

Wolff, Sally. "'How Babies Could Come' and 'How They Could Die': Eudora Welty's Children of the Dark Cradle." *Mississippi Quarterly* 56, no. 2 (spring 2003): 251-67.

Locates autobiographical sources for Welty's concerns with sexuality and motherhood.

Additional coverage of Welty's life and career is contained in the following sources published by Gale: *American Writers*; *American Writers Retrospective Supplement,* Vol. 1; *Authors and Artists for Young Adults,* Vol. 48; *Beacham's Encyclopedia of Popular Fiction: Biography & Resources,* Vol. 3; *Concise Dictionary of American Literary Biography,* 1941-1968; *Concise Major 21st-Century Writers,* Ed. 1; *Contemporary Authors,* Vols. 9-12R, 199; *Contemporary Authors Bibliographical Series,* Vol. 1; *Contemporary Authors New Revision Series,* Vols. 32, 65, 128; *Contemporary Literary Criticism,* Vols. 1, 2, 5, 14, 22, 33, 105, 220; *Contemporary Novelists,* Eds. 1, 2, 3, 4, 5, 6, 7; *Contemporary Southern Writers*; *Dictionary of Literary Biography,* Vols. 2, 102, 143; *Dictionary of Literary Biography Documentary Series,* Vol. 12; *Dictionary of Literary Biography Yearbook,* 1987, 2001; *DISCovering Authors*; *DISCovering Authors: British Edition*; *DISCovering Authors: Canadian Edition*; *DISCovering Authors Modules: Most-Studied Authors* and *Novelists*; *DISCovering Authors 3.0*; *Encyclopedia of World Literature in the 20th Century,* Ed. 3; *Exploring Short Stories*; *Literature and Its Times,* Vol. 3; *Literature Resource Center*; *Major 20th-Century Writers,* Eds. 1, 2; *Major 21st-Century Writers,* eBook 2005; *Modern American Literature,* Ed. 5; *Modern American Women Writers*; *Novels for Students,* Vols. 13, 15; *Reference Guide to American Literature,* Ed. 4; *Reference Guide to Short Fiction,* Ed. 2; *St. James Guide to Horror, Ghost & Gothic Writers*; *Short Stories for Students,* Vols. 2, 10; *Short Story Criticism,* Vols. 1, 27, 51; *Twayne's United States Authors*; *20th Century Romance and Historical Writers*; and *World Literature Criticism,* Vol. 6.

How to Use This Index

The main references

Calvino, Italo 1923-1985 .... **CLC 5, 8, 11, 22, 33, 39, 73; SSC 3, 48**

list all author entries in the following Gale Literary Criticism series:

AAL = *Asian American Literature*
BG = *The Beat Generation: A Gale Critical Companion*
BLC = *Black Literature Criticism*
BLCS = *Black Literature Criticism Supplement*
CLC = *Contemporary Literary Criticism*
CLR = *Children's Literature Review*
CMLC = *Classical and Medieval Literature Criticism*
DC = *Drama Criticism*
FL = *Feminism in Literature: A Gale Critical Companion*
GL = *Gothic Literature: A Gale Critical Companion*
HLC = *Hispanic Literature Criticism*
HLCS = *Hispanic Literature Criticism Supplement*
HR = *Harlem Renaissance: A Gale Critical Companion*
LC = *Literature Criticism from 1400 to 1800*
NCLC = *Nineteenth-Century Literature Criticism*
NNAL = *Native North American Literature*
PC = *Poetry Criticism*
SSC = *Short Story Criticism*
TCLC = *Twentieth-Century Literary Criticism*
WLC = *World Literature Criticism, 1500 to the Present*
WLCS = *World Literature Criticism Supplement*

The cross-references

See also CA 85-88, 116; CANR 23, 61; DAM NOV; DLB 196; EW 13; MTCW 1, 2; RGSF 2; RGWL 2; SFW 4; SSFS 12

list all author entries in the following Gale biographical and literary sources:

AAYA = *Authors & Artists for Young Adults*
AFAW = *African American Writers*
AFW = *African Writers*
AITN = *Authors in the News*
AMW = *American Writers*
AMWR = *American Writers Retrospective Supplement*
AMWS = *American Writers Supplement*
ANW = *American Nature Writers*
AW = *Ancient Writers*
BEST = *Bestsellers*
BPFB = *Beacham's Encyclopedia of Popular Fiction: Biography and Resources*
BRW = *British Writers*
BRWS = *British Writers Supplement*
BW = *Black Writers*
BYA = *Beacham's Guide to Literature for Young Adults*
CA = *Contemporary Authors*
CAAS = *Contemporary Authors Autobiography Series*
CABS = *Contemporary Authors Bibliographical Series*
CAD = *Contemporary American Dramatists*
CANR = *Contemporary Authors New Revision Series*
CAP = *Contemporary Authors Permanent Series*
CBD = *Contemporary British Dramatists*
CCA = *Contemporary Canadian Authors*
CD = *Contemporary Dramatists*
CDALB = *Concise Dictionary of American Literary Biography*

CDALBS = *Concise Dictionary of American Literary Biography Supplement*
CDBLB = *Concise Dictionary of British Literary Biography*
CMW = *St. James Guide to Crime & Mystery Writers*
CN = *Contemporary Novelists*
CP = *Contemporary Poets*
CPW = *Contemporary Popular Writers*
CSW = *Contemporary Southern Writers*
CWD = *Contemporary Women Dramatists*
CWP = *Contemporary Women Poets*
CWRI = *St. James Guide to Children's Writers*
CWW = *Contemporary World Writers*
DA = *DISCovering Authors*
DA3 = *DISCovering Authors 3.0*
DAB = *DISCovering Authors: British Edition*
DAC = *DISCovering Authors: Canadian Edition*
DAM = *DISCovering Authors: Modules*
DRAM: *Dramatists Module;* ***MST:*** *Most-studied Authors Module;*
MULT: *Multicultural Authors Module;* ***NOV:*** *Novelists Module;*
POET: *Poets Module;* ***POP:*** *Popular Fiction and Genre Authors Module*
DFS = *Drama for Students*
DLB = *Dictionary of Literary Biography*
DLBD = *Dictionary of Literary Biography Documentary Series*
DLBY = *Dictionary of Literary Biography Yearbook*
DNFS = *Literature of Developing Nations for Students*
EFS = *Epics for Students*
EXPN = *Exploring Novels*
EXPP = *Exploring Poetry*
EXPS = *Exploring Short Stories*
EW = *European Writers*
FANT = *St. James Guide to Fantasy Writers*
FW = *Feminist Writers*
GFL = *Guide to French Literature,* Beginnings to 1789, 1798 to the Present
GLL = *Gay and Lesbian Literature*
HGG = *St. James Guide to Horror, Ghost & Gothic Writers*
HW = *Hispanic Writers*
IDFW = *International Dictionary of Films and Filmmakers: Writers and Production Artists*
IDTP = *International Dictionary of Theatre: Playwrights*
LAIT = *Literature and Its Times*
LAW = *Latin American Writers*
JRDA = *Junior DISCovering Authors*
MAICYA = *Major Authors and Illustrators for Children and Young Adults*
MAICYAS = *Major Authors and Illustrators for Children and Young Adults Supplement*
MAWW = *Modern American Women Writers*
MJW = *Modern Japanese Writers*
MTCW = *Major 20th-Century Writers*
NCFS = *Nonfiction Classics for Students*
NFS = *Novels for Students*
PAB = *Poets: American and British*
PFS = *Poetry for Students*
RGAL = *Reference Guide to American Literature*
RGEL = *Reference Guide to English Literature*
RGSF = *Reference Guide to Short Fiction*
RGWL = *Reference Guide to World Literature*
RHW = *Twentieth-Century Romance and Historical Writers*
SAAS = *Something about the Author Autobiography Series*
SATA = *Something about the Author*
SFW = *St. James Guide to Science Fiction Writers*
SSFS = *Short Stories for Students*
TCWW = *Twentieth-Century Western Writers*
WLIT = *World Literature and Its Times*
WP = *World Poets*
YABC = *Yesterday's Authors of Books for Children*
YAW = *St. James Guide to Young Adult Writers*

Literary Criticism Series Cumulative Author Index

Aeschines c. 390B.C.-c. 320B.C. .... **CMLC 47**
See also DLB 176

Aeschylus 525(?)B.C.-456(?)B.C. .. **CMLC 11, 51, 94; DC 8; WLCS**
See also AW 1; CDWLB 1; DA; DAB; DAC; DAM DRAM, MST; DFS 5, 10; DLB 176; LMFS 1; RGWL 2, 3; TWA; WLIT 8

Aesop 620(?)B.C.-560(?)B.C. .... **CMLC 24**
See also CLR 14; MAICYA 1, 2; SATA 64

Affable Hawk
See MacCarthy, Sir (Charles Otto) Desmond

Africa, Ben
See Bosman, Herman Charles

Afton, Effie
See Harper, Frances Ellen Watkins

Agapida, Fray Antonio
See Irving, Washington

Agee, James (Rufus) 1909-1955 ...... **TCLC 1, 19, 180**
See also AAYA 44; AITN 1; AMW; CA 148; CAAE 108; CANR 131; CDALB 1941-1968; DAM NOV; DLB 2, 26, 152; DLBY 1989; EWL 3; LAIT 3; LATS 1:2; MAL 5; MTCW 2; MTFW 2005; NFS 22; RGAL 4; TUS

A Gentlewoman in New England
See Bradstreet, Anne

A Gentlewoman in Those Parts
See Bradstreet, Anne

Aghill, Gordon
See Silverberg, Robert

Agnon, S(hmuel) Y(osef Halevi) 1888-1970 .... **CLC 4, 8, 14; SSC 30; TCLC 151**
See also CA 17-18; CAAS 25-28R; CANR 60, 102; CAP 2; DLB 329; EWL 3; MTCW 1, 2; RGHL; RGSF 2; RGWL 2, 3; WLIT 6

Agrippa von Nettesheim, Henry Cornelius 1486-1535 .... **LC 27**

Aguilera Malta, Demetrio 1909-1981 .... **HLCS 1**
See also CA 124; CAAE 111; CANR 87; DAM MULT, NOV; DLB 145; EWL 3; HW 1; RGWL 3

Agustini, Delmira 1886-1914 .... **HLCS 1**
See also CA 166; DLB 290; HW 1, 2; LAW

Aherne, Owen
See Cassill, R(onald) V(erlin)

Ai 1947- .... **CLC 4, 14, 69; PC 72**
See also CA 85-88; 13; CANR 70; CP 6, 7; DLB 120; PFS 16

Aickman, Robert (Fordyce) 1914-1981 .... **CLC 57**
See also CA 5-8R; CANR 3, 72, 100; DLB 261; HGG; SUFW 1, 2

Aidoo, (Christina) Ama Ata 1942- .... **BLCS; CLC 177**
See also AFW; BW 1; CA 101; CANR 62, 144; CD 5, 6; CDWLB 3; CN 6, 7; CWD; CWP; DLB 117; DNFS 1, 2; EWL 3; FW; WLIT 2

Aiken, Conrad (Potter) 1889-1973 .... **CLC 1, 3, 5, 10, 52; PC 26; SSC 9**
See also AMW; CA 5-8R; CAAS 45-48; CANR 4, 60; CDALB 1929-1941; CN 1; CP 1; DAM NOV, POET; DLB 9, 45, 102; EWL 3; EXPS; HGG; MAL 5; MTCW 1, 2; MTFW 2005; PFS 24; RGAL 4; RGSF 2; SATA 3, 30; SSFS 8; TUS

Aiken, Joan (Delano) 1924-2004 ...... **CLC 35**
See also AAYA 1, 25; CA 182; 9-12R, 182; CAAS 223; CANR 4, 23, 34, 64, 121; CLR 1, 19, 90; DLB 161; FANT; HGG; JRDA; MAICYA 1, 2; MTCW 1; RHW; SAAS 1; SATA 2, 30, 73; SATA-Essay 109; SATA-Obit 152; SUFW 2; WYA; YAW

Ainsworth, William Harrison 1805-1882 .... **NCLC 13**
See also DLB 21; HGG; RGEL 2; SATA 24; SUFW 1

Aitmatov, Chingiz (Torekulovich) 1928- .... **CLC 71**
See Aytmatov, Chingiz
See also CA 103; CANR 38; CWW 2; DLB 302; MTCW 1; RGSF 2; SATA 56

Akers, Floyd
See Baum, L(yman) Frank

Akhmadulina, Bella Akhatovna 1937- .... **CLC 53; PC 43**
See also CA 65-68; CWP; CWW 2; DAM POET; EWL 3

Akhmatova, Anna 1888-1966 ..... **CLC 11, 25, 64, 126; PC 2, 55**
See also CA 19-20; CAAS 25-28R; CANR 35; CAP 1; DA3; DAM POET; DLB 295; EW 10; EWL 3; FL 1:5; MTCW 1, 2; PFS 18, 27; RGWL 2, 3

Aksakov, Sergei Timofeevich 1791-1859 .... **NCLC 2, 181**
See also DLB 198

Aksenov, Vasilii (Pavlovich)
See Aksyonov, Vassily (Pavlovich)
See also CWW 2

Aksenov, Vassily
See Aksyonov, Vassily (Pavlovich)

Akst, Daniel 1956- .... **CLC 109**
See also CA 161; CANR 110

Aksyonov, Vassily (Pavlovich) 1932- .... **CLC 22, 37, 101**
See Aksenov, Vasilii (Pavlovich)
See also CA 53-56; CANR 12, 48, 77; DLB 302; EWL 3

Akutagawa Ryunosuke 1892-1927 ... **SSC 44; TCLC 16**
See also CA 154; CAAE 117; DLB 180; EWL 3; MJW; RGSF 2; RGWL 2, 3

Alabaster, William 1568-1640 .... **LC 90**
See also DLB 132; RGEL 2

Alain 1868-1951 .... **TCLC 41**
See also CA 163; EWL 3; GFL 1789 to the Present

Alain de Lille c. 1116-c. 1203 .... **CMLC 53**
See also DLB 208

Alain-Fournier TCLC 6
See Fournier, Henri-Alban
See also DLB 65; EWL 3; GFL 1789 to the Present; RGWL 2, 3

Al-Amin, Jamil Abdullah 1943- ...... **BLC 1:1**
See also BW 1, 3; CA 125; CAAE 112; CANR 82; DAM MULT

Alanus de Insluis
See Alain de Lille

Alarcon, Pedro Antonio de 1833-1891 .... **NCLC 1; SSC 64**

Alas (y Urena), Leopoldo (Enrique Garcia) 1852-1901 .... **TCLC 29**
See also CA 131; CAAE 113; HW 1; RGSF 2

Albee, Edward (III) 1928- ..... **CLC 1, 2, 3, 5, 9, 11, 13, 25, 53, 86, 113; DC 11; WLC 1**
See also AAYA 51; AITN 1; AMW; CA 5-8R; CABS 3; CAD; CANR 8, 54, 74, 124; CD 5, 6; CDALB 1941-1968; DA; DA3; DAB; DAC; DAM DRAM, MST; DFS 2, 3, 8, 10, 13, 14; DLB 7, 266; EWL 3; INT CANR-8; LAIT 4; LMFS 2; MAL 5; MTCW 1, 2; MTFW 2005; RGAL 4; TUS

Alberti (Merello), Rafael
See Alberti, Rafael
See also CWW 2

Alberti, Rafael 1902-1999 .... **CLC 7**
See Alberti (Merello), Rafael
See also CA 85-88; CAAS 185; CANR 81; DLB 108; EWL 3; HW 2; RGWL 2, 3

Albert the Great 1193(?)-1280 ...... **CMLC 16**
See also DLB 115

Alcaeus c. 620B.C.- .... **CMLC 65**
See also DLB 176

Alcala-Galiano, Juan Valera y
See Valera y Alcala-Galiano, Juan

Alcayaga, Lucila Godoy
See Godoy Alcayaga, Lucila

Alciato, Andrea 1492-1550 .... **LC 116**

Alcott, Amos Bronson 1799-1888 ... **NCLC 1, 167**
See also DLB 1, 223

Alcott, Louisa May 1832-1888 . **NCLC 6, 58, 83; SSC 27, 98; WLC 1**
See also AAYA 20; AMWS 1; BPFB 1; BYA 2; CDALB 1865-1917; CLR 1, 38, 109; DA; DA3; DAB; DAC; DAM MST, NOV; DLB 1, 42, 79, 223, 239, 242; DLBD 14; FL 1:2; FW; JRDA; LAIT 2; MAICYA 1, 2; NFS 12; RGAL 4; SATA 100; TUS; WCH; WYA; YABC 1; YAW

Alcuin c. 730-804 .... **CMLC 69**
See also DLB 148

Aldanov, M. A.
See Aldanov, Mark (Alexandrovich)

Aldanov, Mark (Alexandrovich) 1886-1957 .... **TCLC 23**
See also CA 181; CAAE 118; DLB 317

Aldhelm c. 639-709 .... **CMLC 90**

Aldington, Richard 1892-1962 .... **CLC 49**
See also CA 85-88; CANR 45; DLB 20, 36, 100, 149; LMFS 2; RGEL 2

Aldiss, Brian W. 1925- .. **CLC 5, 14, 40; SSC 36**
See also AAYA 42; CA 190; 5-8R, 190; 2; CANR 5, 28, 64, 121, 168; CN 1, 2, 3, 4, 5, 6, 7; DAM NOV; DLB 14, 261, 271; MTCW 1, 2; MTFW 2005; SATA 34; SCFW 1, 2; SFW 4

Aldiss, Brian Wilson
See Aldiss, Brian W.

Aldrich, Bess Streeter 1881-1954 .... **TCLC 125**
See also CLR 70; TCWW 2

Alegria, Claribel
See Alegria, Claribel
See also CWW 2; DLB 145, 283

Alegria, Claribel 1924- .... **CLC 75; HLCS 1; PC 26**
See Alegria, Claribel
See also CA 131; 15; CANR 66, 94, 134; DAM MULT; EWL 3; HW 1; MTCW 2; MTFW 2005; PFS 21

Alegria, Fernando 1918-2005 .... **CLC 57**
See also CA 9-12R; CANR 5, 32, 72; EWL 3; HW 1, 2

Aleixandre, Vicente 1898-1984 .... **HLCS 1; TCLC 113**
See also CANR 81; DLB 108, 329; EWL 3; HW 2; MTCW 1, 2; RGWL 2, 3

Alekseev, Konstantin Sergeivich
See Stanislavsky, Constantin

Alekseyer, Konstantin Sergeyevich
See Stanislavsky, Constantin

Aleman, Mateo 1547-1615(?) .... **LC 81**

Alencar, Jose de 1829-1877 .... **NCLC 157**
See also DLB 307; LAW; WLIT 1

Alencon, Marguerite d'
See de Navarre, Marguerite

Alepoudelis, Odysseus
See Elytis, Odysseus
See also CWW 2

Aleshkovsky, Joseph 1929-
See Aleshkovsky, Yuz
See also CA 128; CAAE 121

Aleshkovsky, Yuz CLC 44
See Aleshkovsky, Joseph
See also DLB 317
Alexander, Barbara
See Ehrenreich, Barbara
Alexander, Lloyd 1924-2007 .... **CLC 35**
See also AAYA 1, 27; BPFB 1; BYA 5, 6, 7, 9, 10, 11; CA 1-4R; CAAS 260; CANR 1, 24, 38, 55, 113; CLR 1, 5, 48; CWRI 5; DLB 52; FANT; JRDA; MAICYA 1, 2; MAICYAS 1; MTCW 1; SAAS 19; SATA 3, 49, 81, 129, 135; SATA-Obit 182; SUFW; TUS; WYA; YAW
Alexander, Lloyd Chudley
See Alexander, Lloyd
Alexander, Meena 1951- .... **CLC 121**
See also CA 115; CANR 38, 70, 146; CP 5, 6, 7; CWP; DLB 323; FW
Alexander, Samuel 1859-1938 .... **TCLC 77**
Alexeiev, Konstantin
See Stanislavsky, Constantin
Alexeyev, Constantin Sergeivich
See Stanislavsky, Constantin
Alexeyev, Konstantin Sergeyevich
See Stanislavsky, Constantin
Alexie, Sherman 1966- .... **CLC 96, 154; NNAL; PC 53; SSC 107**
See also AAYA 28; BYA 15; CA 138; CANR 65, 95, 133; CN 7; DA3; DAM MULT; DLB 175, 206, 278; LATS 1:2; MTCW 2; MTFW 2005; NFS 17; SSFS 18
Alexie, Sherman Joseph, Jr.
See Alexie, Sherman
al-Farabi 870(?)-950 .... **CMLC 58**
See also DLB 115
Alfau, Felipe 1902-1999 .... **CLC 66**
See also CA 137
Alfieri, Vittorio 1749-1803 .... **NCLC 101**
See also EW 4; RGWL 2, 3; WLIT 7
Alfonso X 1221-1284 .... **CMLC 78**
Alfred, Jean Gaston
See Ponge, Francis
Alger, Horatio, Jr. 1832-1899 .... **NCLC 8, 83**
See also CLR 87; DLB 42; LAIT 2; RGAL 4; SATA 16; TUS
Al-Ghazali, Muhammad ibn Muhammad 1058-1111 .... **CMLC 50**
See also DLB 115
Algren, Nelson 1909-1981 ..... **CLC 4, 10, 33; SSC 33**
See also AMWS 9; BPFB 1; CA 13-16R; CAAS 103; CANR 20, 61; CDALB 1941-1968; CN 1, 2; DLB 9; DLBY 1981, 1982, 2000; EWL 3; MAL 5; MTCW 1, 2; MTFW 2005; RGAL 4; RGSF 2
al-Hamadhani 967-1007 .... **CMLC 93**
See also WLIT 6
al-Hariri, al-Qasim ibn 'Ali Abu Muhammad al-Basri 1054-1122 .... **CMLC 63**
See also RGWL 3
Ali, Ahmed 1908-1998 .... **CLC 69**
See also CA 25-28R; CANR 15, 34; CN 1, 2, 3, 4, 5; DLB 323; EWL 3
Ali, Tariq 1943- .... **CLC 173**
See also CA 25-28R; CANR 10, 99, 161
Alighieri, Dante
See Dante
See also WLIT 7
al-Kindi, Abu Yusuf Ya'qub ibn Ishaq c. 801-c. 873 .... **CMLC 80**
Allan, John B.
See Westlake, Donald E.
Allan, Sidney
See Hartmann, Sadakichi
Allan, Sydney
See Hartmann, Sadakichi
Allard, Janet CLC 59
Allen, Edward 1948- .... **CLC 59**
Allen, Fred 1894-1956 .... **TCLC 87**
Allen, Paula Gunn 1939- .... **CLC 84, 202; NNAL**
See also AMWS 4; CA 143; CAAE 112; CANR 63, 130; CWP; DA3; DAM MULT; DLB 175; FW; MTCW 2; MTFW 2005; RGAL 4; TCWW 2
Allen, Roland
See Ayckbourn, Alan
Allen, Sarah A.
See Hopkins, Pauline Elizabeth
Allen, Sidney H.
See Hartmann, Sadakichi
Allen, Woody 1935- .... **CLC 16, 52, 195**
See also AAYA 10, 51; AMWS 15; CA 33-36R; CANR 27, 38, 63, 128, 172; DAM POP; DLB 44; MTCW 1; SSFS 21
Allende, Isabel 1942- ... **CLC 39, 57, 97, 170; HLC 1; SSC 65; WLCS**
See also AAYA 18, 70; CA 130; CAAE 125; CANR 51, 74, 129, 165; CDWLB 3; CLR 99; CWW 2; DA3; DAM MULT, NOV; DLB 145; DNFS 1; EWL 3; FL 1:5; FW; HW 1, 2; INT CA-130; LAIT 5; LAWS 1; LMFS 2; MTCW 1, 2; MTFW 2005; NCFS 1; NFS 6, 18; RGSF 2; RGWL 3; SATA 163; SSFS 11, 16; WLIT 1
Alleyn, Ellen
See Rossetti, Christina
Alleyne, Carla D. CLC 65
Allingham, Margery (Louise) 1904-1966 .... **CLC 19**
See also CA 5-8R; CAAS 25-28R; CANR 4, 58; CMW 4; DLB 77; MSW; MTCW 1, 2
Allingham, William 1824-1889 ...... **NCLC 25**
See also DLB 35; RGEL 2
Allison, Dorothy E. 1949- .... **CLC 78, 153**
See also AAYA 53; CA 140; CANR 66, 107; CN 7; CSW; DA3; FW; MTCW 2; MTFW 2005; NFS 11; RGAL 4
Alloula, Malek CLC 65
Allston, Washington 1779-1843 .... **NCLC 2**
See also DLB 1, 235
Almedingen, E. M. CLC 12
See Almedingen, Martha Edith von
See also SATA 3
Almedingen, Martha Edith von 1898-1971
See Almedingen, E. M.
See also CA 1-4R; CANR 1
Almodovar, Pedro 1949(?)- .... **CLC 114, 229; HLCS 1**
See also CA 133; CANR 72, 151; HW 2
Almqvist, Carl Jonas Love 1793-1866 .... **NCLC 42**
al-Mutanabbi, Ahmad ibn al-Husayn Abu al-Tayyib al-Jufi al-Kindi 915-965 .... **CMLC 66**
See Mutanabbi, Al-
See also RGWL 3
Alonso, Damaso 1898-1990 .... **CLC 14**
See also CA 131; CAAE 110; CAAS 130; CANR 72; DLB 108; EWL 3; HW 1, 2
Alov
See Gogol, Nikolai (Vasilyevich)
al'Sadaawi, Nawal
See El Saadawi, Nawal
See also FW
al-Shaykh, Hanan 1945- .... **CLC 218**
See Shaykh, al- Hanan
See also CA 135; CANR 111; WLIT 6
Al Siddik
See Rolfe, Frederick (William Serafino Austin Lewis Mary)
See also GLL 1; RGEL 2
Alta 1942- .... **CLC 19**
See also CA 57-60
Alter, Robert B. 1935- .... **CLC 34**
See also CA 49-52; CANR 1, 47, 100, 160
Alter, Robert Bernard
See Alter, Robert B.
Alther, Lisa 1944- .... **CLC 7, 41**
See also BPFB 1; CA 65-68; 30; CANR 12, 30, 51; CN 4, 5, 6, 7; CSW; GLL 2; MTCW 1
Althusser, L.
See Althusser, Louis
Althusser, Louis 1918-1990 .... **CLC 106**
See also CA 131; CAAS 132; CANR 102; DLB 242
Altman, Robert 1925-2006 .... **CLC 16, 116, 242**
See also CA 73-76; CAAS 254; CANR 43
Alurista HLCS 1; PC 34
See Urista (Heredia), Alberto (Baltazar)
See also CA 45-48R; DLB 82; LLW
Alvarez, A. 1929- .... **CLC 5, 13**
See also CA 1-4R; CANR 3, 33, 63, 101, 134; CN 3, 4, 5, 6; CP 1, 2, 3, 4, 5, 6, 7; DLB 14, 40; MTFW 2005
Alvarez, Alejandro Rodriguez 1903-1965
See Casona, Alejandro
See also CA 131; CAAS 93-96; HW 1
Alvarez, Julia 1950- .... **CLC 93; HLCS 1**
See also AAYA 25; AMWS 7; CA 147; CANR 69, 101, 133, 166; DA3; DLB 282; LATS 1:2; LLW; MTCW 2; MTFW 2005; NFS 5, 9; SATA 129; WLIT 1
Alvaro, Corrado 1896-1956 .... **TCLC 60**
See also CA 163; DLB 264; EWL 3
Amado, Jorge 1912-2001 ... **CLC 13, 40, 106, 232; HLC 1**
See also CA 77-80; CAAS 201; CANR 35, 74, 135; CWW 2; DAM MULT, NOV; DLB 113, 307; EWL 3; HW 2; LAW; LAWS 1; MTCW 1, 2; MTFW 2005; RGWL 2, 3; TWA; WLIT 1
Ambler, Eric 1909-1998 .... **CLC 4, 6, 9**
See also BRWS 4; CA 9-12R; CAAS 171; CANR 7, 38, 74; CMW 4; CN 1, 2, 3, 4, 5, 6; DLB 77; MSW; MTCW 1, 2; TEA
Ambrose, Stephen E. 1936-2002 .... **CLC 145**
See also AAYA 44; CA 1-4R; CAAS 209; CANR 3, 43, 57, 83, 105; MTFW 2005; NCFS 2; SATA 40, 138
Amichai, Yehuda 1924-2000 .. **CLC 9, 22, 57, 116; PC 38**
See also CA 85-88; CAAS 189; CANR 46, 60, 99, 132; CWW 2; EWL 3; MTCW 1, 2; MTFW 2005; PFS 24; RGHL; WLIT 6
Amichai, Yehudah
See Amichai, Yehuda
Amiel, Henri Frederic 1821-1881 .... **NCLC 4**
See also DLB 217
Amis, Kingsley 1922-1995 . **CLC 1, 2, 3, 5, 8, 13, 40, 44, 129**
See also AAYA 77; AITN 2; BPFB 1; BRWS 2; CA 9-12R; CAAS 150; CANR 8, 28, 54; CDBLB 1945-1960; CN 1, 2, 3, 4, 5, 6; CP 1, 2, 3, 4; DA; DA3; DAB; DAC; DAM MST, NOV; DLB 15, 27, 100, 139, 326; DLBY 1996; EWL 3; HGG; INT CANR-8; MTCW 1, 2; MTFW 2005; RGEL 2; RGSF 2; SFW 4
Amis, Martin 1949- ... **CLC 4, 9, 38, 62, 101, 213**
See also BEST 90:3; BRWS 4; CA 65-68; CANR 8, 27, 54, 73, 95, 132, 166; CN 5, 6, 7; DA3; DLB 14, 194; EWL 3; INT CANR-27; MTCW 2; MTFW 2005
Amis, Martin Louis
See Amis, Martin
Ammianus Marcellinus c. 330-c. 395 .... **CMLC 60**
See also AW 2; DLB 211

Author Index

Bachelard, Gaston 1884-1962 ...... **TCLC 128**
See also CA 97-100; CAAS 89-92; DLB 296; GFL 1789 to the Present
Bachman, Richard
See King, Stephen
Bachmann, Ingeborg 1926-1973 ..... **CLC 69; TCLC 192**
See also CA 93-96; CAAS 45-48; CANR 69; DLB 85; EWL 3; RGHL; RGWL 2, 3
Bacon, Francis 1561-1626 ..... **LC 18, 32, 131**
See also BRW 1; CDBLB Before 1660; DLB 151, 236, 252; RGEL 2; TEA
Bacon, Roger 1214(?)-1294 .... **CMLC 14**
See also DLB 115
Bacovia, George 1881-1957 .... **TCLC 24**
See Vasiliu, Gheorghe
See also CDWLB 4; DLB 220; EWL 3
Badanes, Jerome 1937-1995 .... **CLC 59**
See also CA 234
Bage, Robert 1728-1801 .... **NCLC 182**
See also DLB 39; RGEL 2
Bagehot, Walter 1826-1877 .... **NCLC 10**
See also DLB 55
Bagnold, Enid 1889-1981 .... **CLC 25**
See also AAYA 75; BYA 2; CA 5-8R; CAAS 103; CANR 5, 40; CBD; CN 2; CWD; CWRI 5; DAM DRAM; DLB 13, 160, 191, 245; FW; MAICYA 1, 2; RGEL 2; SATA 1, 25
Bagritsky, Eduard TCLC 60
See Dzyubin, Eduard Georgievich
Bagrjana, Elisaveta
See Belcheva, Elisaveta Lyubomirova
Bagryana, Elisaveta CLC 10
See Belcheva, Elisaveta Lyubomirova
See also CA 178; CDWLB 4; DLB 147; EWL 3
Bailey, Paul 1937- .... **CLC 45**
See also CA 21-24R; CANR 16, 62, 124; CN 1, 2, 3, 4, 5, 6, 7; DLB 14, 271; GLL 2
Baillie, Joanna 1762-1851 ...... **NCLC 71, 151**
See also DLB 93; GL 2; RGEL 2
Bainbridge, Beryl 1934- ...... **CLC 4, 5, 8, 10, 14, 18, 22, 62, 130**
See also BRWS 6; CA 21-24R; CANR 24, 55, 75, 88, 128; CN 2, 3, 4, 5, 6, 7; DAM NOV; DLB 14, 231; EWL 3; MTCW 1, 2; MTFW 2005
Baker, Carlos (Heard)
1909-1987 .... **TCLC 119**
See also CA 5-8R; CAAS 122; CANR 3, 63; DLB 103
Baker, Elliott 1922-2007 .... **CLC 8**
See also CA 45-48; CAAS 257; CANR 2, 63; CN 1, 2, 3, 4, 5, 6, 7
Baker, Elliott Joseph
See Baker, Elliott
Baker, Jean H. TCLC 3, 10
See Russell, George William
Baker, Nicholson 1957- .... **CLC 61, 165**
See also AMWS 13; CA 135; CANR 63, 120, 138; CN 6; CPW; DA3; DAM POP; DLB 227; MTFW 2005
Baker, Ray Stannard 1870-1946 .... **TCLC 47**
See also CAAE 118
Baker, Russell 1925- .... **CLC 31**
See also BEST 89:4; CA 57-60; CANR 11, 41, 59, 137; MTCW 1, 2; MTFW 2005
Bakhtin, M.
See Bakhtin, Mikhail Mikhailovich
Bakhtin, M. M.
See Bakhtin, Mikhail Mikhailovich
Bakhtin, Mikhail
See Bakhtin, Mikhail Mikhailovich
Bakhtin, Mikhail Mikhailovich
1895-1975 .... **CLC 83; TCLC 160**
See also CA 128; CAAS 113; DLB 242; EWL 3
Bakshi, Ralph 1938(?)- .... **CLC 26**
See also CA 138; CAAE 112; IDFW 3
Bakunin, Mikhail (Alexandrovich)
1814-1876 .... **NCLC 25, 58**
See also DLB 277
Bal, Mieke (Maria Gertrudis)
1946- .... **CLC 252**
See also CA 156; CANR 99
Baldwin, James 1924-1987 ...... **BLC 1:1, 2:1; CLC 1, 2, 3, 4, 5, 8, 13, 15, 17, 42, 50, 67, 90, 127; DC 1; SSC 10, 33, 98; WLC 1**
See also AAYA 4, 34; AFAW 1, 2; AMWR 2; AMWS 1; BPFB 1; BW 1; CA 1-4R; CAAS 124; CABS 1; CAD; CANR 3, 24; CDALB 1941-1968; CN 1, 2, 3, 4; CPW; DA; DA3; DAB; DAC; DAM MST, MULT, NOV, POP; DFS 11, 15; DLB 2, 7, 33, 249, 278; DLBY 1987; EWL 3; EXPS; LAIT 5; MAL 5; MTCW 1, 2; MTFW 2005; NCFS 4; NFS 4; RGAL 4; RGSF 2; SATA 9; SATA-Obit 54; SSFS 2, 18; TUS
Baldwin, William c. 1515-1563 .... **LC 113**
See also DLB 132
Bale, John 1495-1563 .... **LC 62**
See also DLB 132; RGEL 2; TEA
Ball, Hugo 1886-1927 .... **TCLC 104**
Ballard, J.G. 1930- .... **CLC 3, 6, 14, 36, 137; SSC 1, 53**
See also AAYA 3, 52; BRWS 5; CA 5-8R; CANR 15, 39, 65, 107, 133; CN 1, 2, 3, 4, 5, 6, 7; DA3; DAM NOV, POP; DLB 14, 207, 261, 319; EWL 3; HGG; MTCW 1, 2; MTFW 2005; NFS 8; RGEL 2; RGSF 2; SATA 93; SCFW 1, 2; SFW 4
Balmont, Konstantin (Dmitriyevich)
1867-1943 .... **TCLC 11**
See also CA 155; CAAE 109; DLB 295; EWL 3
Baltausis, Vincas 1847-1910
See Mikszath, Kalman
Balzac, Honore de 1799-1850 ... **NCLC 5, 35, 53, 153; SSC 5, 59, 102; WLC 1**
See also DA; DA3; DAB; DAC; DAM MST, NOV; DLB 119; EW 5; GFL 1789 to the Present; LMFS 1; RGSF 2; RGWL 2, 3; SSFS 10; SUFW; TWA
Bambara, Toni Cade 1939-1995 ..... **BLC 1:1, 2:1; CLC 19, 88; SSC 35, 107; TCLC 116; WLCS**
See also AAYA 5, 49; AFAW 2; AMWS 11; BW 2, 3; BYA 12, 14; CA 29-32R; CAAS 150; CANR 24, 49, 81; CDALBS; DA; DA3; DAC; DAM MST, MULT; DLB 38, 218; EXPS; MAL 5; MTCW 1, 2; MTFW 2005; RGAL 4; RGSF 2; SATA 112; SSFS 4, 7, 12, 21
Bamdad, A.
See Shamlu, Ahmad
Bamdad, Alef
See Shamlu, Ahmad
Banat, D. R.
See Bradbury, Ray
Bancroft, Laura
See Baum, L(yman) Frank
Banim, John 1798-1842 .... **NCLC 13**
See also DLB 116, 158, 159; RGEL 2
Banim, Michael 1796-1874 .... **NCLC 13**
See also DLB 158, 159
Banjo, The
See Paterson, A(ndrew) B(arton)
Banks, Iain 1954- .... **CLC 34**
See Banks, Iain M.
See also CA 128; CAAE 123; CANR 61, 106; DLB 194, 261; EWL 3; HGG; INT CA-128; MTFW 2005; SFW 4
Banks, Iain M.
See Banks, Iain
See also BRWS 11
Banks, Iain Menzies
See Banks, Iain
Banks, Iain Menzies
See Banks, Iain
Banks, Lynne Reid CLC 23
See Reid Banks, Lynne
See also AAYA 6; BYA 7; CN 4, 5, 6
Banks, Russell 1940- . **CLC 37, 72, 187; SSC 42**
See also AAYA 45; AMWS 5; CA 65-68; 15; CANR 19, 52, 73, 118; CN 4, 5, 6, 7; DLB 130, 278; EWL 3; MAL 5; MTCW 2; MTFW 2005; NFS 13
Banks, Russell Earl
See Banks, Russell
Banville, John 1945- .... **CLC 46, 118, 224**
See also CA 128; CAAE 117; CANR 104, 150; CN 4, 5, 6, 7; DLB 14, 271, 326; INT CA-128
Banville, Theodore (Faullain) de
1832-1891 .... **NCLC 9**
See also DLB 217; GFL 1789 to the Present
Baraka, Amiri 1934- .. **BLC 1:1, 2:1; CLC 1, 2, 3, 5, 10, 14, 33, 115, 213; DC 6; PC 4; WLCS**
See Jones, LeRoi
See also AAYA 63; AFAW 1, 2; AMWS 2; BW 2, 3; CA 21-24R; CABS 3; CAD; CANR 27, 38, 61, 133, 172; CD 3, 5, 6; CDALB 1941-1968; CP 4, 5, 6, 7; CPW; DA; DA3; DAC; DAM MST, MULT, POET, POP; DFS 3, 11, 16; DLB 5, 7, 16, 38; DLBD 8; EWL 3; MAL 5; MTCW 1, 2; MTFW 2005; PFS 9; RGAL 4; TCLE 1:1; TUS; WP
Baratynsky, Evgenii Abramovich
1800-1844 .... **NCLC 103**
See also DLB 205
Barbauld, Anna Laetitia
1743-1825 .... **NCLC 50, 185**
See also DLB 107, 109, 142, 158, 336; RGEL 2
Barbellion, W. N. P. TCLC 24
See Cummings, Bruce F(rederick)
Barber, Benjamin R. 1939- .... **CLC 141**
See also CA 29-32R; CANR 12, 32, 64, 119
Barbera, Jack (Vincent) 1945- .... **CLC 44**
See also CA 110; CANR 45
Barbey d'Aurevilly, Jules-Amedee
1808-1889 .... **NCLC 1; SSC 17**
See also DLB 119; GFL 1789 to the Present
Barbour, John c. 1316-1395 .... **CMLC 33**
See also DLB 146
Barbusse, Henri 1873-1935 .... **TCLC 5**
See also CA 154; CAAE 105; DLB 65; EWL 3; RGWL 2, 3
Barclay, Alexander c. 1475-1552 .... **LC 109**
See also DLB 132
Barclay, Bill
See Moorcock, Michael
Barclay, William Ewert
See Moorcock, Michael
Barea, Arturo 1897-1957 .... **TCLC 14**
See also CA 201; CAAE 111
Barfoot, Joan 1946- .... **CLC 18**
See also CA 105; CANR 141
Barham, Richard Harris
1788-1845 .... **NCLC 77**
See also DLB 159
Baring, Maurice 1874-1945 .... **TCLC 8**
See also CA 168; CAAE 105; DLB 34; HGG
Baring-Gould, Sabine 1834-1924 ... **TCLC 88**
See also DLB 156, 190

Beagle, Peter Soyer
See Beagle, Peter S.
Bean, Normal
See Burroughs, Edgar Rice
Beard, Charles A(ustin) 1874-1948 .... **TCLC 15**
See also CA 189; CAAE 115; DLB 17; SATA 18
Beardsley, Aubrey 1872-1898 .... **NCLC 6**
Beattie, Ann 1947- ..... **CLC 8, 13, 18, 40, 63, 146; SSC 11**
See also AMWS 5; BEST 90:2; BPFB 1; CA 81-84; CANR 53, 73, 128; CN 4, 5, 6, 7; CPW; DA3; DAM NOV, POP; DLB 218, 278; DLBY 1982; EWL 3; MAL 5; MTCW 1, 2; MTFW 2005; RGAL 4; RGSF 2; SSFS 9; TUS
Beattie, James 1735-1803 .... **NCLC 25**
See also DLB 109
Beauchamp, Kathleen Mansfield 1888-1923
See Mansfield, Katherine
See also CA 134; CAAE 104; DA; DA3; DAC; DAM MST; MTCW 2; TEA
Beaumarchais, Pierre-Augustin Caron de 1732-1799 .... **DC 4; LC 61**
See also DAM DRAM; DFS 14, 16; DLB 313; EW 4; GFL Beginnings to 1789; RGWL 2, 3
Beaumont, Francis 1584(?)-1616 .. **DC 6; LC 33**
See also BRW 2; CDBLB Before 1660; DLB 58; TEA
Beauvoir, Simone de 1908-1986 .... **CLC 1, 2, 4, 8, 14, 31, 44, 50, 71, 124; SSC 35; WLC 1**
See also BPFB 1; CA 9-12R; CAAS 118; CANR 28, 61; DA; DA3; DAB; DAC; DAM MST, NOV; DLB 72; DLBY 1986; EW 12; EWL 3; FL 1:5; FW; GFL 1789 to the Present; LMFS 2; MTCW 1, 2; MTFW 2005; RGSF 2; RGWL 2, 3; TWA
Beauvoir, Simone Lucie Ernestine Marie Bertrand de
See Beauvoir, Simone de
Becker, Carl (Lotus) 1873-1945 ..... **TCLC 63**
See also CA 157; DLB 17
Becker, Jurek 1937-1997 .... **CLC 7, 19**
See also CA 85-88; CAAS 157; CANR 60, 117; CWW 2; DLB 75, 299; EWL 3; RGHL
Becker, Walter 1950- .... **CLC 26**
Becket, Thomas a 1118(?)-1170 .... **CMLC 83**
Beckett, Samuel 1906-1989 ... **CLC 1, 2, 3, 4, 6, 9, 10, 11, 14, 18, 29, 57, 59, 83; DC 22; SSC 16, 74; TCLC 145; WLC 1**
See also BRWC 2; BRWR 1; BRWS 1; CA 5-8R; CAAS 130; CANR 33, 61; CBD; CDBLB 1945-1960; CN 1, 2, 3, 4; CP 1, 2, 3, 4; DA; DA3; DAB; DAC; DAM DRAM, MST, NOV; DFS 2, 7, 18; DLB 13, 15, 233, 319, 321, 329; DLBY 1990; EWL 3; GFL 1789 to the Present; LATS 1:2; LMFS 2; MTCW 1, 2; MTFW 2005; RGSF 2; RGWL 2, 3; SSFS 15; TEA; WLIT 4
Beckford, William 1760-1844 .... **NCLC 16**
See also BRW 3; DLB 39, 213; GL 2; HGG; LMFS 1; SUFW
Beckham, Barry (Earl) 1944- .... **BLC 1:1**
See also BW 1; CA 29-32R; CANR 26, 62; CN 1, 2, 3, 4, 5, 6; DAM MULT; DLB 33
Beckman, Gunnel 1910- .... **CLC 26**
See also CA 33-36R; CANR 15, 114; CLR 25; MAICYA 1, 2; SAAS 9; SATA 6
Becque, Henri 1837-1899 .... **DC 21; NCLC 3**
See also DLB 192; GFL 1789 to the Present
Becquer, Gustavo Adolfo 1836-1870 .... **HLCS 1; NCLC 106**
See also DAM MULT
Beddoes, Thomas Lovell 1803-1849 .. **DC 15; NCLC 3, 154**
See also BRWS 11; DLB 96
Bede c. 673-735 .... **CMLC 20**
See also DLB 146; TEA
Bedford, Denton R. 1907-(?) .... **NNAL**
Bedford, Donald F.
See Fearing, Kenneth (Flexner)
Beecher, Catharine Esther 1800-1878 .... **NCLC 30**
See also DLB 1, 243
Beecher, John 1904-1980 .... **CLC 6**
See also AITN 1; CA 5-8R; CAAS 105; CANR 8; CP 1, 2, 3
Beer, Johann 1655-1700 .... **LC 5**
See also DLB 168
Beer, Patricia 1924- .... **CLC 58**
See also CA 61-64; CAAS 183; CANR 13, 46; CP 1, 2, 3, 4, 5, 6; CWP; DLB 40; FW
Beerbohm, Max
See Beerbohm, (Henry) Max(imilian)
Beerbohm, (Henry) Max(imilian) 1872-1956 .... **TCLC 1, 24**
See also BRWS 2; CA 154; CAAE 104; CANR 79; DLB 34, 100; FANT; MTCW 2
Beer-Hofmann, Richard 1866-1945 .... **TCLC 60**
See also CA 160; DLB 81
Beg, Shemus
See Stephens, James
Begiebing, Robert J(ohn) 1946- .... **CLC 70**
See also CA 122; CANR 40, 88
Begley, Louis 1933- .... **CLC 197**
See also CA 140; CANR 98; DLB 299; RGHL; TCLE 1:1
Behan, Brendan (Francis) 1923-1964 .... **CLC 1, 8, 11, 15, 79**
See also BRWS 2; CA 73-76; CANR 33, 121; CBD; CDBLB 1945-1960; DAM DRAM; DFS 7; DLB 13, 233; EWL 3; MTCW 1, 2
Behn, Aphra 1640(?)-1689 .. **DC 4; LC 1, 30, 42, 135; PC 13, 88; WLC 1**
See also BRWS 3; DA; DA3; DAB; DAC; DAM DRAM, MST, NOV, POET; DFS 16, 24; DLB 39, 80, 131; FW; TEA; WLIT 3
Behrman, S(amuel) N(athaniel) 1893-1973 .... **CLC 40**
See also CA 13-16; CAAS 45-48; CAD; CAP 1; DLB 7, 44; IDFW 3; MAL 5; RGAL 4
Bekederemo, J. P. Clark
See Clark Bekederemo, J.P.
See also CD 6
Belasco, David 1853-1931 .... **TCLC 3**
See also CA 168; CAAE 104; DLB 7; MAL 5; RGAL 4
Belcheva, Elisaveta Lyubomirova 1893-1991 .... **CLC 10**
See Bagryana, Elisaveta
Beldone, Phil ''Cheech''
See Ellison, Harlan
Beleno
See Azuela, Mariano
Belinski, Vissarion Grigoryevich 1811-1848 .... **NCLC 5**
See also DLB 198
Belitt, Ben 1911- .... **CLC 22**
See also CA 13-16R; 4; CANR 7, 77; CP 1, 2, 3, 4, 5, 6; DLB 5
Belknap, Jeremy 1744-1798 .... **LC 115**
See also DLB 30, 37
Bell, Gertrude (Margaret Lowthian) 1868-1926 .... **TCLC 67**
See also CA 167; CANR 110; DLB 174
Bell, J. Freeman
See Zangwill, Israel
Bell, James Madison 1826-1902 ..... **BLC 1:1; TCLC 43**
See also BW 1; CA 124; CAAE 122; DAM MULT; DLB 50
Bell, Madison Smartt 1957- ..... **CLC 41, 102, 223**
See also AMWS 10; BPFB 1; CA 183; 111, 183; CANR 28, 54, 73, 134; CN 5, 6, 7; CSW; DLB 218, 278; MTCW 2; MTFW 2005
Bell, Marvin (Hartley) 1937- ...... **CLC 8, 31; PC 79**
See also CA 21-24R; 14; CANR 59, 102; CP 1, 2, 3, 4, 5, 6, 7; DAM POET; DLB 5; MAL 5; MTCW 1; PFS 25
Bell, W. L. D.
See Mencken, H(enry) L(ouis)
Bellamy, Atwood C.
See Mencken, H(enry) L(ouis)
Bellamy, Edward 1850-1898 ..... **NCLC 4, 86, 147**
See also DLB 12; NFS 15; RGAL 4; SFW 4
Belli, Gioconda 1948- .... **HLCS 1**
See also CA 152; CANR 143; CWW 2; DLB 290; EWL 3; RGWL 3
Bellin, Edward J.
See Kuttner, Henry
Bello, Andres 1781-1865 .... **NCLC 131**
See also LAW
Belloc, (Joseph) Hilaire (Pierre Sebastien Rene Swanton) 1870-1953 .... **PC 24; TCLC 7, 18**
See also CA 152; CAAE 106; CLR 102; CWRI 5; DAM POET; DLB 19, 100, 141, 174; EWL 3; MTCW 2; MTFW 2005; SATA 112; WCH; YABC 1
Belloc, Joseph Peter Rene Hilaire
See Belloc, (Joseph) Hilaire (Pierre Sebastien Rene Swanton)
Belloc, Joseph Pierre Hilaire
See Belloc, (Joseph) Hilaire (Pierre Sebastien Rene Swanton)
Belloc, M. A.
See Lowndes, Marie Adelaide (Belloc)
Belloc-Lowndes, Mrs.
See Lowndes, Marie Adelaide (Belloc)
Bellow, Saul 1915-2005 ...... **CLC 1, 2, 3, 6, 8, 10, 13, 15, 25, 33, 34, 63, 79, 190, 200; SSC 14, 101; WLC 1**
See also AITN 2; AMW; AMWC 2; AMWR 2; BEST 89:3; BPFB 1; CA 5-8R; CAAS 238; CABS 1; CANR 29, 53, 95, 132; CDALB 1941-1968; CN 1, 2, 3, 4, 5, 6, 7; DA; DA3; DAB; DAC; DAM MST, NOV, POP; DLB 2, 28, 299, 329; DLBD 3; DLBY 1982; EWL 3; MAL 5; MTCW 1, 2; MTFW 2005; NFS 4, 14, 26; RGAL 4; RGHL; RGSF 2; SSFS 12, 22; TUS
Belser, Reimond Karel Maria de 1929-
See Ruyslinck, Ward
See also CA 152
Bely, Andrey PC 11; TCLC 7
See Bugayev, Boris Nikolayevich
See also DLB 295; EW 9; EWL 3
Belyi, Andrei
See Bugayev, Boris Nikolayevich
See also RGWL 2, 3
Bembo, Pietro 1470-1547 .... **LC 79**
See also RGWL 2, 3
Benary, Margot
See Benary-Isbert, Margot
Benary-Isbert, Margot 1889-1979 .... **CLC 12**
See also CA 5-8R; CAAS 89-92; CANR 4, 72; CLR 12; MAICYA 1, 2; SATA 2; SATA-Obit 21

Benavente (y Martinez), Jacinto 1866-1954 .... **DC 26; HLCS 1; TCLC 3**
See also CA 131; CAAE 106; CANR 81; DAM DRAM, MULT; DLB 329; EWL 3; GLL 2; HW 1, 2; MTCW 1, 2

Benchley, Peter 1940-2006 .... **CLC 4, 8**
See also AAYA 14; AITN 2; BPFB 1; CA 17-20R; CAAS 248; CANR 12, 35, 66, 115; CPW; DAM NOV, POP; HGG; MTCW 1, 2; MTFW 2005; SATA 3, 89, 164

Benchley, Peter Bradford
See Benchley, Peter

Benchley, Robert (Charles) 1889-1945 .... **TCLC 1, 55**
See also CA 153; CAAE 105; DLB 11; MAL 5; RGAL 4

Benda, Julien 1867-1956 .... **TCLC 60**
See also CA 154; CAAE 120; GFL 1789 to the Present

Benedict, Ruth 1887-1948 .... **TCLC 60**
See also CA 158; CANR 146; DLB 246

Benedict, Ruth Fulton
See Benedict, Ruth

Benedikt, Michael 1935- .... **CLC 4, 14**
See also CA 13-16R; CANR 7; CP 1, 2, 3, 4, 5, 6, 7; DLB 5

Benet, Juan 1927-1993 .... **CLC 28**
See also CA 143; EWL 3

Benet, Stephen Vincent 1898-1943 ..... **PC 64; SSC 10, 86; TCLC 7**
See also AMWS 11; CA 152; CAAE 104; DA3; DAM POET; DLB 4, 48, 102, 249, 284; DLBY 1997; EWL 3; HGG; MAL 5; MTCW 2; MTFW 2005; RGAL 4; RGSF 2; SSFS 22; SUFW; WP; YABC 1

Benet, William Rose 1886-1950 ..... **TCLC 28**
See also CA 152; CAAE 118; DAM POET; DLB 45; RGAL 4

Benford, Gregory 1941- .... **CLC 52**
See also BPFB 1; CA 175; 69-72, 175; 27; CANR 12, 24, 49, 95, 134; CN 7; CSW; DLBY 1982; MTFW 2005; SCFW 2; SFW 4

Benford, Gregory Albert
See Benford, Gregory

Bengtsson, Frans (Gunnar) 1894-1954 .... **TCLC 48**
See also CA 170; EWL 3

Benjamin, David
See Slavitt, David R.

Benjamin, Lois
See Gould, Lois

Benjamin, Walter 1892-1940 .... **TCLC 39**
See also CA 164; DLB 242; EW 11; EWL 3

Ben Jelloun, Tahar 1944- .... **CLC 180**
See also CA 135, 162; CANR 100, 166; CWW 2; EWL 3; RGWL 3; WLIT 2

Benn, Gottfried 1886-1956 .. **PC 35; TCLC 3**
See also CA 153; CAAE 106; DLB 56; EWL 3; RGWL 2, 3

Bennett, Alan 1934- .... **CLC 45, 77**
See also BRWS 8; CA 103; CANR 35, 55, 106, 157; CBD; CD 5, 6; DAB; DAM MST; DLB 310; MTCW 1, 2; MTFW 2005

Bennett, (Enoch) Arnold 1867-1931 .... **TCLC 5, 20, 197**
See also BRW 6; CA 155; CAAE 106; CDBLB 1890-1914; DLB 10, 34, 98, 135; EWL 3; MTCW 2

Bennett, Elizabeth
See Mitchell, Margaret (Munnerlyn)

Bennett, George Harold 1930-
See Bennett, Hal
See also BW 1; CA 97-100; CANR 87

Bennett, Gwendolyn B. 1902-1981 .... **HR 1:2**
See also BW 1; CA 125; DLB 51; WP

Bennett, Hal CLC 5
See Bennett, George Harold
See also CA 13; DLB 33

Bennett, Jay 1912- .... **CLC 35**
See also AAYA 10, 73; CA 69-72; CANR 11, 42, 79; JRDA; SAAS 4; SATA 41, 87; SATA-Brief 27; WYA; YAW

Bennett, Louise 1919-2006 .... **BLC 1:1; CLC 28**
See also BW 2, 3; CA 151; CAAS 252; CDWLB 3; CP 1, 2, 3, 4, 5, 6, 7; DAM MULT; DLB 117; EWL 3

Bennett, Louise Simone
See Bennett, Louise

Bennett-Coverley, Louise
See Bennett, Louise

Benoit de Sainte-Maure fl. 12th cent. - .... **CMLC 90**

Benson, A. C. 1862-1925 .... **TCLC 123**
See also DLB 98

Benson, E(dward) F(rederic) 1867-1940 .... **TCLC 27**
See also CA 157; CAAE 114; DLB 135, 153; HGG; SUFW 1

Benson, Jackson J. 1930- .... **CLC 34**
See also CA 25-28R; DLB 111

Benson, Sally 1900-1972 .... **CLC 17**
See also CA 19-20; CAAS 37-40R; CAP 1; SATA 1, 35; SATA-Obit 27

Benson, Stella 1892-1933 .... **TCLC 17**
See also CA 154, 155; CAAE 117; DLB 36, 162; FANT; TEA

Bentham, Jeremy 1748-1832 .... **NCLC 38**
See also DLB 107, 158, 252

Bentley, E(dmund) C(lerihew) 1875-1956 .... **TCLC 12**
See also CA 232; CAAE 108; DLB 70; MSW

Bentley, Eric 1916- .... **CLC 24**
See also CA 5-8R; CAD; CANR 6, 67; CBD; CD 5, 6; INT CANR-6

Bentley, Eric Russell
See Bentley, Eric

ben Uzair, Salem
See Horne, Richard Henry Hengist

Beolco, Angelo 1496-1542 .... **LC 139**

Beranger, Pierre Jean de 1780-1857 .... **NCLC 34**

Berdyaev, Nicolas
See Berdyaev, Nikolai (Aleksandrovich)

Berdyaev, Nikolai (Aleksandrovich) 1874-1948 .... **TCLC 67**
See also CA 157; CAAE 120

Berdyayev, Nikolai (Aleksandrovich)
See Berdyaev, Nikolai (Aleksandrovich)

Berendt, John 1939- .... **CLC 86**
See also CA 146; CANR 75, 83, 151

Berendt, John Lawrence
See Berendt, John

Beresford, J(ohn) D(avys) 1873-1947 .... **TCLC 81**
See also CA 155; CAAE 112; DLB 162, 178, 197; SFW 4; SUFW 1

Bergelson, David (Rafailovich) 1884-1952 .... **TCLC 81**
See Bergelson, Dovid
See also CA 220; DLB 333

Bergelson, Dovid
See Bergelson, David (Rafailovich)
See also EWL 3

Berger, Colonel
See Malraux, (Georges-)Andre

Berger, John 1926- .... **CLC 2, 19**
See also BRWS 4; CA 81-84; CANR 51, 78, 117, 163; CN 1, 2, 3, 4, 5, 6, 7; DLB 14, 207, 319, 326

Berger, John Peter
See Berger, John

Berger, Melvin H. 1927- .... **CLC 12**
See also CA 5-8R; CANR 4, 142; CLR 32; SAAS 2; SATA 5, 88, 158; SATA-Essay 124

Berger, Thomas 1924- .... **CLC 3, 5, 8, 11, 18, 38**
See also BPFB 1; CA 1-4R; CANR 5, 28, 51, 128; CN 1, 2, 3, 4, 5, 6, 7; DAM NOV; DLB 2; DLBY 1980; EWL 3; FANT; INT CANR-28; MAL 5; MTCW 1, 2; MTFW 2005; RHW; TCLE 1:1; TCWW 1, 2

Bergman, Ernst Ingmar
See Bergman, Ingmar

Bergman, Ingmar 1918-2007 ..... **CLC 16, 72, 210**
See also AAYA 61; CA 81-84; CAAS 262; CANR 33, 70; CWW 2; DLB 257; MTCW 2; MTFW 2005

Bergson, Henri(-Louis) 1859-1941 . **TCLC 32**
See also CA 164; DLB 329; EW 8; EWL 3; GFL 1789 to the Present

Bergstein, Eleanor 1938- .... **CLC 4**
See also CA 53-56; CANR 5

Berkeley, George 1685-1753 .... **LC 65**
See also DLB 31, 101, 252

Berkoff, Steven 1937- .... **CLC 56**
See also CA 104; CANR 72; CBD; CD 5, 6

Berlin, Isaiah 1909-1997 .... **TCLC 105**
See also CA 85-88; CAAS 162

Bermant, Chaim (Icyk) 1929-1998 ... **CLC 40**
See also CA 57-60; CANR 6, 31, 57, 105; CN 2, 3, 4, 5, 6

Bern, Victoria
See Fisher, M(ary) F(rances) K(ennedy)

Bernanos, (Paul Louis) Georges 1888-1948 .... **TCLC 3**
See also CA 130; CAAE 104; CANR 94; DLB 72; EWL 3; GFL 1789 to the Present; RGWL 2, 3

Bernard, April 1956- .... **CLC 59**
See also CA 131; CANR 144

Bernard, Mary Ann
See Soderbergh, Steven

Bernard of Clairvaux 1090-1153 .. **CMLC 71**
See also DLB 208

Bernard Silvestris fl. c. 1130-fl. c. 1160 .... **CMLC 87**
See also DLB 208

Bernart de Ventadorn c. 1130-c. 1190 .... **CMLC 98**

Berne, Victoria
See Fisher, M(ary) F(rances) K(ennedy)

Bernhard, Thomas 1931-1989 ..... **CLC 3, 32, 61; DC 14; TCLC 165**
See also CA 85-88; CAAS 127; CANR 32, 57; CDWLB 2; DLB 85, 124; EWL 3; MTCW 1; RGHL; RGWL 2, 3

Bernhardt, Sarah (Henriette Rosine) 1844-1923 .... **TCLC 75**
See also CA 157

Bernstein, Charles 1950- .... **CLC 142,**
See also CA 129; 24; CANR 90; CP 4, 5, 6, 7; DLB 169

Bernstein, Ingrid
See Kirsch, Sarah

Beroul fl. c. 12th cent. - .... **CMLC 75**

Berriault, Gina 1926-1999 .... **CLC 54, 109; SSC 30**
See also CA 129; CAAE 116; CAAS 185; CANR 66; DLB 130; SSFS 7,11

Berrigan, Daniel 1921- .... **CLC 4**
See also CA 187; 33-36R, 187; 1; CANR 11, 43, 78; CP 1, 2, 3, 4, 5, 6, 7; DLB 5

Booth, Philip 1925-2007 .... **CLC 23**
See also CA 5-8R; CAAS 262; CANR 5, 88; CP 1, 2, 3, 4, 5, 6, 7; DLBY 1982
Booth, Philip Edmund
See Booth, Philip
Booth, Wayne C. 1921-2005 .... **CLC 24**
See also CA 1-4R; 5; CAAS 244; CANR 3, 43, 117; DLB 67
Booth, Wayne Clayson
See Booth, Wayne C.
Borchert, Wolfgang 1921-1947 .... **TCLC 5**
See also CA 188; CAAE 104; DLB 69, 124; EWL 3
Borel, Petrus 1809-1859 .... **NCLC 41**
See also DLB 119; GFL 1789 to the Present
Borges, Jorge Luis 1899-1986 ... **CLC 1, 2, 3, 4, 6, 8, 9, 10, 13, 19, 44, 48, 83; HLC 1; PC 22, 32; SSC 4, 41, 100; TCLC 109; WLC 1**
See also AAYA 26; BPFB 1; CA 21-24R; CANR 19, 33, 75, 105, 133; CDWLB 3; DA; DA3; DAB; DAC; DAM MST, MULT; DLB 113, 283; DLBY 1986; DNFS 1, 2; EWL 3; HW 1, 2; LAW; LMFS 2; MSW; MTCW 1, 2; MTFW 2005; PFS 27; RGHL; RGSF 2; RGWL 2, 3; SFW 4; SSFS 17; TWA; WLIT 1
Borne, Ludwig 1786-1837 .... **NCLC 193**
DLB 90
Borowski, Tadeusz 1922-1951 .... **SSC 48; TCLC 9**
See also CA 154; CAAE 106; CDWLB 4; DLB 215; EWL 3; RGHL; RGSF 2; RGWL 3; SSFS 13
Borrow, George (Henry)
1803-1881 .... **NCLC 9**
See also BRWS 12; DLB 21, 55, 166
Bosch (Gavino), Juan 1909-2001 ..... **HLCS 1**
See also CA 151; CAAS 204; DAM MST, MULT; DLB 145; HW 1, 2
Bosman, Herman Charles
1905-1951 .... **TCLC 49**
See Malan, Herman
See also CA 160; DLB 225; RGSF 2
Bosschere, Jean de 1878(?)-1953 ... **TCLC 19**
See also CA 186; CAAE 115
Boswell, James 1740-1795 ... **LC 4, 50; WLC 1**
See also BRW 3; CDBLB 1660-1789; DA; DAB; DAC; DAM MST; DLB 104, 142; TEA; WLIT 3
Bottomley, Gordon 1874-1948 ..... **TCLC 107**
See also CA 192; CAAE 120; DLB 10
Bottoms, David 1949- .... **CLC 53**
See also CA 105; CANR 22; CSW; DLB 120; DLBY 1983
Boucicault, Dion 1820-1890 .... **NCLC 41**
Boucolon, Maryse
See Conde, Maryse
Bourdieu, Pierre 1930-2002 .... **CLC 198**
See also CA 130; CAAS 204
Bourget, Paul (Charles Joseph)
1852-1935 .... **TCLC 12**
See also CA 196; CAAE 107; DLB 123; GFL 1789 to the Present
Bourjaily, Vance (Nye) 1922- .... **CLC 8, 62**
See also CA 1-4R; 1; CANR 2, 72; CN 1, 2, 3, 4, 5, 6, 7; DLB 2, 143; MAL 5
Bourne, Randolph S(illiman)
1886-1918 .... **TCLC 16**
See also AMW; CA 155; CAAE 117; DLB 63; MAL 5
Bova, Ben 1932- .... **CLC 45**
See also AAYA 16; CA 5-8R; 18; CANR 11, 56, 94, 111, 157; CLR 3, 96; DLBY 1981; INT CANR-11; MAICYA 1, 2; MTCW 1; SATA 6, 68, 133; SFW 4
Bova, Benjamin William
See Bova, Ben
Bowen, Elizabeth (Dorothea Cole)
1899-1973 . **CLC 1, 3, 6, 11, 15, 22, 118; SSC 3, 28, 66; TCLC 148**
See also BRWS 2; CA 17-18; CAAS 41-44R; CANR 35, 105; CAP 2; CDBLB 1945-1960; CN 1; DA3; DAM NOV; DLB 15, 162; EWL 3; EXPS; FW; HGG; MTCW 1, 2; MTFW 2005; NFS 13; RGSF 2; SSFS 5, 22; SUFW 1; TEA; WLIT 4
Bowering, George 1935- .... **CLC 15, 47**
See also CA 21-24R; 16; CANR 10; CN 7; CP 1, 2, 3, 4, 5, 6, 7; DLB 53
Bowering, Marilyn R(uthe) 1949- .... **CLC 32**
See also CA 101; CANR 49; CP 4, 5, 6, 7; CWP; DLB 334
Bowers, Edgar 1924-2000 .... **CLC 9**
See also CA 5-8R; CAAS 188; CANR 24; CP 1, 2, 3, 4, 5, 6, 7; CSW; DLB 5
Bowers, Mrs. J. Milton 1842-1914
See Bierce, Ambrose (Gwinett)
Bowie, David CLC 17
See Jones, David Robert
Bowles, Jane (Sydney) 1917-1973 ..... **CLC 3, 68**
See Bowles, Jane Auer
See also CA 19-20; CAAS 41-44R; CAP 2; CN 1; MAL 5
Bowles, Jane Auer
See Bowles, Jane (Sydney)
See also EWL 3
Bowles, Paul 1910-1999 ..... **CLC 1, 2, 19, 53; SSC 3, 98**
See also AMWS 4; CA 1-4R; 1; CAAS 186; CANR 1, 19, 50, 75; CN 1, 2, 3, 4, 5, 6; DA3; DLB 5, 6, 218; EWL 3; MAL 5; MTCW 1, 2; MTFW 2005; RGAL 4; SSFS 17
Bowles, William Lisle 1762-1850 . **NCLC 103**
See also DLB 93
Box, Edgar
See Vidal, Gore
Boyd, James 1888-1944 .... **TCLC 115**
See also CA 186; DLB 9; DLBD 16; RGAL 4; RHW
Boyd, Nancy
See Millay, Edna St. Vincent
See also GLL 1
Boyd, Thomas (Alexander)
1898-1935 .... **TCLC 111**
See also CA 183; CAAE 111; DLB 9; DLBD 16, 316
Boyd, William (Andrew Murray)
1952- .... **CLC 28, 53, 70**
See also CA 120; CAAE 114; CANR 51, 71, 131; CN 4, 5, 6, 7; DLB 231
Boyesen, Hjalmar Hjorth
1848-1895 .... **NCLC 135**
See also DLB 12, 71; DLBD 13; RGAL 4
Boyle, Kay 1902-1992 .... **CLC 1, 5, 19, 58, 121; SSC 5, 102**
See also CA 13-16R; 1; CAAS 140; CANR 29, 61, 110; CN 1, 2, 3, 4, 5; CP 1, 2, 3, 4, 5; DLB 4, 9, 48, 86; DLBY 1993; EWL 3; MAL 5; MTCW 1, 2; MTFW 2005; RGAL 4; RGSF 2; SSFS 10, 13, 14
Boyle, Mark
See Kienzle, William X.
Boyle, Patrick 1905-1982 .... **CLC 19**
See also CA 127
Boyle, T. C.
See Boyle, T. Coraghessan
See also AMWS 8
Boyle, T. Coraghessan 1948- ..... **CLC 36, 55, 90; SSC 16**
See Boyle, T. C.
See also AAYA 47; BEST 90:4; BPFB 1; CA 120; CANR 44, 76, 89, 132; CN 6, 7; CPW; DA3; DAM POP; DLB 218, 278; DLBY 1986; EWL 3; MAL 5; MTCW 2; MTFW 2005; SSFS 13, 19
Boz
See Dickens, Charles (John Huffam)
Brackenridge, Hugh Henry
1748-1816 .... **NCLC 7**
See also DLB 11, 37; RGAL 4
Bradbury, Edward P.
See Moorcock, Michael
See also MTCW 2
Bradbury, Malcolm (Stanley)
1932-2000 .... **CLC 32, 61**
See also CA 1-4R; CANR 1, 33, 91, 98, 137; CN 1, 2, 3, 4, 5, 6, 7; CP 1; DA3; DAM NOV; DLB 14, 207; EWL 3; MTCW 1, 2; MTFW 2005
Bradbury, Ray 1920- ... **CLC 1, 3, 10, 15, 42, 98, 235; SSC 29, 53; WLC 1**
See also AAYA 15; AITN 1, 2; AMWS 4; BPFB 1; BYA 4, 5, 11; CA 1-4R; CANR 2, 30, 75, 125; CDALB 1968-1988; CN 1, 2, 3, 4, 5, 6, 7; CPW; DA; DA3; DAB; DAC; DAM MST, NOV, POP; DLB 2, 8; EXPN; EXPS; HGG; LAIT 3, 5; LATS 1:2; LMFS 2; MAL 5; MTCW 1, 2; MTFW 2005; NFS 1, 22; RGAL 4; RGSF 2; SATA 11, 64, 123; SCFW 1, 2; SFW 4; SSFS 1, 20; SUFW 1, 2; TUS; YAW
Braddon, Mary Elizabeth
1837-1915 .... **TCLC 111**
See also BRWS 8; CA 179; CAAE 108; CMW 4; DLB 18, 70, 156; HGG
Bradfield, Scott 1955- .... **SSC 65**
See also CA 147; CANR 90; HGG; SUFW 2
Bradfield, Scott Michael
See Bradfield, Scott
Bradford, Gamaliel 1863-1932 .... **TCLC 36**
See also CA 160; DLB 17
Bradford, William 1590-1657 .... **LC 64**
See also DLB 24, 30; RGAL 4
Bradley, David, Jr. 1950- ...... **BLC 1:1; CLC 23, 118**
See also BW 1, 3; CA 104; CANR 26, 81; CN 4, 5, 6, 7; DAM MULT; DLB 33
Bradley, David Henry, Jr.
See Bradley, David, Jr.
Bradley, John Ed 1958- .... **CLC 55**
See also CA 139; CANR 99; CN 6, 7; CSW
Bradley, John Edmund, Jr.
See Bradley, John Ed
Bradley, Marion Zimmer
1930-1999 .... **CLC 30**
See Chapman, Lee; Dexter, John; Gardner, Miriam; Ives, Morgan; Rivers, Elfrida
See also AAYA 40; BPFB 1; CA 57-60; 10; CAAS 185; CANR 7, 31, 51, 75, 107; CPW; DA3; DAM POP; DLB 8; FANT; FW; MTCW 1, 2; MTFW 2005; SATA 90, 139; SATA-Obit 116; SFW 4; SUFW 2; YAW
Bradshaw, John 1933- .... **CLC 70**
See also CA 138; CANR 61
Bradstreet, Anne 1612(?)-1672 .... **LC 4, 30, 130; PC 10**
See also AMWS 1; CDALB 1640-1865; DA; DA3; DAC; DAM MST, POET; DLB 24; EXPP; FW; PFS 6; RGAL 4; TUS; WP
Brady, Joan 1939- .... **CLC 86**
See also CA 141
Bragg, Melvyn 1939- .... **CLC 10**
See also BEST 89:3; CA 57-60; CANR 10, 48, 89, 158; CN 1, 2, 3, 4, 5, 6, 7; DLB 14, 271; RHW
Brahe, Tycho 1546-1601 .... **LC 45**
See also DLB 300
Braine, John (Gerard) 1922-1986 . **CLC 1, 3, 41**
See also CA 1-4R; CAAS 120; CANR 1, 33; CDBLB 1945-1960; CN 1, 2, 3, 4; DLB 15; DLBY 1986; EWL 3; MTCW 1

Braithwaite, William Stanley (Beaumont) 1878-1962 ...... **BLC 1:1; HR 1:2; PC 52**
See also BW 1; CA 125; DAM MULT; DLB 50, 54; MAL 5
Bramah, Ernest 1868-1942 .... **TCLC 72**
See also CA 156; CMW 4; DLB 70; FANT
Brammer, Billy Lee
See Brammer, William
Brammer, William 1929-1978 .... **CLC 31**
See also CA 235; CAAS 77-80
Brancati, Vitaliano 1907-1954 .... **TCLC 12**
See also CAAE 109; DLB 264; EWL 3
Brancato, Robin F(idler) 1936- .... **CLC 35**
See also AAYA 9, 68; BYA 6; CA 69-72; CANR 11, 45; CLR 32; JRDA; MAICYA 2; MAICYAS 1; SAAS 9; SATA 97; WYA; YAW
Brand, Dionne 1953- .... **CLC 192**
See also BW 2; CA 143; CANR 143; CWP; DLB 334
Brand, Max
See Faust, Frederick (Schiller)
See also BPFB 1; TCWW 1, 2
Brand, Millen 1906-1980 .... **CLC 7**
See also CA 21-24R; CAAS 97-100; CANR 72
Branden, Barbara CLC 44
See also CA 148
Brandes, Georg (Morris Cohen) 1842-1927 .... **TCLC 10**
See also CA 189; CAAE 105; DLB 300
Brandys, Kazimierz 1916-2000 .... **CLC 62**
See also CA 239; EWL 3
Branley, Franklyn M(ansfield) 1915-2002 .... **CLC 21**
See also CA 33-36R; CAAS 207; CANR 14, 39; CLR 13; MAICYA 1, 2; SAAS 16; SATA 4, 68, 136
Brant, Beth (E.) 1941- .... **NNAL**
See also CA 144; FW
Brant, Sebastian 1457-1521 .... **LC 112**
See also DLB 179; RGWL 2, 3
Brathwaite, Edward Kamau 1930- ..... **BLCS; BLC 2:1; CLC 11; PC 56**
See also BRWS 12; BW 2, 3; CA 25-28R; CANR 11, 26, 47, 107; CDWLB 3; CP 1, 2, 3, 4, 5, 6, 7; DAM POET; DLB 125; EWL 3
Brathwaite, Kamau
See Brathwaite, Edward Kamau
Brautigan, Richard (Gary) 1935-1984 .... **CLC 1, 3, 5, 9, 12, 34, 42; TCLC 133**
See also BPFB 1; CA 53-56; CAAS 113; CANR 34; CN 1, 2, 3; CP 1, 2, 3, 4; DA3; DAM NOV; DLB 2, 5, 206; DLBY 1980, 1984; FANT; MAL 5; MTCW 1; RGAL 4; SATA 56
Brave Bird, Mary NNAL
See Crow Dog, Mary
Braverman, Kate 1950- .... **CLC 67**
See also CA 89-92; CANR 141; DLB 335
Brecht, (Eugen) Bertolt (Friedrich) 1898-1956 ..... **DC 3; TCLC 1, 6, 13, 35, 169; WLC 1**
See also CA 133; CAAE 104; CANR 62; CDWLB 2; DA; DA3; DAB; DAC; DAM DRAM, MST; DFS 4, 5, 9; DLB 56, 124; EW 11; EWL 3; IDTP; MTCW 1, 2; MTFW 2005; RGHL; RGWL 2, 3; TWA
Brecht, Eugen Berthold Friedrich
See Brecht, (Eugen) Bertolt (Friedrich)
Bremer, Fredrika 1801-1865 .... **NCLC 11**
See also DLB 254
Brennan, Christopher John 1870-1932 .... **TCLC 17**
See also CA 188; CAAE 117; DLB 230; EWL 3
Brennan, Maeve 1917-1993 ... **CLC 5; TCLC 124**
See also CA 81-84; CANR 72, 100
Brenner, Jozef 1887-1919
See Csath, Geza
See also CA 240
Brent, Linda
See Jacobs, Harriet A(nn)
Brentano, Clemens (Maria) 1778-1842 .... **NCLC 1, 191**
See also DLB 90; RGWL 2, 3
Brent of Bin Bin
See Franklin, (Stella Maria Sarah) Miles (Lampe)
Brenton, Howard 1942- .... **CLC 31**
See also CA 69-72; CANR 33, 67; CBD; CD 5, 6; DLB 13; MTCW 1
Breslin, James 1930-
See Breslin, Jimmy
See also CA 73-76; CANR 31, 75, 139; DAM NOV; MTCW 1, 2; MTFW 2005
Breslin, Jimmy CLC 4, 43
See Breslin, James
See also AITN 1; DLB 185; MTCW 2
Bresson, Robert 1901(?)-1999 .... **CLC 16**
See also CA 110; CAAS 187; CANR 49
Breton, Andre 1896-1966 .. **CLC 2, 9, 15, 54; PC 15**
See also CA 19-20; CAAS 25-28R; CANR 40, 60; CAP 2; DLB 65, 258; EW 11; EWL 3; GFL 1789 to the Present; LMFS 2; MTCW 1, 2; MTFW 2005; RGWL 2, 3; TWA; WP
Breton, Nicholas c. 1554-c. 1626 .... **LC 133**
See also DLB 136
Breytenbach, Breyten 1939(?)- .. **CLC 23, 37, 126**
See also CA 129; CAAE 113; CANR 61, 122; CWW 2; DAM POET; DLB 225; EWL 3
Bridgers, Sue Ellen 1942- .... **CLC 26**
See also AAYA 8, 49; BYA 7, 8; CA 65-68; CANR 11, 36; CLR 18; DLB 52; JRDA; MAICYA 1, 2; SAAS 1; SATA 22, 90; SATA-Essay 109; WYA; YAW
Bridges, Robert (Seymour) 1844-1930 .... **PC 28; TCLC 1**
See also BRW 6; CA 152; CAAE 104; CDBLB 1890-1914; DAM POET; DLB 19, 98
Bridie, James TCLC 3
See Mavor, Osborne Henry
See also DLB 10; EWL 3
Brin, David 1950- .... **CLC 34**
See also AAYA 21; CA 102; CANR 24, 70, 125, 127; INT CANR-24; SATA 65; SCFW 2; SFW 4
Brink, Andre 1935- .... **CLC 18, 36, 106**
See also AFW; BRWS 6; CA 104; CANR 39, 62, 109, 133; CN 4, 5, 6, 7; DLB 225; EWL 3; INT CA-103; LATS 1:2; MTCW 1, 2; MTFW 2005; WLIT 2
Brinsmead, H. F.
See Brinsmead, H(esba) F(ay)
Brinsmead, H. F(ay)
See Brinsmead, H(esba) F(ay)
Brinsmead, H(esba) F(ay) 1922- ...... **CLC 21**
See also CA 21-24R; CANR 10; CLR 47; CWRI 5; MAICYA 1, 2; SAAS 5; SATA 18, 78
Brittain, Vera (Mary) 1893(?)-1970 . **CLC 23**
See also BRWS 10; CA 13-16; CAAS 25-28R; CANR 58; CAP 1; DLB 191; FW; MTCW 1, 2
Broch, Hermann 1886-1951 .... **TCLC 20**
See also CA 211; CAAE 117; CDWLB 2; DLB 85, 124; EW 10; EWL 3; RGWL 2, 3
Brock, Rose
See Hansen, Joseph
See also GLL 1
Brod, Max 1884-1968 .... **TCLC 115**
See also CA 5-8R; CAAS 25-28R; CANR 7; DLB 81; EWL 3
Brodkey, Harold (Roy) 1930-1996 .. **CLC 56; TCLC 123**
See also CA 111; CAAS 151; CANR 71; CN 4, 5, 6; DLB 130
Brodsky, Iosif Alexandrovich 1940-1996
See Brodsky, Joseph
See also AITN 1; CA 41-44R; CAAS 151; CANR 37, 106; DA3; DAM POET; MTCW 1, 2; MTFW 2005; RGWL 2, 3
Brodsky, Joseph CLC 4, 6, 13, 36, 100; PC 9
See Brodsky, Iosif Alexandrovich
See also AAYA 71; AMWS 8; CWW 2; DLB 285, 329; EWL 3; MTCW 1
Brodsky, Michael 1948- .... **CLC 19**
See also CA 102; CANR 18, 41, 58, 147; DLB 244
Brodsky, Michael Mark
See Brodsky, Michael
Brodzki, Bella CLC 65
Brome, Richard 1590(?)-1652 .... **LC 61**
See also BRWS 10; DLB 58
Bromell, Henry 1947- .... **CLC 5**
See also CA 53-56; CANR 9, 115, 116
Bromfield, Louis (Brucker) 1896-1956 .... **TCLC 11**
See also CA 155; CAAE 107; DLB 4, 9, 86; RGAL 4; RHW
Broner, E(sther) M(asserman) 1930- .... **CLC 19**
See also CA 17-20R; CANR 8, 25, 72; CN 4, 5, 6; DLB 28
Bronk, William (M.) 1918-1999 .... **CLC 10**
See also CA 89-92; CAAS 177; CANR 23; CP 3, 4, 5, 6, 7; DLB 165
Bronstein, Lev Davidovich
See Trotsky, Leon
Bronte, Anne
See Bronte, Anne
Bronte, Anne 1820-1849 ..... **NCLC 4, 71, 102**
See also BRW 5; BRWR 1; DA3; DLB 21, 199; NFS 26; TEA
Bronte, (Patrick) Branwell 1817-1848 .... **NCLC 109**
Bronte, Charlotte
See Bronte, Charlotte
Bronte, Charlotte 1816-1855 ...... **NCLC 3, 8, 33, 58, 105, 155; WLC 1**
See also AAYA 17; BRW 5; BRWC 2; BRWR 1; BYA 2; CDBLB 1832-1890; DA; DA3; DAB; DAC; DAM MST, NOV; DLB 21, 159, 199; EXPN; FL 1:2; GL 2; LAIT 2; NFS 4; TEA; WLIT 4
Bronte, Emily
See Bronte, Emily (Jane)
Bronte, Emily (Jane) 1818-1848 ... **NCLC 16, 35, 165; PC 8; WLC 1**
See also AAYA 17; BPFB 1; BRW 5; BRWC 1; BRWR 1; BYA 3; CDBLB 1832-1890; DA; DA3; DAB; DAC; DAM MST, NOV, POET; DLB 21, 32, 199; EXPN; FL 1:2; GL 2; LAIT 1; TEA; WLIT 3
Brontes
See Bronte, Anne; Bronte, Charlotte; Bronte, Emily (Jane)
Brooke, Frances 1724-1789 .... **LC 6, 48**
See also DLB 39, 99
Brooke, Henry 1703(?)-1783 .... **LC 1**
See also DLB 39

Brooke, Rupert (Chawner) 1887-1915 .. **PC 24; TCLC 2, 7; WLC 1**
See also BRWS 3; CA 132; CAAE 104; CANR 61; CDBLB 1914-1945; DA; DAB; DAC; DAM MST, POET; DLB 19, 216; EXPP; GLL 2; MTCW 1, 2; MTFW 2005; PFS 7; TEA

Brooke-Haven, P.
See Wodehouse, P(elham) G(renville)

Brooke-Rose, Christine 1926(?)- ..... **CLC 40, 184**
See also BRWS 4; CA 13-16R; CANR 58, 118; CN 1, 2, 3, 4, 5, 6, 7; DLB 14, 231; EWL 3; SFW 4

Brookner, Anita 1928- . **CLC 32, 34, 51, 136, 237**
See also BRWS 4; CA 120; CAAE 114; CANR 37, 56, 87, 130; CN 4, 5, 6, 7; CPW; DA3; DAB; DAM POP; DLB 194, 326; DLBY 1987; EWL 3; MTCW 1, 2; MTFW 2005; NFS 23; TEA

Brooks, Cleanth 1906-1994 . **CLC 24, 86, 110**
See also AMWS 14; CA 17-20R; CAAS 145; CANR 33, 35; CSW; DLB 63; DLBY 1994; EWL 3; INT CANR-35; MAL 5; MTCW 1, 2; MTFW 2005

Brooks, George
See Baum, L(yman) Frank

Brooks, Gwendolyn 1917-2000 .... **BLC 1:1, 2:1; CLC 1, 2, 4, 5, 15, 49, 125; PC 7; WLC 1**
See also AAYA 20; AFAW 1, 2; AITN 1; AMWS 3; BW 2, 3; CA 1-4R; CAAS 190; CANR 1, 27, 52, 75, 132; CDALB 1941-1968; CLR 27; CP 1, 2, 3, 4, 5, 6, 7; CWP; DA; DA3; DAC; DAM MST, MULT, POET; DLB 5, 76, 165; EWL 3; EXPP; FL 1:5; MAL 5; MBL; MTCW 1, 2; MTFW 2005; PFS 1, 2, 4, 6; RGAL 4; SATA 6; SATA-Obit 123; TUS; WP

Brooks, Mel 1926-
See Kaminsky, Melvin
See also CA 65-68; CANR 16; DFS 21

Brooks, Peter (Preston) 1938- .... **CLC 34**
See also CA 45-48; CANR 1, 107

Brooks, Van Wyck 1886-1963 .... **CLC 29**
See also AMW; CA 1-4R; CANR 6; DLB 45, 63, 103; MAL 5; TUS

Brophy, Brigid (Antonia) 1929-1995 .... **CLC 6, 11, 29, 105**
See also CA 5-8R; 4; CAAS 149; CANR 25, 53; CBD; CN 1, 2, 3, 4, 5, 6; CWD; DA3; DLB 14, 271; EWL 3; MTCW 1, 2

Brosman, Catharine Savage 1934- ..... **CLC 9**
See also CA 61-64; CANR 21, 46, 149

Brossard, Nicole 1943- .... **CLC 115, 169; PC 80**
See also CA 122; 16; CANR 140; CCA 1; CWP; CWW 2; DLB 53; EWL 3; FW; GLL 2; RGWL 3

Brother Antoninus
See Everson, William (Oliver)

Brothers Grimm
See Grimm, Jacob Ludwig Karl; Grimm, Wilhelm Karl

The Brothers Quay
See Quay, Stephen; Quay, Timothy

Broughton, T(homas) Alan 1936- ..... **CLC 19**
See also CA 45-48; CANR 2, 23, 48, 111

Broumas, Olga 1949- .... **CLC 10, 73**
See also CA 85-88; CANR 20, 69, 110; CP 5, 6, 7; CWP; GLL 2

Broun, Heywood 1888-1939 .... **TCLC 104**
See also DLB 29, 171

Brown, Alan 1950- .... **CLC 99**
See also CA 156

Brown, Charles Brockden 1771-1810 .... **NCLC 22, 74, 122**
See also AMWS 1; CDALB 1640-1865; DLB 37, 59, 73; FW; GL 2; HGG; LMFS 1; RGAL 4; TUS

Brown, Christy 1932-1981 .... **CLC 63**
See also BYA 13; CA 105; CAAS 104; CANR 72; DLB 14

Brown, Claude 1937-2002 ..... **BLC 1:1; CLC 30**
See also AAYA 7; BW 1, 3; CA 73-76; CAAS 205; CANR 81; DAM MULT

Brown, Dan 1964- .... **CLC 209**
See also AAYA 55; CA 217; MTFW 2005

Brown, Dee 1908-2002 .... **CLC 18, 47**
See also AAYA 30; CA 13-16R; 6; CAAS 212; CANR 11, 45, 60, 150; CPW; CSW; DA3; DAM POP; DLBY 1980; LAIT 2; MTCW 1, 2; MTFW 2005; NCFS 5; SATA 5, 110; SATA-Obit 141; TCWW 1, 2

Brown, Dee Alexander
See Brown, Dee

Brown, George
See Wertmueller, Lina

Brown, George Douglas 1869-1902 .... **TCLC 28**
See Douglas, George
See also CA 162

Brown, George Mackay 1921-1996 ... **CLC 5, 48, 100**
See also BRWS 6; CA 21-24R; 6; CAAS 151; CANR 12, 37, 67; CN 1, 2, 3, 4, 5, 6; CP 1, 2, 3, 4, 5, 6; DLB 14, 27, 139, 271; MTCW 1; RGSF 2; SATA 35

Brown, James Wllie
See Komunyakaa, Yusef

Brown, James Wllie, Jr.
See Komunyakaa, Yusef

Brown, Larry 1951-2004 .... **CLC 73**
See also CA 134; CAAE 130; CAAS 233; CANR 117, 145; CSW; DLB 234; INT CA-134

Brown, Moses
See Barrett, William (Christopher)

Brown, Rita Mae 1944- .... **CLC 18, 43, 79**
See also BPFB 1; CA 45-48; CANR 2, 11, 35, 62, 95, 138; CN 5, 6, 7; CPW; CSW; DA3; DAM NOV, POP; FW; INT CANR-11; MAL 5; MTCW 1, 2; MTFW 2005; NFS 9; RGAL 4; TUS

Brown, Roderick (Langmere) Haig-
See Haig-Brown, Roderick (Langmere)

Brown, Rosellen 1939- .... **CLC 32, 170**
See also CA 77-80; 10; CANR 14, 44, 98; CN 6, 7

Brown, Sterling Allen 1901-1989 ... **BLC 1:1; CLC 1, 23, 59; HR 1:2; PC 55**
See also AFAW 1, 2; BW 1, 3; CA 85-88; CAAS 127; CANR 26; CP 3, 4; DA3; DAM MULT, POET; DLB 48, 51, 63; MAL 5; MTCW 1, 2; MTFW 2005; RGAL 4; WP

Brown, Will
See Ainsworth, William Harrison

Brown, William Hill 1765-1793 .... **LC 93**
See also DLB 37

Brown, William Larry
See Brown, Larry

Brown, William Wells 1815-1884 ... **BLC 1:1; DC 1; NCLC 2, 89**
See also DAM MULT; DLB 3, 50, 183, 248; RGAL 4

Browne, Clyde Jackson
See Browne, Jackson

Browne, Jackson 1948(?)- .... **CLC 21**
See also CA 120

Browne, Sir Thomas 1605-1682 .... **LC 111**
See also BRW 2; DLB 151

Browning, Robert 1812-1889 . **NCLC 19, 79; PC 2, 61; WLCS**
See also BRW 4; BRWC 2; BRWR 2; CDBLB 1832-1890; CLR 97; DA; DA3; DAB; DAC; DAM MST, POET; DLB 32, 163; EXPP; LATS 1:1; PAB; PFS 1, 15; RGEL 2; TEA; WLIT 4; WP; YABC 1

Browning, Tod 1882-1962 .... **CLC 16**
See also CA 141; CAAS 117

Brownmiller, Susan 1935- .... **CLC 159**
See also CA 103; CANR 35, 75, 137; DAM NOV; FW; MTCW 1, 2; MTFW 2005

Brownson, Orestes Augustus 1803-1876 .... **NCLC 50**
See also DLB 1, 59, 73, 243

Bruccoli, Matthew J(oseph) 1931- ... **CLC 34**
See also CA 9-12R; CANR 7, 87; DLB 103

Bruce, Lenny CLC 21
See Schneider, Leonard Alfred

Bruchac, Joseph 1942- .... **NNAL**
See also AAYA 19; CA 256; 33-36R, 256; CANR 13, 47, 75, 94, 137, 161; CLR 46; CWRI 5; DAM MULT; JRDA; MAICYA 2; MAICYAS 1; MTCW 2; MTFW 2005; SATA 42, 89, 131, 176; SATA-Essay 176

Bruin, John
See Brutus, Dennis

Brulard, Henri
See Stendhal

Brulls, Christian
See Simenon, Georges (Jacques Christian)

Brunetto Latini c. 1220-1294 .... **CMLC 73**

Brunner, John (Kilian Houston) 1934-1995 .... **CLC 8, 10**
See also CA 1-4R; 8; CAAS 149; CANR 2, 37; CPW; DAM POP; DLB 261; MTCW 1, 2; SCFW 1, 2; SFW 4

Bruno, Giordano 1548-1600 .... **LC 27**
See also RGWL 2, 3

Brutus, Dennis 1924- ...... **BLC 1:1; CLC 43; PC 24**
See also AFW; BW 2, 3; CA 49-52; 14; CANR 2, 27, 42, 81; CDWLB 3; CP 1, 2, 3, 4, 5, 6, 7; DAM MULT, POET; DLB 117, 225; EWL 3

Bryan, C(ourtlandt) D(ixon) B(arnes) 1936- .... **CLC 29**
See also CA 73-76; CANR 13, 68; DLB 185; INT CANR-13

Bryan, Michael
See Moore, Brian
See also CCA 1

Bryan, William Jennings 1860-1925 .... **TCLC 99**
See also DLB 303

Bryant, William Cullen 1794-1878 . **NCLC 6, 46; PC 20**
See also AMWS 1; CDALB 1640-1865; DA; DAB; DAC; DAM MST, POET; DLB 3, 43, 59, 189, 250; EXPP; PAB; RGAL 4; TUS

Bryusov, Valery Yakovlevich 1873-1924 .... **TCLC 10**
See also CA 155; CAAE 107; EWL 3; SFW 4

Buchan, John 1875-1940 .... **TCLC 41**
See also CA 145; CAAE 108; CMW 4; DAB; DAM POP; DLB 34, 70, 156; HGG; MSW; MTCW 2; RGEL 2; RHW; YABC 2

Buchanan, George 1506-1582 .... **LC 4**
See also DLB 132

Buchanan, Robert 1841-1901 .... **TCLC 107**
See also CA 179; DLB 18, 35

Buchheim, Lothar-Guenther 1918-2007 .... **CLC 6**
See also CA 85-88; CAAS 257

Camus, Albert 1913-1960 ...... **CLC 1, 2, 4, 9, 11, 14, 32, 63, 69, 124; DC 2; SSC 9, 76; WLC 1**
See also AAYA 36; AFW; BPFB 1; CA 89-92; CANR 131; DA; DA3; DAB; DAC; DAM DRAM, MST, NOV; DLB 72, 321, 329; EW 13; EWL 3; EXPN; EXPS; GFL 1789 to the Present; LATS 1:2; LMFS 2; MTCW 1, 2; MTFW 2005; NFS 6, 16; RGHL; RGSF 2; RGWL 2, 3; SSFS 4; TWA

Canby, Vincent 1924-2000 .... **CLC 13**
See also CA 81-84; CAAS 191

Cancale
See Desnos, Robert

Canetti, Elias 1905-1994 .. **CLC 3, 14, 25, 75, 86; TCLC 157**
See also CA 21-24R; CAAS 146; CANR 23, 61, 79; CDWLB 2; CWW 2; DA3; DLB 85, 124, 329; EW 12; EWL 3; MTCW 1, 2; MTFW 2005; RGWL 2, 3; TWA

Canfield, Dorothea F.
See Fisher, Dorothy (Frances) Canfield

Canfield, Dorothea Frances
See Fisher, Dorothy (Frances) Canfield

Canfield, Dorothy
See Fisher, Dorothy (Frances) Canfield

Canin, Ethan 1960- .... **CLC 55; SSC 70**
See also CA 135; CAAE 131; DLB 335; MAL 5

Cankar, Ivan 1876-1918 .... **TCLC 105**
See also CDWLB 4; DLB 147; EWL 3

Cannon, Curt
See Hunter, Evan

Cao, Lan 1961- .... **CLC 109**
See also CA 165

Cape, Judith
See Page, P(atricia) K(athleen)
See also CCA 1

Capek, Karel 1890-1938 .... **DC 1; SSC 36; TCLC 6, 37, 192; WLC 1**
See also CA 140; CAAE 104; CDWLB 4; DA; DA3; DAB; DAC; DAM DRAM, MST, NOV; DFS 7, 11; DLB 215; EW 10; EWL 3; MTCW 2; MTFW 2005; RGSF 2; RGWL 2, 3; SCFW 1, 2; SFW 4

Capella, Martianus fl. 4th cent. - .. **CMLC 84**

Capote, Truman 1924-1984 . **CLC 1, 3, 8, 13, 19, 34, 38, 58; SSC 2, 47, 93; TCLC 164; WLC 1**
See also AAYA 61; AMWS 3; BPFB 1; CA 5-8R; CAAS 113; CANR 18, 62; CDALB 1941-1968; CN 1, 2, 3; CPW; DA; DA3; DAB; DAC; DAM MST, NOV, POP; DLB 2, 185, 227; DLBY 1980, 1984; EWL 3; EXPS; GLL 1; LAIT 3; MAL 5; MTCW 1, 2; MTFW 2005; NCFS 2; RGAL 4; RGSF 2; SATA 91; SSFS 2; TUS

Capra, Frank 1897-1991 .... **CLC 16**
See also AAYA 52; CA 61-64; CAAS 135

Caputo, Philip 1941- .... **CLC 32**
See also AAYA 60; CA 73-76; CANR 40, 135; YAW

Caragiale, Ion Luca 1852-1912 ...... **TCLC 76**
See also CA 157

Card, Orson Scott 1951- .... **CLC 44, 47, 50**
See also AAYA 11, 42; BPFB 1; BYA 5, 8; CA 102; CANR 27, 47, 73, 102, 106, 133; CLR 116; CPW; DA3; DAM POP; FANT; INT CANR-27; MTCW 1, 2; MTFW 2005; NFS 5; SATA 83, 127; SCFW 2; SFW 4; SUFW 2; YAW

Cardenal, Ernesto 1925- .... **CLC 31, 161; HLC 1; PC 22**
See also CA 49-52; CANR 2, 32, 66, 138; CWW 2; DAM MULT, POET; DLB 290; EWL 3; HW 1, 2; LAWS 1; MTCW 1, 2; MTFW 2005; RGWL 2, 3

Cardinal, Marie 1929-2001 .... **CLC 189**
See also CA 177; CWW 2; DLB 83; FW

Cardozo, Benjamin N(athan) 1870-1938 .... **TCLC 65**
See also CA 164; CAAE 117

Carducci, Giosue (Alessandro Giuseppe) 1835-1907 .... **PC 46; TCLC 32**
See also CA 163; DLB 329; EW 7; RGWL 2, 3

Carew, Thomas 1595(?)-1640 . **LC 13; PC 29**
See also BRW 2; DLB 126; PAB; RGEL 2

Carey, Ernestine Gilbreth 1908-2006 .... **CLC 17**
See also CA 5-8R; CAAS 254; CANR 71; SATA 2; SATA-Obit 177

Carey, Peter 1943- .... **CLC 40, 55, 96, 183**
See also BRWS 12; CA 127; CAAE 123; CANR 53, 76, 117, 157; CN 4, 5, 6, 7; DLB 289, 326; EWL 3; INT CA-127; MTCW 1, 2; MTFW 2005; RGSF 2; SATA 94

Carleton, William 1794-1869 .... **NCLC 3**
See also DLB 159; RGEL 2; RGSF 2

Carlisle, Henry (Coffin) 1926- .... **CLC 33**
See also CA 13-16R; CANR 15, 85

Carlsen, Chris
See Holdstock, Robert

Carlson, Ron 1947- .... **CLC 54**
See also CA 189; 105, 189; CANR 27, 155; DLB 244

Carlson, Ronald F.
See Carlson, Ron

Carlyle, Jane Welsh 1801-1866 ... **NCLC 181**
See also DLB 55

Carlyle, Thomas 1795-1881 ..... **NCLC 22, 70**
See also BRW 4; CDBLB 1789-1832; DA; DAB; DAC; DAM MST; DLB 55, 144, 254, 338; RGEL 2; TEA

Carman, (William) Bliss 1861-1929 ... **PC 34; TCLC 7**
See also CA 152; CAAE 104; DAC; DLB 92; RGEL 2

Carnegie, Dale 1888-1955 .... **TCLC 53**
See also CA 218

Carossa, Hans 1878-1956 .... **TCLC 48**
See also CA 170; DLB 66; EWL 3

Carpenter, Don(ald Richard) 1931-1995 .... **CLC 41**
See also CA 45-48; CAAS 149; CANR 1, 71

Carpenter, Edward 1844-1929 .... **TCLC 88**
See also BRWS 13; CA 163; GLL 1

Carpenter, John (Howard) 1948- ... **CLC 161**
See also AAYA 2, 73; CA 134; SATA 58

Carpenter, Johnny
See Carpenter, John (Howard)

Carpentier (y Valmont), Alejo 1904-1980 . **CLC 8, 11, 38, 110; HLC 1; SSC 35; TCLC 201**
See also CA 65-68; CAAS 97-100; CANR 11, 70; CDWLB 3; DAM MULT; DLB 113; EWL 3; HW 1, 2; LAW; LMFS 2; RGSF 2; RGWL 2, 3; WLIT 1

Carr, Caleb 1955- .... **CLC 86**
See also CA 147; CANR 73, 134; DA3

Carr, Emily 1871-1945 .... **TCLC 32**
See also CA 159; DLB 68; FW; GLL 2

Carr, John Dickson 1906-1977 .... **CLC 3**
See Fairbairn, Roger
See also CA 49-52; CAAS 69-72; CANR 3, 33, 60; CMW 4; DLB 306; MSW; MTCW 1, 2

Carr, Philippa
See Hibbert, Eleanor Alice Burford

Carr, Virginia Spencer 1929- .... **CLC 34**
See also CA 61-64; DLB 111

Carrere, Emmanuel 1957- .... **CLC 89**
See also CA 200

Carrier, Roch 1937- .... **CLC 13, 78**
See also CA 130; CANR 61, 152; CCA 1; DAC; DAM MST; DLB 53; SATA 105, 166

Carroll, James Dennis
See Carroll, Jim

Carroll, James P. 1943(?)- .... **CLC 38**
See also CA 81-84; CANR 73, 139; MTCW 2; MTFW 2005

Carroll, Jim 1951- .... **CLC 35, 143**
See also AAYA 17; CA 45-48; CANR 42, 115; NCFS 5

Carroll, Lewis NCLC 2, 53, 139; PC 18, 74; WLC 1
See Dodgson, Charles L(utwidge)
See also AAYA 39; BRW 5; BYA 5, 13; CDBLB 1832-1890; CLR 2, 18, 108; DLB 18, 163, 178; DLBY 1998; EXPN; EXPP; FANT; JRDA; LAIT 1; NFS 7; PFS 11; RGEL 2; SUFW 1; TEA; WCH

Carroll, Paul Vincent 1900-1968 ...... **CLC 10**
See also CA 9-12R; CAAS 25-28R; DLB 10; EWL 3; RGEL 2

Carruth, Hayden 1921- ..... **CLC 4, 7, 10, 18, 84; PC 10**
See also AMWS 16; CA 9-12R; CANR 4, 38, 59, 110; CP 1, 2, 3, 4, 5, 6, 7; DLB 5, 165; INT CANR-4; MTCW 1, 2; MTFW 2005; PFS 26; SATA 47

Carson, Anne 1950- .... **CLC 185; PC 64**
See also AMWS 12; CA 203; CP 7; DLB 193; PFS 18; TCLE 1:1

Carson, Ciaran 1948- .... **CLC 201**
See also BRWS 13; CA 153; CAAE 112; CANR 113; CP 6, 7; PFS 26

Carson, Rachel
See Carson, Rachel Louise
See also AAYA 49; DLB 275

Carson, Rachel Louise 1907-1964 .... **CLC 71**
See Carson, Rachel
See also AMWS 9; ANW; CA 77-80; CANR 35; DA3; DAM POP; FW; LAIT 4; MAL 5; MTCW 1, 2; MTFW 2005; NCFS 1; SATA 23

Carter, Angela 1940-1992 ...... **CLC 5, 41, 76; SSC 13, 85; TCLC 139**
See also BRWS 3; CA 53-56; CAAS 136; CANR 12, 36, 61, 106; CN 3, 4, 5; DA3; DLB 14, 207, 261, 319; EXPS; FANT; FW; GL 2; MTCW 1, 2; MTFW 2005; RGSF 2; SATA 66; SATA-Obit 70; SFW 4; SSFS 4, 12; SUFW 2; WLIT 4

Carter, Angela Olive
See Carter, Angela

Carter, Martin (Wylde) 1927- .... **BLC 2:1**
See also BW 2; CA 102; CANR 42; CDWLB 3; CP 1, 2, 3, 4, 5, 6; DLB 117; EWL 3

Carter, Nick
See Smith, Martin Cruz

Carver, Raymond 1938-1988 ..... **CLC 22, 36, 53, 55, 126; PC 54; SSC 8, 51, 104**
See also AAYA 44; AMWS 3; BPFB 1; CA 33-36R; CAAS 126; CANR 17, 34, 61, 103; CN 4; CPW; DA3; DAM NOV; DLB 130; DLBY 1984, 1988; EWL 3; MAL 5; MTCW 1, 2; MTFW 2005; PFS 17; RGAL 4; RGSF 2; SSFS 3, 6, 12, 13, 23; TCLE 1:1; TCWW 2; TUS

Cary, Elizabeth, Lady Falkland 1585-1639 .... **LC 30, 141**

Cary, (Arthur) Joyce (Lunel) 1888-1957 .... **TCLC 1, 29, 196**
See also BRW 7; CA 164; CAAE 104; CDBLB 1914-1945; DLB 15, 100; EWL 3; MTCW 2; RGEL 2; TEA

Casal, Julian del 1863-1893 .... **NCLC 131**
See also DLB 283; LAW

Casanova, Giacomo
See Casanova de Seingalt, Giovanni Jacopo
See also WLIT 7
Casanova de Seingalt, Giovanni Jacopo 1725-1798 .... **LC 13**
See Casanova, Giacomo
Casares, Adolfo Bioy
See Bioy Casares, Adolfo
See also RGSF 2
Casas, Bartolome de las 1474-1566
See Las Casas, Bartolome de
See also WLIT 1
Case, John
See Hougan, Carolyn
Casely-Hayford, J(oseph) E(phraim) 1866-1903 .... **BLC 1:1; TCLC 24**
See also BW 2; CA 152; CAAE 123; DAM MULT
Casey, John (Dudley) 1939- .... **CLC 59**
See also BEST 90:2; CA 69-72; CANR 23, 100
Casey, Michael 1947- .... **CLC 2**
See also CA 65-68; CANR 109; CP 2, 3; DLB 5
Casey, Patrick
See Thurman, Wallace (Henry)
Casey, Warren (Peter) 1935-1988 .... **CLC 12**
See also CA 101; CAAS 127; INT CA-101
Casona, Alejandro CLC 49; TCLC 199
See Alvarez, Alejandro Rodriguez
See also EWL 3
Cassavetes, John 1929-1989 .... **CLC 20**
See also CA 85-88; CAAS 127; CANR 82
Cassian, Nina 1924- .... **PC 17**
See also CWP; CWW 2
Cassill, R(onald) V(erlin) 1919-2002 .... **CLC 4, 23**
See also CA 9-12R; 1; CAAS 208; CANR 7, 45; CN 1, 2, 3, 4, 5, 6, 7; DLB 6, 218; DLBY 2002
Cassiodorus, Flavius Magnus c. 490(?)-c. 583(?) .... **CMLC 43**
Cassirer, Ernst 1874-1945 .... **TCLC 61**
See also CA 157
Cassity, (Allen) Turner 1929- .... **CLC 6, 42**
See also CA 223; 17-20R, 223; 8; CANR 11; CSW; DLB 105
Cassius Dio c. 155-c. 229 .... **CMLC 99**
See also DLB 176
Castaneda, Carlos (Cesar Aranha) 1931(?)-1998 .... **CLC 12, 119**
See also CA 25-28R; CANR 32, 66, 105; DNFS 1; HW 1; MTCW 1
Castedo, Elena 1937- .... **CLC 65**
See also CA 132
Castedo-Ellerman, Elena
See Castedo, Elena
Castellanos, Rosario 1925-1974 .... **CLC 66; HLC 1; SSC 39, 68**
See also CA 131; CAAS 53-56; CANR 58; CDWLB 3; DAM MULT; DLB 113, 290; EWL 3; FW; HW 1; LAW; MTCW 2; MTFW 2005; RGSF 2; RGWL 2, 3
Castelvetro, Lodovico 1505-1571 .... **LC 12**
Castiglione, Baldassare 1478-1529 ...... **LC 12**
See Castiglione, Baldesar
See also LMFS 1; RGWL 2, 3
Castiglione, Baldesar
See Castiglione, Baldassare
See also EW 2; WLIT 7
Castillo, Ana 1953- .... **CLC 151**
See also AAYA 42; CA 131; CANR 51, 86, 128, 172; CWP; DLB 122, 227; DNFS 2; FW; HW 1; LLW; PFS 21
Castillo, Ana Hernandez Del
See Castillo, Ana
Castle, Robert
See Hamilton, Edmond
Castro (Ruz), Fidel 1926(?)- .... **HLC 1**
See also CA 129; CAAE 110; CANR 81; DAM MULT; HW 2
Castro, Guillen de 1569-1631 .... **LC 19**
Castro, Rosalia de 1837-1885 ... **NCLC 3, 78; PC 41**
See also DAM MULT
Cather, Willa (Sibert) 1873-1947 . **SSC 2, 50; TCLC 1, 11, 31, 99, 132, 152; WLC 1**
See also AAYA 24; AMW; AMWC 1; AMWR 1; BPFB 1; CA 128; CAAE 104; CDALB 1865-1917; CLR 98; DA; DA3; DAB; DAC; DAM MST, NOV; DLB 9, 54, 78, 256; DLBD 1; EWL 3; EXPN; EXPS; FL 1:5; LAIT 3; LATS 1:1; MAL 5; MBL; MTCW 1, 2; MTFW 2005; NFS 2, 19; RGAL 4; RGSF 2; RHW; SATA 30; SSFS 2, 7, 16; TCWW 1, 2; TUS
Catherine II
See Catherine the Great
See also DLB 150
Catherine, Saint 1347-1380 ..... **CMLC 27, 95**
Catherine the Great 1729-1796 .... **LC 69**
See Catherine II
Cato, Marcus Porcius 234B.C.-149B.C. .... **CMLC 21**
See Cato the Elder
Cato, Marcus Porcius, the Elder
See Cato, Marcus Porcius
Cato the Elder
See Cato, Marcus Porcius
See also DLB 211
Catton, (Charles) Bruce 1899-1978 . **CLC 35**
See also AITN 1; CA 5-8R; CAAS 81-84; CANR 7, 74; DLB 17; MTCW 2; MTFW 2005; SATA 2; SATA-Obit 24
Catullus c. 84B.C.-54B.C. .... **CMLC 18**
See also AW 2; CDWLB 1; DLB 211; RGWL 2, 3; WLIT 8
Cauldwell, Frank
See King, Francis (Henry)
Caunitz, William J. 1933-1996 .... **CLC 34**
See also BEST 89:3; CA 130; CAAE 125; CAAS 152; CANR 73; INT CA-130
Causley, Charles (Stanley) 1917-2003 .... **CLC 7**
See also CA 9-12R; CAAS 223; CANR 5, 35, 94; CLR 30; CP 1, 2, 3, 4, 5; CWRI 5; DLB 27; MTCW 1; SATA 3, 66; SATA-Obit 149
Caute, (John) David 1936- .... **CLC 29**
See also CA 1-4R; 4; CANR 1, 33, 64, 120; CBD; CD 5, 6; CN 1, 2, 3, 4, 5, 6, 7; DAM NOV; DLB 14, 231
Cavafy, C(onstantine) P(eter) PC 36; TCLC 2, 7
See Kavafis, Konstantinos Petrou
See also CA 148; DA3; DAM POET; EW 8; EWL 3; MTCW 2; PFS 19; RGWL 2, 3; WP
Cavalcanti, Guido c. 1250-c. 1300 .... **CMLC 54**
See also RGWL 2, 3; WLIT 7
Cavallo, Evelyn
See Spark, Muriel
Cavanna, Betty CLC 12
See Harrison, Elizabeth (Allen) Cavanna
See also JRDA; MAICYA 1; SAAS 4; SATA 1, 30
Cavendish, Margaret Lucas 1623-1673 .... **LC 30, 132**
See also DLB 131, 252, 281; RGEL 2
Caxton, William 1421(?)-1491(?) .... **LC 17**
See also DLB 170
Cayer, D. M.
See Duffy, Maureen (Patricia)
Cayrol, Jean 1911-2005 .... **CLC 11**
See also CA 89-92; CAAS 236; DLB 83; EWL 3
Cela (y Trulock), Camilo Jose
See Cela, Camilo Jose
See also CWW 2
Cela, Camilo Jose 1916-2002 .... **CLC 4, 13, 59, 122; HLC 1; SSC 71**
See Cela (y Trulock), Camilo Jose
See also BEST 90:2; CA 21-24R; 10; CAAS 206; CANR 21, 32, 76, 139; DAM MULT; DLB 322; DLBY 1989; EW 13; EWL 3; HW 1; MTCW 1, 2; MTFW 2005; RGSF 2; RGWL 2, 3
Celan, Paul CLC 10, 19, 53, 82; PC 10
See Antschel, Paul
See also CDWLB 2; DLB 69; EWL 3; RGHL; RGWL 2, 3
Celine, Louis-Ferdinand CLC 1, 3, 4, 7, 9, 15, 47, 124
See Destouches, Louis-Ferdinand
See also DLB 72; EW 11; EWL 3; GFL 1789 to the Present; RGWL 2, 3
Cellini, Benvenuto 1500-1571 .... **LC 7**
See also WLIT 7
Cendrars, Blaise CLC 18, 106
See Sauser-Hall, Frederic
See also DLB 258; EWL 3; GFL 1789 to the Present; RGWL 2, 3; WP
Centlivre, Susanna 1669(?)-1723 .... **DC 25; LC 65**
See also DLB 84; RGEL 2
Cernuda (y Bidon), Luis 1902-1963 .... **CLC 54; PC 62**
See also CA 131; CAAS 89-92; DAM POET; DLB 134; EWL 3; GLL 1; HW 1; RGWL 2, 3
Cervantes, Lorna Dee 1954- ..... **HLCS 1; PC 35**
See also CA 131; CANR 80; CP 7; CWP; DLB 82; EXPP; HW 1; LLW
Cervantes (Saavedra), Miguel de 1547-1616 .... **HLCS; LC 6, 23, 93; SSC 12, 108; WLC 1**
See also AAYA 56; BYA 1, 14; DA; DAB; DAC; DAM MST, NOV; EW 2; LAIT 1; LATS 1:1; LMFS 1; NFS 8; RGSF 2; RGWL 2, 3; TWA
Cesaire, Aime 1913- .. **BLC 1:1; CLC 19, 32, 112; DC 22; PC 25**
See also BW 2, 3; CA 65-68; CANR 24, 43, 81; CWW 2; DA3; DAM MULT, POET; DLB 321; EWL 3; GFL 1789 to the Present; MTCW 1, 2; MTFW 2005; WP
Chabon, Michael 1963- ... **CLC 55, 149; SSC 59**
See also AAYA 45; AMWS 11; CA 139; CANR 57, 96, 127, 138; DLB 278; MAL 5; MTFW 2005; NFS 25; SATA 145
Chabrol, Claude 1930- .... **CLC 16**
See also CA 110
Chairil Anwar
See Anwar, Chairil
See also EWL 3
Challans, Mary 1905-1983
See Renault, Mary
See also CA 81-84; CAAS 111; CANR 74; DA3; MTCW 2; MTFW 2005; SATA 23; SATA-Obit 36; TEA
Challis, George
See Faust, Frederick (Schiller)
Chambers, Aidan 1934- .... **CLC 35**
See also AAYA 27; CA 25-28R; CANR 12, 31, 58, 116; JRDA; MAICYA 1, 2; SAAS 12; SATA 1, 69, 108, 171; WYA; YAW
Chambers, James 1948-
See Cliff, Jimmy
See also CAAE 124
Chambers, Jessie
See Lawrence, D(avid) H(erbert Richards)
See also GLL 1

Chambers, Robert W(illiam) 1865-1933 .... **SSC 92; TCLC 41**
See also CA 165; DLB 202; HGG; SATA 107; SUFW 1
Chambers, (David) Whittaker 1901-1961 .... **TCLC 129**
See also CAAS 89-92; DLB 303
Chamisso, Adelbert von 1781-1838 .... **NCLC 82**
See also DLB 90; RGWL 2, 3; SUFW 1
Chance, James T.
See Carpenter, John (Howard)
Chance, John T.
See Carpenter, John (Howard)
Chandler, Raymond (Thornton) 1888-1959 .... **SSC 23; TCLC 1, 7, 179**
See also AAYA 25; AMWC 2; AMWS 4; BPFB 1; CA 129; CAAE 104; CANR 60, 107; CDALB 1929-1941; CMW 4; DA3; DLB 226, 253; DLBD 6; EWL 3; MAL 5; MSW; MTCW 1, 2; MTFW 2005; NFS 17; RGAL 4; TUS
Chang, Diana 1934- .... **AAL**
See also CA 228; CWP; DLB 312; EXPP
Chang, Eileen 1920-1995 .... **AAL; SSC 28; TCLC 184**
See also CA 166; CANR 168; CWW 2; DLB 328; EWL 3; RGSF 2
Chang, Jung 1952- .... **CLC 71**
See also CA 142
Chang Ai-Ling
See Chang, Eileen
Channing, William Ellery 1780-1842 .... **NCLC 17**
See also DLB 1, 59, 235; RGAL 4
Chao, Patricia 1955- .... **CLC 119**
See also CA 163; CANR 155
Chaplin, Charles Spencer 1889-1977 .... **CLC 16**
See Chaplin, Charlie
See also CA 81-84; CAAS 73-76
Chaplin, Charlie
See Chaplin, Charles Spencer
See also AAYA 61; DLB 44
Chapman, George 1559(?)-1634 . **DC 19; LC 22, 116**
See also BRW 1; DAM DRAM; DLB 62, 121; LMFS 1; RGEL 2
Chapman, Graham 1941-1989 .... **CLC 21**
See Monty Python
See also CA 116; CAAS 129; CANR 35, 95
Chapman, John Jay 1862-1933 .... **TCLC 7**
See also AMWS 14; CA 191; CAAE 104
Chapman, Lee
See Bradley, Marion Zimmer
See also GLL 1
Chapman, Walker
See Silverberg, Robert
Chappell, Fred (Davis) 1936- .... **CLC 40, 78, 162**
See also CA 198; 5-8R, 198; 4; CANR 8, 33, 67, 110; CN 6; CP 6, 7; CSW; DLB 6, 105; HGG
Char, Rene(-Emile) 1907-1988 .... **CLC 9, 11, 14, 55; PC 56**
See also CA 13-16R; CAAS 124; CANR 32; DAM POET; DLB 258; EWL 3; GFL 1789 to the Present; MTCW 1, 2; RGWL 2, 3
Charby, Jay
See Ellison, Harlan
Chardin, Pierre Teilhard de
See Teilhard de Chardin, (Marie Joseph) Pierre
Chariton fl. 1st cent. (?)- .... **CMLC 49**
Charlemagne 742-814 .... **CMLC 37**
Charles I 1600-1649 .... **LC 13**
Charriere, Isabelle de 1740-1805 .. **NCLC 66**
See also DLB 313
Chartier, Alain c. 1392-1430 .... **LC 94**
See also DLB 208
Chartier, Emile-Auguste
See Alain
Charyn, Jerome 1937- .... **CLC 5, 8, 18**
See also CA 5-8R; 1; CANR 7, 61, 101, 158; CMW 4; CN 1, 2, 3, 4, 5, 6, 7; DLBY 1983; MTCW 1
Chase, Adam
See Marlowe, Stephen
Chase, Mary (Coyle) 1907-1981 .... **DC 1**
See also CA 77-80; CAAS 105; CAD; CWD; DFS 11; DLB 228; SATA 17; SATA-Obit 29
Chase, Mary Ellen 1887-1973 .... **CLC 2; TCLC 124**
See also CA 13-16; CAAS 41-44R; CAP 1; SATA 10
Chase, Nicholas
See Hyde, Anthony
See also CCA 1
Chase-Riboud, Barbara (Dewayne Tosi) 1939- .... **BLC 2:1**
See also BW 2; CA 113; CANR 76; DAM MULT; DLB 33; MTCW 2
Chateaubriand, Francois Rene de 1768-1848 .... **NCLC 3, 134**
See also DLB 119; EW 5; GFL 1789 to the Present; RGWL 2, 3; TWA
Chatelet, Gabrielle-Emilie Du
See du Chatelet, Emilie
See also DLB 313
Chatterje, Sarat Chandra 1876-1936(?)
See Chatterji, Saratchandra
See also CAAE 109
Chatterji, Bankim Chandra 1838-1894 .... **NCLC 19**
Chatterji, Saratchandra TCLC 13
See Chatterje, Sarat Chandra
See also CA 186; EWL 3
Chatterton, Thomas 1752-1770 .... **LC 3, 54**
See also DAM POET; DLB 109; RGEL 2
Chatwin, (Charles) Bruce 1940-1989 .... **CLC 28, 57, 59**
See also AAYA 4; BEST 90:1; BRWS 4; CA 85-88; CAAS 127; CPW; DAM POP; DLB 194, 204; EWL 3; MTFW 2005
Chaucer, Daniel
See Ford, Ford Madox
See also RHW
Chaucer, Geoffrey 1340(?)-1400 .. **LC 17, 56; PC 19, 58; WLCS**
See also BRW 1; BRWC 1; BRWR 2; CDBLB Before 1660; DA; DA3; DAB; DAC; DAM MST, POET; DLB 146; LAIT 1; PAB; PFS 14; RGEL 2; TEA; WLIT 3; WP
Chavez, Denise 1948- .... **HLC 1**
See also CA 131; CANR 56, 81, 137; DAM MULT; DLB 122; FW; HW 1, 2; LLW; MAL 5; MTCW 2; MTFW 2005
Chaviaras, Strates 1935-
See Haviaras, Stratis
See also CA 105
Chayefsky, Paddy CLC 23
See Chayefsky, Sidney
See also CAD; DLB 7, 44; DLBY 1981; RGAL 4
Chayefsky, Sidney 1923-1981
See Chayefsky, Paddy
See also CA 9-12R; CAAS 104; CANR 18; DAM DRAM
Chedid, Andree 1920- .... **CLC 47**
See also CA 145; CANR 95; EWL 3
Cheever, John 1912-1982 ..... **CLC 3, 7, 8, 11, 15, 25, 64; SSC 1, 38, 57; WLC 2**
See also AAYA 65; AMWS 1; BPFB 1; CA 5-8R; CAAS 106; CABS 1; CANR 5, 27, 76; CDALB 1941-1968; CN 1, 2, 3; CPW; DA; DA3; DAB; DAC; DAM MST, NOV, POP; DLB 2, 102, 227; DLBY 1980, 1982; EWL 3; EXPS; INT CANR-5; MAL 5; MTCW 1, 2; MTFW 2005; RGAL 4; RGSF 2; SSFS 2, 14; TUS
Cheever, Susan 1943- .... **CLC 18, 48**
See also CA 103; CANR 27, 51, 92, 157; DLBY 1982; INT CANR-27
Chekhonte, Antosha
See Chekhov, Anton (Pavlovich)
Chekhov, Anton (Pavlovich) 1860-1904 .... **DC 9; SSC 2, 28, 41, 51, 85, 102; TCLC 3, 10, 31, 55, 96, 163; WLC 2**
See also AAYA 68; BYA 14; CA 124; CAAE 104; DA; DA3; DAB; DAC; DAM DRAM, MST; DFS 1, 5, 10, 12; DLB 277; EW 7; EWL 3; EXPS; LAIT 3; LATS 1:1; RGSF 2; RGWL 2, 3; SATA 90; SSFS 5, 13, 14; TWA
Cheney, Lynne V. 1941- .... **CLC 70**
See also CA 89-92; CANR 58, 117; SATA 152
Chernyshevsky, Nikolai Gavrilovich
See Chernyshevsky, Nikolay Gavrilovich
See also DLB 238
Chernyshevsky, Nikolay Gavrilovich 1828-1889 .... **NCLC 1**
See Chernyshevsky, Nikolai Gavrilovich
Cherry, Carolyn Janice CLC 35
See Cherryh, C.J.
See also AAYA 24; BPFB 1; DLBY 1980; FANT; SATA 93; SCFW 2; SFW 4; YAW
Cherryh, C.J. 1942-
See Cherry, Carolyn Janice
See also CA 65-68; CANR 10, 147; SATA 172
Chesler, Phyllis 1940- .... **CLC 247**
See also CA 49-52; CANR 4, 59, 140; FW
Chesnutt, Charles W(addell) 1858-1932 . **BLC 1:1; SSC 7, 54; TCLC 5, 39**
See also AFAW 1, 2; AMWS 14; BW 1, 3; CA 125; CAAE 106; CANR 76; DAM MULT; DLB 12, 50, 78; EWL 3; MAL 5; MTCW 1, 2; MTFW 2005; RGAL 4; RGSF 2; SSFS 11
Chester, Alfred 1929(?)-1971 .... **CLC 49**
See also CA 196; CAAS 33-36R; DLB 130; MAL 5
Chesterton, G(ilbert) K(eith) 1874-1936 . **PC 28; SSC 1, 46; TCLC 1, 6, 64**
See also AAYA 57; BRW 6; CA 132; CAAE 104; CANR 73, 131; CDBLB 1914-1945; CMW 4; DAM NOV, POET; DLB 10, 19, 34, 70, 98, 149, 178; EWL 3; FANT; MSW; MTCW 1, 2; MTFW 2005; RGEL 2; RGSF 2; SATA 27; SUFW 1
Chettle, Henry 1560-1607(?) .... **LC 112**
See also DLB 136; RGEL 2
Chiang, Pin-chin 1904-1986
See Ding Ling
See also CAAS 118
Chief Joseph 1840-1904 .... **NNAL**
See also CA 152; DA3; DAM MULT
Chief Seattle 1786(?)-1866 .... **NNAL**
See also DA3; DAM MULT
Ch'ien, Chung-shu 1910-1998 .... **CLC 22**
See Qian Zhongshu
See also CA 130; CANR 73; MTCW 1, 2
Chikamatsu Monzaemon 1653-1724 ... **LC 66**
See also RGWL 2, 3
Child, Francis James 1825-1896 . **NCLC 173**
See also DLB 1, 64, 235
Child, L. Maria
See Child, Lydia Maria

Colonna, Vittoria 1492-1547 .... **LC 71**
See also RGWL 2, 3
Colt, Winchester Remington
See Hubbard, L. Ron
Colter, Cyrus J. 1910-2002 .... **CLC 58**
See also BW 1; CA 65-68; CAAS 205; CANR 10, 66; CN 2, 3, 4, 5, 6; DLB 33
Colton, James
See Hansen, Joseph
See also GLL 1
Colum, Padraic 1881-1972 .... **CLC 28**
See also BYA 4; CA 73-76; CAAS 33-36R; CANR 35; CLR 36; CP 1; CWRI 5; DLB 19; MAICYA 1, 2; MTCW 1; RGEL 2; SATA 15; WCH
Colvin, James
See Moorcock, Michael
Colwin, Laurie (E.) 1944-1992 .... **CLC 5, 13, 23, 84**
See also CA 89-92; CAAS 139; CANR 20, 46; DLB 218; DLBY 1980; MTCW 1
Comfort, Alex(ander) 1920-2000 .... **CLC 7**
See also CA 1-4R; CAAS 190; CANR 1, 45; CN 1, 2, 3, 4; CP 1, 2, 3, 4, 5, 6, 7; DAM POP; MTCW 2
Comfort, Montgomery
See Campbell, Ramsey
Compton-Burnett, I(vy)
1892(?)-1969 .... **CLC 1, 3, 10, 15, 34; TCLC 180**
See also BRW 7; CA 1-4R; CAAS 25-28R; CANR 4; DAM NOV; DLB 36; EWL 3; MTCW 1, 2; RGEL 2
Comstock, Anthony 1844-1915 ...... **TCLC 13**
See also CA 169; CAAE 110
Comte, Auguste 1798-1857 .... **NCLC 54**
Conan Doyle, Arthur
See Doyle, Sir Arthur Conan
See also BPFB 1; BYA 4, 5, 11
Conde (Abellan), Carmen
1901-1996 .... **HLCS 1**
See also CA 177; CWW 2; DLB 108; EWL 3; HW 2
Conde, Maryse 1937- .... **BLCS; BLC 2:1; CLC 52, 92, 247**
See also BW 2, 3; CA 190; 110, 190; CANR 30, 53, 76, 171; CWW 2; DAM MULT; EWL 3; MTCW 2; MTFW 2005
Condillac, Etienne Bonnot de
1714-1780 .... **LC 26**
See also DLB 313
Condon, Richard 1915-1996 ...... **CLC 4, 6, 8, 10, 45, 100**
See also BEST 90:3; BPFB 1; CA 1-4R; 1; CAAS 151; CANR 2, 23, 164; CMW 4; CN 1, 2, 3, 4, 5, 6; DAM NOV; INT CANR-23; MAL 5; MTCW 1, 2
Condon, Richard Thomas
See Condon, Richard
Condorcet LC 104
See Condorcet, marquis de Marie-Jean-Antoine-Nicolas Caritat
See also GFL Beginnings to 1789
Condorcet, marquis de Marie-Jean-Antoine-Nicolas Caritat
1743-1794
See Condorcet
See also DLB 313
Confucius 551B.C.-479B.C. ..... **CMLC 19, 65; WLCS**
See also DA; DA3; DAB; DAC; DAM MST
Congreve, William 1670-1729 ... **DC 2; LC 5, 21; WLC 2**
See also BRW 2; CDBLB 1660-1789; DA; DAB; DAC; DAM DRAM, MST, POET; DFS 15; DLB 39, 84; RGEL 2; WLIT 3
Conley, Robert J(ackson) 1940- .... **NNAL**
See also CA 41-44R; CANR 15, 34, 45, 96; DAM MULT; TCWW 2
Connell, Evan S., Jr. 1924- .... **CLC 4, 6, 45**
See also AAYA 7; AMWS 14; CA 1-4R; 2; CANR 2, 39, 76, 97, 140; CN 1, 2, 3, 4, 5, 6; DAM NOV; DLB 2, 335; DLBY 1981; MAL 5; MTCW 1, 2; MTFW 2005
Connelly, Marc(us Cook) 1890-1980 . **CLC 7**
See also CA 85-88; CAAS 102; CAD; CANR 30; DFS 12; DLB 7; DLBY 1980; MAL 5; RGAL 4; SATA-Obit 25
Connor, Ralph TCLC 31
See Gordon, Charles William
See also DLB 92; TCWW 1, 2
Conrad, Joseph 1857-1924 ..... **SSC 9, 67, 69, 71; TCLC 1, 6, 13, 25, 43, 57; WLC 2**
See also AAYA 26; BPFB 1; BRW 6; BRWC 1; BRWR 2; BYA 2; CA 131; CAAE 104; CANR 60; CDBLB 1890-1914; DA; DA3; DAB; DAC; DAM MST, NOV; DLB 10, 34, 98, 156; EWL 3; EXPN; EXPS; LAIT 2; LATS 1:1; LMFS 1; MTCW 1, 2; MTFW 2005; NFS 2, 16; RGEL 2; RGSF 2; SATA 27; SSFS 1, 12; TEA; WLIT 4
Conrad, Robert Arnold
See Hart, Moss
Conroy, Pat 1945- .... **CLC 30, 74**
See also AAYA 8, 52; AITN 1; BPFB 1; CA 85-88; CANR 24, 53, 129; CN 7; CPW; CSW; DA3; DAM NOV, POP; DLB 6; LAIT 5; MAL 5; MTCW 1, 2; MTFW 2005
Constant (de Rebecque), (Henri) Benjamin
1767-1830 .... **NCLC 6, 182**
See also DLB 119; EW 4; GFL 1789 to the Present
Conway, Jill K. 1934- .... **CLC 152**
See also CA 130; CANR 94
Conway, Jill Kathryn Ker
See Conway, Jill K.
Conybeare, Charles Augustus
See Eliot, T(homas) S(tearns)
Cook, Michael 1933-1994 .... **CLC 58**
See also CA 93-96; CANR 68; DLB 53
Cook, Robin 1940- .... **CLC 14**
See also AAYA 32; BEST 90:2; BPFB 1; CA 111; CAAE 108; CANR 41, 90, 109; CPW; DA3; DAM POP; HGG; INT CA-111
Cook, Roy
See Silverberg, Robert
Cooke, Elizabeth 1948- .... **CLC 55**
See also CA 129
Cooke, John Esten 1830-1886 .... **NCLC 5**
See also DLB 3, 248; RGAL 4
Cooke, John Estes
See Baum, L(yman) Frank
Cooke, M. E.
See Creasey, John
Cooke, Margaret
See Creasey, John
Cooke, Rose Terry 1827-1892 ...... **NCLC 110**
See also DLB 12, 74
Cook-Lynn, Elizabeth 1930- .... **CLC 93; NNAL**
See also CA 133; DAM MULT; DLB 175
Cooney, Ray CLC 62
See also CBD
Cooper, Anthony Ashley 1671-1713 .. **LC 107**
See also DLB 101, 336
Cooper, Dennis 1953- .... **CLC 203**
See also CA 133; CANR 72, 86; GLL 1; HGG
Cooper, Douglas 1960- .... **CLC 86**
Cooper, Henry St. John
See Creasey, John
Cooper, J. California (?)- .... **CLC 56**
See also AAYA 12; BW 1; CA 125; CANR 55; DAM MULT; DLB 212
Cooper, James Fenimore
1789-1851 .... **NCLC 1, 27, 54**
See also AAYA 22; AMW; BPFB 1; CDALB 1640-1865; CLR 105; DA3; DLB 3, 183, 250, 254; LAIT 1; NFS 25; RGAL 4; SATA 19; TUS; WCH
Cooper, Susan Fenimore
1813-1894 .... **NCLC 129**
See also ANW; DLB 239, 254
Coover, Robert 1932- .. **CLC 3, 7, 15, 32, 46, 87, 161; SSC 15, 101**
See also AMWS 5; BPFB 1; CA 45-48; CANR 3, 37, 58, 115; CN 1, 2, 3, 4, 5, 6, 7; DAM NOV; DLB 2, 227; DLBY 1981; EWL 3; MAL 5; MTCW 1, 2; MTFW 2005; RGAL 4; RGSF 2
Copeland, Stewart (Armstrong)
1952- .... **CLC 26**
Copernicus, Nicolaus 1473-1543 .... **LC 45**
Coppard, A(lfred) E(dgar)
1878-1957 .... **SSC 21; TCLC 5**
See also BRWS 8; CA 167; CAAE 114; DLB 162; EWL 3; HGG; RGEL 2; RGSF 2; SUFW 1; YABC 1
Coppee, Francois 1842-1908 .... **TCLC 25**
See also CA 170; DLB 217
Coppola, Francis Ford 1939- ... **CLC 16, 126**
See also AAYA 39; CA 77-80; CANR 40, 78; DLB 44
Copway, George 1818-1869 .... **NNAL**
See also DAM MULT; DLB 175, 183
Corbiere, Tristan 1845-1875 .... **NCLC 43**
See also DLB 217; GFL 1789 to the Present
Corcoran, Barbara (Asenath)
1911- .... **CLC 17**
See also AAYA 14; CA 191; 21-24R, 191; 2; CANR 11, 28, 48; CLR 50; DLB 52; JRDA; MAICYA 2; MAICYAS 1; RHW; SAAS 20; SATA 3, 77; SATA-Essay 125
Cordelier, Maurice
See Giraudoux, Jean(-Hippolyte)
Corelli, Marie TCLC 51
See Mackay, Mary
See also DLB 34, 156; RGEL 2; SUFW 1
Corinna c. 225B.C.-c. 305B.C. ...... **CMLC 72**
Corman, Cid CLC 9
See Corman, Sidney
See also CA 2; CP 1, 2, 3, 4, 5, 6, 7; DLB 5, 193
Corman, Sidney 1924-2004
See Corman, Cid
See also CA 85-88; CAAS 225; CANR 44; DAM POET
Cormier, Robert 1925-2000 .... **CLC 12, 30**
See also AAYA 3, 19; BYA 1, 2, 6, 8, 9; CA 1-4R; CANR 5, 23, 76, 93; CDALB 1968-1988; CLR 12, 55; DA; DAB; DAC; DAM MST, NOV; DLB 52; EXPN; INT CANR-23; JRDA; LAIT 5; MAICYA 1, 2; MTCW 1, 2; MTFW 2005; NFS 2, 18; SATA 10, 45, 83; SATA-Obit 122; WYA; YAW
Corn, Alfred (DeWitt III) 1943- .... **CLC 33**
See also CA 179; 179; 25; CANR 44; CP 3, 4, 5, 6, 7; CSW; DLB 120, 282; DLBY 1980
Corneille, Pierre 1606-1684 .. **DC 21; LC 28, 135**
See also DAB; DAM MST; DFS 21; DLB 268; EW 3; GFL Beginnings to 1789; RGWL 2, 3; TWA
Cornwell, David
See le Carre, John
Cornwell, David John Moore
See le Carre, John

Cornwell, Patricia 1956- .... **CLC 155**
See also AAYA 16, 56; BPFB 1; CA 134; CANR 53, 131; CMW 4; CPW; CSW; DAM POP; DLB 306; MSW; MTCW 2; MTFW 2005
Cornwell, Patricia Daniels
See Cornwell, Patricia
Corso, Gregory 1930-2001 .... **CLC 1, 11; PC 33**
See also AMWS 12; BG 1:2; CA 5-8R; CAAS 193; CANR 41, 76, 132; CP 1, 2, 3, 4, 5, 6, 7; DA3; DLB 5, 16, 237; LMFS 2; MAL 5; MTCW 1, 2; MTFW 2005; WP
Cortazar, Julio 1914-1984 ... **CLC 2, 3, 5, 10, 13, 15, 33, 34, 92; HLC 1; SSC 7, 76**
See also BPFB 1; CA 21-24R; CANR 12, 32, 81; CDWLB 3; DA3; DAM MULT, NOV; DLB 113; EWL 3; EXPS; HW 1, 2; LAW; MTCW 1, 2; MTFW 2005; RGSF 2; RGWL 2, 3; SSFS 3, 20; TWA; WLIT 1
Cortes, Hernan 1485-1547 .... **LC 31**
Cortez, Jayne 1936- .... **BLC 2:1**
See also BW 2, 3; CA 73-76; CANR 13, 31, 68, 126; CWP; DLB 41; EWL 3
Corvinus, Jakob
See Raabe, Wilhelm (Karl)
Corwin, Cecil
See Kornbluth, C(yril) M.
Cosic, Dobrica 1921- .... **CLC 14**
See also CA 138; CAAE 122; CDWLB 4; CWW 2; DLB 181; EWL 3
Costain, Thomas B(ertram) 1885-1965 .... **CLC 30**
See also BYA 3; CA 5-8R; CAAS 25-28R; DLB 9; RHW
Costantini, Humberto 1924(?)-1987 . **CLC 49**
See also CA 131; CAAS 122; EWL 3; HW 1
Costello, Elvis 1954- .... **CLC 21**
See also CA 204
Costenoble, Philostene
See Ghelderode, Michel de
Cotes, Cecil V.
See Duncan, Sara Jeannette
Cotter, Joseph Seamon Sr. 1861-1949 .... **BLC 1:1; TCLC 28**
See also BW 1; CA 124; DAM MULT; DLB 50
Couch, Arthur Thomas Quiller
See Quiller-Couch, Sir Arthur (Thomas)
Coulton, James
See Hansen, Joseph
Couperus, Louis (Marie Anne) 1863-1923 .... **TCLC 15**
See also CAAE 115; EWL 3; RGWL 2, 3
Coupland, Douglas 1961- .... **CLC 85, 133**
See also AAYA 34; CA 142; CANR 57, 90, 130, 172; CCA 1; CN 7; CPW; DAC; DAM POP; DLB 334
Coupland, Douglas Campbell
See Coupland, Douglas
Court, Wesli
See Turco, Lewis (Putnam)
Courtenay, Bryce 1933- .... **CLC 59**
See also CA 138; CPW
Courtney, Robert
See Ellison, Harlan
Cousteau, Jacques-Yves 1910-1997 .. **CLC 30**
See also CA 65-68; CAAS 159; CANR 15, 67; MTCW 1; SATA 38, 98
Coventry, Francis 1725-1754 .... **LC 46**
Coverdale, Miles c. 1487-1569 .... **LC 77**
See also DLB 167
Cowan, Peter (Walkinshaw) 1914-2002 .... **SSC 28**
See also CA 21-24R; CANR 9, 25, 50, 83; CN 1, 2, 3, 4, 5, 6, 7; DLB 260; RGSF 2
Coward, Noel (Peirce) 1899-1973 . **CLC 1, 9, 29, 51**
See also AITN 1; BRWS 2; CA 17-18; CAAS 41-44R; CANR 35, 132; CAP 2; CBD; CDBLB 1914-1945; DA3; DAM DRAM; DFS 3, 6; DLB 10, 245; EWL 3; IDFW 3, 4; MTCW 1, 2; MTFW 2005; RGEL 2; TEA
Cowley, Abraham 1618-1667 .... **LC 43**
See also BRW 2; DLB 131, 151; PAB; RGEL 2
Cowley, Malcolm 1898-1989 .... **CLC 39**
See also AMWS 2; CA 5-8R; CAAS 128; CANR 3, 55; CP 1, 2, 3, 4; DLB 4, 48; DLBY 1981, 1989; EWL 3; MAL 5; MTCW 1, 2; MTFW 2005
Cowper, William 1731-1800 ..... **NCLC 8, 94; PC 40**
See also BRW 3; DA3; DAM POET; DLB 104, 109; RGEL 2
Cox, William Trevor 1928-
See Trevor, William
See also CA 9-12R; CANR 4, 37, 55, 76, 102, 139; DAM NOV; INT CANR-37; MTCW 1, 2; MTFW 2005; TEA
Coyne, P. J.
See Masters, Hilary
Coyne, P.J.
See Masters, Hilary
Cozzens, James Gould 1903-1978 . **CLC 1, 4, 11, 92**
See also AMW; BPFB 1; CA 9-12R; CAAS 81-84; CANR 19; CDALB 1941-1968; CN 1, 2; DLB 9, 294; DLBD 2; DLBY 1984, 1997; EWL 3; MAL 5; MTCW 1, 2; MTFW 2005; RGAL 4
Crabbe, George 1754-1832 .... **NCLC 26, 121**
See also BRW 3; DLB 93; RGEL 2
Crace, Jim 1946- .... **CLC 157; SSC 61**
See also CA 135; CAAE 128; CANR 55, 70, 123; CN 5, 6, 7; DLB 231; INT CA-135
Craddock, Charles Egbert
See Murfree, Mary Noailles
Craig, A. A.
See Anderson, Poul
Craik, Mrs.
See Craik, Dinah Maria (Mulock)
See also RGEL 2
Craik, Dinah Maria (Mulock) 1826-1887 .... **NCLC 38**
See Craik, Mrs.; Mulock, Dinah Maria
See also DLB 35, 163; MAICYA 1, 2; SATA 34
Cram, Ralph Adams 1863-1942 ..... **TCLC 45**
See also CA 160
Cranch, Christopher Pearse 1813-1892 .... **NCLC 115**
See also DLB 1, 42, 243
Crane, (Harold) Hart 1899-1932 .... **PC 3; TCLC 2, 5, 80; WLC 2**
See also AMW; AMWR 2; CA 127; CAAE 104; CDALB 1917-1929; DA; DA3; DAB; DAC; DAM MST, POET; DLB 4, 48; EWL 3; MAL 5; MTCW 1, 2; MTFW 2005; RGAL 4; TUS
Crane, R(onald) S(almon) 1886-1967 .... **CLC 27**
See also CA 85-88; DLB 63
Crane, Stephen (Townley) 1871-1900 .... **PC 80; SSC 7, 56, 70; TCLC 11, 17, 32; WLC 2**
See also AAYA 21; AMW; AMWC 1; BPFB 1; BYA 3; CA 140; CAAE 109; CANR 84; CDALB 1865-1917; DA; DA3; DAB; DAC; DAM MST, NOV, POET; DLB 12, 54, 78; EXPN; EXPS; LAIT 2; LMFS 2; MAL 5; NFS 4, 20; PFS 9; RGAL 4; RGSF 2; SSFS 4; TUS; WYA; YABC 2
Cranmer, Thomas 1489-1556 .... **LC 95**
See also DLB 132, 213
Cranshaw, Stanley
See Fisher, Dorothy (Frances) Canfield
Crase, Douglas 1944- .... **CLC 58**
See also CA 106
Crashaw, Richard 1612(?)-1649 .. **LC 24; PC 84**
See also BRW 2; DLB 126; PAB; RGEL 2
Cratinus c. 519B.C.-c. 422B.C. ..... **CMLC 54**
See also LMFS 1
Craven, Margaret 1901-1980 .... **CLC 17**
See also BYA 2; CA 103; CCA 1; DAC; LAIT 5
Crawford, F(rancis) Marion 1854-1909 .... **TCLC 10**
See also CA 168; CAAE 107; DLB 71; HGG; RGAL 4; SUFW 1
Crawford, Isabella Valancy 1850-1887 .... **NCLC 12, 127**
See also DLB 92; RGEL 2
Crayon, Geoffrey
See Irving, Washington
Creasey, John 1908-1973 .... **CLC 11**
See Marric, J. J.
See also CA 5-8R; CAAS 41-44R; CANR 8, 59; CMW 4; DLB 77; MTCW 1
Crebillon, Claude Prosper Jolyot de (fils) 1707-1777 .... **LC 1, 28**
See also DLB 313; GFL Beginnings to 1789
Credo
See Creasey, John
Credo, Alvaro J. de
See Prado (Calvo), Pedro
Creeley, Robert 1926-2005 .... **CLC 1, 2, 4, 8, 11, 15, 36, 78; PC 73**
See also AMWS 4; CA 1-4R; 10; CAAS 237; CANR 23, 43, 89, 137; CP 1, 2, 3, 4, 5, 6, 7; DA3; DAM POET; DLB 5, 16, 169; DLBD 17; EWL 3; MAL 5; MTCW 1, 2; MTFW 2005; PFS 21; RGAL 4; WP
Creeley, Robert White
See Creeley, Robert
Crenne, Helisenne de 1510-1560 .... **LC 113**
See also DLB 327
Crevecoeur, Hector St. John de
See Crevecoeur, Michel Guillaume Jean de
See also ANW
Crevecoeur, Michel Guillaume Jean de 1735-1813 .... **NCLC 105**
See Crevecoeur, Hector St. John de
See also AMWS 1; DLB 37
Crevel, Rene 1900-1935 .... **TCLC 112**
See also GLL 2
Crews, Harry 1935- .... **CLC 6, 23, 49**
See also AITN 1; AMWS 11; BPFB 1; CA 25-28R; CANR 20, 57; CN 3, 4, 5, 6, 7; CSW; DA3; DLB 6, 143, 185; MTCW 1, 2; MTFW 2005; RGAL 4
Crichton, Michael 1942- .... **CLC 2, 6, 54, 90, 242**
See also AAYA 10, 49; AITN 2; BPFB 1; CA 25-28R; CANR 13, 40, 54, 76, 127; CMW 4; CN 2, 3, 6, 7; CPW; DA3; DAM NOV, POP; DLB 292; DLBY 1981; INT CANR-13; JRDA; MTCW 1, 2; MTFW 2005; SATA 9, 88; SFW 4; YAW
Crispin, Edmund CLC 22
See Montgomery, (Robert) Bruce
See also DLB 87; MSW
Cristina of Sweden 1626-1689 .... **LC 124**
Cristofer, Michael 1945(?)- .... **CLC 28**
See also CA 152; CAAE 110; CAD; CANR 150; CD 5, 6; DAM DRAM; DFS 15; DLB 7
Cristofer, Michael Ivan
See Cristofer, Michael
Criton
See Alain

Croce, Benedetto 1866-1952 .... **TCLC 37**
See also CA 155; CAAE 120; EW 8; EWL 3; WLIT 7
Crockett, David 1786-1836 .... **NCLC 8**
See also DLB 3, 11, 183, 248
Crockett, Davy
See Crockett, David
Crofts, Freeman Wills 1879-1957 .. **TCLC 55**
See also CA 195; CAAE 115; CMW 4; DLB 77; MSW
Croker, John Wilson 1780-1857 .... **NCLC 10**
See also DLB 110
Crommelynck, Fernand 1885-1970 .. **CLC 75**
See also CA 189; CAAS 89-92; EWL 3
Cromwell, Oliver 1599-1658 .... **LC 43**
Cronenberg, David 1943- .... **CLC 143**
See also CA 138; CCA 1
Cronin, A(rchibald) J(oseph)
1896-1981 .... **CLC 32**
See also BPFB 1; CA 1-4R; CAAS 102; CANR 5; CN 2; DLB 191; SATA 47; SATA-Obit 25
Cross, Amanda
See Heilbrun, Carolyn G(old)
See also BPFB 1; CMW; CPW; DLB 306; MSW
Crothers, Rachel 1878-1958 .... **TCLC 19**
See also CA 194; CAAE 113; CAD; CWD; DLB 7, 266; RGAL 4
Croves, Hal
See Traven, B.
Crow Dog, Mary (?)- .... **CLC 93**
See Brave Bird, Mary
See also CA 154
Crowfield, Christopher
See Stowe, Harriet (Elizabeth) Beecher
Crowley, Aleister TCLC 7
See Crowley, Edward Alexander
See also GLL 1
Crowley, Edward Alexander 1875-1947
See Crowley, Aleister
See also CAAE 104; HGG
Crowley, John 1942- .... **CLC 57**
See also AAYA 57; BPFB 1; CA 61-64; CANR 43, 98, 138; DLBY 1982; FANT; MTFW 2005; SATA 65, 140; SFW 4; SUFW 2
Crowne, John 1641-1712 .... **LC 104**
See also DLB 80; RGEL 2
Crud
See Crumb, R.
Crumarums
See Crumb, R.
Crumb, R. 1943- .... **CLC 17**
See also CA 106; CANR 107, 150
Crumb, Robert
See Crumb, R.
Crumbum
See Crumb, R.
Crumski
See Crumb, R.
Crum the Bum
See Crumb, R.
Crunk
See Crumb, R.
Crustt
See Crumb, R.
Crutchfield, Les
See Trumbo, Dalton
Cruz, Victor Hernandez 1949- ... **HLC 1; PC 37**
See also BW 2; CA 65-68; 17; CANR 14, 32, 74, 132; CP 1, 2, 3, 4, 5, 6, 7; DAM MULT, POET; DLB 41; DNFS 1; EXPP; HW 1, 2; LLW; MTCW 2; MTFW 2005; PFS 16; WP
Cryer, Gretchen (Kiger) 1935- .... **CLC 21**
See also CA 123; CAAE 114
Csath, Geza TCLC 13
See Brenner, Jozef
See also CAAE 111
Cudlip, David R(ockwell) 1933- .... **CLC 34**
See also CA 177
Cullen, Countee 1903-1946 ..... **BLC 1:1; HR 1:2; PC 20; TCLC 4, 37; WLCS**
See also AFAW 2; AMWS 4; BW 1; CA 124; CAAE 108; CDALB 1917-1929; DA; DA3; DAC; DAM MST, MULT, POET; DLB 4, 48, 51; EWL 3; EXPP; LMFS 2; MAL 5; MTCW 1, 2; MTFW 2005; PFS 3; RGAL 4; SATA 18; WP
Culleton, Beatrice 1949- .... **NNAL**
See also CA 120; CANR 83; DAC
Cum, R.
See Crumb, R.
Cumberland, Richard
1732-1811 .... **NCLC 167**
See also DLB 89; RGEL 2
Cummings, Bruce F(rederick) 1889-1919
See Barbellion, W. N. P.
See also CAAE 123
Cummings, E(dward) E(stlin)
1894-1962 .. **CLC 1, 3, 8, 12, 15, 68; PC 5; TCLC 137; WLC 2**
See also AAYA 41; AMW; CA 73-76; CANR 31; CDALB 1929-1941; DA; DA3; DAB; DAC; DAM MST, POET; DLB 4, 48; EWL 3; EXPP; MAL 5; MTCW 1, 2; MTFW 2005; PAB; PFS 1, 3, 12, 13, 19; RGAL 4; TUS; WP
Cummins, Maria Susanna
1827-1866 .... **NCLC 139**
See also DLB 42; YABC 1
Cunha, Euclides (Rodrigues Pimenta) da
1866-1909 .... **TCLC 24**
See also CA 219; CAAE 123; DLB 307; LAW; WLIT 1
Cunningham, E. V.
See Fast, Howard
Cunningham, J(ames) V(incent)
1911-1985 .... **CLC 3, 31**
See also CA 1-4R; CAAS 115; CANR 1, 72; CP 1, 2, 3, 4; DLB 5
Cunningham, Julia (Woolfolk)
1916- .... **CLC 12**
See also CA 9-12R; CANR 4, 19, 36; CWRI 5; JRDA; MAICYA 1, 2; SAAS 2; SATA 1, 26, 132
Cunningham, Michael 1952- .... **CLC 34, 243**
See also AMWS 15; CA 136; CANR 96, 160; CN 7; DLB 292; GLL 2; MTFW 2005; NFS 23
Cunninghame Graham, R. B.
See Cunninghame Graham, Robert (Gallnigad) Bontine
Cunninghame Graham, Robert (Gallnigad) Bontine 1852-1936 .... **TCLC 19**
See Graham, R(obert) B(ontine) Cunninghame
See also CA 184; CAAE 119
Curnow, (Thomas) Allen (Monro)
1911-2001 .... **PC 48**
See also CA 69-72; CAAS 202; CANR 48, 99; CP 1, 2, 3, 4, 5, 6, 7; EWL 3; RGEL 2
Currie, Ellen 19(?)- .... **CLC 44**
Curtin, Philip
See Lowndes, Marie Adelaide (Belloc)
Curtin, Phillip
See Lowndes, Marie Adelaide (Belloc)
Curtis, Price
See Ellison, Harlan
Cusanus, Nicolaus 1401-1464 .... **LC 80**
See Nicholas of Cusa
Cutrate, Joe
See Spiegelman, Art
Cynewulf c. 770- .... **CMLC 23**
See also DLB 146; RGEL 2
Cyrano de Bergerac, Savinien de
1619-1655 .... **LC 65**
See also DLB 268; GFL Beginnings to 1789; RGWL 2, 3
Cyril of Alexandria c. 375-c. 430 . **CMLC 59**
Czaczkes, Shmuel Yosef Halevi
See Agnon, S(hmuel) Y(osef Halevi)
Dabrowska, Maria (Szumska)
1889-1965 .... **CLC 15**
See also CA 106; CDWLB 4; DLB 215; EWL 3
Dabydeen, David 1955- .... **CLC 34**
See also BW 1; CA 125; CANR 56, 92; CN 6, 7; CP 5, 6, 7
Dacey, Philip 1939- .... **CLC 51**
See also CA 231; 37-40R, 231; 17; CANR 14, 32, 64; CP 4, 5, 6, 7; DLB 105
Dacre, Charlotte c. 1772-1825(?) . **NCLC 151**
Dafydd ap Gwilym c. 1320-c. 1380 ..... **PC 56**
Dagerman, Stig (Halvard)
1923-1954 .... **TCLC 17**
See also CA 155; CAAE 117; DLB 259; EWL 3
D'Aguiar, Fred 1960- ..... **BLC 2:1; CLC 145**
See also CA 148; CANR 83, 101; CN 7; CP 5, 6, 7; DLB 157; EWL 3
Dahl, Roald 1916-1990 ...... **CLC 1, 6, 18, 79; TCLC 173**
See also AAYA 15; BPFB 1; BRWS 4; BYA 5; CA 1-4R; CAAS 133; CANR 6, 32, 37, 62; CLR 1, 7, 41, 111; CN 1, 2, 3, 4; CPW; DA3; DAB; DAC; DAM MST, NOV, POP; DLB 139, 255; HGG; JRDA; MAICYA 1, 2; MTCW 1, 2; MTFW 2005; RGSF 2; SATA 1, 26, 73; SATA-Obit 65; SSFS 4; TEA; YAW
Dahlberg, Edward 1900-1977 .. **CLC 1, 7, 14**
See also CA 9-12R; CAAS 69-72; CANR 31, 62; CN 1, 2; DLB 48; MAL 5; MTCW 1; RGAL 4
Daitch, Susan 1954- .... **CLC 103**
See also CA 161
Dale, Colin TCLC 18
See Lawrence, T(homas) E(dward)
Dale, George E.
See Asimov, Isaac
d'Alembert, Jean Le Rond
1717-1783 .... **LC 126**
Dalton, Roque 1935-1975(?) ..... **HLCS 1; PC 36**
See also CA 176; DLB 283; HW 2
Daly, Elizabeth 1878-1967 .... **CLC 52**
See also CA 23-24; CAAS 25-28R; CANR 60; CAP 2; CMW 4
Daly, Mary 1928- .... **CLC 173**
See also CA 25-28R; CANR 30, 62, 166; FW; GLL 1; MTCW 1
Daly, Maureen 1921-2006 .... **CLC 17**
See also AAYA 5, 58; BYA 6; CAAS 253; CANR 37, 83, 108; CLR 96; JRDA; MAICYA 1, 2; SAAS 1; SATA 2, 129; SATA-Obit 176; WYA; YAW
Damas, Leon-Gontran 1912-1978 .... **CLC 84**
See also BW 1; CA 125; CAAS 73-76; EWL 3
Dana, Richard Henry Sr.
1787-1879 .... **NCLC 53**
Dangarembga, Tsitsi 1959- .... **BLC 2:1**
See also BW 3; CA 163; WLIT 2
Daniel, Samuel 1562(?)-1619 .... **LC 24**
See also DLB 62; RGEL 2
Daniels, Brett
See Adler, Renata

Defoe, Daniel 1660(?)-1731 .... **LC 1, 42, 108; WLC 2**
See also AAYA 27; BRW 3; BRWR 1; BYA 4; CDBLB 1660-1789; CLR 61; DA; DA3; DAB; DAC; DAM MST, NOV; DLB 39, 95, 101, 336; JRDA; LAIT 1; LMFS 1; MAICYA 1, 2; NFS 9, 13; RGEL 2; SATA 22; TEA; WCH; WLIT 3
de Gouges, Olympe
See de Gouges, Olympe
de Gouges, Olympe 1748-1793 .... **LC 127**
See also DLB 313
de Gourmont, Remy(-Marie-Charles)
See Gourmont, Remy(-Marie-Charles) de
de Gournay, Marie le Jars
1566-1645 .... **LC 98**
See also DLB 327; FW
de Hartog, Jan 1914-2002 .... **CLC 19**
See also CA 1-4R; CAAS 210; CANR 1; DFS 12
de Hostos, E. M.
See Hostos (y Bonilla), Eugenio Maria de
de Hostos, Eugenio M.
See Hostos (y Bonilla), Eugenio Maria de
Deighton, Len CLC 4, 7, 22, 46
See Deighton, Leonard Cyril
See also AAYA 6; BEST 89:2; BPFB 1; CDBLB 1960 to Present; CMW 4; CN 1, 2, 3, 4, 5, 6, 7; CPW; DLB 87
Deighton, Leonard Cyril 1929-
See Deighton, Len
See also AAYA 57; CA 9-12R; CANR 19, 33, 68; DA3; DAM NOV, POP; MTCW 1, 2; MTFW 2005
Dekker, Thomas 1572(?)-1632 ..... **DC 12; LC 22**
See also CDBLB Before 1660; DAM DRAM; DLB 62, 172; LMFS 1; RGEL 2
de Laclos, Pierre Ambroise Franois
See Laclos, Pierre-Ambroise Francois
Delacroix, (Ferdinand-Victor-)Eugene
1798-1863 .... **NCLC 133**
See also EW 5
Delafield, E. M. TCLC 61
See Dashwood, Edmee Elizabeth Monica de la Pasture
See also DLB 34; RHW
de la Mare, Walter (John)
1873-1956 ..... **PC 77; SSC 14; TCLC 4, 53; WLC 2**
See also CA 163; CDBLB 1914-1945; CLR 23; CWRI 5; DA3; DAB; DAC; DAM MST, POET; DLB 19, 153, 162, 255, 284; EWL 3; EXPP; HGG; MAICYA 1, 2; MTCW 2; MTFW 2005; RGEL 2; RGSF 2; SATA 16; SUFW 1; TEA; WCH
de Lamartine, Alphonse (Marie Louis Prat)
See Lamartine, Alphonse (Marie Louis Prat) de
Delaney, Franey
See O'Hara, John (Henry)
Delaney, Shelagh 1939- .... **CLC 29**
See also CA 17-20R; CANR 30, 67; CBD; CD 5, 6; CDBLB 1960 to Present; CWD; DAM DRAM; DFS 7; DLB 13; MTCW 1
Delany, Martin Robison
1812-1885 .... **NCLC 93**
See also DLB 50; RGAL 4
Delany, Mary (Granville Pendarves)
1700-1788 .... **LC 12**
Delany, Samuel R., Jr. 1942- .... **BLC 1:1; CLC 8, 14, 38, 141**
See also AAYA 24; AFAW 2; BPFB 1; BW 2, 3; CA 81-84; CANR 27, 43, 116, 172; CN 2, 3, 4, 5, 6, 7; DAM MULT; DLB 8, 33; FANT; MAL 5; MTCW 1, 2; RGAL 4; SATA 92; SCFW 1, 2; SFW 4; SUFW 2
Delany, Samuel Ray
See Delany, Samuel R., Jr.
de la Parra, (Ana) Teresa (Sonojo)
1890(?)-1936 .... **TCLC 185**
See Parra Sanojo, Ana Teresa de la
See also CA 178; HW 2
De La Ramee, Marie Louise 1839-1908
See Ouida
See also CA 204; SATA 20
de la Roche, Mazo 1879-1961 .... **CLC 14**
See also CA 85-88; CANR 30; DLB 68; RGEL 2; RHW; SATA 64
De La Salle, Innocent
See Hartmann, Sadakichi
de Laureamont, Comte
See Lautreamont
Delbanco, Nicholas 1942- ..... **CLC 6, 13, 167**
See also CA 189; 17-20R, 189; 2; CANR 29, 55, 116, 150; CN 7; DLB 6, 234
Delbanco, Nicholas Franklin
See Delbanco, Nicholas
del Castillo, Michel 1933- .... **CLC 38**
See also CA 109; CANR 77
Deledda, Grazia (Cosima)
1875(?)-1936 .... **TCLC 23**
See also CA 205; CAAE 123; DLB 264, 329; EWL 3; RGWL 2, 3; WLIT 7
Deleuze, Gilles 1925-1995 .... **TCLC 116**
See also DLB 296
Delgado, Abelardo (Lalo) B(arrientos)
1930-2004 .... **HLC 1**
See also CA 131; 15; CAAS 230; CANR 90; DAM MST, MULT; DLB 82; HW 1, 2
Delibes, Miguel CLC 8, 18
See Delibes Setien, Miguel
See also DLB 322; EWL 3
Delibes Setien, Miguel 1920-
See Delibes, Miguel
See also CA 45-48; CANR 1, 32; CWW 2; HW 1; MTCW 1
DeLillo, Don 1936- ..... **CLC 8, 10, 13, 27, 39, 54, 76, 143, 210, 213**
See also AMWC 2; AMWS 6; BEST 89:1; BPFB 1; CA 81-84; CANR 21, 76, 92, 133, 173; CN 3, 4, 5, 6, 7; CPW; DA3; DAM NOV, POP; DLB 6, 173; EWL 3; MAL 5; MTCW 1, 2; MTFW 2005; RGAL 4; TUS
de Lisser, H. G.
See De Lisser, H(erbert) G(eorge)
See also DLB 117
De Lisser, H(erbert) G(eorge)
1878-1944 .... **TCLC 12**
See de Lisser, H. G.
See also BW 2; CA 152; CAAE 109
Deloire, Pierre
See Peguy, Charles (Pierre)
Deloney, Thomas 1543(?)-1600 .... **LC 41; PC 79**
See also DLB 167; RGEL 2
Deloria, Ella (Cara) 1889-1971(?) ..... **NNAL**
See also CA 152; DAM MULT; DLB 175
Deloria, Vine, Jr. 1933-2005 .... **CLC 21, 122; NNAL**
See also CA 53-56; CAAS 245; CANR 5, 20, 48, 98; DAM MULT; DLB 175; MTCW 1; SATA 21; SATA-Obit 171
Deloria, Vine Victor, Jr.
See Deloria, Vine, Jr.
del Valle-Inclan, Ramon (Maria)
See Valle-Inclan, Ramon (Maria) del
See also DLB 322
Del Vecchio, John M(ichael) 1947- .. **CLC 29**
See also CA 110; DLBD 9
de Man, Paul (Adolph Michel)
1919-1983 .... **CLC 55**
See also CA 128; CAAS 111; CANR 61; DLB 67; MTCW 1, 2
DeMarinis, Rick 1934- .... **CLC 54**
See also CA 184; 57-60, 184; 24; CANR 9, 25, 50, 160; DLB 218; TCWW 2
de Maupassant, (Henri Rene Albert) Guy
See Maupassant, (Henri Rene Albert) Guy de
Dembry, R. Emmet
See Murfree, Mary Noailles
Demby, William 1922- ...... **BLC 1:1; CLC 53**
See also BW 1, 3; CA 81-84; CANR 81; DAM MULT; DLB 33
de Menton, Francisco
See Chin, Frank (Chew, Jr.)
Demetrius of Phalerum c. 307B.C.- .... **CMLC 34**
Demijohn, Thom
See Disch, Thomas M.
De Mille, James 1833-1880 .... **NCLC 123**
See also DLB 99, 251
Deming, Richard 1915-1983
See Queen, Ellery
See also CA 9-12R; CANR 3, 94; SATA 24
Democritus c. 460B.C.-c. 370B.C. . **CMLC 47**
de Montaigne, Michel (Eyquem)
See Montaigne, Michel (Eyquem) de
de Montherlant, Henry (Milon)
See Montherlant, Henry (Milon) de
Demosthenes 384B.C.-322B.C. ...... **CMLC 13**
See also AW 1; DLB 176; RGWL 2, 3; WLIT 8
de Musset, (Louis Charles) Alfred
See Musset, Alfred de
de Natale, Francine
See Malzberg, Barry N(athaniel)
de Navarre, Marguerite 1492-1549 ... **LC 61; SSC 85**
See Marguerite d'Angouleme; Marguerite de Navarre
See also DLB 327
Denby, Edwin (Orr) 1903-1983 .... **CLC 48**
See also CA 138; CAAS 110; CP 1
de Nerval, Gerard
See Nerval, Gerard de
Denham, John 1615-1669 .... **LC 73**
See also DLB 58, 126; RGEL 2
Denis, Julio
See Cortazar, Julio
Denmark, Harrison
See Zelazny, Roger
Dennis, John 1658-1734 .... **LC 11**
See also DLB 101; RGEL 2
Dennis, Nigel (Forbes) 1912-1989 ...... **CLC 8**
See also CA 25-28R; CAAS 129; CN 1, 2, 3, 4; DLB 13, 15, 233; EWL 3; MTCW 1
Dent, Lester 1904-1959 .... **TCLC 72**
See also CA 161; CAAE 112; CMW 4; DLB 306; SFW 4
De Palma, Brian 1940- .... **CLC 20, 247**
See also CA 109
De Palma, Brian Russell
See De Palma, Brian
de Pizan, Christine
See Christine de Pizan
See also FL 1:1
De Quincey, Thomas 1785-1859 ..... **NCLC 4, 87**
See also BRW 4; CDBLB 1789-1832; DLB 110, 144; RGEL 2
Deren, Eleanora 1908(?)-1961
See Deren, Maya
See also CA 192; CAAS 111
Deren, Maya CLC 16, 102
See Deren, Eleanora

Dobell, Sydney Thompson 1824-1874 .... **NCLC 43**
See also DLB 32; RGEL 2
Doblin, Alfred TCLC 13
See Doeblin, Alfred
See also CDWLB 2; EWL 3; RGWL 2, 3
Dobroliubov, Nikolai Aleksandrovich
See Dobrolyubov, Nikolai Alexandrovich
See also DLB 277
Dobrolyubov, Nikolai Alexandrovich 1836-1861 .... **NCLC 5**
See Dobroliubov, Nikolai Aleksandrovich
Dobson, Austin 1840-1921 .... **TCLC 79**
See also DLB 35, 144
Dobyns, Stephen 1941- .... **CLC 37, 233**
See also AMWS 13; CA 45-48; CANR 2, 18, 99; CMW 4; CP 4, 5, 6, 7; PFS 23
Doctorow, Edgar Laurence
See Doctorow, E.L.
Doctorow, E.L. 1931- . **CLC 6, 11, 15, 18, 37, 44, 65, 113, 214**
See also AAYA 22; AITN 2; AMWS 4; BEST 89:3; BPFB 1; CA 45-48; CANR 2, 33, 51, 76, 97, 133, 170; CDALB 1968-1988; CN 3, 4, 5, 6, 7; CPW; DA3; DAM NOV, POP; DLB 2, 28, 173; DLBY 1980; EWL 3; LAIT 3; MAL 5; MTCW 1, 2; MTFW 2005; NFS 6; RGAL 4; RGHL; RHW; TCLE 1:1; TCWW 1, 2; TUS
Dodgson, Charles L(utwidge) 1832-1898
See Carroll, Lewis
See also CLR 2; DA; DA3; DAB; DAC; DAM MST, NOV, POET; MAICYA 1, 2; SATA 100; YABC 2
Dodsley, Robert 1703-1764 .... **LC 97**
See also DLB 95; RGEL 2
Dodson, Owen (Vincent) 1914-1983 .... **BLC 1:1; CLC 79**
See also BW 1; CA 65-68; CAAS 110; CANR 24; DAM MULT; DLB 76
Doeblin, Alfred 1878-1957 .... **TCLC 13**
See Doblin, Alfred
See also CA 141; CAAE 110; DLB 66
Doerr, Harriet 1910-2002 .... **CLC 34**
See also CA 122; CAAE 117; CAAS 213; CANR 47; INT CA-122; LATS 1:2
Domecq, H(onorio Bustos)
See Bioy Casares, Adolfo
Domecq, H(onorio) Bustos
See Bioy Casares, Adolfo; Borges, Jorge Luis
Domini, Rey
See Lorde, Audre
See also GLL 1
Dominique
See Proust, (Valentin-Louis-George-Eugene) Marcel
Don, A
See Stephen, Sir Leslie
Donaldson, Stephen R. 1947- ... **CLC 46, 138**
See also AAYA 36; BPFB 1; CA 89-92; CANR 13, 55, 99; CPW; DAM POP; FANT; INT CANR-13; SATA 121; SFW 4; SUFW 1, 2
Donleavy, J(ames) P(atrick) 1926- .... **CLC 1, 4, 6, 10, 45**
See also AITN 2; BPFB 1; CA 9-12R; CANR 24, 49, 62, 80, 124; CBD; CD 5, 6; CN 1, 2, 3, 4, 5, 6, 7; DLB 6, 173; INT CANR-24; MAL 5; MTCW 1, 2; MTFW 2005; RGAL 4
Donnadieu, Marguerite
See Duras, Marguerite
Donne, John 1572-1631 ... **LC 10, 24, 91; PC 1, 43; WLC 2**
See also AAYA 67; BRW 1; BRWC 1; BRWR 2; CDBLB Before 1660; DA; DAB; DAC; DAM MST, POET; DLB 121, 151; EXPP; PAB; PFS 2, 11; RGEL 3; TEA; WLIT 3; WP
Donnell, David 1939(?)- .... **CLC 34**
See also CA 197
Donoghue, Denis 1928- .... **CLC 209**
See also CA 17-20R; CANR 16, 102
Donoghue, Emma 1969- .... **CLC 239**
See also CA 155; CANR 103, 152; DLB 267; GLL 2; SATA 101
Donoghue, P.S.
See Hunt, E. Howard
Donoso (Yanez), Jose 1924-1996 ... **CLC 4, 8, 11, 32, 99; HLC 1; SSC 34; TCLC 133**
See also CA 81-84; CAAS 155; CANR 32, 73; CDWLB 3; CWW 2; DAM MULT; DLB 113; EWL 3; HW 1, 2; LAW; LAWS 1; MTCW 1, 2; MTFW 2005; RGSF 2; WLIT 1
Donovan, John 1928-1992 .... **CLC 35**
See also AAYA 20; CA 97-100; CAAS 137; CLR 3; MAICYA 1, 2; SATA 72; SATA-Brief 29; YAW
Don Roberto
See Cunninghame Graham, Robert (Gallnigad) Bontine
Doolittle, Hilda 1886-1961 . **CLC 3, 8, 14, 31, 34, 73; PC 5; WLC 3**
See H. D.
See also AAYA 66; AMWS 1; CA 97-100; CANR 35, 131; DA; DAC; DAM MST, POET; DLB 4, 45; EWL 3; FW; GLL 1; LMFS 2; MAL 5; MBL; MTCW 1, 2; MTFW 2005; PFS 6; RGAL 4
Doppo, Kunikida TCLC 99
See Kunikida Doppo
Dorfman, Ariel 1942- .... **CLC 48, 77, 189; HLC 1**
See also CA 130; CAAE 124; CANR 67, 70, 135; CWW 2; DAM MULT; DFS 4; EWL 3; HW 1, 2; INT CA-130; WLIT 1
Dorn, Edward (Merton) 1929-1999 .... **CLC 10, 18**
See also CA 93-96; CAAS 187; CANR 42, 79; CP 1, 2, 3, 4, 5, 6, 7; DLB 5; INT CA-93-96; WP
Dor-Ner, Zvi CLC 70
Dorris, Michael 1945-1997 .... **CLC 109; NNAL**
See also AAYA 20; BEST 90:1; BYA 12; CA 102; CAAS 157; CANR 19, 46, 75; CLR 58; DA3; DAM MULT, NOV; DLB 175; LAIT 5; MTCW 2; MTFW 2005; NFS 3; RGAL 4; SATA 75; SATA-Obit 94; TCWW 2; YAW
Dorris, Michael A.
See Dorris, Michael
Dorsan, Luc
See Simenon, Georges (Jacques Christian)
Dorsange, Jean
See Simenon, Georges (Jacques Christian)
Dorset
See Sackville, Thomas
Dos Passos, John (Roderigo) 1896-1970 ... **CLC 1, 4, 8, 11, 15, 25, 34, 82; WLC 2**
See also AMW; BPFB 1; CA 1-4R; CAAS 29-32R; CANR 3; CDALB 1929-1941; DA; DA3; DAB; DAC; DAM MST, NOV; DLB 4, 9, 274, 316; DLBD 1, 15; DLBY 1996; EWL 3; MAL 5; MTCW 1, 2; MTFW 2005; NFS 14; RGAL 4; TUS
Dossage, Jean
See Simenon, Georges (Jacques Christian)
Dostoevsky, Fedor Mikhailovich 1821-1881 .. **NCLC 2, 7, 21, 33, 43, 119, 167; SSC 2, 33, 44; WLC 2**
See Dostoevsky, Fyodor
See also AAYA 40; DA; DA3; DAB; DAC; DAM MST, NOV; EW 7; EXPN; NFS 3, 8; RGSF 2; RGWL 2, 3; SSFS 8; TWA
Dostoevsky, Fyodor
See Dostoevsky, Fedor Mikhailovich
See also DLB 238; LATS 1:1; LMFS 1, 2
Doty, Mark 1953(?)- .... **CLC 176; PC 53**
See also AMWS 11; CA 183; 161, 183; CANR 110, 173; CP 7
Doty, Mark A.
See Doty, Mark
Doty, Mark Alan
See Doty, Mark
Doty, M.R.
See Doty, Mark
Doughty, Charles M(ontagu) 1843-1926 .... **TCLC 27**
See also CA 178; CAAE 115; DLB 19, 57, 174
Douglas, Ellen CLC 73
See Haxton, Josephine Ayres; Williamson, Ellen Douglas
See also CN 5, 6, 7; CSW; DLB 292
Douglas, Gavin 1475(?)-1522 .... **LC 20**
See also DLB 132; RGEL 2
Douglas, George
See Brown, George Douglas
See also RGEL 2
Douglas, Keith (Castellain) 1920-1944 .... **TCLC 40**
See also BRW 7; CA 160; DLB 27; EWL 3; PAB; RGEL 2
Douglas, Leonard
See Bradbury, Ray
Douglas, Michael
See Crichton, Michael
Douglas, (George) Norman 1868-1952 .... **TCLC 68**
See also BRW 6; CA 157; CAAE 119; DLB 34, 195; RGEL 2
Douglas, William
See Brown, George Douglas
Douglass, Frederick 1817(?)-1895 .. **BLC 1:1; NCLC 7, 55, 141; WLC 2**
See also AAYA 48; AFAW 1, 2; AMWC 1; AMWS 3; CDALB 1640-1865; DA; DA3; DAC; DAM MST, MULT; DLB 1, 43, 50, 79, 243; FW; LAIT 2; NCFS 2; RGAL 4; SATA 29
Dourado, (Waldomiro Freitas) Autran 1926- .... **CLC 23, 60**
See also CA 25-28R, 179; CANR 34, 81; DLB 145, 307; HW 2
Dourado, Waldomiro Freitas Autran
See Dourado, (Waldomiro Freitas) Autran
Dove, Rita 1952- . **BLCS; BLC 2:1; CLC 50, 81; PC 6**
See also AAYA 46; AMWS 4; BW 2; CA 109; 19; CANR 27, 42, 68, 76, 97, 132; CDALBS; CP 5, 6, 7; CSW; CWP; DA3; DAM MULT, POET; DLB 120; EWL 3; EXPP; MAL 5; MTCW 2; MTFW 2005; PFS 1, 15; RGAL 4
Dove, Rita Frances
See Dove, Rita
Doveglion
See Villa, Jose Garcia
Dowell, Coleman 1925-1985 .... **CLC 60**
See also CA 25-28R; CAAS 117; CANR 10; DLB 130; GLL 2
Downing, Major Jack
See Smith, Seba
Dowson, Ernest (Christopher) 1867-1900 .... **TCLC 4**
See also CA 150; CAAE 105; DLB 19, 135; RGEL 2
Doyle, A. Conan
See Doyle, Sir Arthur Conan

Dunlap, William 1766-1839 .... **NCLC 2**
See also DLB 30, 37, 59; RGAL 4
Dunn, Douglas (Eaglesham) 1942- .... **CLC 6, 40**
See also BRWS 10; CA 45-48; CANR 2, 33, 126; CP 1, 2, 3, 4, 5, 6, 7; DLB 40; MTCW 1
Dunn, Katherine 1945- .... **CLC 71**
See also CA 33-36R; CANR 72; HGG; MTCW 2; MTFW 2005
Dunn, Stephen 1939- .... **CLC 36, 206**
See also AMWS 11; CA 33-36R; CANR 12, 48, 53, 105; CP 3, 4, 5, 6, 7; DLB 105; PFS 21
Dunn, Stephen Elliott
See Dunn, Stephen
Dunne, Finley Peter 1867-1936 ...... **TCLC 28**
See also CA 178; CAAE 108; DLB 11, 23; RGAL 4
Dunne, John Gregory 1932-2003 ..... **CLC 28**
See also CA 25-28R; CAAS 222; CANR 14, 50; CN 5, 6, 7; DLBY 1980
Dunsany, Lord **TCLC 2, 59**
See Dunsany, Edward John Moreton Drax Plunkett
See also DLB 77, 153, 156, 255; FANT; IDTP; RGEL 2; SFW 4; SUFW 1
Dunsany, Edward John Moreton Drax Plunkett 1878-1957
See Dunsany, Lord
See also CA 148; CAAE 104; DLB 10; MTCW 2
Duns Scotus, John 1266(?)-1308 ... **CMLC 59**
See also DLB 115
du Perry, Jean
See Simenon, Georges (Jacques Christian)
Durang, Christopher 1949- .... **CLC 27, 38**
See also CA 105; CAD; CANR 50, 76, 130; CD 5, 6; MTCW 2; MTFW 2005
Durang, Christopher Ferdinand
See Durang, Christopher
Duras, Claire de 1777-1832 .... **NCLC 154**
Duras, Marguerite 1914-1996 . **CLC 3, 6, 11, 20, 34, 40, 68, 100; SSC 40**
See also BPFB 1; CA 25-28R; CAAS 151; CANR 50; CWW 2; DFS 21; DLB 83, 321; EWL 3; FL 1:5; GFL 1789 to the Present; IDFW 4; MTCW 1, 2; RGWL 2, 3; TWA
Durban, (Rosa) Pam 1947- .... **CLC 39**
See also CA 123; CANR 98; CSW
Durcan, Paul 1944- .... **CLC 43, 70**
See also CA 134; CANR 123; CP 1, 5, 6, 7; DAM POET; EWL 3
d'Urfe, Honore
See Urfe, Honore d'
Durfey, Thomas 1653-1723 .... **LC 94**
See also DLB 80; RGEL 2
Durkheim, Emile 1858-1917 .... **TCLC 55**
See also CA 249
Durrell, Lawrence (George) 1912-1990 ..... **CLC 1, 4, 6, 8, 13, 27, 41**
See also BPFB 1; BRWS 1; CA 9-12R; CAAS 132; CANR 40, 77; CDBLB 1945-1960; CN 1, 2, 3, 4; CP 1, 2, 3, 4, 5; DAM NOV; DLB 15, 27, 204; DLBY 1990; EWL 3; MTCW 1, 2; RGEL 2; SFW 4; TEA
Durrenmatt, Friedrich
See Duerrenmatt, Friedrich
See also CDWLB 2; EW 13; EWL 3; RGHL; RGWL 2, 3
Dutt, Michael Madhusudan 1824-1873 .... **NCLC 118**
Dutt, Toru 1856-1877 .... **NCLC 29**
See also DLB 240
Dwight, Timothy 1752-1817 .... **NCLC 13**
See also DLB 37; RGAL 4
Dworkin, Andrea 1946-2005 ..... **CLC 43, 123**
See also CA 77-80; 21; CAAS 238; CANR 16, 39, 76, 96; FL 1:5; FW; GLL 1; INT CANR-16; MTCW 1, 2; MTFW 2005
Dwyer, Deanna
See Koontz, Dean R.
Dwyer, K. R.
See Koontz, Dean R.
Dybek, Stuart 1942- .... **CLC 114; SSC 55**
See also CA 97-100; CANR 39; DLB 130; SSFS 23
Dye, Richard
See De Voto, Bernard (Augustine)
Dyer, Geoff 1958- .... **CLC 149**
See also CA 125; CANR 88
Dyer, George 1755-1841 .... **NCLC 129**
See also DLB 93
Dylan, Bob 1941- .... **CLC 3, 4, 6, 12, 77; PC 37**
See also CA 41-44R; CANR 108; CP 1, 2, 3, 4, 5, 6, 7; DLB 16
Dyson, John 1943- .... **CLC 70**
See also CA 144
Dzyubin, Eduard Georgievich 1895-1934
See Bagritsky, Eduard
See also CA 170
E. V. L.
See Lucas, E(dward) V(errall)
Eagleton, Terence (Francis) 1943- .. **CLC 63, 132**
See also CA 57-60; CANR 7, 23, 68, 115; DLB 242; LMFS 2; MTCW 1, 2; MTFW 2005
Eagleton, Terry
See Eagleton, Terence (Francis)
Early, Jack
See Scoppettone, Sandra
See also GLL 1
East, Michael
See West, Morris L(anglo)
Eastaway, Edward
See Thomas, (Philip) Edward
Eastlake, William (Derry) 1917-1997 .... **CLC 8**
See also CA 5-8R; 1; CAAS 158; CANR 5, 63; CN 1, 2, 3, 4, 5, 6; DLB 6, 206; INT CANR-5; MAL 5; TCWW 1, 2
Eastman, Charles A(lexander) 1858-1939 .... **NNAL; TCLC 55**
See also CA 179; CANR 91; DAM MULT; DLB 175; YABC 1
Eaton, Edith Maude 1865-1914 .... **AAL**
See Far, Sui Sin
See also CA 154; DLB 221, 312; FW
Eaton, (Lillie) Winnifred 1875-1954 .... **AAL**
See also CA 217; DLB 221, 312; RGAL 4
Eberhart, Richard 1904-2005 ...... **CLC 3, 11, 19, 56; PC 76**
See also AMW; CA 1-4R; CAAS 240; CANR 2, 125; CDALB 1941-1968; CP 1, 2, 3, 4, 5, 6, 7; DAM POET; DLB 48; MAL 5; MTCW 1; RGAL 4
Eberhart, Richard Ghormley
See Eberhart, Richard
Eberstadt, Fernanda 1960- .... **CLC 39**
See also CA 136; CANR 69, 128
Ebner, Margaret c. 1291-1351 ...... **CMLC 98**
Echegaray (y Eizaguirre), Jose (Maria Waldo) 1832-1916 .... **HLCS 1; TCLC 4**
See also CAAE 104; CANR 32; DLB 329; EWL 3; HW 1; MTCW 1
Echeverria, (Jose) Esteban (Antonino) 1805-1851 .... **NCLC 18**
See also LAW
Echo
See Proust, (Valentin-Louis-George-Eugene) Marcel
Eckert, Allan W. 1931- .... **CLC 17**
See also AAYA 18; BYA 2; CA 13-16R; CANR 14, 45; INT CANR-14; MAICYA 2; MAICYAS 1; SAAS 21; SATA 29, 91; SATA-Brief 27
Eckhart, Meister 1260(?)-1327(?) .. **CMLC 9, 80**
See also DLB 115; LMFS 1
Eckmar, F. R.
See de Hartog, Jan
Eco, Umberto 1932- .... **CLC 28, 60, 142, 248**
See also BEST 90:1; BPFB 1; CA 77-80; CANR 12, 33, 55, 110, 131; CPW; CWW 2; DA3; DAM NOV, POP; DLB 196, 242; EWL 3; MSW; MTCW 1, 2; MTFW 2005; NFS 22; RGWL 3; WLIT 7
Eddison, E(ric) R(ucker) 1882-1945 .... **TCLC 15**
See also CA 156; CAAE 109; DLB 255; FANT; SFW 4; SUFW 1
Eddy, Mary (Ann Morse) Baker 1821-1910 .... **TCLC 71**
See also CA 174; CAAE 113
Edel, (Joseph) Leon 1907-1997 .. **CLC 29, 34**
See also CA 1-4R; CAAS 161; CANR 1, 22, 112; DLB 103; INT CANR-22
Eden, Emily 1797-1869 .... **NCLC 10**
Edgar, David 1948- .... **CLC 42**
See also CA 57-60; CANR 12, 61, 112; CBD; CD 5, 6; DAM DRAM; DFS 15; DLB 13, 233; MTCW 1
Edgerton, Clyde (Carlyle) 1944- ...... **CLC 39**
See also AAYA 17; CA 134; CAAE 118; CANR 64, 125; CN 7; CSW; DLB 278; INT CA-134; TCLE 1:1; YAW
Edgeworth, Maria 1768-1849 ... **NCLC 1, 51, 158; SSC 86**
See also BRWS 3; DLB 116, 159, 163; FL 1:3; FW; RGEL 2; SATA 21; TEA; WLIT 3
Edmonds, Paul
See Kuttner, Henry
Edmonds, Walter D(umaux) 1903-1998 .... **CLC 35**
See also BYA 2; CA 5-8R; CANR 2; CWRI 5; DLB 9; LAIT 1; MAICYA 1, 2; MAL 5; RHW; SAAS 4; SATA 1, 27; SATA-Obit 99
Edmondson, Wallace
See Ellison, Harlan
Edson, Margaret 1961- ...... **CLC 199; DC 24**
See also CA 190; DFS 13; DLB 266
Edson, Russell 1935- .... **CLC 13**
See also CA 33-36R; CANR 115; CP 2, 3, 4, 5, 6, 7; DLB 244; WP
Edwards, Bronwen Elizabeth
See Rose, Wendy
Edwards, G(erald) B(asil) 1899-1976 .... **CLC 25**
See also CA 201; CAAS 110
Edwards, Gus 1939- .... **CLC 43**
See also CA 108; INT CA-108
Edwards, Jonathan 1703-1758 .... **LC 7, 54**
See also AMW; DA; DAC; DAM MST; DLB 24, 270; RGAL 4; TUS
Edwards, Sarah Pierpont 1710-1758 .. **LC 87**
See also DLB 200
Efron, Marina Ivanovna Tsvetaeva
See Tsvetaeva (Efron), Marina (Ivanovna)
Egeria fl. 4th cent. - .... **CMLC 70**
Eggers, Dave 1970- .... **CLC 241**
See also AAYA 56; CA 198; CANR 138; MTFW 2005
Egoyan, Atom 1960- .... **CLC 151**
See also AAYA 63; CA 157; CANR 151
Ehle, John (Marsden, Jr.) 1925- ...... **CLC 27**
See also CA 9-12R; CSW
Ehrenbourg, Ilya (Grigoryevich)
See Ehrenburg, Ilya (Grigoryevich)

Ehrenburg, Ilya (Grigoryevich) 1891-1967 .... **CLC 18, 34, 62**
See Erenburg, Il'ia Grigor'evich
See also CA 102; CAAS 25-28R; EWL 3
Ehrenburg, Ilyo (Grigoryevich)
See Ehrenburg, Ilya (Grigoryevich)
Ehrenreich, Barbara 1941- .... **CLC 110**
See also BEST 90:4; CA 73-76; CANR 16, 37, 62, 117, 167; DLB 246; FW; MTCW 1, 2; MTFW 2005
Ehrlich, Gretel 1946- .... **CLC 249**
See also ANW; CA 140; CANR 74, 146; DLB 212, 275; TCWW 2
Eich, Gunter
See Eich, Gunter
See also RGWL 2, 3
Eich, Gunter 1907-1972 .... **CLC 15**
See Eich, Gunter
See also CA 111; CAAS 93-96; DLB 69, 124; EWL 3
Eichendorff, Joseph 1788-1857 .... **NCLC 8**
See also DLB 90; RGWL 2, 3
Eigner, Larry CLC 9
See Eigner, Laurence (Joel)
See also CA 23; CP 1, 2, 3, 4, 5, 6; DLB 5; WP
Eigner, Laurence (Joel) 1927-1996
See Eigner, Larry
See also CA 9-12R; CAAS 151; CANR 6, 84; CP 7; DLB 193
Eilhart von Oberge c. 1140-c. 1195 .... **CMLC 67**
See also DLB 148
Einhard c. 770-840 .... **CMLC 50**
See also DLB 148
Einstein, Albert 1879-1955 .... **TCLC 65**
See also CA 133; CAAE 121; MTCW 1, 2
Eiseley, Loren
See Eiseley, Loren Corey
See also DLB 275
Eiseley, Loren Corey 1907-1977 .... **CLC 7**
See Eiseley, Loren
See also AAYA 5; ANW; CA 1-4R; CAAS 73-76; CANR 6; DLBD 17
Eisenstadt, Jill 1963- .... **CLC 50**
See also CA 140
Eisenstein, Sergei (Mikhailovich) 1898-1948 .... **TCLC 57**
See also CA 149; CAAE 114
Eisner, Simon
See Kornbluth, C(yril) M.
Eisner, Will 1917-2005 .... **CLC 237**
See also AAYA 52; CA 108; CAAS 235; CANR 114, 140; MTFW 2005; SATA 31, 165
Eisner, William Erwin
See Eisner, Will
Ekeloef, (Bengt) Gunnar 1907-1968 .... **CLC 27; PC 23**
See Ekelof, (Bengt) Gunnar
See also CA 123; CAAS 25-28R; DAM POET
Ekelof, (Bengt) Gunnar 1907-1968
See Ekeloef, (Bengt) Gunnar
See also DLB 259; EW 12; EWL 3
Ekelund, Vilhelm 1880-1949 .... **TCLC 75**
See also CA 189; EWL 3
Ekwensi, C. O. D.
See Ekwensi, Cyprian
Ekwensi, Cyprian 1921-2007 .... **BLC 1:1; CLC 4**
See also AFW; BW 2, 3; CA 29-32R; CANR 18, 42, 74, 125; CDWLB 3; CN 1, 2, 3, 4, 5, 6; CWRI 5; DAM MULT; DLB 117; EWL 3; MTCW 1, 2; RGEL 2; SATA 66; WLIT 2
Ekwensi, Cyprian Odiatu Duaka
See Ekwensi, Cyprian
Elaine TCLC 18
See Leverson, Ada Esther
El Crummo
See Crumb, R.
Elder, Lonne III 1931-1996 .. **BLC 1:1; DC 8**
See also BW 1, 3; CA 81-84; CAAS 152; CAD; CANR 25; DAM MULT; DLB 7, 38, 44; MAL 5
Eleanor of Aquitaine 1122-1204 ... **CMLC 39**
Elia
See Lamb, Charles
Eliade, Mircea 1907-1986 .... **CLC 19**
See also CA 65-68; CAAS 119; CANR 30, 62; CDWLB 4; DLB 220; EWL 3; MTCW 1; RGWL 3; SFW 4
Eliot, A. D.
See Jewett, (Theodora) Sarah Orne
Eliot, Alice
See Jewett, (Theodora) Sarah Orne
Eliot, Dan
See Silverberg, Robert
Eliot, George 1819-1880 ...... **NCLC 4, 13, 23, 41, 49, 89, 118, 183; PC 20; SSC 72; WLC 2**
See Evans, Mary Ann
See also BRW 5; BRWC 1, 2; BRWR 2; CDBLB 1832-1890; CN 7; CPW; DA; DA3; DAB; DAC; DAM MST, NOV; DLB 21, 35, 55; FL 1:3; LATS 1:1; LMFS 1; NFS 17, 20; RGEL 2; RGSF 2; SSFS 8; TEA; WLIT 3
Eliot, John 1604-1690 .... **LC 5**
See also DLB 24
Eliot, T(homas) S(tearns) 1888-1965 ...... **CLC 1, 2, 3, 6, 9, 10, 13, 15, 24, 34, 41, 55, 57, 113; DC 28; PC 5, 31; WLC 2**
See also AAYA 28; AMW; AMWC 1; AMWR 1; BRW 7; BRWR 2; CA 5-8R; CAAS 25-28R; CANR 41; CBD; CDALB 1929-1941; DA; DA3; DAB; DAC; DAM DRAM, MST, POET; DFS 4, 13; DLB 7, 10, 45, 63, 245, 329; DLBY 1988; EWL 3; EXPP; LAIT 3; LATS 1:1; LMFS 2; MAL 5; MTCW 1, 2; MTFW 2005; NCFS 5; PAB; PFS 1, 7, 20; RGAL 4; RGEL 2; TUS; WLIT 4; WP
Elisabeth of Schonau c. 1129-1165 .... **CMLC 82**
Elizabeth 1866-1941 .... **TCLC 41**
Elizabeth I 1533-1603 .... **LC 118**
See also DLB 136
Elkin, Stanley L. 1930-1995 ...... **CLC 4, 6, 9, 14, 27, 51, 91; SSC 12**
See also AMWS 6; BPFB 1; CA 9-12R; CAAS 148; CANR 8, 46; CN 1, 2, 3, 4, 5, 6; CPW; DAM NOV, POP; DLB 2, 28, 218, 278; DLBY 1980; EWL 3; INT CANR-8; MAL 5; MTCW 1, 2; MTFW 2005; RGAL 4; TCLE 1:1
Elledge, Scott CLC 34
Eller, Scott
See Shepard, Jim
Elliott, Don
See Silverberg, Robert
Elliott, George P(aul) 1918-1980 .... **CLC 2**
See also CA 1-4R; CAAS 97-100; CANR 2; CN 1, 2; CP 3; DLB 244; MAL 5
Elliott, Janice 1931-1995 .... **CLC 47**
See also CA 13-16R; CANR 8, 29, 84; CN 5, 6, 7; DLB 14; SATA 119
Elliott, Sumner Locke 1917-1991 ..... **CLC 38**
See also CA 5-8R; CAAS 134; CANR 2, 21; DLB 289
Elliott, William
See Bradbury, Ray
Ellis, A. E. CLC 7
Ellis, Alice Thomas CLC 40
See Haycraft, Anna
See also CN 4, 5, 6; DLB 194
Ellis, Bret Easton 1964- ..... **CLC 39, 71, 117, 229**
See also AAYA 2, 43; CA 123; CAAE 118; CANR 51, 74, 126; CN 6, 7; CPW; DA3; DAM POP; DLB 292; HGG; INT CA-123; MTCW 2; MTFW 2005; NFS 11
Ellis, (Henry) Havelock 1859-1939 .... **TCLC 14**
See also CA 169; CAAE 109; DLB 190
Ellis, Landon
See Ellison, Harlan
Ellis, Trey 1962- .... **CLC 55**
See also CA 146; CANR 92; CN 7
Ellison, Harlan 1934- .... **CLC 1, 13, 42, 139; SSC 14**
See also AAYA 29; BPFB 1; BYA 14; CA 5-8R; CANR 5, 46, 115; CPW; DAM POP; DLB 8, 335; HGG; INT CANR-5; MTCW 1, 2; MTFW 2005; SCFW 2; SFW 4; SSFS 13, 14, 15, 21; SUFW 1, 2
Ellison, Ralph 1914-1994 .... **BLC 1:1, 2:2; CLC 1, 3, 11, 54, 86, 114; SSC 26, 79; WLC 2**
See also AAYA 19; AFAW 1, 2; AMWC 2; AMWR 2; AMWS 2; BPFB 1; BW 1, 3; BYA 2; CA 9-12R; CAAS 145; CANR 24, 53; CDALB 1941-1968; CN 1, 2, 3, 4, 5; CSW; DA; DA3; DAB; DAC; DAM MST, MULT, NOV; DLB 2, 76, 227; DLBY 1994; EWL 3; EXPN; EXPS; LAIT 4; MAL 5; MTCW 1, 2; MTFW 2005; NCFS 3; NFS 2, 21; RGAL 4; RGSF 2; SSFS 1, 11; YAW
Ellmann, Lucy 1956- .... **CLC 61**
See also CA 128; CANR 154
Ellmann, Lucy Elizabeth
See Ellmann, Lucy
Ellmann, Richard (David) 1918-1987 .... **CLC 50**
See also BEST 89:2; CA 1-4R; CAAS 122; CANR 2, 28, 61; DLB 103; DLBY 1987; MTCW 1, 2; MTFW 2005
Elman, Richard (Martin) 1934-1997 .... **CLC 19**
See also CA 17-20R; 3; CAAS 163; CANR 47; TCLE 1:1
Elron
See Hubbard, L. Ron
El Saadawi, Nawal 1931- ...... **BLC 2:2; CLC 196**
See al'Sadaawi, Nawal; Sa'adawi, al-Nawal; Saadawi, Nawal El; Sa'dawi, Nawal al-
See also CA 118; 11; CANR 44, 92
Eluard, Paul PC 38; TCLC 7, 41
See Grindel, Eugene
See also EWL 3; GFL 1789 to the Present; RGWL 2, 3
Elyot, Thomas 1490(?)-1546 .... **LC 11, 139**
See also DLB 136; RGEL 2
Elytis, Odysseus 1911-1996 .... **CLC 15, 49, 100; PC 21**
See Alepoudelis, Odysseus
See also CA 102; CAAS 151; CANR 94; CWW 2; DAM POET; DLB 329; EW 13; EWL 3; MTCW 1, 2; RGWL 2, 3
Emecheta, Buchi 1944- ... **BLC 1:2; CLC 14, 48, 128, 214**
See also AAYA 67; AFW; BW 2, 3; CA 81-84; CANR 27, 81, 126; CDWLB 3; CN 4, 5, 6, 7; CWRI 5; DA3; DAM MULT; DLB 117; EWL 3; FL 1:5; FW; MTCW 1, 2; MTFW 2005; NFS 12, 14; SATA 66; WLIT 2

Emerson, Mary Moody 1774-1863 .... **NCLC 66**
Emerson, Ralph Waldo 1803-1882 . **NCLC 1, 38, 98; PC 18; WLC 2**
See also AAYA 60; AMW; ANW; CDALB 1640-1865; DA; DA3; DAB; DAC; DAM MST, POET; DLB 1, 59, 73, 183, 223, 270; EXPP; LAIT 2; LMFS 1; NCFS 3; PFS 4, 17; RGAL 4; TUS; WP
Eminem 1972- .... **CLC 226**
See also CA 245
Eminescu, Mihail 1850-1889 .. **NCLC 33, 131**
Empedocles 5th cent. B.C.- .... **CMLC 50**
See also DLB 176
Empson, William 1906-1984 ... **CLC 3, 8, 19, 33, 34**
See also BRWS 2; CA 17-20R; CAAS 112; CANR 31, 61; CP 1, 2, 3; DLB 20; EWL 3; MTCW 1, 2; RGEL 2
Enchi, Fumiko (Ueda) 1905-1986 ..... **CLC 31**
See Enchi Fumiko
See also CA 129; CAAS 121; FW; MJW
Enchi Fumiko
See Enchi, Fumiko (Ueda)
See also DLB 182; EWL 3
Ende, Michael (Andreas Helmuth) 1929-1995 .... **CLC 31**
See also BYA 5; CA 124; CAAE 118; CAAS 149; CANR 36, 110; CLR 14; DLB 75; MAICYA 1, 2; MAICYAS 1; SATA 61, 130; SATA-Brief 42; SATA-Obit 86
Endo, Shusaku 1923-1996 ..... **CLC 7, 14, 19, 54, 99; SSC 48; TCLC 152**
See Endo Shusaku
See also CA 29-32R; CAAS 153; CANR 21, 54, 131; DA3; DAM NOV; MTCW 1, 2; MTFW 2005; RGSF 2; RGWL 2, 3
Endo Shusaku
See Endo, Shusaku
See also CWW 2; DLB 182; EWL 3
Engel, Marian 1933-1985 .... **CLC 36; TCLC 137**
See also CA 25-28R; CANR 12; CN 2, 3; DLB 53; FW; INT CANR-12
Engelhardt, Frederick
See Hubbard, L. Ron
Engels, Friedrich 1820-1895 .. **NCLC 85, 114**
See also DLB 129; LATS 1:1
Enright, D(ennis) J(oseph) 1920-2002 .... **CLC 4, 8, 31**
See also CA 1-4R; CAAS 211; CANR 1, 42, 83; CN 1, 2; CP 1, 2, 3, 4, 5, 6, 7; DLB 27; EWL 3; SATA 25; SATA-Obit 140
Ensler, Eve 1953- .... **CLC 212**
See also CA 172; CANR 126, 163; DFS 23
Enzensberger, Hans Magnus 1929- .... **CLC 43; PC 28**
See also CA 119; CAAE 116; CANR 103; CWW 2; EWL 3
Ephron, Nora 1941- .... **CLC 17, 31**
See also AAYA 35; AITN 2; CA 65-68; CANR 12, 39, 83, 161; DFS 22
Epicurus 341B.C.-270B.C. .... **CMLC 21**
See also DLB 176
Epinay, Louise d' 1726-1783 .... **LC 138**
See also DLB 313
Epsilon
See Betjeman, John
Epstein, Daniel Mark 1948- .... **CLC 7**
See also CA 49-52; CANR 2, 53, 90
Epstein, Jacob 1956- .... **CLC 19**
See also CA 114
Epstein, Jean 1897-1953 .... **TCLC 92**
Epstein, Joseph 1937- .... **CLC 39, 204**
See also AMWS 14; CA 119; CAAE 112; CANR 50, 65, 117, 164
Epstein, Leslie 1938- .... **CLC 27**
See also AMWS 12; CA 215; 73-76, 215; 12; CANR 23, 69, 162; DLB 299; RGHL
Equiano, Olaudah 1745(?)-1797 ..... **BLC 1:2; LC 16, 143**
See also AFAW 1, 2; CDWLB 3; DAM MULT; DLB 37, 50; WLIT 2
Erasmus, Desiderius 1469(?)-1536 ..... **LC 16, 93**
See also DLB 136; EW 2; LMFS 1; RGWL 2, 3; TWA
Erdman, Paul E. 1932-2007 .... **CLC 25**
See also AITN 1; CA 61-64; CAAS 259; CANR 13, 43, 84
Erdman, Paul Emil
See Erdman, Paul E.
Erdrich, Karen Louise
See Erdrich, Louise
Erdrich, Louise 1954- .... **CLC 39, 54, 120, 176; NNAL; PC 52**
See also AAYA 10, 47; AMWS 4; BEST 89:1; BPFB 1; CA 114; CANR 41, 62, 118, 138; CDALBS; CN 5, 6, 7; CP 6, 7; CPW; CWP; DA3; DAM MULT, NOV, POP; DLB 152, 175, 206; EWL 3; EXPP; FL 1:5; LAIT 5; LATS 1:2; MAL 5; MTCW 1, 2; MTFW 2005; NFS 5; PFS 14; RGAL 4; SATA 94, 141; SSFS 14, 22; TCWW 2
Erenburg, Ilya (Grigoryevich)
See Ehrenburg, Ilya (Grigoryevich)
Erickson, Stephen Michael
See Erickson, Steve
Erickson, Steve 1950- .... **CLC 64**
See also CA 129; CANR 60, 68, 136; MTFW 2005; SFW 4; SUFW 2
Erickson, Walter
See Fast, Howard
Ericson, Walter
See Fast, Howard
Eriksson, Buntel
See Bergman, Ingmar
Eriugena, John Scottus c. 810-877 .... **CMLC 65**
See also DLB 115
Ernaux, Annie 1940- .... **CLC 88, 184**
See also CA 147; CANR 93; MTFW 2005; NCFS 3, 5
Erskine, John 1879-1951 .... **TCLC 84**
See also CA 159; CAAE 112; DLB 9, 102; FANT
Erwin, Will
See Eisner, Will
Eschenbach, Wolfram von
See von Eschenbach, Wolfram
See also RGWL 3
Eseki, Bruno
See Mphahlele, Ezekiel
Esenin, S.A.
See Esenin, Sergei
See also EWL 3
Esenin, Sergei 1895-1925 .... **TCLC 4**
See Esenin, S.A.
See also CAAE 104; RGWL 2, 3
Esenin, Sergei Aleksandrovich
See Esenin, Sergei
Eshleman, Clayton 1935- .... **CLC 7**
See also CA 212; 33-36R, 212; 6; CANR 93; CP 1, 2, 3, 4, 5, 6, 7; DLB 5
Espada, Martin 1957- .... **PC 74**
See also CA 159; CANR 80; CP 7; EXPP; LLW; MAL 5; PFS 13, 16
Espriella, Don Manuel Alvarez
See Southey, Robert
Espriu, Salvador 1913-1985 .... **CLC 9**
See also CA 154; CAAS 115; DLB 134; EWL 3
Espronceda, Jose de 1808-1842 ..... **NCLC 39**
Esquivel, Laura 1950(?)- ... **CLC 141; HLCS 1**
See also AAYA 29; CA 143; CANR 68, 113, 161; DA3; DNFS 2; LAIT 3; LMFS 2; MTCW 2; MTFW 2005; NFS 5; WLIT 1
Esse, James
See Stephens, James
Esterbrook, Tom
See Hubbard, L. Ron
Esterhazy, Peter 1950- .... **CLC 251**
See also CA 140; CANR 137; CDWLB 4; CWW 2; DLB 232; EWL 3; RGWL 3
Estleman, Loren D. 1952- .... **CLC 48**
See also AAYA 27; CA 85-88; CANR 27, 74, 139; CMW 4; CPW; DA3; DAM NOV, POP; DLB 226; INT CANR-27; MTCW 1, 2; MTFW 2005; TCWW 1, 2
Etherege, Sir George 1636-1692 . **DC 23; LC 78**
See also BRW 2; DAM DRAM; DLB 80; PAB; RGEL 2
Euclid 306B.C.-283B.C. .... **CMLC 25**
Eugenides, Jeffrey 1960(?)- .... **CLC 81, 212**
See also AAYA 51; CA 144; CANR 120; MTFW 2005; NFS 24
Euripides c. 484B.C.-406B.C. .... **CMLC 23, 51; DC 4; WLCS**
See also AW 1; CDWLB 1; DA; DA3; DAB; DAC; DAM DRAM, MST; DFS 1, 4, 6; DLB 176; LAIT 1; LMFS 1; RGWL 2, 3; WLIT 8
Evan, Evin
See Faust, Frederick (Schiller)
Evans, Caradoc 1878-1945 ... **SSC 43; TCLC 85**
See also DLB 162
Evans, Evan
See Faust, Frederick (Schiller)
Evans, Marian
See Eliot, George
Evans, Mary Ann
See Eliot, George
See also NFS 20
Evarts, Esther
See Benson, Sally
Evelyn, John 1620-1706 .... **LC 144**
See also BRW 2; RGEL 2
Everett, Percival
See Everett, Percival L.
See also CSW
Everett, Percival L. 1956- .... **CLC 57**
See Everett, Percival
See also BW 2; CA 129; CANR 94, 134; CN 7; MTFW 2005
Everson, R(onald) G(ilmour) 1903-1992 .... **CLC 27**
See also CA 17-20R; CP 1, 2, 3, 4; DLB 88
Everson, William (Oliver) 1912-1994 .... **CLC 1, 5, 14**
See Antoninus, Brother
See also BG 1:2; CA 9-12R; CAAS 145; CANR 20; CP 2, 3, 4, 5; DLB 5, 16, 212; MTCW 1
Evtushenko, Evgenii Aleksandrovich
See Yevtushenko, Yevgeny (Alexandrovich)
See also CWW 2; RGWL 2, 3
Ewart, Gavin (Buchanan) 1916-1995 .... **CLC 13, 46**
See also BRWS 7; CA 89-92; CAAS 150; CANR 17, 46; CP 1, 2, 3, 4, 5, 6; DLB 40; MTCW 1
Ewers, Hanns Heinz 1871-1943 ..... **TCLC 12**
See also CA 149; CAAE 109
Ewing, Frederick R.
See Sturgeon, Theodore (Hamilton)

Exley, Frederick (Earl) 1929-1992 .... **CLC 6, 11**
See also AITN 2; BPFB 1; CA 81-84; CAAS 138; CANR 117; DLB 143; DLBY 1981
Eynhardt, Guillermo
See Quiroga, Horacio (Sylvestre)
Ezekiel, Nissim (Moses) 1924-2004 .. **CLC 61**
See also CA 61-64; CAAS 223; CP 1, 2, 3, 4, 5, 6, 7; DLB 323; EWL 3
Ezekiel, Tish O'Dowd 1943- .... **CLC 34**
See also CA 129
Fadeev, Aleksandr Aleksandrovich
See Bulgya, Alexander Alexandrovich
See also DLB 272
Fadeev, Alexandr Alexandrovich
See Bulgya, Alexander Alexandrovich
See also EWL 3
Fadeyev, A.
See Bulgya, Alexander Alexandrovich
Fadeyev, Alexander TCLC 53
See Bulgya, Alexander Alexandrovich
Fagen, Donald 1948- .... **CLC 26**
Fainzil'berg, Il'ia Arnol'dovich
See Fainzilberg, Ilya Arnoldovich
Fainzilberg, Ilya Arnoldovich
1897-1937 .... **TCLC 21**
See Il'f, Il'ia
See also CA 165; CAAE 120; EWL 3
Fair, Ronald L. 1932- .... **CLC 18**
See also BW 1; CA 69-72; CANR 25; DLB 33
Fairbairn, Roger
See Carr, John Dickson
Fairbairns, Zoe (Ann) 1948- .... **CLC 32**
See also CA 103; CANR 21, 85; CN 4, 5, 6, 7
Fairfield, Flora
See Alcott, Louisa May
Fairman, Paul W. 1916-1977
See Queen, Ellery
See also CAAS 114; SFW 4
Falco, Gian
See Papini, Giovanni
Falconer, James
See Kirkup, James
Falconer, Kenneth
See Kornbluth, C(yril) M.
Falkland, Samuel
See Heijermans, Herman
Fallaci, Oriana 1930-2006 .... **CLC 11, 110**
See also CA 77-80; CAAS 253; CANR 15, 58, 134; FW; MTCW 1
Faludi, Susan 1959- .... **CLC 140**
See also CA 138; CANR 126; FW; MTCW 2; MTFW 2005; NCFS 3
Faludy, George 1913- .... **CLC 42**
See also CA 21-24R
Faludy, Gyoergy
See Faludy, George
Fanon, Frantz 1925-1961 ...... **BLC 1:2; CLC 74; TCLC 188**
See also BW 1; CA 116; CAAS 89-92; DAM MULT; DLB 296; LMFS 2; WLIT 2
Fanshawe, Ann 1625-1680 .... **LC 11**
Fante, John (Thomas) 1911-1983 .... **CLC 60; SSC 65**
See also AMWS 11; CA 69-72; CAAS 109; CANR 23, 104; DLB 130; DLBY 1983
Far, Sui Sin SSC 62
See Eaton, Edith Maude
See also SSFS 4
Farah, Nuruddin 1945- .. **BLC 1:2, 2:2; CLC 53, 137**
See also AFW; BW 2, 3; CA 106; CANR 81, 148; CDWLB 3; CN 4, 5, 6, 7; DAM MULT; DLB 125; EWL 3; WLIT 2
Fargue, Leon-Paul 1876(?)-1947 .... **TCLC 11**
See also CAAE 109; CANR 107; DLB 258; EWL 3
Farigoule, Louis
See Romains, Jules
Farina, Richard 1936(?)-1966 .... **CLC 9**
See also CA 81-84; CAAS 25-28R
Farley, Walter (Lorimer)
1915-1989 .... **CLC 17**
See also AAYA 58; BYA 14; CA 17-20R; CANR 8, 29, 84; DLB 22; JRDA; MAICYA 1, 2; SATA 2, 43, 132; YAW
Farmer, Philip Jose 1918- .... **CLC 1, 19**
See also AAYA 28; BPFB 1; CA 1-4R; CANR 4, 35, 111; DLB 8; MTCW 1; SATA 93; SCFW 1, 2; SFW 4
Farquhar, George 1677-1707 .... **LC 21**
See also BRW 2; DAM DRAM; DLB 84; RGEL 2
Farrell, J(ames) G(ordon)
1935-1979 .... **CLC 6**
See also CA 73-76; CAAS 89-92; CANR 36; CN 1, 2; DLB 14, 271, 326; MTCW 1; RGEL 2; RHW; WLIT 4
Farrell, James T(homas) 1904-1979 . **CLC 1, 4, 8, 11, 66; SSC 28**
See also AMW; BPFB 1; CA 5-8R; CAAS 89-92; CANR 9, 61; CN 1, 2; DLB 4, 9, 86; DLBD 2; EWL 3; MAL 5; MTCW 1, 2; MTFW 2005; RGAL 4
Farrell, Warren (Thomas) 1943- ...... **CLC 70**
See also CA 146; CANR 120
Farren, Richard J.
See Betjeman, John
Farren, Richard M.
See Betjeman, John
Fassbinder, Rainer Werner
1946-1982 .... **CLC 20**
See also CA 93-96; CAAS 106; CANR 31
Fast, Howard 1914-2003 .... **CLC 23, 131**
See also AAYA 16; BPFB 1; CA 181; 1-4R, 181; 18; CAAS 214; CANR 1, 33, 54, 75, 98, 140; CMW 4; CN 1, 2, 3, 4, 5, 6, 7; CPW; DAM NOV; DLB 9; INT CANR-33; LATS 1:1; MAL 5; MTCW 2; MTFW 2005; RHW; SATA 7; SATA-Essay 107; TCWW 1, 2; YAW
Faulcon, Robert
See Holdstock, Robert
Faulkner, William (Cuthbert)
1897-1962 .... **CLC 1, 3, 6, 8, 9, 11, 14, 18, 28, 52, 68; SSC 1, 35, 42, 92, 97; TCLC 141; WLC 2**
See also AAYA 7; AMW; AMWR 1; BPFB 1; BYA 5, 15; CA 81-84; CANR 33; CDALB 1929-1941; DA; DA3; DAB; DAC; DAM MST, NOV; DLB 9, 11, 44, 102, 316, 330; DLBD 2; DLBY 1986, 1997; EWL 3; EXPN; EXPS; GL 2; LAIT 2; LATS 1:1; LMFS 2; MAL 5; MTCW 1, 2; MTFW 2005; NFS 4, 8, 13, 24; RGAL 4; RGSF 2; SSFS 2, 5, 6, 12; TUS
Fauset, Jessie Redmon
1882(?)-1961 ...... **BLC 1:2; CLC 19, 54; HR 1:2**
See also AFAW 2; BW 1; CA 109; CANR 83; DAM MULT; DLB 51; FW; LMFS 2; MAL 5; MBL
Faust, Frederick (Schiller)
1892-1944 .... **TCLC 49**
See Brand, Max; Dawson, Peter; Frederick, John
See also CA 152; CAAE 108; CANR 143; DAM POP; DLB 256; TUS
Faust, Irvin 1924- .... **CLC 8**
See also CA 33-36R; CANR 28, 67; CN 1, 2, 3, 4, 5, 6, 7; DLB 2, 28, 218, 278; DLBY 1980
Fawkes, Guy
See Benchley, Robert (Charles)
Fearing, Kenneth (Flexner)
1902-1961 .... **CLC 51**
See also CA 93-96; CANR 59; CMW 4; DLB 9; MAL 5; RGAL 4
Fecamps, Elise
See Creasey, John
Federman, Raymond 1928- .... **CLC 6, 47**
See also CA 208; 17-20R, 208; 8; CANR 10, 43, 83, 108; CN 3, 4, 5, 6; DLBY 1980
Federspiel, J.F. 1931-2007 .... **CLC 42**
See also CA 146; CAAS 257
Federspiel, Juerg F.
See Federspiel, J.F.
Federspiel, Jurg F.
See Federspiel, J.F.
Feiffer, Jules 1929- .... **CLC 2, 8, 64**
See also AAYA 3, 62; CA 17-20R; CAD; CANR 30, 59, 129, 161; CD 5, 6; DAM DRAM; DLB 7, 44; INT CANR-30; MTCW 1; SATA 8, 61, 111, 157
Feiffer, Jules Ralph
See Feiffer, Jules
Feige, Hermann Albert Otto Maximilian
See Traven, B.
Feinberg, David B. 1956-1994 .... **CLC 59**
See also CA 135; CAAS 147
Feinstein, Elaine 1930- .... **CLC 36**
See also CA 69-72; 1; CANR 31, 68, 121, 162; CN 3, 4, 5, 6, 7; CP 2, 3, 4, 5, 6, 7; CWP; DLB 14, 40; MTCW 1
Feke, Gilbert David CLC 65
Feldman, Irving (Mordecai) 1928- ..... **CLC 7**
See also CA 1-4R; CANR 1; CP 1, 2, 3, 4, 5, 6, 7; DLB 169; TCLE 1:1
Felix-Tchicaya, Gerald
See Tchicaya, Gerald Felix
Fellini, Federico 1920-1993 .... **CLC 16, 85**
See also CA 65-68; CAAS 143; CANR 33
Felltham, Owen 1602(?)-1668 .... **LC 92**
See also DLB 126, 151
Felsen, Henry Gregor 1916-1995 ..... **CLC 17**
See also CA 1-4R; CAAS 180; CANR 1; SAAS 2; SATA 1
Felski, Rita CLC 65
Fenelon, Francois de Pons de Salignac de la Mothe- 1651-1715 .... **LC 134**
See also DLB 268; EW 3; GFL Beginnings to 1789
Fenno, Jack
See Calisher, Hortense
Fenollosa, Ernest (Francisco)
1853-1908 .... **TCLC 91**
Fenton, James 1949- .... **CLC 32, 209**
See also CA 102; CANR 108, 160; CP 2, 3, 4, 5, 6, 7; DLB 40; PFS 11
Fenton, James Martin
See Fenton, James
Ferber, Edna 1887-1968 .... **CLC 18, 93**
See also AITN 1; CA 5-8R; CAAS 25-28R; CANR 68, 105; DLB 9, 28, 86, 266; MAL 5; MTCW 1, 2; MTFW 2005; RGAL 4; RHW; SATA 7; TCWW 1, 2
Ferdowsi, Abu'l Qasem
940-1020(?) .... **CMLC 43**
See Firdawsi, Abu al-Qasim
See also RGWL 2, 3
Ferguson, Helen
See Kavan, Anna
Ferguson, Niall 1964- .... **CLC 134, 250**
See also CA 190; CANR 154
Ferguson, Niall Campbell
See Ferguson, Niall
Ferguson, Samuel 1810-1886 .... **NCLC 33**
See also DLB 32; RGEL 2
Fergusson, Robert 1750-1774 .... **LC 29**
See also DLB 109; RGEL 2

Ferling, Lawrence
See Ferlinghetti, Lawrence
Ferlinghetti, Lawrence 1919(?)- .... **CLC 2, 6, 10, 27, 111; PC 1**
See also AAYA 74; BG 1:2; CA 5-8R; CAD; CANR 3, 41, 73, 125, 172; CDALB 1941-1968; CP 1, 2, 3, 4, 5, 6, 7; DA3; DAM POET; DLB 5, 16; MAL 5; MTCW 1, 2; MTFW 2005; RGAL 4; WP
Ferlinghetti, Lawrence Monsanto
See Ferlinghetti, Lawrence
Fern, Fanny
See Parton, Sara Payson Willis
Fernandez, Vicente Garcia Huidobro
See Huidobro Fernandez, Vicente Garcia
Fernandez-Armesto, Felipe CLC 70
See Fernandez-Armesto, Felipe Fermin Ricardo
See also CANR 153
Fernandez-Armesto, Felipe Fermin Ricardo 1950-
See Fernandez-Armesto, Felipe
See also CA 142; CANR 93
Fernandez de Lizardi, Jose Joaquin
See Lizardi, Jose Joaquin Fernandez de
Ferre, Rosario 1938- ...... **CLC 139; HLCS 1; SSC 36, 106**
See also CA 131; CANR 55, 81, 134; CWW 2; DLB 145; EWL 3; HW 1, 2; LAWS 1; MTCW 2; MTFW 2005; WLIT 1
Ferrer, Gabriel (Francisco Victor) Miro
See Miro (Ferrer), Gabriel (Francisco Victor)
Ferrier, Susan (Edmonstone) 1782-1854 .... **NCLC 8**
See also DLB 116; RGEL 2
Ferrigno, Robert 1948(?)- .... **CLC 65**
See also CA 140; CANR 125, 161
Ferron, Jacques 1921-1985 .... **CLC 94**
See also CA 129; CAAE 117; CCA 1; DAC; DLB 60; EWL 3
Feuchtwanger, Lion 1884-1958 .... **TCLC 3**
See also CA 187; CAAE 104; DLB 66; EWL 3; RGHL
Feuerbach, Ludwig 1804-1872 ..... **NCLC 139**
See also DLB 133
Feuillet, Octave 1821-1890 .... **NCLC 45**
See also DLB 192
Feydeau, Georges (Leon Jules Marie) 1862-1921 .... **TCLC 22**
See also CA 152; CAAE 113; CANR 84; DAM DRAM; DLB 192; EWL 3; GFL 1789 to the Present; RGWL 2, 3
Fichte, Johann Gottlieb 1762-1814 .... **NCLC 62**
See also DLB 90
Ficino, Marsilio 1433-1499 .... **LC 12**
See also LMFS 1
Fiedeler, Hans
See Doeblin, Alfred
Fiedler, Leslie A(aron) 1917-2003 ..... **CLC 4, 13, 24**
See also AMWS 13; CA 9-12R; CAAS 212; CANR 7, 63; CN 1, 2, 3, 4, 5, 6; DLB 28, 67; EWL 3; MAL 5; MTCW 1, 2; RGAL 4; TUS
Field, Andrew 1938- .... **CLC 44**
See also CA 97-100; CANR 25
Field, Eugene 1850-1895 .... **NCLC 3**
See also DLB 23, 42, 140; DLBD 13; MAICYA 1, 2; RGAL 4; SATA 16
Field, Gans T.
See Wellman, Manly Wade
Field, Michael 1915-1971 .... **TCLC 43**
See also CAAS 29-32R
Fielding, Helen 1958- .... **CLC 146, 217**
See also AAYA 65; CA 172; CANR 127; DLB 231; MTFW 2005
Fielding, Henry 1707-1754 .... **LC 1, 46, 85; WLC 2**
See also BRW 3; BRWR 1; CDBLB 1660-1789; DA; DA3; DAB; DAC; DAM DRAM, MST, NOV; DLB 39, 84, 101; NFS 18; RGEL 2; TEA; WLIT 3
Fielding, Sarah 1710-1768 .... **LC 1, 44**
See also DLB 39; RGEL 2; TEA
Fields, W. C. 1880-1946 .... **TCLC 80**
See also DLB 44
Fierstein, Harvey (Forbes) 1954- ..... **CLC 33**
See also CA 129; CAAE 123; CAD; CD 5, 6; CPW; DA3; DAM DRAM, POP; DFS 6; DLB 266; GLL; MAL 5
Figes, Eva 1932- .... **CLC 31**
See also CA 53-56; CANR 4, 44, 83; CN 2, 3, 4, 5, 6, 7; DLB 14, 271; FW; RGHL
Filippo, Eduardo de
See de Filippo, Eduardo
Finch, Anne 1661-1720 ..... **LC 3, 137; PC 21**
See also BRWS 9; DLB 95
Finch, Robert (Duer Claydon) 1900-1995 .... **CLC 18**
See also CA 57-60; CANR 9, 24, 49; CP 1, 2, 3, 4, 5, 6; DLB 88
Findley, Timothy (Irving Frederick) 1930-2002 .... **CLC 27, 102**
See also CA 25-28R; CAAS 206; CANR 12, 42, 69, 109; CCA 1; CN 4, 5, 6, 7; DAC; DAM MST; DLB 53; FANT; RHW
Fink, William
See Mencken, H(enry) L(ouis)
Firbank, Louis 1942-
See Reed, Lou
See also CAAE 117
Firbank, (Arthur Annesley) Ronald 1886-1926 .... **TCLC 1**
See also BRWS 2; CA 177; CAAE 104; DLB 36; EWL 3; RGEL 2
Firdawsi, Abu al-Qasim
See Ferdowsi, Abu'l Qasem
See also WLIT 6
Fish, Stanley
See Fish, Stanley Eugene
Fish, Stanley E.
See Fish, Stanley Eugene
Fish, Stanley Eugene 1938- .... **CLC 142**
See also CA 132; CAAE 112; CANR 90; DLB 67
Fisher, Dorothy (Frances) Canfield 1879-1958 .... **TCLC 87**
See also CA 136; CAAE 114; CANR 80; CLR 71; CWRI 5; DLB 9, 102, 284; MAICYA 1, 2; MAL 5; YABC 1
Fisher, M(ary) F(rances) K(ennedy) 1908-1992 .... **CLC 76, 87**
See also AMWS 17; CA 77-80; CAAS 138; CANR 44; MTCW 2
Fisher, Roy 1930- .... **CLC 25**
See also CA 81-84; 10; CANR 16; CP 1, 2, 3, 4, 5, 6, 7; DLB 40
Fisher, Rudolph 1897-1934 ...... **BLC 1:2; HR 1:2; SSC 25; TCLC 11**
See also BW 1, 3; CA 124; CAAE 107; CANR 80; DAM MULT; DLB 51, 102
Fisher, Vardis (Alvero) 1895-1968 .... **CLC 7; TCLC 140**
See also CA 5-8R; CAAS 25-28R; CANR 68; DLB 9, 206; MAL 5; RGAL 4; TCWW 1, 2
Fiske, Tarleton
See Bloch, Robert (Albert)
Fitch, Clarke
See Sinclair, Upton
Fitch, John IV
See Cormier, Robert
Fitzgerald, Captain Hugh
See Baum, L(yman) Frank
FitzGerald, Edward 1809-1883 ...... **NCLC 9, 153; PC 79**
See also BRW 4; DLB 32; RGEL 2
Fitzgerald, F(rancis) Scott (Key) 1896-1940 ... **SSC 6, 31, 75; TCLC 1, 6, 14, 28, 55, 157; WLC 2**
See also AAYA 24; AITN 1; AMW; AMWC 2; AMWR 1; BPFB 1; CA 123; CAAE 110; CDALB 1917-1929; DA; DA3; DAB; DAC; DAM MST, NOV; DLB 4, 9, 86, 219, 273; DLBD 1, 15, 16; DLBY 1981, 1996; EWL 3; EXPN; EXPS; LAIT 3; MAL 5; MTCW 1, 2; MTFW 2005; NFS 2, 19, 20; RGAL 4; RGSF 2; SSFS 4, 15, 21, 25; TUS
Fitzgerald, Penelope 1916-2000 . **CLC 19, 51, 61, 143**
See also BRWS 5; CA 85-88; 10; CAAS 190; CANR 56, 86, 131; CN 3, 4, 5, 6, 7; DLB 14, 194, 326; EWL 3; MTCW 2; MTFW 2005
Fitzgerald, Robert (Stuart) 1910-1985 .... **CLC 39**
See also CA 1-4R; CAAS 114; CANR 1; CP 1, 2, 3, 4; DLBY 1980; MAL 5
FitzGerald, Robert D(avid) 1902-1987 .... **CLC 19**
See also CA 17-20R; CP 1, 2, 3, 4; DLB 260; RGEL 2
Fitzgerald, Zelda (Sayre) 1900-1948 .... **TCLC 52**
See also AMWS 9; CA 126; CAAE 117; DLBY 1984
Flanagan, Thomas (James Bonner) 1923-2002 .... **CLC 25, 52**
See also CA 108; CAAS 206; CANR 55; CN 3, 4, 5, 6, 7; DLBY 1980; INT CA-108; MTCW 1; RHW; TCLE 1:1
Flaubert, Gustave 1821-1880 .... **NCLC 2, 10, 19, 62, 66, 135, 179, 185; SSC 11, 60; WLC 2**
See also DA; DA3; DAB; DAC; DAM MST, NOV; DLB 119, 301; EW 7; EXPS; GFL 1789 to the Present; LAIT 2; LMFS 1; NFS 14; RGSF 2; RGWL 2, 3; SSFS 6; TWA
Flavius Josephus
See Josephus, Flavius
Flecker, Herman Elroy
See Flecker, (Herman) James Elroy
Flecker, (Herman) James Elroy 1884-1915 .... **TCLC 43**
See also CA 150; CAAE 109; DLB 10, 19; RGEL 2
Fleming, Ian 1908-1964 ... **CLC 3, 30; TCLC 193**
See also AAYA 26; BPFB 1; CA 5-8R; CANR 59; CDBLB 1945-1960; CMW 4; CPW; DA3; DAM POP; DLB 87, 201; MSW; MTCW 1, 2; MTFW 2005; RGEL 2; SATA 9; TEA; YAW
Fleming, Ian Lancaster
See Fleming, Ian
Fleming, Thomas 1927- .... **CLC 37**
See also CA 5-8R; CANR 10, 102, 155; INT CANR-10; SATA 8
Fleming, Thomas James
See Fleming, Thomas
Fletcher, John 1579-1625 .... **DC 6; LC 33**
See also BRW 2; CDBLB Before 1660; DLB 58; RGEL 2; TEA
Fletcher, John Gould 1886-1950 .... **TCLC 35**
See also CA 167; CAAE 107; DLB 4, 45; LMFS 2; MAL 5; RGAL 4
Fleur, Paul
See Pohl, Frederik
Flieg, Helmut
See Heym, Stefan
Flooglebuckle, Al
See Spiegelman, Art

Frank, Anne(lies Marie) 1929-1945 .... **TCLC 17; WLC 2**
See also AAYA 12; BYA 1; CA 133; CAAE 113; CANR 68; CLR 101; DA; DA3; DAB; DAC; DAM MST; LAIT 4; MAICYA 2; MAICYAS 1; MTCW 1, 2; MTFW 2005; NCFS 2; RGHL; SATA 87; SATA-Brief 42; WYA; YAW
Frank, Bruno 1887-1945 .... **TCLC 81**
See also CA 189; DLB 118; EWL 3
Frank, Elizabeth 1945- .... **CLC 39**
See also CA 126; CAAE 121; CANR 78, 150; INT CA-126
Frankl, Viktor E(mil) 1905-1997 ...... **CLC 93**
See also CA 65-68; CAAS 161; RGHL
Franklin, Benjamin
See Hasek, Jaroslav (Matej Frantisek)
Franklin, Benjamin 1706-1790 .. **LC 25, 134; WLCS**
See also AMW; CDALB 1640-1865; DA; DA3; DAB; DAC; DAM MST; DLB 24, 43, 73, 183; LAIT 1; RGAL 4; TUS
Franklin, Madeleine
See L'Engle, Madeleine
Franklin, Madeleine L'Engle
See L'Engle, Madeleine
Franklin, Madeleine L'Engle Camp
See L'Engle, Madeleine
Franklin, (Stella Maria Sarah) Miles (Lampe) 1879-1954 .... **TCLC 7**
See also CA 164; CAAE 104; DLB 230; FW; MTCW 2; RGEL 2; TWA
Franzen, Jonathan 1959- .... **CLC 202**
See also AAYA 65; CA 129; CANR 105, 166
Fraser, Antonia 1932- .... **CLC 32, 107**
See also AAYA 57; CA 85-88; CANR 44, 65, 119, 164; CMW; DLB 276; MTCW 1, 2; MTFW 2005; SATA-Brief 32
Fraser, George MacDonald 1925-2008 .... **CLC 7**
See also AAYA 48; CA 180; 45-48, 180; CANR 2, 48, 74; MTCW 2; RHW
Fraser, Sylvia 1935- .... **CLC 64**
See also CA 45-48; CANR 1, 16, 60; CCA 1
Frayn, Michael 1933- .... **CLC 3, 7, 31, 47, 176; DC 27**
See also AAYA 69; BRWC 2; BRWS 7; CA 5-8R; CANR 30, 69, 114, 133, 166; CBD; CD 5, 6; CN 1, 2, 3, 4, 5, 6, 7; DAM DRAM, NOV; DFS 22; DLB 13, 14, 194, 245; FANT; MTCW 1, 2; MTFW 2005; SFW 4
Fraze, Candida (Merrill) 1945- .... **CLC 50**
See also CA 126
Frazer, Andrew
See Marlowe, Stephen
Frazer, J(ames) G(eorge) 1854-1941 .... **TCLC 32**
See also BRWS 3; CAAE 118; NCFS 5
Frazer, Robert Caine
See Creasey, John
Frazer, Sir James George
See Frazer, J(ames) G(eorge)
Frazier, Charles 1950- .... **CLC 109, 224**
See also AAYA 34; CA 161; CANR 126, 170; CSW; DLB 292; MTFW 2005; NFS 25
Frazier, Charles R.
See Frazier, Charles
Frazier, Charles Robinson
See Frazier, Charles
Frazier, Ian 1951- .... **CLC 46**
See also CA 130; CANR 54, 93
Frederic, Harold 1856-1898 ... **NCLC 10, 175**
See also AMW; DLB 12, 23; DLBD 13; MAL 5; NFS 22; RGAL 4
Frederick, John
See Faust, Frederick (Schiller)
See also TCWW 2
Frederick the Great 1712-1786 .... **LC 14**
Fredro, Aleksander 1793-1876 .... **NCLC 8**
Freeling, Nicolas 1927-2003 .... **CLC 38**
See also CA 49-52; 12; CAAS 218; CANR 1, 17, 50, 84; CMW 4; CN 1, 2, 3, 4, 5, 6; DLB 87
Freeman, Douglas Southall 1886-1953 .... **TCLC 11**
See also CA 195; CAAE 109; DLB 17; DLBD 17
Freeman, Judith 1946- .... **CLC 55**
See also CA 148; CANR 120; DLB 256
Freeman, Mary E(leanor) Wilkins 1852-1930 .... **SSC 1, 47; TCLC 9**
See also CA 177; CAAE 106; DLB 12, 78, 221; EXPS; FW; HGG; MBL; RGAL 4; RGSF 2; SSFS 4, 8; SUFW 1; TUS
Freeman, R(ichard) Austin 1862-1943 .... **TCLC 21**
See also CAAE 113; CANR 84; CMW 4; DLB 70
French, Albert 1943- .... **CLC 86**
See also BW 3; CA 167
French, Antonia
See Kureishi, Hanif
French, Marilyn 1929- .. **CLC 10, 18, 60, 177**
See also BPFB 1; CA 69-72; CANR 3, 31, 134, 163; CN 5, 6, 7; CPW; DAM DRAM, NOV, POP; FL 1:5; FW; INT CANR-31; MTCW 1, 2; MTFW 2005
French, Paul
See Asimov, Isaac
Freneau, Philip Morin 1752-1832 .. **NCLC 1, 111**
See also AMWS 2; DLB 37, 43; RGAL 4
Freud, Sigmund 1856-1939 .... **TCLC 52**
See also CA 133; CAAE 115; CANR 69; DLB 296; EW 8; EWL 3; LATS 1:1; MTCW 1, 2; MTFW 2005; NCFS 3; TWA
Freytag, Gustav 1816-1895 .... **NCLC 109**
See also DLB 129
Friedan, Betty 1921-2006 .... **CLC 74**
See also CA 65-68; CAAS 248; CANR 18, 45, 74; DLB 246; FW; MTCW 1, 2; MTFW 2005; NCFS 5
Friedan, Betty Naomi
See Friedan, Betty
Friedlander, Saul 1932- .... **CLC 90**
See also CA 130; CAAE 117; CANR 72; RGHL
Friedman, B(ernard) H(arper) 1926- .... **CLC 7**
See also CA 1-4R; CANR 3, 48
Friedman, Bruce Jay 1930- ...... **CLC 3, 5, 56**
See also CA 9-12R; CAD; CANR 25, 52, 101; CD 5, 6; CN 1, 2, 3, 4, 5, 6, 7; DLB 2, 28, 244; INT CANR-25; MAL 5; SSFS 18
Friel, Brian 1929- .. **CLC 5, 42, 59, 115, 253; DC 8; SSC 76**
See also BRWS 5; CA 21-24R; CANR 33, 69, 131; CBD; CD 5, 6; DFS 11; DLB 13, 319; EWL 3; MTCW 1; RGEL 2; TEA
Friis-Baastad, Babbis Ellinor 1921-1970 .... **CLC 12**
See also CA 17-20R; CAAS 134; SATA 7
Frisch, Max 1911-1991 ...... **CLC 3, 9, 14, 18, 32, 44; TCLC 121**
See also CA 85-88; CAAS 134; CANR 32, 74; CDWLB 2; DAM DRAM, NOV; DLB 69, 124; EW 13; EWL 3; MTCW 1, 2; MTFW 2005; RGHL; RGWL 2, 3
Fromentin, Eugene (Samuel Auguste) 1820-1876 .... **NCLC 10, 125**
See also DLB 123; GFL 1789 to the Present
Frost, Frederick
See Faust, Frederick (Schiller)
Frost, Robert 1874-1963 . **CLC 1, 3, 4, 9, 10, 13, 15, 26, 34, 44; PC 1, 39, 71; WLC 2**
See also AAYA 21; AMW; AMWR 1; CA 89-92; CANR 33; CDALB 1917-1929; CLR 67; DA; DA3; DAB; DAC; DAM MST, POET; DLB 54, 284; DLBD 7; EWL 3; EXPP; MAL 5; MTCW 1, 2; MTFW 2005; PAB; PFS 1, 2, 3, 4, 5, 6, 7, 10, 13; RGAL 4; SATA 14; TUS; WP; WYA
Frost, Robert Lee
See Frost, Robert
Froude, James Anthony 1818-1894 .... **NCLC 43**
See also DLB 18, 57, 144
Froy, Herald
See Waterhouse, Keith (Spencer)
Fry, Christopher 1907-2005 ... **CLC 2, 10, 14**
See also BRWS 3; CA 17-20R; 23; CAAS 240; CANR 9, 30, 74, 132; CBD; CD 5, 6; CP 1, 2, 3, 4, 5, 6, 7; DAM DRAM; DLB 13; EWL 3; MTCW 1, 2; MTFW 2005; RGEL 2; SATA 66; TEA
Frye, (Herman) Northrop 1912-1991 .... **CLC 24, 70; TCLC 165**
See also CA 5-8R; CAAS 133; CANR 8, 37; DLB 67, 68, 246; EWL 3; MTCW 1, 2; MTFW 2005; RGAL 4; TWA
Fuchs, Daniel 1909-1993 .... **CLC 8, 22**
See also CA 81-84; 5; CAAS 142; CANR 40; CN 1, 2, 3, 4, 5; DLB 9, 26, 28; DLBY 1993; MAL 5
Fuchs, Daniel 1934- .... **CLC 34**
See also CA 37-40R; CANR 14, 48
Fuentes, Carlos 1928- .. **CLC 3, 8, 10, 13, 22, 41, 60, 113; HLC 1; SSC 24; WLC 2**
See also AAYA 4, 45; AITN 2; BPFB 1; CA 69-72; CANR 10, 32, 68, 104, 138; CDWLB 3; CWW 2; DA; DA3; DAB; DAC; DAM MST, MULT, NOV; DLB 113; DNFS 2; EWL 3; HW 1, 2; LAIT 3; LATS 1:2; LAW; LAWS 1; LMFS 2; MTCW 1, 2; MTFW 2005; NFS 8; RGSF 2; RGWL 2, 3; TWA; WLIT 1
Fuentes, Gregorio Lopez y
See Lopez y Fuentes, Gregorio
Fuertes, Gloria 1918-1998 .... **PC 27**
See also CA 178, 180; DLB 108; HW 2; SATA 115
Fugard, (Harold) Athol 1932- . **CLC 5, 9, 14, 25, 40, 80, 211; DC 3**
See also AAYA 17; AFW; CA 85-88; CANR 32, 54, 118; CD 5, 6; DAM DRAM; DFS 3, 6, 10, 24; DLB 225; DNFS 1, 2; EWL 3; LATS 1:2; MTCW 1; MTFW 2005; RGEL 2; WLIT 2
Fugard, Sheila 1932- .... **CLC 48**
See also CA 125
Fujiwara no Teika 1162-1241 .... **CMLC 73**
See also DLB 203
Fukuyama, Francis 1952- .... **CLC 131**
See also CA 140; CANR 72, 125, 170
Fuller, Charles (H.), (Jr.) 1939- ..... **BLC 1:2; CLC 25; DC 1**
See also BW 2; CA 112; CAAE 108; CAD; CANR 87; CD 5, 6; DAM DRAM, MULT; DFS 8; DLB 38, 266; EWL 3; INT CA-112; MAL 5; MTCW 1
Fuller, Henry Blake 1857-1929 .... **TCLC 103**
See also CA 177; CAAE 108; DLB 12; RGAL 4
Fuller, John (Leopold) 1937- .... **CLC 62**
See also CA 21-24R; CANR 9, 44; CP 1, 2, 3, 4, 5, 6, 7; DLB 40
Fuller, Margaret
See Ossoli, Sarah Margaret (Fuller)
See also AMWS 2; DLB 183, 223, 239; FL 1:3

Garnett, David 1892-1981 .... **CLC 3**
See also CA 5-8R; CAAS 103; CANR 17, 79; CN 1, 2; DLB 34; FANT; MTCW 2; RGEL 2; SFW 4; SUFW 1
Garnier, Robert c. 1545-1590 .... **LC 119**
See also DLB 327; GFL Beginnings to 1789
Garrett, George (Palmer, Jr.) 1929- . **CLC 3, 11, 51; SSC 30**
See also AMWS 7; BPFB 2; CA 202; 1-4R, 202; 5; CANR 1, 42, 67, 109; CN 1, 2, 3, 4, 5, 6, 7; CP 1, 2, 3, 4, 5, 6, 7; CSW; DLB 2, 5, 130, 152; DLBY 1983
Garrick, David 1717-1779 .... **LC 15**
See also DAM DRAM; DLB 84, 213; RGEL 2
Garrigue, Jean 1914-1972 .... **CLC 2, 8**
See also CA 5-8R; CAAS 37-40R; CANR 20; CP 1; MAL 5
Garrison, Frederick
See Sinclair, Upton
Garrison, William Lloyd
1805-1879 .... **NCLC 149**
See also CDALB 1640-1865; DLB 1, 43, 235
Garro, Elena 1920(?)-1998 .. **HLCS 1; TCLC 153**
See also CA 131; CAAS 169; CWW 2; DLB 145; EWL 3; HW 1; LAWS 1; WLIT 1
Garth, Will
See Hamilton, Edmond; Kuttner, Henry
Garvey, Marcus (Moziah, Jr.)
1887-1940 ..... **BLC 1:2; HR 1:2; TCLC 41**
See also BW 1; CA 124; CAAE 120; CANR 79; DAM MULT
Gary, Romain CLC 25
See Kacew, Romain
See also DLB 83, 299; RGHL
Gascar, Pierre CLC 11
See Fournier, Pierre
See also EWL 3; RGHL
Gascoigne, George 1539-1577 .... **LC 108**
See also DLB 136; RGEL 2
Gascoyne, David (Emery)
1916-2001 .... **CLC 45**
See also CA 65-68; CAAS 200; CANR 10, 28, 54; CP 1, 2, 3, 4, 5, 6, 7; DLB 20; MTCW 1; RGEL 2
Gaskell, Elizabeth Cleghorn
1810-1865 .... **NCLC 5, 70, 97, 137; SSC 25, 97**
See also BRW 5; CDBLB 1832-1890; DAB; DAM MST; DLB 21, 144, 159; RGEL 2; RGSF 2; TEA
Gass, William H. 1924- . **CLC 1, 2, 8, 11, 15, 39, 132; SSC 12**
See also AMWS 6; CA 17-20R; CANR 30, 71, 100; CN 1, 2, 3, 4, 5, 6, 7; DLB 2, 227; EWL 3; MAL 5; MTCW 1, 2; MTFW 2005; RGAL 4
Gassendi, Pierre 1592-1655 .... **LC 54**
See also GFL Beginnings to 1789
Gasset, Jose Ortega y
See Ortega y Gasset, Jose
Gates, Henry Louis, Jr. 1950- ... **BLCS; CLC 65**
See also BW 2, 3; CA 109; CANR 25, 53, 75, 125; CSW; DA3; DAM MULT; DLB 67; EWL 3; MAL 5; MTCW 2; MTFW 2005; RGAL 4
Gatos, Stephanie
See Katz, Steve
Gautier, Theophile 1811-1872 .. **NCLC 1, 59; PC 18; SSC 20**
See also DAM POET; DLB 119; EW 6; GFL 1789 to the Present; RGWL 2, 3; SUFW; TWA
Gay, John 1685-1732 .... **LC 49**
See also BRW 3; DAM DRAM; DLB 84, 95; RGEL 2; WLIT 3
Gay, Oliver
See Gogarty, Oliver St. John
Gay, Peter 1923- .... **CLC 158**
See also CA 13-16R; CANR 18, 41, 77, 147; INT CANR-18; RGHL
Gay, Peter Jack
See Gay, Peter
Gaye, Marvin (Pentz, Jr.)
1939-1984 .... **CLC 26**
See also CA 195; CAAS 112
Gebler, Carlo 1954- .... **CLC 39**
See also CA 133; CAAE 119; CANR 96; DLB 271
Gee, Maggie 1948- .... **CLC 57**
See also CA 130; CANR 125; CN 4, 5, 6, 7; DLB 207; MTFW 2005
Gee, Maurice 1931- .... **CLC 29**
See also AAYA 42; CA 97-100; CANR 67, 123; CLR 56; CN 2, 3, 4, 5, 6, 7; CWRI 5; EWL 3; MAICYA 2; RGSF 2; SATA 46, 101
Gee, Maurice Gough
See Gee, Maurice
Geiogamah, Hanay 1945- .... **NNAL**
See also CA 153; DAM MULT; DLB 175
Gelbart, Larry
See Gelbart, Larry (Simon)
See also CAD; CD 5, 6
Gelbart, Larry (Simon) 1928- .... **CLC 21, 61**
See Gelbart, Larry
See also CA 73-76; CANR 45, 94
Gelber, Jack 1932-2003 ...... **CLC 1, 6, 14, 79**
See also CA 1-4R; CAAS 216; CAD; CANR 2; DLB 7, 228; MAL 5
Gellhorn, Martha (Ellis)
1908-1998 .... **CLC 14, 60**
See also CA 77-80; CAAS 164; CANR 44; CN 1, 2, 3, 4, 5, 6 7; DLBY 1982, 1998
Genet, Jean 1910-1986 .. **CLC 1, 2, 5, 10, 14, 44, 46; DC 25; TCLC 128**
See also CA 13-16R; CANR 18; DA3; DAM DRAM; DFS 10; DLB 72, 321; DLBY 1986; EW 13; EWL 3; GFL 1789 to the Present; GLL 1; LMFS 2; MTCW 1, 2; MTFW 2005; RGWL 2, 3; TWA
Genlis, Stephanie-Felicite Ducrest
1746-1830 .... **NCLC 166**
See also DLB 313
Gent, Peter 1942- .... **CLC 29**
See also AITN 1; CA 89-92; DLBY 1982
Gentile, Giovanni 1875-1944 .... **TCLC 96**
See also CAAE 119
Geoffrey of Monmouth c. 1100-1155 .... **CMLC 44**
See also DLB 146; TEA
George, Jean
See George, Jean Craighead
George, Jean Craighead 1919- .... **CLC 35**
See also AAYA 8, 69; BYA 2, 4; CA 5-8R; CANR 25; CLR 1; 80; DLB 52; JRDA; MAICYA 1, 2; SATA 2, 68, 124, 170; WYA; YAW
George, Stefan (Anton) 1868-1933 . **TCLC 2, 14**
See also CA 193; CAAE 104; EW 8; EWL 3
Georges, Georges Martin
See Simenon, Georges (Jacques Christian)
Gerald of Wales c. 1146-c. 1223 ... **CMLC 60**
Gerhardi, William Alexander
See Gerhardie, William Alexander
Gerhardie, William Alexander
1895-1977 .... **CLC 5**
See also CA 25-28R; CAAS 73-76; CANR 18; CN 1, 2; DLB 36; RGEL 2
Gerson, Jean 1363-1429 .... **LC 77**
See also DLB 208
Gersonides 1288-1344 .... **CMLC 49**
See also DLB 115
Gerstler, Amy 1956- .... **CLC 70**
See also CA 146; CANR 99
Gertler, T. CLC 34
See also CA 121; CAAE 116
Gertsen, Aleksandr Ivanovich
See Herzen, Aleksandr Ivanovich
Ghalib NCLC 39, 78
See Ghalib, Asadullah Khan
Ghalib, Asadullah Khan 1797-1869
See Ghalib
See also DAM POET; RGWL 2, 3
Ghelderode, Michel de 1898-1962 ..... **CLC 6, 11; DC 15; TCLC 187**
See also CA 85-88; CANR 40, 77; DAM DRAM; DLB 321; EW 11; EWL 3; TWA
Ghiselin, Brewster 1903-2001 .... **CLC 23**
See also CA 13-16R; 10; CANR 13; CP 1, 2, 3, 4, 5, 6, 7
Ghose, Aurabinda 1872-1950 .... **TCLC 63**
See Ghose, Aurobindo
See also CA 163
Ghose, Aurobindo
See Ghose, Aurabinda
See also EWL 3
Ghose, Zulfikar 1935- .... **CLC 42, 200**
See also CA 65-68; CANR 67; CN 1, 2, 3, 4, 5, 6, 7; CP 1, 2, 3, 4, 5, 6, 7; DLB 323; EWL 3
Ghosh, Amitav 1956- .... **CLC 44, 153**
See also CA 147; CANR 80, 158; CN 6, 7; DLB 323; WWE 1
Giacosa, Giuseppe 1847-1906 .... **TCLC 7**
See also CAAE 104
Gibb, Lee
See Waterhouse, Keith (Spencer)
Gibbon, Edward 1737-1794 .... **LC 97**
See also BRW 3; DLB 104, 336; RGEL 2
Gibbon, Lewis Grassic TCLC 4
See Mitchell, James Leslie
See also RGEL 2
Gibbons, Kaye 1960- .... **CLC 50, 88, 145**
See also AAYA 34; AMWS 10; CA 151; CANR 75, 127; CN 7; CSW; DA3; DAM POP; DLB 292; MTCW 2; MTFW 2005; NFS 3; RGAL 4; SATA 117
Gibran, Kahlil 1883-1931 . **PC 9; TCLC 1, 9**
See also CA 150; CAAE 104; DA3; DAM POET, POP; EWL 3; MTCW 2; WLIT 6
Gibran, Khalil
See Gibran, Kahlil
Gibson, Mel 1956- .... **CLC 215**
Gibson, William 1914- .... **CLC 23**
See also CA 9-12R; CAD; CANR 9, 42, 75, 125; CD 5, 6; DA; DAB; DAC; DAM DRAM, MST; DFS 2; DLB 7; LAIT 2; MAL 5; MTCW 2; MTFW 2005; SATA 66; YAW
Gibson, William 1948- .... **CLC 39, 63, 186, 192; SSC 52**
See also AAYA 12, 59; AMWS 16; BPFB 2; CA 133; CAAE 126; CANR 52, 90, 106, 172; CN 6, 7; CPW; DA3; DAM POP; DLB 251; MTCW 2; MTFW 2005; SCFW 2; SFW 4
Gibson, William Ford
See Gibson, William
Gide, Andre (Paul Guillaume)
1869-1951 ...... **SSC 13; TCLC 5, 12, 36, 177; WLC 3**
See also CA 124; CAAE 104; DA; DA3; DAB; DAC; DAM MST, NOV; DLB 65, 321, 330; EW 8; EWL 3; GFL 1789 to the Present; MTCW 1, 2; MTFW 2005; NFS 21; RGSF 2; RGWL 2, 3; TWA

Gogol, Nikolai (Vasilyevich) 1809-1852 .... **DC 1; NCLC 5, 15, 31, 162; SSC 4, 29, 52; WLC 3**
See also DA; DAB; DAC; DAM DRAM, MST; DFS 12; DLB 198; EW 6; EXPS; RGSF 2; RGWL 2, 3; SSFS 7; TWA

Goines, Donald 1937(?)-1974 .... **BLC 1:2; CLC 80**
See also AITN 1; BW 1, 3; CA 124; CAAS 114; CANR 82; CMW 4; DA3; DAM MULT, POP; DLB 33

Gold, Herbert 1924- ... **CLC 4, 7, 14, 42, 152**
See also CA 9-12R; CANR 17, 45, 125; CN 1, 2, 3, 4, 5, 6, 7; DLB 2; DLBY 1981; MAL 5

Goldbarth, Albert 1948- .... **CLC 5, 38**
See also AMWS 12; CA 53-56; CANR 6, 40; CP 3, 4, 5, 6, 7; DLB 120

Goldberg, Anatol 1910-1982 .... **CLC 34**
See also CA 131; CAAS 117

Goldemberg, Isaac 1945- .... **CLC 52**
See also CA 69-72; 12; CANR 11, 32; EWL 3; HW 1; WLIT 1

Golding, Arthur 1536-1606 .... **LC 101**
See also DLB 136

Golding, William 1911-1993 . **CLC 1, 2, 3, 8, 10, 17, 27, 58, 81; WLC 3**
See also AAYA 5, 44; BPFB 2; BRWR 1; BRWS 1; BYA 2; CA 5-8R; CAAS 141; CANR 13, 33, 54; CD 5; CDBLB 1945-1960; CLR 94, 130; CN 1, 2, 3, 4; DA; DA3; DAB; DAC; DAM MST, NOV; DLB 15, 100, 255, 326, 330; EWL 3; EXPN; HGG; LAIT 4; MTCW 1, 2; MTFW 2005; NFS 2; RGEL 2; RHW; SFW 4; TEA; WLIT 4; YAW

Golding, William Gerald
See Golding, William

Goldman, Emma 1869-1940 .... **TCLC 13**
See also CA 150; CAAE 110; DLB 221; FW; RGAL 4; TUS

Goldman, Francisco 1954- .... **CLC 76**
See also CA 162

Goldman, William 1931- .... **CLC 1, 48**
See also BPFB 2; CA 9-12R; CANR 29, 69, 106; CN 1, 2, 3, 4, 5, 6, 7; DLB 44; FANT; IDFW 3, 4

Goldman, William W.
See Goldman, William

Goldmann, Lucien 1913-1970 .... **CLC 24**
See also CA 25-28; CAP 2

Goldoni, Carlo 1707-1793 .... **LC 4**
See also DAM DRAM; EW 4; RGWL 2, 3; WLIT 7

Goldsberry, Steven 1949- .... **CLC 34**
See also CA 131

Goldsmith, Oliver 1730(?)-1774 .... **DC 8; LC 2, 48, 122; PC 77; WLC 3**
See also BRW 3; CDBLB 1660-1789; DA; DAB; DAC; DAM DRAM, MST, NOV, POET; DFS 1; DLB 39, 89, 104, 109, 142, 336; IDTP; RGEL 2; SATA 26; TEA; WLIT 3

Goldsmith, Peter
See Priestley, J(ohn) B(oynton)

Goldstein, Rebecca 1950- .... **CLC 239**
See also CA 144; CANR 99, 165; TCLE 1:1

Goldstein, Rebecca Newberger
See Goldstein, Rebecca

Gombrowicz, Witold 1904-1969 .... **CLC 4, 7, 11, 49**
See also CA 19-20; CAAS 25-28R; CANR 105; CAP 2; CDWLB 4; DAM DRAM; DLB 215; EW 12; EWL 3; RGWL 2, 3; TWA

Gomez de Avellaneda, Gertrudis 1814-1873 .... **NCLC 111**
See also LAW

Gomez de la Serna, Ramon 1888-1963 .... **CLC 9**
See also CA 153; CAAS 116; CANR 79; EWL 3; HW 1, 2

Goncharov, Ivan Alexandrovich 1812-1891 .... **NCLC 1, 63**
See also DLB 238; EW 6; RGWL 2, 3

Goncourt, Edmond (Louis Antoine Huot) de 1822-1896 .... **NCLC 7**
See also DLB 123; EW 7; GFL 1789 to the Present; RGWL 2, 3

Goncourt, Jules (Alfred Huot) de 1830-1870 .... **NCLC 7**
See also DLB 123; EW 7; GFL 1789 to the Present; RGWL 2, 3

Gongora (y Argote), Luis de 1561-1627 .... **LC 72**
See also RGWL 2, 3

Gontier, Fernande 19(?)- .... **CLC 50**

Gonzalez Martinez, Enrique
See Gonzalez Martinez, Enrique
See also DLB 290

Gonzalez Martinez, Enrique 1871-1952 .... **TCLC 72**
See Gonzalez Martinez, Enrique
See also CA 166; CANR 81; EWL 3; HW 1, 2

Goodison, Lorna 1947- .... **BLC 2:2; PC 36**
See also CA 142; CANR 88; CP 5, 6, 7; CWP; DLB 157; EWL 3; PFS 25

Goodman, Allegra 1967- .... **CLC 241**
See also CA 204; CANR 162; DLB 244

Goodman, Paul 1911-1972 ..... **CLC 1, 2, 4, 7**
See also CA 19-20; CAAS 37-40R; CAD; CANR 34; CAP 2; CN 1; DLB 130, 246; MAL 5; MTCW 1; RGAL 4

GoodWeather, Hartley
See King, Thomas

Googe, Barnabe 1540-1594 .... **LC 94**
See also DLB 132; RGEL 2

Gordimer, Nadine 1923- ...... **CLC 3, 5, 7, 10, 18, 33, 51, 70, 123, 160, 161; SSC 17, 80; WLCS**
See also AAYA 39; AFW; BRWS 2; CA 5-8R; CANR 3, 28, 56, 88, 131; CN 1, 2, 3, 4, 5, 6, 7; DA; DA3; DAB; DAC; DAM MST, NOV; DLB 225, 326, 330; EWL 3; EXPS; INT CANR-28; LATS 1:2; MTCW 1, 2; MTFW 2005; NFS 4; RGEL 2; RGSF 2; SSFS 2, 14, 19; TWA; WLIT 2; YAW

Gordon, Adam Lindsay 1833-1870 .... **NCLC 21**
See also DLB 230

Gordon, Caroline 1895-1981 . **CLC 6, 13, 29, 83; SSC 15**
See also AMW; CA 11-12; CAAS 103; CANR 36; CAP 1; CN 1, 2; DLB 4, 9, 102; DLBD 17; DLBY 1981; EWL 3; MAL 5; MTCW 1, 2; MTFW 2005; RGAL 4; RGSF 2

Gordon, Charles William 1860-1937
See Connor, Ralph
See also CAAE 109

Gordon, Mary 1949- .. **CLC 13, 22, 128, 216; SSC 59**
See also AMWS 4; BPFB 2; CA 102; CANR 44, 92, 154; CN 4, 5, 6, 7; DLB 6; DLBY 1981; FW; INT CA-102; MAL 5; MTCW 1

Gordon, Mary Catherine
See Gordon, Mary

Gordon, N. J.
See Bosman, Herman Charles

Gordon, Sol 1923- .... **CLC 26**
See also CA 53-56; CANR 4; SATA 11

Gordone, Charles 1925-1995 .... **BLC 2:2; CLC 1, 4; DC 8**
See also BW 1, 3; CA 180; 93-96, 180; CAAS 150; CAD; CANR 55; DAM DRAM; DLB 7; INT CA-93-96; MTCW 1

Gore, Catherine 1800-1861 .... **NCLC 65**
See also DLB 116; RGEL 2

Gorenko, Anna Andreevna
See Akhmatova, Anna

Gorky, Maxim SSC 28; TCLC 8; WLC 3
See Peshkov, Alexei Maximovich
See also DAB; DFS 9; DLB 295; EW 8; EWL 3; TWA

Goryan, Sirak
See Saroyan, William

Gosse, Edmund (William) 1849-1928 .... **TCLC 28**
See also CAAE 117; DLB 57, 144, 184; RGEL 2

Gotlieb, Phyllis (Fay Bloom) 1926- .. **CLC 18**
See also CA 13-16R; CANR 7, 135; CN 7; CP 1, 2, 3, 4; DLB 88, 251; SFW 4

Gottesman, S. D.
See Kornbluth, C(yril) M.; Pohl, Frederik

Gottfried von Strassburg fl. c. 1170-1215 .... **CMLC 10, 96**
See also CDWLB 2; DLB 138; EW 1; RGWL 2, 3

Gotthelf, Jeremias 1797-1854 .... **NCLC 117**
See also DLB 133; RGWL 2, 3

Gottschalk, Laura Riding
See Jackson, Laura (Riding)

Gould, Lois 1932(?)-2002 .... **CLC 4, 10**
See also CA 77-80; CAAS 208; CANR 29; MTCW 1

Gould, Stephen Jay 1941-2002 .... **CLC 163**
See also AAYA 26; BEST 90:2; CA 77-80; CAAS 205; CANR 10, 27, 56, 75, 125; CPW; INT CANR-27; MTCW 1, 2; MTFW 2005

Gourmont, Remy(-Marie-Charles) de 1858-1915 .... **TCLC 17**
See also CA 150; CAAE 109; GFL 1789 to the Present; MTCW 2

Gournay, Marie le Jars de
See de Gournay, Marie le Jars

Govier, Katherine 1948- .... **CLC 51**
See also CA 101; CANR 18, 40, 128; CCA 1

Gower, John c. 1330-1408 .... **LC 76; PC 59**
See also BRW 1; DLB 146; RGEL 2

Goyen, (Charles) William 1915-1983 .... **CLC 5, 8, 14, 40**
See also AITN 2; CA 5-8R; CAAS 110; CANR 6, 71; CN 1, 2, 3; DLB 2, 218; DLBY 1983; EWL 3; INT CANR-6; MAL 5

Goytisolo, Juan 1931- .... **CLC 5, 10, 23, 133; HLC 1**
See also CA 85-88; CANR 32, 61, 131; CWW 2; DAM MULT; DLB 322; EWL 3; GLL 2; HW 1, 2; MTCW 1, 2; MTFW 2005

Gozzano, Guido 1883-1916 .... **PC 10**
See also CA 154; DLB 114; EWL 3

Gozzi, (Conte) Carlo 1720-1806 .... **NCLC 23**

Grabbe, Christian Dietrich 1801-1836 .... **NCLC 2**
See also DLB 133; RGWL 2, 3

Grace, Patricia Frances 1937- .... **CLC 56**
See also CA 176; CANR 118; CN 4, 5, 6, 7; EWL 3; RGSF 2

Gracian y Morales, Baltasar 1601-1658 .... **LC 15**

Gracq, Julien 1910-2007 .... **CLC 11, 48**
See also CA 126; CAAE 122; CANR 141; CWW 2; DLB 83; GFL 1789 to the present

Grenville, Kate 1950- .... **CLC 61**
See also CA 118; CANR 53, 93, 156; CN 7; DLB 325
Grenville, Pelham
See Wodehouse, P(elham) G(renville)
Greve, Felix Paul (Berthold Friedrich) 1879-1948
See Grove, Frederick Philip
See also CA 141, 175; CAAE 104; CANR 79; DAC; DAM MST
Greville, Fulke 1554-1628 .... **LC 79**
See also BRWS 11; DLB 62, 172; RGEL 2
Grey, Lady Jane 1537-1554 .... **LC 93**
See also DLB 132
Grey, Zane 1872-1939 .... **TCLC 6**
See also BPFB 2; CA 132; CAAE 104; DA3; DAM POP; DLB 9, 212; MTCW 1, 2; MTFW 2005; RGAL 4; TCWW 1, 2; TUS
Griboedov, Aleksandr Sergeevich 1795(?)-1829 .... **NCLC 129**
See also DLB 205; RGWL 2, 3
Grieg, (Johan) Nordahl (Brun) 1902-1943 .... **TCLC 10**
See also CA 189; CAAE 107; EWL 3
Grieve, C(hristopher) M(urray) 1892-1978 .... **CLC 11, 19**
See MacDiarmid, Hugh; Pteleon
See also CA 5-8R; CAAS 85-88; CANR 33, 107; DAM POET; MTCW 1; RGEL 2
Griffin, Gerald 1803-1840 .... **NCLC 7**
See also DLB 159; RGEL 2
Griffin, John Howard 1920-1980 ..... **CLC 68**
See also AITN 1; CA 1-4R; CAAS 101; CANR 2
Griffin, Peter 1942- .... **CLC 39**
See also CA 136
Griffith, D(avid Lewelyn) W(ark) 1875(?)-1948 .... **TCLC 68**
See also CA 150; CAAE 119; CANR 80
Griffith, Lawrence
See Griffith, D(avid Lewelyn) W(ark)
Griffiths, Trevor 1935- .... **CLC 13, 52**
See also CA 97-100; CANR 45; CBD; CD 5, 6; DLB 13, 245
Griggs, Sutton (Elbert) 1872-1930 .... **TCLC 77**
See also CA 186; CAAE 123; DLB 50
Grigson, Geoffrey (Edward Harvey) 1905-1985 .... **CLC 7, 39**
See also CA 25-28R; CAAS 118; CANR 20, 33; CP 1, 2, 3, 4; DLB 27; MTCW 1, 2
Grile, Dod
See Bierce, Ambrose (Gwinett)
Grillparzer, Franz 1791-1872 .... **DC 14; NCLC 1, 102; SSC 37**
See also CDWLB 2; DLB 133; EW 5; RGWL 2, 3; TWA
Grimble, Reverend Charles James
See Eliot, T(homas) S(tearns)
Grimke, Angelina (Emily) Weld 1880-1958 .... **HR 1:2**
See Weld, Angelina (Emily) Grimke
See also BW 1; CA 124; DAM POET; DLB 50, 54
Grimke, Charlotte L(ottie) Forten 1837(?)-1914
See Forten, Charlotte L.
See also BW 1; CA 124; CAAE 117; DAM MULT, POET
Grimm, Jacob Ludwig Karl 1785-1863 .... **NCLC 3, 77; SSC 36**
See Grimm Brothers
See also CLR 112; DLB 90; MAICYA 1, 2; RGSF 2; RGWL 2, 3; SATA 22; WCH
Grimm, Wilhelm Karl 1786-1859 .. **NCLC 3, 77; SSC 36**
See Grimm Brothers
See also CDWLB 2; CLR 112; DLB 90; MAICYA 1, 2; RGSF 2; RGWL 2, 3; SATA 22; WCH
Grimm and Grim
See Grimm, Jacob Ludwig Karl; Grimm, Wilhelm Karl
Grimm Brothers SSC 88
See Grimm, Jacob Ludwig Karl; Grimm, Wilhelm Karl
See also CLR 112
Grimmelshausen, Hans Jakob Christoffel von
See Grimmelshausen, Johann Jakob Christoffel von
See also RGWL 2, 3
Grimmelshausen, Johann Jakob Christoffel von 1621-1676 .... **LC 6**
See Grimmelshausen, Hans Jakob Christoffel von
See also CDWLB 2; DLB 168
Grindel, Eugene 1895-1952
See Eluard, Paul
See also CA 193; CAAE 104; LMFS 2
Grisham, John 1955- .... **CLC 84**
See also AAYA 14, 47; BPFB 2; CA 138; CANR 47, 69, 114, 133; CMW 4; CN 6, 7; CPW; CSW; DA3; DAM POP; MSW; MTCW 2; MTFW 2005
Grosseteste, Robert 1175(?)-1253 . **CMLC 62**
See also DLB 115
Grossman, David 1954- .... **CLC 67, 231**
See also CA 138; CANR 114; CWW 2; DLB 299; EWL 3; RGHL; WLIT 6
Grossman, Vasilii Semenovich
See Grossman, Vasily (Semenovich)
See also DLB 272
Grossman, Vasily (Semenovich) 1905-1964 .... **CLC 41**
See Grossman, Vasilii Semenovich
See also CA 130; CAAE 124; MTCW 1; RGHL
Grove, Frederick Philip TCLC 4
See Greve, Felix Paul (Berthold Friedrich)
See also DLB 92; RGEL 2; TCWW 1, 2
Grubb
See Crumb, R.
Grumbach, Doris 1918- .... **CLC 13, 22, 64**
See also CA 5-8R; 2; CANR 9, 42, 70, 127; CN 6, 7; INT CANR-9; MTCW 2; MTFW 2005
Grundtvig, Nikolai Frederik Severin 1783-1872 .... **NCLC 1, 158**
See also DLB 300
Grunge
See Crumb, R.
Grunwald, Lisa 1959- .... **CLC 44**
See also CA 120; CANR 148
Gryphius, Andreas 1616-1664 .... **LC 89**
See also CDWLB 2; DLB 164; RGWL 2, 3
Guare, John 1938- .... **CLC 8, 14, 29, 67; DC 20**
See also CA 73-76; CAD; CANR 21, 69, 118; CD 5, 6; DAM DRAM; DFS 8, 13; DLB 7, 249; EWL 3; MAL 5; MTCW 1, 2; RGAL 4
Guarini, Battista 1538-1612 .... **LC 102**
See also DLB 339
Gubar, Susan 1944- .... **CLC 145**
See also CA 108; CANR 45, 70, 139; FW; MTCW 1; RGAL 4
Gubar, Susan David
See Gubar, Susan
Gudjonsson, Halldor Kiljan 1902-1998
See Halldor Laxness
See also CA 103; CAAS 164
Guenter, Erich
See Eich, Gunter
Guest, Barbara 1920-2006 ... **CLC 34; PC 55**
See also BG 1:2; CA 25-28R; CAAS 248; CANR 11, 44, 84; CP 1, 2, 3, 4, 5, 6, 7; CWP; DLB 5, 193
Guest, Edgar A(lbert) 1881-1959 ... **TCLC 95**
See also CA 168; CAAE 112
Guest, Judith 1936- .... **CLC 8, 30**
See also AAYA 7, 66; CA 77-80; CANR 15, 75, 138; DA3; DAM NOV, POP; EXPN; INT CANR-15; LAIT 5; MTCW 1, 2; MTFW 2005; NFS 1
Guevara, Che CLC 87; HLC 1
See Guevara (Serna), Ernesto
Guevara (Serna), Ernesto 1928-1967 .... **CLC 87; HLC 1**
See Guevara, Che
See also CA 127; CAAS 111; CANR 56; DAM MULT; HW 1
Guicciardini, Francesco 1483-1540 ..... **LC 49**
Guido delle Colonne c. 1215-c. 1290 .... **CMLC 90**
Guild, Nicholas M. 1944- .... **CLC 33**
See also CA 93-96
Guillemin, Jacques
See Sartre, Jean-Paul
Guillen, Jorge 1893-1984 . **CLC 11; HLCS 1; PC 35**
See also CA 89-92; CAAS 112; DAM MULT, POET; DLB 108; EWL 3; HW 1; RGWL 2, 3
Guillen, Nicolas (Cristobal) 1902-1989 .... **BLC 1:2; CLC 48, 79; HLC 1; PC 23**
See also BW 2; CA 125; CAAE 116; CAAS 129; CANR 84; DAM MST, MULT, POET; DLB 283; EWL 3; HW 1; LAW; RGWL 2, 3; WP
Guillen y Alvarez, Jorge
See Guillen, Jorge
Guillevic, (Eugene) 1907-1997 .... **CLC 33**
See also CA 93-96; CWW 2
Guillois
See Desnos, Robert
Guillois, Valentin
See Desnos, Robert
Guimaraes Rosa, Joao 1908-1967 .... **HLCS 2**
See Rosa, Joao Guimaraes
See also CA 175; LAW; RGSF 2; RGWL 2, 3
Guiney, Louise Imogen 1861-1920 .... **TCLC 41**
See also CA 160; DLB 54; RGAL 4
Guinizelli, Guido c. 1230-1276 ...... **CMLC 49**
See Guinizzelli, Guido
Guinizzelli, Guido
See Guinizelli, Guido
See also WLIT 7
Guiraldes, Ricardo (Guillermo) 1886-1927 .... **TCLC 39**
See also CA 131; EWL 3; HW 1; LAW; MTCW 1
Gumilev, Nikolai (Stepanovich) 1886-1921 .... **TCLC 60**
See Gumilyov, Nikolay Stepanovich
See also CA 165; DLB 295
Gumilyov, Nikolay Stepanovich
See Gumilev, Nikolai (Stepanovich)
See also EWL 3
Gump, P. Q.
See Card, Orson Scott
Gunesekera, Romesh 1954- .... **CLC 91**
See also BRWS 10; CA 159; CANR 140, 172; CN 6, 7; DLB 267, 323
Gunn, Bill CLC 5
See Gunn, William Harrison
See also DLB 38

Hamilton, Eugene (Jacob) Lee
See Lee-Hamilton, Eugene (Jacob)
Hamilton, Franklin
See Silverberg, Robert
Hamilton, Gail
See Corcoran, Barbara (Asenath)
Hamilton, (Robert) Ian 1938-2001 . **CLC 191**
See also CA 106; CAAS 203; CANR 41, 67; CP 1, 2, 3, 4, 5, 6, 7; DLB 40, 155
Hamilton, Jane 1957- .... **CLC 179**
See also CA 147; CANR 85, 128; CN 7; MTFW 2005
Hamilton, Mollie
See Kaye, M.M.
Hamilton, (Anthony Walter) Patrick 1904-1962 .... **CLC 51**
See also CA 176; CAAS 113; DLB 10, 191
Hamilton, Virginia 1936-2002 .... **CLC 26**
See also AAYA 2, 21; BW 2, 3; BYA 1, 2, 8; CA 25-28R; CAAS 206; CANR 20, 37, 73, 126; CLR 1, 11, 40, 127; DAM MULT; DLB 33, 52; DLBY 2001; INT CANR-20; JRDA; LAIT 5; MAICYA 1, 2; MAICYAS 1; MTCW 1, 2; MTFW 2005; SATA 4, 56, 79, 123; SATA-Obit 132; WYA; YAW
Hammett, (Samuel) Dashiell 1894-1961 .... **CLC 3, 5, 10, 19, 47; SSC 17; TCLC 187**
See also AAYA 59; AITN 1; AMWS 4; BPFB 2; CA 81-84; CANR 42; CDALB 1929-1941; CMW 4; DA3; DLB 226, 280; DLBD 6; DLBY 1996; EWL 3; LAIT 3; MAL 5; MSW; MTCW 1, 2; MTFW 2005; NFS 21; RGAL 4; RGSF 2; TUS
Hammon, Jupiter 1720(?)-1800(?) . **BLC 1:2; NCLC 5; PC 16**
See also DAM MULT, POET; DLB 31, 50
Hammond, Keith
See Kuttner, Henry
Hamner, Earl (Henry), Jr. 1923- ...... **CLC 12**
See also AITN 2; CA 73-76; DLB 6
Hampton, Christopher 1946- .... **CLC 4**
See also CA 25-28R; CD 5, 6; DLB 13; MTCW 1
Hampton, Christopher James
See Hampton, Christopher
Hamsun, Knut TCLC 2, 14, 49, 151, 203
See Pedersen, Knut
See also DLB 297, 330; EW 8; EWL 3; RGWL 2, 3
Handke, Peter 1942- .... **CLC 5, 8, 10, 15, 38, 134; DC 17**
See also CA 77-80; CANR 33, 75, 104, 133; CWW 2; DAM DRAM, NOV; DLB 85, 124; EWL 3; MTCW 1, 2; MTFW 2005; TWA
Handy, W(illiam) C(hristopher) 1873-1958 .... **TCLC 97**
See also BW 3; CA 167; CAAE 121
Hanley, James 1901-1985 ..... **CLC 3, 5, 8, 13**
See also CA 73-76; CAAS 117; CANR 36; CBD; CN 1, 2, 3; DLB 191; EWL 3; MTCW 1; RGEL 2
Hannah, Barry 1942- .. **CLC 23, 38, 90; SSC 94**
See also BPFB 2; CA 110; CAAE 108; CANR 43, 68, 113; CN 4, 5, 6, 7; CSW; DLB 6, 234; INT CA-110; MTCW 1; RGSF 2
Hannon, Ezra
See Hunter, Evan
Hansberry, Lorraine (Vivian) 1930-1965 ... **BLC 1:2; CLC 17, 62; DC 2; TCLC 192**
See also AAYA 25; AFAW 1, 2; AMWS 4; BW 1, 3; CA 109; CAAS 25-28R; CABS 3; CAD; CANR 58; CDALB 1941-1968; CWD; DA; DA3; DAB; DAC; DAM DRAM, MST, MULT; DFS 2; DLB 7, 38; EWL 3; FL 1:6; FW; LAIT 4; MAL 5; MTCW 1, 2; MTFW 2005; RGAL 4; TUS
Hansen, Joseph 1923-2004 .... **CLC 38**
See Brock, Rose; Colton, James
See also BPFB 2; CA 29-32R; 17; CAAS 233; CANR 16, 44, 66, 125; CMW 4; DLB 226; GLL 1; INT CANR-16
Hansen, Karen V. 1955- .... **CLC 65**
See also CA 149; CANR 102
Hansen, Martin A(lfred) 1909-1955 .... **TCLC 32**
See also CA 167; DLB 214; EWL 3
Hanson, Kenneth O(stlin) 1922- .... **CLC 13**
See also CA 53-56; CANR 7; CP 1, 2, 3, 4, 5
Hardwick, Elizabeth 1916-2007 .... **CLC 13**
See also AMWS 3; CA 5-8R; CANR 3, 32, 70, 100, 139; CN 4, 5, 6; CSW; DA3; DAM NOV; DLB 6; MBL; MTCW 1, 2; MTFW 2005; TCLE 1:1
Hardwick, Elizabeth Bruce
See Hardwick, Elizabeth
Hardy, Thomas 1840-1928 .... **PC 8; SSC 2, 60; TCLC 4, 10, 18, 32, 48, 53, 72, 143, 153; WLC 3**
See also AAYA 69; BRW 6; BRWC 1, 2; BRWR 1; CA 123; CAAE 104; CDBLB 1890-1914; DA; DA3; DAB; DAC; DAM MST, NOV, POET; DLB 18, 19, 135, 284; EWL 3; EXPN; EXPP; LAIT 2; MTCW 1, 2; MTFW 2005; NFS 3, 11, 15, 19; PFS 3, 4, 18; RGEL 2; RGSF 2; TEA; WLIT 4
Hare, David 1947- . **CLC 29, 58, 136; DC 26**
See also BRWS 4; CA 97-100; CANR 39, 91; CBD; CD 5, 6; DFS 4, 7, 16; DLB 13, 310; MTCW 1; TEA
Harewood, John
See Van Druten, John (William)
Harford, Henry
See Hudson, W(illiam) H(enry)
Hargrave, Leonie
See Disch, Thomas M.
Hariri, Al- al-Qasim ibn 'Ali Abu Muhammad al-Basri
See al-Hariri, al-Qasim ibn 'Ali Abu Muhammad al-Basri
Harjo, Joy 1951- ..... **CLC 83; NNAL; PC 27**
See also AMWS 12; CA 114; CANR 35, 67, 91, 129; CP 6, 7; CWP; DAM MULT; DLB 120, 175; EWL 3; MTCW 2; MTFW 2005; PFS 15; RGAL 4
Harlan, Louis R(udolph) 1922- .... **CLC 34**
See also CA 21-24R; CANR 25, 55, 80
Harling, Robert 1951(?)- .... **CLC 53**
See also CA 147
Harmon, William (Ruth) 1938- .... **CLC 38**
See also CA 33-36R; CANR 14, 32, 35; SATA 65
Harper, F. E. W.
See Harper, Frances Ellen Watkins
Harper, Frances E. W.
See Harper, Frances Ellen Watkins
Harper, Frances E. Watkins
See Harper, Frances Ellen Watkins
Harper, Frances Ellen
See Harper, Frances Ellen Watkins
Harper, Frances Ellen Watkins 1825-1911 .. **BLC 1:2; PC 21; TCLC 14**
See also AFAW 1, 2; BW 1, 3; CA 125; CAAE 111; CANR 79; DAM MULT, POET; DLB 50, 221; MBL; RGAL 4
Harper, Michael S(teven) 1938- ..... **BLC 2:2; CLC 7, 22**
See also AFAW 2; BW 1; CA 224; 33-36R, 224; CANR 24, 108; CP 2, 3, 4, 5, 6, 7; DLB 41; RGAL 4; TCLE 1:1
Harper, Mrs. F. E. W.
See Harper, Frances Ellen Watkins
Harpur, Charles 1813-1868 .... **NCLC 114**
See also DLB 230; RGEL 2
Harris, Christie
See Harris, Christie (Lucy) Irwin
Harris, Christie (Lucy) Irwin 1907-2002 .... **CLC 12**
See also CA 5-8R; CANR 6, 83; CLR 47; DLB 88; JRDA; MAICYA 1, 2; SAAS 10; SATA 6, 74; SATA-Essay 116
Harris, Frank 1856-1931 .... **TCLC 24**
See also CA 150; CAAE 109; CANR 80; DLB 156, 197; RGEL 2
Harris, George Washington 1814-1869 .... **NCLC 23, 165**
See also DLB 3, 11, 248; RGAL 4
Harris, Joel Chandler 1848-1908 ..... **SSC 19, 103; TCLC 2**
See also CA 137; CAAE 104; CANR 80; CLR 49, 128; DLB 11, 23, 42, 78, 91; LAIT 2; MAICYA 1, 2; RGSF 2; SATA 100; WCH; YABC 1
Harris, John (Wyndham Parkes Lucas) Beynon 1903-1969
See Wyndham, John
See also CA 102; CAAS 89-92; CANR 84; SATA 118; SFW 4
Harris, MacDonald CLC 9
See Heiney, Donald (William)
Harris, Mark 1922-2007 .... **CLC 19**
See also CA 5-8R; 3; CAAS 260; CANR 2, 55, 83; CN 1, 2, 3, 4, 5, 6, 7; DLB 2; DLBY 1980
Harris, Norman CLC 65
Harris, (Theodore) Wilson 1921- ... **BLC 2:2; CLC 25, 159**
See also BRWS 5; BW 2, 3; CA 65-68; 16; CANR 11, 27, 69, 114; CDWLB 3; CN 1, 2, 3, 4, 5, 6, 7; CP 1, 2, 3, 4, 5, 6, 7; DLB 117; EWL 3; MTCW 1; RGEL 2
Harrison, Barbara Grizzuti 1934-2002 .... **CLC 144**
See also CA 77-80; CAAS 205; CANR 15, 48; INT CANR-15
Harrison, Elizabeth (Allen) Cavanna 1909-2001
See Cavanna, Betty
See also CA 9-12R; CAAS 200; CANR 6, 27, 85, 104, 121; MAICYA 2; SATA 142; YAW
Harrison, Harry (Max) 1925- .... **CLC 42**
See also CA 1-4R; CANR 5, 21, 84; DLB 8; SATA 4; SCFW 2; SFW 4
Harrison, James
See Harrison, Jim
Harrison, James Thomas
See Harrison, Jim
Harrison, Jim 1937- .... **CLC 6, 14, 33, 66, 143; SSC 19**
See also AMWS 8; CA 13-16R; CANR 8, 51, 79, 142; CN 5, 6; CP 1, 2, 3, 4, 5, 6; DLBY 1982; INT CANR-8; RGAL 4; TCWW 2; TUS
Harrison, Kathryn 1961- .... **CLC 70, 151**
See also CA 144; CANR 68, 122
Harrison, Tony 1937- .... **CLC 43, 129**
See also BRWS 5; CA 65-68; CANR 44, 98; CBD; CD 5, 6; CP 2, 3, 4, 5, 6, 7; DLB 40, 245; MTCW 1; RGEL 2
Harriss, Will(ard Irvin) 1922- .... **CLC 34**
See also CA 111
Hart, Ellis
See Ellison, Harlan
Hart, Josephine 1942(?)- .... **CLC 70**
See also CA 138; CANR 70, 149; CPW; DAM POP

Hoffman, Alice 1952- .... **CLC 51**
See also AAYA 37; AMWS 10; CA 77-80; CANR 34, 66, 100, 138, 170; CN 4, 5, 6, 7; CPW; DAM NOV; DLB 292; MAL 5; MTCW 1, 2; MTFW 2005; TCLE 1:1
Hoffman, Daniel (Gerard) 1923- . **CLC 6, 13, 23**
See also CA 1-4R; CANR 4, 142; CP 1, 2, 3, 4, 5, 6, 7; DLB 5; TCLE 1:1
Hoffman, Eva 1945- .... **CLC 182**
See also AMWS 16; CA 132; CANR 146
Hoffman, Stanley 1944- .... **CLC 5**
See also CA 77-80
Hoffman, William 1925- .... **CLC 141**
See also CA 21-24R; CANR 9, 103; CSW; DLB 234; TCLE 1:1
Hoffman, William M.
See Hoffman, William M(oses)
See also CAD; CD 5, 6
Hoffman, William M(oses) 1939- ..... **CLC 40**
See Hoffman, William M.
See also CA 57-60; CANR 11, 71
Hoffmann, E(rnst) T(heodor) A(madeus) 1776-1822 ..... **NCLC 2, 183; SSC 13, 92**
See also CDWLB 2; DLB 90; EW 5; GL 2; RGSF 2; RGWL 2, 3; SATA 27; SUFW 1; WCH
Hofmann, Gert 1931-1993 .... **CLC 54**
See also CA 128; CANR 145; EWL 3; RGHL
Hofmannsthal, Hugo von 1874-1929 ... **DC 4; TCLC 11**
See also CA 153; CAAE 106; CDWLB 2; DAM DRAM; DFS 17; DLB 81, 118; EW 9; EWL 3; RGWL 2, 3
Hogan, Linda 1947- ..... **CLC 73; NNAL; PC 35**
See also AMWS 4; ANW; BYA 12; CA 226; 120, 226; CANR 45, 73, 129; CWP; DAM MULT; DLB 175; SATA 132; TCWW 2
Hogarth, Charles
See Creasey, John
Hogarth, Emmett
See Polonsky, Abraham (Lincoln)
Hogarth, William 1697-1764 .... **LC 112**
See also AAYA 56
Hogg, James 1770-1835 .... **NCLC 4, 109**
See also BRWS 10; DLB 93, 116, 159; GL 2; HGG; RGEL 2; SUFW 1
Holbach, Paul-Henri Thiry 1723-1789 .... **LC 14**
See also DLB 313
Holberg, Ludvig 1684-1754 .... **LC 6**
See also DLB 300; RGWL 2, 3
Holcroft, Thomas 1745-1809 .... **NCLC 85**
See also DLB 39, 89, 158; RGEL 2
Holden, Ursula 1921- .... **CLC 18**
See also CA 101; 8; CANR 22
Holderlin, (Johann Christian) Friedrich 1770-1843 .... **NCLC 16, 187; PC 4**
See also CDWLB 2; DLB 90; EW 5; RGWL 2, 3
Holdstock, Robert 1948- .... **CLC 39**
See also CA 131; CANR 81; DLB 261; FANT; HGG; SFW 4; SUFW 2
Holdstock, Robert P.
See Holdstock, Robert
Holinshed, Raphael fl. 1580- .... **LC 69**
See also DLB 167; RGEL 2
Holland, Isabelle (Christian) 1920-2002 .... **CLC 21**
See also AAYA 11, 64; CA 181; 21-24R; CAAS 205; CANR 10, 25, 47; CLR 57; CWRI 5; JRDA; LAIT 4; MAICYA 1, 2; SATA 8, 70; SATA-Essay 103; SATA-Obit 132; WYA
Holland, Marcus
See Caldwell, (Janet Miriam) Taylor (Holland)
Hollander, John 1929- .... **CLC 2, 5, 8, 14**
See also CA 1-4R; CANR 1, 52, 136; CP 1, 2, 3, 4, 5, 6, 7; DLB 5; MAL 5; SATA 13
Hollander, Paul
See Silverberg, Robert
Holleran, Andrew CLC 38
See Garber, Eric
See also CA 144; GLL 1
Holley, Marietta 1836(?)-1926 .... **TCLC 99**
See also CAAE 118; DLB 11; FL 1:3
Hollinghurst, Alan 1954- .... **CLC 55, 91**
See also BRWS 10; CA 114; CN 5, 6, 7; DLB 207, 326; GLL 1
Hollis, Jim
See Summers, Hollis (Spurgeon, Jr.)
Holly, Buddy 1936-1959 .... **TCLC 65**
See also CA 213
Holmes, Gordon
See Shiel, M(atthew) P(hipps)
Holmes, John
See Souster, (Holmes) Raymond
Holmes, John Clellon 1926-1988 ...... **CLC 56**
See also BG 1:2; CA 9-12R; CAAS 125; CANR 4; CN 1, 2, 3, 4; DLB 16, 237
Holmes, Oliver Wendell, Jr. 1841-1935 .... **TCLC 77**
See also CA 186; CAAE 114
Holmes, Oliver Wendell 1809-1894 .... **NCLC 14, 81; PC 71**
See also AMWS 1; CDALB 1640-1865; DLB 1, 189, 235; EXPP; PFS 24; RGAL 4; SATA 34
Holmes, Raymond
See Souster, (Holmes) Raymond
Holt, Victoria
See Hibbert, Eleanor Alice Burford
See also BPFB 2
Holub, Miroslav 1923-1998 .... **CLC 4**
See also CA 21-24R; CAAS 169; CANR 10; CDWLB 4; CWW 2; DLB 232; EWL 3; RGWL 3
Holz, Detlev
See Benjamin, Walter
Homer c. 8th cent. B.C.- .... **CMLC 1, 16, 61; PC 23; WLCS**
See also AW 1; CDWLB 1; DA; DA3; DAB; DAC; DAM MST, POET; DLB 176; EFS 1; LAIT 1; LMFS 1; RGWL 2, 3; TWA; WLIT 8; WP
Hongo, Garrett Kaoru 1951- .... **PC 23**
See also CA 133; 22; CP 5, 6, 7; DLB 120, 312; EWL 3; EXPP; PFS 25; RGAL 4
Honig, Edwin 1919- .... **CLC 33**
See also CA 5-8R; 8; CANR 4, 45, 144; CP 1, 2, 3, 4, 5, 6, 7; DLB 5
Hood, Hugh (John Blagdon) 1928- . **CLC 15, 28; SSC 42**
See also CA 49-52; 17; CANR 1, 33, 87; CN 1, 2, 3, 4, 5, 6, 7; DLB 53; RGSF 2
Hood, Thomas 1799-1845 .... **NCLC 16**
See also BRW 4; DLB 96; RGEL 2
Hooker, (Peter) Jeremy 1941- .... **CLC 43**
See also CA 77-80; CANR 22; CP 2, 3, 4, 5, 6, 7; DLB 40
Hooker, Richard 1554-1600 .... **LC 95**
See also BRW 1; DLB 132; RGEL 2
Hooker, Thomas 1586-1647 .... **LC 137**
See also DLB 24
hooks, bell 1952(?)- .... **BLCS; CLC 94**
See also BW 2; CA 143; CANR 87, 126; DLB 246; MTCW 2; MTFW 2005; SATA 115, 170
Hooper, Johnson Jones 1815-1862 .... **NCLC 177**
See also DLB 3, 11, 248; RGAL 4
Hope, A(lec) D(erwent) 1907-2000 .... **CLC 3, 51; PC 56**
See also BRWS 7; CA 21-24R; CAAS 188; CANR 33, 74; CP 1, 2, 3, 4, 5; DLB 289; EWL 3; MTCW 1, 2; MTFW 2005; PFS 8; RGEL 2
Hope, Anthony 1863-1933 .... **TCLC 83**
See also CA 157; DLB 153, 156; RGEL 2; RHW
Hope, Brian
See Creasey, John
Hope, Christopher (David Tully) 1944- .... **CLC 52**
See also AFW; CA 106; CANR 47, 101; CN 4, 5, 6, 7; DLB 225; SATA 62
Hopkins, Gerard Manley 1844-1889 .... **NCLC 17, 189; PC 15; WLC 3**
See also BRW 5; BRWR 2; CDBLB 1890-1914; DA; DA3; DAB; DAC; DAM MST, POET; DLB 35, 57; EXPP; PAB; PFS 26; RGEL 2; TEA; WP
Hopkins, John (Richard) 1931-1998 .. **CLC 4**
See also CA 85-88; CAAS 169; CBD; CD 5, 6
Hopkins, Pauline Elizabeth 1859-1930 .... **BLC 1:2; TCLC 28**
See also AFAW 2; BW 2, 3; CA 141; CANR 82; DAM MULT; DLB 50
Hopkinson, Francis 1737-1791 .... **LC 25**
See also DLB 31; RGAL 4
Hopley-Woolrich, Cornell George 1903-1968
See Woolrich, Cornell
See also CA 13-14; CANR 58, 156; CAP 1; CMW 4; DLB 226; MTCW 2
Horace 65B.C.-8B.C. .... **CMLC 39; PC 46**
See also AW 2; CDWLB 1; DLB 211; RGWL 2, 3; WLIT 8
Horatio
See Proust, (Valentin-Louis-George-Eugene) Marcel
Horgan, Paul (George Vincent O'Shaughnessy) 1903-1995 .. **CLC 9, 53**
See also BPFB 2; CA 13-16R; CAAS 147; CANR 9, 35; CN 1, 2, 3, 4, 5; DAM NOV; DLB 102, 212; DLBY 1985; INT CANR-9; MTCW 1, 2; MTFW 2005; SATA 13; SATA-Obit 84; TCWW 1, 2
Horkheimer, Max 1895-1973 .... **TCLC 132**
See also CA 216; CAAS 41-44R; DLB 296
Horn, Peter
See Kuttner, Henry
Hornby, Nick 1957(?)- .... **CLC 243**
See also AAYA 74; CA 151; CANR 104, 151; CN 7; DLB 207
Horne, Frank (Smith) 1899-1974 ...... **HR 1:2**
See also BW 1; CA 125; CAAS 53-56; DLB 51; WP
Horne, Richard Henry Hengist 1802(?)-1884 .... **NCLC 127**
See also DLB 32; SATA 29
Horne Tooke, John 1736-1812 ..... **NCLC 195**
Hornem, Horace Esq.
See Byron, George Gordon (Noel)
Horney, Karen (Clementine Theodore Danielsen) 1885-1952 .... **TCLC 71**
See also CA 165; CAAE 114; DLB 246; FW
Hornung, E(rnest) W(illiam) 1866-1921 .... **TCLC 59**
See also CA 160; CAAE 108; CMW 4; DLB 70
Horovitz, Israel (Arthur) 1939- .... **CLC 56**
See also CA 33-36R; CAD; CANR 46, 59; CD 5, 6; DAM DRAM; DLB 7; MAL 5
Horton, George Moses 1797(?)-1883(?) .... **NCLC 87**
See also DLB 50

Author Index

Horvath, odon von 1901-1938
See von Horvath, Odon
See also EWL 3
Horvath, Oedoen von -1938
See von Horvath, Odon
Horwitz, Julius 1920-1986 .... **CLC 14**
See also CA 9-12R; CAAS 119; CANR 12
Horwitz, Ronald
See Harwood, Ronald
Hospital, Janette Turner 1942- .... **CLC 42, 145**
See also CA 108; CANR 48, 166; CN 5, 6, 7; DLB 325; DLBY 2002; RGSF 2
Hosseini, Khaled 1965- .... **CLC 254**
See also CA 225; SATA 156
Hostos, E. M. de
See Hostos (y Bonilla), Eugenio Maria de
Hostos, Eugenio M. de
See Hostos (y Bonilla), Eugenio Maria de
Hostos, Eugenio Maria
See Hostos (y Bonilla), Eugenio Maria de
Hostos (y Bonilla), Eugenio Maria de 1839-1903 .... **TCLC 24**
See also CA 131; CAAE 123; HW 1
Houdini
See Lovecraft, H. P.
Houellebecq, Michel 1958- .... **CLC 179**
See also CA 185; CANR 140; MTFW 2005
Hougan, Carolyn 1943-2007 .... **CLC 34**
See also CA 139; CAAS 257
Household, Geoffrey (Edward West) 1900-1988 .... **CLC 11**
See also CA 77-80; CAAS 126; CANR 58; CMW 4; CN 1, 2, 3, 4; DLB 87; SATA 14; SATA-Obit 59
Housman, A(lfred) E(dward) 1859-1936 .... **PC 2, 43; TCLC 1, 10; WLCS**
See also AAYA 66; BRW 6; CA 125; CAAE 104; DA; DA3; DAB; DAC; DAM MST, POET; DLB 19, 284; EWL 3; EXPP; MTCW 1, 2; MTFW 2005; PAB; PFS 4, 7; RGEL 2; TEA; WP
Housman, Laurence 1865-1959 .... **TCLC 7**
See also CA 155; CAAE 106; DLB 10; FANT; RGEL 2; SATA 25
Houston, Jeanne Wakatsuki 1934- .... **AAL**
See also AAYA 49; CA 232; 103, 232; 16; CANR 29, 123, 167; LAIT 4; SATA 78, 168; SATA-Essay 168
Hove, Chenjerai 1956- .... **BLC 2:2**
See also CP 7
Howard, Elizabeth Jane 1923- ..... **CLC 7, 29**
See also BRWS 11; CA 5-8R; CANR 8, 62, 146; CN 1, 2, 3, 4, 5, 6, 7
Howard, Maureen 1930- .... **CLC 5, 14, 46, 151**
See also CA 53-56; CANR 31, 75, 140; CN 4, 5, 6, 7; DLBY 1983; INT CANR-31; MTCW 1, 2; MTFW 2005
Howard, Richard 1929- .... **CLC 7, 10, 47**
See also AITN 1; CA 85-88; CANR 25, 80, 154; CP 1, 2, 3, 4, 5, 6, 7; DLB 5; INT CANR-25; MAL 5
Howard, Robert E 1906-1936 .... **TCLC 8**
See also BPFB 2; BYA 5; CA 157; CAAE 105; CANR 155; FANT; SUFW 1; TCWW 1, 2
Howard, Robert Ervin
See Howard, Robert E
Howard, Warren F.
See Pohl, Frederik
Howe, Fanny (Quincy) 1940- .... **CLC 47**
See also CA 187; 117, 187; 27; CANR 70, 116; CP 6, 7; CWP; SATA-Brief 52
Howe, Irving 1920-1993 .... **CLC 85**
See also AMWS 6; CA 9-12R; CAAS 141; CANR 21, 50; DLB 67; EWL 3; MAL 5; MTCW 1, 2; MTFW 2005
Howe, Julia Ward 1819-1910 . **PC 81; TCLC 21**
See also CA 191; CAAE 117; DLB 1, 189, 235; FW
Howe, Susan 1937- .... **CLC 72, 152; PC 54**
See also AMWS 4; CA 160; CP 5, 6, 7; CWP; DLB 120; FW; RGAL 4
Howe, Tina 1937- .... **CLC 48**
See also CA 109; CAD; CANR 125; CD 5, 6; CWD
Howell, James 1594(?)-1666 .... **LC 13**
See also DLB 151
Howells, W. D.
See Howells, William Dean
Howells, William D.
See Howells, William Dean
Howells, William Dean 1837-1920 ... **SSC 36; TCLC 7, 17, 41**
See also AMW; CA 134; CAAE 104; CDALB 1865-1917; DLB 12, 64, 74, 79, 189; LMFS 1; MAL 5; MTCW 2; RGAL 4; TUS
Howes, Barbara 1914-1996 .... **CLC 15**
See also CA 9-12R; 3; CAAS 151; CANR 53; CP 1, 2, 3, 4, 5, 6; SATA 5; TCLE 1:1
Hrabal, Bohumil 1914-1997 ...... **CLC 13, 67; TCLC 155**
See also CA 106; 12; CAAS 156; CANR 57; CWW 2; DLB 232; EWL 3; RGSF 2
Hrabanus Maurus 776(?)-856 .... **CMLC 78**
See also DLB 148
Hrotsvit of Gandersheim c. 935-c. 1000 .... **CMLC 29**
See also DLB 148
Hsi, Chu 1130-1200 .... **CMLC 42**
Hsun, Lu
See Lu Hsun
Hubbard, L. Ron 1911-1986 .... **CLC 43**
See also AAYA 64; CA 77-80; CAAS 118; CANR 52; CPW; DA3; DAM POP; FANT; MTCW 2; MTFW 2005; SFW 4
Hubbard, Lafayette Ronald
See Hubbard, L. Ron
Huch, Ricarda (Octavia) 1864-1947 .... **TCLC 13**
See also CA 189; CAAE 111; DLB 66; EWL 3
Huddle, David 1942- .... **CLC 49**
See also CA 57-60, 261; 20; CANR 89; DLB 130
Hudson, Jeffrey
See Crichton, Michael
Hudson, W(illiam) H(enry) 1841-1922 .... **TCLC 29**
See also CA 190; CAAE 115; DLB 98, 153, 174; RGEL 2; SATA 35
Hueffer, Ford Madox
See Ford, Ford Madox
Hughart, Barry 1934- .... **CLC 39**
See also CA 137; FANT; SFW 4; SUFW 2
Hughes, Colin
See Creasey, John
Hughes, David (John) 1930-2005 ..... **CLC 48**
See also CA 129; CAAE 116; CAAS 238; CN 4, 5, 6, 7; DLB 14
Hughes, Edward James
See Hughes, Ted
See also DA3; DAM MST, POET
Hughes, (James Mercer) Langston 1902-1967 .. **BLC 1:2; CLC 1, 5, 10, 15, 35, 44, 108; DC 3; HR 1:2; PC 1, 53; SSC 6, 90; WLC 3**
See also AAYA 12; AFAW 1, 2; AMWR 1; AMWS 1; BW 1, 3; CA 1-4R; CAAS 25-28R; CANR 1, 34, 82; CDALB 1929-1941; CLR 17; DA; DA3; DAB; DAC; DAM DRAM, MST, MULT, POET; DFS 6, 18; DLB 4, 7, 48, 51, 86, 228, 315; EWL 3; EXPP; EXPS; JRDA; LAIT 3; LMFS 2; MAICYA 1, 2; MAL 5; MTCW 1, 2; MTFW 2005; NFS 21; PAB; PFS 1, 3, 6, 10, 15; RGAL 4; RGSF 2; SATA 4, 33; SSFS 4, 7; TUS; WCH; WP; YAW
Hughes, Richard (Arthur Warren) 1900-1976 .... **CLC 1, 11**
See also CA 5-8R; CAAS 65-68; CANR 4; CN 1, 2; DAM NOV; DLB 15, 161; EWL 3; MTCW 1; RGEL 2; SATA 8; SATA-Obit 25
Hughes, Ted 1930-1998 . **CLC 2, 4, 9, 14, 37, 119; PC 7**
See Hughes, Edward James
See also BRWC 2; BRWR 2; BRWS 1; CA 1-4R; CAAS 171; CANR 1, 33, 66, 108; CLR 3, 131; CP 1, 2, 3, 4, 5, 6; DAB; DAC; DLB 40, 161; EWL 3; EXPP; MAICYA 1, 2; MTCW 1, 2; MTFW 2005; PAB; PFS 4, 19; RGEL 2; SATA 49; SATA-Brief 27; SATA-Obit 107; TEA; YAW
Hugo, Richard
See Huch, Ricarda (Octavia)
Hugo, Richard F(ranklin) 1923-1982 .... **CLC 6, 18, 32; PC 68**
See also AMWS 6; CA 49-52; CAAS 108; CANR 3; CP 1, 2, 3; DAM POET; DLB 5, 206; EWL 3; MAL 5; PFS 17; RGAL 4
Hugo, Victor (Marie) 1802-1885 .... **NCLC 3, 10, 21, 161, 189; PC 17; WLC 3**
See also AAYA 28; DA; DA3; DAB; DAC; DAM DRAM, MST, NOV, POET; DLB 119, 192, 217; EFS 2; EW 6; EXPN; GFL 1789 to the Present; LAIT 1, 2; NFS 5, 20; RGWL 2, 3; SATA 47; TWA
Huidobro, Vicente
See Huidobro Fernandez, Vicente Garcia
See also DLB 283; EWL 3; LAW
Huidobro Fernandez, Vicente Garcia 1893-1948 .... **TCLC 31**
See Huidobro, Vicente
See also CA 131; HW 1
Hulme, Keri 1947- .... **CLC 39, 130**
See also CA 125; CANR 69; CN 4, 5, 6, 7; CP 6, 7; CWP; DLB 326; EWL 3; FW; INT CA-125; NFS 24
Hulme, T(homas) E(rnest) 1883-1917 .... **TCLC 21**
See also BRWS 6; CA 203; CAAE 117; DLB 19
Humboldt, Alexander von 1769-1859 .... **NCLC 170**
See also DLB 90
Humboldt, Wilhelm von 1767-1835 .... **NCLC 134**
See also DLB 90
Hume, David 1711-1776 .... **LC 7, 56**
See also BRWS 3; DLB 104, 252, 336; LMFS 1; TEA
Humphrey, William 1924-1997 .... **CLC 45**
See also AMWS 9; CA 77-80; CAAS 160; CANR 68; CN 1, 2, 3, 4, 5, 6; CSW; DLB 6, 212, 234, 278; TCWW 1, 2
Humphreys, Emyr Owen 1919- .... **CLC 47**
See also CA 5-8R; CANR 3, 24; CN 1, 2, 3, 4, 5, 6, 7; DLB 15
Humphreys, Josephine 1945- ..... **CLC 34, 57**
See also CA 127; CAAE 121; CANR 97; CSW; DLB 292; INT CA-127
Huneker, James Gibbons 1860-1921 .... **TCLC 65**
See also CA 193; DLB 71; RGAL 4
Hungerford, Hesba Fay
See Brinsmead, H(esba) F(ay)
Hungerford, Pixie
See Brinsmead, H(esba) F(ay)
Hunt, E. Howard 1918-2007 .... **CLC 3**
See also AITN 1; CA 45-48; CAAS 256; CANR 2, 47, 103, 160; CMW 4

Jarvis, E. K.
See Ellison, Harlan
Jawien, Andrzej
See John Paul II, Pope
Jaynes, Roderick
See Coen, Ethan
Jeake, Samuel, Jr.
See Aiken, Conrad (Potter)
Jean Paul 1763-1825 .... **NCLC 7**
Jefferies, (John) Richard
1848-1887 .... **NCLC 47**
See also DLB 98, 141; RGEL 2; SATA 16; SFW 4
Jeffers, John Robinson
See Jeffers, Robinson
Jeffers, Robinson 1887-1962 .... **CLC 2, 3, 11, 15, 54; PC 17; WLC 3**
See also AMWS 2; CA 85-88; CANR 35; CDALB 1917-1929; DA; DAC; DAM MST, POET; DLB 45, 212; EWL 3; MAL 5; MTCW 1, 2; MTFW 2005; PAB; PFS 3, 4; RGAL 4
Jefferson, Janet
See Mencken, H(enry) L(ouis)
Jefferson, Thomas 1743-1826 . **NCLC 11, 103**
See also AAYA 54; ANW; CDALB 1640-1865; DA3; DLB 31, 183; LAIT 1; RGAL 4
Jeffrey, Francis 1773-1850 .... **NCLC 33**
See Francis, Lord Jeffrey
Jelakowitch, Ivan
See Heijermans, Herman
Jelinek, Elfriede 1946- .... **CLC 169**
See also AAYA 68; CA 154; CANR 169; DLB 85, 330; FW
Jellicoe, (Patricia) Ann 1927- .... **CLC 27**
See also CA 85-88; CBD; CD 5, 6; CWD; CWRI 5; DLB 13, 233; FW
Jelloun, Tahar ben
See Ben Jelloun, Tahar
Jemyma
See Holley, Marietta
Jen, Gish AAL; CLC 70, 198
See Jen, Lillian
See also AMWC 2; CN 7; DLB 312
Jen, Lillian 1955-
See Jen, Gish
See also CA 135; CANR 89, 130
Jenkins, (John) Robin 1912- .... **CLC 52**
See also CA 1-4R; CANR 1, 135; CN 1, 2, 3, 4, 5, 6, 7; DLB 14, 271
Jennings, Elizabeth (Joan)
1926-2001 .... **CLC 5, 14, 131**
See also BRWS 5; CA 61-64; 5; CAAS 200; CANR 8, 39, 66, 127; CP 1, 2, 3, 4, 5, 6, 7; CWP; DLB 27; EWL 3; MTCW 1; SATA 66
Jennings, Waylon 1937-2002 .... **CLC 21**
Jensen, Johannes V(ilhelm)
1873-1950 .... **TCLC 41**
See also CA 170; DLB 214, 330; EWL 3; RGWL 3
Jensen, Laura (Linnea) 1948- .... **CLC 37**
See also CA 103
Jerome, Saint 345-420 .... **CMLC 30**
See also RGWL 3
Jerome, Jerome K(lapka)
1859-1927 .... **TCLC 23**
See also CA 177; CAAE 119; DLB 10, 34, 135; RGEL 2
Jerrold, Douglas William
1803-1857 .... **NCLC 2**
See also DLB 158, 159; RGEL 2
Jewett, (Theodora) Sarah Orne
1849-1909 . **SSC 6, 44, 110; TCLC 1, 22**
See also AAYA 76; AMW; AMWC 2; AMWR 2; CA 127; CAAE 108; CANR 71; DLB 12, 74, 221; EXPS; FL 1:3; FW; MAL 5; MBL; NFS 15; RGAL 4; RGSF 2; SATA 15; SSFS 4
Jewsbury, Geraldine (Endsor)
1812-1880 .... **NCLC 22**
See also DLB 21
Jhabvala, Ruth Prawer 1927- . **CLC 4, 8, 29, 94, 138; SSC 91**
See also BRWS 5; CA 1-4R; CANR 2, 29, 51, 74, 91, 128; CN 1, 2, 3, 4, 5, 6, 7; DAB; DAM NOV; DLB 139, 194, 323, 326; EWL 3; IDFW 3, 4; INT CANR-29; MTCW 1, 2; MTFW 2005; RGSF 2; RGWL 2; RHW; TEA
Jibran, Kahlil
See Gibran, Kahlil
Jibran, Khalil
See Gibran, Kahlil
Jiles, Paulette 1943- .... **CLC 13, 58**
See also CA 101; CANR 70, 124, 170; CP 5; CWP
Jimenez (Mantecon), Juan Ramon
1881-1958 .... **HLC 1; PC 7; TCLC 4, 183**
See also CA 131; CAAE 104; CANR 74; DAM MULT, POET; DLB 134, 330; EW 9; EWL 3; HW 1; MTCW 1, 2; MTFW 2005; RGWL 2, 3
Jimenez, Ramon
See Jimenez (Mantecon), Juan Ramon
Jimenez Mantecon, Juan
See Jimenez (Mantecon), Juan Ramon
Jin, Ba 1904-2005
See Pa Chin
See also CAAS 244; CWW 2; DLB 328
Jin, Xuefei
See Ha Jin
Jodelle, Etienne 1532-1573 .... **LC 119**
See also DLB 327; GFL Beginnings to 1789
Joel, Billy CLC 26
See Joel, William Martin
Joel, William Martin 1949-
See Joel, Billy
See also CA 108
John, St.
See John of Damascus, St.
John of Damascus, St. c. 675-749 .... **CMLC 27, 95**
John of Salisbury c. 1115-1180 ..... **CMLC 63**
John of the Cross, St. 1542-1591 .... **LC 18, 146**
See also RGWL 2, 3
John Paul II, Pope 1920-2005 .... **CLC 128**
See also CA 133; CAAE 106; CAAS 238
Johnson, B(ryan) S(tanley William)
1933-1973 .... **CLC 6, 9**
See also CA 9-12R; CAAS 53-56; CANR 9; CN 1; CP 1, 2; DLB 14, 40; EWL 3; RGEL 2
Johnson, Benjamin F., of Boone
See Riley, James Whitcomb
Johnson, Charles (Richard) 1948- . **BLC 1:2; CLC 7, 51, 65, 163**
See also AFAW 2; AMWS 6; BW 2, 3; CA 116; 18; CANR 42, 66, 82, 129; CN 5, 6, 7; DAM MULT; DLB 33, 278; MAL 5; MTCW 2; MTFW 2005; RGAL 4; SSFS 16
Johnson, Charles S(purgeon)
1893-1956 .... **HR 1:3**
See also BW 1, 3; CA 125; CANR 82; DLB 51, 91
Johnson, Denis 1949- . **CLC 52, 160; SSC 56**
See also CA 121; CAAE 117; CANR 71, 99; CN 4, 5, 6, 7; DLB 120
Johnson, Diane 1934- ...... **CLC 5, 13, 48, 244**
See also BPFB 2; CA 41-44R; CANR 17, 40, 62, 95, 155; CN 4, 5, 6, 7; DLBY 1980; INT CANR-17; MTCW 1
Johnson, E(mily) Pauline 1861-1913 . **NNAL**
See also CA 150; CCA 1; DAC; DAM MULT; DLB 92, 175; TCWW 2
Johnson, Eyvind (Olof Verner)
1900-1976 .... **CLC 14**
See also CA 73-76; CAAS 69-72; CANR 34, 101; DLB 259, 330; EW 12; EWL 3
Johnson, Fenton 1888-1958 .... **BLC 2**
See also BW 1; CA 124; CAAE 118; DAM MULT; DLB 45, 50
Johnson, Georgia Douglas (Camp)
1880-1966 .... **HR 1:3**
See also BW 1; CA 125; DLB 51, 249; WP
Johnson, Helene 1907-1995 .... **HR 1:3**
See also CA 181; DLB 51; WP
Johnson, J. R.
See James, C(yril) L(ionel) R(obert)
Johnson, James Weldon
1871-1938 .... **BLC 1:2; HR 1:3; PC 24; TCLC 3, 19, 175**
See also AAYA 73; AFAW 1, 2; BW 1, 3; CA 125; CAAE 104; CANR 82; CDALB 1917-1929; CLR 32; DA3; DAM MULT, POET; DLB 51; EWL 3; EXPP; LMFS 2; MAL 5; MTCW 1, 2; MTFW 2005; NFS 22; PFS 1; RGAL 4; SATA 31; TUS
Johnson, Joyce 1935- .... **CLC 58**
See also BG 1:3; CA 129; CAAE 125; CANR 102
Johnson, Judith (Emlyn) 1936- .... **CLC 7, 15**
See Sherwin, Judith Johnson
See also CA 25-28R, 153; CANR 34; CP 6, 7
Johnson, Lionel (Pigot)
1867-1902 .... **TCLC 19**
See also CA 209; CAAE 117; DLB 19; RGEL 2
Johnson, Marguerite Annie
See Angelou, Maya
Johnson, Mel
See Malzberg, Barry N(athaniel)
Johnson, Pamela Hansford
1912-1981 .... **CLC 1, 7, 27**
See also CA 1-4R; CAAS 104; CANR 2, 28; CN 1, 2, 3; DLB 15; MTCW 1, 2; MTFW 2005; RGEL 2
Johnson, Paul 1928- .... **CLC 147**
See also BEST 89:4; CA 17-20R; CANR 34, 62, 100, 155
Johnson, Paul Bede
See Johnson, Paul
Johnson, Robert CLC 70
Johnson, Robert 1911(?)-1938 .... **TCLC 69**
See also BW 3; CA 174
Johnson, Samuel 1709-1784 . **LC 15, 52, 128; PC 81; WLC 3**
See also BRW 3; BRWR 1; CDBLB 1660-1789; DA; DAB; DAC; DAM MST; DLB 39, 95, 104, 142, 213; LMFS 1; RGEL 2; TEA
Johnson, Uwe 1934-1984 .. **CLC 5, 10, 15, 40**
See also CA 1-4R; CAAS 112; CANR 1, 39; CDWLB 2; DLB 75; EWL 3; MTCW 1; RGWL 2, 3
Johnston, Basil H. 1929- .... **NNAL**
See also CA 69-72; CANR 11, 28, 66; DAC; DAM MULT; DLB 60
Johnston, George (Benson) 1913- .... **CLC 51**
See also CA 1-4R; CANR 5, 20; CP 1, 2, 3, 4, 5, 6, 7; DLB 88
Johnston, Jennifer (Prudence)
1930- .... **CLC 7, 150, 228**
See also CA 85-88; CANR 92; CN 4, 5, 6, 7; DLB 14
Joinville, Jean de 1224(?)-1317 ..... **CMLC 38**
Jolley, Elizabeth 1923-2007 ..... **CLC 46; SSC 19**
See also CA 127; 13; CAAS 257; CANR 59; CN 4, 5, 6, 7; DLB 325; EWL 3; RGSF 2
Jolley, Monica Elizabeth
See Jolley, Elizabeth

Kaiser, Georg 1878-1945 .... **TCLC 9**
See also CA 190; CAAE 106; CDWLB 2; DLB 124; EWL 3; LMFS 2; RGWL 2, 3
Kaledin, Sergei CLC 59
Kaletski, Alexander 1946- .... **CLC 39**
See also CA 143; CAAE 118
Kalidasa fl. c. 400-455 .... **CMLC 9; PC 22**
See also RGWL 2, 3
Kallman, Chester (Simon) 1921-1975 .... **CLC 2**
See also CA 45-48; CAAS 53-56; CANR 3; CP 1, 2
Kaminsky, Melvin CLC 12, 217
See Brooks, Mel
See also AAYA 13, 48; DLB 26
Kaminsky, Stuart M. 1934- .... **CLC 59**
See also CA 73-76; CANR 29, 53, 89, 161; CMW 4
Kaminsky, Stuart Melvin
See Kaminsky, Stuart M.
Kamo no Chomei 1153(?)-1216 .... **CMLC 66**
See also DLB 203
Kamo no Nagaakira
See Kamo no Chomei
Kandinsky, Wassily 1866-1944 .... **TCLC 92**
See also AAYA 64; CA 155; CAAE 118
Kane, Francis
See Robbins, Harold
Kane, Henry 1918-
See Queen, Ellery
See also CA 156; CMW 4
Kane, Paul
See Simon, Paul
Kane, Sarah 1971-1999 .... **DC 31**
See also BWS 8; CA 190; CD 5, 6; DLB 310
Kanin, Garson 1912-1999 .... **CLC 22**
See also AITN 1; CA 5-8R; CAAS 177; CAD; CANR 7, 78; DLB 7; IDFW 3, 4
Kaniuk, Yoram 1930- .... **CLC 19**
See also CA 134; DLB 299; RGHL
Kant, Immanuel 1724-1804 ..... **NCLC 27, 67**
See also DLB 94
Kantor, MacKinlay 1904-1977 .... **CLC 7**
See also CA 61-64; CAAS 73-76; CANR 60, 63; CN 1, 2; DLB 9, 102; MAL 5; MTCW 2; RHW; TCWW 1, 2
Kanze Motokiyo
See Zeami
Kaplan, David Michael 1946- .... **CLC 50**
See also CA 187
Kaplan, James 1951- .... **CLC 59**
See also CA 135; CANR 121
Karadzic, Vuk Stefanovic 1787-1864 .... **NCLC 115**
See also CDWLB 4; DLB 147
Karageorge, Michael
See Anderson, Poul
Karamzin, Nikolai Mikhailovich 1766-1826 .... **NCLC 3, 173**
See also DLB 150; RGSF 2
Karapanou, Margarita 1946- .... **CLC 13**
See also CA 101
Karinthy, Frigyes 1887-1938 .... **TCLC 47**
See also CA 170; DLB 215; EWL 3
Karl, Frederick R(obert) 1927-2004 .... **CLC 34**
See also CA 5-8R; CAAS 226; CANR 3, 44, 143
Karr, Mary 1955- .... **CLC 188**
See also AMWS 11; CA 151; CANR 100; MTFW 2005; NCFS 5
Kastel, Warren
See Silverberg, Robert
Kataev, Evgeny Petrovich 1903-1942
See Petrov, Evgeny
See also CAAE 120
Kataphusin
See Ruskin, John
Katz, Steve 1935- .... **CLC 47**
See also CA 25-28R; 14, 64; CANR 12; CN 4, 5, 6, 7; DLBY 1983
Kauffman, Janet 1945- .... **CLC 42**
See also CA 117; CANR 43, 84; DLB 218; DLBY 1986
Kaufman, Bob (Garnell) 1925-1986 .... **CLC 49; PC 74**
See also BG 1:3; BW 1; CA 41-44R; CAAS 118; CANR 22; CP 1; DLB 16, 41
Kaufman, George S. 1889-1961 ...... **CLC 38; DC 17**
See also CA 108; CAAS 93-96; DAM DRAM; DFS 1, 10; DLB 7; INT CA-108; MTCW 2; MTFW 2005; RGAL 4; TUS
Kaufman, Moises 1964- .... **DC 26**
See also CA 211; DFS 22; MTFW 2005
Kaufman, Sue CLC 3, 8
See Barondess, Sue K(aufman)
Kavafis, Konstantinos Petrou 1863-1933
See Cavafy, C(onstantine) P(eter)
See also CAAE 104
Kavan, Anna 1901-1968 .... **CLC 5, 13, 82**
See also BRWS 7; CA 5-8R; CANR 6, 57; DLB 255; MTCW 1; RGEL 2; SFW 4
Kavanagh, Dan
See Barnes, Julian
Kavanagh, Julie 1952- .... **CLC 119**
See also CA 163
Kavanagh, Patrick (Joseph) 1904-1967 .... **CLC 22; PC 33**
See also BRWS 7; CA 123; CAAS 25-28R; DLB 15, 20; EWL 3; MTCW 1; RGEL 2
Kawabata, Yasunari 1899-1972 ..... **CLC 2, 5, 9, 18, 107; SSC 17**
See Kawabata Yasunari
See also CA 93-96; CAAS 33-36R; CANR 88; DAM MULT; DLB 330; MJW; MTCW 2; MTFW 2005; RGSF 2; RGWL 2, 3
Kawabata Yasunari
See Kawabata, Yasunari
See also DLB 180; EWL 3
Kaye, Mary Margaret
See Kaye, M.M.
Kaye, M.M. 1908-2004 .... **CLC 28**
See also CA 89-92; CAAS 223; CANR 24, 60, 102, 142; MTCW 1, 2; MTFW 2005; RHW; SATA 62; SATA-Obit 152
Kaye, Mollie
See Kaye, M.M.
Kaye-Smith, Sheila 1887-1956 .... **TCLC 20**
See also CA 203; CAAE 118; DLB 36
Kaymor, Patrice Maguilene
See Senghor, Leopold Sedar
Kazakov, Iurii Pavlovich
See Kazakov, Yuri Pavlovich
See also DLB 302
Kazakov, Yuri Pavlovich 1927-1982 . **SSC 43**
See Kazakov, Iurii Pavlovich; Kazakov, Yury
See also CA 5-8R; CANR 36; MTCW 1; RGSF 2
Kazakov, Yury
See Kazakov, Yuri Pavlovich
See also EWL 3
Kazan, Elia 1909-2003 .... **CLC 6, 16, 63**
See also CA 21-24R; CAAS 220; CANR 32, 78
Kazantzakis, Nikos 1883(?)-1957 .... **TCLC 2, 5, 33, 181**
See also BPFB 2; CA 132; CAAE 105; DA3; EW 9; EWL 3; MTCW 1, 2; MTFW 2005; RGWL 2, 3
Kazin, Alfred 1915-1998 ..... **CLC 34, 38, 119**
See also AMWS 8; CA 1-4R; 7; CANR 1, 45, 79; DLB 67; EWL 3
Keane, Mary Nesta (Skrine) 1904-1996
See Keane, Molly
See also CA 114; CAAE 108; CAAS 151; RHW
Keane, Molly CLC 31
See Keane, Mary Nesta (Skrine)
See also CN 5, 6; INT CA-114; TCLE 1:1
Keates, Jonathan 1946(?)- .... **CLC 34**
See also CA 163; CANR 126
Keaton, Buster 1895-1966 .... **CLC 20**
See also CA 194
Keats, John 1795-1821 ...... **NCLC 8, 73, 121; PC 1; WLC 3**
See also AAYA 58; BRW 4; BRWR 1; CDBLB 1789-1832; DA; DA3; DAB; DAC; DAM MST, POET; DLB 96, 110; EXPP; LMFS 1; PAB; PFS 1, 2, 3, 9, 17; RGEL 2; TEA; WLIT 3; WP
Keble, John 1792-1866 .... **NCLC 87**
See also DLB 32, 55; RGEL 2
Keene, Donald 1922- .... **CLC 34**
See also CA 1-4R; CANR 5, 119
Keillor, Garrison 1942- ..... **CLC 40, 115, 222**
See also AAYA 2, 62; AMWS 16; BEST 89:3; BPFB 2; CA 117; CAAE 111; CANR 36, 59, 124; CPW; DA3; DAM POP; DLBY 1987; EWL 3; MTCW 1, 2; MTFW 2005; SATA 58; TUS
Keith, Carlos
See Lewton, Val
Keith, Michael
See Hubbard, L. Ron
Keller, Gottfried 1819-1890 .... **NCLC 2; SSC 26, 107**
See also CDWLB 2; DLB 129; EW; RGSF 2; RGWL 2, 3
Keller, Nora Okja 1965- .... **CLC 109**
See also CA 187
Kellerman, Jonathan 1949- .... **CLC 44**
See also AAYA 35; BEST 90:1; CA 106; CANR 29, 51, 150; CMW 4; CPW; DA3; DAM POP; INT CANR-29
Kelley, William Melvin 1937- .... **BLC 2:2; CLC 22**
See also BW 1; CA 77-80; CANR 27, 83; CN 1, 2, 3, 4, 5, 6, 7; DLB 33; EWL 3
Kellogg, Marjorie 1922-2005 .... **CLC 2**
See also CA 81-84; CAAS 246
Kellow, Kathleen
See Hibbert, Eleanor Alice Burford
Kelly, Lauren
See Oates, Joyce Carol
Kelly, M(ilton) T(errence) 1947- ...... **CLC 55**
See also CA 97-100; 22; CANR 19, 43, 84; CN 6
Kelly, Robert 1935- .... **SSC 50**
See also CA 17-20R; 19; CANR 47; CP 1, 2, 3, 4, 5, 6, 7; DLB 5, 130, 165
Kelman, James 1946- .... **CLC 58, 86**
See also BRWS 5; CA 148; CANR 85, 130; CN 5, 6, 7; DLB 194, 319, 326; RGSF 2; WLIT 4
Kemal, Yasar
See Kemal, Yashar
See also CWW 2; EWL 3; WLIT 6
Kemal, Yashar 1923(?)- .... **CLC 14, 29**
See also CA 89-92; CANR 44
Kemble, Fanny 1809-1893 .... **NCLC 18**
See also DLB 32
Kemelman, Harry 1908-1996 .... **CLC 2**
See also AITN 1; BPFB 2; CA 9-12R; CAAS 155; CANR 6, 71; CMW 4; DLB 28
Kempe, Margery 1373(?)-1440(?) ... **LC 6, 56**
See also BRWS 12; DLB 146; FL 1:1; RGEL 2

Lacan, Jacques (Marie Emile) 1901-1981 .... **CLC 75**
See also CA 121; CAAS 104; DLB 296; EWL 3; TWA
Laclos, Pierre-Ambroise Francois 1741-1803 .... **NCLC 4, 87**
See also DLB 313; EW 4; GFL Beginnings to 1789; RGWL 2, 3
Lacolere, Francois
See Aragon, Louis
La Colere, Francois
See Aragon, Louis
La Deshabilleuse
See Simenon, Georges (Jacques Christian)
Lady Gregory
See Gregory, Lady Isabella Augusta (Persse)
Lady of Quality, A
See Bagnold, Enid
La Fayette, Marie-(Madelaine Pioche de la Vergne) 1634-1693 .... **LC 2, 144**
See Lafayette, Marie-Madeleine
See also GFL Beginnings to 1789; RGWL 2, 3
Lafayette, Marie-Madeleine
See La Fayette, Marie-(Madelaine Pioche de la Vergne)
See also DLB 268
Lafayette, Rene
See Hubbard, L. Ron
La Flesche, Francis 1857(?)-1932 ...... **NNAL**
See also CA 144; CANR 83; DLB 175
La Fontaine, Jean de 1621-1695 .... **LC 50**
See also DLB 268; EW 3; GFL Beginnings to 1789; MAICYA 1, 2; RGWL 2, 3; SATA 18
LaForet, Carmen 1921-2004 .... **CLC 219**
See also CA 246; CWW 2; DLB 322; EWL 3
LaForet Diaz, Carmen
See LaForet, Carmen
Laforgue, Jules 1860-1887 . **NCLC 5, 53; PC 14; SSC 20**
See also DLB 217; EW 7; GFL 1789 to the Present; RGWL 2, 3
Lagerkvist, Paer (Fabian) 1891-1974 ..... **CLC 7, 10, 13, 54; TCLC 144**
See Lagerkvist, Par
See also CA 85-88; CAAS 49-52; DA3; DAM DRAM, NOV; MTCW 1, 2; MTFW 2005; TWA
Lagerkvist, Par SSC 12
See Lagerkvist, Paer (Fabian)
See also DLB 259, 331; EW 10; EWL 3; RGSF 2; RGWL 2, 3
Lagerloef, Selma (Ottiliana Lovisa) TCLC 4, 36
See Lagerlof, Selma (Ottiliana Lovisa)
See also CAAE 108; MTCW 2
Lagerlof, Selma (Ottiliana Lovisa) 1858-1940
See Lagerloef, Selma (Ottiliana Lovisa)
See also CA 188; CLR 7; DLB 259, 331; RGWL 2, 3; SATA 15; SSFS 18
La Guma, Alex 1925-1985 .. **BLCS; CLC 19; TCLC 140**
See also AFW; BW 1, 3; CA 49-52; CAAS 118; CANR 25, 81; CDWLB 3; CN 1, 2, 3; CP 1; DAM NOV; DLB 117, 225; EWL 3; MTCW 1, 2; MTFW 2005; WLIT 2; WWE 1
Lahiri, Jhumpa 1967- .... **SSC 96**
See also AAYA 56; CA 193; CANR 134; DLB 323; MTFW 2005; SSFS 19
Laidlaw, A. K.
See Grieve, C(hristopher) M(urray)
Lainez, Manuel Mujica
See Mujica Lainez, Manuel
See also HW 1
Laing, R(onald) D(avid) 1927-1989 . **CLC 95**
See also CA 107; CAAS 129; CANR 34; MTCW 1
Laishley, Alex
See Booth, Martin
Lamartine, Alphonse (Marie Louis Prat) de 1790-1869 .... **NCLC 11, 190; PC 16**
See also DAM POET; DLB 217; GFL 1789 to the Present; RGWL 2, 3
Lamb, Charles 1775-1834 ..... **NCLC 10, 113; WLC 3**
See also BRW 4; CDBLB 1789-1832; DA; DAB; DAC; DAM MST; DLB 93, 107, 163; RGEL 2; SATA 17; TEA
Lamb, Lady Caroline 1785-1828 ... **NCLC 38**
See also DLB 116
Lamb, Mary Ann 1764-1847 .... **NCLC 125**
See also DLB 163; SATA 17
Lame Deer 1903(?)-1976 .... **NNAL**
See also CAAS 69-72
Lamming, George (William) 1927- .... **BLC 1:2; CLC 2, 4, 66, 144**
See also BW 2, 3; CA 85-88; CANR 26, 76; CDWLB 3; CN 1, 2, 3, 4, 5, 6, 7; CP 1; DAM MULT; DLB 125; EWL 3; MTCW 1, 2; MTFW 2005; NFS 15; RGEL 2
L'Amour, Louis 1908-1988 .... **CLC 25, 55**
See also AAYA 16; AITN 2; BEST 89:2; BPFB 2; CA 1-4R; CAAS 125; CANR 3, 25, 40; CPW; DA3; DAM NOV, POP; DLB 206; DLBY 1980; MTCW 1, 2; MTFW 2005; RGAL 4; TCWW 1, 2
Lampedusa, Giuseppe (Tomasi) di TCLC 13
See Tomasi di Lampedusa, Giuseppe
See also CA 164; EW 11; MTCW 2; MTFW 2005; RGWL 2, 3
Lampman, Archibald 1861-1899 .. **NCLC 25, 194**
See also DLB 92; RGEL 2; TWA
Lancaster, Bruce 1896-1963 .... **CLC 36**
See also CA 9-10; CANR 70; CAP 1; SATA 9
Lanchester, John 1962- .... **CLC 99**
See also CA 194; DLB 267
Landau, Mark Alexandrovich
See Aldanov, Mark (Alexandrovich)
Landau-Aldanov, Mark Alexandrovich
See Aldanov, Mark (Alexandrovich)
Landis, Jerry
See Simon, Paul
Landis, John 1950- .... **CLC 26**
See also CA 122; CAAE 112; CANR 128
Landolfi, Tommaso 1908-1979 .... **CLC 11, 49**
See also CA 127; CAAS 117; DLB 177; EWL 3
Landon, Letitia Elizabeth 1802-1838 .... **NCLC 15**
See also DLB 96
Landor, Walter Savage 1775-1864 .... **NCLC 14**
See also BRW 4; DLB 93, 107; RGEL 2
Landwirth, Heinz
See Lind, Jakov
Lane, Patrick 1939- .... **CLC 25**
See also CA 97-100; CANR 54; CP 3, 4, 5, 6, 7; DAM POET; DLB 53; INT CA-97-100
Lane, Rose Wilder 1887-1968 ...... **TCLC 177**
See also CA 102; CANR 63; SATA 29; SATA-Brief 28; TCWW 2
Lang, Andrew 1844-1912 .... **TCLC 16**
See also CA 137; CAAE 114; CANR 85; CLR 101; DLB 98, 141, 184; FANT; MAICYA 1, 2; RGEL 2; SATA 16; WCH
Lang, Fritz 1890-1976 .... **CLC 20, 103**
See also AAYA 65; CA 77-80; CAAS 69-72; CANR 30
Lange, John
See Crichton, Michael
Langer, Elinor 1939- .... **CLC 34**
See also CA 121
Langland, William 1332(?)-1400(?) .... **LC 19, 120**
See also BRW 1; DA; DAB; DAC; DAM MST, POET; DLB 146; RGEL 2; TEA; WLIT 3
Langstaff, Launcelot
See Irving, Washington
Lanier, Sidney 1842-1881 . **NCLC 6, 118; PC 50**
See also AMWS 1; DAM POET; DLB 64; DLBD 13; EXPP; MAICYA 1; PFS 14; RGAL 4; SATA 18
Lanyer, Aemilia 1569-1645 .... **LC 10, 30, 83; PC 60**
See also DLB 121
Lao-Tzu
See Lao Tzu
Lao Tzu c. 6th cent. B.C.-3rd cent. B.C. .... **CMLC 7**
Lapine, James (Elliot) 1949- .... **CLC 39**
See also CA 130; CAAE 123; CANR 54, 128; INT CA-130
Larbaud, Valery (Nicolas) 1881-1957 .... **TCLC 9**
See also CA 152; CAAE 106; EWL 3; GFL 1789 to the Present
Larcom, Lucy 1824-1893 .... **NCLC 179**
See also AMWS 13; DLB 221, 243
Lardner, Ring
See Lardner, Ring(gold) W(ilmer)
See also BPFB 2; CDALB 1917-1929; DLB 11, 25, 86, 171; DLBD 16; MAL 5; RGAL 4; RGSF 2
Lardner, Ring W., Jr.
See Lardner, Ring(gold) W(ilmer)
Lardner, Ring(gold) W(ilmer) 1885-1933 .... **SSC 32; TCLC 2, 14**
See Lardner, Ring
See also AMW; CA 131; CAAE 104; MTCW 1, 2; MTFW 2005; TUS
Laredo, Betty
See Codrescu, Andrei
Larkin, Maia
See Wojciechowska, Maia (Teresa)
Larkin, Philip (Arthur) 1922-1985 ... **CLC 3, 5, 8, 9, 13, 18, 33, 39, 64; PC 21**
See also BRWS 1; CA 5-8R; CAAS 117; CANR 24, 62; CDBLB 1960 to Present; CP 1, 2, 3, 4; DA3; DAB; DAM MST, POET; DLB 27; EWL 3; MTCW 1, 2; MTFW 2005; PFS 3, 4, 12; RGEL 2
La Roche, Sophie von 1730-1807 .... **NCLC 121**
See also DLB 94
La Rochefoucauld, Francois 1613-1680 .... **LC 108**
Larra (y Sanchez de Castro), Mariano Jose de 1809-1837 .... **NCLC 17, 130**
Larsen, Eric 1941- .... **CLC 55**
See also CA 132
Larsen, Nella 1893(?)-1963 ... **BLC 1:2; CLC 37; HR 1:3; TCLC 200**
See also AFAW 1, 2; BW 1; CA 125; CANR 83; DAM MULT; DLB 51; FW; LATS 1:1; LMFS 2
Larson, Charles R(aymond) 1938- ... **CLC 31**
See also CA 53-56; CANR 4, 121
Larson, Jonathan 1960-1996 .... **CLC 99**
See also AAYA 28; CA 156; DFS 23; MTFW 2005
La Sale, Antoine de c. 1386-1460(?) . **LC 104**
See also DLB 208

Author Index

Lee, Li-Young 1957- .... **CLC 164; PC 24**
See also AMWS 15; CA 153; CANR 118; CP 6, 7; DLB 165, 312; LMFS 2; PFS 11, 15, 17

Lee, Manfred B. 1905-1971 .... **CLC 11**
See Queen, Ellery
See also CA 1-4R; CAAS 29-32R; CANR 2, 150; CMW 4; DLB 137

Lee, Manfred Bennington
See Lee, Manfred B.

Lee, Nathaniel 1645(?)-1692 .... **LC 103**
See also DLB 80; RGEL 2

Lee, Nelle Harper
See Lee, Harper

Lee, Shelton Jackson
See Lee, Spike

Lee, Sophia 1750-1824 .... **NCLC 191**
See also DLB 39

Lee, Spike 1957(?)- .... **BLCS; CLC 105**
See also AAYA 4, 29; BW 2, 3; CA 125; CANR 42, 164; DAM MULT

Lee, Stan 1922- .... **CLC 17**
See also AAYA 5, 49; CA 111; CAAE 108; CANR 129; INT CA-111; MTFW 2005

Lee, Tanith 1947- .... **CLC 46**
See also AAYA 15; CA 37-40R; CANR 53, 102, 145, 170; DLB 261; FANT; SATA 8, 88, 134, 185; SFW 4; SUFW 1, 2; YAW

Lee, Vernon SSC 33, 98; TCLC 5
See Paget, Violet
See also DLB 57, 153, 156, 174, 178; GLL 1; SUFW 1

Lee, William
See Burroughs, William S.
See also GLL 1

Lee, Willy
See Burroughs, William S.
See also GLL 1

Lee-Hamilton, Eugene (Jacob)
1845-1907 .... **TCLC 22**
See also CA 234; CAAE 117

Leet, Judith 1935- .... **CLC 11**
See also CA 187

Le Fanu, Joseph Sheridan
1814-1873 .... **NCLC 9, 58; SSC 14, 84**
See also CMW 4; DA3; DAM POP; DLB 21, 70, 159, 178; GL 3; HGG; RGEL 2; RGSF 2; SUFW 1

Leffland, Ella 1931- .... **CLC 19**
See also CA 29-32R; CANR 35, 78, 82; DLBY 1984; INT CANR-35; SATA 65; SSFS 24

Leger, Alexis
See Leger, (Marie-Rene Auguste) Alexis Saint-Leger

Leger, (Marie-Rene Auguste) Alexis Saint-Leger 1887-1975 .. **CLC 4, 11, 46; PC 23**
See Perse, Saint-John; Saint-John Perse
See also CA 13-16R; CAAS 61-64; CANR 43; DAM POET; MTCW 1

Leger, Saintleger
See Leger, (Marie-Rene Auguste) Alexis Saint-Leger

Le Guin, Ursula K. 1929- ...... **CLC 8, 13, 22, 45, 71, 136; SSC 12, 69**
See also AAYA 9, 27; AITN 1; BPFB 2; BYA 5, 8, 11, 14; CA 21-24R; CANR 9, 32, 52, 74, 132; CDALB 1968-1988; CLR 3, 28, 91; CN 2, 3, 4, 5, 6, 7; CPW; DA3; DAB; DAC; DAM MST, POP; DLB 8, 52, 256, 275; EXPS; FANT; FW; INT CANR-32; JRDA; LAIT 5; MAICYA 1, 2; MAL 5; MTCW 1, 2; MTFW 2005; NFS 6, 9; SATA 4, 52, 99, 149; SCFW 1, 2; SFW 4; SSFS 2; SUFW 1, 2; WYA; YAW

Lehmann, Rosamond (Nina)
1901-1990 .... **CLC 5**
See also CA 77-80; CAAS 131; CANR 8, 73; CN 1, 2, 3, 4; DLB 15; MTCW 2; RGEL 2; RHW

Leiber, Fritz (Reuter, Jr.)
1910-1992 .... **CLC 25**
See also AAYA 65; BPFB 2; CA 45-48; CAAS 139; CANR 2, 40, 86; CN 2, 3, 4, 5; DLB 8; FANT; HGG; MTCW 1, 2; MTFW 2005; SATA 45; SATA-Obit 73; SCFW 1, 2; SFW 4; SUFW 1, 2

Leibniz, Gottfried Wilhelm von
1646-1716 .... **LC 35**
See also DLB 168

Leino, Eino TCLC 24
See Lonnbohm, Armas Eino Leopold
See also EWL 3

Leiris, Michel (Julien) 1901-1990 ..... **CLC 61**
See also CA 128; CAAE 119; CAAS 132; EWL 3; GFL 1789 to the Present

Leithauser, Brad 1953- .... **CLC 27**
See also CA 107; CANR 27, 81, 171; CP 5, 6, 7; DLB 120, 282

le Jars de Gournay, Marie
See de Gournay, Marie le Jars

Lelchuk, Alan 1938- .... **CLC 5**
See also CA 45-48; 20; CANR 1, 70, 152; CN 3, 4, 5, 6, 7

Lem, Stanislaw 1921-2006 ..... **CLC 8, 15, 40, 149**
See also AAYA 75; CA 105; 1; CAAS 249; CANR 32; CWW 2; MTCW 1; SCFW 1, 2; SFW 4

Lemann, Nancy (Elise) 1956- .... **CLC 39**
See also CA 136; CAAE 118; CANR 121

Lemonnier, (Antoine Louis) Camille
1844-1913 .... **TCLC 22**
See also CAAE 121

Lenau, Nikolaus 1802-1850 .... **NCLC 16**

L'Engle, Madeleine 1918-2007 .... **CLC 12**
See also AAYA 28; AITN 2; BPFB 2; BYA 2, 4, 5, 7; CA 1-4R; CAAS 264; CANR 3, 21, 39, 66, 107; CLR 1, 14, 57; CPW; CWRI 5; DA3; DAM POP; DLB 52; JRDA; MAICYA 1, 2; MTCW 1, 2; MTFW 2005; SAAS 15; SATA 1, 27, 75, 128; SATA-Obit 186; SFW 4; WYA; YAW

L'Engle, Madeleine Camp Franklin
See L'Engle, Madeleine

Lengyel, Jozsef 1896-1975 .... **CLC 7**
See also CA 85-88; CAAS 57-60; CANR 71; RGSF 2

Lenin 1870-1924
See Lenin, V. I.
See also CA 168; CAAE 121

Lenin, V. I. TCLC 67
See Lenin

Lennon, John (Ono) 1940-1980 .. **CLC 12, 35**
See also CA 102; SATA 114

Lennox, Charlotte Ramsay
1729(?)-1804 .... **NCLC 23, 134**
See also DLB 39; RGEL 2

Lentricchia, Frank, Jr.
See Lentricchia, Frank

Lentricchia, Frank 1940- .... **CLC 34**
See also CA 25-28R; CANR 19, 106, 148; DLB 246

Lenz, Gunter CLC 65

Lenz, Jakob Michael Reinhold
1751-1792 .... **LC 100**
See also DLB 94; RGWL 2, 3

Lenz, Siegfried 1926- .... **CLC 27; SSC 33**
See also CA 89-92; CANR 80, 149; CWW 2; DLB 75; EWL 3; RGSF 2; RGWL 2, 3

Leon, David
See Jacob, (Cyprien-)Max

Leonard, Elmore 1925- .... **CLC 28, 34, 71, 120, 222**
See also AAYA 22, 59; AITN 1; BEST 89:1, 90:4; BPFB 2; CA 81-84; CANR 12, 28, 53, 76, 96, 133; CMW 4; CN 5, 6, 7; CPW; DA3; DAM POP; DLB 173, 226; INT CANR-28; MSW; MTCW 1, 2; MTFW 2005; RGAL 4; SATA 163; TCWW 1, 2

Leonard, Hugh CLC 19
See Byrne, John Keyes
See also CBD; CD 5, 6; DFS 13, 24; DLB 13

Leonov, Leonid (Maximovich)
1899-1994 .... **CLC 92**
See Leonov, Leonid Maksimovich
See also CA 129; CANR 76; DAM NOV; EWL 3; MTCW 1, 2; MTFW 2005

Leonov, Leonid Maksimovich
See Leonov, Leonid (Maximovich)
See also DLB 272

Leopardi, (Conte) Giacomo
1798-1837 .... **NCLC 22, 129; PC 37**
See also EW 5; RGWL 2, 3; WLIT 7; WP

Le Reveler
See Artaud, Antonin (Marie Joseph)

Lerman, Eleanor 1952- .... **CLC 9**
See also CA 85-88; CANR 69, 124

Lerman, Rhoda 1936- .... **CLC 56**
See also CA 49-52; CANR 70

Lermontov, Mikhail Iur'evich
See Lermontov, Mikhail Yuryevich
See also DLB 205

Lermontov, Mikhail Yuryevich
1814-1841 .... **NCLC 5, 47, 126; PC 18**
See Lermontov, Mikhail Iur'evich
See also EW 6; RGWL 2, 3; TWA

Leroux, Gaston 1868-1927 .... **TCLC 25**
See also CA 136; CAAE 108; CANR 69; CMW 4; MTFW 2005; NFS 20; SATA 65

Lesage, Alain-Rene 1668-1747 .... **LC 2, 28**
See also DLB 313; EW 3; GFL Beginnings to 1789; RGWL 2, 3

Leskov, N(ikolai) S(emenovich) 1831-1895
See Leskov, Nikolai (Semyonovich)

Leskov, Nikolai (Semyonovich)
1831-1895 ... **NCLC 25, 174; SSC 34, 96**
See Leskov, Nikolai Semenovich

Leskov, Nikolai Semenovich
See Leskov, Nikolai (Semyonovich)
See also DLB 238

Lesser, Milton
See Marlowe, Stephen

Lessing, Doris 1919- .. **CLC 1, 2, 3, 6, 10, 15, 22, 40, 94, 170, 254; SSC 6, 61; WLCS**
See also AAYA 57; AFW; BRWS 1; CA 9-12R; 14; CANR 33, 54, 76, 122; CBD; CD 5, 6; CDBLB 1960 to Present; CN 1, 2, 3, 4, 5, 6, 7; CWD; DA; DA3; DAB; DAC; DAM MST, NOV; DFS 20; DLB 15, 139; DLBY 1985; EWL 3; EXPS; FL 1:6; FW; LAIT 4; MTCW 1, 2; MTFW 2005; RGEL 2; RGSF 2; SFW 4; SSFS 1, 12, 20; TEA; WLIT 2, 4

Lessing, Doris May
See Lessing, Doris

Lessing, Gotthold Ephraim
1729-1781 .... **DC 26; LC 8, 124**
See also CDWLB 2; DLB 97; EW 4; RGWL 2, 3

Lester, Julius 1939- .... **BLC 2:2**
See also AAYA 12, 51; BW 2; BYA 3, 9, 11, 12; CA 17-20R; CANR 8, 23, 43, 129; CLR 2, 41; JRDA; MAICYA 1, 2; MAICYAS 1; MTFW 2005; SATA 12, 74, 112, 157; YAW

Lester, Richard 1932- .... **CLC 20**

Levenson, Jay CLC 70

Linney, Romulus 1930- .... **CLC 51**
See also CA 1-4R; CAD; CANR 40, 44, 79; CD 5, 6; CSW; RGAL 4
Linton, Eliza Lynn 1822-1898 .... **NCLC 41**
See also DLB 18
Li Po 701-763 .... **CMLC 2, 86; PC 29**
See also PFS 20; WP
Lipsius, Justus 1547-1606 .... **LC 16**
Lipsyte, Robert 1938- .... **CLC 21**
See also AAYA 7, 45; CA 17-20R; CANR 8, 57, 146; CLR 23, 76; DA; DAC; DAM MST, NOV; JRDA; LAIT 5; MAICYA 1, 2; SATA 5, 68, 113, 161; WYA; YAW
Lipsyte, Robert Michael
See Lipsyte, Robert
Lish, Gordon 1934- .... **CLC 45; SSC 18**
See also CA 117; CAAE 113; CANR 79, 151; DLB 130; INT CA-117
Lish, Gordon Jay
See Lish, Gordon
Lispector, Clarice 1925(?)-1977 .... **CLC 43; HLCS 2; SSC 34, 96**
See also CA 139; CAAS 116; CANR 71; CDWLB 3; DLB 113, 307; DNFS 1; EWL 3; FW; HW 2; LAW; RGSF 2; RGWL 2, 3; WLIT 1
Littell, Robert 1935(?)- .... **CLC 42**
See also CA 112; CAAE 109; CANR 64, 115, 162; CMW 4
Little, Malcolm 1925-1965
See Malcolm X
See also BW 1, 3; CA 125; CAAS 111; CANR 82; DA; DA3; DAB; DAC; DAM MST, MULT; MTCW 1, 2; MTFW 2005
Littlewit, Humphrey Gent.
See Lovecraft, H. P.
Litwos
See Sienkiewicz, Henryk (Adam Alexander Pius)
Liu, E. 1857-1909 .... **TCLC 15**
See also CA 190; CAAE 115; DLB 328
Lively, Penelope 1933- .... **CLC 32, 50**
See also BPFB 2; CA 41-44R; CANR 29, 67, 79, 131, 172; CLR 7; CN 5, 6, 7; CWRI 5; DAM NOV; DLB 14, 161, 207, 326; FANT; JRDA; MAICYA 1, 2; MTCW 1, 2; MTFW 2005; SATA 7, 60, 101, 164; TEA
Lively, Penelope Margaret
See Lively, Penelope
Livesay, Dorothy (Kathleen) 1909-1996 .... **CLC 4, 15, 79**
See also AITN 2; CA 25-28R; 8; CANR 36, 67; CP 1, 2, 3, 4, 5; DAC; DAM MST, POET; DLB 68; FW; MTCW 1; RGEL 2; TWA
Livy c. 59B.C.-c. 12 .... **CMLC 11**
See also AW 2; CDWLB 1; DLB 211; RGWL 2, 3; WLIT 8
Lizardi, Jose Joaquin Fernandez de 1776-1827 .... **NCLC 30**
See also LAW
Llewellyn, Richard
See Llewellyn Lloyd, Richard Dafydd Vivian
See also DLB 15
Llewellyn Lloyd, Richard Dafydd Vivian 1906-1983 .... **CLC 7, 80**
See Llewellyn, Richard
See also CA 53-56; CAAS 111; CANR 7, 71; SATA 11; SATA-Obit 37
Llosa, Jorge Mario Pedro Vargas
See Vargas Llosa, Mario
See also RGWL 3
Llosa, Mario Vargas
See Vargas Llosa, Mario
Lloyd, Manda
See Mander, (Mary) Jane
Lloyd Webber, Andrew 1948-
See Webber, Andrew Lloyd
See also AAYA 1, 38; CA 149; CAAE 116; DAM DRAM; SATA 56
Llull, Ramon c. 1235-c. 1316 .... **CMLC 12**
Lobb, Ebenezer
See Upward, Allen
Locke, Alain (Le Roy) 1886-1954 .... **BLCS; HR 1:3; TCLC 43**
See also AMWS 14; BW 1, 3; CA 124; CAAE 106; CANR 79; DLB 51; LMFS 2; MAL 5; RGAL 4
Locke, John 1632-1704 .... **LC 7, 35, 135**
See also DLB 31, 101, 213, 252; RGEL 2; WLIT 3
Locke-Elliott, Sumner
See Elliott, Sumner Locke
Lockhart, John Gibson 1794-1854 .. **NCLC 6**
See also DLB 110, 116, 144
Lockridge, Ross (Franklin), Jr. 1914-1948 .... **TCLC 111**
See also CA 145; CAAE 108; CANR 79; DLB 143; DLBY 1980; MAL 5; RGAL 4; RHW
Lockwood, Robert
See Johnson, Robert
Lodge, David 1935- .... **CLC 36, 141**
See also BEST 90:1; BRWS 4; CA 17-20R; CANR 19, 53, 92, 139; CN 1, 2, 3, 4, 5, 6, 7; CPW; DAM POP; DLB 14, 194; EWL 3; INT CANR-19; MTCW 1, 2; MTFW 2005
Lodge, Thomas 1558-1625 .... **LC 41**
See also DLB 172; RGEL 2
Loewinsohn, Ron(ald William) 1937- .... **CLC 52**
See also CA 25-28R; CANR 71; CP 1, 2, 3, 4
Logan, Jake
See Smith, Martin Cruz
Logan, John (Burton) 1923-1987 .... **CLC 5**
See also CA 77-80; CAAS 124; CANR 45; CP 1, 2, 3, 4; DLB 5
Lo Kuan-chung 1330(?)-1400(?) .... **LC 12**
Lombard, Nap
See Johnson, Pamela Hansford
Lombard, Peter 1100(?)-1160(?) ... **CMLC 72**
Lombino, Salvatore
See Hunter, Evan
London, Jack 1876-1916 .. **SSC 4, 49; TCLC 9, 15, 39; WLC 4**
See London, John Griffith
See also AAYA 13; AITN 2; AMW; BPFB 2; BYA 4, 13; CDALB 1865-1917; CLR 108; DLB 8, 12, 78, 212; EWL 3; EXPS; LAIT 3; MAL 5; NFS 8; RGAL 4; RGSF 2; SATA 18; SFW 4; SSFS 7; TCWW 1, 2; TUS; WYA; YAW
London, John Griffith 1876-1916
See London, Jack
See also AAYA 75; CA 119; CAAE 110; CANR 73; DA; DA3; DAB; DAC; DAM MST, NOV; JRDA; MAICYA 1, 2; MTCW 1, 2; MTFW 2005; NFS 19
Long, Emmett
See Leonard, Elmore
Longbaugh, Harry
See Goldman, William
Longfellow, Henry Wadsworth 1807-1882 .... **NCLC 2, 45, 101, 103; PC 30; WLCS**
See also AMW; AMWR 2; CDALB 1640-1865; CLR 99; DA; DA3; DAB; DAC; DAM MST, POET; DLB 1, 59, 235; EXPP; PAB; PFS 2, 7, 17; RGAL 4; SATA 19; TUS; WP
Longinus c. 1st cent. - .... **CMLC 27**
See also AW 2; DLB 176
Longley, Michael 1939- .... **CLC 29**
See also BRWS 8; CA 102; CP 1, 2, 3, 4, 5, 6, 7; DLB 40
Longstreet, Augustus Baldwin 1790-1870 .... **NCLC 159**
See also DLB 3, 11, 74, 248; RGAL 4
Longus fl. c. 2nd cent. - .... **CMLC 7**
Longway, A. Hugh
See Lang, Andrew
Lonnbohm, Armas Eino Leopold 1878-1926
See Leino, Eino
See also CAAE 123
Lonnrot, Elias 1802-1884 .... **NCLC 53**
See also EFS 1
Lonsdale, Roger CLC 65
Lopate, Phillip 1943- .... **CLC 29**
See also CA 97-100; CANR 88, 157; DLBY 1980; INT CA-97-100
Lopez, Barry (Holstun) 1945- .... **CLC 70**
See also AAYA 9, 63; ANW; CA 65-68; CANR 7, 23, 47, 68, 92; DLB 256, 275, 335; INT CANR-7, CANR-23; MTCW 1; RGAL 4; SATA 67
Lopez de Mendoza, Inigo
See Santillana, Inigo Lopez de Mendoza, Marques de
Lopez Portillo (y Pacheco), Jose 1920-2004 .... **CLC 46**
See also CA 129; CAAS 224; HW 1
Lopez y Fuentes, Gregorio 1897(?)-1966 .... **CLC 32**
See also CA 131; EWL 3; HW 1
Lorca, Federico Garcia TCLC 197
See Garcia Lorca, Federico
See also DFS 4; EW 11; PFS 20; RGWL 2, 3; WP
Lord, Audre
See Lorde, Audre
See also EWL 3
Lord, Bette Bao 1938- .... **AAL; CLC 23**
See also BEST 90:3; BPFB 2; CA 107; CANR 41, 79; INT CA-107; SATA 58
Lord Auch
See Bataille, Georges
Lord Brooke
See Greville, Fulke
Lord Byron
See Byron, George Gordon (Noel)
Lorde, Audre 1934-1992 . **BLC 1:2; CLC 18, 71; PC 12; TCLC 173**
See Domini, Rey; Lord, Audre
See also AFAW 1, 2; BW 1, 3; CA 25-28R; CAAS 142; CANR 16, 26, 46, 82; CP 2, 3, 4, 5; DA3; DAM MULT, POET; DLB 41; FW; MAL 5; MTCW 1, 2; MTFW 2005; PFS 16; RGAL 4
Lorde, Audre Geraldine
See Lorde, Audre
Lord Houghton
See Milnes, Richard Monckton
Lord Jeffrey
See Jeffrey, Francis
Loreaux, Nichol CLC 65
Lorenzini, Carlo 1826-1890
See Collodi, Carlo
See also MAICYA 1, 2; SATA 29, 100
Lorenzo, Heberto Padilla
See Padilla (Lorenzo), Heberto
Loris
See Hofmannsthal, Hugo von
Loti, Pierre TCLC 11
See Viaud, (Louis Marie) Julien
See also DLB 123; GFL 1789 to the Present
Lou, Henri
See Andreas-Salome, Lou

MacDonald, John D. 1916-1986 .. **CLC 3, 27, 44**
See also BPFB 2; CA 1-4R; CAAS 121; CANR 1, 19, 60; CMW 4; CPW; DAM NOV, POP; DLB 8, 306; DLBY 1986; MSW; MTCW 1, 2; MTFW 2005; SFW 4
Macdonald, John Ross
See Millar, Kenneth
Macdonald, Ross CLC 1, 2, 3, 14, 34, 41
See Millar, Kenneth
See also AMWS 4; BPFB 2; CN 1, 2, 3; DLBD 6; MAL 5; MSW; RGAL 4
MacDougal, John
See Blish, James (Benjamin)
MacDougal, John
See Blish, James (Benjamin)
MacDowell, John
See Parks, Tim(othy Harold)
MacEwen, Gwendolyn (Margaret)
1941-1987 .... **CLC 13, 55**
See also CA 9-12R; CAAS 124; CANR 7, 22; CP 1, 2, 3, 4; DLB 53, 251; SATA 50; SATA-Obit 55
MacGreevy, Thomas 1893-1967 .... **PC 82**
See also CA 262
Macha, Karel Hynek 1810-1846 .... **NCLC 46**
Machado (y Ruiz), Antonio
1875-1939 .... **TCLC 3**
See also CA 174; CAAE 104; DLB 108; EW 9; EWL 3; HW 2; PFS 23; RGWL 2, 3
Machado de Assis, Joaquim Maria
1839-1908 . **BLC 1:2; HLCS 2; SSC 24; TCLC 10**
See also CA 153; CAAE 107; CANR 91; DLB 307; LAW; RGSF 2; RGWL 2, 3; TWA; WLIT 1
Machaut, Guillaume de c.
1300-1377 .... **CMLC 64**
See also DLB 208
Machen, Arthur SSC 20; TCLC 4
See Jones, Arthur Llewellyn
See also CA 179; DLB 156, 178; RGEL 2; SUFW 1
Machiavelli, Niccolo 1469-1527 ... **DC 16; LC 8, 36, 140; WLCS**
See also AAYA 58; DA; DAB; DAC; DAM MST; EW 2; LAIT 1; LMFS 1; NFS 9; RGWL 2, 3; TWA; WLIT 7
MacInnes, Colin 1914-1976 .... **CLC 4, 23**
See also CA 69-72; CAAS 65-68; CANR 21; CN 1, 2; DLB 14; MTCW 1, 2; RGEL 2; RHW
MacInnes, Helen (Clark)
1907-1985 .... **CLC 27, 39**
See also BPFB 2; CA 1-4R; CAAS 117; CANR 1, 28, 58; CMW 4; CN 1, 2; CPW; DAM POP; DLB 87; MSW; MTCW 1, 2; MTFW 2005; SATA 22; SATA-Obit 44
Mackay, Mary 1855-1924
See Corelli, Marie
See also CA 177; CAAE 118; FANT; RHW
Mackay, Shena 1944- .... **CLC 195**
See also CA 104; CANR 88, 139; DLB 231, 319; MTFW 2005
Mackenzie, Compton (Edward Montague)
1883-1972 .... **CLC 18; TCLC 116**
See also CA 21-22; CAAS 37-40R; CAP 2; CN 1; DLB 34, 100; RGEL 2
Mackenzie, Henry 1745-1831 .... **NCLC 41**
See also DLB 39; RGEL 2
Mackey, Nathaniel 1947- .... **BLC 2:3; PC 49**
See also CA 153; CANR 114; CP 6, 7; DLB 169
Mackey, Nathaniel Ernest
See Mackey, Nathaniel
MacKinnon, Catharine A. 1946- .... **CLC 181**
See also CA 132; CAAE 128; CANR 73, 140; FW; MTCW 2; MTFW 2005
Mackintosh, Elizabeth 1896(?)-1952
See Tey, Josephine
See also CAAE 110; CMW 4
Macklin, Charles 1699-1797 .... **LC 132**
See also DLB 89; RGEL 2
MacLaren, James
See Grieve, C(hristopher) M(urray)
MacLaverty, Bernard 1942- ..... **CLC 31, 243**
See also CA 118; CAAE 116; CANR 43, 88, 168; CN 5, 6, 7; DLB 267; INT CA-118; RGSF 2
MacLean, Alistair (Stuart)
1922(?)-1987 .... **CLC 3, 13, 50, 63**
See also CA 57-60; CAAS 121; CANR 28, 61; CMW 4; CP 2, 3, 4, 5, 6, 7; CPW; DAM POP; DLB 276; MTCW 1; SATA 23; SATA-Obit 50; TCWW 2
Maclean, Norman (Fitzroy)
1902-1990 .... **CLC 78; SSC 13**
See also AMWS 14; CA 102; CAAS 132; CANR 49; CPW; DAM POP; DLB 206; TCWW 2
MacLeish, Archibald 1892-1982 ... **CLC 3, 8, 14, 68; PC 47**
See also AMW; CA 9-12R; CAAS 106; CAD; CANR 33, 63; CDALBS; CP 1, 2; DAM POET; DFS 15; DLB 4, 7, 45; DLBY 1982; EWL 3; EXPP; MAL 5; MTCW 1, 2; MTFW 2005; PAB; PFS 5; RGAL 4; TUS
MacLennan, (John) Hugh
1907-1990 .... **CLC 2, 14, 92**
See also CA 5-8R; CAAS 142; CANR 33; CN 1, 2, 3, 4; DAC; DAM MST; DLB 68; EWL 3; MTCW 1, 2; MTFW 2005; RGEL 2; TWA
MacLeod, Alistair 1936- .. **CLC 56, 165; SSC 90**
See also CA 123; CCA 1; DAC; DAM MST; DLB 60; MTCW 2; MTFW 2005; RGSF 2; TCLE 1:2
Macleod, Fiona
See Sharp, William
See also RGEL 2; SUFW
MacNeice, (Frederick) Louis
1907-1963 .... **CLC 1, 4, 10, 53; PC 61**
See also BRW 7; CA 85-88; CANR 61; DAB; DAM POET; DLB 10, 20; EWL 3; MTCW 1, 2; MTFW 2005; RGEL 2
MacNeill, Dand
See Fraser, George MacDonald
Macpherson, James 1736-1796 .... **LC 29**
See Ossian
See also BRWS 8; DLB 109, 336; RGEL 2
Macpherson, (Jean) Jay 1931- .... **CLC 14**
See also CA 5-8R; CANR 90; CP 1, 2, 3, 4, 6, 7; CWP; DLB 53
Macrobius fl. 430- .... **CMLC 48**
MacShane, Frank 1927-1999 .... **CLC 39**
See also CA 9-12R; CAAS 186; CANR 3, 33; DLB 111
Macumber, Mari
See Sandoz, Mari(e Susette)
Madach, Imre 1823-1864 .... **NCLC 19**
Madden, (Jerry) David 1933- .... **CLC 5, 15**
See also CA 1-4R; 3; CANR 4, 45; CN 3, 4, 5, 6, 7; CSW; DLB 6; MTCW 1
Maddern, Al(an)
See Ellison, Harlan
Madhubuti, Haki R. 1942- .... **BLC 1:2; CLC 6, 73; PC 5**
See Lee, Don L.
See also BW 2, 3; CA 73-76; CANR 24, 51, 73, 139; CP 6, 7; CSW; DAM MULT, POET; DLB 5, 41; DLBD 8; EWL 3; MAL 5; MTCW 2; MTFW 2005; RGAL 4
Madison, James 1751-1836 .... **NCLC 126**
See also DLB 37
Maepenn, Hugh
See Kuttner, Henry
Maepenn, K. H.
See Kuttner, Henry
Maeterlinck, Maurice 1862-1949 ..... **TCLC 3**
See also CA 136; CAAE 104; CANR 80; DAM DRAM; DLB 192, 331; EW 8; EWL 3; GFL 1789 to the Present; LMFS 2; RGWL 2, 3; SATA 66; TWA
Maginn, William 1794-1842 .... **NCLC 8**
See also DLB 110, 159
Mahapatra, Jayanta 1928- .... **CLC 33**
See also CA 73-76; 9; CANR 15, 33, 66, 87; CP 4, 5, 6, 7; DAM MULT; DLB 323
Mahfouz, Nagib
See Mahfouz, Naguib
Mahfouz, Naguib 1911(?)-2006 ..... **CLC 153; SSC 66**
See Mahfuz, Najib
See also AAYA 49; BEST 89:2; CA 128; CAAS 253; CANR 55, 101; DA3; DAM NOV; MTCW 1, 2; MTFW 2005; RGWL 2, 3; SSFS 9
Mahfouz, Naguib Abdel Aziz Al-Sabilgi
See Mahfouz, Naguib
Mahfouz, Najib
See Mahfouz, Naguib
Mahfuz, Najib CLC 52, 55
See Mahfouz, Naguib
See also AFW; CWW 2; DLB 331; DLBY 1988; EWL 3; RGSF 2; WLIT 6
Mahon, Derek 1941- .... **CLC 27; PC 60**
See also BRWS 6; CA 128; CAAE 113; CANR 88; CP 1, 2, 3, 4, 5, 6, 7; DLB 40; EWL 3
Maiakovskii, Vladimir
See Mayakovski, Vladimir (Vladimirovich)
See also IDTP; RGWL 2, 3
Mailer, Norman 1923-2007 ... **CLC 1, 2, 3, 4, 5, 8, 11, 14, 28, 39, 74, 111, 234**
See also AAYA 31; AITN 2; AMW; AMWC 2; AMWR 2; BPFB 2; CA 9-12R; CAAS 266; CABS 1; CANR 28, 74, 77, 130; CDALB 1968-1988; CN 1, 2, 3, 4, 5, 6, 7; CPW; DA; DA3; DAB; DAC; DAM MST, NOV, POP; DLB 2, 16, 28, 185, 278; DLBD 3; DLBY 1980, 1983; EWL 3; MAL 5; MTCW 1, 2; MTFW 2005; NFS 10; RGAL 4; TUS
Mailer, Norman Kingsley
See Mailer, Norman
Maillet, Antonine 1929- .... **CLC 54, 118**
See also CA 120; CAAE 115; CANR 46, 74, 77, 134; CCA 1; CWW 2; DAC; DLB 60; INT CA-120; MTCW 2; MTFW 2005
Maimonides, Moses 1135-1204 ..... **CMLC 76**
See also DLB 115
Mais, Roger 1905-1955 .... **TCLC 8**
See also BW 1, 3; CA 124; CAAE 105; CANR 82; CDWLB 3; DLB 125; EWL 3; MTCW 1; RGEL 2
Maistre, Joseph 1753-1821 .... **NCLC 37**
See also GFL 1789 to the Present
Maitland, Frederic William
1850-1906 .... **TCLC 65**
Maitland, Sara (Louise) 1950- .... **CLC 49**
See also BRWS 11; CA 69-72; CANR 13, 59; DLB 271; FW
Major, Clarence 1936- ...... **BLC 1:2; CLC 3, 19, 48**
See also AFAW 2; BW 2, 3; CA 21-24R; 6; CANR 13, 25, 53, 82; CN 3, 4, 5, 6, 7; CP 2, 3, 4, 5, 6, 7; CSW; DAM MULT; DLB 33; EWL 3; MAL 5; MSW
Major, Kevin (Gerald) 1949- .... **CLC 26**
See also AAYA 16; CA 97-100; CANR 21, 38, 112; CLR 11; DAC; DLB 60; INT CANR-21; JRDA; MAICYA 1, 2; MAICYAS 1; SATA 32, 82, 134; WYA; YAW

Marivaux, Pierre Carlet de Chamblain de 1688-1763 .... **DC 7; LC 4, 123**
See also DLB 314; GFL Beginnings to 1789; RGWL 2, 3; TWA
Markandaya, Kamala CLC 8, 38
See Taylor, Kamala
See also BYA 13; CN 1, 2, 3, 4, 5, 6, 7; DLB 323; EWL 3
Markfield, Wallace (Arthur) 1926-2002 .... **CLC 8**
See also CA 69-72; 3; CAAS 208; CN 1, 2, 3, 4, 5, 6, 7; DLB 2, 28; DLBY 2002
Markham, Edwin 1852-1940 .... **TCLC 47**
See also CA 160; DLB 54, 186; MAL 5; RGAL 4
Markham, Robert
See Amis, Kingsley
Marks, J.
See Highwater, Jamake (Mamake)
Marks-Highwater, J.
See Highwater, Jamake (Mamake)
Markson, David M. 1927- .... **CLC 67**
See also AMWS 17; CA 49-52; CANR 1, 91, 158; CN 5, 6
Markson, David Merrill
See Markson, David M.
Marlatt, Daphne (Buckle) 1942- .... **CLC 168**
See also CA 25-28R; CANR 17, 39; CN 6, 7; CP 4, 5, 6, 7; CWP; DLB 60; FW
Marley, Bob CLC 17
See Marley, Robert Nesta
Marley, Robert Nesta 1945-1981
See Marley, Bob
See also CA 107; CAAS 103
Marlowe, Christopher 1564-1593 . **DC 1; LC 22, 47, 117; PC 57; WLC 4**
See also BRW 1; BRWR 1; CDBLB Before 1660; DA; DA3; DAB; DAC; DAM DRAM, MST; DFS 1, 5, 13, 21; DLB 62; EXPP; LMFS 1; PFS 22; RGEL 2; TEA; WLIT 3
Marlowe, Stephen 1928-2008 .... **CLC 70**
See Queen, Ellery
See also CA 13-16R; CANR 6, 55; CMW 4; SFW 4
Marmion, Shakerley 1603-1639 .... **LC 89**
See also DLB 58; RGEL 2
Marmontel, Jean-Francois 1723-1799 .. **LC 2**
See also DLB 314
Maron, Monika 1941- .... **CLC 165**
See also CA 201
Marot, Clement c. 1496-1544 .... **LC 133**
See also DLB 327; GFL Beginnings to 1789
Marquand, John P(hillips) 1893-1960 .... **CLC 2, 10**
See also AMW; BPFB 2; CA 85-88; CANR 73; CMW 4; DLB 9, 102; EWL 3; MAL 5; MTCW 2; RGAL 4
Marques, Rene 1919-1979 .. **CLC 96; HLC 2**
See also CA 97-100; CAAS 85-88; CANR 78; DAM MULT; DLB 305; EWL 3; HW 1, 2; LAW; RGSF 2
Marquez, Gabriel Garcia
See Garcia Marquez, Gabriel
Marquis, Don(ald Robert Perry) 1878-1937 .... **TCLC 7**
See also CA 166; CAAE 104; DLB 11, 25; MAL 5; RGAL 4
Marquis de Sade
See Sade, Donatien Alphonse Francois
Marric, J. J.
See Creasey, John
See also MSW
Marryat, Frederick 1792-1848 .... **NCLC 3**
See also DLB 21, 163; RGEL 2; WCH
Marsden, James
See Creasey, John
Marsh, Edward 1872-1953 .... **TCLC 99**
Marsh, (Edith) Ngaio 1895-1982 .. **CLC 7, 53**
See also CA 9-12R; CANR 6, 58; CMW 4; CN 1, 2, 3; CPW; DAM POP; DLB 77; MSW; MTCW 1, 2; RGEL 2; TEA
Marshall, Allen
See Westlake, Donald E.
Marshall, Garry 1934- .... **CLC 17**
See also AAYA 3; CA 111; SATA 60
Marshall, Paule 1929- ..... **BLC 1:3; CLC 27, 72, 253; SSC 3**
See also AFAW 1, 2; AMWS 11; BPFB 2; BW 2, 3; CA 77-80; CANR 25, 73, 129; CN 1, 2, 3, 4, 5, 6, 7; DA3; DAM MULT; DLB 33, 157, 227; EWL 3; LATS 1:2; MAL 5; MTCW 1, 2; MTFW 2005; RGAL 4; SSFS 15
Marshallik
See Zangwill, Israel
Marsten, Richard
See Hunter, Evan
Marston, John 1576-1634 .... **LC 33**
See also BRW 2; DAM DRAM; DLB 58, 172; RGEL 2
Martel, Yann 1963- .... **CLC 192**
See also AAYA 67; CA 146; CANR 114; DLB 326, 334; MTFW 2005
Martens, Adolphe-Adhemar
See Ghelderode, Michel de
Martha, Henry
See Harris, Mark
Marti, Jose PC 76
See Marti (y Perez), Jose (Julian)
See also DLB 290
Marti (y Perez), Jose (Julian) 1853-1895 .... **HLC 2; NCLC 63**
See Marti, Jose
See also DAM MULT; HW 2; LAW; RGWL 2, 3; WLIT 1
Martial c. 40-c. 104 .... **CMLC 35; PC 10**
See also AW 2; CDWLB 1; DLB 211; RGWL 2, 3
Martin, Ken
See Hubbard, L. Ron
Martin, Richard
See Creasey, John
Martin, Steve 1945- .... **CLC 30, 217**
See also AAYA 53; CA 97-100; CANR 30, 100, 140; DFS 19; MTCW 1; MTFW 2005
Martin, Valerie 1948- .... **CLC 89**
See also BEST 90:2; CA 85-88; CANR 49, 89, 165
Martin, Violet Florence 1862-1915 .. **SSC 56; TCLC 51**
Martin, Webber
See Silverberg, Robert
Martindale, Patrick Victor
See White, Patrick (Victor Martindale)
Martin du Gard, Roger 1881-1958 .... **TCLC 24**
See also CAAE 118; CANR 94; DLB 65, 331; EWL 3; GFL 1789 to the Present; RGWL 2, 3
Martineau, Harriet 1802-1876 ...... **NCLC 26, 137**
See also DLB 21, 55, 159, 163, 166, 190; FW; RGEL 2; YABC 2
Martines, Julia
See O'Faolain, Julia
Martinez, Enrique Gonzalez
See Gonzalez Martinez, Enrique
Martinez, Jacinto Benavente y
See Benavente (y Martinez), Jacinto
Martinez de la Rosa, Francisco de Paula 1787-1862 .... **NCLC 102**
See also TWA
Martinez Ruiz, Jose 1873-1967
See Azorin; Ruiz, Jose Martinez
See also CA 93-96; HW 1
Martinez Sierra, Gregorio
See Martinez Sierra, Maria
Martinez Sierra, Gregorio 1881-1947 .... **TCLC 6**
See also CAAE 115; EWL 3
Martinez Sierra, Maria 1874-1974 .. **TCLC 6**
See also CA 250; CAAS 115; EWL 3
Martinsen, Martin
See Follett, Ken
Martinson, Harry (Edmund) 1904-1978 .... **CLC 14**
See also CA 77-80; CANR 34, 130; DLB 259, 331; EWL 3
Martyn, Edward 1859-1923 .... **TCLC 131**
See also CA 179; DLB 10; RGEL 2
Marut, Ret
See Traven, B.
Marut, Robert
See Traven, B.
Marvell, Andrew 1621-1678 .... **LC 4, 43; PC 10, 86; WLC 4**
See also BRW 2; BRWR 2; CDBLB 1660-1789; DA; DAB; DAC; DAM MST, POET; DLB 131; EXPP; PFS 5; RGEL 2; TEA; WP
Marx, Karl (Heinrich) 1818-1883 .... **NCLC 17, 114**
See also DLB 129; LATS 1:1; TWA
Masaoka, Shiki -1902 .... **TCLC 18**
See Masaoka, Tsunenori
See also RGWL 3
Masaoka, Tsunenori 1867-1902
See Masaoka, Shiki
See also CA 191; CAAE 117; TWA
Masefield, John (Edward) 1878-1967 .... **CLC 11, 47; PC 78**
See also CA 19-20; CAAS 25-28R; CANR 33; CAP 2; CDBLB 1890-1914; DAM POET; DLB 10, 19, 153, 160; EWL 3; EXPP; FANT; MTCW 1, 2; PFS 5; RGEL 2; SATA 19
Maso, Carole 1955(?)- .... **CLC 44**
See also CA 170; CANR 148; CN 7; GLL 2; RGAL 4
Mason, Bobbie Ann 1940- ... **CLC 28, 43, 82, 154; SSC 4, 101**
See also AAYA 5, 42; AMWS 8; BPFB 2; CA 53-56; CANR 11, 31, 58, 83, 125, 169; CDALBS; CN 5, 6, 7; CSW; DA3; DLB 173; DLBY 1987; EWL 3; EXPS; INT CANR-31; MAL 5; MTCW 1, 2; MTFW 2005; NFS 4; RGAL 4; RGSF 2; SSFS 3, 8, 20; TCLE 1:2; YAW
Mason, Ernst
See Pohl, Frederik
Mason, Hunni B.
See Sternheim, (William Adolf) Carl
Mason, Lee W.
See Malzberg, Barry N(athaniel)
Mason, Nick 1945- .... **CLC 35**
Mason, Tally
See Derleth, August (William)
Mass, Anna CLC 59
Mass, William
See Gibson, William
Massinger, Philip 1583-1640 .... **LC 70**
See also BRWS 11; DLB 58; RGEL 2
Master Lao
See Lao Tzu
Masters, Edgar Lee 1868-1950 ...... **PC 1, 36; TCLC 2, 25; WLCS**
See also AMWS 1; CA 133; CAAE 104; CDALB 1865-1917; DA; DAC; DAM MST, POET; DLB 54; EWL 3; EXPP; MAL 5; MTCW 1, 2; MTFW 2005; RGAL 4; TUS; WP

Author Index

McCourt, Frank 1930- .... **CLC 109**
See also AAYA 61; AMWS 12; CA 157; CANR 97, 138; MTFW 2005; NCFS 1
McCourt, James 1941- .... **CLC 5**
See also CA 57-60; CANR 98, 152
McCourt, Malachy 1931- .... **CLC 119**
See also SATA 126
McCoy, Horace (Stanley) 1897-1955 .... **TCLC 28**
See also AMWS 13; CA 155; CAAE 108; CMW 4; DLB 9
McCrae, John 1872-1918 .... **TCLC 12**
See also CAAE 109; DLB 92; PFS 5
McCreigh, James
See Pohl, Frederik
McCullers, (Lula) Carson (Smith) 1917-1967 .... **CLC 1, 4, 10, 12, 48, 100; SSC 9, 24, 99; TCLC 155; WLC 4**
See also AAYA 21; AMW; AMWC 2; BPFB 2; CA 5-8R; CAAS 25-28R; CABS 1, 3; CANR 18, 132; CDALB 1941-1968; DA; DA3; DAB; DAC; DAM MST, NOV; DFS 5, 18; DLB 2, 7, 173, 228; EWL 3; EXPS; FW; GLL 1; LAIT 3, 4; MAL 5; MBL; MTCW 1, 2; MTFW 2005; NFS 6, 13; RGAL 4; RGSF 2; SATA 27; SSFS 5; TUS; YAW
McCulloch, John Tyler
See Burroughs, Edgar Rice
McCullough, Colleen 1937- ...... **CLC 27, 107**
See also AAYA 36; BPFB 2; CA 81-84; CANR 17, 46, 67, 98, 139; CPW; DA3; DAM NOV, POP; MTCW 1, 2; MTFW 2005; RHW
McCunn, Ruthanne Lum 1946- .... **AAL**
See also CA 119; CANR 43, 96; DLB 312; LAIT 2; SATA 63
McDermott, Alice 1953- .... **CLC 90**
See also CA 109; CANR 40, 90, 126; CN 7; DLB 292; MTFW 2005; NFS 23
McElroy, Joseph 1930- .... **CLC 5, 47**
See also CA 17-20R; CANR 149; CN 3, 4, 5, 6, 7
McElroy, Joseph Prince
See McElroy, Joseph
McEwan, Ian 1948- ... **CLC 13, 66, 169; SSC 106**
See also BEST 90:4; BRWS 4; CA 61-64; CANR 14, 41, 69, 87, 132; CN 3, 4, 5, 6, 7; DAM NOV; DLB 14, 194, 319, 326; HGG; MTCW 1, 2; MTFW 2005; RGSF 2; SUFW 2; TEA
McFadden, David 1940- .... **CLC 48**
See also CA 104; CP 1, 2, 3, 4, 5, 6, 7; DLB 60; INT CA-104
McFarland, Dennis 1950- .... **CLC 65**
See also CA 165; CANR 110
McGahern, John 1934-2006 .... **CLC 5, 9, 48, 156; SSC 17**
See also CA 17-20R; CAAS 249; CANR 29, 68, 113; CN 1, 2, 3, 4, 5, 6, 7; DLB 14, 231, 319; MTCW 1
McGinley, Patrick (Anthony) 1937- . **CLC 41**
See also CA 127; CAAE 120; CANR 56; INT CA-127
McGinley, Phyllis 1905-1978 .... **CLC 14**
See also CA 9-12R; CAAS 77-80; CANR 19; CP 1, 2; CWRI 5; DLB 11, 48; MAL 5; PFS 9, 13; SATA 2, 44; SATA-Obit 24
McGinniss, Joe 1942- .... **CLC 32**
See also AITN 2; BEST 89:2; CA 25-28R; CANR 26, 70, 152; CPW; DLB 185; INT CANR-26
McGivern, Maureen Daly
See Daly, Maureen
McGivern, Maureen Patricia Daly
See Daly, Maureen
McGrath, Patrick 1950- .... **CLC 55**
See also CA 136; CANR 65, 148; CN 5, 6, 7; DLB 231; HGG; SUFW 2
McGrath, Thomas (Matthew) 1916-1990 .... **CLC 28, 59**
See also AMWS 10; CA 9-12R; CAAS 132; CANR 6, 33, 95; CP 1, 2, 3, 4, 5; DAM POET; MAL 5; MTCW 1; SATA 41; SATA-Obit 66
McGuane, Thomas 1939- .. **CLC 3, 7, 18, 45, 127**
See also AITN 2; BPFB 2; CA 49-52; CANR 5, 24, 49, 94, 164; CN 2, 3, 4, 5, 6, 7; DLB 2, 212; DLBY 1980; EWL 3; INT CANR-24; MAL 5; MTCW 1; MTFW 2005; TCWW 1, 2
McGuane, Thomas Francis III
See McGuane, Thomas
McGuckian, Medbh 1950- .... **CLC 48, 174; PC 27**
See also BRWS 5; CA 143; CP 4, 5, 6, 7; CWP; DAM POET; DLB 40
McHale, Tom 1942(?)-1982 .... **CLC 3, 5**
See also AITN 1; CA 77-80; CAAS 106; CN 1, 2, 3
McHugh, Heather 1948- .... **PC 61**
See also CA 69-72; CANR 11, 28, 55, 92; CP 4, 5, 6, 7; CWP; PFS 24
McIlvanney, William 1936- .... **CLC 42**
See also CA 25-28R; CANR 61; CMW 4; DLB 14, 207
McIlwraith, Maureen Mollie Hunter
See Hunter, Mollie
See also SATA 2
McInerney, Jay 1955- .... **CLC 34, 112**
See also AAYA 18; BPFB 2; CA 123; CAAE 116; CANR 45, 68, 116; CN 5, 6, 7; CPW; DA3; DAM POP; DLB 292; INT CA-123; MAL 5; MTCW 2; MTFW 2005
McIntyre, Vonda N. 1948- .... **CLC 18**
See also CA 81-84; CANR 17, 34, 69; MTCW 1; SFW 4; YAW
McIntyre, Vonda Neel
See McIntyre, Vonda N.
McKay, Claude BLC 1:3; HR 1:3; PC 2; TCLC 7, 41; WLC 4
See McKay, Festus Claudius
See also AFAW 1, 2; AMWS 10; DAB; DLB 4, 45, 51, 117; EWL 3; EXPP; GLL 2; LAIT 3; LMFS 2; MAL 5; PAB; PFS 4; RGAL 4; WP
McKay, Festus Claudius 1889-1948
See McKay, Claude
See also BW 1, 3; CA 124; CAAE 104; CANR 73; DA; DAC; DAM MST, MULT, NOV, POET; MTCW 1, 2; MTFW 2005; TUS
McKuen, Rod 1933- .... **CLC 1, 3**
See also AITN 1; CA 41-44R; CANR 40; CP 1
McLoughlin, R. B.
See Mencken, H(enry) L(ouis)
McLuhan, (Herbert) Marshall 1911-1980 .... **CLC 37, 83**
See also CA 9-12R; CAAS 102; CANR 12, 34, 61; DLB 88; INT CANR-12; MTCW 1, 2; MTFW 2005
McManus, Declan Patrick Aloysius
See Costello, Elvis
McMillan, Terry 1951- .. **BLCS; CLC 50, 61, 112**
See also AAYA 21; AMWS 13; BPFB 2; BW 2, 3; CA 140; CANR 60, 104, 131; CN 7; CPW; DA3; DAM MULT, NOV, POP; MAL 5; MTCW 2; MTFW 2005; RGAL 4; YAW
McMurtry, Larry 1936- .... **CLC 2, 3, 7, 11, 27, 44, 127, 250**
See also AAYA 15; AITN 2; AMWS 5; BEST 89:2; BPFB 2; CA 5-8R; CANR 19, 43, 64, 103, 170; CDALB 1968-1988; CN 2, 3, 4, 5, 6, 7; CPW; CSW; DA3; DAM NOV, POP; DLB 2, 143, 256; DLBY 1980, 1987; EWL 3; MAL 5; MTCW 1, 2; MTFW 2005; RGAL 4; TCWW 1, 2
McMurtry, Larry Jeff
See McMurtry, Larry
McNally, Terrence 1939- ... **CLC 4, 7, 41, 91, 252; DC 27**
See also AAYA 62; AMWS 13; CA 45-48; CAD; CANR 2, 56, 116; CD 5, 6; DA3; DAM DRAM; DFS 16, 19; DLB 7, 249; EWL 3; GLL 1; MTCW 2; MTFW 2005
McNally, Thomas Michael
See McNally, T.M.
McNally, T.M. 1961- .... **CLC 82**
See also CA 246
McNamer, Deirdre 1950- .... **CLC 70**
See also CA 188; CANR 163
McNeal, Tom CLC 119
See also CA 252
McNeile, Herman Cyril 1888-1937
See Sapper
See also CA 184; CMW 4; DLB 77
McNickle, (William) D'Arcy 1904-1977 .... **CLC 89; NNAL**
See also CA 9-12R; CAAS 85-88; CANR 5, 45; DAM MULT; DLB 175, 212; RGAL 4; SATA-Obit 22; TCWW 1, 2
McPhee, John 1931- .... **CLC 36**
See also AAYA 61; AMWS 3; ANW; BEST 90:1; CA 65-68; CANR 20, 46, 64, 69, 121, 165; CPW; DLB 185, 275; MTCW 1, 2; MTFW 2005; TUS
McPhee, John Angus
See McPhee, John
McPherson, James Alan 1943- . **BLCS; CLC 19, 77; SSC 95**
See also BW 1, 3; CA 25-28R; 17; CANR 24, 74, 140; CN 3, 4, 5, 6; CSW; DLB 38, 244; EWL 3; MTCW 1, 2; MTFW 2005; RGAL 4; RGSF 2; SSFS 23
McPherson, William (Alexander) 1933- .... **CLC 34**
See also CA 69-72; CANR 28; INT CANR-28
McTaggart, J. McT. Ellis
See McTaggart, John McTaggart Ellis
McTaggart, John McTaggart Ellis 1866-1925 .... **TCLC 105**
See also CAAE 120; DLB 262
Mda, Zakes 1948- .... **BLC 2:3**
See also CA 205; CANR 151; CD 5, 6; DLB 225
Mead, George Herbert 1863-1931 . **TCLC 89**
See also CA 212; DLB 270
Mead, Margaret 1901-1978 .... **CLC 37**
See also AITN 1; CA 1-4R; CAAS 81-84; CANR 4; DA3; FW; MTCW 1, 2; SATA-Obit 20
Meaker, Marijane 1927-
See Kerr, M. E.
See also CA 107; CANR 37, 63, 145; INT CA-107; JRDA; MAICYA 1, 2; MAICYAS 1; MTCW 1; SATA 20, 61, 99, 160; SATA-Essay 111; YAW
Mechthild von Magdeburg c. 1207-c. 1282 .... **CMLC 91**
See also DLB 138
Medoff, Mark (Howard) 1940- .... **CLC 6, 23**
See also AITN 1; CA 53-56; CAD; CANR 5; CD 5, 6; DAM DRAM; DFS 4; DLB 7; INT CANR-5

Miles, Josephine (Louise) 1911-1985 .... **CLC 1, 2, 14, 34, 39**
See also CA 1-4R; CAAS 116; CANR 2, 55; CP 1, 2, 3, 4; DAM POET; DLB 48; MAL 5; TCLE 1:2

Militant
See Sandburg, Carl (August)

Mill, Harriet (Hardy) Taylor 1807-1858 .... **NCLC 102**
See also FW

Mill, John Stuart 1806-1873 ... **NCLC 11, 58, 179**
See also CDBLB 1832-1890; DLB 55, 190, 262; FW 1; RGEL 2; TEA

Millar, Kenneth 1915-1983 .... **CLC 14**
See Macdonald, Ross
See also CA 9-12R; CAAS 110; CANR 16, 63, 107; CMW 4; CPW; DA3; DAM POP; DLB 2, 226; DLBD 6; DLBY 1983; MTCW 1, 2; MTFW 2005

Millay, E. Vincent
See Millay, Edna St. Vincent

Millay, Edna St. Vincent 1892-1950 ..... **PC 6, 61; TCLC 4, 49, 169; WLCS**
See Boyd, Nancy
See also AMW; CA 130; CAAE 104; CDALB 1917-1929; DA; DA3; DAB; DAC; DAM MST, POET; DLB 45, 249; EWL 3; EXPP; FL 1:6; MAL 5; MBL; MTCW 1, 2; MTFW 2005; PAB; PFS 3, 17; RGAL 4; TUS; WP

Miller, Arthur 1915-2005 ..... **CLC 1, 2, 6, 10, 15, 26, 47, 78, 179; DC 1, 31; WLC 4**
See also AAYA 15; AITN 1; AMW; AMWC 1; CA 1-4R; CAAS 236; CABS 3; CAD; CANR 2, 30, 54, 76, 132; CD 5, 6; CDALB 1941-1968; DA; DA3; DAB; DAC; DAM DRAM, MST; DFS 1, 3, 8; DLB 7, 266; EWL 3; LAIT 1, 4; LATS 1:2; MAL 5; MTCW 1, 2; MTFW 2005; RGAL 4; RGHL; TUS; WYAS 1

Miller, Henry (Valentine) 1891-1980 .... **CLC 1, 2, 4, 9, 14, 43, 84; WLC 4**
See also AMW; BPFB 2; CA 9-12R; CAAS 97-100; CANR 33, 64; CDALB 1929-1941; CN 1, 2; DA; DA3; DAB; DAC; DAM MST, NOV; DLB 4, 9; DLBY 1980; EWL 3; MAL 5; MTCW 1, 2; MTFW 2005; RGAL 4; TUS

Miller, Hugh 1802-1856 .... **NCLC 143**
See also DLB 190

Miller, Jason 1939(?)-2001 .... **CLC 2**
See also AITN 1; CA 73-76; CAAS 197; CAD; CANR 130; DFS 12; DLB 7

Miller, Sue 1943- .... **CLC 44**
See also AMWS 12; BEST 90:3; CA 139; CANR 59, 91, 128; DA3; DAM POP; DLB 143

Miller, Walter M(ichael, Jr.) 1923-1996 .... **CLC 4, 30**
See also BPFB 2; CA 85-88; CANR 108; DLB 8; SCFW 1, 2; SFW 4

Millett, Kate 1934- .... **CLC 67**
See also AITN 1; CA 73-76; CANR 32, 53, 76, 110; DA3; DLB 246; FW; GLL 1; MTCW 1, 2; MTFW 2005

Millhauser, Steven 1943- ... **CLC 21, 54, 109; SSC 57**
See also AAYA 76; CA 111; CAAE 110; CANR 63, 114, 133; CN 6, 7; DA3; DLB 2; FANT; INT CA-111; MAL 5; MTCW 2; MTFW 2005

Millhauser, Steven Lewis
See Millhauser, Steven

Millin, Sarah Gertrude 1889-1968 ... **CLC 49**
See also CA 102; CAAS 93-96; DLB 225; EWL 3

Milne, A. A. 1882-1956 .... **TCLC 6, 88**
See also BRWS 5; CA 133; CAAE 104; CLR 1, 26, 108; CMW 4; CWRI 5; DA3; DAB; DAC; DAM MST; DLB 10, 77, 100, 160; FANT; MAICYA 1, 2; MTCW 1, 2; MTFW 2005; RGEL 2; SATA 100; WCH; YABC 1

Milne, Alan Alexander
See Milne, A. A.

Milner, Ron(ald) 1938-2004 .. **BLC 1:3; CLC 56**
See also AITN 1; BW 1; CA 73-76; CAAS 230; CAD; CANR 24, 81; CD 5, 6; DAM MULT; DLB 38; MAL 5; MTCW 1

Milnes, Richard Monckton 1809-1885 .... **NCLC 61**
See also DLB 32, 184

Milosz, Czeslaw 1911-2004 .... **CLC 5, 11, 22, 31, 56, 82, 253; PC 8; WLCS**
See also AAYA 62; CA 81-84; CAAS 230; CANR 23, 51, 91, 126; CDWLB 4; CWW 2; DA3; DAM MST, POET; DLB 215, 331; EW 13; EWL 3; MTCW 1, 2; MTFW 2005; PFS 16; RGHL; RGWL 2, 3

Milton, John 1608-1674 ..... **LC 9, 43, 92; PC 19, 29; WLC 4**
See also AAYA 65; BRW 2; BRWR 2; CDBLB 1660-1789; DA; DA3; DAB; DAC; DAM MST, POET; DLB 131, 151, 281; EFS 1; EXPP; LAIT 1; PAB; PFS 3, 17; RGEL 2; TEA; WLIT 3; WP

Min, Anchee 1957- .... **CLC 86**
See also CA 146; CANR 94, 137; MTFW 2005

Minehaha, Cornelius
See Wedekind, Frank

Miner, Valerie 1947- .... **CLC 40**
See also CA 97-100; CANR 59; FW; GLL 2

Minimo, Duca
See D'Annunzio, Gabriele

Minot, Susan (Anderson) 1956- ...... **CLC 44, 159**
See also AMWS 6; CA 134; CANR 118; CN 6, 7

Minus, Ed 1938- .... **CLC 39**
See also CA 185

Mirabai 1498(?)-1550(?) .... **LC 143; PC 48**
See also PFS 24

Miranda, Javier
See Bioy Casares, Adolfo
See also CWW 2

Mirbeau, Octave 1848-1917 .... **TCLC 55**
See also CA 216; DLB 123, 192; GFL 1789 to the Present

Mirikitani, Janice 1942- .... **AAL**
See also CA 211; DLB 312; RGAL 4

Mirk, John (?)-c. 1414 .... **LC 105**
See also DLB 146

Miro (Ferrer), Gabriel (Francisco Victor) 1879-1930 .... **TCLC 5**
See also CA 185; CAAE 104; DLB 322; EWL 3

Misharin, Alexandr CLC 59

Mishima, Yukio CLC 2, 4, 6, 9, 27; DC 1; SSC 4; TCLC 161; WLC 4
See Hiraoka, Kimitake
See also AAYA 50; BPFB 2; GLL 1; MJW; RGSF 2; RGWL 2, 3; SSFS 5, 12

Mistral, Frederic 1830-1914 .... **TCLC 51**
See also CA 213; CAAE 122; DLB 331; GFL 1789 to the Present

Mistral, Gabriela
See Godoy Alcayaga, Lucila
See also DLB 283, 331; DNFS 1; EWL 3; LAW; RGWL 2, 3; WP

Mistry, Rohinton 1952- ... **CLC 71, 196; SSC 73**
See also BRWS 10; CA 141; CANR 86, 114; CCA 1; CN 6, 7; DAC; DLB 334; SSFS 6

Mitchell, Clyde
See Ellison, Harlan

Mitchell, Emerson Blackhorse Barney 1945- .... **NNAL**
See also CA 45-48

Mitchell, James Leslie 1901-1935
See Gibbon, Lewis Grassic
See also CA 188; CAAE 104; DLB 15

Mitchell, Joni 1943- .... **CLC 12**
See also CA 112; CCA 1

Mitchell, Joseph (Quincy) 1908-1996 .... **CLC 98**
See also CA 77-80; CAAS 152; CANR 69; CN 1, 2, 3, 4, 5, 6; CSW; DLB 185; DLBY 1996

Mitchell, Margaret (Munnerlyn) 1900-1949 .... **TCLC 11, 170**
See also AAYA 23; BPFB 2; BYA 1; CA 125; CAAE 109; CANR 55, 94; CDALBS; DA3; DAM NOV, POP; DLB 9; LAIT 2; MAL 5; MTCW 1, 2; MTFW 2005; NFS 9; RGAL 4; RHW; TUS; WYAS 1; YAW

Mitchell, Peggy
See Mitchell, Margaret (Munnerlyn)

Mitchell, S(ilas) Weir 1829-1914 .... **TCLC 36**
See also CA 165; DLB 202; RGAL 4

Mitchell, W(illiam) O(rmond) 1914-1998 .... **CLC 25**
See also CA 77-80; CAAS 165; CANR 15, 43; CN 1, 2, 3, 4, 5, 6; DAC; DAM MST; DLB 88; TCLE 1:2

Mitchell, William (Lendrum) 1879-1936 .... **TCLC 81**
See also CA 213

Mitford, Mary Russell 1787-1855 ... **NCLC 4**
See also DLB 110, 116; RGEL 2

Mitford, Nancy 1904-1973 .... **CLC 44**
See also BRWS 10; CA 9-12R; CN 1; DLB 191; RGEL 2

Miyamoto, (Chujo) Yuriko 1899-1951 .... **TCLC 37**
See Miyamoto Yuriko
See also CA 170, 174

Miyamoto Yuriko
See Miyamoto, (Chujo) Yuriko
See also DLB 180

Miyazawa, Kenji 1896-1933 .... **TCLC 76**
See Miyazawa Kenji
See also CA 157; RGWL 3

Miyazawa Kenji
See Miyazawa, Kenji
See also EWL 3

Mizoguchi, Kenji 1898-1956 .... **TCLC 72**
See also CA 167

Mo, Timothy (Peter) 1950- .... **CLC 46, 134**
See also CA 117; CANR 128; CN 5, 6, 7; DLB 194; MTCW 1; WLIT 4; WWE 1

Modarressi, Taghi (M.) 1931-1997 ... **CLC 44**
See also CA 134; CAAE 121; INT CA-134

Modiano, Patrick (Jean) 1945- .... **CLC 18, 218**
See also CA 85-88; CANR 17, 40, 115; CWW 2; DLB 83, 299; EWL 3; RGHL

Mofolo, Thomas (Mokopu) 1875(?)-1948 .... **BLC 1:3; TCLC 22**
See also AFW; CA 153; CAAE 121; CANR 83; DAM MULT; DLB 225; EWL 3; MTCW 2; MTFW 2005; WLIT 2

Mohr, Nicholasa 1938- .... **CLC 12; HLC 2**
See also AAYA 8, 46; CA 49-52; CANR 1, 32, 64; CLR 22; DAM MULT; DLB 145; HW 1, 2; JRDA; LAIT 5; LLW; MAICYA 2; MAICYAS 1; RGAL 4; SAAS 8; SATA 8, 97; SATA-Essay 113; WYA; YAW

Moi, Toril 1953- .... **CLC 172**
See also CA 154; CANR 102; FW

Mojtabai, A(nn) G(race) 1938- ..... **CLC 5, 9, 15, 29**
See also CA 85-88; CANR 88

Moliere 1622-1673 ..... **DC 13; LC 10, 28, 64, 125, 127; WLC 4**
See also DA; DA3; DAB; DAC; DAM DRAM, MST; DFS 13, 18, 20; DLB 268; EW 3; GFL Beginnings to 1789; LATS 1:1; RGWL 2, 3; TWA

Molin, Charles
See Mayne, William (James Carter)

Molnar, Ferenc 1878-1952 .... **TCLC 20**
See also CA 153; CAAE 109; CANR 83; CDWLB 4; DAM DRAM; DLB 215; EWL 3; RGWL 2, 3

Momaday, N. Scott 1934- ...... **CLC 2, 19, 85, 95, 160; NNAL; PC 25; WLCS**
See also AAYA 11, 64; AMWS 4; ANW; BPFB 2; BYA 12; CA 25-28R; CANR 14, 34, 68, 134; CDALBS; CN 2, 3, 4, 5, 6, 7; CPW; DA; DA3; DAB; DAC; DAM MST, MULT, NOV, POP; DLB 143, 175, 256; EWL 3; EXPP; INT CANR-14; LAIT 4; LATS 1:2; MAL 5; MTCW 1, 2; MTFW 2005; NFS 10; PFS 2, 11; RGAL 4; SATA 48; SATA-Brief 30; TCWW 1, 2; WP; YAW

Monette, Paul 1945-1995 .... **CLC 82**
See also AMWS 10; CA 139; CAAS 147; CN 6; GLL 1

Monroe, Harriet 1860-1936 .... **TCLC 12**
See also CA 204; CAAE 109; DLB 54, 91

Monroe, Lyle
See Heinlein, Robert A.

Montagu, Elizabeth 1720-1800 .... **NCLC 7, 117**
See also FW

Montagu, Mary (Pierrepont) Wortley 1689-1762 .... **LC 9, 57; PC 16**
See also DLB 95, 101; FL 1:1; RGEL 2

Montagu, W. H.
See Coleridge, Samuel Taylor

Montague, John (Patrick) 1929- ..... **CLC 13, 46**
See also CA 9-12R; CANR 9, 69, 121; CP 1, 2, 3, 4, 5, 6, 7; DLB 40; EWL 3; MTCW 1; PFS 12; RGEL 2; TCLE 1:2

Montaigne, Michel (Eyquem) de 1533-1592 .... **LC 8, 105; WLC 4**
See also DA; DAB; DAC; DAM MST; DLB 327; EW 2; GFL Beginnings to 1789; LMFS 1; RGWL 2, 3; TWA

Montale, Eugenio 1896-1981 ... **CLC 7, 9, 18; PC 13**
See also CA 17-20R; CAAS 104; CANR 30; DLB 114, 331; EW 11; EWL 3; MTCW 1; PFS 22; RGWL 2, 3; TWA; WLIT 7

Montesquieu, Charles-Louis de Secondat 1689-1755 .... **LC 7, 69**
See also DLB 314; EW 3; GFL Beginnings to 1789; TWA

Montessori, Maria 1870-1952 ...... **TCLC 103**
See also CA 147; CAAE 115

Montgomery, (Robert) Bruce 1921(?)-1978
See Crispin, Edmund
See also CA 179; CAAS 104; CMW 4

Montgomery, L(ucy) M(aud) 1874-1942 .... **TCLC 51, 140**
See also AAYA 12; BYA 1; CA 137; CAAE 108; CLR 8, 91; DA3; DAC; DAM MST; DLB 92; DLBD 14; JRDA; MAICYA 1, 2; MTCW 2; MTFW 2005; RGEL 2; SATA 100; TWA; WCH; WYA; YABC 1

Montgomery, Marion, Jr. 1925- .... **CLC 7**
See also AITN 1; CA 1-4R; CANR 3, 48, 162; CSW; DLB 6

Montgomery, Marion H. 1925-
See Montgomery, Marion, Jr.

Montgomery, Max
See Davenport, Guy (Mattison, Jr.)

Montherlant, Henry (Milon) de 1896-1972 .... **CLC 8, 19**
See also CA 85-88; CAAS 37-40R; DAM DRAM; DLB 72, 321; EW 11; EWL 3; GFL 1789 to the Present; MTCW 1

Monty Python
See Chapman, Graham; Cleese, John (Marwood); Gilliam, Terry; Idle, Eric; Jones, Terence Graham Parry; Palin, Michael (Edward)
See also AAYA 7

Moodie, Susanna (Strickland) 1803-1885 .... **NCLC 14, 113**
See also DLB 99

Moody, Hiram 1961-
See Moody, Rick
See also CA 138; CANR 64, 112; MTFW 2005

Moody, Minerva
See Alcott, Louisa May

Moody, Rick CLC 147
See Moody, Hiram

Moody, William Vaughan 1869-1910 .... **TCLC 105**
See also CA 178; CAAE 110; DLB 7, 54; MAL 5; RGAL 4

Mooney, Edward 1951-
See Mooney, Ted
See also CA 130

Mooney, Ted CLC 25
See Mooney, Edward

Moorcock, Michael 1939- ...... **CLC 5, 27, 58, 236**
See Bradbury, Edward P.
See also AAYA 26; CA 45-48; 5; CANR 2, 17, 38, 64, 122; CN 5, 6, 7; DLB 14, 231, 261, 319; FANT; MTCW 1, 2; MTFW 2005; SATA 93, 166; SCFW 1, 2; SFW 4; SUFW 1, 2

Moorcock, Michael John
See Moorcock, Michael

Moorcock, Michael John
See Moorcock, Michael

Moore, Alan 1953- .... **CLC 230**
See also AAYA 51; CA 204; CANR 138; DLB 261; MTFW 2005; SFW 4

Moore, Brian 1921-1999 ... **CLC 1, 3, 5, 7, 8, 19, 32, 90**
See Bryan, Michael
See also BRWS 9; CA 1-4R; CAAS 174; CANR 1, 25, 42, 63; CCA 1; CN 1, 2, 3, 4, 5, 6; DAB; DAC; DAM MST; DLB 251; EWL 3; FANT; MTCW 1, 2; MTFW 2005; RGEL 2

Moore, Edward
See Muir, Edwin
See also RGEL 2

Moore, G. E. 1873-1958 .... **TCLC 89**
See also DLB 262

Moore, George Augustus 1852-1933 .... **SSC 19; TCLC 7**
See also BRW 6; CA 177; CAAE 104; DLB 10, 18, 57, 135; EWL 3; RGEL 2; RGSF 2

Moore, Lorrie CLC 39, 45, 68
See Moore, Marie Lorena
See also AMWS 10; CN 5, 6, 7; DLB 234; SSFS 19

Moore, Marianne (Craig) 1887-1972 .... **CLC 1, 2, 4, 8, 10, 13, 19, 47; PC 4, 49; WLCS**
See also AMW; CA 1-4R; CAAS 33-36R; CANR 3, 61; CDALB 1929-1941; CP 1; DA; DA3; DAB; DAC; DAM MST, POET; DLB 45; DLBD 7; EWL 3; EXPP; FL 1:6; MAL 5; MBL; MTCW 1, 2; MTFW 2005; PAB; PFS 14, 17; RGAL 4; SATA 20; TUS; WP

Moore, Marie Lorena 1957- .... **CLC 165**
See Moore, Lorrie
See also CA 116; CANR 39, 83, 139; DLB 234; MTFW 2005

Moore, Michael 1954- .... **CLC 218**
See also AAYA 53; CA 166; CANR 150

Moore, Thomas 1779-1852 .... **NCLC 6, 110**
See also DLB 96, 144; RGEL 2

Moorhouse, Frank 1938- .... **SSC 40**
See also CA 118; CANR 92; CN 3, 4, 5, 6, 7; DLB 289; RGSF 2

Mora, Pat 1942- .... **HLC 2**
See also AMWS 13; CA 129; CANR 57, 81, 112, 171; CLR 58; DAM MULT; DLB 209; HW 1, 2; LLW; MAICYA 2; MTFW 2005; SATA 92, 134, 186

Moraga, Cherrie 1952- ... **CLC 126, 250; DC 22**
See also CA 131; CANR 66, 154; DAM MULT; DLB 82, 249; FW; GLL 1; HW 1, 2; LLW

Morand, Paul 1888-1976 .... **CLC 41; SSC 22**
See also CA 184; CAAS 69-72; DLB 65; EWL 3

Morante, Elsa 1918-1985 .... **CLC 8, 47**
See also CA 85-88; CAAS 117; CANR 35; DLB 177; EWL 3; MTCW 1, 2; MTFW 2005; RGHL; RGWL 2, 3; WLIT 7

Moravia, Alberto CLC 2, 7, 11, 27, 46; SSC 26
See Pincherle, Alberto
See also DLB 177; EW 12; EWL 3; MTCW 2; RGSF 2; RGWL 2, 3; WLIT 7

More, Hannah 1745-1833 ...... **NCLC 27, 141**
See also DLB 107, 109, 116, 158; RGEL 2

More, Henry 1614-1687 .... **LC 9**
See also DLB 126, 252

More, Sir Thomas 1478(?)-1535 ... **LC 10, 32, 140**
See also BRWC 1; BRWS 7; DLB 136, 281; LMFS 1; RGEL 2; TEA

Moreas, Jean TCLC 18
See Papadiamantopoulos, Johannes
See also GFL 1789 to the Present

Moreton, Andrew Esq.
See Defoe, Daniel

Morgan, Berry 1919-2002 .... **CLC 6**
See also CA 49-52; CAAS 208; DLB 6

Morgan, Claire
See Highsmith, Patricia
See also GLL 1

Morgan, Edwin 1920- .... **CLC 31**
See also BRWS 9; CA 5-8R; CANR 3, 43, 90; CP 1, 2, 3, 4, 5, 6, 7; DLB 27

Morgan, Edwin George
See Morgan, Edwin

Morgan, (George) Frederick 1922-2004 .... **CLC 23**
See also CA 17-20R; CAAS 224; CANR 21, 144; CP 2, 3, 4, 5, 6, 7

Morgan, Harriet
See Mencken, H(enry) L(ouis)

Morgan, Jane
See Cooper, James Fenimore

Morgan, Janet 1945- .... **CLC 39**
See also CA 65-68

Morgan, Lady 1776(?)-1859 .... **NCLC 29**
See also DLB 116, 158; RGEL 2

Ohiyesa
See Eastman, Charles A(lexander)
Okada, John 1923-1971 .... **AAL**
See also BYA 14; CA 212; DLB 312; NFS 25
Okigbo, Christopher 1930-1967 ..... **BLC 1:3; CLC 25, 84; PC 7; TCLC 171**
See also AFW; BW 1, 3; CA 77-80; CANR 74; CDWLB 3; DAM MULT, POET; DLB 125; EWL 3; MTCW 1, 2; MTFW 2005; RGEL 2
Okigbo, Christopher Ifenayichukwu
See Okigbo, Christopher
Okri, Ben 1959- .... **BLC 2:3; CLC 87, 223**
See also AFW; BRWS 5; BW 2, 3; CA 138; CAAE 130; CANR 65, 128; CN 5, 6, 7; DLB 157, 231, 319, 326; EWL 3; INT CA-138; MTCW 2; MTFW 2005; RGSF 2; SSFS 20; WLIT 2; WWE 1
Olds, Sharon 1942- .. **CLC 32, 39, 85; PC 22**
See also AMWS 10; CA 101; CANR 18, 41, 66, 98, 135; CP 5, 6, 7; CPW; CWP; DAM POET; DLB 120; MAL 5; MTCW 2; MTFW 2005; PFS 17
Oldstyle, Jonathan
See Irving, Washington
Olesha, Iurii
See Olesha, Yuri (Karlovich)
See also RGWL 2
Olesha, Iurii Karlovich
See Olesha, Yuri (Karlovich)
See also DLB 272
Olesha, Yuri (Karlovich) 1899-1960 . **CLC 8; SSC 69; TCLC 136**
See Olesha, Iurii; Olesha, Iurii Karlovich; Olesha, Yury Karlovich
See also CA 85-88; EW 11; RGWL 3
Olesha, Yury Karlovich
See Olesha, Yuri (Karlovich)
See also EWL 3
Oliphant, Mrs.
See Oliphant, Margaret (Oliphant Wilson)
See also SUFW
Oliphant, Laurence 1829(?)-1888 .. **NCLC 47**
See also DLB 18, 166
Oliphant, Margaret (Oliphant Wilson) 1828-1897 .... **NCLC 11, 61; SSC 25**
See Oliphant, Mrs.
See also BRWS 10; DLB 18, 159, 190; HGG; RGEL 2; RGSF 2
Oliver, Mary 1935- ... **CLC 19, 34, 98; PC 75**
See also AMWS 7; CA 21-24R; CANR 9, 43, 84, 92, 138; CP 4, 5, 6, 7; CWP; DLB 5, 193; EWL 3; MTFW 2005; PFS 15
Olivier, Laurence (Kerr) 1907-1989 . **CLC 20**
See also CA 150; CAAE 111; CAAS 129
Olsen, Tillie 1912-2007 .... **CLC 4, 13, 114; SSC 11, 103**
See also AAYA 51; AMWS 13; BYA 11; CA 1-4R; CAAS 256; CANR 1, 43, 74, 132; CDALBS; CN 2, 3, 4, 5, 6, 7; DA; DA3; DAB; DAC; DAM MST; DLB 28, 206; DLBY 1980; EWL 3; EXPS; FW; MAL 5; MTCW 1, 2; MTFW 2005; RGAL 4; RGSF 2; SSFS 1; TCLE 1:2; TCWW 2; TUS
Olson, Charles (John) 1910-1970 .. **CLC 1, 2, 5, 6, 9, 11, 29; PC 19**
See also AMWS 2; CA 13-16; CAAS 25-28R; CABS 2; CANR 35, 61; CAP 1; CP 1; DAM POET; DLB 5, 16, 193; EWL 3; MAL 5; MTCW 1, 2; RGAL 4; WP
Olson, Toby 1937- .... **CLC 28**
See also CA 65-68; 11; CANR 9, 31, 84; CP 3, 4, 5, 6, 7
Olyesha, Yuri
See Olesha, Yuri (Karlovich)
Olympiodorus of Thebes c. 375-c. 430 .... **CMLC 59**
Omar Khayyam
See Khayyam, Omar
See also RGWL 2, 3
Ondaatje, Michael 1943- ..... **CLC 14, 29, 51, 76, 180; PC 28**
See also AAYA 66; CA 77-80; CANR 42, 74, 109, 133, 172; CN 5, 6, 7; CP 1, 2, 3, 4, 5, 6, 7; DA3; DAB; DAC; DAM MST; DLB 60, 323, 326; EWL 3; LATS 1:2; LMFS 2; MTCW 2; MTFW 2005; NFS 23; PFS 8, 19; TCLE 1:2; TWA; WWE 1
Ondaatje, Philip Michael
See Ondaatje, Michael
Oneal, Elizabeth 1934-
See Oneal, Zibby
See also CA 106; CANR 28, 84; MAICYA 1, 2; SATA 30, 82; YAW
Oneal, Zibby CLC 30
See Oneal, Elizabeth
See also AAYA 5, 41; BYA 13; CLR 13; JRDA; WYA
O'Neill, Eugene (Gladstone) 1888-1953 ... **DC 20; TCLC 1, 6, 27, 49; WLC 4**
See also AAYA 54; AITN 1; AMW; AMWC 1; CA 132; CAAE 110; CAD; CANR 131; CDALB 1929-1941; DA; DA3; DAB; DAC; DAM DRAM, MST; DFS 2, 4, 5, 6, 9, 11, 12, 16, 20; DLB 7, 331; EWL 3; LAIT 3; LMFS 2; MAL 5; MTCW 1, 2; MTFW 2005; RGAL 4; TUS
Onetti, Juan Carlos 1909-1994 ... **CLC 7, 10; HLCS 2; SSC 23; TCLC 131**
See also CA 85-88; CAAS 145; CANR 32, 63; CDWLB 3; CWW 2; DAM MULT, NOV; DLB 113; EWL 3; HW 1, 2; LAW; MTCW 1, 2; MTFW 2005; RGSF 2
O Nuallain, Brian 1911-1966
See O'Brien, Flann
See also CA 21-22; CAAS 25-28R; CAP 2; DLB 231; FANT; TEA
Ophuls, Max
See Ophuls, Max
Ophuls, Max 1902-1957 .... **TCLC 79**
See also CAAE 113
Opie, Amelia 1769-1853 .... **NCLC 65**
See also DLB 116, 159; RGEL 2
Oppen, George 1908-1984 ..... **CLC 7, 13, 34; PC 35; TCLC 107**
See also CA 13-16R; CAAS 113; CANR 8, 82; CP 1, 2, 3; DLB 5, 165
Oppenheim, E(dward) Phillips 1866-1946 .... **TCLC 45**
See also CA 202; CAAE 111; CMW 4; DLB 70
Oppenheimer, Max
See Ophuls, Max
Opuls, Max
See Ophuls, Max
Orage, A(lfred) R(ichard) 1873-1934 .... **TCLC 157**
See also CAAE 122
Origen c. 185-c. 254 .... **CMLC 19**
Orlovitz, Gil 1918-1973 .... **CLC 22**
See also CA 77-80; CAAS 45-48; CN 1; CP 1, 2; DLB 2, 5
Orosius c. 385-c. 420 .... **CMLC 100**
O'Rourke, Patrick Jake
See O'Rourke, P.J.
O'Rourke, P.J. 1947- .... **CLC 209**
See also CA 77-80; CANR 13, 41, 67, 111, 155; CPW; DAM POP; DLB 185
Orris
See Ingelow, Jean
Ortega y Gasset, Jose 1883-1955 ...... **HLC 2; TCLC 9**
See also CA 130; CAAE 106; DAM MULT; EW 9; EWL 3; HW 1, 2; MTCW 1, 2; MTFW 2005
Ortese, Anna Maria 1914-1998 .... **CLC 89**
See also DLB 177; EWL 3
Ortiz, Simon
See Ortiz, Simon J.
Ortiz, Simon J. 1941- . **CLC 45, 208; NNAL; PC 17**
See also AMWS 4; CA 134; CANR 69, 118, 164; CP 3, 4, 5, 6, 7; DAM MULT, POET; DLB 120, 175, 256; EXPP; MAL 5; PFS 4, 16; RGAL 4; SSFS 22; TCWW 2
Ortiz, Simon Joseph
See Ortiz, Simon J.
Orton, Joe CLC 4, 13, 43; DC 3; TCLC 157
See Orton, John Kingsley
See also BRWS 5; CBD; CDBLB 1960 to Present; DFS 3, 6; DLB 13, 310; GLL 1; RGEL 2; TEA; WLIT 4
Orton, John Kingsley 1933-1967
See Orton, Joe
See also CA 85-88; CANR 35, 66; DAM DRAM; MTCW 1, 2; MTFW 2005
Orwell, George SSC 68; TCLC 2, 6, 15, 31, 51, 128, 129; WLC 4
See Blair, Eric (Arthur)
See also BPFB 3; BRW 7; BYA 5; CDBLB 1945-1960; CLR 68; DAB; DLB 15, 98, 195, 255; EWL 3; EXPN; LAIT 4, 5; LATS 1:1; NFS 3, 7; RGEL 2; SCFW 1, 2; SFW 4; SSFS 4; TEA; WLIT 4; YAW
Osborne, David
See Silverberg, Robert
Osborne, Dorothy 1627-1695 .... **LC 141**
Osborne, George
See Silverberg, Robert
Osborne, John 1929-1994 .... **CLC 1, 2, 5, 11, 45; TCLC 153; WLC 4**
See also BRWS 1; CA 13-16R; CAAS 147; CANR 21, 56; CBD; CDBLB 1945-1960; DA; DAB; DAC; DAM DRAM, MST; DFS 4, 19, 24; DLB 13; EWL 3; MTCW 1, 2; MTFW 2005; RGEL 2
Osborne, Lawrence 1958- .... **CLC 50**
See also CA 189; CANR 152
Osbourne, Lloyd 1868-1947 .... **TCLC 93**
Osgood, Frances Sargent 1811-1850 .... **NCLC 141**
See also DLB 250
Oshima, Nagisa 1932- .... **CLC 20**
See also CA 121; CAAE 116; CANR 78
Oskison, John Milton 1874-1947 .... **NNAL; TCLC 35**
See also CA 144; CANR 84; DAM MULT; DLB 175
Ossian c. 3rd cent. - .... **CMLC 28**
See Macpherson, James
Ossoli, Sarah Margaret (Fuller) 1810-1850 .... **NCLC 5, 50**
See Fuller, Margaret; Fuller, Sarah Margaret
See also CDALB 1640-1865; FW; LMFS 1; SATA 25
Ostriker, Alicia 1937- .... **CLC 132**
See also CA 25-28R; 24; CANR 10, 30, 62, 99, 167; CWP; DLB 120; EXPP; PFS 19, 26
Ostriker, Alicia Suskin
See Ostriker, Alicia
Ostrovsky, Aleksandr Nikolaevich
See Ostrovsky, Alexander
See also DLB 277
Ostrovsky, Alexander 1823-1886 .. **NCLC 30, 57**
See Ostrovsky, Aleksandr Nikolaevich

Osundare, Niyi 1947- .... **BLC 2:3**
See also AFW; BW 3; CA 176; CDWLB 3; CP 7; DLB 157
Otero, Blas de 1916-1979 .... **CLC 11**
See also CA 89-92; DLB 134; EWL 3
O'Trigger, Sir Lucius
See Horne, Richard Henry Hengist
Otto, Rudolf 1869-1937 .... **TCLC 85**
Otto, Whitney 1955- .... **CLC 70**
See also CA 140; CANR 120
Otway, Thomas 1652-1685 ... **DC 24; LC 106**
See also DAM DRAM; DLB 80; RGEL 2
Ouida TCLC 43
See De La Ramee, Marie Louise
See also DLB 18, 156; RGEL 2
Ouologuem, Yambo 1940- .... **CLC 146**
See also CA 176; CAAE 111
Ousmane, Sembene 1923-2007 .... **BLC 1:3; CLC 66**
See Sembene, Ousmane
See also BW 1, 3; CA 125; CAAE 117; CAAS 261; CANR 81; CWW 2; MTCW 1
Ovid 43B.C.-17 .... **CMLC 7; PC 2**
See also AW 2; CDWLB 1; DA3; DAM POET; DLB 211; PFS 22; RGWL 2, 3; WLIT 8; WP
Owen, Hugh
See Faust, Frederick (Schiller)
Owen, Wilfred (Edward Salter) 1893-1918 ... **PC 19; TCLC 5, 27; WLC 4**
See also BRW 6; CA 141; CAAE 104; CDBLB 1914-1945; DA; DAB; DAC; DAM MST, POET; DLB 20; EWL 3; EXPP; MTCW 2; MTFW 2005; PFS 10; RGEL 2; WLIT 4
Owens, Louis (Dean) 1948-2002 .... **NNAL**
See also CA 179; 137, 179; 24; CAAS 207; CANR 71
Owens, Rochelle 1936- .... **CLC 8**
See also CA 17-20R; 2; CAD; CANR 39; CD 5, 6; CP 1, 2, 3, 4, 5, 6, 7; CWD; CWP
Oz, Amos 1939- ...... **CLC 5, 8, 11, 27, 33, 54; SSC 66**
See also CA 53-56; CANR 27, 47, 65, 113, 138; CWW 2; DAM NOV; EWL 3; MTCW 1, 2; MTFW 2005; RGHL; RGSF 2; RGWL 3; WLIT 6
Ozick, Cynthia 1928- .... **CLC 3, 7, 28, 62, 155; SSC 15, 60**
See also AMWS 5; BEST 90:1; CA 17-20R; CANR 23, 58, 116, 160; CN 3, 4, 5, 6, 7; CPW; DA3; DAM NOV, POP; DLB 28, 152, 299; DLBY 1982; EWL 3; EXPS; INT CANR-23; MAL 5; MTCW 1, 2; MTFW 2005; RGAL 4; RGHL; RGSF 2; SSFS 3, 12, 22
Ozu, Yasujiro 1903-1963 .... **CLC 16**
See also CA 112
Pabst, G. W. 1885-1967 .... **TCLC 127**
Pacheco, C.
See Pessoa, Fernando (Antonio Nogueira)
Pacheco, Jose Emilio 1939- .... **HLC 2**
See also CA 131; CAAE 111; CANR 65; CWW 2; DAM MULT; DLB 290; EWL 3; HW 1, 2; RGSF 2
Pa Chin CLC 18
See Jin, Ba
See also EWL 3
Pack, Robert 1929- .... **CLC 13**
See also CA 1-4R; CANR 3, 44, 82; CP 1, 2, 3, 4, 5, 6, 7; DLB 5; SATA 118
Padgett, Lewis
See Kuttner, Henry
Padilla (Lorenzo), Heberto 1932-2000 .... **CLC 38**
See also AITN 1; CA 131; CAAE 123; CAAS 189; CWW 2; EWL 3; HW 1
Page, James Patrick 1944-
See Page, Jimmy
See also CA 204
Page, Jimmy 1944- .... **CLC 12**
See Page, James Patrick
Page, Louise 1955- .... **CLC 40**
See also CA 140; CANR 76; CBD; CD 5, 6; CWD; DLB 233
Page, P(atricia) K(athleen) 1916- ...... **CLC 7, 18; PC 12**
See Cape, Judith
See also CA 53-56; CANR 4, 22, 65; CP 1, 2, 3, 4, 5, 6, 7; DAC; DAM MST; DLB 68; MTCW 1; RGEL 2
Page, Stanton
See Fuller, Henry Blake
Page, Stanton
See Fuller, Henry Blake
Page, Thomas Nelson 1853-1922 .... **SSC 23**
See also CA 177; CAAE 118; DLB 12, 78; DLBD 13; RGAL 4
Pagels, Elaine
See Pagels, Elaine Hiesey
Pagels, Elaine Hiesey 1943- .... **CLC 104**
See also CA 45-48; CANR 2, 24, 51, 151; FW; NCFS 4
Paget, Violet 1856-1935
See Lee, Vernon
See also CA 166; CAAE 104; GLL 1; HGG
Paget-Lowe, Henry
See Lovecraft, H. P.
Paglia, Camille 1947- .... **CLC 68**
See also CA 140; CANR 72, 139; CPW; FW; GLL 2; MTCW 2; MTFW 2005
Paige, Richard
See Koontz, Dean R.
Paine, Thomas 1737-1809 .... **NCLC 62**
See also AMWS 1; CDALB 1640-1865; DLB 31, 43, 73, 158; LAIT 1; RGAL 4; RGEL 2; TUS
Pakenham, Antonia
See Fraser, Antonia
Palamas, Costis
See Palamas, Kostes
Palamas, Kostes 1859-1943 .... **TCLC 5**
See Palamas, Kostis
See also CA 190; CAAE 105; RGWL 2, 3
Palamas, Kostis
See Palamas, Kostes
See also EWL 3
Palazzeschi, Aldo 1885-1974 .... **CLC 11**
See also CA 89-92; CAAS 53-56; DLB 114, 264; EWL 3
Pales Matos, Luis 1898-1959 .... **HLCS 2**
See Pales Matos, Luis
See also DLB 290; HW 1; LAW
Paley, Grace 1922-2007 ... **CLC 4, 6, 37, 140; SSC 8**
See also AMWS 6; CA 25-28R; CAAS 263; CANR 13, 46, 74, 118; CN 2, 3, 4, 5, 6, 7; CPW; DA3; DAM POP; DLB 28, 218; EWL 3; EXPS; FW; INT CANR-13; MAL 5; MBL; MTCW 1, 2; MTFW 2005; RGAL 4; RGSF 2; SSFS 3, 20
Paley, Grace Goodside
See Paley, Grace
Palin, Michael (Edward) 1943- .... **CLC 21**
See Monty Python
See also CA 107; CANR 35, 109; SATA 67
Palliser, Charles 1947- .... **CLC 65**
See also CA 136; CANR 76; CN 5, 6, 7
Palma, Ricardo 1833-1919 .... **TCLC 29**
See also CA 168; LAW
Pamuk, Orhan 1952- .... **CLC 185**
See also CA 142; CANR 75, 127, 172; CWW 2; WLIT 6
Pancake, Breece Dexter 1952-1979
See Pancake, Breece D'J
See also CA 123; CAAS 109
Pancake, Breece D'J CLC 29; SSC 61
See Pancake, Breece Dexter
See also DLB 130
Panchenko, Nikolai CLC 59
Pankhurst, Emmeline (Goulden) 1858-1928 .... **TCLC 100**
See also CAAE 116; FW
Panko, Rudy
See Gogol, Nikolai (Vasilyevich)
Papadiamantis, Alexandros 1851-1911 .... **TCLC 29**
See also CA 168; EWL 3
Papadiamantopoulos, Johannes 1856-1910
See Moreas, Jean
See also CA 242; CAAE 117
Papini, Giovanni 1881-1956 .... **TCLC 22**
See also CA 180; CAAE 121; DLB 264
Paracelsus 1493-1541 .... **LC 14**
See also DLB 179
Parasol, Peter
See Stevens, Wallace
Pardo Bazan, Emilia 1851-1921 .... **SSC 30; TCLC 189**
See also EWL 3; FW; RGSF 2; RGWL 2, 3
Paredes, Americo 1915-1999 .... **PC 83**
See also CA 37-40R; CAAS 179; DLB 209; EXPP; HW 1
Pareto, Vilfredo 1848-1923 .... **TCLC 69**
See also CA 175
Paretsky, Sara 1947- .... **CLC 135**
See also AAYA 30; BEST 90:3; CA 129; CAAE 125; CANR 59, 95; CMW 4; CPW; DA3; DAM POP; DLB 306; INT CA-129; MSW; RGAL 4
Paretsky, Sara N.
See Paretsky, Sara
Parfenie, Maria
See Codrescu, Andrei
Parini, Jay (Lee) 1948- .... **CLC 54, 133**
See also CA 229; 97-100, 229; 16; CANR 32, 87
Park, Jordan
See Kornbluth, C(yril) M.; Pohl, Frederik
Park, Robert E(zra) 1864-1944 ..... **TCLC 73**
See also CA 165; CAAE 122
Parker, Bert
See Ellison, Harlan
Parker, Dorothy (Rothschild) 1893-1967 . **CLC 15, 68; PC 28; SSC 2, 101; TCLC 143**
See also AMWS 9; CA 19-20; CAAS 25-28R; CAP 2; DA3; DAM POET; DLB 11, 45, 86; EXPP; FW; MAL 5; MBL; MTCW 1, 2; MTFW 2005; PFS 18; RGAL 4; RGSF 2; TUS
Parker, Robert B. 1932- .... **CLC 27**
See also AAYA 28; BEST 89:4; BPFB 3; CA 49-52; CANR 1, 26, 52, 89, 128, 165; CMW 4; CPW; DAM NOV, POP; DLB 306; INT CANR-26; MSW; MTCW 1; MTFW 2005
Parker, Robert Brown
See Parker, Robert B.
Parker, Theodore 1810-1860 .... **NCLC 186**
See also DLB 1, 235
Parkin, Frank 1940- .... **CLC 43**
See also CA 147
Parkman, Francis, Jr. 1823-1893 .. **NCLC 12**
See also AMWS 2; DLB 1, 30, 183, 186, 235; RGAL 4

Peguy, Charles (Pierre) 1873-1914 .... **TCLC 10**
See also CA 193; CAAE 107; DLB 258; EWL 3; GFL 1789 to the Present
Peirce, Charles Sanders 1839-1914 .... **TCLC 81**
See also CA 194; DLB 270
Pelecanos, George P. 1957- .... **CLC 236**
See also CA 138; CANR 122, 165; DLB 306
Pelevin, Victor 1962- .... **CLC 238**
See Pelevin, Viktor Olegovich
See also CA 154; CANR 88, 159
Pelevin, Viktor Olegovich
See Pelevin, Victor
See also DLB 285
Pellicer, Carlos 1897(?)-1977 .... **HLCS 2**
See also CA 153; CAAS 69-72; DLB 290; EWL 3; HW 1
Pena, Ramon del Valle y
See Valle-Inclan, Ramon (Maria) del
Pendennis, Arthur Esquir
See Thackeray, William Makepeace
Penn, Arthur
See Matthews, (James) Brander
Penn, William 1644-1718 .... **LC 25**
See also DLB 24
PEPECE
See Prado (Calvo), Pedro
Pepys, Samuel 1633-1703 ... **LC 11, 58; WLC 4**
See also BRW 2; CDBLB 1660-1789; DA; DA3; DAB; DAC; DAM MST; DLB 101, 213; NCFS 4; RGEL 2; TEA; WLIT 3
Percy, Thomas 1729-1811 .... **NCLC 95**
See also DLB 104
Percy, Walker 1916-1990 .... **CLC 2, 3, 6, 8, 14, 18, 47, 65**
See also AMWS 3; BPFB 3; CA 1-4R; CAAS 131; CANR 1, 23, 64; CN 1, 2, 3, 4; CPW; CSW; DA3; DAM NOV, POP; DLB 2; DLBY 1980, 1990; EWL 3; MAL 5; MTCW 1, 2; MTFW 2005; RGAL 4; TUS
Percy, William Alexander 1885-1942 .... **TCLC 84**
See also CA 163; MTCW 2
Perec, Georges 1936-1982 .... **CLC 56, 116**
See also CA 141; DLB 83, 299; EWL 3; GFL 1789 to the Present; RGHL; RGWL 3
Pereda (y Sanchez de Porrua), Jose Maria de 1833-1906 .... **TCLC 16**
See also CAAE 117
Pereda y Porrua, Jose Maria de
See Pereda (y Sanchez de Porrua), Jose Maria de
Peregoy, George Weems
See Mencken, H(enry) L(ouis)
Perelman, S(idney) J(oseph) 1904-1979 .. **CLC 3, 5, 9, 15, 23, 44, 49; SSC 32**
See also AITN 1, 2; BPFB 3; CA 73-76; CAAS 89-92; CANR 18; DAM DRAM; DLB 11, 44; MTCW 1, 2; MTFW 2005; RGAL 4
Peret, Benjamin 1899-1959 .... **PC 33; TCLC 20**
See also CA 186; CAAE 117; GFL 1789 to the Present
Peretz, Isaac Leib
See Peretz, Isaac Loeb
See also CA 201; DLB 333
Peretz, Isaac Loeb 1851(?)-1915 .... **SSC 26; TCLC 16**
See Peretz, Isaac Leib
See also CAAE 109
Peretz, Yitzkhok Leibush
See Peretz, Isaac Loeb
Perez Galdos, Benito 1843-1920 .... **HLCS 2; TCLC 27**
See Galdos, Benito Perez
See also CA 153; CAAE 125; EWL 3; HW 1; RGWL 2, 3
Peri Rossi, Cristina 1941- .. **CLC 156; HLCS 2**
See also CA 131; CANR 59, 81; CWW 2; DLB 145, 290; EWL 3; HW 1, 2
Perlata
See Peret, Benjamin
Perloff, Marjorie G(abrielle) 1931- .... **CLC 137**
See also CA 57-60; CANR 7, 22, 49, 104
Perrault, Charles 1628-1703 .... **LC 2, 56**
See also BYA 4; CLR 79; DLB 268; GFL Beginnings to 1789; MAICYA 1, 2; RGWL 2, 3; SATA 25; WCH
Perry, Anne 1938- .... **CLC 126**
See also CA 101; CANR 22, 50, 84, 150; CMW 4; CN 6, 7; CPW; DLB 276
Perry, Brighton
See Sherwood, Robert E(mmet)
Perse, St.-John
See Leger, (Marie-Rene Auguste) Alexis Saint-Leger
Perse, Saint-John
See Leger, (Marie-Rene Auguste) Alexis Saint-Leger
See also DLB 258, 331; RGWL 3
Persius 34-62 .... **CMLC 74**
See also AW 2; DLB 211; RGWL 2, 3
Perutz, Leo(pold) 1882-1957 .... **TCLC 60**
See also CA 147; DLB 81
Peseenz, Tulio F.
See Lopez y Fuentes, Gregorio
Pesetsky, Bette 1932- .... **CLC 28**
See also CA 133; DLB 130
Peshkov, Alexei Maximovich 1868-1936
See Gorky, Maxim
See also CA 141; CAAE 105; CANR 83; DA; DAC; DAM DRAM, MST, NOV; MTCW 2; MTFW 2005
Pessoa, Fernando (Antonio Nogueira) 1888-1935 .... **HLC 2; PC 20; TCLC 27**
See also CA 183; CAAE 125; DAM MULT; DLB 287; EW 10; EWL 3; RGWL 2, 3; WP
Peterkin, Julia Mood 1880-1961 .... **CLC 31**
See also CA 102; DLB 9
Peters, Joan K(aren) 1945- .... **CLC 39**
See also CA 158; CANR 109
Peters, Robert L(ouis) 1924- .... **CLC 7**
See also CA 13-16R; 8; CP 1, 5, 6, 7; DLB 105
Petofi, Sandor 1823-1849 .... **NCLC 21**
See also RGWL 2, 3
Petrakis, Harry Mark 1923- .... **CLC 3**
See also CA 9-12R; CANR 4, 30, 85, 155; CN 1, 2, 3, 4, 5, 6, 7
Petrarch 1304-1374 .... **CMLC 20; PC 8**
See also DA3; DAM POET; EW 2; LMFS 1; RGWL 2, 3; WLIT 7
Petronius c. 20-66 .... **CMLC 34**
See also AW 2; CDWLB 1; DLB 211; RGWL 2, 3; WLIT 8
Petrov, Evgeny TCLC 21
See Kataev, Evgeny Petrovich
Petry, Ann (Lane) 1908-1997 .. **CLC 1, 7, 18; TCLC 112**
See also AFAW 1, 2; BPFB 3; BW 1, 3; BYA 2; CA 5-8R; 6; CAAS 157; CANR 4, 46; CLR 12; CN 1, 2, 3, 4, 5, 6; DLB 76; EWL 3; JRDA; LAIT 1; MAICYA 1, 2; MAICYAS 1; MTCW 1; RGAL 4; SATA 5; SATA-Obit 94; TUS
Petursson, Halligrimur 1614-1674 .... **LC 8**
Peychinovich
See Vazov, Ivan (Minchov)
Phaedrus c. 15B.C.-c. 50 .... **CMLC 25**
See also DLB 211
Phelps (Ward), Elizabeth Stuart
See Phelps, Elizabeth Stuart
See also FW
Phelps, Elizabeth Stuart 1844-1911 .... **TCLC 113**
See Phelps (Ward), Elizabeth Stuart
See also CA 242; DLB 74
Philips, Katherine 1632-1664 .... **LC 30, 145; PC 40**
See also DLB 131; RGEL 2
Philipson, Ilene J. 1950- .... **CLC 65**
See also CA 219
Philipson, Morris H. 1926- .... **CLC 53**
See also CA 1-4R; CANR 4
Phillips, Caryl 1958- .... **BLCS; CLC 96, 224**
See also BRWS 5; BW 2; CA 141; CANR 63, 104, 140; CBD; CD 5, 6; CN 5, 6, 7; DA3; DAM MULT; DLB 157; EWL 3; MTCW 2; MTFW 2005; WLIT 4; WWE 1
Phillips, David Graham 1867-1911 .... **TCLC 44**
See also CA 176; CAAE 108; DLB 9, 12, 303; RGAL 4
Phillips, Jack
See Sandburg, Carl (August)
Phillips, Jayne Anne 1952- .... **CLC 15, 33, 139; SSC 16**
See also AAYA 57; BPFB 3; CA 101; CANR 24, 50, 96; CN 4, 5, 6, 7; CSW; DLBY 1980; INT CANR-24; MTCW 1, 2; MTFW 2005; RGAL 4; RGSF 2; SSFS 4
Phillips, Richard
See Dick, Philip K.
Phillips, Robert (Schaeffer) 1938- .... **CLC 28**
See also CA 17-20R; 13; CANR 8; DLB 105
Phillips, Ward
See Lovecraft, H. P.
Philo c. 20 B.C.-50 A.D. .... **CMLC 100**
See also DLB 176
Philostratus, Flavius c. 179-c. 244 .... **CMLC 62**
Piccolo, Lucio 1901-1969 .... **CLC 13**
See also CA 97-100; DLB 114; EWL 3
Pickthall, Marjorie L(owry) C(hristie) 1883-1922 .... **TCLC 21**
See also CAAE 107; DLB 92
Pico della Mirandola, Giovanni 1463-1494 .... **LC 15**
See also LMFS 1
Piercy, Marge 1936- .... **CLC 3, 6, 14, 18, 27, 62, 128; PC 29**
See also BPFB 3; CA 187; 21-24R, 187; 1; CANR 13, 43, 66, 111; CN 3, 4, 5, 6, 7; CP 1, 2, 3, 4, 5, 6, 7; CWP; DLB 120, 227; EXPP; FW; MAL 5; MTCW 1, 2; MTFW 2005; PFS 9, 22; SFW 4
Piers, Robert
See Anthony, Piers
Pieyre de Mandiargues, Andre 1909-1991
See Mandiargues, Andre Pieyre de
See also CA 103; CAAS 136; CANR 22, 82; EWL 3; GFL 1789 to the Present
Pilnyak, Boris 1894-1938 . **SSC 48; TCLC 23**
See Vogau, Boris Andreyevich
See also EWL 3
Pinchback, Eugene
See Toomer, Jean
Pincherle, Alberto 1907-1990 .... **CLC 11, 18**
See Moravia, Alberto
See also CA 25-28R; CAAS 132; CANR 33, 63, 142; DAM NOV; MTCW 1; MTFW 2005
Pinckney, Darryl 1953- .... **CLC 76**
See also BW 2, 3; CA 143; CANR 79

Pritchett, V(ictor) S(awdon) 1900-1997 ... **CLC 5, 13, 15, 41; SSC 14**
See also BPFB 3; BRWS 3; CA 61-64; CAAS 157; CANR 31, 63; CN 1, 2, 3, 4, 5, 6; DA3; DAM NOV; DLB 15, 139; EWL 3; MTCW 1, 2; MTFW 2005; RGEL 2; RGSF 2; TEA
Private 19022
See Manning, Frederic
Probst, Mark 1925- .... **CLC 59**
See also CA 130
Procaccino, Michael
See Cristofer, Michael
Proclus c. 412-c. 485 .... **CMLC 81**
Prokosch, Frederic 1908-1989 ...... **CLC 4, 48**
See also CA 73-76; CAAS 128; CANR 82; CN 1, 2, 3, 4; CP 1, 2, 3, 4; DLB 48; MTCW 2
Propertius, Sextus c. 50B.C.-c. 16B.C. .... **CMLC 32**
See also AW 2; CDWLB 1; DLB 211; RGWL 2, 3; WLIT 8
Prophet, The
See Dreiser, Theodore
Prose, Francine 1947- .... **CLC 45, 231**
See also AMWS 16; CA 112; CAAE 109; CANR 46, 95, 132; DLB 234; MTFW 2005; SATA 101, 149
Protagoras c. 490B.C.-420B.C. ...... **CMLC 85**
See also DLB 176
Proudhon
See Cunha, Euclides (Rodrigues Pimenta) da
Proulx, Annie
See Proulx, E. Annie
Proulx, E. Annie 1935- ...... **CLC 81, 158, 250**
See also AMWS 7; BPFB 3; CA 145; CANR 65, 110; CN 6, 7; CPW 1; DA3; DAM POP; DLB 335; MAL 5; MTCW 2; MTFW 2005; SSFS 18, 23
Proulx, Edna Annie
See Proulx, E. Annie
Proust, (Valentin-Louis-George-Eugene) Marcel 1871-1922 ..... **SSC 75; TCLC 7, 13, 33; WLC 5**
See also AAYA 58; BPFB 3; CA 120; CAAE 104; CANR 110; DA; DA3; DAB; DAC; DAM MST, NOV; DLB 65; EW 8; EWL 3; GFL 1789 to the Present; MTCW 1, 2; MTFW 2005; RGWL 2, 3; TWA
Prowler, Harley
See Masters, Edgar Lee
Prudentius, Aurelius Clemens 348-c. 405 .... **CMLC 78**
See also EW 1; RGWL 2, 3
Prudhomme, Rene Francois Armand 1839-1907
See Sully Prudhomme, Rene-Francois-Armand
See also CA 170
Prus, Boleslaw 1845-1912 .... **TCLC 48**
See also RGWL 2, 3
Prynne, William 1600-1669 .... **LC 148**
Pryor, Aaron Richard
See Pryor, Richard
Pryor, Richard 1940-2005 .... **CLC 26**
See also CA 152; CAAE 122; CAAS 246
Pryor, Richard Franklin Lenox Thomas
See Pryor, Richard
Przybyszewski, Stanislaw 1868-1927 .... **TCLC 36**
See also CA 160; DLB 66; EWL 3
Pseudo-Dionysius the Areopagite fl. c. 5th cent. - .... **CMLC 89**
See also DLB 115
Pteleon
See Grieve, C(hristopher) M(urray)
See also DAM POET
Puckett, Lute
See Masters, Edgar Lee
Puig, Manuel 1932-1990 .... **CLC 3, 5, 10, 28, 65, 133; HLC 2**
See also BPFB 3; CA 45-48; CANR 2, 32, 63; CDWLB 3; DA3; DAM MULT; DLB 113; DNFS 1; EWL 3; GLL 1; HW 1, 2; LAW; MTCW 1, 2; MTFW 2005; RGWL 2, 3; TWA; WLIT 1
Pulitzer, Joseph 1847-1911 .... **TCLC 76**
See also CAAE 114; DLB 23
Pullman, Philip 1946- .... **CLC 245**
See also AAYA 15, 41; BRWS 13; BYA 8, 13; CA 127; CANR 50, 77, 105, 134; CLR 20, 62, 84; JRDA; MAICYA 1, 2; MAICYAS 1; MTFW 2005; SAAS 17; SATA 65, 103, 150; SUFW 2; WYAS 1; YAW
Purchas, Samuel 1577(?)-1626 .... **LC 70**
See also DLB 151
Purdy, A(lfred) W(ellington) 1918-2000 .... **CLC 3, 6, 14, 50**
See also CA 81-84; 17; CAAS 189; CANR 42, 66; CP 1, 2, 3, 4, 5, 6, 7; DAC; DAM MST, POET; DLB 88; PFS 5; RGEL 2
Purdy, James (Amos) 1923- .... **CLC 2, 4, 10, 28, 52**
See also AMWS 7; CA 33-36R; 1; CANR 19, 51, 132; CN 1, 2, 3, 4, 5, 6, 7; DLB 2, 218; EWL 3; INT CANR-19; MAL 5; MTCW 1; RGAL 4
Pure, Simon
See Swinnerton, Frank Arthur
Pushkin, Aleksandr Sergeevich
See Pushkin, Alexander (Sergeyevich)
See also DLB 205
Pushkin, Alexander (Sergeyevich) 1799-1837 .... **NCLC 3, 27, 83; PC 10; SSC 27, 55, 99; WLC 5**
See Pushkin, Aleksandr Sergeevich
See also DA; DA3; DAB; DAC; DAM DRAM, MST, POET; EW 5; EXPS; RGSF 2; RGWL 2, 3; SATA 61; SSFS 9; TWA
P'u Sung-ling 1640-1715 .... **LC 49; SSC 31**
Putnam, Arthur Lee
See Alger, Horatio, Jr.
Puttenham, George 1529(?)-1590 ...... **LC 116**
See also DLB 281
Puzo, Mario 1920-1999 .... **CLC 1, 2, 6, 36, 107**
See also BPFB 3; CA 65-68; CAAS 185; CANR 4, 42, 65, 99, 131; CN 1, 2, 3, 4, 5, 6; CPW; DA3; DAM NOV, POP; DLB 6; MTCW 1, 2; MTFW 2005; NFS 16; RGAL 4
Pygge, Edward
See Barnes, Julian
Pyle, Ernest Taylor 1900-1945
See Pyle, Ernie
See also CA 160; CAAE 115
Pyle, Ernie TCLC 75
See Pyle, Ernest Taylor
See also DLB 29; MTCW 2
Pyle, Howard 1853-1911 .... **TCLC 81**
See also AAYA 57; BYA 2, 4; CA 137; CAAE 109; CLR 22, 117; DLB 42, 188; DLBD 13; LAIT 1; MAICYA 1, 2; SATA 16, 100; WCH; YAW
Pym, Barbara (Mary Crampton) 1913-1980 .... **CLC 13, 19, 37, 111**
See also BPFB 3; BRWS 2; CA 13-14; CAAS 97-100; CANR 13, 34; CAP 1; DLB 14, 207; DLBY 1987; EWL 3; MTCW 1, 2; MTFW 2005; RGEL 2; TEA
Pynchon, Thomas 1937- .. **CLC 2, 3, 6, 9, 11, 18, 33, 62, 72, 123, 192, 213; SSC 14, 84; WLC 5**
See also AMWS 2; BEST 90:2; BPFB 3; CA 17-20R; CANR 22, 46, 73, 142; CN 1, 2, 3, 4, 5, 6, 7; CPW 1; DA; DA3; DAB; DAC; DAM MST, NOV, POP; DLB 2, 173; EWL 3; MAL 5; MTCW 1, 2; MTFW 2005; NFS 23; RGAL 4; SFW 4; TCLE 1:2; TUS
Pythagoras c. 582B.C.-c. 507B.C. . **CMLC 22**
See also DLB 176
Q
See Quiller-Couch, Sir Arthur (Thomas)
Qian, Chongzhu
See Ch'ien, Chung-shu
Qian, Sima 145B.C.-c. 89B.C. .... **CMLC 72**
Qian Zhongshu
See Ch'ien, Chung-shu
See also CWW 2; DLB 328
Qroll
See Dagerman, Stig (Halvard)
Quarles, Francis 1592-1644 .... **LC 117**
See also DLB 126; RGEL 2
Quarrington, Paul 1953- .... **CLC 65**
See also CA 129; CANR 62, 95
Quarrington, Paul Lewis
See Quarrington, Paul
Quasimodo, Salvatore 1901-1968 .... **CLC 10; PC 47**
See also CA 13-16; CAAS 25-28R; CAP 1; DLB 114, 332; EW 12; EWL 3; MTCW 1; RGWL 2, 3
Quatermass, Martin
See Carpenter, John (Howard)
Quay, Stephen 1947- .... **CLC 95**
See also CA 189
Quay, Timothy 1947- .... **CLC 95**
See also CA 189
Queen, Ellery CLC 3, 11
See Dannay, Frederic; Davidson, Avram (James); Deming, Richard; Fairman, Paul W.; Flora, Fletcher; Hoch, Edward D.; Kane, Henry; Lee, Manfred B.; Marlowe, Stephen; Powell, (Oval) Talmage; Sheldon, Walter J(ames); Sturgeon, Theodore (Hamilton); Tracy, Don(ald Fiske); Vance, Jack
See also BPFB 3; CMW 4; MSW; RGAL 4
Queen, Ellery, Jr.
See Dannay, Frederic; Lee, Manfred B.
Queneau, Raymond 1903-1976 ..... **CLC 2, 5, 10, 42**
See also CA 77-80; CAAS 69-72; CANR 32; DLB 72, 258; EW 12; EWL 3; GFL 1789 to the Present; MTCW 1, 2; RGWL 2, 3
Quevedo, Francisco de 1580-1645 .... **LC 23**
Quiller-Couch, Sir Arthur (Thomas) 1863-1944 .... **TCLC 53**
See also CA 166; CAAE 118; DLB 135, 153, 190; HGG; RGEL 2; SUFW 1
Quin, Ann 1936-1973 .... **CLC 6**
See also CA 9-12R; CAAS 45-48; CANR 148; CN 1; DLB 14, 231
Quin, Ann Marie
See Quin, Ann
Quincey, Thomas de
See De Quincey, Thomas
Quindlen, Anna 1953- .... **CLC 191**
See also AAYA 35; AMWS 17; CA 138; CANR 73, 126; DA3; DLB 292; MTCW 2; MTFW 2005
Quinn, Martin
See Smith, Martin Cruz
Quinn, Peter 1947- .... **CLC 91**
See also CA 197; CANR 147
Quinn, Peter A.
See Quinn, Peter
Quinn, Simon
See Smith, Martin Cruz
Quintana, Leroy V. 1944- ...... **HLC 2; PC 36**
See also CA 131; CANR 65, 139; DAM MULT; DLB 82; HW 1, 2

Quintilian c. 40-c. 100 .... **CMLC 77**
See also AW 2; DLB 211; RGWL 2, 3
Quintillian 0035-0100 .... **CMLC 77**
Quiroga, Horacio (Sylvestre) 1878-1937 ... **HLC 2; SSC 89; TCLC 20**
See also CA 131; CAAE 117; DAM MULT; EWL 3; HW 1; LAW; MTCW 1; RGSF 2; WLIT 1
Quoirez, Francoise 1935-2004 .... **CLC 9**
See Sagan, Francoise
See also CA 49-52; CAAS 231; CANR 6, 39, 73; MTCW 1, 2; MTFW 2005; TWA
Raabe, Wilhelm (Karl) 1831-1910 . **TCLC 45**
See also CA 167; DLB 129
Rabe, David (William) 1940- .. **CLC 4, 8, 33, 200; DC 16**
See also CA 85-88; CABS 3; CAD; CANR 59, 129; CD 5, 6; DAM DRAM; DFS 3, 8, 13; DLB 7, 228; EWL 3; MAL 5
Rabelais, Francois 1494-1553 .... **LC 5, 60; WLC 5**
See also DA; DAB; DAC; DAM MST; DLB 327; EW 2; GFL Beginnings to 1789; LMFS 1; RGWL 2, 3; TWA
Rabi'a al-'Adawiyya c. 717-c. 801 .... **CMLC 83**
See also DLB 311
Rabinovitch, Sholem 1859-1916
See Sholom Aleichem
See also CAAE 104
Rabinyan, Dorit 1972- .... **CLC 119**
See also CA 170; CANR 147
Rachilde
See Vallette, Marguerite Eymery; Vallette, Marguerite Eymery
See also EWL 3
Racine, Jean 1639-1699 .... **LC 28, 113**
See also DA3; DAB; DAM MST; DLB 268; EW 3; GFL Beginnings to 1789; LMFS 1; RGWL 2, 3; TWA
Radcliffe, Ann (Ward) 1764-1823 ... **NCLC 6, 55, 106**
See also DLB 39, 178; GL 3; HGG; LMFS 1; RGEL 2; SUFW; WLIT 3
Radclyffe-Hall, Marguerite
See Hall, Radclyffe
Radiguet, Raymond 1903-1923 ...... **TCLC 29**
See also CA 162; DLB 65; EWL 3; GFL 1789 to the Present; RGWL 2, 3
Radishchev, Aleksandr Nikolaevich 1749-1802
See Radishchev, Alexander
See also DLB 150
Radishchev, Alexander NCLC 190
See Radishchev, Aleksandr Nikolaevich
Radnoti, Miklos 1909-1944 .... **TCLC 16**
See also CA 212; CAAE 118; CDWLB 4; DLB 215; EWL 3; RGHL; RGWL 2, 3
Rado, James 1939- .... **CLC 17**
See also CA 105
Radvanyi, Netty 1900-1983
See Seghers, Anna
See also CA 85-88; CAAS 110; CANR 82
Rae, Ben
See Griffiths, Trevor
Raeburn, John (Hay) 1941- .... **CLC 34**
See also CA 57-60
Ragni, Gerome 1942-1991 .... **CLC 17**
See also CA 105; CAAS 134
Rahv, Philip CLC 24
See Greenberg, Ivan
See also DLB 137; MAL 5
Raimund, Ferdinand Jakob 1790-1836 .... **NCLC 69**
See also DLB 90
Raine, Craig 1944- .... **CLC 32, 103**
See also BRWS 13; CA 108; CANR 29, 51, 103, 171; CP 3, 4, 5, 6, 7; DLB 40; PFS 7
Raine, Craig Anthony
See Raine, Craig
Raine, Kathleen (Jessie) 1908-2003 .. **CLC 7, 45**
See also CA 85-88; CAAS 218; CANR 46, 109; CP 1, 2, 3, 4, 5, 6, 7; DLB 20; EWL 3; MTCW 1; RGEL 2
Rainis, Janis 1865-1929 .... **TCLC 29**
See also CA 170; CDWLB 4; DLB 220; EWL 3
Rakosi, Carl CLC 47
See Rawley, Callman
See also CA 5; CAAS 228; CP 1, 2, 3, 4, 5, 6, 7; DLB 193
Ralegh, Sir Walter
See Raleigh, Sir Walter
See also BRW 1; RGEL 2; WP
Raleigh, Richard
See Lovecraft, H. P.
Raleigh, Sir Walter 1554(?)-1618 .... **LC 31, 39; PC 31**
See Ralegh, Sir Walter
See also CDBLB Before 1660; DLB 172; EXPP; PFS 14; TEA
Rallentando, H. P.
See Sayers, Dorothy L(eigh)
Ramal, Walter
See de la Mare, Walter (John)
Ramana Maharshi 1879-1950 .... **TCLC 84**
Ramoacn y Cajal, Santiago 1852-1934 .... **TCLC 93**
Ramon, Juan
See Jimenez (Mantecon), Juan Ramon
Ramos, Graciliano 1892-1953 .... **TCLC 32**
See also CA 167; DLB 307; EWL 3; HW 2; LAW; WLIT 1
Rampersad, Arnold 1941- .... **CLC 44**
See also BW 2, 3; CA 133; CAAE 127; CANR 81; DLB 111; INT CA-133
Rampling, Anne
See Rice, Anne
See also GLL 2
Ramsay, Allan 1686(?)-1758 .... **LC 29**
See also DLB 95; RGEL 2
Ramsay, Jay
See Campbell, Ramsey
Ramuz, Charles-Ferdinand 1878-1947 .... **TCLC 33**
See also CA 165; EWL 3
Rand, Ayn 1905-1982 ...... **CLC 3, 30, 44, 79; WLC 5**
See also AAYA 10; AMWS 4; BPFB 3; BYA 12; CA 13-16R; CAAS 105; CANR 27, 73; CDALBS; CN 1, 2, 3; CPW; DA; DA3; DAC; DAM MST, NOV, POP; DLB 227, 279; MTCW 1, 2; MTFW 2005; NFS 10, 16; RGAL 4; SFW 4; TUS; YAW
Randall, Dudley (Felker) 1914-2000 .... **BLC 1:3; CLC 1, 135; PC 86**
See also BW 1, 3; CA 25-28R; CAAS 189; CANR 23, 82; CP 1, 2, 3, 4, 5; DAM MULT; DLB 41; PFS 5
Randall, Robert
See Silverberg, Robert
Ranger, Ken
See Creasey, John
Rank, Otto 1884-1939 .... **TCLC 115**
Ransom, John Crowe 1888-1974 .. **CLC 2, 4, 5, 11, 24; PC 61**
See also AMW; CA 5-8R; CAAS 49-52; CANR 6, 34; CDALBS; CP 1, 2; DA3; DAM POET; DLB 45, 63; EWL 3; EXPP; MAL 5; MTCW 1, 2; MTFW 2005; RGAL 4; TUS
Rao, Raja 1908-2006 .... **CLC 25, 56; SSC 99**
See also CA 73-76; CAAS 252; CANR 51; CN 1, 2, 3, 4, 5, 6; DAM NOV; DLB 323; EWL 3; MTCW 1, 2; MTFW 2005; RGEL 2; RGSF 2
Raphael, Frederic (Michael) 1931- ... **CLC 2, 14**
See also CA 1-4R; CANR 1, 86; CN 1, 2, 3, 4, 5, 6, 7; DLB 14, 319; TCLE 1:2
Raphael, Lev 1954- .... **CLC 232**
See also CA 134; CANR 72, 145; GLL 1
Ratcliffe, James P.
See Mencken, H(enry) L(ouis)
Rathbone, Julian 1935-2008 .... **CLC 41**
See also CA 101; CANR 34, 73, 152
Rattigan, Terence (Mervyn) 1911-1977 .... **CLC 7; DC 18**
See also BRWS 7; CA 85-88; CAAS 73-76; CBD; CDBLB 1945-1960; DAM DRAM; DFS 8; DLB 13; IDFW 3, 4; MTCW 1, 2; MTFW 2005; RGEL 2
Ratushinskaya, Irina 1954- .... **CLC 54**
See also CA 129; CANR 68; CWW 2
Raven, Simon (Arthur Noel) 1927-2001 .... **CLC 14**
See also CA 81-84; CAAS 197; CANR 86; CN 1, 2, 3, 4, 5, 6; DLB 271
Ravenna, Michael
See Welty, Eudora
Rawley, Callman 1903-2004
See Rakosi, Carl
See also CA 21-24R; CAAS 228; CANR 12, 32, 91
Rawlings, Marjorie Kinnan 1896-1953 .... **TCLC 4**
See also AAYA 20; AMWS 10; ANW; BPFB 3; BYA 3; CA 137; CAAE 104; CANR 74; CLR 63; DLB 9, 22, 102; DLBD 17; JRDA; MAICYA 1, 2; MAL 5; MTCW 2; MTFW 2005; RGAL 4; SATA 100; WCH; YABC 1; YAW
Ray, Satyajit 1921-1992 .... **CLC 16, 76**
See also CA 114; CAAS 137; DAM MULT
Read, Herbert Edward 1893-1968 ..... **CLC 4**
See also BRW 6; CA 85-88; CAAS 25-28R; DLB 20, 149; EWL 3; PAB; RGEL 2
Read, Piers Paul 1941- .... **CLC 4, 10, 25**
See also CA 21-24R; CANR 38, 86, 150; CN 2, 3, 4, 5, 6, 7; DLB 14; SATA 21
Reade, Charles 1814-1884 .... **NCLC 2, 74**
See also DLB 21; RGEL 2
Reade, Hamish
See Gray, Simon
Reading, Peter 1946- .... **CLC 47**
See also BRWS 8; CA 103; CANR 46, 96; CP 5, 6, 7; DLB 40
Reaney, James 1926- .... **CLC 13**
See also CA 41-44R; 15; CANR 42; CD 5, 6; CP 1, 2, 3, 4, 5, 6, 7; DAC; DAM MST; DLB 68; RGEL 2; SATA 43
Rebreanu, Liviu 1885-1944 .... **TCLC 28**
See also CA 165; DLB 220; EWL 3
Rechy, John 1934- ..... **CLC 1, 7, 14, 18, 107; HLC 2**
See also CA 195; 5-8R, 195; 4; CANR 6, 32, 64, 152; CN 1, 2, 3, 4, 5, 6, 7; DAM MULT; DLB 122, 278; DLBY 1982; HW 1, 2; INT CANR-6; LLW; MAL 5; RGAL 4
Rechy, John Francisco
See Rechy, John
Redcam, Tom 1870-1933 .... **TCLC 25**
Reddin, Keith 1956- .... **CLC 67**
See also CAD; CD 6
Redgrove, Peter (William) 1932-2003 .... **CLC 6, 41**
See also BRWS 6; CA 1-4R; CAAS 217; CANR 3, 39, 77; CP 1, 2, 3, 4, 5, 6, 7; DLB 40; TCLE 1:2

Redmon, Anne CLC 22
See Nightingale, Anne Redmon
See also DLBY 1986
Reed, Eliot
See Ambler, Eric
Reed, Ishmael 1938- . **BLC 1:3; CLC 2, 3, 5, 6, 13, 32, 60, 174; PC 68**
See also AFAW 1, 2; AMWS 10; BPFB 3; BW 2, 3; CA 21-24R; CANR 25, 48, 74, 128; CN 1, 2, 3, 4, 5, 6, 7; CP 1, 2, 3, 4, 5, 6, 7; CSW; DA3; DAM MULT; DLB 2, 5, 33, 169, 227; DLBD 8; EWL 3; LMFS 2; MAL 5; MSW; MTCW 1, 2; MTFW 2005; PFS 6; RGAL 4; TCWW 2
Reed, John (Silas) 1887-1920 .... **TCLC 9**
See also CA 195; CAAE 106; MAL 5; TUS
Reed, Lou CLC 21
See Firbank, Louis
Reese, Lizette Woodworth 1856-1935 .... **PC 29; TCLC 181**
See also CA 180; DLB 54
Reeve, Clara 1729-1807 .... **NCLC 19**
See also DLB 39; RGEL 2
Reich, Wilhelm 1897-1957 .... **TCLC 57**
See also CA 199
Reid, Christopher (John) 1949- .... **CLC 33**
See also CA 140; CANR 89; CP 4, 5, 6, 7; DLB 40; EWL 3
Reid, Desmond
See Moorcock, Michael
Reid Banks, Lynne 1929-
See Banks, Lynne Reid
See also AAYA 49; CA 1-4R; CANR 6, 22, 38, 87; CLR 24, 86; CN 1, 2, 3, 7; JRDA; MAICYA 1, 2; SATA 22, 75, 111, 165; YAW
Reilly, William K.
See Creasey, John
Reiner, Max
See Caldwell, (Janet Miriam) Taylor (Holland)
Reis, Ricardo
See Pessoa, Fernando (Antonio Nogueira)
Reizenstein, Elmer Leopold
See Rice, Elmer (Leopold)
See also EWL 3
Remarque, Erich Maria 1898-1970 . **CLC 21**
See also AAYA 27; BPFB 3; CA 77-80; CAAS 29-32R; CDWLB 2; DA; DA3; DAB; DAC; DAM MST, NOV; DLB 56; EWL 3; EXPN; LAIT 3; MTCW 1, 2; MTFW 2005; NFS 4; RGHL; RGWL 2, 3
Remington, Frederic S(ackrider) 1861-1909 .... **TCLC 89**
See also CA 169; CAAE 108; DLB 12, 186, 188; SATA 41; TCWW 2
Remizov, A.
See Remizov, Aleksei (Mikhailovich)
Remizov, A. M.
See Remizov, Aleksei (Mikhailovich)
Remizov, Aleksei (Mikhailovich) 1877-1957 .... **TCLC 27**
See Remizov, Alexey Mikhaylovich
See also CA 133; CAAE 125; DLB 295
Remizov, Alexey Mikhaylovich
See Remizov, Aleksei (Mikhailovich)
See also EWL 3
Renan, Joseph Ernest 1823-1892 . **NCLC 26, 145**
See also GFL 1789 to the Present
Renard, Jules(-Pierre) 1864-1910 .. **TCLC 17**
See also CA 202; CAAE 117; GFL 1789 to the Present
Renart, Jean fl. 13th cent. - .... **CMLC 83**
Renault, Mary CLC 3, 11, 17
See Challans, Mary
See also BPFB 3; BYA 2; CN 1, 2, 3; DLBY 1983; EWL 3; GLL 1; LAIT 1; RGEL 2; RHW
Rendell, Ruth 1930- .... **CLC 28, 48**
See Vine, Barbara
See also BPFB 3; BRWS 9; CA 109; CANR 32, 52, 74, 127, 162; CN 5, 6, 7; CPW; DAM POP; DLB 87, 276; INT CANR-32; MSW; MTCW 1, 2; MTFW 2005
Rendell, Ruth Barbara
See Rendell, Ruth
Renoir, Jean 1894-1979 .... **CLC 20**
See also CA 129; CAAS 85-88
Rensie, Willis
See Eisner, Will
Resnais, Alain 1922- .... **CLC 16**
Revard, Carter 1931- .... **NNAL**
See also CA 144; CANR 81, 153; PFS 5
Reverdy, Pierre 1889-1960 .... **CLC 53**
See also CA 97-100; CAAS 89-92; DLB 258; EWL 3; GFL 1789 to the Present
Rexroth, Kenneth 1905-1982 .... **CLC 1, 2, 6, 11, 22, 49, 112; PC 20**
See also BG 1:3; CA 5-8R; CAAS 107; CANR 14, 34, 63; CDALB 1941-1968; CP 1, 2, 3; DAM POET; DLB 16, 48, 165, 212; DLBY 1982; EWL 3; INT CANR-14; MAL 5; MTCW 1, 2; MTFW 2005; RGAL 4
Reyes, Alfonso 1889-1959 .... **HLCS 2; TCLC 33**
See also CA 131; EWL 3; HW 1; LAW
Reyes y Basoalto, Ricardo Eliecer Neftali
See Neruda, Pablo
Reymont, Wladyslaw (Stanislaw) 1868(?)-1925 .... **TCLC 5**
See also CAAE 104; DLB 332; EWL 3
Reynolds, John Hamilton 1794-1852 .... **NCLC 146**
See also DLB 96
Reynolds, Jonathan 1942- .... **CLC 6, 38**
See also CA 65-68; CANR 28
Reynolds, Joshua 1723-1792 .... **LC 15**
See also DLB 104
Reynolds, Michael S(hane) 1937-2000 .... **CLC 44**
See also CA 65-68; CAAS 189; CANR 9, 89, 97
Reznikoff, Charles 1894-1976 .... **CLC 9**
See also AMWS 14; CA 33-36; CAAS 61-64; CAP 2; CP 1, 2; DLB 28, 45; RGHL; WP
Rezzori, Gregor von
See Rezzori d'Arezzo, Gregor von
Rezzori d'Arezzo, Gregor von 1914-1998 .... **CLC 25**
See also CA 136; CAAE 122; CAAS 167
Rhine, Richard
See Silverstein, Alvin; Silverstein, Virginia B(arbara Opshelor)
Rhodes, Eugene Manlove 1869-1934 .... **TCLC 53**
See also CA 198; DLB 256; TCWW 1, 2
R'hoone, Lord
See Balzac, Honore de
Rhys, Jean 1890-1979 .... **CLC 2, 4, 6, 14, 19, 51, 124; SSC 21, 76**
See also BRWS 2; CA 25-28R; CAAS 85-88; CANR 35, 62; CDBLB 1945-1960; CDWLB 3; CN 1, 2; DA3; DAM NOV; DLB 36, 117, 162; DNFS 2; EWL 3; LATS 1:1; MTCW 1, 2; MTFW 2005; NFS 19; RGEL 2; RGSF 2; RHW; TEA; WWE 1
Ribeiro, Darcy 1922-1997 .... **CLC 34**
See also CA 33-36R; CAAS 156; EWL 3
Ribeiro, Joao Ubaldo (Osorio Pimentel) 1941- .... **CLC 10, 67**
See also CA 81-84; CWW 2; EWL 3
Ribman, Ronald (Burt) 1932- .... **CLC 7**
See also CA 21-24R; CAD; CANR 46, 80; CD 5, 6
Ricci, Nino (Pio) 1959- .... **CLC 70**
See also CA 137; CANR 130; CCA 1
Rice, Anne 1941- .... **CLC 41, 128**
See Rampling, Anne
See also AAYA 9, 53; AMWS 7; BEST 89:2; BPFB 3; CA 65-68; CANR 12, 36, 53, 74, 100, 133; CN 6, 7; CPW; CSW; DA3; DAM POP; DLB 292; GL 3; GLL 2; HGG; MTCW 2; MTFW 2005; SUFW 2; YAW
Rice, Elmer (Leopold) 1892-1967 ...... **CLC 7, 49**
See Reizenstein, Elmer Leopold
See also CA 21-22; CAAS 25-28R; CAP 2; DAM DRAM; DFS 12; DLB 4, 7; IDTP; MAL 5; MTCW 1, 2; RGAL 4
Rice, Tim(othy Miles Bindon) 1944- .... **CLC 21**
See also CA 103; CANR 46; DFS 7
Rich, Adrienne 1929- ..... **CLC 3, 6, 7, 11, 18, 36, 73, 76, 125; PC 5**
See also AAYA 69; AMWR 2; AMWS 1; CA 9-12R; CANR 20, 53, 74, 128; CDALBS; CP 1, 2, 3, 4, 5, 6, 7; CSW; CWP; DA3; DAM POET; DLB 5, 67; EWL 3; EXPP; FL 1:6; FW; MAL 5; MBL; MTCW 1, 2; MTFW 2005; PAB; PFS 15; RGAL 4; RGHL; WP
Rich, Barbara
See Graves, Robert
Rich, Robert
See Trumbo, Dalton
Richard, Keith CLC 17
See Richards, Keith
Richards, David Adams 1950- .... **CLC 59**
See also CA 93-96; CANR 60, 110, 156; CN 7; DAC; DLB 53; TCLE 1:2
Richards, I(vor) A(rmstrong) 1893-1979 .... **CLC 14, 24**
See also BRWS 2; CA 41-44R; CAAS 89-92; CANR 34, 74; CP 1, 2; DLB 27; EWL 3; MTCW 2; RGEL 2
Richards, Keith 1943-
See Richard, Keith
See also CA 107; CANR 77
Richardson, Anne
See Roiphe, Anne
Richardson, Dorothy Miller 1873-1957 .... **TCLC 3, 203**
See also BRWS 13; CA 192; CAAE 104; DLB 36; EWL 3; FW; RGEL 2
Richardson (Robertson), Ethel Florence Lindesay 1870-1946
See Richardson, Henry Handel
See also CA 190; CAAE 105; DLB 230; RHW
Richardson, Henry Handel TCLC 4
See Richardson (Robertson), Ethel Florence Lindesay
See also DLB 197; EWL 3; RGEL 2; RGSF 2
Richardson, John 1796-1852 .... **NCLC 55**
See also CCA 1; DAC; DLB 99
Richardson, Samuel 1689-1761 ...... **LC 1, 44, 138; WLC 5**
See also BRW 3; CDBLB 1660-1789; DA; DAB; DAC; DAM MST, NOV; DLB 39; RGEL 2; TEA; WLIT 3
Richardson, Willis 1889-1977 .... **HR 1:3**
See also BW 1; CA 124; DLB 51; SATA 60
Richler, Mordecai 1931-2001 .... **CLC 3, 5, 9, 13, 18, 46, 70, 185**
See also AITN 1; CA 65-68; CAAS 201; CANR 31, 62, 111; CCA 1; CLR 17; CN 1, 2, 3, 4, 5, 7; CWRI 5; DAC; DAM MST, NOV; DLB 53; EWL 3; MAICYA 1, 2; MTCW 1, 2; MTFW 2005; RGEL 2; RGHL; SATA 44, 98; SATA-Brief 27; TWA

Richter, Conrad (Michael) 1890-1968 .... **CLC 30**
See also AAYA 21; BYA 2; CA 5-8R; CAAS 25-28R; CANR 23; DLB 9, 212; LAIT 1; MAL 5; MTCW 1, 2; MTFW 2005; RGAL 4; SATA 3; TCWW 1, 2; TUS; YAW
Ricostranza, Tom
See Ellis, Trey
Riddell, Charlotte 1832-1906 .... **TCLC 40**
See Riddell, Mrs. J. H.
See also CA 165; DLB 156
Riddell, Mrs. J. H.
See Riddell, Charlotte
See also HGG; SUFW
Ridge, John Rollin 1827-1867 ...... **NCLC 82; NNAL**
See also CA 144; DAM MULT; DLB 175
Ridgeway, Jason
See Marlowe, Stephen
Ridgway, Keith 1965- .... **CLC 119**
See also CA 172; CANR 144
Riding, Laura CLC 3, 7
See Jackson, Laura (Riding)
See also CP 1, 2, 3, 4, 5; RGAL 4
Riefenstahl, Berta Helene Amalia 1902-2003
See Riefenstahl, Leni
See also CA 108; CAAS 220
Riefenstahl, Leni CLC 16, 190
See Riefenstahl, Berta Helene Amalia
Riffe, Ernest
See Bergman, Ingmar
Riffe, Ernest Ingmar
See Bergman, Ingmar
Riggs, (Rolla) Lynn 1899-1954 .... **NNAL; TCLC 56**
See also CA 144; DAM MULT; DLB 175
Riis, Jacob A(ugust) 1849-1914 ..... **TCLC 80**
See also CA 168; CAAE 113; DLB 23
Riley, James Whitcomb 1849-1916 .... **PC 48; TCLC 51**
See also CA 137; CAAE 118; DAM POET; MAICYA 1, 2; RGAL 4; SATA 17
Riley, Tex
See Creasey, John
Rilke, Rainer Maria 1875-1926 .... **PC 2; TCLC 1, 6, 19, 195**
See also CA 132; CAAE 104; CANR 62, 99; CDWLB 2; DA3; DAM POET; DLB 81; EW 9; EWL 3; MTCW 1, 2; MTFW 2005; PFS 19, 27; RGWL 2, 3; TWA; WP
Rimbaud, (Jean Nicolas) Arthur 1854-1891 ... **NCLC 4, 35, 82; PC 3, 57; WLC 5**
See also DA; DA3; DAB; DAC; DAM MST, POET; DLB 217; EW 7; GFL 1789 to the Present; LMFS 2; RGWL 2, 3; TWA; WP
Rinehart, Mary Roberts 1876-1958 .... **TCLC 52**
See also BPFB 3; CA 166; CAAE 108; RGAL 4; RHW
Ringmaster, The
See Mencken, H(enry) L(ouis)
Ringwood, Gwen(dolyn Margaret) Pharis 1910-1984 .... **CLC 48**
See also CA 148; CAAS 112; DLB 88
Rio, Michel 1945(?)- .... **CLC 43**
See also CA 201
Rios, Alberto 1952- .... **PC 57**
See also AAYA 66; AMWS 4; CA 113; CANR 34, 79, 137; CP 6, 7; DLB 122; HW 2; MTFW 2005; PFS 11
Ritsos, Giannes
See Ritsos, Yannis
Ritsos, Yannis 1909-1990 .... **CLC 6, 13, 31**
See also CA 77-80; CAAS 133; CANR 39, 61; EW 12; EWL 3; MTCW 1; RGWL 2, 3
Ritter, Erika 1948(?)- .... **CLC 52**
See also CD 5, 6; CWD
Rivera, Jose Eustasio 1889-1928 ... **TCLC 35**
See also CA 162; EWL 3; HW 1, 2; LAW
Rivera, Tomas 1935-1984 .... **HLCS 2**
See also CA 49-52; CANR 32; DLB 82; HW 1; LLW; RGAL 4; SSFS 15; TCWW 2; WLIT 1
Rivers, Conrad Kent 1933-1968 .... **CLC 1**
See also BW 1; CA 85-88; DLB 41
Rivers, Elfrida
See Bradley, Marion Zimmer
See also GLL 1
Riverside, John
See Heinlein, Robert A.
Rizal, Jose 1861-1896 .... **NCLC 27**
Roaag, Ole Edvart
See Rolvaag, O.E.
Roa Bastos, Augusto 1917-2005 ...... **CLC 45; HLC 2**
See also CA 131; CAAS 238; CWW 2; DAM MULT; DLB 113; EWL 3; HW 1; LAW; RGSF 2; WLIT 1
Roa Bastos, Augusto Jose Antonio
See Roa Bastos, Augusto
Robbe-Grillet, Alain 1922-2008 ..... **CLC 1, 2, 4, 6, 8, 10, 14, 43, 128**
See also BPFB 3; CA 9-12R; CANR 33, 65, 115; CWW 2; DLB 83; EW 13; EWL 3; GFL 1789 to the Present; IDFW 3, 4; MTCW 1, 2; MTFW 2005; RGWL 2, 3; SSFS 15
Robbins, Harold 1916-1997 .... **CLC 5**
See also BPFB 3; CA 73-76; CAAS 162; CANR 26, 54, 112, 156; DA3; DAM NOV; MTCW 1, 2
Robbins, Thomas Eugene 1936-
See Robbins, Tom
See also CA 81-84; CANR 29, 59, 95, 139; CN 7; CPW; CSW; DA3; DAM NOV, POP; MTCW 1, 2; MTFW 2005
Robbins, Tom CLC 9, 32, 64
See Robbins, Thomas Eugene
See also AAYA 32; AMWS 10; BEST 90:3; BPFB 3; CN 3, 4, 5, 6, 7; DLBY 1980
Robbins, Trina 1938- .... **CLC 21**
See also AAYA 61; CA 128; CANR 152
Robert de Boron fl. 12th cent. - .... **CMLC 94**
Roberts, Charles G(eorge) D(ouglas) 1860-1943 .... **SSC 91; TCLC 8**
See also CA 188; CAAE 105; CLR 33; CWRI 5; DLB 92; RGEL 2; RGSF 2; SATA 88; SATA-Brief 29
Roberts, Elizabeth Madox 1886-1941 .... **TCLC 68**
See also CA 166; CAAE 111; CLR 100; CWRI 5; DLB 9, 54, 102; RGAL 4; RHW; SATA 33; SATA-Brief 27; TCWW 2; WCH
Roberts, Kate 1891-1985 .... **CLC 15**
See also CA 107; CAAS 116; DLB 319
Roberts, Keith (John Kingston) 1935-2000 .... **CLC 14**
See also BRWS 10; CA 25-28R; CANR 46; DLB 261; SFW 4
Roberts, Kenneth (Lewis) 1885-1957 .... **TCLC 23**
See also CA 199; CAAE 109; DLB 9; MAL 5; RGAL 4; RHW
Roberts, Michele 1949- .... **CLC 48, 178**
See also CA 115; CANR 58, 120, 164; CN 6, 7; DLB 231; FW
Roberts, Michele Brigitte
See Roberts, Michele
Robertson, Ellis
See Ellison, Harlan; Silverberg, Robert
Robertson, Thomas William 1829-1871 .... **NCLC 35**
See Robertson, Tom
See also DAM DRAM
Robertson, Tom
See Robertson, Thomas William
See also RGEL 2
Robeson, Kenneth
See Dent, Lester
Robinson, Edwin Arlington 1869-1935 .... **PC 1, 35; TCLC 5, 101**
See also AAYA 72; AMW; CA 133; CAAE 104; CDALB 1865-1917; DA; DAC; DAM MST, POET; DLB 54; EWL 3; EXPP; MAL 5; MTCW 1, 2; MTFW 2005; PAB; PFS 4; RGAL 4; WP
Robinson, Henry Crabb 1775-1867 .... **NCLC 15**
See also DLB 107
Robinson, Jill 1936- .... **CLC 10**
See also CA 102; CANR 120; INT CA-102
Robinson, Kim Stanley 1952- ... **CLC 34, 248**
See also AAYA 26; CA 126; CANR 113, 139, 173; CN 6, 7; MTFW 2005; SATA 109; SCFW 2; SFW 4
Robinson, Lloyd
See Silverberg, Robert
Robinson, Marilynne 1944- ...... **CLC 25, 180**
See also AAYA 69; CA 116; CANR 80, 140; CN 4, 5, 6, 7; DLB 206; MTFW 2005; NFS 24
Robinson, Mary 1758-1800 .... **NCLC 142**
See also BRWS 13; DLB 158; FW
Robinson, Smokey CLC 21
See Robinson, William, Jr.
Robinson, William, Jr. 1940-
See Robinson, Smokey
See also CAAE 116
Robison, Mary 1949- .... **CLC 42, 98**
See also CA 116; CAAE 113; CANR 87; CN 4, 5, 6, 7; DLB 130; INT CA-116; RGSF 2
Roches, Catherine des 1542-1587 ...... **LC 117**
See also DLB 327
Rochester
See Wilmot, John
See also RGEL 2
Rod, Edouard 1857-1910 .... **TCLC 52**
Roddenberry, Eugene Wesley 1921-1991
See Roddenberry, Gene
See also CA 110; CAAS 135; CANR 37; SATA 45; SATA-Obit 69
Roddenberry, Gene CLC 17
See Roddenberry, Eugene Wesley
See also AAYA 5; SATA-Obit 69
Rodgers, Mary 1931- .... **CLC 12**
See also BYA 5; CA 49-52; CANR 8, 55, 90; CLR 20; CWRI 5; INT CANR-8; JRDA; MAICYA 1, 2; SATA 8, 130
Rodgers, W(illiam) R(obert) 1909-1969 .... **CLC 7**
See also CA 85-88; DLB 20; RGEL 2
Rodman, Eric
See Silverberg, Robert
Rodman, Howard 1920(?)-1985 .... **CLC 65**
See also CAAS 118
Rodman, Maia
See Wojciechowska, Maia (Teresa)
Rodo, Jose Enrique 1871(?)-1917 .... **HLCS 2**
See also CA 178; EWL 3; HW 2; LAW
Rodolph, Utto
See Ouologuem, Yambo
Rodriguez, Claudio 1934-1999 .... **CLC 10**
See also CA 188; DLB 134

Rodriguez, Richard 1944- .... **CLC 155; HLC 2**
See also AMWS 14; CA 110; CANR 66, 116; DAM MULT; DLB 82, 256; HW 1, 2; LAIT 5; LLW; MTFW 2005; NCFS 3; WLIT 1
Roethke, Theodore 1908-1963 ... **CLC 1, 3, 8, 11, 19, 46, 101; PC 15**
See also AMW; CA 81-84; CABS 2; CDALB 1941-1968; DA3; DAM POET; DLB 5, 206; EWL 3; EXPP; MAL 5; MTCW 1, 2; PAB; PFS 3; RGAL 4; WP
Roethke, Theodore Huebner
See Roethke, Theodore
Rogers, Carl R(ansom)
1902-1987 .... **TCLC 125**
See also CA 1-4R; CAAS 121; CANR 1, 18; MTCW 1
Rogers, Samuel 1763-1855 .... **NCLC 69**
See also DLB 93; RGEL 2
Rogers, Thomas 1927-2007 .... **CLC 57**
See also CA 89-92; CAAS 259; CANR 163; INT CA-89-92
Rogers, Thomas Hunton
See Rogers, Thomas
Rogers, Will(iam Penn Adair)
1879-1935 .... **NNAL; TCLC 8, 71**
See also CA 144; CAAE 105; DA3; DAM MULT; DLB 11; MTCW 2
Rogin, Gilbert 1929- .... **CLC 18**
See also CA 65-68; CANR 15
Rohan, Koda
See Koda Shigeyuki
Rohlfs, Anna Katharine Green
See Green, Anna Katharine
Rohmer, Eric CLC 16
See Scherer, Jean-Marie Maurice
Rohmer, Sax TCLC 28
See Ward, Arthur Henry Sarsfield
See also DLB 70; MSW; SUFW
Roiphe, Anne 1935- .... **CLC 3, 9**
See also CA 89-92; CANR 45, 73, 138, 170; DLBY 1980; INT CA-89-92
Roiphe, Anne Richardson
See Roiphe, Anne
Rojas, Fernando de 1475-1541 ... **HLCS 1, 2; LC 23**
See also DLB 286; RGWL 2, 3
Rojas, Gonzalo 1917- .... **HLCS 2**
See also CA 178; HW 2; LAWS 1
Roland (de la Platiere), Marie-Jeanne
1754-1793 .... **LC 98**
See also DLB 314
Rolfe, Frederick (William Serafino Austin Lewis Mary) 1860-1913 .... **TCLC 12**
See Al Siddik
See also CA 210; CAAE 107; DLB 34, 156; RGEL 2
Rolland, Romain 1866-1944 .... **TCLC 23**
See also CA 197; CAAE 118; DLB 65, 284, 332; EWL 3; GFL 1789 to the Present; RGWL 2, 3
Rolle, Richard c. 1300-c. 1349 ...... **CMLC 21**
See also DLB 146; LMFS 1; RGEL 2
Rolvaag, O.E.
See Rolvaag, O.E.
Rolvaag, O.E. 1876-1931 .... **TCLC 17**
See also AAYA 75; CA 171; CAAE 117; DLB 9, 212; MAL 5; NFS 5; RGAL 4; TCWW 1,2
Romain Arnaud, Saint
See Aragon, Louis
Romains, Jules 1885-1972 .... **CLC 7**
See also CA 85-88; CANR 34; DLB 65, 321; EWL 3; GFL 1789 to the Present; MTCW 1
Romero, Jose Ruben 1890-1952 .... **TCLC 14**
See also CA 131; CAAE 114; EWL 3; HW 1; LAW
Ronsard, Pierre de 1524-1585 . **LC 6, 54; PC 11**
See also DLB 327; EW 2; GFL Beginnings to 1789; RGWL 2, 3; TWA
Rooke, Leon 1934- .... **CLC 25, 34**
See also CA 25-28R; CANR 23, 53; CCA 1; CPW; DAM POP
Roosevelt, Franklin Delano
1882-1945 .... **TCLC 93**
See also CA 173; CAAE 116; LAIT 3
Roosevelt, Theodore 1858-1919 ..... **TCLC 69**
See also CA 170; CAAE 115; DLB 47, 186, 275
Roper, Margaret c. 1505-1544 .... **LC 147**
Roper, William 1498-1578 .... **LC 10**
Roquelaure, A. N.
See Rice, Anne
Rosa, Joao Guimaraes 1908-1967 ... **CLC 23; HLCS 1**
See Guimaraes Rosa, Joao
See also CAAS 89-92; DLB 113, 307; EWL 3; WLIT 1
Rose, Wendy 1948- . **CLC 85; NNAL; PC 13**
See also CA 53-56; CANR 5, 51; CWP; DAM MULT; DLB 175; PFS 13; RGAL 4; SATA 12
Rosen, R. D.
See Rosen, Richard (Dean)
Rosen, Richard (Dean) 1949- .... **CLC 39**
See also CA 77-80; CANR 62, 120; CMW 4; INT CANR-30
Rosenberg, Isaac 1890-1918 .... **TCLC 12**
See also BRW 6; CA 188; CAAE 107; DLB 20, 216; EWL 3; PAB; RGEL 2
Rosenblatt, Joe CLC 15
See Rosenblatt, Joseph
See also CP 3, 4, 5, 6, 7
Rosenblatt, Joseph 1933-
See Rosenblatt, Joe
See also CA 89-92; CP 1, 2; INT CA-89-92
Rosenfeld, Samuel
See Tzara, Tristan
Rosenstock, Sami
See Tzara, Tristan
Rosenstock, Samuel
See Tzara, Tristan
Rosenthal, M(acha) L(ouis)
1917-1996 .... **CLC 28**
See also CA 1-4R; 6; CAAS 152; CANR 4, 51; CP 1, 2, 3, 4, 5, 6; DLB 5; SATA 59
Ross, Barnaby
See Dannay, Frederic; Lee, Manfred B.
Ross, Bernard L.
See Follett, Ken
Ross, J. H.
See Lawrence, T(homas) E(dward)
Ross, John Hume
See Lawrence, T(homas) E(dward)
Ross, Martin 1862-1915
See Martin, Violet Florence
See also DLB 135; GLL 2; RGEL 2; RGSF 2
Ross, (James) Sinclair 1908-1996 ... **CLC 13; SSC 24**
See also CA 73-76; CANR 81; CN 1, 2, 3, 4, 5, 6; DAC; DAM MST; DLB 88; RGEL 2; RGSF 2; TCWW 1, 2
Rossetti, Christina 1830-1894 ... **NCLC 2, 50, 66, 186; PC 7; WLC 5**
See also AAYA 51; BRW 5; BYA 4; CLR 115; DA; DA3; DAB; DAC; DAM MST, POET; DLB 35, 163, 240; EXPP; FL 1:3; LATS 1:1; MAICYA 1, 2; PFS 10, 14, 27; RGEL 2; SATA 20; TEA; WCH
Rossetti, Christina Georgina
See Rossetti, Christina
Rossetti, Dante Gabriel 1828-1882 . **NCLC 4, 77; PC 44; WLC 5**
See also AAYA 51; BRW 5; CDBLB 1832-1890; DA; DAB; DAC; DAM MST, POET; DLB 35; EXPP; RGEL 2; TEA
Rossi, Cristina Peri
See Peri Rossi, Cristina
Rossi, Jean-Baptiste 1931-2003
See Japrisot, Sebastien
See also CA 201; CAAS 215
Rossner, Judith 1935-2005 .... **CLC 6, 9, 29**
See also AITN 2; BEST 90:3; BPFB 3; CA 17-20R; CAAS 242; CANR 18, 51, 73; CN 4, 5, 6, 7; DLB 6; INT CANR-18; MAL 5; MTCW 1, 2; MTFW 2005
Rossner, Judith Perelman
See Rossner, Judith
Rostand, Edmond (Eugene Alexis)
1868-1918 .... **DC 10; TCLC 6, 37**
See also CA 126; CAAE 104; DA; DA3; DAB; DAC; DAM DRAM, MST; DFS 1; DLB 192; LAIT 1; MTCW 1; RGWL 2, 3; TWA
Roth, Henry 1906-1995 ..... **CLC 2, 6, 11, 104**
See also AMWS 9; CA 11-12; CAAS 149; CANR 38, 63; CAP 1; CN 1, 2, 3, 4, 5, 6; DA3; DLB 28; EWL 3; MAL 5; MTCW 1, 2; MTFW 2005; RGAL 4
Roth, (Moses) Joseph 1894-1939 ... **TCLC 33**
See also CA 160; DLB 85; EWL 3; RGWL 2, 3
Roth, Philip 1933- ... **CLC 1, 2, 3, 4, 6, 9, 15, 22, 31, 47, 66, 86, 119, 201; SSC 26, 102; WLC 5**
See also AAYA 67; AMWR 2; AMWS 3; BEST 90:3; BPFB 3; CA 1-4R; CANR 1, 22, 36, 55, 89, 132, 170; CDALB 1968-1988; CN 3, 4, 5, 6, 7; CPW 1; DA; DA3; DAB; DAC; DAM MST, NOV, POP; DLB 2, 28, 173; DLBY 1982; EWL 3; MAL 5; MTCW 1, 2; MTFW 2005; NFS 25; RGAL 4; RGHL; RGSF 2; SSFS 12, 18; TUS
Roth, Philip Milton
See Roth, Philip
Rothenberg, Jerome 1931- .... **CLC 6, 57**
See also CA 45-48; CANR 1, 106; CP 1, 2, 3, 4, 5, 6, 7; DLB 5, 193
Rotter, Pat CLC 65
Roumain, Jacques (Jean Baptiste)
1907-1944 .... **BLC 1:3; TCLC 19**
See also BW 1; CA 125; CAAE 117; DAM MULT; EWL 3
Rourke, Constance Mayfield
1885-1941 .... **TCLC 12**
See also CA 200; CAAE 107; MAL 5; YABC 1
Rousseau, Jean-Baptiste 1671-1741 ...... **LC 9**
Rousseau, Jean-Jacques 1712-1778 .... **LC 14, 36, 122; WLC 5**
See also DA; DA3; DAB; DAC; DAM MST; DLB 314; EW 4; GFL Beginnings to 1789; LMFS 1; RGWL 2, 3; TWA
Roussel, Raymond 1877-1933 .... **TCLC 20**
See also CA 201; CAAE 117; EWL 3; GFL 1789 to the Present
Rovit, Earl (Herbert) 1927- .... **CLC 7**
See also CA 5-8R; CANR 12
Rowe, Elizabeth Singer 1674-1737 ..... **LC 44**
See also DLB 39, 95
Rowe, Nicholas 1674-1718 .... **LC 8**
See also DLB 84; RGEL 2
Rowlandson, Mary 1637(?)-1678 .... **LC 66**
See also DLB 24, 200; RGAL 4
Rowley, Ames Dorrance
See Lovecraft, H. P.
Rowley, William 1585(?)-1626 ... **LC 100, 123**
See also DFS 22; DLB 58; RGEL 2

Sagan, Carl 1934-1996 .... **CLC 30, 112**
See also AAYA 2, 62; CA 25-28R; CAAS 155; CANR 11, 36, 74; CPW; DA3; MTCW 1, 2; MTFW 2005; SATA 58; SATA-Obit 94
Sagan, Francoise CLC 3, 6, 9, 17, 36
See Quoirez, Francoise
See also CWW 2; DLB 83; EWL 3; GFL 1789 to the Present; MTCW 2
Sahgal, Nayantara (Pandit) 1927- .... **CLC 41**
See also CA 9-12R; CANR 11, 88; CN 1, 2, 3, 4, 5, 6, 7; DLB 323
Said, Edward W. 1935-2003 .... **CLC 123**
See also CA 21-24R; CAAS 220; CANR 45, 74, 107, 131; DLB 67; MTCW 2; MTFW 2005
Saikaku, Ihara 1642-1693 .... **LC 141**
See also RGWL 3
Saikaku Ihara
See Saikaku, Ihara
Saint, H(arry) F. 1941- .... **CLC 50**
See also CA 127
St. Aubin de Teran, Lisa 1953-
See Teran, Lisa St. Aubin de
See also CA 126; CAAE 118; CN 6, 7; INT CA-126
Saint Birgitta of Sweden c. 1303-1373 .... **CMLC 24**
Sainte-Beuve, Charles Augustin 1804-1869 .... **NCLC 5**
See also DLB 217; EW 6; GFL 1789 to the Present
Saint-Exupery, Antoine de 1900-1944 .... **TCLC 2, 56, 169; WLC**
See also AAYA 63; BPFB 3; BYA 3; CA 132; CAAE 108; CLR 10; DA3; DAM NOV; DLB 72; EW 12; EWL 3; GFL 1789 to the Present; LAIT 3; MAICYA 1, 2; MTCW 1, 2; MTFW 2005; RGWL 2, 3; SATA 20; TWA
Saint-Exupery, Antoine Jean Baptiste Marie Roger de
See Saint-Exupery, Antoine de
St. John, David
See Hunt, E. Howard
St. John, J. Hector
See Crevecoeur, Michel Guillaume Jean de
Saint-John Perse
See Leger, (Marie-Rene Auguste) Alexis Saint-Leger
See also EW 10; EWL 3; GFL 1789 to the Present; RGWL 2
Saintsbury, George (Edward Bateman) 1845-1933 .... **TCLC 31**
See also CA 160; DLB 57, 149
Sait Faik TCLC 23
See Abasiyanik, Sait Faik
Saki SSC 12; TCLC 3; WLC 5
See Munro, H(ector) H(ugh)
See also BRWS 6; BYA 11; LAIT 2; RGEL 2; SSFS 1; SUFW
Sala, George Augustus 1828-1895 . **NCLC 46**
Saladin 1138-1193 .... **CMLC 38**
Salama, Hannu 1936- .... **CLC 18**
See also CA 244; EWL 3
Salamanca, J(ack) R(ichard) 1922- .. **CLC 4, 15**
See also CA 193; 25-28R, 193
Salas, Floyd Francis 1931- .... **HLC 2**
See also CA 119; 27; CANR 44, 75, 93; DAM MULT; DLB 82; HW 1, 2; MTCW 2; MTFW 2005
Sale, J. Kirkpatrick
See Sale, Kirkpatrick
Sale, John Kirkpatrick
See Sale, Kirkpatrick
Sale, Kirkpatrick 1937- .... **CLC 68**
See also CA 13-16R; CANR 10, 147
Salinas, Luis Omar 1937- ... **CLC 90; HLC 2**
See also AMWS 13; CA 131; CANR 81, 153; DAM MULT; DLB 82; HW 1, 2
Salinas (y Serrano), Pedro 1891(?)-1951 .... **TCLC 17**
See also CAAE 117; DLB 134; EWL 3
Salinger, J.D. 1919- . **CLC 1, 3, 8, 12, 55, 56, 138, 243; SSC 2, 28, 65; WLC 5**
See also AAYA 2, 36; AMW; AMWC 1; BPFB 3; CA 5-8R; CANR 39, 129; CDALB 1941-1968; CLR 18; CN 1, 2, 3, 4, 5, 6, 7; CPW 1; DA; DA3; DAB; DAC; DAM MST, NOV, POP; DLB 2, 102, 173; EWL 3; EXPN; LAIT 4; MAICYA 1, 2; MAL 5; MTCW 1, 2; MTFW 2005; NFS 1; RGAL 4; RGSF 2; SATA 67; SSFS 17; TUS; WYA; YAW
Salisbury, John
See Caute, (John) David
Sallust c. 86B.C.-35B.C. .... **CMLC 68**
See also AW 2; CDWLB 1; DLB 211; RGWL 2, 3
Salter, James 1925- .. **CLC 7, 52, 59; SSC 58**
See also AMWS 9; CA 73-76; CANR 107, 160; DLB 130; SSFS 25
Saltus, Edgar (Everton) 1855-1921 . **TCLC 8**
See also CAAE 105; DLB 202; RGAL 4
Saltykov, Mikhail Evgrafovich 1826-1889 .... **NCLC 16**
See also DLB 238:
Saltykov-Shchedrin, N.
See Saltykov, Mikhail Evgrafovich
Samarakis, Andonis
See Samarakis, Antonis
See also EWL 3
Samarakis, Antonis 1919-2003 .... **CLC 5**
See Samarakis, Andonis
See also CA 25-28R; 16; CAAS 224; CANR 36
Sanchez, Florencio 1875-1910 .... **TCLC 37**
See also CA 153; DLB 305; EWL 3; HW 1; LAW
Sanchez, Luis Rafael 1936- .... **CLC 23**
See also CA 128; DLB 305; EWL 3; HW 1; WLIT 1
Sanchez, Sonia 1934- . **BLC 1:3; CLC 5, 116, 215; PC 9**
See also BW 2, 3; CA 33-36R; CANR 24, 49, 74, 115; CLR 18; CP 2, 3, 4, 5, 6, 7; CSW; CWP; DA3; DAM MULT; DLB 41; DLBD 8; EWL 3; MAICYA 1, 2; MAL 5; MTCW 1, 2; MTFW 2005; PFS 26; SATA 22, 136; WP
Sancho, Ignatius 1729-1780 .... **LC 84**
Sand, George 1804-1876 .... **DC 29; NCLC 2, 42, 57, 174; WLC 5**
See also DA; DA3; DAB; DAC; DAM MST, NOV; DLB 119, 192; EW 6; FL 1:3; FW; GFL 1789 to the Present; RGWL 2, 3; TWA
Sandburg, Carl (August) 1878-1967 . **CLC 1, 4, 10, 15, 35; PC 2, 41; WLC 5**
See also AAYA 24; AMW; BYA 1, 3; CA 5-8R; CAAS 25-28R; CANR 35; CDALB 1865-1917; CLR 67; DA; DA3; DAB; DAC; DAM MST, POET; DLB 17, 54, 284; EWL 3; EXPP; LAIT 2; MAICYA 1, 2; MAL 5; MTCW 1, 2; MTFW 2005; PAB; PFS 3, 6, 12; RGAL 4; SATA 8; TUS; WCH; WP; WYA
Sandburg, Charles
See Sandburg, Carl (August)
Sandburg, Charles A.
See Sandburg, Carl (August)
Sanders, (James) Ed(ward) 1939- .... **CLC 53**
See Sanders, Edward
See also BG 1:3; CA 13-16R; 21; CANR 13, 44, 78; CP 1, 2, 3, 4, 5, 6, 7; DAM POET; DLB 16, 244
Sanders, Edward
See Sanders, (James) Ed(ward)
See also DLB 244
Sanders, Lawrence 1920-1998 .... **CLC 41**
See also BEST 89:4; BPFB 3; CA 81-84; CAAS 165; CANR 33, 62; CMW 4; CPW; DA3; DAM POP; MTCW 1
Sanders, Noah
See Blount, Roy (Alton), Jr.
Sanders, Winston P.
See Anderson, Poul
Sandoz, Mari(e Susette) 1900-1966 .. **CLC 28**
See also CA 1-4R; CAAS 25-28R; CANR 17, 64; DLB 9, 212; LAIT 2; MTCW 1, 2; SATA 5; TCWW 1, 2
Sandys, George 1578-1644 .... **LC 80**
See also DLB 24, 121
Saner, Reg(inald Anthony) 1931- .... **CLC 9**
See also CA 65-68; CP 3, 4, 5, 6, 7
Sankara 788-820 .... **CMLC 32**
Sannazaro, Jacopo 1456(?)-1530 .... **LC 8**
See also RGWL 2, 3; WLIT 7
Sansom, William 1912-1976 . **CLC 2, 6; SSC 21**
See also CA 5-8R; CAAS 65-68; CANR 42; CN 1, 2; DAM NOV; DLB 139; EWL 3; MTCW 1; RGEL 2; RGSF 2
Santayana, George 1863-1952 .... **TCLC 40**
See also AMW; CA 194; CAAE 115; DLB 54, 71, 246, 270; DLBD 13; EWL 3; MAL 5; RGAL 4; TUS
Santiago, Danny CLC 33
See James, Daniel (Lewis)
See also DLB 122
Santillana, Inigo Lopez de Mendoza, Marques de 1398-1458 .... **LC 111**
See also DLB 286
Santmyer, Helen Hooven 1895-1986 .... **CLC 33; TCLC 133**
See also CA 1-4R; CAAS 118; CANR 15, 33; DLBY 1984; MTCW 1; RHW
Santoka, Taneda 1882-1940 .... **TCLC 72**
Santos, Bienvenido N(uqui) 1911-1996 ... **AAL; CLC 22; TCLC 156**
See also CA 101; CAAS 151; CANR 19, 46; CP 1; DAM MULT; DLB 312; EWL; RGAL 4; SSFS 19
Sapir, Edward 1884-1939 .... **TCLC 108**
See also CA 211; DLB 92
Sapper TCLC 44
See McNeile, Herman Cyril
Sapphire 1950- .... **CLC 99**
See also CA 262
Sapphire, Brenda
See Sapphire
Sappho fl. 6th cent. B.C.- ... **CMLC 3, 67; PC 5**
See also CDWLB 1; DA3; DAM POET; DLB 176; FL 1:1; PFS 20; RGWL 2, 3; WLIT 8; WP
Saramago, Jose 1922- ..... **CLC 119; HLCS 1**
See also CA 153; CANR 96, 164; CWW 2; DLB 287, 332; EWL 3; LATS 1:2; SSFS 23
Sarduy, Severo 1937-1993 .... **CLC 6, 97; HLCS 2; TCLC 167**
See also CA 89-92; CAAS 142; CANR 58, 81; CWW 2; DLB 113; EWL 3; HW 1, 2; LAW
Sargeson, Frank 1903-1982 ..... **CLC 31; SSC 99**
See also CA 25-28R; CAAS 106; CANR 38, 79; CN 1, 2, 3; EWL 3; GLL 2; RGEL 2; RGSF 2; SSFS 20
Sarmiento, Domingo Faustino 1811-1888 .... **HLCS 2; NCLC 123**
See also LAW; WLIT 1
Sarmiento, Felix Ruben Garcia
See Dario, Ruben

Seton, Ernest (Evan) Thompson 1860-1946 .... **TCLC 31**
See also ANW; BYA 3; CA 204; CAAE 109; CLR 59; DLB 92; DLBD 13; JRDA; SATA 18

Seton-Thompson, Ernest
See Seton, Ernest (Evan) Thompson

Settle, Mary Lee 1918-2005 .... **CLC 19, 61**
See also BPFB 3; CA 89-92; 1; CAAS 243; CANR 44, 87, 126; CN 6, 7; CSW; DLB 6; INT CA-89-92

Seuphor, Michel
See Arp, Jean

Sevigne, Marie (de Rabutin-Chantal) 1626-1696 .... **LC 11, 144**
See Sevigne, Marie de Rabutin Chantal
See also GFL Beginnings to 1789; TWA

Sevigne, Marie de Rabutin Chantal
See Sevigne, Marie (de Rabutin-Chantal)
See also DLB 268

Sewall, Samuel 1652-1730 .... **LC 38**
See also DLB 24; RGAL 4

Sexton, Anne (Harvey) 1928-1974 ..... **CLC 2, 4, 6, 8, 10, 15, 53, 123; PC 2, 79; WLC 5**
See also AMWS 2; CA 1-4R; CAAS 53-56; CABS 2; CANR 3, 36; CDALB 1941-1968; CP 1, 2; DA; DA3; DAB; DAC; DAM MST, POET; DLB 5, 169; EWL 3; EXPP; FL 1:6; FW; MAL 5; MBL; MTCW 1, 2; MTFW 2005; PAB; PFS 4, 14; RGAL 4; RGHL; SATA 10; TUS

Shaara, Jeff 1952- .... **CLC 119**
See also AAYA 70; CA 163; CANR 109, 172; CN 7; MTFW 2005

Shaara, Michael 1929-1988 .... **CLC 15**
See also AAYA 71; AITN 1; BPFB 3; CA 102; CAAS 125; CANR 52, 85; DAM POP; DLBY 1983; MTFW 2005; NFS 26

Shackleton, C.C.
See Aldiss, Brian W.

Shacochis, Bob CLC 39
See Shacochis, Robert G.

Shacochis, Robert G. 1951-
See Shacochis, Bob
See also CA 124; CAAE 119; CANR 100; INT CA-124

Shadwell, Thomas 1641(?)-1692 .... **LC 114**
See also DLB 80; IDTP; RGEL 2

Shaffer, Anthony 1926-2001 .... **CLC 19**
See also CA 116; CAAE 110; CAAS 200; CBD; CD 5, 6; DAM DRAM; DFS 13; DLB 13

Shaffer, Anthony Joshua
See Shaffer, Anthony

Shaffer, Peter 1926- ... **CLC 5, 14, 18, 37, 60; DC 7**
See also BRWS 1; CA 25-28R; CANR 25, 47, 74, 118; CBD; CD 5, 6; CDBLB 1960 to Present; DA3; DAB; DAM DRAM, MST; DFS 5, 13; DLB 13, 233; EWL 3; MTCW 1, 2; MTFW 2005; RGEL 2; TEA

Shakespeare, William 1564-1616 .... **PC 84; WLC 5**
See also AAYA 35; BRW 1; CDBLB Before 1660; DA; DA3; DAB; DAC; DAM DRAM, MST, POET; DFS 20, 21; DLB 62, 172, 263; EXPP; LAIT 1; LATS 1:1; LMFS 1; PAB; PFS 1, 2, 3, 4, 5, 8, 9; RGEL 2; TEA; WLIT 3; WP; WS; WYA

Shakey, Bernard
See Young, Neil

Shalamov, Varlam (Tikhonovich) 1907-1982 .... **CLC 18**
See also CA 129; CAAS 105; DLB 302; RGSF 2

Shamloo, Ahmad
See Shamlu, Ahmad

Shamlou, Ahmad
See Shamlu, Ahmad

Shamlu, Ahmad 1925-2000 .... **CLC 10**
See also CA 216; CWW 2

Shammas, Anton 1951- .... **CLC 55**
See also CA 199

Shandling, Arline
See Berriault, Gina

Shange, Ntozake 1948- ...... **BLC 1:3; CLC 8, 25, 38, 74, 126; DC 3**
See also AAYA 9, 66; AFAW 1, 2; BW 2; CA 85-88; CABS 3; CAD; CANR 27, 48, 74, 131; CD 5, 6; CP 5, 6, 7; CWD; CWP; DA3; DAM DRAM, MULT; DFS 2, 11; DLB 38, 249; FW; LAIT 4, 5; MAL 5; MTCW 1, 2; MTFW 2005; NFS 11; RGAL 4; SATA 157; YAW

Shanley, John Patrick 1950- .... **CLC 75**
See also AAYA 74; AMWS 14; CA 133; CAAE 128; CAD; CANR 83, 154; CD 5, 6; DFS 23

Shapcott, Thomas W(illiam) 1935- .. **CLC 38**
See also CA 69-72; CANR 49, 83, 103; CP 1, 2, 3, 4, 5, 6, 7; DLB 289

Shapiro, Jane 1942- .... **CLC 76**
See also CA 196

Shapiro, Karl 1913-2000 ... **CLC 4, 8, 15, 53; PC 25**
See also AMWS 2; CA 1-4R; 6; CAAS 188; CANR 1, 36, 66; CP 1, 2, 3, 4, 5, 6; DLB 48; EWL 3; EXPP; MAL 5; MTCW 1, 2; MTFW 2005; PFS 3; RGAL 4

Sharp, William 1855-1905 .... **TCLC 39**
See Macleod, Fiona
See also CA 160; DLB 156; RGEL 2

Sharpe, Thomas Ridley 1928-
See Sharpe, Tom
See also CA 122; CAAE 114; CANR 85; INT CA-122

Sharpe, Tom CLC 36
See Sharpe, Thomas Ridley
See also CN 4, 5, 6, 7; DLB 14, 231

Shatrov, Mikhail CLC 59

Shaw, Bernard
See Shaw, George Bernard
See also DLB 10, 57, 190

Shaw, G. Bernard
See Shaw, George Bernard

Shaw, George Bernard 1856-1950 ..... **DC 23; TCLC 3, 9, 21, 45; WLC 5**
See Shaw, Bernard
See also AAYA 61; BRW 6; BRWC 1; BRWR 2; CA 128; CAAE 104; CDBLB 1914-1945; DA; DA3; DAB; DAC; DAM DRAM, MST; DFS 1, 3, 6, 11, 19, 22; DLB 332; EWL 3; LAIT 3; LATS 1:1; MTCW 1, 2; MTFW 2005; RGEL 2; TEA; WLIT 4

Shaw, Henry Wheeler 1818-1885 .. **NCLC 15**
See also DLB 11; RGAL 4

Shaw, Irwin 1913-1984 .... **CLC 7, 23, 34**
See also AITN 1; BPFB 3; CA 13-16R; CAAS 112; CANR 21; CDALB 1941-1968; CN 1, 2, 3; CPW; DAM DRAM, POP; DLB 6, 102; DLBY 1984; MAL 5; MTCW 1, 21; MTFW 2005

Shaw, Robert (Archibald) 1927-1978 .... **CLC 5**
See also AITN 1; CA 1-4R; CAAS 81-84; CANR 4; CN 1, 2; DLB 13, 14

Shaw, T. E.
See Lawrence, T(homas) E(dward)

Shawn, Wallace 1943- .... **CLC 41**
See also CA 112; CAD; CD 5, 6; DLB 266

Shaykh, al- Hanan
See al-Shaykh, Hanan
See also CWW 2; EWL 3

Shchedrin, N.
See Saltykov, Mikhail Evgrafovich

Shea, Lisa 1953- .... **CLC 86**
See also CA 147

Sheed, Wilfrid (John Joseph) 1930- . **CLC 2, 4, 10, 53**
See also CA 65-68; CANR 30, 66; CN 1, 2, 3, 4, 5, 6, 7; DLB 6; MAL 5; MTCW 1, 2; MTFW 2005

Sheehy, Gail 1937- .... **CLC 171**
See also CA 49-52; CANR 1, 33, 55, 92; CPW; MTCW 1

Sheldon, Alice Hastings Bradley 1915(?)-1987
See Tiptree, James, Jr.
See also CA 108; CAAS 122; CANR 34; INT CA-108; MTCW 1

Sheldon, John
See Bloch, Robert (Albert)

Sheldon, Walter J(ames) 1917-1996
See Queen, Ellery
See also AITN 1; CA 25-28R; CANR 10

Shelley, Mary Wollstonecraft (Godwin) 1797-1851 .... **NCLC 14, 59, 103, 170; SSC 92; WLC 5**
See also AAYA 20; BPFB 3; BRW 3; BRWC 2; BRWS 3; BYA 5; CDBLB 1789-1832; DA; DA3; DAB; DAC; DAM MST, NOV; DLB 110, 116, 159, 178; EXPN; FL 1:3; GL 3; HGG; LAIT 1; LMFS 1, 2; NFS 1; RGEL 2; SATA 29; SCFW 1, 2; SFW 4; TEA; WLIT 3

Shelley, Percy Bysshe 1792-1822 .. **NCLC 18, 93, 143, 175; PC 14, 67; WLC 5**
See also AAYA 61; BRW 4; BRWR 1; CDBLB 1789-1832; DA; DA3; DAB; DAC; DAM MST, POET; DLB 96, 110, 158; EXPP; LMFS 1; PAB; PFS 2, 27; RGEL 2; TEA; WLIT 3; WP

Shepard, James R.
See Shepard, Jim

Shepard, Jim 1956- .... **CLC 36**
See also AAYA 73; CA 137; CANR 59, 104, 160; SATA 90, 164

Shepard, Lucius 1947- .... **CLC 34**
See also CA 141; CAAE 128; CANR 81, 124; HGG; SCFW 2; SFW 4; SUFW 2

Shepard, Sam 1943- .... **CLC 4, 6, 17, 34, 41, 44, 169; DC 5**
See also AAYA 1, 58; AMWS 3; CA 69-72; CABS 3; CAD; CANR 22, 120, 140; CD 5, 6; DA3; DAM DRAM; DFS 3, 6, 7, 14; DLB 7, 212; EWL 3; IDFW 3, 4; MAL 5; MTCW 1, 2; MTFW 2005; RGAL 4

Shepherd, Jean (Parker) 1921-1999 .... **TCLC 177**
See also AAYA 69; AITN 2; CA 77-80; CAAS 187

Shepherd, Michael
See Ludlum, Robert

Sherburne, Zoa (Lillian Morin) 1912-1995 .... **CLC 30**
See also AAYA 13; CA 1-4R; CAAS 176; CANR 3, 37; MAICYA 1, 2; SAAS 18; SATA 3; YAW

Sheridan, Frances 1724-1766 .... **LC 7**
See also DLB 39, 84

Sheridan, Richard Brinsley 1751-1816 . **DC 1; NCLC 5, 91; WLC 5**
See also BRW 3; CDBLB 1660-1789; DA; DAB; DAC; DAM DRAM, MST; DFS 15; DLB 89; WLIT 3

Sherman, Jonathan Marc 1968- .... **CLC 55**
See also CA 230

Sherman, Martin 1941(?)- .... **CLC 19**
See also CA 123; CAAE 116; CAD; CANR 86; CD 5, 6; DFS 20; DLB 228; GLL 1; IDTP; RGHL

Sherwin, Judith Johnson
See Johnson, Judith (Emlyn)
See also CANR 85; CP 2, 3, 4, 5; CWP

Sherwood, Frances 1940- .... **CLC 81**
See also CA 220; 146, 220; CANR 158
Sherwood, Robert E(mmet) 1896-1955 .... **TCLC 3**
See also CA 153; CAAE 104; CANR 86; DAM DRAM; DFS 11, 15, 17; DLB 7, 26, 249; IDFW 3, 4; MAL 5; RGAL 4
Shestov, Lev 1866-1938 .... **TCLC 56**
Shevchenko, Taras 1814-1861 .... **NCLC 54**
Shiel, M(atthew) P(hipps) 1865-1947 .... **TCLC 8**
See Holmes, Gordon
See also CA 160; CAAE 106; DLB 153; HGG; MTCW 2; MTFW 2005; SCFW 1, 2; SFW 4; SUFW
Shields, Carol 1935-2003 .. **CLC 91, 113, 193**
See also AMWS 7; CA 81-84; CAAS 218; CANR 51, 74, 98, 133; CCA 1; CN 6, 7; CPW; DA3; DAC; DLB 334; MTCW 2; MTFW 2005; NFS 23
Shields, David 1956- .... **CLC 97**
See also CA 124; CANR 48, 99, 112, 157
Shields, David Jonathan
See Shields, David
Shiga, Naoya 1883-1971 .... **CLC 33; SSC 23; TCLC 172**
See Shiga Naoya
See also CA 101; CAAS 33-36R; MJW; RGWL 3
Shiga Naoya
See Shiga, Naoya
See also DLB 180; EWL 3; RGWL 3
Shilts, Randy 1951-1994 .... **CLC 85**
See also AAYA 19; CA 127; CAAE 115; CAAS 144; CANR 45; DA3; GLL 1; INT CA-127; MTCW 2; MTFW 2005
Shimazaki, Haruki 1872-1943
See Shimazaki Toson
See also CA 134; CAAE 105; CANR 84; RGWL 3
Shimazaki Toson TCLC 5
See Shimazaki, Haruki
See also DLB 180; EWL 3
Shirley, James 1596-1666 .... **DC 25; LC 96**
See also DLB 58; RGEL 2
Shirley Hastings, Selina
See Hastings, Selina
Sholokhov, Mikhail (Aleksandrovich) 1905-1984 .... **CLC 7, 15**
See also CA 101; CAAS 112; DLB 272, 332; EWL 3; MTCW 1, 2; MTFW 2005; RGWL 2, 3; SATA-Obit 36
Sholom Aleichem 1859-1916 .... **SSC 33; TCLC 1, 35**
See Rabinovitch, Sholem
See also DLB 333; TWA
Shone, Patric
See Hanley, James
Showalter, Elaine 1941- .... **CLC 169**
See also CA 57-60; CANR 58, 106; DLB 67; FW; GLL 2
Shreve, Susan
See Shreve, Susan Richards
Shreve, Susan Richards 1939- .... **CLC 23**
See also CA 49-52; 5; CANR 5, 38, 69, 100, 159; MAICYA 1, 2; SATA 46, 95, 152; SATA-Brief 41
Shue, Larry 1946-1985 .... **CLC 52**
See also CA 145; CAAS 117; DAM DRAM; DFS 7
Shu-Jen, Chou 1881-1936
See Lu Hsun
See also CAAE 104
Shulman, Alix Kates 1932- .... **CLC 2, 10**
See also CA 29-32R; CANR 43; FW; SATA 7
Shuster, Joe 1914-1992 .... **CLC 21**
See also AAYA 50
Shute, Nevil CLC 30
See Norway, Nevil Shute
See also BPFB 3; DLB 255; NFS 9; RHW; SFW 4
Shuttle, Penelope (Diane) 1947- .... **CLC 7**
See also CA 93-96; CANR 39, 84, 92, 108; CP 3, 4, 5, 6, 7; CWP; DLB 14, 40
Shvarts, Elena 1948- .... **PC 50**
See also CA 147
Sidhwa, Bapsi 1939-
See Sidhwa, Bapsy (N.)
See also CN 6, 7; DLB 323
Sidhwa, Bapsy (N.) 1938- .... **CLC 168**
See Sidhwa, Bapsi
See also CA 108; CANR 25, 57; FW
Sidney, Mary 1561-1621 .... **LC 19, 39**
See Sidney Herbert, Mary
Sidney, Sir Philip 1554-1586 .... **LC 19, 39, 131; PC 32**
See also BRW 1; BRWR 2; CDBLB Before 1660; DA; DA3; DAB; DAC; DAM MST, POET; DLB 167; EXPP; PAB; RGEL 2; TEA; WP
Sidney Herbert, Mary
See Sidney, Mary
See also DLB 167
Siegel, Jerome 1914-1996 .... **CLC 21**
See Siegel, Jerry
See also CA 169; CAAE 116; CAAS 151
Siegel, Jerry
See Siegel, Jerome
See also AAYA 50
Sienkiewicz, Henryk (Adam Alexander Pius) 1846-1916 .... **TCLC 3**
See also CA 134; CAAE 104; CANR 84; DLB 332; EWL 3; RGSF 2; RGWL 2, 3
Sierra, Gregorio Martinez
See Martinez Sierra, Gregorio
Sierra, Maria de la O'LeJarraga Martinez
See Martinez Sierra, Maria
Sigal, Clancy 1926- .... **CLC 7**
See also CA 1-4R; CANR 85; CN 1, 2, 3, 4, 5, 6, 7
Siger of Brabant 1240(?)-1284(?) . **CMLC 69**
See also DLB 115
Sigourney, Lydia H.
See Sigourney, Lydia Howard (Huntley)
See also DLB 73, 183
Sigourney, Lydia Howard (Huntley) 1791-1865 .... **NCLC 21, 87**
See Sigourney, Lydia H.; Sigourney, Lydia Huntley
See also DLB 1
Sigourney, Lydia Huntley
See Sigourney, Lydia Howard (Huntley)
See also DLB 42, 239, 243
Siguenza y Gongora, Carlos de 1645-1700 .... **HLCS 2; LC 8**
See also LAW
Sigurjonsson, Johann
See Sigurjonsson, Johann
Sigurjonsson, Johann 1880-1919 ... **TCLC 27**
See also CA 170; DLB 293; EWL 3
Sikelianos, Angelos 1884-1951 .... **PC 29; TCLC 39**
See also EWL 3; RGWL 2, 3
Silkin, Jon 1930-1997 .... **CLC 2, 6, 43**
See also CA 5-8R; 5; CANR 89; CP 1, 2, 3, 4, 5, 6; DLB 27
Silko, Leslie 1948- ...... **CLC 23, 74, 114, 211; NNAL; SSC 37, 66; WLCS**
See also AAYA 14; AMWS 4; ANW; BYA 12; CA 122; CAAE 115; CANR 45, 65, 118; CN 4, 5, 6, 7; CP 4, 5, 6, 7; CPW 1; CWP; DA; DA3; DAC; DAM MST, MULT, POP; DLB 143, 175, 256, 275; EWL 3; EXPP; EXPS; LAIT 4; MAL 5; MTCW 2; MTFW 2005; NFS 4; PFS 9, 16; RGAL 4; RGSF 2; SSFS 4, 8, 10, 11; TCWW 1, 2
Sillanpaa, Frans Eemil 1888-1964 ... **CLC 19**
See also CA 129; CAAS 93-96; DLB 332; EWL 3; MTCW 1
Sillitoe, Alan 1928- .. **CLC 1, 3, 6, 10, 19, 57, 148**
See also AITN 1; BRWS 5; CA 191; 9-12R, 191; 2; CANR 8, 26, 55, 139; CDBLB 1960 to Present; CN 1, 2, 3, 4, 5, 6; CP 1, 2, 3, 4, 5; DLB 14, 139; EWL 3; MTCW 1, 2; MTFW 2005; RGEL 2; RGSF 2; SATA 61
Silone, Ignazio 1900-1978 .... **CLC 4**
See also CA 25-28; CAAS 81-84; CANR 34; CAP 2; DLB 264; EW 12; EWL 3; MTCW 1; RGSF 2; RGWL 2, 3
Silone, Ignazione
See Silone, Ignazio
Silver, Joan Micklin 1935- .... **CLC 20**
See also CA 121; CAAE 114; INT CA-121
Silver, Nicholas
See Faust, Frederick (Schiller)
Silverberg, Robert 1935- .... **CLC 7, 140**
See also AAYA 24; BPFB 3; BYA 7, 9; CA 186; 1-4R, 186; 3; CANR 1, 20, 36, 85, 140; CLR 59; CN 6, 7; CPW; DAM POP; DLB 8; INT CANR-20; MAICYA 1, 2; MTCW 1, 2; MTFW 2005; SATA 13, 91; SATA-Essay 104; SCFW 1, 2; SFW 4; SUFW 2
Silverstein, Alvin 1933- .... **CLC 17**
See also CA 49-52; CANR 2; CLR 25; JRDA; MAICYA 1, 2; SATA 8, 69, 124
Silverstein, Shel 1932-1999 .... **PC 49**
See also AAYA 40; BW 3; CA 107; CAAS 179; CANR 47, 74, 81; CLR 5, 96; CWRI 5; JRDA; MAICYA 1, 2; MTCW 2; MTFW 2005; SATA 33, 92; SATA-Brief 27; SATA-Obit 116
Silverstein, Virginia B(arbara Opshelor) 1937- .... **CLC 17**
See also CA 49-52; CANR 2; CLR 25; JRDA; MAICYA 1, 2; SATA 8, 69, 124
Sim, Georges
See Simenon, Georges (Jacques Christian)
Simak, Clifford D(onald) 1904-1988 . **CLC 1, 55**
See also CA 1-4R; CAAS 125; CANR 1, 35; DLB 8; MTCW 1; SATA-Obit 56; SCFW 1, 2; SFW 4
Simenon, Georges (Jacques Christian) 1903-1989 .... **CLC 1, 2, 3, 8, 18, 47**
See also BPFB 3; CA 85-88; CAAS 129; CANR 35; CMW 4; DA3; DAM POP; DLB 72; DLBY 1989; EW 12; EWL 3; GFL 1789 to the Present; MSW; MTCW 1, 2; MTFW 2005; RGWL 2, 3
Simic, Charles 1938- .... **CLC 6, 9, 22, 49, 68, 130; PC 69**
See also AMWS 8; CA 29-32R; 4; CANR 12, 33, 52, 61, 96, 140; CP 2, 3, 4, 5, 6, 7; DA3; DAM POET; DLB 105; MAL 5; MTCW 2; MTFW 2005; PFS 7; RGAL 4; WP
Simmel, Georg 1858-1918 .... **TCLC 64**
See also CA 157; DLB 296
Simmons, Charles (Paul) 1924- .... **CLC 57**
See also CA 89-92; INT CA-89-92
Simmons, Dan 1948- .... **CLC 44**
See also AAYA 16, 54; CA 138; CANR 53, 81, 126; CPW; DAM POP; HGG; SUFW 2
Simmons, James (Stewart Alexander) 1933- .... **CLC 43**
See also CA 105; 21; CP 1, 2, 3, 4, 5, 6, 7; DLB 40

Simmons, Richard
See Simmons, Dan
Simms, William Gilmore 1806-1870 .... **NCLC 3**
See also DLB 3, 30, 59, 73, 248, 254; RGAL 4
Simon, Carly 1945- .... **CLC 26**
See also CA 105
Simon, Claude 1913-2005 ... **CLC 4, 9, 15, 39**
See also CA 89-92; CAAS 241; CANR 33, 117; CWW 2; DAM NOV; DLB 83, 332; EW 13; EWL 3; GFL 1789 to the Present; MTCW 1
Simon, Claude Eugene Henri
See Simon, Claude
Simon, Claude Henri Eugene
See Simon, Claude
Simon, Marvin Neil
See Simon, Neil
Simon, Myles
See Follett, Ken
Simon, Neil 1927- .... **CLC 6, 11, 31, 39, 70, 233; DC 14**
See also AAYA 32; AITN 1; AMWS 4; CA 21-24R; CAD; CANR 26, 54, 87, 126; CD 5, 6; DA3; DAM DRAM; DFS 2, 6, 12, 18,, 24; DLB 7, 266; LAIT 4; MAL 5; MTCW 1, 2; MTFW 2005; RGAL 4; TUS
Simon, Paul 1941(?)- .... **CLC 17**
See also CA 153; CAAE 116; CANR 152
Simon, Paul Frederick
See Simon, Paul
Simonon, Paul 1956(?)- .... **CLC 30**
Simonson, Rick CLC 70
Simpson, Harriette
See Arnow, Harriette (Louisa) Simpson
Simpson, Louis 1923- ... **CLC 4, 7, 9, 32, 149**
See also AMWS 9; CA 1-4R; 4; CANR 1, 61, 140; CP 1, 2, 3, 4, 5, 6, 7; DAM POET; DLB 5; MAL 5; MTCW 1, 2; MTFW 2005; PFS 7, 11, 14; RGAL 4
Simpson, Mona 1957- .... **CLC 44, 146**
See also CA 135; CAAE 122; CANR 68, 103; CN 6, 7; EWL 3
Simpson, Mona Elizabeth
See Simpson, Mona
Simpson, N(orman) F(rederick) 1919- .... **CLC 29**
See also CA 13-16R; CBD; DLB 13; RGEL 2
Sinclair, Andrew (Annandale) 1935- . **CLC 2, 14**
See also CA 9-12R; 5; CANR 14, 38, 91; CN 1, 2, 3, 4, 5, 6, 7; DLB 14; FANT; MTCW 1
Sinclair, Emil
See Hesse, Hermann
Sinclair, Iain 1943- .... **CLC 76**
See also CA 132; CANR 81, 157; CP 5, 6, 7; HGG
Sinclair, Iain MacGregor
See Sinclair, Iain
Sinclair, Irene
See Griffith, D(avid Lewelyn) W(ark)
Sinclair, Julian
See Sinclair, May
Sinclair, Mary Amelia St. Clair (?)-
See Sinclair, May
Sinclair, May 1865-1946 .... **TCLC 3, 11**
See also CA 166; CAAE 104; DLB 36, 135; EWL 3; HGG; RGEL 2; RHW; SUFW
Sinclair, Roy
See Griffith, D(avid Lewelyn) W(ark)
Sinclair, Upton 1878-1968 ...... **CLC 1, 11, 15, 63; TCLC 160; WLC 5**
See also AAYA 63; AMWS 5; BPFB 3; BYA 2; CA 5-8R; CAAS 25-28R; CANR 7; CDALB 1929-1941; DA; DA3; DAB; DAC; DAM MST, NOV; DLB 9; EWL 3; INT CANR-7; LAIT 3; MAL 5; MTCW 1, 2; MTFW 2005; NFS 6; RGAL 4; SATA 9; TUS; YAW
Sinclair, Upton Beall
See Sinclair, Upton
Singe, (Edmund) J(ohn) M(illington) 1871-1909 .... **WLC**
Singer, Isaac
See Singer, Isaac Bashevis
Singer, Isaac Bashevis 1904-1991 .. **CLC 1, 3, 6, 9, 11, 15, 23, 38, 69, 111; SSC 3, 53, 80; WLC 5**
See also AAYA 32; AITN 1, 2; AMW; AMWR 2; BPFB 3; BYA 1, 4; CA 1-4R; CAAS 134; CANR 1, 39, 106; CDALB 1941-1968; CLR 1; CN 1, 2, 3, 4; CWRI 5; DA; DA3; DAB; DAC; DAM MST, NOV; DLB 6, 28, 52, 278, 332, 333; DLBY 1991; EWL 3; EXPS; HGG; JRDA; LAIT 3; MAICYA 1, 2; MAL 5; MTCW 1, 2; MTFW 2005; RGAL 4; RGHL; RGSF 2; SATA 3, 27; SATA-Obit 68; SSFS 2, 12, 16; TUS; TWA
Singer, Israel Joshua 1893-1944 .... **TCLC 33**
See also CA 169; DLB 333; EWL 3
Singh, Khushwant 1915- .... **CLC 11**
See also CA 9-12R; 9; CANR 6, 84; CN 1, 2, 3, 4, 5, 6, 7; DLB 323; EWL 3; RGEL 2
Singleton, Ann
See Benedict, Ruth
Singleton, John 1968(?)- .... **CLC 156**
See also AAYA 50; BW 2, 3; CA 138; CANR 67, 82; DAM MULT
Siniavskii, Andrei
See Sinyavsky, Andrei (Donatevich)
See also CWW 2
Sinjohn, John
See Galsworthy, John
Sinyavsky, Andrei (Donatevich) 1925-1997 .... **CLC 8**
See Siniavskii, Andrei; Sinyavsky, Andrey Donatovich; Tertz, Abram
See also CA 85-88; CAAS 159
Sinyavsky, Andrey Donatovich
See Sinyavsky, Andrei (Donatevich)
See also EWL 3
Sirin, V.
See Nabokov, Vladimir (Vladimirovich)
Sissman, L(ouis) E(dward) 1928-1976 .... **CLC 9, 18**
See also CA 21-24R; CAAS 65-68; CANR 13; CP 2; DLB 5
Sisson, C(harles) H(ubert) 1914-2003 .... **CLC 8**
See also BRWS 11; CA 1-4R; 3; CAAS 220; CANR 3, 48, 84; CP 1, 2, 3, 4, 5, 6, 7; DLB 27
Sitting Bull 1831(?)-1890 .... **NNAL**
See also DA3; DAM MULT
Sitwell, Dame Edith 1887-1964 ..... **CLC 2, 9, 67; PC 3**
See also BRW 7; CA 9-12R; CANR 35; CDBLB 1945-1960; DAM POET; DLB 20; EWL 3; MTCW 1, 2; MTFW 2005; RGEL 2; TEA
Siwaarmill, H. P.
See Sharp, William
Sjoewall, Maj 1935- .... **CLC 7**
See Sjowall, Maj
See also CA 65-68; CANR 73
Sjowall, Maj
See Sjoewall, Maj
See also BPFB 3; CMW 4; MSW
Skelton, John 1460(?)-1529 ..... **LC 71; PC 25**
See also BRW 1; DLB 136; RGEL 2
Skelton, Robin 1925-1997 .... **CLC 13**
See Zuk, Georges
See also AITN 2; CA 5-8R; 5; CAAS 160; CANR 28, 89; CCA 1; CP 1, 2, 3, 4, 5, 6; DLB 27, 53
Skolimowski, Jerzy 1938- .... **CLC 20**
See also CA 128
Skram, Amalie (Bertha) 1847-1905 .... **TCLC 25**
See also CA 165
Skvorecky, Josef 1924- . **CLC 15, 39, 69, 152**
See also CA 61-64; 1; CANR 10, 34, 63, 108; CDWLB 4; CWW 2; DA3; DAC; DAM NOV; DLB 232; EWL 3; MTCW 1, 2; MTFW 2005
Slade, Bernard 1930- .... **CLC 11, 46**
See Newbound, Bernard Slade
See also CA 9; CCA 1; CD 6; DLB 53
Slaughter, Carolyn 1946- .... **CLC 56**
See also CA 85-88; CANR 85, 169; CN 5, 6, 7
Slaughter, Frank G(ill) 1908-2001 ... **CLC 29**
See also AITN 2; CA 5-8R; CAAS 197; CANR 5, 85; INT CANR-5; RHW
Slavitt, David R. 1935- .... **CLC 5, 14**
See also CA 21-24R; 3; CANR 41, 83, 166; CN 1, 2; CP 1, 2, 3, 4, 5, 6, 7; DLB 5, 6
Slavitt, David Rytman
See Slavitt, David R.
Slesinger, Tess 1905-1945 .... **TCLC 10**
See also CA 199; CAAE 107; DLB 102
Slessor, Kenneth 1901-1971 .... **CLC 14**
See also CA 102; CAAS 89-92; DLB 260; RGEL 2
Slowacki, Juliusz 1809-1849 .... **NCLC 15**
See also RGWL 3
Smart, Christopher 1722-1771 .... **LC 3, 134; PC 13**
See also DAM POET; DLB 109; RGEL 2
Smart, Elizabeth 1913-1986 .... **CLC 54**
See also CA 81-84; CAAS 118; CN 4; DLB 88
Smiley, Jane 1949- ...... **CLC 53, 76, 144, 236**
See also AAYA 66; AMWS 6; BPFB 3; CA 104; CANR 30, 50, 74, 96, 158; CN 6, 7; CPW 1; DA3; DAM POP; DLB 227, 234; EWL 3; INT CANR-30; MAL 5; MTFW 2005; SSFS 19
Smiley, Jane Graves
See Smiley, Jane
Smith, A(rthur) J(ames) M(arshall) 1902-1980 .... **CLC 15**
See also CA 1-4R; CAAS 102; CANR 4; CP 1, 2, 3; DAC; DLB 88; RGEL 2
Smith, Adam 1723(?)-1790 .... **LC 36**
See also DLB 104, 252, 336; RGEL 2
Smith, Alexander 1829-1867 .... **NCLC 59**
See also DLB 32, 55
Smith, Anna Deavere 1950- ...... **CLC 86, 241**
See also CA 133; CANR 103; CD 5, 6; DFS 2, 22
Smith, Betty (Wehner) 1904-1972 .... **CLC 19**
See also AAYA 72; BPFB 3; BYA 3; CA 5-8R; CAAS 33-36R; DLBY 1982; LAIT 3; RGAL 4; SATA 6
Smith, Charlotte (Turner) 1749-1806 .... **NCLC 23, 115**
See also DLB 39, 109; RGEL 2; TEA
Smith, Clark Ashton 1893-1961 .... **CLC 43**
See also AAYA 76; CA 143; CANR 81; FANT; HGG; MTCW 2; SCFW 1, 2; SFW 4; SUFW
Smith, Dave CLC 22, 42
See Smith, David (Jeddie)
See also CA 7; CP 3, 4, 5, 6, 7; DLB 5
Smith, David (Jeddie) 1942-
See Smith, Dave
See also CA 49-52; CANR 1, 59, 120; CSW; DAM POET

Smith, Iain Crichton 1928-1998 .... **CLC 64**
See also BRWS 9; CA 21-24R; CAAS 171; CN 1, 2, 3, 4, 5, 6; CP 1, 2, 3, 4, 5, 6; DLB 40, 139, 319; RGSF 2
Smith, John 1580(?)-1631 .... **LC 9**
See also DLB 24, 30; TUS
Smith, Johnston
See Crane, Stephen (Townley)
Smith, Joseph, Jr. 1805-1844 .... **NCLC 53**
Smith, Kevin 1970- .... **CLC 223**
See also AAYA 37; CA 166; CANR 131
Smith, Lee 1944- .... **CLC 25, 73**
See also CA 119; CAAE 114; CANR 46, 118, 173; CN 7; CSW; DLB 143; DLBY 1983; EWL 3; INT CA-119; RGAL 4
Smith, Martin
See Smith, Martin Cruz
Smith, Martin Cruz 1942- .. **CLC 25; NNAL**
See also BEST 89:4; BPFB 3; CA 85-88; CANR 6, 23, 43, 65, 119; CMW 4; CPW; DAM MULT, POP; HGG; INT CANR-23; MTCW 2; MTFW 2005; RGAL 4
Smith, Patti 1946- .... **CLC 12**
See also CA 93-96; CANR 63, 168
Smith, Pauline (Urmson)
1882-1959 .... **TCLC 25**
See also DLB 225; EWL 3
Smith, Rosamond
See Oates, Joyce Carol
Smith, Seba 1792-1868 .... **NCLC 187**
See also DLB 1, 11, 243
Smith, Sheila Kaye
See Kaye-Smith, Sheila
Smith, Stevie 1902-1971 .... **CLC 3, 8, 25, 44; PC 12**
See also BRWS 2; CA 17-18; CAAS 29-32R; CANR 35; CAP 2; CP 1; DAM POET; DLB 20; EWL 3; MTCW 1, 2; PAB; PFS 3; RGEL 2; TEA
Smith, Wilbur 1933- .... **CLC 33**
See also CA 13-16R; CANR 7, 46, 66, 134; CPW; MTCW 1, 2; MTFW 2005
Smith, William Jay 1918- .... **CLC 6**
See also AMWS 13; CA 5-8R; CANR 44, 106; CP 1, 2, 3, 4, 5, 6, 7; CSW; CWRI 5; DLB 5; MAICYA 1, 2; SAAS 22; SATA 2, 68, 154; SATA-Essay 154; TCLE 1:2
Smith, Woodrow Wilson
See Kuttner, Henry
Smith, Zadie 1975- .... **CLC 158**
See also AAYA 50; CA 193; MTFW 2005
Smolenskin, Peretz 1842-1885 .... **NCLC 30**
Smollett, Tobias (George) 1721-1771 ... **LC 2, 46**
See also BRW 3; CDBLB 1660-1789; DLB 39, 104; RGEL 2; TEA
Snodgrass, W.D. 1926- .... **CLC 2, 6, 10, 18, 68; PC 74**
See also AMWS 6; CA 1-4R; CANR 6, 36, 65, 85; CP 1, 2, 3, 4, 5, 6, 7; DAM POET; DLB 5; MAL 5; MTCW 1, 2; MTFW 2005; RGAL 4; TCLE 1:2
Snorri Sturluson 1179-1241 .... **CMLC 56**
See also RGWL 2, 3
Snow, C(harles) P(ercy) 1905-1980 ... **CLC 1, 4, 6, 9, 13, 19**
See also BRW 7; CA 5-8R; CAAS 101; CANR 28; CDBLB 1945-1960; CN 1, 2; DAM NOV; DLB 15, 77; DLBD 17; EWL 3; MTCW 1, 2; MTFW 2005; RGEL 2; TEA
Snow, Frances Compton
See Adams, Henry (Brooks)
Snyder, Gary 1930- . **CLC 1, 2, 5, 9, 32, 120; PC 21**
See also AAYA 72; AMWS 8; ANW; BG 1:3; CA 17-20R; CANR 30, 60, 125; CP 1, 2, 3, 4, 5, 6, 7; DA3; DAM POET; DLB 5, 16, 165, 212, 237, 275; EWL 3; MAL 5; MTCW 2; MTFW 2005; PFS 9, 19; RGAL 4; WP
Snyder, Zilpha Keatley 1927- .... **CLC 17**
See also AAYA 15; BYA 1; CA 252; 9-12R, 252; CANR 38; CLR 31, 121; JRDA; MAICYA 1, 2; SAAS 2; SATA 1, 28, 75, 110, 163; SATA-Essay 112, 163; YAW
Soares, Bernardo
See Pessoa, Fernando (Antonio Nogueira)
Sobh, A.
See Shamlu, Ahmad
Sobh, Alef
See Shamlu, Ahmad
Sobol, Joshua 1939- .... **CLC 60**
See Sobol, Yehoshua
See also CA 200; RGHL
Sobol, Yehoshua 1939-
See Sobol, Joshua
See also CWW 2
Socrates 470B.C.-399B.C. .... **CMLC 27**
Soderberg, Hjalmar 1869-1941 ...... **TCLC 39**
See also DLB 259; EWL 3; RGSF 2
Soderbergh, Steven 1963- .... **CLC 154**
See also AAYA 43; CA 243
Soderbergh, Steven Andrew
See Soderbergh, Steven
Sodergran, Edith (Irene) 1892-1923
See Soedergran, Edith (Irene)
See also CA 202; DLB 259; EW 11; EWL 3; RGWL 2, 3
Soedergran, Edith (Irene)
1892-1923 .... **TCLC 31**
See Sodergran, Edith (Irene)
Softly, Edgar
See Lovecraft, H. P.
Softly, Edward
See Lovecraft, H. P.
Sokolov, Alexander V(sevolodovich) 1943-
See Sokolov, Sasha
See also CA 73-76
Sokolov, Raymond 1941- .... **CLC 7**
See also CA 85-88
Sokolov, Sasha CLC 59
See Sokolov, Alexander V(sevolodovich)
See also CWW 2; DLB 285; EWL 3; RGWL 2, 3
Solo, Jay
See Ellison, Harlan
Sologub, Fyodor TCLC 9
See Teternikov, Fyodor Kuzmich
See also EWL 3
Solomons, Ikey Esquir
See Thackeray, William Makepeace
Solomos, Dionysios 1798-1857 .... **NCLC 15**
Solwoska, Mara
See French, Marilyn
Solzhenitsyn, Aleksandr I. 1918- .. **CLC 1, 2, 4, 7, 9, 10, 18, 26, 34, 78, 134, 235; SSC 32, 105; WLC 5**
See Solzhenitsyn, Aleksandr Isayevich
See also AAYA 49; AITN 1; BPFB 3; CA 69-72; CANR 40, 65, 116; DA; DA3; DAB; DAC; DAM MST, NOV; DLB 302, 332; EW 13; EXPS; LAIT 4; MTCW 1, 2; MTFW 2005; NFS 6; RGSF 2; RGWL 2, 3; SSFS 9; TWA
Solzhenitsyn, Aleksandr Isayevich
See Solzhenitsyn, Aleksandr I.
See also CWW 2; EWL 3
Somers, Jane
See Lessing, Doris
Somerville, Edith Oenone
1858-1949 .... **SSC 56; TCLC 51**
See also CA 196; DLB 135; RGEL 2; RGSF 2
Somerville & Ross
See Martin, Violet Florence; Somerville, Edith Oenone
Sommer, Scott 1951- .... **CLC 25**
See also CA 106
Sommers, Christina Hoff 1950- ...... **CLC 197**
See also CA 153; CANR 95
Sondheim, Stephen 1930- .. **CLC 30, 39, 147; DC 22**
See also AAYA 11, 66; CA 103; CANR 47, 67, 125; DAM DRAM; LAIT 4
Sondheim, Stephen Joshua
See Sondheim, Stephen
Sone, Monica 1919- .... **AAL**
See also DLB 312
Song, Cathy 1955- .... **AAL; PC 21**
See also CA 154; CANR 118; CWP; DLB 169, 312; EXPP; FW; PFS 5
Sontag, Susan 1933-2004 ... **CLC 1, 2, 10, 13, 31, 105, 195**
See also AMWS 3; CA 17-20R; CAAS 234; CANR 25, 51, 74, 97; CN 1, 2, 3, 4, 5, 6, 7; CPW; DA3; DAM POP; DLB 2, 67; EWL 3; MAL 5; MBL; MTCW 1, 2; MTFW 2005; RGAL 4; RHW; SSFS 10
Sophocles 496(?)B.C.-406(?)B.C. .... **CMLC 2, 47, 51, 86; DC 1; WLCS**
See also AW 1; CDWLB 1; DA; DA3; DAB; DAC; DAM DRAM, MST; DFS 1, 4, 8, 24; DLB 176; LAIT 1; LATS 1:1; LMFS 1; RGWL 2, 3; TWA; WLIT 8
Sordello 1189-1269 .... **CMLC 15**
Sorel, Georges 1847-1922 .... **TCLC 91**
See also CA 188; CAAE 118
Sorel, Julia
See Drexler, Rosalyn
Sorokin, Vladimir CLC 59
See Sorokin, Vladimir Georgievich
See also CA 258
Sorokin, Vladimir Georgievich
See Sorokin, Vladimir
See also DLB 285
Sorrentino, Gilbert 1929-2006 .... **CLC 3, 7, 14, 22, 40, 247**
See also CA 77-80; CAAS 250; CANR 14, 33, 115, 157; CN 3, 4, 5, 6, 7; CP 1, 2, 3, 4, 5, 6, 7; DLB 5, 173; DLBY 1980; INT CANR-14
Soseki
See Natsume, Soseki
See also MJW
Soto, Gary 1952- ... **CLC 32, 80; HLC 2; PC 28**
See also AAYA 10, 37; BYA 11; CA 125; CAAE 119; CANR 50, 74, 107, 157; CLR 38; CP 4, 5, 6, 7; DAM MULT; DLB 82; EWL 3; EXPP; HW 1, 2; INT CA-125; JRDA; LLW; MAICYA 2; MAICYAS 1; MAL 5; MTCW 2; MTFW 2005; PFS 7; RGAL 4; SATA 80, 120, 174; WYA; YAW
Soupault, Philippe 1897-1990 .... **CLC 68**
See also CA 147; CAAE 116; CAAS 131; EWL 3; GFL 1789 to the Present; LMFS 2
Souster, (Holmes) Raymond 1921- .... **CLC 5, 14**
See also CA 13-16R; 14; CANR 13, 29, 53; CP 1, 2, 3, 4, 5, 6, 7; DA3; DAC; DAM POET; DLB 88; RGEL 2; SATA 63
Southern, Terry 1924(?)-1995 .... **CLC 7**
See also AMWS 11; BPFB 3; CA 1-4R; CAAS 150; CANR 1, 55, 107; CN 1, 2, 3, 4, 5, 6; DLB 2; IDFW 3, 4
Southerne, Thomas 1660-1746 .... **LC 99**
See also DLB 80; RGEL 2
Southey, Robert 1774-1843 .... **NCLC 8, 97**
See also BRW 4; DLB 93, 107, 142; RGEL 2; SATA 54
Southwell, Robert 1561(?)-1595 .... **LC 108**
See also DLB 167; RGEL 2; TEA

Southworth, Emma Dorothy Eliza Nevitte 1819-1899 .... **NCLC 26**
See also DLB 239
Souza, Ernest
See Scott, Evelyn
Soyinka, Wole 1934- ..... **BLC 1:3; CLC 3, 5, 14, 36, 44, 179; DC 2; WLC 5**
See also AFW; BW 2, 3; CA 13-16R; CANR 27, 39, 82, 136; CD 5, 6; CDWLB 3; CN 6, 7; CP 1, 2, 3, 4, 5, 6 ,7; DA; DA3; DAB; DAC; DAM DRAM, MST, MULT; DFS 10; DLB 125, 332; EWL 3; MTCW 1, 2; MTFW 2005; PFS 27; RGEL 2; TWA; WLIT 2; WWE 1
Spackman, W(illiam) M(ode) 1905-1990 .... **CLC 46**
See also CA 81-84; CAAS 132
Spacks, Barry (Bernard) 1931- .... **CLC 14**
See also CA 154; CANR 33, 109; CP 3, 4, 5, 6, 7; DLB 105
Spanidou, Irini 1946- .... **CLC 44**
See also CA 185
Spark, Muriel 1918-2006 .... **CLC 2, 3, 5, 8, 13, 18, 40, 94, 242; PC 72; SSC 10**
See also BRWS 1; CA 5-8R; CAAS 251; CANR 12, 36, 76, 89, 131; CDBLB 1945-1960; CN 1, 2, 3, 4, 5, 6, 7; CP 1, 2, 3, 4, 5, 6, 7; DA3; DAB; DAC; DAM MST, NOV; DLB 15, 139; EWL 3; FW; INT CANR-12; LAIT 4; MTCW 1, 2; MTFW 2005; NFS 22; RGEL 2; TEA; WLIT 4; YAW
Spark, Muriel Sarah
See Spark, Muriel
Spaulding, Douglas
See Bradbury, Ray
Spaulding, Leonard
See Bradbury, Ray
Speght, Rachel 1597-c. 1630 .... **LC 97**
See also DLB 126
Spence, J. A. D.
See Eliot, T(homas) S(tearns)
Spencer, Anne 1882-1975 ...... **HR 1:3; PC 77**
See also BW 2; CA 161; DLB 51, 54
Spencer, Elizabeth 1921- .... **CLC 22; SSC 57**
See also CA 13-16R; CANR 32, 65, 87; CN 1, 2, 3, 4, 5, 6, 7; CSW; DLB 6, 218; EWL 3; MTCW 1; RGAL 4; SATA 14
Spencer, Leonard G.
See Silverberg, Robert
Spencer, Scott 1945- .... **CLC 30**
See also CA 113; CANR 51, 148; DLBY 1986
Spender, Stephen 1909-1995 ..... **CLC 1, 2, 5, 10, 41, 91; PC 71**
See also BRWS 2; CA 9-12R; CAAS 149; CANR 31, 54; CDBLB 1945-1960; CP 1, 2, 3, 4, 5, 6; DA3; DAM POET; DLB 20; EWL 3; MTCW 1, 2; MTFW 2005; PAB; PFS 23; RGEL 2; TEA
Spengler, Oswald (Arnold Gottfried) 1880-1936 .... **TCLC 25**
See also CA 189; CAAE 118
Spenser, Edmund 1552(?)-1599 ...... **LC 5, 39, 117; PC 8, 42; WLC 5**
See also AAYA 60; BRW 1; CDBLB Before 1660; DA; DA3; DAB; DAC; DAM MST, POET; DLB 167; EFS 2; EXPP; PAB; RGEL 2; TEA; WLIT 3; WP
Spicer, Jack 1925-1965 .... **CLC 8, 18, 72**
See also BG 1:3; CA 85-88; DAM POET; DLB 5, 16, 193; GLL 1; WP
Spiegelman, Art 1948- .... **CLC 76, 178**
See also AAYA 10, 46; CA 125; CANR 41, 55, 74, 124; DLB 299; MTCW 2; MTFW 2005; RGHL; SATA 109, 158; YAW
Spielberg, Peter 1929- .... **CLC 6**
See also CA 5-8R; CANR 4, 48; DLBY 1981
Spielberg, Steven 1947- .... **CLC 20, 188**
See also AAYA 8, 24; CA 77-80; CANR 32; SATA 32
Spillane, Frank Morrison
See Spillane, Mickey
See also BPFB 3; CMW 4; DLB 226; MSW
Spillane, Mickey 1918-2006 .. **CLC 3, 13, 241**
See Spillane, Frank Morrison
See also CA 25-28R; CAAS 252; CANR 28, 63, 125; DA3; MTCW 1, 2; MTFW 2005; SATA 66; SATA-Obit 176
Spinoza, Benedictus de 1632-1677 .. **LC 9, 58**
Spinrad, Norman (Richard) 1940- ... **CLC 46**
See also BPFB 3; CA 233; 37-40R, 233; 19; CANR 20, 91; DLB 8; INT CANR-20; SFW 4
Spitteler, Carl 1845-1924 .... **TCLC 12**
See also CAAE 109; DLB 129, 332; EWL 3
Spitteler, Karl Friedrich Georg
See Spitteler, Carl
Spivack, Kathleen (Romola Drucker) 1938- .... **CLC 6**
See also CA 49-52
Spivak, Gayatri Chakravorty 1942- .... **CLC 233**
See also CA 154; CAAE 110; CANR 91; FW; LMFS 2
Spofford, Harriet (Elizabeth) Prescott 1835-1921 .... **SSC 87**
See also CA 201; DLB 74, 221
Spoto, Donald 1941- .... **CLC 39**
See also CA 65-68; CANR 11, 57, 93, 173
Springsteen, Bruce 1949- .... **CLC 17**
See also CA 111
Springsteen, Bruce F.
See Springsteen, Bruce
Spurling, Hilary 1940- .... **CLC 34**
See also CA 104; CANR 25, 52, 94, 157
Spurling, Susan Hilary
See Spurling, Hilary
Spyker, John Howland
See Elman, Richard (Martin)
Squared, A.
See Abbott, Edwin A.
Squires, (James) Radcliffe 1917-1993 .... **CLC 51**
See also CA 1-4R; CAAS 140; CANR 6, 21; CP 1, 2, 3, 4, 5
Srivastava, Dhanpat Rai 1880(?)-1936
See Premchand
See also CA 197; CAAE 118
Ssu-ma Ch'ien c. 145B.C.-c. 86B.C. .... **CMLC 96**
Ssu-ma T'an (?)-c. 110B.C. .... **CMLC 96**
Stacy, Donald
See Pohl, Frederik
Stael
See Stael-Holstein, Anne Louise Germaine Necker
See also EW 5; RGWL 2, 3
Stael, Germaine de
See Stael-Holstein, Anne Louise Germaine Necker
See also DLB 119, 192; FL 1:3; FW; GFL 1789 to the Present; TWA
Stael-Holstein, Anne Louise Germaine Necker 1766-1817 .... **NCLC 3, 91**
See Stael; Stael, Germaine de
Stafford, Jean 1915-1979 .. **CLC 4, 7, 19, 68; SSC 26, 86**
See also CA 1-4R; CAAS 85-88; CANR 3, 65; CN 1, 2; DLB 2, 173; MAL 5; MTCW 1, 2; MTFW 2005; RGAL 4; RGSF 2; SATA-Obit 22; SSFS 21; TCWW 1, 2; TUS
Stafford, William (Edgar) 1914-1993 .... **CLC 4, 7, 29; PC 71**
See also AMWS 11; CA 5-8R; 3; CAAS 142; CANR 5, 22; CP 1, 2, 3, 4, 5; DAM POET; DLB 5, 206; EXPP; INT CANR-22; MAL 5; PFS 2, 8, 16; RGAL 4; WP
Stagnelius, Eric Johan 1793-1823 . **NCLC 61**
Staines, Trevor
See Brunner, John (Kilian Houston)
Stairs, Gordon
See Austin, Mary (Hunter)
Stalin, Joseph 1879-1953 .... **TCLC 92**
Stampa, Gaspara c. 1524-1554 .. **LC 114; PC 43**
See also RGWL 2, 3; WLIT 7
Stampflinger, K. A.
See Benjamin, Walter
Stancykowna
See Szymborska, Wislawa
Standing Bear, Luther 1868(?)-1939(?) .... **NNAL**
See also CA 144; CAAE 113; DAM MULT
Stanislavsky, Constantin 1863(?)-1938 .... **TCLC 167**
See also CAAE 118
Stanislavsky, Konstantin
See Stanislavsky, Constantin
Stanislavsky, Konstantin Sergeievich
See Stanislavsky, Constantin
Stanislavsky, Konstantin Sergeivich
See Stanislavsky, Constantin
Stanislavsky, Konstantin Sergeyevich
See Stanislavsky, Constantin
Stannard, Martin 1947- .... **CLC 44**
See also CA 142; DLB 155
Stanton, Elizabeth Cady 1815-1902 .... **TCLC 73**
See also CA 171; DLB 79; FL 1:3; FW
Stanton, Maura 1946- .... **CLC 9**
See also CA 89-92; CANR 15, 123; DLB 120
Stanton, Schuyler
See Baum, L(yman) Frank
Stapledon, (William) Olaf 1886-1950 .... **TCLC 22**
See also CA 162; CAAE 111; DLB 15, 255; SCFW 1, 2; SFW 4
Starbuck, George (Edwin) 1931-1996 .... **CLC 53**
See also CA 21-24R; CAAS 153; CANR 23; CP 1, 2, 3, 4, 5, 6; DAM POET
Stark, Richard
See Westlake, Donald E.
Statius c. 45-c. 96 .... **CMLC 91**
See also AW 2; DLB 211
Staunton, Schuyler
See Baum, L(yman) Frank
Stead, Christina (Ellen) 1902-1983 ... **CLC 2, 5, 8, 32, 80**
See also BRWS 4; CA 13-16R; CAAS 109; CANR 33, 40; CN 1, 2, 3; DLB 260; EWL 3; FW; MTCW 1, 2; MTFW 2005; RGEL 2; RGSF 2; WWE 1
Stead, William Thomas 1849-1912 .... **TCLC 48**
See also BRWS 13; CA 167
Stebnitsky, M.
See Leskov, Nikolai (Semyonovich)
Steele, Richard 1672-1729 .... **LC 18**
See also BRW 3; CDBLB 1660-1789; DLB 84, 101; RGEL 2; WLIT 3
Steele, Timothy (Reid) 1948- .... **CLC 45**
See also CA 93-96; CANR 16, 50, 92; CP 5, 6, 7; DLB 120, 282
Steffens, (Joseph) Lincoln 1866-1936 .... **TCLC 20**
See also CA 198; CAAE 117; DLB 303; MAL 5

Stegner, Wallace (Earle) 1909-1993 .. **CLC 9, 49, 81; SSC 27**
See also AITN 1; AMWS 4; ANW; BEST 90:3; BPFB 3; CA 1-4R; 9; CAAS 141; CANR 1, 21, 46; CN 1, 2, 3, 4, 5; DAM NOV; DLB 9, 206, 275; DLBY 1993; EWL 3; MAL 5; MTCW 1, 2; MTFW 2005; RGAL 4; TCWW 1, 2; TUS
Stein, Gertrude 1874-1946 .... **DC 19; PC 18; SSC 42, 105; TCLC 1, 6, 28, 48; WLC 5**
See also AAYA 64; AMW; AMWC 2; CA 132; CAAE 104; CANR 108; CDALB 1917-1929; DA; DA3; DAB; DAC; DAM MST, NOV, POET; DLB 4, 54, 86, 228; DLBD 15; EWL 3; EXPS; FL 1:6; GLL 1; MAL 5; MBL; MTCW 1, 2; MTFW 2005; NCFS 4; RGAL 4; RGSF 2; SSFS 5; TUS; WP
Steinbeck, John (Ernst) 1902-1968 ... **CLC 1, 5, 9, 13, 21, 34, 45, 75, 124; SSC 11, 37, 77; TCLC 135; WLC 5**
See also AAYA 12; AMW; BPFB 3; BYA 2, 3, 13; CA 1-4R; CAAS 25-28R; CANR 1, 35; CDALB 1929-1941; DA; DA3; DAB; DAC; DAM DRAM, MST, NOV; DLB 7, 9, 212, 275, 309, 332; DLBD 2; EWL 3; EXPS; LAIT 3; MAL 5; MTCW 1, 2; MTFW 2005; NFS 1, 5, 7, 17, 19; RGAL 4; RGSF 2; RHW; SATA 9; SSFS 3, 6, 22; TCWW 1, 2; TUS; WYA; YAW
Steinem, Gloria 1934- .... **CLC 63**
See also CA 53-56; CANR 28, 51, 139; DLB 246; FL 1:1; FW; MTCW 1, 2; MTFW 2005
Steiner, George 1929- .... **CLC 24, 221**
See also CA 73-76; CANR 31, 67, 108; DAM NOV; DLB 67, 299; EWL 3; MTCW 1, 2; MTFW 2005; RGHL; SATA 62
Steiner, K. Leslie
See Delany, Samuel R., Jr.
Steiner, Rudolf 1861-1925 .... **TCLC 13**
See also CAAE 107
Stendhal 1783-1842 .... **NCLC 23, 46, 178; SSC 27; WLC 5**
See also DA; DA3; DAB; DAC; DAM MST, NOV; DLB 119; EW 5; GFL 1789 to the Present; RGWL 2, 3; TWA
Stephen, Adeline Virginia
See Woolf, (Adeline) Virginia
Stephen, Sir Leslie 1832-1904 .... **TCLC 23**
See also BRW 5; CAAE 123; DLB 57, 144, 190
Stephen, Sir Leslie
See Stephen, Sir Leslie
Stephen, Virginia
See Woolf, (Adeline) Virginia
Stephens, James 1882(?)-1950 .... **SSC 50; TCLC 4**
See also CA 192; CAAE 104; DLB 19, 153, 162; EWL 3; FANT; RGEL 2; SUFW
Stephens, Reed
See Donaldson, Stephen R.
Stephenson, Neal 1959- .... **CLC 220**
See also AAYA 38; CA 122; CANR 88, 138; CN 7; MTFW 2005; SFW 4
Steptoe, Lydia
See Barnes, Djuna
See also GLL 1
Sterchi, Beat 1949- .... **CLC 65**
See also CA 203
Sterling, Brett
See Bradbury, Ray; Hamilton, Edmond
Sterling, Bruce 1954- .... **CLC 72**
See also CA 119; CANR 44, 135; CN 7; MTFW 2005; SCFW 2; SFW 4
Sterling, George 1869-1926 .... **TCLC 20**
See also CA 165; CAAE 117; DLB 54
Stern, Gerald 1925- .... **CLC 40, 100**
See also AMWS 9; CA 81-84; CANR 28, 94; CP 3, 4, 5, 6, 7; DLB 105; PFS 26; RGAL 4
Stern, Richard (Gustave) 1928- ... **CLC 4, 39**
See also CA 1-4R; CANR 1, 25, 52, 120; CN 1, 2, 3, 4, 5, 6, 7; DLB 218; DLBY 1987; INT CANR-25
Sternberg, Josef von 1894-1969 .... **CLC 20**
See also CA 81-84
Sterne, Laurence 1713-1768 .... **LC 2, 48; WLC 5**
See also BRW 3; BRWC 1; CDBLB 1660-1789; DA; DAB; DAC; DAM MST, NOV; DLB 39; RGEL 2; TEA
Sternheim, (William Adolf) Carl 1878-1942 .... **TCLC 8**
See also CA 193; CAAE 105; DLB 56, 118; EWL 3; IDTP; RGWL 2, 3
Stevens, Margaret Dean
See Aldrich, Bess Streeter
Stevens, Mark 1951- .... **CLC 34**
See also CA 122
Stevens, Wallace 1879-1955 . **PC 6; TCLC 3, 12, 45; WLC 5**
See also AMW; AMWR 1; CA 124; CAAE 104; CDALB 1929-1941; DA; DA3; DAB; DAC; DAM MST, POET; DLB 54; EWL 3; EXPP; MAL 5; MTCW 1, 2; PAB; PFS 13, 16; RGAL 4; TUS; WP
Stevenson, Anne (Katharine) 1933- .. **CLC 7, 33**
See also BRWS 6; CA 17-20R; 9; CANR 9, 33, 123; CP 3, 4, 5, 6, 7; CWP; DLB 40; MTCW 1; RHW
Stevenson, Robert Louis (Balfour) 1850-1894 ...... **NCLC 5, 14, 63, 193; PC 84; SSC 11, 51; WLC 5**
See also AAYA 24; BPFB 3; BRW 5; BRWC 1; BRWR 1; BYA 1, 2, 4, 13; CDBLB 1890-1914; CLR 10, 11, 107; DA; DA3; DAB; DAC; DAM MST, NOV; DLB 18, 57, 141, 156, 174; DLBD 13; GL 3; HGG; JRDA; LAIT 1, 3; MAICYA 1, 2; NFS 11, 20; RGEL 2; RGSF 2; SATA 100; SUFW; TEA; WCH; WLIT 4; WYA; YABC 2; YAW
Stewart, J(ohn) I(nnes) M(ackintosh) 1906-1994 .... **CLC 7, 14, 32**
See Innes, Michael
See also CA 85-88; 3; CAAS 147; CANR 47; CMW 4; CN 1, 2, 3, 4, 5; MTCW 1, 2
Stewart, Mary (Florence Elinor) 1916- .... **CLC 7, 35, 117**
See also AAYA 29, 73; BPFB 3; CA 1-4R; CANR 1, 59, 130; CMW 4; CPW; DAB; FANT; RHW; SATA 12; YAW
Stewart, Mary Rainbow
See Stewart, Mary (Florence Elinor)
Stifle, June
See Campbell, Maria
Stifter, Adalbert 1805-1868 .. **NCLC 41; SSC 28**
See also CDWLB 2; DLB 133; RGSF 2; RGWL 2, 3
Still, James 1906-2001 .... **CLC 49**
See also CA 65-68; 17; CAAS 195; CANR 10, 26; CSW; DLB 9; DLBY 01; SATA 29; SATA-Obit 127
Sting 1951-
See Sumner, Gordon Matthew
See also CA 167
Stirling, Arthur
See Sinclair, Upton
Stitt, Milan 1941- .... **CLC 29**
See also CA 69-72
Stockton, Francis Richard 1834-1902
See Stockton, Frank R.
See also AAYA 68; CA 137; CAAE 108; MAICYA 1, 2; SATA 44; SFW 4
Stockton, Frank R. TCLC 47
See Stockton, Francis Richard
See also BYA 4, 13; DLB 42, 74; DLBD 13; EXPS; SATA-Brief 32; SSFS 3; SUFW; WCH
Stoddard, Charles
See Kuttner, Henry
Stoker, Abraham 1847-1912
See Stoker, Bram
See also CA 150; CAAE 105; DA; DA3; DAC; DAM MST, NOV; HGG; MTFW 2005; SATA 29
Stoker, Bram SSC 62; TCLC 8, 144; WLC 6
See Stoker, Abraham
See also AAYA 23; BPFB 3; BRWS 3; BYA 5; CDBLB 1890-1914; DAB; DLB 304; GL 3; LATS 1:1; NFS 18; RGEL 2; SUFW; TEA; WLIT 4
Stolz, Mary 1920-2006 .... **CLC 12**
See also AAYA 8, 73; AITN 1; CA 5-8R; CAAS 255; CANR 13, 41, 112; JRDA; MAICYA 1, 2; SAAS 3; SATA 10, 71, 133; SATA-Obit 180; YAW
Stolz, Mary Slattery
See Stolz, Mary
Stone, Irving 1903-1989 .... **CLC 7**
See also AITN 1; BPFB 3; CA 1-4R; 3; CAAS 129; CANR 1, 23; CN 1, 2, 3, 4; CPW; DA3; DAM POP; INT CANR-23; MTCW 1, 2; MTFW 2005; RHW; SATA 3; SATA-Obit 64
Stone, Oliver 1946- .... **CLC 73**
See also AAYA 15, 64; CA 110; CANR 55, 125
Stone, Oliver William
See Stone, Oliver
Stone, Robert 1937- .... **CLC 5, 23, 42, 175**
See also AMWS 5; BPFB 3; CA 85-88; CANR 23, 66, 95, 173; CN 4, 5, 6, 7; DLB 152; EWL 3; INT CANR-23; MAL 5; MTCW 1; MTFW 2005
Stone, Robert Anthony
See Stone, Robert
Stone, Ruth 1915- .... **PC 53**
See also CA 45-48; CANR 2, 91; CP 5, 6, 7; CSW; DLB 105; PFS 19
Stone, Zachary
See Follett, Ken
Stoppard, Tom 1937- ... **CLC 1, 3, 4, 5, 8, 15, 29, 34, 63, 91; DC 6, 30; WLC 6**
See also AAYA 63; BRWC 1; BRWR 2; BRWS 1; CA 81-84; CANR 39, 67, 125; CBD; CD 5, 6; CDBLB 1960 to Present; DA; DA3; DAB; DAC; DAM DRAM, MST; DFS 2, 5, 8, 11, 13, 16; DLB 13, 233; DLBY 1985; EWL 3; LATS 1:2; MTCW 1, 2; MTFW 2005; RGEL 2; TEA; WLIT 4
Storey, David (Malcolm) 1933- . **CLC 2, 4, 5, 8**
See also BRWS 1; CA 81-84; CANR 36; CBD; CD 5, 6; CN 1, 2, 3, 4, 5, 6; DAM DRAM; DLB 13, 14, 207, 245, 326; EWL 3; MTCW 1; RGEL 2
Storm, Hyemeyohsts 1935- ... **CLC 3; NNAL**
See also CA 81-84; CANR 45; DAM MULT
Storm, (Hans) Theodor (Woldsen) 1817-1888 ... **NCLC 1, 195; SSC 27, 106**
See also CDWLB 2; DLB 129; EW; RGSF 2; RGWL 2, 3
Storni, Alfonsina 1892-1938 . **HLC 2; PC 33; TCLC 5**
See also CA 131; CAAE 104; DAM MULT; DLB 283; HW 1; LAW
Stoughton, William 1631-1701 .... **LC 38**
See also DLB 24

Taylor, Kamala 1924-2004
See Markandaya, Kamala
See also CA 77-80; CAAS 227; MTFW 2005; NFS 13

Taylor, Mildred D. 1943- .... **CLC 21**
See also AAYA 10, 47; BW 1; BYA 3, 8; CA 85-88; CANR 25, 115, 136; CLR 9, 59, 90; CSW; DLB 52; JRDA; LAIT 3; MAICYA 1, 2; MTFW 2005; SAAS 5; SATA 135; WYA; YAW

Taylor, Peter (Hillsman) 1917-1994 .. **CLC 1, 4, 18, 37, 44, 50, 71; SSC 10, 84**
See also AMWS 5; BPFB 3; CA 13-16R; CAAS 147; CANR 9, 50; CN 1, 2, 3, 4, 5; CSW; DLB 218, 278; DLBY 1981, 1994; EWL 3; EXPS; INT CANR-9; MAL 5; MTCW 1, 2; MTFW 2005; RGSF 2; SSFS 9; TUS

Taylor, Robert Lewis 1912-1998 .... **CLC 14**
See also CA 1-4R; CAAS 170; CANR 3, 64; CN 1, 2; SATA 10; TCWW 1, 2

Tchekhov, Anton
See Chekhov, Anton (Pavlovich)

Tchicaya, Gerald Felix 1931-1988 .. **CLC 101**
See Tchicaya U Tam'si
See also CA 129; CAAS 125; CANR 81

Tchicaya U Tam'si
See Tchicaya, Gerald Felix
See also EWL 3

Teasdale, Sara 1884-1933 .... **PC 31; TCLC 4**
See also CA 163; CAAE 104; DLB 45; GLL 1; PFS 14; RGAL 4; SATA 32; TUS

Tecumseh 1768-1813 .... **NNAL**
See also DAM MULT

Tegner, Esaias 1782-1846 .... **NCLC 2**

Teilhard de Chardin, (Marie Joseph) Pierre 1881-1955 .... **TCLC 9**
See also CA 210; CAAE 105; GFL 1789 to the Present

Temple, Ann
See Mortimer, Penelope (Ruth)

Tennant, Emma 1937- .... **CLC 13, 52**
See also BRWS 9; CA 65-68; 9; CANR 10, 38, 59, 88; CN 3, 4, 5, 6, 7; DLB 14; EWL 3; SFW 4

Tenneshaw, S. M.
See Silverberg, Robert

Tenney, Tabitha Gilman 1762-1837 .... **NCLC 122**
See also DLB 37, 200

Tennyson, Alfred 1809-1892 ... **NCLC 30, 65, 115; PC 6; WLC 6**
See also AAYA 50; BRW 4; CDBLB 1832-1890; DA; DA3; DAB; DAC; DAM MST, POET; DLB 32; EXPP; PAB; PFS 1, 2, 4, 11, 15, 19; RGEL 2; TEA; WLIT 4; WP

Teran, Lisa St. Aubin de CLC 36
See St. Aubin de Teran, Lisa

Terence c. 184B.C.-c. 159B.C. ...... **CMLC 14; DC 7**
See also AW 1; CDWLB 1; DLB 211; RGWL 2, 3; TWA; WLIT 8

Teresa de Jesus, St. 1515-1582 .... **LC 18, 149**

Teresa of Avila, St.
See Teresa de Jesus, St.

Terkel, Louis CLC 38
See Terkel, Studs
See also AAYA 32; AITN 1; MTCW 2; TUS

Terkel, Studs 1912-
See Terkel, Louis
See also CA 57-60; CANR 18, 45, 67, 132; DA3; MTCW 1, 2; MTFW 2005

Terry, C. V.
See Slaughter, Frank G(ill)

Terry, Megan 1932- .... **CLC 19; DC 13**
See also CA 77-80; CABS 3; CAD; CANR 43; CD 5, 6; CWD; DFS 18; DLB 7, 249; GLL 2

Tertullian c. 155-c. 245 .... **CMLC 29**

Tertz, Abram
See Sinyavsky, Andrei (Donatevich)
See also RGSF 2

Tesich, Steve 1943(?)-1996 .... **CLC 40, 69**
See also CA 105; CAAS 152; CAD; DLBY 1983

Tesla, Nikola 1856-1943 .... **TCLC 88**

Teternikov, Fyodor Kuzmich 1863-1927
See Sologub, Fyodor
See also CAAE 104

Tevis, Walter 1928-1984 .... **CLC 42**
See also CA 113; SFW 4

Tey, Josephine TCLC 14
See Mackintosh, Elizabeth
See also DLB 77; MSW

Thackeray, William Makepeace 1811-1863 ...... **NCLC 5, 14, 22, 43, 169; WLC 6**
See also BRW 5; BRWC 2; CDBLB 1832-1890; DA; DA3; DAB; DAC; DAM MST, NOV; DLB 21, 55, 159, 163; NFS 13; RGEL 2; SATA 23; TEA; WLIT 3

Thakura, Ravindranatha
See Tagore, Rabindranath

Thames, C. H.
See Marlowe, Stephen

Tharoor, Shashi 1956- .... **CLC 70**
See also CA 141; CANR 91; CN 6, 7

Thelwall, John 1764-1834 .... **NCLC 162**
See also DLB 93, 158

Thelwell, Michael Miles 1939- .... **CLC 22**
See also BW 2; CA 101

Theobald, Lewis, Jr.
See Lovecraft, H. P.

Theocritus c. 310B.C.- .... **CMLC 45**
See also AW 1; DLB 176; RGWL 2, 3

Theodorescu, Ion N. 1880-1967
See Arghezi, Tudor
See also CAAS 116

Theriault, Yves 1915-1983 .... **CLC 79**
See also CA 102; CANR 150; CCA 1; DAC; DAM MST; DLB 88; EWL 3

Theroux, Alexander 1939- .... **CLC 2, 25**
See also CA 85-88; CANR 20, 63; CN 4, 5, 6, 7

Theroux, Alexander Louis
See Theroux, Alexander

Theroux, Paul 1941- .... **CLC 5, 8, 11, 15, 28, 46, 159**
See also AAYA 28; AMWS 8; BEST 89:4; BPFB 3; CA 33-36R; CANR 20, 45, 74, 133; CDALBS; CN 1, 2, 3, 4, 5, 6, 7; CP 1; CPW 1; DA3; DAM POP; DLB 2, 218; EWL 3; HGG; MAL 5; MTCW 1, 2; MTFW 2005; RGAL 4; SATA 44, 109; TUS

Thesen, Sharon 1946- .... **CLC 56**
See also CA 163; CANR 125; CP 5, 6, 7; CWP

Thespis fl. 6th cent. B.C.- .... **CMLC 51**
See also LMFS 1

Thevenin, Denis
See Duhamel, Georges

Thibault, Jacques Anatole Francois 1844-1924
See France, Anatole
See also CA 127; CAAE 106; DA3; DAM NOV; MTCW 1, 2; TWA

Thiele, Colin 1920-2006 .... **CLC 17**
See also CA 29-32R; CANR 12, 28, 53, 105; CLR 27; CP 1, 2; DLB 289; MAICYA 1, 2; SAAS 2; SATA 14, 72, 125; YAW

Thiong'o, Ngugi Wa
See Ngugi wa Thiong'o

Thistlethwaite, Bel
See Wetherald, Agnes Ethelwyn

Thomas, Audrey (Callahan) 1935- .... **CLC 7, 13, 37, 107; SSC 20**
See also AITN 2; CA 237; 21-24R, 237; 19; CANR 36, 58; CN 2, 3, 4, 5, 6, 7; DLB 60; MTCW 1; RGSF 2

Thomas, Augustus 1857-1934 .... **TCLC 97**
See also MAL 5

Thomas, D.M. 1935- ..... **CLC 13, 22, 31, 132**
See also BPFB 3; BRWS 4; CA 61-64; 11; CANR 17, 45, 75; CDBLB 1960 to Present; CN 4, 5, 6, 7; CP 1, 2, 3, 4, 5, 6, 7; DA3; DLB 40, 207, 299; HGG; INT CANR-17; MTCW 1, 2; MTFW 2005; RGHL; SFW 4

Thomas, Dylan (Marlais) 1914-1953 .... **PC 2, 52; SSC 3, 44; TCLC 1, 8, 45, 105; WLC 6**
See also AAYA 45; BRWS 1; CA 120; CAAE 104; CANR 65; CDBLB 1945-1960; DA; DA3; DAB; DAC; DAM DRAM, MST, POET; DLB 13, 20, 139; EWL 3; EXPP; LAIT 3; MTCW 1, 2; MTFW 2005; PAB; PFS 1, 3, 8; RGEL 2; RGSF 2; SATA 60; TEA; WLIT 4; WP

Thomas, (Philip) Edward 1878-1917 . **PC 53; TCLC 10**
See also BRW 6; BRWS 3; CA 153; CAAE 106; DAM POET; DLB 19, 98, 156, 216; EWL 3; PAB; RGEL 2

Thomas, Joyce Carol 1938- .... **CLC 35**
See also AAYA 12, 54; BW 2, 3; CA 116; CAAE 113; CANR 48, 114, 135; CLR 19; DLB 33; INT CA-116; JRDA; MAICYA 1, 2; MTCW 1, 2; MTFW 2005; SAAS 7; SATA 40, 78, 123, 137; SATA-Essay 137; WYA; YAW

Thomas, Lewis 1913-1993 .... **CLC 35**
See also ANW; CA 85-88; CAAS 143; CANR 38, 60; DLB 275; MTCW 1, 2

Thomas, M. Carey 1857-1935 .... **TCLC 89**
See also FW

Thomas, Paul
See Mann, (Paul) Thomas

Thomas, Piri 1928- .... **CLC 17; HLCS 2**
See also CA 73-76; HW 1; LLW

Thomas, R(onald) S(tuart) 1913-2000 .... **CLC 6, 13, 48**
See also CA 89-92; 4; CAAS 189; CANR 30; CDBLB 1960 to Present; CP 1, 2, 3, 4, 5, 6, 7; DAB; DAM POET; DLB 27; EWL 3; MTCW 1; RGEL 2

Thomas, Ross (Elmore) 1926-1995 .. **CLC 39**
See also CA 33-36R; CAAS 150; CANR 22, 63; CMW 4

Thompson, Francis (Joseph) 1859-1907 .... **TCLC 4**
See also BRW 5; CA 189; CAAE 104; CDBLB 1890-1914; DLB 19; RGEL 2; TEA

Thompson, Francis Clegg
See Mencken, H(enry) L(ouis)

Thompson, Hunter S. 1937(?)-2005 .. **CLC 9, 17, 40, 104, 229**
See also AAYA 45; BEST 89:1; BPFB 3; CA 17-20R; CAAS 236; CANR 23, 46, 74, 77, 111, 133; CPW; CSW; DA3; DAM POP; DLB 185; MTCW 1, 2; MTFW 2005; TUS

Thompson, James Myers
See Thompson, Jim (Myers)

Thompson, Jim (Myers) 1906-1977(?) .... **CLC 69**
See also BPFB 3; CA 140; CMW 4; CPW; DLB 226; MSW

Thompson, Judith (Clare Francesca) 1954- .... **CLC 39**
See also CA 143; CD 5, 6; CWD; DFS 22; DLB 334

Thomson, James 1700-1748 .... **LC 16, 29, 40**
See also BRWS 3; DAM POET; DLB 95; RGEL 2

Thomson, James 1834-1882 .... **NCLC 18**
See also DAM POET; DLB 35; RGEL 2
Thoreau, Henry David 1817-1862 .. **NCLC 7, 21, 61, 138; PC 30; WLC 6**
See also AAYA 42; AMW; ANW; BYA 3; CDALB 1640-1865; DA; DA3; DAB; DAC; DAM MST; DLB 1, 183, 223, 270, 298; LAIT 2; LMFS 1; NCFS 3; RGAL 4; TUS
Thorndike, E. L.
See Thorndike, Edward L(ee)
Thorndike, Edward L(ee)
1874-1949 .... **TCLC 107**
See also CAAE 121
Thornton, Hall
See Silverberg, Robert
Thorpe, Adam 1956- .... **CLC 176**
See also CA 129; CANR 92, 160; DLB 231
Thorpe, Thomas Bangs
1815-1878 .... **NCLC 183**
See also DLB 3, 11, 248; RGAL 4
Thubron, Colin 1939- .... **CLC 163**
See also CA 25-28R; CANR 12, 29, 59, 95, 171; CN 5, 6, 7; DLB 204, 231
Thubron, Colin Gerald Dryden
See Thubron, Colin
Thucydides c. 455B.C.-c. 395B.C. . **CMLC 17**
See also AW 1; DLB 176; RGWL 2, 3; WLIT 8
Thumboo, Edwin Nadason 1933- .... **PC 30**
See also CA 194; CP 1
Thurber, James (Grover)
1894-1961 .. **CLC 5, 11, 25, 125; SSC 1, 47**
See also AAYA 56; AMWS 1; BPFB 3; BYA 5; CA 73-76; CANR 17, 39; CDALB 1929-1941; CWRI 5; DA; DA3; DAB; DAC; DAM DRAM, MST, NOV; DLB 4, 11, 22, 102; EWL 3; EXPS; FANT; LAIT 3; MAICYA 1, 2; MAL 5; MTCW 1, 2; MTFW 2005; RGAL 4; RGSF 2; SATA 13; SSFS 1, 10, 19; SUFW; TUS
Thurman, Wallace (Henry)
1902-1934 .. **BLC 1:3; HR 1:3; TCLC 6**
See also BW 1, 3; CA 124; CAAE 104; CANR 81; DAM MULT; DLB 51
Tibullus c. 54B.C.-c. 18B.C. .... **CMLC 36**
See also AW 2; DLB 211; RGWL 2, 3; WLIT 8
Ticheburn, Cheviot
See Ainsworth, William Harrison
Tieck, (Johann) Ludwig
1773-1853 ..... **NCLC 5, 46; SSC 31, 100**
See also CDWLB 2; DLB 90; EW 5; IDTP; RGSF 2; RGWL 2, 3; SUFW
Tiger, Derry
See Ellison, Harlan
Tilghman, Christopher 1946- .... **CLC 65**
See also CA 159; CANR 135, 151; CSW; DLB 244
Tillich, Paul (Johannes)
1886-1965 .... **CLC 131**
See also CA 5-8R; CAAS 25-28R; CANR 33; MTCW 1, 2
Tillinghast, Richard (Williford)
1940- .... **CLC 29**
See also CA 29-32R; 23; CANR 26, 51, 96; CP 2, 3, 4, 5, 6, 7; CSW
Tillman, Lynne (?)- .... **CLC 231**
See also CA 173; CANR 144, 172
Timrod, Henry 1828-1867 .... **NCLC 25**
See also DLB 3, 248; RGAL 4
Tindall, Gillian (Elizabeth) 1938- ...... **CLC 7**
See also CA 21-24R; CANR 11, 65, 107; CN 1, 2, 3, 4, 5, 6, 7
Tiptree, James, Jr. CLC 48, 50
See Sheldon, Alice Hastings Bradley
See also DLB 8; SCFW 1, 2; SFW 4
Tirone Smith, Mary-Ann 1944- .... **CLC 39**
See also CA 136; CAAE 118; CANR 113; SATA 143
Tirso de Molina 1580(?)-1648 .... **DC 13; HLCS 2; LC 73**
See also RGWL 2, 3
Titmarsh, Michael Angelo
See Thackeray, William Makepeace
Tocqueville, Alexis (Charles Henri Maurice Clerel Comte) de 1805-1859 .. **NCLC 7, 63**
See also EW 6; GFL 1789 to the Present; TWA
Toer, Pramoedya Ananta
1925-2006 .... **CLC 186**
See also CA 197; CAAS 251; CANR 170; RGWL 3
Toffler, Alvin 1928- .... **CLC 168**
See also CA 13-16R; CANR 15, 46, 67; CPW; DAM POP; MTCW 1, 2
Toibin, Colm 1955- .... **CLC 162**
See also CA 142; CANR 81, 149; CN 7; DLB 271
Tolkien, John Ronald Reuel
See Tolkien, J.R.R
Tolkien, J.R.R 1892-1973 ...... **CLC 1, 2, 3, 8, 12, 38; TCLC 137; WLC 6**
See also AAYA 10; AITN 1; BPFB 3; BRWC 2; BRWS 2; CA 17-18; CAAS 45-48; CANR 36, 134; CAP 2; CDBLB 1914-1945; CLR 56; CN 1; CPW 1; CWRI 5; DA; DA3; DAB; DAC; DAM MST, NOV, POP; DLB 15, 160, 255; EFS 2; EWL 3; FANT; JRDA; LAIT 1; LATS 1:2; LMFS 2; MAICYA 1, 2; MTCW 1, 2; MTFW 2005; NFS 8, 26; RGEL 2; SATA 2, 32, 100; SATA-Obit 24; SFW 4; SUFW; TEA; WCH; WYA; YAW
Toller, Ernst 1893-1939 .... **TCLC 10**
See also CA 186; CAAE 107; DLB 124; EWL 3; RGWL 2, 3
Tolson, M. B.
See Tolson, Melvin B(eaunorus)
Tolson, Melvin B(eaunorus)
1898(?)-1966 .... **BLC 1:3; CLC 36, 105; PC 88**
See also AFAW 1, 2; BW 1, 3; CA 124; CAAS 89-92; CANR 80; DAM MULT, POET; DLB 48, 76; MAL 5; RGAL 4
Tolstoi, Aleksei Nikolaevich
See Tolstoy, Alexey Nikolaevich
Tolstoi, Lev
See Tolstoy, Leo (Nikolaevich)
See also RGSF 2; RGWL 2, 3
Tolstoy, Aleksei Nikolaevich
See Tolstoy, Alexey Nikolaevich
See also DLB 272
Tolstoy, Alexey Nikolaevich
1882-1945 .... **TCLC 18**
See Tolstoy, Aleksei Nikolaevich
See also CA 158; CAAE 107; EWL 3; SFW 4
Tolstoy, Leo (Nikolaevich)
1828-1910 . **SSC 9, 30, 45, 54; TCLC 4, 11, 17, 28, 44, 79, 173; WLC 6**
See Tolstoi, Lev
See also AAYA 56; CA 123; CAAE 104; DA; DA3; DAB; DAC; DAM MST, NOV; DLB 238; EFS 2; EW 7; EXPS; IDTP; LAIT 2; LATS 1:1; LMFS 1; NFS 10; SATA 26; SSFS 5; TWA
Tolstoy, Count Leo
See Tolstoy, Leo (Nikolaevich)
Tomalin, Claire 1933- .... **CLC 166**
See also CA 89-92; CANR 52, 88, 165; DLB 155
Tomasi di Lampedusa, Giuseppe 1896-1957
See Lampedusa, Giuseppe (Tomasi) di
See also CAAE 111; DLB 177; EWL 3; WLIT 7
Tomlin, Lily 1939(?)-
See Tomlin, Mary Jean
See also CAAE 117
Tomlin, Mary Jean CLC 17
See Tomlin, Lily
Tomline, F. Latour
See Gilbert, W(illiam) S(chwenck)
Tomlinson, (Alfred) Charles 1927- .... **CLC 2, 4, 6, 13, 45; PC 17**
See also CA 5-8R; CANR 33; CP 1, 2, 3, 4, 5, 6, 7; DAM POET; DLB 40; TCLE 1:2
Tomlinson, H(enry) M(ajor)
1873-1958 .... **TCLC 71**
See also CA 161; CAAE 118; DLB 36, 100, 195
Tonna, Charlotte Elizabeth
1790-1846 .... **NCLC 135**
See also DLB 163
Tonson, Jacob fl. 1655(?)-1736 .... **LC 86**
See also DLB 170
Toole, John Kennedy 1937-1969 ..... **CLC 19, 64**
See also BPFB 3; CA 104; DLBY 1981; MTCW 2; MTFW 2005
Toomer, Eugene
See Toomer, Jean
Toomer, Eugene Pinchback
See Toomer, Jean
Toomer, Jean 1894-1967 ... **BLC 1:3; CLC 1, 4, 13, 22; HR 1:3; PC 7; SSC 1, 45; TCLC 172; WLCS**
See also AFAW 1, 2; AMWS 3, 9; BW 1; CA 85-88; CDALB 1917-1929; DA3; DAM MULT; DLB 45, 51; EWL 3; EXPP; EXPS; LMFS 2; MAL 5; MTCW 1, 2; MTFW 2005; NFS 11; RGAL 4; RGSF 2; SSFS 5
Toomer, Nathan Jean
See Toomer, Jean
Toomer, Nathan Pinchback
See Toomer, Jean
Torley, Luke
See Blish, James (Benjamin)
Tornimparte, Alessandra
See Ginzburg, Natalia
Torre, Raoul della
See Mencken, H(enry) L(ouis)
Torrence, Ridgely 1874-1950 .... **TCLC 97**
See also DLB 54, 249; MAL 5
Torrey, E. Fuller 1937- .... **CLC 34**
See also CA 119; CANR 71, 158
Torrey, Edwin Fuller
See Torrey, E. Fuller
Torsvan, Ben Traven
See Traven, B.
Torsvan, Benno Traven
See Traven, B.
Torsvan, Berick Traven
See Traven, B.
Torsvan, Berwick Traven
See Traven, B.
Torsvan, Bruno Traven
See Traven, B.
Torsvan, Traven
See Traven, B.
Tourneur, Cyril 1575(?)-1626 .... **LC 66**
See also BRW 2; DAM DRAM; DLB 58; RGEL 2
Tournier, Michel 1924- .... **CLC 6, 23, 36, 95, 249; SSC 88**
See also CA 49-52; CANR 3, 36, 74, 149; CWW 2; DLB 83; EWL 3; GFL 1789 to the Present; MTCW 1, 2; SATA 23
Tournier, Michel Edouard
See Tournier, Michel
Tournimparte, Alessandra
See Ginzburg, Natalia

Author Index

Virgil
See Vergil
See also CDWLB 1; DLB 211; LAIT 1; RGWL 2, 3; WLIT 8; WP
Visconti, Luchino 1906-1976 .... **CLC 16**
See also CA 81-84; CAAS 65-68; CANR 39
Vitry, Jacques de
See Jacques de Vitry
Vittorini, Elio 1908-1966 .... **CLC 6, 9, 14**
See also CA 133; CAAS 25-28R; DLB 264; EW 12; EWL 3; RGWL 2, 3
Vivekananda, Swami 1863-1902 .... **TCLC 88**
Vizenor, Gerald Robert 1934- .... **CLC 103; NNAL**
See also CA 205; 13-16R, 205; 22; CANR 5, 21, 44, 67; DAM MULT; DLB 175, 227; MTCW 2; MTFW 2005; TCWW 2
Vizinczey, Stephen 1933- .... **CLC 40**
See also CA 128; CCA 1; INT CA-128
Vliet, R(ussell) G(ordon) 1929-1984 .... **CLC 22**
See also CA 37-40R; CAAS 112; CANR 18; CP 2, 3
Vogau, Boris Andreyevich 1894-1938
See Pilnyak, Boris
See also CA 218; CAAE 123
Vogel, Paula A. 1951- .... **CLC 76; DC 19**
See also CA 108; CAD; CANR 119, 140; CD 5, 6; CWD; DFS 14; MTFW 2005; RGAL 4
Voigt, Cynthia 1942- .... **CLC 30**
See also AAYA 3, 30; BYA 1, 3, 6, 7, 8; CA 106; CANR 18, 37, 40, 94, 145; CLR 13, 48; INT CANR-18; JRDA; LAIT 5; MAICYA 1, 2; MAICYAS 1; MTFW 2005; SATA 48, 79, 116, 160; SATA-Brief 33; WYA; YAW
Voigt, Ellen Bryant 1943- .... **CLC 54**
See also CA 69-72; CANR 11, 29, 55, 115, 171; CP 5, 6, 7; CSW; CWP; DLB 120; PFS 23
Voinovich, Vladimir 1932- .. **CLC 10, 49, 147**
See also CA 81-84; 12; CANR 33, 67, 150; CWW 2; DLB 302; MTCW 1
Voinovich, Vladimir Nikolaevich
See Voinovich, Vladimir
Vollmann, William T. 1959- ...... **CLC 89, 227**
See also AMWS 17; CA 134; CANR 67, 116; CN 7; CPW; DA3; DAM NOV, POP; MTCW 2; MTFW 2005
Voloshinov, V. N.
See Bakhtin, Mikhail Mikhailovich
Voltaire 1694-1778 . **LC 14, 79, 110; SSC 12; WLC 6**
See also BYA 13; DA; DA3; DAB; DAC; DAM DRAM, MST; DLB 314; EW 4; GFL Beginnings to 1789; LATS 1:1; LMFS 1; NFS 7; RGWL 2, 3; TWA
von Aschendrof, Baron Ignatz
See Ford, Ford Madox
von Chamisso, Adelbert
See Chamisso, Adelbert von
von Daeniken, Erich 1935- .... **CLC 30**
See also AITN 1; CA 37-40R; CANR 17, 44
von Daniken, Erich
See von Daeniken, Erich
von Eschenbach, Wolfram c. 1170-c. 1220 .... **CMLC 5**
See Eschenbach, Wolfram von
See also CDWLB 2; DLB 138; EW 1; RGWL 2
von Hartmann, Eduard 1842-1906 .... **TCLC 96**
von Hayek, Friedrich August
See Hayek, F(riedrich) A(ugust von)
von Heidenstam, (Carl Gustaf) Verner
See Heidenstam, (Carl Gustaf) Verner von
von Heyse, Paul (Johann Ludwig)
See Heyse, Paul (Johann Ludwig von)
von Hofmannsthal, Hugo
See Hofmannsthal, Hugo von
von Horvath, Odon
See von Horvath, Odon
von Horvath, Odon
See von Horvath, Odon
von Horvath, Odon 1901-1938 .... **TCLC 45**
See von Horvath, Oedoen
See also CA 194; CAAE 118; DLB 85, 124; RGWL 2, 3
von Horvath, Oedoen
See von Horvath, Odon
See also CA 184
von Kleist, Heinrich
See Kleist, Heinrich von
Vonnegut, Kurt, Jr.
See Vonnegut, Kurt
Vonnegut, Kurt 1922-2007 .... **CLC 1, 2, 3, 4, 5, 8, 12, 22, 40, 60, 111, 212, 254; SSC 8; WLC 6**
See also AAYA 6, 44; AITN 1; AMWS 2; BEST 90:4; BPFB 3; BYA 3, 14; CA 1-4R; CAAS 259; CANR 1, 25, 49, 75, 92; CDALB 1968-1988; CN 1, 2, 3, 4, 5, 6, 7; CPW 1; DA; DA3; DAB; DAC; DAM MST, NOV, POP; DLB 2, 8, 152; DLBD 3; DLBY 1980; EWL 3; EXPN; EXPS; LAIT 4; LMFS 2; MAL 5; MTCW 1, 2; MTFW 2005; NFS 3; RGAL 4; SCFW; SFW 4; SSFS 5; TUS; YAW
Von Rachen, Kurt
See Hubbard, L. Ron
von Sternberg, Josef
See Sternberg, Josef von
Vorster, Gordon 1924- .... **CLC 34**
See also CA 133
Vosce, Trudie
See Ozick, Cynthia
Voznesensky, Andrei (Andreievich) 1933- .... **CLC 1, 15, 57**
See Voznesensky, Andrey
See also CA 89-92; CANR 37; CWW 2; DAM POET; MTCW 1
Voznesensky, Andrey
See Voznesensky, Andrei (Andreievich)
See also EWL 3
Wace, Robert c. 1100-c. 1175 .... **CMLC 55**
See also DLB 146
Waddington, Miriam 1917-2004 .... **CLC 28**
See also CA 21-24R; CAAS 225; CANR 12, 30; CCA 1; CP 1, 2, 3, 4, 5, 6, 7; DLB 68
Wagman, Fredrica 1937- .... **CLC 7**
See also CA 97-100; CANR 166; INT CA-97-100
Wagner, Linda W.
See Wagner-Martin, Linda (C.)
Wagner, Linda Welshimer
See Wagner-Martin, Linda (C.)
Wagner, Richard 1813-1883 ..... **NCLC 9, 119**
See also DLB 129; EW 6
Wagner-Martin, Linda (C.) 1936- .... **CLC 50**
See also CA 159; CANR 135
Wagoner, David (Russell) 1926- .... **CLC 3, 5, 15; PC 33**
See also AMWS 9; CA 1-4R; 3; CANR 2, 71; CN 1, 2, 3, 4, 5, 6, 7; CP 1, 2, 3, 4, 5, 6, 7; DLB 5, 256; SATA 14; TCWW 1, 2
Wah, Fred(erick James) 1939- .... **CLC 44**
See also CA 141; CAAE 107; CP 1, 6, 7; DLB 60
Wahloo, Per 1926-1975 .... **CLC 7**
See also BPFB 3; CA 61-64; CANR 73; CMW 4; MSW
Wahloo, Peter
See Wahloo, Per
Wain, John (Barrington) 1925-1994 . **CLC 2, 11, 15, 46**
See also CA 5-8R; 4; CAAS 145; CANR 23, 54; CDBLB 1960 to Present; CN 1, 2, 3, 4, 5; CP 1, 2, 3, 4, 5; DLB 15, 27, 139, 155; EWL 3; MTCW 1, 2; MTFW 2005
Wajda, Andrzej 1926- .... **CLC 16, 219**
See also CA 102
Wakefield, Dan 1932- .... **CLC 7**
See also CA 211; 21-24R, 211; 7; CN 4, 5, 6, 7
Wakefield, Herbert Russell 1888-1965 .... **TCLC 120**
See also CA 5-8R; CANR 77; HGG; SUFW
Wakoski, Diane 1937- ...... **CLC 2, 4, 7, 9, 11, 40; PC 15**
See also CA 216; 13-16R, 216; 1; CANR 9, 60, 106; CP 1, 2, 3, 4, 5, 6, 7; CWP; DAM POET; DLB 5; INT CANR-9; MAL 5; MTCW 2; MTFW 2005
Wakoski-Sherbell, Diane
See Wakoski, Diane
Walcott, Derek 1930- .... **BLC 1:3; CLC 2, 4, 9, 14, 25, 42, 67, 76, 160; DC 7; PC 46**
See also BW 2; CA 89-92; CANR 26, 47, 75, 80, 130; CBD; CD 5, 6; CDWLB 3; CP 1, 2, 3, 4, 5, 6, 7; DA3; DAB; DAC; DAM MST, MULT, POET; DLB 117, 332; DLBY 1981; DNFS 1; EFS 1; EWL 3; LMFS 2; MTCW 1, 2; MTFW 2005; PFS 6; RGEL 2; TWA; WWE 1
Waldman, Anne (Lesley) 1945- .... **CLC 7**
See also BG 1:3; CA 37-40R; 17; CANR 34, 69, 116; CP 1, 2, 3, 4, 5, 6, 7; CWP; DLB 16
Waldo, E. Hunter
See Sturgeon, Theodore (Hamilton)
Waldo, Edward Hamilton
See Sturgeon, Theodore (Hamilton)
Walker, Alice 1944- ... **BLC 1:3; CLC 5, 6, 9, 19, 27, 46, 58, 103, 167; PC 30; SSC 5; WLCS**
See also AAYA 3, 33; AFAW 1, 2; AMWS 3; BEST 89:4; BPFB 3; BW 2, 3; CA 37-40R; CANR 9, 27, 49, 66, 82, 131; CDALB 1968-1988; CN 4, 5, 6, 7; CPW; CSW; DA; DA3; DAB; DAC; DAM MST, MULT, NOV, POET, POP; DLB 6, 33, 143; EWL 3; EXPN; EXPS; FL 1:6; FW; INT CANR-27; LAIT 3; MAL 5; MBL; MTCW 1, 2; MTFW 2005; NFS 5; RGAL 4; RGSF 2; SATA 31; SSFS 2, 11; TUS; YAW
Walker, Alice Malsenior
See Walker, Alice
Walker, David Harry 1911-1992 ...... **CLC 14**
See also CA 1-4R; CAAS 137; CANR 1; CN 1, 2; CWRI 5; SATA 8; SATA-Obit 71
Walker, Edward Joseph 1934-2004
See Walker, Ted
See also CA 21-24R; CAAS 226; CANR 12, 28, 53
Walker, George F(rederick) 1947- .. **CLC 44, 61**
See also CA 103; CANR 21, 43, 59; CD 5, 6; DAB; DAC; DAM MST; DLB 60
Walker, Joseph A. 1935-2003 .... **CLC 19**
See also BW 1, 3; CA 89-92; CAD; CANR 26, 143; CD 5, 6; DAM DRAM, MST; DFS 12; DLB 38
Walker, Margaret 1915-1998 .... **BLC 1:3; CLC 1, 6; PC 20; TCLC 129**
See also AFAW 1, 2; BW 2, 3; CA 73-76; CAAS 172; CANR 26, 54, 76, 136; CN 1, 2, 3, 4, 5, 6; CP 1, 2, 3, 4, 5, 6; CSW; DAM MULT; DLB 76, 152; EXPP; FW; MAL 5; MTCW 1, 2; MTFW 2005; RGAL 4; RHW

Walker, Ted CLC 13
See Walker, Edward Joseph
See also CP 1, 2, 3, 4, 5, 6, 7; DLB 40
Wallace, David Foster 1962- ... **CLC 50, 114; SSC 68**
See also AAYA 50; AMWS 10; CA 132; CANR 59, 133; CN 7; DA3; MTCW 2; MTFW 2005
Wallace, Dexter
See Masters, Edgar Lee
Wallace, (Richard Horatio) Edgar 1875-1932 .... **TCLC 57**
See also CA 218; CAAE 115; CMW 4; DLB 70; MSW; RGEL 2
Wallace, Irving 1916-1990 .... **CLC 7, 13**
See also AITN 1; BPFB 3; CA 1-4R; 1; CAAS 132; CANR 1, 27; CPW; DAM NOV, POP; INT CANR-27; MTCW 1, 2
Wallant, Edward Lewis 1926-1962 ... **CLC 5, 10**
See also CA 1-4R; CANR 22; DLB 2, 28, 143, 299; EWL 3; MAL 5; MTCW 1, 2; RGAL 4; RGHL
Wallas, Graham 1858-1932 .... **TCLC 91**
Waller, Edmund 1606-1687 .... **LC 86; PC 72**
See also BRW 2; DAM POET; DLB 126; PAB; RGEL 2
Walley, Byron
See Card, Orson Scott
Walpole, Horace 1717-1797 .... **LC 2, 49**
See also BRW 3; DLB 39, 104, 213; GL 3; HGG; LMFS 1; RGEL 2; SUFW 1; TEA
Walpole, Hugh (Seymour) 1884-1941 .... **TCLC 5**
See also CA 165; CAAE 104; DLB 34; HGG; MTCW 2; RGEL 2; RHW
Walrond, Eric (Derwent) 1898-1966 . **HR 1:3**
See also BW 1; CA 125; DLB 51
Walser, Martin 1927- .... **CLC 27, 183**
See also CA 57-60; CANR 8, 46, 145; CWW 2; DLB 75, 124; EWL 3
Walser, Robert 1878-1956 ..... **SSC 20; TCLC 18**
See also CA 165; CAAE 118; CANR 100; DLB 66; EWL 3
Walsh, Gillian Paton
See Paton Walsh, Jill
Walsh, Jill Paton CLC 35
See Paton Walsh, Jill
See also CLR 2, 65, 128; WYA
Walter, Villiam Christian
See Andersen, Hans Christian
Walters, Anna L(ee) 1946- .... **NNAL**
See also CA 73-76
Walther von der Vogelweide c. 1170-1228 .... **CMLC 56**
Walton, Izaak 1593-1683 .... **LC 72**
See also BRW 2; CDBLB Before 1660; DLB 151, 213; RGEL 2
Walzer, Michael (Laban) 1935- ...... **CLC 238**
See also CA 37-40R; CANR 15, 48, 127
Wambaugh, Joseph, Jr. 1937- ...... **CLC 3, 18**
See also AITN 1; BEST 89:3; BPFB 3; CA 33-36R; CANR 42, 65, 115, 167; CMW 4; CPW 1; DA3; DAM NOV, POP; DLB 6; DLBY 1983; MSW; MTCW 1, 2
Wambaugh, Joseph Aloysius
See Wambaugh, Joseph, Jr.
Wang Wei 699(?)-759(?) . **CMLC 100; PC 18**
See also TWA
Warburton, William 1698-1779 .... **LC 97**
See also DLB 104
Ward, Arthur Henry Sarsfield 1883-1959
See Rohmer, Sax
See also CA 173; CAAE 108; CMW 4; HGG
Ward, Douglas Turner 1930- .... **CLC 19**
See also BW 1; CA 81-84; CAD; CANR 27; CD 5, 6; DLB 7, 38
Ward, E. D.
See Lucas, E(dward) V(errall)
Ward, Mrs. Humphry 1851-1920
See Ward, Mary Augusta
See also RGEL 2
Ward, Mary Augusta 1851-1920 ... **TCLC 55**
See Ward, Mrs. Humphry
See also DLB 18
Ward, Nathaniel 1578(?)-1652 .... **LC 114**
See also DLB 24
Ward, Peter
See Faust, Frederick (Schiller)
Warhol, Andy 1928(?)-1987 .... **CLC 20**
See also AAYA 12; BEST 89:4; CA 89-92; CAAS 121; CANR 34
Warner, Francis (Robert Le Plastrier) 1937- .... **CLC 14**
See also CA 53-56; CANR 11; CP 1, 2, 3, 4
Warner, Marina 1946- .... **CLC 59, 231**
See also CA 65-68; CANR 21, 55, 118; CN 5, 6, 7; DLB 194; MTFW 2005
Warner, Rex (Ernest) 1905-1986 ...... **CLC 45**
See also CA 89-92; CAAS 119; CN 1, 2, 3, 4; CP 1, 2, 3, 4; DLB 15; RGEL 2; RHW
Warner, Susan (Bogert) 1819-1885 .... **NCLC 31, 146**
See also DLB 3, 42, 239, 250, 254
Warner, Sylvia (Constance) Ashton
See Ashton-Warner, Sylvia (Constance)
Warner, Sylvia Townsend 1893-1978 .. **CLC 7, 19; SSC 23; TCLC 131**
See also BRWS 7; CA 61-64; CAAS 77-80; CANR 16, 60, 104; CN 1, 2; DLB 34, 139; EWL 3; FANT; FW; MTCW 1, 2; RGEL 2; RGSF 2; RHW
Warren, Mercy Otis 1728-1814 ..... **NCLC 13**
See also DLB 31, 200; RGAL 4; TUS
Warren, Robert Penn 1905-1989 .. **CLC 1, 4, 6, 8, 10, 13, 18, 39, 53, 59; PC 37; SSC 4, 58; WLC 6**
See also AITN 1; AMW; AMWC 2; BPFB 3; BYA 1; CA 13-16R; CAAS 129; CANR 10, 47; CDALB 1968-1988; CN 1, 2, 3, 4; CP 1, 2, 3, 4; DA; DA3; DAB; DAC; DAM MST, NOV, POET; DLB 2, 48, 152, 320; DLBY 1980, 1989; EWL 3; INT CANR-10; MAL 5; MTCW 1, 2; MTFW 2005; NFS 13; RGAL 4; RGSF 2; RHW; SATA 46; SATA-Obit 63; SSFS 8; TUS
Warrigal, Jack
See Furphy, Joseph
Warshofsky, Isaac
See Singer, Isaac Bashevis
Warton, Joseph 1722-1800 ... **LC 128; NCLC 118**
See also DLB 104, 109; RGEL 2
Warton, Thomas 1728-1790 .... **LC 15, 82**
See also DAM POET; DLB 104, 109, 336; RGEL 2
Waruk, Kona
See Harris, (Theodore) Wilson
Warung, Price TCLC 45
See Astley, William
See also DLB 230; RGEL 2
Warwick, Jarvis
See Garner, Hugh
See also CCA 1
Washington, Alex
See Harris, Mark
Washington, Booker T(aliaferro) 1856-1915 .... **BLC 1:3; TCLC 10**
See also BW 1; CA 125; CAAE 114; DA3; DAM MULT; LAIT 2; RGAL 4; SATA 28
Washington, George 1732-1799 .... **LC 25**
See also DLB 31
Wassermann, (Karl) Jakob 1873-1934 .... **TCLC 6**
See also CA 163; CAAE 104; DLB 66; EWL 3
Wasserstein, Wendy 1950-2006 . **CLC 32, 59, 90, 183; DC 4**
See also AAYA 73; AMWS 15; CA 129; CAAE 121; CAAS 247; CABS 3; CAD; CANR 53, 75, 128; CD 5, 6; CWD; DA3; DAM DRAM; DFS 5, 17; DLB 228; EWL 3; FW; INT CA-129; MAL 5; MTCW 2; MTFW 2005; SATA 94; SATA-Obit 174
Waterhouse, Keith (Spencer) 1929- . **CLC 47**
See also BRWS 13; CA 5-8R; CANR 38, 67, 109; CBD; CD 6; CN 1, 2, 3, 4, 5, 6, 7; DLB 13, 15; MTCW 1, 2; MTFW 2005
Waters, Frank (Joseph) 1902-1995 .. **CLC 88**
See also CA 5-8R; 13; CAAS 149; CANR 3, 18, 63, 121; DLB 212; DLBY 1986; RGAL 4; TCWW 1, 2
Waters, Mary C. CLC 70
Waters, Roger 1944- .... **CLC 35**
Watkins, Frances Ellen
See Harper, Frances Ellen Watkins
Watkins, Gerrold
See Malzberg, Barry N(athaniel)
Watkins, Gloria Jean
See hooks, bell
Watkins, Paul 1964- .... **CLC 55**
See also CA 132; CANR 62, 98
Watkins, Vernon Phillips 1906-1967 .... **CLC 43**
See also CA 9-10; CAAS 25-28R; CAP 1; DLB 20; EWL 3; RGEL 2
Watson, Irving S.
See Mencken, H(enry) L(ouis)
Watson, John H.
See Farmer, Philip Jose
Watson, Richard F.
See Silverberg, Robert
Watts, Ephraim
See Horne, Richard Henry Hengist
Watts, Isaac 1674-1748 .... **LC 98**
See also DLB 95; RGEL 2; SATA 52
Waugh, Auberon (Alexander) 1939-2001 .... **CLC 7**
See also CA 45-48; CAAS 192; CANR 6, 22, 92; CN 1, 2, 3; DLB 14, 194
Waugh, Evelyn (Arthur St. John) 1903-1966 .. **CLC 1, 3, 8, 13, 19, 27, 44, 107; SSC 41; WLC 6**
See also BPFB 3; BRW 7; CA 85-88; CAAS 25-28R; CANR 22; CDBLB 1914-1945; DA; DA3; DAB; DAC; DAM MST, NOV, POP; DLB 15, 162, 195; EWL 3; MTCW 1, 2; MTFW 2005; NFS 13, 17; RGEL 2; RGSF 2; TEA; WLIT 4
Waugh, Harriet 1944- .... **CLC 6**
See also CA 85-88; CANR 22
Ways, C. R.
See Blount, Roy (Alton), Jr.
Waystaff, Simon
See Swift, Jonathan
Webb, Beatrice (Martha Potter) 1858-1943 .... **TCLC 22**
See also CA 162; CAAE 117; DLB 190; FW
Webb, Charles (Richard) 1939- .... **CLC 7**
See also CA 25-28R; CANR 114
Webb, Frank J. NCLC 143
See also DLB 50
Webb, James, Jr.
See Webb, James
Webb, James 1946- .... **CLC 22**
See also CA 81-84; CANR 156
Webb, James H.
See Webb, James

Webb, James Henry
See Webb, James
Webb, Mary Gladys (Meredith) 1881-1927 .... **TCLC 24**
See also CA 182; CAAS 123; DLB 34; FW; RGEL 2
Webb, Mrs. Sidney
See Webb, Beatrice (Martha Potter)
Webb, Phyllis 1927- .... **CLC 18**
See also CA 104; CANR 23; CCA 1; CP 1, 2, 3, 4, 5, 6, 7; CWP; DLB 53
Webb, Sidney (James) 1859-1947 .. **TCLC 22**
See also CA 163; CAAE 117; DLB 190
Webber, Andrew Lloyd CLC 21
See Lloyd Webber, Andrew
See also DFS 7
Weber, Lenora Mattingly 1895-1971 .... **CLC 12**
See also CA 19-20; CAAS 29-32R; CAP 1; SATA 2; SATA-Obit 26
Weber, Max 1864-1920 .... **TCLC 69**
See also CA 189; CAAE 109; DLB 296
Webster, John 1580(?)-1634(?) ...... **DC 2; LC 33, 84, 124; WLC 6**
See also BRW 2; CDBLB Before 1660; DA; DAB; DAC; DAM DRAM, MST; DFS 17, 19; DLB 58; IDTP; RGEL 2; WLIT 3
Webster, Noah 1758-1843 .... **NCLC 30**
See also DLB 1, 37, 42, 43, 73, 243
Wedekind, Benjamin Franklin
See Wedekind, Frank
Wedekind, Frank 1864-1918 .... **TCLC 7**
See also CA 153; CAAE 104; CANR 121, 122; CDWLB 2; DAM DRAM; DLB 118; EW 8; EWL 3; LMFS 2; RGWL 2, 3
Wehr, Demaris CLC 65
Weidman, Jerome 1913-1998 .... **CLC 7**
See also AITN 2; CA 1-4R; CAAS 171; CAD; CANR 1; CD 1, 2, 3, 4, 5; DLB 28
Weil, Simone (Adolphine) 1909-1943 .... **TCLC 23**
See also CA 159; CAAE 117; EW 12; EWL 3; FW; GFL 1789 to the Present; MTCW 2
Weininger, Otto 1880-1903 .... **TCLC 84**
Weinstein, Nathan
See West, Nathanael
Weinstein, Nathan von Wallenstein
See West, Nathanael
Weir, Peter (Lindsay) 1944- .... **CLC 20**
See also CA 123; CAAE 113
Weiss, Peter (Ulrich) 1916-1982 .. **CLC 3, 15, 51; TCLC 152**
See also CA 45-48; CAAS 106; CANR 3; DAM DRAM; DFS 3; DLB 69, 124; EWL 3; RGHL; RGWL 2, 3
Weiss, Theodore (Russell) 1916-2003 .... **CLC 3, 8, 14**
See also CA 189; 9-12R, 189; 2; CAAS 216; CANR 46, 94; CP 1, 2, 3, 4, 5, 6, 7; DLB 5; TCLE 1:2
Welch, (Maurice) Denton 1915-1948 .... **TCLC 22**
See also BRWS 8, 9; CA 148; CAAE 121; RGEL 2
Welch, James (Phillip) 1940-2003 ..... **CLC 6, 14, 52, 249; NNAL; PC 62**
See also CA 85-88; CAAS 219; CANR 42, 66, 107; CN 5, 6, 7; CP 2, 3, 4, 5, 6, 7; CPW; DAM MULT, POP; DLB 175, 256; LATS 1:1; NFS 23; RGAL 4; TCWW 1, 2
Weldon, Fay 1931- . **CLC 6, 9, 11, 19, 36, 59, 122**
See also BRWS 4; CA 21-24R; CANR 16, 46, 63, 97, 137; CDBLB 1960 to Present; CN 3, 4, 5, 6, 7; CPW; DAM POP; DLB 14, 194, 319; EWL 3; FW; HGG; INT CANR-16; MTCW 1, 2; MTFW 2005; RGEL 2; RGSF 2
Wellek, Rene 1903-1995 .... **CLC 28**
See also CA 5-8R; 7; CAAS 150; CANR 8; DLB 63; EWL 3; INT CANR-8
Weller, Michael 1942- .... **CLC 10, 53**
See also CA 85-88; CAD; CD 5, 6
Weller, Paul 1958- .... **CLC 26**
Wellershoff, Dieter 1925- .... **CLC 46**
See also CA 89-92; CANR 16, 37
Welles, (George) Orson 1915-1985 .. **CLC 20, 80**
See also AAYA 40; CA 93-96; CAAS 117
Wellman, John McDowell 1945-
See Wellman, Mac
See also CA 166; CD 5
Wellman, Mac CLC 65
See Wellman, John McDowell; Wellman, John McDowell
See also CAD; CD 6; RGAL 4
Wellman, Manly Wade 1903-1986 ... **CLC 49**
See also CA 1-4R; CAAS 118; CANR 6, 16, 44; FANT; SATA 6; SATA-Obit 47; SFW 4; SUFW
Wells, Carolyn 1869(?)-1942 .... **TCLC 35**
See also CA 185; CAAE 113; CMW 4; DLB 11
Wells, H(erbert) G(eorge) 1866-1946 . **SSC 6, 70; TCLC 6, 12, 19, 133; WLC 6**
See also AAYA 18; BPFB 3; BRW 6; CA 121; CAAE 110; CDBLB 1914-1945; CLR 64; DA; DA3; DAB; DAC; DAM MST, NOV; DLB 34, 70, 156, 178; EWL 3; EXPS; HGG; LAIT 3; LMFS 2; MTCW 1, 2; MTFW 2005; NFS 17, 20; RGEL 2; RGSF 2; SATA 20; SCFW 1, 2; SFW 4; SSFS 3; SUFW; TEA; WCH; WLIT 4; YAW
Wells, Rosemary 1943- .... **CLC 12**
See also AAYA 13; BYA 7, 8; CA 85-88; CANR 48, 120; CLR 16, 69; CWRI 5; MAICYA 1, 2; SAAS 1; SATA 18, 69, 114, 156; YAW
Wells-Barnett, Ida B(ell) 1862-1931 .... **TCLC 125**
See also CA 182; DLB 23, 221
Welsh, Irvine 1958- .... **CLC 144**
See also CA 173; CANR 146; CN 7; DLB 271
Welty, Eudora 1909-2001 .... **CLC 1, 2, 5, 14, 22, 33, 105, 220; SSC 1, 27, 51, 111; WLC 6**
See also AAYA 48; AMW; AMWR 1; BPFB 3; CA 9-12R; CAAS 199; CABS 1; CANR 32, 65, 128; CDALB 1941-1968; CN 1, 2, 3, 4, 5, 6, 7; CSW; DA; DA3; DAB; DAC; DAM MST, NOV; DLB 2, 102, 143; DLBD 12; DLBY 1987, 2001; EWL 3; EXPS; HGG; LAIT 3; MAL 5; MBL; MTCW 1, 2; MTFW 2005; NFS 13, 15; RGAL 4; RGSF 2; RHW; SSFS 2, 10; TUS
Welty, Eudora Alice
See Welty, Eudora
Wen I-to 1899-1946 .... **TCLC 28**
See also EWL 3
Wentworth, Robert
See Hamilton, Edmond
Werfel, Franz (Viktor) 1890-1945 ... **TCLC 8**
See also CA 161; CAAE 104; DLB 81, 124; EWL 3; RGWL 2, 3
Wergeland, Henrik Arnold 1808-1845 .... **NCLC 5**
Werner, Friedrich Ludwig Zacharias 1768-1823 .... **NCLC 189**
See also DLB 94
Werner, Zacharias
See Werner, Friedrich Ludwig Zacharias
Wersba, Barbara 1932- .... **CLC 30**
See also AAYA 2, 30; BYA 6, 12, 13; CA 182; 29-32R, 182; CANR 16, 38; CLR 3, 78; DLB 52; JRDA; MAICYA 1, 2; SAAS 2; SATA 1, 58; SATA-Essay 103; WYA; YAW
Wertmueller, Lina 1928- .... **CLC 16**
See also CA 97-100; CANR 39, 78
Wescott, Glenway 1901-1987 .. **CLC 13; SSC 35**
See also CA 13-16R; CAAS 121; CANR 23, 70; CN 1, 2, 3, 4; DLB 4, 9, 102; MAL 5; RGAL 4
Wesker, Arnold 1932- .... **CLC 3, 5, 42**
See also CA 1-4R; 7; CANR 1, 33; CBD; CD 5, 6; CDBLB 1960 to Present; DAB; DAM DRAM; DLB 13, 310, 319; EWL 3; MTCW 1; RGEL 2; TEA
Wesley, Charles 1707-1788 .... **LC 128**
See also DLB 95; RGEL 2
Wesley, John 1703-1791 .... **LC 88**
See also DLB 104
Wesley, Richard (Errol) 1945- .... **CLC 7**
See also BW 1; CA 57-60; CAD; CANR 27; CD 5, 6; DLB 38
Wessel, Johan Herman 1742-1785 .... **LC 7**
See also DLB 300
West, Anthony (Panther) 1914-1987 .... **CLC 50**
See also CA 45-48; CAAS 124; CANR 3, 19; CN 1, 2, 3, 4; DLB 15
West, C. P.
See Wodehouse, P(elham) G(renville)
West, Cornel 1953- .... **BLCS; CLC 134**
See also CA 144; CANR 91, 159; DLB 246
West, Cornel Ronald
See West, Cornel
West, Delno C(loyde), Jr. 1936- .... **CLC 70**
See also CA 57-60
West, Dorothy 1907-1998 ...... **HR 1:3; TCLC 108**
See also BW 2; CA 143; CAAS 169; DLB 76
West, (Mary) Jessamyn 1902-1984 ... **CLC 7, 17**
See also CA 9-12R; CAAS 112; CANR 27; CN 1, 2, 3; DLB 6; DLBY 1984; MTCW 1, 2; RGAL 4; RHW; SATA-Obit 37; TCWW 2; TUS; YAW
West, Morris L(anglo) 1916-1999 ..... **CLC 6, 33**
See also BPFB 3; CA 5-8R; CAAS 187; CANR 24, 49, 64; CN 1, 2, 3, 4, 5, 6; CPW; DLB 289; MTCW 1, 2; MTFW 2005
West, Nathanael 1903-1940 .. **SSC 16; TCLC 1, 14, 44**
See also AAYA 77; AMW; AMWR 2; BPFB 3; CA 125; CAAE 104; CDALB 1929-1941; DA3; DLB 4, 9, 28; EWL 3; MAL 5; MTCW 1, 2; MTFW 2005; NFS 16; RGAL 4; TUS
West, Owen
See Koontz, Dean R.
West, Paul 1930- .... **CLC 7, 14, 96, 226**
See also CA 13-16R; 7; CANR 22, 53, 76, 89, 136; CN 1, 2, 3, 4, 5, 6, 7; DLB 14; INT CANR-22; MTCW 2; MTFW 2005
West, Rebecca 1892-1983 ... **CLC 7, 9, 31, 50**
See also BPFB 3; BRWS 3; CA 5-8R; CAAS 109; CANR 19; CN 1, 2, 3; DLB 36; DLBY 1983; EWL 3; FW; MTCW 1, 2; MTFW 2005; NCFS 4; RGEL 2; TEA
Westall, Robert (Atkinson) 1929-1993 .... **CLC 17**
See also AAYA 12; BYA 2, 6, 7, 8, 9, 15; CA 69-72; CAAS 141; CANR 18, 68; CLR 13; FANT; JRDA; MAICYA 1, 2; MAICYAS 1; SAAS 2; SATA 23, 69; SATA-Obit 75; WYA; YAW

Westermarck, Edward 1862-1939 . **TCLC 87**
Westlake, Donald E. 1933- .... **CLC 7, 33**
See also BPFB 3; CA 17-20R; 13; CANR 16, 44, 65, 94, 137; CMW 4; CPW; DAM POP; INT CANR-16; MSW; MTCW 2; MTFW 2005
Westlake, Donald Edwin
See Westlake, Donald E.
Westmacott, Mary
See Christie, Agatha (Mary Clarissa)
Weston, Allen
See Norton, Andre
Wetcheek, J. L.
See Feuchtwanger, Lion
Wetering, Janwillem van de
See van de Wetering, Janwillem
Wetherald, Agnes Ethelwyn
1857-1940 .... **TCLC 81**
See also CA 202; DLB 99
Wetherell, Elizabeth
See Warner, Susan (Bogert)
Whale, James 1889-1957 .... **TCLC 63**
See also AAYA 75
Whalen, Philip (Glenn) 1923-2002 .... **CLC 6, 29**
See also BG 1:3; CA 9-12R; CAAS 209; CANR 5, 39; CP 1, 2, 3, 4, 5, 6, 7; DLB 16; WP
Wharton, Edith (Newbold Jones)
1862-1937 ... **SSC 6, 84; TCLC 3, 9, 27, 53, 129, 149; WLC 6**
See also AAYA 25; AMW; AMWC 2; AMWR 1; BPFB 3; CA 132; CAAE 104; CDALB 1865-1917; DA; DA3; DAB; DAC; DAM MST, NOV; DLB 4, 9, 12, 78, 189; DLBD 13; EWL 3; EXPS; FL 1:6; GL 3; HGG; LAIT 2, 3; LATS 1:1; MAL 5; MBL; MTCW 1, 2; MTFW 2005; NFS 5, 11, 15, 20; RGAL 4; RGSF 2; RHW; SSFS 6, 7; SUFW; TUS
Wharton, James
See Mencken, H(enry) L(ouis)
Wharton, William (a pseudonym)
1925- .... **CLC 18, 37**
See also CA 93-96; CN 4, 5, 6, 7; DLBY 1980; INT CA-93-96
Wheatley (Peters), Phillis
1753(?)-1784 .... **BLC 1:3; LC 3, 50; PC 3; WLC 6**
See also AFAW 1, 2; CDALB 1640-1865; DA; DA3; DAC; DAM MST, MULT, POET; DLB 31, 50; EXPP; FL 1:1; PFS 13; RGAL 4
Wheelock, John Hall 1886-1978 .... **CLC 14**
See also CA 13-16R; CAAS 77-80; CANR 14; CP 1, 2; DLB 45; MAL 5
Whim-Wham
See Curnow, (Thomas) Allen (Monro)
Whisp, Kennilworthy
See Rowling, J.K.
Whitaker, Rod 1931-2005
See Trevanian
See also CA 29-32R; CAAS 246; CANR 45, 153; CMW 4
White, Babington
See Braddon, Mary Elizabeth
White, E. B. 1899-1985 .... **CLC 10, 34, 39**
See also AAYA 62; AITN 2; AMWS 1; CA 13-16R; CAAS 116; CANR 16, 37; CDALBS; CLR 1, 21, 107; CPW; DA3; DAM POP; DLB 11, 22; EWL 3; FANT; MAICYA 1, 2; MAL 5; MTCW 1, 2; MTFW 2005; NCFS 5; RGAL 4; SATA 2, 29, 100; SATA-Obit 44; TUS
White, Edmund 1940- .... **CLC 27, 110**
See also AAYA 7; CA 45-48; CANR 3, 19, 36, 62, 107, 133, 172; CN 5, 6, 7; DA3; DAM POP; DLB 227; MTCW 1, 2; MTFW 2005
White, Edmund Valentine III
See White, Edmund
White, Elwyn Brooks
See White, E. B.
White, Hayden V. 1928- .... **CLC 148**
See also CA 128; CANR 135; DLB 246
White, Patrick (Victor Martindale)
1912-1990 ...... **CLC 3, 4, 5, 7, 9, 18, 65, 69; SSC 39; TCLC 176**
See also BRWS 1; CA 81-84; CAAS 132; CANR 43; CN 1, 2, 3, 4; DLB 260, 332; EWL 3; MTCW 1; RGEL 2; RGSF 2; RHW; TWA; WWE 1
White, Phyllis Dorothy James 1920-
See James, P. D.
See also CA 21-24R; CANR 17, 43, 65, 112; CMW 4; CN 7; CPW; DA3; DAM POP; MTCW 1, 2; MTFW 2005; TEA
White, T(erence) H(anbury)
1906-1964 .... **CLC 30**
See also AAYA 22; BPFB 3; BYA 4, 5; CA 73-76; CANR 37; DLB 160; FANT; JRDA; LAIT 1; MAICYA 1, 2; RGEL 2; SATA 12; SUFW 1; YAW
White, Terence de Vere 1912-1994 ... **CLC 49**
See also CA 49-52; CAAS 145; CANR 3
White, Walter
See White, Walter F(rancis)
White, Walter F(rancis)
1893-1955 ..... **BLC 1:3; HR 1:3; TCLC 15**
See also BW 1; CA 124; CAAE 115; DAM MULT; DLB 51
White, William Hale 1831-1913
See Rutherford, Mark
See also CA 189; CAAE 121
Whitehead, Alfred North
1861-1947 .... **TCLC 97**
See also CA 165; CAAE 117; DLB 100, 262
Whitehead, Colson 1969- ...... **BLC 2:3; CLC 232**
See also CA 202; CANR 162
Whitehead, E(dward) A(nthony)
1933- .... **CLC 5**
See Whitehead, Ted
See also CA 65-68; CANR 58, 118; CBD; CD 5; DLB 310
Whitehead, Ted
See Whitehead, E(dward) A(nthony)
See also CD 6
Whiteman, Roberta J. Hill 1947- ...... **NNAL**
See also CA 146
Whitemore, Hugh (John) 1936- .... **CLC 37**
See also CA 132; CANR 77; CBD; CD 5, 6; INT CA-132
Whitman, Sarah Helen (Power)
1803-1878 .... **NCLC 19**
See also DLB 1, 243
Whitman, Walt(er) 1819-1892 .. **NCLC 4, 31, 81; PC 3; WLC 6**
See also AAYA 42; AMW; AMWR 1; CDALB 1640-1865; DA; DA3; DAB; DAC; DAM MST, POET; DLB 3, 64, 224, 250; EXPP; LAIT 2; LMFS 1; PAB; PFS 2, 3, 13, 22; RGAL 4; SATA 20; TUS; WP; WYAS 1
Whitney, Isabella fl. 1565-fl. 1575 ..... **LC 130**
See also DLB 136
Whitney, Phyllis A. 1903-2008 .... **CLC 42**
See also AAYA 36; AITN 2; BEST 90:3; CA 1-4R; CANR 3, 25, 38, 60; CLR 59; CMW 4; CPW; DA3; DAM POP; JRDA; MAICYA 1, 2; MTCW 2; RHW; SATA 1, 30; YAW
Whitney, Phyllis Ayame
See Whitney, Phyllis A.
Whittemore, (Edward) Reed, Jr.
1919- .... **CLC 4**
See also CA 219; 9-12R, 219; 8; CANR 4, 119; CP 1, 2, 3, 4, 5, 6, 7; DLB 5; MAL 5
Whittier, John Greenleaf
1807-1892 .... **NCLC 8, 59**
See also AMWS 1; DLB 1, 243; RGAL 4
Whittlebot, Hernia
See Coward, Noel (Peirce)
Wicker, Thomas Grey 1926-
See Wicker, Tom
See also CA 65-68; CANR 21, 46, 141
Wicker, Tom CLC 7
See Wicker, Thomas Grey
Wicomb, Zoe 1948- .... **BLC 2:3**
See also CA 127; CANR 106, 167; DLB 225
Wideman, John Edgar 1941- .... **BLC 1:3; CLC 5, 34, 36, 67, 122; SSC 62**
See also AFAW 1, 2; AMWS 10; BPFB 4; BW 2, 3; CA 85-88; CANR 14, 42, 67, 109, 140; CN 4, 5, 6, 7; DAM MULT; DLB 33, 143; MAL 5; MTCW 2; MTFW 2005; RGAL 4; RGSF 2; SSFS 6, 12, 24; TCLE 1:2
Wiebe, Rudy 1934- .... **CLC 6, 11, 14, 138**
See also CA 37-40R; CANR 42, 67, 123; CN 1, 2, 3, 4, 5, 6, 7; DAC; DAM MST; DLB 60; RHW; SATA 156
Wiebe, Rudy Henry
See Wiebe, Rudy
Wieland, Christoph Martin
1733-1813 .... **NCLC 17, 177**
See also DLB 97; EW 4; LMFS 1; RGWL 2, 3
Wiene, Robert 1881-1938 .... **TCLC 56**
Wieners, John 1934- .... **CLC 7**
See also BG 1:3; CA 13-16R; CP 1, 2, 3, 4, 5, 6, 7; DLB 16; WP
Wiesel, Elie 1928- ...... **CLC 3, 5, 11, 37, 165; WLCS**
See also AAYA 7, 54; AITN 1; CA 5-8R; 4; CANR 8, 40, 65, 125; CDALBS; CWW 2; DA; DA3; DAB; DAC; DAM MST, NOV; DLB 83, 299; DLBY 1987; EWL 3; INT CANR-8; LAIT 4; MTCW 1, 2; MTFW 2005; NCFS 4; NFS 4; RGHL; RGWL 3; SATA 56; YAW
Wiesel, Eliezer
See Wiesel, Elie
Wiggins, Marianne 1947- .... **CLC 57**
See also AAYA 70; BEST 89:3; CA 130; CANR 60, 139; CN 7; DLB 335
Wigglesworth, Michael 1631-1705 .... **LC 106**
See also DLB 24; RGAL 4
Wiggs, Susan CLC 70
See also CA 201; CANR 173
Wight, James Alfred 1916-1995
See Herriot, James
See also CA 77-80; SATA 55; SATA-Brief 44
Wilbur, Richard 1921- .. **CLC 3, 6, 9, 14, 53, 110; PC 51**
See also AAYA 72; AMWS 3; CA 1-4R; CABS 2; CANR 2, 29, 76, 93, 139; CDALBS; CP 1, 2, 3, 4, 5, 6, 7; DA; DAB; DAC; DAM MST, POET; DLB 5, 169; EWL 3; EXPP; INT CANR-29; MAL 5; MTCW 1, 2; MTFW 2005; PAB; PFS 11, 12, 16; RGAL 4; SATA 9, 108; WP
Wilbur, Richard Purdy
See Wilbur, Richard
Wild, Peter 1940- .... **CLC 14**
See also CA 37-40R; CP 1, 2, 3, 4, 5, 6, 7; DLB 5

Literary Criticism Series Cumulative Topic Index

This index lists all topic entries in Gale's *Children's Literature Review* (CLR), *Classical and Medieval Literature Criticism* (CMLC), *Contemporary Literary Criticism* (CLC), *Drama Criticism* (DC), *Literature Criticism from 1400 to 1800* (LC), *Nineteenth-Century Literature Criticism* (NCLC), *Short Story Criticism* (SSC), and *Twentieth-Century Literary Criticism* (TCLC). The index also lists topic entries in the Gale Critical Companion Collection, which includes the following publications: *The Beat Generation* (BG), *Feminism in Literature* (FL), *Gothic Literature* (GL), and *Harlem Renaissance* (HR).

Topic Index

Topic Index

Topic Index

SSC Cumulative Nationality Index

Ross, Martin **56**
Somerville, Edith **56**
Stephens, James **50**
Stoker, Abraham **55, 62**
Trevor, William **21, 58**
Wilde, Oscar (Fingal O'Flahertie Wills) **11, 77**

ISRAELI

Agnon, S(hmuel) Y(osef Halevi) **30**
Appelfeld, Aharon **42**
Oz, Amos **66**

ITALIAN

Boccaccio, Giovanni **10, 87**
Calvino, Italo **3, 48**
Ginzburg, Natalia **65**
Levi, Primo **12**
Moravia, Alberto **26**
Pavese, Cesare **19**
Pirandello, Luigi **22**
Svevo, Italo (Schmitz, Aron Hector) **25**
Verga, Giovanni (Carmelo) **21, 87**

JAMAICAN

Senior, Olive (Marjorie) **78**

JAPANESE

Abe, Kobo **61**
Akutagawa, Ryunosuke **44**
Dazai Osamu **41**
Endo, Shūsaku **48**
Kawabata, Yasunari **17**
Oe, Kenzaburo **20**
Shiga, Naoya **23**
Tanizaki, Junichirō **21**

MEXICAN

Arreola, Juan José **38**
Castellanos, Rosario **39, 68**
Fuentes, Carlos **24**
Rulfo, Juan **25**

NEW ZEALANDER

Frame, Janet **29**
Mansfield, Katherine **9, 23, 38, 81**
Sargeson, Frank **99**

NIGERIAN

Achebe, Chinua **105**

POLISH

Agnon, S(hmuel) Y(osef Halevi) **30**
Borowski, Tadeusz **48**
Conrad, Joseph **9, 71**
Peretz, Isaac Loeb **26**
Schulz, Bruno **13**
Singer, Isaac Bashevis **3, 53, 80**

PUERTO RICAN

Ferré, Rosario **36, 106**

RUSSIAN

Babel, Isaak (Emmanuilovich) **16, 78**
Bulgakov, Mikhail (Afanas'evich) **18**
Bunin, Ivan Alexeyevich **5**
Chekhov, Anton (Pavlovich) **2, 28, 41, 51, 85, 102**
Dostoevsky, Fedor Mikhailovich **2, 33, 44**
Gogol, Nikolai (Vasilyevich) **4, 29, 52**
Gorky, Maxim **28**
Kazakov, Yuri Pavlovich **43**
Leskov, Nikolai (Semyonovich) **34, 96**
Nabokov, Vladimir (Vladimirovich) **11, 86**
Olesha, Yuri **69**
Pasternak, Boris (Leonidovich) **31**
Pilnyak, Boris **48**
Platonov, Andrei (Klimentov, Andrei Platonovich) **42**
Pushkin, Alexander (Sergeyevich) **27, 55, 99**
Solzhenitsyn, Aleksandr I(sayevich) **32, 105**
Tolstoy, Leo (Nikolaevich) **9, 30, 45, 54**
Turgenev, Ivan (Sergeevich) **7, 57**
Zamyatin, Yevgeny **89**
Zoshchenko, Mikhail (Mikhailovich) **15**

SCOTTISH

Davie, Elspeth **52**
Doyle, Arthur Conan **12**
Oliphant, Margaret (Oliphant Wilson) **25**
Scott, Walter **32**
Spark, Muriel (Sarah) **10**
Stevenson, Robert Louis (Balfour) **11, 51**

SOUTH AFRICAN

Gordimer, Nadine **17, 80**
Head, Bessie **52**

SPANISH

Alarcón, Pedro Antonio de **64**
Cela, Camilo José **71**
Cervantes (Saavedra), Miguel de **12, 108**
Pardo Bazán, Emilia **30**
Unamuno (y Jugo), Miguel de **11, 69**
de Zayas y Sotomayor, María **94**

SWEDISH

Lagervist, Par **12**

SWISS

Hesse, Hermann **9, 49**
Keller, Gottfried **26, 107**
Meyer, Conrad Ferdinand **30**
Walser, Robert **20**

TRINIDADIAN

Naipaul, V(idiadhar) S(urajprasad) **38**

UKRAINIAN

Aleichem, Sholom **33**

URUGUAYAN

Onetti, Juan Carlos **23**
Quiroga, Horacio **89**

WELSH

Evans, Caradoc **43**
Lewis, Alun **40**
Machen, Arthur **20**
Thomas, Dylan (Marlais) **3, 44**

YUGOSLAVIAN

Andrić, Ivo **36**

SSC-111 Title Index

ISBN-13: 978-1-4144-1895-7
ISBN-10: 1-4144-1895-7